M|P|W

Mander Portman Woodward

UNIVERSITY DEGREE COURSE OFFERS

HEAP 2011

The essential guide to winning your place at university

Brian Heap

41st edition

UNIVERSITY DEGREE COURSE OFFERS – HEAP 2011

In order to ensure that *University Degree Course Offers* retains its reputation as the definitive guide for students wishing to study at UK universities and other higher education institutions, thousands of questionnaires are distributed, months of research and analysis are undertaken, and painstaking data checking and proofing are carried out.

Every effort has been made to maintain absolute accuracy in providing course information and to ensure that the entire book is as up-to-date as possible. However, changes are constantly taking place in higher education so it is important for readers to check carefully with prospectuses and websites before submitting their applications. The author, compilers and publishers cannot be held responsible for any inaccuracies in information supplied to them by third parties or contained in resources and websites listed in the book.

We hope you find this 41st edition useful, and would welcome your feedback as to how we can ensure the 42nd edition is even better.

Author Brian Heap
Compilation and Data Processing Dianah Ellis, Henry Ellis
Advertising Sales Crimson Publishing Services. Contact Lee Scott or Simon Connor on 020 8334 1781 or email info@crimsonpublishingservices.co.uk

This 41st edition published in 2010 by Trotman Publishing an imprint of Crimson Publishing Ltd
Westminster House, Kew Road,
Richmond, Surrey, TW9 2ND
www.trotman.co.uk

A CIP record for this book is available from the British Library

ISBN 978 1 84455 246 7

Typeset by RefineCatch Limited, Bungay, Suffolk
Printed and bound in the UK by Ashford Colour Press, Gosport, Hants

Founded in 1973, **Mander Portman Woodward (MPW)** is one of the UK's best known groups of independent sixth-form colleges with centres in London, Birmingham and Cambridge. It offers over 40 subjects at AS and A2 with no restrictions on subject combinations and a maximum class size of eight.

MPW has one of the highest numbers of university placements each year of any independent school in the country. It has developed considerable expertise over the years in the field of applications strategy and is frequently consulted by students facing some of the more daunting challenges that may arise in areas such as getting into Oxbridge, Medicine or Law. This expertise is available to a wider audience in the form of **Getting Into** guides on higher education and the seminars that are run for sixth-formers at its London centre. We are grateful to Trotman for publishing the Guides and hope that this latest edition of **University Degree Course Offers** will prove as popular and useful as ever.

If you would like to know more about MPW or Getting Into guides, please telephone us on 020 7835 1355 or visit our website, www.mpw.co.uk.

University Centre Doncaster
A joint development between Doncaster College and The University of Hull
The latest figures show people with a higher education earn, on average, about £160,000 more in a lifetime than those without a higher education.
And you could receive up to £2400 towards your degree* by studying at University Centre Doncaster.
We offer courses in:
Business
Childcare
Creative Arts
Criminolgy
Education
Humanities
Performing Arts
Social Sciences
Sport
Technology
Call us now to find out more or 0800 358 7474
or click on our website www.don.ac.uk
DONCASTER COLLEGE
UNIVERSITY OF Hull
* terms and conditions apply

Higher Education
at Hull & Harrogate College:
HC UK
Hull College Group
Higher Education
Hull College Group is one of the largest and most successful providers of Higher Education within the Further Education sector. Our growing Higher Education provision includes a wide choice of Foundation Degrees and BA (Hons) Degrees in many specialist subjects; including options to study at our campuses in Hull and Harrogate.
Opportunities for work placements are extensive with 'live' employer projects leading to many students achieving national recognition and awards.
For information, advice and guidance call:
Hull College: 01482 598744
www.hull-college.ac.uk
Harrogate College: 01423 878211
www.harrogate.ac.uk

QUOTES

'The guru of university choice'
The Times, 2007

'For those of you going through Clearing, an absolute must is the Degree Course Offers book. This guide operates subject by subject and gives you each university's requirements, standard offers and, most importantly, "course features"'
The Independent, August 2007

'Brian Heap, the guru of university admissions'
The Independent, September 2007

I would like to take this opportunity to congratulate you in maintaining the quality and currency of the information in your guide. We are aware of its wide range and its reputation for impartiality'
University Senior Assistant Registrar, 2007

'Degree Course Offers is probably the UK's longest running and best known reference work on the subject'
www.universityadvice.co.uk, 2005

'This guide contains useful, practical information for all university applicants and those advising them. I heartily recommend it'
Dr John Dunford, General Secretary, Association of School and College Leaders, 2005

'An invaluable guide to helping students and their advisers find their way through the maze of degree courses currently on offer'
Kath Wright, President, Association for Careers Education and Guidance, 2005

'No one is better informed or more experienced than Brian Heap in mediating this range of information to university and college applicants'
Careers Education and Guidance, October 2005

'The course-listings bible'
The Guardian, June 2005

'After consulting this you won't be able to say "I didn't know!" For every school library'
The Teacher, Nov 2003

'A must buy . . . one of the best single reference sources to degree course offers available'
Career Guidance Today, July 2003

'The most comprehensive guide is Degree Course Offers by Brian Heap'
John Clare in The Daily Telegraph, April 2003

'Degree Course Offers is an excellent resource and contains the type of information that prospective students and their parents need to know when making decisions about degree courses'
Mandy Telford, NUS National President, April 2003

'This guide gives a valuable and objective insight into the country's universities'
Will Straw, President, Oxford University Student Union, April 2003

'The Bible for university applicants provides detailed information on pretty much every course in the land'
The Northern Echo, April 2003

'Going to university is one of the biggest investment decisions you will ever make in your own future. In order to make the right choices, you need to be armed with fair and accurate information of the wide variety of institutions and courses open to you. Brian Heap's Degree Course Offers is an excellent source of information'
Rt Hon Charles Clarke MP, Secretary of State for Education and Skills, March 2003'

CONTENTS

AUTHOR'S ACKNOWLEDGEMENTS

This year, again, I must record my gratitude for the invaluable and extended support received from my daughter Jane Heap of Putney High School (staff), who has provided additional research and advice in the compilation of this edition.

I acknowledge gratefully the efforts of the many university and college registrars, schools liaison staff, faculty and departmental heads and admissions tutors in providing information about their admissions policies and courses. I appreciate, especially, the information and generosity of time given by admissions staff in the many universities and colleges who respond each year to the questionnaire research for *The Heap Guide*.

In particular, I should like to thank Tony Charlton, Caroline Russell and Jenny Vowles at UCAS, Sarah Hannaford of the University of Cambridge Admissions Office, Clare Woodcock of the University of Oxford Public Relations Office and Lee Hennessy, Head of Admissions at the University of Bath, for providing me with up-to-date information on admissions procedures. Additionally, my thanks are due to the Engineering Council UK for information about engineering courses and professional training, and to the Higher Education Statistics Agency (HESA) for the use of data in *Destinations of Leavers from Higher Education 2007/8*.

My thanks are due also to those admissions tutors, teachers and their pupils who have sent me interview reports and other information which has provided useful supplementary data for the book.

I also wish to thank Dianah Ellis for her continuing editorial work, advice and attention to detail, and also the many readers who have written to me about the problems they have encountered in choosing courses and places to study. Such information adds to a valuable store of knowledge which can be passed on, thereby creating a better understanding of mutual difficulties.

Finally, I should like to thank my wife Rita for her administrative help (and patience!) through 41 years of publication.

Brian Heap
March 2010

ABOUT THIS BOOK

University Degree Course Offers for 40 years has been a first-stop reference for university and college applicants choosing their courses in higher education by providing information from official sources about how to choose courses and how admissions tutors select students.

For 2010/11 higher education applicants, this new annual edition of ***University Degree Course Offers*** again aims to provide the latest possible information from universities to help equip them to obtain a degree course place in a fiercely competitive applications process. This level of competition will make it essential for every applicant to research carefully courses and institutions: latest statistics show that large numbers of even well-qualified applicants are not able to obtain university places and, because of the huge and increasing number of applicants and cuts in the number of places, the same will happen to applicants planning entry in 2011.

This creates problems for applicants. Because many universities and colleges are setting their offers higher for places on their courses in 2010 and 2011, how do applicants decide on a strategy to find a place on a degree course? There are more than 350 separate degree subjects and over 18,000 Joint and Combined Honours courses so how can applicants choose a course that is right for them, especially at a time of recession and employment difficulties? What can applicants do to find a course place and a university or college that is right for them?

University Degree Course Offers 2011 is intended to help applicants find their way through these problems by providing the latest possible information about university course offers from official sources, and by giving guidance and information about:

- **Degree courses** – what Honours level courses involve, the range and differences between them, and what applicants need to consider when choosing and deciding on subjects and courses
- **Universities and higher education colleges** – the range and differences between universities and colleges, and the questions applicants might ask when deciding where to study
- **Typical A/AS grade/UCAS points offers** (listed in points order in the Subject Tables in **Chapter 8**) for 2011 entry to Honours degree courses in universities and colleges, with additional Appendix data for applicants with IB, the Progression and Advanced Diplomas, the Extended Project, Scottish Highers, the Welsh Baccalaureate, the Irish Leaving Certificate and international qualifications
- **The UCAS applications process** – what to do, when to do it and how to prepare the personal statement in the UCAS Application
- **Universities' and colleges' admissions policies** – how admissions tutors select students
- **Which universities, colleges and courses use admissions tests for entry**
- **Finance, fees and sources of help**
- **Graduate destinations data for each subject area**
- **Action after Results Day** – and what to do if your grades don't match your offer
- **Entry to UK universities and higher education colleges for international students**

University Degree Course Offers provides essential information for all students preparing to go into higher education in 2011, covering all stages of researching, planning, deciding and applying to courses and universities. To provide the latest possible information the book is compiled each year between October and March for publication in May and includes important data from the many universities and colleges responding to questionnaires each year.

Every effort is made to ensure the book is as up to date as possible. Because many changes have occurred throughout the preparation of this year's edition, **Chapter 10** has been allocated to include late-coming admissions information, including newly-released information for applicants planning degree course entry with Advanced Diplomas and the new Cambridge Pre-U qualification.

Nevertheless, the increased demand for places and cuts in the number of places available are expected to lead to offers changes during 2010/11, and after prospectuses have been published. It will be essential for applicants to check institutions' websites **frequently** to find out any changes in offers, course availability and requirements. If you have any queries, contact admissions staff without delay to find out the latest information as institutions, for many courses, will be looking for a very close, if not precise, match between their requirements and what you offer in your application, qualifications and grades.

University Degree Course Offers 2011 is your starting point for moving on into higher education. Used in conjunction with *Choosing Your Degree Course & University* and *University Scholarships, Awards and Bursaries* (see Appendix 5) it will take you through all the stages in choosing the course and place of study which is right for you.

Brian Heap
March 2010

Every effort has been made to maintain absolute accuracy in providing course information and to ensure that the entire book is as up-to-date as possible. However, changes are constantly taking place in higher education so it is important for readers to check carefully with prospectuses and websites before submitting their applications.

1 | YOUR FIRST DECISIONS

HIGHER EDUCATION OR NOT?

Why do you want to go on to higher education? If you are taking GCE Advanced (AL) and Advanced Subsidiary (AS) qualifications, the International Baccalaureate, Scottish Highers and Advanced Highers, the Welsh Baccalaureate or the new Advanced Diploma this is an important question to ask. Last year (2009) there were approximately 630,000 applicants, with over 470,000 acceptances, for full-time first degree and diploma courses in the United Kingdom. However, higher education is just one of two options you have. The other is employment, and perhaps it is important to note that higher education is not necessarily the best option for everyone. It is one which is appropriate for many and, therefore, should not be rejected lightly. Higher education is likely to open many doors and give you opportunities for work and leisure that otherwise you might not have. Also, very often and quite accidentally, it can lead into careers that you might not have considered before.

Choosing your AS/A-levels (or equivalent qualifications) is done on the basis of your best subjects and those which you find most interesting. However, leading universities (and, especially, those with popular and competitive courses) will seek a grouping of subjects with 'academic weight'. Usually at least two AS/A-level academic subjects are required which are **not** on the following list:

Accounting, art and design, business studies, communication studies, dance, design and technology, drama/theatre studies, film studies, health and social care, home economics, information and communication, leisure studies, media studies, music technology, performance studies, performing arts, photography, physical education, sports studies, technology, travel and tourism.

If you are taking two or more of these subjects at AS/A-level you should check with your preferred universities.

Most courses in higher education lead to a degree or a diploma and for either you will have to make a subject choice. This can be difficult because the universities alone offer over 1200 degree subjects and over 50,000 courses within the UCAS scheme. You have two main options:

A Choosing a course that is either similar to, or the same as, one (or more) of your examination subjects, or related to an interest outside the school curriculum, such as Anthropology, American Studies, Archaeology. See **Section A** below.

B Choosing a course in preparation for a future career, for example Medicine, Architecture, Engineering. See **Section B** below and also **Appendix 2**.

SECTION A

Choosing your course by examination subjects

Deciding your degree or diploma course on the basis of your A-level (or equivalent) subjects is a reasonably safe option since already you are familiar with the subjects themselves and what they involve. Inevitably, long-term career prospects will be of some concern, especially in a period of economic recession. However, it is important to remember that a degree in higher education gives you many skills, including for example, those for critical thinking, assessment and research and, for many occupations, the degree subject is often not as important as the degree itself. If you are taking science subjects, they can lead naturally on to a range of scientific careers, although many scientists follow non-science careers such as law and accountancy. If you are taking arts or social science subjects, remember that specialist training for most non-scientific careers often starts once you have your degree.

When choosing your degree course by examination subjects it is important to consider the subjects you are taking at A-level (or equivalent) as universities may 'require' or 'prefer' certain subjects for entry to some courses. To make sure you have the right subjects, check the course subject requirements in university/college prospectuses and on their websites. Many universities, especially those giving high-level offers, have increasingly detailed A-level requirements, so it is very important that you find out the latest information. This also applies to GCSE subjects and grade requirements. When choosing AS-level subjects, students sometimes prefer to select those with a similar subject base, for example four science subjects, or four arts, or four humanities subjects. However, some institutions welcome one, or even two, contrasting subjects, even for specialist courses such as Medicine, providing the required subjects are also offered.

Subjects do not stand on their own, in isolation. Each subject you are taking is one of a much larger family. Each has many similarities to subjects studied in degree and diploma courses that you might never have considered, so before you decide finally on taking a subject to degree level read through the lists of A-level subjects below, each followed by examples of degree courses in the same subject field which will give you some idea of degree courses with similarities to the subjects you might be taking. (These lists are also useful if you have to consider alternative courses after the examination results are published!)

Accounting Accountancy, Accounting, Actuarial Mathematics, Banking and Finance, Business Studies (Finance), Economics, Finance Investment and Risk, Financial Mathematics, Financial Software Engineering, Management Sciences, Mathematics. See also **Section B**.

Ancient history Archaeology, Biblical Studies, Classical Greek, Classics and Classical Civilisation, Latin, Middle and Near Eastern Studies.

Arabic Arabic. See also **Languages** below.

Archaeology Ancient History, Anthropology, Archaeological Sciences, Archaeology, Bioarchaeology, Classical Civilisation, Conservation of Objects in Museums and Archaeology, Egyptology, Geology, History, Marine Archaeology, Viking Studies. See also **Section B**.

Art and design Art, Fine Art, Furniture Design, Graphic Design, Photography, Textile Design, Theatre Design, Three Dimensional Design, Typography and Graphic Communication. See also **Section B**.

Bengali Bengali. See also **Languages** below.

Biblical Hebrew Hebrew, Religious Studies, Theology.

Biology Agricultural Sciences, Animal Behaviour, Bioinformatics, Biological Sciences, Biology, Biomedical Sciences, Biotechnology, Ecology and Conservation, Environmental Sciences, Genetics, Human Embryology, Infection and Immunity, Life Sciences, Medicine, Microbiology, Molecular Sciences, Natural Sciences, Physiology, Plant Biology, Veterinary Science, Zoology. See also **Section B**.

Business Accounting, Banking, Business Management, Business Statistics, Computing, Economics, Entrepreneurship, Finance, Hospitality Management, Human Resource Management, Information Systems, Logistics, Management Sciences, Marketing, Mathematics, Publishing, Retail Management, Transport Management, Web Design and Development. See also **Section B**.

Chemistry Biochemistry, Chemical Engineering, Chemical Physics, Chemistry, Environmental Sciences, Fire Engineering, Forensic Sciences, Medicinal Chemistry, Natural Sciences, Nutritional Biochemistry, Pharmacology, Pharmacy. See also **Section B**.

Chinese Chinese. See also **Languages** below.

Classics and classical civilisation Ancient History, Archaeology, Classical Studies, Classics, Greek (Classical), Latin.

Communication studies Advertising, Communications Studies, Drama, Education, English Language, Information and Library Studies, Journalism, Languages, Linguistics, Media and Communications, Psychology, Public Relations, Publishing, Speech Sciences. See also **Section B**.

Computing Artificial Intelligence, Business Information Systems, Computer Engineering, Computer Science, Computing, Cybernetics, E-Commerce, Electronic Engineering, Games Technology, Intelligent Product Design, Multimedia Systems Engineering, Network Management and Security, Robotics, Software Engineering. See also **Section B**.

Critical thinking (Check acceptability with universities and colleges: subject may not be included in offers.)

Dance Arts Management, Ballet Education, Choreography, Dance, Drama, Education, Music, Musical Theatre, Performance Management, Performing Arts, Sport and Exercise, Street Arts, Theatre and Performance, Theatre Arts, Writing Directing and Performance. See also **Section B**.

Design technology Food Technology, Manufacturing Engineering, Product Design, Sport Equipment Design, Systems and Control. See also **Section B**.

Drama and theatre studies Acting, Community Drama, Costume Production, Creative Writing, Dance, Drama, Education Studies, English Comedy: Writing and Performance, International Theatre, Music, Performing Arts, Scenic Arts, Scriptwriting, Set Design, Stage Management, Theatre Arts, Theatre Practice. See also **Section B**.

Dutch Dutch. See also **Languages** below.

Economics Accountancy, Banking, Business Administration, Business Economics, Business Studies, Development Studies, Economics, Estate Management, Finance, Management Science, Mathematics, Political Economy, Politics, Quantity Surveying, Sociology, Statistics.

Electronics Computing, Electronics, Engineering (Aeronautical, Aerospace, Communication, Computer, Software, Systems), Mechatronics, Medical Electronics, Multimedia Technology, Technology. See also **Section B**.

English language and literature Communications Studies, Comparative Literature, Creative Writing, Drama, Education, English Language, English Literature, Information and Library Studies/Management, Journalism, Linguistics, Media Writing, Publishing, Scottish Literature, Scriptwriting, Theatre Studies.

Environmental sciences Biological Sciences, Biology, Earth Sciences, Ecology, Environment and Planning, Environmental Management, Environmental Sciences, Forestry, Geography, Geology, Land Management, Marine Biology, Meteorology, Oceanography, Outdoor Education, Plant Sciences, Sustainable Development, Wastes Management, Water Science, Wildlife Biology, Wildlife Conservation, Zoology.

French French, International Business Studies, International Hospitality Management, Law with French Law. See also **Languages** below.

General studies (Check acceptability with universities and colleges: subject may not be included in offers.)

Geography Development Studies, Earth Sciences, Environmental Policy, Environmental Sciences, Estate Management, Forestry, Geographical Information Science, Geography, Geology, Land Economy, Meteorology, Oceanography, Surveying, Town and Country Planning, Urban Studies, Water Science.

Geology Earth Sciences, Geography, Geology, Geophysical Sciences, Geosciences, Meteorology, Mining Engineering, Natural Sciences, Oceanography, Palaeontology and Evolution, Planetary Sciences, Water and Environmental Management. See also **Section B**.

German German, International Business Studies, International Hospitality Management, Law with German Law. See also **Languages** below.

Government/Politics Development Studies, Economics, Global Politics, Government, History, Human Rights, Industrial Relations, International Politics, Law, Peace Studies, Politics, Public Administration, Social and Political Science, Social Policy, Sociology, Strategic Studies, War Studies.

Gujarati Gujarati. See also **Languages** below.

Health and social care Early Childhood Studies, Environmental Health, Health and Social Care, Health Promotion, Health Psychology, Health Sciences, Health Studies, Nursing, Nutrition, Public Health, Social Sciences, Social Work, Sport and Health, Working with Children and Young People, Youth and Community Work. See also **Section B**.

History African Studies, American Studies, Archaeology, Art History, Classical Civilisations, Education, Egyptology, Fashion and Dress History, History, International Relations, Law, Literature, Medieval Studies, Museum and Heritage Studies, Philosophy, Politics, Russian Studies, Scandinavian Studies, Scottish History, Social and Economic History, Victorian Studies.

Home economics Culinary Arts Management, Design and Technology Education, Food and Consumer Management, Food Science, Home Economics (Food Design and Technology), Hospitality Management, Nutrition.

Information and communication technology Business Information Systems, Communications Systems Design, Communications Technology, Digital Communications, Electrical and Electronic Engineering, Geographic Information Science, Information and Library Studies, Information Management, Information Sciences, Information Systems, Internet Engineering, Mobile Computing, Multimedia Computing, Telecommunications Engineering. See also **Section B**.

Italian Italian. See also **Languages** below.

Japanese Japanese. See also **Languages** below.

Languages Languages, Modern Languages, Translating and Interpreting. **NB** Apart from French and German – and Spanish for some universities – it is not usually necessary to have completed an A-level language course before studying the many languages (over 60) offered at degree level. Many universities provide opportunities to study a language in a wide range of degree courses. See also **the Erasmus programme** details below.

Law Criminal Justice, Criminology, European Business Law, Human Rights, International Business, International Relations, Law, Legal Studies, Police Sciences, Social Sciences, Sociology, Youth Justice. See also **Section B**.

Leisure studies Adventure Tourism Management, Countryside Recreation and Tourism, Equine Business Management, Events Management, Fitness and Health, Health and Leisure Studies, Hospitality and Leisure Management, Leisure Marketing, Outdoor Leadership, Personal Fitness Training, Sport and Leisure Management, Sport Leisure and Culture, Sports Education, Tourism Management, Tourism Marketing.

Mathematics Accountancy, Actuarial Mathematics, Aeronautical Engineering, Astrophysics, Business Management, Chemical Engineering, Civil Engineering, Computational Science, Computer Systems Engineering, Control Systems Engineering, Cybernetics, Economics, Engineering Science, Ergonomics, Financial Mathematics, Further and Additional Mathematics, Geophysics, Management Science, Materials Science and Technology, Mechanical Engineering, Meteorology, Naval Architecture, Physics, Quantity Surveying, Statistics, Systems Analysis, Telecommunications.

Media studies Advertising, Animation, Broadcasting, Communication Studies, Creative Writing, English, Film and Television Studies, Journalism, Mass Communication, Media courses, Media Culture and Society, Media Production, Media Technology, Multimedia, Photography, Publishing, Radio Production and Communication, Society Culture and Media, Translation Media and French/Spanish, Web and Broadcasting. See also **Section B**.

Modern Greek Greek. See also **Languages** above.

Modern Hebrew Hebrew. See also **Languages** above.

Music Actor, Audio and Music Production, Creative Music Technology, Education, Music, Music Broadcasting, Music Informatics, Music Management, Music Systems Engineering, Musical Theatre, Musician, Performance Arts, Popular and World Music, Sonic Arts. See also **Section B**.

Persian Persian. See also **Languages** above.

Philosophy Classical Studies, Cultural Studies, Divinity, Educational Studies, Ethics, History of Ideas, History of Science, Law, Mathematics, Natural Sciences, Philosophy, Politics, Philosophy and Economics, Psychology, Religious Studies, Social Sciences, Theology.

Physics Aeronautical Engineering, Architecture, Astronomy, Astrophysics, Automotive Engineering, Biomedical Engineering, Biophysics, Chemical Physics, Civil Engineering, Communications Engineering, Computer Science, Cybernetics, Education, Electrical/Electronic Engineering, Engineering Science, Ergonomics, Geophysics, Materials Science and Technology, Mechanical Engineering, Medical Physics,

Meteorology, Nanotechnology, Naval Architecture, Oceanography, Optometry, Photonics, Planetary Science, Quantum Informatics, Radiography, Renewable Energy, Telecommunications Engineering.

Polish Polish. See also **Languages** above.

Portuguese Portuguese. See also **Languages** above.

Psychology Advertising, Animal Behaviour, Anthropology, Artificial Intelligence, Behavioural Science, Childhood Strudies, Cognitive Science, Counselling Studies, Criminology, Education, Human Resource Management, Marketing, Neuroscience, Nursing, Politics, Psychology, Social Sciences, Sociology, Speech and Language Therapy. See also **Section B**.

Punjabi Punjabi. See also **Languages** above.

Religious studies Abrahamic Religions (Christianity, Islam and Judaism), Anthropology, Archaeology, Biblical Studies, Christian Youth Work, Comparative Religion, Divinity, Education, Ethics, History of Art, International Relations, Islamic Studies, Jewish Studies, Philosophy, Psychology, Religious Studies, Social Policy, Theology.

Russian Russian. See also **Languages** above.

Sport and physical education Chiropractic, Coaching Science, Community Sport Development, Dance Studies, Exercise and Health, Exercise Science, Fitness Science, Football Studies, Golf Studies, Osteopathy, Outdoor Pursuits, Physical Education, Physiotherapy, Sport and Exercise Science, Sport and Health, Sport Coaching, Sport Equipment Design, Sport Management, Sport Marketing, Teaching (Primary) (Secondary).

Statistics Actuarial Studies, Business Analysis, Business Studies, Informatics, Management Sciences, Statistics. See also Mathematics above and **Section B** Mathematics-related careers.

Travel and tourism See **Section B**.

Turkish Turkish. See also **Languages** above.

Urdu Urdu. See also **Languages** above.

SECTION B

Choosing your course by career interests

An alternative strategy for deciding on the subject of your degree or diploma course is to relate it to your career interests. However, even though you may have set your mind on a particular career, it is important to remember that sometimes there are others which are very similar to your planned career. The following lists give examples of career areas, each followed by examples of degree subjects in the subject field.

Accountancy Accountancy, Accounting, Actuarial Science, Banking, Business Studies, Economics, Finance and Business, Finance and Investment, Financial Services, Management Science, Real Estate Management, Risk Management.

Actuarial work Actuarial Mathematics, Actuarial Science, Actuarial Studies, Financial Mathematics, Risk Analysis and Insurance.

Agricultural careers Agri-Business, Agricultural Engineering, Agriculture, Animal Sciences, Aquaculture and Fishery Sciences, Conservation and Habitat Management, Countryside Management, Crop Science, Ecology, Environmental Science, Estate Management, Forestry, Horticulture, Landscape Management, Plant Sciences, Rural Resource Management, Soil Science, Wildlife Management.

Animal careers Agricultural Sciences, Animal Behaviour and Welfare, Biological Sciences, Bioveterinary Science, Equine Management/Science/Studies, Veterinary Nursing, Veterinary Practice Management, Veterinary Science, Zoology.

Archaeology Ancient History, Anthropology, Archaeology, Bioarchaeology, Classical Civilisation and Classics, Egyptology, Geography, History, History of Art and Architecture, Viking Studies.

Architecture Architectural Design, Architectural Technology, Architecture, Building, Building Conservation, City and Regional Planning, Civil Engineering, Conservation and Restoration, Construction Engineering and Management, Interior Architecture, Stained Glass Restoration and Conservation, Structural Engineering.

Art and Design careers Advertising, Animation, Architecture, Art, Design, Digital Media Design, Education (Art), Fashion and Textiles, Fine Art, Games Art and Design, Glassware, Graphic Design, Illustration, Industrial Design, Jewellery, Landscape Architecture, Photography, Stained Glass, Three Dimensional Design.

Astronomy Astronomy, Astrophysics, Mathematics, Natural Sciences, Planetary Geology, Physics, Quantum and Cosmological Physics, Space Science, Space Technology and Planetary Exploration.

Audiology Audiology, Education of the Deaf, Human Communication, Nursing, Speech and Language Therapy.

Banking/Insurance Accountancy, Actuarial Sciences, Banking, Business Studies, Economics, Financial Services, Insurance, Real Estate Management, Risk Management.

Biology-related careers Agricultural Sciences, Animal Sciences, Biochemistry, Biological Sciences, Biology, Biomedical Sciences, Biotechnology, Cell Biology, Ecology, Education, Environmental Biology, Environmental Sciences, Freshwater Science, Genetics, Immunology, Life Sciences, Marine Biology, Medical Biochemistry, Medicine, Microbiology, Molecular Biology, Natural Sciences, Oceanography, Pharmacy, Plant Science, Physiology, Wildlife Conservation.

Book Publishing Advertising, Business Studies, Communications, Creative Writing, Illustration, Journalism, Media Communication, Photography, Printing, Publishing, Science Communication, Web and Multimedia.

Brewing and Distilling Biochemistry, Brewing and Distilling, Chemistry, Food Science and Technology, Viticulture and Oenology.

Broadcasting Audio Video and Digital Broadcast Engineering, Broadcast Documentary, Broadcast Media, Broadcast Technology and Production, Digital Media, Electronic Engineering (Broadcast Systems), Film and TV Broadcasting, Media and Communications Studies, Media Production, Multimedia, Music Broadcasting, Outside Broadcast Technology, Radio Journalism, Television Studio Production, TV Production, Video and Broadcasting.

Building Architecture, Building Conservation, Building Services Engineering, Building Studies, Building Surveying, Civil Engineering, Estate Management, General Practice Surveying, Land Surveying, Quantity Surveying.

Business Accountancy, Advertising, Banking, Business Administration, Business Analysis, Business Studies, Business Systems, E-Commerce, Economics, Estate Management, European Business, Hospitality Management, Housing Management, Human Resource Management, Industrial Relations, Insurance, Logistics, Management Sciences, Marketing, Property Development, Public Relations, Publishing, Supply Chain Management, Transport Management, Tourism

Cartography Geographic Information Systems, Geographical Information Science, Geography, Land Surveying.

Catering Consumer Studies, Culinary Arts Management, Dietetics, Food Science, Hospitality Management, International and Hospitality Business Management, Nutrition.

Chemistry-related careers Agricultural Science, Biochemistry, Botany, Ceramics, Chemical Engineering, Chemistry, Colour Chemistry, Education, Environmental Sciences, Geochemistry, Materials Science and Technology, Medical Chemistry, Nanotechnology, Natural Sciences, Pharmacology, Pharmacy, Physiology, Technologies (for example Food, Plastics).

Computing Artificial Intelligence, Bioinformatics, Business Computing, Business Studies, Computer Engineering, Computer Games Development, Computer Science, Computers, Electronics and Communications, Digital Forensics and System Security, Electronic Engineering, Games Design, Information and Communication Technology, Internet Computing, Mathematics, Multimedia Computing, Physics, Software Systems, Telecommunications, Virtual Reality Design.

Construction Architectural Technology, Architecture, Building, Building Services Engineering, Civil Engineering, Construction Management, Fire Risk Engineering, Landscape Architecture, Quantity Surveying, Surveying, Town and Country Planning.

Dance Ballet Education, Choreography, Dance, Drama, Movement Studies, Performance/Performing Arts, Physical Education, Theatre Studies.

Dentistry Biochemistry, Dental Materials, Dental Technician, Dentistry, Equine Dentistry, Medicine, Nursing, Oral Health Sciences, Pharmacy.

Drama Dance, Drama, Education, Movement Studies, Musical Theatre, Scenic Arts, Teaching, Theatre Management.

Education Ballet Education, British Sign Language, Childhood Studies, Coach Education, Deaf Studies, Early Years Education, Education Studies, Education with QTS, Education without QTS, Music Education, Physical Education, Primary Education, Psychology, Secondary Education, Social Work, Special Educational Needs, Speech and Language Therapy, Sport and Exercise, Teaching, Technology for Teaching and Learning, Youth Studies.

Electronics Automotive Electronics, Avionics, Computer Systems, Computer Technology, Computing, Digital Electronics, Digital Media Technology, Electronic Design, Electronic Engineering, Electronics, Information Systems, Internet Engineering, Mechatronics, Medical Electronics, Motorsport Electronic Systems, Multimedia Computing, Software Development, Sound Engineering.

Engineering Engineering (including Aeronautical, Aerospace, Chemical, Civil, Computing, Control, Electrical, Electronics, Energy, Environmental, Food Process, Manufacturing, Mechanical, Motorsport, Nuclear, Product Design, Software, Telecommunications Electronics), Geology and Geotechnics, Horology, Mathematics, Physics.

Estate Management Architecture, Building, Civil Engineering, Economics, Estate Management, Forestry, Housing Studies, Landscape Architecture, Property Development, Real Estate Management, Town and Country Planning.

Food Science and Technology Biochemistry, Brewing and Distilling, Chemistry, Culinary Arts, Dietetics, Food and Consumer Studies, Food Safety Management, Food Science and Technology, Food Supply Chain Management, Fresh Produce Management, Hospitality and Food Management, Nutrition, Public Health Nutrition, Viticulture and Oenology.

Forestry Arboriculture, Biological Sciences, Countryside Management, Ecology, Environmental Science, Forestry, Horticulture, Plant Sciences, Rural Resource Management, Tropical Forestry, Urban Forestry.

Furniture Design Furniture Design, Furniture Production, History of Art and Design, Three Dimensional Design, Timber Technology.

Geology-related careers Chemistry, Earth Sciences, Engineering (Civil, Minerals), Environmental Sciences, Geochemistry, Geography, Geology, Land Surveying, Oceanography, Soil Science.

Graphic Design Advertising, Graphic Design, Photography, Printing, Web Design.

Health and Safety careers Biomedical Informatics, Biomedical Sciences, Community and Health Studies, Environmental Health, Exercise and Health Science, Fire Science Engineering, Health and Social Care, Health Management, Health Promotion, Health Psychology, Health Sciences, Holistic Therapy, Nursing, Occupational Safety and Health, Paramedic Science, Public Health, Public Services Management. (See also Medical careers.)

Horticulture Agriculture, Botany, Crop Science, Horticulture, Landscape Architecture, Plant Science, Soil Science.

Hospitality Management Business and Management, Culinary Arts Management, Events and Facilities Management, Food Science, Food Technology, Heritage Management, Hospitality Management, Human Resource Management, International Hospitality Management, Leisure Services Management, Licensed Retail Management, Spa Management, Travel and Tourism Management.

Housing Architecture, Estate Management, General Practice Surveying, Housing, Social Administration, Town and Country Planning.

Law Business Law, Commercial Law, Consumer Law, Criminal Justice, Criminology, European Law, Government and Politics, International History, Land Management, Law, Legal Studies, Politics, Sociology.

Leisure and Recreation Adventure Tourism, Airline and Airport Management, Business Travel and Tourism, Community Arts, Countryside Management, Dance, Drama, Event Management, Fitness Science, Hospitality Management, International Tourism Management, Leisure Management, Movement Studies, Music, Physical Education, Sport and Leisure Management, Sport Development, Sports Management, Theatre Studies, Travel and Tourism.

Library and Information Management Administration, Business Information Systems, Digital Media, Education Studies, Information and Communication Studies, Information and Library Studies, Information Management, Information Sciences and Technology, Management and Marketing, Media and Cultural Studies, Media Communications, Museum and Galleries Studies, Publishing.

Marketing Advertising, Business Studies, Consumer Science, E-Marketing, Health Promotion, International Business, Marketing, Psychology, Public Relations, Retail Management, Sports Development, Travel and Tourism.

Materials Science/Metallurgy Automotive Materials, Chemistry, Engineering, Glass Science and Technology, Materials Science and Technology, Mineral Surveying, Physics, Polymer Science, Sports Materials, Textile Science.

Mathematics-related careers Accountancy, Actuarial Science, Astronomy, Banking, Business Decision Mathematics, Business Studies, Computer Studies, Economics, Education, Engineering, Financial Mathematics, Mathematical Physics, Mathematics, Physics, Quantity Surveying, Statistics.

Media careers Advertising, Broadcasting, Communications, Computer Graphics, Creative Writing, Film/Video Production, Journalism, Media, Multimedia, Photography, Public Relations, Psychology, Visual Communication.

Medical careers Anatomy, Biochemistry, Biological Sciences, Biomedical Sciences, Chiropractic, Dentistry, Genetics, Human Physiology, Immunology, Medical Engineering, Medical Sciences/Medicine, Nursing, Occupational Therapy, Orthoptics, Osteopathy, Pathology and Microbiology, Pharmacology, Pharmacy, Physiotherapy, Radiography, Speech and Language Therapy, Sports Biomedicine, Virology.

Music Commercial Music, Creative Music Technology, Digital Music, Drama, Folk and Traditional Music, Music, Music Composition, Music Education, Music Industry Management, Music Performance, Music Production, Music Studies, Musical Theatre, Performance/Performing Arts, Popular Music, Sonic Arts, Sound and Multimedia Technology, Theatre Studies.

Nautical careers Marine Engineering, Marine Studies, Nautical Studies, Naval Architecture, Oceanography, Offshore Engineering, Ship Science.

Naval Architecture Boat Design, Marine Engineering, Marine Studies, Naval Architecture, Offshore Engineering, Ship Science, Yacht and Powercraft Design, Yacht Production.

Nursing Anatomy, Applied Biology, Biochemistry, Biological Sciences, Biology, Dentistry, Education, Environmental Health and Community Studies, Health Studies, Human Biology, Medicine, Midwifery, Nursing, Occupational Therapy, Orthoptics, Physiotherapy, Podiatry, Psychology, Radiography, Social Administration, Speech and Language Therapy, Veterinary Nursing. (See also **Medical careers**.)

Nutrition Dietetics, Food Science and Technology, Health Promotion, Human Nutrition, Nursing, Nutrition, Sport and Fitness.

Occupational Therapy Art, Nursing, Occupational Therapy, Orthoptics, Physiotherapy, Psychology, Social Sciences, Speech and Language Therapy.

Optometry Applied Physics, Optometry, Orthoptics, Physics.

Photography/Film/TV Animation, Communication Studies (some courses), Digital Video Design, Documentary Communications, Film and Media, Graphic Art, Media Studies, Moving Image, Multimedia, Photography.

Physics-related careers Applied Physics, Astronomy, Astrophysics, Avionics and Space Systems, Education, Electronics, Engineering (Civil, Electrical, Mechanical), Laser Physics, Mathematical Physics, Medical Instrumentation, Molecular Physics, Nanotechnology, Natural Sciences, Optometry, Physics, Planetary and Space Physics, Quantum and Cosmological Physics, Theoretical Physics.

Physiotherapy Chiropractic, Exercise Science, Nursing, Orthoptics, Osteopathy, Physical Education, Physiotherapy, Sport and Exercise, Sports Rehabilitation.

Production Technology Engineering (Mechanical, Manufacturing), Materials Science.

Property and Valuation Management Architecture, Building Surveying, Estate Agency, Property Investment and Finance, Property Management and Valuation, Quantity Surveying, Real Estate Management, Residential Property, Urban Land Economics.

Psychology Advertising, Animal Sciences, Anthropology, Applied Social Studies, Behavioural Science, Business, Cognitive Science, Criminology, Early Childhood Studies, Education, Human Resource Management, Human Sciences, Linguistics, Marketing, Neuroscience, Occupational Therapy, Psychology (Clinical, Developmental, Educational, Experimental, Forensic, Health, Occupational, Social, Sports), Psychosocial Sciences, Public Relations, Social Sciences, Sociology.

Public Administration Applied Social Studies, Business Studies, Public Administration, Public Policy Investment and Management, Public Services, Social Administration, Social Policy, Youth Studies.

Quantity Surveying Accountancy, Architecture, Building, Civil Engineering, Construction and Commercial Management Surveying Technology, Environmental Construction Surveying, Quantity Surveying, Surveying (Building, Land, Quantity and Valuation).

Radiography Anatomy, Audiology, Biological Sciences, Clinical Photography, Diagnostic Imaging, Diagnostic Radiography, Digital Imaging, Imaging Science and Technology, Medical Imaging, Moving Image, Nursing, Orthoptics, Photography, Physics, Physiology, Physiotherapy, Radiography, Radiotherapy, Therapeutic Radiography.

Silversmithing/Jewellery Design Silversmithing and Jewellery, Silversmithing Goldsmithing and Jewellery, Silversmithing Metalwork and Jewellery, Three Dimensional Design.

Social Work Abuse Studies, Applied Social Science, Community Work, Counselling Studies, Early Childhood Studies, Education, Health and Social Care, Human Rights, Journalism, Law, Nursing, Playwork, Politics and Government, Psychology, Public Administration, Religious Studies, Social Administration, Social Policy, Social Work, Sociology, Town and Country Planning, Youth Studies.

Speech and Language Therapy Audiology, Education (Special Education), Linguistics, Nursing, Occupational Therapy, Psychology, Radiography, Speech and Language Therapy.

Sport and Physical Education Coaching Sciences, Exercise Sciences, Fitness Science, Health and Fitness Management, Leisure and Recreation Management, Physical Education, Sport and Recreational Studies, Sport Journalism, Sports Psychology, Sports Science; Sports Studies.

Statistics Business Studies, Economics, Informatics, Mathematics, Operational Research, Population Sciences, Statistics.

Surveying Building Surveying, General Practice Surveying, Property Development, Quantity Surveying, Real Estate Management.

Technology Audio Technology, Dental Technology, Design Technology, Food Science and Technology, Football Technology, Logistics Technology, Medical Technology, Music Studio Technology, Paper Science, Polymer Science, Product Design Technology, Sports Technology, Technology for Teaching and Learning, Timber Technology.

Textile Design Applied Art and Design, Art, Clothing Studies, Fashion Design, Interior Design, Textile Design (Embroidery, Constructive Textiles, Printed Textiles), Textile Management.

Theatre Design Drama, Interior Design, Leisure and Recreational Studies, Theatre Design, Theatre Management, Theatre Studies.

Three Dimensional Design Architecture, Industrial Design, Interior Design, Theatre Design, Three Dimensional Design.

Town and Regional Planning Architecture, Architecture and Planning, City and Regional Planning, Environmental Planning, Estate Management, Geography, Housing, Land Economy, Planning and Development, Population Sciences, Property Planning and Development, Spatial Planning, Statistics, Sustainable Development, Town and Regional Planning, Transport Management, Urban and Regional Planning.

Transport Air Transport Engineering, Air Transport Operations, Air Transport with Pilot Training, Business Studies, Civil and Transportation Engineering, Cruise Operations Management, Industrial Design Transport, Logistics, Planning with Transport, Supply Chain Management, Sustainable Transport Design, Town and Regional Planning, Urban Planning Design and Management.

Typography and Graphic Communication Design (Graphic and Typographic Design), Digital Graphics, Fine Art (Print and Digital Media), Graphic Communication and Typography, Graphic Design, Illustration, Illustration and Print, Printmaking, Publication Design, Publishing, Visual Communication.

Veterinary careers Agricultural Sciences, Agriculture, Anatomical Science, Animal Behaviour and Welfare, Animal Sciences, Bioveterinary Sciences, Equine Dentistry, Equine Science, Medicine, Pharmacology, Pharmacy, Veterinary Medicine, Veterinary Nursing, Veterinary Practice Management, Zoology.

COURSE TYPES AND DIFFERENCES

You will then need to decide on the type of course you want to follow. The way in which Honours degree courses are arranged differs between institutions. For example, a subject might be offered as a single subject course (a Single Honours degree), or as a two-subject course (a Joint Honours degree), or as one of two, three or four subjects (a Combined Honours degree) or a major-minor degree (75% and 25% of each subject respectively). The chapter **University Course Profiles** gives more information about the different types of courses and provides for each university a resumé of the ways their courses are structured and the range of courses they offer.

Courses in the same subject at different universities and colleges can have different subject requirements so it is important to check the acceptability of your GCE A/AS and GCSE subjects (or equivalent) for all your preferred courses. Specific GCE A/AS-levels, and in some cases, GCSE subjects, may be stipulated. (See also **Chapter 7** and **Appendix 1** for information on the International Baccalaureate, Scottish Highers/Advanced Highers, the Welsh Baccalaureate, the Cambridge Pre-U Diploma, the Advanced Diploma, the Extended Project and the Irish Leaving Certificate, and **Appendix 1** for international qualifications.)

SANDWICH COURSES AND PROFESSIONAL PLACEMENTS

One variation on Single Honours courses is that of the sandwich course, in which students will spend part of their degree course on professional, industrial or commercial placements. Media coverage on student debt and the introduction of tuition fees (see **Chapter 2**) highlight the importance of sandwich courses. Many sandwich and placement courses are on offer, in which industrial, commercial and public sector placements take place in the third year of a four-year degree course. For example, there is the Work-Based Learning (WBL) programme which Chester University established several years ago, with some other institutions following suit, in which students take a WBL module in the second year of their degree course. This involves a placement lasting a few weeks when students can have the opportunity to try out possible careers. Other universities and colleges may offer longer placements of periods of six months with different employers for students taking vocational courses.

However, the most structured arrangements are known as 'professional placements' which a number of universities offer and which are very advantageous to students (see the subject tables in **Chapter 8** and university/college websites and prospectuses). Although placements in some fields such as health, social care, education may be unpaid, in most cases a salary is paid. Where a placement is unpaid the placement period is shorter – 30 weeks – to allow students time to undertake paid work. It is important to note that during the placement year students' tuition fees will be reduced by 50% except for those on one-year courses on the Erasmus programme (see below) when no fees are paid but student loans will still apply.

The advantages of sandwich courses are quite considerable although students should be aware that in the present period of recession safeguards are necessary when selecting courses and universities. While students can arrange their own placement, with the approval of their Head of Department, it is more usual for university staff to make contacts with firms and to recommend students. With the present cutbacks, however, some firms may be less likely to take on students or to pay them during their placement. Consequently, this is an important issue to raise with admissions tutors before applying and it is important also to find out how your studies would continue if placements are not possible.

To help you to consider the advantages of sandwich courses, included below are views of some students, employers and university staff. They could well help you decide whether a four-year sandwich course is, for you, preferable to a three-year full-time degree.

Students report . . .

'I was able to earn £15,000 during my year out and £4000 during my three-month vacation with the same firm.' (**Bath** Engineering)

'There's really no other better way to find out what you want to do for your future career than having tried it for a year.' (**Aston** Human Resources Management)

'It was a welcome break in formal university education: I met some great people including students from other universities.' (**Kingston** Biochemistry)

'Having experienced a year in a working environment, I am more confident and more employable than students without this experience.' (**Aston** Business Studies)

'At Sanolfi in Toulouse, I learned to think on my feet – no two days were the same.' (**Aston** European Studies)

'I have seen how an organisation works at first-hand, learned how academic skills may be applied in a working environment, become proficient in the use of various software, acquired new skills in interpersonal relationships and communications and used my period away to realign my career perspectives.' (**Aston** European Studies)

'I was working alongside graduate employees and the firm offered me a job when I graduated.' (**Bath** Mathematics)

Employers, too, gain from having students . . .

'We meet a lot of enthusiastic potential recruits who bring new ideas into the firm, and we can offer them commercially sponsored help for their final year project.'

'The quality of this student has remained high throughout the year. He will do well for his next employer, whoever that may be. However, I sincerely hope that it will be with us.'

University staff advise . . .

'We refer to sandwich courses as professional placements, not "work experience" which is a phrase we reserve for short non-professional experiences, for example summer or pre-university jobs. The opportunity is available to all students but their success in gaining a good placement depends on academic ability.' (**Bath**)

'Where a placement year is optional, those who opt for it are more likely to be awarded a First or an Upper Second compared to those who don't, not because they are given more marks for doing it, but because they always seem to have added context and motivation for their final year.' (**Aston**)

When choosing your sandwich course, check with the university (a) that the institution will guarantee a list of employers (b) whether placement experience counts towards the final degree result (c) that placements are paid (d) that placements are validated by professional bodies.

Finally, once you start on the course, remember that your first-year academic performance will be taken into account by potential employers. Now read on!

What do employers require when considering students?

Aston (Biol) Successful second year undergraduates; (Bus) Number of UCAS points, degree programme, any prior experience; (Eng) UCAS points scores and expected degree classification; (Mech Eng) Students interviewed and selected by the company according to student ability, what they are studying and specific needs of the job. **Bath** (Chem) 'Good students': Upper Second or above and non-international students (those without work visas). Students with strong vivisection views rejected; (Mech Elec Eng) Subject-based, eg electronics, aerospace, computing and electrical engineering; (Mech Eng) Good communication, IT and social skills; (Maths) Interest in positions of responsibility, teamwork, integrity, self-motivation, analytical ability, communication, recent work experience, knowledge of the company, desire to work for the company; GCSE maths/English A/B, AL 300 UCAS points minimum (excluding general studies), predicted 2.1; (Phys) Many organisations have cut-offs regarding students' first-year performance (eg must be heading for a 2.1 although some require better than this), some need students to be particularly good in some areas (eg lab work, computer programming), many require UK nationality with minimum residency condition. **Brunel** Requirements not usually specified except for IT jobs since they need technical skills. **Cardiff (UWIC)** (Clsrm Asst) Criminal Records Bureau (CRB) checks. **Kingston** (Bus Law) Theoretical knowledge and a stated interest in certain areas (eg finance, human resources, marketing, sales, IT), excellent communication skills, teamwork, ability to prioritise, time management and a professional attitude; (Sci) Grades are rarely mentioned: it's usually a specific module or course requirement undertaken by the students that they are looking for, as well as a good attitude, motivation, initiative: a good all-rounder. **Loughborough** (Civ Eng) Target specific courses.

What are the advantages of placements to the students?

Aston (Biol) Many take jobs with their placement employers (eg NHS), gaining valuable research and clinical experience; (Bus) Graduate job offers, sponsorship through the final year of the course, gym membership, staff discounts; (Eng) Some students are fast-tracked into full-time employment and, in some cases, have been given higher starting salaries as a result of the placement with the company; (Mech Eng) Offers of full-time employment on graduation, bursaries for their final year of study, final year projects following placements, better class of degree. **Bath** (Chem) Sponsorships for final year project work, offers of full-time employment, PhD offers and work-to-study courses, industrial references, establishment of prizes; (Maths) Sponsorship in the second year, graduate employment, bonuses during placement, travel abroad during placement, sponsorship during final year; (Phys) Job offers on graduation, sponsored final year, improved study skills for final year, job market awareness, career decisions. **Brunel** Higher percentage of students get Firsts, many students get a job offer from the placement provider, higher salaries often paid to sandwich course students, some students get exemptions from professional exams, eg ACCA, ACA and IMechE. **Cardiff (UWIC)** (Clsrm Asst) Good experience in team work, classroom experience, coaching, mentoring: decisions made whether or not to follow a teaching career. **Kingston** (Bus Law) Sponsorships fewer these days but students return with more confidence and maturity and better able to complete their final year; 60% receive job offers on completion of a successful placement; (Sci) Full-time employment on graduation and occasionally part-time work in the final year; many students are encouraged to write their final year dissertation whilst on placement and benefit from the company's support, subject matter and validation. **Loughborough** (Civ Eng) Most students are sponsored by their firms and perform better in their final examinations; (Prod Des) Final year bursary for some students, offer of employment by the sponsor and a final year design project for the sponsor.

MODULAR COURSES AND CREDIT ACCUMULATION AND TRANSFER SCHEMES (CATS)

Courses can also differ considerably not only in their content but in how they are organised. Many universities and colleges of higher education have modularised their courses which means you can choose modules of different subjects, and 'build' your course within specified 'pathways' with the help and approval of your course tutor. It also means that you are likely to be assessed after completing each module, rather than in your last year for all your previous years' learning. In almost every course the options and modules offered include some which reflect the research interests of individual members of staff. In some courses subsidiary subjects are available as minor courses alongside a Single Honours course. In an increasing number of courses these additional subjects include a European language, and the importance of this cannot be over-emphasised with the United Kingdom's membership of the European Union. Such links are also reinforced by way of the Erasmus Programme (see below) which enables university students to apply for courses in Europe for periods of up to a year, some of the courses being taught in English.

Many institutions have introduced credit accumulation and transfer schemes (CATS). These allow students to be awarded credits for modules or units of study they have successfully completed which are accumulated towards a certificate, diploma or degree. They can also put their completed modules towards higher education study in other universities or colleges. Students wanting to transfer their credits should talk to the admissions office of the university they want to enter as there may be additional special subjects or module requirements for the degree they want to study.

THE ERASMUS PROGRAMME

Many universities in the UK have formal agreements with partner institutions in Europe through the Erasmus Programme which enables UK university students to apply for courses in Europe for periods up to one year. Some of these courses are taught in English and students can receive help with accommodation and other expenses through the Erasmus Student Grant scheme.

The Erasmus Programme is for undergraduates in all subject areas who would like to study or do a work placement for three to twelve months as part of their degree course in one of 30 other European countries. Most universities offer it although it is not available with every course so students are advised to check with their chosen universities before making an application. Students do not pay any fees to the European university they visit and those who go for the full academic year (24 weeks) have their UK tuition fees waived.

NEXT STEPS

When choosing your course it is important to remember that one course is not better than another – it is just different. The best course for you is the one which best suits you. To give some indication of the differences between courses, see **Chapter 3** and also *Choosing Your Degree Course and University*, the companion book to *Heap 2011: University Degree Course Offers* (see **Appendix 5**). After provisionally choosing your courses, read the prospectuses again carefully to be sure that you understand what is included in the three, four or more years of study. Each institution differs in its course content even though the course titles may be the same and courses differ in other ways, for example, in their:

- methods of assessment (eg unseen examinations, continuous assessment, project work, dissertations)
- contact time with tutors
- how they are taught (for example, frequency and size of lectures, seminars)
- practicals; field work requirements
- library, computing, laboratory and studio facilities
- amount of free study time available.

These are useful points of comparison between courses in different institutions when you are making final course choices. Other important factors to consider when comparing courses include the availability of opportunities for studying and working abroad during your course, professional body accreditation of courses leading to certain professional careers (see **Appendix 4**) and in the career destinations of their graduates.

Once you have chosen your course subject(s) and the type of course you want to follow, the next step is to find out about the universities and colleges offering courses in your subject area, how much a higher education course will cost you and what financial help is available. The next chapter, **University Choice and Finance** provides information to help you do this.

2 | UNIVERSITY CHOICE AND FINANCE

CHOOSING YOUR UNIVERSITY OR COLLEGE

Location, reputation and Open Days

For many applicants the choice of university or college is probably the main priority, with location being a key factor. However, many students have little or no knowledge of regional geography and have no concept of where universities are located: one student thought that Bangor University (situated in North Wales) was located at Bognor on England's south coast!

Some institutions – probably those nearest home or those farthest away – will be rejected quickly. In addition to the region, location and immediate surroundings of a university or college, applicants have their own individual priorities – perhaps a hectic city life or, alternatively, a quiet life in the country! But university isn't all about studying, so it's not a bad idea to link your leisure interests with what the university or college can offer or with the opportunities available in the locality. Many applicants have theatrical, musical or artistic interests while others have sporting interests and achievements ranging from basketball, cricket and football to riding, rowing, sailing, mountaineering, and even fishing for England!

Some other decisions about your choice of university or college, however, could be made for the wrong reasons. Many students, for example, talk about 'reputation' or base their decisions on league tables. Reputations are fairly clear-cut in the case of some institutions. Oxford and Cambridge are both top world-class universities in which all courses have been established for many years and are supported by first class facilities. In other universities certain subjects are predominant, such as the social sciences at the London School of Economics, and the sciences and technologies at Imperial London.

Many other leading universities in the UK are also very strong in some subjects but not necessarily in all. This is why it is wrong to conclude that a 'university has a good reputation' – most universities are not necessarily good at everything! In seeking advice, you should also be a little wary of school staff who will usually always claim that their own university or college has a 'good reputation'. Teachers obviously can provide good advice on the courses and the general atmosphere of their own institution, but they are not in a good position to make comparisons with other universities.

The best way to find out about universities and colleges and the courses that interest you is to visit your preferred institutions. Open Days provide the opportunity to talk to staff and students although, with thousands of students wandering round campuses, it may be difficult to meet and talk to the right people. Also, many institutions hold Open Days during vacations when many students are away which means that you may only hear talks from the staff, and not have any opportunity to meet students. However, it is often possible to visit a university or college in your own time and simply 'walk in'. Alternatively, a letter to the head of department requesting a visit could enable you to get a closer look at the subject facilities. But failing this, you will be invited automatically to visit when you receive an offer and then you can meet the students in the department.

ACTION POINTS

Before deciding on your preferred universities and courses it is important to check out the following points:

Teaching staff

How do the students react to their tutors? Do staff have a flair and enthusiasm for their subject? Are they approachable? Do they mark your work regularly and is the feedback helpful, or are you left to get on with your own work with very little direction? What are the research interests of the staff?

Teaching styles

How will you be taught, for example, lectures, seminars, tutorials? Are lectures popular? If not, why not? How much on-line learning will you have? How much time will you be expected to work on your own? If there are field courses, how often are they arranged and are they compulsory? How much will they cost?

Facilities

Are the facilities of a high standard and easily available? Is the laboratory equipment 'state of the art' or just adequate? Are the libraries well-stocked with software packages, books and journals? What are the computing facilities? Is there plenty of space to study or do rooms and workspaces become overcrowded? Do students have to pay for any materials?

New students

Are there induction courses for new students? What student services and facilities are available? Is it possible to buy second-hand copies of set books?

Work placements

Are work placements an optional or compulsory part of the course? Who arranges them? Are the placements popular? Do they count towards your degree? Are work placements paid? How long are they?

Transferable skills

Transferable skills are now regarded as important by all future employers. Does the department provide training in communication skills, teamwork, time-management and information technology as part of the degree course?

Accommodation

How easy is it to find accommodation? Where are the halls of residence? Are they conveniently located for libraries and lecture theatres? Are they self-catering? Alternatively, what is the cost of meals in the university refectory? Which types of student accommodation are the most popular? What is the annual cost of accommodation? If there is more than one campus, is a shuttle-bus service provided?

Costs

Find out the costs of materials, accommodation and travel in addition to tuition fees (see below) and your own personal needs. What are the opportunities for earning money, on or off campus? Does the department or faculty have any rules about part-time employment?

FINANCE: WHAT WILL IT COST AND WHAT HELP IS THERE?

Tuition fees and other costs

Tuition fees are charged for Honours and Ordinary degree courses in England, Wales and Northern Ireland. The level of tuition fees charged for courses is decided annually by each individual university or college, and may vary between courses as well as between institutions. Most universities in England, Wales and Northern Ireland have set their annual fees for first degree courses at £3225 for 2010/11. Students domiciled in Scotland received free tuition (2009/10) but Scottish students studying in universities elsewhere in the UK paid up to £3225 a year. Students from England, Wales and Northern Ireland studying in Scotland paid a fee of £1775 (except for Medicine for which the fee is £2825). Students domiciled in Wales studying in Welsh institutions paid an annual fee of £3225 and can apply for a non-means tested fee grant of up to £1940.

Students starting their courses in 2011 should check university and college websites, and websites listed below, for the latest information about fees, as this was not available at the time this book went to press. Note that from 2012 it is likely that students will pay more towards the cost of their courses following the current student finance review.

You may also have additional charges, depending on your course of study. For example, studio fees for Art courses could reach £250 per year, while for other courses, such as Architecture, Science and Engineering, there could be charges for equipment. Additionally, there could also be charges for fieldwork trips, study abroad and vacation courses. To find out your likely yearly course costs, in addition to your tuition fees, check with your subject department.

It is also important to check your fee status if you are planning a sandwich course involving either unpaid or paid placements. You can receive a salary of up to £12,000 doing a one-year placement but if you earn more than this you'll need to check your fee status carefully with your finance officer and consult the relevant websites listed below.

Loans Students will not have to pay tuition fees before starting their courses or while they are studying. Depending on their household income, students either have their tuition fees paid or they will be able to take out a student loan to pay for their fees. Loan and fee repayments are made only after graduation and when annual earnings are more than (currently) £15,000.

University scholarships These are usually merit-based and are often competitive although some universities offer valuable scholarships to any new entrant who has achieved top grades at A-level. Scholarships vary considerably and are often subject-specific, offered through faculties or departments, so check the availability of any awards with the subject departmental head. Additionally, there are often music, choral and organ awards, and scholarships and bursaries for sporting achievement.

Entry scholarships are offered by several universities which normally stipulate that the applicant must place the university as their first choice and achieve the specified high grades. Changes in bursaries and scholarships take place every year so it is important to check university and college websites.

University bursaries These are usually paid in cases of financial need: all universities charging course fees are obliged to offer some bursaries to students receiving maintenance grants. The term 'bursary' is usually used to denote an award to students requiring financial assistance or who are disadvantaged in various ways. Universities are committed to fair access to all students from lower income backgrounds and individual universities and colleges have bursaries, trust funds and sponsorships for those students receiving maintenance grants, although reports suggest that many such students fail to claim the money due to them. These non-repayable awards are linked to the size of the maintenance grant students receive and vary between universities.

Living costs

Most students spend their first year in university accommodation. This is usually the highest single cost in a typical weekly budget and the costs will vary considerably between universities. Rooms may be single or shared and include catering or self-catering arrangements. Outside university in the private sector additional costs are likely to include heating, electricity, hot water and water rates.

In addition, other living expenses will need to be considered. These include insurance, healthcare, food, books and stationery, photocopying, computing and telephone calls, clothes and toiletries, local travel, travel to and from university, entertainment, socialising and sport or leisure activities.

Help towards living costs

Maintenance grants These government grants are available but depend on the student's household income. They are paid on a sliding scale to students where the family income is (currently) between £25,000 and £50,000: the maximum grant is £2906 per annum for 2010/11. These grants are not repayable.

Loans to help towards living costs are also available, and details of these are found on the websites listed below, and also in *University Scholarships, Awards and Bursaries* (see **Appendix 5**). Finally, remember that price reductions are often available for students at some shops, restaurants, cinemas, museums and galleries. Contact the university's Student Union before or when you arrive to find out more about these arrangements.

Other financial support

Many major organisations also provide financial help to those in various categories. These include the Lawrence Atwell's Charity for refugee young people from low income backgrounds, the Prince's Trust for disadvantaged young people aged between 14 and 25, and grants of up to £2000 for the disabled from the Snowdon Award Scheme.

Similarly, many scholarships are also offered by professional, commercial and other organisations. These include the armed services and the Engineering professional organisations, particularly those specialising in Civil or Mechanical Engineering, and also the Institute of Materials, Minerals and Mining. There are also sponsorships in which the student joins a firm on leaving school, combining university study with work experience and with an almost guaranteed offer of full-time employment on graduation. And there is the alternative route of taking a sandwich course and being placed with a firm for a year on full pay, often up to £14,000 (see **Chapter 1**).

Some universities also offer additional bursaries to encourage applications from the locality. These may be available to students applying from partner schools or colleges and living in certain postcode areas, in some cases to the brothers and sisters of current students at the university, or to students who have been in care or are homeless. These awards are not repayable.

In addition, students on some Health-related courses, for example Dental Hygiene, Nursing, Occupational Therapy, Physiotherapy, Radiography will be eligible for NHS bursaries. Other bursaries are also payable for programmes funded through the General Social Care Council and also for shortage subjects for those on teacher training courses.

After starting the course, Access to Learning funds are available to help students in financial hardship or through emergency payments for unexpected financial crises. Hardship funds are also offered in very special cases, particularly to students with children or to single parents, mature students and, in particular, to students with disabilities who may also claim Disability Living Allowance. These payments are made in instalments or as a lump sum or as a short-term loan.

Useful websites Students from England www.direct.gov.uk/studentfinance
Students from Scotland www.student-support-saas.gov.uk
Students from Wales www.studentfinancewales.co.uk
Students from Northern Ireland www.studentfinanceni.co.uk

For comprehensive finance information see the useful websites above, *University Scholarships, Awards and Bursaries* and other sources listed in **Appendix 5**.

INFORMATION SOURCES

Prospectuses, websites and Open Days are key sources of the information you need to decide where to study and at the back of this book a **Directory of Institutions** is provided, with full contact details, for you to use in your research. Other sources of information include the books and websites listed in **Appendix 5**, the professional associations listed in **Appendix 4**, and the websites given in the subject tables in **Chapter 8**. It is important to take time to find out as much as you can about your preferred universities, colleges and courses, and to explore their similarities and differences.

The following chapter **University Course Profiles** gives you information about the types of courses offered by each university and how they are organised. This is important information that you need to know when choosing your university or college because those factors affect, for example, the amount of choice you have in what you study, and the opportunities you have for sandwich placements (see **Chapter 1**). You therefore need to read **Chapter 3** to give you an insight into universities so that you can find the one that is right for you.

3 UNIVERSITY COURSE PROFILES

UNIVERSITIES AND THEIR COURSES

Choosing a degree subject is one step of the way to higher education (see **Chapter 1**), choosing a university or college is the next stage (see **Chapter 2** and **Directory of Institutions on** page 567). However, in addition to such features as location, entry requirements, accommodation, students' facilities and the subjects offered, many universities differ in the way they organise and teach their courses. The course profiles which follow below aim to identify the main course features of each of the universities and to provide some brief notes about the types of courses they offer and how they differ.

There are five main types of degree courses. Single Honours courses offer one main subject with a range of specialist subject options from which to choose in Years 2 and 3. Joint Honours courses involve the study of two subjects whilst Combined Honours courses may involve a study of two or three subjects. Some institutions also offer major/minor courses in which the split between the time spent on each subject may be divided as much as 75/25. Finally, many universities and colleges offer sandwich courses in which students are involved in a work placement often lasting up to a year on full pay (see **Chapter 1**).

The ways in which students are taught differ between universities and often between subjects, even at the same university. Modularisation is now quite common because of the flexibility it offers the student to choose a range of topics within their subject choice. Each course comprises modules of study, some are compulsory, some are optional, and some are 'free units' which allow the student to study a subject totally unrelated to their chosen course, for example a foreign language or management. Each module often has a credit rating and students are awarded this value of credits for each module they successfully complete (ie, they pass the assessment). For a three-year Honours degree students usually need 360 credits. Courses which are not modular are often those for vocational subjects which must conform to the course requirements of professional bodies.

Although universities have their own distinct identities and course characteristics, they have many similarities. Apart from full-time and sandwich courses, one-year foundation courses are also offered in many subjects which can help the student to either convert or build on existing qualifications to enable them to start an Honours degree programme. All universities also offer one-year International foundation courses for overseas students to provide a preliminary introduction to courses and often to provide English language tuition.

Foundation courses, however, must not be confused with Foundation degrees which normally require two years' full-time study, or longer for part-time study. They are also often taught in local colleges and may be taken part-time to allow students to continue to work. Successful completion of a Foundation degree can lead into the second or final year of related Honours degree courses when offered by the university validating the Foundation degree. Two-year Higher National Diplomas will also qualify for entry into the second or final year of degree courses. These, too, are often offered at universities as well as colleges of further education and partnership colleges linked to universities.

Part-time degrees and courses in lifelong learning or distance learning are also often available and details of these can be found on university websites and in prospectuses. Some universities publish separate prospectuses for part-time courses.

The following is a list of universities and a brief outline (profile) for each of the ways in which their undergraduate courses are structured and provided, and of the range of courses they provide. For full details see university websites and prospectuses.

COURSE PROFILES

Aberdeen Students applying for the MA degree in Arts and Social Sciences are admitted to a degree rather than a subject. Students select from a range of courses in the first year, leading up to the final choice of subject and Honours course in the fourth year. The BSc degree is also flexible but within the Science framework. Engineering students follow a common core course in Years 1 and 2, specialising in Year 3. There is less flexibility, however, in some vocational courses such as Accountancy, Law, Medicine and Dentistry. For some degree programmes, highly qualified applicants may be admitted to the second year of the course. Other courses cover Divinity and Theology, Education and Music.

Abertay Dundee Courses have a strong vocational bias and are offered in the Schools of Computing and Creative Technologies, Business, Contemporary Sciences and Social and Health Sciences. Four-year courses are offered on a modular basis. Sandwich courses may be either thick (one-year placement) or thin (two six-month placements) and placements are usually at the end of the second and/or third years.

Aberystwyth The University offers Single, Joint and major-minor Honours courses on a modular basis. In Part 1 (Year 1) core topics related to the chosen subject are studied alongside optional subjects. This arrangement allows some flexibility for change when choosing final degree subjects in Part 2 (Years 2 and 3). Some students take a year in industry or commerce between Years 2 and 3. Courses include Accountancy, Business, Economics, Management and Marketing, Agriculture, the Arts and Humanities, Computer Science, Education, Law, Languages, Mathematics, the Sciences, Sport, Theatre and TV Studies and Welsh and Celtic Studies.

Anglia Ruskin Courses are modular which enables students to choose from a range of subject topics in addition to the compulsory subject core modules. Single and Combined Honours courses are offered in the Faculties of Arts, Law and Social Sciences, Science and Technology, Health and Social Care, Education, and in the Business School. Many programmes have a strong vocational focus, with some opportunities to study abroad.

Arts London The University is Europe's largest institution offering courses in Art and Design, Communication and Performing Arts, focusing on creativity and practice in a large number of specialist fields.

Aston The University offers modular courses in Single Honours degrees (one subject), Joint Honours (two subjects, usually in related areas) and in Combined Honours and interdisciplinary studies in which programmes are organised across different subjects. Combined Honours courses may be weighted 50%–50%, and major/minor programmes weighted 67% for the major element and 33% for the minor. A distinctive feature of Aston is that most degrees allow students to spend the third year on a one-year sandwich placement; 70% of students follow sandwich courses or study-abroad programmes, leading to a high percentage of employed graduates. Courses are taught in the Schools of Engineering and Applied Science, Languages and Social Sciences, Life and Health Sciences and in the Aston Business School.

Bangor Modular courses are offered in Single and Joint Honours programmes. A broad and flexible programme is taken in Level 1 (Year 1) with the opportunity to study modules outside the chosen subject including a language. This is followed by greater specialisation in Levels 2 and 3. Courses include Agriculture and Forestry, Arts subjects, Business and Management, Computer Science and Electronics, Creative Studies, Education, Archaeology, History, Law, Health Studies, Languages, Music, Psychology, Biological Sciences, Chemistry, Ocean Sciences, Geography, Social Sciences, Sport and Religious Studies. Contrary to popular belief, two-thirds of the students come from outside Wales and all courses are taught in English.

Bath The academic year is divided into two semesters with Single and Combined Honours degrees composed of core units and optional units, allowing students some flexibility in shaping their courses with 10–12 units taken each year. A central feature of all programmes is the opportunity to take a sandwich course as part of the degree: this is usually taken as either one 12-month placement or two periods of six months. Courses are offered in the Faculties of Engineering and Design, Humanities and Social Sciences, Science, Sport and the School of Management.

Bath Spa Most courses – for single awards, specialised awards and combined awards – are part of a flexible modular scheme with students taking six modules each year. Some modules are compulsory but there is a good range of optional modules. The wide range of courses on offer include Biology, Business and Management, Creative Studies, Cultural Studies, Dance, Drama, Education, English Literature, Food Studies, Geography, Health Studies, History, Media Communications, Music, Psychology, Sociology and Study of Religions.

Bedfordshire This university offers BA and BSc undergraduate, Foundation and Extended degrees in Advertising, Marketing and Communications, Art and Design, Biosciences, Business, Computing, Journalism, Law, Media, Nursing, Psychology, Social Sciences, Sport and Leisure and Tourism. Most of the courses are vocational, some of which offer a placement year in industry or commerce.

Birmingham Courses cover Arts subjects (including Drama), Social Sciences, Business and Commerce, Education, Engineering, Law, Life and Environmental Sciences, Medicine and Dentistry and Health Sciences. Single subject and Joint Honours courses are offered. In Joint Honours courses the two chosen subjects may have common ground or can be very disparate, for example technology and a modern language. Some major/minor combinations are also possible. The modular system provides opportunities for students to study a subject outside their main degree.

Birmingham City Courses are offered through the Birmingham Institute of Art and Design, the Business School, the School of Computing, the School of Jewellery and the Faculties of the Built Environment, Education, Health and Community Care, Law, Humanities and Social Sciences and the Technology Innovation Centre. Many courses have a vocational focus and include sandwich placements. Music is offered through the Birmingham Conservatoire, a music college of international standing. There is also an extensive International Exchange Programme, with many courses abroad being taught in English.

Bolton Modular Single and Combined Honours courses are available, with many offering vocational or professional content and work experience elements. Courses include Art and Design, Built Environment, Business Studies, Computing and Electronics, Cultural and Creative Studies, Education, Engineering, Health and Social Studies, Product Design, Psychology and Sport, Leisure and Tourism. Teaching and learning take place through a mixture of lectures, practicals, seminars and small tutorial groups.

Bournemouth The University offers undergraduate degrees leading to BA, BSc and LLB. The programmes, which are mainly vocational and include sandwich placements, often carry professional recognition. The academic schools cover Arts and Humanities, Business and Management, Design, Food and Nutrition, Law, Media and Communications, Technology, Tourism, Sport and Hospitality.

Bradford Single, Joint and major/minor Honours degree courses are offered, many of which are vocational, leading to professional accreditation, and include sandwich placements in industry and commerce. Other courses offer work-shadowing placements. Language options are available to all students irrespective of their chosen degree course. Subjects are taught in the Schools of Computing, Informatics and Media, The School of Engineering Design and Technology, The School of Health Studies, The School of Life Sciences, The School of Management, The School of Social and International Studies and The School of Lifelong Education and Development.

Brighton BA, BSc and BEng courses are offered, 90% with industrial placements including some in Europe, the USA and Canada. Courses include Accounting, Art and Architecture, Business, Education and

Sport, Health, Law, Information Sciences and Science and Engineering. Brighton and Sussex Medical School students are based at the Falmer campus for the first two years, with academic and clinical studies integrated from Year 1, and thereafter in the education centre at the Royal Sussex County Hospital in Brighton.

Bristol The University offers Single and Joint Honours programmes, mostly of three or four years and, except for Dentistry, Medicine and Veterinary Science, they are based on a modular structure. Students on Single Honours courses have open units allowing optional choices from a range of subjects. Lectures play an important part in teaching and are supported by tutorials and seminars which, in Arts and Social Sciences, tend to dominate the final year. Other subject areas offered in Sciences and Engineering (some courses include a year abroad), Arts, Social Sciences and Law.

Bristol UWE The University offers Single and Joint Honours courses organised on a modular basis which gives flexibility in the choice of options. Many courses include sandwich placements and, in addition, students have the opportunity to undertake a period of study in another EU country. The language centre is open to all students. Courses cover a full range of subjects in the Faculties of Media and Design, Applied Sciences, Built Environment, Computing, Education, Engineering and Mathematical Sciences, Health and Social Care, Humanities, Law, Languages and Social Sciences, the Bristol Business School and Hartpury College (offering Agricultural and Equine Business courses).

Brunel All courses are made up of self-contained modules enabling students, within their scheme of studies, to choose a broad range of topics or greater specialisation as they prefer. Some modern language modules may be taken, depending on the timetable of the chosen subjects. Almost all degree courses are available in a three-year full-time mode or in four-year thick or thin sandwich courses which combine academic work with industrial experience. Some exchange schemes also operate in Europe and the USA. Degree programmes are offered in the Schools of Arts (Drama, English, Media), Business, Engineering and Design, Health Sciences and Social Care, Information Systems, Law, Social Sciences and Sport and Education.

Buckingham The University is an educational charity with its main income provided by the students who pay full tuition fees. A unique feature is the two-year degree programme which starts in January although some courses start in September and may extend to 2¼ years, and some last three years. Courses are offered in Business, Humanities, Law, International Studies and Sciences.

Bucks New Courses are focused on vocational studies in a wide range of subjects in three main groups. These cover Creativity and Culture (Art, Design, Music and Media), Enterprise and Innovation (Business, Computing, Law, Human Sciences and Sport) and Society and Health (Health and Social Care and Nursing).

Cambridge The University offers undergraduate courses in Arts and Sciences and postgraduate degree programmes. Three-year degree courses (Triposes) provide a broad introduction to the subject followed by options at a later stage, and are divided into Part 1 (one or two years) and Part 2. In some Science and Engineering courses there is a fourth year (Part 3). In college-based teaching sessions (supervisions), essays are set for discussion to support university lectures, seminars and practicals.

Canterbury Christ Church A wide range of BA and BSc courses are on offer in addition to a wide choice of combined courses. Most of these courses are offered at the Canterbury campus and include Primary Education and Law, Arts and Social Science and Science subjects. Nursing and other paramedical courses are also offered at the Medway campus at Chatham, Visual and Performing Arts are studied at Folkestone and Music and some Business courses are taken at the Broadstairs campus.

Cardiff All students taking the very flexible BA degree study three subjects in the first year and then follow a Single or Joint Honours course in their chosen subject(s), or a degree in the additional subject. Similarly, BSc Econ courses offer the option to transfer to an alternative degree course at the end of Year

1, depending on the subjects originally chosen. Many degree schemes have a vocational and professional content with a period of attachment in industry, and there are well established links with universities abroad. Degrees schemes are offered by 26 Schools covering Architecture and Planning, Arts and Humanities subjects, Business, Computer Science, Earth, Ocean and Planetary Sciences, Engineering, Healthcare Studies, Law, Media Studies, Medicine, Dentistry and Nursing, Music, Optometry, Pharmacy, Psychology, Religious Studies, Sciences, Social Sciences and Welsh Studies.

Central Lancashire The University has five Faculties (Cultural, Legal, Social Studies, Health, Science). Subjects are taught in a series of modules which gives maximum flexibility in the final choice of degree course. Students may specialise or keep their options open with a choice of Single Honours, Joint or Combined Honours, or they can choose three subjects in Year 1 and reduce to two in the second and third years. Some sandwich courses are offered.

Chester Single and Combined Honours courses are offered in a wide range of subjects on the Chester campus. Subjects offered include Art and Design, Drama and Theatre Studies, Business and Social Studies courses and Nutrition and Health Care. The Warrington campus offers well established courses in Media (Radio, TV, Music) and Journalism in addition to Computer Science and Sports courses.

Chichester Degree subjects can be studied in major, joint or minor programmes. All undergraduate courses comprise a number of individual short course units/modules, taught and assessed separately. Each degree course consists of compulsory and optional modules enabling students to follow their own interests. BA courses are offered in a range of subjects covering Dance, English, Fine Art, History, Media Studies, Music, Performing Arts, Sports Studies and Theology at Chichester, and Business, Education and Tourism at the Bognor Regis campus.

City The University offers a wide range of three-year and four-year programmes leading to degrees in Business and Management, Communication, Computing, Engineering and Mathematical Sciences, Health Sciences, Law, Nursing and Social Sciences. Some Schools and Departments provide a common first year, allowing students to make a final decision on their degree course at the end of the first year. Some sandwich courses are optional, others compulsory. Students in some subject areas may apply to study abroad.

Coventry Courses are offered in the Schools of Art and Design, Business, Engineering and Computing, Environment and Society (including Law, Geography and Social Science), Health and Life Sciences, Mathematical and Information Sciences and Science and the Environment. Many courses are industry-linked and offer sandwich placements in industry and commerce, with some opportunities to study abroad. Individual programmes of study are usually made up of compulsory modules, core options from a prescribed list and free choice modules.

Creative Arts Foundation and Honours degree courses are offered covering art and design, architecture, media and communications.

Cumbria Courses cover Art, Design, Media and Performance, Arts, Humanities and Social Science, Business, IT and Law, Education, Health and Social Care, Natural Resources and Outdoor Studies and Sport.

De Montfort Courses cover Art and Design, Business and Management, Computing Sciences, Creative Technologies, Dance and Drama, Engineering, Health and Society, Humanities, Law, Life Sciences and Music. Single Honours programmes are offered together with sandwich courses and an extensive Joint Honours programme in which two subjects are chosen to be studied equally. Courses are modular, some assessed by coursework only, or by a combination of coursework and examination and a few by examination only. It is possible to change a selected module early in the year.

Derby Courses in Derby are offered across three subject areas – Arts, Design and Technology, Business and Education, Health and Sciences, whilst at the Buxton campus Foundation degrees and Higher

National Diploma courses are offered as well as some BA and BSc degrees. There is also a comprehensive Joint Honours programme offering two subjects and Combined Honours courses with a choice of up to three subjects. Major/minor courses are also available.

Dundee Courses are offered in Accountancy, Architecture and Planning, Art and Design, Arts, Education, Engineering, Law, Medicine and Dentistry, Nursing, Sciences and Social Sciences. A flexible modular system is offered in which Arts and Social Science students have a choice of up to three or four subjects in Year 1 leading to greater specialisation as students progress through the next three years. A similar system applies to courses in Life Sciences and Physical Sciences. In Engineering a common core curriculum operates in Level 1 and in the first half of Level 2.

Durham A collegiate university with 15 colleges including two colleges at the Queen's campus at Stockton. Degree options include Single and Joint Honours courses to which subsidiary subjects can be added. There are named routes in Natural Sciences and courses in Combined Arts and Social Sciences in which students may design their own degree course by choosing several subjects from a wide range. Courses include the Arts, Business, Computer Science, Education, Engineering, Law, Medicine, Science and Social Science.

East Anglia There are 24 Schools of Study spanning the Arts, Humanities, Biological Sciences, Business, Computing Sciences, Social Sciences, Health Professions, Mathematics, World Art Studies and Meteorology. Many Schools are interdisciplinary or multidisciplinary, allowing students to combine a specialist study with complementary subjects and optional units. Some courses include study abroad in Europe, North America and Australasia. There is also a 'Languages for All' programme offering a choice from eight modern languages.

East London The University offers Single Honours and Combined Honours programmes. Courses provide a flexibility of choice and are based on a modular structure with compulsory and optional course units. Courses include Architecture, Art and Design, Business, Computing, Engineering, Health Sciences, Humanities, Law, Media, Social Sciences, Sciences and Sport. A very large number of extended degrees are also available for applicants who do not have the normal university entrance requirements.

Edge Hill The University has three-year programmes including Business, English, Film, Geographical Sciences, History, Law, Media, Midwifery, Nursing, Performance Studies, Social and Psychological Sciences, Sport and Teacher Training.

Edinburgh Courses are offered in Humanities and the Social Sciences, Medicine and Veterinary Medicine and in Science and Engineering. Depending on the choice of degree, three or more subjects are taken in the first year followed by second level courses in at least two of these subjects in Year 2, thus allowing a range of subjects to be studied at degree level. There is a considerable choice of subjects although there may be restrictions in the case of high-demand subjects such as English and Psychology. General or Ordinary degrees take three years and Honours degrees take four years. Joint Honours degrees are also offered.

Edinburgh Napier Students choose between Single and Joint (two subject) degrees and customised degrees which can include a range of subjects. Courses are offered in Accounting, Economics and Financial Services, Business, Management, Languages and Law, Computing, Creative Industries, Engineering and the Built Environment, Life Sciences, Nursing, Social Sciences and Tourism and Hospitality.

Essex Undergraduate departments are grouped in Schools of Study covering Humanities and Comparative Studies, Social Sciences, Law and Sciences and Engineering. In Year 1 students take four or five courses including modules for their chosen degree. In Year 2 they may follow their chosen degree or choose another degree, including combined and joint courses. The four-year BA and some Law degrees include a year abroad and/or industrial placements. Degree schemes in Health, Business and the Performing Arts are also offered at the Southend campus.

Exeter Subjects are offered in the Schools of Biological Sciences, Business and Economics, Classics, Ancient History and Theology, Education and Lifelong Learning, Engineering, Computer Science and Mathematics, English, Geography, Archaeology and Earth Resources, Historical, Political and Sociological Studies, Law, Modern Languages, the Institute of Arab and Islamic Studies and the Peninsula Medical School. In some courses it is possible to study for up to a year in Europe, North America, Australia or New Zealand. Some subjects including Mining Engineering, Geology and Law can be taken at the Cornwall campus at Penrhyn.

Glamorgan Many of the courses are vocational and can be studied as Single or Joint Honours courses or major-minor degrees. Courses are offered in the fields of Art and Design, Built Environment, Business, Computing and Mathematics, Education, Engineering, English and Creative Writing, Geography and the Environment, Health Sciences, Life and Physical Sciences, Humanities and Social Sciences, Law, Policing and Crime, Media and Drama Studies and Sport.

Glasgow Applicants choose a Faculty and a degree from the Faculties of Arts, Education, Engineering, Law, Business and Social Sciences, Medicine, Science and Veterinary Medicine. Flexible arrangements allow students to build their own degree programme from all the courses on offer. Honours degrees normally take four years, with the decision for Honours taken at the end of Year 2 (not automatic). General degrees take three years except for those involving a foreign language. Creative, Cultural Environmental, Health and Scottish Studies can also be taken at the Crichton campus in Dumfries.

Glasgow Caledonian The University offers a wide range of vocational full-time and sandwich courses organised in the Schools of the Built and Natural Environment, Computing and Engineering, Health and Social Care, Law and Social Sciences, Life Sciences, Nursing, Midwifery and Community Health and the Caledonian Business School.

Gloucestershire Courses are made up of individual study units (modules). Some are compulsory for the chosen course but other modules can be chosen from other subjects. There are three main Faculties: Arts and Education, Business and Social Sciences and Environment and Leisure. Modular, Single and Joint Honours courses are offered, many with work placements and some with exchange schemes with institutions in the USA. Many students are home-based.

Glyndŵr This new university in North Wales (Wrexham) offers a range of courses covering Art and Design, Business, Computing and Communications Technology, Education and Community, Health, Social Sciences, Social Care and Sport and Exercise Sciences, Humanities and Science and Technology.

Greenwich Courses include Architecture and Construction, Business, Chemical and Life Sciences, Computing and Mathematical Sciences, Earth and Environmental Sciences, Education and Training, Engineering, Languages, Health and Social Care, Humanities and Social Sciences and Law. There is also a flexible and comprehensive Combined Honours degree programme offering two joint subjects of equal weight or, alternatively, major-minor combinations.

Heriot-Watt The year is divided into three ten-week terms with four modules taken each term. The six Schools cover the Built Environment, Engineering and Physical Sciences, Management and Languages, Mathematical and Computer Sciences, Textiles and Design and Life Sciences.

Hertfordshire Honours degree courses, including sandwich degrees, are offered including Art and Design, Astronomy and Astrophysics, Business, Computer Science, Education, Engineering, Humanities, Law, Life and Physical Sciences, Geography, Music, Sport, Nursing and Health subjects, Psychology and Social Studies and many courses are vocational. There is also an extensive combined modular programme in which students choose three subjects in Year 1, followed by specialisation in Years 2 and 3.

Huddersfield The modular approach to study provides a flexible structure to all courses which are offered as full-time or sandwich options. All students also have the opportunity to study a modern language either as a minor option or by studying part-time through the Modern Languages Centre. Most courses are vocational and include such subjects as Accountancy and Business, Architecture, Art and Design, Computing, Education, Engineering, Geography and Environmental Sciences, Food Sciences, Hospitality and Tourism, Human and Health Sciences, Law, Marketing, Music and Sciences.

Hull All full-time courses are made up of core and optional modules with a free elective scheme which allows students to take one module each year outside their main subject. A 'Languages for All' programme is available for all students irrespective of their degree course subject. The wide range of subjects offered include Arts and Humanities, Business, Computing, Drama, Economics, Education, Engineering, Law, Medicine (Hull York Medical School), Music, Nursing, Physical Sciences, Social Sciences and Sport. The Scarborough campus also offers a wide range of courses.

Imperial London The University offers world-class programmes in Science, Medicine, Engineering and Management. Joint Honours courses and degree courses abroad with a year abroad are also available. Science courses are offered primarily in one principal subject, but flexibility is provided by the possibility to transfer at the end of the first year and by the choice of optional subjects in the later years of the course. A Humanities programme is also open to all students with a wide range of options whilst the Tanaka Business School offers Management courses which form an integral part of undergraduate degrees.

Keele Flexibility is provided through either interdisciplinary Single Honours degrees, bringing together a number of topics in an integrated form, or Dual Honours degrees in which two principal subjects are studied to degree level to the same depth as a Single Honours course. In addition, all students take a first-year course in Complementary Studies and may also study a foreign language. Courses are offered in Arts subjects, Biosciences and Physical Sciences, Economics, Education, Law, Management Science, Media, Music and Social Sciences.

Kent Single Honours courses can include the option of taking up to 25% of the degree in another subject, or to change the focus of a degree at the end of the year. Two subjects are studied on a 50/50 basis in Joint Honours courses and there are also major/minor Honours degrees. Degrees include Accountancy and Business courses, Arts subjects, Biological and Physical Sciences, Computer Science, Drama and Theatre and Film Studies, Languages, Law, Music Technology, Pharmacy, Psychology, Religious Studies and Social Sciences.

Kingston Single and Joint Honours courses are offered within a modular structure, with the opportunity to take a language option in French, German, Italian, Japanese, Mandarin Chinese, Russian or Spanish. Several courses are available as a minor field, for example, Business, which adds an extra dimension to the chosen degree. Subjects are offered in Architecture, Art, Design and Music, Arts and Social Sciences, Business, Computing, Earth Sciences, Economics, Education, Engineering, Humanities, Law Life Sciences, Mathematics, Health and Social Care Sciences, Media, Performance Studies, Pharmacy, Social Sciences and Surveying. Exchange schemes are offered with 72 universities in Europe and five in the USA.

Lancaster The University is collegiate with each student being a member of one of the eight colleges. Each college has its own social activities and events. The degree programme is split into Part 1 (Year 1) and Part 2 (Years 2 and 3). Students study up to three subjects in Year 1 and then choose to major in one or a combination of subjects in Years 2 and 3. Single and joint courses are offered in a wide range of subjects, for example, Business, Computer Science, Engineering, Finance, Languages, Mathematics, Medicine, Natural Sciences, Music, Politics and Psychology. There are study opportunities abroad in the USA and Canada, the Far East and Australasia.

Leeds A very wide range of courses are on offer in most subject areas (Leeds is a pioneer of Joint Honours degrees). In the first year, Joint Honours students normally divide their time equally between three subjects, with a wide choice of the third or elective subject in the first year. In many cases, students can transfer to a different course at the end of the first year and delay their final choice of degree. A wide range of subjects is offered in Arts and Humanities, Medicine and Dentistry, Theatre and Performance, Science and Engineering, Social Sciences and in the Business School.

Leeds Metropolitan Many of the degrees are vocational with links to industry and commerce. Courses are modular with core studies and optional modules. Degree programmes are offered in the Faculties of Arts and Society, Information and Technology, Health, Sport and Recreation, the Leslie Silver International Faculty and the Leeds Business School.

Leicester The Single Honours courses are offered in all the main disciplines and are taken by 75% of students. The main subject of study may be supported by one or two supplementary subjects taken in the first, and sometimes the second, year. Joint Honours courses are also offered. A three-year Combined Studies degree is also available in which three subjects are studied, one taken for two years only. Apart from Medicine, all programmes have a common modular structure with compulsory modules and a wide choice of optional modules.

Lincoln There are Faculties of Art, Architecture and Design, Business and Law, Health, Life and Social Sciences, Media, Humanities and Technology. Single and joint subject degrees are offered on a modular basis, with some subjects offering the chance to study abroad.

Liverpool The University offers degrees in the Faculties of Arts, Engineering, Medicine, Science, Social and Environmental Studies and Veterinary Science. Apart from courses with a clinical component, programmes are modular. In some cases they include placements in industry or in another country whilst a 'Languages for All' scheme offers European languages. A Combined Honours programme in Arts gives students the chance to choose three subjects in Year 1, reducing to two subjects in Years 2 and 3. A similar Combined Honours course in Social and Environmental Studies is also offered.

Liverpool Hope Single Honours courses leading to degrees of BA and BSc are offered and there is also a wide range of options by way of two combined subjects. Courses include Business, Computing, Dance, Drama, Education, English, Environmental Management, Film Studies, Fine Art and Design, Geography, Health, History, Human Biology, Law, Leisure, Marketing, Mathematics, Media, Music, Politics, Psychology, Sports Studies, Theology and Religious Studies and Tourism.

Liverpool John Moores Courses are offered in the Faculties of Business, Law and Languages, Education, Community and Leisure, Health and Applied Social Sciences, Media, Arts and Social Science, Science and Technology and the Environment. The majority of courses provide the opportunity for work-based learning or for a year-long industrial placement.

London (Birkbeck) Part-time evening courses are offered for mature students wishing to read for first and higher degrees. Courses are offered in the Faculties of Arts, Science, Social Science and Continuing Education.

London (Central School of Speech and Drama) The School offers a broad range of courses in the Theatre Arts. It is also linked to the Webber Douglas Academy of Dramatic Art to provide a range of courses leading to careers in classical and contemporary theatre, film and TV. Courses include Acting, Costume Construction, Stage Design, Prop Making, Puppetry, Stage Management, Theatre Lighting and Sound Design.

London (Courtauld) A leading centre for the study of the history of art and conservation located in central London. Small class-size teaching.

London (Goldsmiths) Programmes include Art, Drama and Media, the Arts, Education and Social Sciences. Like most London University degrees, the majority of undergraduate degrees are made up of course units giving some flexibility. Twelve units are taken over three years.

London (Heythrop) Nine BA courses are offered in Philosophy and Theology. The supportive and learning environment is enhanced by one-to-one tutorials for all students throughout their courses.

London (Institute in Paris) A Single Honours course in French Studies is offered to English-speaking applicants who study in France for the whole of their course. The course is taught almost entirely in French. Students graduate after their three-year course with a University of London BA.

London (King's) The College offers more than 200 degree programmes in the Faculties of Arts and Humanities, Biomedical and Health Sciences, Law, Nursing and Midwifery, and Physical Sciences; Social Science and Public Policy, and Medicine and Dentistry at the Guy's or King's Denmark Hill and St Thomas's campuses. The degree course structure varies with the subject chosen and consists of Single Honours (one subject), Joint Honours (two subjects), Combined Honours (a choice of over 60 programmes) and major/minor courses.

London (Queen Mary) The College offers courses in the Arts and Humanities, Biological and Physical Sciences, Business Management and Economics, Computer Science, Engineering, Languages, Materials Science, Mathematics, Medicine and Social Sciences. In most subjects, students choose compulsory and optional course units which allow for some flexibility in planning a course to suit individual interests.

London (Royal Holloway) The College offers Single, Joint and major/minor Honours degrees in three Faculties – Arts, History and Social Sciences, and Science. Study abroad is a feature of many courses and all students can compete for international exchanges.

London (Royal Veterinary College) Courses are offered in Veterinary Medicine and Bioveterinary Sciences; the latter does not qualify graduates to practise as veterinary surgeons. There is also a Veterinary Gateway course and a four-year Veterinary Nursing programme.

London (St George's) A 'Health Sciences' university located in south London. Courses are offered in Biomedical Informatics, Biomedical Science, Medicine, Physiotherapy and Diagnostic and Therapeutic Radiography.

London (School of Oriental and African Studies) This is the only higher education institution in the UK specialising in the study of Asia, Africa and the Near and Middle East. Single subject degrees include compulsory and optional units, with two-thirds of the total units studied in the chosen subject and the remaining units or 'floaters' from a complementary course offered at SOAS or another college of the University. In addition, two-subject degrees give great flexibility in the choice of units, enabling students to personalise their degrees to match their interests.

London (School of Pharmacy) The School offers the Master of Pharmacy degree. Except for hospital and extra-mural projects, all the teaching takes place on the Bloomsbury campus.

London (University College) Subjects are organised in Faculties – Arts and Humanities, Social and Historical Sciences (with a flexible course unit system), Fine Art (the Slade School), Law, Built Environment (the Bartlett), Engineering Sciences, Mathematical and Physical Sciences and Life Sciences. In addition, there is the School of Medicine. The School of Slavonic and East European Studies also offers degrees which focus on developing a high level of proficiency in speaking, writing and understanding the chosen language.

London Metropolitan Single and Joint Honours courses are made up of compulsory and optional modules allowing students some flexibility to follow their particular interests. Courses are offered in Accountancy and Business, Art and Architecture, Arts, Humanities and Languages, Computing, Economics and Finance, Education, Health and Human Sciences and Law.

London School of Economics and Political Science The School offers courses not only in Economics and Political Science but also in a wide range of other Social Science subjects taught in 19 Departments.

Programmes are offered as Single Honours, Joint Honours or major/minor courses. From 2010 all undergraduates study a compulsory course (LSE 100) in Year 1.

London South Bank Subject areas cover Arts and Human Sciences including Law and Psychology, Business, Computing and Information Management, Engineering, Science and the Built Environment and Health and Social Care. All courses have flexible modes of study and many vocational courses offer sandwich placements.

Loughborough Academic programmes cover Art and Design, Business, Chemistry, Computer Science, Economics, Engineering, Mathematics, Politics and International Relations, Humanities, Sciences, Social Science and Sport. Degree programmes combine compulsory and optional modules and some transfers between courses are possible. Additional language study is possible in French, German or Spanish (including beginners' courses), for students on most courses. Sandwich degree courses with a year's paid work experience in industry result in high graduate employment. World-class sporting facilities and an unrivalled reputation in sporting success attract applicants at junior international level and above.

Manchester The University offers Single and Joint Honours courses which are divided into course units, some of which are compulsory and others optional, and some are taken from a choice of subjects offered by other Schools and Faculties. A comprehensive Combined Studies degree enables students to choose course units from Arts, Humanities, Social Sciences and Sciences, and this provides the flexibility for students to alter the emphasis of their studies from year to year. Degree programmes are offered in the Faculties of Engineering and Physical Sciences, Humanities, Life Sciences and Medical and Human Sciences.

Manchester Metropolitan Degree programmes are offered in the Faculties of Art and Design, Community Studies and Education, Food, Clothing and Hospitality Management, Humanities, Law and Social Science, Science and Engineering and the Manchester Metropolitan Business School. A large number of courses involve industrial and commercial placements. It is also possible to take Combined Honours degrees selecting a combination of two or three subjects. Many programmes have a modular structure with compulsory and optional core modules.

Middlesex Single and Joint Honours courses are offered on a modular basis, most programmes having an optional work placement. Courses cover Art and Design, Arts subjects, Biological and Health Sciences, Business and Management, Computing and IT, Dance, Drama and Music, Social Sciences and Teaching and Education.

Newcastle Degree programmes are available in the Faculties of Arts, Biological Sciences, Business and Law, Engineering, Medical Sciences, Physical Sciences and Social Sciences. Single, Joint and Combined Honours programmes are offered, in some cases providing students with the opportunity either to defer their choice of final degree or to transfer to other subjects at a later stage. In the Combined Studies BA and BSc courses it is possible to combine the study of up to three different subjects which can be studied over two or three years.

Newport The University consists of seven Schools – Art and Design, Humanities, Business, Computing and Engineering, Social Studies, Education and the Centre for Community and Lifelong Learning. Courses include Single and Joint Honours and major/minor studies; they vary in structure but many are based on a modular system.

Northampton Courses are offered in seven schools: Applied Sciences (Computing, Mechanical and Electrical/Electronic Engineering), Business, Education, Health, Social Sciences, Arts (including Fine Art and Design) and Land-based subjects at Moulton College. Courses are offered as Single, Combined and Joint Honours programmes.

Northumbria A wide range of courses is offered with an emphasis on vocational studies, including Art and Design, Arts subjects, Built Environment, Business and Financial Management, Computing, Education and Sport, Engineering, Health and Social Care, Humanities, Languages, Law, Mathematics, Nursing and Midwifery, Psychology and Sciences. Single and Joint Honours courses are offered, and a Combined Honours course allows a choice of up to three subjects.

Nottingham Single and Joint Honours courses are available, with some sandwich courses. Programmes are modular with compulsory and optional modules, the latter giving some flexibility in the selection of topics from outside the chosen subject field. Degree programmes are offered in the Faculties of Arts, Business, Engineering, Law, Medicine and Health Sciences, Science and Social Sciences.

Nottingham Trent Degree programmes are offered in a range of subjects covering Animal, Rural and Environmental Sciences, Architecture, Arts and Humanities, Art and Design, Business, Education, Law, Sciences and Technology and Social Sciences. Many courses are vocational with industrial and commercial placements and some students are also able to spend a semester (half an academic year) studying at a partner university in Europe, the USA or Australia.

Open University Degree and diploma courses are offered in the following subject areas: Arts and Humanities, Business and Management, Childhood and Youth, Computing and ICT, Education, Engineering and Technology, Environmental Development and International Studies, Health and Social Care, Languages, Law, Mathematics and Statistics, Psychology, Science and Social Sciences. Students study at home and are sent learning materials by the OU maintaining contact with their tutors by email, post and telephone.

Oxford Candidates apply to a college and for a Single or Joint Honours programme. Courses are offered with a core element plus a variety of options. Weekly contact with a college tutor assists students to tailor their courses to suit personal interests. Arts students are examined twice, once in the first year (Preliminary examinations) and at the end of the course (Final Honours School). Science students are similarly examined although in some subjects examinations also take place in the second year.

Oxford Brookes Single Honours courses are offered with modules chosen from a field of study or, alternatively, Combined Honours courses in which two subjects are chosen. These subjects may be in related or unrelated subjects. There is also a Combined Studies degree in which students 'build' their own degree by taking approved modules from a range of the subjects offered by the University.

Plymouth A broad portfolio of degree courses is available including Medicine at the Peninsula Medical School – a partnership with Exeter University. Other courses cover Agriculture, Art and Design, Biological and Physical Sciences, Built Environment, Business and Financial Management, Computing, Drama, Education, Engineering, Health and Social Sciences, Humanities, Languages, Law, Marine Studies, Mathematics and Sport Studies. Single Honours courses are offered with many vocational programmes offering work placements.

Portsmouth The Faculties of Creative and Cultural Industries, Humanities and Social Sciences, Science, Technology and the Portsmouth Business School offer Single and Joint Honours courses. Sandwich programmes are also available in many subjects and there is also an opportunity for all students to learn a foreign language. Many courses are planned on a modular basis which allows students to defer specialisation until after their first year.

Queen Margaret The five main areas at this new university (2007) now based on a purpose-built campus outside Edinburgh, cover Business and Enterprise, Health, Media and Social Sciences, Drama and the Creative Industries. All courses focus on vocational careers.

Queen's Belfast The academic year is divided into two semesters of 15 weeks each (12 teaching weeks and three examination weeks), with degree courses (pathways) normally taken over three years of full-time study. Six modules are taken each year (three in each semester) and, in theory, a degree can involve any combination of six Level 1 modules. Single, Joint and Combined Honours courses are offered and, in addition, major-minor combinations; some courses include sandwich placements. Courses cover

Agriculture and Food Science, Education, Engineering, Humanities and Social Sciences, Management and Economics, Law and Medicine and Health Sciences.

Reading Faculties of Arts and Humanities and Economics and Social Sciences provide flexible arrangements for students. A teaching system operates in Year 1 in which students can take modules in their chosen subject and in two or three other subjects. At the end of the first year they may transfer from Single Honours to Joint Honours courses or change to another subject.

Robert Gordon The University offers a wide range of vocational courses including Accountancy and Business, Architecture, Art and Design, Computer Science, Engineering, Law, Nursing, Occupational Therapy, Pharmacy, Physiotherapy, Radiography, Sciences, Social Sciences and Sports Science. Many courses offer work placements and there are some opportunities to study abroad in Europe, Canada and the USA.

Roehampton London's only campus university, managing its academic programmes in eight Schools – Arts and Business, Social Sciences and Computing, Education Studies, English and Modern Languages, Humanities and Cultural Studies, Initial Teacher Education, Sports Science and Psychological and Therapeutic Studies. All programmes operate within a modular and semester-based structure.

St Andrews A very wide range of subjects is offered across the Faculties of Arts, Divinity, Medicine and Science. A flexible programme is offered in the first two years when students take several subjects. The decision of Honours degree subject is made at the end of Year 2 when students choose between Single or Joint Honours degrees for the next two years. A broadly-based General degree programme is also offered lasting three years.

Salford The University offers BA, BSc and BEng degrees with teaching methods depending on the degree (they are equally likely to accept students with BTECs and Access qualifications as well as those with A-levels). There is a wide range of professionally accredited programmes many involving work placements. All undergraduates may study a foreign language. Subjects include Accountancy and Business, Art and Design, Computer Science, Drama, Engineering, Humanities, Journalism, Leisure and Tourism, Languages, Music, Nursing, Physiotherapy, Psychology, Sciences, Social Sciences and Sport Science.

Sheffield The teaching year consists of two semesters (two periods of 15 weeks). Courses are fully modular, with the exceptions of Dentistry and Medicine. Students register for a named degree course which has a number of core modules, some optional modules chosen from a prescribed range of topics and some unrestricted modules chosen from any at the University. Programmes offered include Accounting and Business, Arts and Humanities, Computer Science, Engineering and Materials Science, Languages, Law, Nursing, Psychology, Sciences, Social Sciences and Town and Country Planning.

Sheffield Hallam A large number of vocational courses are offered in addition to those in Arts, Humanities and Social Sciences. The University is the largest provider of sandwich courses in the UK with most courses offering work placements, usually between the second and third years. Most students are able to study an additional language from French, German, Italian, Spanish and Japanese.

Southampton A wide range of courses is offered in the Faculties of Law, Arts and Social Sciences, Engineering, Science and Mathematics and Medicine, Health and Life Sciences. Programmes are generally for three years. All students have the chance to study a language as part of their degree and there are many opportunities for students to study abroad or on Erasmus-Socrates exchange programmes whether or not they are studying modern languages.

Southampton Solent Courses are offered in the Faculties of Technology, Media, Arts and Society and the Southampton Business School. Subjects cover Art and Design, Business and Finance including Accountancy, Marketing and Personnel, Computing, Construction, Engineering and Technology, the Environment, Human and Social Sciences and Law, Leisure, Sport and Tourism, Maritime Studies and Media, Film and Journalism.

Staffordshire The Stafford campus focuses on courses in Computing, Engineering, Technology and Health Studies whilst at Stoke programmes are offered in Art and Design, Law, Business, Humanities, Social Sciences and Science subjects. Single and Joint Honours awards are available, some of which are for four years and include a work placement year. Part-time courses are also offered.

Stirling A flexible system operates in which students can delay their final degree choice until midway through the course. The University year is divided into two 15-week semesters, from September to December and February to May with a reading/study block and exams at the end of each semester. Innovative February entry is possible to some degree programmes. There are 250 degree combinations with the opportunity to study a range of disciplines in the first two years. In addition to Single and Combined Honours degrees, there is a General degree which allows for greater breadth of choice. Subjects range across the Arts, Social Sciences and Sciences.

Strathclyde A credit-based modular system operates with a good degree of flexibility in course choices. The University offers many vocational courses in the Faculties of Engineering, Science and the Strathclyde Business School. There are also degree programmes in Arts subjects, Education, Law and the Social Sciences.

Sunderland There are two campuses, Sunderland and Gateshead, and five Schools of study: Arts, Media and Culture, Business, Computer Science and Technology and Single, Joint Honours and sandwich courses with strong links with industry. A modular programme provides maximum flexibility in choosing appropriate subjects. Some placements are possible in Canada, USA, Australia, New Zealand, India and Europe and there is a large number of mature and local students.

Surrey Degree programmes are offered in the Arts, Biomedical and Molecular Sciences, Electronics and Physical Sciences, Engineering, Health and Medical Sciences, Human Sciences and Management. Some 80% of students spend a professional training year as part of their course and in some cases there are placements abroad. There is also a part-time BSc degree in Professional Development through work-based learning.

Sussex Teaching is structured around five Schools of study, the Brighton and Sussex Medical School and the Science and Technology Policy Research Unit. Courses cover a wide range of subjects in Humanities, Life Sciences, Science and Technology, Social Sciences and Cultural Studies. Students are registered in a School depending on the degree taken. The flexible structure allows students to interrupt their degree programme to take a year out.

Swansea Courses are offered in Arts and Social Sciences, Business, Economics and Law, Engineering, Languages, Medicine and Health Sciences and Science. Degree courses are modular with the opportunity to take some subjects outside the chosen degree course. Part-time degrees are available and study-abroad arrangements are possible in several subject areas.

Swansea Metropolitan This new university consists of three main faculties. The faculty of Applied Design and Engineering offers a broad spectrum of courses from Automotive Engineering to Multimedia. The Faculty of Art and Design established 150 years ago is a major centre for art and crafts in Wales. The Faculty of Humanities comprises Schools of Business, Education, Health Sciences, Humanities, the Performing Arts, Leisure, Tourism and Recreation.

Teesside Single and Combined Honours degrees are offered with the major subject occupying two thirds of the course and the minor option one third. There is a wide choice of vocational courses, many with sandwich arrangements in industry, commerce and the professions. Courses are offered in the Arts, Business, Engineering, Law, Media, Social Sciences and Sport with large Schools of Health and Social Care and Computing and Mathematics. There is a high mature student intake.

Thames Valley Subjects offered cover Business, Management and Law, Tourism, Hospitality and Leisure, Music, Media and Creative Technologies and Health and Human Sciences. Credit-rated Single and Joint

Honours courses are offered, many with year-long work placements between Years 2 and 3. There are some study-abroad arrangements in Europe, Canada and the USA and there is a large mature student intake.

Trinity Saint David A new university, to be created in 2010 by the merger of the University of Wales, Lampeter and Trinity University College, it offers courses in the Humanities, Business and Management. Courses also include Education, Art, Design and the Performing Arts, and the Social Sciences. Check the University website for the latest information (www.lamp.ac.uk).

Ulster Faculties of Arts, Business and Management, Engineering and Built Environment, Life and Health Sciences and Social Sciences offer a wide range of courses. There are various styles of learning supported by formal lectures and many courses include periods of work placement.

Warwick Courses are offered by Departments in the Faculty of Arts, Science and Social Studies, the Warwick Business School, the Warwick Institute of Education and the Warwick Medical School. Students may choose single subject degrees or combine several subjects in a joint degree. Options offered in each course provide flexibility in the choice of subjects although courses are not fully modularised. Many degrees offer the opportunity to study abroad and work placements on some science courses.

West of Scotland The University is located on four campuses at Ayr, Dumfries, Hamilton and Paisley and is a leading provider of vocational education in the region. It offers industry-relevant and career-focused courses, and many programmes include periods of paid work placements. There are also some European and US study opportunities. Courses are offered in the Business School and the Schools of Computing, Education, Engineering and Science, Health, Nursing and Midwifery and Media, Language and Music.

Westminster Courses include Architecture and the Built Environment, Biosciences, Business Management, Complementary Therapies, Computer Sciences, Electronics, English and Linguistics, Languages, Law, Media and Arts and Design and Psychology and Social Sciences. Undergraduate courses are modular and taught over two semesters. The University has a broad network of partnerships within the EU which enables students to include a period of study abroad as part of their degree.

Winchester Single and two-subject courses are offered consisting of either one subject, or two subjects studied equally (a Joint Honours degree) or a 75%–25% split by way of a main and subsidiary subject Honours degree. Courses are offered in American Studies, Archaeology, Business, Dance, Drama and Performance, Education, English and Creative Writing, Film Studies, History, Journalism and Media Studies, Psychology, Sport Science, Theology and Tourism.

Wolverhampton A large number of specialist and Joint Honours degrees are offered and many have work placements at home or abroad. Except for courses linked to specific professional requirements, programmes are modular providing flexibility of choice. Courses include Art and Design, Arts and Humanities, Business Studies, Computer Science, Education, Engineering, Environmental Studies, Health Studies, Law, Media, Nursing, Sciences and Social Studies.

Worcester The courses are grouped into six institutes: Health and Society, Humanities and Creative Arts, Science and the Environment, Sport and Exercise Science, the Worcester Business School and Education.

York Thirty departments and centres cover a range of subjects in the arts, social sciences, technology and medicine. The 'Languages for All' programme enables any student to take a course in any one of 14 languages, in addition to which there are several opportunities to build a period abroad into a degree course. Courses offered include Archaeology, Arts subjects, Computer Science, Economics, Education, Electronics, Health Sciences, Languages, Management, Medicine, Music, Psychology, Sciences and Social Sciences.

York St John The Faculties of Education and Theology, Business and Communication, Health and Life Sciences and Art offer a range of specialist degrees and Joint Honours courses are offered in Business, Management, Languages and Linguistics, Peace Studies, Health Studies, Counselling, Design, Education, Information Technology, Occupational Therapy, Physiotherapy, Psychology, Sport and Theology.

COLLEGES AND THEIR COURSES

In addition to the large numbers of universities offering degree courses, there are over 100 colleges admitting several thousands of students, each on full degree courses. These include University Colleges, University Centres, Colleges of Further and Higher Education and specialist colleges of Agriculture and Horticulture, Art, Drama, and Music: see the Directory of Institutions at the back of the book.

Larger institutions will offer a range of Single subject, Joint and Combined Honours degree courses leading to BA, BSc and BEd degrees whilst the smaller colleges may only offer one or two degree programmes. A large number, however, also provide full or part-time Foundation degrees which can lead to Honours degree courses. These colleges are listed in the subject tables.

The next chapter **University Admissions** outlines how universities select applicants for their courses and it provides information for each university relating to key points of their admissions policies.

4 | UNIVERSITY ADMISSIONS

ADMISSIONS POLICIES

Although the UCAS application process is standard for all undergraduate Honours degree courses (see **Chapter 6**) the admissions policies adopted by individual departments in universities and colleges often differ, depending on the popularity of the course and the quality of applicants.

There are, however, common areas of agreement concerning applications, in particular the acceptance of the different qualifying examinations being offered. Apart from a diverse range of international qualifications, A-level grades and the International Baccalaureate (IB), have been the common currency of selection linked with the UCAS Tariff points system for many years, although some very popular universities and courses do not make points offers, preferring to set their entry standards in the grades awarded in specific subjects.

Most universities are still making decisions on the timing and introduction of the new A* grades. Most, if not all, institutions accept recent qualifications such as the Advanced Diplomas, the Extended Project and the Cambridge Pre-U Diploma although there may be some additional requirements depending on the degrees applied for when specified subjects may be required. A-levels in general studies and critical thinking are nearly always taken into account when selecting applicants although they rarely form part of an offer. Key Skills may also be noted by selectors and for some courses they could be worth up to 20 Tariff points. BTEC is also acceptable with two passes for some Foundation courses to full distinction for some competitive degree programmes. However, it should also be noted that a number of universities and degree courses also have general entry requirements which include GCSE grade C or above in English and Mathematics.

Interview policies vary considerably and, in most cases, simply will be based on the information on the UCAS application with the personal statement being highly important for many courses. Candidates receiving offers will be invited to visit their universities. Interviews are usual for Medicine, Dentistry, Veterinary Science, Art, Social Work and for Teaching courses and inevitable for Dance, Drama and Music (see **Chapter 5**). Mature students (defined as those over 21 on entry) are often interviewed. Normal published offers may not apply to mature students. In all universities certain courses require Criminal Records Bureau (CRB) checks or medical examinations; students should check these requirements before applying for courses.

Deferred entry is acceptable in almost all cases although many universities ask that the intention to take a Gap Year should be included on the application if firm arrangements have been made. It is worth noting, however, that there may well be fewer places available on a subsequent course for students wanting to defer. Several universities have advised that if a student fails to achieve the grades required for an offer, they may still be awarded a place; however they may receive a changed offer for an alternative course. Many universities are also prepared to provide feedback on the results of unsuccessful applications.

In addition, all universities have a number of schemes in place to enable admissions tutors to identify and make offers to applicants who, for example, may have had their education affected by circumstances outside their control. A major initiative is Widening Participation in which various schemes can assist school and college students in getting into university. These programmes focus on specific groups of students and communities including:

- Students from low participation areas
- Low-performing schools and colleges or those without a strong history of progression to higher education
- Students with disabilities
- People living in deprived geographical areas, including deprived rural areas
- Students from black or ethnic minority backgrounds
- Students from the lower socio-economic groups 4-8 including mature learners
- Students requiring financial assistance or who are disadvantaged in various ways
- Families with little or no experience of higher education
- Students from homes with low household incomes
- Students returning to study after a period of time spent away
- Students from state schools.

Students who feel that they might qualify for Widening Participation programmes should find out from their school or college about the schemes offered by universities including their local university.

In addition to the general information above, universities have emphasised certain aspects of their selection procedures and these are listed below. Even so, applicants are strongly advised to check prospectuses and websites for up-to-date information on admissions and, in particular, any entrance test to be taken (see also **Chapter 5**).

UNIVERSITIES' ADMISSIONS INFORMATION

The following information provides a selection of relevant aspects of universities' admissions policies and practice. Although the information on alternative qualifications to A-levels such as the Cambridge Pre-U Diploma, the Advanced Diploma, BTEC qualifications, Key Skills and Access courses is not always published in prospectuses, it is usually available on universities' websites. While it can be assumed that applicants will be considered and accepted with these alternative qualifications, depending on the requirements for individual degree programmes, it is important to check with university admissions staff **before** you make your application that your qualifications will meet their requirements. Non-EU applicants should refer to **Chapter 9** for details of the English Language entry requirements.

Aberdeen Selectors look for evidence of subject knowledge and understanding, commitment, motivation and responsibility, and the ability to cope with a university education.

Abertay Dundee The University will not use admissions tests for entry in 2011, and only some applicants are interviewed – for courses in Nursing, Ethical Hacking and Computer Arts.

Aberystwyth The University states that it is important that applications are made by the initial closing date of 15 January. They cannot guarantee to consider late applications. Some interviews take place although the majority of offers will be made on the basis of the application form. Decisions are made within four weeks of receiving the application and all those receiving an offer will be invited to visit the University.

Anglia Ruskin The University interviews all applicants for Art and Design, Education, Nursing, Social Work, Midwifery and Television and Media Studies. Some applicants are interviewed for Business. A maths test is also used for some Education (ITT) courses. The University is happy to give advice and guidance about the admissions process: email admissions@anglia.ac.uk. A second semester point for some courses is being considered.

Arts London In addition to formally qualified applicants, the University welcomes applications from candidates without formal qualifications who can demonstrate equivalent skills, knowledge and ability gained from work or life experience.

Aston There are no entrance tests in the selection process and offers are not normally made simply on the basis of UCAS points. Applications from high-achieving students taking Applied A-levels are welcomed and all degree programmes will consider a single award Applied A-level in place of a third A-level subject. For all degree programmes, except those in the School of Health and Life Sciences, a relevant Applied A-level double award plus one relevant A-level will normally be accepted. BTEC awards are acceptable and a mix of BTEC and A-levels welcomed. High-achieving Level 3 Diploma students in relevant subjects will be considered. Key skills will be taken into account but will not be included in offers; Access course applications are accepted.

Bangor Applications welcomed from students taking validated Access courses and 14–19 Diplomas in specified subjects.

Bath Some departments interview promising applicants; those not receiving an offer can obtain feedback on the reasons for their rejection. Students are encouraged to take the Extended Project and to provide details on their personal statement. Students taking the Advanced Diploma should check the requirements of individual degree courses.

Bath Spa Some candidates will be interviewed but all will be invited to visit the University after receiving an offer. Gap Years are acceptable.

Birmingham Courses are academic and 75% of the personal statement should relate to the proposed course of study. General studies A-level is accepted for some degree courses. Most subjects of the Advanced Diploma will be acceptable for most courses, although an A-level will also be required for some courses. The Extended Project will not be included in the University's offers. Some applicants are interviewed, for example for Medicine, Dentistry and for Social Work. The University uses LNAT (see **Chapter 5**) as its admissions test for Law applicants. Gap Years are acceptable and should be mentioned on the UCAS application or as soon as arrangements have been made. Decisions on offers are normally made within four to six weeks of receiving the application.

Birmingham City Some applicants will be called to interview and others invited to the Department before an offer is made. If the required grades of an offer are not achieved it may still be possible to be accepted on to a course. Deferred entry is acceptable.

Bolton The University welcomes the AL and AS general studies and also Key Skills at Level 3. If admissions staff consider that the course applied for is not suitable then an offer for an alternative course may be made. The academic reference should highlight academic skills, attendance and punctuality, time management skills and any contributions to extra-curricular activities. Dissatisfied applicants should contact the Head of Marketing and Recruitment with details of their application.

Bournemouth The personal statement is regarded as an important aspect of the application process. Some subject areas may require applicants to attend for interview. Deferred entry is acceptable.

Bradford It is not anticipated that the A* grade will be used in any offers. Candidates will not be accepted on to any degree course purely on the basis of AS-level results (including the double award) although two AS-levels or an AS double award may be accepted instead of a non-essential A-level. Low offers may be made to applicants showing considerable promise in academic or in other areas. Offers are normally based on the UCAS Tariff. The University accepts a range of alternative qualifications and takes a very positive view on the value of the new Advanced Diploma. These qualifications will be considered on a course-by-course basis.

Brighton The University welcomes applications from students with qualifications and experience other than traditional A-levels. The Advanced Diploma, Access courses and BTEC are acceptable alternative qualifications.

Bristol Decisions on applications may be delayed due to the volume of applications. A* grades may be included in the offers for some applicants depending on the application, the subject and the competition for places. Students choosing to take the Extended Project may receive two offers, one which includes the Extended Project, for example, AAA, or AAB plus the Extended Project. Requirements for the Advanced Diploma will be set by individual departments. Up to two Applied A-levels will be accepted with an A-level. Some admissions tutors take unit grade information into account in making an offer while others may specify unit grades in their offers. Deferred entry is acceptable but intention to defer should be indicated in the personal statement, giving information about your plans. However, in some cases the number of places available might be limited and higher offers may be made. An interview is required for an offer for Medicine, Dentistry, Veterinary Science, Drama, Engineering Design and Veterinary Nursing, but not all applicants are interviewed. LNAT (see **Chapter 5**) is used for admission to the Law programmes. Advice to applicants can be found on www.bristol.ac.uk/study.

Bristol UWE Typical offers are made for each degree programme although these offers may vary between applicants since selection is based on individual merit. Students applying for courses 'subject to approval' or ' subject to validation' will be kept informed of the latest developments. Many offers will be made in terms of Tariff points.

Brunel All offers for degree courses are for three A-levels and either one AS-level or the Extended Project. If an applicant has not been able to take a fourth subject at AS-level, or complete a Project, this should be indicated in the application; offers will then be made for three A-levels (or equivalent). The University accepts relevant Advanced Diplomas (see www.brunel.ac.uk).

Buckingham Candidates apply through UCAS in the normal way or directly with a paper application obtainable from the University.

Bucks New It may be possible to transfer to the University from another university under the Credit Accumulation and Transfer Scheme (CATS), and to gain exemptions from part of the course if the student has CATS credit points from their relevant previous study. Transfers from full-time to part-time study is possible. BTEC qualifications are acceptable.

Cambridge Currently, the standard offer is A*AA but the subject in which the A* is to be achieved in unlikely to be specified. All Colleges modify offers to take account of individual circumstances, for example, lower offers may be made to students applying through the Cambridge Special Access Scheme – see the University's website. Self-discipline, motivation and commitment are required together with the ability to think critically and independently, plus passion or, at the very least, real enthusiasm for the chosen course. If examination predictions are good then the chance of admission may be better than one in four.

Applicants are encouraged to take the Extended Project although it will not be a requirement of any offer. Although AS and AL critical thinking and general studies are acceptable as a fourth AS or A-level subject, neither is considered acceptable as a third A-level. The Advanced Engineering Diploma is the only Advanced Diploma with adequate preparation for a Cambridge course and will be accepted for Engineering if applicants have an AL physics and the new Level 3 Certificate in Mathematics for Engineering within the Specialist Learning component. For many courses admissions tests are used – and written work may be required – so it is very important to check the university website and prospectus well before completing the application to find out exactly what is needed for entry.

See **Chapter 5**, and also www.cam.ac.uk/admissions/undergraduate/tests and www.admissionstests.cambridgeassment.org.uk.

Canterbury Christ Church The personal statement is regarded as highly important. Applicants for Teaching and Health-related courses must show evidence on their application of relevant experience. If they do not, they will be rejected without interview. Some subjects, including Geography, History and Music interview candidates.

Cardiff Applicants are required to take only three A-levels for degree courses. Deferred entry is acceptable. The 14–19 Diploma is an acceptable qualification for entry. Key Skills should be mentioned in an application but will not form part of an offer.

Central Lancashire The University looks for grades C/D plus Additional Specialist Learning for applicants with the new Advanced Diplomas. Grades B/C will be required from students with the Progression Diploma.

Chester Interviews and workshops are required for some courses to support applications. General studies at A-level is acceptable for entry to courses in addition to other A-levels.

Chichester Early application is advised for popular courses such as Dance, Physical Education, Primary Education, Teaching and Sports Therapy. Deferred entry applications are not considered for PGCE courses. Teaching applicants should have spent a minimum of two weeks observing/helping out in a state school within two years of applying. Significant experience is also required for applicants for Social Work courses. Applicants taking a Level 3 Diploma will be considered for entry to the relevant course. Dance, Music and Performing Arts applicants will be required to prepare a set piece in advance and to perform it in front of a group. Decisions on applications are normally made within two weeks, and, except for some courses where interviews are required (see **Chapter 5**) most decisions are made on the basis of the application form.

City It is hoped that applicants will have taken four AS-level subjects in Year 13, one of which is a contrasting subject.

Coventry The University welcomes applications from those with significant work or life experience who do not necessarily meet the published academic requirements for the course. Applicants will be required to demonstrate evidence of motivation, potential and knowledge of the subject. Some candidates will be required to attend interviews depending on their course choice. Deferred entry is acceptable.

Creative Arts There is no minimum age requirement for entry to undergraduate courses.

Cumbria Candidates without GCSE English, Mathematics or Science at Grade C or above (which are required for some courses) take an equivalency test at the University. The new Diploma qualification is acceptable for some subjects and will be recognised as equivalent to 3.5 A-levels with a possible total Tariff score of 300 points. Key Skills at Level 3 may be allowed to contribute up to 20 UCAS Tariff points towards meeting the conditions of an offer.

De Montfort Selection criteria depend on the chosen course. Some courses require a personal interview and/or examination of portfolios.

Derby The Level 2 Diploma is regarded as equivalent to GCSEs and the Level 3 Diploma to A-levels. Students without formal qualifications can take an Access course or the Modular Foundation course to gain entry to degree programmes.

Dundee Decisions for non-interviewing courses are usually made within five working days. Applicants taking qualifications in subjects other than A-levels should contact the subject department for details of entry requirements. The University considers applicants re-sitting A-levels on an individual basis.

Durham The main factor in selection is academic performance and potential. The personal statement is important and is likely to be used as the basis for questions at interview. The statement should focus on your reasons for choosing the subject, your understanding of what its study involves, why you think you are suitable for the course, and on other aspects such as 'why you are an interesting and unique individual'. Durham does not use interviews as a means for selection except for Teacher Training courses and Medicine, for applicants to foundation courses and for those who have had a break in their education.

East Anglia Offers are normally made in terms of three A-levels although applicants with two A-levels and AS-levels are welcome. Most offers are made without an interview. Deferred entry is acceptable.

East London Candidates are advised to apply as soon as possible and results are normally announced within seven days. Some students may be called for interview and in some cases an essay or a portfolio may be required. The interviewers will be looking for evidence of a real interest in the chosen subject. Rejected applicants may receive an offer of a place on an Extended degree or another course.

Edge Hill With the exception of courses in Journalism, Animation, Media (Film and TV), TV Production courses, Performing Arts and Social and Psychological Sciences, Teacher Training, Nursing and Midwifery, most decisions are made without an interview, those applicants made offers being invited to visit the University. The new Advanced Diploma is accepted as equivalent to three A-levels.

Edinburgh The results of applications may be delayed until the deadline and all applications have been received. All offers will be expressed in grades not Tariff points. Decisions have yet to be made on the timing of the introduction of the new A* grade. Applicants offering the new Advanced Diploma in Engineering, IT or Society, Health and Development may be considered for entry to programmes in Engineering, Computing, Nursing or Social Work.

Edinburgh Napier Offers are normally based on the UCAS Tariff point system. The normal offers may not apply to candidates over 21 who should contact the admissions tutor for details. Interviews may be required for some courses.

Essex Candidates are required to have two full A-levels or equivalent although students taking two A-levels, or re-sitting some subjects may get a higher offer. All departments accept general studies and critical thinking. Key Skills at Level 3 can be used as part of the points total providing they do not overlap with other qualifications (eg numeracy or A-level Mathematics). Unit grades are not used as standard procedure. Additional aptitude tests are not used. Interviews may be required for some subjects.

Exeter The University welcomes applications that offer a greater breadth of experience both academically and vocationally. Key indicators include predicted and achieved academic performance in Level 2 and 3 qualifications; candidates normally would be expected to take four AS-levels followed by three A-levels in Year 13. The personal statement should cover the reasons for your course choice and how the course relates to your current or previous studies and experience. It should also give evidence of your motivation to study at a higher level, details of work experience or positions of responsibility and what you have gained from these. The University supports the introduction of the new qualifications including the Advanced Diplomas, the Extended Project and the Cambridge Pre-U Diploma. Deferred applications are acceptable but the number of places for deferred applicants for popular courses can be limited and in some cases higher offers may be made.

Glamorgan Candidates applying for the Excellence Award must submit their applications by the 15 January deadline. Key Skills points can contribute to the overall Tariff point requirement.

Glasgow Candidates are strongly advised to meet the deadlines for applications. Normally all subjects apart from Dentistry, Education (for the BEd Primary programme), Medicine, Veterinary Medicine, Social Sciences and Law accept applications after the 15 January deadline, but this is not guaranteed and will depend on the pressure on places and the academic qualifications of the applicant. Offers are made from early to late March. The University does not interview students to all faculties, some exceptions being the Medical and Veterinary Sciences, Music, Education and Technological Education. Deferrred entry is not guaranteed for all subjects (eg Dentistry, Veterinary Medicine and Primary Education): check with the University.

Glasgow Caledonian Some courses interview applicants. Applicants who are considering deferred entry should contact the admissions tutor before applying.

Gloucestershire Students failing to meet the UCAS Tariff requirements may be eligible for entry based on life or work experience following an interview. Entry with the Advanced Diploma, BTEC, NVQ Level 3 and Access to Higher Education qualifications is acceptable.

Glyndŵr The general requirement for entry to most degree courses is 200 UCAS points and 100 points for Foundation degrees. UCAS points may be counted from a wide variety of qualifications. Applications are also welcomed from candidates who do not possess the standard qualifications but who can demonstrate their capacity to pursue the course successfully. Entrance can be based on past experience, skills, organisational capabilities and the potential to succeed. Interviews for some courses are essential including Education, Nursing and Social Work. Portfolios are required for Art and Design courses and an audition is required for Theatre and Performance.

Greenwich The University operates a Credit Accumulation and Transfer Scheme (CATS). This means that normally a full-time undergraduate student earns 120 credits for each academic year they successfully complete, and most degrees require a total of 360 credits. CATS make it easier for students to transfer their credits from one university to another, and to move between programmes of the University. Candidates are reminded to apply early since popular courses fill up quickly. Interviews are held for some courses. Those who are rejected may receive an offer for an alternative course.

Heriot-Watt In order to give candidates as much flexibility as possible, many will receive offers for both first and second year entry. Although one of these will be the main offer, candidates accepting this can easily change their main offer to the alternative year if they subsequently want to do so. Applicants are interviewed for some programmes.

Hertfordshire Applicants wanting to take a Gap Year should finalise their arrangements before asking for deferment and accepting a place. Once a place has been accepted for the following year it will not be possible to change their application for entry to the current year. They would need to withdraw their application and apply again through Clearing.

Huddersfield The University welcomes a wide range of qualifications. Some students will be called for interview. Students wishing to defer entry should state their intention on their application. It is advisable to have finalised arrangements for a Gap Year before accepting an offer for deferment.

Hull The University will not be using the A-level A* grade or unit grade information for entry to courses in 2011. A wide range of qualifications are accepted for entry to degree courses. Applications are also welcomed from those who can demonstrate Level 3 work-based learning such as Advanced Apprenticeships and NVQ 3. Bridging study may be recommended by way of a foundation year. Most courses welcome applications for deferred entry although this should be stated on the application. Deferred entry is not available for Nursing courses.

Imperial London Except for courses where three specific A-levels are required for admission, candidates with two A-levels and two AS-levels will normally be considered equally with other candidates offering three A-levels. The College considers candidates with the Advanced Engineering Diploma if they also have A levels in specified subjects which meet the College's entry requirements. Applicants for entry to Year 2 of some courses can also be considered if they have completed the first year of a comparable degree at another institution with a high level of achievement, but they need to contact the relevant department before applying. A College Admissions and Appeals and Complaints procedure is available to applicants dissatisfied with the way their application has been considered. Applicants should note the College's policy on dress, health and safety published on its website. An offer for an alternative course may be made to rejected applicants.

Keele Conditional offers are normally made in grades for Medicine, Pharmacy and Physiotherapy. For other subjects offers are usually made in Tariff points and include points for Key Skills at Level 3, stand-alone AS-levels and Advanced Extension Awards. The Advanced Diploma is accepted as equivalent to three A-levels and general studies is also accepted as a condition of an offer. Applicants are normally required to be currently undertaking some formal study before starting a course, but if this is not possible the University may make an offer for a Foundation course.

Kent The University accepts a wide range of qualifications. For mature students and those without the required qualifications Foundation course offers may be made. Applicants returning to study after a long break are advised to contact the admissions staff before making a UCAS application. Deferred entry is acceptable but should be mentioned on the application. The University regards the personal statement as important and recommends that applicants research their chosen courses thoroughly, and show an understanding of the curriculum.

Kingston Admissions staff look carefully at each applicant's academic record, references and personal statement. Some courses require interviews where selectors look for evidence of the applicant's intellectual capacity, course knowledge and enthusiasm. Punctuality and a smart appearance could be important.

Lancaster The University welcomes applications from students wishing to defer entry. General studies is acceptable for the majority of courses. Schools and colleges should include clearly in their references the range of programmes available to their students, whether students are required to sit AS-level examinations if they are continuing the subject to A-level, and whether it is school policy to list AS-level results on the UCAS application. Admissions tutors accept a range of qualifications for entry. Some candidates are interviewed before an offer is made, but most are invited to an informal post-offer Open Day which can involve an interview or discussion with an admissions tutor.

Leeds The University welcomes students who do not come straight from school or college or who wish to defer entry. It also welcomes the increased breadth of post-16 qualifications. Some courses do not accept AL general studies or critical thinking.

Leeds Metropolitan Most offers are made in UCAS points, and interviews are held before an offer is made for some courses. Deferred entry is acceptable although applicants should be aware that some courses may change slightly each year. Students without the required qualifications may provide a 'portfolio of achievement', giving, for example, information about their work experience and their reasons for applying for the course, and also providing references.

Leicester Most courses do not interview applicants although invitations to visit the University will follow any offers made. Most offers are made on the basis of three A-levels although in some cases two A-levels and two AS-levels may be accepted. The University welcomes the Extended Project which should be mentioned in the personal statement. The Advanced Diploma and the Cambridge Pre-U Diploma are also acceptable qualifications. Applications from suitably qualified students are also considered for second year entry. Contact the subject department for further information.

Lincoln On some courses, notably Art and Design and Architecture, an interview with a portfolio is sometimes required before an offer can be made. The University accepts a wide range of qualifications but students without the standard entry requirements may still be offered a place on the basis of prior experience and qualifications.

Liverpool Most departments will invite applicants to visit the University before or after an offer is made. Some departments require interviews. Offers are normally based on three A-levels or equivalent (a wide range of qualifications is accepted). Some programmes will accept two A-levels and two AS-levels.

Liverpool Hope Students who are invited for audition or interview are encouraged to bring their Records of Achievement.

Liverpool John Moores The personal statement is regarded as highly important and students are advised to include all relevant interests and work experience. The University welcomes a wide range of entry qualifications. If an applicant fails to receive an offer for their chosen course then an offer for an alternative course may be made.

London (Birkbeck) Applications are made on-line. For details contact the Registry at www.bbk.ac.uk.

London (Courtauld) History, history of art, English and modern European languages are the most relevant A-level subjects for the one BA course in History of Art, but applications will be considered from those studying other subjects. Art offered at A-level should normally include a history of art paper. The ability to read foreign languages is a particular asset. The offer of BBB is flexible.

London (Goldsmiths) While offers are stipulated for courses, candidates are assessed individually and may receive an offer lower than the published grades. Some applicants are interviewed, in particular those for Art and Design degrees for which examples of current art and design work are required before interview. Applicants requiring deferred entry (which may or may not be acceptable depending on the course) should contact the admissions tutor before applying. International students applying for the BA in Design, or the MEng/BEng in Design and Innovation who are unable to attend for interview are asked to send photographs and explanations of their work.

London (Heythrop) When considering applications Heythrop takes note of applicants' current and predicted performance at A-level, their ability to study at the relevant level, to take increasing responsibility for their own learning and their motivation to engage intellectually with issues in theology and philosophy.

London (King's) Applicants will normally have taken four AS-level subjects and pursued three of these at A-level. However, departments will also consider those who have taken five AS levels and passed only two of these at A-level. Applicants may take all their examinations at the end of Year 13 without prejudice. Conditional offers may include the fourth AS-level, a high grade possibly compensating for a failure to obtain the right grade in one of the A-level subjects. AS and A-level general studies and critical thinking are not accepted although the grade achieved may be considered when the required grades of an offer have not been met. Applicants are not required to take aptitude tests, except for Dentistry, Law and Medicine. Deferred entry is acceptable.

London (Queen Mary) It is possible for students to join undergraduate degree programmes at the beginning of the second and sometimes the third year. Those wishing to transfer their degree studies from another UK higher education institution may be considered but should contact the subject department before applying to obtain approval.

London (Royal Holloway) Applicants likely to meet the entry requirements may be called for interview or invited to an Open Day. International students may be asked to submit an example of academic work or other exercise although it would be preferable if they could visit the campus. Interviews are not intended to be nerve-wracking or daunting but rather a chance to assess the candidate's potential. In Music there may be an audition, in Drama a workshop session, and in Modern Languages some conversation in the appropriate language. Candidates who fail to meet the requirements of their offer may still be offered a place, particularly if they shone at interview.

London (Royal Veterinary College) Applications for deferred entry are considered but the offer conditions must be met in the same academic year as the application. Applicants holding offers from RVC who fall slightly below the grades required are always reconsidered and may be offered entry if places are available.

London (St George's) Once admitted students are not allowed to change courses.

London (School of Oriental and African Studies) Offers may be made without an interview and particular attention is paid to past and predicted academic performance. SOAS is happy to consider deferred entry which should be stated on the UCAS application.

London (School of Pharmacy) Applicants are recommended to write a supplementary personal statement explaining their interest in studying Pharmacy. The statement should be sent directly to the admissions tutor before the interview. Qualified applicants are required to attend for interview.

London (University College) UCL welcomes applications from students proposing to spend a pre-university year engaged in constructive activity in the UK or abroad. About 9% of UCL's undergraduates take a Gap Year. Those wanting to enter the second or third year of a degree programme should make early contact with the relevant subject department to obtain approval. Applications are assessed on the basis of the personal statement, the referee's report and the predicted academic performance. UCL is one of the few universities that interviews a significant proportion of its applicants. The programme for the day varies but will include a talk about the subject, a tour of the campus, a discussion with current students and the interview itself. Interviews vary, some being subject-based, others focusing on motivation and communication skills. Decisions on admission are final and there is normally no right of appeal.

London Metropolitan Applicants may be required to sit a test or to submit a portfolio of work.

London School of Economics and Political Science (LSE) While many other qualifications are considered in the selection of applicants, the vast majority of applicants are expected to have taken four AS-level subjects, followed by three at A-level. Applicants will not be penalised if they have not been able to take the normal number of AS and AL subjects but referees should advise on such circumstances. Applicants normally offer A-levels in LSE's preferred subjects which do **not** include AS/AL accounting, art and design, business studies, communication studies, design and technology, drama and theatre studies (for some departments), home economics, ICT, law, media studies, music technology, sports studies, travel and tourism. The A* grade (not used for the 2010 entry) may be used for the 2011 entry – check with departments. The Advanced Diploma in Society Health and Development will be considered with one A-level in the additional/specialist learning component plus one free-standing additional A-level in a preferred subject. Competition is particularly high for the Accounting and Finance, Economics, Law, and Management courses. Predicted grades on the application will not guarantee an offer of a place. Applications are often held in a 'gathered field' (candidates are informed) and decisions made only when all on-time applications have been received.

Some applicants will be asked to take an entrance examination (held in March each year), which lasts for three hours and consists of a précis of an English language text, essays on general discussion topics and tests of mathematical understanding. Sample papers are available from web pages from January to March. It is unlikely that there will be any course vacancies when the A-level results are published. From 2010 all undergraduates study a compulsory course (LSE 100) in Year 1.

London South Bank Applicants not achieving the grades required for their chosen course should contact the University which may still be able to make an offer of a place.

Loughborough The University will not use admissions tests for entry in 2011. It does not differentiate between applicants taking A-levels for the first time or re-sitting subjects. The Advanced Diploma is acceptable for most undergraduate degrees (see below) although for some degrees applicants may be asked to achieve an A-level in an appropriate subject or relevant Additional Specialist Learning. In most cases offers are based on the application following an invitation to visit the University. Transfers between courses may be possible providing that the required entry requirements have been achieved.

Acceptable Advanced Diploma subjects for the University's courses:

Business, Administration and Finance Diploma Business and Management, Economics, History and International Relations, Information Science, Politics.
Construction Diploma Architectural Engineering, Commercial Management and Quantity Surveying, Geography.

Creative and Media Diploma Business and Management, Design and Technology, Drama, English, Ergonomics, History and International Relations, Information Science, Politics, Psychology, Social Sciences.
Engineering Diploma Chemistry, Computer Science, Design and Technology, all Engineering subjects, Mathematics.
Environmental and Land-Based Studies Diploma Architectural Engineering, Commercial Management and Quantity Surveying, Geography.
IT Diploma Architectural Engineering, Business and Management, Chemistry, Commercial Management and Quantity Surveying, Computer Science, Design and Technology, Drama, Economics, Electronic and Electrical Engineering, English, Ergonomics, Geography, History and International Relations, Information Science, Mathematics, Politics, Psychology, Social Sciences.
Manufacturing and Product Design Diploma Design and Technology, Manufacturing Engineering, Materials Engineering.

The University's admissions and associated policies are available on its website: www.lboro.ac.uk/admin/ar/admissions/sacop/index.htm.

Manchester Entry requirements are set at course level: check course requirements at www.manchester.ac.uk/undergraduate/courses for latest information. Methods of assessing applications vary between courses and may involve interviews, supporting information and aptitude tests. Unit grades normally will not form part of the offer, except for Mathematics programmes. Candidates who fail to achieve the required grades of an offer should not automatically assume that they have been rejected. In the case of failure to obtain a place on a course it should not be assumed that a department will consider a re-application for a course.

Manchester Metropolitan Admissions staff look for personal statements showing evidence of the applicants' motivation and commitment to their chosen courses, work or voluntary experience relevant to any chosen career, and extra-curricular activities, achievements and interests which are relevant to the chosen courses.

Middlesex Some courses start in January (see www.mdx.uk/janstart).

Newcastle In general, offers will be made in grades to be achieved, not in Tariff points. A- and AS-level critical thinking and in some cases general studies will be considered. The Advanced Diploma is welcomed although it may not be acceptable for some courses. Offers will also be made for the Cambridge Pre-U Diploma, together with other specified subjects.

Newport Interviews and auditions are held for applicants to Art, Media and Design courses.

Northampton Achievement in Key Skills units counts towards the final UCAS Tariff points score.

Northumbria Interviews are compulsory for courses in Architecture, most courses in Art and Design and courses in Health and Teaching. There are no admissions tests.

Nottingham Although grade predictions may match the offers published for the course there is no guarantee that an offer can be made.

Nottingham Trent The UCAS personal statement is seen as a key part of the application process; the University website provides a guide on its possible content and preparation.

Open University There are no formal entry qualifications for admission to courses.

Oxford The University will not use the A* grade when making offers for 2011 entry but will review this policy in time to advise those applying for 2012 entry. All A-levels except general studies are approved for admissions purposes but specific subject requirements must be met. If applicants have taken the Extended Project (EP), the University will not make it a condition for an offer but it does recognise its potential value to applicants for study at the University and encourages applicants to use their experience of the EP when writing their personal statements, especially if their EP topic is related to their chosen degree course. The Advanced Diploma in Engineering will be accepted for Engineering courses provided candidates obtain both an A-level in Physics and the new Level 3 Certificate in Mathematics for Engineering.

Interviews normally take place in December except for international interviews which are arranged in October and November, either in Oxford or in international interview centres in North America, India, Hong Kong, Singapore, China and Malaysia. All interviews for Medicine and Fine Art are held in Oxford and not in any international centres or by telephone. For most courses over 75% of applicants are interviewed. Admissions tests are required for a number of subjects and applicants are responsible for checking and registering for any such tests. Examples of written work undertaken at school or college are also required for some subjects or by some colleges and these are submitted before interview with a completed cover sheet. The purpose is to allow candidates to demonstrate analytical, reasoning, language and written skills. See **Chapter 5**, and also www.admissions.ox.ac.uk/tests and the 'How to apply' sections of the course pages of the University website.

Oxford Brookes For all applications considerable emphasis is placed on the personal statement. Referees are requested to give reasons for their statements, for example, whether predicted grades are based on the results of studies at the end of Year 12, how applicants' skills have been assessed. Fine Art applicants wishing to take a Gap Year should contact the admissions tutor before applying.

Plymouth The University looks for evidence in the UCAS personal statement of your understanding of the course, good numeracy and literacy skills, motivation and commitment, work experience or placement or volunary work, especially if it is relevant to your course, any sponsorships or placements you have applied for, and your possible plans for a Gap Year.

Portsmouth For some courses applicants will be expected to attend an interview as part of the selection process. The University accepts the principle of credit tranfer and wherever possible, recognition will be given to prior learning in order to facilitate admission with advanced standing. It also welcomes applications from those taking the Advanced Diploma: one A-level will be required in most cases. The Extended Project is not a requirement but may be taken into consideration.

Queen's Belfast Applications for admission to full-time undergraduate courses are made through UCAS except for courses in Midwifery and Nursing. These should be made direct to the University's School of Nursing and Midwifery (see www.qub.ac.uk).

Queen Margaret Applicants are not usually interviewed.

Reading For some courses admissions tutors may interview before making an offer, and in a few programmes, they may make an offer of a place which is dependent on passing the interview. The University welcomes evidence of Key Skills in students' portfolios, and will take them into account when making offers, although points from Key Skills will not be included in the standard offers.

Robert Gordon Interviews are held for some courses, for example Social Work.

Roehampton Applicants successfully achieving the new Level 3 Advanced Diplomas will be considered for entry on to degrees in closely related subjects. For entry to other subjects, each application will be judged taking the applicant's entire academic record into account and on its own merit.

Salford The University is committed to widening participation; it does not make lower offers on the basis of educational or social disadvantage.

St Andrews The University highlights the importance of the personal statement and the quality of this is likely to decide which applicants receive offers. It looks for well-organised, well-written statements which include information about the applicants, their interests, relevant work experience, any voluntary work, ideas about career choice and, importantly, their reasons for their choice of course. Admissions tutors prefer candidates to achieve their grades at the first sitting, and if they re-apply, to upgrade their academic attainment if that was the main reason for UCAS rejection. Only candidates for Medicine A100 are interviewed; no other subjects interview as a matter of course.

Sheffield Hallam An intensive six-week preparation course in mathematics is offered, equivalent to GCSE maths, to applicants who are unable to meet the entrance requirements for their chosen course.

Southampton The University looks for a well-considered personal statement, focusing on your reasons for choosing a particular course, the skills you would bring to it, information about any relevant work experience, your career ideas, your personal interests related to the course, and your thoughts about 'what makes you stand out in a crowd'.

Southampton Solent Admissions staff look for applicants' reasons for their course choice, and for evidence of their abilities and ambitions.

Staffordshire The University provides an on-line workbook for helping applicants to prepare their personal statements.

Stirling It is essential to include in the personal statement your reasons for choosing your specified course. The University also looks for evidence of your transferable skills, for example communication skills, teamwork, and how you acquired these, for example through work experience, voluntary work, academic studies, hobbies and general life experience.

Strathclyde Formal interviews are required for some Faculty of Education courses; informal interviews are held by some Science and Engineering courses.

Sunderland The University holds informal interviews for certain courses, when applicants will be asked to present their portfolio, or to give an audition, or to talk about themselves and why they want to study for that particular course.

Surrey The University is willing to consider deferring an application for one year, providing it considers that this will benefit the applicant's studies. Contact the admissions staff if you are considering deferred entry.

Sussex Apart from Social Work and Medicine, interviews at Sussex are increasingly unusual, but some departments may ask for examples of written work or for an additional reference. Mature students submitting a strong application but without the relevant qualifications will probably be asked to attend an interview and submit an essay of up to 1500 words on their chosen subject.

Swansea Selectors also take into account the candidate's ability to contribute to the cultural, sporting and social life of the University.

Swansea Metropolitan For many courses an interview is an important part of the selection process.

Teesside Interviews are held for a wide range of courses, and successful applicants are given an individualised offer. Each course accepts a minimum of 20 UCAS Tariff points for Level 3 Key Skills.

Thames Valley The University accepts each of the new 14–19 Diplomas as qualification for entry on to all of its undergraduate courses, providing the UCAS Tariff points achieved by applicants match or exceed the UCAS Tariff points listed in the course entry requirements. The University welcomes applicants with the Extended Project, and offers an Extended Project module to students in Years 12 and 13 in the school holidays. It is also possible to transfer credits achieved at another university to a course at Thames Valley.

Trinity Saint David (created from the merger (2010) of University of Wales, Lampeter and Trinity University College) The University guarantees to give equal consideration to all applicants irrespective of when their applications are received. Applicants who successfully complete the residential Wales

Summer School at Lampeter, Aberystwyth or Carmarthen are offered a place on an appropriate course of study on completion of their current school or college course.

Ulster Applicants seeking admission to any of the following courses should use the University's direct entry form: BSc courses in Community Nursing, Specialist Nursing Practice, Nursing Sciences, and Health Sciences, the Certificate in Information Technology and Professional Development for Women and the Diploma in Telematics and Management Studies.

Warwick The University welcomes the introduction of the A* grade and is monitoring developments. Students taking the Advanced Diploma will be considered if they are taking subjects closely aligned to the chosen degree courses, and they must also take appropriate additional specialised learning options: they are advised to contact the admissions team before making their application. Advice on the completion of the application is available on www.warwick.ac.uk/go/study. Feedback can be provided if requested for candidates whose application has been rejected.

West of Scotland Applications to Nursing and Midwifery courses are not made through UCAS but through the Centralised Applications to Nursing and Midwifery Training Clearing House (CATCH): contact the University for details.

Westminster Interviews are usually only required for Media, Art and Design and Complementary Therapy courses. The University accepts transfers into Years 1, 2 or 3 of a full-time degree programme if students have studied similar units to the chosen Westminster course, and have passed Year 1 and Year 2, each with 120 credits.

Winchester The following programmes require applicants to take a second subject at Level 1: Childhood, Youth and Community Studies; Education Studies; Education Studies (Early Childhood); Film Studies; Media Studies; Politics and Global Studies; Psychology; Theology and Religious Studies. Second subjects can be contrasting or complementary.

Wolverhampton Admissions staff make decisions on the basis of the application, and may invite applicants for interview or audition. If an applicant cannot meet the entry requirements for the chosen course, the University may offer an alternative course, or give the applicant feedback about why it was unable to offer a place.

Worcester The University advises applicants to consider their personal statements carefully. It advises them to include their reasons for their choice of degree programme, their career plans, their outside interests and work experience, and any other information they consider relevant. Applicants who are not accepted are not necessarily rejected: they may receive a 'changed programme' offer which they need not accept if they prefer to enter Clearing.

York The University welcomes applicants with the Advanced Diploma, and Departments will consider applicants studying any of the following Diplomas: Construction and the Built Environment, Creative and Media, IT, and Society, Health and Development.

York St John Interviews are compulsory for the following courses: Primary Education, Occupational Therapy, Physiotherapy, Product Design, Fine Art and Counselling.

The following chapter provides details of admissions tests used for the selection of applicants by a number of universities and colleges. It also gives an insight into the ways in which universities select applicants and into the interview process and how you can prepare yourself for this.

5 | ADMISSIONS TESTS, SELECTION OF APPLICANTS AND INTERVIEWS

The selection of applicants by universities and colleges takes many forms. However, with rising numbers of applicants for places (especially in the popular subjects) and increasing numbers of students with high grades, greater importance is now attached not only to applicants' predicted A-level grades and GCSE attainments, but also to other aspects of their applications, especially the school reference and the personal statement and, for some courses and some institutions, performance at interview, and performance in admissions tests.

ADMISSIONS TESTS

Admissions tests are now increasingly used for undergraduate entry to specific courses and specific institutions. These include national subject-based tests such as LNAT, BMAT and UKCAT (see below) which are used for selecting applicants for entry to specified courses at particular institutions in subjects such as Law, Medicine, Dentistry and Veterinary Sciences. Admissions tests are also set by individual universities and colleges (or commercial organisations on their behalf) for entry, again, to particular courses in the individual institutions. Examples of these include the Thinking Skills Assessment (TSA) used by, for example, many Cambridge University colleges, and the Health Professions Aptitude Test (HPAT) used by Ulster University for entry to some health-related courses. Other examples include the subject-based admissions tests used by many universities and colleges for entry to particular courses in subjects such as Art, Dance, Construction, Design, Drama and other Performance-based courses, Education and Teacher Training, Economics, Engineering, Journalism, Languages, Music, Nursing and Social Work.

Admissions tests are usually taken before or at interview and, except for courses requiring auditions or portfolio inspections, they are generally timed, unseen, written, or on-line tests. They can be used on their own, or alongside other selection methods used by university and college admissions staff, including:

- Questionnaires or tests to be completed by applicants prior to interview and/or offer.
- Examples of school work to be submitted prior to interview and/or offer.
- Written tests at interview.
- Mathematical tests at interview.
- Practical tests at interview.
- A response to a passage at interview.
- Performance-based tests (for example, for Music, Dance, Drama).

Applicants should find out early from university prospectuses and websites whether admissions tests are required for entry to their preferred courses, and if so, what these will be, and the arrangements for taking them. This is important, especially for Oxford and Cambridge applicants as many of their courses and colleges also require submission of marked written work done in Years 12 or 13 at school or college.

The next section provides a list of commonly used admissions tests, and this is followed by degree subject lists showing subject-based and individual institutions' admissions tests.

English

English Literature Admissions Test (ELAT)

The ELAT is a pre-interview admissions test for applicants to English courses at the University of Oxford (see the ELAT pages on the Cambridge Assessment website www.admissionstests.cambridgeassessment.org.uk).

Health Professions

Health Professions Admissions Test (HPAT)

The HPAT is used by the University of Ulster for entry to Dietetics, Occupational Therapy, Physiotherapy, Podiatry, Radiography and Speech and Language Therapies.

History

History Aptitude Test (HAT)

The HAT is a two-hour test sat by all candidates applying for History courses at Oxford University (see ***History*** below). See www.history.ox.ac.uk.

Law

Cambridge Law Test

This is a new paper-based, one-hour, one-question, test designed and used by most of the Cambridge University Colleges with Law applicants who are called for interview. No prior knowledge of law is required for the test. See www.law.cam.ac.uk/admissions/cambridge-law-test.php for full details.

National Admissions Test for Law (LNAT)

The LNAT is an on-screen test for applicants to specified undergraduate Law programmes at the Birmingham, Bristol, Durham, Glasgow, Leeds, London (King's), (UCL), Nottingham and Oxford universities. (See ***Law*** below, and **Law** in the subject tables in **Chapter 8**.) Applicants need to check universities' websites and the LNAT website (www.lnat.ac.uk) for the UCAS codes for courses requiring applicants to sit the LNAT. (**NB** Cambridge does not now require Law applicants to take the LNAT but see above and the Cambridge entry under ***Law*** below.) Details of LNAT (which includes multiple-choice and essay questions), practice papers, registration dates, test dates, test centres and fees are all available on the LNAT website.

Mathematics

Sixth Term Examination Paper (STEP)

Applicants with offers for Mathematics courses at Cambridge and Warwick Universities are usually required to take STEP. Bristol and Oxford Universities, and Imperial London also encourage applicants for their Mathematics courses to take STEP. For details, see the STEP pages on the Cambridge Assessment website (www.admissionstests.cambridgeassesssment.org.uk).

Medicine, Dentistry, Veterinary Science/Medicine, and related subjects

The BioMedical Admissions Test (BMAT)

This is a pen-and-paper admissions test taken by undergraduate applicants to specified Medicine, Veterinary Science/Medicine courses at Cambridge, and Oxford universities, and at Imperial London, London (RVC) and London (UCL). Imperial London also requires BMAT for entry to Biomedical Science, and Pharmacology with Translational Medical Science; BMAT is also a requirement for entry to Physiological Sciences at Oxford University but note that this course will be replaced for 2011 entry by Biomedical Sciences (see **Oxford** below). A list of the courses requiring BMAT is available on the BMAT pages of the Cambridge Assessment website (www.admissionstests.cambridgeassessment.org.uk) and also on university websites and in their prospectuses. It is important to note BMAT's early closing date for entries and also the test dates. The two-hour test consists of three sections:

- Aptitude and skills
- Scientific knowledge and application
- Writing task.

Applicants sit the test only once and pay one entry fee no matter how many courses they apply for. However, if they re-apply to universities the following year they will need to re-take the BMAT and pay another fee. Past question papers are available (see website) and an official study guide *Preparing for the BMAT* is also available at www.pearsonschoolsandfecolleges.co.uk. Results of the BMAT are first sent to the universities, and then to the BMAT test centres. Candidates need to contact their test centres direct for their results. See ***Dentistry***, ***Medicine*** and ***Veterinary Science/Medicine*** below and relevant subject tables in **Chapter 8**.

The UK Clinical Aptitude Test (UKCAT)

The UKCAT is a clinical aptitude test used by the majority of medical and dental schools in the selection of applicants for Medicine and Dentistry, alongside their existing selection processes, for undergraduate entry. The tests are not curriculum-based and do not have a science component. No revision is necessary; there is no textbook and no course of instruction. In the first instance, the UKCAT is a test of cognitive skills involving problem-solving and critical reasoning. With over 150 test centres, it is an on-screen test (not paper-based), and is marked electronically. Some bursaries are available to help towards the cost of the test. Further details (including the most recent list of universities requiring applicants to sit the UKCAT) are found on the website www.ukcat.ac.uk. See also the **Dentistry** and **Medicine** subject tables in **Chapter 8**, the entries for ***Dentistry*** and ***Medicine*** below, and **Chapter 6** for application details. See www.ukcat.ac.uk.

Modern and Medieval Languages

The Modern and Medieval Languages Test (MML)

This written test is used by the University of Cambridge for selecting applicants for entry to courses involving modern and medieval languages. See www.mml.cam.ac.uk/prospectus/undergrad/applying/test.html.

General Admissions Test

Thinking Skills Assessment (TSA)

The TSA is a 90-minute multiple choice test consisting of 50 questions which test applicants' critical thinking and problem-solving skills. It is used at or before interview by applicants for some courses at Cambridge University by some colleges, by University College London for applicants to European Social and Political Studies, and by Oxford University for entry to several courses (see below and see the TSA web pages on www.admissionstests.cambridgeassessment.org.uk).

DEGREE SUBJECT LISTS OF UNIVERSITIES AND COLLEGES USING TESTS AND ASSESSMENTS

Many universities and colleges set their own tests for specific subjects so it is important to check the websites for your preferred institutions and courses for the latest information about their applications and selection processes. The following list provides a guide to the subjects and institutions requiring admissions tests and other forms of assessment.

Accountancy

Buckingham Written test for non-English-speaking applicants.

Anglo Saxon, Norse and Celtic

Cambridge *Interview only*: Fitzwilliam, Girton, Murray Edwards, St Edmund's, St John's, Wolfson; *Test at interview:* Hughes Hall, Lucy Cavendish; *School/College essays:* all other colleges offering the subject. Check www.cam.ac.uk/admissions/undergraduate/apply/tests.html.

Anthropology

Cambridge See ***Archaeology***.

Oxford See ***Archaeology***.

Arabic

Salford (Arbc Engl Transl Interp – for native speakers of Arabic) Applicants may be required to sit Arabic or English language tests.

Archaeology

Bournemouth Test for mature applicants.

Cambridge (Arch Anth) *Interview only:* Jesus; *College-set Essay:* St Catharine's, Wolfson; *Test at interview:* Clare, Emmanuel, Girton, Hughes Hall, King's, Lucy Cavendish, Robinson, St Edmunds; *Preparatory study/assignment before interview:* Churchill, Robinson, Trinity; *College-set Essay:* St Catharine's; *School/college essays*: Christ's, Churchill, Corpus Christi, Downing, Fitzwilliam, Gonville & Caius, Homerton, Magdalene, Murray Edwards, Newnham, Pembroke, Peterhouse, Queens', Robinson, St John's, Selwyn, Sidney Sussex, Trinity Hall. Check www.cam.ac.uk/admissions/undergraduate/apply/tests.html.

Oxford (Arch Anth) *All colleges offering the subject* Two recent marked essays are required, preferably in different subjects, plus a statement of no more than 300 words setting out your understanding of the relations between archaeology and social, cultural and biological anthropology required before interview. No written test at interview. Check www.admissions.ox.ac.uk/tests.

Oxford (Class Arch Anc Hist) *All colleges offering the subject*: Two recent marked essays are required. No written test at interview. Check www.admissions.ox.ac.uk/tests.

Architecture

Some universities may require applicants to complete drawing tests at the time of application and prior to interview. Most universities require art portfolios at interview.

Bradford (Coll) Questionnaire and samples of work before interview. Literacy and numeracy test at interview.

Cambridge *Interview only:* Downing, Girton, King's, Queens', Robinson, St Edmund's, Sidney Sussex, Trinity Hall; *Test at interview:* Jesus, Lucy Cavendish, Pembroke, Trinity; *Preparatory study/assignment at/before interview:* Clare, Emmanuel, Fitzwilliam, Magdalene, Murray Edwards, Selwyn, Wolfson; *Project:* Peterhouse; *School/college essays:* Churchill, Clare, Gonville & Caius, Newnham, St John's. **NB All colleges offering course require a portfolio of recent work at interview.** Check www.cam.ac.uk/admissions/undergraduate/apply/tests.html.

Cardiff Samples of work to be sent before interview.

Dundee Samples of work required before interview.

Huddersfield, **London Met** Portfolio of work required.

Liverpool The interview will be based on the portfolio of work.

London South Bank Samples of work to be sent before interview.

Nottingham Trent Examples of work are required.

Sheffield Art portfolio required for applicants without A-level art.

Westminster Samples of work required before interview.

Art and Design

All institutions will require candidates to provide a portfolio of work for discussion at interview.

Bournemouth (Comp Vis Animat) Maths, logic and life-drawing tests.

Bournemouth Arts (UC) Practical test.

Creative Arts Tests.

Oxford (Fine Art) *All colleges offering the subject* No written work required. Portfolio to be submitted by mid-November. Drawing examination. Two drawings in pencil or pencil and ink from a number of possible subjects. Check www.admissions.ox.ac.uk/tests.

Oxford and Cherwell Valley (Coll) A drawing examination is taken by all candidates who are interviewed (two drawings in pencil or pen and ink).

Ravensbourne (CDC) Verbal examination.

Westminster (Fash Mrchnds Mgt) Interview and numeracy test.

Asian and Middle Eastern Studies

Cambridge *Interview only:* St Edmund's; *Test at interview:* Clare, Downing (depending on subject), Girton (depending on subject), Hughes Hall, Lucy Cavendish, Magdalene (depending on subject), Murray Edwards (depending on subject), Robinson, St John's; *Preparatory study at/before interview:* Robinson, St John's, Selwyn; *School/college essays*: Christ's, Churchill, Clare, Corpus Christie, Downing, Emmanuel, Fitzwilliam, Girton, Gonville & Caius, Homerton, Jesus, King's, Magdalene, Murray Edwards, Newnham, Pembroke, Peterhouse, Queens', St Catharine's, St John's, Trinity, Trinity Hall, Wolfson. Check www.cam.ac.uk/admissions/undergraduate/apply/tests.html.

Biochemistry

London South Bank Degree subject-based test at interview.

Oxford *All colleges offering the subject* No written work required. No written tests. Check www.admissions.ox.ac.uk/tests

Biological Sciences

London South Bank Degree subject-based test at interview.

Nottingham Trent Essay set.

Oxford *All colleges offering the subject:* No written work or written tests required. Check www.ox.ac.uk/tests.

Biomedical Sciences

Imperial London BMAT.

Nottingham Trent Essay.

Oxford New course 2011. Check www.medsci.ox.ac.uk/study/bms.

Portsmouth Test of motivation and knowledge of the subject, the degree and careers to which it leads.

Bioveterinary Science

London (RVC) BMAT is not required for entry but applicants wanting to be considered for Merit Scholarships will have to take BMAT.

Broadcast Technology

Birmingham City Mature students to take English and mathematics tests.

Building/Construction

Bradford (Coll) Questionnaire before interview, literacy and numeracy tests at interview.

London South Bank (Bld Serv Eng) Degree subject-based test and numeracy test at interview.

Business Courses

Arts London (CFash) School work to be submitted before interview. Degree subject-based test and numeracy test at interview.

Bolton Literacy and numeracy tests.

Buckingham English test for applicants without English as a first language.

Newcastle Some short-listed applicants will be given a variety of assessment tests at interview.

Nottingham Trent Short-listed applicants are invited to a day-long business style assessment.

Westminster (Fash Mrchnds Mgt) Interview and numeracy test.

Chemistry

London South Bank Degree subject-based test.

Oxford *All colleges offering the subject:* No written work and no written tests required. Check www.admissions.ox.ac.uk/tests.

Classical Studies

Birmingham Language aptitude test for students without a language at GCSE.

Classics (See also *Archaeology*)

Cambridge *Interview only:* Wolfson; *Test at interview:* Clare, Corpus Christi, Fitzwilliam, Girton, Lucy Cavendish, Peterhouse, St Catharine's, St Edmund's, St John's, Trinity Hall; *Preparatory study at/before interview:* Downing, Jesus, Murray Edwards, Newnham, Sidney Sussex; *School/college essays:* Christ's, Churchill, Clare, Corpus Christi, Downing, Emmanuel, Fitzwilliam, Girton, Gonville & Caius, Homerton, Jesus, King's, Magdalene, Murray Edwards, Newnham, Pembroke, Peterhouse, Queen's, Robinson, St Catharine's, St Edmund's, St John's, Selwyn, Sidney Sussex, Trinity, Trinity Hall. Check www.cam.ac.uk/admissions/undergraduate/apply/tests.html.

Oxford *All colleges offering the subject*: Two recently marked essays required, normally in areas related to Classics. Written tests at interview. Check www.admissions.ox.ac.uk/tests.

Classics and English

Oxford *All colleges offering the subject:* The ELAT (see above) and the Classics test. Two pieces of written work, relevant to either Classics or English also required. Check www.admissions.ox.ac.uk/tests.

Classics and Modern Languages

Oxford *All colleges offering the subject*: Classics and Modern Languages tests; two Classics essays and two modern language essays also required, one in the chosen language. Check with www.admissions.ox.ac.uk/tests.

Classics and Oriental Studies

Oxford *All colleges offering the subject*: Classics test; also language aptitude test for applicants planning to study Arabic, Hebrew, Persian or Turkish as main language; two pieces written work also required, at least one on classical topic. Check www.admissions.ox.ac.uk/tests.

Communication Studies

Buckingham English test for non-native-English-speaking applicants.

Cardiff Short essay.

Computer Science

Abertay Dundee (Comp Arts) Portfolio of work required. Practical tests at interview.

Blackburn (Coll Univ Centre) Questionnaire and test before interview.

Cambridge *Interview only:* Magdalene, St Catharine's; *Test at interview:* Churchill, Downing, Homerton, Hughes Hall, Trinity; *Thinking Skills Assessment at interview:* Christ's, Clare, Corpus Christi, Emmanuel, Fitzwilliam, Girton, Gonville & Caius, Jesus, King's, Lucy Cavendish, Murray Edwards, Newnham, Pembroke, Peterhouse, Queens', Robinson, St Edmund's, St John's, Selwyn, Sidney Sussex, Trinity Hall, Wolfson; *Preparatory study at/before interview:* Clare, Gonville & Caius, King's, Robinson. **NB** STEP used for conditional offers. Check www.cam.ac.uk/admissions/undergraduate/apply/tests.html.

Central Lancashire Test for Foundation course applicants.

Cumbria Literacy test at interview.

Liverpool John Moores Questionnaire before interview. Literacy test at interview.

London (Gold) Degree subject-based test.

London (QM) Mathematical test at interview.

Oxford *All colleges offering the subject*: Maths aptitude test. See also ***Mathematics*** below. Check www.admissions.ox.ac.uk/tests.

West Thames (Coll) Degree subject-based test and numeracy test.

Dance

All institutions with courses in which performance is involved will require an audition.

Chichester (Perf Arts) Group practical test.

Liverpool (LIPA) See **Dance/Dance Studies** in **Chapter 8** (**Interview advice and questions**).

Dental Nursing

Portsmouth (Dntl Nurs; Dntl Hyg Dntl Thera) Interview.

Dentistry

UKCAT for undergraduate courses at the following universities and dental schools: Check www.ukcat.ac.uk and universities' websites for latest admissions information. **Barts and the London School of Medicine and Dentistry, Birmingham, Bristol, Cardiff, Dundee, Glasgow, Leeds, Liverpool, London (King's), (UCL), Manchester, Newcastle, Peninsula College of Medicine and Dentistry, Queen's Belfast, Sheffield.**

Dietetics

London Met Interview and essay.

Ulster Health Professions Admissions Test: see above, www.hpat.org.uk and www.ulster.ac.uk before completing the UCAS application.

Drama

Liverpool (LIPA) (Perf Arts (Actg)) Applicants will be expected to perform one devised piece, one Shakespearean piece and a song plus a short review of a performance they have seen recently.

London (Central Sch SpDr), **Central Lancashire**, **De Montfort**, **London (RH)** Written papers and/or tests.

London (Gold) Written work required at interview.

London (RH) At interview the University looks for students who are mentally agile and versatile who enjoy reading as well as taking part in productions.

London Mountview (Ac Thea Arts) Voice, movement and singing sessions plus acting pieces.

Royal Welsh (CMusDr) Written papers and/or tests.

Earth Sciences (Geology)

Oxford *All Colleges offering the subject:* No essays required. No written tests at interview; no written work for interview. Check www.admissions.ox.ac.uk/tests.

Economics

Buckingham English test for non-native-English-speaking applicants.

Cambridge *Interview only:* Clare; *Test at interview*: Downing (mathematical test), Homerton, Hughes Hall, Lucy Cavendish, Robinson, Sidney Sussex; *Thinking Skills Assessment*: Corpus Christi, Emmanuel, Fitzwilliam, Girton, Gonville & Caius, Jesus, King's, Newnham, Pembroke, Peterhouse, Queens', St Edmund's. St John's, Selwyn, Trinity Hall, Wolfson; *Preparatory study at/before interview:* Christ's, Churchill, Emmanuel, Fitzwilliam, Jesus, Lucy Cavendish, Magdalene, Murray Edwards, Newnham, St John's, *College-set essay/work,* Peterhouse, St John's, Trinity Hall; *School/college essays:* Christ's, Churchill, Homerton, Magdalene, Newnham, Robinson. Check www.cam.ac.uk/admissions/undergraduate/apply/tests.html.

Lancaster Workshop.

London LSE Has its own admissions test (the LSE Entrance Examination) which is used for some applicants with non-standard backgrounds. The test is not subject or course-specific.

Oxford (Econ Mgt) *All colleges offering the subject*: Thinking Skills Assessment (Oxford University). Check www.admissions.ox.ac.uk/tests, and also www.admissionstests.cambridgeassessment.org.uk.

Education Studies (See also *Teacher Training*)

Cambridge *Interview only:* Fitzwilliam, Girton, Jesus, Murray Edwards, St Edmund's, Wolfson; *Test at interview:* Churchill (depending on subject), Hughes Hall, Lucy Cavendish, Trinity Hall; *Preparatory study at/before interview:* Churchill, Magdalene, Robinson; *College-set essay*: Emmanuel; *School/college essays:* Christ's, Churchill, Gonville & Caius, Homerton, Magdalene, Queens', St John's, Trinity Hall. Check www.cam.ac.uk/admissions/undergraduate/apply/tests.html.

Cumbria (Science and Education) Literacy test.

Durham (Primary Teaching) Key skills tests at interview.

Engineering

Birmingham City Mature students without GCSE English and/or mathematics are required to take a literacy and/or numeracy test. (Snd Eng Prod) Mature students to take English and mathematics tests.

Blackburn (Coll Univ Centre) Questionnaire and tests before interview.

Bristol (Eng Des) A-level-based test.

Cambridge *Interview only:* Corpus Christi, Girton, Murray Edwards; *Test at interview:* Churchill, Fitzwilliam, Gonville & Caius, King's (problem-solving), Lucy Cavendish, Newham, Peterhouse, Robinson, St Edmund's, St John's (maths test), Trinity; *Thinking Skills Assessment:* Christ's, Clare, Downing, Emmanuel, Gonville & Caius, Homerton, Jesus, King's, Lucy Cavendish, Newnham, Pembroke, Queens', St Catharine's, St Edmund's, Selwyn, Sidney Sussex, Trinity Hall, Wolfson; *Preparatory study at/before interview:* Clare. Check www.cam.ac.uk/admissions/undergraduate/apply/tests.html.

London South Bank (Bld Serv Eng; Civ Eng; Elec Eng; Mech Eng) Degree subject-based test and numeracy test at interview.

Oxford (Eng Sci; Eng Comp Sci; Eng Econ Mgt) *All colleges offering the subjects:* No written work or written tests required. Check www.admissions.ox.ac.uk/tests.

Southampton Literacy and numeracy tests for foundation course applicants.

Southampton Solent Mathematical test at interview.

Suffolk (Univ Campus) (Civ Eng, Elec Electron Eng, Mech Eng courses) Interviews.

English

Anglia Ruskin Samples of written work required.

Birmingham City, **Bristol** Samples of work required.

Blackpool and Fylde (Coll) Samples of work before interview.

Buckingham English test for non-native-English-speaking applicants.

Cambridge *Test at interview:* Clare, Corpus Christi, Downing, Emmanuel, Girton, Homerton, Hughes Hall, Jesus, King's, Lucy Cavendish, Magdalene, Murray Edwards, Newnham, Pembroke, Peterhouse, Queens', Robinson, St Catharine's, St Edmund's, St John's, Selwyn, Sidney Sussex, Trinity, Trinity Hall, Wolfson; *Preparatory study at/before interview:* Christ's, Churchill, Clare, Corpus Christi, Emmanuel, Fitzwilliam, Jesus, Newnham, Robinson, Sidney Sussex; *School/college essays:* Christ's, Churchill, Clare, Corpus Christi, Emmanuel, Fitzwilliam, Girton, Homerton, Jesus, King's, Magdalene, Murray Edwards, Newnham, Peterhouse, Queens', Robinson, St Catharine's, St John's, Selwyn, Sidney Sussex, Trinity, Trinity Hall. Check www.cam.ac.uk/admissions/undergraduate/apply/tests.html.

Cardiff Short essay.

London (King's) Applicants to prepare a short literary text before interview.

London (UCL) After interview applicants are asked to write a critical commentary on an unseen passage of prose or verse.

Newport (Crea Writ) Samples of creative writing before interview.

Oxford Check www.admissions.ox.ac.uk/tests.

(Engl Lang Lit) *All colleges offering the subject:* ELAT (see above) and one recent marked essay.

(Engl Modn Langs) *All colleges offering the subject*: ELAT (see above), Modern Language(s) test, one recent marked essay.

Portsmouth (Engl Crea Writ; Crea Writ Dr) All applicants will be required to submit a short piece of creative writing to the admissions office. This should be between 400 and 500 words long and should include the following words and use each one twice: shell, flicker, knit, coin, compose, lark, stream, root. All the words must be used and each word must be used in a different context and/or with a different meaning on each occasion. Language should be used imaginatively and accurately.

Southampton Examples of written work required from Access students.

Equine Science

Lincoln Applicants are required to show that they can ride to BHS Level 2 or equivalent.

European and Middle Eastern Languages (See also *Modern and Medieval Languages*)

Oxford *All colleges offering the subject:* Language aptitude test, modern language test, TSA. Check www.admissions.ox.ac.uk/tests.

European Studies

London (Gold) Informal conversation in the relevant language (French, German or Spanish).

Film Production

Birmingham City (Film Prod Tech) Mature students to take English and mathematics tests.

Film Studies

Bournemouth A 20-page screen-play required before interview.
Bournemouth Arts (UC) Portfolio. Practical test of short film stills.
Creative Arts Portfolio at interview.
Liverpool John Moores Questionnaire and test before interview.
Newport Portfolio of work.
Roehampton Essays taken to interview and discussed.
Westminster Questionnaire to be completed and samples of work required before interview.

Fine Art

Oxford *All colleges offering the subject*: Specimen drawing examination paper available on website. Check www.admissions.ox.ac.uk/tests.

French (See also *Modern and Medieval Languages*)

Geography

Cambridge *Interview only:* Christ's, Downing, St Edmund's, St John's, Trinity, Wolfson; *Test at interview:* Hughes Hall, Lucy Cavendish, Murray Edwards; *Preparatory study at/before interview:* Churchill, Clare, Corpus Christi, Emmanuel, Fitzwilliam, Girton, Homerton, King's, Newnham, Robinson, St Catharine's, Selwyn; *School/college essays:* Churchill, Clare, Corpus Christi, Emmanuel, Fitzwilliam, Girton, Gonville & Caius, Homerton, Jesus, King's, Magdalene, Murray Edwards, Newnham, Queens', Robinson, Sidney Sussex, Trinity Hall. Check www.cam.ac.uk/admissions/undergraduate/apply/tests.html.
Cardiff Test for some joint courses.
Oxford *All colleges offering the subject*: No test. Check www.admissions.ox.ac.uk/tests.

German (See also *Modern and Medieval Languages*)

Aston, **Liverpool John Moores** Written test at interview.

History

Bangor Samples of work only required from mature applicants without conventional qualifications.
Buckingham English test for non-native-English-speaking applicants.
Cambridge *Test at interview:* Hughes Hall, King's, Lucy Cavendish, Newnham, Peterhouse, Robinson, St Edmund's, St John's, Selwyn, Sidney Sussex, Wolfson; *Thinking Skills Assessment:* St John's; *Preparatory study at/before interview:* Christ's, Churchill, Clare, Corpus Christi, Downing, Emmanuel, Fitzwilliam, Girton, Homerton, Murray Edwards, Newnham, Pembroke, Queens', Robinson, St Catharine's, Selwyn, Sidney Sussex; *School/college essays:* Christ's, Churchill, Clare, Corpus Christi, Downing, Emmanuel, Fitzwilliam, Girton, Gonville & Caius, Homerton, Jesus, King's, Magdalene, Murray Edwards, Newnham, Pembroke, Peterhouse, Queens', Robinson, St Catharine's, Selwyn, Sidney Sussex, Trinity, Trinity Hall, Wolfson. Check www.cam.ac.uk/admissions/undergraduate/apply/tests.html.

Liverpool Test for mature applicants.

Liverpool John Moores Mature students not in education must submit an essay.

London (Gold) Samples of written work from non-standard applicants and from those without academic qualifications.

Oxford Check www.admissions.ox.ac.uk/tests.

(Hist (Anc Modn)(Hist Econ)) *All colleges offering the subject*: History Aptitude Test.

(Hist Modn Langs) History Aptitude Test and Modern Language Test. (Hist Pol) No test.

Those called for interview send an essay by end of November.

Roehampton Essays taken to interview and discussed.

History of Art

Cambridge *Interview only:* Fitzwilliam, Selwyn; *Test at interview:* Hughes Hall, St Edmund's, Wolfson; *School/college essays:* Christ's, Churchill, Clare, Corpus Christie, Downing, Emmanuel, Girton, Gonville & Caius, Homerton, Jesus, King's, Magdalene, Murray Edwards, Newnham, Pembroke, Peterhouse, Queens', St John's, Sidney Sussex, Trinity, Trinity Hall. Check www.cam.ac.uk.admissions/undergraduate/apply/tests.html.

Oxford *All colleges offering the subject*: Two pieces required: (a) a marked essay from an A-level or equivalent course, and (b) a brief account of no more than 750 words responding to an item of art or design to which the applicant has had first-hand access with a photograph or photocopy of the item provided if possible. No written test at interview although the applicant may be presented with photographs or artefacts for discussion at interview. Submitted written work may also be discussed at interview. Check www.admissions.ox.ac.uk/tests.

Human Sciences

Oxford *All colleges offering the subject*: Two recent marked essays or project reports, relevant to the Human Sciences course, written as part of the school or college course. No written test at interview.

Italian (see *Medieval and Modern Languages*)

Cardiff Test for some joint courses.

Journalism (see also *Media Studies*)

West Scotland Tests on public affairs and writing skills.

Land Economy

Cambridge *Interview only:* Christ's, Girton, Gonville & Caius, Queens', St Catharine's, St Edmund's, St John's, Selwyn, Sidney Sussex, Trinity Hall, Wolfson; *Test at interview:* Hughes Hall, Lucy Cavendish; *Thinking Skills Assessment:* Jesus, Lucy Cavendish, Newnham, Robinson; *Preparatory study at/before interview:* Fitzwilliam (written test prior to interview), Jesus, Magdalene, Trinity; *School/college essays:* Clare, Fitzwilliam, Homerton, Magdalene, Murray Edwards, Newnham, Pembroke. Check www.cam.ac.uk/admissions/undergraduate/apply/tests.html.

Law

The following universities require applicants to take the LNAT for specified Law courses: **Birmingham**, **Bristol**, **Durham**, **Glasgow**, **Leeds**, **London (King's)**, **(UCL), Nottingham**, **Oxford.** Check university websites and www.lnat.ac.uk; see also **Chapter 6** and the **Law** subject table in **Chapter 8**. (**NB** After 2009, LNAT is not required for entry to **Cambridge**.)

Birmingham City Questionnaire to be completed and an IQ test.

Bolton Own diagnostic test used (logic and reasoning).

Bradford (Coll) Academic tests at interview for mature students.

Bristol Check with the Law Department for LNAT requirements.

Cambridge *Test at interview:* Churchill, Wolfson; *Cambridge Law Test:* Christ's, Clare, Corpus Christi, Downing, Emmanuel, Fitzwilliam, Girton, Gonville & Caius, Homerton, Hughes Hall, Jesus, King's, Lucy

Cavendish, Magdalene, Murray Edwards, Newnham, Pembroke, Peterhouse, Queens', Robinson, St Catharine's, St Edmund's, St John's, Selwyn, Sidney Sussex, Trinity, Trinity Hall; *Preparatory study at/before interview:* Clare, Corpus Christi, Emmanuel, Homerton, Jesus, King's, Magdalene, Selwyn, Sidney Sussex, Trinity, Trinity Hall. *School/college essays:* Emmanuel, Magdalene, Wolfson. Check www.cam.ac.uk/admissions/undergraduate/apply/tests.html.

Oxford *All colleges offering the subject*: All applicants take the LNAT. (Law Law St Euro) LNAT plus, at interview, a short oral test in the modern language for students taking a joint language, except for those taking European Legal Studies. No other written work required except for Harris Manchester College. Check www.admissions.ox.ac.uk/tests.

Linguistics

Cambridge *Interview only:* Christ's, Homerton, King's; *Test at interview:* Churchill, Fitzwilliam, Jesus, Robinson, Wolfson; *Preparatory study at/before interview:* Churchill, Robinson, Sidney Sussex, Trinity. *School/college essays:* Churchill, Corpus Christi, Downing, Emmanuel, Murray Edwards, Newnham, Peterhouse, Robinson, Selwyn, Sidney Sussex, Trinity Hall; *Contact the College:* Clare, Girton, Gonville & Caius, Hughes Hall, Lucy Cavendish, Magdalene, Pembroke, Queens', St Catharine's, St Edmund's, St John's. Check www.cam.ac.uk/admissions/undergraduate/apply/tests.html.

Materials Science

Oxford (Mat Sci) (Mat Econ Mgt) No written work required. No written test at interview. Check www.admissions.ox.ac.uk/tests.

Mathematics

Cambridge *Test at interview:* Christ's, Churchill, Corpus Christi, Girton, Homerton, Hughes Hall, King's, Lucy Cavendish, Magdalene, Murray Edwards, Robinson, St John's, Trinity; *Maths STEP:* Christ's, Churchill, Clare, Corpus Christi, Downing, Emmanuel, Fitzwilliam, Girton, Gonville & Caius, Homerton, Jesus, King's, Magdalene, Murray Edwards, Newnham, Pembroke, Peterhouse, Queens', Robinson, St Catharine's, St Edmund's, St John's, Selwyn, Sidney Sussex, Trinity, Trinity Hall; *Preparatory study at/before interview:* Downing, King's, Newnham. Check www.cam.ac.uk/admissions/undergraduate/apply/tests.html.

Liverpool John Moores Literacy and numeracy tests.

Oxford (Maths; Maths Comp Sci; Maths Stats) *All colleges offering the subjects*: Mathematics Aptitude Test. Overseas candidates unable to attend for interview may be required to submit written work; (Maths Phil) *All colleges offering the subject*: Mathematics Aptitude Test; two essays showing capacity for reasoned argument and clear writing, not expected to be on a philosophical subject. Check www.admissions.ox.ac.uk/interviews/tests.

Media Studies

Blackpool and Fylde (Coll) Samples of work before interview.

Bournemouth 250-word essay.

Bournemouth and Poole (Coll) Degree subject-based test at interview.

City Spelling, punctuation, grammar, general knowledge tests and an essay assignment. Tests on current affairs and use of English.

Bolton Samples of work at interview.

Brighton (Spo Jrnl) Test for those called to interview: contact admissions tutor.

Coventry Interview and portfolio.

Edinburgh Napier (Jrnl) Samples of work before interview.

Glasgow Caledonian Written test at interview.

Hull (Coll) Essay required before interview.

Liverpool John Moores Questionnaire to be completed before interview. Degree subject-based test at interview.

London Met Mathematics and written English test.

Newport Portfolio of work.
West Scotland (Jrnl) Test covers public affairs and writing ability.
Westminster Questionnaire to be completed before interview.

Medicine

NB Most medical schools require applicants to sit the UK Clinical Aptitude Test (UKCAT) or the BioMedical Admissions Test (BMAT) or, for graduate entry, the Graduate Australian Medical Schools Admissions Test (GAMSAT) for specified Medicine courses. Applicants are advised to check the websites of all universities and medical schools offering Medicine for their latest admissions requirements, including admissions and aptitude tests, to check the UKCAT website www.ukcat.ac.uk or the BMAT pages on www.admissionstests.cambridgeassessment.org.uk, (and for graduate entry www.gamsat.co.uk) for the latest information.

BMAT is required by:
Cambridge Christ's, Churchill, Clare, Corpus Christi, Downing, Emmanuel, Fitzwilliam, Girton, Gonville & Caius, Jesus, King's, Lucy Cavendish, Magdalene, Murray Edwards, Newnham, Pembroke, Peterhouse, Queens', Robinson, St Catharine's, St Edmund's, St John's, Selwyn, Sidney Sussex, Trinity, Trinity Hall, Wolfson. Check www.cam.ac.uk/admissions/undergraduate/apply/tests.html.
Imperial London (Six-year course)
London (UCL)
Oxford.

UKCAT is required by the following universities and medical schools for undergraduate entry to Medicine: **Aberdeen, Brighton and Sussex, Cardiff, Dundee, Durham, East Anglia, Edinburgh, Glasgow, Hull York, Keele, Leeds, Leicester, London (King's), (St George's), Manchester, Newcastle, Nottingham, Peninsula, Queen's Belfast, Sheffield, Southampton, St Andrews.**

(**NB** UKCAT is also required for graduate entry to Medicine at Oxford and Warwick Universities; GAMSAT is required for graduate entry to **Keele**, **London (St George's), Nottingham, Swansea**.)

Modern and Medieval Languages (See also *Asian and Middle Eastern Studies*, *Oriental Studies* and separate languages.)

Bangor Offer may be lowered after interview.
Cambridge *Test at interview:* Christ's, Churchill, Clare, Corpus Christi, Downing, Emmanuel, Fitzwilliam, Girton, Gonville & Caius, Homerton, Hughes Hall, Jesus, King's, Lucy Cavendish, Magdalene, Murray Edwards, Newnham, Pembroke, Peterhouse, Queens', Robinson, St Catharine's, St Edmund's, St John's, Selwyn, Wolfson; *Preparatory study at/before interview:* Churchill, Clare, Emmanuel, Homerton, Jesus, Magdalene, Murray Edwards, Newnham, Queens', Robinson, St Edmund's, St John's, Selwyn, Trinity, Trinity Hall; *School/college essays:* Christ's, Churchill, Corpus Christi, Downing, Emmanuel, Gonville & Caius, Homerton, Jesus, King's, Magdalene, Murray Edwards, Newnham, Pembroke, Peterhouse, Queens', Robinson, St Catharine's, St Edmund's, St John's, Selwyn, Trinity, Trinity Hall. Check www.cam.ac.uk/admissions/undergraduate/apply/tests.html.
Liverpool The interview lasts approximately 20 minutes with part in the language(s) to be studied. Occasionally the applicant may be asked to sit a short grammar test.
Oxford Check course requirements carefully on the University website and check test requirements on www.admissions.ox.ac.uk/tests.

(Modn Langs) *All colleges offering the subjects* Modern Languages Test(s). Two marked essays for each language being studied.

(Modn Lang Ling) *All colleges offering the subject* Language Aptitude Test and Modern Language Test.

(Euro Mid E Langs) *All colleges offering the subject*: Language Aptitude Test and Modern Language Test. Two recent marked essays, one in the European language.

Music

(See also **Chapter 8 Music**)

NB All institutions organise auditions for applicants.

Bangor Candidates offered the option of an audition.
Birmingham City Some subject-based and practical tests.
Cambridge *Test at interview:* Clare, Downing, Fitzwilliam, Girton, Gonville & Caius, Homerton, Hughes Hall, Jesus, King's, Lucy Cavendish, Magdalene, Murray Edwards, Newnham, Pembroke, Peterhouse, Queens', Robinson, St Catharine's, St Edmunds, St John's (possible keyboard test), Selwyn, Trinity, Trinity Hall; *Preparatory study at/before interview:* Churchill, Clare, Emmanuel, Newnham, Robinson, St Edmund's, Sidney Sussex, Wolfson; *School/college essays:* Christ's, Churchill, Corpus Christi, Downing, Emmanuel, Fitzwilliam, Girton, Gonville & Caius, Homerton, Jesus, King's, Magdalene, Murray Edwards, Newnham, Pembroke, Peterhouse, Queens', Robinson, St Catharine's, St John's, Selwyn, Sidney Sussex, Trinity, Trinity Hall. Check www.cam.ac.uk/admissions/undergraduate/apply/tests.html.
Coventry Proforma used prior to interview. Some students rejected at this stage.
Edinburgh Napier Audition and theory test.
Leeds (CMus) (Jazz; Mus; Pop Mus St) In-house theory test to determine level of musical theory ability.
Liverpool Candidates may be asked to undertake a variety of aural tests, the performance of a prepared piece of music and some sight-reading when called for interview.

TABLE OF INTERVIEW REQUIREMENTS FOR MUSIC COURSES

Key
P = Performance
K = Keyboard tests
E = Essay
S = Sight-singing
A = Aural
H = Harmony and Counterpoint (Written)
X = Extracts for analysis or 'guessing the composer', dates etc.

Bangor* PAX (bring example)
Barnsley (Coll) A
Bath Spa PKXA
Birmingham PSKHXA
Birmingham City PAH
Bristol PSKHEXA
Cambridge (Hom)* PKE (bring example)
Cardiff PE
Chichester P
City PASKE
Colchester (Inst) PKSX
Derby PE
Durham PKXA
East Anglia PKHEXA
Edinburgh PKHEA
Glasgow PS
Huddersfield PH
Lancaster PAH
Leeds PX
Liverpool PK
Liverpool Hope PKH
London (Gold) PKH
London (King's) PASK
London (RAcMus) PKHX
London (RCMus) PKEXH
London (RH) PHEXA
Oxford PHAK
Roehampton PKH
Royal Scottish (RSAMD) PSA
Royal Welsh (CMus/Dr) PSA
Salford PKEH
Sheffield PEAH
South Birmingham (Coll) P
Southampton P
Surrey PH or X
Ulster P
Wolverhampton PE
York PEKHX

* Examples may include essays, harmony and counterpoint compositions. Performance tests/auditions are standard practice for Music courses in all universities and colleges.

London (Gold) Degree subject-based test.

London (RAcMus) (BMus) 50-minute written test; possible keyboard and aural skills test.

London Met Performance tests and essay.

Oxford *All colleges offering the subject:* One marked sample of harmony and/or counterpoint and two marked essays on any areas or aspects of music. Candidates may submit a portfolio of compositions (these are non-returnable). Performance tests at interview; Check www.admissions.ox.ac.uk/tests.

Thames Valley (Mus Tech) Students required to produce a portfolio of work. (Mus Perf) Students attend an audition: see www.tvu.ac.uk.

Natural Sciences (Biological Sciences)

Cambridge *Interview only:* Churchill, Corpus Christi, Downing, Fitzwilliam, Girton, Jesus, King's, Newnham, Pembroke, St Catharine's, Selwyn; *Test at interview:* Homerton, Hughes Hall, Lucy Cavendish, Magdalene, Murray Edwards, Robinson, St Edmund's, St John's, Trinity; *Thinking Skills Assessment:* Clare, Emmanuel, Gonville & Caius, Peterhouse, Queens', St Edmund's, Trinity Hall, Wolfson; *Preparatory study at/before interview:* Emmanuel, Homerton, Magdalene, Robinson; *School/college essays:* Christ's (or project work), Peterhouse, Robinson. Check www.cam.ac.uk/admissions/undergraduate/apply/tests.html.

Natural Sciences (Physical Sciences)

Cambridge *Interview only:* Christ's, Churchill, Fitzwilliam, Girton, Jesus, Pembroke, St Catharine's, Selwyn; *Test at interview:* Corpus Christi, Downing (mathematical test), Homerton, Hughes Hall, Lucy Cavendish, Magdalene, Robinson, St John's, Trinity; *Thinking Skills Assessment:* Clare, Emmanuel, Gonville & Caius, King's, Murray Edwards, Newnham, Peterhouse, Queens', St Edmund's, Trinity Hall, Wolfson; *Preparatory study at/before interview:* Emmanuel (for Chemistry), Homerton; *School/college essays:* Murray Edwards. Check www.cam.ac.uk/admissions/undergraduate/apply/tests.html.

Nursing

Most institutions will interview.

Birmingham City Literacy and numeracy tests at interview.

Bolton Literacy test.

Bristol UWE Questionnaire/test before interview.

Bucks New Tests for BSc and DipHE Nursing.

City Written test.

Derby Literacy and numeracy tests at interview.

Dundee Literacy test.

East Anglia Tests.

Liverpool A group of candidates is given a task to undertake during which applicants are assessed for their ability to work in a team, maturity, communication skills and their level of involvement.

London South Bank (Nurs A, C, MH) Literacy and numeracy tests at interview.

Suffolk (Univ Campus) Interview and tests.

Wolverhampton Tests.

York Literacy and numeracy tests.

Occupational Therapy

Bristol UWE Questionnaire/test before interview.

Ulster Health Professions Admissions Test: see www.hpat.org.uk and www.ulster.ac.uk before completing the UCAS application.

Optometry

Bradford (Coll) Literacy and numeracy tests.

Oriental Studies

Cambridge See ***Asian and Middle Eastern Studies***

Oxford *All colleges offering the subject*: Language Aptitude Test. Two essays, preferably of different kinds. Essays in a European language are acceptable. No prior knowledge of Oriental languages required. Occasional written tests. Check the University website and prospectuses and www.admissions.ox.ac.uk/tests.

Osteopathy

British Sch of Ost At interview, A-level, literacy, numeracy, logic and reasoning-based tests plus a practical aptitude test.

Paramedic Science

Coventry Stress Test.

Performing Arts (See ***Dance and Drama***)

Pharmacology/Pharmaceutical Sciences

Imperial London (Pharmacology and Translational Medical Sciences) BMAT.

Portsmouth Test of motivation, knowledge of the subject, of the degree course and the careers to which it leads.

Pharmacy

Liverpool John Moores Literacy and numeracy tests.

Portsmouth (A-level students) Test of motivation and knowledge of Pharmacy as a profession. (Other applicants) Test of chemistry and biology, plus literacy and numeracy tests.

Philosophy

Cambridge *Test at interview:* Christ's, Churchill, Clare, Corpus Christi, Downing, Emmanuel, Fitzwilliam, Girton, Gonville & Caius, Homerton, Hughes Hall, Jesus, King's, Lucy Cavendish, Magdalene, Newnham, Pembroke, Peterhouse, Queens', Robinson, St Catharine's, St Edmund's, St John's, Selwyn, Sidney Sussex, Trinity, Trinity Hall, Wolfson; *School/college essays:* Churchill, Downing, Emmanuel, Homerton, King's, Magdalene, Peterhouse, Trinity. Check www.cam.ac.uk/admissions/undergraduate/apply/tests.html.

Leeds Written test at interview.

Liverpool Samples of written work may be requested in cases where there is a question of the applicant's ability to cope with the academic skills required of them.

London (UCL) Written test at interview.

Oxford *All colleges offering the subjects*: (Phil Modn Langs) Philosophy and Modern Languages tests; two pieces of written work required. (Phil Theol) Philosophy test and two pieces of written work; (Phil Pol Econ (PPE)) Thinking Skills Assessment (Oxford University); no written work required. Check course pages on University website and www.admissions.ox.ac.uk/tests.

Warwick Written test at interview.

Physical Education

All institutions require practical tests at interview.

Chichester Physical test.

Liverpool John Moores Literacy and numeracy tests and gym assessment.

Manchester (Coll) Communications test.

Physics

Oxford *All colleges offering the subject:* Physics Aptitude test; no written work required. Check www.admissions.ox.ac.uk/tests.

Physics and Philosophy

Oxford *All colleges offering the subject:* Physics Aptitude test; two pieces of written work required.

Physiological Sciences/Physiology

Oxford From 2011 entry Physiological Sciences, Physiology and Philosophy, and Physiology and Psychology will be replaced by the new Biomedical Sciences course. For details of how to apply and admissions test check the course pages on the University website and www.admissions.ox.ac.uk/tests.

Physiotherapy

East Anglia Tests.

Liverpool A group of candidates is given a task to undertake, during which they are assessed for their ability to work in a team, maturity, communication skills and their level of involvement.

Robert Gordon Practical testing varies from year to year.

Ulster Health Professions Admissions Test (see www.hpat.org.uk and www.ulster.ac.uk before completing the UCAS application).

Podiatry

Ulster Health Professions Admissions Test (see www.hpat.ac.uk and www.ulster.ac.uk before completing the UCAS application).

Politics

Cambridge (Pol Psy Sociol) *Test at interview:* Churchill, Clare, Homerton, Hughes Hall, Jesus, Lucy Cavendish, Robinson, St John's, Sidney Sussex; *Thinking Skills Assessment:* Gonville & Caius, King's, Newnham, Queens', St Catharine's, St John's; *Preparatory work at/before interview:* Emmanuel, Magdalene, Murray Edwards, Newnham, Robinson, Sidney Sussex; *School/college essays:* Christ's, Churchill, Corpus Christi, Downing, Emmanuel, Fitzwilliam, Girton, Gonville & Caius, Homerton, Jesus, King's, Magdalene, Murray Edwards, Newnham, Pembroke, Robinson, St Edmund's, St John's, Selwyn, Sidney Sussex, Trinity, Trinity Hall (College-set essay), Wolfson. Check www.cam.ac.uk/admissions/undergraduate/apply/tests.html.

Buckingham English test for non-native-English-speaking applicants.

Liverpool John Moores Mature students not in education must submit an essay.

London (Gold) Essays from current A/AS-level course to be submitted before interview.

Oxford See (Philosopy, Politics and Economics PPE) under ***Philosophy*** above.

Psychology

Bangor Access course entry students may be asked to submit an essay.

Birmingham Written tests at interview.

Liverpool John Moores Written tests at interview.

London (UCL) Questionnaire to be completed.

Manchester Written tests at interview.

Oxford (Expmtl Psy) *All colleges offering the subject*: Thinking Skills Assessment test (Oxford University); no written work required. See www.admissions.ox.ac.uk/tests.

Oxford (Psy Phil Physiol) From 2011 this course is replaced by the Biomedical Sciences course. For details of admissions requirements see the course pages on the University website and also www.admissions.ox.ac.uk/tests.

Roehampton Questionnaire before interview; test at interview.

Radiography

Bangor A short essay will be set at interview.

Liverpool (Diag Radiog Radiothera) The group of candidates is given a task to undertake, during which they are assessed for their ability to work in a team, maturity, communication skills and their level of involvement.

Ulster Health Professions Admissions Test: see www.hpat.org.uk and www.ulster.ac.uk before completing the UCAS application.

Russian (See ***Modern and Medieval Languages***)

Social Policy

London (LSE) Two essays to be submitted before interview.

Social Work

Anglia Ruskin Samples of written work required.

Bangor, **Birmingham**, **Brunel**, **De Montfort**, **Durham New (Coll)**, **London (Gold)**, **Worcestershire New (Coll)** Written test at interview.

Birmingham City Some tests are set at interview.

Bristol UWE Questionnaire before interview.

Bucks New Tests.

De Montfort Test.

Derby Literacy and numeracy tests at interview.

Dundee Literacy test.

Durham New (Coll) Test.

East Anglia Test.

London (Gold) Questions on social work practice and the applicant's experience of working in the social work/social care field.

London Met Pre-interview literacy test and if successful, an interview.

London South Bank Literacy and numeracy tests.

Manchester Met (Yth Commun Wk) Tests.

NEW (Coll) Test.

Newman (UC) (Yth Commun Wk) Written test.

Portsmouth Test.

Sheffield Literacy and numeracy tests.

Stirling Tests.

Suffolk (Univ Campus) Interview and test.

Wolverhampton Tests.

Sociology

Leeds Copy of written work requested.

London Met Where appropriate separate tests in comprehension and mathematical skills that will be used to help us reach a decision.

Spanish (See ***Modern and Medieval Languages***)

Speech Sciences

Manchester Met Two essays and a questionnaire.

Sheffield Listening test and problem-solving.

Ulster Health Professions Admissions Test: see www.hpat.org.uk and www.ulster.ac.uk before completing the UCAS application.

Sports Sciences/Studies

Nottingham Trent (Spo Hrs Mgt) Riding test.

Teacher Training

Anglia Ruskin Literacy test at interview; maths test for some courses.

Bath Spa, **Brighton**, **Chichester**, **Cumbria, De Montfort**, **Gloucestershire**, **Liverpool John Moores**, **Nottingham Trent**, **Plymouth**, **Roehampton**, **Sunderland**, **Trinity Saint David**, **Worcester**, **York St John** Written test at interview.

Bristol UWE, **Newport**, **St Mary's Twickenham (UC)** Literacy and mathematical tests at interview.

Brunel Literacy, mathematical and practical tests depending on subject.

Chester Literacy and numeracy tests.

Dundee Literacy and numeracy tests.

Durham Key skills test.

Gloucestershire Mathematical test at interview.

Liverpool John Moores Mathematical and diagnostic tests on interview day.

London South Bank Literacy and numeracy tests.

Newman (UC) Basic literacy and numeracy tests for QTS and other courses.

Nottingham Trent Practical presentation.

Plymouth Mathematical test at interview.

St Mary's Twickenham (UC) Practical tests for PE applicants.

Wigan and Leigh (Coll) Mathematical test at interview.

Winchester Literacy test at interview.

Theology and Religious Studies

Cambridge (Theol Relig St) *Test at interview:* Clare, Fitzwilliam, Hughes Hall, Lucy Cavendish, St Edmund's; *Preparatory work at/before interview:* Clare, Corpus Christi, Emmanuel, Jesus, Magdalene, Newnham, Selwyn; *School/college essays:* Christ's, Corpus Christi, Downing, Emmanuel, Fitzwilliam, Girton, Gonville & Caius, Homerton, Jesus, King's, Magdalene, Murray Edwards, Newnham, Pembroke, Peterhouse, Queens', Robinson, St Catharine's, St John's, Selwyn, Sidney Sussex, Trinity, Trinity Hall, Wolfson. Check www.cam.ac.uk/admissions/undergraduate/apply/tests.html.

Oxford *All colleges offering the subject*: (Theol) No test; two pieces written work required. (Theol Orntl St) Oriental Studies Language Aptitude Test for candidates planning to study Islam or Judaism; two pieces written work required. Check www.admissions.ox.ac.uk/tests.

Veterinary Science/Medicine

Cambridge BMAT: Churchill, Clare, Downing, Emmanuel, Fitzwilliam, Girton, Jesus, Lucy Cavendish, Magdalene, Murray Edwards, Newnham, Pembroke, Queens', Robinson, St Catharine's, St Edmund's, St John's, Selwyn, Sidney Sussex, Trinity Hall, Wolfson; *Preparatory work at/before interview:* Emmanuel, Robinson. Check www.cam.ac.uk/admissions/undergraduate/apply/tests.html.

Liverpool Candidates are asked to write an essay on a veterinary topic prior to interview.

London (RVC) BMAT (see www.admissionstests.cambridgeassessment.org.uk and www.rvc.ac.uk).

Myerscough (Coll) (Vet Nurs) Subject-based test at interview.

Nottingham Trent (Vet Nurs) Evidence of 1-2 weeks work experience in a veterinary practice.

SELECTION OF APPLICANTS

University and college departmental admissions tutors are responsible for selecting candidates, basing their decisions on the policies of acceptable qualifications established by each institution and, where required, applicants' performance in admissions tests. There is little doubt that academic achievement, aptitude and promise are the most important factors although other subsidiary factors may be taken into consideration. The outline which follows provides information on the way in which candidates are selected for degree and diploma courses:

* Grades obtained by the applicant in GCE, A-level and AS-level examinations and the range of subjects studied may be considered.
* Applicant's performance in aptitude and admissions tests, as required by universities and colleges.
* Academic record of the applicant throughout his or her school career, especially up to A-level and AS-levels, Highers, Advanced Highers or other qualifications and the choice of subjects. If you

are taking general studies at A-level or AS-level confirm with the admissions tutor that this is acceptable.

* Time taken by the applicant to obtain good grades at GCSE/Standard Grade and A-level and AS-levels/Highers/Advanced Highers.
* Forecast or the examination results of the applicant at A-level and AS-level and head teacher's report.
* The applicant's intellectual development; evidence of ability and motivation to follow the chosen course.
* The applicant's range of interests, both in and out of school; aspects of character and personality.
* The vocational interests, knowledge and experience of the applicant particularly if they are choosing vocational courses.

INTERVIEWS

Fewer applicants are now interviewed than in the past but even if you are not called you should make an effort to visit your chosen universities and/or colleges before you accept any offer. Interviews may be arranged simply to give you a chance to see the institution and the department and to meet the staff and students. Alternatively, interviews may be an important part of the selection procedure for specific courses such as Law, Medicine and Teaching. If they are, you need to prepare yourself well.

Most interviews last approximately 20–30 minutes and you may be interviewed by more than one person. For practical subjects such as Music and Drama almost certainly you will be asked to perform, and for artistic subjects, to take examples of your work. For some courses you may also have a written or other test at interview (see above).

How best can you prepare yourself?

Firstly, as one applicant advised, 'Go to the interview – at least you'll see the place.'

Secondly, on the question of dress, try to turn up looking smart (it may not matter, but it can't be wrong). Two previous applicants were more specific: 'Dress smartly but sensibly so you are comfortable for travelling and walking round the campus.'

More general advice is also important:

* 'Prepare well – interviewers are never impressed by applicants who only sit there with no willingness to take part.'
* 'Read up the prospectus and course details. Know how their course differs from any others you have applied for and be able to say why you prefer theirs.'
* 'They always ask if you have any questions to ask them: prepare some!' For example, How many students are admitted to the course each year? What are the job prospects for graduates? How easy is it to change from your chosen course to a related course?

Questions which you could ask might focus on the ways in which work is assessed, the content of the course, field work, work experience, teaching methods, accommodation and, especially for vocational courses, contacts with industry, commerce or the professions. However, don't ask questions which are already answered in the prospectus!

These are only a few suggestions and other questions may come to mind during the interview which, above all, should be a two-way flow of information. It is also important to keep a copy of your UCAS application (especially Section 10) for reference since your interview will probably start with a question about something you have written.

Usually interviewers will want to know why you have chosen the subject and why you have chosen their particular institution. They will want to see how motivated you are, how much care you have taken in choosing your subject, how much you know about your subject, what books you have read. If you have chosen a vocational course they will want to find out how much you know about the career it leads to, and whether you have visited any places of work or had any work experience. If your chosen subject is also an A-level subject you will be asked about your course and the aspects of the course you like the most.

Try to relax. For some people interviews can be an ordeal; most interviewers know this and will make allowances. The following extract from the Oxford prospectus will give you some idea of what admissions tutors look for:

* 'Interviews serve various purposes and no two groups of tutors will conduct them in the same way or give them exactly the same weight. Most tutors wish to discover whether a candidate has done more than absorb passively what he/she has been taught. They try to ascertain the nature and strength of candidates' intellectual interests and their capacity for independent development. They are also likely to ask about applicants' other interests outside their school curriculum. This is partly because between two candidates of equal academic merit, preference will be given to the one who has the livelier interests or activities, and partly because it is easier to learn about candidates when they talk about what interests them most.'
* 'Interviews are in no sense hostile interrogations. Those candidates who show themselves to be honest, thoughtful and unpretentious will be regarded more favourably than those who try to impress or take the view that it is safest to say as little as possible. We do not expect candidates to be invariably mature and judicious.'

In the tables in **Chapter 8** (**Selection interviews**, **Interview advice and questions** and **Reasons for rejection**) you will also find examples of questions which have been asked in recent years for which you might prepare, and non-academic reasons why applicants have been rejected!

The following chapter **Applications** provides a guide through the process of applying to your chosen universities and courses and highlights key points for your action.

6 | APPLICATIONS

ENTRY REQUIREMENTS

Before applying to universities and colleges, be sure that you have the required subjects and qualifications for entry to your chosen course. Details of entry requirements are available direct from the universities and colleges. You will need to check:

(i) the general entry requirements for courses.

(ii) any specific subject requirements to enter a particular course, for example, study of specified GCE A- and/or AS-levels, Scottish Highers/Advanced Highers, GCSEs, Scottish Standard Grades, or BTEC qualifications (for example, National Diploma, National Certificate). The course requirements are set out in prospectuses and on websites.

(iii) any age, health, Criminal Records Bureau (CRB) clearance or other requirements for entry to particular courses and universities and colleges. For entry to some specific courses such as Medicine and Nursing, offers are made subject to health screening for hepatitis B, for example, and immunisation requirements. Owing to Government regulations, some universities will insist on a minimum age at entry of 18 years. Check university and college websites and prospectuses for these particular course requirements.

(iv) admissions tests required by a number of universities for a range of subjects, including Dentistry, Law, Medicine and Veterinary Science/Medicine. Offers of places made by these universities are dependent on an applicant's performance in the relevant test. It is important to find out full details about universities' course requirements for possible admissions tests well before submitting the UCAS application and to make all the necessary arrangements for registering and taking any required admissions tests. See **Chapter 5** and check university/college and admissions tests websites for the latest information.

Potential applicants should ask the advice of teachers, careers advisers and university and college advisers before submitting their application.

APPLICATIONS FOR UNIVERSITY AND COLLEGE COURSES THROUGH UCAS

UCAS, the organisation responsible for managing applications to higher education courses in the UK, deals with applications for admission to full-time and sandwich first degrees, Foundation degrees, Diploma of Higher Education and Higher National Diploma courses and some full-time Higher National Certificate courses in nearly all universities (but not the Open University), university colleges, colleges and institutes of higher education, specialist colleges and some further education colleges.

The UCAS Application Process

Full details of application procedures and all course information can be found on the UCAS website. Information is also available in the UCAS publication *Big Guide* (available from www.ucasbooks.com or from Publication Services, PO Box 130, Cheltenham GL52 3ZF, email publicationservices@ucas.ac.uk or fax 01242 544806).

Applications are made online at www.ucas.com using **UCAS Apply**. This is a secure web-based application system, which has been designed for all applicants whether they are applying through a UCAS-registered centre, such as a school or college, or applying independently from anywhere in the world.

Applications can be sent to UCAS from mid-September. The first deadline is 15 October for applications to Oxford or Cambridge Universities and applications for courses in Medicine, Dentistry and Veterinary Science/Medicine. January 15 is the deadline for UK and EU applicants to apply for all other courses, except for some Art and Design courses that have a 24 March deadline. You can still apply after these deadlines up to 30 June, but institutions may not be able to consider you.

On the UCAS application, you have up to five course choices unless you are applying for Dentistry (courses A200, A203, A204, A205 and A206), Medicine (courses A100, A101, A102, A103, A104 and A106) or Veterinary Science/Medicine (courses D100 and D101). For these courses only four choices are permitted.

It is important to note that some universities (for example, Birmingham and Cambridge) now require their applicants to complete a Supplementary Application Questionnaire after they have received your UCAS application. Check the websites of your listed universities for their latest application information.

Each university or college makes any offer through the UCAS system. UCAS does not make offers, or recruit on behalf of universities and colleges. It does not advise applicants on their choice of subject although it does publish material which applicants may find useful.

Applicants may receive an 'unconditional' offer in the case of those who already hold the required qualifications, or, for those awaiting examination results, a 'conditional' offer or a rejection. When all decisions have been received from universities or colleges, applicants may finally hold up to two offers: a first choice (firm) offer and an insurance offer. Applicants who have made five choices and have no offers or have declined any offers received can use **UCAS Extra**. Applicants are told when they become eligible for **UCAS Extra** and can apply online for one further course at a time using **UCAS Track** at www.ucas.com. **UCAS Extra** runs from 25 February until 6 July. Courses available in **UCAS Extra** will be highlighted on **Course Search** at www.ucas.com. Applicants not placed through this system will be eligible to contact institutions with vacancies in **Clearing** from mid-August.

Confirmation starts on the day when the A-level examination results are released. **Clearing** vacancy lists are also published on A-level results day. Applicants meeting the conditions of their offers for their firm choice will receive confirmation from their university or college and may still be accepted even if their results are slightly lower than those stipulated in the original offer. If rejected by their firm choice university/college, applicants will have their places confirmed by their insurance choice institution providing they have obtained the right grades. Applicants who are unsuccessful with both their institutions will be eligible to go into **Clearing** in which they can select an appropriate course in the same or a different institution where places are available. Each year up to 40,000 applicants obtain places through **Clearing**, and over 5,500 applicants found a place though **Extra** last year.

UCAS timetable

Mid-September 2010	UCAS begins accepting applications.
15 October	Deadline for UCAS to receive applications to Oxford University or the University of Cambridge, and applications to courses in Medicine, Dentistry or Veterinary Medicine/Science.
15 January 2011	Deadline for UCAS to receive applications from UK and EU applicants for all other courses, except for some Art and Design courses that have a 24 March deadline. Visit **Course Search** at www.ucas.com to find out whether Art and Design courses have a 15 January or 24 March deadline.
16 January–30 June	Applications received by UCAS are forwarded to the institutions for consideration at their discretion. Applications received after 30 June are processed through **Clearing**.
25 February–6 July	Applicants who have made five choices and have no offers or who have declined any offers received can use **UCAS Extra** to apply for one further course at a time on **UCAS Track** at www.ucas.com. Institutions will show which courses have

	vacancies in **UCAS Extra** on the UCAS website. Details of the **UCAS Extra** service will be included in the *Applicant Welcome Guide* sent to applicants.
24 March	Deadline for UCAS to receive applications for some Art and Design courses. Visit **Course Search** at www.ucas.com to find out whether Art and Design courses have a 15 January or 24 March deadline.
9 May	Applicants who have received all their decisions from universities and colleges by the end of March are asked to reply to their offers by this date.
7 June	Applicants receiving decisions from all their choices by 9 May must reply to their offers by this date.
30 June	Last date for receiving applications. Applications received after this date are entered directly into **Clearing**. In mid-July **Clearing** starts.
5 August	Scottish SQA results published.
18 August	GCE A-level and AS-level results published. **Clearing** vacancy information available. (See **What To Do on Results Day . . . and After** below.)

PLEASE NOTE

- You are not required to reply to any university/college offers until you have received your last decision.
- Do not send a firm acceptance to more than one offer.
- Do not try to alter a firm acceptance.
- Send a Cancel slip to, or 'phone, UCAS at once if you decide not to go to university/college this year.
- Remember to tell the institutions and UCAS if you change your address, or change your examination board(s), subjects or arrangements.

APPLICATIONS FOR ART AND DESIGN COURSES

NB For entry to courses in 2010 and beyond, all Art and Design courses come under the main UCAS scheme (see above **Applications for University and College Courses through UCAS**).

Universities and colleges offering Art and Design courses will choose an 'equal consideration' application deadline of either 15 January or 24 March to suit their own individual institution's admissions process. Students will be able to choose five Art and Design courses in no order of preference, regardless of the application deadline date.

Check with the UCAS website (www.ucas.com) and university and college websites for full details for entry in 2011.

APPLICATIONS FOR LAW COURSES

Applicants for some specified undergraduate Law programmes at Birmingham, Bristol, Durham, Glasgow (4 yr course), Leeds, London (King's), (UCL), Nottingham and Oxford will have to sit the National Admissions Test for Law (LNAT) (see **Chapter 5**). See the LNAT website (www.lnat.ac.uk) for full details of which Law courses require applicants to sit the LNAT and for information about registration fees, sample papers, test dates and test centres. Applicants are advised to fill in their UCAS application before registering or taking the LNAT but it is important to check the deadlines for registering for, and sitting, the test. If you apply for an LNAT-specified Law course but fail to take the test in time, your application will be rejected by the university. It is important to note that applicants must enter their UCAS number on the LNAT registration form by specified deadlines (check for 2010/11 dates). Applicants' LNAT scores cannot be sent to the universities to which they have applied until this has been done and all LNAT fees have been paid.

If you are applying for Law courses not listed on the LNAT website, or by the universities themselves with the LNAT as a requirement, there is no need for you to sit the LNAT.

APPLICATIONS FOR MEDICINE AND DENTISTRY COURSES

It is essential that you check university websites for their latest information for entry to their medical and dental schools. Check, especially, their subject and grade requirements for GCSEs as well as for A-levels (or their equivalents). They are very specific in their conditions for entry which usually include either the UK Clinical Aptitude Test (UKCAT) or the BioMedical Admissions Test (BMAT). You will need the most up-to-date information about these admissions tests (for example, about registration deadlines, universities/medical schools, test dates, test centres, practice papers) so check their websites frequently (www.ukcat.ac.uk and www.bmat.org.uk). You must make the necessary arrangements well in advance of completing your UCAS application. See also **Chapter 5**.

APPLICATIONS FOR VETERINARY SCIENCE/MEDICINE COURSES

The BioMedical Admissions Test (BMAT) is required for entry to specified Veterinary Science/Medicine courses at Bristol, Cambridge and London (RVC). Applicants have to register for the BMAT and must check the website (www.bmat.org.uk) for details, including entry closing dates, test centres, fees and test dates. It is essential that you make your arrangements well before completing your UCAS application. See also **Chapter 5**.

APPLICATIONS FOR BIOMEDICAL SCIENCES AND PHARMACOLOGY AND TRANSLATIONAL MEDICAL SCIENCE

Oxford and Imperial London require applicants to take the BMAT for their Biomedical Sciences and (for Imperial London) the Pharmacology and Translational Medical Sciences courses. See the universties' websites, **Chapter 5** and www.bmat.org.uk.

APPLICATIONS FOR MUSIC COURSES AT CONSERVATOIRES

The Conservatoires UK Admissions Service (CUKAS) handles applications for practical Music courses. Applications can be made simultaneously to a maximum of six of the conservatoires listed below and simultaneous applications can also be made to both UCAS and CUKAS. Full details of CUKAS are given on www.cukas.ac.uk. The Conservatoires taking part in this online admissions system are:

- Birmingham Conservatoire www.conservatoire.uce.ac.uk
- Leeds College of Music www.lcm.ac.uk
- Royal College of Music www.rcm.ac.uk
- Royal Northern College of Music www.rncm.ac.uk
- Royal Scottish Academy of Music and Drama www.rsamd.ac.uk
- Royal Welsh College of Music and Drama www.rwcmd.ac.uk
- Trinity Laban Conservatoire of Music and Dance www.tcm.ac.uk

See also the **Music** table of interview requirements/tests in **Chapter 5**.

APPLICATIONS FOR TEACHER TRAINING COURSES

Applicants intending to start a course of initial teacher training in England leading to Qualified Teacher Status have to be provisionally registered with the General Teaching Council of England (GTCE). Check www.gtce.org.uk for full details. See also www.gttr.ac.uk/students/beforeyouapply and www.tda.gov.uk for full details of applying for undergraduate (and postgraduate) training courses. Students in Wales and Northern Ireland should also check with this website; Scottish students should check www.gtcs.org.uk.

THE UCAS APPLICATION

Two important aspects of the UCAS application concern Sections 3 and 10. In Section 3 all your university/college choices (a maximum of five) are to be listed, but remember that you should not mix your subjects. For example, in popular subject areas such as English, History or Physiotherapy, it is safer to show total commitment by applying for all courses in the same subject and not to include second and/or third subject alternatives on the form. (See advice in separate tables in **Chapter 8** for **Medicine**, **Dentistry** and **Veterinary Science/Medicine**.)

A brief glance at the subject tables in **Chapter 8** will give you some idea of the popularity of various courses. In principle, institutions want the best applicants available so if there are large numbers of applicants the offers made will be higher. For Medicine and a number of other courses offers in terms of A-level grades are now reaching AAA or A* grades, and often with additional AS-levels. Conversely, for the less popular subjects such as Chemistry or Manufacturing Engineering, the offers can be much lower – down to CCC, but with many more applicants expected in 2010, for entry in 2011, typical offers for many courses have increased significantly.

Similarly, some institutions are more popular (not necessarily better) than others. Again, this popularity can be judged easily in the tables in **Chapter 8**: the higher the offer, the more popular the institution. Popular universities often are located in attractive towns or cities such as Bristol, Exeter, Warwick, Bath or York. Additionally, some institutions have established a good 'reputation' for various reasons, for example, Oxford, Cambridge and Durham. Conversely and unfortunately, some universities have confused applicants with unfamiliar names and no immediate identity as to their location, such as De Montfort and Brunel. More students would apply to these excellent institutions if they knew where they were situated.

When you have chosen your courses and your institutions, look again at the offers the latter usually make and compare these with the grades projected by your teachers on your UCAS reference. It is most important to maximise your chances of a place by choosing institutions which might make you a range of offers. When all universities have considered your application you can hold only two offers (one firm and one insurance offer) and naturally it is preferable for one to be lower than the other in case you do not achieve the offer grades or equivalent points for your first choice of university or college.

The other section of the UCAS application that deserves careful thought is Section 10 (Personal Statement). This seems simple enough but it is the only part of the application where you can put in a personal bid for a place! In short, you are asked to give relevant background information about yourself, your interests and your choice of course and career. Give yourself plenty of time to prepare Section 10 – if you have a Record of Achievement you could use it as a guide – as this part of your application could make all the difference to getting an offer or not.

Motivation to undertake your chosen course is very important. You can show this by giving details of any work experience and work shadowing you have done (and for History courses, for example, details of visits to places of historical interest). It is a good idea to begin your statement with such evidence and explain how your interest in your chosen subject has developed. In the subject tables in **Chapter 8** under **Advice to applicants and planning the UCAS personal statement**, advice is given on what you might include in Section 10. You should also include various activities in which you have been involved in the last three or four years. Get your parents and other members of the family to refresh your memory – it is easy to forget something quite important. You might consider planning out this section in a series of sub-sections – and if you have a lot to say, be brief. The sub-sections can include:

- **School activities** Are you a prefect, chairperson or treasurer of a society? Are you involved in supervisory duties of any kind? Are you in a school team? Which team? For how long? (Remember, team means any team: sports, chess, debating, even business.)
- **Intellectual activities** Have you attended any field or lecture courses in your main subjects? Where? When? Have you taken part in any school visits? Do you play in the school orchestra or have you taken part in a school drama production – on or off stage? Do you go to the theatre, art galleries or concerts?

- **Out-of-school activities** This category might cover many of the topics above, but it could also include any community or voluntary work you do, or Duke of Edinburgh's Awards, the Combined Cadet Force (CCF), sport, music and drama activities etc. The countries you have visited might also be mentioned – for example, any exchange visits with friends living abroad.
- **Work experience** Details of part-time, holiday or Saturday jobs could be included here, particularly if they have some connection with your chosen course. Some applicants plan ahead and arrange to visit firms and discuss career interests with various people who already work in their chosen field. For some courses such as Veterinary Science, work experience is essential, and it certainly helps for others, for example Medicine and Business courses.
- **Key Skills** These cover numeracy, communication and information technology (the basics) and also advanced skills involving teamwork, problem solving and improving your own learning. If you are not offering the Key Skills Certificate then evidence of your strengths in these areas may be mentioned in the school or college reference or you may include examples in your personal statement relating to your out-of-school activities.

Finally, plan your UCAS application carefully. You may write short statements if you wish. It is not essential to write in prose except perhaps if you are applying for English or language courses in which case your statement will be judged grammatically! Take a copy to use as a trial and a copy of your complete application to keep by you for reference if you are called for interview. Almost certainly you will be questioned on what you have written.

Admissions tutors always stress the importance of the confidential report from your head teacher or form tutors. Most schools and colleges will make some effort to find out why you want to apply for a particular course, but if they do not ask, do not take it for granted that they will know! Consequently, although you have the opportunity to write about your interests on the form, it is still a good idea to tell your teachers about them. Also, if you have to work at home under difficult conditions or if you have any medical problem, your teachers must be told since these points should be mentioned on the report.

Deferred entry

Although application is usually made in the autumn of the year preceding the proposed year of entry, admissions tutors may be prepared to consider an application made two years before entry, so that the applicant can, perhaps, gain work experience or spend a period abroad. Policies on deferred entry may differ from department to department, so you should check with admissions tutors before applying. Simply remember that there is no guarantee that you will get the grades you need or a place at the university of your first choice at the first attempt! If not, you may need to repeat A-levels and try again. It may be better not to apply for deferred entry until you are certain in August of your grades and your place.

APPLICATIONS TO THE UNIVERSITY OF CAMBRIDGE

The University recently announced changes to its applications process so you will need to check with its Admissions Office or on www.cam.ac.uk/admissions/undergraduate/apply for the latest information. If you are a UK or EU applicant, you now need only complete the UCAS application. You will then receive an email from the University, confirming the arrival of your application and giving you the website address of their online Supplementary Application Questionnaire (SAQ) which you will then need to complete and return by the specified date.

Your UCAS application listing Cambridge as one of your university choices must be sent to UCAS by 15 October. If you are applying for Medicine or Veterinary Medicine you must include your BMAT registration with your application. You can indicate your choice of college or make an Open application if you have no preference. Open applicants are allocated by a computer program to colleges that have had fewer applicants per place for your chosen subject.

The Cambridge Special Access Scheme (CSAS) is also available for applicants whose schooling has been disrupted or disadvantaged. You need to complete a CSAS application by 15 October but discuss this with your school/college higher education adviser and check with the UCAS website for more information.

Interviews take place in Cambridge in the first three weeks of December, although some may be a little earlier. Many of the University's colleges use tests as part of the selection process for specific courses and written work also may be requested before interview. This practice, however, varies between colleges and subjects. See the University website and **Chapter 5** for information you need to know before completing and submitting your application.

In January applicants receive either an offer conditional upon certain grades in examinations to be taken the following summer, or a rejection. Alternatively, you may be placed in a pool for further consideration. About one in five applicants are pooled and one in four receive an offer. Decisions are made on the basis of academic record, reference, personal statement, submitted work/test results and interviews. The conditions set are grades to be obtained in examinations such as A-levels, Scottish Highers/Advanced Highers or the International Baccalaureate. Offers made by some Cambridge University colleges may also include Sixth Term Examination Papers (STEP) in mathematics (see **Chapter 5** under ***Mathematics***). The STEPs are taken in June and copies of past papers and full details are available from www.admissionstests.cambridgeassessment.org.uk.

College policies

All colleges which admit undergraduates use the selection procedures described in **Chapter 5**. However, there will be some minor variations between the various colleges, within each college and also between subjects. Further information about the policies of any particular college can be found in the Cambridge Undergraduate Prospectus and may also be obtained from the admissions tutor of the college concerned. No college operates a quota system for any subject except Medicine and Veterinary Medicine, for which there are strict quotas for the University from which places are allocated to each college.

Full details of the admissions procedures are contained in the current Cambridge Undergraduate Prospectus. Copies of the prospectus are available from Cambridge Admissions Office, Fitzwilliam House, 32 Trumpington Street, Cambridge CB2 1QY, or via the website www.cam.ac.uk/admissions.

APPLICATIONS TO THE UNIVERSITY OF OXFORD

Application procedures to Oxford are similar to all other universities except that candidates applying to Oxford must submit a UCAS application by 15 October 2010 for those applying for entry in October 2011 or for deferred entry in October 2012. Admissions are carried out on a college basis: candidates can name a college of preference and may be allocated second and third preference colleges, but if they do not have a specific college in mind, they can make an open application. This means that they will be allocated a college by the Admissions Office computer which takes account of their chosen course and the approximate number of applicants per place that each college has received that year (and gender in the case of the one women-only college).

For some subjects at some colleges at Oxford, applicants are required to sit aptitude or admissions tests (for example, the History Aptitude Test, the National Admissions Test for Law (LNAT) and the BioMedical Admissions Test (BMAT)) or to provide essays or a portfolio for interview. Specimen test questions are published on the website. See **Chapter 5** for more information and see www.ox.ac.uk/admissions/undergraduatecourses/howtoapply for full details. All candidates are considered carefully on their individual merits. Tutors take into account a range of information from the candidate's application including details of their academic record and the reference in order to assess a candidate's suitability and potential for his or her proposed course. Candidates applying for some courses may be required to submit samples of marked school work by early November, and/or to take a short written test when they are in Oxford for interview (see **Chapter 5**). The majority of candidates applying to Oxford are invited for interview at the beginning of December and this is an integral part of the selection procedure. Candidates will be interviewed at their college of preference and also may be interviewed by other colleges. Colleges co-operate and pool candidates to ensure that the most able candidates are offered places. Successful candidates who have not completed their school-leaving examinations will be made conditional offers based on their forthcoming examinations such as A-levels, Scottish Highers, Advanced Highers, International Baccalaureate, European Baccalaureate and other European and international qualifications. Decisions are notified to candidates via UCAS by the end of January. Candidates are welcome to attend Open Days which are held at all of the colleges and a number of departments, usually during the summer term or in September.

Common Framework

The University and Colleges have agreed to a Common Framework for Colleges and Faculties (see www.admissions.ox.ac.uk/news/common_framework.shtml) which lays down key principles and procedures for undergraduate admissions. The Common Framework is designed to make admissions more transparent, improve methods of assessing candidates and ensure that selection is unaffected by the applicant's choice of college.

Colleges will continue to have the final say over whom they admit but they will be guided by the central banding of candidates by faculties based on the whole range of information arising from the selection process. This information may include results from pre-interview test, written work, school qualifications and/or predicted school-leaving grades, interviews and contextual information about a candidate's educational background.

Where a college wishes to offer a place to a candidate below the 'selection threshold', it will be required to explain the reasons to the relevant faculty with reference to the agreed admissions criteria.

APPLICATIONS TO SCOTTISH UNIVERSITIES

Another point worth noting concerns the older Scottish universities in which admission is generally to a faculty and not to a specific course or department. Students often study three subjects in Year 1 and either two or three in Year 2. Honours courses normally take four years although admission to the second year of the course is sometimes possible (see **Chapter 7**).

APPLICATIONS TO IRISH UNIVERSITIES

All applications to universities in the Republic of Ireland are made through the Central Application Office, Tower House, Eglinton Street, Galway, Ireland; see www.cao.ie or telephone 091 509 800.

The Central Application Office website gives full details of all 44 institutions and details of the application procedure. Applications are made by 1 February. Individual institutions publish details of their entry requirements for courses, but unlike applications through UCAS in the UK, no conditional offers are made. Applicants are judged purely on their academic ability except for the Royal College of Surgeons which also requires a school reference and a personal statement. The results are published in August when institutions make their offers and when successful students are required to accept or decline the offer.

APPLICATIONS TO AMERICAN UNIVERSITIES

There are over 2000 universities and colleges offering degree course programmes in the USA; some institutions are independent and others state-controlled. Unlike the UK, however, where UCAS control nearly all university and college applications, it is necessary to apply separately to all American universities.

Most American universities will expect applicants to have A-levels or IB qualifications and in addition, usually require students to complete a School Assessment Test (SAT) covering mathematical and verbal reasoning abilities. In some cases applicants may be required to take SAT II tests which are based on specific subjects. Tests can be taken at centres in the UK: see www.collegeboard.com.

Unlike the usual specialised subject degrees at UK universities, 'Liberal Arts programmes' in the USA have considerable breadth and flexibility, although subjects requiring greater specialised knowledge such as Medicine and Law require further study at Medical or Law School.

Because of the complexities of an application to American universities, such as financial implications, visas etc, students should initially refer to www.fulbright.co.uk. It is also important to be able to identify the differences between and the quality of institutions and a valuable guide can be sourced through www.petersons.com (*General Guides to Colleges, Scholarships and Admissions*).

MATURE APPLICANTS

There are a great many mature students following first degree courses in UK universities and colleges. The following is a list of key points a group of mature students found useful in exploring and deciding on a university course.

- Check with your nearest university or college to find out about the courses they can offer, for example degrees, diplomas, full-time, part-time.
- Some institutions will require examination passes in some subjects, others may not.
- An age limit may apply for some vocational courses, for example Medicine, Dentistry and Teaching.
- If entry requirements are an obstacle, prospective students should approach their local colleges for information on Access or Open College courses. These courses are fast-growing in number and popularity, offering adults an alternative route into higher education other than A-levels. They are usually developed jointly by colleges of further education and the local higher education institution.
- Demands of the course – how much time will be required for study? What are the assignments and the deadlines to be met? How is your work assessed – unseen examinations, continuous assessment, practicals?
- The demands on finance – cost of the course – loan needed – loss of earnings – drop in income if changing to another career – travel requirements – accommodation – need to work part-time for income?
- The availability and suitability of the course – geographical location – competition for places – where it will lead – student support services, for example childcare, library.
- What benefits will you derive? Fulfilment, transferable skills, social contacts, sense of achievement, enjoyment, self-esteem, career enhancement?
- Why would employers want to recruit you? Ability to adapt to the work scene, realistic and balanced approach, mature attitude to work?
- Why would employers not want to recruit you? Salary expectations, inability to fit in with younger colleagues, limited mobility? However, some employers particularly welcome older graduates: Civil Service, local authorities, Health Service, religious, charitable and voluntary organisations, teaching, social/probation work, careers work, housing.

AND FINALLY . . . BEFORE YOU SEND IN YOUR APPLICATION

CHECK that you have passes at Grade C or higher in the GCSE (or equivalent) subjects required for the course at the institutions to which you are applying. FAILURE TO HAVE THE RIGHT GCSE SUBJECTS OR THE RIGHT NUMBER OF GRADE C PASSES OR HIGHER IN GCSE WILL RESULT IN A REJECTION.

CHECK that you are taking (or have taken) the GCE A- and AS-level (or equivalent) subjects required for the course at the institution to which you are applying. FAILURE TO BE TAKING OR HAVE TAKEN THE RIGHT A-LEVELS WILL ALSO RESULT IN A REJECTION.

CHECK that the GCE A-levels and other qualifications you are taking will be accepted for the course for which you are applying. Some subjects and institutions do not stipulate any specific A-levels, only that you are required to offer two or three subjects at GCE A-level. In the view of some admissions tutors NOT ALL GCE A-LEVELS CARRY THE SAME WEIGHT (see **Chapter 1**).

CHECK that you can meet the requirements for all relevant admissions/interview tests.

CHECK that you have made all the necessary arrangements for sitting any required admissions tests.

CHECK that you can meet any age, health and CRB requirements for entry to your listed courses.

WHAT TO DO ON RESULTS DAY . . . AND AFTER

BE AT HOME! Do not arrange to be away when your results are published. If you do not achieve the grades you require, you will need to follow an alternative course of action and make decisions that could affect your life during the next few years. Do not expect others to make these decisions for you.

If you achieve the grades or points which have been offered you will receive confirmation of a place, but this may take a few days to reach you. Once your place is confirmed contact the accommodation office at the university or college and inform them that you will need a place in a hall of residence or other accommodation.

If you achieve grades or points higher than your conditional firm (CF) choice you can reconsider where and what to study by registering with UCAS to use the **Adjustment in Track** process. This is available from A-level results day until 31 August and you have five days to register and secure an alternative course. You must check very carefully all the **Adjustment** information on the UCAS website before changing your CF choice to make sure you are eligible and that a vacancy is available. There is no guarantee of a vacancy on a course you are aiming for, and it is very unlikely that competitive courses will have places. If you decide definitely to change courses advise the university or college immediately, but check with www.ucas.com and your school/college adviser for the latest information.

If your grades or points are higher than you expected and you are not holding any offers you can telephone or e-mail the admissions tutor at the universities and colleges which rejected you and request that they might reconsider you.

If you just miss your offers then telephone or email the universities and colleges to see if they can still offer you a place. ALWAYS HAVE YOUR UCAS REFERENCE NUMBER AVAILABLE WHEN YOU CALL. Their decisions may take a few days. You should check the universities and colleges in your order of preference. Your first choice must reject you before you contact your second choice.

If you have not applied to any university or college earlier in the year then you can apply through the **Clearing** scheme which runs from the middle of July. Check the tables in **Chapter 8** to identify which institutions normally make offers matching your results, then telephone or email the institution to see if they have any vacancies before completing your **Clearing** form.

If you learn finally that you do not have a place you will receive automatically a **Clearing** form to enable you to re-apply. Before you complete this form follow the instructions above.

If an institution has vacancies they will ask you for your grades. If they can consider you they will ask you for your **Clearing** form. You can only be considered by one institution at a time.

If you have to re-apply for a place, check the vacancies on the UCAS website (www.ucas.com), in the national press and through your local careers office. If there are vacancies in your subject, check with the university or college that these vacancies have not been taken.

REMEMBER – There are many thousands of students just like you. Admissions tutors have a mammoth task checking how many students will be taking up their places since not all students whose grades match their offers finally decide to do so!

IF YOU HAVE AN OFFER AND THE RIGHT GRADES BUT ARE NOT ACCEPTING THAT OR AN ALTERNATIVE PLACE – TELL THE UNIVERSITY OR COLLEGE. Someone else is waiting for your place!

You may have to make many telephone calls to institutions before you are successful. It may even be late September before you know you have a place so BE PATIENT AND STAY CALM!

TAKING A GAP YEAR

Choosing your course is the first decision you need to make, the second is choosing your university and then, for an increasing number, the third is deciding whether or not to take a gap year. But there lies the problem. Because of the very large number of things to do and places to go, you'll find that you almost need a gap year to choose the right one (although a read through *Your Gap Year* by Susan Griffith (see **Appendix 5**) is a good place to start)!

Planning ahead is important but, in the end, bear in mind that you might be overtaken by events, not least in failing to get the grades you need for a place on the course or at the university you were counting on. This could mean repeating A-levels and re-applying, which in turn could mean waiting for interviews and offers and, possibly, deferring the start of your 'gap' until February or March.

Once you have decided to go, however, it's a question of whether you will go under your own steam or through a gap year agency. Unless you are streetwise, or preferably 'world wise', then an agency offers several advantages. Some agencies may cover a broad field of opportunities whilst others will focus on a specific region and activity, such as the African Conservation Experience, offering animal and plant conservation work in game and nature reserves in southern Africa.

When making the choice, some students will always prefer a 'do-it-yourself' arrangement. However, there are many advantages to going through specialist agencies. Not only can they offer a choice of destinations and opportunities but also they can provide a lot of essential and helpful advice before your departure on issues such as health precautions and insurance. Support is also available in the case of accidents or illnesses when a link can be established between the agency and parents.

Good luck!

7 HOW TO USE THE SUBJECT TABLES

The subject tables in the next chapter represent the core of the book, listing degree courses offered by all UK universities and colleges. These tables are designed to provide you with the information you need so that you can match your abilities and interests with your chosen degree subject, prepare your application and find out how applicants are selected for courses.

At the top of each table there is a brief overview of the subject area, together with a selection of websites for organisations that can provide relevant careers or course information. This is then followed by the subject tables themselves in which information is provided in sequence under the following headings.

Course offers information
- Subject requirements/preferences (GCSE/A-level/other requirements)
- NB Offers statement
- Your target offers and examples of courses provided by each institution
- Alternative offers

Examples of Foundation degrees in the subject field

Choosing your course
- Some course features
- Universities and colleges teaching quality
- Top universities and colleges (research)
- Examples of sandwich degree courses

Admissions information
- Number of applicants per place
- Advice to applicants and planning the UCAS personal statement
- Misconceptions about this course
- Selection interviews
- Interview advice and questions
- Reasons for rejection (non-academic)

After-results advice
- Offers to applicants repeating A-levels

Graduate destinations and employment
- Career note

Other degree subjects for consideration

When selecting a degree course it is important to try to judge the points score or grades that you are likely to achieve and compare them with the offers listed under **Your target offers and examples of courses provided by each institution**. However, even though you might be capable of achieving the indicated grades or UCAS Tariff points, it is important to note that these are likely to be the minimum grades or points required and that there is no guarantee that you will receive an offer: other factors in your application, such as the personal statement, references, and admissions test performance will be taken into consideration (see also **Chapters 4** and **5**).

University departments frequently adjust their offers, depending on the numbers of candidates applying, so you must not assume that the offers and policies published now will necessarily apply to courses starting in 2011 or thereafter. In 2010 there are many more changes than usual because of the high number of applicants to universities and colleges, and competition for places in 2011 for many courses is likely to be keen. Nevertheless, even though offers may change during the 2010/11 application cycle, you can assume that the offers published in this book represent the general academic levels at which you should aim.

Below are explanations of the information given under the headings in the subject tables. It is important that you read these carefully so that you understand how they can help you to choose and apply for courses that are right for you.

COURSE OFFERS INFORMATION

Subject requirements/preferences

Brief information is given on the GCSE and A-level requirements. Note that for the Dentistry, Medicine and Veterinary Sciences/Medicine courses A-level subject requirements are stated, on the individual institutions' offers line as their A-level requirements are more complex than for other subjects. Other requirements are sometimes specified, where these are relevant to the course subject area, for example, medical requirements for health-related courses and Criminal Records Bureau (CRB) clearance. Check prospectuses and websites of universities and colleges for course requirements.

The following statement appears in all subject tables:

NB It is important to note that in 2011 universities and colleges will differ in their use of GCE AL/AS unit grade information, A* grades, the Extended Project (EPQ), the Advanced Diploma and the Cambridge Pre-U when considering applicants and making offers. An EPQ may be accepted in place of an AS subject. Check websites of universities and colleges for the latest offers information.

Your target offers and examples of courses provided by each institution

Universities and colleges offering degree courses in the subject area are listed in descending order according to the number of UCAS Tariff points and/or A-level grades they are likely to require applicants to achieve. The UCAS Tariff points total is listed down the left-hand side of the page, and to the right appear all the institutions (in alphabetical order) likely to make offers in this Tariff point range. (Information on the UCAS Tariff is given in **Appendix 1** and guidance on how to calculate your offers is provided on the inside back cover of this book. Please also read the information in the **Important Note** box below.)

The courses included on the offers line are examples of the courses available in the subject field at that university or college. You will need to check prospectuses and websites for a complete list of the institution's single, joint, combined or major/minor degree courses available in the subject.

For each institution listed, the following information may be given.

Name of institution

Note that the name of an institution's university college or campus may be given in brackets after the institution title, for example London (King's) or Kent (Medway Sch Pharm). Where the institution is not a university, further information about its status may also be given to indicate the type of college – for example (UC) to mean University College or (CAg) to mean College of Agriculture. This is to help readers to differentiate between the types of colleges and to help them identify any specialisation a college may have, for example art or agriculture. A full list of abbreviations used is given under the heading **INSTITUTION ABBREVIATIONS** towards the end of this chapter and see the **Directory of Institutions** at the back of the book.

Grades/points offer

After the institution's name, a line of offers information is given, showing a typical offer made by the institution for the courses indicated in brackets at the end of the line. Offers, however, may vary between applicants and the published grades and/or points offers should be regarded as targets to aim for and not necessarily the actual grades or points required. Offers may be reduced after the publication of A-level results, particularly if a university or college is left with spare places. However, individual course offers listed in the Tables in **Chapter 8** are abridged and should be used as a first source of reference and comparison only. It is not possible to publish all the variables relevant to each offer: applicants must check prospectuses and websites for full details of all offers and courses.

Depending on the details given by institutions, the offers may provide information as follows:

- **Grades** The specific grades, or average grades, required at GCE A-level or at A-level plus AS-level or, if specified, EPQ for the listed courses. A-level grades are always presented in capital letters;

AS-levels and EPQ grades are shown in lower case – so the offer BBBc would indicate three grade Bs at A-level, plus an additional EPQ or AS-level at grade c. Where necessary, the abbreviation 'AL' is used to indicate A-level; 'AS' to indicate AS-level and EPQ to indicate that an Extended Project Qualification is part of the offer. Offers are usually shown in terms of three A-level grades although some institutions accept two grades with the same points total or, alternatively, two A-level grades accompanied by AS-level grades. Two AS-levels may generally be regarded as equivalent to one A-level, and one Double Award A-level as equivalent to two standard A-levels.

NB Unit grade and module information, now introduced into the admissions system, is most likely to be required by universities where a course is competitive, or where taking a specific unit is necessary or desirable for entry. Check with institutions' websites for their latest information.

* **UCAS Tariff points** The number (or range) of A-level, AS-level UCAS Tariff points required for the listed courses. A, AS-levels, International Baccalaureate (IB), Scottish Highers, the Advanced Diploma and a range of other qualifications have a unit value in the UCAS Tariff system (see **The UCAS Tariff Points Table** in **Appendix 1**). Where a range of Tariff points is shown, for example 220–180 points, offers are usually made within this points range for these specified courses. Note that, in some cases, an institution may require a points score which is higher than the specified grade offer given. This can be for a number of reasons – for example, you may not be offering the standard subjects that would have been stipulated in a grades offer. In such cases additional points may be added by way of AS-levels, Key Skills etc.

  It is important to note that the UCAS Tariff is constantly updated and new qualifications are introduced each year. However, universities and colleges will specify on their websites the qualifications that applicants can offer for entry to specific courses as not all qualifications can be counted towards a Tariff point offer.

  Check with prospectuses and websites or contact the university or college for further information.

See **Chapter 4** for information from universities about their admissions policies including, for example, information about their expected use of A*, unit grades, the Advanced Diploma, the Extended Project and the Cambridge Pre-U in their offers for applicants. See **Appendix 3** for information about the Cambridge Pre-U and **Appendix 1** for **The UCAS 2011 Entry Tariff Points** tables.

* **Admissions tests for Law, Medicine and Veterinary Science/Medicine** Where admissions tests form part of a university's offer for any of these subjects, this is indicated on the offers line in the subject tables for the relevant university. This is shown by '+LNAT' (for Law), '+BMAT' or '+UKCAT' (for Medicine), and '+BMAT' (for Veterinary Science/Medicine). For example, the offers lines could read as follows:

  Edinburgh – AAAb +UKCAT (inc AL chem+1 from maths/phys/biol; AS biol min) (Medicine 5/6 yrs) (IB 37 pts HL 766)
  London (King's) – AAAb +LNAT (Law) (IB 38 pts HL 555–554)
  London (RVC) – AAA +BMAT (inc AL chem+biol+1 other) (Vet Med)

  Entry and admissions tests will be required for 2011 by a number of institutions for a wide range of subjects: see **Chapter 5** and the subject tables in **Chapter 8** for more information and check university websites and prospectuses.

COURSE TITLE(S)

After the offer, an abbreviated form of the course title(s) to which the offers information refers is provided, also in brackets. The abbreviations used (see **COURSE ABBREVIATIONS** at the end of this chapter) closely relate to the course titles shown in the institutions' prospectuses. When the course gives the opportunity to study abroad (for example, in Continental Europe, Australia, North America) the abbreviated name of the relevant country is shown after the abbreviated course title. For example:

Lancaster – AAB 340 pts (Env Sci N Am/Aus; MChem Env Chem Abrd) (IB 30 pts)

When experience in industry is provided as part of the course (not necessarily a sandwich course) this can be indicated on the offers line by including 'Ind' after the abbreviated course title. For example:

Bristol – ABB (Pharmacol; Pharmacol Ind) (IB 34 pts)

Sometimes the information in the offers line relates to more than one course (see **Plymouth** below). In such cases, each course title is separated with a semicolon.

Plymouth – 300 pts (MEng Civ Eng; Civ Cstl Eng)

When a number of joint courses exist in combination with a major subject, they may be presented using a list separated by slashes – for example '(Euro Mgt with Fr/Ger/Ital/Span)' indicates European Management with French or German or Italian or Spanish.

Some titles may be followed by the word 'courses' – for example, (Geog courses):

St Andrews – AAB (Theol St; Bib St courses) (IB 30 pts)

This means that the information on the offers line refers not only to the Single Honours course in Theological Studies, but also to the range of Biblical Studies courses. For some institutions with extensive Combined Honours programmes, the information given on the offers line may specify (Comb Hons) or (Comb courses).

Courses awaiting validation are usually publicised in prospectuses and on websites. However, these are not included in the tables in **Chapter 8** since there is no guarantee that they will run. You should check with the university that a non-validated course will be available.

To help you understand the information provided under the 'UCAS Tariff points requirements' heading, the box below provides a few examples with their meaning explained underneath.

OFFERS LINES EXPLAINED

320 pts [University/College name] – BBCc **or** BBccc (Fr Ger)
For the joint course in French and German, the University requires grades of BBC (280 pts) at A-level plus AS-level grade c (40 pts) making a total of 320 points or, alternatively, BB (200 pts) at A-level plus AS-level grades ccc (120 pts), making the same total.

320 pts [University/College name] – 320 pts BBC +AS/EPQ c (Biomed Sci (Genet))
For the Biomedical Sciences course specialising in Genetics the University requires 320 pts, typically from 3 A-levels, together with either one AS-level or Extended Project Qualification (EPQ). The typical offer will be BBC at A-level plus c in either an AS-level or an EPQ.

220 pts [University/College name] – 220–280 pts (Geography)
For Geography, the University usually requires 220 UCAS tariff points, but offers may range up to 280 UCAS tariff points.

IB offers

A selection of IB points offers appears at the end of some university/subject entries. For comparison of entry requirements, applicants with IB qualifications should check the A-level offers required for their course and then refer to **Appendix 1** which gives the revised IB UCAS points Tariff for 2011 entry. The figures under this subheading indicate the number or range of International Baccalaureate (IB) Diploma points likely to be requested in an offer. A range of points indicates variations between Single and Joint

Honours courses. Applicants should check with the universities for any requirements for points gained from specific Higher Level subjects.

Applicants offering the IB should check with prospectuses and websites and, if in doubt, contact admissions tutors for the latest information on IB offers.

Alternative offers

In each of the subject tables, offers are shown in A-level grades or equivalent UCAS Tariff points, and in some cases as points offers of the International Baccalaureate Diploma (see above). However, applicants taking Scottish Highers/Advanced Highers, the Welsh Baccalaureate, Advanced Diploma, the IB Diploma, the Irish Leaving Certificate, the Advanced Diploma, the Extended Project and the Cambridge Pre-U should refer to the **Appendix 1 UCAS 2011 Entry Tariff Points**. For more information, see www.ucas.com/students/ucas_Tariff/Tarifftables or contact the institution direct.

Scottish offers

Scottish Honours degrees normally take four years. However, students with very good qualifications may be admitted into the second year of courses (Advanced entry). In some cases it may even be possible to enter the third year.

320 pts **Dundee** – ABB 2nd yr entry (MEng Electron Eng Microcomp Sys)
260 pts **Dundee** – BCC 1st yr entry (MEng Electron Eng Microcomp Sys)

The policies at each of the universities are as follows:

Aberdeen Advanced entry possible for many courses, but not for Education, Law or Medicine.
Abertay Dundee No advanced entry.
Dundee Advanced entry possible for many courses, but not Art, Education, Law or Medicine.
Edinburgh Only in very unusual cases is entry to the second year accepted.
Edinburgh Napier Advanced entry to Stages 2, 3 or 4 of a programme, particularly for those with an HNC/HND or those with (or expecting to obtain) good grades in Advanced Highers or A-levels.
Glasgow No advanced entry except in some cases for Engineering and Sciences, but not for Accountancy, Arts or Social Science courses.
Glasgow Caledonian No advanced entry.
Queen Margaret Advanced entry for some courses.
St Andrews Advanced entry for some courses.
Stirling Advanced entry for some courses.
Strathclyde Advanced entry for some courses.
West Scotland Advanced entry for some courses.

IMPORTANT NOTE ON THE COURSE OFFERS INFORMATION

The information provided in **Chapter 8** is presented as a first reference source as to the target levels required. Institutions may alter their standard offers in the light of the qualifications offered by applicants.

The offers they publish do not constitute a contract and are not binding on prospective students: changes may occur between the time of publication and the time of application in line with market and student demand.

The points levels shown on the left-hand side of the offers listings are for ease of reference for the reader: not all universities will be making offers using the UCAS tariff points system and it cannot be assumed that they will accept a points equivalent to the grades they have stipulated.

Check university and college prospectuses, and also their websites, for their latest information before submitting your application.

EXAMPLES OF FOUNDATION DEGREES IN THE SUBJECT FIELD

This section lists examples of universities and colleges offering Foundation degrees in the subject field. Foundation degrees are employment-related higher education qualifications bringing higher education and business closer together to meet the needs of employers. The degrees are at a lower level than Honours degrees and can be studied on a part-time basis or full-time over two years. Entry requirements for these courses vary, but many institutions request between 60 and 140 UCAS Tariff points. Increasingly, universities and university colleges – and now university centres – provide one-year top-up degree courses for Foundation degree graduates to obtain an Honours degree. Full details of institutions offering Foundation degrees can be obtained from www.ucas.com and www.findfoundationdegree.co.uk.

CHOOSING YOUR COURSE

The information under this heading (to be read in conjunction with **Chapter 1**) covers factors that are important to consider in order to make an informed decision on which courses to apply for. The information is organised under the following subheadings.

Some course features

The purpose of this section is to alert you to the diversity of courses on offer and the importance of checking the content of your chosen course. It should be noted that many departments provide a common first year in the same subject, for example Biological Sciences, with a choice of specialisation in Year 2. (The courses listed have not been selected on the basis of academic reputation or course quality.)

Universities and colleges teaching quality

The Unistats website (www.unistats.com) provides official information where available for different subjects and universities and colleges in the United Kingdom to help prospective students and their advisers make comparisons between them and so make informed choices about what and where to study. Information is updated annually and is available for each subject taught at each university and college (and for some further education colleges). The Quality Assurance Agency (www.qaa.ac.uk) reviews the quality and standards of all universities and colleges and official reports of their reviews are available on their website but it is important to note their dates of publication.

Top research universities and colleges (RAE 2008)

In December 2008 the latest research assessment exercise took place covering certain subject areas. The leading universities in the relevant subject areas are listed in the order of achievement. It should be noted that not all subjects were assessed.

Examples of sandwich degree courses

This section lists examples of institutions that offer sandwich placements for some of their courses in the subject field shown. The courses listed are of one-year duration and do not include language courses or work experience or other short-term placements. Check with the institutions too, since new courses may be introduced and others withdrawn depending on industrial or commercial arrangements. Further information on sandwich courses with specific information on the placements of students appears at the end of **Chapter 1**.

NB During a period of recession, universities and colleges may have problems placing students on sandwich courses. Applicants applying for courses are therefore advised to check with admissions tutors that these courses will run, and that placements will be available.

ADMISSIONS INFORMATION

Under this heading, information gathered from the institutions has been provided. This will be useful when planning your application.

Number of applicants per place (approx)

These figures show the approximate number of applicants initially applying for each place before any offers are made. It should be noted that any given number of applicants represents candidates who have also applied for up to four other university and college courses. In some subject areas some universities have provided details of the actual breakdown of numbers of applicants under the following headings: UK, EU (non-UK), non-EU (overseas), mature (over 21).

Advice to applicants and planning the UCAS personal statement

This section offers guidelines on information that could be included in the personal statement section of your UCAS application. In most cases, applicants will be required to indicate why they wish to follow a particular course and, if possible, to provide positive evidence of their interest. See also **Chapters 5** and **6**.

Misconceptions about this course

Admissions tutors are given the opportunity in the research for this book to set the record straight by clarifying aspects of their course they feel are often misunderstood by students, and in some cases, advisers!

Selection interviews

Institutions that normally use the interview as part of their selection procedure are listed here. Those institutions adopting the interview procedure will usually interview only a small proportion of applicants. It is important to use this section in conjunction with **Chapter 5**.

Interview advice and questions

This section includes information from institutions on what candidates might expect in an interview to cover, and examples of the types of interview questions posed in recent years. Also refer to **Chapter 5**: this provides information on tests and assessments which are used in selecting students.

Reasons for rejection (non-academic)

Academic ability and potential to suceed on the course are the major factors in the selection (or rejection) of applicants. Under this subheading, admissions tutors give other reasons for rejecting applicants.

AFTER-RESULTS ADVICE

Under this heading, information for helping you decide what to do after the examination results are published is provided (see also the section on **What to do on Results Day . . . and After** in **Chapter 6**). Details refer to the main subject area unless otherwise stated in brackets.

Offers to applicants repeating A-levels

This section gives details of whether second-time offers made to applicants repeating their exams may be 'higher', 'possibly higher' or the 'same' as those made to first-time applicants. The information refers to single Honours courses. It should be noted that circumstances may differ between candidates – some will be repeating the same subjects taken in the previous year, while others may be taking different subjects. Offers will also be dictated by the grades you achieved on your first sitting of the examinations. Remember, if you were rejected by all your universities and have achieved good grades, contact them by telephone on results day – they may be prepared to revise their decision. This applies particularly to medical schools.

GRADUATE DESTINATIONS AND EMPLOYMENT

The information under this heading has been provided by the Higher Education Statistics Agency (HESA) and is taken from their report *Destinations of Leavers from Higher Education 2007/8*. The report can be obtained from HESA, 95 Promenade, Cheltenham, Gloucestershire GL50 1HZ; Tel 01242 211155; e-mail customer.services@hesa.ac.uk.

Details are given of the total number of graduates surveyed whose destinations have been recorded – not the total number who graduated in that subject. Employment figures relate to those in full-time permanent paid employment after six months in a variety of occupations not necessarily related to their degree subject (short-term and unpaid employment figures are not included). 'Further Study' includes research into a subject-related field, higher degrees, private study or, alternatively, career training involving work and further study. The 'Assumed unemployed' category refers to those students who were believed to be unemployed for various reasons (eg travelling, personal reasons) or those students still seeking permanent employment six months after graduating.

Career note
Short descriptions of the career destinations of graduates in the subject area are provided.

OTHER DEGREE SUBJECTS FOR CONSIDERATION

This heading includes some suggested alternative courses that have similarities to the courses listed in the subject table.

ABBREVIATIONS USED IN THE SUBJECT TABLES CHAPTER 8

INSTITUTION ABBREVIATIONS

The following abbreviations are used to indicate specific institutions or types of institution:

Ac	Academy
AI	Arts Institute
ALRA	Academy of Live and Recorded Arts
AMD	Academy of Music and Drama
Birk	Birkbeck (London University)
CA	College of Art(s)
CAD	College of Art and Design
CAFRE	College of Agriculture, Food and Rural Enterprise
CAg	College of Agriculture
CAgH	College of Agriculture and Horticulture
CAT	College of Advanced Technology or Arts and Technology
CComm	College of Communication
CDC	College of Design and Communication
CECOS	London College of IT and Management
CFash	College of Fashion
CHort	College of Horticulture
CmC	Community College
CMus	College of Music
CMusDr	College of Music and Drama
Coll	College
Consv	Conservatoire (Birmingham)
Court	Courtauld Institute (London University)
CT	College of Technology
CTA	College of Technology and Arts
Gold	Goldsmiths (London University)
Hey	Heythrop College (London University)
IA	Institute of Art(s)

IFHE	Institute of Further and Higher Education
Inst	Institute
King's	King's College (London University)
LIPA	Liverpool Institute of Performing Arts
LSE	London School of Economics and Political Science
Met	Metropolitan
MS	Medical School
QM	Queen Mary (London University)
RAcMus	Royal Academy of Music
RCMus	Royal College of Music
Reg Coll	Regional College
Reg Fed	Regional Federation (Staffordshire)
RH	Royal Holloway (London University)
RNCM	Royal Northern College of Music
RSAMD	Royal Scottish Academy of Music and Drama
RVC	Royal Veterinary College (London University)
SA	School of Art
SAC	Scottish Agricultural College
SAD	School of Art and Design
Sch	School
Sch SpDr	School of Speech and Drama
SOAS	School of Oriental and African Studies (London University)
UC	University College
UCL	University College (London University)
UCP	Marjon University College Plymouth St Mark and St John
Univ	University
UWIC	University of Wales Institute (Cardiff)

COURSE ABBREVIATIONS

The following abbreviations are used to indicate course titles:

Ab	Abrahamic
Abrd	Abroad
Acc	Accountancy/Accounting
Accs	Accessories
Acoust	Acoustics/Acoustical
Acu	Acupuncture
Acq	Acquisition
Act	Actuarial
Actg	Acting
Actn	Action
Actr	Actor
Actv	Active
Actvt(s)	Activity/Activities
Add	Additional
Adlscn	Adolescence
Adlt	Adult
Admin	Administration/ Administrative
Adt	Audit
Adv	Advertising
Advc	Advice
Advnc	Advanced
Advntr	Adventure
Aero	Aeronautical/Aeronautics
Aerodyn	Aerodynamics
Aeromech	Aeromechanical
Aerosp	Aerospace
Aeroth	Aerothermal
Af	Africa(n)
Affrs	Affairs
Age	Ageing
Agncy	Agency
Agric	Agriculture/Agricultural
Agrofor	Agroforestry
Agron	Agronomy
Aircft	Aircraft
Airln	Airline
Airpt	Airport
Am	American
Amen	Amenity

Analys	Analysis
Analyt	Analytical
Anat	Anatomy/Anatomical
Anim	Animal
Animat	Animation
Animatron	Animatronics
Anth	Anthropology
Antq	Antique(s)
App(s)	Applied/Applicable/ Applications
Appr	Appropriate
Apprsl	Appraisal
Aqua	Aquaculture/Aquatic
Ar	Area(s)
Arbc	Arabic
Arbor	Arboriculture
Arch	Archaeology
Archit	Architecture
Archvl	Archival
Aroma	Aromatherapy
Arst	Artist
Artfcts	Artefacts
Artif	Artificial
As	Asian
Ass	Assessment
Assoc	Associated
Asst	Assistant
Assyr	Assyriology
Ast	Asset
Astnaut	Astronautics/Astronautical
Astro	Astrophysics
Astron	Astronomy
A-Sxn	Anglo-Saxon
Ated	Accelerated
Atel	Atelier
Atlan	Atlantic
Atmos	Atmospheric
Attrctns	Attractions
Auc	Auctioneering
Aud	Audio
Audiol	Audiology
Audtech	Audiotechnology
Aus	Australia(n)
Austr	Australasia
Auth	Author/Authoring/Authorship
Auto	Automotive
Autom	Automated/Automation
Automat	Automatic
Autombl	Automobile
AV	Audio Video
Avion	Avionics
Avn	Aviation
Ay St	Ayurvedic Studies

Bch	Beach
Bd	Based
Bdwk	Bodywork
Bhv	Behaviourial
Bib	Biblical
Bio Ins	Bio Instrumentation
Bioarch	Bioarchaeology
Bioch	Biochemistry/Biochemical
Biodiv	Biodiversity
Bioelectron	Bioelectronics
Biogeog	Biogeography
Biogeosci	Biogeoscience
Bioinform	Bioinformatics
Biokin	Biokinetics
Biol	Biological/Biology
Biom	Biometry
Biomed	Biomedical/Biomedicine
Biomol	Biomolecular
Biophys	Biophysics
Bioproc	Bioprocess
Biorg	Bio-organic
Biotech	Biotechnology
Bkbnd	Bookbinding
Bld	Build/Building
Blt	Built
Bngli	Bengali
Br	British
Braz	Brazilian
Brew	Brewing
Brit	British
Brnd	Brand/Branding
Broad	Broadcast
Bspk	Bespoke
Bty	Beauty
Bulg	Bulgarian
Burm	Burmese
Bus	Business
Buy	Buying
Byz	Byzantine

Callig	Calligraphy
Can	Canada/Canadian
Cap	Capital
Cardio	Cardiology
Carib	Caribbean
Cart	Cartography

Cat	Catering
CATS	Credit Accumulation and Transfer Scheme
Cdtng	Conditioning
Cell	Cellular
Celt	Celtic
Cent	Century
Ceram	Ceramics
Cert	Certificate
Ch Mgt	Chain Management
Chc	Choice
Chch	Church
Chem	Chemistry
Cheml	Chemical
Chin	Chinese
Chld	Child/Children/Childhood
Chn	Chain
Chng	Change
Choreo	Choreography
Chr	Christian(ity)
Chtls	Chattels
Cits	Cities
Civ	Civilisation/Civil
Class	Classical
Clim	Climate/Climatic
Clin	Clinical
Cllct	Collect/Collecting
Clnl	Colonial
Cloth	Clothing
Clsrm	Classroom
Cmbt	Combat
Cmdy	Comedy
Cmn	Common
Cmnd	Command
Cmplrs	Compilers
Cmpn	Companion
Cmpsn	Composition
Cmpste	Composite
Cmwlth	Commonwealth
Cncr	Cancer
Cnflct	Conflict
Cnma	Cinema/Cinematics
Cnslg	Counselling
Cnsltncy	Consultancy
Cnt	Central
Cntnt	Content
Cntrms	Countermeasures
Cntry	Country/Countryside
Cntxt	Context
Cnty	Century
Coach	Coaching
Cog	Cognitive
Col	Colour
Comb	Combined
Combus	Combustion
Comm(s)	Communication(s)
Commer	Commerce/Commercial
Commun	Community
Comp	Computer/Computerised/ Computing
Compar	Comparative
Complem	Complementary
Comput	Computation/al
Con	Context
Concur	Concurrent
Cond	Conductive
Condit	Conditioning
Cons	Conservation
Constr	Construction
Consum	Consumer
Cont	Contour
Contemp	Contemporary
Contnl	Continental
Contr	Control
Conv	Conveyancing
Corn	Cornish
Corp	Corporate/Corporation
Cos	Cosmetic
Cosmo	Cosmology
Cr	Care
Crcs	Circus
Crdc	Cardiac
Crea	Creative/Creation
Crfts	Crafts/Craftsmanship
Crim	Criminal
Crimin	Criminological/Criminology
Crit	Criticism/Critical
Crm	Crime
Cro	Croatian
Crr	Career
Crs	Course
Crsn	Corrosion
Cru	Cruise
Crypt	Cryptography
Cstl	Coastal
Cstm	Costume
Cstmd	Customised
Ctln	Catalan
Ctlys	Catalysis
Ctzn	Citizenship

Culn	Culinary
Cult	Culture/Cultural
Cur	Curation
Cy	Cyber
Cyber	Cybernetics/Cyberspace
Cybertron	Cybertronics
Cym	Cymraeg
Cz	Czech
Dan	Danish
Decn	Decision
Decr	Decoration/Decorative
Def	Defence
Defer	Deferred Choice
Deg	Degree
Demcr	Democratic
Dept	Department
Des	Design(er)
Desr	Desirable
Dev	Development/Developmental
Devsg	Devising
Df	Deaf
Diag	Diagnostic
Diet	Dietetics/Dietitian
Dif	Difficulties
Dig	Digital
Dip Ing	Diplom Ingeneur
Dir	Direct/Direction/Director/ Directing
Dis	Diseases
Disab	Disability
Disas	Disaster
Discip	Disciplinary
Diso	Disorders
Disp	Dispensing
Dist	Distributed/Distribution
Distil	Distillation/Distilling
Div	Divinity
d/l	distance learning
Dlvry	Delivery
Dnstry	Dentistry
Dntl	Dental
Doc	Document/Documentary
Dom	Domestic/Domesticated
Dr	Drama
Drg	Drawing
Drs	Dress
Dscrt	Discrete
Dscvry	Discovery
Dsply	Display
Dtbs	Databases
Dth	Death
Dvc	Device
Dvnc	Deviance
Dynmcs	Dynamics
Ecol	Ecology/Ecological
Ecomet	Econometrics
e-Commer	E-Commerce
Econ	Economics
Econy	Economy/ies
Ecosys	Ecosystem(s)
Ecotech	Ecotechnology
Ecotour	Ecotourism
Ecotox	Ecotoxicology
Edit	Editorial
Educ	Education
Educr	Educare
Efcts	Effects
EFL	English as a Foreign Language
Egypt	Egyptian/Egyptology
Elec	Electrical
Elecacoust	Electroacoustics
Electromech	Electromechanical
Electron	Electronics
ELT	English Language Teaching
Ely	Early
Emb	Embryo
Embd	Embedded
Embr	Embroidery
Emer	Emergency
Emp	Employment
Ener	Energy
Eng	Engineering
Engl	English
Engn	Engine
Ent	Enterprise
Enter	Entertainment
Entre	Entrepreneur/ Entrepreneurship
Env	Environment/Environmental
Eql	Equal
Eqn	Equine
Eqstrn	Equestrian
Equip	Equipment
Equit	Equitation
Ergon	Ergonomics
Est	Estate
Eth	Ethics

Ethl	Ethical
Eth-Leg	Ethico-Legal
Ethn	Ethnic
Ethnol	Ethnology
Ethnomus	Ethnomusicology
EU	European Union
Euro	European
Eval	Evaluation
Evnglstc	Evangelistic
Evnt(s)	Event(s)
Evol	Evolution/Evolutionary
Ex	Executing
Excl	Excellence
Exer	Exercise
Exhib	Exhibition
Exp	Export
Explor	Exploration
Explsn	Explosion
Expltn	Exploitation
Expmtl	Experimental
Expnc	Experience
Expr	Expressive
Ext	Extended
Extr	Exterior
Extrm	Extreme
Fabs	Fabric(s)
Fac	Faculty
Facil	Facilities
Fash	Fashion
Fbr	Fibre
Fctn	Fiction
Fd	Food
Fdn	Foundation
Fin	Finance/Financial
Finn	Finnish
Fish	Fisheries
Fit	Fitness
Fl	Fluid
Fld	Field
Flex	Flexible
Flor	Floristry
FMaths	Further Mathematics
Fmly	Family
Fn	Fine
Foot	Footwear
For	Foreign
Foren	Forensic
Foss	Fossil(s)
Fr	French
Frchd	Franchised
Frcst	Forecasting
Frm	Farm
Frmwk	Framework
Frshwtr	Freshwater
Frst	Forest
Frsty	Forestry
Frtlty	Fertility
Fst Trk	Fast Track
Fstvl	Festival
Ftbl	Football
Ftre	Feature(s)
Ftwr	Footwear
Furn	Furniture
Fut	Futures
Gael	Gaelic
Gam	Gambling
Gdn	Garden
Gdnc	Guidance
Gem	Gemmology
Gen	General
Genet	Genetics
Geochem	Geochemistry
Geoinform	Geoinformatics
Geophys	Geophysics
Geophysl	Geophysical
Geopol	Geopolitics
Geosptl	Geospatial
Geotech	Geotechnics
Ger	German/Germany
Gerc	Germanic
Gk	Greek
GIS	Geographical Information Systems
Glf	Golf
Glf Crs	Golf Course
Gllry	Gallery/Galleries
Glob	Global/Globalisation
Gls	Glass
Gmg	Gaming
Gmnt	Garment
Gms	Games
Gmtc	Geomatic
Gndr	Gender
Gnm	Genome/Genomics
Gov	Government
Govn	Governance
Graph	Graphic
Grgn	Georgian

Grn	Green
gs	General Studies
Guj	Gujerati
Hab	Habitat
Hack	Hacking
Hard	Hardware
Haz	Hazard
Heal	Healing
Heb	Hebrew
Herb	Herbal
Herit	Heritage
Hisp	Hispanic
Hist	History/Historical
HL	IB Higher level
Hlcst	Holocaust
Hlnds	Highlands
Hlth	Health
Hlthcr	Healthcare
HlthSC	Health and Social Care
Hm	Home
Hol	Holistic
Hom	Homeopathic
Homin	Hominid
Horol	Horology
Hort	Horticulture
Hosp	Hospital
Hous	Housing
HR	Human Resources
Hrdrs	Hairdressing
Hrs	Horse
Hse	House
Hspty	Hospitality
Htl	Hotel
Hum	Human(ities)
Hung	Hungarian
Hydrog	Hydrography
Hydrol	Hydrology
Hyg	Hygiene
Iber	Iberian
Ice	Icelandic
ICT	Information and Communications Technology
Id	Ideas
Idnty	Identity
Illus	Illustration
Imag	Image/Imaging/Imaginative
Immun	Immunology/Immunity
Impair	Impairment
Inc	Including
Incln	Inclusion
Inclsv	Inclusive
Ind	Industrial/Industry
Indep St	Independent Study
Indsn	Indonesian
Inf	Information
Infec	Infectious/Infection
Infml	Informal
Inform	Informatics
Infra	Infrastructure
Inftq	Informatique
Injry	Injury
Innov	Innovation
Ins	Insurance
Inst	Institution(al)
Instln	Installation
Instr	Instrument/Instrumentation
Int	International
Intcult	Intercultural
Integ	Integrated/Integration
Intel	Intelligent/Intelligence
Inter	Interior
Interact	Interaction/Interactive
Interd	Interdisciplinary
Interp	Interpretation
Intlctl	Intellectual
Intnet	Internet
Intrmdl	Intermodal
Inv	Investment
Invn	Innovation
Invstg	Investigating/Investigation
Ir	Irish
Is	Issues
Isl	Islands
Islam	Islamic
Isrl	Israel/Israeli
IT	Information Technology
Ital	Italian
ITE	Initial Teacher Education
ITT	Initial Teacher Training
Jap	Japanese
Jew	Jewish
Jewel	Jewellery
Jrnl	Journalism
Jud	Judaism
Juris	Jurisprudence
Just	Justice

Kntwr	Knitwear
Knwl	Knowledge
Kor	Korean
KS	Key Stage
Lab	Laboratory
Lang(s)	Language(s)
Las	Laser
Lat	Latin
Lcl	Local
LD	Learning Disabilities
Ldrshp	Leadership
Lea	Leather
Leg	Legal
Legis	Legislative
Leis	Leisure
Lf	Life
Lfstl	Lifestyle
Lgc	Logic
Lib	Library
Libshp	Librarianship
Lic	Licensed
Lic de Geog	Licence de Geographie
Lic de Let	Licence de Lettres
Ling	Linguistics
Lit	Literature/Literary
Litcy	Literacy
Lnd	Land(scape)
Lndbd	Land-based
Lns	Lens
Log	Logistics
Lrng	Learning
Ls	Loss
Lsr	Laser
Ltg	Lighting
Ltr	Later
Lv	Live
Lvstk	Livestock
Mach	Machine(ry)
Mait	Maitrise Internationale
Mak	Making
Mand	Mandarin
Manuf	Manufacturing
Map	Map/Mapping
Mar	Marine
Marit	Maritime
Mark	Market(ing)
Masch	Maschinenbau
Mat	Materials
Mathem	Mathematical
Maths	Mathematics
Mbl	Mobile
Mdl	Modelling
Measur	Measurement
Mech	Mechanical
Mecha	Mechatronics
Mechn	Mechanisation
Mechnsms	Mechanisms
Med	Medicine/cal
Medcnl	Medicinal
Mediev	Medieval
Medit	Mediterranean
Metal	Metallurgy/Metallurgical
Meteor	Meteorology/Meteorological
Meth	Method(s)
Mgr	Manager
Mgrl	Managerial
Mgt	Management
Microbiol	Microbiology/Microbiological
Microbl	Microbial
Microcomp	Microcomputer/ Microcomputing
Microelec	Microelectronics
Mid E	Middle Eastern
Midwif	Midwifery
Min	Mining
Miner	Minerals
Mkup	Make-up
Mling	Multilingual
Mltry	Military
MML	Master of Modern Languages
Mnd	Mind
Mndrn	Mandarin
Mnrts	Minorities
Mnstry	Ministry
Mnswr	Menswear
Mntl Hlth	Mental Health
Mntn	Mountain
Mntnce	Maintenance
Mny	Money
Mod	Modular
Modl	Modelling/Modelmaking
Modn	Modern
Modnty	Modernity
Mol	Molecular
Monit	Monitoring
Mov	Movement/Moving
Mrchnds	Merchandise
Mrchnt	Merchant

Mrl	Moral
Msg	Massage
Mslm	Muslim
Mtl	Metal(s)
Mtlsmth	Metalsmithing
Mtn	Motion
Mtr	Motor
Mtrcycl	Motorcycle
Mtrg	Motoring
Mtrspo	Motorsports
Multid	Multidisciplinary
Multim	Multimedia
Mus	Music(ian)
Muscskel	Musculoskeletal
Musl	Musical
Musm	Museum
Mushp	Musicianship
N	New
N Am	North America
Nano	Nanoscience
Nanotech	Nanotechnology
Nat	Nature/Natural
Navig	Navigation
Nds	Needs
Neg	Negotiated
Net	Network
Neuro	Neuroscience
Neuropsy	Neuropsychology
News	Newspaper
NGO	Non-Governmental Organisation(s)
NI	Northern Ireland/ Northern Irish
NMedia	New Media
Nnl	National
Norw	Norwegian
Npli	Nepali
Nrs	Norse
Ntv	Native
Nucl	Nuclear
Nurs	Nursing
Nursy	Nursery
Nutr	Nutrition(al)
Nvl	Naval
NZ	New Zealand
Objs	Objects
Obs	Observational
Occ	Occupational
Ocean	Oceanography
Ocn	Ocean
Ocnc	Oceanic
Oeno	Oenology
Ofce	Office
Off	Offshore
Offrd	Off-road
Okl	Oklahoma
Onc	Oncology
Onln	On-Line
Op(s)	Operation(s)
Oph	Ophthamic
Oprtg	Operating
Opt	Optical
Optim	Optimisation
Optn/s	Optional/Options
Optoel	Optoelectronics
Optom	Optometry
OR	Operational Research
Ord	Ordinary
Org	Organisation
Orgnc	Organic
Orgnsms	Organisms
Orn	Ornithology
Orntl	Oriental
Orth	Orthoptics
Orthot	Orthotics
Oseas	Overseas
Ost	Osteopathy
Out	Outdoor
Out Act	Outdoor Activity
Outsd	Outside
Ovrs	Overseas
P	Primary
P Cr	Primary Care
Pacif	Pacific
Pack	Packaging
PActv	Physical Activity
Pal	Palaeobiology
Palae	Palaeoecology/ Palaeontology
Palaeoenv	Palaeoenvironments
Paramed	Paramedic(al)
Parasit	Parasitology
Parl	Parliamentary
Pat	Patent
Path	Pathology
Pathobiol	Pathobiological
Pathogen	Pathogenesis

Patt	Pattern
Pblc	Public
Pce	Peace
PE	Physical Education
Per	Person/Personal
Perf	Performance
Perfum	Perfumery
Pers	Personnel
Persn	Persian
Petrol	Petroleum
PGCE	Postgraduate Certificate in Education
Pharm	Pharmacy
Pharmacol	Pharmacology
Pharml	Pharmaceutical
Phil	Philosophy
Philgy	Philology
Phn	Phone
Phon	Phonetics
Photo	Photography/ Photographic
Photojrnl	Photojournalism
PhotoM	Photomedia
Photon	Photonic(s)
Phys	Physics
Physio	Physiotherapy
Physiol	Physiology/Physiological
Physl	Physical
Pks	Parks
Plan	Planning
Planet	Planetary
Plas	Plastics
Play	Playwork
Plcg	Police/Policing
Plcy	Policy
Plmt	Placement
Plnt	Plant
Plntsmn	Plantsmanship
Plt	Pilot
Pltry	Poultry
PMaths	Pure Mathematics
Pntg	Painting
Pod	Podiatry/Podiatric
Pol	Politics/Political
Polh	Polish
Pollut	Pollution
Poly	Polymer/Polymeric
Pop	Popular
Popn	Population
Port	Portuguese
PPE	Philosophy, Politics and Economics or Politics, Philosophy and Economics
PPI	Private Pilot Instruction
Ppl	People
Ppr	Paper
Pptry	Puppetry
PR	Public Relations
Prac	Practice/Practical
Practnr	Practitioner
Prchsng	Purchasing
Prcrmt	Procurement
Prdcl	Periodical
Precsn	Precision
Pref	Preferable/Preferred
Prehist	Prehistory
Prem	Premises
Proc	Process/Processing
Prod	Product/Production/Produce
Prof	Professional/Professions
Prodg	Producing
Prog	Programme/Programming
Proj	Project
Prom	Promotion
Prop	Property/ies
Pros	Prosthetics
Prot	Protection/Protected
Prplsn	Propulsion
Prsts	Pursuits
Prt	Print
Prtcl	Particle
Prtd	Printed
Prtg	Printing/Printmaking
Prvntn	Prevention
Pst	Post
Pstcolnl	Postcolonial
Pstrl	Pastoral
Psy	Psychology
Psybiol	Psychobiology
Psyling	Psycholinguistics
Psysoc	Psychosocial
p/t	part-time
Ptcl	Particle
Pub	Publishing
Pvt	Private
Pwr	Power
Pwrcft	Powercraft
Qntm	Quantum
Qry	Quarry

Qtrnry	Quaternary
QTS	Qualified Teacher Status
Qual	Quality
Qualif	Qualification
Quant	Quantity/Quantitative

Rad	Radio
Radiog	Radiography
Radiothera	Radiotherapy
Rbr	Rubber
Rce	Race
Rcycl	Recycling
Rdtn	Radiation
Realsn	Realisation
Rec	Recording
Reclam	Reclamation
Recr	Recreation
Reg	Regional
Regn	Regeneration
Rehab	Rehabilitation
Rel	Relations
Relgn	Religion
Relig	Religious
Reltd	Related
Rem Sens	Remote Sensing
Ren	Renaissance
Renew	Renewable
Rep	Representation
Reqd	Required
Res	Resources
Resid	Residential
Resoln	Resolution
Resp	Response
Restor	Restoration
Rev	Revenue
Rflxgy	Reflexology
Rgby	Rugby
Rgstrn	Registration
Rl	Real
Rlblty	Reliability
Rlwy	Railway
Rmnc	Romance
Rnwl	Renewal
Robot	Robotics
Rom	Roman
Romn	Romanian
Rsch	Research
Rspnsb	Responsibility
Rsprty	Respiratory
Rsrt	Resort
Rstrnt	Restaurant
Rtl	Retail
Rts	Rights
Rur	Rural
Russ	Russian
Rvr	River

S	Secondary
Sansk	Sanskrit
S As	South Asian
Sat	Satellite
Sbstnce	Substance
Scand	Scandinavian
Schlstc	Scholastic
Schm	Scheme
Sci	Science/Scientific
Scnc	Scenic
Scngrph	Scenographic/Scenography
Scot	Scottish
Scr	Secure
Script	Scriptwriting
Scrn	Screen
Scrnwrit	Sreenwriting
Scrts	Securities
Scrty	Security
Sctr	Sector
Sculp	Sculpture
Sdlry	Saddlery
SE	South East
Sec	Secretarial
Semicond	Semiconductor
SEN	Special Educational Needs
Serb Cro	Serbo-Croat
Serv	Services
Set	Settings
Sfc	Surface
Sfty	Safety
Sgnl	Signal
Ship	Shipping
Simul	Simulation
Sit Lrng	Situated Learning
Sk	Skills
Slf	Self
Sln	Salon
Slov	Slovak/Slovene/Slavonic
Sls	Sales
Sml	Small
Smt	Smart
Smtc	Semitic
Snc	Sonic

Snd	Sound
Sndtrk	Soundtrack
Sndwch	Sandwich
Sng	Song
Soc	Social
Sociol	Sociology
SocioLeg	Socio-Legal
Socling	Sociolinguistics
Soft	Software
Sol	Solution(s)
Soty	Society
Sov	Soviet
Sp	Speech
Span	Spanish
Spat	Spatial
Spc	Space
SPD	Surface Pattern Design
Spec	Special/Specialisms/ Specialist
Spec Efcts	Special Effects
Sply	Supply
Spn	Spain
Spo	Sports
Spowr	Sportswear
Sprtd	Supported
Sprtng	Supporting
Sqntl	Sequential
Srf	Surf/Surfing
Srgy	Surgery
SS	Solid-state
St	Studies
St Reg	State Registration
Stats	Statistics
Std	Studio
Stg	Stage
Stgs	Settings
Stnds	Standards
STQ	Scottish Teaching Qualification
Str	Stringed
Strat	Strategic/Strategy
Strg	Strength
Strt	Street
Struct	Structural/Structures
Stt	State
Surf	Surface
Surv	Surveying
Sust	Sustainability/Sustainable
Swed	Swedish
Swli	Swahili
Sxlty	Sexuality
Sys	System(s)
Systmtc	Systematic
Tap	Tapestry
Tax Rev	Taxation and Revenue
Tbtn	Tibetan
Tcnqs	Techniques
Teach	Teaching
Tech	Technology/Technician
Technol	Technological
TEFL	Teaching English as a Foreign Language
Telecomm	Telecommunications
Ter	Terrestial
TESOL	Teaching English to Speakers of Other Languages
Testmt	Testament
Tex	Textiles
Thea	Theatre
Theol	Theology
Theor	Theory/Theoretical
Ther	Therapeutic
Thera	Therapy
Tht	Thought
Tiss	Tissue
Tlrg	Tailoring
Tm	Time
Tmbr	Timber
Tnnl	Tunnel/Tunnelling
Tns	Tennis
Topog	Topographical
Tour	Tourism
Tox	Toxicology
TQ	Teaching Qualification
Tr	Trade
Tr Stands	Trading Standards
Trad	Traditional
Trans	Transport(ation)
Transat	Transatlantic
Transnl Med Sci	Translational Medical Science
Transl	Translation
Trav	Travel
Trfgrs	Turfgrass
Trg	Training
Trnrs	Trainers
Trpcl	Tropical
Trpl	Triple
Trstrl	Terrestrial
Tstmnt	Testament
Ttl	Total

Turk Turkish
Twn Town
Typo Typographical/Typography

Ukr Ukrainian
Un Union
Undwtr Underwater
Unif Unified
Up Upland
Urb Urban
USA United States of America
Util Utilities/Utilisation

Val Valuation
Vcl Vocal
Veh Vehicle
Vntr Venture
Vib Vibration
Vict Victorian
Vid Video
Viet Vietnamese
Virol Virology
Vis Visual/Visualisation
Vit Viticulture
Vkg Viking
Vnu Venue
Voc Vocational
Vol Voluntary
Vrtbrt Vertebrate
Vrtl Rlty Virtual Reality
Vsn Vision
Vstr Visitor

Wdlnd Woodland
Welf Welfare
Wk Work
Wkg Working
Wlbng Well-being
Wldlf Wildlife
Wls Wales
Wmnswr Womenswear
Wn Wine
Wrbl Wearable
Writ Writing/Writer
Wrld World
Wrlss Wireless
Wst Waste(s)
Wstn Western
Wtr Water
Wtrspo Watersports
Wvn Woven
www World Wide Web

Ycht Yacht
Ychtg Yachting
Yng Young
Yth Youth

Zool Zoology

3D Three-dimensional

ACCOUNTANCY/ACCOUNTING

(see also **Finance**)

Accounting and Accountancy degree courses include accounting, finance, economics, law, management, qualitative methods and information technology. Many, but not all, Accountancy and Accounting degrees give exemptions from the examinations of some or all of the accountancy professional bodies. Single Honours courses are more likely to give full exemptions, while Joint Honours courses are more likely to lead to partial exemptions. Students should check with universities and colleges which professional bodies offer exemptions for their courses before applying. Most courses are strongly vocational and many offer sandwich placements or opportunities to study Accountancy/Accounting with a second subject. Many graduates entering careers in accountancy will do so after taking degree courses in other subjects although in all cases further study is necessary to qualify as an accountant.

Useful websites www.acca.co.uk; www.cimaglobal.org.uk; www.cipfa.org.uk; www.tax.org.uk; www.icaew.com; www.bized.co.uk.

NB The points totals shown to the left of the institutions are for ease of reference only. It must not be assumed that Tariff points are always used by institutions or that they can be substituted for an offer in grades. The level of an offer is not necessarily indicative of the quality of a course.

COURSE OFFERS INFORMATION

Subject requirements/preferences **GCSE** English and mathematics required: popular universities may specify grades. **AL** Mathematics or accounting required or preferred for some courses. Business studies accepted for some courses.

NB In 2011 universities and colleges will differ in their use of GCE AL/AS unit grade information, A* grades, the Extended Project (EPQ), the Advanced Diploma and the Cambridge Pre-U examination when considering applicants and making offers. An EPQ may be accepted in place of an AS subject. Check websites of universities and colleges for the latest offers information.

Your target offers and examples of courses provided by each institution

390 pts **Warwick** – AABb (Acc Fin) (IB 36 pts)
380 pts **Nottingham** – AABc (Fin Acc Mgt) (IB 32 pts)
370 pts **Keele** – 370 pts inc BB (Accounting) (IB 28–30 pts)
360 pts **Bath** – AAA–AAB (Acc Fin) (IB 36 pts HL maths 5–6)
Bristol – AAA–ABB (Econ Acc; Acc Fin) (IB 37–34 pts)
City – AAA (Econ Acc; Acc Fin) (IB 35 pts)
Exeter – AAA–AAB (Acc Fin; Acc Ldrshp; Bus Acc) (IB 36–33 pts)
Lancaster – AAA (Acc; Acc Adt Fin)
Manchester – AAA (Accounting) (IB 37–35 pts)
Newcastle – AAA–AAB (Bus Acc Fin; Acc Fin) (IB 36–34 pts)
Ulster – AAA–AAB+AS 360 pts (Acc Law)
340 pts **Aston** – AAB–ABB 340–320 pts (Acc Mgt) (IB 36 pts)
Birmingham – AAB–ABBc (Acc Fin;) (IB 33–36 pts)
Cardiff – AAB (Acc; Acc Mgt; Acc Econ; Acc Fin)
Glasgow – AAB–AAA (Acc Fin) (IB 34 pts)

Lancaster – AAB (Acc Econ; Acc Mgt St; Acc Fin Comp Sci) (IB 30 pts)
Leeds – AAB (Acc Fin; Acc Mgt; Acc Law) (IB 35 pts HL 17 pts)
London (RH) – AAB 340 pts (Mgt Acc) (IB 35 pts)
London LSE – AAB (Acc Fin) (IB 37 pts HL 666)
Loughborough – AAB (Acc Fin Mgt; Econ Acc; Maths Acc Fin Mgt) (IB 36–34 pts)
Manchester – AAB (Mgt (Acc Fin); Acc Econ; Acc Fin) (IB 35 pts)
Queen's Belfast – AAB–ABBa (Acc; Acc Fr/Ger/Span)
Reading – AAB (Acc Mgt; Acc Econ) (IB 34 pts)
Southampton – AAB (Acc Fin; Acc Econ; Mgt Sci Acc) (IB 34 pts)
Ulster – 340 pts (Accounting)

320 pts **Brunel** – BBC+AS/EPQ c 320 pts (Fin Acc) (IB 30 pts)
Durham (Stockton) – ABB (Acc Fin)
Keele – 320–360 pts inc BB/AB (Acc; Acc Fin)
Kent – 320 pts inc BB (Acc Fin; Brit Fr Acc; Acc Fin Comp) (IB 35 pts HL 16 pts)
Kingston – 320 pts (Acc Fin)
Lancaster – ABB (Acc Fin Maths) (IB 30 pts)
Liverpool – ABB (Accounting) (IB 32 pts)
Newcastle – ABB (Acc Maths; Acc Stats) (IB 32–34 pts)
Queen's Belfast – ABB–BBBb (Econ Acc)
Sheffield – ABB–BBB (Acc Fin Mgt; Acc Fin Mgt Econ) (IB 33–32 pts)
Strathclyde – ABB (Accounting) (IB 32 pts)
Surrey – ABB 320 pts (Acc Fin) (IB 34 pts)
Ulster – ABB (Law Acc)
York – ABB (Acc Bus Fin Mgt) (IB 32 pts)

300 pts **Bournemouth** – 300 pts (Acc Fin; Acc Tax; Acc Law; Acc Bus)
Brunel – 300 pts 3AL **or** 350 pts 3AL+AS (Bus Mgt (Acc))
Coventry – 300 pts (Accountancy)
Edinburgh – BBB/AAA (Bus St Acc; Econ Acc; Law Acc; Acc Fin)
Essex – 300 pts (Acc; Acc Fin) (IB 29 pts)
Heriot-Watt – BBB 2nd yr entry (Acc Fin)
Portsmouth – 300 pts (Accounting)
Sheffield – BBB (Acc Fin Maths)
Westminster – BBB (Acc Bus Mgt) (IB 26 pts)

280 pts **Birmingham City** – 280–260 pts (Acc; Acc joint courses)
Brighton – BBC 280 pts (Acc Fin) (IB 26 pts)
De Montfort – 280 pts (Acc Fin)
East Anglia – BBC (Acc Fin; Acc Mgt) (IB 30 pts)
Gloucestershire – 280 pts (Acc Fin Mgt)
Hertfordshire – 280–260 pts (Acc Fin; Acc; Acc Langs)
Huddersfield – 280 pts (Acc Fin Serv; Acc)
Northumbria – 280 pts (Accounting)
Oxford Brookes – BBC (Acc Fin) (IB 30 pts)
Portsmouth – 280 pts (Acc Fin; Acc Bus)
Salford – 280 pts (Fin Acc) (IB 28 pts)
Swansea – 280 pts (Bus Mgt Acc)

260 pts **Aberdeen** – BCC 2nd yr entry (Accounting)
Aberystwyth – 260 pts (Acc Fin) (IB 27 pts)
Bristol UWE – 260–300 pts (Acc Fin) (IB 24–28 pts)
Central Lancashire – 260–280 pts (Acc; Acc Fin St; Acc Int Bus)
Chichester – 260 pts (Accounting)
Coventry – 260–280 pts (Acc Econ; Acc Fin)
Glasgow Caledonian – BCC (Accountancy)
Heriot-Watt – BCC 260 pts 1st yr entry (Acc Fin; Acc Bus Law)
Hull – 260 pts (Acc; Acc (Int); Acc (Prof Exp); Acc Fin Mgt)
Lincoln – 260 pts (Acc Fin; Acc Mark)

Liverpool John Moores – 260 pts (Acc Fin)
Staffordshire – BCC 260 pts (Acc Leg St; Acc Inf Sys; Acc Bus) (IB 26 pts)
240 pts **Aberdeen** – CCC **or** aabb 1st yr entry (Accounting) (IB 30 pts)
Bangor – 240–280 pts (Acc Fin; Acc Bank; Acc Econ)
Bradford – 240 pts (Acc Fin)
Buckingham – CCC (Acc Fin Mgt)
Cardiff (UWIC) – 240 pts (Acc; Acc Fin)
Cumbria – 240 pts (Acc Fin; Acc Law)
De Montfort – 240 pts (Acc Mark; Acc; Acc Law)
Dundee – CCC (Acc; Int Acc; Acc App Comp) (IB 29 pts)
East London – 240 pts (Acc Law)
Edinburgh Napier – 240 pts (Acc courses)
Glamorgan – 240–280 pts (Acc Fin; Foren Acc; Int Acc)
Liverpool Hope – 240–280 pts (Accounting)
London South Bank – 240 pts (Acc Law)
Manchester Met – 240 pts (Acc Fin) (IB 24 pts)
Middlesex – 240 pts (Acc; Acc Fin; Acc Bus Econ; Acc Stats; Bus Acc)
Newport – 240 pts (Acc; Acc Law; Acc Econ)
Nottingham Trent – 240 pts (Acc Fin)
Plymouth – 240 pts (Acc Fin; Acc Langs)
Robert Gordon – CCC 240 pts (Acc Fin)
Sheffield Hallam – 240 pts (Acc; Acc Fin Mgt; Bus Acc; Foren Acc)
Stirling – CCC (Acc courses) (IB 30 pts)
Teesside – 240 pts (Acc Fin)
Ulster – 240 pts (Acc Mark)
Worcester – 240 pts (Bus Innov Acc)
220 pts **Bolton** – 220 pts (Acc courses)
Chester – 220–260 pts (Acc; Acc Fin)
Edge Hill – 220–240 pts (Accountancy)
Greenwich – 220–260 pts (Acc Fin; Acc Adt Ass)
Leeds Met – 220 pts (Acc Fin)
London Met – 220 pts (Acc Fin; Acc Bank; Acc Fin Serv; Acc Bus Law)
Northampton – 220–260 pts (Acc courses)
Southampton Solent – 220 pts (Accountancy)
Wolverhampton – 220 pts (Bus Acc; Acc Fin)
200 pts **Bedfordshire** – 200 pts (Accounting)
Bucks New – 200–240 pts (Acc Fin)
Canterbury Christ Church – 200 pts (Bus St Acc; Mark Acc)
Chichester – CDD 200–240 pts (Acc Fin)
Derby – 200–280 pts (Acc courses)
East London – 200 pts (Acc; Acc Bus Econ)
Glyndŵr – 200 pts (Bus Acc)
Thames Valley – 200 pts (Acc Fin)
160 pts **Anglia Ruskin** – 160 pts (Acc Fin)
London South Bank – 160 pts (Acc Fin; Acc Mark)
Swansea Met – 160 pts (Acc; Bus Fin)
West Scotland – CC (Accounting)
Wolverhampton – 160–220 pts (Acc Law)
120 pts **Blackburn (Coll Univ Centre)** – 120 pts (Bus Acc)
100 pts **Bradford (Coll)** – 100–140 pts (Accountancy)
80 pts **Holborn (Coll)** – 80 pts (Accountancy)
London (Birk) – 80 pts (p/t Acc Mgt)

Regents Bus Sch London – check with Business School (Int Fin Acc)

Alternative offers
See **Chapter 7** and **Appendix 1** for grades/UCAS Tariff points information for the International Baccalaureate, Scottish Highers/Advanced Highers, the Welsh Baccalaureate, the Irish Leaving Certificate, the Cambridge Pre-U Diploma, the Advanced Diploma and the Extended Project.

EXAMPLES OF FOUNDATION DEGREES IN THE SUBJECT FIELD

Aberdeen (Coll); Adam Smith (Coll); Anniesland (Coll); Ayr (Coll); Banff and Buchan (Coll); Blackburn (Coll Univ Centre); Blackpool and Fylde (Coll); Bournemouth; Cardiff (UWIC); Central Lancashire; Cornwall (Coll); Croydon (Coll); Darlington (Coll); Doncaster (Coll); Glamorgan; Glyndŵr; Hertfordshire; Highbury (Coll); Kensington Bus (Coll); Lambeth (Coll); Langside Glasgow (Coll); Leeds Met; London Met; London South Bank; Manchester (CAT); Manchester City (Coll); Northampton; Northbrook (Coll); Plymouth; Salford; Southampton Solent; Suffolk (Univ Campus); West Cheshire (Coll); Westminster Kingsway (Coll); Wirral Met (Coll).

CHOOSING YOUR COURSE (SEE ALSO CH.1)

Some course features
Anglia Ruskin Course can be started in February.
Aston Third year spent in paid professional placement; experience can count towards professional recognition by major accounting bodies.
Exeter Courses can include a year of study or a combination of study and work placement in Europe or in North America, Japan or China.
Lancaster (Acc Adt Fin) Up to 18 months spent on salaried placement with Ernst & Young; first year bursary paid to all students.
London LSE A broad course, focusing on both accounting and its applications in different management areas. Options in first year depend on students' level of mathematics.
Portsmouth Professional mentoring scheme, pairing level 2 and 3 students with practising accountant.

Universities and colleges teaching quality See www.qaa.ac.uk; www.unistats.com.

Top research universities and colleges (RAE 2008) (Accounting and Finance) Bangor; Essex; Exeter; Bristol; Glasgow; Stirling; Bristol UWE; Dundee; Huddersfield.

Examples of sandwich degree courses Aston; Bath; Birmingham City; Bournemouth; Bradford; Brighton; Bristol UWE; Brunel; City; Coventry; De Montfort; Derby; Exeter; Glamorgan; Gloucestershire; Greenwich; Hertfordshire; Huddersfield; Lancaster; Leeds Met; Loughborough; Middlesex; Nottingham Trent; Plymouth; Portsmouth; Sheffield Hallam; Staffordshire; Swansea Met; Teesside; Ulster; West Scotland; Westminster; Wolverhampton; Worcester.

ADMISSIONS INFORMATION

Number of applicants per place (approx) Bath 7; Birmingham 14; Bristol 23; Dundee 5; East Anglia 17; Essex 7; Exeter 18; Glasgow 10; Heriot-Watt 7; Hull 8; Kent 10; Lancaster 20; Leeds 25; London LSE 19; Loughborough 12; Manchester (Acc courses) 22–23; Oxford Brookes 9; Salford 8; Sheffield 40; Southampton 13; Staffordshire 3; Stirling 20; Strathclyde 10; Ulster 10; Warwick 14.

Advice to applicants and planning the UCAS personal statement Universities look for good numerical and communication skills, interest in the business and financial world, teamwork, problem-solving and computing experience. On the UCAS application you should be able to demonstrate your interest and understanding of accountancy and to give details of any work experience or work shadowing undertaken. Try to arrange meetings with accountants, or work shadowing or work experience in accountants' offices, commercial or industrial firms, town halls, banks or insurance companies and describe the work you have done. Obtain information from the main accountancy professional bodies (see **Appendix 4**). Refer to current affairs which have stimulated your interest from articles in the *Financial Times*, *The Economist* or the business and financial sections of the weekend press. **Bath** Gap year welcomed. Extra-curricular activities important and should be described on the personal statement. There should be no gaps in your chronological history. **Brunel** (Bus Mgt (Acc)) Extended Project qualification accepted in place of AS-level; AL critical thinking and general studies acceptable. **Lancaster** (Acc Adt Fin) Selected UCAS applicants complete supplementary application form and on-line test. They may then be invited to a selection workshop.

Misconceptions about this course Many students believe incorrectly that you need to be a brilliant mathematician. However, you do have to be numerate and enjoy numbers (see **Subject requirements/preferences**). Many under-estimate the need for a high level of attention to detail. **Buckingham** Some students think it's a maths course. **Salford** Some applicants believe the course is limited to financial knowledge when it also provides an all-round training in management skills.

Selection interviews Thames Valley; **Some** Abertay Dundee, Aberystwyth, Anglia Ruskin, Buckingham, Cardiff, Cardiff (UWIC), De Montfort, Dundee, East Anglia, Kent, Lincoln, Liverpool John Moores, London LSE, Staffordshire, Stirling, Sunderland, Wolverhampton; **No** Bristol.

Interview advice and questions Be prepared to answer questions about why you have chosen the course, the qualities needed to be an accountant, and why you think you have these qualities! You should also be able to discuss any work experience you have done and to describe the differences in the work of chartered, certified, public finance and management accountants. **Buckingham** If students are from a non-English-speaking background, they are asked to write an essay. If their maths results are weak they may be asked to do a simple arithmetic test. Mature students with no formal qualifications are usually interviewed and questioned about their work experience. See also **Chapter 5**.

Reasons for rejection (non-academic) Poor English. Lack of interest in the subject because they realise they have chosen the wrong course! No clear motivation. Course details not researched. **London South Bank** Punctuality, neatness, enthusiasm and desire to come to London South Bank not evident.

AFTER-RESULTS ADVICE

Offers to applicants repeating A-levels **Higher** Brunel, Glasgow (AAA), Hull, Manchester Met; **Possibly higher** Brighton, Central Lancashire, East Anglia, Leeds, Newcastle, Oxford Brookes, Sheffield Hallam; **Same** Aberystwyth, Anglia Ruskin, Bangor, Birmingham City, Bradford, Buckingham, Cardiff, De Montfort, Derby, Dundee, Durham, East London, Edinburgh Napier, Heriot-Watt, Huddersfield, Liverpool John Moores, Loughborough, Northumbria, Salford, Staffordshire, Stirling, Thames Valley, Wolverhampton.

GRADUATE DESTINATIONS AND EMPLOYMENT (2007/8 HESA)

Graduates surveyed 2710 **Employed** 1155 **In further study** 225 **Assumed unemployed** 280.

Career note Most Accounting/Accountancy graduates enter careers in finance. Further study is required to qualify as accountants.

OTHER DEGREE SUBJECTS FOR CONSIDERATION

Actuarial Studies; Banking; Business Studies; Economics; Financial Services; Insurance; International Securities and Investment Banking; Mathematics; Quantity Surveying; Statistics.

ACTUARIAL SCIENCE/STUDIES

Actuaries deal with the evaluation and management of financial risks, particularly those associated with insurance companies and pension funds. Although Actuarial Science/Studies degrees are vocational and give full or partial exemptions from some of the examinations of the Institute and Faculty of Actuaries, students are not necessarily committed to a career as an actuary on graduation. However, many graduates go on to be actuary trainees, leading to one of the highest-paid careers.

Useful websites www.actuaries.org.uk; www.soa.org; www.beanactuary.org

NB The points totals shown to the left of the institutions are for ease of reference only. It must not be assumed that Tariff points are always used by institutions or that they can be substituted for an offer in grades. The level of an offer is not necessarily indicative of the quality of a course.

COURSE OFFERS INFORMATION

Subject requirements/preferences **GCSE** Most institutions require grades A or B in mathematics. **AL** Mathematics at a specified grade required.

NB In 2011 universities and colleges will differ in their use of GCE AL/AS unit grade information, A* grades, the Extended Project (EPQ), the Advanced Diploma and the Cambridge Pre-U examination when considering applicants and making offers. An EPQ may be accepted in place of an AS subject. Check websites of universities and colleges for the latest offers information.

Your target offers and examples of courses provided by each institution

420 pts **Queen's Belfast** – AAAa (Act Sci Rsk Mgt)
360 pts **City** – AAA (Act Sci) (IB 35 pts)
London LSE – AAA (Act Sci) (IB 38 pts HL 17 pts)
Manchester – AAA–AAB (maths A+AB in modules C3/C4) (Act Sci Maths)
Southampton – AAA inc A maths **or** AAB inc f.maths (Maths Act Sci) (IB 36 pts HL 6)
340 pts **East Anglia** – AAB–AAC inc A maths (Act Sci) (IB 33 pts HL maths 7)
Heriot-Watt – AAB inc A maths 2nd yr entry (Act Sci)
Keele – AAB (Act Sci)
Kent – 340–360 pts (Act Sci; Act Sci Ind) (IB 35 pts HL maths 6)
Leeds – AAB (Act Maths)
Southampton – AAB (Econ Act Sci) (IB 34 pts HL 17 pts)
320 pts **Heriot-Watt** – ABB inc A maths 1st yr entry (Act Sci)
300 pts **Swansea** – 300 pts (Act St; Act St Acc; Act St Abrd)
260 pts **Kingston** – 260 pts (Act Maths Stats)
240 pts **City** – CCC (Act Sci 4 yr inc Fdn)

Alternative offers

See **Chapter 7** and **Appendix 1** for grades/UCAS Tariff points information for the International Baccalaureate, Scottish Highers/Advanced Highers, the Welsh Baccalaureate, the Irish Leaving Certificate, the Cambridge Pre-U Diploma, the Advanced Diploma and the Extended Project.

CHOOSING YOUR COURSE (SEE ALSO CH.1)

Some course features

Heriot-Watt Opportunities for industrial placements or year abroad. University has active Students' Actuarial Society.
Kent Core actuarial modules taught by qualified actuaries. Optional year in industry in Year 3.
London LSE The Actuarial Science degree and the BSc Business Mathematics and Statistics degree have the same first year. Transfer between the two courses possible in Year 2.
Queen's Belfast Nine-month placement in Year 3 in either an actuarial or risk management setting in mainland UK, Ireland, the US or mainland Europe.
Southampton Both courses offer some exemptions from the examinations of the Institute of Actuaries.

Universities and colleges teaching quality See www.unistats.com; www.qaa.ac.uk.

Examples of sandwich degree courses City; East Anglia; Kent; Queen's Belfast.

ADMISSIONS INFORMATION

Number of applicants per place (approx) City 6; Heriot-Watt 5; Kent 6; London LSE 9; Southampton (Maths Act Sci) 9, (Econ Act Sci) 7; Swansea 9.

Advice to applicants and planning the UCAS personal statement Demonstrate your knowledge of this career and its training, and mention any contacts you have made with an actuary. (See **Appendix 4** for contact details of professional associations for further information.) Any work experience or shadowing in insurance companies should be mentioned, together with what you have learned about the problems facing actuaries. It is important to show motivation and sheer determination for training as an actuary which is long and tough (up to three or four years after graduation). Mathematical flair, an ability to communicate and an interest in business are paramount.

Misconceptions about this course There is a general lack of understanding of actuaries' career training and of the career itself.

Selection interviews **Some** Heriot-Watt, Kent, Southampton, Swansea.

Interview advice and questions In view of the demanding nature of the training, it is important to have spent some time discussing this career with an actuary in practice. Questions, therefore, may focus on the roles of the actuary and the qualities you have to succeed. You should also be ready to field questions about your Advanced Level mathematics course and the aspects of it you most enjoy. **Swansea** The interview does not determine who will be accepted or rejected, only the level of the offer made. See also **Chapter 5**.

Reasons for rejection (non-academic) **Kent** Poor language skills.

AFTER-RESULTS ADVICE

Offers to applicants repeating A-levels **Higher** City; **Same** Heriot-Watt, Southampton.

GRADUATE DESTINATIONS AND EMPLOYMENT (2007/8 HESA)

No data available. See **Finance**.

Career note Graduates commonly enter careers in finance, many taking further examinations to qualify as actuaries.

OTHER DEGREE COURSE SUBJECTS FOR CONSIDERATION

Accountancy; Banking; Business Studies; Economics; Financial Risk Management; Financial Services; Insurance; Mathematics; Money, Banking and Finance; Statistics.

AFRICAN and CARIBBEAN STUDIES

African Studies courses tend to be multi-disciplinary, covering several subject areas and can include anthropology, history, geography, sociology, social psychology and languages. Most courses focus on Africa and African languages (Amharic (Ethiopia), Hausa (Nigeria), Somali (Horn of Africa), Swahili (Somalia and Mozambique), Yoruba (Nigeria, Sierra Leone, Ghana and Senegal), and Zulu (South Africa)).

Useful websites www.britishmuseum.org; www.africanstudies.org; www.black-history-month.co.uk.

NB The points totals shown to the left of the institutions are for ease of reference only. It must not be assumed that Tariff points are always used by institutions or that they can be substituted for an offer in grades. The level of an offer is not necessarily indicative of the quality of a course.

COURSE OFFERS INFORMATION

Subject requirements/preferences **GCSE** Grade A–C in mathematics and English may be required. **AL** For language courses a language subject or demonstrated proficiency in a language is required.

NB In 2011 universities and colleges will differ in their use of GCE AL/AS unit grade information, A* grades, the Extended Project (EPQ), the Advanced Diploma and the Cambridge Pre-U examination when considering applicants and making offers. An EPQ may be accepted in place of an AS subject. Check websites of universities and colleges for the latest offers information.

Your target offers and examples of courses provided by each institution

320 pts **Birmingham** – ABB–BBB (Af St joint courses) (IB 32 pts)
London (SOAS) – ABB (Af Lang Cult; Af St) (IB 34 pts HL 555)
300 pts **Birmingham** – BBB–BCC (Af St) (IB 30–32 pts)
240 pts **London Met** – 240 pts (Carib St Int Tour Mgt; Carib St Educ St) (IB 28 pts)

Alternative offers
See **Chapter 7** and **Appendix 1** for grades/UCAS Tariff points information for the International Baccalaureate, Scottish Highers/Advanced Highers, the Welsh Baccalaureate, the Irish Leaving Certificate, the Cambridge Pre-U Diploma, the Advanced Diploma and the Extended Project.

CHOOSING YOUR COURSE (SEE ALSO CH.1)

Some course features
Birmingham A broad multi-disciplinary degree, offering Single and Joint Honours courses.
London (SOAS) Six African languages taught at undergraduate level; students have some flexibility in constructing their own course of study.
London Met One-semester or one-year placement in the West Indies.

Universities and colleges teaching quality See www.qaa.ac.uk; www.unistats.com.

Top research universities and colleges (RAE 2008) (Middle Eastern and African Studies) Cambridge; Oxford; Edinburgh; London (SOAS); Durham.

ADMISSIONS INFORMATION

Number of applicants per place (approx) Birmingham 5.

Advice to applicants and planning the UCAS personal statement Describe any visits you have made to African or Caribbean countries, and why you wish to study this subject. Embassies in London may be able to provide information about the history, geography, politics, economics and the culture of the countries in which you are interested. Keep up-to-date with political developments in Africa or Caribbean countries. Discuss any aspects which interest you.

Interview advice and questions Questions are likely on your choice of country or geographical region, your knowledge of it and your awareness of some of the political, economic and social problems that exist. See also **Chapter 5**.

AFTER-RESULTS ADVICE

Offers to applicants repeating A-levels Information not available from institutions.

GRADUATE DESTINATIONS AND EMPLOYMENT (2007/8 HESA)

Graduates surveyed 20 **Employed** 10 **In further study** 5 **Assumed unemployed** none.

Career note The language skills and knowledge acquired in African Studies courses, particularly when combined with periods of study in Africa, are relevant to a wide range of careers.

OTHER DEGREE SUBJECTS FOR CONSIDERATION

Anthropology; Geography; History; Languages; Sociology.

AGRICULTURAL SCIENCES/AGRICULTURE

(including **Agricultural Business Management, Aquaculture, Countryside Conservation, Crop Science** and **Rural Resources Management;** see also **Animal Sciences, Forestry, Horticulture, Landscape Architecture** and **Surveying**)

Courses in Agriculture recognise that modern farming practice requires sound technical and scientific knowledge, together with appropriate management skills, and most courses focus to a greater or lesser extent on all these requirements. Your choice of course depends on your particular interest and aims: some courses will give greater priority than others to practical application. Many students will come from an agricultural background and work experience will be necessary for most institutions.

Useful websites www.defra.gov.uk; www.naturalengland.org.uk; www.ccw.gov.uk; www.rase.org.uk; www.scienceyear.com; www.iah.bbsrc.ac.uk; www.lantra.co.uk; www.nfuonline.com; www.nfyfc.org.uk; www.iagre.org; www.afuturein.com.

NB The points totals shown to the left of the institutions are for ease of reference only. It must not be assumed that Tariff points are always used by institutions or that they can be substituted for an offer in grades. The level of an offer is not necessarily indicative of the quality of a course.

COURSE OFFERS INFORMATION

Subject requirements/preferences **GCSE** English and mathematics usually required; chemistry sometimes required. Practical experience may be required. **AL** One or two maths/biological science subjects may be required or preferred. Geography may be accepted as a science subject. Similar requirements apply for Agricultural Business Management courses. (Crop Science) Two science subjects may be required. (Countryside Management) Geography or biology preferred.

NB In 2011 universities and colleges will differ in their use of GCE AL/AS unit grade information, A* grades, the Extended Project (EPQ), the Advanced Diploma and the Cambridge Pre-U examination when considering applicants and making offers. An EPQ may be accepted in place of an AS subject. Check websites of universities and colleges for the latest offers information.

Note that many agricultural courses are offered at colleges on sites separate from the universities.

Your target offers and examples of courses provided by each institution

320 pts **Newcastle** – ABB (Agri-Bus Mgt) (IB 34 pts)

300 pts **Newcastle** – BBB–BBC (Cntry Mgt; Rur St) (IB 30 pts)
Reading – 300 pts (Agric Bus Mgt; Agric) (IB 29pts)
Royal (CAg) – 300 pts (Rur Lnd Mgt)
Stirling – BBB 2nd yr entry (Frshwtr Sci; Cons Mgt; Cons Sci; Aquacult) (IB 26 pts)

280 pts **CAFRE** – BBC (Agric Tech)
Harper Adams (UC) – 280 pts (Rur Ent Lnd Mgt)

Queen's Belfast – BBC–BBB (Lnd Use Env Mgt; Agric Tech)
Reading – 280 pts (Rur Res Mgt)
260 pts **Newcastle** –BCC (Agric; Rur Res Mgt; Frm Bus Mgt; Agron; Anim Prod Sci) (IB 28 pts)
Nottingham – BCC (Agric; Crop Sci) (IB 28 pts)
240 pts **Bangor** – 240–260 pts (Agric Cons Env)
Harper Adams (UC) – 240 pts (Agric; Agric Anim Sci; Agric Frm Bus Mgt; Agric Mark; Agric Mechn; Agric Eng; Agric Crop Mgt; Agric Env Mgt)
Royal (CAg) – 240 pts (Agric; Agric (Orgnc Frm) (Anim Mgt) (Lnd Mgt) (Crop Prod); Int Eqn Agric Bus Mgt) (IB 26–28 pts)
220 pts **Harper Adams (UC)** – 220–240 pts (Cntry Env Mgt)
Myerscough (Coll) – 220 pts (Agriculture)
Nottingham Trent – 220 pts (Env Cons Cntry Mgt; Wldlf Cons)
Stirling – CCD 1st yr entry (Aquaculture)
210 pts **Aberystwyth** – 210 pts (Agric Bus St) (IB 28 pts)
200 pts **Aberystwyth** – 200 pts (Cntry Recr Tour; Cntry Mgt; Cntry Cons) (IB 26 pts)
180 pts **Aberystwyth** – 180 pts (Agric; Agric Cntry Mgt; Agric Anim Sci) (IB 24 pts)
Harper Adams (UC) – 180–220 pts (Agri-Business)
160 pts **Bristol UWE (Hartpury)** – 160–200 pts (Agric Bus Mgt; Cons Cntry Mgt; Dairy Herd Mgt) (IB 28–30 pts)
Derby – 160–240 pts (Cntry Mgt)
Greenwich – 160 pts (Sust Lnd Mgt; Int Agric)
SAC (Scottish CAg) – CC (Agri Sci; Agric; Rur Bus Mgt (Agric); Cntry Mgt; Grn Tech; Rur Bus Mgt courses)
140 pts **Writtle (Coll)** – 140–180 pts (Agric; Agric Bus Mgt courses; Agric Crp Prod courses; Frm Lvst Prod courses; Cons Env Mgt courses)
120 pts **Sparsholt (Coll)** – DD (Aquacult Fish Mgt; Cons Wldlf Mgt; Anim Mgt)

Alternative offers
See **Chapter 7** and **Appendix 1** for grades/UCAS Tariff points information for the International Baccalaureate, Scottish Highers/Advanced Highers, the Welsh Baccalaureate, the Irish Leaving Certificate, the Cambridge Pre-U Diploma, the Advanced Diploma and the Extended Project.

EXAMPLES OF FOUNDATION DEGREES IN THE SUBJECT FIELD
Aberystwyth; Askham Bryan (Coll); Bath; Bath (Coll); Bath Spa; Berkshire (CAg); Bishop Burton (Coll); Bournemouth; Bridgend (Coll); Brighton; Bristol UWE (Hartpury); Bucks New; CAFRE; Capel Manor (Coll); Cumbria; Duchy (Coll); East Anglia; Easton (Coll); Greenwich; Guildford (Coll); Hadlow (Coll); Harper Adams (UC); Hertfordshire; Kingston Maurward (Coll); Lincoln; Manchester City (Coll); Moulton (Coll); Myerscough (Coll); Northampton; Nottingham Trent; Oatridge (Coll); Oxford Brookes; Plymouth; Reaseheath (Coll); Rodbaston (Coll); Royal (CAg); Sparsholt (Coll); Suffolk (Univ Campus); Sunderland; Warwickshire (Coll); Welsh (CHort); Wiltshire (Coll); Wolverhampton; Writtle (Coll).

CHOOSING YOUR COURSE (SEE ALSO CH.1)
Some course features
Aberystwyth (Agric) Nine months of work experience in third year.
Bristol UWE (Hartpury) (Cons Cntry Mgt) Range of optional modules allow students to develop interests in, for example, woodland management.
Greenwich (Int Agric) Worldwide focus on agriculture science and practice, business, trade, development and sustainability; placement opportunities in the UK, Europe and the US, with study tours in UK and Europe.
Harper Adams (UC) (Rur Ent Lnd Mgt) Course includes surveying, valuation, law, taxation, the rural economy (including woodlands and field sports management), business finance, and agriculture and the environment. Options include languages and property investment.
Newcastle Choice of degree deferred to third year.
Nottingham During optional fourth year students can take a Certificate in European Studies. Second modern language at Grade B required.

Reading Wide range of optional modules in every year includes subjects from other departments, for example languages, business entrepreneurship, international development.
Royal (CAg) (Int Eqn Agric Bus Mgt) Twenty-week work placement in second year; links with the Westphalian Riding School.

Other universities offer a very wide choice of courses including many specialisms associated with land use including Forest and Woodland Management (**Cumbria**, **Worcester**), Garden Design (**Greenwich**), Wildlife Conservation (**Kent**, **Plymouth**).

Universities and colleges teaching quality See www.qaa.ac.uk; www.unistats.com.

Top research universities and colleges (RAE 2008) (Agriculture, Veterinary and Food Science) Warwick; Aberdeen; Nottingham; Leeds; Reading (Food Biosciences); London (RVC); Aberystwyth; Glasgow; Edinburgh; Stirling; Cambridge; Liverpool; Newcastle; Bristol UWE; Bangor.

Examples of sandwich degree courses Aberystwyth; Bangor; Harper Adams (UC); Nottingham Trent; Plymouth; Royal (CAg); Sparsholt (Coll).

ADMISSIONS INFORMATION

Number of applicants per place (approx) Aberystwyth (Agric courses) 2–3; Bangor (Agric Cons Env) 4; Newcastle 6; Nottingham 4; Royal (CAg) (Agric) 2.

Advice to applicants and planning the UCAS personal statement First-hand farming experience is essential for some courses and obviously important for all. Check prospectuses and websites. Describe the work done. Details of experience of work with agricultural or food farms (production and laboratory work), garden centres, even with landscape architects, could be appropriate. Keep up-to-date with European agricultural and fishing policies and mention any interests you have in these areas. Read farming magazines and discuss any articles which have interested you. You may even have had first-hand experience of the serious problems facing farmers. Interest or experience in practical conservation work. Ability to work both independently or as a member of a team is important. (See **Appendix 4**.)

Selection interviews **Yes** Bristol UWE (Hartpury); **Some** Bangor, Bishop Burton (Coll), Derby, Edinburgh, Harper Adams (UC), Queen's Belfast, Royal (CAg).

Interview advice and questions Agriculture is in the news, especially in relation to the use of farming land for growing bio-fuel crops, the rapidly rising prices of fertilisers, world food shortages and the problems faced by UK dairy farmers. You should be up-to-date with political and scientific issues concerning the farming community in general and how these problems might be resolved. You are likely to be questioned on your own farming background (if relevant) and your farming experience. Questions asked in the past have included: What special agricultural interests do you have? What types of farms have you worked on? What farming publications do you read and which agricultural shows have you visited? What is meant by the term 'sustainable development'? What is the UK Biodiversity Action Plan? Are farmers custodians of the countryside? What are the potential sources of non-fossil-fuel electricity generation? **Bangor** (Agric Cons Env) No tests at interview. **Derby** (Cntry Mgt) Discussion about fieldwork experience. See also **Chapter 5**.

Reasons for rejection (non-academic) Insufficient motivation. Too immature. Unlikely to integrate well. Lack of practical experience with crops or animals.

AFTER-RESULTS ADVICE

Offers to applicants repeating A-levels **Possibly higher** Newcastle (Agric); **Same** Bangor (Agric Cons Env), Bristol UWE (Hartpury), Derby, Harper Adams (UC), Nottingham, Royal (CAg), Writtle (Coll).

GRADUATE DESTINATIONS AND EMPLOYMENT (2007/8 HESA)

Agriculture graduates surveyed 735 **Employed** 420 **In further study** 55 **Assumed unemployed** 60. **Agricultural Science graduates surveyed** 20 **Employed** 10 **In further study** none **Assumed unemployed** 5.

Career note The majority of graduates entered the agricultural industry whilst others moved into manufacturing, the wholesale and retail trades and property development.

OTHER DEGREE SUBJECTS FOR CONSIDERATION

Agroforestry; Animal Sciences; Biochemistry; Biological Sciences; Biology; Biotechnology; Chemistry; Conservation Management; Crop Science; Ecology (Biological Sciences); Environmental Sciences; Estate Management (Surveying); Food Science and Technology; Forestry; Horticulture; Land Surveying; Landscape Architecture; Plant Sciences; Veterinary Science; Zoology.

AMERICAN STUDIES

(see also **Latin American Studies**)

Courses normally cover American history, politics and literature, although there are opportunities to study specialist fields such as drama, film studies, history of art, linguistics, politics or sociology. In some universities a year, term or semester spent in the USA (or Canada) is compulsory or optional whilst at other institutions the course lasts three years without a placement abroad.

Useful websites www.historynet.com; www.americansc.org.uk; www.theasa.net.

NB The points totals shown to the left of the institutions are for ease of reference only. It must not be assumed that Tariff points are always used by institutions or that they can be substituted for an offer in grades. The level of an offer is not necessarily indicative of the quality of a course.

COURSE OFFERS INFORMATION

Subject requirements/preferences **GCSE** Specific grades in some subjects may be specified by some popular universities. **AL** English, a modern language, humanities or social science subjects preferred.

NB In 2011 universities and colleges will differ in their use of GCE AL/AS unit grade information, A* grades, the Extended Project (EPQ), the Advanced Diploma and the Cambridge Pre-U examination when considering applicants and making offers. An EPQ may be accepted in place of an AS subject. Check websites of universities and colleges for the latest offers information.

Your target offers and examples of courses provided by each institution

320 pts **Birmingham** – ABB (Am Can St; Engl Am St) (IB 34 pts)
East Anglia – ABB–BBB (Am Lit Crea Writ) (IB 30–31 pts)
Leicester – ABB (Am St Yr USA; Engl Am St) (IB 34 pts)
Loughborough – 320 pts (Engl N Am Lit Film) (IB 34 pts)
Manchester – ABB (Am St) (IB 33 pts)
Nottingham – ABB (Am St Hist; Am Engl St) (IB 32–34 pts)
Sussex – ABB–BBB (Am St courses) (IB 32–34 pts)
Warwick – ABB/BBBc (Hist Lit Cult Am) (IB 32–36 pts)

300 pts **Dundee** – BBB 2nd yr entry (Am St courses; Transat St courses)
East Anglia – BBB (Am Engl Lit; Am St Mus; Am St) (IB 30–31 pts)
Essex – BBB 300 pts (Am (US) St; Am (US St) Film) (IB 32 pts)
Hull – 300 pts (Am St Dr)
Leicester – BBB (Am St; Hist Am St) (IB 34 pts)
Liverpool – BBB–BBC (Compar Am St) (IB 30 pts)
London (Gold) – BBB (Engl Am Lit)
Manchester – BBB (Am Lat Am St) (IB 32 pts)
Nottingham – ABC–BBB (Am St Chin St; Am St Lat Am St) (IB 32 pts)

280 pts **East Anglia** – BBC–BCC (Am Hist Engl Hist; Am Hist Pol) (IB 30–31 pts)
Kent – 280 pts (Am St; Am St (Hist) (Lit)) (IB 36 pts HL 16 pts)
Manchester Met – BBC 280 pts (Am Lit) (IB 29 pts)
Swansea – 280 pts (Am St courses)

260 pts **Hull** – 260–280 pts (Am St Hist; Am St Phil; Am St Fr/Ger/Ital/Span)
Keele – 260–320 pts (Am St) (IB 28–32 pts)
Winchester – 260–300 pts (Am St Media St; Am St Am Film)
240 pts **Central Lancashire** – 240–200 pts (Am St Comb Hons; Am St)
Dundee – CCC 1st yr entry (Am St courses; Transat St courses) (IB 29 pts)
Hull – 240–280 pts (Am St Relig)
London Met – 240 pts (Am St courses; Carib St courses)
Portsmouth – 240–300 pts (Am St courses)
Ulster – 240 pts (Am St courses)
Winchester – 240–280 pts (Am St Dr; Am St Engl) (IB 24 pts)
220 pts **Glamorgan** – 220–260 pts (Am St Comb Hons)
Lincoln – 220–260 pts (Am St courses)
Sunderland – 220 pts (Am St courses)
Winchester – 220–260 pts (Am St Bus Mgt; Am St Film Cnma Tech; Am Hist)
200 pts **Canterbury Christ Church** – 200 pts (Am St courses)
Worcester – 200–240 pts (Am St courses)
York St John – 200–220 pts (Am St courses)
180 pts **Derby** – 180–240 pts (Am St courses)

Alternative offers

See **Chapter 7** and **Appendix 1** for grades/UCAS Tariff points information for the International Baccalaureate, Scottish Highers/Advanced Highers, the Welsh Baccalaureate, the Irish Leaving Certificate, the Cambridge Pre-U Diploma, the Advanced Diploma and the Extended Project.

CHOOSING YOUR COURSE (SEE ALSO CH.1)

Some course features

Canterbury Christ Church American Studies is available as Single Honours and Joint or Combined Honours courses. Opportunity to spend either a semester or a year in the US.
East Anglia Students on four-year programme spend third year at American, Australian or Canadian university and are eligible for local education authority financial support.
Kent (Am St courses) Students spending a third year at an American university do not pay American tuition fees – only travel and living costs.
Liverpool An inter-disciplinary course covering North America, Latin America and the Caribbean. Option to learn Spanish or Portuguese from scratch, or to combine study of AL French, Spanish or Portuguese to degree level.
Manchester (Am St) Course covers the history, literature, film, politics and popular culture of the United States. Opportunity to study in US university for one or two semesters.
Nottingham (Am St courses) Part-time (4–7 yrs) study is also available.
Ulster Programme combines study of American history, literature, film, politics, music and cultural studies in an area study of the US.

One-year placements abroad

Compulsory: Birmingham, Derby (one semester), East Anglia, Essex, Hull, Sussex, Ulster (one semester), Warwick.
Optional: Aberystwyth, Canterbury Christ Church, Dundee, Keele (one semester or one year), Kent, Liverpool (one semester), Manchester, Nottingham, Portsmouth (one semester), Swansea.

Universities and colleges teaching quality See www.qaa.ac.uk; www.unistats.com.

Top research universities and colleges (RAE 2008) Sussex; Birmingham; East Anglia; Nottingham; London (King's).

ADMISSIONS INFORMATION

Number of applicants per place (approx) Birmingham 4; Dundee 5; East Anglia 7; Essex 6; Hull 15; Keele 7; Leicester 5; Manchester 8; Nottingham 12; Swansea 2; Warwick 14.

Advice to applicants and planning the UCAS personal statement Visits to America should be described, and any knowledge or interests you have of the history, politics, economics and the culture of the USA should be included on the UCAS application. The US Embassy in London may be a useful source of information. American magazines and newspapers are good reference sources and also give a good insight to life in the USA. Applicants should demonstrate an intelligent interest in both North American literature and history in their personal statement. Tell us why you are excited and interested in the subject: at least half of your personal statement should focus on how and why your interest has developed, for example through extra-curricular reading, projects, films, academic study. **Manchester** Due to the detailed nature of entry requirements for American Studies course, we are unable to include full details in the prospectus. For complete and up-to-date information on our entry requirements for these courses, please visit our website at www.manchester.ac.uk/ugcourses.

Misconceptions about this course **Swansea** Some candidates feel that American Studies is a soft option. While we study many topics which students find interesting, we are very much a humanities-based degree course incorporating more traditional subjects like history, literature and English. Our graduates also find that they are employable in the same jobs as those students taking other degrees.

Selection interviews **Yes** Birmingham, Derby, East Anglia, Hull, Sussex, Winchester; **Some** Birmingham, Dundee, Kent, Warwick.

Interview advice and questions Courses often focus on history and literature so expect some questions on any American literature you have read and also on aspects of American history, arts and culture. You may also be questioned on visits you have made to America (or Canada) and your impressions. Current political issues might also be raised, so keep up-to-date with the political scene. **Birmingham** Access course and mature students are interviewed and also those students with strong applications but whose achieved grades do not meet entrance requirements. **Derby** The purpose of the interview is to help applicants understand the interdisciplinary nature of the course. **East Anglia** Admissions tutors want to see how up-to-date is the applicant's knowledge of American culture. **Swansea** Our interviews are very informal, giving students the chance to ask questions about the course. See also **Chapter 5**.

Reasons for rejection (non academic) If personal reasons prevent year of study in America. **Birmingham** Lack of commitment to the course. **Swansea** Lack of knowledge covering literature, history and politics.

AFTER-RESULTS ADVICE

Offers to applicants repeating A-levels **Higher** Essex, Warwick, Winchester; **Possibly higher** Nottingham; **Same** Birmingham, Derby, Dundee, East Anglia, Hull, Swansea.

GRADUATE DESTINATIONS AND EMPLOYMENT (2007/8 HESA)

Graduates surveyed 640 **Employed** 300 **In further study** 105 **Assumed unemployed** 70.

Career note All non-scientific careers are open to graduates. Start your career planning during your degree course and obtain work experience.

OTHER DEGREE SUBJECTS FOR CONSIDERATION

Business Studies; Cultural Studies; English Literature; Film Studies; Government; History; International History; International Relations; Latin-American Literature/Studies; Politics.

ANATOMICAL SCIENCE/ANATOMY

(see also **Physiology**)

Anatomy is the study of the structures of living creatures, from the sub-cellular level to the whole individual, and relates structure to function in the adult and during embryonic development.

Useful websites www.scienceyear.com; www.innerbody.com; www.instantanatomy.net

NB The points totals shown to the left of the institutions are for ease of reference only. It must not be assumed that Tariff points are always used by institutions or that they can be substituted for an offer in grades. The level of an offer is not necessarily indicative of the quality of a course.

COURSE OFFERS INFORMATION

Subject requirements/preferences **GCSE** Mathematics usually required. **AL** One or two mathematics/science subjects usually required; biology and chemistry preferred.

NB In 2011 universities and colleges will differ in their use of GCE AL/AS unit grade information, A* grades, the Extended Project (EPQ), the Advanced Diploma and the Cambridge Pre-U examination when considering applicants and making offers. An EPQ may be accepted in place of an AS subject. Check websites of universities and colleges for the latest offers information.

Your target offers and examples of courses provided by each institution

360 pts **London (UCL)** – AABe 2nd yr entry only from Biomed Sci (Anat Dev Biol) (IB 34–36 pts)
340 pts **Cardiff** – AAB–ABB 340–320 pts (Biomed Sci (Anat))
London (King's) – ABBe (Hum Sci) (IB 34 pts)
Manchester – AAB–BBB (Anat Sci; Anat Sci Ind/Prof Exp/Modn Lang) (IB 35–32 pts)
320 pts **Bristol** – ABB (Anat Sci; Hum Muscskel Sci; Anat Sci Vet Anat) (IB 32–34 pts HL 665)
Glasgow – ABB (Anatomy) (IB 32 pts)
Liverpool – ABB–AAB (Anat Hum Biol) (IB 32 pts)
300 pts **Dundee** – BBB 2nd yr entry (Anat Sci; Anat Physiol Sci) (IB 34 pts)
240 pts **Dundee** – CCC 1st yr entry (Anat Sci; Anat Physiol Sci) (IB 28 pts)

Alternative offers
See **Chapter 7** and **Appendix 1** for grades/UCAS Tariff points information for the International Baccalaureate, Scottish Highers/Advanced Highers, the Welsh Baccalaureate, the Irish Leaving Certificate, the Cambridge Pre-U Diploma, the Advanced Diploma and the Extended Project.

CHOOSING YOUR COURSE (SEE ALSO CH.1)

Some course features
Bristol (Anat Sci; Hum Muscskel Sci) Focus on mammalian anatomy involving dissection. (Anat Sci Vet Anat) Focus on anatomy and physiology of domestic mammals (eg dogs, horses). All courses can lead to further study in, for example, medicine, veterinary medicine.
Cardiff A common Biosciences first year programme (with the chance to change degrees) with following years centred on human anatomy, with dissection.
Dundee Emphasis on human anatomy.
Glasgow Students may be eligible for one-year research placement, registering for an MSci degree in Anatomy.
Liverpool Practical degree involving dissection and module choices from Biomedical and Biological Sciences and Psychology.
Manchester Anatomy part of Life Sciences programme, with common first year and options to change between degree courses.

Universities and colleges teaching quality See www.qaa.ac.uk; www.unistats.com.

Top research universities and colleges (RAE 2008) See **Biological Sciences**.

Examples of sandwich degree courses Bristol; Cardiff; Glasgow; Manchester.

ADMISSIONS INFORMATION

Number of applicants per place (approx) Bristol 8; Cardiff 8; Dundee 6; Liverpool 7.

Advice to applicants and planning the UCAS personal statement Give reasons for your interest in this subject (usually stemming from school work in biology). Discuss any articles in medical and other scientific journals which have attracted your attention and any new developments in medicine related to anatomical science.

Selection interviews **Liverpool** Offer subject to interview; **Some** Cardiff, Dundee; **No** Bristol.

Interview advice and questions Questions are likely on your particular interests in biology and anatomy, why you wish to study the subject and your future career intentions. See also **Chapter 5**.

Reasons for rejection (non-academic) **Liverpool** Unfocused applications with no evidence of basic knowledge of the course.

AFTER-RESULTS ADVICE

Offers to applicants repeating A-levels **Higher** Bristol, Dundee; **Possibly higher** Liverpool; **Same** Cardiff.

GRADUATE DESTINATIONS AND EMPLOYMENT (2007/8 HESA)

(Including **Pathology** and **Physiology**)
Graduates surveyed 2730 **Employed** 1620 **In further study** 480 **Assumed unemployed** 160.

Career note The subject leads to a range of careers in various laboratories, in government establishments, the NHS, pharmaceutical and food industries. It can also lead to postgraduate studies in physiotherapy, nursing, osteopathy and, in exceptional cases, in medicine, dentistry and veterinary science.

OTHER DEGREE SUBJECTS FOR CONSIDERATION

Biological Sciences; Biology; Genetics; Microbiology; Neuroscience; Osteopathy; Physiology; Physiotherapy.

ANIMAL SCIENCES

(including **Equine Science/Studies** and **Wildlife Conservation**; see also **Agricultural Sciences/Agriculture, Biological Sciences, Biology, Psychology, Veterinary Science/Medicine, Zoology**)

Animal Sciences is a broad-based subject involving both farm and companion animals. The range of specialisms is reflected in the table of courses below and can focus on animal nutrition and health, animal biology, behaviour, ecology and welfare. In addition, many courses specialise in equine science, studies and management. **NB** It is important to note that Bioveterinary Science graduates are not qualified to practise as vets (see **Veterinary Sciences/Medicine**).

Useful websites www.rspca.org.uk; www.iah.bbsrc.ac.uk; www.bhs.org.uk; www.wwf.org.uk; www.bsas.org.uk.

NB The points totals shown to the left of the institutions are for ease of reference only. It must not be assumed that Tariff points are always used by institutions or that they can be substituted for an offer in grades. The level of an offer is not necessarily indicative of the quality of a course.

COURSE OFFERS INFORMATION

Subject requirements/preferences **GCSE** Mathematics/science subjects required. Also check any weight limits on equitation modules. **AL** One or two science subjects required for scientific courses, biology and chemistry preferred.

NB In 2011 universities and colleges will differ in their use of GCE AL/AS unit grade information, A* grades, the Extended Project (EPQ), the Advanced Diploma and the Cambridge Pre-U examination when considering applicants and making offers. An EPQ may be accepted in place of an AS subject. Check websites of universities and colleges for the latest offers information.

Your target offers and examples of courses provided by each institution
380 pts **Cambridge** – A*AA college offers may vary (Nat Sci) (IB 38–42 pts)
340 pts **Sheffield** – AAB (MBiol Sci Anim Bhv) (IB 35 pts)

320 pts **Bristol** – ABB (Anim Bhv Welf; Anat Sci Vet Anat) (IB 34 pts HL 665)
Exeter – ABB–BBB (Anim Bhv) (IB 32–29 pts)
Sheffield – ABB (BSc Anim Bhv)

300 pts **Aberdeen** – BBB 2nd yr entry (Anim Ecol; Wldlf Mgt) (IB 26–28 pts)
Glasgow – BBB (Vet Biosci) (IB 28 pts)
Harper Adams (UC) – BBB (Anim Sci; Biovet Sci)
London (RVC) – BBB (BSc Biovet Sci) See **Advice to applicants and planning the UCAS personal statement** below
Newcastle – BBB–BBC (Anim Sci (Cmpn Anim St) (Lvstk Tech)) (IB 30–32 pts)
Reading – 300 pts min (Anim Sci) (IB 30 pts HL 655)

280 pts **Aberystwyth** – 280 pts (Anim Bhv) (IB 26 pts)
Bristol – BBC (Vet Nurs Biovet Sci) (IB 30 pts)
Gloucestershire – 280 pts (Anim Biol)
Kent – 280 pts (Wldlf Cons)
Lincoln – 280 pts (Biovet Sci)
Nottingham – BBC–BCC (Anim Sci) (IB 28–30 pts)
Oxford Brookes – BBC 280 pts (Eqn Sci (Anim Biol Cons)) (IB 30 pts)
Plymouth – 280–320 pts (Anim Sci (Bhv Welf))

260 pts **Newcastle** – BCC (Anim Prod Sci) (IB 28 pts)
Staffordshire – 260 pts (Anim Biol Cons) (IB 28 pts)

240 pts **Aberdeen** – CCC 1st yr entry (Anim Ecol; Wldlf Mgt)
Aberystwyth – 240 pts (Eqn Sci; Anim Sci; Eqn Hum Spo Sci) (IB 28 pts)
CAFRE – 240 pts (Eqn Mgt)
Chester – 240 pts (Anim Bhv courses)

Cumbria – 240 pts (Anim Cons Sci)
Glamorgan – 240–280 pts (Int Wldlf Biol)
Harper Adams (UC) – 240 pts (Anim Hlth Welf)
Lincoln – 240 pts (Eqn Sci; Anim Bhv Sci) (IB 30 pts)
Royal (CAg) – 240 pts (Agric (Anim Mgt); Eqn Mgt)

220 pts **Anglia Ruskin** – CCD 220 pts (Anim Welf Psy)
Askham Bryan (Coll) – 220 pts (Anim Mgt Sci)
Edinburgh Napier – CCD 220 pts (Anim Biol)
Lincoln – 220 pts (Eqn Spo Sci; Anim Mgt Welf)
Liverpool John Moores – 220–260 pts (Anim Bhv; Wldlf Cons)
Myerscough (Coll) – 220 pts (Anim Bhv Welf)
Northampton – 220–260 pts (Anim St; Eqn St)
Nottingham Trent (Brackenhurst) – 220 pts (Eqn Spo Sci; Eqn Spo Sci (Eqstrn Psy); Wldlf Cons; Zoo Biol)
Warwickshire (Coll) – 220 (Eqn Sci; Eqn St; Spo Sci (Eqn Hum))

200 pts **Anglia Ruskin** – 200–220 pts (Anim Bhv Psy; Anim Bhv; Anim Welf)
Bristol UWE (Hartpury) – 200–240 pts (Eqn Spo Sci; Eqn Sci; Eqn Dntl Sci; Biovet Sci) (IB 24 pts)
Canterbury Christ Church – 200 pts (Anim Sci)
Chester – 200 pts (Anim Bhv Welf)
Nottingham Trent (Brackenhurst) – 200 pts (Anim Biol)
Reaseheath (CFHE) – 200–240 pts (Anim Mgt)
Salford – 200 pts (Wldlf Prac Cons; Wldlf Cons Zoo Biol)
Wolverhampton – 200–260 pts (Anim Bhv Wldlf Cons; Anim Mgt; Eqn Spo Sci; Zoo Anim Mgt)
Worcester – 200 pts (Anim Biol)

180 pts **Aberystwyth** – 180 pts (Agric Anim Sci) (IB 26 pts)
Writtle (Coll) – 180 pts (Anim Sci; Anim Mgt; Eqn Sci (Bhv Welf); Eqn St; Eqn Spo Thera)

160 pts **Bristol UWE (Hartpury)** – 160–200 pts (Anim Sci; Eqn Mgt) (IB 28–30 pts)
Bristol UWE (Hartpury) – 160–220 pts (Anim Bhv Welf)
Greenwich – 160 pts (Anim Mgt; Eqn Mgt; Anim Cons Biodiv)
Hadlaw (Coll) – CC 160 pts (Equ Sci; Equ Mgt; Anim Bhv; Sci Welf; Anim Cons Biodiv)
SAC (Scottish CAg) – CC (App Anim Sci)

140 pts **Bishop Burton (Coll)** – 140 pts (Eqn Sci; App Anim Sci)

120 pts **Sparsholt (Coll)** – DD (Anim Mgt; Eqn St; Cons Wldlf Mgt)

Alternative offers

See **Chapter 7** and **Appendix 1** for grades/UCAS Tariff points information for the International Baccalaureate, Scottish Highers/Advanced Highers, the Welsh Baccalaureate, the Irish Leaving Certificate, the Cambridge Pre-U Diploma, the Advanced Diploma and the Extended Project.

EXAMPLES OF FOUNDATION DEGREES IN THE SUBJECT FIELD

Aberystwyth; Abingdon and Witney (Coll); Askham Bryan (Coll); Berkshire (CAg); Bicton (Coll); Bishop Burton (Coll); Bournemouth; Bridgwater (Coll); Brighton; Bristol UWE (Hartpury); Brooksby Melton (Coll); Bucks New; CAFRE; Capel Manor (Coll); Chester; Cornwall (Coll); Craven (Coll); Derby; Duchy (Coll); East Anglia; Easton (Coll); Greenwich; Guildford (Coll); Hadlow (Coll); Harper Adams (UC); Kingston Maurward (Coll); Leeds City (Coll); Lincoln; Moulton (Coll); Myerscough (Coll); Northampton; Nottingham Trent; Otley (Coll); Plymouth; Reaseheath (Coll); Shuttleworth (Coll); Solihull (Coll); Sparsholt (Coll); Warwickshire (Coll); Weston (Coll); Wiltshire (Coll); Worcester; Writtle (Coll).

CHOOSING YOUR COURSE (SEE ALSO CH.1)

Some course features

Aberdeen Field courses in land use and zoology compulsory. Opportunities for expeditions, volunteering work overseas and year-out placements. All students carry out work experience.
Bristol UWE (Anim Sci) A science-based programme focusing on anatomy, physiology, health,

nutrition and welfare, and including, eg animal management, equine husbandry, animal psychology with work experience.

Newcastle Range of Animal Science courses with a common first year followed by specialisation in, eg Companion Animal Studies or Livestock Technology.

Nottingham Trent First animal degree in UK specialising in exotic animals.

Oxford Brookes (Eqn Sci) Practical and vocational course with range of opportunities in second year to study in Europe or the US or Canada or Australia.

Writtle (Coll) (Anim Sci) Common first year with Animal Management degree focusing on development of practical husbandry in each of the three major animal groups (farm animals, horses and companion animals). Business skills also important.

Universities and colleges teaching quality See www.qaa.ac.uk; www.unistats.com.

Top research universities and colleges (RAE 2008) See **Agricultural Sciences/Agriculture** and **Biological Sciences**.

Examples of sandwich degree courses Aberystwyth; Edinburgh Napier; Harper Adams (UC); Nottingham Trent; Royal (CAg); Warwickshire (Coll).

ADMISSIONS INFORMATION

Number of applicants per place (approx) Aberystwyth 6; Bristol 10; Harper Adams (UC) 5; Leeds 6; Newcastle 9 (all courses); Nottingham 6; Nottingham Trent (Eqn Spo Sci) 4; Reading 10; Royal (CAg) 4.

Advice to applicants and planning the UCAS personal statement Describe any work you have done with animals which generated your interest in this subject. Work experience in veterinary practices, on farms or with agricultural firms would be useful. Read agricultural/scientific journals for updates on animal nutrition or breeding. For Equine courses, details of practical experience with horses (eg BHS examinations, Pony Club tests) should be included. **London (RVC)** BMAT is not required for entry **but** applicants wanting to be considered for the Merit Scholarships will have to take BMAT.

Misconceptions about this course Students are not always aware that horse studies courses cover science, business management, nutrition, health and breeding. **Bishop Burton (Coll)** (Eqn Sci) Some students wrongly believe that riding skills and a science background are not required for this course which, in fact, is heavily focused on the scientific principles and practice of horse management.

Selection interviews **Yes** Bristol, Cumbria (usually), Lincoln, Newcastle, Nottingham (depends on application), Plymouth, Royal (CAg), SAC (Scottish CAg), Writtle (Coll); **Some** Anglia Ruskin, Bishop Burton (Coll), Bristol UWE (Hartpury), Harper Adams (UC), Stirling.

Interview advice and questions Questions are likely about your experience with animals and your reasons for wishing to follow this science-based subject. Other questions asked in recent years have included: What do your parents think about your choice of course? What are your views on battery hens and the rearing of veal calves? The causes of blue-tongue disease, foot and mouth disease and BSE may also feature. **Equine courses** Students should check the level of riding ability expected (eg BHS Level 2 or PC B-test level). Check the amount of riding, jumping and competition work on the course. **Lincoln** (Eqn Spo Sci) Applicants required to show that they can ride to BHS Level 2. Experience with animals in general (see also **Chapter 5**).

Reasons for rejection (non-academic) Uncertainty as to why applicants chose the course. Too immature. Unlikely to integrate well.

AFTER-RESULTS ADVICE

Offers to applicants repeating A-levels **Possibly higher** Nottingham; **Same** Anglia Ruskin, Bishop Burton (Coll), Bristol UWE (Hartpury), Chester, Harper Adams (UC), Liverpool John Moores, Royal (CAg), Stirling.

GRADUATE DESTINATIONS AND EMPLOYMENT (2007/8 HESA)

Graduates surveyed 465 **Employed** 215 **In further study** 70 **Assumed unemployed** 40.

Career note The majority of graduates obtained work with animals whilst others moved towards business and administration careers. This is a specialised subject area and undergraduates should start early to make contacts with organisations and gain work experience.

OTHER DEGREE SUBJECTS FOR CONSIDERATION

Agriculture; Biological Sciences; Biology; Food Science; Natural Sciences; Veterinary Science; Zoology.

ANTHROPOLOGY

(including **Social Anthropology**; see also **Archaeology**)

Anthropology is the study of people's behaviour, beliefs and institutions and the diverse societies in which they live, and is concerned with the biological evolution of human beings. It also involves our relationships with other primates, the structure of communities and the effects of diet and disease on human groups. Alternatively, social or cultural anthropology covers aspects of social behaviour in respect of family, kinship, marriage, gender, religion, political structures, law, psychology and language.

Useful websites www.britishmuseum.org; www.therai.org.uk.

NB The points totals shown to the left of the institutions are for ease of reference only. It must not be assumed that Tariff points are always used by institutions or that they can be substituted for an offer in grades. The level of an offer is not necessarily indicative of the quality of a course.

COURSE OFFERS INFORMATION

Subject requirements/preferences GCSE English and mathematics usually required. A foreign language may be required. **AL** Biology and geography preferred for some Biological Anthropological courses. (Social Anthropology) No specific subjects required except **London LSE** See prospectus and website.

NB In 2011 universities and colleges will differ in their use of GCE AL/AS unit grade information, A* grades, the Extended Project (EPQ), the Advanced Diploma and the Cambridge Pre-U examination when considering applicants and making offers. An EPQ may be accepted in place of an AS subject. Check websites of universities and colleges for the latest offers information.

Your target offers and examples of courses provided by each institution

380 pts **Cambridge** – A*AA college offers may vary (Arch Anth) (IB 38–42 pts)
360 pts **Durham** – AAA (Nat Sci (Anth Arch)) (IB 34 pts HL 17–19 pts)
London (UCL) – AABe–ABBe (Anth; Arch Anth) (IB 34–36 pts)
Oxford – AAA (Arch Anth) (IB 38–42 pts)
350 pts **Brunel** – BBB +AS/EPQ b 350 pts (Psy Anth)
340 pts **Bristol** – AAB–BBB (MSci Arch Anth) (IB 35–32 pts HL 666–665)
Durham – AAB (Anthropology) (IB 34 pts HL 17–19 pts)
East Anglia – AAB–BBB (Arch Anth Art Hist) (IB 32–34 pts)
Exeter – AAB–BBB (Arch Anth) (IB 34–29 pts)
Kent – AAB (Anth N Am) (IB 36 pts HL 16 pts)
London (SOAS) – AAB (Soc Anth) (IB 36 pts HL 666)
St Andrews – AAB–ABB (Soc Anth courses) (IB 32–36 pts)
Sussex – AAB–BBB (Anth courses) (IB 32 pts)
320 pts **Dundee** – ABB 2nd yr entry (Foren Anth)
Durham – ABB (Anth Arch; Anth Sociol) (IB 34 pts HL 17–19 pts)
Glasgow – ABB (Sociol Anth)
London LSE – ABB (Anth Law; Soc Anth) (IB 37 pts HL 666)

Manchester – ABB (Soc Anth; Soc Anth Sociol; Soc Anth Crimin; Arch Anth) (IB 34 pts)
Southampton – ABB (App Soc Sci (Anth)) (IB 30 pts)
300 pts **Birmingham** – BBB–BBC (Af St Anth; Anth Pol Sci; Anth Hist Art joint courses) (IB 30–32 pts)
Bristol – BBB–BCC (BSc Arch Anth Sci) (IB 32–29 pts)
Brunel – BCC +AS/EPQ c 300 pts (Anth courses except under **350 pts**) (IB 32 pts)
Durham – BBB (Biol Anth)
Edinburgh – BBB (Soc Anth courses) (IB 35 pts HL 555)
Liverpool – BBB (Evol Anth) (IB 34 pts)
London (Gold) – BBB (Anth; Anth Media; Anth Sociol; Hist Anth) (IB 32 pts)
Queen's Belfast – BBB–BBCb (Soc Anth courses)
280 pts **Kent** – 280 pts (Biol Anth; Med Anth; Anth; Soc Anth) (IB 31 pts)
Oxford Brookes – BBC (Anth courses)
Roehampton – 280–340 pts (Anth; Biol Anth courses)
260 pts **Dundee** – BCC 1st yr entry (Foren Anth)
Hull – 260–300 pts (Sociol Anth courses)
240 pts **Aberdeen** – CCC (Anth courses) (IB 30 pts)
220 pts **Liverpool John Moores** – 220–260 pts (Foren Anth)
200 pts **East London** – 200 pts (Anth Comb courses)
London Met – 200 pts (Soc Anth)
180 pts **Trinity Saint David** – 180–240 pts (Anthropology)

Alternative offers
See **Chapter 7** and **Appendix 1** for grades/UCAS Tariff points information for the International Baccalaureate, Scottish Highers/Advanced Highers, the Welsh Baccalaureate, the Irish Leaving Certificate, the Cambridge Pre-U Diploma, the Advanced Diploma and the Extended Project.

CHOOSING YOUR COURSE (SEE ALSO CH.1)

Some course features
Birmingham A broad course taught in the Centre of West African Studies.
Durham A wide choice of social and biological anthropology courses including Joint and Combined Honours and a route via Natural Sciences.
East London (Anth Ntv Am St) The degree includes one year in the University of New Mexico.
Kent The course covers both biological and social aspects of anthropology.
Liverpool (Evol Anth) Unique course focusing on human evolution, evolutionary psychology and hominid palaeontology.
Sussex Opportunities for overseas placements.

Universities and colleges teaching quality See www.qaa.ac.uk; www.unistats.com.

Top research universities and colleges (RAE 2008) Cambridge; London (SOAS); London LSE; Roehampton; London (UCL); Sussex; Queen's Belfast; Aberdeen; London (Gold); Oxford; Edinburgh; St Andrews; Manchester.

Examples of sandwich degree courses Brunel; Liverpool John Moores; Oxford Brookes.

ADMISSIONS INFORMATION

Number of applicants per place (approx) Cambridge 2; Durham 14; Hull 11; Kent 6; Liverpool John Moores 4; London (Gold) 7, (SOAS) 10, (UCL) 3; London LSE (Anth Law) 10, (Soc Anth) 10; Manchester 27; Oxford Brookes 8; Queen's Belfast 10; Southampton 6; Sussex 10.

Advice to applicants and planning the UCAS personal statement Visits to museums should be discussed, for example, museums of anthropology (London, Cambridge). Describe any aspect of the subject which interests you (including books you have read) and how you have pursued this interest. Give details of any overseas travel. Give reasons for choosing course: since this is not a school subject, you will need to convince the selectors of your knowledge and interest. **Oxford** See **Archaeology**.

Selection interviews **Yes** Cambridge, Dundee (Foren Anth), East Anglia, Hull, London (Gold), (UCL) mature students, Oxford, Oxford Brookes; **Some** London LSE, Roehampton; **No** Bristol.

Interview advice and questions This is a broad subject and questions will tend to emerge as a result of your interests in aspects of anthropology or social anthropology and your comments on your personal statement. Past questions have included: What stresses are there among the nomads of the North African desert? What is a society? What is speech? If you dug up a stone axe what could you learn from it? What are the values created by a capitalist society? Discuss the role of women since the beginning of this century. **Cambridge**, **Oxford** See **Chapter 5** and **Archaeology**.

Reasons for rejection (non-academic) Lack of commitment. Inability to deal with a more philosophical (less positivist) approach to knowledge.

AFTER-RESULTS ADVICE

Offers to applicants repeating A-levels **Possibly higher** Oxford Brookes; **Same** Cambridge, Durham, East Anglia, Liverpool John Moores, London (UCL), Roehampton.

GRADUATE DESTINATIONS AND EMPLOYMENT (2007/8 HESA)

Graduates surveyed 515 **Employed** 200 **In further study** 110 **Assumed unemployed** 45.

Career note All non-scientific careers are open to graduates. However, career planning should start early and efforts made to contact employers and gain work experience.

OTHER DEGREE SUBJECTS FOR CONSIDERATION

Archaeology; Egyptology; Heritage Studies; History; Human Sciences; Political Science; Psychology; Religious Studies; Social Science; Sociology.

ARABIC AND ANCIENT NEAR AND MIDDLE EASTERN STUDIES

Arabic is one of the world's most widely-used languages, spoken by more than 300 million people in 21 countries in the Middle East. Links between Britain and Arabic-speaking countries have increased considerably in recent years and most of the larger UK organisations with offices in the Middle East have only a relatively small pool of Arabic-speaking graduates from which to recruit future employees each year. Islamic Studies focuses on a faith which has much in common with Christianity and Judaism, is the second largest religion in the world, extending from Africa to the East Indies, and is focused on the Middle East.

Useful websites www.cilt.org.uk; www.iol.org.uk; www.bbc.co.uk/languages; www.languageadvantage.com; www.languagematters.co.uk; www.reed.co.uk/multilingual; www.metimes.com; www.merip.org; www.memri.org; www.mei.edu.

NB The points totals shown to the left of the institutions are for ease of reference only. It must not be assumed that Tariff points are always used by institutions or that they can be substituted for an offer in grades. The level of an offer is not necessarily indicative of the quality of a course.

COURSE OFFERS INFORMATION

Subject requirements/preferences **GCSE** English, mathematics and a foreign language usually required. A high grade in Arabic may be required. **AL** A modern language is usually required or preferred.

NB In 2011 universities and colleges will differ in their use of GCE AL/AS unit grade information, A* grades, the Extended Project (EPQ), the Advanced Diploma and the Cambridge Pre-U examination when considering applicants and making offers. An EPQ may be accepted in place of an AS subject. Check websites of universities and colleges for the latest offers information.

Your target offers and examples of courses provided by each institution

380 pts **Cambridge** – A*AA college offers may vary (As Mid E St; As Mid E St (Arbc) (Persn)) (IB 38–42 pts)

360 pts **Durham** – AAA (Comb Arts (Arbc)) (IB 38 pts)

Oxford – AAA (Orntl St (Arbc) (Arbc Islam St) (Arbc Lang); Persn Lang; Persn Islam St Hist; Persn Islam Art Arch; Turk courses) (IB 38–40 pts)

St Andrews – AAA (Arbc Econ; Arbc Int Rel)

340 pts **Durham** – AAB (Modn Langs (Arbc))

London (King's) – ABBe (Turk Modn Gk St) (IB 30 pts)

320 pts **Exeter** – ABB–BBB (Arbc courses; Mid E St; Arbc Persn) (IB 32–29 pts)

Leeds – ABB (Arbc Int Dev; Arbc Chin; Arbc Class Lit)

London (SOAS) – ABB (Arbc; Islam St; Anc Near E St; Persn; Heb Isrl St) (IB 34 pts HL 555)

Manchester – ABB–BBC (Arbc St; Turk St; Islam St Arbc; Persn St; Mid E St; Jew St Heb St) (IB 32–30 pts)

St Andrews – ABB (Arbc Mid E St) (IB 32 pts)

300 pts **Edinburgh** – BBB (Arbc courses; Persn Pol; Mid E St) (IB 34 pts)

Leeds – BBB (Islam St; Mid E St) (IB 32 pts HL 15 pts)

Liverpool – BBB (Egyptology) (IB 34 pts)

280 pts **Salford** – 280 pts (Arbc Engl Transl Interp (for native Arabic speakers: contact admissions tutor))

Westminster – BBC (Arbc Engl Lang; Arbc Ling)

260 pts **Swansea** – 260–300 pts (Egyptology)

240 pts **Central Lancashire** – 240 pts (Arbc comb courses)

Manchester Met – 240 pts (Arbc Modn Lang)

London (Birk) – Check with admissions tutor (Arbc courses)

Alternative offers

See **Chapter 7** and **Appendix 1** for grades/UCAS Tariff points information for the International Baccalaureate, Scottish Highers/Advanced Highers, the Welsh Baccalaureate, the Irish Leaving Certificate, the Cambridge Pre-U Diploma, the Advanced Diploma and the Extended Project.

CHOOSING YOUR COURSE (SEE ALSO CH.1)

Some course features

Edinburgh (Arbc) Students usually spend part of their third year in Cairo.

Exeter Single and Combined Honours Arabic courses provide a strong language base combined with study of the culture, literature and history. All four-year Arabic students spend their second year in, eg Morocco, Egypt, Damascus or Jordan.

Leeds (Mid E St) Course focuses on the culture, politics and economy of the region. No knowledge is needed; an Arabic option is available.

Liverpool (Egypt) Course covers the language, archaeology and history of Ancient Egypt, together with a study of Egyptian art, religion and society.

Salford The only Arabic/English translation and interpreting course.

Universities and colleges teaching quality See www.qaa.ac.uk; www.unistats.com.

Top research universities and colleges (RAE 2008) (Middle Eastern and African Studies) Cambridge; Oxford; Edinburgh; London (SOAS); Durham.

ADMISSIONS INFORMATION

Number of applicants per place (approx) Cambridge 3; Leeds 6; London (SOAS) 5; Salford 5.

Advice to applicants and planning the UCAS personal statement Describe any visits to, or your experience of living in, Arabic-speaking countries. Develop a knowledge of Middle Eastern cultures, history and politics and mention these topics on the UCAS application. Provide evidence of language-learning skills and experience. **Salford** Arab applicants are normally expected to have passed their secondary school leaving certificate and to demonstrate an acceptable command of English. English-speaking and European applicants should also be able to speak Arabic.

Selection interviews **Yes** Cambridge, Exeter, Leeds, Oxford; **Some** Salford.

Interview advice and questions You will need to be able to justify your reasons for wanting to study Arabic or other languages and to discuss your interest in, and awareness of, cultural, social and political aspects of the Middle East. **Cambridge**, **Oxford** See **Chapter 5** under **Modern and Medieval Languages**. **Salford** (Arbc Engl Transl Interp) Applicants may be required to sit Arabic language tests. See also **Chapter 5**.

AFTER-RESULTS ADVICE

Offers to applicants repeating A-levels **Higher** Leeds, St Andrews; **Same** Exeter, Salford.

GRADUATE DESTINATIONS AND EMPLOYMENT (2007/8 HESA)

Graduates surveyed 70 **Employed** 20 **In further study** 15 **Assumed unemployed** 10.

Career note Most graduates entered business and administrative work, in some cases closely linked to their language studies.

OTHER DEGREE SUBJECTS FOR CONSIDERATION

Anthropology; Archaeology; Classical Studies; Hebrew; History; Persian; Politics; Turkish.

ARCHAEOLOGY

Courses in Archaeology differ between institutions but the majority focus on the archaeology of Europe, the Mediterranean and Middle Eastern countries and on the close examination of discoveries of pre-historic communities and ancient, medieval and post-medieval societies. Hands-on experience is involved in all courses as well as a close study of the history of the artefacts themselves and, in some courses, an appreciation of the application of science.

Useful websites www.britarch.ac.uk; www.english-heritage.org.uk; www.prehistoric.org.uk; www.britishmuseum.org; www.archaeologists.net.

NB The points totals shown to the left of the institutions are for ease of reference only. It must not be assumed that Tariff points are always used by institutions or that they can be substituted for an offer in grades. The level of an offer is not necessarily indicative of the quality of a course.

COURSE OFFERS INFORMATION

Subject requirements/preferences **GCSE** English and mathematics or science usually required for BSc courses. **AL** History, geography, English or a science subject may be preferred for some courses and two science subjects for Archaeological Science courses.

NB In 2011 universities and colleges will differ in their use of GCE AL/AS unit grade information, A* grades, the Extended Project (EPQ), the Advanced Diploma and the Cambridge Pre-U examination when considering applicants and making offers. An EPQ may be accepted in place of an AS subject. Check websites of universities and colleges for the latest offers information.

Your target offers and examples of courses provided by each institution

380 pts **Cambridge** – A*AA college offers may vary (Arch Anth) (IB 38–42 pts)
London (UCL) – AAAe–ABBe (Palaeobiology) (IB 34–38 pts)

360 pts **Durham** – AAA (Nat Sci (Arch); Comb Soc Sci (Arch)) (IB 38 pts)
London (UCL) – AABe–BBBe (Arch Anth) (IB 36 pts)
Oxford – AAA (Arch Anth; Class Arch Anc Hist) (IB 38–42 pts)
Warwick – ABBc–BBBc (Anc Hist Class Arch) (IB 32–36 pts)

340 pts **Bristol** – AAB–BBB (Arch Anth; Palae Evol) (IB 36 pts HL 665–666)
Durham – AAB–ABB (Arch; Anth Arch; Anc Hist Arch) (IB 32 pts)
East Anglia – AAB–BBB (Arch Anth Art Hist; Hist Land Arch) (IB 32–33 pts)
Newcastle – AAB–BBC (Arch; Anc Hist Arch) (IB 30–35 pts)
St Andrews – AAB (Anc Hist Arch; Mediev Hist Arch) (IB 36 pts)

320 pts **Birmingham** – ABB–BBC (Pal; Arch joint courses)
Cardiff – ABB–BBB (BA/BSc Arch courses) (IB 30 pts)
Exeter – ABB–BBB (Arch courses) (IB 32–29 pts)
Glasgow – ABB–BBB (Arch courses) (IB 32–30 pts)
Kent – 320–300 pts (Class Arch St courses; Arch Anth) (IB 31 pts)
Leicester – ABB (Geog Arch)
London (King's) – ABB+AS (Class Arch) (IB 34 pts)
London (UCL) – BBBe (Arch; Vkg St; Class Arch Class Civ; Egypt Arch) (IB 32–34 pts)
Manchester – ABB–BBB (Arch; Anc Hist Arch) (IB 33–32 pts)
Nottingham – ABB (Arch Engl Lang) (IB 30–34 pts)
Nottingham – ABB–BBC (Arch Geog; Arch; Arch His)
Sheffield – ABB–BBB (Arch courses) (IB 32 pts)
York – ABB (Arch; Bioarch; Hist Arch) (IB 32 pts)

300 pts **Birmingham** – BBB (Arch; Arch Anc Hist) (IB 30–32 pts)
Bristol – BBB–BCC (Arch Anth Sci) (IB 29–32 pts)
Edinburgh – BBB (one sitting) (Arch; Celt Arch; Scot Ethnol Arch) (IB 34 pts HL 555)
Hull – 300 pts (Hist Arch)
Kent – 300–320 pts (Class Arch St) (IB 35 pts HL 16 pts)
Leicester – BBB (Anc Hist Arch; Hist Arch; Arch) (IB 28–30 pts)
Liverpool – BBB (Arch (Sci) (Arts); Egypt Arch; Egypt) (IB 30 pts)
Nottingham – BBB (Vkg St) (IB 30 pts)
Queen's Belfast – BBB–BCCb (Arch; Env Arch; Arch Ir Celt) (IB 29 pts)
Southampton – BBB–BBC (Arch; Arch Geog; Arch Hist) (IB 30–28 pts)
Swansea – BBB (Egyptology)

280 pts **Leicester** – BBC–BCC (Arch Comb courses)
Reading – 280–360 pts (Arch courses) (IB 30 pts)

260 pts **Bournemouth** – 260 pts (Arch Foren Sci)
Bradford – 260–280 pts (Arch Sci; Arch; Bioarch; Foren Arch Sci) (IB 28 pts)
Hull – 260–320 pts (Geog Arch)
London (SOAS) – BCC (Hist Art Arch courses) (IB 34 pts)

240 pts **Aberdeen** – CCC 240 pts (Arch; Scot Arch) (IB 28 pts)
Bangor – 240–260 pts (Herit Arch Hist; Wls Hist Arch) (IB 28 pts)
Central Lancashire – 240–220 pts (Arch courses) (IB 26 pts)
Chester – 240 pts (Arch courses) (IB 30 pts)
Portsmouth – 240–300 pts (Pal Evol)
Swansea – 240–280 pts (Egypt Anc Hist; Egypt Class Civ courses)

220 pts **Bournemouth** – 220 pts (Fld Arch; Mar Arch; Rom Arch; Arch Foren Sci)
Winchester – 220–260 pts (Arch courses) (IB 24 pts)

200 pts **Trinity Saint David** – 200–260 pts (Arch; Arch (Prac) (Wrld Cult)) (IB 26 pts)
Worcester – 200–260 pts (Arch Herit St courses)

180 pts **Trinity Saint David** – 180–240 pts (Arch (Env); Arch Anth; Islam St Arch) (IB 26 pts)

160 pts **Trinity Saint David** – 160 pts (Welsh St Arch)

120 pts **Peterborough Reg (Coll)** – 120 pts (Arch Land Hist)

80 pts **London (Birk)** – (p/t Archaeology)

Alternative offers

See **Chapter 7** and **Appendix 1** for grades/UCAS Tariff points information for the International Baccalaureate, Scottish Highers/Advanced Highers, the Welsh Baccalaureate, the Irish Leaving Certificate, the Cambridge Pre-U Diploma, the Advanced Diploma and the Extended Project.

EXAMPLES OF FOUNDATION DEGREES IN THE SUBJECT FIELD

Bournemouth; Cornwall (Coll).

CHOOSING YOUR COURSE (SEE ALSO CH.1)

Some course features

Bangor (Herit Arch Hist) Focus on historical and archaeological evidence and its use in the heritage industry.

Bournemouth (Fld Arch) Focuses on a practical training for a career in archaeology.

Glasgow (Arch) A study of Scottish archaeology and field projects in Britain, Europe and the Mediterranean.

Leicester (Arch) Option to study another subject outside Archaeology in Year 1.

London (SOAS) Wide range of Archaeology courses, many with languages and History of Art.

York Archaeology courses provide wide range of options and opportunity to spend a term in another discipline, for example History, Biology.

Universities and colleges teaching quality See www.qaa.ac.uk; www.unistats.com.

Top research universities and colleges (RAE 2008) Durham; Reading; Oxford; Cambridge; Liverpool; London (UCL); Leicester; Southampton; Sheffield; York; Queen's Belfast; Exeter; Nottingham.

Examples of sandwich degree courses Bradford.

ADMISSIONS INFORMATION

Number of applicants per place (approx) Birmingham 5; Bradford 4; Bristol 7; Cambridge 2; Cardiff 6; Durham 6; Leicester 4; Liverpool 12, (Egypt) 5; London (UCL) 5; Manchester (Anc Hist Arch) 15, (Arch) 4; Newcastle 14; Nottingham 11; Sheffield 5; Southampton 6; Trinity Saint David 2; York 3.

Advice to applicants and planning the UCAS personal statement First-hand experience of 'digs' and other field work should be described. The Council for British Archaeology (see **Appendix 4**) can provide information on where digs are taking place. Describe any interests in fossils and museum visits as well as details of visits to current archaeological sites. Your local university archaeological department or central library will also provide information on contacts in your local area (each county council employs an archaeological officer). Since this is not a school subject, the selectors will be looking for good reasons for your choice of subject. Gain practical field experience and discuss this in the personal statement. Show your serious commitment to archaeology through your out-of-school activities (fieldwork, museum experience). **Cambridge** Most colleges require a school/college essay (see **Chapter 5**). (See also **Anthropology** and **Appendix 4**.)

Misconceptions about this course **Bristol** We are not an élitist course: 75% of applicants and students come from state schools and non-traditional backgrounds. **Liverpool** (Egypt) Some students would have been better advised looking at courses in Archaeology or Ancient History and Archaeology which offer major pathways in the study of Ancient Egypt.

Selection interviews **Yes** Bangor, Bournemouth, Bradford, Cambridge, Durham, East Anglia, Glasgow, Liverpool (Egypt), London (UCL), Newcastle, Nottingham, Oxford, Southampton, Swansea, Trinity Saint David; **Some** Birmingham, Bristol, Cardiff, York.

Interview advice and questions Questions will be asked about any experience you have had in visiting archaeological sites or taking part in digs. Past questions have included: How would you interpret archaeological evidence, for example a pile of flints, coins? What is stratification? How would you date archaeological remains? What recent archaeological discoveries have been made? How did you become interested in archaeology? With which archaeological sites in the UK are you familiar? **Birmingham** Questions may cover recent archaeological events. **Cambridge**, **Oxford** (see **Chapter 5**). **Oxford** Interviews involve artefacts, maps and other material to be interpreted. Successful entrants average 30.7%. **York** What are your views on the archaeology programmes on TV? What would you do with a spare weekend? See also **Chapter 5**.

Reasons for rejection (non-academic) (Mature students) Inability to cope with essay-writing and exams. **Bournemouth** Health and fitness important for excavations. **Liverpool** (Egypt) Applicant misguided on choice of course – Egyptology used to fill a gap on the UCAS application.

AFTER-RESULTS ADVICE

Offers to applicants repeating A-levels **Same** Birmingham, Bradford, Cambridge, Chester, Durham, East Anglia, Leicester, Liverpool (Egypt), London (UCL), Sheffield, Trinity Saint David, Winchester.

GRADUATE DESTINATIONS AND EMPLOYMENT (2007/8 HESA)

Graduates surveyed 720 **Employed** 270 **In further study** 160 **Assumed unemployed** 95.

Career note Vocational opportunities closely linked to this subject are limited. However, some graduates aim for positions in local authorities, libraries and museums. A number of organisations covering Water Boards, forestry, civil engineering and surveying also employ field archaeologists.

OTHER DEGREE SUBJECTS FOR CONSIDERATION

Ancient History; Anthropology; Classical Studies; Classics; Geology; Heritage Studies; History; History of Art and Architecture; Medieval History.

ARCHITECTURE

(including **Architectural Technology** and **Architectural Engineering**; see also **Building and Construction**)

Courses in Architecture provide a broad education consisting of technological subjects covering structures, construction, materials and environmental studies. Project-based design work is an integral part of all courses and in addition, history and social studies will also be incorporated into degree programmes. After completing the first three years leading to a BA (Hons), students aiming for full professional status take a further two-year course leading to eg, the BArch, MArch degrees or Diploma and after a year in an architect's practice, the final professional examinations are taken.

Useful websites www.ciat.org.uk; www.architecture.com; www.rias.org.uk; www.archrecord.construction.com.

NB The points totals shown to the left of the institutions are for ease of reference only. It must not be assumed that Tariff points are always used by institutions or that they can be substituted for an offer in grades. The level of an offer is not necessarily indicative of the quality of a course.

COURSE OFFERS INFORMATION

Subject requirements/preferences **GCSE** English and mathematics, in some cases at certain grades, are required in all cases. A science subject may also be required. **AL** Mathematics and/or physics required or preferred for some courses. Art and design may be preferable to design and technology. Art is sometimes a requirement and many schools of architecture prefer it; a portfolio of art work is often requested and, in some cases, a drawing test will be set.

NB In 2011 universities and colleges will differ in their use of GCE AL/AS unit grade information, A* grades, the Extended Project (EPQ), the Advanced Diploma and the Cambridge Pre-U examination when considering applicants and making offers. An EPQ may be accepted in place of an AS subject. Check websites of universities and colleges for the latest offers information.

Your target offers and examples of courses provided by each institution

380 pts **Cambridge** – A*AA college offers may vary (Architecture) (IB 38–42 pts)
360 pts **Bath** – AAA (Architecture) (IB 36–38 pts HL maths 6)
Cardiff – AAA (Archit St) (IB 35 pts)
Glasgow (SA) – AAA–ABB (Architecture)
Liverpool – AAA (Architecture) (IB 35 pts)
Manchester – AAA (Architecture) (IB 36 pts)
Manchester Met – AAA (Architecture) (IB 36 pts)
Newcastle – AAA (Archit St) (IB 37 pts HL art 6)
Nottingham – AAA (Arch; Arch Env Des) (IB 36 pts)

Sheffield – AAA–AAaa (Archit; Archit Land) (IB 37 pts)
Sheffield – AAA (Struct Eng Archit) (IB 37 pts)
Southampton – AAA (Civ Eng Archit) (IB 34 pts HL 18 pts)

340 pts **Leeds** – AAB (Archit Eng; Int Archit Eng)
London (UCL) – ABBe (Architecture) (IB 34 pts)
Oxford Brookes – AAB (Architecture) (IB 32–34 pts)
Sheffield – AAB (Struct Eng Archit St) (IB 35 pts)
Strathclyde – AAB (MEng Archit Eng) (IB 36 pts HL maths phys 6))

320 pts **Birmingham City** – 320 pts (Architecture) (IB 31 pts)
Brighton – ABB offers may vary (Architecture) (IB 34pts)
City – 320 pts (MEng Civ Eng Archit) (IB 34 pts)
Heriot-Watt – ABB 2nd yr entry (MEng/BEng/BSc Archit Eng) (IB 35 pts)
Kent – 320 pts (Archit; Inter Archit) (IB 33 pts HL 15 pts)
Kingston – 320 pts (Architecture)
Lincoln – 320 pts (Architecture)
Plymouth – 320 pts (Architecture) (IB 30 pts)
Queen's Belfast – ABB (Architecture) (IB 29 pts HL 655)
Strathclyde – ABB (Archit St) (IB 34 pts)
Westminster – ABB 320 pts (Archit; Archit Eng; Archit Urb Des) (IB 28 pts)

300 pts **Archit Assoc Sch London** – BBB 300 pts (Architecture)
Bristol UWE – 300–360 pts (Archit Plan) (IB 24–32 pts)
Central Lancashire – 300 pts (Architecture) (IB 32 pts)
Dundee – 300 pts (Archit; Archit St) (IB 30 pts)
Edinburgh/Edinburgh (CA) – BBB (Archit Hist courses; Archit; Archit Crea Cult Env) (IB 30 pts)
Glasgow – BBB (BEng Civ Eng Archit)
Huddersfield – 300 pts (Archit (Int); Archit; Archit Tech) (IB 28–26 pts)
Leeds Met – 300 pts (Architecture)
Liverpool John Moores – 300 pts (Architecture) (IB 30 pts)
Northumbria – BBB (Architecture) (IB 26 pts)
Nottingham Trent – 300 pts (Architecture) (IB 28 pts)
Sheffield Hallam – 300 pts (Archit Env Des; Archit Tech)
Strathclyde – BBB (BEng Archit Eng) (IB 32 pts HL maths phys 55)
Ulster – 300 pts (Architecture) (IB 25 pts)

285 pts **Cardiff (UWIC)** – 285 pts (Archit Des Tech)

280 pts **Brighton** – BBC offers may vary (Archit Tech)
Bristol UWE – 280–320 pts (Archit Env Eng)
City – 280 pts (BEng Civ Eng Archit) (IB 30 pts)
De Montfort – 280 pts (Architecture)
Heriot-Watt – BBC 1st yr entry (MEng/BEng/BSc Archit Eng) (IB 29 pts)
London Met – 280 pts (Archit; Archit St) (IB 32 pts) (IB 32 pts)
Salford – 280 pts (Archit Tech)
Westminster – BBC (Archit Tech) (IB 26 pts)

260 pts **Central Lancashire** – 260 pts (Archit Tech) (IB 26 pts)
Coventry – 260 pts (Architecture)
Creative Arts – 260 pts (Architecture)
Northumbria – 260 pts (Archit Tech) (IB 26 pts)
Nottingham Trent – 260 pts (Archit Tech) (IB 28 pts)
Plymouth – 260 pts (Archit Tech Env)
Portsmouth – 260–320 pts (Architecture) (IB 28 pts)
Ulster – 260 pts (Archit Tech Mgt) (IB 24 pts)

240 pts **Anglia Ruskin** – 240 pts (Architecture) (IB 26 pts)
Bolton – 240 pts (Archit Tech) (IB 30 pts)
Bristol UWE – 240–280 pts (Archit Tech Des) (IB 24–28 pts)
De Montfort – 240 pts (Archit Des Tech Prod) (IB 28 pts)

	Edinburgh Napier – 240 pts (Archit Tech)
	Greenwich – 240 pts (Architecture) (IB 24 pts)
	Leeds Met – 240 pts (Archit Tech)
	Liverpool John Moores – 240 pts (Archit Tech)
	Plymouth – 240 pts (Archit Des Struct) (IB 28 pts)
	Robert Gordon – CCC (Architecture) (IB 24 pts)
	Sheffield Hallam – 240 pts (Archit Tech)
220 pts	**Anglia Ruskin** – 220 pts (Archit Tech) (IB 26 pts)
	Birmingham City – 220 pts (Archit Tech)
	Coventry – 220 pts (Archit Des Tech)
	East London – 220 pts (Architecture)
	London South Bank – 220 pts (Archit Tech) (IB 24 pts)
	Northampton – 220–260 pts (Archit Tech) (IB 24 pts)
200 pts	**Glyndŵr** – 200 pts (Archit Des Tech)
180 pts	**Derby** – 180–240 pts (Archit Vnu Des; Archit Tech Prac) (IB 26 pts)
160 pts	**London South Bank** – 160 pts (Archit; Archit Eng) (IB 24 pts)
120 pts	**Southampton Solent** – 120 pts (Archit Tech)
80 pts	**Bournemouth Arts (UC)** – 80 pts (Architecture)
	London Arts – 80 pts (Archit (Spc Objs))

Alternative offers
See **Chapter 7** and **Appendix 1** for grades/UCAS Tariff points information for the International Baccalaureate, Scottish Highers/Advanced Highers, the Welsh Baccalaureate, the Irish Leaving Certificate, the Cambridge Pre-U Diploma, the Advanced Diploma and the Extended Project.

EXAMPLES OF FOUNDATION DEGREES IN THE SUBJECT FIELD
Bolton; Bournemouth; Brighton; Derby; Huddersfield; Northumbria; Oldham (Coll); Thames Valley.

CHOOSING YOUR COURSE (SEE ALSO CH.1)
Some course features
Architecture is a broad subject combining the vocational with the academic. To practise as an architect it is important to check that your chosen courses follow the requirements of the Royal Institute of British Architects (see **Appendix 4**).

Bath Four-year full-time thin sandwich BSc degree with second and third-year placements, and opportunity for third-year Erasmus exchange at a European school of architecture.
Edinburgh Wide range of Architecture-related courses delivered jointly by University and Edinburgh College of Art. Choice of three-year BA or four-year MA Architecture course, both with options to proceed to MArch degree which completes RIBA/ARB Part 2 qualification for architects.
Huddersfield (Archit (Int)) Course focuses on the built environment in the developing world, with extensive overseas field work.
Northumbria Project work, management skills in architectural design, field study visits and strong links with Interior Design programme central to this full-time course.
Oxford Brookes (Archit) Wide-ranging three-year full-time course, with teaching centred on the design studio, technology, practice and historical and theoretical approaches to architecture. Department has open-studio culture.
Westminster Modular course with 75% core modules, 25% options. Choice of modules determines choice of a general or special pathway degree.

Universities and colleges teaching quality See www.qaa.ac.uk; www.unistats.com.

Top research universities and colleges (RAE 2008) (Architecture and Built Environment) Cambridge; London (UCL); Sheffield; Liverpool; Loughborough; Bath; Reading; Edinburgh/Edinburgh (CA).

Examples of sandwich degree courses Bath; Brighton; Bristol UWE; Cardiff; De Montfort; Dundee; Glasgow (SA); Huddersfield; Leeds Met; London South Bank; Northumbria; Nottingham Trent; Plymouth; Queen's Belfast; Sheffield Hallam; Ulster.

ADMISSIONS INFORMATION

Number of applicants per place (approx) Archit Assoc Sch London 2; Bath 13; Cambridge 8; Cardiff 12; Cardiff (UWIC) 2; Creative Arts 4; Dundee 6; Edinburgh 18; Glasgow 16; London (UCL) 16; London Met 13; Manchester Met 25; Newcastle 11; Nottingham 30; Oxford Brookes 15; Queen's Belfast 9; Robert Gordon 8; Sheffield 20; Southampton 10; Strathclyde 10.

Advice to applicants and planning the UCAS personal statement You should describe any visits to historical or modern architectural sites and give your opinions. Contact architects in your area and try to obtain work shadowing or work experience in their practices. Describe any such work you have done. Develop a portfolio of drawings and sketches of buildings and parts of buildings (you will probably need this for your interview). Show evidence of your reading on the history of architecture in Britain and modern architecture throughout the world. Discuss your preferences among the work of leading 20th century world architects. **Cambridge** Check college requirement for preparatory work (see **Chapter 5**). (See **Appendix 4**.)

Misconceptions about this course Some applicants believe that Architectural Technology is the same as Architecture. Some students confuse Architecture with Architectural Engineering.

Selection interviews The majority of universities and colleges interview or inspect portfolios for Architecture and most require a portfolio of art work. **Yes** Archit Assoc Sch London, Bradford, Brighton, Cambridge, Cardiff, Coventry, Derby, Dundee, East London, Edinburgh, Huddersfield, Kingston, Liverpool, London (UCL), London South Bank, Newcastle, Nottingham, Sheffield; **Some** Anglia Ruskin, Cardiff (UWIC).

Interview advice and questions Most Architecture departments will expect to see evidence of your ability to draw; portfolios are often requested at interview and, in some cases, drawing tests are set prior to the interview. You should have a real awareness of architecture with some knowledge of historical styles as well as examples of modern architecture. If you have gained some work experience then you will be asked to describe the work done in the architect's office and any site visits you have made. Questions in the past have included the following: What is the role of the architect in society? Is the London Eye an eyesore? Discuss one historic and one 20th century building you admire. Who is your favourite architect? What sort of buildings do you want to design? How do you make a place peaceful? How would you reduce crime through architecture? Do you like the University buildings? Do you read any architectural journals? Which? What is the role of an architectural technologist? **Archit Assoc Sch London** The interview assesses the student's potential and ability to benefit from the course. Every portfolio we see at interview will be different; sketches, models, photographs and paintings all help to build up a picture of the student's interests. Detailed portfolio guidelines are available on the website. **Cambridge** How do you make a place peaceful? How do you reduce crime through architecture? (Robinson) Candidates who have taken, or are going to take, A-level art should bring with them their portfolio of work (GCSE work is not required). All candidates, including those who are not taking A-level art, should bring photographs of any three-dimensional material. Those not taught art should bring a sketch book (for us to assess drawing abilities) and analytical drawings of a new and old (pre-1900) building and a natural and human-made artefact. We are interested to see any graphic work in any medium that you would like to show us – please do not feel you should restrict your samples to only those with architectural reference. All evidence of sketching ability is helpful to us. (**NB** All colleges at **Cambridge** and other university Departments of Architecture will seek similar evidence.) **Sheffield** Art portfolio required for those without AL/GCSE art. See also **Chapter 5**.

Reasons for rejection (non-academic) Weak evidence of creative skills. Folio of art work does not give sufficient evidence of design creativity. Insufficient evidence of interest in architecture. Unwillingness to try freehand sketching. **Archit Assoc Sch London** Poor standard of work in the portfolio.

AFTER-RESULTS ADVICE

Offers to applicants repeating A-levels **Higher** Huddersfield; **Possibly higher** Brighton, De Montfort, Glasgow, Newcastle; **Same** Archit Assoc Sch London, Bath, Birmingham City, Cambridge, Cardiff,

Cardiff (UWIC), Creative Arts, Derby, Dundee, Greenwich, Kingston, Liverpool John Moores, London Met, London South Bank, Manchester Met, Nottingham, Nottingham Trent, Oxford Brookes, Queen's Belfast, Robert Gordon, Sheffield.

GRADUATE DESTINATIONS AND EMPLOYMENT (2007/8 HESA)

Graduates surveyed 1670 **Employed** 830 **In further study** 235 **Assumed unemployed** 175.

Career note Further study is needed to enter architecture as a profession. Opportunities exist in local government or private practice – areas include planning, housing, environmental and conservation fields. Architectural technicians support the work of architects and may be involved in project management, design presentations and submissions to planning authorities.

OTHER DEGREE SUBJECTS FOR CONSIDERATION

Architectural Engineering; Building; Building Surveying; Civil Engineering; Construction; Heritage Management; History of Art and Architecture; Housing; Interior Architecture; Interior Design; Landscape Architecture; Property Development; Quantity Surveying; Surveying; Town and Country Planning; Urban Studies.

ART and DESIGN (General)

(including **Animation, Conservation** and **Restoration**; see also **Combined Courses**)

Art and Design and all specialisms remain one of the most popular subjects. This table provides a list of Art and Design courses that cover a wide range of creative activities. Many of the courses listed in this table cover aspects of fine art, graphic or three dimensional design, but to a less specialised extent than those listed in the other Art and Design tables. Travel and visits to art galleries and museums are strongly recommended by many universities and colleges. Note that for entry to Art and Design courses it is often necessary to follow an Art and Design Foundation course first: check with your chosen institution.

Art and Design degree courses cover a wide range of subjects. These are grouped together in the following six tables:

Art and Design (General)
Art and Design (Fashion and Textiles)
Art and Design (Fine Art)
Art and Design (Graphic Design)
Art and Design (Product and Industrial Design)
Art and Design (Three Dimensional Design)
(**History of Art** and **Photography** are listed in separate tables)

Useful websites www.artscouncil.org.uk; www.designcouncil.org.uk; www.britart.com; www.theatredesign.org.uk; www.worldofinteriors.co.uk; www.artefactantiques.com; www.arts.ac.uk; www.dandad.org; www.csd.org.uk; www.yourcreativefuture.org.uk.

NB The points totals shown to the left of the institutions are for ease of reference only. It must not be assumed that Tariff points are always used by institutions or that they can be substituted for an offer in grades. The level of an offer is not necessarily indicative of the quality of a course.

COURSE OFFERS INFORMATION

Subject requirements/preferences Entry requirements for Art and Design courses vary between institutions and courses (check prospectuses and websites). Most courses require an Art and Design Foundation course. AL grades or points may be required plus five **GCSE** subjects at grades A–C, or a recognised equivalent. A portfolio of work demonstrating potential and visual awareness will also be required. **AL** (Design Technology) Design technology or a physical science may be required or preferred. (Creative Arts courses) Music/art/drama may be required.

NB In 2011 universities and colleges will differ in their use of GCE AL/AS unit grade information, A* grades, the Extended Project (EPQ), the Advanced Diploma and the Cambridge Pre-U examination when considering applicants and making offers. An EPQ may be accepted in place of an AS subject. Check websites of universities and colleges for the latest offers information.

Your target offers and examples of courses provided by each institution

360 pts **Glasgow (SA)** – AAA–ABB (Des (Vis Comm))
340 pts **Bournemouth** – 340 pts (Comp Animat Arts)
Reading – AAB (Art Psy) (IB inc HL 666)
320 pts **Lancaster** – ABB–BCC 320–260 pts (Crea Arts courses) (IB 27–30 pts)
300 pts **Dundee** – BBB 2nd yr entry (Art Des Engl; Art Phil Contemp Prac)
Reading – 300 pts 3AL **or** 320 pts 3AL+AS (Art Phil) (IB inc HL 655)
280 pts **Kent** – 280 pts (Art Film; Vis Perf Arts; Crea Evnts (Des Prod))
Leeds – BBC (Des Col Tech) (IB 30 pts HL art 5–6)
London (Gold) – BBC (Design)
Newman (UC) – 280–320 pts (P Educ Arts (QTS); Art Des Educ)
Reading – 280–300 pts (Art Film Thea)
260 pts **Bath Spa** – 260 pts (Crea Arts; Art)
240 pts **Cumbria** – 240 pts (Contemp App Arts)
De Montfort – 240 pts (Animat Des)
Edinburgh Napier – 240 pts (Crea Ind)
Glamorgan – 240–280 pts (Animation)
Lincoln – 240 pts (Animat; Cons Restor)
Manchester Met – 240 pts (Interact Arts; Illus Animat)
Newport – 240–260 pts (Crea Thera Educ; Animat)
Teesside – 240–280 pts (Des Sust Fut; Decr Arts Inter)
Wolverhampton – 240 pts (App Arts; Animat)
220 pts **Dundee** – CCD 220 pts 1st yr entry (Art Des Engl; Art Phil Contemp Prac)
Falmouth (UC) – 220 pts (Crea Evnts Mgt)
Worcester – 220–260 pts (Art Des; Animat)
200 pts **Bolton** – 200 pts (Art Des; Animat Illus)
Glyndŵr – 200 pts (Des; Animat; App Arts)
Hereford (CA) – 200 pts (Animat; Contemp App Arts; Illus)
Hull – 200–240 pts (Des Dig Media; Dig Arts)
Portsmouth – 200–280 pts (Comp Animat; Animat)
Salford – 200 pts (Des Dig Media; Des Fut; Vis Arts)
Southampton Solent – 200 pts (Animation)
Staffordshire – 200 pts (Animation) (IB 28 pts)
Suffolk (Univ Campus) – 200 pts (Des (Des Cfts))
Swansea Met – 200 pts (Des Adv)
180 pts **Kingston** – 180–220 pts (Des St)
Northampton – 180–220 pts (Crea Des Mark)
Sunderland – 180 pts (Arts Des)
160 pts **Bishop Grosseteste (UC)** – CC (Educ St Art QTS)
Bournemouth Arts (UC) – 160 pts (Arts Evnts Mgt)
Creative Arts – 160–200 pts (App Arts; Animat Arts)
Glasgow (SA) – CC (Vis Comm)
Middlesex – 160 pts (Des Inter App Arts; Animat)
Thames Valley – 160 pts (Dig Animat)
Ulster – 160 pts (Des Vis Comm; Art Des)
Westminster – 160 pts (Illus; Animat)
100 pts **and below or other selection criteria (Foundation course, interview and portfolio inspection)**
Anglia Ruskin; Archit Assoc Sch London; Arts London (Camberwell CA), (Central Saint Martins CAD), (Chelsea CAD), (CFash); Bath Spa; Bedfordshire; Bournemouth Arts (UC); Brighton;

Bristol UWE; Carmarthenshire (Coll); Chester (Coll); Colchester (Inst); Creative Arts; Cumbria; Derby; Doncaster (Coll); Dundee; East London; Edge Hill; Edinburgh (CA); Falmouth (UC); Glamorgan; Gloucestershire; Hull (Coll); Kingston (Illus Animat); Leeds (CAD); Leeds Met; Lincoln; London (Gold); London Met; London South Bank; Loughborough (Vis Comm courses); Manchester City (Coll); Middlesex; NEW (Coll); Newcastle (Coll); Northbrook (Coll); Norwich Arts (UC); Nottingham New (Coll); Nottingham Trent; Portsmouth; Reading (2–3 good A-levels or equiv); Sheffield Hallam; Suffolk (Univ Campus); Swansea Met; Warwickshire (Coll); Westminster.

Central Lancashire – contact University (Contemp Vis Arts)

Alternative offers
See **Chapter 7** and **Appendix 1** for grades/UCAS Tariff points information for the International Baccalaureate, Scottish Highers/Advanced Highers, the Welsh Baccalaureate, the Irish Leaving Certificate, the Cambridge Pre-U Diploma, the Advanced Diploma and the Extended Project.

EXAMPLES OF FOUNDATION DEGREES IN THE SUBJECT FIELD

Arts London (Coll); Blackburn (Coll Univ Centre); Blackpool and Fylde (Coll); Bournemouth; Bournemouth Arts (UC); Brighton; Bristol City (Coll); Burnley (Coll); Cardiff (Coll); Cavendish (Coll); Chesterfield (Coll); Cleveland (CAD); Colchester (Inst); Cornwall (Coll); Creative Arts; Croydon (Coll); Darlington (CT); De Montfort; Derby; Doncaster (Coll); Dunstable (Coll); Glyndŵr; Grimsby (IFHE); Hastings (Coll); Hereford (CA); Hertfordshire; Hopwood Hall (Coll); Huddersfield; Hull (Coll); Hugh Baird (Coll); Huntingdon (Coll); Kirklees (Coll); Leeds (CAD); Leeds Met; Leicester (Coll); London Met; Manchester City (Coll); Mid-Cheshire (Coll); Milton Keynes (Coll); Newcastle (Coll); Newham (Coll); Newport; North West Kent (Coll); Northumberland (Coll); Norwich Arts (UC); Nottingham New (Coll); Oldham (Coll); Plymouth (CAD); Preston (Coll); Ravensbourne (CDC); Richmond (CmC); Runshaw (Coll); St Helens (Coll); Salisbury (Coll); Shrewsbury (CAT); South Devon (Coll); South Nottingham (Coll); South Tyneside (Coll); Southend Campus Essex; Stafford (Coll); Staffordshire (Reg Fed); Sussex Downs (Coll); Tameside (Coll); Thames Valley; Truro (Coll); West Anglia (Coll); West Herts (Coll); West Kent (Coll); Weston (Coll); Weymouth (Coll); Wiltshire (Coll); Winchester; Writtle (Coll); York St John; Yorkshire Coast (CFHE).

CHOOSING YOUR COURSE (SEE ALSO CH.1)

Some course features
Bournemouth Course includes specialist units in art practice, visual studies and aesthetic theory.
Dundee Course includes digital film making, photography, sound design, sonic art, performance, web art and interactive media.
Lancaster Two arts disciplines chosen from art, creative writing, music and theatre studies.
London (Gold) This interdisciplinary course includes contemporary design practice, design and art theory, literature, sociology, philosophy, anthropology and material culture with strong emphasis on studio practice.
Loughborough Graphic communication and illustration are two alternative routes in the Visual Communication course.
Teesside (Decr Arts Inter) Unique studio-based course focussing on decorative interior crafts and surface application working with paint, glass, ceramics, wood, metal and plastics; also includes project management and developing software applications for production processes.

Top research universities and colleges (RAE 2008) Loughborough (Design Technology); Reading (Typographic/Graphic Communication); Lancaster; Newcastle; Westminster; London (UCL); Brighton; Bournemouth; Oxford; Cardiff (UWIC); Newport.

ADMISSIONS INFORMATION

Number of applicants per place (approx) Arts London (Camberwell CA) 2; (Chelsea CAD) 2; Birmingham 20; Birmingham City/Birmingham (IAD) 10; Colchester (Inst) 4; Cumbria 5; Derby 4; Dundee 5; Falmouth (UC) 4; Glamorgan 7; Gloucestershire 8; Leeds (CAD) 5; London (Gold) 10; Manchester Met 10; Newman (UC) 5; Northampton (Crea Des Mark) 5; Norwich Arts (UC) 3;

Nottingham Trent 25; Portsmouth 3; Sheffield Hallam 15; Southampton Solent 1; Sunderland 8; Teesside 2; York St John 3.

Advice to applicants and planning the UCAS personal statement Admissions tutors look for a wide interest in aspects of art and design. Discuss the type of work and the range of media you have explored through your studies to date. Refer to visits to art galleries and museums and give your opinions of the styles of painting and sculpture, both historical and present-day. Mention art-related hobbies. Good drawing skills and sketchbook work, creative and analytical thinking will be needed. See also **Appendix 4**.

Misconceptions about this course **Kent** (Vis Perf Arts) It is not a fine arts course. **Nottingham Trent** School sixth formers are often unaware of the importance of a level zero or Foundation course preceding BA Art and Design courses.

Selection interviews **Yes** Creative Arts, Dundee, Nottingham Trent, Thames Valley, and most courses (see under **Interview advice and questions**); **Some** Staffordshire.

Interview advice and questions All courses require a portfolio inspection. Admissions tutors will want to see both breadth and depth in the applicant's work and evidence of strong self-motivation. They will also be interested to see any sketchbooks or notebooks. However, they do not wish to see similar work over and over again! A logical, ordered presentation helps considerably. Large work, especially three-dimensional work, can be presented by way of photographs. Video or film work should be edited to a running time of no more than 15 minutes. Examples of written work may also be provided. Past questions have included: How often do you visit art galleries and exhibitions? Discuss the last exhibition you visited. What are the reactions of your parents to your choice of course and career? How do they link up with art? Do you feel that modern art has anything to contribute to society compared with earlier art? Is a brick a work of art? Show signs of life – no apathy! Be eager and enthusiastic. **Ulster** Candidates should be able to communicate clearly and through discussion, to show an awareness of current developments, and to convey enthusiasm for their chosen subject. See also **Chapter 5**.

Reasons for rejection (non-academic) Lack of enthusiasm for design issues or to acquire design skills. Poorly presented practical work. Lack of interest or enthusiasm in contemporary visual arts. Lack of knowledge and experience of the art and design industry.

AFTER-RESULTS ADVICE

Offers to applicants repeating A-levels **Possibly higher** Brighton; **Same** Birmingham City/Birmingham (IAD), Canterbury Christ Church, Chester, Colchester (Inst), Dundee, Leeds, Lincoln, Liverpool Hope, Newcastle, Nottingham Trent, Staffordshire, Sunderland, Thames Valley, Wolverhampton, York St John.

GRADUATE DESTINATIONS AND EMPLOYMENT (2007/8 HESA)

Graduates surveyed 8870 **Employed** 4805 **In further study** 495 **Assumed unemployed** 1175.

Career note Many Art and Design courses are linked to specific career paths which are achieved through freelance consultancy work or studio work. Some enter teaching and many find other areas such as retail and management fields. Opportunities for fashion and graphic design specialists exceed those of the other areas of art and design. Opportunities in industrial and product design and 3D design are likely to be limited and dependent on the contacts that students establish during their degree courses. Only a very limited number of students committed to painting and sculpture can expect to succeed without seeking alternative employment.

OTHER DEGREE SUBJECTS FOR CONSIDERATION

Animation; Architecture; Art Gallery Management; Communication Studies; Computer Studies; Education; Film Studies; History of Art; Media Studies; Photography; see other **Art and Design** tables.

ART and DESIGN (Fashion and Textiles)

(including **Surface Design**)

Fashion Design courses involve drawing and design, research, pattern cutting and garment construction for clothing for men, women and children. Courses may also cover design for textiles, commercial production and marketing. Some institutions have particularly good contacts with industry and are able to arrange sponsorships for students.

Useful websites www.fashion.net; www.londonfashionweek.co.uk; www.texi.org; www.yourcreativefuture.org.uk.

NB The points totals shown to the left of the institutions are for ease of reference only. It must not be assumed that Tariff points are always used by institutions or that they can be substituted for an offer in grades. The level of an offer is not necessarily indicative of the quality of a course.

COURSE OFFERS INFORMATION

Subject requirements/preferences **AL** Textiles or textile science and technology may be required.

NB In 2011 universities and colleges will differ in their use of GCE AL/AS unit grade information, A* grades, the Extended Project (EPQ), the Advanced Diploma and the Cambridge Pre-U examination when considering applicants and making offers. An EPQ may be accepted in place of an AS subject. Check websites of universities and colleges for the latest offers information.

Your target offers and examples of courses provided by each institution

360 pts **Glasgow (SA)** – AAA–AAB (Fash Des; Tex Fash)

320 pts **Manchester** – ABB–ABC (Tex Des Des Mgt; Fash Tex Rtl; Tex Sci Tech; Tex Tech (Bus Mgt)) (IB 34–33 pts)

Southampton/Winchester (SA) – ABB (Fash Tex Des; Fash Mark) (IB 32 pts)
300 pts **Leeds** – BBB–BBC (Fash Des; Tex Des) (IB 30 pts)
Nottingham Trent – 300 pts (Fash Comm Prom; Fash Mark Brnd)
280 pts **Birmingham City/Birmingham (IAD)** – 280 pts (Fash Des courses; Fash Rtl Mgt)
London (Central Sch SpDr) – BBC 280 pts (Thea Prac (Cstm Constr))
Manchester Met – 280 pts (Fash Buy; Int Fash Mark)
Northumbria – 280 pts (Fash; Fash Mark)
Nottingham Trent – 280 pts (Fash Des)
Westminster – BBC 280 pts (Fash Merch Mgt)
260 pts **Brighton** – BCC (Fash Drs Hist)
Huddersfield – 260 pts (Fash Des Mark Prod; Fash Des Tex; Fash Tex Buy; Fash Tex Mgt)
Sheffield Hallam – 260 pts (Fash Des)
240 pts **Coventry** – 240 pts (Fash; Fash Accs)
De Montfort – 240 pts (Fash Cont Des; Rtl Buy (Fash) (Tex); Fash Des; Fash Tech; Tex Des courses; Fash Fabs Accs)
Glamorgan – 240–280 pts (Fash Des; Fash Prom; Cstm Constr Stg Scrn)
Glasgow Caledonian – CCC (Fash Mark)
Hertfordshire – 240 pts (Fashion)
Lincoln – 240 pts (Fash St)
Manchester Met – 240 pts (Fash; Tex Des Fash; Cloth Des Tech; Embr; Tex)
Newport – 240–260 pts (Fash Des)
Nottingham Trent – 240–280 pts (Fash Tex Mgt; Fash Des; Fash Knit Des Knit Tex; Tex Des)
Southampton Solent – 240 pts (Writ Fash Cult)
Wolverhampton – 240 pts (Fash Accs; Tex Des)
230 pts **Queen Margaret** – 230 pts (Cstm Des Constr)
220 pts **Anglia Ruskin** – 220 pts (Fash Des)
Bath Spa – 220–260 pts (Tex Des St)
Glasgow Caledonian – CCD (Fash Bus)
Heriot-Watt – CCD (Fash Comm; Fash Wmnswr; Fash Mnswr; Fash Tech; Fash)
Northampton – 220–260 pts (Fash; Fash (Ftwr Accs) (Tex Fash) (Fash Mark); Sfc Des; Prntd Tex)
200 pts **Bolton** – 200 pts (Tex Sfc Des)
Creative Arts – 200 pts (Fash Atel; Fash Jrnl; Tex Fash Int; Fash Prom Imag)
Hereford (CA) – 200 pts (Tex Des)
Portsmouth – 200–280 pts (Fash Tex Des Ent)
Salford – 200 pts (Fashion) (IB 26 pts)
Staffordshire – 200 pts (Tex Sfc; Sfc Pattn Des)
Swansea Met – 200–340 pts (Sfc Pattn (Tex Fash) (Tex Inter))
180 pts **Derby** – 180–240 pts (Tex Des; Fash St)
Dundee – 180 pts (Tex Des)
160 pts **Bournemouth Arts (UC)** – 160 pts (Fash St)
Cardiff (UWIC) – 160 pts (Fash Inter Art Tex)
Central Lancashire – 160–200 pts (Dig Des Fash; E Fash Des; Fash Prom Styl; Fash Brnd Mgt)
East London – 160 pts (Prtd Tex Des)
Leeds Met – 160 pts (Des App Tex)
Robert Gordon – 160–180 pts (Tex Sfc Des; Fash Des; Fash Mgt)
South Essex (Coll) – 160 pts (Fash Des)
Southampton Solent – 160 pts (Fash Graph; Fash PR)
Thames Valley – 160 pts (Fash Tex)
UHI Millennium Inst – CC (Contemp Tex)
Ulster – 160 pts (Tex Fash Des)
120 pts **Basingstoke (CT)** – 120 pts (Tex Fash)
Bradford (Coll) – 120 pts (Fash Des)
Cleveland (CAD) – 120–100 pts (Tex Sfc Des)

Northbrook (Coll) – 120 pts (Fash Des; Fash Media Prom; Tex Des)
Stockport (CFHE) – 120–240 pts (Des Vis Arts (Sfc Des))

100 pts and below or other selection criteria (Foundation course, interview and portfolio inspection)

Arts London (Central Saint Martins CAD), (CFash), (Wimbledon CA); Bath Spa; Bournemouth; Birmingham City (Tex Des courses); Birmingham City (Coll); Brighton; Bristol UWE; Bucks New; Carmarthenshire (Coll); Chesterfield (Coll); Colchester (Inst); Coventry; Croydon (Coll); Doncaster (Coll); Dudley (Coll); East London; Edinburgh (CA); Falmouth (UC); Glamorgan; Great Yarmouth (Coll); Havering (Coll); Kingston; Leeds (CAD); Leeds Met; Leicester (Coll); Lincoln; Liverpool John Moores; Loughborough; Manchester (Coll); Menai (Col); Mid-Cheshire (Coll); Middlesex; NEW (Coll); Newcastle (Coll); Northampton; Nottingham New (Coll); Plymouth; Ravensbourne (CDC); Robert Gordon; Somerset (Coll); Southampton/Winchester (SA); Staffordshire (Reg Fed); Thames Valley; West Anglia (Coll); Westminster; York (Coll); Yorkshire Coast (CFHE).

Loughborough – Pre-degree course preferred prior to entry but direct entry applicants with A-levels considered (Tex (Multim Tex) (Prntd Tex) (Wvn Tex))

Alternative offers
See **Chapter 7** and **Appendix 1** for grades/UCAS Tariff points information for the International Baccalaureate, Scottish Highers/Advanced Highers, the Welsh Baccalaureate, the Irish Leaving Certificate, the Cambridge Pre-U Diploma, the Advanced Diploma and the Extended Project.

EXAMPLES OF FOUNDATION DEGREES IN THE SUBJECT FIELD

Arts London (CFash); Barnfield (Coll); Bath City (Coll); Bath Spa; Bedfordshire; Blackburn (Coll Univ Centre), Bournemouth Arts (UC); Brighton; Bristol UWE; Chesterfield (Coll); Cleveland (CAD); Colchester (Inst); Cornwall (Coll); Creative Arts; Croydon (Coll); Derby; Exeter (Coll); Hereford (CT); Hertfordshire; Hull (Coll); Kent; Kirklees (Coll); Leeds Met; Leicester (Coll); Liverpool (CmC); Llandrillo (Coll); London Met; Manchester (Coll); Mid-Cheshire (Coll); Newcastle (Coll); Newport; Nottingham New (Coll); Plymouth (Coll); Sheffield (Coll); South Essex (Coll); Suffolk (Univ Campus); West Anglia (Coll).

CHOOSING YOUR COURSE (SEE ALSO CH.1)

Some course features
Universities and colleges offer a very wide range of specialist and individual subjects. In each case programmes will differ, often depending on the specialist interests of teaching staff. When considering specialist courses, eg Fashion Retail Management, Fashion Embroidery, Fashion Journalism choose only named courses since a number of institutions claim to offer these subjects but only as a minor study.

Universities and colleges teaching quality See www.qaa.ac.uk; www.unistats.com.

Top research universities and colleges (RAE 2008) See **Art and Design (General)**.

Examples of sandwich degree courses Brighton; Central Lancashire; De Montfort; Glasgow Caledonian; Huddersfield; Leeds; Manchester Met; Northumbria; Nottingham Trent; Southampton Solent; Westminster.

ADMISSIONS INFORMATION

Number of applicants per place (approx) Arts London (Central Saint Martins CAD) 5, (CFash) (Fash Mgt) 20; Birmingham City/Birmingham (IAD) (Tex Des) 4; Bournemouth Arts (UC) 6; Brighton 6; Bristol UWE 4; Central Lancashire 4; Creative Arts 8; De Montfort 5; Derby (Tex Des) 2; Heriot-Watt 6; Huddersfield 4; Kingston 5; Leeds (CAD) 4; Liverpool John Moores 6; London (Gold) 5; Loughborough 5; Manchester Met 3; Middlesex 5; Northampton 4; Northumbria 8; Nottingham Trent 8, (Tex Des) 3; Southampton/Winchester (SA) 3; Southend Campus Essex 2; Staffordshire 3; Wolverhampton 2.

Advice to applicants and planning the UCAS personal statement A well-written legible statement is sought, clearly stating an interest in fashion and how prior education and work experience relate to your application. You should describe any visits to exhibitions, and importantly, your views and opinions. Describe any work you have done ('making' and 'doing' skills, if any, for example, pattern cutting, sewing) or work observation in textile firms, fashion houses, even visits to costume departments in theatres can be useful. These contacts and visits should be described in detail, showing your knowledge of the types of fabrics and production processes. Give opinions on trends in haute couture, and show awareness of the work of others. Provide evidence of materials handling (see also **Appendix 4**). Show good knowledge of the contemporary fashion scene. See also **Art and Design (Graphic Design)**.

Misconceptions about this course Some students expect the Fashion degree to include textiles; (Tex) Some applicants feel that it's necessary to have experience in textiles – this is not the case. The qualities sought in the portfolio are analytical drawing, good colour sense and a sensitivity to materials.

Selection interviews Most institutions interview and require a portfolio of work. You should be familiar with current fashion trends and the work of leading designers.

Interview advice and questions Questions mostly originate from student's portfolio. **Birmingham City/Birmingham (IAD)** (Tex Des) What do you expect to achieve from a degree in Fashion? **Creative Arts** Describe in detail a specific item in your portfolio and why it was selected. See also **Art and Design (General)** and **Chapter 5**.

Reasons for rejection (non-academic) Portfolio work not up to standard. Not enough research. Not articulate at interview. Lack of sense of humour and inflexibility. Narrow perspective. Lack of resourcefulness, self-motivation and organisation. Complacency, lack of verbal, written and self-presentation skills. Not enough experience in designing or making clothes. See also **Art and Design (General)**.

AFTER-RESULTS ADVICE

Offers to applicants repeating A-levels **Same** Birmingham City/Birmingham (IAD), Bournemouth Arts (UC), Creative Arts, Huddersfield, Manchester Met, Nottingham Trent, South Essex (Coll), Staffordshire.

GRADUATE DESTINATIONS AND EMPLOYMENT (2007/8 HESA)

See **Art and Design (General)**.

Career note See **Art and Design (General)**.

OTHER DEGREE SUBJECTS FOR CONSIDERATION

History of Art; Retail Management; Theatre Design.

ART and DESIGN (Fine Art)

(including **Printing, Printmaking** and **Sculpture**)

Fine Art courses can involve a range of activities such as painting, illustration and sculpture and often fine art media – electronic media, film, video, photography and print – although course options will vary between institutions. As in the case of most Art degrees, admission to courses usually requires a one-year Foundation Art course before applying.

Useful websites www.artcyclopedia.com; www.fine-art.com; www.nationalgallery.org.uk; www.britisharts.co.uk; www.tate.org.uk; www.yourcreativefuture.org.uk.

NB The points totals shown to the left of the institutions are for ease of reference only. It must not be assumed that Tariff points are always used by institutions or that they can be substituted for an offer in grades. The level of an offer is not necessarily indicative of the quality of a course.

COURSE OFFERS INFORMATION

Subject requirements/preferences See **Art and Design (General)** **Course offers information**.

NB In 2011 universities and colleges will differ in their use of GCE AL/AS unit grade information, A* grades, the Extended Project (EPQ), the Advanced Diploma and the Cambridge Pre-U examination when considering applicants and making offers. An EPQ may be accepted in place of an AS subject. Check websites of universities and colleges for the latest offers information.

Your target offers and examples of courses provided by each institution

360 pts **Glasgow (SA)** – AAA–AAB (Fine Art (Env Art Sculp) (Pntg/Prtg) (Photo))
Oxford – AAA (Fine Art) (IB 38–40 pts)

320 pts **London (UCL/Slade CA)** – BBBe (Fine Art) (IB 34 pts)
Southampton – ABB (Fine Art)

300 pts **Dundee** – BBB 300 pts 2nd yr entry (Art Phil Contemp Prac)
Edinburgh/Edinburgh (CA) – BBB min /AAA (Fine Art) (IB 34 pts)
Leeds – BBB (Fine Art) (IB 32 pts)
Newcastle – BBB–BCC (Fine Art) (IB 28–30 pts HL 555+)

280 pts **Birmingham City/Birmingham (IAD)** – 280 pts (Fine Art)
Kent – 280 pts inc BC (Fine Art)
Reading – 280–300 pts (Art Hist Art Archit)

260 pts **Bolton** – 260 pts (Fine Arts Psy)
Gloucestershire – 260 pts (Fine Art; Fine Art Pntg Drg; Fine Art Photo)
Lancaster – BCC 260 pts (Fine Art) (IB 27 pts)
Liverpool Hope – 260 pts (Fine Art)
Northumbria – 260 pts (Fine Art)

240 pts **Aberystwyth** – 240 pts (Fine Art courses) (IB 29 pts)
Chichester – BCD (Fine Art courses) (IB 28 pts)
Coventry – 240 pts (Fine Art)
Cumbria – 240 pts (Fine Art)
De Montfort – 240 pts (Fine Art)
Hertfordshire – 240 pts (Fine Art)
Huddersfield – 240–300 pts (Fine Art courses)
Lincoln – 240 pts (Fine Art)
London Met – 240 pts (Fine Art courses)
Newport – 240–260 pts (Fine Art)
Nottingham Trent – 240 pts (Fine Art)
Plymouth – 240 pts (Fine Art; Fine Art Art Hist)
Sheffield Hallam – 240 pts (Contemp Fine Art)
Wolverhampton – 240 pts (Fine Art (Photo))
York St John – 240–220 pts (Fine Art courses)

220 pts **Anglia Ruskin** – 220 pts (Fine Art)
Blackburn (Coll Univ Centre) – CCD (Fine Art (Integ Media))
Chester – 220–260 pts (Fine Art) (IB 24 pts)
Dundee – CCD 220 pts 1st yr entry (Art Phil Contemp Prac)
Falmouth (UC) – 220 pts (Fine Art)
Northampton – 220 pts (Fine Art; Fine Art Pntg Drg)
Oxford Brookes – CCD (Fine Art)
Teesside – 220–260 pts (Fine Art)
Worcester – 220–260 pts (Fine Art Prac)

205 pts **Reading** – 205 pts (Fine Art)

200 pts **Bolton** – 200 pts (Fine Arts)
Canterbury Christ Church – 200 pts (Fine App Arts)
Glyndŵr – 200 pts (Fine Art)
Hereford (CA) – 200 pts (Fine Art)
Middlesex – 200–240 pts (Fine Art; Crit Theor)
Portsmouth – 200–280 pts (Fine Art)
Southampton Solent – 200 pts (Fine Art)

Suffolk (Univ Campus) – 200 pts (Fine Art)
Swansea Met – 200 pts (Fine Art (Comb Media) (Pntg Drg) (Ceram))
180 pts **Derby** – 180–240 pts (Fine Art)
Stamford New (Coll) – 180 pts (Fine Art)
165 pts **Staffordshire** – 165–200 pts (Fine Art joint courses) (IB 28 pts)
160 pts **Blackpool and Fylde (Coll)** – 160 pts (Fine Art Prof Prac)
Bournemouth Arts (UC) – 160 pts (Fine Art)
Colchester (Inst) – 160 pts (Art Des (Fine Art))
Creative Arts – 160 pts (Fine Art courses)
Grimsby (IFHE) – 160 pts (Fine App Arts)
Kingston – 160 pts (Fine Art)
Robert Gordon – 160–180 pts (Pntg; Prtg; Sculp)
South Essex (Coll) – 160 pts (Fine Art)
Suffolk (Univ Campus) – 160 pts (Fine Art Prac)
Swindon (Coll) – 160–200 pts (Fine Art)
Ulster – 160 pts (Fine App Arts)
Yorkshire Coast (CFHE) – 160 pts (Fine Art)
140 pts **Sunderland** – 140 pts (Fine Art)
100 pts **and below or other selection criteria (Foundation course, interview and portfolio inspection)**

Arts London (Camberwell CA), (Central Saint Martins CAD), (Chelsea CAD), (Wimbledon CA); Barking (Coll); Bath Spa (80–160 pts); Bedfordshire; Bradford (Coll); Brighton; Bristol UWE; Bucks New; Cardiff (UWIC); Carmarthenshire (Coll)/Sir Gâr (Col); Central Lancashire; Colchester (Inst); Cornwall (Coll); Coventry; Creative Arts; Croydon (Coll); De Montfort; Doncaster (Coll); East London; Edinburgh (CA); Glamorgan; Glyndŵr; Havering (Coll); Hopwood Hall (Coll); Kingston (+ A-levels); Kirklees (Coll); Leeds (CAD); Leeds Met; Liverpool John Moores; Liverpool (CmC); London (Gold); Loughborough (A-level entry applicants considered but pre-degree course qualifications preferred); Manchester Met; Middlesex; NEW (Coll); North Warwickshire (Coll); Northbrook (Coll); Norwich Arts (UC); Nottingham (p/t only); Reading; St Helens (Coll); Salford; Sheffield (Coll); Solihull (Coll); South Essex (Coll); South Nottingham (Coll); Southport (Coll); Staffordshire (Reg Fed); Stourbridge (Coll); Stranmillis (UC); Suffolk (Univ Campus); Swansea Met; Swindon (Coll); Thames Valley; Trinity Saint David; Tyne Met (Coll); UHI Millennium Inst (MC); Walsall (Coll); Warwickshire (Coll); West Anglia (Coll); West Thames (Coll); Westminster; Wimbledon (CA); Wirral Met (Coll).

Brighton – offers may vary (Crit Fine Art Prac)

Alternative offers
See **Chapter 7** and **Appendix 1** for grades/UCAS Tariff points information for the International Baccalaureate, Scottish Highers/Advanced Highers, the Welsh Baccalaureate, the Irish Leaving Certificate, the Cambridge Pre-U Diploma, the Advanced Diploma and the Extended Project.

EXAMPLES OF FOUNDATION DEGREES IN THE SUBJECT FIELD

Arts London (Central Saint Martins CAD); Bath Spa; Bedfordshire; Blackpool and Fylde (Coll); Brighton; Bristol UWE; Cornwall (Coll); Creative Arts; De Montfort; Dunstable (Coll); Exeter (Coll); Glyndŵr; Greenwich; Hereford (CA); Huddersfield; Leeds Met; Leicester (Coll); Liverpool (CmC); Llandrillo (Coll); Newcastle (Coll); Plymouth; Plymouth (CAD); Sheffield (Coll); Somerset (CAT); South Tyneside (Coll); Southport (Coll); Suffolk (Univ Campus); Sunderland; Sunderland City (Coll); Thames Valley; Tyne Met (Coll).

CHOOSING YOUR COURSE (SEE ALSO CH.1)

Some course features
All are practical workshop courses.

Universities and colleges teaching quality See www.qaa.ac.uk; www.unistats.com.

Top research universities and colleges (RAE 2008) See **Art and Design (General)**.

ADMISSIONS INFORMATION

Number of applicants per place (approx) Arts London (Chelsea CAD) 5, (Wimbledon CA) (Sculp) 3; Bath Spa 8; Birmingham City/Birmingham (IAD) 6; Bournemouth Arts (UC) 6; Bristol UWE 3; Cardiff (UWIC) 3; Central Lancashire 4; Cleveland (CAD) 2; Creative Arts 2; Cumbria 4; De Montfort 5; Derby 3; Dundee 5; Gloucestershire 5; Hertfordshire 6; Hull (Scarborough) 2; Kingston 9; Lincoln 4; Liverpool John Moores 3; London (Gold) 10, (UCL/Slade SA) 26; London Met 11; Loughborough 4; Manchester Met 4; Middlesex 3; Newcastle 30; Northampton 3; Northumbria 4; Norwich Arts (UC) 3; Nottingham Trent 5; Portsmouth 6; Robert Gordon 5; Sheffield Hallam 4; Solihull (Coll) 4; Southampton 3; Staffordshire 3; Sunderland 3; UHI Millennium Inst (MC) 2; Wirral Met (Coll) 3.

Advice to applicants and planning the UCAS personal statement Since this is a subject area that can be researched easily in art galleries, you should discuss not only your own style of work and your preferred subjects but also your opinions on various art forms, styles and periods. Keep up-to-date with public opinion on controversial issues. Give your reasons for wishing to pursue a course in Fine Art. Visits to galleries and related hobbies, for example reading, cinema, music, literature should be mentioned. Show the nature of your external involvement in art. **Oxford** No deferred applications are accepted for this course; successful applicants average 11.5%. (See also **Appendix 4**.)

Misconceptions about this course That Fine Art is simply art and design. Sixth form applicants are often unaware of the importance of a Foundation Art course before starting a degree programme. **Bournemouth Arts (UC)** Applicants need to make the distinction between fine art and illustration.

Selection interviews Most institutions interview and require a portfolio of work. **Arts London (Chelsea CAD)** Interviews with portfolios and essays. **Oxford** Portfolio to be submitted by 15th November. Drawing examination taken by all interviewed candidates (two drawings in pencil or pen and ink).

Interview advice and questions Questions asked on portfolio of work. Be prepared to answer questions on your stated opinions on your UCAS application and on current art trends and controversial topics reported in the press. Discussion covering the applicant's engagement with contemporary fine art practice. Visits to exhibitions, galleries etc. Ambitions for their own work. How do you perceive the world in a visual sense? Who is your favourite living artist and why? **UHI Millennium Inst (MC)** Applicants are asked to produce a drawing in response to a set topic. See also **Art and Design (General)** and **Chapter 5**.

Reasons for rejection (non-academic) Lack of a fine art specialist portfolio. No intellectual grasp of the subject – only interested in techniques.

AFTER-RESULTS ADVICE

Offers to applicants repeating A-levels **Same** Anglia Ruskin, Arts London (Central Saint Martins CAD), Birmingham City/Birmingham (IAD), Cumbria, Manchester Met, Nottingham Trent, Staffordshire, Sunderland, UHI Millennium Inst (MC).

GRADUATE DESTINATIONS AND EMPLOYMENT (2007/8 HESA)

Graduates surveyed 2725 **Employed** 1010 **In further study** 355 **Assumed unemployed** 315.

Career note See **Art and Design (General)**.

OTHER DEGREE SUBJECTS FOR CONSIDERATION

Art Gallery Management; History of Art; see other **Art and Design** tables.

ART and DESIGN (Graphic Design)

(including **Advertising, Design, Graphic Communication, Illustration** and **Visual Communication**; see also **Art and Design (General), (Fine Art)** and **Film, Radio, Video and TV Studies**)

Graphic Design ranges from the design of websites, books, magazines and newspapers to packaging and advertisements. Visual communication uses symbols as teaching aids and also includes TV graphics. An Art Foundation course is usually taken before entry to degree courses.

Useful websites www.graphicdesign.about.com; www.graphic-design.com; www.allgraphicdesign.com; www.yourcreativefuture.org.uk.

NB The points totals shown to the left of the institutions are for ease of reference only. It must not be assumed that Tariff points are always used by institutions or that they can be substituted for an offer in grades. The level of an offer is not necessarily indicative of the quality of a course.

COURSE OFFERS INFORMATION

Subject requirements/preferences See **Art and Design (General)** **Course offers information**.

NB In 2011 universities and colleges will differ in their use of GCE AL/AS unit grade information, A* grades, the Extended Project (EPQ), the Advanced Diploma and the Cambridge Pre-U examination when considering applicants and making offers. An EPQ may be accepted in place of an AS subject. Check websites of universities and colleges for the latest offers information.

Your target offers and examples of courses provided by each institution

360 pts **Glasgow (SA)** – AAA–ABB (Vis Comm)
320 pts **Southampton** – ABB (Graph Arts) (IB 32 pts)
300 pts **Leeds** – BBB (Graph Comm Des; NMedia) (IB 32 pts)
Reading – 300–330 pts (Graph Comm)
280 pts **Birmingham City** – 280 pts (Vis Comm (Graph Des) (Illus) (Photo) (Mov Imag))
Northumbria – 280 pts (Graph Des)
Nottingham Trent – 280 pts (Graph Des)
260 pts **Gloucestershire** – 260 pts (Adv; Graph Des)
Sheffield Hallam – 260 pts (Graph Des courses)
240 pts **Coventry** – 240 pts (Graph Des; Illus Animat; Illus Graph)
Cumbria – 240 pts (Graph Des)
De Montfort – 240 pts (Graph Des; Graph Des Illus; Graph Des Photo; Graph Des Interact Media)
Edinburgh Napier – 240 pts (Graph Des)
Glamorgan – 240–280 pts (Graph Comm)
Hertfordshire – 240 pts (Graph Des Illus)
Huddersfield – 240 pts (Crea Imag (Graph Des) (Adv) (Illus))
Lincoln – 240 pts (Graph Des; Graph Des Illus; Graph Des Contemp Lns Media)
London Met – 240 pts (Graph Des)
Manchester Met – 240 pts (Illus Animat)
Newport – 240–260 pts (Graph Des; Adv Des)
Plymouth – 240 pts (Des (Graph Comm Typo))
Salford – 240 pts (Graph Des)
Teesside – 240–280 pts (Graph Des (Adv) (Illus) (Multim Web Pub))
Wolverhampton – 240 pts (Graph Comm; Graph Comm Illus)
230 pts **Greenwich** – 230 pts (Graph Dig Des)
220 pts **Anglia Ruskin** – 220 pts (Graph Des; Illus Animat; Graph Web Des)
Chester (Warrington) – 220–260 pts (Graph Des courses) (IB 24 pts)
Northampton – 220–260 pts (Graph Comm; Illus)
Teesside – 220–260 pts (Graph Arts (Mtn Graph))
200 pts **Glyndŵr** – 200 pts (Des (Graph Des); Illus; Illus Graph NVls; Illus Child Pub Dig Art)
Hereford (CA) – 200 pts (Illus; Graph Media Des)
Hull (Coll) – 200 pts (Graph Des; Illus)
Portsmouth – 200–280 pts (Illus; Graph Des)
Salford – 200 pts (Adv Des)
Staffordshire – 200 pts (Graph Des)

Suffolk (Univ Campus) – 200 pts (Graph Des; Graph Des Graph Illus; Graph Des Mtn Graph)
Swansea Met – 200 pts (Graph Des; Illus)
Westminster – BB (Graph Inf Des)

180 pts **Derby** – 180–240 pts (Vis Comm (Graph Des))
Dundee – 180 pts (Graph Des) (IB 24 pts)
Stamford New (Coll) – 180 pts (Graph Des)

160 pts **Bedfordshire** – 160 pts (Graph Des; Adv Des)
Blackpool and Fylde (Coll) – 160 pts (Graph Des; Inf Illus; Sci Nat Hist Illus)
Bournemouth Arts (UC) – 160 pts (Graph Des; Illus)
Colchester (Inst) – 160 pts (Art Des (Graph Media))
Creative Arts – 160 pts (Graph Des; Graph Comm; Adv Brnd Comm)
East London – 160 pts (Graph Des; Illus)
Glasgow (SA) – 160 pts (Vis Comm)
Middlesex – 160 pts offers may vary (Graph Des; Illus)
Robert Gordon – 160–180 pts (Graph Des) (IB 24 pts)
South Essex (Coll) – 160–180 pts (Graph Des)
Southampton Solent – 160 pts (Graph Des)
Sunderland – 160 pts (Graph Comm Des; Illus Des)
Swindon (Coll) – 160–200 pts (Graph Des; Illus)
Ulster – 160 pts (Des Vis Comm)

120 pts **Bradford (Coll)** – 120 pts (Graph Des Illus Dig Media)
Northbrook (Coll) – 120 pts (Comm Des)

100 pts **and below or other selection criteria (Foundation course, interview and portfolio inspection)**

Anglia Ruskin; Arts London; Bath Spa; Blackburn (Coll Univ Centre); Bradford; Bristol UWE; Bristol City (Coll); Bucks New; Cardiff (UWIC); Carmarthenshire (Coll); Central Lancashire; Colchester (Inst); Coventry; Croydon (Coll); Cumbria; Doncaster (Coll); Edinburgh (CA); Falmouth (UC); Gloucestershire (Coll); Greenwich; Grimsby (IFHE); Havering (Coll); Hertfordshire; Hopwood Hall (Coll); Kent; Kingston; Leeds (CAD); Leeds Met; Liverpool John Moores; Llandrillo (Coll); Manchester (Coll); Mid-Cheshire (Coll); NEW (Coll); Northbrook (Coll); Norwich Arts (UC); Plymouth (CAD); Ravensbourne (CDC); Rotherham (CAT); St Helens (Coll); Solihull (Coll); Somerset (CAT); South Essex (Coll); South Nottingham (Coll); Southampton/Winchester (SA); Southwark (Coll); Stockport (Coll); Suffolk (Univ Campus); Swansea Met; Thames Valley; Tyne Met (Coll); Warwickshire (Coll); West Anglia (Coll); West Thames (Coll); Westminster; Wigan and Leigh (Coll); Wiltshire (Coll); Worcester; Yorkshire Coast (CFHE).

Brighton – offers vary; AL entrants usually need Art Foundation diploma (Graph Des Illus)
Loughborough – A-level entry students considered but the University prefers applicants to complete a relevant pre-degree course first (Vis Comm (Graph Comm))

Alternative offers

See **Chapter 7** and **Appendix 1** for grades/UCAS Tariff points information for the International Baccalaureate, Scottish Highers/Advanced Highers, the Welsh Baccalaureate, the Irish Leaving Certificate, the Cambridge Pre-U Diploma, the Advanced Diploma and the Extended Project.

EXAMPLES OF FOUNDATION DEGREES IN THE SUBJECT FIELD

Arts London; Bath Spa; Bedfordshire; Bournemouth; Brighton; Bristol City (Coll); Bucks New; Cardiff (UWIC); Chichester; Cleveland (CAD); Cornwall (Coll); Creative Arts; Cumbria; Durham New (Coll); Exeter (Coll); Greenwich; Hereford (CA); Hertfordshire; Kingston; Kirklees (Coll); Leeds (CAD); Llandrillo (Coll); Mid-Cheshire (Coll); Middlesex; Newcastle (Coll); Norwich Arts (UC); Plymouth (CAD); Rotherham (CAT); St Helens (Coll); Sheffield (Coll); Somerset (CAT); South Tyneside (Coll); Southwark (Coll); Staffordshire (Reg Fed); Suffolk (Univ Campus).

CHOOSING YOUR COURSE (SEE ALSO CH.1)

Some course features

These courses offer a wide range of specialisms; check the course contents before selecting.

Universities and colleges teaching quality See www.qaa.ac.uk; www.unistats.com.

Top research universities and colleges (RAE 2008) See **Art and Design (General)**.

Examples of sandwich degree courses Aberystwyth; Arts London; Huddersfield; Kingston; Northumbria; Sheffield Hallam; Staffordshire; Teesside.

ADMISSIONS INFORMATION

Number of applicants per place (approx) Anglia Ruskin (Illus) 3; Arts London (Central Saint Martins CAD) 4; Bath Spa 9; Blackburn (Coll Univ Centre) 2; Bournemouth Arts (UC) 6; Bristol UWE 4; Cardiff (UWIC) 5; Central Lancashire 5; Colchester (Inst) 3; Coventry 6; Creative Arts 5; Derby 5; Edinburgh Napier 7; Glamorgan 3; Hertfordshire 6; Kingston 8; Lincoln 5; Liverpool John Moores 7; Loughborough 5; Manchester Met 8; Middlesex 3; Northampton 3; Northumbria 8; Norwich Arts (UC) 4; Nottingham Trent 6; Ravensbourne (CDC) 9; Solihull (Coll) 3; South Essex (Coll) 2; Southampton 6; Staffordshire 3; Swansea Met 10; Teesside 5; Wolverhampton 5.

Advice to applicants and planning the UCAS personal statement Discuss your special interest in this field and any commercial applications that have impressed you. Discuss the work you are enjoying at present and the range of media that you have explored. Show your interests in travel, architecture, the arts, literature, film, current affairs (see also **Appendix 4** for contact details of relevant professional associations). Awareness of the place of design in society.

Misconceptions about this course **Bath Spa** Some students think that they can start the course from A-levels, that a course in Illustration is simply 'doing small drawings' and that Graphic Design is a soft option with little academic work.

Selection interviews All institutions interview and require a portfolio of work.

Interview advice and questions Questions may be asked on recent trends in graphic design from the points of view of methods and designers and, particularly, art and the computer. Questions usually are asked on applicant's portfolio of work. **Nottingham Trent** Why Graphic Design? Why this course? Describe a piece of graphic design which has succeeded. See also **Art and Design (General)** and **Chapter 5**.

Reasons for rejection (non-academic) Not enough work in portfolio. Inability to think imaginatively. Lack of interest in the arts in general. Lack of drive. Tutor's statement indicating problems. Poorly constructed personal statement. Inability to talk about your work. Lack of knowledge about the chosen course. See also **Art and Design (General)**.

AFTER-RESULTS ADVICE

Offers to applicants repeating A-levels **Same** Bath Spa, Bournemouth Arts (UC), Blackpool and Fylde (Coll), Cardiff (UWIC), Creative Arts, Lincoln, Manchester Met, Nottingham Trent, Salford, South Essex (Coll), Staffordshire.

GRADUATE DESTINATIONS AND EMPLOYMENT (2007/8 HESA)

See **Art and Design (General)**.

Career note Graphic Design students are probably the most fortunate in terms of the range of career opportunities open to them on graduation. These include advertising, book and magazine illustration, film, interactive media design, typography, packaging, photography and work in publishing and television. See also **Art and Design (General)**.

OTHER DEGREE SUBJECTS FOR CONSIDERATION

Art Gallery Management; Film and Video Production; History of Art; Multimedia Design, Photography and Digital Imaging. See also other **Art and Design** tables.

ART and DESIGN (Product and Industrial Design)

(including **Design Technology, Footwear Design, Furniture Design, Interior Architecture, Interior Design, Product Design, Theatre Design** and **Transport Design**; see also **Art and Design (3D Design)**)

The field of industrial design is extensive and degree studies are usually preceded by an Art Foundation course. Product Design is one of the most common courses in which technological studies (involving materials and methods of production) are integrated with creative design in the production of a range of household and industrial products. Other courses on offer include Furniture Design, Interior, Theatre, Museum and Exhibition, Automotive and Transport Design. It should be noted that some Product Design courses have an engineering bias: see **Subject requirements/preferences** below.

These are stimulating courses but graduate opportunities in this field are very limited. Good courses will have good industrial contacts for sandwich courses or shorter work placements – check with course leaders (or students) before applying.

Useful websites www.ergonomics.org.uk; www.yourcreativefuture.org.uk; wwwproductdesignforums.com; www.carbodydesign.com; www.shoe-design.com.

NB The points totals shown to the left of the institutions are for ease of reference only. It must not be assumed that Tariff points are always used by institutions or that they can be substituted for an offer in grades. The level of an offer is not necessarily indicative of the quality of a course.

COURSE OFFERS INFORMATION

Subject requirements/preferences AL Check Product Design, Industrial Design and Engineering Design course requirements since these will often require mathematics and/or physics.

NB In 2011 universities and colleges will differ in their use of GCE AL/AS unit grade information, A* grades, the Extended Project (EPQ), the Advanced Diploma and the Cambridge Pre-U examination when considering applicants and making offers. An EPQ may be accepted in place of an AS subject. Check websites of universities and colleges for the latest offers information.

Your target offers and examples of courses provided by each institution

360 pts **Glasgow (SA)** – AAA–ABB (Prod Des; Inter Des)
320 pts **Brunel** – BBC +AS/EPQ c 320 pts (Ind Des Tech; Prod Des Eng; Prod Des) (IB 31 pts)
Kent – 320 pts (Interiors) (IB 33 pts)
Leeds – ABB (Prod Des) (IB 34 pts HL 16 pts)
Nottingham – ABB (Prod Des Manuf) (IB 30–32 pts)
Sussex – ABB–BBC (Prod Des) (IB 30–34 pts)
300 pts **Aston** – BBB (Auto Prod Des; Sust Prod Des; Eng Prod Des; Med Prod Des)
Bournemouth – 300 pts (Ind Des; Soft Prod Des; Prod Des)
Brighton – BBB 300 pts offers may vary (Prod Des Tech; Spo Prod Des; Sust Prod Des) (IB 32 pts)
Glasgow – BBB (BEng Prod Des Eng)
Liverpool – BBB (4yr Eng Prod Des)
Nottingham Trent – 300 pts (Inter Archit Des)
Queen's Belfast – BBB (MEng Prod Des Dev)
Strathclyde – BBB (MEng Prod Des Eng; Prod Eng Mgt)
280 pts **Birmingham City/Birmingham (IAD)** – 280 pts (Inter Des)
Leeds – BBC (Des Tech Mgt)
Leeds Met – 280–300 pts (Inter Archit Des)
London Met – 280 pts (Inter Archit Des)

Northumbria – 280 pts (Trans Des)
Nottingham – BBC (BEng Prod Des Eng) (IB 30–32 pts)
Nottingham Trent – 280 pts (Furn Prod Des; Prod Des)
Staffordshire – 280 pts (Prod Des Med Dvcs; Prod Des Tech) (IB 28 pts)

260 pts **Aston** – 260–300 pts (Electron Prod Des)
De Montfort – 260 pts (Des Prod)
Loughborough – 260–300 pts (Prod Des Tech; Ind Des Tech) (IB 30–32 pts)
Manchester Met – 260–300 pts (Inter Des)
Northumbria – 260 pts (Prod Des Tech)
Queen's Belfast – BCC (BEng Prod Des Dev)
Salford – 260 pts (Prod Des) (IB 26 pts)
Swansea – 260–300 pts (Prod Des Eng; Prod Des Tech)

240 pts **Bolton** – 240 pts (Prod Des courses)
Bristol UWE – 240–300 pts (Prod Des Tech; Crea Prod Des) (IB 24–28 pts)
Coventry – 240 pts (Auto Trans Des; Ind Prod Des; Consum Prod Des; Spo Prod Des; Toy Prod Des)
De Montfort – 240 pts (Prod Des; Inter Des; Prod Furn Des; Ftwr Des)
Dundee – CCC (Prod Des)
Edinburgh Napier – 240 pts (Inter Archit; Prod Des; Prod Des Eng)
Glamorgan – 240–280 pts (Inter Des)
Hertfordshire – 240 pts (Prod Des; Ind Des)
Huddersfield – 240–300 pts (Inter Des; Prod Des (3D Animat); Exhib Rtl Des; Prod Des (Child Prod Toys) (Sust Des); Prod Innov Des Dev)
Kingston – 240 pts (Prod Des)
Edinburgh Napier – 240 pts (Inter Archit; Prod Des; Prod Des Eng)
Liverpool John Moores – 240 pts (Inter Des; Prod Des Dig Modl)
London Met – 240 pts (Inter Des Tech; Prod Des)
Manchester Met – 240 pts (Prod Des Tech)
Middlesex – 240–260 pts (Prod Des; Inter Archit Des; Des Tech)
Sheffield Hallam – 240–260 pts (Furn Prod Des; Prod Des)
Teesside – 240–280 pts (Inter Archit Des; Prod Des (Contemp Lfstl Furn) (Ind Trans))
Wolverhampton – 240 pts (Inter Des; Prod Des)

230 pts **Creative Arts** – 230–260 pts (Inter Archit Des)

220 pts **Anglia Ruskin** – 220 pts (Inter Des)
Hull – 220–260 pts (Med Prod Des)
Northampton – 220–260 pts (Prod Des; Inter Des)
Portsmouth – 220–320 pts (Inter Des)
Teesside – 220–260 pts (Prod Des (Mark))
Ulster – 220 pts (Tech Des)

200 pts **Bangor** – 200–220 pts (Prod Des)
Bolton – 200 pts (Inter Des)
Bradford – 200–240 pts (Prod Des)
Creative Arts – 200 pts (Prod Des Sust Fut; Prod Des)
East London – 200 pts (Prod Des; Prod Des Fut)
Glyndŵr – 200 pts (Mtrspo Des Mgt)
London Met – 200 pts (Furn Prod Des)
Portsmouth – 200 pts (Inter Des; Prod Des Innov; Prod Des Modn Mat)
Salford – 200 pts (Inter Des)
Suffolk (Univ Campus) – 200 pts (Inter Des)
York St John – 200–220 pts (Prod Des courses)

180 pts **Cardiff (UWIC)** – BC (Prod Des)
Derby – 180–240 pts (Prod Des)
Greenwich – 180 pts (Educ Des Tech)
Sunderland – 180 pts (Inter Des)

160 pts **Bedfordshire** – 160–240 pts (Inter Des)
Central Lancashire – 160 pts (Prod Des; Inter Des)
Liverpool (LIPA) – 160 pts (Thea Perf Des)
London (Gold) – CC (Des Tech Educ QTS)
London South Bank – 160 pts (Spo Prod Des)
Robert Gordon – 160–180 pts (Prod Des)
South Essex (Coll) – 160 pts (Inter Des)
Southampton Solent – 160 pts (Prod Des; Inter Des (Stg Film) (Decr); Prod Des Mark)
Strathclyde – CC (BEng Prod Des Eng; Prod Eng Mgt)

140 pts **Sheffield Hallam** – 140 pts (Des Tech)
Swansea Met – 140 pts (Prod Des)
West Scotland – CD (Prod Des Dev)

120 pts **London South Bank** – 120 pts (Prod Des)

100 pts **and below or other selection criteria (Foundation course, interview and portfolio inspection)**
Arts London (Central Saint Martins CAD), (Chelsea CAD), (Wimbledon CA); Barking (Coll); Bath Spa; Bolton; Bournemouth Arts (UC); Brighton; Bucks New; Cardiff (UWIC); Cleveland (CAD); Colchester (Inst); Croydon (Coll); De Montfort; Derby; Dundee; Easton (Coll); Edinburgh (CA); Falmouth (UC); Forth Valley (Coll); Glasgow Caledonian; Glasgow Met (Coll); Hereford (CA)/(CT); Heriot-Watt; Hertfordshire; Huddersfield; Kingston; Kirklees (Coll); Leeds (CAD); Lincoln; London South Bank; Ravensbourne (CDC); Royal Welsh (CMusDr); Shrewsbury (CAT); South Essex (Coll); Southampton Solent; Teesside; West Scotland; Worcestershire New (Coll).

Alternative offers

See **Chapter 7** and **Appendix 1** for grades/UCAS Tariff points information for the International Baccalaureate, Scottish Highers/Advanced Highers, the Welsh Baccalaureate, the Irish Leaving Certificate, the Cambridge Pre-U Diploma, the Advanced Diploma and the Extended Project.

EXAMPLES OF FOUNDATION DEGREES IN THE SUBJECT FIELD

Arts London; Barking (Coll); Bath Spa; Bedfordshire; Bishop Burton (Coll); Blackburn (Coll Univ Centre); Bournemouth Arts (UC); Bristol City (Coll); Bristol UWE; Bucks New; Capel Manor (Coll); Cornwall (Coll); Croydon (Coll); Greenwich; Kirklees (Coll); Leeds (CAD); Leicester (Coll); London Met; Plymouth (CAD); Rose Bruford (Coll); Somerset (CAT); South Devon (Coll); Swansea Met; Thames Valley.

CHOOSING YOUR COURSE (SEE ALSO CH.1)

Some course features

Note that there is an engineering element in some Product Design courses, and several specifically lead to an Engineering degree. Many are accredited by the Institution of Engineering Designers (see **Appendix 4**).

Universities and colleges teaching quality See www.qaa.ac.uk; www.unistats.com.

Top research universities and colleges (RAE 2008) See **Art and Design (General)**.

Examples of sandwich degree courses Aston; Bournemouth; Bradford; Brighton; Bristol UWE; Brunel; De Montfort; East London; Hertfordshire; Huddersfield; Lincoln; Liverpool John Moores; London South Bank; Manchester Met; Middlesex; Nottingham Trent; Portsmouth; Robert Gordon; Sheffield Hallam; Staffordshire; Sunderland; Sussex; West Scotland.

ADMISSIONS INFORMATION

Number of applicants per place (approx) Arts London (Central Saint Martins CAD) 2, (Chelsea CAD) 2; (Wimbledon CA) 2; Aston 6; Bath Spa 4; Birmingham City/Birmingham (IAD) (Inter Des) 9; Bolton 1; Brunel 4; Cardiff (UWIC) 6; Central Lancashire 7; Colchester (Inst) 4; Coventry 5; Creative Arts 4; De Montfort 5; Derby 2; Edinburgh Napier 6; Loughborough 9; Manchester Met 2; Middlesex (Inter Archit Des) 4; Northampton (Prod Des) 2; Northumbria 4; Nottingham Trent (Inter Archit Des) 7, (Prod Des) 5; Portsmouth 3; Ravensbourne (CDC) (Inter Des) 4, (Prod Des) 7; Salford 6; Sheffield 4; Shrewsbury (CAT) 6; Staffordshire 3; Swansea Met 3; Teesside 3.

Advice to applicants and planning the UCAS personal statement Your knowledge of design in all fields should be described, including any special interests you may have, for example in domestic, rail and road aspects of design, and visits to exhibitions, motor shows. **School/College reference** Tutors should make it clear that the applicant's knowledge, experience and attitude match the chosen course – not simply higher education in general. Admissions tutors look for knowledge of interior design and interior architecture, experience in 3D-design projects (which include problem-solving and sculptural demands), model-making experience in diverse materials, experience with 2D illustration and colour work, and knowledge of computer-aided design. Photography is also helpful, and also model-making and CAD/computer skills. See also **Art and Design (Graphic Design)**.

Misconceptions about this course Theatre Design is sometimes confused with Theatre Architecture or an academic course in Theatre Studies. **Birmingham City/Birmingham (IAD)** (Inter Des) Some applicants believe that it is an interior decorating course (carpets and curtains). **Lincoln** (Musm Exhib Des) This is a design course, not a museum course. **Portsmouth** (Inter Des) Some students think that this is about interior decorating after Laurence Llewelyn-Bowen!

Selection interviews **Yes** Brunel, Cardiff (UWIC), Dundee; most institutions will interview and require a portfolio of work. **Some** Salford, Staffordshire.

Interview advice and questions Applicants' portfolios of art work form an important talking-point throughout the interview. Applicants should be able to discuss examples of current design and new developments in the field and answer questions on the aspects of industrial design which interest them. **Creative Arts** No tests. Discuss any visits to modern buildings and new developments, eg British Museum Great Court or the Louvre Pyramid. See also **Art and Design (General)** and **Chapter 5**.

Reasons for rejection (non-academic) Not hungry enough! Mature students without formal qualifications may not be able to demonstrate the necessary mathematical or engineering skills. Poor quality and organisation of portfolio. Lack of interest. Inappropriate dress. Lack of enthusiasm. Insufficient portfolio work (eg exercises instead of projects). Lack of historical knowledge of interior design. Weak oral communication. **Creative Arts** Not enough 3D model-making. Poor sketching and drawing. See also **Art and Design (General)**.

AFTER-RESULTS ADVICE

Offers to applicants repeating A-levels **Same** Birmingham City/Birmingham (IAD), Bournemouth, Creative Arts, Nottingham Trent, Salford, Staffordshire.

GRADUATE DESTINATIONS AND EMPLOYMENT (2007/8 HESA)

See **Art and Design (General)**.

Career note See **Art and Design (General)**.

OTHER DEGREE SUBJECTS FOR CONSIDERATION

Architectural Studies; Architecture; Art Gallery Management; Design (Manufacturing Systems); History of Art; Manufacturing Engineering; Multimedia and Communication Design and subjects in other **Art and Design** tables.

ART and DESIGN (3D Design)

(including **Ceramics, Design Crafts, Glassmaking, Jewellery, Metalwork, Silversmithing, Plastics** and **Woodwork**; see also **Art and Design (General)** and **(Industrial and Product Design)**)

This group of courses covers mainly three dimensional design work, focusing on creative design involving jewellery, silverware, ceramics, glass, wood and plastics. Some institutions offer broad three dimensional studies courses while others provide the opportunity to study very specialised subjects such as stained glass, gemology and horology. Students normally take an Art Foundation course before their degree level studies.

Useful websites www.ergonomics.org.uk; www.yourcreativefuture.org.uk; www.top3D.net; www.glassassociation.org.uk; www.bja.org.uk; www.cpaceramics.com.

NB The points totals shown to the left of the institutions are for ease of reference only. It must not be assumed that Tariff points are always used by institutions or that they can be substituted for an offer in grades. The level of an offer is not necessarily indicative of the quality of a course.

COURSE OFFERS INFORMATION

Subject requirements/preferences See **Art and Design (General) Course offers information**.

NB In 2011 universities and colleges will differ in their use of GCE AL/AS unit grade information, A* grades, the Extended Project (EPQ), the Advanced Diploma and the Cambridge Pre-U examination when considering applicants and making offers. An EPQ may be accepted in place of an AS subject. Check websites of universities and colleges for the latest offers information.

Your target offers and examples of courses provided by each institution

360 pts **Glasgow (SA)** – AAA–ABB (Silver Jewel)
280 pts **Birmingham City/Birmingham (IAD)** – 280 pts (Jewel Silver)
Northumbria – 280 pts (3D Furn Prod Des)
260 pts **Huddersfield** – 260 pts (3D Des: Fine Prod Crea Enter)
240 pts **Coventry** – 240 pts (3D Des)
De Montfort – 240 pts (Furn Des)
Hertfordshire – 240 pts (3D Gms Art)
Manchester Met – 240 pts (3D Des)
Plymouth – 240 pts (3D Des; 3D Des (Des Mkr) (Furn Inter Des))
Sheffield Hallam – 240 pts (Mtl Jewel)
Staffordshire – 240–280 pts (Dig Film 3D Animat Tech)
Wolverhampton – 240 pts (App Arts)
200 pts **Glyndŵr** – 200 pts (Des Decr Arts; App Arts)
Hereford (CA) – 200 pts (Jewel Des)
Portsmouth – 200–280 pts (3D Des)
Suffolk (Univ Campus) – 200 pts (Des (Des Crfts))
Swansea Met – 200 pts (Fine Art (Ceram))
180 pts **Swansea Met** – 180 pts (3D Comp Animat)
Sunderland – 180–360 pts (Glass Archit Glass Ceram)
160 pts **Bournemouth Arts (UC)** – 160 pts (Modelmaking)
Bucks New – 160–200 pts (Ceram Gls)
Leeds Met – 160 pts (Des Furn)
Robert Gordon – 160–180 pts (3D Des (Ceram Gls Jewel))
Swansea Met – 160–360 pts (Archit Gls)
100 pts **and below or other selection criteria (Foundation course, interview and portfolio inspection)**
Anglia Ruskin; Arts London (Camberwell CA), (Central Saint Martins CAD); Barking (Coll); Bath Spa; Bedfordshire; Bradford (Coll); Brighton; Bucks New; Central Lancashire; Colchester (Inst); Cornwall (Coll); Creative Arts; Croydon (Coll); Dundee; East London; Edinburgh (CA); Falmouth (UC); Greenwich; Havering (Coll); Hereford (CA); Leeds (CAD); Lincoln; Loughborough; Manchester (Coll); Menai (Coll); Middlesex; NEW (Coll); Northampton; Northbrook (Coll); Northumbria; Nottingham New (Coll); Ravensbourne (CDC); Robert Gordon; Staffordshire (Reg Fed); Stockport (Coll); Teesside; Warwickshire (Coll); York St John.

Alternative offers

See **Chapter 7** and **Appendix 1** for grades/UCAS Tariff points information for the International Baccalaureate, Scottish Highers/Advanced Highers, the Welsh Baccalaureate, the Irish Leaving Certificate, the Cambridge Pre-U Diploma, the Advanced Diploma and the Extended Project.

EXAMPLES OF FOUNDATION DEGREES IN THE SUBJECT FIELD

Barking (Coll); Bedfordshire; Bournemouth Arts (UC); Brighton; Cleveland (CAD); Croydon (Coll); Cumbria; East Anglia; East London; Hereford (CA); Hertfordshire; London Met; Manchester (Coll); Newcastle (Coll); Plymouth; Plymouth (CAD); South Devon (Coll); South Essex (Coll); Truro (Coll); Writtle (Coll).

CHOOSING YOUR COURSE (SEE ALSO CH.1)

Some course features

Manchester Met Four-year course offers a business option.
Plymouth Opportunity for European study exchange or work placement for 12 weeks in Year 2.
Sheffield Hallam Students work with precious and non-precious metals, mixed media, wood, plastics and paper; opportunities to learn a language.
Staffordshire (Dig Film 3D Animat Tech) Course covers 3D modelling, creating and editing digital video, animation, 2D graphics, post-production work and a year-long project merging filmed footage with 3D objects.
Ulster Live projects undertaken in all three years of course. Furniture Design covers public, contract, domestic and street furniture.
Wolverhampton Seven specialised courses.

Other courses specialise in ceramics, glassware, jewellery and silversmithing.

Universities and colleges teaching quality See www.qaa.ac.uk; www.unistats.com.

Top research universities and colleges (RAE 2008) See **Art and Design (General)**.

ADMISSIONS INFORMATION

Number of applicants per place (approx) Arts London (Camberwell CA) 2, (Ceram) 3, (Central Saint Martins CAD) (Ceram) 2, (Jewel) 2; Bath Spa 3; Birmingham City/Birmingham (IAD) 4, (Jewel) 5; Brighton 3; De Montfort 3; Dundee 5; Creative Arts 4; Manchester Met 5; Middlesex (3D Des) 4, (Jewel) 4; Portsmouth 3; Ravensbourne (CDC) total of 110 first-choice applicants.

Advice to applicants and planning the UCAS personal statement Describe your art studies and your experience of different types of materials used. Discuss your special interest in your chosen field. Compare your work with that of professional artists and designers and describe your visits to museums, art galleries, exhibitions etc. Submit a portfolio of recent work to demonstrate drawing skills, visual awareness, creativity and innovation, showing examples of 3D work in photographic or model form. See also **Art and Design (Graphic Design)**.

Selection interviews All institutions will interview and require a portfolio of work.

Interview advice and questions Questions focus on the art work presented in the student's portfolio. See also **Art and Design (General)** and **Chapter 5**.

Reasons for rejection (non-academic) Lack of pride in their work. No ideas. See also **Art and Design (General)**.

AFTER-RESULTS ADVICE

Offers to applicants repeating A-levels **Same** Birmingham City/Birmingham (IAD), Brighton, Creative Arts, Dundee, Manchester Met.

GRADUATE DESTINATIONS AND EMPLOYMENT (2007/8 HESA)

See **Art and Design (General)**.

Career note See **Art and Design (General)**.

OTHER DEGREE SUBJECTS FOR CONSIDERATION

Design Technology; see other **Art and Design** tables.

ASIA-PACIFIC STUDIES

(including **East and South Asian Studies**; see also **Chinese, Japanese** and **Languages**)

These courses focus on the study of the cultures and the languages of this region of the world, such as Korean, Sanskrit, Thai, Vietnamese.

Useful websites www.dur.ac.uk/oriental.museum; www.bubl.ac.uk; www.asia-alliance.org; www.bacsuk.org.uk.

NB The points totals shown to the left of the institutions are for ease of reference only. It must not be assumed that Tariff points are always used by institutions or that they can be substituted for an offer in grades. The level of an offer is not necessarily indicative of the quality of a course.

COURSE OFFERS INFORMATION

Subject requirements/preferences **GCSE** A language subject grade A–C. **AL** A language or a second joint subject may be required.

NB In 2011 universities and colleges will differ in their use of GCE AL/AS unit grade information, A* grades, the Extended Project (EPQ), the Advanced Diploma and the Cambridge Pre-U examination when considering applicants and making offers. An EPQ may be accepted in place of an AS subject. Check websites of universities and colleges for the latest offers information.

Your target offers and examples of courses provided by each institution

380 pts **Cambridge** – A*AA college offers may vary (As Mid E St)

360 pts **Oxford** – AAA (Orntl St Class; Sansk; Chin; Jap) (IB 38–40 pts)

320 pts **Leeds** – ABB (As Pacif St Econ; As Pacif St Int Rel; As Pacif St Chin/Jap) (IB 32 pts HL 15 pts)

London (SOAS) – ABB (S As St courses; SE As St courses; Sansk/Burm/Hindi/Nepali/Thai/Viet/Chin/Jap/Kor courses) (IB 34 pts HL 555)

Manchester – ABB–BBB (St Relig Theol (S As St))

300 pts **Edinburgh** – BBB 300 pts (Soc Anth S As St; Sansk; Sansk Gk; Sansk Lat; Sansk Ling) (IB 34 pts)

Leeds – BBB (As Pacif St) (IB 32 pts HL 15 pts)

280 pts **Sheffield** – BBC (E As St; Chin St courses; Jap St; Kor St) (IB 32–33 pts)

200 pts **Central Lancashire** – 200–240 pts (As Pacif St)

Alternative offers

See **Chapter 7** and **Appendix 1** for grades/UCAS Tariff points information for the International Baccalaureate, Scottish Highers/Advanced Highers, the Welsh Baccalaureate, the Irish Leaving Certificate, the Cambridge Pre-U Diploma, the Advanced Diploma and the Extended Project.

CHOOSING YOUR COURSE (SEE ALSO CH.1)

Some course features

Central Lancashire A sandwich course covering business, politics and Asian languages – Chinese and Japanese.

Leeds (As Pacif St courses) Courses deal mainly with the region's politics, economics and culture. Single Honours, major and Joint courses available.

Manchester Course focuses on religious, social and cultural traditions and issues in South Asia and provides an opportunity to learn a South Asian language.

Universities and colleges teaching quality See www.qaa.ac.uk; www.unistats.com.

Top research universities and colleges (RAE 2008) London (SOAS); Oxford; Cambridge; Leeds; Manchester; Sheffield.

Examples of sandwich degree courses Central Lancashire.

ADMISSIONS INFORMATION

Number of applicants per place (approx) London (SOAS) 4, (Thai) 2, (Burm) 1.

Advice to applicants and planning the UCAS personal statement Connections with, and visits to, South and South East Asia should be mentioned. You should give some indication of what impressed you and your reasons for wishing to study these subjects. An awareness of the geography, culture and politics of the area also should be shown on the UCAS application. Show your skills in learning a foreign language (if choosing a language course), interest in current affairs of the region, experience of travel and self-discipline.

Selection interviews **Yes** Cambridge, Manchester, Oxford.

Interview advice and questions General questions are usually asked that relate to applicants' reasons for choosing degree courses in this subject area and to their background knowledge of the various cultures. See also **Chapter 5**.

AFTER-RESULTS ADVICE

Offers to applicants repeating A-levels Information not available from institutions.

GRADUATE DESTINATIONS AND EMPLOYMENT (2007/8 HESA)

Graduates surveyed 40 **Employed** 20 **In further study** 5 **Assumed unemployed** 5.

Career note Graduates enter a wide range of careers covering business and administration, retail work, education, transport, finance, community and social services. Work experience during undergraduate years will help students to focus their interests. Many courses have a language bias or are taught jointly with other subjects. Graduates may have opportunities of using their languages in a range of occupations.

OTHER DEGREE SUBJECTS FOR CONSIDERATION

Anthropology; Development Studies; Far Eastern Languages; Geography; History; International Relations; Politics; Social Studies.

ASTRONOMY and ASTROPHYSICS

(including **Planetary Science** and **Space Science**; see also **Geology/Geological Sciences** and **Physics**)

All Astronomy-related degrees are built on a core of mathematics and physics which, in the first two years, is augmented by an introduction to the theory and practice of astronomy or astrophysics. Astronomy emphasises observational aspects of the science and includes a study of the planetary system whilst Astrophysics tends to pursue the subject from a more theoretical stand-point. Courses often combine Mathematics or Physics with Astronomy.

Useful websites www.ras.org.uk; www.scicentral.com; www.iop.org.

NB The points totals shown to the left of the institutions are for ease of reference only. It must not be assumed that Tariff points are always used by institutions or that they can be substituted for an offer in grades. The level of an offer is not necessarily indicative of the quality of a course.

COURSE OFFERS INFORMATION

Subject requirements/preferences **GCSE** English and a foreign language may be required by some universities; specified grades may be stipulated for some subjects. **AL** Mathematics and physics usually required.

NB In 2011 universities and colleges will differ in their use of GCE AL/AS unit grade information, A* grades, the Extended Project (EPQ), the Advanced Diploma and the Cambridge Pre-U examination when considering applicants and making offers. An EPQ may be accepted in place of an AS subject. Check websites of universities and colleges for the latest offers information.

Your target offers and examples of courses provided by each institution

380 pts **Cambridge** – A*AA college offers may vary (Nat Sci (Astro)) (IB 38–42 pts HL 776–777)
London (UCL) – AAAe–ABBe (Planet Sci) (IB 34–38 pts)

360 pts **Bristol** – AAA–AAB (Phys Astro) (IB 37–35 pts HL maths phys 6)
Durham – AAA–AAB (Phys Astron) (IB 36–38 pts)
Leeds – AAA–AAB (MPhys Phys Astro) (IB 33pts)
Liverpool – AAA–ABB (MPhys Astro) (IB 27 pts HL maths phys 6)
London (King's) – AABe (Phys Astro) (IB 36 pts HL maths phys 5)
London (UCL) – AABe–ABBe (Astrophysics) (IB 34–36 pts)
Manchester – AAA–AAB (Phys Astro) (IB 33–37 pts)
St Andrews – AAA (Astrophysics) (IB 36 pts)

340 pts **Birmingham** – AAB–ABB (Phys Astro; Phys Prtcl Phys Cosmo) (IB 32–36 pts)
Cardiff – AAB 340 pts (MPhys Phys Astron; MPhys Astro) (IB 32pts)
Edinburgh – AAB (MPhys Astro) (IB 36 pts)
Exeter – AAB–ABB (Phys Astro) (IB 30 pts) (IB 34–31 pts)
Lancaster – AAB 340 pts (MPhys Phys Prtcl Phys Cosmo; Phys Spc Sci) (IB 31 pts)
Leicester – AAB (MPhys Phys Astro; Phys Planet Sci; MPhys Phys Spc Sci Tech) (IB 32–34 pts)
London (QM) – 340 pts (MSci Astro)
London (RH) – AAB–ABB 340–320 pts (Astrophysics) (IB 34 pts HL maths phys 6–7)
Nottingham – AAB–ABB (Phys Theor Astro; Phys Astron) (IB HL maths 6 +65)
Queen's Belfast – AAB (MSci Phys Astro)
Southampton – AAB (Phys Astron; Phys Spc Sci) (IB 36–34 pts)
Surrey – AAB 340 pts (MEng Spc Tech Planet Explor)
Sussex – AAB–BBB (Phys Astro; Astro) (IB 32–36 pts)
York – AAB 340 pts (MPhys Phys Astro) (IB 32–30 pts)

320 pts **Edinburgh** – ABB (BSc Astro)
Glasgow – ABB (Astro Phys; Astron) (IB 32 pts)
Lancaster – ABB 320 pts (BSc Phys Astro Cosmo; Phys Spc Sci; Phys Prtcl Phys Cosmo) (IB 30 pts)
Liverpool – ABB–BBB (Phys Astron) (IB HL maths phys 6)
Sheffield – ABB (Phys Astro; Maths Astron) (IB 32–33 pts)
Surrey – ABB (BEng Spc Tech Planet Explor) (IB 28 pts)
York – ABB (BSc Phys Astro)

300 pts **Cardiff** – 300 pts (BSc Phys Astron) (IB 28 pts)
Keele – 300–320 pts (Astrophysics)
Kent – 300 pts (Astron Spc Sci Astro) (IB 33 pts)
Leicester – BBB (BSc Phys Astro; Phys Planet Sci Tech; Phys Spc Sci Tech)
Liverpool John Moores – BBB 300–280 pts (Phys Astron; Astro) (IB 24–28 pts)
London (QM) – 300 pts (BSc Astro) (IB 30–32 pts)
Salford – 300 pts (MPhys Phys Spc Tech)

280 pts **Central Lancashire** – 280–320 pts (Astrophysics)
Hertfordshire – 280 pts (Astrophysics) (IB 24 pts)
Queen's Belfast – BBC (BSc Phys Astro)

260 pts **Salford** – 260 pts (BSc Phys Spc Tech) (IB 27 pts)

240 pts **Aberystwyth** – 240–280 pts (Phys Planet Spc Phys; Spc Sci Robot; Astro) (IB 27 pts)
Hull – 240–300 pts (Phys Astro)

200 pts **Glamorgan** – 200–240 pts (Astron Spc) (IB 28 pts)

120 pts **Sussex** – DD (Phys Astron 4 yr inc Fdn Yr)

Alternative offers

See **Chapter 7** and **Appendix 1** for grades/UCAS Tariff points information for the International Baccalaureate, Scottish Highers/Advanced Highers, the Welsh Baccalaureate, the Irish Leaving Certificate, the Cambridge Pre-U Diploma, the Advanced Diploma and the Extended Project.

CHOOSING YOUR COURSE (SEE ALSO CH.1)

Some course features

Aberystwyth New Astrophysics course designed for students with a general interest in astronomy; it includes core physics modules and broader modules in cosmology and galactic astronomy; progression possible to MPhys degree.
Glamorgan Course provides practical experience of observational astronomy and training in astrophysical techniques, with an astronomy field school in the Algarve.
Kent Course includes involvment in space missions and work on Hubble Telescope data and an exchange programme in Year 3 in the USA.
London (QM) Astronomy and Astrophysics programmes are similar and transfer is possible up to the final year.
Surrey (Spc Tech Planet Explor) Courses include hands-on spacecraft engineering, have a strong international focus with close ties with space industries and European Space Agency; opportunities for a professional training year. Surrey is the only university building complete satellites.

Universities and colleges teaching quality See www.qaa.ac.uk; www.unistats.com.

Top research universities and colleges (RAE 2008) See **Physics**.

Examples of sandwich degree courses Hertfordshire; Kingston; Nottingham Trent; Surrey.

ADMISSIONS INFORMATION

Number of applicants per place (approx) Bristol 9; Cardiff 6; Durham 3; Hertfordshire 5; Leicester 12; London (QM) 6, (RH) 6, (UCL) 5; Newcastle 7; Southampton 6.

Advice to applicants and planning the UCAS personal statement Books and magazines you have read on astronomy and astrophysics are an obvious source of information. Describe your interests and why you have chosen this subject. Visits to observatories would also be important. **York** Advanced Diploma not generally accepted. (See also **Appendix 4**.)

Misconceptions about this course Career opportunities are not as limited as some students think. These courses involve an extensive study of maths and physics, opening many opportunities for graduates such as geodesy, rocket and satellite studies and engineering specialisms.

Selection interviews **Yes** Bristol, Cambridge, London (UCL), Newcastle; **Some** Cardiff.

Interview advice and questions You will probably be questioned on your study of physics and the aspects of the subject you most enjoy. Questions in the past have included: Can you name a recent development in physics which will be important in the future? Describe a physics experiment, indicating any errors and exactly what it was intended to prove. Explain weightlessness. What is a black hole? What are the latest discoveries in space? **Southampton** Entrance examination for year abroad courses. See also **Chapter 5**.

AFTER-RESULTS ADVICE

Offers to applicants repeating A-levels **Higher** St Andrews; **Same** Cardiff, Durham, London (UCL), Newcastle; **No offers made** Cambridge.

GRADUATE DESTINATIONS AND EMPLOYMENT (2007/8 HESA)

Graduates surveyed 165 **Employed** 50 **In further study** 65 **Assumed unemployed** 20.

Career note The number of posts for professional astronomers is limited although some technological posts are occasionally offered in observatories. However, degree courses include extensive mathematics and physics so many graduates can look towards related fields including telecommunications and electronics.

OTHER DEGREE SUBJECTS FOR CONSIDERATION

Aeronautical/Aerospace Engineering; Computer Science; Earth Sciences; Geology; Geophysics; Mathematics; Meteorology; Mineral Sciences; Oceanography; Physics.

BIOCHEMISTRY

Biochemistry is the study of life processes at molecular level. Most courses are extremely flexible and have common first years. Modules could include genetics, immunology, blood biochemistry, physiology and biotechnology. The option to choose other courses in the subject field features at many universities. Many courses allow for a placement in industry in the UK or in Europe or North America.

Useful websites www.biochemistry.org; www.scienceyear.com; www.bioworld.com; www.arjournals.annualreviews.org; see also **Biological Sciences** and **Biology**.

NB The points totals shown to the left of the institutions are for ease of reference only. It must not be assumed that Tariff points are always used by institutions or that they can be substituted for an offer in grades. The level of an offer is not necessarily indicative of the quality of a course.

COURSE OFFERS INFORMATION

Subject requirements/preferences **GCSE** English, mathematics and science usually required; leading universities often stipulate A-B grades. **AL** Chemistry required and biology usually preferred; one or two mathematics/science subjects required.

NB In 2011 universities and colleges will differ in their use of GCE AL/AS unit grade information, A* grades, the Extended Project (EPQ), the Advanced Diploma and the Cambridge Pre-U examination when considering applicants and making offers. An EPQ may be accepted in place of an AS subject. Check websites of universities and colleges for the latest offers information.

Your target offers and examples of courses provided by each institution

380 pts **Cambridge** – A*AA College offers may vary (Nat Sci (Bioch)) (IB 38–42 pts HL 766–777)

360 pts **Bath** – AAA–AAB (Bioch; Biochem Eng) (IB 34 pts HL chem 6)
East Anglia – AAA–AAB (Bioch Aus/N Am) (IB 33–34 pts HL 666)
Edinburgh – AAA 2nd yr entry (Biochemistry) (IB 36 pts)
London (UCL) – AABe–ABBe (Biochemistry) (IB 34–36 pts)
Oxford – AAA (Mol Cell Bioch) (IB 39 pts)

340 pts **Birmingham** – AAB–BBBb (Bioch; Bioch Euro; Med Bioch) (IB 32–34 pts)
Bristol – AAB (Bioch; Bioch Med Bioch; Bioch Mol Biol Biotech) (IB 35 pts)
Cardiff – AAB–ABB 340–320 pts (Biochemistry) (IB 34 pts)
Exeter – AAB–BBB (Biochemistry) (IB 34–29 pts)
Heriot-Watt – AAB 2nd yr entry (Chem Bioch; Brew Distil)
Imperial London – AAB (Bioch; Bioch Mgt; Bioch Rsch Abrd; Bioch Yr Ind) (IB 38 pts)
Leeds – AAB–BBB 340–300 pts (Bioch; Bioch Mol Biol; Med Bioch) (IB 36–32 pts HL 15–17 pts)
London (King's) – ABB+AS (Biochemistry) (IB 34 pts HL chem 5)
Manchester – AAB–BBB (Bioch Ind Exp; Bioch; Med Bioch) (IB 32–35 pts)
Nottingham – AAB–BBB (Bioch; Bioch Mol Med; Bioch Biol Chem; Neuro Bioch) (IB 32–34 pts)
Sheffield – AAB–ABB (Bioch; Bioch Genet; Bioch Mol Cell Biol; Med Bioch) (IB 33 pts)

320 pts **Birmingham** – ABB–BBBb (Bioch (Genet); Bioch Biotech; Med Bioch)
Brunel – 320 pts BBC +AS/EPQ c (Biomed Sci (Bioch)) (IB 32 pts)
Durham – ABB (Mol Biol Bioch) (IB 34 pts H chem/biol 5)
East Anglia – ABB–BBB (Bioch; Bioch Ind; Bioch Euro) (IB 31–32 pts HL 555)
Edinburgh – ABB 1st yr entry (Biochemistry) (IB 32 pts)
Glasgow – ABB (Bioch; Med Bioch) (IB 30 pts)
Lancaster – ABB 320 pts (Biochemistry)
Leicester – ABB (Biol Sci (Bioch); Med Bioch) (IB 32–34 pts)
Liverpool – ABB–BBB (Bioch; Bioch Yr Ind) (IB 33–30 pts)
London (RH) – ABB (Mol Biosci (Bioch); Med Bioch) (IB 34 pts)

Newcastle – ABB (Bioch Immun; Bioch) (IB 32–35 pts HL biol chem 6)
Reading – 320 pts (Biochemistry) (IB 30 pts)
St Andrews – ABB (Biochemistry) (IB 32 pts)
Southampton – ABB–BBB (Biochemistry) (IB 32 pts)
Surrey – ABB–BBB 320–300 pts (Bioch; Bioch (Med) (Neuro) (Pharmacol) (Tox)) (IB 24–30 pts)
Sussex – ABB–BBB 320–300 pts (Biochemistry) (IB 34 pts)
Warwick – ABB–BBB (Biochemistry) (IB 32–34 pts)
York – ABB (Bioch; Bioch Yr Euro) (IB 32 pts)

300 pts **Aberdeen** – BBB 300 pts 2nd yr entry (Bioch; Bioch Yr Ind; Bioch Innov) (IB 28 pts)
Aston – BBB (Biol Chem)
Dundee – BBB 2nd yr entry (Bioch; Bioch Pharmacol; Bioch Physiol Sci) (IB 34 pts)
Heriot-Watt – BBB 1st yr entry (Chem Bioch; Brew Distil)
Keele – 300 pts inc BC (Bioch courses) (IB 26–28 pts)
Lancaster – BBB 300 pts (Bioch; Bioch Biomed; Bioch Genet) (IB 29–30 pts)
Nottingham – BBB–BBC (Nutr Biochem) (IB 28–32 pts)

280 pts **Essex** – 280–240 pts (Biochemistry) (IB 30–26 pts)
Kent – BBC–BBB (Bioch; Bioch Euro) (IB 31–33 pts HL 14–15 pts)
London (QM) – 280 pts (Biochemistry) (IB 30–32 pts)
Queen's Belfast – BBC (Biochemistry) (IB 28 pts HL 555)
Strathclyde – BBC 2nd yr entry (Bioch Immun; Bioch Microbiol; Bioch Pharmacol; Nat Sci (Bioch))
Swansea – 280–300 pts (Bioch; Med Bioch)

260 pts **Bradford** – 260 pts (Med Bioch)
Nottingham Trent – 260 pts (Biochemistry)
Portsmouth – 260–300 pts (Bioch Gnm Sci)
Sheffield Hallam – 260 pts (Biochemistry)
Staffordshire – 260 pts (Bioch Microbiol) (IB 28 pts)
Strathclyde – BCC 1st yr entry (Bioch Immun; Bioch Microbiol; Bioch Pharmacol)

240 pts **Aberdeen** – 240 pts 1st yr entry (Bioch; Bioch (Immun))
Aberystwyth – 240–280 pts (Bioch (Genet Bioch)) (IB 26 pts HL chem 5)
Dundee – CCC 240 pts 1st yr entry (Bioch; Bioch Pharmacol; Bioch Physiol Sci) (IB 28 pts)
Hertfordshire – 240 pts (Bioch; Bioch Euro)
Huddersfield – 240 pts (Bioch; Med Bioch)
Liverpool John Moores – 240 pts (Bioch; Bioch Foren Sci; App Bioch; Med Bioch)
Salford – 240 pts (Bioch; Bioch USA) (IB 34 pts)

220 pts **Westminster** – CCD (Biochemistry) (IB 26 pts)

200 pts **East London** – 200 pts (Biochemistry)
Kingston – 200–280 pts (Bioch; Med Bioch)
Wolverhampton – 200–260 pts (Biochemistry)

160 pts **London Met** – 160 pts (Biochemistry)
Sussex – CC (Biosci inc Fdn Yr)

140 pts **West Scotland** – CD (App Bioch)

120 pts **London South Bank** – 120 pts (Biosci (Bioch))

80 pts **London (Birk)** – 80 pts for under 21s (over 21s offer varies) (p/t Bioch Sci)

Alternative offers

See **Chapter 7** and **Appendix 1** for grades/UCAS Tariff points information for the International Baccalaureate, Scottish Highers/Advanced Highers, the Welsh Baccalaureate, the Irish Leaving Certificate, the Cambridge Pre-U Diploma, the Advanced Diploma and the Extended Project.

EXAMPLES OF FOUNDATION DEGREES IN THE SUBJECT FIELD

Truro (Coll).

CHOOSING YOUR COURSE (SEE ALSO CH.1)

Some course features

Birmingham (Bioch) A range of Biochemistry programmes offers specialisation in several fields.
Bristol (Bioch) A choice to include a period of industrial placement is made in Year 2 from any one of the Biochemistry courses.
East Anglia (Bioch) Options to study for a year in Australasia, Europe or North America.
Imperial London Biochemistry and Biotechnology students follow a similar programme with specialisations in Year 3.
Lancaster (Bioch) Option to study one other non-scientific subject in Year 1.
Leeds Biochemistry and the course with Molecular Biology have a common first year, with the choice of degree made in Year 2.
Sussex (Bioch) Option to study French, German or Spanish.
Wolverhampton (Bioch) Joint courses and an optional year's placement are offered.

Universities and colleges teaching quality See www.qaa.ac.uk; www.unistats.com.

Top research universities and colleges (RAE 2008) See **Biological Sciences**.

Examples of sandwich degree courses Bath; Bristol; Bristol UWE; Brunel; Cardiff; East London; Essex; Hertfordshire; Huddersfield; Kent; Kingston; Leeds; Liverpool John Moores; London South Bank; Manchester; Nottingham Trent; Salford; Sheffield Hallam; Surrey; Sussex; West Scotland; Wolverhampton; York.

ADMISSIONS INFORMATION

Number of applicants per place (approx) Aberystwyth 5; Bath 7; Birmingham 5; Bradford 7; Bristol 8; Cardiff 6; Dundee 6; Durham 6; East Anglia 10; East London 5; Edinburgh 8; Essex 5; Imperial London 6; Keele 7; Leeds 10; Leicester (Med Bioch) 5; London (RH) 8, (UCL) 8; Newcastle 7; Nottingham 14; Salford 4; Southampton 8; Staffordshire 6; Strathclyde 7; Surrey 3; Warwick 6; York 6.

Advice to applicants and planning the UCAS personal statement It is important to show by reading scientific journals that you have interests in chemistry and biology beyond the exam syllabus. Focus on one or two aspects of biochemistry that interest you. Attend scientific lectures (often arranged by universities on Open Days), find some work experience if possible, and use these to show your understanding of what biochemistry is. Give evidence of your communication skills and time management. **Oxford** No written or work tests; successful entrants 42.7%. Further information may be obtained from the Institute of Biology and the Royal Society of Chemistry (see **Appendix 4**).

Misconceptions about this course **York** Students feel that being taught by two departments could be a problem but actually it increases their options.

Selection interviews **Yes** Birmingham (Clearing only), Bradford, Brunel, Cambridge, East London, Keele (mature students only), Kingston, Leeds, London (RH), (UCL), London South Bank, Oxford, Portsmouth (mature students only), Surrey, Warwick; **Some** Aberystwyth (mature students only), Bath, Cardiff, East Anglia, Liverpool John Moores, Salford, Sheffield, Staffordshire, Wolverhampton.

Interview advice and questions Questions will be asked on your study of chemistry and biology and any special interests. They will also probe your understanding of what a course in Biochemistry involves and the special features offered by the university. In the past questions have been asked covering Mendel, genetics, RNA and DNA. **Liverpool John Moores** Informal interviews. It would be useful to bring samples of coursework to the interview. See also **Chapter 5**.

Reasons for rejection (non-academic) Borderline grades plus poor motivation. Failure to turn up for interviews or answer correspondence. Inability to discuss subject. Not compatible with A-level predictions or references. **Birmingham** Lack of total commitment to Biochemistry, for example intention to transfer to Medicine without completing the course.

AFTER-RESULTS ADVICE

Offers to applicants repeating A-levels **Higher** East Anglia, Leeds, Leicester, Nottingham,

St Andrews, Strathclyde, Surrey, Warwick; **Possibly higher** Bath, Bristol, Brunel, Keele, Kent, Lancaster, Newcastle; **Same** Aberystwyth, Birmingham, Bradford, Cardiff, Dundee, Durham, Heriot-Watt, Hull, Liverpool, Liverpool John Moores, London (RH), (UCL), Salford, Sheffield, Staffordshire, Wolverhampton, York; **No offers made** Cambridge.

GRADUATE DESTINATIONS AND EMPLOYMENT (2007/8 HESA)

(Including **Biophysics** and **Molecular Biology**)
Graduates surveyed 1260 **Employed** 455 **In further study** 455 **Assumed unemployed** 125.

Career note Biochemistry courses involve several specialities which offer a range of job opportunities. These include the application of biochemistry in industrial, medical and clinical areas with additional openings in pharmaceuticals and agricultural work, environmental science and in toxicology.

OTHER DEGREE SUBJECTS FOR CONSIDERATION

Agricultural Sciences; Agriculture; Biological Sciences; Biology; Biotechnology; Botany; Brewing; Chemistry; Food Science; Genetics; Medical Sciences; Medicine; Microbiology; Neuroscience; Nursing; Nutrition; Pharmaceutical Sciences; Pharmacology; Pharmacy; Plant Science.

BIOLOGICAL SCIENCES

(including **Biomedical Science, Ecology, Forensic Science, Immunology, Neurosciences** and **Virology**; see also **Anatomical Science/Anatomy, Biochemistry, Biology, Biotechnology, Environmental Sciences/Studies, Genetics, Human Sciences, Microbiology, Plant Sciences, Zoology**)

Biological Science (in some universities referred to as Biosciences) is a fast-moving, rapidly expanding and wide subject area, ranging from, for example, conservation biology to molecular genetics. Boundaries between separate subjects are blurring and this is reflected in the content and variety of the courses offered. Many universities offer a common first year allowing final decisions to be made later in the course. Since most subjects are research-based, students undertake their own projects in the final year.

Useful websites http://bsi.immunology.org; www.ibms.org; www.scienceyear.com; www.scicentral.com; www.forensic.gov.uk; www.bbsrc.ac.uk; see also **Biochemistry** and **Biology**.

NB The points totals shown to the left of the institutions are for ease of reference only. It must not be assumed that Tariff points are always used by institutions or that they can be substituted for an offer in grades. The level of an offer is not necessarily indicative of the quality of a course.

COURSE OFFERS INFORMATION

Subject requirements/preferences GCSE English, mathematics and science usually required. Grades A-B often stipulated by popular universities. **AL** Chemistry required plus one or two other mathematics/science subjects, biology preferred. (Ecology) Biology and one other science subject may be required or preferred. (Neuroscience) Mathematics/science subjects with chemistry and/or biology required or preferred. **London (St George's)** (Biol Inform) Computer science, mathematics and/or science advantageous.

NB In 2011 universities and colleges will differ in their use of GCE AL/AS unit grade information, A* grades, the Extended Project (EPQ), the Advanced Diploma and the Cambridge Pre-U examination when considering applicants and making offers. An EPQ may be accepted in place of an AS subject. Check websites of universities and colleges for the latest offers information.

Your target offers and examples of courses provided by each institution
410 pts **Imperial London** – AAAb (Biomed Sci)
380 pts **Cambridge** – A*AA college offers may vary (Nat Sci (Biol Biomed Sci) (Neuro) (Path) (Plant Sci); Educ Biol Sci) (IB 38–42 pts)

360 pts **Bristol** – AAA–ABB (Biol Sci courses) (IB 34 pts HL 666)
East Anglia – AAA–AAB (Biol Sci N Am/Aus; Ecol N Am/Aus) (IB 33–34 pts)
Edinburgh – AAA–ABB 2nd yr entry (Biol Sci; Neuro; Biol Sci Mgt; Ecol Sci; Ecol; Immun) (IB 36 pts)
London (UCL) – AAB+AS–ABB+AS (Biomed Sci; Biol Sci; Neuro) (IB 34–36 pts)
Oxford – AAA (Biol Sci) (IB 38–42 pts)

340 pts **Birmingham** – AAB–BBB (Biol Sci; Biol Sci (Biotech) (Env Biol) (Genet); Med Sci)
Cardiff – AAB–ABB (Biomed Sci; Biomed Sci (Anat) (Neuro) (Physiol); Ecol)
Exeter – AAB–BBB (Biol Sci; Hum Biosci) (IB 34 pts)
Heriot-Watt – AAB 2nd yr entry (Biol Sci; Brew Distil)
Imperial London – AAB (Ecol Env Biol)
Leicester – AAB (MBiol Biol Sci) (IB 34 pts)
London (King's) – ABB+AS (Biomed Sci; Neuro) (IB 34 pts)
Manchester – AAB–BBB (Neuro; Cog Neuro Psy; Biomed Sci; Biol Comp Sci (Bioinform)) (IB 35–32 pts)
Manchester – AAB–ABC (Biomed Mat Sci courses) (IB 32 pts)
Newcastle – AAB (Biol Sci; Biomed Sci; Med Microbiol Immun) (IB 34 pts)
St Andrews – AAB–ABB (Mol Biol; Ecol Cons)
Sheffield – AAB–ABB (Ecology)
Sussex – AAB–ABB (Biomed Sci; Mol Med; Med Neuro) (IB 32–36 pts)

320 pts **Bristol** – ABB (Neuro; Immun; Virol Immun) (IB 33–30 pts HL 665)
Brunel – 320 pts BBC +AS/EPQ c (Biomed Sci courses) (IB 32 pts)
Dundee – ABB 2nd yr entry (Foren Anth)
Durham – ABB (Biomed Sci; Ecol) (IB 28 pts)
East Anglia – ABB–BBB (Biol Sci Euro/Ind; Biol Sci; Ecol; Biomed) (IB 31–32 pts)
Edinburgh – ABB–BBB 1st yr entry (Biol Sci; Neuro; Biol Sci Mgt; Ecol Sci; Ecol; Immun) (IB 32 pts)
Glasgow – ABB (Biomol Sci; Biomed Sci; Neuro) (IB 32 pts)
Lancaster – ABB 320 pts (Ecol N Am/USA; Biol Sci N Am/USA) (IB 30 pts)
Leeds – ABB–BBB (Neuro; Hum Physiol; Nanotech; Med Sci; Biol Sci; Ecol) (IB 32 pts)
Leicester – ABB (BSc Biol Sci; Biol Sci (Genet) (Microbiol) (Physiol Pharmacol); Med Genet) (IB 32–34 pts)
Liverpool – ABB–BBB (Biol Sci; Biol Med Sci; Lf Sci App Med; Biovet Sci) (IB 33–30 pts HL 6/5 biol chem)
London (QM) – 320 pts (Biomed Sci) (IB 30 pts)
London (RH) – ABB 320 pts (Biomed Sci; Ecol Env) (IB 34 pts)
Reading – 320 pts (Biol Sci; Biol Sci Ind; Biomed Sci) (IB 30–32 pts)
Sheffield – ABB (Biomed Sci) (IB 33 pts inc HL chem)
Southampton – ABB–BBB 320–300 pts (Biomed Sci) (IB 32 pts)
Surrey – ABB–BBB 320–300 pts (Biomed Sci; Bioch Neuro; Vet Biosci) (IB 34–30 pts)
Sussex – ABB (Neuroscience) (IB 34 pts)
Warwick – ABB–BBB (Biomed Sci) (IB 32–36 pts)
York – ABB (Ecol Cons Env) (IB 32 pts)

300 pts **Aberdeen** – BBB (Sci (Biol Sci) (Ecol) (Biomed Sci)) (IB 32 pts)
Aston – BBB (Biomed Sci) (IB 33 pts)
Birmingham – BBB (Biomed Mat Sci) (IB 32–34 pts)
Bournemouth – 300 pts (Foren Crime Scn Sci)
Dundee – BBB 2nd yr entry (Mol Genet; Biomol Drug Dscvry; Neuro; Biomed Sci)
Essex – 300–260 pts (Biol Sci) (IB 32–28 pts)
Heriot-Watt – BBB 1st yr entry (Biol Sci; Brew Distil)
Keele – 300 pts inc BC (Biomed Sci; Neuro)
Lancaster – BBB 300–260 pts (Biol Sci; Biol Sci Biomed; Biomed Sci; Ecol) (IB 29 pts)
London (RVC) – BBB (Biovet Sci)
London (St George's) – BBB (Biomed Sci; Biomed Inform)
Nottingham – BBB (Neuro Bioch; Neuro; Neuro Pharmacol) (IB 32 pts)

Queen's Belfast – BBB–BBC (Biol Sci)
Stirling – BBB 2nd yr entry (Ecol; Aquacult)
Sussex – BBB–BBC (Mol Genet)
Warwick – BBB (Biol Sci; Biomed Sci) (IB 32–34 pts)

280 pts **Aberystwyth** – 280 pts (Biol Sci) (IB 24–26 pts)
Aston – BBC 280 pts (Infec Immun)
Bangor – 280–320 pts (Biomed Sci)
Bradford – 280 pts (Clin Sci – transfer to Medicine poss)
Essex – 280–240 pts (Biomed Sci) (IB 28–26 pts)
Kent – 280 pts (Biol Anth)
Kent – BBC–BBB (Foren Sci courses; Biomed Sci) (IB 31–34 pts HL 14–15 pts)
Lincoln – 280 pts (Biovet Sci)
London Met – 280 pts (Biomed Sci)
Northumbria – 280–300 pts (Foren Sci; Biomed Sci)
Oxford Brookes – BBC 280 pts (Biomed Sci; Biol Sci) (IB 30 pts)
Plymouth – 280–320 pts (Hum Biosci; Biomed Sci; Biol Sci)
Queen's Belfast – BBC/BCCb (Biomed Sci)
Strathclyde – BBC 2nd yr entry (Biomed Sci; Biol Sci; Foren Biol) (IB 26 pts)
Swansea – 280–300 pts (Biol Sci Joint Hons; Med Sci Hum)
Teesside – 280 pts (Foren Biol)
Ulster – 280 pts (Biomed Sci)

260 pts **Bradford** – 260–280 pts (Biomed Sci; Foren Sci; Foren Med Sci; Bioarch)
Brighton – BCC 260 pts (Biol Sci; Biomed St) (IB 28 pts)
Bristol UWE – 260–300 pts (Biol Sci; Biomed courses; Foren Sci)
Central Lancashire – 260–300 pts (Foren Biol; Foren Sci)
Dundee – BCC 1st yr entry (Foren Anth)
Keele – 260–300 pts inc BB/BC (Foren Sci) (IB 26–28 pts)
Nottingham Trent – 260 pts (Foren Biol)
Portsmouth – 260 pts (Biomed Sci; App Biomed Sci)
Staffordshire – 260 pts (Biomed Sci; Foren Biol) (IB 28 pts)
Strathclyde – BCC 1st yr entry (Biomed Sci; Biol Sci; Foren Biol)
Wolverhampton – 260–320 pts (Biomed Sci)

240 pts **Aberdeen** – 240 pts 1st yr entry (Sci (Biol Sci) (Biomed Sci) (Ecol))
Bangor – 240–280 pts (Ecology)
Brighton – CCC/BCD (Ecol Biogeog)
Bristol UWE – 240–300 pts (App Biomed Sci)
Cardiff (UWIC) – 240 pts (Spo Biomed Nutr; Biomed Sci)
Central Lancashire – 240–260 pts (Neuro; Biomed Sci; Biol Sci)
Coventry – 240 pts (Biomed Sci; Biol Foren Sci)

De Montfort – 240 pts (Biomed Sci)
Dundee – CCC 1st yr entry (Mol Genet; Neuro; Biomed Sci)
Glamorgan – 240–280 pts (Foren Sci)
Greenwich – 240–300 pts (Biomed Sci)
Hertfordshire – 240 pts (Biol Sci; Biol N Am; Biomed Sci)
Huddersfield – 240 pts (Foren Analyt Sci)
Hull – 240–300 pts (Biomed Sci; Foren Sci Crim)
Leeds Trinity (UC) – 240 pts (Foren Psy)
Lincoln – 240 pts (Foren Sci; App Biomed Sci)
Liverpool John Moores – 240 pts (Biomed Sci)
London (St George's) – 240 pts (Biomed Inform)
Manchester Met – 240 pts (Ecol Cons; Biomed Sci; Biomed Sci Foren Biol; Biol Biomed Psy) (IB 27 pts)
Nescot – 240 pts (App Biol Sci; App Biomed Sci; Biomed Sci)
Nottingham Trent – 240 pts (Biol Sci)
Portsmouth – 240–280 pts (Foren Biol)
Robert Gordon – CCC (Foren Sci)
Roehampton – 240–300 pts (Biol Sci; Biomed Sci; Hum Biosci)

220 pts **Abertay Dundee** – CCD (Foren Sci; Biomed Sci)
Edge Hill – 220 pts (Biogeography)
Edinburgh Napier – 220 pts (Biol Sci; Immun Tox)
Hull – 220–280 pts (Ecology)
Lincoln – 220 pts (Biomed Sci)
Liverpool John Moores – 220–260 pts (Foren Sci)
Manchester Met – 220 pts (Foren Sci) (IB 26 pts)
Northampton – 220–260 pts (Biol Cons)
Nottingham Trent – 220 pts (Biol Sci)
Sheffield Hallam – 220 pts (Foren Biosci; Biomed Sci; Biol Sci Bus)
Stirling – CCD/BC 1st yr entry (Ecol; Aquacult) (IB 26 pts)
Sunderland – 220 pts (Biomed Sci)
Westminster – CCD (Biol Sci; Biomed Sci) (IB 26 pts)
Worcester – 220–240 pts (Ecology)

200 pts **Anglia Ruskin** – 200 pts (Foren Sci; App Biomed Sci; Biomed Sci; Biol Sci (Med Biol Microbiol); Ecol Cons)
Bedfordshire – 200 pts (Biomed Sci; Med Sci; Foren Sci)
Canterbury Christ Church – 200 pts (Biosci courses; Foren Sci)
Chester – 200–240 pts (Foren Biol; Biomed Sci) (IB 30 pts)
Derby – 200–240 pts (Foren Sci)
East London – 200 pts (Biomed Sci; Foren Sci)
Edinburgh Napier – 200 pts (Biomed Sci)
Glyndŵr – 200 pts (Foren Sci; Foren Sci Crim Just)
Kingston – 200–280 pts (Biomed Sci)
London Met – 200 pts (Foren Med Sci)
Middlesex – 200–240 pts (Spo Biomed; Biomed Sci)
Salford – 200 pts (Biomed Sci) (IB 24 pts)
Thames Valley – 200 pts (Foren Sci)
Wolverhampton – 200–260 pts (Foren Sci; Foren Mol Biol)

180 pts **De Montfort** – 180 pts (Foren Sci) (IB 24 pts)
Glasgow Caledonian – DDD (Foren Invstg; Cell Mol Biol; Biomed Sci)
Kingston – 180–280 pts (Foren Biol)
Sunderland – 180 pts (Foren Pharml Sci)

160 pts **Abertay Dundee** – CC (Foren Psychobiol)
Leeds Met – 160 pts (Biomed Sci courses)
London Met – 160 pts (Biol Sci)
London South Bank – 160 pts (Foren Sci)

Robert Gordon – CC (App Biomed Sci)
SAC (Scottish CAg) – CC (App Biosci)
140 pts **West Scotland** – CD (App Biosci; Foren Sci)
80 pts **Glasgow Caledonian** – EE (Biol Sci)
London (Birk) – 80 pts for under 21s (over 21 varies) (p/t Biol Sci Biomed)

Alternative offers
See **Chapter 7** and **Appendix 1** for grades/UCAS Tariff points information for the International Baccalaureate, Scottish Highers/Advanced Highers, the Welsh Baccalaureate, the Irish Leaving Certificate, the Cambridge Pre-U Diploma, the Advanced Diploma and the Extended Project.

EXAMPLES OF FOUNDATION DEGREES IN THE SUBJECT FIELD

Aston; Brighton; Bristol UWE; Cornwall (Coll); Glyndŵr; Hertfordshire; Hull (Coll); Kent; London (QM); Myerscough (Coll); Nescot; North Devon (Coll); Nottingham Trent; Plymouth; Plymouth City (Coll); Preston (Coll); Riverside Halton (Coll); Sheffield (Coll); Staffordshire; Thames Valley; Truro (Coll); Weymouth (Coll); Wigan and Leigh (Coll); Worcester; Writtle (Coll); York (Coll).

CHOOSING YOUR COURSE (SEE ALSO CH.1)

Some course features
Brighton (Biol Sci) A sandwich placement in Year 3 is optional. Specialist fields include animal sciences, ecology, forestry and countryside management.
Bristol (Immun) One of eight Cellular and Molecular Medicine courses, with flexibility to transfer between programmes as students' scientific interests develop. All have option for a year in industry.
Lancaster (Biol Sci) Opportunity to mix and match subjects such as genetics, biomedicine, land environment and ecology.
Leeds (Biol Sci) Students may transfer to any other course in the Faculty in Year 2.
Leicester The Biological Sciences programme offers specialist options in biochemistry, genetics, microbiology, physiology with pharmacology or zoology. All courses have a common first year with specialist decisions made in year 2.
Liverpool (Biol Sci) A broad programme, with option in first two years to specialise by transferring to any one of a range of courses in the subject field, eg Ecology, Genetics, Molecular Biology.
Warwick (Biol Sci) Specialisations in genetics, microbiology, cell biology, virology and environmental resources.
Westminster (Biol Sci) Students plan their programme with tutors through the course, combining core subjects (eg cell science, physiology) with option modules from a wide range of bioscience modules.

Universities and colleges teaching quality See www.qaa.ac.uk; www.unistats.com.

Top research universities and colleges (RAE 2008) Oxford (Biochemistry); Manchester; Oxford (Plant Sciences); Sheffield; Dundee; Bristol (Biochemistry); London (RH); York; Imperial London; London (King's); Leeds; Oxford (Zoology); Cambridge; Edinburgh.

Examples of sandwich degree courses Brighton; Bristol UWE; see also **Biology**.

ADMISSIONS INFORMATION

Number of applicants per place (approx) Aston (Biomed Sci) 8; Bristol 8, (Neuro) 10; Cardiff 8; Durham 11; East Anglia (Biol Sci) 15; Edinburgh 8; Essex 8; Lancaster (Biol Sci) 12; Leeds (Med Sci) 25; Leicester 7; London (King's) 7, (QM) 8, (St George's) 15; Newcastle 14; Nottingham 11; Southampton 8; Stirling 7; York 9.

Advice to applicants and planning the UCAS personal statement Read scientific journals and try to extend your knowledge beyond the A-level syllabus. Discuss your special interests, for example, ecology, microbiology, genetics or zoology (read up thoroughly on your interests since questions could be asked at interview). Voluntary attendance on courses, work experience, voluntary work, holiday jobs. Demonstrate good oral and written communication skills and be competent at handling numerical data. Interest in the law for forensic science courses. See **Appendix 4**.

Misconceptions about this course **Anglia Ruskin** (Foren Sci) Students are not aware that modules in management and quality assurance are taken as part of the course. **Birmingham** We offer a range of degree labels each with different UCAS codes, for example Biol Sci Genet, Biol Sci Microbiol: all have the same first year and students can freely transfer between them. It is not necessary to apply for more than one except Biol Sci Euro. (Med Sci) Applicants often use this course as an insurance for a vocational course (usually Medicine). If they are unsuccessful for their first choice, they occasionally find it difficult to commit themselves to Medical Sciences and do not perform as well as their academic performance would predict. **Cardiff** Some students mistakenly believe that they can transfer to Medicine. **De Montfort** (Foren Sci) Students are often unaware of how much of the work is analytical biology and chemistry: they think they spend their time visiting crime scenes. **London (St George's)** It is not possible to transfer to Medicine after the first year of the Biomedical Science course. Students may be able to transfer to Year 3 of the Medical course on completion of the BSc degree. **Swansea** (Med Sci Hum) Some applicants think the course is a form of medical training – it isn't, but it is relevant to anyone planning graduate entry for courses in Medicine or paramedical careers. (Biol Sci deferred entry) Some applicants think that this is a degree in its own right. In fact, after the first year, students have to choose one of the other degrees offered by the School of Biological Sciences. This course allows students an extra year in which to consider their final specialisation.

Selection interviews **Yes** Bangor, Bristol UWE, Durham, Essex, Greenwich, Hull, London (RH), (UCL), London South Bank, Manchester, Newcastle, Nottingham, Nottingham Trent, Oxford, Oxford Brookes, Stirling, Strathclyde, Sunderland, Surrey (Biomed Sci), Sussex, Swansea (Med Sci Hum), Warwick; **Some** Anglia Ruskin, Aston, Birmingham, Bristol, Cardiff, Cardiff (UWIC), De Montfort, Derby, East Anglia, Kent, Liverpool John Moores, London (St George's), Roehampton, Salford, Sheffield, Sheffield Hallam, Staffordshire, Wolverhampton, York.

Interview advice and questions You are likely to be asked about your main interests in biology and your choice of specialisation in the field of biological sciences or, for example, about the role of the botanist, specialist microbiologist in industry, your understanding of biotechnology or genetic engineering. Questions likely to be asked on field courses attended. If you have a field course workbook, take it to interview. **London (St George's)** (Biomed Sci) What career path do you envisage for yourself with this degree? **Oxford** No written or work tests. Interviews are rigorous but sympathetic; successful entrant average 38.8%. Applicants are expected to demonstrate their ability to understand whatever facts they have encountered and to discuss a particular aspect of biology in which they are interested (interviews rigorous but sympathetic). What problems does a fish face under water? Are humans still evolving? See also **Chapter 5**.

Reasons for rejection (non-academic) **Oxford** He appeared to have so much in his head that he tended to express his ideas in too much of a rush. He needs to slow down a bit and take more time to select points that are really pertinent to the questions.

AFTER-RESULTS ADVICE

Offers to applicants repeating A-levels **Higher** Bristol, Bristol UWE, Hull, London (St George's), Newcastle, St Andrews, Sheffield; **Possibly higher** Aston, Essex, Lancaster, Manchester Met; **Same** Anglia Ruskin, Birmingham, Cardiff, Chester, De Montfort, Derby, Durham, East Anglia, Edinburgh Napier, Exeter, Heriot-Watt, Kingston, Leeds, Lincoln, Liverpool Hope, Liverpool John Moores, London (RH), Oxford Brookes, Plymouth, Robert Gordon, Roehampton, Salford, Sheffield Hallam, Stirling, Thames Valley, Wolverhampton, Worcester, York; **No offers made** Cambridge.

GRADUATE DESTINATIONS AND EMPLOYMENT (2007/8 HESA)

See **Biology**.

Career note Degrees in Biological Science subjects often lead graduates into medical, pharmaceutical, veterinary, food and environmental work, research and education, in both the public and private sectors (see also **Biology**). Sandwich courses are offered at a number of institutions enabling students to gain paid experience in industry and commerce, often resulting in permanent employment on graduation. In recent years there has been a considerable increase in the number of

Biomedical Science courses designed for students interested in taking a hands-on approach to studying the biology of disease. However, students should be warned that the ever-popular Forensic Science courses may not always pave the way to jobs in this highly specialised field.

OTHER DEGREE SUBJECTS FOR CONSIDERATION

Biochemistry; Biology; Biotechnology; Botany; Chemistry; Consumer Sciences; Ecology; Environmental Health; Environmental Science; Genetics; Genomics; Immunology; Microbiology; Pharmaceutical Sciences; Pharmacology; Pharmacy; Physiology; Plant Sciences; Psychology; Sport and Exercise Science; Toxicology; Virology; Zoology.

BIOLOGY

(including **Applied, Cancer, Conservation, Environmental, Forensic, Human, Marine** and **Molecular Biology**; see also **Biological Sciences, Biotechnology, Microbiology** and **Zoology**)

The science of biology is a broad and rapidly developing subject that increasingly affects our lives. Biologists address the challenges faced by human populations such as disease, conservation and food production, and the continuing advances in such areas as genetics and molecular biology that have applications in medicine and agriculture.

Useful websites www.societyofbiology.org; www.scienceyear.com; www.bbsrc.ac.uk; see also Biochemistry.

NB The points totals shown to the left of the institutions are for ease of reference only. It must not be assumed that Tariff points are always used by institutions or that they can be substituted for an offer in grades. The level of an offer is not necessarily indicative of the quality of a course.

COURSE OFFERS INFORMATION

Subject requirements/preferences **GCSE** Mathematics and English stipulated in some cases. **AL** Biology and chemistry important, other science subjects may be accepted. Two and sometimes three mathematics/science subjects required including biology.

NB In 2011 universities and colleges will differ in their use of GCE AL/AS unit grade information, A* grades, the Extended Project (EPQ), the Advanced Diploma and the Cambridge Pre-U examination when considering applicants and making offers. An EPQ may be accepted in place of an AS subject. Check websites of universities and colleges for the latest offers information.

Your target offers and examples of courses provided by each institution

380 pts **Cambridge** – A*AA college offers may vary (Nat Sci (Biol Biomed Sci)) (IB 38–42 pts)
London (UCL) – AAA+AS–AAB+AS (Palaeobiology) (IB 34–38 pts)

360 pts **Bristol** – AAA–AAB (Biol; Biol Maths) (IB 34 pts HL 666)
Durham – AAA (Nat Sci (Biol))
Edinburgh – AAA 2nd yr entry (Med Biol; Mol Biol; Evol Biol) (IB 36 pts)
London (UCL) – AAB+AS–ABB+AS (Biol Sci (Env Biol))

340 pts **Bath** – AAB–ABB (Biol; Mol Cell Biol) (IB 34 pts)
Cardiff – AAB–ABB 340–320 pts (Biology)
Exeter (Cornwall) – AAB–BBB (Evol Biol; Cons Biol Ecol; Mol Biol; Biol Anim Bhv) (IB 34–29 pts)
Heriot-Watt – AAB 2nd yr entry (Brew Distil; Biol Sci (Microbiol))
Imperial London – AAB 340 pts (Biol; Ecol Env Biol; Biol Mgt; Biol Yr Euro/Ind/Rsch; Biol Microbiol; Biol Fr/Ger/Span Sci) (IB 38 pts)
Leeds – AAB (Nanotechnology) (IB 35 pts)
Manchester – AAB–BBB (Biol courses; Cell Biol courses; Dev Biol courses) (IB 32–35 pts)
Reading – AAB–ABBb (Psy Biol)
Sheffield – AAB (MBiol Sci Biol; Biol Cons Biodiv; BSc Biol Yr Abrd)
Southampton – ABB (Mar Biol; Mar Biol Ocean) (IB 36–30 pts HL 18–16 pts)

320 pts **Birmingham** – ABB–BBB (Hum Biol; Biol Sci (Env Biol) (Plant Biol); Palaeobiol; Palaeoenv) (IB 32–34 pts)
Bristol – ABB (Geol Maths; Palae Evol; Cncr Biol) (IB 33 pts HL 665)
Durham – ABB (Biol; Cell Biol; Biol Ind) (IB 34 pts)
East Anglia – ABB–BBB (Cell Biol; Microbiol; Plnt Biol) (IB 30 pts)
Glasgow – ABB (Mar Frshwtr Biol) (IB 32 pts)
Lancaster – ABB 320 pts (Cell Biol; Env Biol Abrd; Cons Biol Abrd) (IB 29–30 pts)
Leeds – ABB–BBB 320–300 pts (Biol; Ecol Env Biol; Biol Hist Phil Sci; Biol Mgt) (IB 34–32 pts)
Leicester – ABB (Med Microbiol)
Liverpool – ABB–BBB (Mar Biol; Trpcl Dis Biol; Biol Yr Ind/Rsch; Microbiol) (IB 33–30 pts)
London (RH) – ABB (Biol; Biol Psy; Biol Sci Comm; Mol Biol) (IB 34 pts)
Nottingham – ABB–BBB (Biol; Microbiol) (IB 31–32 pts)
St Andrews – ABB (Biol courses) (IB 32 pts)
Sheffield – ABB (BSc Biol; Biol Cons Biol Lang) (IB 33 pts)
Southampton – ABB 320 pts 3 AL inc 2 sci BBB 300 pts 3AL sci (Biology) (IB 32 pts)
Sussex – ABB (Biology) (IB 34 pts)
Warwick – ABB (Chem Biol) (IB 34 pts)
York – ABB (Biol; Biol Yr Ind/Euro; Mol Cell Biol) (IB 32 pts)

300 pts **Aberdeen** – BBB 2nd yr entry (Mar Biol; Cons Biol; Biol)
Aston – BBB (Cell Mol Biol; Infec Immun; App Hum Biol) (IB 33 pts)
Dundee – BBB 2nd yr entry (Biol; Mol Biol; Microbiol; Mathem Biol) (IB 32 pts)
Edinburgh – BBB 1st yr entry (Med Biol; Mol Biol; Evol Biol) (IB 32 pts)
Essex – 300–260 pts (Mar Frshwtr Biol; Mol Cell Biol) (IB 32–28 pts)
Heriot-Watt – BBB 1st yr entry (Brew Distil; App Mar Biol; Biol Sci (Microbiol))
Keele – 300 pts inc BC (Biol courses) (IB 26–28 pts)
Lancaster – BBB 300 pts (Env Biol; Cell Biol Biomed; Biol Psy) (IB 29–30 pts)
London (QM) – 300 pts (Biol Psy)
Loughborough – 300–320 pts (Hum Biol) (IB 32–34 pts)
Newcastle – BBB (Biol; App Biol; Mar Biol; Biol Chem; Mar Biol Ocean) (IB 32–35 pts HL biol 6)
Nottingham – BBB–BCC (App Biol) (IB 32 pts)
Plymouth – 300–360 pts (Mar Biol courses)
Queen's Belfast – BBB–BBC (Env Biol; Mol Biol)
Sheffield – BBB (Biol Arch)
Stirling – BBB 2nd yr entry (Biol; Mar Biol; Cell Biol; Anim Biol) (IB 26 pts)
Warwick – BBB (Env Biol) (IB 32 pts)

280 pts **Aberystwyth** – 280 pts (Biol; Env Biol; Biol Bioinform; Mar Frshwtr Biol; Hum Biol Spo Sci; Plnt Biol) (IB 26 pts)
Bangor – 280–340 pts (MBiol Biol)
Gloucestershire – 280 pts (Biol; Anim Biol)
London (QM) – 280 pts (Biology) (IB 30–32 pts)
Northumbria – 280 pts (App Biol; Biol Foren Biol)
Oxford Brookes – BBC 280 pts (Biol courses; Hum Biol; Cell Mol Biol) (IB 30 pts)
Plymouth – 280–320 pts (Env Biol) (IB 26 pts)
Queen's Belfast – BBC/BCCb (Hum Biol; Mar Biol)
Staffordshire – 280 pts (Bioinformatics)
Strathclyde – BBC 2nd yr entry (Foren Biol)
Swansea – 280–300 pts (Biol; Mar Biol)
Teesside – 280 pts (Foren Biol)

260 pts **Bangor** – 260–320 pts (App Mar Biol; Mar Biol; Mar Biol Zool)
Bournemouth – 260–240 pts (App Biol Hlth; App Biol)
Bristol UWE – 260–300 pts (Foren Biol; Spo Biol; Hum Biol; Cons Biol)
Central Lancashire – 260–300 pts (Foren Biol)
Kent – BCC–BBC (Biol courses) (IB 28–30 pts HL 13–14 pts)
Liverpool Hope – 260–300 pts (Hum Biol)

Nottingham – BCC–CCC (Env Biol)
Nottingham Trent – 260 pts (Foren Biol)
Portsmouth – 260–300 pts (Biol; Foren Biol; Mar Biol)
Sheffield Hallam – 260 pts (Hum Biol; Biol)
Strathclyde – BCC (Foren Biol)
Ulster – 260 pts (Biology) (IB 28 pts)

240 pts **Aberdeen** – CCC 1st yr entry (Biol; Cons Biol)
Bangor – 240–280 pts (Biol; Mar Biol Ocean; App Ter Mar Ecol; Cancr Biol; Mol Biol) (IB 28 pts)
Brighton – CCC/BCD (Env Biol Educ)
Cardiff (UWIC) – 240 pts (Biomed Sci (Mol Biol))
Cumbria – 240 pts (Cons Biol)
Dundee – 240 pts 1st yr entry (Biol; Mathem Biol; Microbiol; Mol Biol) (IB 29 pts)
Glamorgan – 240–280 pts (Int Wldlf Biol)
Hertfordshire – 240 pts (Mol Biol Genet)
Huddersfield – 240 pts (Med Biol; Biol (Mol Cell))
Hull – 240–280 pts (Biol; Hum Biol; Mar Frshwtr Biol; Aqua)
Lincoln – 240 pts (Cons Biol)
Roehampton – 240–300 pts (Cons Biol)

220 pts **Bath Spa** – 220–260 pts (Biol courses)
Edge Hill – 220–260 pts (Biology)
Edinburgh Napier – 220 pts (Mar Frshwtr Biol; Foren Biol; Anim Biol)
Glamorgan – 220–260 pts (Biol; Hum Biol; Foren Biol)
Hull – 220–280 pts (Cstl Mar Biol)
Liverpool John Moores – 220–260 pts (Mol Biol Genet; Biol; Psy Biol)
Manchester Met – 220–260pts (Biol courses; Cell Mol Biol; Cons Biol) (IB 28 pts)
Northampton – 220–260 pts (Biol; App Cons Biol)
Stirling – CCD 1st yr entry (Biol; Mar Biol; Cell Biol; Anim Biol) (IB 26 pts)
Westminster – CCD (Foren Biol; Mol Biol Genet) (IB 26 pts)

200 pts **Anglia Ruskin** – 200 pts (Biol courses)
Bolton – 200 pts (Biol courses)
Canterbury Christ Church – 200 pts (Env Biol courses)
Chester – 200–240 pts (Biol; Foren Biol) (IB 30 pts)
Derby – 200–240 pts (Biol; Cons Biol)
East London – 200 pts (App Biol; Hum Biol courses)
Nottingham Trent – 200–220 pts (Anim Biol; Zoo Biol)
Salford – 200 pts (Biol courses)
Staffordshire – 200–260 pts (Biol courses; Hum Biol) (IB 28 pts)
Wolverhampton – 200–260 pts (Genet Mol Biol; Microbiol)
Worcester – 200 pts (Hum Biol; Biol)

180 pts **Glasgow Caledonian** – CC–DDD (Hum Biol Sociol Psy)
Greenwich – 180 pts (App Biol; Cell Mol Biol; Hum Biosci)
Kingston – 180–280 pts (Biol; Foren Biol; Hum Biol courses; Cell Mol Biol)

160 pts **Essex** – 160 pts (Mar Frshwtr Biol 4 yr)
Leeds Met – 160 pts (Biomed Sci (Hum Biol))
London South Bank – CC (Biosci (Hum Biol) (Microbiol))
Queen Margaret – 160–165 pts (Hum Biol)

120 pts **Strathclyde** – DD (Nat Sci (Biol))
West Scotland – DD (Biol courses; Env Biol)

80 pts **London (Birk)** – 80 pts for under 21s (over 21 varies) (p/t Mol Biol)

Alternative offers

See **Chapter 7** and **Appendix 1** for grades/UCAS Tariff points information for the International Baccalaureate, Scottish Highers/Advanced Highers, the Welsh Baccalaureate, the Irish Leaving Certificate, the Cambridge Pre-U Diploma, the Advanced Diploma and the Extended Project.

EXAMPLES OF FOUNDATION DEGREES IN THE SUBJECT FIELD

Anglia Ruskin; Bedfordshire; Blackpool and Fylde (Coll); Bournemouth; Cornwall (Coll); Harlow (Coll); Nottingham Trent; Truro (Coll). See also **Biological Sciences**.

CHOOSING YOUR COURSE (SEE ALSO CH.1)

Some course features

Bangor (Biol) Some students take a 3–6-month exchange programme in Europe or the USA.
Cardiff Biochemistry, Biological Sciences and Biology courses have a common first year with the option to change at the end of Year 1.
Gloucestershire A hands-on Biology course with an emphasis on laboratory projects and field work. A short placement is included.
Leeds (Biol) An optional year in industry is offered.
London (UCL) The degrees in Biology, Environmental Biology, Human Genetics and Zoology have a common first year with the opportunity to change degrees within the department.
Nottingham (Biol) A comprehensive modern treatment of microbial, plant, animal and human biology.
Swansea (Biol) A deferred choice course enables students to choose their final degree subjects in Year 2.

Universities and colleges teaching quality See www.qaa.ac.uk; www.unistats.com.

Top research universities and colleges (RAE 2008) See **Biological Sciences**.

Examples of sandwich degree courses Aston; Bath; Bradford; Bristol; Bristol UWE; Cardiff; Coventry; De Montfort; East London; Edinburgh Napier; Glamorgan; Harper Adams (UC); Hertfordshire; Huddersfield; Kent; Kingston; Leeds; Liverpool John Moores; London South Bank; Loughborough; Manchester; Manchester Met; Middlesex; Northumbria; Nottingham Trent; Plymouth; Reading; Sheffield Hallam; Surrey; Teesside; Ulster; West Scotland; York.

ADMISSIONS INFORMATION

Number of applicants per place (approx) Aberdeen 8; Aberystwyth 5; Aston 6; Bath 7; Birmingham 3; Bradford 7; Bristol 9; Cardiff 8; Dundee 6; Durham 11; Exeter 6; Hull 4; Imperial London 4; Kent 10; Leeds 6; Leicester 15; London (King's) 5; (RH) 5; Newcastle (Mar Biol) 15, (App Biol) 9; Nottingham 9; Oxford Brookes 13; Salford 3; Southampton (Mar Biol Ocean) 6, (Biol) 7; Stirling 15; Sussex 4; Swansea (Mar Biol) 8, (Biol) 4; York 5.

Advice to applicants and planning the UCAS personal statement **York** Advanced Diploma not generally accepted. See **Biochemistry**, **Biological Sciences** and **Appendix 4**.

Misconceptions about this course **Sussex** Many students think that a Biology degree limits you to being a professional scientist which is not the case. **York** Some fail to realise that chemistry beyond GCSE is essential. Mature students often lack the confidence to consider the course.

Selection interviews **Yes** Bangor, Bath, Birmingham, Bradford (informal, after offer), Cambridge, Durham, East Anglia, Essex, Hertfordshire, Imperial London, Kent, Kingston, London (RH), (UCL), London South Bank, Nottingham (depends on application), SAC (Scottish CAg), Sheffield Hallam, Southampton, Staffordshire, Surrey, Swansea, Writtle (Coll); **Some** Anglia Ruskin, Aston, Bath Spa, Derby, Dundee, Liverpool John Moores, London (King's), Roehampton, Salford, Sheffield, Stirling, Wolverhampton, York.

Interview advice and questions Questions are likely to focus on your studies in biology, on any work experience or any special interests you may have in biology outside school. In the past, questions have included: Is the computer like a brain and, if so, could it ever be taught to think? What do you think the role of the environmental biologist will be in the next 40–50 years? Have you any strong views on vivisection? You have a micro-organism in the blood: you want to make a culture. What conditions should be borne in mind? What is a pacemaker? What problems will a giraffe experience? How does water enter a flowering plant? Compare an egg and a potato. Discuss a family tree of human genotypes. Discuss fish farming in Britain today. **Liverpool John Moores**

Informal interview. It is useful to bring samples of coursework to the interview. **York** Why Biology? How do you see your future? See also **Chapter 5**.

Reasons for rejection (non-academic) **Bath Spa** Poor mathematical and scientific knowledge.

AFTER-RESULTS ADVICE

Offers to applicants repeating A-levels **Higher** Cardiff, East London, London (King's), St Andrews, Strathclyde; **Possibly higher** Aston, Bath, Bradford, Durham, Leeds, London (RH), Nottingham, Portsmouth; **Same** Aberystwyth, Anglia Ruskin, Bangor, Bedfordshire, Brunel, Chester, Derby, Dundee, Edinburgh Napier, Heriot-Watt, Hull, Liverpool John Moores, London (UCL), London South Bank, Loughborough, Manchester Met, Newcastle, Oxford Brookes, Plymouth, Roehampton, Salford, Sheffield, Southampton, Staffordshire, Stirling, Teesside, Ulster, Wolverhampton, York.

GRADUATE DESTINATIONS AND EMPLOYMENT (2007/8 HESA)

Graduates surveyed 3205 **Employed** 1270 **In further study** 835 **Assumed unemployed** 310.

Career note Some graduates go into research, but many will go into laboratory work in hospitals, food laboratories, agriculture, the environment and pharmaceuticals. Others go into teaching, management and other professional and technical areas.

OTHER DEGREE SUBJECTS FOR CONSIDERATION

Anatomy; Biochemistry; Biological Sciences; Biotechnology; Chemistry; Dentistry; Ecology; Environmental Health; Environmental Science/Studies; Food Science; Genomics; Health Studies; Medicine; Midwifery; Nursing; Nutrition; Optometry; Orthoptics; Pharmaceutical Sciences; Pharmacology; Pharmacy; Physiology; Physiotherapy; Plant Sciences; Radiography; Speech and Language Therapy; Zoology.

BIOTECHNOLOGY

(including **Medical Engineering**)

Biotechnology is a multidisciplinary subject which can include chemistry, biological sciences, microbiology, genetics and chemical engineering. Medical engineering involves the design, installation, maintenance and provision of technical support for diagnostic, therapeutic and other clinical equipment used by doctors, nurses and other clinical healthcare workers.

Biomedical engineering applies the principles of engineering, medicine and science to medical technologies used in the diagnosis, prognosis, monitoring and treatment of ill and injured people.

Useful websites www.bbsrc.ac.uk; www.scienceyear.com; www.abcinformation.org.

NB The points totals shown to the left of the institutions are for ease of reference only. It must not be assumed that Tariff points are always used by institutions or that they can be substituted for an offer in grades. The level of an offer is not necessarily indicative of the quality of a course.

COURSE OFFERS INFORMATION

Subject requirements/preferences **GCSE** Mathematics and science subjects required. **AL** Courses vary but one, two or three subjects from chemistry, biology, physics and mathematics may be required.

NB In 2011 universities and colleges will differ in their use of GCE AL/AS unit grade information, A* grades, the Extended Project (EPQ), the Advanced Diploma and the Cambridge Pre-U examination when considering applicants and making offers. An EPQ may be accepted in place of an AS subject. Check websites of universities and colleges for the latest offers information.

Your target offers and examples of courses provided by each institution

360 pts **Edinburgh** – AAA 2nd yr entry (Biotechnology) (IB 36 pts)
London (UCL) – AAB+AS–ABB+AS (Biotechnology) (IB 34–36 pts)

340 pts **Birmingham** – AAB–BBB (Biol Sci (Biotech); Mech Eng (Biomed); Bioch Biotech) (IB 32–34 pts)
Bristol – AAB (Bioch Mol Biol Biotech) (IB 35 pts HL 666)
Cardiff – AAB 340 pts (MEng Med Eng)
Imperial London – AAB 340 pts (BSc Biotech; Biotech Mgt Yr Ind/Rsch; BEng Biomat Tiss Eng; Bioeng) (IB 34 pts HL chem biol 6)
Leeds – AAB (MEng Med Eng) (IB 36 pts HL 17 pts)
Manchester – AAB–BBB (Biotech (Ent) (Ent Ind)) (IB 35–32 pts)
Newcastle – AAB–ABB (Biotech; Bioproc Eng) (IB 33 pts)
Surrey – AAB 340 pts (MEng Med Eng) (IB 34–32 pts)

320 pts **Edinburgh** – ABB 1st yr entry (Biotechnology) (IB 32 pts)
Glasgow – ABB (Biotechnology) (IB 32 pts)
Liverpool – ABB–BBB (Microbl Biotech) (IB 33–30 pts)
Newcastle – ABB (Biotech; Biotech Ind) (IB 30–32 pts)
Sheffield – ABB–BBC (Med Sys Eng Mgt; Biomat Sci Tiss Eng; Biomed Eng) (IB 33–30 pts)

300 pts **Aberdeen** – 2nd yr entry BBB (Biotechnology)
Birmingham – BBB (Biomed Mat Sci) (IB 30 pts)
Bradford – 300 pts (MEng Med Eng)
Cardiff – BBB 300 pts (BEng Med Eng)
Nottingham – BBB–BCC (Biomed Mat Sci; Biotech Cert Euro St; Biotech) (IB 32 pts)
Surrey – BBB 300 pts (BEng Med Eng) (IB 30–32 pts)

280 pts **Bradford** – 280 pts (Clin Sci)
City – BBC 280 pts (BEng Biomed Eng) (IB 28 pts)
Northumbria – 280 pts (Biotechnology) (IB 28 pts)
Oxford Brookes – BBC (Biotechnology) (IB 30 pts)
Reading – 280 pts (Biomed Eng Cyber)
Salford – 280 pts (Pros Orthot) (IB 28 pts)
Strathclyde – BBC (Pros Orthot) (IB 32 pts)

260 pts **Bradford** – 260 pts (App Biotech)
Bristol UWE – 260–300 pts (Biotechnology)
London (QM) – 260–340 pts (MEng/BEng Med Eng; Biomed Mat Sci Eng; Biomat) (IB 30–32 pts)

240 pts **Aberdeen** – CCC 1st yr entry (Biotechnology)
Bradford – 240 pts (BEng Med Eng)
Hertfordshire – 240 pts (Biotechnology)
Ulster – 240 pts (Biomed Eng)

220 pts **Edinburgh Napier** – 220 pts (Microbiol Biotech)
Westminster – CCD (Biotechnology) (IB 26 pts)

200 pts **Bradford** – 200 pts (Fdn Clin Tech)
East London – 200 pts (Med Biotech)

160 pts **SAC (Scottish CAg)** – CC (App Biosci)
Wolverhampton – 160–220 pts (Biotechnology)

140 pts **West Scotland** – CD 140 pts (App Biosci; Phys Med Tech)

Alternative offers

See **Chapter 7** and **Appendix 1** for grades/UCAS Tariff points information for the International Baccalaureate, Scottish Highers/Advanced Highers, the Welsh Baccalaureate, the Irish Leaving Certificate, the Cambridge Pre-U Diploma, the Advanced Diploma and the Extended Project.

EXAMPLES OF FOUNDATION DEGREES IN THE SUBJECT FIELD

Edinburgh Napier.

CHOOSING YOUR COURSE (SEE ALSO CH.1)

Some course features

Leeds (Med Eng) The course combines engineering science, biological science and medicine. It has study abroad and work placement opportunities and strong links with industry.

Manchester (Biotech) A common first year covering several Life Science subjects provides the opportunity to change at a later stage.
Newcastle Twelve degrees covering the biomedical and biomolecular sciences have a common first year allowing the flexibility to make a final choice at the end of Stage 1.
Northumbria (Biotech) Main focus of course is on molecular biotechnology, including molecular biology, immunology and bioinformatics.
Wolverhampton (Biotech) Specialisation in gene manipulation, plant or microbial biotechnology.

Universities and colleges teaching quality See www.qaa.ac.uk; www.unistats.com.

Examples of sandwich degree courses Bradford; Bristol; Bristol UWE; Cardiff; Edinburgh Napier; Manchester; Northumbria; Reading; Sussex.

ADMISSIONS INFORMATION

Number of applicants per place (approx) Bristol 9; Cardiff 4; Imperial London 4; Leeds 7; London (UCL) 4; Strathclyde 4.

Advice to applicants and planning the UCAS personal statement See **Biological Sciences** and **Biochemistry**. See also **Appendix 4**.

Selection interviews **Yes** Imperial London, Leeds, Strathclyde, Surrey; **Some** Cardiff, Wolverhampton.

Interview advice and questions See **Biology** and **Biological Sciences**. See also **Chapter 5**.

AFTER-RESULTS ADVICE

Offers to applicants repeating A-levels **Possibly higher** Nottingham; **Same** Cardiff, Leeds, Liverpool John Moores, Wolverhampton.

GRADUATE DESTINATIONS AND EMPLOYMENT (2006/7 HESA)

Graduates surveyed 35 **Employed** 15 **In further study** 10 **Assumed unemployed** None.

Career note Biotechnology, biomedical and biochemical engineering opportunities exist in medical, agricultural, food science and pharmaceutical laboratories. Some Bioengineering graduates apply for graduate medical courses and obtain both engineering and medical qualifications.

OTHER DEGREE SUBJECTS FOR CONSIDERATION

Agriculture; Biochemistry; Biological Sciences; Biomedicine; Chemistry; Food Technology; Genetics; Materials Science and Technology; Microbiology; Molecular Biology; Pharmacology.

BUILDING and CONSTRUCTION

(including **Building Design, Building Services Engineering, Building Surveying, Construction, Fire Risk Engineering, Fire Safety Management**; for Architectural Technology see **Architecture**; see also **Property Management/Development**)

The building and construction industry covers a wide range of activities and is closely allied to civil, municipal and structural engineering and quantity surveying. One branch of the industry covers building services engineering, a career which involves specialised areas such as heating, acoustics, lighting, refrigeration and air conditioning. Many Building, Construction, Building Surveying and Building Services Engineering courses include industrial placements and are accredited by professional bodies such as the Chartered Institute of Building, the Royal Institution of Chartered Surveyors and the Engineering Council.

Useful websites www.ciob.org.uk; www.cibse.org; www.cskills.org.

NB The points totals shown to the left of the institutions are for ease of reference only. It must not be assumed that Tariff points are always used by institutions or that they can be substituted for an offer in grades. The level of an offer is not necessarily indicative of the quality of a course.

COURSE OFFERS INFORMATION

Subject requirements/preferences **GCSE** English, mathematics and science usually required. **AL** Physics, mathematics or a technical subject may be required for some courses.

NB In 2011 universities and colleges will differ in their use of GCE AL/AS unit grade information, A* grades, the Extended Project (EPQ), the Advanced Diploma and the Cambridge Pre-U examination when considering applicants and making offers. An EPQ may be accepted in place of an AS subject. Check websites of universities and colleges for the latest offers information.

Your target offers and examples of courses provided by each institution

340 pts **Heriot-Watt** – AAB 2nd yr entry (Constr Proj Mgt; Bld Surv) (IB 35 pts)
Leeds – AAB (Civ Eng Constr Mgt courses) (IB 36 pts)
Manchester – AAB-BBB (Blt Nat Env Comb St) (IB 35–32 pts)
320 pts **Brunel** – 320 pts 3AL +AS/EPQ c (MEng/BEng Mech Eng Bld Serv) (IB 32 pts)
London (UCL) – BBB+AS (Proj Mgt Constr) (IB 32 pts)
300 pts **Kingston** – 300 pts (Bld Surv) (IB 28 pts)
Loughborough – 300 pts (Commer Mgt Quant Surv) (IB 32 pts)
Newcastle – BBB (Surv Map Sci) (IB 32 pts)
Reading – 300–320 pts pts (Bld Constr Mgt; Bld Surv; Constr Mgt Surv)
Ulster – 300 pts (Bld Surv; Constr Eng Mgt)
280 pts **Aston** – 280 pts (Constr Mgt; Constr Proj Mgt) (IB 29 pts)
Brighton – BBC 260 pts (Bld Surv; Constr Mgt) (IB 28 pts)
Central Lancashire – 280 pts (Fire Ldrshp St)
Heriot-Watt – BBC 1st yr entry (Constr Proj Mgt; Bld Surv) (IB 29 pts)
Loughborough – 280 pts (Constr Eng Mgt) (IB 30 pts)
Northumbria – 280 pts (Bld Surv) (IB 30 pts)
Nottingham – BBC (Sust Blt Env) (IB 30 pts)
Nottingham Trent – 280 pts (Bld Surv) (IB 31 pts)
Salford – 280 pts (Constr Mgt; Constr Proj Mgt; Bld Surv)
Westminster – BBC (Bld Eng; Bld Surv; Constr Mgt; Constr Surv) (IB 26 pts)
270 pts **Anglia Ruskin** – 270 pts (Bld Surv)
Glasgow Caledonian – 270 pts (Bld Surv; Bld Serv Eng; Constr Mgt; Fire Rsk Eng)
Liverpool John Moores – 270 pts (Bld Serv Eng)
Sheffield Hallam – 270 pts (Bld Surv)
260 pts **Birmingham City** – 260 pts (Bld Surv)
Oxford Brookes – BCC (Constr Mgt) (IB 28 pts)
Plymouth – 260 pts (Bld Surv Env) (IB 27 pts)
Ulster – 260 pts (Bld Mats Eng) (IB 32 pts)
240 pts **Anglia Ruskin** – 240 pts (Constr Mgt)
Bolton – 240 pts (Constr Mgt; Bld Surv Prop Mgt; Constr)
Central Lancashire – 240–260 pts (Bld Serv Sust Eng; Fire Eng)
Coventry – 240 pts (BEng Bld Serv Eng)
Edinburgh Napier – 240 pts (Bld Surv; Constr Proj Mgt)
Glamorgan – 240–280 pts (Bld Serv Eng)
Greenwich – 240 pts (Constr Surv Mgt; Constr Bus Mgt)
Leeds Met – 240–230 pts (Constr Mgt; Bld Surv)
Liverpool John Moores – 240 pts (Bld Serv Eng Proj Mgt; Constr Mgt)
Newport – 240 pts (Bld St)
Northumbria – 240–280 pts (Bld Des Mgt; Constr Mgt; Bld Surv; Bld Proj Mgt) (IB 25 pts)
Nottingham Trent – 240 pts (Constr Mgt; Constr Prop Mgt)
Plymouth – 240 pts (Constr Mgt Env)
Portsmouth – 240 pts (Bld Serv Tech)
230 pts **Central Lancashire** – 230 pts (Bld Surv)
Coventry – 230 pts (Bld Surv; Quant Surv Commer Mgt; Constr Mgt)

Liverpool John Moores – 230 pts (Bld Surv; Bld Serv Eng Proj Mgt) (IB 25 pts)
Sheffield Hallam – 230 pts (Constr Mgt)
Wolverhampton – 230 pts (Bld Surv)

220 pts **Bristol UWE** – 220–260 pts (Blt Nat Env; Constr Commer Mgt; Constr Prop Mgt; Constr Mgt)
Central Lancashire – 220 pts (Constr Proj Mgt)
Glamorgan – 220–260 pts (Proj Mgt (Constr))
London South Bank – 220 pts (Constr Mgt; Prop Mgt (Bld Surv))

200 pts **Glyndŵr** – 200 pts (Bld St (Constr) (Mntnce Mgt))

180 pts **Derby** – 180–240 pts (Constr Mgt)
Greenwich – 180 pts (Bld Surv)
Liverpool John Moores – 180 pts (Constr Mgt)
Plymouth – 180 pts (Env Constr Surv)
Portsmouth – 180 pts (Constr Eng Mgt)

160 pts **Central Lancashire** – 160 pts (Fire Sfty Risk Mgt)
Kingston – 160 pts (Constr Mgt)
Robert Gordon – 160 pts (Constr Des Mgt)
Swansea Met – 160–360 pts (Proj Constr Mgt; Constr Mgt; Bld Cons Mgt)
Wolverhampton – 160–220 pts (Constr Mgt)

150 pts **Portsmouth** – 150 pts (Constr Eng Mgt)
Thames Valley – 150 pts (Blt Env courses)

120 pts **Colchester (Inst)** – 120 pts (Constr Mgt)
Huddersfield – 120 pts (Constr Proj Mgt)
Southampton Solent – 120 pts (Constr Mgt)

Alternative offers
See **Chapter 7** and **Appendix 1** for grades/UCAS Tariff points information for the International Baccalaureate, Scottish Highers/Advanced Highers, the Welsh Baccalaureate, the Irish Leaving Certificate, the Cambridge Pre-U Diploma, the Advanced Diploma and the Extended Project.

EXAMPLES OF FOUNDATION DEGREES IN THE SUBJECT FIELD
Bedfordshire; Blackburn (Coll Univ Centre); Bolton; Bournemouth; Bradford (Coll); Brighton; Central Lancashire; Colchester (Inst); Cornwall (Coll); Cumbria; Derby; Ealing, Hammersmith and West London (Coll); East London; Glamorgan; Glyndŵr; Greenwich; Huddersfield; Kent; Kingston; Northampton; Northumbria; Suffolk (Univ Campus); Swansea Met; Thames Valley; West Nottinghamshire (Coll); Westminster City (Coll); Weymouth (Coll); Wolverhampton.

CHOOSING YOUR COURSE (SEE ALSO CH.1)
Some course features
Aston Construction and Construction Project Management courses have a common first year; sandwich course has good industrial contacts.
Heriot-Watt (Constr Proj Mgt) Three options are offered in Project Management, Surveying or Building Services.
Loughborough (Constr Eng Mgt) Course sponsored by industry. Two six-month placements of industrial training.
Northumbria The Foundation degree route enables entry to Architectural Technology, Building Services Engineering or Surveying, Construction Management, Estate Management or Quantity Surveying.
Plymouth The course is accredited by the Chartered Institute of Building and focuses on the environmental and sustainability performance of buildings.
Reading Students taking Construction Management, Quantity Surveying and Building Surveying follow the same course for two years, choosing the specialism in Year 3.

Universities and colleges teaching quality See www.qaa.ac.uk; www.unistats.com.

Top research universities and colleges (RAE 2008) See **Architecture**.

Examples of sandwich degree courses Aston; Bristol UWE; Brunel; Cardiff; Edinburgh Napier; Glasgow Caledonian; Kingston; Leeds Met; London South Bank; Loughborough; Northumbria; Nottingham Trent; Oxford Brookes; Plymouth; Sheffield Hallam; Ulster; Wolverhampton.

ADMISSIONS INFORMATION

Number of applicants per place (approx) Bristol UWE (Constr Mgt) 5; Edinburgh Napier 8; Glamorgan 3; Glasgow Caledonian 6; Heriot-Watt 6; Kingston 4; London (UCL) 4; Loughborough 4; Northumbria 6; Salford (Bld Surv) 6; Strathclyde 5.

Advice to applicants and planning the UCAS personal statement Details of work experience with any levels of responsibility should be included. Make contact with any building organisation to arrange a meeting with staff to discuss careers in building. Give evidence of your ability to work in a team and give details of any personal achievements in technological areas and work experience. Building also covers civil engineering, surveying, quantity surveying etc and these areas should also be explored. See also **Appendix 2**.

Misconceptions about this course **Loughborough** Some students fail to realise that the degree includes law, finance, economics and management plus constructional technology.

Selection interviews **Yes** Brunel, Derby, Glamorgan, Glasgow Caledonian, Greenwich, Kingston, Liverpool John Moores, London South Bank, Loughborough, Plymouth, Robert Gordon, Sheffield Hallam, Staffordshire, Westminster; **Some** Anglia Ruskin, Birmingham City, Brighton, Salford.

Interview advice and questions Work experience in the building and civil engineering industries is important and you could be expected to describe any building project you have visited and any problems experienced in its construction. A knowledge of the range of activities to be found on a building site will be expected, for example the work of quantity and land surveyors and of the various building trades. **Loughborough** The applicant should show an understanding of the role of the quantity surveyor. See also **Chapter 5**.

Reasons for rejection (non-academic) Inability to communicate. Lack of motivation. Indecisiveness about reasons for choosing the course. **Loughborough** Applicant more suited to hands-on rather than an academic course.

AFTER-RESULTS ADVICE

Offers to applicants repeating A-levels **Higher** Liverpool John Moores, Strathclyde; **Possibly higher** Bristol UWE; **Same** Birmingham City, Bolton, Brighton, Coventry, Heriot-Watt, Huddersfield, Kingston, London (UCL), Loughborough, Northumbria, Robert Gordon.

GRADUATE DESTINATIONS AND EMPLOYMENT (2007/8 HESA)

Graduates surveyed 1265 **Employed** 820 **In further study** 55 **Assumed unemployed** 140.

Career note There is a wide range of opportunities within the building and construction industry for building technologists and managers, particularly stemming from the construction projects for the 2012 Olympic Games in London. This subject area also overlaps into surveying, quantity surveying, civil engineering, architecture and planning and graduates from all these subjects commonly work together as members of construction teams.

OTHER DEGREE SUBJECTS FOR CONSIDERATION

Architectural Technology; Architecture; Civil Engineering; Property Planning and Development; Quantity Surveying; Surveying.

BUSINESS COURSES

(**Section A:** Business and Management Courses; **Section B:** International and European Business and Management Courses, Business and Management Courses with Languages; **Section C:** Specialised Business and Management Courses including Advertising, E-Commerce, Entrepreneurship, Operations Management, Public Relations and Publishing; see also **Hospitality and Hotel Management, Human Resource Management, Leisure and Recreation Management/Studies, Marketing, Retail Management** and **Tourism and Travel**)

Business degrees attract more applicants than any other degree subject, with a further rise in the past year for places on a wide range of programmes. Financial studies form part of most courses, in addition to sales, marketing, human resources management and general management. Since this is a vocational subject, some work experience in the field is generally required prior to application. Many courses offer industrial placements, in some cases in the USA, Australia and New Zealand and, for those students with an A-level in a language (and in some cases a good GCSE), placements abroad in Europe are possible.

Useful websites www.civilservicem.gov.uk/jobs/faststream; www.bized.co.uk; www.icsa.org.uk; www.oft.gov.uk; www.adassoc.org.uk; www.cipr.co.uk; www.ismm.co.uk; www.export.org.uk; www.ipsos-mori.com; www.capitaresourcing.co.uk; www.tax.org.uk; www.hmrc.gov.uk; www.camfoundation.com; www.shell-livewire.org; www.ibconsulting.org.uk; www.managers.org.uk; www.cipd.co.uk; www.inprad.org; www.managementhelp.com.

NB The points totals shown to the left of the institutions are for ease of reference only. It must not be assumed that Tariff points are always used by institutions or that they can be substituted for an offer in grades. The level of an offer is not necessarily indicative of the quality of a course.

COURSE OFFERS INFORMATION

Subject requirements/preferences **GCSE** Mathematics and English often at grade A or B required. **AL** Mathematics required for some courses and a language will be stipulated for most courses in Section B. In some cases grades A, B or C may be required. (**Publishing**) English required for some courses.

NB In 2011 universities and colleges will differ in their use of GCE AL/AS unit grade information, A* grades, the Extended Project (EPQ), the Advanced Diploma and the Cambridge Pre-U examination when considering applicants and making offers. An EPQ may be accepted in place of an AS subject. Check websites of universities and colleges for the latest offers information.

SECTION A: BUSINESS AND MANAGEMENT COURSES

(Refer to **Section B** and **Section C** for other Business courses)

Your target offers and examples of courses provided by each institution

390 pts **London (King's)** – AABb (Bus Mgt) (IB 36 pts HL 665)
Warwick – AABb (Management) (IB 36 pts)

360 pts **Bath** – AAA (Bus Admin) (IB 38 pts)
Bristol – AAA–ABB inc A maths (Mgt Acc; Mgt Econ) (IB 37–34 pts)
Cambridge – competitive entry after 2 or 3 yrs or another Cambridge Tripos course (Mgt St) (IB 38–42 pts)
Durham – AAA–ABB (Bus Econ)
Exeter – AAA–AAB (Bus Mgt; Mgt courses) (IB 36–33 pts)
Imperial London – AAA–AAB (Mgt Joint Hons with Bioch/Biol/Biotech/Chem/Elec Electron Eng courses – contact the subj dept)
St Andrews – AAA (Mgt courses; Mgt Sci) (IB 36 pts)

340 pts **Aston** – 340–320 pts (Bus Mgt; Mgt Strat) (IB 34 pts)
Birmingham – AAB–ABB (Bus Mgt courses) (IB 34 pts)
Cardiff – AAB (Bus Mgt)
City – AAB (Bus St; Mgt) (IB 35 pts)

Glasgow – AAB–ABB (Bus Mgt courses) (IB 30 pts)
Lancaster – AAB (Bus St; Mgt courses) (IB 34–36 pts)
Leeds – AAB (Mgt Trans St; Mgt Mark; Mgt) (IB 35 pts HL 17 pts)
London (RH) – AAB (Management) (IB 35 pts)
London LSE – AAB (Mgt; Mgt Sci) (IB 37 pts HL 766)
Loughborough – AAB (Mgt Sci; Maths Mgt) (IB 36 pts)
Manchester – AAB–ABB (Bus St; Mgt courses) (IB 33–35 pts)
Newcastle – AAB (Bus Mgt) (IB 34 pts)
Nottingham – AAB (Mgt St) (IB 32 pts)
Southampton – AAB (Mgt; Mgt Sci courses) (IB 34 pts)

320 pts **Bournemouth** – 320 pts (Bus St; Bus St courses)
Durham – ABB (Bus; Bus Fin) (IB 28 pts)
Leicester – ABB (Mgt St; Mgt St Pol) (IB 30 pts)
Liverpool – ABB (Bus St; Bus St Ind) (IB 32 pts)
London (QM) – 320 pts (Bus Mgt) (IB 32 pts)
Loughborough – ABB (Geog Mgt)
Northumbria – ABB 320 pts (Bus St; Bus Mgt)
Queen's Belfast – ABB–BBBb (Bus Mgt)
Reading – 320–350 pts (Mgt IT) (IB 33 pts)
Sheffield – ABB (Bus Mgt; Bus Mgt Econ; Bus Mgt Inf Mgt) (IB 33pts)
Strathclyde – ABB (Bus; Bus Ent courses; Mgt) (IB 32 pts)
Surrey – ABB 320 pts (Bus Mgt) (IB 34–32 pts)
Sussex – ABB (Bus Mgt St; Bus (Fin) (Mark)) (IB 34 pts)
York – ABB (Mgt; Acc Bus Fin Mgt) (IB 32 pts)

300 pts **Brunel** – 300–350 pts (Bus Mgt; Bus Mgt (Acc) (Mark))
Edinburgh – BBB (Bus St courses)
Essex – 300 pts (Bus Serv Ind Mgt; Bus Mgt; NTech Dig Ent Mgt; NVntr Crea Ent Mgt) (IB 32 pts)
Kent – 300 pts (Bus Admin courses; Mgt Sci) (IB 33 pts HL 15 pts)
Oxford Brookes – BBB–BBC (Bus; Bus Mgt; Bus Comb Hons) (IB 31 pts)
Stirling – BBB 2nd yr entry (Bus St; Mgt; Mgt Sci)
Westminster – BBB 300 pts (Bus Mgt courses; Bus St courses) (IB 28 pts)

280 pts **Brighton** – BBC 280 pts (Law Bus; Bus Mgt courses) (IB 30 pts)
East Anglia – BBC (Bus Mgt; Acc Mgt) (IB 30–32 pts)
Gloucestershire – 280 pts (Bus Mgt)
Heriot-Watt – BBC 2nd yr entry (Bus Mgt Ind)
Keele – 280–320 pts inc BB/AB (Bus Mgt) (IB 28–32 pts)
Kent – 280 pts (Bus St)
Kingston – 280–320 pts (Bus Sys Mgt; Bus Mgt; Bus St; Bus Ops Mgt)
Loughborough – 280 pts (Trans Bus Mgt; Air Trans Mgt) (IB 30 pts)
Newport – 280 pts (Bus Ldrshp Bus Ent 2yrs)
Northumbria – 280 pts (Bus joint courses)
Oxford Brookes – BBC (Bus Mgt Comb) (IB 30 pts)
Portsmouth – 280–300 pts (Bus Admin; Bus St)
Swansea – 280 pts (Bus Mgt courses)

260 pts **Aberystwyth** – 260 pts (Bus Mgt) (IB 27 pts)
Bristol UWE – 260–300 pts (Bus St; Bus Ent; Bus Prop)
Chichester – CCD 260–240 pts (Bus St) (IB 26 pts)
Coventry – 260–280 pts (Bus St; Bus Mgt) (IB 24 pts)
Heriot-Watt – BCC (Management)
Hertfordshire – 260–300 pts (Bus St; Mgt)
Hull – 260 pts (Bus; Bus Fin Mgt; Mgt)
Lincoln – 260 pts (Bus Mgt; Bus St; Mgt)
Liverpool Hope – 260 pts (Bus Mgt)
Liverpool John Moores – 260–240 pts (Bus St; Marit Bus Mgt)

Mander Portman Woodward
Business Economics and Management Courses
Consult the Specialist
MPW is one of the UK's best known groups of independent sixth-form colleges. We offer a range of specialist services to those who have chosen a career in business- or finance-related fields.
Two-year and one-year A level courses
Seminars on applications procedures
Detailed UCAS advice
Interview training
London 020 7835 1355
Birmingham 0121 454 9637
Cambridge 01223 350158
MPW's handbook "Getting into Business, Economics and Management Courses" is published by Trotman Group

Plymouth – 260–240 pts (Bus St; Bus Ent; Marit Bus courses)
Portsmouth – 260–280 pts (Bus Ent Dev)
Salford – BCC 260 pts (Bus Mgt St) (IB 28–32 pts)
Staffordshire – 260 pts (Bus St courses) (IB 26 pts)
Stirling – BCC 1st yr entry (Bus St; Mgt; Mgt Sci) (IB 28–30 pts)
Ulster – 260 pts (Bus joint courses; Bus St courses)

240 pts **Aberdeen** – CCC (Mgt St courses) (IB 30 pts)
Anglia Ruskin – 240 pts (Mgt Prac)
Bangor – 240–280 pts (Bus St courses; Bus Soc Admin) (IB 28 pts)
Birmingham City – 240–280 pts (Bus courses)
Bolton – 260 pts (Bus Mgt)
Bradford – 240 pts (Bus Mgt St; Bus St Law)
Bristol UWE – 240–300 pts (Bus courses; Mgt) (IB 26–32 pts)
Buckingham – 240 pts (Bus Mgt courses; Bus Ent)
Chester – 240–260 pts (Bus Comb courses; Mgt courses) (IB 30 pts)
Cumbria – 240 pts (Bus Mark)
De Montfort – 240–280 pts (Bus Mgt; Bus Mgt Ent)
Derby – 240 pts (Bus St)
Dundee – CCC (Bus Mgt)
Edinburgh Napier – 240 pts (Bus courses)
Glamorgan – 240–280 pts (Mgt Bus; Bus Ent)
Glasgow Caledonian – CCC (Bus Mgt; Bus St)
Huddersfield – 240–280 pts (Bus St)
Liverpool John Moores – 240 pts (Bus Inf Sys; Bus PR; Bus Econ; Bus Fin)
Manchester Met – 240 pts (Mgt Sys courses; Bus Sys Mgt; Bus courses) (IB 24–28 pts)
Newport – 240 pts (Bus Law; Bus St; Bus Inf Sys Mgt)
Nottingham Trent – 240–280 pts (Bus; Bus Mgt Acc Fin; Bus Mgt Ops)
Robert Gordon – CCC (Mgt courses) (IB 26 pts)
Roehampton – 240–280 pts (Bus Mgt courses)
Sheffield Hallam – 240 pts (Bus courses)
Westminster – CCC (Business) (IB 28 pts)
Winchester – 240–280 pts (Bus Mgt courses) (IB 24 pts)
Wolverhampton – 240 pts (Bus Mgt)
Worcester – 240 pts (Bus courses)

230 pts **Edinburgh Napier** – 230 pts (Bus St courses)

220 pts **Bath Spa** – 220–260 pts (Bus Mgt courses)
Central Lancashire – 220–280 pts (Bus courses)
Chester – 220–260 pts (Bus; Mgt)
Edge Hill – 220–260 pts (Bus Mgt St; Bus Mgt (Acc) (HR Mgt) (Int Bus) (Mark))
Heriot-Watt – CCD 1st yr entry (Bus Mgt Ind; Bus Admin)
Huddersfield – 220–280 pts (Bus Mgt; Entre Bus)
Leeds Met – 220 pts (Bus St; Bus Mgt)
London Met – 220–200 pts (Bus courses; Mgt)
Northampton – 220–260 pts (Bus Comp Sys; Bus St; Bus Entre)
Oldham (Coll Univ Centre) – 220–280 pts (Bus Mgt)
Southampton Solent – 220 pts (Bus Mgt Entre; Bus St)
Sunderland – 220 pts (Bus St; Bus Acc; Bus Econ; Bus HR Mgt; App Mgt Bus Mark)
Teesside – 220 pts (Bus Mgt; Bus St)

200 pts **Bedfordshire** – 200 pts (Bus Mgt)
Bucks New – 200–240 pts (Bus courses; Int Mgt)
Canterbury Christ Church – 200 pts (Bus St; Bus Mgt)
Central Lancashire – 200–260 pts (Bus St)
Coventry – 200 pts (Bus Inf Sys)
De Montfort – 200 pts (Crea Ldrshp Mgt)
East London – 200 pts (Bus Econ; Bus Inf Sys; Bus Mgt)

Glyndŵr – 200 pts (Bus Mgt)
Hull (Scarborough) – 200 pts (Bus Mgt IT)
Leeds Trinity (UC) – 200 pts (Bus Mgt; Bus)
Middlesex – 200–280 pts (Bus Mgt; Bus Admin; Bus HR Mgt; Bus Mark)
Suffolk (Univ Campus) – 200 pts (Bus Mgt)
Swansea Met – 200–240 pts (Bus St)
Thames Valley – 200 pts (Bus St)
York St John – 200–240 pts (Bus Mgt courses)
195 pts **Queen Margaret** – 195 pts (Bus Mgt)
180 pts **Abertay Dundee** – DDD (Bus St Ops Mgt; Mgt)
Cardiff (UWIC) – BC 180 pts (Bus Mgt St courses)
Greenwich – 180–160 pts (Bus Admin; Bus St)
Harper Adams (UC) – 180–220 pts (Bus courses)
Trinity Saint David – 180–240 pts (Bus Mgt courses)
Writtle (Coll) – 180 pts (Bus Mgt)
160 pts **Anglia Ruskin** – 160 pts (Bus Mgt; Bus St; Bus Econ)
Bedfordshire – 160 pts (Bus St)
Doncaster (Coll) – 160 pts (Bus Mgt)
Farnborough (CT) – 160–200 pts (Bus Mgt)
London South Bank – 160 pts (Bus St; Bus Admin; Mgt Comb courses)
Newman (UC) – 160–240 pts (Mgt St courses)
Royal (CAg) – 160–220 pts (Bus Mgt)
SAC (Scottish CAg) – CC (Rur Bus Mgt)
St Mary's Twickenham (UC) – 160–200 pts (Mgt St)
South Essex (Coll) – 160 pts (Bus St)
West Scotland (Ayr/Hamilton/Paisley) – CC (Bus; Ent St; Mgt)
120 pts **Blackburn (Coll Univ Centre)** – 120 pts (Bus St)
Grimsby (IFHE) – 120–240 pts (Bus courses)
Llandrillo Cymru (Col) – 120 pts (Mgt Bus)
Northbrook (Coll) – 120 pts (Bus Admin)
Norwich City (Coll) – 120–240 pts (Bus Mgt)
Peterborough Reg (Coll) – 120 pts (Bus Law)
Swansea Met – DD (Bus St; Mgt St Psy)
100 pts **Bradford (Coll)** – 100–140 pts (Bus St)
80 pts **Croydon (Coll)** – 80–100 pts (Bus courses)
Greenwich (Sch Mgt) – 80–120 pts (Bus Mgt IT)
Holborn (Coll) – 80 pts (Bus Admin)
Kensington Bus (Coll) – 80 pts (Bus St)
London (Birk) – 80 pts under 21s (over 21 varies) (p/t Mgt)
UHI Millennium Inst (IC) – 80 pts (Bus Mgt)

Open University – (Bus St – contact +44 (0)845 300 6090 or www.openuniversity.co.uk/you)
Regents Bus Sch London – check with School (Bus courses)

SECTION B: INTERNATIONAL AND EUROPEAN BUSINESS AND MANAGEMENT COURSES, BUSINESS AND MANAGEMENT COURSES WITH LANGUAGES

(Refer to **Section A** and **Section C** for other Business courses)

Your target offers and examples of courses provided by each institution

390 pts **Warwick** – AABb (Int Bus; Int Mgt) (IB 36 pts)
360 pts **Bath** – AAA–ABB 340 pts (Int Mgt Fr/Ger/Span) (IB 34–36 HL lang 6)
Lancaster – AAA (Bus St N Am/Aus; Mgt Org N Am/Aus)
Manchester – AAA–ABB (Int Bus Fin Econ; Mgt (Int St); Int Mgt; Int Mgt Am Bus St) (IB 35–34 pts)
350 pts **Brunel** – 350 pts (Int Bus) (IB 32 pts)

Liverpool Business School, Liverpool John Moores University

ONLY A FIVE minute walk from the centre of Liverpool you'll find Liverpool Business School (LBS). A modern and dynamic educational establishment, the School is set around tranquil gardens and boasts an award-winning, state-of-the-art learning resource centre.

At undergraduate level, LBS offers:

- **BA Business Studies**
- **BA Accounting and Finance**
- **BA Business and Economics**
- **BA Human Resource Management**
- **BA Marketing**
- **BA International Business and Languages**
- **BA Public Relations and Languages**
- **BA Business and Public Relations**
- **BSc Business Information Systems**
- **BA Retail Management**

LBS is continually exploring new ways in which it can improve the employability of its graduates and it places considerable emphasis on the practical nature of its programmes. For example, a number of students were this year able to study for the Chartered Management Institute (CMI) Level 5 Certificate in Management and Leadership alongside their sandwich year placement. Through this initiative the students were able to gain new and invaluable skills, making them more attractive to future employers.

If you want to have a great university experience, graduate with a respected qualification and secure the skills and 'know-how' that will help you climb the professional career ladder, then you should choose LBS.

For more information about Liverpool Business School contact the BLW Admissions Team:

tel: 0151 231 3999
email: blwadmissions@ljmu.ac.uk
website: www.ljmu.ac.uk/lbs

340 pts **Birmingham** – AAB–ABB (Int Bus; Euro Bus Mgt)
Cardiff – AAB (Bus Mgt (Int Mgt); Euro Mgt; Bus Mgt Euro Lang/Jap)
Lancaster – AAB 340 pts (Euro St Mgt Langs)
Leicester – AAB (Maths Mgt St)
London (RH) – AAB 340 pts (Mgt Fr/Ger/Ital/Span; Mgt Int Bus) (IB 35 pts)
Loughborough – AAB 340 pts (Int Bus) (IB 36 pts)
Newcastle – AAB (Int Bus Mgt) (IB 34 pts)
Nottingham – AAB (Mgt St Chin St/Fr/Ger/Span; Mgt As St; Int Bus – China campus)
Reading – AAB (Int Mgt Bus Admin Fr/Ger/Ital) (IB HL 666)
Southampton – AAB–ABB (Mgt Sci Fr/Ger/Span)

320 pts **Aston** – 320–340 pts (Int Bus Fr/Ger/Span)
Bournemouth – 320 pts (Int Bus)
Liverpool – ABB (Int Bus) (IB 32 pts)
London (QM) – 320 pts (Bus Mgt Fr/Ger/Hisp St/Russ)
Queen's Belfast – ABB–BBBb (Int Bus Lang)
Sheffield – ABB–BBC (Kor St Bus Mgt; E As St Bus Mgt; Chin St Bus Mgt; Fr/Ger/Russ Bus Mgt) (IB 33–30 pts)
Surrey – ABB 320 pts (Bus Mgt Fr/Ger/Span)
Sussex – ABB (Bus (Int Bus))

300 pts **Dundee** – 300 pts 2nd yr entry (Int Bus 3yrs; Int Bus Fin; Int Bus Mark; Int Bus Lang) (IB 34 pts)
Edinburgh – BBB (Bus St Fr/Ger/Span; Int Bus; Int Bus Langs)
Essex – 300 pts (Int Ent Bus Dev; Bus Mgt Mdn Lang) (IB 28–29 pts)

REGENT'S COLLEGE LONDON
REGENT'S COLLEGE
LONDON
Private Higher Education
Study business in central London – British and American degrees available
Courses commence February and September
Scholarships available – apply today!
• Business Foundation Course
• BA (Hons) International Business
• BA (Hons) International Events Management
• BA (Hons) Global Management
• BA (Hons) Leisure Management
• BA Management (with Marketing or Business)
Beautiful central London campus • Small class sizes • Study abroad opportunities
Personalised careers support • Evening foreign language classes
Regent's College, Inner Circle, Regent's Park, London NW1 4NS, UK
Tel: +44 (0) 20 7487 7505 Fax: +44 (0) 20 7487 7425 Email: exrel@regents.ac.uk Web: www.regents.ac.uk

Hertfordshire – 300 pts (Int Mgt)
Kent – 300 pts (Int Bus; Hisp St Bus Admin)
Liverpool – BBB (Bus St Fr/Ger/Ital; Bus St Hisp St) (IB 30 pts HL lang 6)
Stirling – BBB 2nd yr entry (Bus St Fr/Span) (IB 30 pts)
Strathclyde – BBB–BBC (Int Bus Modn Lang; Int Bus)
Westminster – BBB 300 pts (Int Bus Arbc/Chin/Fr/Russ/Span; Int Bus) (IB 28 pts)

280 pts **Brighton** – BBC 280 pts (Int Bus)
Heriot-Watt – BBC (Int Mgt Fr/Ger/Span)
Kingston – 280–320 pts (Int Bus; Int Bus Fr/Span; Int Bus Law)
Northumbria – 280 pts (Int Bus Mgt)
Portsmouth – 280–300 pts (Int Bus St; Euro Bus courses)
Swansea – 280–300 pts (Int Bus; Int Mgt Sci N Am/Euro; Int Mgt Sci Lang; Int Bus Mgt; Int Bus Mgt (Austr) (Euro) (Lang) (N Am))

260 pts **Aberystwyth** – 260 pts (Mgt Span) (IB 27 pts)
Bristol UWE – 260–300 pts (Int Bus St Span; Int Bus St)
Coventry – 260–280 pts (Int Bus Mgt)
Hertfordshire – 260 pts (Int Bus; Bus Mand/Euro Langs)
Lincoln – 260 pts (Euro Bus; Int Bus)
Oxford Brookes – BCC (Int Bus Fin Econ) (IB 29 pts)
Staffordshire – 260 pts (Int Bus Mgt)
Stirling – BCC 1st yr entry (Bus St Fr/Span) (IB 30 pts)

240 pts **Aberdeen** – CCC (Euro Mgt St)
Bangor – 240–280 pts (Bus St Fr/Ger)
Bradford – 240 pts (Int Bus Mgt)
Cardiff (UWIC) – 240 pts (Int Bus Mgt)
Central Lancashire – 240–280 pts (Bus Mgt Chin)
Dundee – CCC 240 pts 1st yr entry (Int Bus; Int Bus Fin; Int Bus Mark; Int Bus Lang)
Glasgow Caledonian – CCC (Int Bus)
Gloucestershire – 240–220 pts (Int Bus Mark; Int Bus St)
Liverpool John Moores – 240 pts (Int Mgt; Int Bus St Chin/Fr/Jap/Span)
Manchester Met – 240 pts (Int Bus; Int Bus (Euro Mgt))
Nottingham Trent – CCC 240 pts (Int Bus; Int Bus Fr)
Plymouth – 240 pts (Int Bus; Int Bus Fr/Ger/Span; Marit Bus Fr/Ger/Span; Int Bus Econ)
Robert Gordon – CCC (Int Bus Mgt)
Roehampton – 240–380 pts (Int Bus)
Salford – 240–260 pts (Bus St Int Bus Mgt; Bus Mgt (Int))
Sheffield Hallam – 240 pts (Int Bus St; Int Bus St Lang; Int Bus St Tour)
Stirling – CCC (Int Mgt St)
Ulster – CCC (Bus St Fr/Ger/Span; Bus Am St; Euro St Bus)
Wolverhampton – 240 pts (Int Bus Mgt; Bus Fr)

230 pts **Edinburgh Napier** – 230 pts (Bus St Lang; Int Bus)

220 pts **Central Lancashire** – 220–240 pts (Int Bus)
Chester – 220–260 pts (Int Bus)
Edge Hill – 220–260 pts (Bus Mgt (Int Bus); Chin Bus)
Leeds Met – 220 pts (Int Bus; Langs Int Bus)
London Met – 220 pts (Int Bus Mgt)
Northampton – 220–260 pts (Bus Fr/Ger)
Southampton Solent – 220 pts (Int Bus Mgt; Int Bus Mgt Engl)
Teesside – 220 pts (Int Bus Mgt)
York St John – 220 pts (Int Bus)

200 pts **Central Lancashire** – 200–240 pts (Int Bus Mgt)
De Montfort – 200–240 pts (Int Bus Glob)
East London – 200 pts (Int Bus courses)
Greenwich – 200 pts (Bus Euro; Int Bus; Bus Mgt)
Hull (Scarborough) – 200 pts (Int Bus)

Middlesex – 200–280 pts (Bus St Fr/Ger/Ital/Span; Int Bus; Int Bus (Arbc) (Mand) (Russ) (Span))
180 pts **Abertay Dundee** – DDD (Int Mgt)
Anglia Ruskin – 180–200 pts (Int Bus Strat; Int Mgt)
160 pts **Bedfordshire** – 160 pts (Int Bus St)

Euro Bus Sch London – contact School (Int Bus courses)
Open University – (Bus St Fr/Span – contact +44 (0)845 300 6090 or www.openuniversity.co.uk/you)
Regents Bus Sch London – check with School (Int Bus; Int Bus Des Mgt)

SECTION C: SPECIALISED BUSINESS AND MANAGEMENT COURSES INCLUDING:

Advertising, **Air Transport Management**, **Arts Management**, **Entrepreneurship**, **Industrial Relations**, **Operations Management**, **Public Relations**, **Publishing**, **Quality Management**. (Refer to **Section A** and **Section B** for other Business courses); for other **Advertising** courses see also **Art and Design (Graphic Design)**, and for **Events Management** see also **Hospitality and Hotel Management**.

Your target offers and examples of courses provided by each institution

360 pts **Ulster** – AAA 360 pts (Comm Adv Mark)
340 pts **Lancaster** – AAB 340 pts (Adv Mark)
Southampton – AAB (Mgt Entre) (IB 34 pts)
320 pts **Lancaster** – ABB 320 pts (Ops Mgt; Org St Psy)
Newcastle – ABB (Agri-Bus Mgt)
Northumbria – 320 pts (Adv Mgt)
300 pts **Aston** – BBB 300 pts (Tech Ent Mgt) (IB 32 pts)
Bournemouth – 300 pts (PR)
Manchester – ABC (Tex Tech (Bus Mgt)) (IB 32 pts)
280 pts **Coventry** – 280–300 pts (Disas Mgt Emer Plan)
De Montfort – 280 pts (Advertising)
Huddersfield – 280 pts (PR)
Loughborough – 280 pts (Air Trans Mgt; Pub Engl; E-Bus) (IB 30–28 pts)
Loughborough – BBC–ABB (BSc Comp Sci Bus) (IB 36 pts)
Oxford Brookes – BBC (Pub Media) (IB 29 pts)
260 pts **Birmingham City** – 260 pts (Bus PR; Bus Adv; Adv Mgt; Bus Psy Bus)
Central Lancashire – 260 pts (PR)
Coventry – 260–280 pts (Disas Mgt; Disas Reconstr; Disas Emer Plan; Adv Bus; Adv Media)
Gloucestershire – 260 pts (Evnts Mgt)
Hertfordshire – 260 pts (Evnt Mgt)
Leeds Met – 260 pts (PR courses)
Lincoln – 260 pts (Adv courses)
Portsmouth – 260–300 pts (Bus Ent Dev; Bus Ent Sys)
Winchester – 260–280 pts (Arts Mgt Perf Arts)
240 pts **Aberdeen** – CCC (Entrepreneurship)
Central Lancashire – 240 pts (Advertising)
City – CCC 240 pts (Air Trans Op) (IB 26 pts)
De Montfort – 240 pts (Des Mgt Innov)
Edinburgh Napier – 240 pts (Comm Adv PR)
Kingston – 240–280 pts (Env Haz Disas Mgt)
Liverpool John Moores – 240 pts (Mgt Trans Log)
London Met – 240 pts (Avn Mgt)
Manchester Met – 240 pts (Adv Mgt Brnd Mgt; Adv Mgt PR; Bus Ent PR)
Robert Gordon – CCC (Comm PR)
Sheffield Hallam – 240 pts (PR courses; Evnts Mgt)
Southampton Solent – 240 pts (Adv; PR)
Stirling – CCC (Pblc Mgt Admin)

Sunderland – 240 pts (PR)
Ulster – 240 pts (Adv courses)
Winchester – 240–280 pts (Arts Mgt) (IB 24 pts)
Worcester – 240 pts (Mark Adv PR; Mark Adv Wb Des)

220 pts **Chester (Warrington)** – 220–260 pts (Advertising) (IB 24 pts)
Edge Hill – 220–260 pts (PR)
Falmouth (UC) – 220 pts (Crea Evnts Mgt)
Huddersfield – 220–280 pts (Adv Mark Comm)
Huddersfield – 220 pts (Adv Media Rel)
London Met – 220 pts (Arts Mgt; Adv Mark Comm)
Northampton – 220–260 pts (Bus Entre; Adv courses)
Plymouth – 220 pts (Cru Mgt)
Queen Margaret – 220 pts (PR Media; PR Mark)
Southampton Solent – 220–240 pts (Extrm Spo Mgt; Arts Ind Mgt; Evnts Mgt courses; Cru Ind Mgt)
Teesside – 220–280 pts (PR)

200 pts **Birmingham (UC)** – 200 pts (Evnt Mgt; Advntr Tour Mgt; Culn Arts Mgt; Bus Ent; Enter Mgt; Fd Consum Mgt; Fd Media Commun Mgt)
Bucks New – 200–240 pts (Bus Adv Mgt; PR Mark Comm)
Central Lancashire – 200–260 pts (Adv Mark Comm)
De Montfort – 200 pts (Crea Mgt Mark)
East London – 200 pts (Advertising)
Huddersfield – 200–280 pts (Air Trans Log Mgt)
Liverpool John Moores – 200 pts (PR Fr/Chin/Jap/Span)
Middlesex – 200–240 pts (Adv PR Media)
Salford – 200 pts (Adv Des)
Suffolk (Univ Campus) – 200 pts (Crea Ind Mgt)
Swansea Met – 200 pts (Pblc Admin)
Thames Valley – 200 pts (Airln Airpt Mgt; Adv; PR)

180 pts **Greenwich** – 180 pts (Adv Mark Comm)
Liverpool (LIPA) – BC 180 pts (Mus Thea Enter Mgt)
Staffordshire – 180–220 pts (Adv Brnd Mgt)
Sunderland – 180 pts (Adv Des)
UCP Marjon – 180 pts (PR courses)

160 pts **Bedfordshire** – 160–240 pts (PR; Adv Mark)
Bucks New – 160–200 pts (Adv Crea)
Central Lancashire – 160 pts (Fire Sfty Risk Mgt)
London South Bank – CC (Arts Mgt)
Southampton Solent – 160 pts (Fash Mgt Mark)
Wolverhampton – 160–220 pts (PR courses)

80 pts **Arts London** – 80 pts (PR)

Open University – (Bus Law – contact +44 (0)845 300 6090 or www.openuniversity.co.uk/you)

Alternative offers

See **Chapter 7** and **Appendix 1** for grades/UCAS Tariff points information for the International Baccalaureate, Scottish Highers/Advanced Highers, the Welsh Baccalaureate, the Irish Leaving Certificate, the Cambridge Pre-U Diploma, the Advanced Diploma and the Extended Project.

EXAMPLES OF FOUNDATION DEGREES IN THE SUBJECT FIELD

Askham Bryan (CAg); Bedfordshire; Bexley (Coll); Birmingham (UC); Blackburn (Coll Univ Centre); Blackpool and Fylde (Coll); Bolton; Bournemouth; Bradford; Brighton; Bristol City (Coll); Bristol UWE; Central Lancashire; Colchester (Inst); Cornwall (Coll); Croydon (Coll); De Montfort; Doncaster (Coll); Duchy (Coll); Durham New (Coll); Ealing, Hammersmith and West London (Coll); East London; Edge Hill; Farnborough (CT); Glamorgan; Gloucestershire; Glyndŵr; Greenwich; Grimsby (IFHE); Harper

Adams (UC); Hertfordshire; Kingston (Coll); Kirklees (Coll); Knowsley (Coll); Lakes (Coll); Leeds Met; Liverpool John Moores; London South Bank; Manchester (Coll); Mid-Cheshire (Coll); Middlesex; NEW (Coll); Newcastle (Coll); North Lindsey (Coll); Northampton; Northbrook (Coll); Nottingham New (Coll); Plymouth; Riverside Halton (Coll); Royal (CAg); St Helens (Coll); Sheffield (Coll); Sheffield Hallam; Somerset (CAT); South Devon (Coll); South Essex (Coll); Southampton Solent; Suffolk (Univ Campus); Wakefield (Coll); Warwickshire (Coll); Westminster Kingsway (Coll); Writtle (Coll); York (Coll).

CHOOSING YOUR COURSE (SEE ALSO CH.1)

Some course features

Bath (Bus Admin) A popular and highly respected sandwich course with placements in the UK and abroad.
Brunel (Bus Mgt) Three-year or four-year sandwich courses allowing for specialisation in management, accounting, business systems or marketing.
De Montfort (Bus Mgt Ent) Course focuses on entrepreneurship and business practice, researching and developing new business opportunities and ideas, with an optional paid placement year.
London LSE (Mgt) Course has compulsory modules in economics, psychology, accounting and finance and marketing. (Mgt Sci) Course focuses on quantitative analysis, decision-making and economic and social issues. Operational research and statistics are taken in Years 2 and 3.
Nottingham (Mgt St) Core modules include organisation studies, entrepreneurship, accounting, business computing, business, business ethics, human resource management and economics. French, German, Spanish or Chinese Studies can be selected as major/minor combinations.
Oxford Brookes (Bus Mgt) Course aimed at students not wanting to specialise in any particular area of business or are undecided. At the end of the first year, students can opt for one of the named Business degrees.
Southampton (Mgt Sci) Courses allow for specialisation in mathematical or non-mathematical aspects of management including accounting and finance, languages, entrepreneurship and music.
Winchester (Bus Mgt) Optional pathway to BA in Business Management with Public Service Management. Modules include quality management and customer care, local government, public administration and European culture and institutions.

Universities and colleges teaching quality See www.qaa.ac.uk; www.unistats.com.

Top research universities and colleges (RAE 2008) (Business and Management Studies) Imperial London; Cambridge; Cardiff; Bath; London (King's); London LSE; Oxford; Lancaster; Warwick; Manchester; Strathclyde; Leeds; Nottingham; Aston; Loughborough; Sheffield.

Examples of sandwich degree courses Abertay Dundee; Aberystwyth; Aston; Bath; Birmingham (UC); Birmingham City; Bournemouth; Bradford; Brighton; Bristol UWE; Brunel; Central Lancashire; City; Coventry; De Montfort; Edinburgh Napier; Glamorgan; Glasgow Caledonian; Gloucestershire; Greenwich; Harper Adams (UC); Hertfordshire; Huddersfield; Hull; Kingston; Lancaster; Leeds Met; Lincoln; Liverpool John Moores; London (QM); Loughborough; Manchester; Manchester Met; Middlesex; Newcastle; Northumbria; Nottingham Trent; Oxford Brookes; Plymouth; Portsmouth; Reading; Royal (CAg); Sheffield Hallam; Southampton Solent; Staffordshire; Surrey; Swansea Met; Teesside; Ulster; Warwickshire (Coll); West Scotland; Westminster; Wolverhampton.

ADMISSIONS INFORMATION

Number of applicants per place (approx) Abertay Dundee (Bus St) 4; Aberystwyth 3; Anglia Ruskin 5; Aston (Bus Mgt) 12, (Int Bus) 6, (Mgt) 5, (Int Bus Econ) 8; Bangor 4; Bath (Bus Admin) 7, (Int Mgt Lang) 14; Birmingham 28; Birmingham (UC) 5; Blackpool and Fylde (Coll) 2; Bolton 3; Bournemouth 30, (PR) 10; Bradford 12; Bristol 28; Brunel 12; Canterbury Christ Church 20; Cardiff 8; Central Lancashire 15; City (Bus St) 17, (Mgt Sys) 6; Colchester (Inst) 2; De Montfort (Bus Mgt) 5; Derby (Int Bus) 4; Edge Hill 4; Edinburgh Napier (Pub) 7; Glasgow Caledonian 18; Heriot-Watt 5; Hertfordshire 10; Huddersfield 5; Hull (Bus St) 19, (Mgt) 10; Hull (Scarborough) 3; Kent 30; Kingston 50; Leeds 27, (Mgt St) 16; Leeds Trinity (UC) 3; Liverpool John Moores (Int Bus) 16; Llandrillo Cymru (Col) 2; London (King's) 25, (Mgt Sci) 12, (RH) 9; London LSE (Mgt) 23; London Met 10; London South Bank 4; Loughborough 5; Manchester Met (Bus St) 26, (Int Bus) 8; Middlesex 12; Newcastle 27, (Int Bus Mgt)

25, (Bus Mgt) 40; Northumbria 10; Oxford Brookes 40; Plymouth 4; Portsmouth 10; (Bus Admin) 7, (Bus St) 6, (Int Bus) 5; Regents Bus Sch London 25; Robert Gordon 5; Salford (Bus St) 9, (Mgt Sci) 2; Sheffield Hallam (Int Bus) 6; Southampton Solent 13; Strathclyde 12, (Int Bus Modn Lang) 6; Sunderland 20; Surrey (Bus Mgt) 6; Swansea Met 7; Teesside (Bus St) 4; Thames Valley 4; Warwick 22; West Scotland 5; Westminster 12; Winchester 4; Wolverhampton 7; York 6; York St John 3.

Advice to applicants and planning the UCAS personal statement There are many different kinds of businesses and any work experience is almost essential for these courses. This should be described in detail: for example, size of firm, turnover, managerial problems, sales and marketing aspects, customers' attitudes. Any special interests in business management should also be included, for example, personnel work, purchasing, marketing. Give details of travel or work experience abroad and, for international courses, language expertise and examples of leadership and organising skills. Reference can be made to any particular business topics you have studied in the *Financial Times*, *The Economist* and the business sections in the weekend press. Applicants need to be sociable, ambitious, team players. Say why you are interested in the course, identify your academic strengths, your personal strengths and interests. Check information on the Chartered Institute of Public Relations, the Chartered Institute of Marketing and the Chartered Institute of Personnel and Development. See **Appendix 4**; see also **Accountancy/Accounting**.

Misconceptions about this course **Aberystwyth** Students are unaware that the course addresses practical aspects of business. **Aston** (Int Bus Fr) Not two separate disciplines – the two subjects are integrated involving the study of language in a business and management context. **Loughborough** (Pub Engl) That this is a course in Journalism: it is not! **Salford** (Mgt Sci) Students should appreciate that the courses are fairly mathematical. **York** A previous study of management, IT or languages at A-level is necessary.

Selection interviews **Yes** Birmingham City, Bradford, Carmarthenshire (Coll), Coventry, Doncaster (Coll), Durham, Edge Hill, Euro Bus Sch London, Glamorgan, Glasgow Caledonian, Hull, Kent (mature and Access students), London Met, Middlesex, Northumbria, Nottingham Trent, Plymouth, Robert Gordon, Roehampton, Sheffield Hallam, Strathclyde, Swansea, Teesside, Thames Valley, Trinity Saint David, West Thames (Coll), York; **Some** Abertay Dundee, Aberystwyth, Anglia Ruskin, Bath, Bath Spa, Blackpool and Fylde (Coll), Brighton, Buckingham, Cardiff (UWIC), Chichester, City, De Montfort, Derby (Int Bus), East Anglia, Greenwich, Kent, Leeds, Lincoln, Liverpool John Moores, Manchester Met, Salford, South Kent (Coll), Staffordshire, Stirling, Sunderland, Warwick, Winchester, Wolverhampton.

Interview advice and questions Any work experience you describe on the UCAS application probably will be the focus of questions which could include topics covering marketing, selling, store organisation and management and customer problems. Personal qualities are naturally important in a career in business, so be ready for such questions as: What qualities do you have which are suitable and important for this course? Describe your strengths and weaknesses. Why should we give you a place on this course? Is advertising fair? What qualities does a person in business require to be successful? What makes a good manager? What is a cash-flow system? What problems can it cause? How could supermarkets improve customer relations? **Int Bus courses** Why can you be expected to be sent to China by your company when you only have French as a second language? Do you consider that knowing a foreign language makes you a good international manager? **Buckingham** Why Business? How do you see yourself in five years' time? Have you had any work experience? If so, discuss. **Loughborough** (Pub Engl) No tests at interview. We seek students with an interest in information issues within society. **Wolverhampton** Mature students with no qualifications will be asked about their work experience. See also **Chapter 5**.

Reasons for rejection (non-academic) Hadn't read the prospectus. Lack of communication skills. Limited commercial interest. Weak on numeracy and problem-solving. Lack of interview preparation (no questions). Lack of outside interests. Inability to cope with a year abroad. The candidate brought his parent who answered all the questions. **Aberystwyth** Would have trouble fitting into the unique environment of Aberystwyth. Casual approach to learning. **Bournemouth** The Business Studies course is very popular. **Surrey** Hesitation about the period abroad. See also **Marketing**.

AFTER-RESULTS ADVICE

Offers to applicants repeating A-levels **Higher** Bradford, Bristol UWE, Brunel, Greenwich, Hertfordshire, Kingston, Lancaster, Liverpool, Manchester Met, St Andrews, Sheffield, Strathclyde, Teesside; **Same** Aberystwyth, Anglia Ruskin, Aston, Bath, Birmingham City, Bournemouth, Brighton, Buckingham, Cardiff, Cardiff (UWIC), Chester, Chichester, De Montfort, Derby, Durham, East Anglia, Gloucestershire, Huddersfield, Hull, Kent, Leeds, Lincoln, Liverpool Hope, Liverpool John Moores, Loughborough, Northumbria, Oxford Brookes, Robert Gordon, Roehampton, Royal (CAg), Salford, Sheffield Hallam, Staffordshire, Stirling, Sunderland, Suffolk (Univ Campus), Surrey, Thames Valley, Ulster, Winchester, Wolverhampton, Worcester, York, York St John; **Rare** Queen Margaret, Warwick.

GRADUATE DESTINATIONS AND EMPLOYMENT (2007/8 HESA)

Business Studies graduates surveyed 8130 **Employed** 4730 **In further study** 650 **Assumed unemployed** 775.
Management Sciences graduates surveyed 3380 **Employed** 1935 **In further study** 310 **Assumed unemployed** 325.
Public Relations graduates surveyed 515 **Employed** 370 **In further study** 30 **Assumed unemployed** 30.
Publishing graduates surveyed 100 **Employed** 60 **In further study** 10 **Assumed unemployed** 10.

Career note The majority of graduates enter trainee management roles in business-related and administrative careers, many specialising in some of the areas listed below. In 2005/6 the main graduate destinations were in finance, property development, wholesale, retail and manufacturing.

OTHER DEGREE SUBJECTS FOR CONSIDERATION

Accountancy; Banking; Business Information Technology; E-Business; Economics; Estate Management; Finance; Hospitality Management; Housing Management; Human Resource Management; Insurance; Leisure Management; Logistics; Marketing; Public Administration; Retail Management; Sports Management; Surveying.

CELTIC, IRISH, SCOTTISH AND WELSH STUDIES

(including **Cornish Studies** and **Gaelic Studies**; see also **History** and **Literature**)

Irish, Scottish, Gaelic, Welsh, Breton, Manx, Cornish, Gaulish and Celtiberian languages are all included in this subject area. Courses may also include the history and civilisation of the Celtic peoples.

Useful websites www.byig-wlb.org.uk; http://new.wales.gov.uk; www.bbc.co.uk/wales; www.daltai.com; www.eisteddfod.org.uk; www.digitalmedievalist.com; www.gaelic-scotland.co.uk.

NB The points totals shown to the left of the institutions are for ease of reference only. It must not be assumed that Tariff points are always used by institutions or that they can be substituted for an offer in grades. The level of an offer is not necessarily indicative of the quality of a course.

COURSE OFFERS INFORMATION

Subject requirements/preferences **GCSE** A foreign language or Welsh may be required. **AL** Welsh may be required for some courses.

NB In 2011 universities and colleges will differ in their use of GCE AL/AS unit grade information, A* grades, the Extended Project (EPQ), the Advanced Diploma and the Cambridge Pre-U examination when considering applicants and making offers. An EPQ may be accepted in place of an AS subject. Check websites of universities and colleges for the latest offers information.

Your target offers and examples of courses provided by each institution
380 pts **Cambridge** – A*AA college offers may vary (A-Sxn Nrs Celt) (IB 38–42 pts)
360 pts **Oxford** – AAA (Celt courses)

340 pts **Glasgow** – AAB (Celt Civ; Celt St courses; Gael courses) (IB 34 pts)
320 pts **Exeter** – ABB–BBB (Modn Celt St Hum; Corn St Hum) (IB 32–29 pts)
300 pts **Cardiff** – 300 pts (Welsh)
Edinburgh – BBB (Celt; Celt Arch; Celt Scand St; Celt Scot Hist; Scot Ethnol) (IB 34 pts HL 555)
Queen's Belfast – BBB–BBCb (Irish Celt courses)
280 pts **Cardiff** – BBC (Welsh Ital/Span; Welsh Relig St)
260 pts **Liverpool** – BCC (Ir St; Ir St Pol) (IB 27 pts)
240 pts **Aberdeen** – CCC (Celt Civ courses; Celt St courses; Gael St courses)
Aberystwyth – 240 pts (Celt St; Ir courses; Welsh courses; Welsh Celt Langs) (IB 28 pts)
Bangor – 240–260 pts (Welsh Hist Arch; Welsh Hist – also available in Welsh)
Swansea – 240–300 pts (Welsh courses)
Ulster – 240 pts (Ir courses)
220 pts **Cardiff (UWIC)** – 220 pts (Educ St Welsh)
200 pts **Glamorgan** – 200–240 pts (Prof Welsh courses)
Glyndŵr – 200 pts (Educ P Welsh)
180 pts **St Mary's Twickenham (UC)** – 180–200 pts (Ir St courses)
UHI Millennium Inst – DDD 180 pts (Gael; Gael Lang Cult; Gael Trad Mus; Gael Media St)
160 pts **Trinity Saint David** – 160 pts (Welsh St Anc Hist; Welsh St Lat)

Alternative offers
See **Chapter 7** and **Appendix 5** for grades/UCAS Tariff points information for the International Baccalaureate, Scottish Highers/Advanced Highers, the Welsh Baccalaureate, the Irish Leaving Certificate, the Cambridge Pre-U Diploma, the Advanced Diploma and the Extended Project.

CHOOSING YOUR COURSE (SEE ALSO CH.1)

Some course features
Aberystwyth There are beginners' courses for those with no previous knowledge of Welsh or Celtic languages. (Welsh Celt Langs) One or more Celtic languages, together with Welsh, are studied, with a semester spent in Brittany or Ireland.
Bangor (Welsh Hist Arch) The course focuses on the development of Wales over the centuries, the changing nature of society and settlements, and the historical context of contemporary Wales.
Edinburgh In addition to studying the cultures of Ireland and Wales, Scottish Gaelic is offered on the course in Celtic Studies.
Queen's Belfast (Ir Celt) The course focuses on modern Irish language and literature and contemporary Irish culture and society, but also provides a study of Old and Middle Irish, Scottish Gaelic, Welsh and Cornish. Students spend at least six weeks in the Gaeltacht.
UHI Millennium Inst The only degree in Scotland delivered entirely through Gaelic.

Universities and colleges teaching quality See www.qaa.ac.uk; www.unistats.com.

Top research universities and colleges (RAE 2008) (Celtic studies) Cambridge; Ulster; Aberystwyth; Swansea; Cardiff; Glasgow; Bangor; Edinburgh.

ADMISSIONS INFORMATION

Number of applicants per place (approx) Aberystwyth 6; Bangor 8; Cambridge 2; Cardiff 2; Exeter 5; St Mary's Twickenham (UC) 3; Swansea 7.

Advice to applicants and planning the UCAS personal statement Interests in this field largely develop through literature, museum visits or archaeology which should be fully described in the UCAS application.

Selection interviews **Yes** Aberystwyth; **No** St Mary's Twickenham (UC).

Interview advice and questions Past questions have included: Why do you want to study this subject? What specific areas of Celtic culture interest you? What do you expect to gain by studying unusual subjects? See **Chapter 5**.

AFTER-RESULTS ADVICE

Offers to applicants repeating A-levels **Higher** Glasgow (AAA); **Same** Aberystwyth, Bangor, Cardiff, Swansea.

GRADUATE DESTINATIONS AND EMPLOYMENT (2007/8 HESA)

Graduates surveyed 145 **Employed** 55 **In further study** 60 **Assumed unemployed** 10.

Career note See **Combined Courses** and **Languages**.

OTHER DEGREE SUBJECTS FOR CONSIDERATION

Anthropology; Archaeology; History.

CHEMISTRY

(see also **Biochemistry** and **Engineering (Chemical)**)

There is a shortage of applicants for this subject despite the fact that it is the basis of a wide range of careers in the manufacturing industries. These focus on such areas as pharmaceuticals, medicine, veterinary science and health, agriculture, petroleum, cosmetics, plastics, the food industry, colour chemistry and aspects of the environment such as pollution and recycling.

Useful websites www.rsc.org; www.chem.ox.ac.uk/vrchemistry.

NB The points totals shown to the left of the institutions are for ease of reference only. It must not be assumed that Tariff points are always used by institutions or that they can be substituted for an offer in grades. The level of an offer is not necessarily indicative of the quality of a course.

COURSE OFFERS INFORMATION

Subject requirements/preferences **GCSE** English, mathematics/science subjects usually required. A/B grades often stipulated by popular universities. **AL** Two science subjects including chemistry required.

NB In 2011 universities and colleges will differ in their use of GCE AL/AS unit grade information, A* grades, the Extended Project (EPQ), the Advanced Diploma and the Cambridge Pre-U examination when considering applicants and making offers. An EPQ may be accepted in place of an AS subject. Check websites of universities and colleges for the latest offers information.

Your target offers and examples of courses provided by each institution

380 pts **Cambridge** – A*AA college offers may vary (Nat Sci (Chem)) (IB 38–42 pts HL 766–777)
360 pts **Bristol** – AAA–ABB (Chem courses) (IB 35–33 pts HL 665)
Durham – AAA (Nat Sci (Chem))
Imperial London – AAA (MSci/BSc Chem; Chem Rsch Abrd; Chem Mgt; Chem Fr/Ger/Span Sci; Chem Medcnl Chem; Chem Mol Phys) (IB 38 pts HL chem 7 maths 6)
London (UCL) – AABe–BBBe (Chem; Chem Maths; Chem Mgt Sci; Chem Euro Lang; Medcnl Chem) (IB 32–36 pts)
Oxford – AAA (Chemistry) (IB 38–40 pts)
340 pts **Aston** – AAB (MChem; App Chem)
Cardiff – AAB–ABB 340–320 pts (MChem Chem courses)
Durham – AAB–ABB (Chem; Chem Ind; Chem Int)
Edinburgh – AAB 2nd yr entry (Chem courses) (IB 36 pts)
Exeter – AAB–ABB (Biol Med Chem)
Lancaster – AAB 340 pts (MChem Env Chem courses)
Leeds – AAB (Nanotechnology) (IB 36 pts HL 17 pts)
Nottingham – AAB–BBB (Bioch Biol Chem; Chem Ind; Medcnl Biol Chem) (IB 34–32 pts)
St Andrews – AAB 2nd yr entry (Chem; Chem Medcnl Chem; Chem Maths) (IB 31–34 pts)
Sheffield – AAB (Chem Ind; Chem Aus; Chem Jap; Chem USA) (IB 35–32 pts)

Southampton – AAB–ABB (BSc Chem; Chem Medcnl Sci; Chem Maths) (IB 34–32 pts)
Sussex – AAB–ABB (MChem Chem) (IB 34–36 pts)

320 pts **Bath** – ABB (Chem; Chem Mgt; Chem Educ; Chem Drug Dscvry) (IB 34 pts HL chem 6)
Birmingham – ABB–BBB (MSci Chem; Chem Analyt Chem; Chem Biorg Chem; Chem Psy; Chem Pharmacol)
Cardiff – ABB–BBB 320–300 pts (BSc Chem; Chem Phys)
East Anglia – ABB (MChem Chem; Chem Analyt Foren Sci; Biol Medcnl Chem; Cheml Phys) (IB 32 pts)
Glasgow – ABB (Chem; Chem Foren St; Chem Medcnl Chem) (IB 32 pts)
Leeds – ABB (Chem; Chem Analyt Chem; Chem Col Sci; Medcnl Chem; Chem joint Hons) (IB 34 pts HL chem 6 pts)
Leicester – ABB (MChem Chem Pharml Chem; Chem Foren Sci) (IB 30 pts)
Liverpool – ABB (Chem Nano; MChem Chem; Medcnl Chem Pharmacol) (IB 33 pts HL chem 6)
Manchester – ABB–ABC (Chem; Chem Pat Law; Chem Foren Analyt Chem; Chem Bus Mgt; Medcnl Chem) (IB 33–32 pts)
Newcastle – ABB (MChem Chem; Chem Ind; Chem Medcnl Chem; Chem Mgt; Chem N Am/Euro) (IB 34 pts HL chem 6)
Reading – ABB–BBB (MChem Chem courses)
St Andrews – ABB 1st yr entry (Chem Geosci; Chem; Chem Mat Chem; Chem Sci) (IB 31–34 pts)
Sussex – ABB–BBB (BSc Chem) (IB 32–34 pts)
Warwick – ABB (Chem; Chem Mgt; Chem Medcnl Chem; Biomed Chem; Cheml Biol) (IB 34 pts)

300 pts **Aberdeen** – BBB 2nd yr entry (Chem; Biomed Mat Chem; Chem Off Ind; Env Chem; Medcnl Chem)
Aston – BBB (BSc Chem)
Birmingham – BBB–BBC (BSc Chem; Chem Analyt Sci; Chem Biorg Chem; Chem Modn Lang; Chem Env Sci; Chem Pharmacol; Chem Psy) (IB 31 pts)
Bradford – BBB 300 pts (Chem Foren Sci; Chem Drug Dscvry; Chem)
Dundee – BBB 2nd yr entry (Biol Chem Drug Dscvry)
East Anglia – BBB (BSc Chem; Chem Analyt Sci; Biol Chem; Env Chem; Cheml Phys) (IB 31 pts)
Edinburgh – BBB 1st yr entry (Chem courses) (IB 34 pts)
Kent – BBB–BBC (Foren Chem) (IB 33–31 pts)
Lancaster – BBB (BSc Env Chem)
Liverpool – BBB (Chem Ocean) (IB 31 pts)
Loughborough – 300 pts (MChem Chem; BSc Chem Spo Sci) (IB 34 pts)
Newcastle – BBB (BSc Chem; Chem Ind; Chem Medcnl Chem) (IB 32 pts HL chem 6)
Northumbria – 300 pts (MChem Chem) (IB 26 pts)
Plymouth – 300 pts (Analyt Chem)
Queen's Belfast – BBB (MSci Chem) (IB 27–30 pts HL 655)
Sheffield – BBB (Chem; Chem Maths; Chem Euro) (IB 32–35 pts)
Surrey – BBB (MChem Chem; Chem Foren Invstg; Medcnl Chem) (IB 30 pts)
York – BBB (Chem; Chem Biol Medcnl Chem; Chem Mgt Ind; Chem Res Env) (IB 32 pts)

280 pts **Keele** – 280–300 pts (Chem courses) (IB 26–28 pts)
Liverpool – BBC (BSc Chem; Medcnl Chem; Chem Foren Analys) (IB 28 pts HL chem 5)
London (QM) – 280 pts (Chem courses) (IB 26–28 pts)
Loughborough – 280 pts (BSc Chem; Chem Analyt Chem; Medcnl Pharml Chem; Chem Foren Analys) (IB 32 pts)
Northumbria – 280 pts (Chem Biomed Sci; Chem Foren Chem; Pharml Chem) (IB 25 pts)
Nottingham Trent – 280–260 pts (MChem/BSc Chem; Pharml Medcnl Chem)
Queen's Belfast – BBC (Medcnl Chem; Chem Foren Analys)
Strathclyde – BBC 2nd yr entry (Chem; Chem Teach; Chem Analyt Chem; Foren Chem; Chem Drug Dscvry) (IB 28 pts)
Teesside – 280 pts (Chemistry)

260 pts **Aston** – BCC–BBC (BSc App Chem)
Bradford – 260 pts (Chem Pharml Foren Sci)
Brighton – BCC 260 pts (Pharml Chem Sci; Analyt Chem Bus) (IB 28 pts)
Bristol UWE – 260–300 pts (Foren Chem)
Heriot-Watt – BCC 2nd yr entry (Chem courses)
Leicester – BCC (BSc Chem) (IB 30–28 pts)
Manchester Met – 260 pts (MChem Chem)
Plymouth – 260 pts (Chemistry)
Queen's Belfast – BCC (BSc Chem; Chem Euro)
Reading – 260–290 pts (BSc Chem; Chem Arch; Chem Educ)

240 pts **Aberdeen** – CCC 1st yr entry (Chem; Biomed Mat Chem; Chem Off Ind; Env Chem; Medcnl Chem)
Bangor – 240–300 pts (Chem; Env Chem; Mar Chem; Chem Biomol Sci; Chem Euro; Chem Ind)
Central Lancashire – 240–260 pts (Chem; Foren Chem)
Dundee – CCC 1st yr entry (Biol Chem)
Greenwich – 240 pts (Chemistry)
Huddersfield – 240–220 pts (Chem; Chem Bioch; Chem Medcnl Chem)
Hull – 240–300 pts (Chem Analyt Chem Tox; Chem Bus; Chem Mol Med; Chem Nano)
Manchester Met – 240–220 pts (Chem; Chem Comb Hons; Medcnl Biol Chem; Pharml Chem; Foren Chem) (IB 24 pts)

220 pts **Glamorgan** – 220–260 pts (Chem; Foren Chem)
Heriot-Watt – CCD 1st yr entry (Chem courses)
Liverpool John Moores – 220–240 pts (App Chem Pharml Sci)

200 pts **Derby** – 200–240 pts (Chem Biol)
Huddersfield – 200 pts (Chem Analyt Chem)
Kingston – 200–280 pts (MChem Chem; BSc Chem; App Chem; Medcnl Chem)

160 pts **London Met** – 160 pts (Chem; Cos Sci)

140 pts **West Scotland** – CD (Chem; Medcnl Chem)

120 pts **London Arts** – 120 pts (Cos Sci)

80 pts **London (Birk)** – 80 pts under 21s (over 21s varies) (p/t Chemistry)

Open University – (Mol Sci – contact +44 (0)845 300 6090 or www.openuniversity.co.uk/you)

Alternative offers

See **Chapter 7** and **Appendix 1** for grades/UCAS Tariff points information for the International Baccalaureate, Scottish Highers/Advanced Highers, the Welsh Baccalaureate, the Irish Leaving Certificate, the Cambridge Pre-U Diploma, the Advanced Diploma and the Extended Project.

EXAMPLES OF FOUNDATION DEGREES IN THE SUBJECT FIELD

London Met; Sunderland.

CHOOSING YOUR COURSE (SEE ALSO CH.1)

Some course features

Birmingham Single Honours or major/minor courses which link chemistry with business, environmental science, pharmacology or psychology.
Durham Chemistry is offered as a Single or Joint Honours course or as part of the Natural Sciences programme.
Leeds Industrial bursary scheme for students.
London (UCL), Warwick MSc and BSc courses are common in the first two years after which a choice can be made. MSc courses provide greater depth and are aimed at those wishing to follow a scientific career.
Loughborough Strong links with industry for sandwich courses.
Manchester A range of course options inlcuding placements in industry, Europe and North America.
York Sponsorships and sandwich courses available.

Universities and colleges teaching quality See www.qaa.ac.uk; www.unistats.com.

Top research universities and colleges (RAE 2008) Cambridge; Nottingham; Oxford; Edinburgh; St Andrews; Bristol; Imperial London; Leeds; Warwick; York; Liverpool; Manchester; Sheffield.

Examples of sandwich degree courses Aston; Bangor; Bath; Bradford; Cardiff; Dundee; Glamorgan; Kingston; Liverpool John Moores; Loughborough; Manchester; Manchester Met; Northumbria; Nottingham Trent; Queen's Belfast; St Andrews; Surrey; Sussex; Teesside; West Scotland; York.

ADMISSIONS INFORMATION

Number of applicants per place (approx) Bangor (Mar Chem) 3, (Chem) 6; Bath 7; Bradford (Chem Pharml Foren Sci) 10; Bristol 7; Durham 6; Edinburgh 5; Heriot-Watt 6; Hull 7; Imperial London 3; Kingston 4; Leeds 3; Leicester 6; London (QM) 3, (UCL) 5; Newcastle 5; Nottingham (Chem Mol Phys) 4, (Chem) 8; Oxford (success rate 63%); Southampton 7; Surrey 3; York 5.

Advice to applicants and planning the UCAS personal statement Extend your knowledge beyond your exam studies by reading scientific journals and keeping abreast of scientific developments in the news. Discuss any visits to chemical firms and laboratories, for example, pharmaceutical, food science, rubber and plastic, paper, photographic, environmental health. See also **Appendix 4**.

Misconceptions about this course Many students do not fully appreciate the strengths of a Chemistry degree for any career despite the fact that graduates regularly go into a diverse range of careers. **Durham** Students fail to realise that they require mathematics and that physics is useful.

Selection interviews **Yes** Bangor, Bath, Bristol, Cambridge, Coventry, Durham, Greenwich, Huddersfield, Hull, Keele (mature students only), Kingston, London (UCL), London Met, Loughborough, Newcastle, Northumbria, Nottingham, Nottingham Trent, Oxford (success rate 66%), Sheffield, Southampton, Surrey, Warwick, York; **Some** Aston, Cardiff, Dundee, East Anglia, Liverpool John Moores, Plymouth.

Interview advice and questions Be prepared for questions on your chemistry syllabus and aspects that you enjoy the most. In the past a variety of questions have been asked, for example: Why is carbon a special element? Discuss the nature of forces between atoms with varying intermolecular distances. Describe recent practicals. What is acid rain? What other types of pollution are caused by the human race? What is an enzyme? What are the general properties of benzene? Why might sciences be less popular among girls at school? What can a mass spectrometer be used for? What would you do if a river turned bright blue and you were asked how to test a sample? What would be the difference between metal and non-metal pollution? **Bath** Why Chemistry? Discuss the practical work you are doing. **Oxford** No written or work tests. Evidence required of motivation and further potential and a capacity to analyse and use information to form opinions and a willingness to discuss them. **York** Discuss your favourite areas of chemistry, some of your extra-curricular activities, your preferred learning styles – for example, small tutorials of four or fewer, lectures. See also **Chapter 5**.

Reasons for rejection (non-academic) Didn't attend interview. Rude and unco-operative. Arrived under influence of drink. Poor attitude and poor commitment to chemistry. Incomplete, inappropriate, illegible, illiterate personal statements. **Southampton** Applicants called for interview are not normally rejected.

AFTER-RESULTS ADVICE

Offers to applicants repeating A-levels **Higher** Bangor, Dundee, Hull, Leeds, Northumbria, Nottingham, St Andrews, Warwick; **Possibly higher** Coventry, Edinburgh, Newcastle; **Same** Aston, Bath, Bristol (no offer if first-time grades are low), Cardiff, Derby, Durham, East Anglia, Greenwich, Heriot-Watt, Huddersfield, Keele, Kingston, Liverpool John Moores, London (UCL), London Met, Loughborough, Plymouth, Sheffield, Surrey; **No offers made** Cambridge.

GRADUATE DESTINATIONS AND EMPLOYMENT (2007/8 HESA)

Graduates surveyed 1710; **Employed** 710; **In further study** 700; **Assumed unemployed** 170.

Career note A large number of chemistry graduates choose to go on to further study as well as into scientific careers in research, analysis or development. Significant numbers also follow careers in a wide range of areas in management, teaching and retail work.

OTHER DEGREE SUBJECTS FOR CONSIDERATION

Agriculture; Biochemistry; Biological Sciences; Biomedical Science; Chemical Engineering; Environmental Science; Forensic Science; Genetics; Materials Science; Medicine; Microbiology; Oceanography; Pharmacology; Pharmacy.

CHINESE

(including **Korean**; see also **Asia-Pacific Studies, Business Courses** and **Languages**)

Oriental languages are not necessarily difficult languages but they differ considerably in their writing systems which present their own problems for the new student. Even so, Chinese is not a language to be chosen for its novelty and students should have a strong interest in China and its people. It is a country with a high economic growth rate and there are good opportunities for graduates, an increasing number being recruited by firms based in East Asia. Other opportunities exist in diplomacy, aid work and tourism throughout China, Taiwan and Mongolia as well as most non-scientific career areas in the UK.

Useful websites www.cilt.org.uk; www.iol.org.uk; www.bbc.co.uk/languages; www.china.org.cn/english; www.languageadvantage.com; www.languagematters.co.uk; www.reed.co.uk/multilingual; www.chineseculture.about.com.

NB The points totals shown to the left of the institutions are for ease of reference only. It must not be assumed that Tariff points are always used by institutions or that they can be substituted for an offer in grades. The level of an offer is not necessarily indicative of the quality of a course.

COURSE OFFERS INFORMATION

Subject requirements/preferences **GCSE** A language is required. **AL** A modern language is usually required.

NB In 2011 universities and colleges will differ in their use of GCE AL/AS unit grade information, A* grades, the Extended Project (EPQ), the Advanced Diploma and the Cambridge Pre-U examination when considering applicants and making offers. An EPQ may be accepted in place of an AS subject. Check websites of universities and colleges for the latest offers information.

Your target offers and examples of courses provided by each institution

380 pts **Cambridge** – A*AA college offers may vary (As Mid E St (Chin St)) (IB 38–42 pts)
360 pts **Manchester** – AAA–AAB (MML Chin Jap)
Nottingham – AAA–AAB (Maths Chin St; Econ Chin St)
Oxford – AAA (Chinese) (IB 38–42 pts)
340 pts **Birmingham** – AAB–ABB (Int Bus Mand Chin) (IB 33–36 pts)
London (SOAS) – AAB (Chin (Modn Class)) (IB 36 pts HL 666)
Manchester – AAB–BBB (Chin St; Chin Ling) (IB 35–30 pts)
Nottingham – AAB–ABB (Glob Iss Contemp Chin St; Geog Chin St; Mgt St Chin St)
320 pts **Leeds** – ABB (Chin (Modn); As Pacif St Chin; 21 joint Hons Chin courses) (IB 34 pts)
London (SOAS) – ABB (Korean) (IB 34 pts)
Manchester – ABB–BBC (BA Chin Jap)
Newcastle – ABB (Chin/Jap Cult St) (IB 32 pts)
Sheffield – ABB (Chin St Hist)
300 pts **Edinburgh** – BBB (Chin; Econ Chin; Chin Hist; Chin Ling; Int Bus Chin) (IB 34 pts HL 555)
Manchester – BBB–BBC (Chin Scrn St) (IB 30 pts)
Newcastle – ABC/BBB (Ling Chin/Jap) (IB 32 pts)
Nottingham – BBB (Contemp Chin St; Bus Econ Contemp Chin) (IB 32 pts)

Sheffield – BBB–BBC (Chin St Bus Mgt; Chin St Fr/Ger/Jap/Russ/Span)
Westminster – BBB (Jrnl Contemp Chin St) (IB 32 pts)
280 pts **Sheffield** – BBC (Mus Chin St; Kor St)
Westminster – BBC (Chin Engl Lang; Int Rel Chin)
260 pts **Nottingham Trent** – 260 pts (Chin (Mand) courses)
240 pts **Central Lancashire** – 240–280 pts (Bus Mgt Chin)
Liverpool John Moores – 240 pts (Int Bus St Chin; PR Chin)
Manchester Met – 240 pts (Modn Lang (Chin))
220 pts **Edge Hill** – 220–260 pts (Chin St Bus; Engl Chin St)
180 pts **Greenwich** – 180 pts (Chin Int Bus)
Trinity Saint David – 180–240 pts (Chin St Anth; Chin St Arch; Chin St Class St; Chin St Engl; Chin St Phil St; Chin St Relig St; Chin St Welsh St)

London (Birk) – check with admissions tutor (Chin Hist Art; Chin Ling)

Alternative offers
See **Chapter 7** and **Appendix 1** for grades/UCAS Tariff points information for the International Baccalaureate, Scottish Highers/Advanced Highers, the Welsh Baccalaureate, the Irish Leaving Certificate, the Cambridge Pre-U Diploma, the Advanced Diploma and the Extended Project.

CHOOSING YOUR COURSE (SEE ALSO CH.1)

Some course features
Edinburgh (Chin) This is an intensive language course in Mandarin Chinese and Modern Standard (colloquial) Chinese. Year 3 is spent in China.
Leeds (Chin Int Rel) Year 2 spent in China taking language courses at a university in Beijing, Tianjin or Taipei. Students expected to reach a high standard of language ability.
London (SOAS) (Chin (Modn Class)) Course designed to give broad understanding of Chinese culture, past and present, through its language, history and literature. In Years 3 and 4 students can choose to specialise in either modern or classical China.
Manchester (Chin St) Course covers both language (Mandarin) and culture, society, economics, politics and international relations.
Newcastle (Chin/Jap Cult St) Course provides language tuition in either language.
Sheffield (Mus Chin St) Dual Honours course allows students to design their own Music programme, specialising in composition, dissertation or performance. Chinese Studies involves intensive language learning (from scratch or with some prior knowledge). Year 2 at Nanjing University, and modules in Chinese business, literature, history and the environment.
Trinity Saint David (Chin St) A broad course covering the language, culture, politics, economics, philosophy and religions of China. There is a four-month placement at a Chinese university.

Universities and colleges teaching quality See www.qaa.ac.uk; www.unistats.com.

Top research universities and colleges (RAE 2008) (Asian Studies) London (SOAS); Oxford; Cambridge; Leeds; Manchester; Nottingham; Westminster.

Examples of sandwich degree courses Westminster.

ADMISSIONS INFORMATION

Number of applicants per place (approx) Leeds 5; London (SOAS) 8; Westminster 18.

Advice to applicants and planning the UCAS personal statement It will be necessary to demonstrate a knowledge of China, its culture, political and economic background. Visits to the Far East should be mentioned, with reference to any features which have influenced your choice of degree course. See also **Appendix 4** under **Languages**.

Selection interviews **Yes** Cambridge, Leeds, London (SOAS), Oxford.

Interview advice and questions You will be expected to convince the admissions tutor why you want to study the language. Your knowledge of Chinese culture, politics and society in general, and of Far Eastern problems, could also be tested. See also **Chapter 5**.

Reasons for rejection (non-academic) **Oxford** His language background seemed a little weak and his written work not as strong as that of other applicants. At interview he showed himself to be a dedicated hard-working young man but lacking in the imagination, flexibility and the intellectual liveliness needed to succeed on the course.

AFTER-RESULTS ADVICE

Offers to applicants repeating A-levels **Higher** Leeds; **No offers made** Cambridge.

GRADUATE DESTINATIONS AND EMPLOYMENT (2007/8 HESA)

Graduates surveyed 60; **Employed** 25; **In further study** 15; **Assumed unemployed** 5.

Career note See **Languages**.

OTHER DEGREE SUBJECTS FOR CONSIDERATION

Traditional Chinese Medicine; other Oriental languages.

CLASSICAL STUDIES/CLASSICAL CIVILISATION

(see also **Archaeology, Classics** and **History (Ancient)**)

Classical Studies and Classical Civilisation courses cover the literature, history, philosophy and archaeology of Ancient Greece and Rome. A knowledge of Latin or Greek is not necessary for many courses, but check subject requirements carefully.

Useful websites www.britishmuseum.org; see also **History** and **History (Ancient)**.

NB The points totals shown to the left of the institutions are for ease of reference only. It must not be assumed that Tariff points are always used by institutions or that they can be substituted for an offer in grades. The level of an offer is not necessarily indicative of the quality of a course.

COURSE OFFERS INFORMATION

Subject requirements/preferences **GCSE** English and a foreign language often required. **AL** A modern language is required for joint language courses. Relevant subjects include classical civilisation, English literature, archaeology, Latin, Greek.

NB In 2011 universities and colleges will differ in their use of GCE AL/AS unit grade information, A* grades, the Extended Project (EPQ), the Advanced Diploma and the Cambridge Pre-U examination when considering applicants and making offers. An EPQ may be accepted in place of an AS subject. Check websites of universities and colleges for the latest offers information.

Your target offers and examples of courses provided by each institution

360 pts **Exeter** – AAA–ABB (Class St courses) (IB 36–31 pts)
London (King's) – AAB+AS (Class St; Class St Byz Modn Gk St; Class St Film St) (IB 36 pts HL 665)
Warwick – ABBc **or** ABbbc (Class Civ Phil; Class Civ) (IB 36–32 pts)

340 pts **Bristol** – AAB (Class St; Class St Euro; Class St Phil) (IB 35 pts HL 666)
Durham – AAB (Class Past)
Exeter – AAB–ABB (Class St Fr/Ger/Ital/Span; Class St Phil) (IB 34–29 pts)
Glasgow – AAB (Class Class Civ) (IB 30 pts)
London (UCL) – ABB+AS (Anc Wrld St) (IB 34 pts)
Manchester – AAB–BBB (Class Civ Art Hist App Engl Lang St; Class Civ Art Hist Sci Psy; Comb St courses) (IB 35–32 pts)
Newcastle – AAB (Class St Engl) (IB 35 pts HL Engl 6)
St Andrews – AAB (Class St courses) (IB 36 pts)

320 pts **Birmingham** – ABB (Class Lit Civ) (IB 32 pts)
Birmingham – ABB-BBB (Anth Class Lit Civ; Class Lit Civ joint courses) (IB 32 pts)

Kent – 320–300 pts (Class Arch St courses) (IB 32 pts)
Leeds – ABB (Class Civ; Class Lit Russ Civ; Rom Civ Russ Civ; Gk Civ courses)
London (RH) – ABB (Class St; Class St Ital; Class St Dr) (IB 34 pts)
Manchester – ABB–BBB (Class St) (IB 33–32 pts)
Newcastle – ABB (Class St) (IB 32 pts)
Nottingham – ABB (Class Civ; Class Civ Engl St; Class Civ Fr/Ger; Class Civ Phil) (IB 34 pts)
300 pts **Edinburgh** – BBB (Class St; Class Arch Gk)
Leeds – BBB (Rom Civ Theol Relig St) (IB 32 pts)
Liverpool – BBB (Class St; Class St Modn Lang) (IB 30 pts)
Nottingham – ABC/BBB (Arch Class Civ; Class Civ Art Hist) (IB 32 pts)
Reading – 300–320 pts (Class St; Class Mediev St; Class St Engl Lit) (IB 30 pts)
260 pts **Swansea** – 260–300 pts (Class Civ joint courses; Egypt Class Civ)
240 pts **Roehampton** – 240–320 pts (Class Civ courses)
180 pts **Trinity Saint David** – 180–240 pts (Class St courses)
80 pts **London (Birk)** – 80 pts (p/t Class St)

Alternative offers
See **Chapter 7** and **Appendix 1** for grades/UCAS Tariff points information for the International Baccalaureate, Scottish Highers/Advanced Highers, the Welsh Baccalaureate, the Irish Leaving Certificate, the Cambridge Pre-U Diploma, the Advanced Diploma and the Extended Project.

CHOOSING YOUR COURSE (SEE ALSO CH.1)

Some course features
Birmingham (Class Lit Civ) Broad course covering literature, history, drama, politics, philosophy, art, religion and science.
Durham Three courses (Classical Past, Ancient History and Classics) have a common first year.
London (King's) (Class St) One language option module (Greek or Latin) to be taken in Year 1.
London (RH) (Class St) Option courses in Year 1 include Greek law, Roman Egypt, the built environment and women in classical antiquity.
Manchester (Class St) Greek or Latin options available including beginners' courses.

Universities and colleges teaching quality See www.qaa.ac.uk; www.unistats.com.

Top research universities and colleges (RAE 2008) See **Classics**.

ADMISSIONS INFORMATION

Number of applicants per place (approx) Birmingham 3; Bristol 10; Durham (Class Past) 10; Exeter 3; Leeds 7; London (RH) 4; Manchester (Class St) 4; Newcastle 8; Nottingham 6; Reading 10; Swansea 5; Trinity Saint David 2; Warwick 23.

Advice to applicants and planning the UCAS personal statement Discuss any A-level work and what has attracted you to this subject. Describe visits to classical sites or museums and what impressed you.

Misconceptions about this course **Birmingham** (Class Lit Civ) A study of classics at school is not necessary although while many people catch the classics bug by doing classical civilisation at A-level, others come to classics through reading the myths or seeing the plays and being fascinated by them. For others the inter-disciplinary nature of the subject attracts them – literature, drama, history, politics and philosophy. **Exeter** (Class St) This is not a language degree. There is no requirement for either A-level Latin or Greek.

Selection interviews **Yes** Birmingham, Durham, Kent, London (RH), Newcastle, Nottingham, Trinity Saint David; **Some** Bristol, Warwick.

Interview advice and questions In the past questions have included: What special interests do you have in Classical Studies/Classics? Have you visited Greece, Rome or any other classical sites or museums and what were your impressions? These are the types of questions to expect, along with those to explore your knowledge of the culture, theatre and architecture of the period. **Birmingham**

(Class Lit Civ) The programme includes some language study and, if applicants do not have a GCSE in a foreign language, we ask them to do a short language aptitude test. Interview questions are likely to focus on your reading interests (not necessarily classical texts!) and your own reflections on them. We are interested in your ability to think for yourself and we want to be sure that you are someone who will enjoy three years of reading and talking about books. **Swansea** Reasons for choosing the subject and how the student hopes to benefit from the course. See also **Chapter 5**.

Reasons for rejection (non-academic) **Birmingham** Lukewarm interest in the subject. Lack of clear idea why they wanted to do this degree.

AFTER-RESULTS ADVICE

Offers to applicants repeating A-levels **Higher** Glasgow (AAA), Nottingham, St Andrews, Warwick; **Same** Birmingham, Bristol, Durham, Exeter, Leeds, London (RH), Newcastle.

GRADUATE DESTINATIONS AND EMPLOYMENT (2007/8 HESA)

Graduates surveyed 680; **Employed** 285; **In further study** 180; **Assumed unemployed** 65.

Career note As with other non-vocational subjects, graduates enter a wide range of careers. In a small number of cases this may be subject-related with work in museums and art galleries. However, much will depend on how the student's interests develop during the undergraduate years and career planning should start early.

OTHER DEGREE SUBJECTS FOR CONSIDERATION

Archaeology; Ancient History; Classics; Greek; History; History of Art; Latin; Philosophy.

CLASSICS

(see also **Classical Studies/Classical Civilisation, Greek** and **Latin**)

Classics courses focus on a study of Greek and Latin but may also include topics related to ancient history, art and architecture, drama and philosophy. These subjects are also frequently offered in joint courses.

Useful websites www.classicspage.com; www.classics.ac.uk; www.cambridgescp.com; www.bbc.co.uk/history/ancient/greeks; www.bbc.co.uk/history/ancient/romans.

NB The points totals shown to the left of the institutions are for ease of reference only. It must not be assumed that Tariff points are always used by institutions or that they can be substituted for an offer in grades. The level of an offer is not necessarily indicative of the quality of a course.

COURSE OFFERS INFORMATION

Subject requirements/preferences **GCSE** English and a foreign language usually required. Grades A*/A/B may be stipulated. **AL** Check courses for Latin/Greek requirements.

NB In 2011 universities and colleges will differ in their use of GCE AL/AS unit grade information, A* grades, the Extended Project (EPQ), the Advanced Diploma and the Cambridge Pre-U examination when considering applicants and making offers. An EPQ may be accepted in place of an AS subject. Check websites of universities and colleges for the latest offers information.

Your target offers and examples of courses provided by each institution

380 pts **Cambridge** – A*AA college offers may vary (Class Gk Lat; Class Educ; Modn Mediev Langs (Class Lat) (Class Gk)) (IB 38–42 pts)

360 pts **Bristol** – AAA–AAB (Class; Class Euro) (IB 37–35 pts)
Exeter – AAA–ABB (Classics) (IB 36–31 pts HL Lat/Gk 6)
London (King's) – AAB+AS (Classics) (IB 36 pts HL 665)
Oxford – AAA (Class Engl; Class Modn Langs; Class I; Class II; Class Orntl St) (IB 38–40 pts)

	Warwick – ABBc–BBBc (Classics) (IB 36–32 pts)
340 pts	**Durham** – AAB (Class; Class Past)
	London (UCL) – ABBe (Class; Class Abrd) (IB 34 pts)
	St Andrews – AAB (Class courses) (IB 36 pts)
320 pts	**Leeds** – ABB (Classics A/B)
	London (RH) – ABB (Classics) (IB 34 pts)
	Manchester – ABB–BBB (Class; Class Anc Hist) (IB 33–32 pts)
	Newcastle – ABB (Classics) (IB 32 pts)
	Nottingham – ABB (Class (Gk Lat)) (IB 34 pts)
	Reading – 320 pts (Classics) (IB 30 pts)
300 pts	**Edinburgh** – BBB (Class; Class Engl Lang; Hist Class)
	Liverpool – BBB (Classics) (IB 30 pts)
260 pts	**Swansea** – 260–300 pts (Classics)
200 pts	**Trinity Saint David** – 200 pts (Classics)
80 pts	**London (Birk)** – 80 pts for under 21s (over 21s varies) (p/t Classics)

Alternative offers

See **Chapter 7** and **Appendix 1** for grades/UCAS Tariff points information for the International Baccalaureate, Scottish Highers/Advanced Highers, the Welsh Baccalaureate, the Irish Leaving Certificate, the Cambridge Pre-U Diploma, the Advanced Diploma and the Extended Project.

CHOOSING YOUR COURSE (SEE ALSO CH.1)

Some course features

Bristol (Class) Greek and Latin languages are studied for the first two years plus option topics from literature, art, philosophy, political, social and cultural history.
Cambridge (Class Gk Lat) Latin or Greek A-levels not required for the four-year course.
Liverpool (Class) 50% of the course consists of language study (Greek or Latin) including beginners' level. The remainder is a study of literature, art, history and archaeology.
Newcastle (Class) A concentration on the study of Greek and Latin languages and literature.
Oxford Course II (Latin or Greek) requires no formal qualifications. (**NB** Several other universities do not require a classical language qualification.)
St Andrews (Class) A wide range of related subjects is offered as part of the Single Honours course and a wide choice of complementary courses from other departments.

Universities and colleges teaching quality See www.qaa.ac.uk; www.unistats.com.

Top research universities and colleges (RAE 2008) (including Classics, Ancient History, Byzantine and Modern Greek Studies) Cambridge; Oxford; London (UCL), (King's); Durham; Warwick; Exeter; Manchester; Bristol; St Andrews.

ADMISSIONS INFORMATION

Number of applicants per place (approx) Bristol 15; Cambridge 2; Durham (Class) 8, (Class Past) 10; Leeds 4; London (King's) 6, (RH) 6; Manchester (Class) 7, (Class Anc Hist) 8; Newcastle 14; Nottingham 6; Oxford 2; Swansea 6; Trinity Saint David 5.

Advice to applicants and planning the UCAS personal statement Describe any visits made to classical sites or museums, or literature which you have read and enjoyed. Discuss any significant aspects which impressed you. Classics is an interdisciplinary subject and universities are looking for people who are versatile, imaginative and independently minded, so all types of extra-curricular activities (drama, music, philosophy, creative arts, politics, other languages and cultures) will be relevant. See also **Classical Studies/Classical Civilisation**.

Misconceptions about this course While Classics can appear irrelevant and élitist, universities aim to assist students to leave with a range of transferable skills that are of importance to employers.

Selection interviews Yes Cambridge, London (RH), (UCL), Newcastle, Oxford, Swansea; **Some** Bristol, Warwick; **No** Durham, Leeds, St Andrews.

Interview advice and questions What do you think it means to study Classics? Do you think Classics is still a vital and central cultural discipline? What made you apply to study Classics at this university? There are often detailed questions on the texts which the students have read, to find out how reflective they are in their reading. **Cambridge** What would happen if the Classics department burned down? Do you think feminism is dead? 'Emma has become a different person since she took up yoga. Therefore she is not responsible for anything she did before she took up yoga'. Discuss. **Oxford** Written tests to demonstrate ability in linguistics, competence in translation. Use of dictionaries not permitted. Classics and English applicants take the English Admissions Test. See also **Classical Studies/Classical Civilisation** and **Chapter 5**.

Reasons for rejection (non-academic) Did not demonstrate a clear sense of why they wanted to study Classics rather than anything else.

AFTER-RESULTS ADVICE

Offers to applicants repeating A-levels **Higher** Leeds, Nottingham, St Andrews; **Same** Cambridge, Durham, Newcastle; Swansea.

GRADUATE DESTINATIONS AND EMPLOYMENT (2007/8 HESA)

See **Classical Studies/Classical Civilisation**.

Career note See **Classical Studies/Classical Civilisation**.

OTHER DEGREE SUBJECTS FOR CONSIDERATION

See **Classical Studies/Classical Civilisation**.

COMBINED COURSES

(including **Arts Management** and **Cultural Studies**)

Many different subjects are offered in combined or modular arrangements. These courses are particularly useful for those applicants who have difficulty in deciding on one specialist subject to follow, allowing students to 'mix and match' according to their interests and often enabling them to embark on new subjects.

Useful websites www.artscouncil.org.uk; www.scottisharts.org.uk; www.arts.org.uk; www.artsprofessional.co.uk; www.culturalstudies.net.

NB The points totals shown to the left of the institutions are for ease of reference only. It must not be assumed that Tariff points are always used by institutions or that they can be substituted for an offer in grades. The level of an offer is not necessarily indicative of the quality of a course.

COURSE OFFERS INFORMATION

Subject requirements/preferences **GCSE** English, mathematics or science and foreign language may be required by some universities. **AL** Some joint courses may require a specified subject.

NB In 2011 universities and colleges will differ in their use of GCE AL/AS unit grade information, A* grades, the Extended Project (EPQ), the Advanced Diploma and the Cambridge Pre-U examination when considering applicants and making offers. An EPQ may be accepted in place of an AS subject. Check websites of universities and colleges for the latest offers information.

Your target offers and examples of courses provided by each institution
The offers listed below are average offers. Specific offers will vary depending on the popularity of the subjects in combination.

360 pts **Durham** – AAA (BA Comb Arts/Soc Sci) (IB 38 pts)
Exeter – AAA–ABB (Flex Comb Hons)
340 pts **Glasgow** – AAB (Humanities) (IB 32 pts)

Imperial London – AAB (Comb Chem/Biol Fr/Ger/Span; NB: Hum subjs and lang courses can be taken alongside main subjs)
Liverpool – AAB–BBB (Comb Hons) (IB 30–35 pts)
Manchester – AAB–BBB (Comb St courses) (IB 35–32 pts)
Newcastle – AAB (BA Comb St) (IB 34 pts HL 555+)

320 pts **Birmingham** – ABB (Media Cult Soty) (IB 32–34 pts)
Cardiff – ABB 320 pts (Cult Crit joint Hons)
East Anglia – ABB–BBB (Cult Lit Pol)
Newcastle – ABB (Chin Cult St) (IB 32 pts)

300 pts **Aston** – 300–320 pts (Comb Hons)
Edinburgh – BBB (Hum Soc Sci)
Kent – 300 pts (Cult St) (IB 33 pts HL 15 pts)
Leeds – BBB (Cult St Fr/Ger/Ital/Jap/Port/Russ) (IB 32 pts)
Nottingham – ABC–BBB (Cult Sociol) (IB 32 pts)
Oxford Brookes – BBB (Dr Comb Hons) (IB 33 pts)
St Andrews – BBB (MA General) (IB 32 pts)
Strathclyde – BBB (Arts Soc Sci)
Surrey – BBB (Sociol Cult Media) (IB 32 pts)

280 pts **Birmingham City** – 280 pts (Comb St)
Bristol UWE – 280–340 pts (Media Cult St)
Essex – 280 pts (Humanities)
Lancaster – BBC (Comb Sci)
Leicester – BBC–BCC (Comb St courses) (IB 30 pts)
London (Gold) – BBC (Soc Cult St)

260 pts **Bournemouth Arts (UC)** – BCC (Arts Evnt Mgt)
Brighton – BCC (Glob Hist Pol Cult) (IB 28 pts)
Coventry – 260–280 pts (Comb St)
Glamorgan – 260 pts (Comb St)
Hertfordshire – 260 pts (Humanities) (IB 24–26 pts)
Hull – 260 pts (Media Cult Soty)
Keele – 260–320 pts (Dual Hons)
Nottingham – 260 pts BCC (Humanities)
Strathclyde – BCC–BB (Arts Soc Sci)
Westminster – BCC (Comb Soc Sci (Cult St)) (IB 28 pts)
Winchester – 260–300 pts (Arts Mgt Perf Arts; Arts Mgt Dr; Arts Mgt Choreo Dance)

240 pts **Aberdeen** – CCC (Arts Soc Sci) (B 28 pts)
Bath Spa – 240–280 pts (Dance Comb Hons)
Cardiff (UWIC) – 240 pts (Engl Pop Cult)
Central Lancashire – 240–280 pts (Comb Hons Comm St Pop Cult)
Chester – 240 pts (Comb Hons)
Cumbria – 240 pts (Contemp App Arts)
Dundee – CCC 240 pts (Arts Soc Sci) (IB 29 pts)
Edinburgh Napier – 240 pts (Cstmd Prog Cult St)
Heriot-Watt – CCC–BCE (Comb St) (IB 25 pts)
Manchester Met – 240–260 pts (Cult St Comb Hons)
Surrey – 240 pts (Humanities) (IB 26 pts)
Worcester – 240 pts (Media Cult St Sociol) (IB 26 pts)

220 pts **Bath Spa** – 220–260 pts (Cult St Hist; Crea Arts courses)
Bradford – 220 pts (Comb St) (IB 24 pts)
De Montfort – 220–240 pts (Arts Fstvl Mgt Dance; Arts Fstvl Mgt Dr St)
Kingston – 220 pts (Vis Mat Cult)
Liverpool LIPA – 220–240 pts (Mus Thea Enter Mgt)
London Met – 220–240 pts (Arts Mgt; Arts Mgt Evnts Mgt; Arts Mgt Thea St)
Northampton – 220 pts (Joint Hons)

200 pts **Canterbury Christ Church** – 200 pts (Media Cult St Comb Hons) (IB 24 pts)

East London – 200 pts (Cult St courses) (IB 27 pts)
Hertfordshire – 200–240 pts (Joint Hons Open Prog)
London Met – 200 pts (Arts Mgt joint courses)
Middlesex – 200–300 pts (Mus Arts Mgt)
Roehampton – 200–280 pts (Hum; Comb Hons)
Trinity Saint David – 200 pts (Comb Hons)
180 pts **Derby** – 180–240 pts (Joint Hons)
Leeds Trinity (UC) – 180 pts (Humanities)
160 pts **Central Lancashire** – 160–240 pts (Comb Hons) (IB 26–28 pts)
Greenwich – 160 pts (Comb Hons)
Keele – 160 pts (Fdn Yr)
London South Bank – 160 pts (Arts Mgt)
St Mary's Twickenham (UC) – 160–200 pts (Cult St courses)
120 pts **Wirral Met (Coll)** – DD 120 pts (Cult St (Comb St))
100 pts **Bradford (Coll)** – 100 pts (Comb St)
80 pts **London (Birk)** – 80 pts for under 21s (over 21 varies) (p/t Hum Engl/Fr/Ger; Hum Hisp St; Hum Hist Art; Hum Hist; Hum Media St; Hum Phil)

Open University – (Hum Engl/Fr/Ger/Span – contact +44 (0)845 300 6090 or www.openuniversity.co.uk/you)
Wigan and Leigh (Coll) – (Comb Hons)

Alternative offers
See **Chapter 7** and **Appendix 1** for grades/UCAS Tariff points information for the International Baccalaureate, Scottish Highers/Advanced Highers, the Welsh Baccalaureate, the Irish Leaving Certificate, the Cambridge Pre-U Diploma, the Advanced Diploma and the Extended Project.

EXAMPLES OF FOUNDATION DEGREES IN THE SUBJECT FIELD
Bedfordshire; Canterbury Christ Church; Colchester (Inst); Norwich Arts (UC); Suffolk (Univ Campus); Truro (Coll).

CHOOSING YOUR COURSE (SEE ALSO CH.1)
Some course features
Birmingham (Media Cult Soty) A study of media and cultural analysis covering national and transnational interests in Europe today.
Cardiff (Cult Crit) Course covers all aspects of society's practices, for example literature, entertainment, buildings, artefacts.
East London (Cult St) Exploration of social and political issues and the media.
Kent (Cult St) A study of popular culture, the arts and everyday life in the context of the social sciences and humanities.
Leeds (Cult St) Course focuses on languages of texts, images, bodies, technologies, spaces and power, the possibilities for radical changes and the constraints and failures of modernity.
Manchester Met (Cult St Comb Hons) Opportunity for exchange study visit to USA in second year.
Nottingham (Cult Sociol) Course based on aspects of philosophy, sociology, history, linguistics and politics.

Universities and colleges teaching quality See www.qaa.ac.uk; www.unistats.com.

Top research universities and colleges (RAE 2008) (Cultural Studies) See **Communication Studies/Communication**.

ADMISSIONS INFORMATION
Number of applicants per place (approx) Birmingham 9; Dundee 13 (average); Durham (Comb Arts) 7; Heriot-Watt 3; Leeds 15; Liverpool 6; Newcastle 7; Strathclyde 9.

Advice to applicants and planning the UCAS personal statement Refer to chosen subject tables.
Bath Spa (Crea Arts) Looks for personal statements which clarify relevant work done outside the

school syllabus (eg creative writing). **De Montfort** Give information about practical experience and a personal interest in one or more areas of the arts. Show a mature attitude on arts/culture and be an original thinker. **Liverpool** (Comb Hons) We look for evidence of a broad interest across a range of subjects.

Misconceptions about this course **Bath Spa** (Crea Arts) Some applicants wish to specialise in one subject not realising it is a Joint Honours course. **Liverpool** (Comb Hons) Some students deterred because they believe that the course is too general. This is not so. The degree certificate shows the names of the two subjects taken to Honours degree level.

Selection interviews **Yes** Aberdeen, Bath Spa, Bristol UWE, De Montfort, Dundee, Durham, London Met, Manchester Met, Roehampton, St Mary's Twickenham (UC), Worcester; **Some** Birmingham (Comb courses inc Drama), Bournemouth Arts (UC), Liverpool.

Interview advice and questions Questions will focus on your chosen subjects. See under separate subject tables. **De Montfort** What do you understand to be the role of the Arts Council of England? What recent arts events have you seen/enjoyed? See also **Chapter 5**.

Reasons for rejection (non-academic) Lack of clarity of personal goals.

AFTER-RESULTS ADVICE

Offers to applicants repeating A-levels **Higher** Glamorgan, St Andrews; **Possibly higher** Bristol UWE, Leeds, Newcastle, Roehampton, St Mary's Twickenham (UC); **Same** Bath Spa, Birmingham, De Montfort, Derby, Durham, Greenwich, Leicester, Liverpool, London Met, Manchester Met, Worcester.

GRADUATE DESTINATIONS AND EMPLOYMENT (2007/8 HESA)

No data available.

Career note Graduates enter a wide range of careers covering business and administration, retail work, education, transport, finance, community and social services. Work experience during undergraduate years will help students to focus their interests.

OTHER DEGREE SUBJECTS FOR CONSIDERATION

See **Social Sciences/Studies**.

COMMUNICATION STUDIES/COMMUNICATION

(see also **Art and Design (General), Business Courses (Section C), Computer Courses, Engineering (Communications), Film, Radio, Video and TV Studies, Media Studies** and **Speech Pathology/Sciences/Therapy**)

Some courses combine academic and vocational studies, whilst others may be wholly academic or strictly vocational. The subject thus covers a very wide range of approaches concerning 'communication' which should be carefully researched before applying.

Useful websites www.camfoundation.com; www.coi.gov.uk; www.aejmc.org.

NB The points totals shown to the left of the institutions are for ease of reference only. It must not be assumed that Tariff points are always used by institutions or that they can be substituted for an offer in grades. The level of an offer is not necessarily indicative of the quality of a course.

COURSE OFFERS INFORMATION

Subject requirements/preferences **GCSE** English and mathematics grade A–C may be required. **AL** No specific subjects required.

NB In 2011 universities and colleges will differ in their use of GCE AL/AS unit grade information, A* grades, the Extended Project (EPQ), the Advanced Diploma and the Cambridge Pre-U examination when considering applicants and making offers. An EPQ may be accepted in

place of an AS subject. Check websites of universities and colleges for the latest offers information.

Your target offers and examples of courses provided by each institution

360 pts **London (UCL)** – AABe–BBBe (Sci Comm Plcy)
Ulster – AAA (Comm Adv Mark)
340 pts **Liverpool** – AAB (Engl Comm St) (IB 36 pts HL Engl 7)
London (Gold) – AAB (Media Comm)
Newcastle – AAB (Media Comm Cult St) (IB 30–32 pts)
320 pts **Cardiff** – ABB (Comm; Engl Lang Comm) (IB 32 pts)
Leeds – ABB (Comm St) (IB 32 pts)
Leicester – ABB 320 pts (Comm Media Soty) (IB 30 pts)
Liverpool – ABB (Comm Media Pop Mus; Comm Bus St; Pol Comm St) (IB 33 pts)
London (King's) – BBB+AS (Engl Lang Comm)
Loughborough – ABB (Comm Media St) (IB 34 pts)
300 pts **Bournemouth** – 300 pts (Comm Media)
City – BBB (Hum Comm) (IB 32 pts)
Brunel – 300 pts 3AL+AS/EPQ c (Comm Media St) (IB 31 pts)
Essex – 300 pts (Lang Comm) (IB 29 pts)
Sheffield – BBB (Hum Comm Sci) (IB 32 pts)
280 pts **Birmingham City** – 280 pts (Media Comm courses)
De Montfort – 280 pts (Hum Comm (Sp Lang Thera))
Glamorgan – 280–320 pts (Media Comm courses)
Hertfordshire – 280 pts (Mass Comm)
Manchester – BBC–BCC (Lang Litcy Comm) (IB 30–28 pts)
Oxford Brookes – BBC (Comm Media Cult courses; Comm Engl Lang; Pub Media) (IB 30 pts)
260 pts **Bristol UWE** – 260–300 pts (Comm Mark)
Glasgow Caledonian – BCC (Media Comm)
Gloucestershire – 260 pts (Media Comms Cult; Mark Adv Comms)
Keele – 260–320 pts (Media Comm Cult courses)
Northumbria – 260–280 pts (Comm PR; Fash Comm) (IB 24 pts)
Nottingham Trent – 260 pts (Comm Soty)
Ulster – BCC 260 pts (Comm courses) (IB 24 pts)
240 pts **Coventry** – 240 pts (Comm Cult Media)
Edinburgh Napier – 240 pts (Comm Adv PR)
Robert Gordon – CCC (Comm PR)
Sheffield Hallam – 240 pts (Communication)
Southampton Solent – 240 pts (Media Comm; Corp Comm)
220 pts **Bath Spa** – 220–260 pts (Media Comms)
Chester – 220–260 pts (Comm St) (IB 24 pts)
Huddersfield – 220–280 pts (Adv Mark Comm)
Manchester Met – 220 pts (Inf Comms)
200 pts **Central Lancashire** – 200 pts (Comm St Pop Cult Comb courses)
East London – 200 pts (Comm St)
Glyndŵr – 200 pts (Media Comms courses)
Middlesex – 200–240 pts (Jrnl Comm)
190 pts **Buckingham** – 190 pts (Comm Media Jrnl) (IB 24 pts)
180 pts **Anglia Ruskin** – 180–220 pts (Comm St courses)
Newman (UC) – 180 pts (Media Comm courses)
160 pts **Bedfordshire** – 160–240 pts (Adv Mark Comm)
Greenwich – 160 pts (Media Comm)
Wolverhampton – 160–220 pts (Media Comm St)

Alternative offers

See **Chapter 7** and **Appendix 1** for grades/UCAS Tariff points information for the International Baccalaureate, Scottish Highers/Advanced Highers, the Welsh Baccalaureate, the Irish Leaving

Certificate, the Cambridge Pre-U Diploma, the Advanced Diploma and the Extended Project.

EXAMPLES OF FOUNDATION DEGREES IN THE SUBJECT FIELD

Blackpool and Fylde (Coll); Oxford Brookes; Ravensbourne (CDC); Truro (Coll); see also **Film, Radio, Video and TV Studies** and **Media Studies**.

CHOOSING YOUR COURSE (SEE ALSO CH.1)

Some course features

Anglia Ruskin Pathways in Communications Studies and Media Studies.
Chester A theoretical and partly practical course with a six-week placement in Year 2.
Middlesex A communications course with a strong media focus.
Sheffield Hallam Focus on concepts and theories in cultural studies, linguistics, psychology and sociology. Professional expertise is possible by choosing modules in film, media and fine art.
Ulster Course includes one-to-one communication, language and communication, communication within and between social groups, mass communication and communication research. Course emphasis on students' own communication skills and inter-personal effectiveness.

Universities and colleges teaching quality See www.qaa.ac.uk; www.unistats.com.

Top research universities and colleges (RAE 2008) (Communication, Cultural and Media Studies) Westminster; East Anglia; London (Gold), (LSE); Cardiff; East London; London (RH); Sussex; Nottingham Trent; Ulster; Lincoln; Sunderland; Stirling.

Examples of sandwich degree courses Birmingham City; Bournemouth; Bristol UWE; Brunel; Central Lancashire; Edinburgh Napier; Gloucestershire; Greenwich; Hertfordshire; Huddersfield; Leeds Met; Nottingham Trent; Ulster.

ADMISSIONS INFORMATION

Number of applicants per place (approx) Brunel 9; Cardiff 6; Leicester 9; Manchester 5.

Advice to applicants and planning the UCAS personal statement Applicants should be able to give details of any work experience/work shadowing/discussions they have had in the media including, for example, in newspaper offices, advertising agencies, local radio stations or film companies (see also **Media Studies**). **Huddersfield** Critical awareness. Willingness to develop a range of communication skills including new technologies. **London (Gold)** Interest in a study in depth of media theory plus some experience in media practice. **Manchester Met** Motivation more important than grades.

Selection interviews **Yes** Brunel, Buckingham, Coventry, Glamorgan, Glasgow Caledonian, Leicester, Middlesex, Southampton Solent, Ulster; **Some** Anglia Ruskin, Cardiff, Chester, Huddersfield (rarely), London (Gold) (mature students), Sheffield Hallam (mature students).

Interview advice and questions Courses differ in this subject and, depending on your choice, the questions will focus on the type of course, either biased towards the media, or towards human communication by way of language, psychology, sociology or linguistics. See also separate subject tables. See also **Chapter 5**.

Reasons for rejection (non-academic) Unlikely to work well in groups. Poor writing. Misguided application, for example more practical work wanted. Poor motivation. Inability to give reasons for choosing the course. More practice needed in academic writing skills. Wrong course choice, wanted more practical work.

AFTER-RESULTS ADVICE

Offers to applicants repeating A-levels **Possibly higher** Coventry; **Same** Brunel, Cardiff, Chester, Huddersfield, Loughborough, Nottingham Trent, Robert Gordon, Sheffield Hallam.

GRADUATE DESTINATIONS AND EMPLOYMENT (2007/8 HESA)

See **Marketing** and **Media Studies**.

Career note Graduates have developed a range of transferable skills in their courses which open up opportunities in several areas. There are obvious links with openings in the media, public relations and advertising.

OTHER DEGREE SUBJECTS FOR CONSIDERATION

Advertising; Art and Design; Cultural Studies; Digital Communications; English; Film, Radio, Video and TV Studies; Information Studies; Journalism; Languages; Linguistics; Marketing; Media Studies; Psychology; Public Relations; Speech Sciences.

COMMUNITY STUDIES/DEVELOPMENT

(see also **Education Studies, Health Sciences/Studies, Nursing and Midwifery, Social and Public Policy and Administration** and **Social Work**)

These courses cover aspects of community social issues, for example housing, food, health, the elderly, welfare rights and counselling and features of community development such as education, arts, sport and leisure. Work experience is very important. Most courses will lead to professional qualifications.

Useful websites www.csv.org.uk; www.infed.org/community.

NB The points totals shown to the left of the institutions are for ease of reference only. It must not be assumed that Tariff points are always used by institutions or that they can be substituted for an offer in grades. The level of an offer is not necessarily indicative of the quality of a course.

COURSE OFFERS INFORMATION

Subject requirements/preferences **GCSE** English and mathematics grade A–C may be required at some institutions. **AL** No specific subjects required. **Other** Minimum age 19 plus youth work experience for some courses. Health and CRB checks required for some courses

NB In 2011 universities and colleges will differ in their use of GCE AL/AS unit grade information, A* grades, the Extended Project (EPQ), the Advanced Diploma and the Cambridge Pre-U examination when considering applicants and making offers. An EPQ may be accepted in place of an AS subject. Check websites of universities and colleges for the latest offers information.

Your target offers and examples of courses provided by each institution

320 pts **Birmingham** – ABB–BBB (Spo PE Commun St)
300 pts **Edinburgh** – BBB (Commun Educ)
Glasgow – BBB (Commun Dev)
280 pts **Newport** – 280 pts (Yth Commun St; Spo Yth Commun St)
260 pts **Manchester Met** – 260 pts (Commun Arts courses) (IB 26 pts)
Strathclyde – BCC (Commun Arts; Commun Educ) (IB 28 pts)
240 pts **Birmingham City** – 240 pts (Commun App Thea; Commun App Dance Thea)
Bournemouth – 240 pts (Commun Dev)
Liverpool John Moores – 240–280 pts (Commun Nutr)
Winchester – 240–280 pts (Chld Yth Commun St courses) (IB 24 pts)
220 pts **Coventry** – 220 pts (App Commun Soc St)
Sunderland – 220 pts (Commun Yth Wk St)
200 pts **Dundee** – BB (Commun Lrng Dev) (IB 29 pts)
East London – 200 pts (Educ Commun Dev; Commun Serv Ent; Yth Commun Wk)
Gloucestershire – 200 pts (Hlth Commun Soc Cr courses)
Huddersfield – 200–220 pts (Hlth Commun St)
London Met – 200 pts (Commun Sctr Mgt)
Sheffield Hallam – 200 pts (Spo Commun Dev)
Ulster – 200 pts (Commun Yth Wk)

180 pts **Bolton** – 180 pts (Commun Hlth Wlbng; Commun St; App Commun St)
UCP Marjon – 180 pts (Commun Prac courses; Commun Wk; Yth Commun Wk)
160 pts **Cardiff (UWIC)** – 160 pts (Yth Commun Educ)
Central Lancashire – 160 pts (Commun Ldrshp)
De Montfort – 160 pts (Yth Commun Dev)
Manchester Met – 160 pts (Yth Commun Wk)
140 pts **Bishop Grosseteste (UC)** – 140 pts (Dr Commun)
Leeds Met – 140 pts (Yth Wk Commun Dev)
100 pts **Newport** – 100–120 pts (Commun Hlth Soc Cr)
80 pts **Bolton** – 80 pts (Commun St Educ St inc Fdn)
Cumbria – 80 pts (Yth Commun Wk)
Derby – 80–120 pts (App Commun Yth St)

London (Birk) – (p/t Commun St)
Manchester – contact admissions tutor (App Commun Yth Wk St)

Alternative offers
See **Chapter 7** and **Appendix 1** for grades/UCAS Tariff points information for the International Baccalaureate, Scottish Highers/Advanced Highers, the Welsh Baccalaureate, the Irish Leaving Certificate, the Cambridge Pre-U Diploma, the Advanced Diploma and the Extended Project.

EXAMPLES OF FOUNDATION DEGREES IN THE SUBJECT FIELD

Bradford; Bradford (Coll); Cornwall (Coll); De Montfort; Derby; Durham New (Coll); Glyndŵr; Grimsby (IFHE); Kent; Leeds Met; Lincoln; Llandrillo (Col); Newcastle (Coll); Newport; Northampton; Northumberland (Coll); Norwich Arts (UC); Sheffield Hallam; Somerset (CAT); South Devon (Coll); Staffordshire (Reg Fed); Truro (Coll); Walsall (Coll); Warwickshire (Coll); Wirral Met (Coll); Wolverhampton; Worcester; York (Coll).

CHOOSING YOUR COURSE (SEE ALSO CH.1)

Some course features
Bolton A wide range of specialist modules and work experience in Years 2 and 3.
Derby A vocational course leading to careers in community and youth work.
Edinburgh Course focuses on adult education, community work, community arts and youth work and people's participation in all aspects of community life. Practice placement blocks in Years 2 and 3, and concurrent practice placements in Year 4.
Newport An initial qualifying course leading to a recognised youth work programme.

Universities and colleges teaching quality See www.qaa.ac.uk; www.unistats.com.

ADMISSIONS INFORMATION

Number of applicants per place (approx) Liverpool John Moores 2; Manchester Met 8; UCP Marjon 7.

Advice to applicants and planning the UCAS personal statement You should describe work you have done with people (elderly or young), particularly in a caring capacity, such as social work, or with the elderly or young children in schools, nursing, hospital work, youth work, community or charity work. You should also describe any problems arising and how staff dealt with them. See **Appendix 4**.

Advice for overseas applicants **UCP Marjon** Strong multi-cultural policy. English as a Foreign Language teaching offered.

Selection interviews **Yes** Bradford (Coll), Derby, Huddersfield (in groups), Manchester Met, Strathclyde; **Some** Liverpool John Moores.

Interview advice and questions This subject has a vocational emphasis and work experience, or even full-time work in the field, will be expected. Community work varies considerably so, depending on your experiences, you could be asked about the extent of your work and how you would solve the problems which occur. **Derby** Take us through your experience of youth and community work. What are the problems facing young people today? See also **Chapter 5**.

Reasons for rejection (non-academic) Insufficient experience. Lack of understanding of community and youth work. Uncertain career aspirations. Incompatibility with values, methods and aims of the course. No work experience.

AFTER-RESULTS ADVICE

Offers to applicants repeating A-levels **Same** Liverpool John Moores, UCP Marjon.

GRADUATE DESTINATIONS AND EMPLOYMENT (2007/8 HESA)

See **Social Work**.

Career note Social and welfare areas of employment provide openings for those wanting to specialise in their chosen field of social work. Other opportunities will also exist in educational administration, leisure and outdoor activities.

OTHER DEGREE SUBJECTS FOR CONSIDERATION

Communication Studies; Education; Health and Social Care; Nursing; Politics; Psychology; Social Policy and Administration; Social Work; Sociology; Youth Studies.

COMPUTER COURSES

(including **Artificial Intelligence, Business Information Systems, Computer Networks, Computer Science, Digital Computing, E-Commerce, Information Technology** and **Web Management**; see also **Engineering (Computer, Control, Software and Systems)** and **Technologies**)

Computer courses are popular and provide graduates with good career prospects. Courses vary in content and in the specialisations offered which may include software engineering, programming languages, artificial intelligence, data processing and graphics. Many universities offer sandwich placements in industry and commerce.

Useful websites www.bcs.org; www.intellectuk.org; www.e-skills.com; www.iap.org.uk.

NB The points totals shown to the left of the institutions are for ease of reference only. It must not be assumed that Tariff points are always used by institutions or that they can be substituted for an offer in grades. The level of an offer is not necessarily indicative of the quality of a course.

COURSE OFFERS INFORMATION

Subject requirements/preferences **GCSE** Mathematics usually required. A*/A/B grades may be stipulated for some subjects. **AL** Mathematics, a science subject or computer science required for some courses. **Cambridge** (Churchill, Magdalene) Uses STEP as part of offers; (Gonville and Caius) AEA mathematics required (see **Chapter 5**).

NB In 2011 universities and colleges will differ in their use of GCE AL/AS unit grade information, A* grades, the Extended Project (EPQ), the Advanced Diploma and the Cambridge Pre-U examination when considering applicants and making offers. An EPQ may be accepted in place of an AS subject. Check websites of universities and colleges for the latest offers information.

Your target offers and examples of courses provided by each institution

390 pts **Warwick** – AABb **or** AAbbb (Phil Comp Sci)

380 pts **Cambridge** – A*AA college offers may vary (Comp Sci) (IB 38–42 pts HL 766–777)

Imperial London – A*mathsAA (Comp; Comp (Artif Intel) (Biol Med) (Gms Vis Interact) (Soft Eng)) (IB 38 pts)

London (UCL) – AAA+AS–AAB+AS (Comp Sci; Comp Sci Int) (IB 36–38 pts)

360 pts **Bristol** – AAA–AAB (Comp Sci; Comp Sci Euro; Comp Sci Electron Abrd) (IB 35 pts HL 665)
Durham – AAA (Nat Sci (Comp Sci))
Edinburgh – AAA 2nd yr entry (Artif Intel courses; Comp Sci courses) (IB 36 pts)
Manchester – AAA–AAB (Comp Sci courses; Artif Intel courses; Comp Sci Bus Mgt; Soft Eng) (IB 37–35 pts)
Oxford – AAA (Comp Sci) (IB 38–42 pts)
St Andrews – AAA (Intnet Comp Sci Econ; Comp Sci Mgt Sci; Comp Sci Bus) (IB 36–40 pts)
Southampton – AAA (Comp Sci; Comp Sci Artif Intel; Comp Sci Imag Multim Sys) (IB 33 pts)

340 pts **Aston** – AAB–ABB 340–320 pts (Bus Comp IT) (IB 34 pts)
Bath – AAB 340 pts (Comp Sci; Comp Sci Jap; Comp Bus; Comp Sci Maths; Comp Sci Fr/Ger/Mand Chin/Span) (IB 36 pts HL maths 6)
Birmingham – AAB–ABB (Comp Interact Sys Bus Mgt)
Birmingham – AAB–BBB (Comp St Joint Hons)
Bournemouth – 340 pts (Comp Vis Animat)
Brighton – AAB (Comp Sci 4 yr; Bus Comp Sys 4 yr)
Durham – AAB (Comp Sci) (IB 36 pts)
Exeter – AAB–BBB (IT Mgt Bus; Comp Sci Artif Intel) (IB 34–29 pts HL Maths 6)
Lancaster – AAB 340 pts (Comp Sci Innov) (IB 31 pts)
Leeds – AAB (Artif Intel; Comp Sci; Comp Sci Maths; Maths Comp) (IB 36 pts HL 17 pts)
London (King's) – ABB+AS **or** AAC+AS (Comp Sci; Comp Sci Mgt; Comp Sci Abrd) (IB 34 pts)
St Andrews – AAB (Intnet Comp Sci; Comp Sci Lgc Phil Sci; Comp Sci) (IB 31–36 pts)
Sheffield – AAB (Inf Tech Mgt Bus; Ent Comp; IT Mgt Bus) (IB 35 pts)
Warwick – AAB **or** AAbb (Comp Sci; Comp Sys; Comp Bus St; Comp Mgt Sci) (IB 36 pts)
York – AAB (Comp Sys Soft Eng; Comp Sci courses) (IB 36 pts)

320 pts **Aston** – ABB (Comp Bus) (IB 32 pts)
Birmingham – ABB (Comp Sci courses; Artif Intel Comp Sci) (IB 34–32 pts)
Brunel – BBC +AS/EPQ c 320 pts (Comp Sci (Artif Intel); Inf Sys; Net Comp; Comp Sci (Soft Eng)) (IB 32 pts)
Cardiff – ABB–BBB (Comp Sci; Comp Sci Comp Vis Comp Graph; Comp Sci Dist Mbl Sys; Comp Sci Knwl Inf Sys; Comp Maths) (IB 32 pts)
City – 320–300 pts (Comp Sci Mus Tech; Comp Sci; Inf Sys; Soft Eng; Bus Comp Sys) (IB 28 pts)
Durham – ABB (Soft Eng; Comp; Comp (Euro St))
East Anglia – ABB 320 pts (MComp Comp Sci; Comp Graph) (IB 30–32 pts)
Edinburgh – ABB 1st yr entry (Artif Intel courses; Comp Sci courses) (IB 34 pts)
Glasgow – ABB (Comp Sci Physiol (Neuroinform); Comp Sci) (IB 32 pts)
Kent – 320 pts (Comp Sci courses; Web Comp) (IB 32 pts)
Lancaster – ABB (Comp Sci Maths) (IB 33–35 pts)
Leicester – ABB (Maths Comp Sci; Comp Sci; Comput Maths) (IB 28–30 pts)
Liverpool – ABB (MEng/BSc Comp Sci courses; Comp Inf Sys; Comp; Intnet Comp) (IB 33 pts)
Queen's Belfast – ABB (MEng Comp Sci; Comp IT; Comp Gms Des Dev)
Reading – 320 pts (MEng: Artif Intel Cyber; Cyber; Comp Sci Cyber; IT Tech Mgt) (IB 33 pts)
Sheffield – ABB (Comp Sci; Artif Intel Comp Sci; Soft Eng) (IB 33 pts)
Strathclyde – ABB 2nd yr entry (Comp Sci; Bus Inf Sys) (IB 28 pts)
Surrey – ABB 320 pts (Comp IT; Comp Sci; Comp Sci Eng) (IB 34 pts)
Sussex – ABB–BBB (IT E-Comm; Comp Sci; Comp Artif Intel; Gms Multim Env; Mus Inform)

300 pts **Aberdeen** – BBB 2nd yr entry (Artif Intel) (IB 28–29 pts)
Aston – BBB 300 pts (Comp Sci; Multim Comp) (IB 32 pts)
Bournemouth – 300 pts (Soft Eng Mgt; Comp; Web Sys; Foren Comp Scrty)
Brunel – BCC +AS/EPQ c 300 pts (Gms Des courses; Fin Comp) (IB 30 pts)
Dundee – BBB 2nd yr entry (App Comp courses; Comp Sci; Comp Cog Sci)
East Anglia – BBB 300 pts (BSc Comp Sci courses)
Essex – 300 pts (Comp Sci; Comp Net; Comp Gms; Comp Maths) (IB 29 pts)
Keele – 300 pts inc BC (Comp Sci courses) (IB 26–28 pts)

Lancaster – BBB 300 pts (Comp Sci Multim Sys; Comp Sci Soft Eng)
Leicester – BBB (Comp Ind; Comp Sci)
Lincoln – 300 pts (MComp Comp Sci; Comp Inf Sys; Comp Gms Prod)
London (Gold) – BBB (Crea Comp; Comp Sci; Interact Des)
London (QM) – 300 pts (MSci Comp Sci)
London (RH) – ABC/BBB (Comp Sci (Artif Intel) (Inf Scrty)) (IB 30 pts)
Loughborough – BBB–ABB 300–340 pts (MComp Comp Sci; Artif Intel; Comp Sci eBus; Comp Sci) (IB 34 pts)
Newcastle – ABC (Comp Sci (Gms Vrtl Envs) (Net Sys Intnet Tech)) (IB 30 pts HL maths 6)
Nottingham – BBB (Comp Sci 3 yrs; Comp Sci Artif Intel; Comp Sci Mgt St; Soft Sys) (IB 32 pts)
Oldham (Coll Univ Centre) – 300 pts (Dig Jrnl)
Reading – 300 pts (BSc Comput Sci; Comp Sci; App Comp Sci; IT courses)
Swansea – 300 pts (MEng Comp)

280 pts **Abertay Dundee** – BBC (Comp Arts; Comp Gms Tech)
Aberystwyth – 280 pts (Comp Sci; Comp Graph Vsn Gms; Comp Sci Artif Intel; Mbl Wrbl Comp) (IB 26–28 pts)
Brighton – BBC 280 pts (Comp Sci (Gms); Comp Sci; Bus Comp Sys; Dig Media; Soft Eng) (IB 28 pts)
Bristol UWE – 280–300 pts (Comp Sci; Gms Tech Prog; IT Mgt Bus; Web Des)
De Montfort – 280 pts (Foren Comp; Comp Scrty)
Glamorgan – 280–320 pts (Comp Gms Dev)
Glasgow Caledonian – BBC (Net Sys Sprt)
Heriot-Watt – BBC 2nd yr entry (IT; Comp Sci (Artif Intel) (Gms Prog))

Leicester – BBC (Comp Mgt; Comp)
Loughborough – BBC–ABB 280–320 pts (BSc Comp Sci Artif Intel; Comp Mgt; Comp Sci eBus; Comp Sci) (IB 30 pts)
Newcastle – BBC (Inf Sys; Inf Sys Mgt) (IB 28 pts)
Plymouth – 280 pts (Comp; Comp Sci; Comp Inf Scrty; Comp Sys Net; Web Apps Dev)
Queen's Belfast – BBC (BEng Comp Sci)
Reading – 280 pts (BSc Artif Intel Cyber)
Salford – 280 pts (Comp Sci; Comp; Intnet Comp)
Staffordshire – 280 pts (Comp Gms Prog)
Strathclyde – BBC (Comp Sci Law)
Swansea – 280 pts (Comp Sci Fr/Ger/Ital/Span/Welsh; Comp Comm; Comp Sci)

260 pts **Birmingham City** – 260–280 pts (Comp Net Scrty; Comp Sci; Foren Comp)
Bolton – 260 pts (Gms Des; Intnet Comm Net)
Brighton – BCC (Maths Comp) (IB 28 pts)
Bristol UWE – 260 pts (Comp Sys Integ; Foren Comp)
Glamorgan – 260–280 pts (Comp Foren)
Kent – 260 pts (Soft Eng) (IB 28–32 pts)
Kingston – 260 pts (Comp Sci Joint Hons courses; Cy Scrty Comp Foren; Web Dev; Inf Sys (Intnet Bus); Mbl Comp)
Lincoln – 260 pts (BSc Comp Gms Prod; Comp Inf Sys; Comp Sci)
Liverpool Hope – 260 pts (Comp courses)
London (QM) – 260 pts (BSc Comp Sci courses; Multim Comp; Bus Comp courses) (IB 32 pts)
Manchester Met – 260 pts (Mbl Comp; Comp Sci; Artif Intel)
Newport – 260 pts (Inf Scrty)
Northumbria – 260 pts (Comp Net Tech; Comp Sci; Comp Sci Gms Prod; Comp Foren; Ethl Hack Comp Scrty)
Portsmouth – 260 pts (Comp Sci; Comp; Web Tech)
Teesside – 260–320 pts (Comp Gms Prog; Comp Gms Des; Comp Gms Art)
Ulster – 260 pts (Comp Sci; Comp Sci (Embd Comp) (Intel Sys) (Mbl Comp) (Robot))

240 pts **Aberdeen** – CCC (Comp Sci; Comput Sci; Artif Intel (1st yr entry); Inf Sys Mgt)
Abertay Dundee – CCC (Ethl Hack Cntrms)
Bangor – 240–280 pts (Comp Sci; Comp Sci Bus; Intnet Sys E-Commer)
Bradford – 240 pts (Bus Comp; Comp Sci; Intnet Comp; Mbl Comp; Multim Comp; Intel Sys Robot)
Bristol UWE – 240–200 pts (Foren Comp; Comp Sys Integ; Comp App Maths) (IB 28–30 pts)
Buckingham – CCC 240 pts (App Comp)
Cardiff (UWIC) – 240 pts (Int Inf Sys Mgt)
Central Lancashire – 240 pts (Comp Net Tech; Mbl Interact Tech; Comp Gms Dev; Comp; Foren Comp)
Cumbria – 240 pts (App Comp)
De Montfort – 240 pts (Comp; Comp Sci; Multim Comp; Comp Gms Prog; Artif Intel Robot)
Derby – 240 pts (Mathem Comp St)
Dundee – CCC 240 pts 2nd yr entry (App Comp courses; Comp Cog Sci; Comp Sci) (IB 28 pts)
Edinburgh Napier – 240 pts (Comp Scrty Foren; Comp Net Distr Sys; Comp)
Glamorgan – 240–280 pts (Comp Sys Scrty; Comp Net; Intnet Comp)
Heriot-Watt – CCC 1st yr entry (Comp Sci (Gms Des))
Huddersfield – 240–260 pts (Comp Sci; Comp Gms Prog; Comp)
Liverpool John Moores – 240 pts (Comp Foren; Comp Gms Tech)
London (St George's) – 240 pts (Biomed Inform)
London Met – 240–200 pts (Comp Foren; Comp Net; Comp Sci; Comp)
Manchester Met – 240 pts (Comp Net Tech)
Newport – 240–260 pts (Comp; Net Web Dev; Comp Gms Des; Inf Scrty)
Nottingham Trent – 240–280 pts (Comp Sci courses; Comp Sys (Foren Scrty); Comp St)

Oxford Brookes – CCC (Comp Sci courses; Net Comp) (IB 29 pts)
Roehampton – 240–320 pts (Comp St Films)
Salford – 240–260 pts (Comp Sci; Comp Net) (IB 25–30 pts)
Sheffield Hallam – 240 pts (Comp Inf Scrty; Web Sys Des)
Staffordshire – 240 pts (Comp Sci; Comp Scrty; Comp Apps Bus; Foren Comp)
Sunderland – 240 pts (Comp Foren; Comp Sci; Ethl Hack Scrty Sys Des; Net Comp; Bus Comp)
Westminster – 240 pts (Mbl Web Comp; Comp Gms Dev; Comp Sci) (IB 28 pts)

220 pts **Bristol UWE** – 220–240 pts (Comp Scrty)
Chichester – CCD (IT Mgt Bus) (IB 28 pts)
Derby – 220 pts (Comp Net; Comp Foren Scrty)
Edge Hill – 220 pts (Web Sys Dev; Comp Inf Sys)
Gloucestershire – 220 pts (Computing)
Heriot-Watt – CCD 1st yr entry (Comp Sci (Artif Intel))
Manchester Met – 220 pts (Web Dev; Comp Mus Tech) (IB 26 pts)
Northampton – 220–260 pts (Comp; Comp (Intnet Tech Scrty))
Stirling – CCD (Bus Comp; Comp Sci) (IB 26–30 pts)
Teesside – 220–280 pts (Comp Sci; Comp Web; i-Comp)
West Scotland – CCD (Comp Gms Tech)

200 pts **Bristol UWE** – 200–240 pts (Computing)
Bucks New – 200–240 pts (Gms Dev)
Canterbury Christ Church – 200 pts (Bus Comp; Foren Comp; Comp)
Chester – 200–240 pts (Comp Sci; Comp; Intnet Tech) (IB 24 pts)
Coventry – 200–240 pts (Comp; Comp Net Comm Tech; Crea Comp; Ethl Hack Net Scrty)
Cumbria – 200 pts (Educ ICT)
East London – 200 pts (Bus Inf Sys; IT; Comp Net; Comp)
Glyndŵr – 200 pts (Comp Net Mgt Scrty; Comp; Comp Gms Dev)
Hertfordshire – 200 pts (Comp Sci (Artif Intel) (Net); Dig Foren Tech; Dig Rts Tech)
Hull – 200–280 pts (Comp Sci; Comp Bus Inform; Web Des Dev)
Kingston – 200–280 pts (Comp Graph Tech)
Liverpool John Moores – 200 pts (IT Multim Comp)
Middlesex – 200–280 pts (Foren Comp; Comp Sci; Comp Net)
Portsmouth – 200 pts (Cyber Scrty; Comp Gms Ent; Comp Net Mgt Des)
Suffolk (Univ Campus) – 200 pts (Comp Gms Prog)
Worcester – 200 pts (Comp; Web Dev)
York St John – 200 pts (IT (Web Tech))

180 pts **Bangor** – 180–200 pts (ICT)
Newman (UC) – 180–240 pts (IT courses)
Sheffield Hallam – 180 pts (Comp St)
Swansea Met – 180 pts (Comp Animat (3D))

160 pts **Bedfordshire** – 160 pts (Comp Sci; Comp Net; Mbl Comp)
Birmingham City – 160–180 pts (Computing)
Greenwich – 160–180 pts (Comp; Bus Comps; Intnet Comp; Web Bus Sys)
Kingston – 160 pts (Comp St)
Leeds Met – 160 pts (Comp; Comp Foren; Gms Des)
London South Bank – 160 pts (Comp courses)
Robert Gordon – CC 160–180 pts (Comp Sci; Inf Sys Tech) (IB 24 pts)
Roehampton – 160–240 pts (Computing Single/Comb Hons)
South Essex (Coll) – 160 pts (Net Tech)
Southampton Solent – 160 pts (Comp Net Web Des; Comp Sys Net)
Strathclyde – CC 1st yr entry (Nat Sci (Comp Sci))
West Scotland (Paisley) – CC–CD (Comp; Multim Tech; Comp Net)
Wolverhampton – 160–220 pts (Comp Sci courses; Comp courses; IT Scrty)

150 pts **Anglia Ruskin** – 150 pts (Comp Net; Comp Sci Intnet Tech)

140 pts **Blackpool and Fylde (Coll)** – 140 pts (Intnet Media Tech)

120 pts **Colchester (Inst)** – 120 pts (Comp Sol (Net) (Intnet))
Swansea Met – 120–340 pts (Comp Gms Dev)
80 pts **Bradford (Coll)** – 80 pts (Bus Comp courses)
Farnborough (CT) – 80–160 pts (Computing)
Havering (Coll) – 80–120 pts (Comp Sci courses)
London (Birk) – 80 pts for under 21s (over 21s varies) (p/t Inf Sys Mgt; Comp Biol/Chem)
West Anglia (Coll) – 80–160 pts (Comp Sc)

Open University – (Comp; Comp Maths; Comp Stats; Comp Psy St; Comp Sys; Comp Bus; Comp Des; IT Comp; ICT – contact +44 (0)845 300 6090 or www.openuniversity.co.uk/you)

Alternative offers
See **Chapter 7** and **Appendix 1** for grades/UCAS Tariff points information for the International Baccalaureate, Scottish Highers/Advanced Highers, the Welsh Baccalaureate, the Irish Leaving Certificate, the Cambridge Pre-U Diploma, the Advanced Diploma and the Extended Project.

EXAMPLES OF FOUNDATION DEGREES IN THE SUBJECT FIELD

Bath City (Coll); Bath Spa; Bedfordshire; Blackpool and Fyde (Coll); Bournemouth; Bradford; Bradford (Coll); Brighton; Bristol City (Coll); Bucks New; Central Lancashire; Chesterfield (Coll); Colchester (Inst); Cornwall (Coll); Croydon (Coll); Cumbria; De Montfort; Doncaster (Coll); Dunstable (Coll); Durham New (Coll); Ealing, Hammersmith and West London (Coll); East Anglia; East Berkshire (Coll); East London; Edge Hill; Farnborough (CT); Glamorgan; Glyndŵr; Greenwich; Grimsby (IFHE); Highbury (Coll); Huddersfield; Kent; Kingston; Kirklees (Coll); Lakes (Coll); Leeds (CAD); Leeds Met; Llandrillo Cymru (Col); London Met; London South Bank; Manchester (Coll); Merton (Coll); Mid-Cheshire (Coll); NEW (Coll); Newcastle (Coll); Newport; Northbrook (Coll); Northumbria; Nottingham New (Coll); Oxford Brookes; Plymouth; Queen's Belfast; Ravensbourne (CDC); Riverside Halton (Coll); St Helens (Coll); Salford; Sheffield (Coll); Sheffield Hallam; Shrewsbury (Coll); Somerset (CAT); South Cheshire (Coll); South Devon (Coll); South Essex (Coll); Southampton Solent; Staffordshire (Reg Fed); Stockport (CFHE); Stockton Riverside (Coll); Stoke on Trent (Coll); Suffolk (Univ Campus); Sunderland; Teesside; Truro (Coll); Tyne Met (Coll); Warrington (Coll); West Cheshire (Coll); Westminster Kingsway (Coll); Wigan and Leigh (Coll); Wiltshire (Coll); Wolverhampton; York (Coll).

CHOOSING YOUR COURSE (SEE ALSO CH.1)

Some course features
Abertay Dundee (Ethl Hack Cntrms) An unusual course, designed in collaboration with computer security companies and is expected to be accredited by the British Computer Society.
Brighton The Computing programme offers a wide range of different degrees with the final choice being made at the end of the first semester.
Reading A course is offered in Computer Science and Cybernetics involving applications with human activities and systems.
Salford The degree courses in Computer Science, Computing, Information and Intelligent Systems and Software Engineering share a common first year with final decisions on specialisation taking place in Year 2.
Southampton Transfer between Computing courses is possible up to the end of Year 2.
Warwick Students can apply for a place in the Erasmus programme or similar programme for study in an overseas university or salaried employment in industry.

Universities and colleges teaching quality See www.qaa.ac.uk; www.unistats.com.

Top research universities and colleges (RAE 2008) (Computer Science and Informatics) Cambridge; Imperial London; Southampton; Edinburgh; Oxford; London (UCL); Manchester; Nottingham; Glasgow; Liverpool; Lancaster; Leeds.

Examples of sandwich degree courses Aberystwyth; Aston; Bath; Birmingham City; Bournemouth; Bradford; Brighton; Bristol UWE; Brunel; Cardiff; City; Coventry; De Montfort; Derby; East London; Edinburgh Napier; Glamorgan; Glasgow Caledonian; Gloucestershire; Greenwich; Hertfordshire;

Huddersfield; Kent; Kingston; Leeds Met; Lincoln; Liverpool John Moores; London South Bank; Loughborough; Manchester; Manchester Met; Northumbria; Nottingham Trent; Oxford Brookes; Plymouth; Portsmouth; Queen's Belfast; Reading; Salford; Sheffield Hallam; Southampton Solent; Staffordshire; Surrey; Teesside; Ulster; West Scotland; Westminster; Wolverhampton; Worcester; York.

ADMISSIONS INFORMATION

Number of applicants per place (approx) Abertay Dundee 2; Aberystwyth 8; Aston (Bus Comp IT) 12; Bath 5; Birmingham 7; Bournemouth 8; Bradford 13; Bristol 9; Bristol UWE 4; Brunel 10; Buckingham 6; Cambridge 3; Cardiff 5; City 10; Coventry 10; Derby 3; Dundee 6; Durham 10; East Anglia (Maths Comp) 7; Edinburgh 4; Essex 2; Exeter 10; Glasgow Caledonian 8; Glyndŵr 3; Heriot-Watt 6; Hull (Comp Sci) 6; Imperial London 6; Kent 8; Kingston 10; Lancaster 5; Leeds 10; Leicester 22; Lincoln 5; Liverpool John Moores 3; London (King's) 20, (QM) 6, (RH) 5; Loughborough (CT) 2; Manchester Met 10, (Bus IT) 8; Newcastle 7; Northumbria 4; Nottingham 8; Nottingham Trent 4; Oxford Brookes 18; Plymouth 12; Portsmouth 6; Robert Gordon 3; Roehampton 3; Sheffield Hallam 5; Southampton 9; Staffordshire 4; Stirling 6; Strathclyde 16; Surrey 9; Swansea 5; Teesside 4; Warwick 11; York 9.

Advice to applicants and planning the UCAS personal statement Your computer and programming interests in and outside school or college should be described. It is also useful to give details of any visits, work experience and work shadowing relating to industrial or commercial organisations and their computer systems. (See **Appendix 4**.) Give details of your interests in, and knowledge of computer hardware, software and multimedia packages. Contact the BCS The Chartered Institute for IT for information. **Oxford** Successful entrants average 29.8%.

Misconceptions about this course That anyone who plays computer games or uses a word processor can do a degree in Computer Studies. Some think Computing degrees are just about programming; in reality, programming is only one, albeit essential, part of computing. **Aston** (Bus Comp IT) 60% business, 40% computing and IT; compulsory placement year in industry. **City** (Bus Comp Sys) Some applicants think that it is a Business degree: it is a Computing degree focused on computing in business. **London (QM)** There are many misconceptions – among students, teachers and careers advisers – about what computer science entails. The main one is to confuse it with what schools call information and communication technology which is about the use of computer applications. Computer science is all about software – ie programming – and will generally only cover a limited study of hardware.

Selection interviews **Yes** Bath, Blackburn (Coll Univ Centre), Bradford, Bristol, Bristol UWE, Brunel, Buckingham, Cambridge, Cardiff, City, Coventry, Cumbria, Durham, Edinburgh, Edinburgh Napier, Glamorgan, Hertfordshire, Hull, Imperial London, Kingston, Liverpool Hope, London (Gold), (QM), (UCL), London South Bank, Loughborough, Newcastle, Newport, Northampton, Northbrook (Coll), Nottingham, Nottingham Trent, Oxford, Plymouth, Portsmouth, Sheffield Hallam, Southampton, Surrey, Thames Valley, Wigan and Leigh (Coll), York; **Some** Abertay Dundee, Aberystwyth, Anglia Ruskin, Birmingham City, Blackpool and Fylde (Coll), Brighton, Chichester, Dundee, East Anglia, Exeter, Liverpool John Moores, London Met, Manchester Met, Salford, Staffordshire, Sunderland; Warwick 5–10%.

Interview advice and questions While A-level computer studies is not usually required, you will be questioned on your use of computers and aspects of the subject which interest you. How do you organise your homework/social life? What are your strengths and weaknesses? Do you have any idea of the type of career you would like? **Cambridge** Why is the pole-vaulting world record about 6.5m and why can't it be broken? **City** The aim of the interview is to obtain a full picture of the applicant's background, life experiences etc, before making an offer. **York** No tests. Questions for discussion at the whiteboard are usually mathematical or are about fundamental computer science such as sorting. See also **Chapter 5**.

Reasons for rejection (non-academic) Little practical interest in computers/electronics. Inability to work as part of a small team. Mismatch between referee's description and performance at interview. Unsatisfactory English. Can't communicate. Inability to convince interviewer of the candidate's worth.

Incoherent, unmotivated, arrogant and without any evidence of good reason. **London (QM)** Misunderstanding of what computer science involves as an academic subject – especially in personal statements where some suggest that they are interested in a course with business and administrative skills. Lack of sufficient mathematics. Computer science is a mathematical subject and we cannot accept applicants who are unable to demonstrate good mathematical skills. **Southampton** Lack of motivation; incoherence; carelessness.

AFTER-RESULTS ADVICE

Offers to applicants repeating A-levels **Higher** Brighton, De Montfort, Greenwich, Kingston, St Andrews, Surrey, Sussex, Warwick; **Possibly higher** Bath, Bristol UWE, Edinburgh, Lancaster, Leeds, Newcastle, Oxford Brookes, Portsmouth, Sheffield, Teesside; **Same** Anglia Ruskin, Aston, Blackpool and Fylde (Coll), Brunel, Buckingham, Cambridge, Cardiff, Chichester, City, Derby, Dundee, Durham, East Anglia, Exeter, Farnborough (CT), Huddersfield, Hull, Kent, Lincoln, Liverpool, Liverpool Hope, Liverpool John Moores, London (RH), (UCL), London South Bank, Loughborough, Manchester Met, Newman (UC), Northumbria, Nottingham Trent, Robert Gordon, Salford, Sheffield Hallam, Staffordshire, Sunderland, Suffolk (Univ Campus), Thames Valley, Ulster, Wolverhampton, Worcester, York.

GRADUATE DESTINATIONS AND EMPLOYMENT (2007/8 HESA)

Computer Science graduates surveyed 5525 **Employed** 3125 **In further study** 590 **Assumed unemployed** 815.
Information Systems graduates surveyed 1775 **Employed** 960 **In further stud**y 200 **Assumed unemployed** 245.
Artificial Intelligence graduates surveyed 75 **Employed** 35 **In further study** 20 **Assumed unemployed** 10.

Career note A high proportion of graduates go to work in the IT sector with some degrees leading towards particular fields (usually indicated by the course title). Significant areas include software design and engineering, web and internet-based fields, programming, systems analysis and administration.

OTHER DEGREE SUBJECTS FOR CONSIDERATION

Business Studies; Communications Engineering; Computer Engineering; Electrical and Electronic Engineering; Geographical Information Systems; Information Studies; Mathematics; Physics; Software Engineering.

CONSUMER STUDIES/SCIENCES

(including **Consumer Product Design** and **Trading Standards**; see also **Food Science/Studies and Technology** and **Hospitality and Hotel Management**)

Consumer Studies courses involve topics such as food and nutrition, shelter, clothing, community studies and consumer behaviour and marketing. Trading Standards courses focus on consumer law, contract law, food law, weights and measures, criminal investigation, fraud, counterfeit and fairtrading. Accredited by the Trading Standards Institute, they can lead to careers as trading standards officers.

Useful websites www.which.co.uk; www.tradingstandards.gov.uk

NB The points totals shown to the left of the institutions are for ease of reference only. It must not be assumed that Tariff points are always used by institutions or that they can be substituted for an offer in grades. The level of an offer is not necessarily indicative of the quality of a course.

COURSE OFFERS INFORMATION

Subject requirements/preferences **GCSE** Mathematics and English usually required. **AL** No specific subjects required.

NB In 2011 universities and colleges will differ in their use of GCE AL/AS unit grade information, A* grades, the Extended Project (EPQ), the Advanced Diploma and the Cambridge Pre-U examination when considering applicants and making offers. An EPQ may be accepted in place of an AS subject. Check websites of universities and colleges for the latest offers information.

Your target offers and examples of courses provided by each institution

300 pts	**Edinburgh Napier** – 300 pts (inc bus st/econ) 2nd yr entry (Mark Mgt Consum St)
	Reading – 300 pts (Consum Bhv Mark)
260 pts	**Reading** – 260 pts (Consum Electron)
240 pts	**Coventry** – 240 pts (Consum Prod Des)
	Manchester Met – 240 pts (Int Consum Mark; Consum Mark; Tr Stnds) (IB 24 pts)
	Teesside – 240 pts (Tr Stnds Consum Prot)
	Ulster – CCC 240 pts (Consum St)
230 pts	**Edinburgh Napier** – 230 pts 1st yr entry (Mark Mgt Consum St)
200 pts	**Birmingham (UC)** – 200 pts (Fd Consum Mgt) (IB 24 pts)
195 pts	**Queen Margaret** – 195 pts (Consum St)
180 pts	**Abertay Dundee** – DDD (Fd Consum Sci)
	Cardiff (UWIC) – 180 pts (Consum Tr Stnds) (IB 28 pts)
	Harper Adams (UC) – 180–220 pts (Fd Consum St)
160 pts	**London Met** – 160 pts (Fd Consum St courses)

Alternative offers

See **Chapter 7** and **Appendix 1** for grades/UCAS Tariff points information for the International Baccalaureate, Scottish Highers/Advanced Highers, the Welsh Baccalaureate, the Irish Leaving Certificate, the Cambridge Pre-U Diploma, the Advanced Diploma and the Extended Project.

CHOOSING YOUR COURSE (SEE ALSO CH.1)

Some course features

Cardiff (UWIC) The theme of the course (accredited by Trading Standards Institute) is of consumer protection, quality, law and trading standards. Graduates with a 2:2 degree are eligible for training as trading standards officers via the Diploma in Consumer Affairs and Trading Standards.
Coventry (Consum Prod Des) The four-year course covers the field of industrial design related to household products with an emphasis on styling and ergonomics. Towards the end of Year 3 students may apply for an industrial placement.
Manchester Met (Consum Mark) Course covers communications, brand design, consumer behaviour, retailing and buying. The course is validated by the Chartered Institute of Marketing.
Reading (Consum Bhv Mark) Course focuses on marketing, psychology, economics and research methods, with a wide range of optional modules from across the University including management, languages, politics and sociology.

Universities and colleges teaching quality See www.qaa.ac.uk; www.unistats.com.

Examples of sandwich degree courses Birmingham (UC); Cardiff (UWIC); Harper Adams (UC); Manchester Met.

ADMISSIONS INFORMATION

Number of applicants per place (approx) Birmingham (UC) 2; Cardiff (UWIC) 5; London Met 5; Manchester Met 4; Queen Margaret 3.

Advice to applicants and planning the UCAS personal statement Relevant work experience or work shadowing in, for example, business organisations, restaurants, cafes, or the school meals service, would be appropriate. (See also **Hospitality and Hotel Management** and **Dietetics**.) Details may be obtained from the Institute of Consumer Sciences – see **Appendix 4**.

Selection interviews Teesside; **Some** Manchester Met.

Interview advice and questions Questions will stem from your special interests in this subject and in the past have included: What interests you in consumer behaviour? What are the advantages and disadvantages? What is ergonomics? What do you understand by the term 'sustainable consumption'? What world or national news has annoyed, pleased or upset you? What relevance do textiles and dress have to home economics? How would you react in a room full of fools? **Queen Margaret** Very informal interviews covering work experience and career aspirations. See also **Chapter 5**.

AFTER-RESULTS ADVICE

Offers to applicants repeating A-levels **Same** Manchester Met, Queen Margaret, Ulster.

GRADUATE DESTINATIONS AND EMPLOYMENT (2007/8 HESA)

No data available.

Career note The various specialisms involved in these courses allow graduates to look for openings in several career areas, for example, food quality assurance, trading standards, consumer education and advice. Many graduates enter business administration and careers in particularly retailing, evaluating new products and liaising with the public.

OTHER DEGREE SUBJECTS FOR CONSIDERATION

Biological Sciences; Business Studies; Dietetics; Environmental Health; Food Science; Health Studies; Hospitality Management; Marketing; Nutrition; Psychology; Retail Management.

DANCE/DANCE STUDIES

(see also **Drama**)

Every aspect of dance can be studied in the various courses on offer as well as the theoretical, educational, historical and social aspects of the subject.

Useful websites www.arts.org.uk; www.cdet.org.uk; www.ballet.co.uk; www.ndta.org.uk.

NB The points totals shown to the left of the institutions are for ease of reference only. It must not be assumed that Tariff points are always used by institutions or that they can be substituted for an offer in grades. The level of an offer is not necessarily indicative of the quality of a course.

COURSE OFFERS INFORMATION

Subject requirements/preferences **GCSE** English usually required. Practical dance experience essential. **AL** No specific subjects required. **Other** CRB checks required for some courses: check websites.

NB In 2011 universities and colleges will differ in their use of GCE AL/AS unit grade information, A* grades, the Extended Project (EPQ), the Advanced Diploma and the Cambridge Pre-U examination when considering applicants and making offers. An EPQ may be accepted in place of an AS subject. Check websites of universities and colleges for the latest offers information.

Your target offers and examples of courses provided by each institution

340 pts **Leeds** – AAB (Thea Perf) (IB 36 pts)

300 pts **Leeds** – BBB (Perf Des; Dance) (IB 32 pts)

Surrey – BBB–BBC 300–280 pts (Dance Cult; Dance Cult Prof Trg) (IB 30–28 pts)

280 pts **Cumbria** – BBC 280 pts (Dance Perf Tech Thea; Dance Perf Musl Thea Perf; Dance Perf Dr Perf)

Kingston – 280–320 pts (Dance)

Roehampton – 280–340 pts (Dance St)

Salford – 280–300 pts (Perf Arts) (IB 31 pts)

260 pts **Brighton** – BCC 260 pts +Fdn Dip (Perf Vis Arts (Thea) (Dance))

Chichester – BCC 260–300 pts (Dance) (IB 28 pts)

Lincoln – 260 pts (Dance; Dance Dr)

Liverpool Hope – 260 pts (Dance courses; Crea Perf Arts)

London Met – 260 pts (Perf Arts)
Manchester Met – 260 pts (Dance; Dance Comb Hons) (IB 28 pts)
Northumbria – 260 pts (Dance Choreo)
Winchester – 260–300 pts (Choreo Dance) (IB 24 pts)

240 pts **Bath Spa** – 240–280 pts (Dance; Crea Writ Dance; Dance Comb Hons)
Cardiff (UWIC) – 240 pts (Dance)
Chester – 240–280 pts (Dance) (IB 24 pts)
Coventry – 240 pts (Dance Thea Prof Prac; Dance Prof Prac)
De Montfort – 240 pts (Dance; Dance Arts Fstvls Mgt; Dance Dr; Dance Educ St; Perf Arts)
Falmouth (UC) – 240 pts (Dance Choreo)
Liverpool John Moores – 240–280 pts (Dance)

220 pts **Edge Hill** – 220–280 pts based on audition (Dance; Dance Dr courses)
Middlesex – 220–240 pts (Dance St; Dance Perf)
Northampton – 220–260 pts (Dance; Dance Joint Hons)
Plymouth – 220 pts (Dance Thea) (IB 24 pts)
Sunderland – 220 pts (Dance)
Teesside – 220–260 pts (Dance)
Ulster – 220 pts (Dance; Dance Dr; Dance Ir; Dance Mus)
York St John – 220 pts (Dance)

200 pts **Bucks New** – 200–240 pts (Dance Perf)
Canterbury Christ Church – 200 pts (Dance Educ)
East London – 200 pts (Dance Urb Prac; Prof Dance Musl Thea)
Thames Valley – 200 pts (Musl Thea)

180 pts **Derby** – 180–240 pts (Dance Mov St courses)
Liverpool (LIPA) – BC 180 pts (Dance (Perf Arts))
Wolverhampton – 180 pts (Dance)
160 pts **Central Lancashire** – 160 pts (Dance Perf Teach)
Colchester (Inst) – 160 pts (Musl Thea)
Doncaster (Coll) – 160 pts (Dance Prac Dig Perf)
Greenwich – 160 pts (Dance Thea Perf)
Trinity Laban Consv – CC (Dance Thea – apply early, course validated by City Univ)
80 pts **Grimsby (IFHE)** – 80 pts (Perf Dance)
London (RAc Dance) – 80 pts (Ballet Educ)
Royal Scottish (RSAMD) – 80 pts min (Modn Ballet)

London (Arts Educ Sch) – (Musl Thea)
Northern (Sch Contemp Dance) – (Dance)

Alternative offers
See **Chapter 7** and **Appendix 1** for grades/UCAS Tariff points information for the International Baccalaureate, Scottish Highers/Advanced Highers, the Welsh Baccalaureate, the Irish Leaving Certificate, the Cambridge Pre-U Diploma, the Advanced Diploma and the Extended Project.

EXAMPLES OF FOUNDATION DEGREES IN THE SUBJECT FIELD

Bath Spa; Bedfordshire; Blackpool and Fylde (Coll); Bournemouth; Bournemouth Arts (UC); Bradford (Coll); Brighton; Bristol City (Coll); Bucks New; Colchester (Inst); Cornwall (Coll); Craven (Coll); Cumbria; Exeter (Coll); Farnborough (CT); Hereford (CA); Hertfordshire; Huddersfield; Hull (Coll); Kirklees (Coll); Leeds City (Coll); Leeds Met; Manchester (Coll); Middlesex; NEW (Coll); Newcastle (Coll); Northbrook (Coll); Norwich City (Coll); Nottingham New (Coll); Plymouth; Rotherham (CAT); St Helens (Coll); Sheffield (Coll); South Devon (Coll); Staffordshire (Reg Fed); Suffolk (Univ Campus); Teesside; Thames Valley; Truro (Coll); Wigan and Leigh (Coll).

CHOOSING YOUR COURSE (SEE ALSO CH.1)

Some course features
Edge Hill (Dance) Topics covered include dance analysis, applied dance, dance production and dance techniques.
Kingston (Dance) Two themes – movement improvisation and key dance skills and a study of British dance in modern muticultural Britain.
Leeds (Dance) Contemporary choreography is a key area of the course to provide a focus on making and performing dance.
Surrey (Dance Cult) Focus on dance of the 20th and 21st centuries, on dance techniques (including ballet, kathak, contemporary, and African people's dance), together with choreography and dance policy and practice.

Universities and colleges teaching quality See www.qaa.ac.uk; www.unistats.com.

Top research universities and colleges (RAE 2008) See **Drama**.

ADMISSIONS INFORMATION

Number of applicants per place (approx) Chichester 6; De Montfort (Dance) 13, (Perf Arts) 9; Derby 12; Liverpool (LIPA) 24; Liverpool John Moores 3; Middlesex 12; Northern (Sch Contemp Dance) 6; Roehampton 17; Surrey 5; Trinity Laban Consv 5; York St John 3.

Advice to applicants and planning the UCAS personal statement Full details should be given of examinations taken and practical experience in contemporary dance or ballet. Refer to your visits to the theatre and your impressions. You should list the dance projects in which you have worked, productions in which you have performed and the roles. State any formal dance training you have had and the grades achieved. Applicants need to have dedication, versatility, inventiveness and individuality, practical experience of dance, theoretical ability and language competency. **Bath Spa** Dance experience outside education should be mentioned.

Misconceptions about this course That Performing Arts is only an acting course: it also includes music.

Interview advice and questions Nearly all institutions will require auditions or interviews or attendance at a workshop. The following scheme required by **Liverpool (LIPA)** may act as a guide:

1 Write a short essay (500 words) on your own views and experience of dance. You should take into account the following:
   * Your history and how you have developed physically and intellectually in your run-up to applying to LIPA.
   * Your main influences and what inspires you.
   * What you want to gain from training as a dancer.
   * Your ideas on health and nutrition as a dancer, taking into account gender and physicality.

2 All candidates must prepare **two** practical audition pieces:
   * Whatever you like, in whatever style you wish, as long as the piece does not exceed two minutes (please note: panel will stop anyone exceeding this time-limit). There will be no pianist at this part of the session, so if you're using music please bring it with you on a cassette tape. This devised piece should be created through you and this means that you should feel comfortable with it and that it expresses something personal about you. You should wear your regular practice clothes for your presentation.
   * You must prepare a song of your own choice. An accompanist is provided, but you must provide the sheet music for your song, fully written out for piano accompaniment and in the key you wish to sing (the accompanist will **not** transpose at sight). **Important** Do NOT choreograph your song. You should expect to sit on a high stool or stand when singing for the audition.

3 Additionally, all candidates will participate in a class given on the day of audition:
   * Please ensure that you are dressed appropriately for class with clothing you are comfortable in but allows your movement to be seen. In preparing the practical elements of the audition, please remember that audition panels are not looking for a 'polished' performance. The panel will be looking for candidates' ability to make a genuine emotional and physical connection with the material that they are presenting which shows clear intent and focus.

Remember that it is in your best interest to prepare thoroughly. Nerves inevitably play a part in any audition and can undermine even the best-prepared candidate. Your best defence is to feel confident in your preparation. **Chichester** Applicants will be asked to prepare a set-piece in advance and to perform the piece in front of a group. **De Montfort** (Perf Arts) Practical workshops in dance and theatre plus a written paper. **Salford** (Perf Arts) Audition and interview. **Surrey** Applicants invited to spend a day at the university for interview and a practical class to assess dance skills. An audition fee may be charged. **Wolverhampton** Audition in the form of a dance class. See also **Chapter 5**.

Reasons for rejection (non-academic) Applicants more suitable for an acting or dance school course than a degree course. No experience of dance on the UCAS application. Limited dance skills. **Surrey** Inadequate dance background. Had not seen/read about/done any dance.

AFTER-RESULTS ADVICE

Offers to applicants repeating A-levels **Same** Chester, Chichester, De Montfort (Perf Arts), Liverpool John Moores, Salford, Surrey, Trinity Laban Consv, Winchester, Wolverhampton, York St John.

GRADUATE DESTINATIONS AND EMPLOYMENT (2007/8 HESA)

Graduates surveyed 530 **Employed** 255 **In further study** 85 **Assumed unemployed** 30.

Career note Teaching is the most popular career destination for the majority of graduates. Other opportunities exist as dance animators working in education or in the community to encourage activity and participation in dance. There is a limited number of openings for dance or movement therapists who work with the emotionally disturbed, the elderly or physically disadvantaged.

OTHER DEGREE SUBJECTS FOR CONSIDERATION

Arts Management; Drama; Education (Primary); Music; Performance Studies; Physical Education; Sport and Exercise Science.

DENTISTRY

(including **Dental Technology, Dental Hygiene, Equine Dental Science** and **Oral Health Science**)

Dentistry involves the treatment and prevention of a wide range of mouth diseases from tooth decay and gum disease to mouth cancer. Courses in Dentistry/Dental Surgery cover the basic medical sciences, human disease, clinical studies and clinical dentistry. The amount of patient contact will vary between institutions but will be considerable in all Dental Schools. Intercalated courses in other science subjects are offered on most courses.

Useful websites www.bda.org; www.bdha.org.uk; www.dla.org.uk.

NB The points totals shown to the left of the institutions are for ease of reference only. It must not be assumed that Tariff points are always used by institutions or that they can be substituted for an offer in grades. The level of an offer is not necessarily indicative of the quality of a course.

COURSE OFFERS INFORMATION

Subject requirements/preferences GCSE English, mathematics and science subjects required in most cases for Dentistry courses. A*/A/B grades stipulated in certain subjects by many Dental Schools. **AL** Chemistry plus biology or a science subject usually required for Dentistry: see offers lines below. (Dntl Tech, Oral Hlth Sci) Science subject required or preferred. **Other** Many Dental Schools use admissions tests (eg UKCAT: see **Chapter 5**). Evidence of non-infectivity or hepatitis-B immunisation required and all new dental students screened for hepatitis-C. CRB check at enhanced level is also required.

NB In 2011 universities and colleges will differ in their use of GCE AL/AS unit grade information, A* grades, the Extended Project (EPQ), the Advanced Diploma and the Cambridge Pre-U examination when considering applicants and making offers. An EPQ may be accepted in place of an AS subject. Check websites of universities and colleges for the latest offers information.

Your target offers and examples of courses provided by each institution

420 pts **Queen's Belfast** – AAAa (inc AL/AS chem A+1 subj from biol, maths, phys (must inc AS biol)) (Dentistry) (IB 37 pts HL 666)

400 pts **Birmingham** – AABa/b (inc 300 pts 3AL inc 2AL AB chem+biol) (Dentistry) (IB 36 pts)

390 pts **London (King's)** – AABb +UKCAT (inc AL chem/biol) (Dentistry) (IB 36 pts HL 665)

London (QM) – AABb +UKCAT (inc 2ALs chem/biol/sci subj or chem/biol bb) (Dentistry) (IB 36 pts HL 665)

Manchester – AABb +UKCAT (Dentistry) (IB 34 pts)

360 pts **Dundee** – AAA +UKCAT (inc biol+2 subj from chem/phys/maths) (Dnstry courses)

Liverpool – AAA–AAB (inc chem/biol+1 subj from chem, biol, maths, phys, stats) (Dntl Srgy) (IB 36 pts HL chem biol 6)

340 pts **Bristol** – AAB (inc chem+biol pref+biol if 3rd AL is non-sci) (Dentistry A206) (IB 35 pts HL 666)

Bristol – AAB (inc 3 non-sci subjs or 1 sci+2 non-sci) (Dentistry A204) (IB 35 pts HL 666)

Cardiff – AAB +UKCAT (inc chem/biol+2 sci subj (5yr course); inc no more than one sci subj from chem/biol/phys (6yr course)) (Dnstry; Fdn Dnstry) (IB 34 pts HL chem 5)

Glasgow – AAB (AS bbb min) +UKCAT (inc chem+phys/maths/biol) (Dentistry) (IB 34 pts)

Leeds – AAB (inc AL chem, biol) (Dentistry) (IB 35 pts HL chem biol 6)

Newcastle – AAB +UKCAT (inc AL chem and/or biol) (Dentistry) (IB 35 pts HL chem biol 6)

Sheffield – AAB +UKCAT (inc AL chem AB+1 sci B) (Dentistry) (IB 35 pts)

320 pts **London (QM)** – 320–280 pts 3AL (Dntl Mat) (IB 28 pts)

Manchester – ABB +UKCAT (2 arts+sci subj) (Dnstry pre-dental entry) (IB 33 pts)

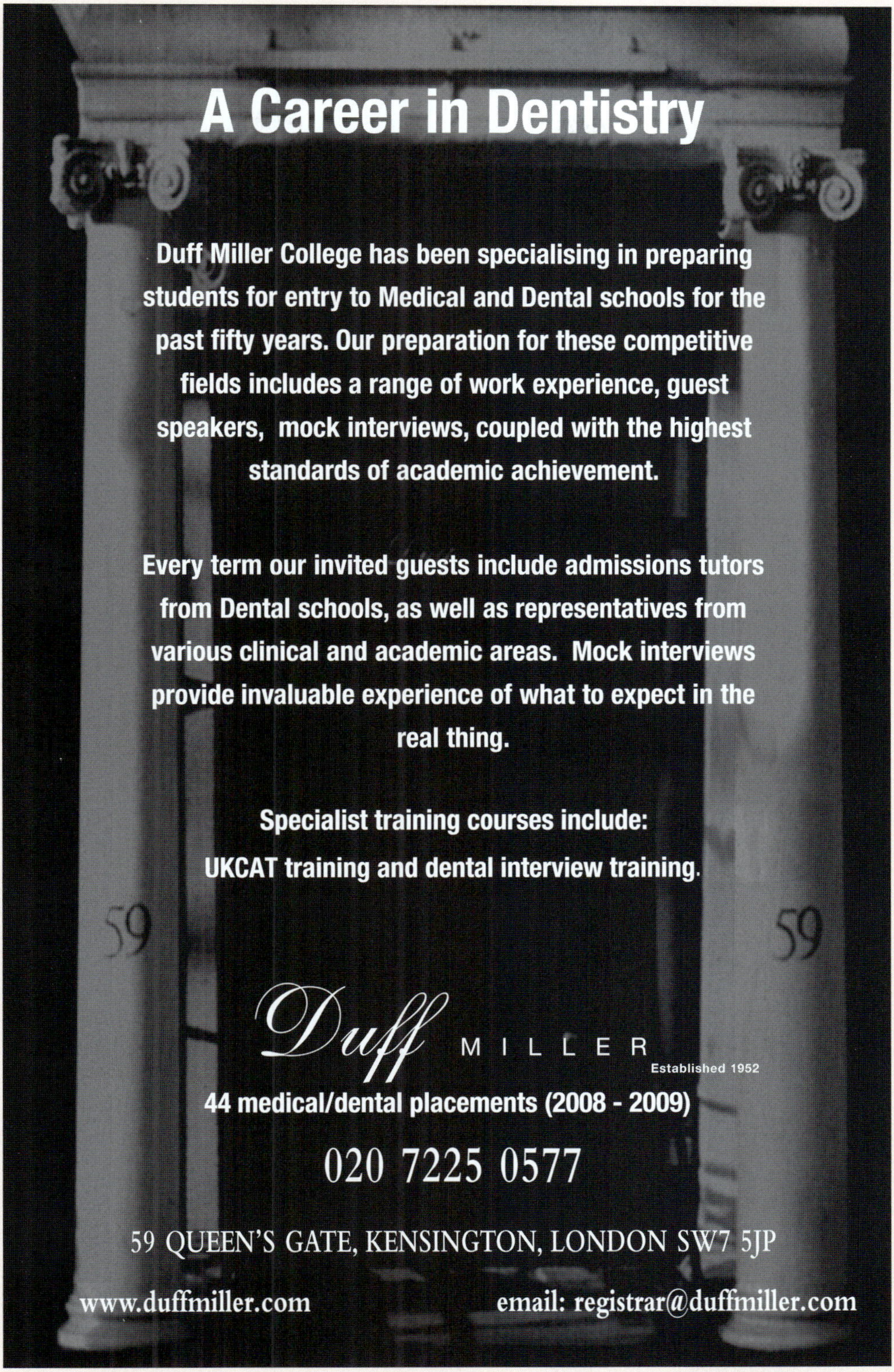
A Career in Dentistry
Duff Miller College has been specialising in preparing students for entry to Medical and Dental schools for the past fifty years. Our preparation for these competitive fields includes a range of work experience, guest speakers, mock interviews, coupled with the highest standards of academic achievement.
Every term our invited guests include admissions tutors from Dental schools, as well as representatives from various clinical and academic areas. Mock interviews provide invaluable experience of what to expect in the real thing.
Specialist training courses include:
UKCAT training and dental interview training.
59
59
Duff MILLER
Established 1952
44 medical/dental placements (2008 - 2009)
020 7225 0577
59 QUEEN'S GATE, KENSINGTON, LONDON SW7 5JP
www.duffmiller.com
email: registrar@duffmiller.com

300 pts **Birmingham** – BBB (Dntl Hyg Thera) (IB 30 pts)
Edinburgh – BBB (Oral Hlth Sci) (IB 32 pts)
240 pts **Dundee** – CCC 240 pts (Oral Hlth Sci)
Liverpool – CCC (Dntl Hyg Dntl Thera) (IB 27 pts)
Manchester Met – 240 pts inc 2AL inc sci/tech (Dntl Tech)
Portsmouth – 240 pts (Dntl Hyg Dntl Thera)
200 pts **Bristol UWE** – 200–240 pts (Eqn Dntl Sci)
180 pts **Cardiff (UWIC)** – 180 pts (inc sci subj) (Dntl Tech)

NB The following universities/dental schools offer shortened (usually four years) courses in Dentistry/Dental Surgery for graduates with at least 2.1 degrees in specified subjects. GCE A-level subjects and grades are also specified. Check with universities: **Aberdeen**, **Central Lancashire**, **Liverpool**, **London (King's), (QM)**, **Peninsula (MS)**.

Diploma courses
160 pts **Cardiff** – CC (Dntl Hyg; Dntl Thera)
Sheffield – CC (Dntl Hyg; Dntl Thera)

Alternative offers
See **Chapter 7** and **Appendix 1** for grades/UCAS Tariff points information for the International Baccalaureate, Scottish Highers/Advanced Highers, the Welsh Baccalaureate, the Irish Leaving Certificate, the Cambridge Pre-U Diploma, the Advanced Diploma and the Extended Project.

EXAMPLES OF FOUNDATION DEGREES IN THE SUBJECT FIELD
Bedfordshire (Dntl Nurs; Dntl Prac Mgt); Bristol UWE (Eqn Dntl St); De Montfort (Dntl Tech); Essex (Oral Hlth Sci); Northampton (Dntl Nurs).

CHOOSING YOUR COURSE (SEE ALSO CH.1)
Mature students A-level standard necessary. Graduates require 2:1 degree plus A-level grades close to the normal requirement.

Some course features
Birmingham, **Bristol**, **Newcastle**, **Queen's Belfast** Basic sciences are covered in Years 1 and 2, and clinical studies in Years 3, 4 and 5.
Cardiff Clinical teaching starts at an early stage.
Leeds Focus on clinical dentistry from the outset.
London (King's), **Sheffield** Main components cover the basic sciences, diagnosis and treatment of oral and dental conditions and clinical dentistry. These are vertically integrated with a larger component of basic sciences at the beginning and a larger clinical component at the end.
Liverpool, **London (QM)**, **Manchester** Clinical skills introduced from Year 2.

Universities and colleges teaching quality See www.qaa.ac.uk; www.unistats.com.

Top research universities and colleges (RAE 2008) Manchester; London (QM), (King's); Sheffield; Bristol; Cardiff; Leeds; Newcastle; London (UCL).

ADMISSIONS INFORMATION
Number of applicants per place (approx) Birmingham 10, (Dntl Hyg Thera) 17; Bristol 16; Cardiff 14; Cardiff (UWIC) (Dntl Tech) 1; Dundee 8, (Pre-Dental) 5; Edinburgh (Oral Hlth Sci) 10 places every 2nd yr; Glasgow 7; Leeds 11.5; Liverpool 15; London (King's) 128 places (offers to 1 in 5 applicants), (QM) 18, (300 interviewed and 200 offers made); Manchester 11, (Pre-Dental) 21, (Oral Hlth Sci) 18; Manchester Met 16; Newcastle 12; Portsmouth 2; Queen's Belfast 5; Sheffield 16 (interviews not held for non-EU students: 3 accepted each year). International applicants Birmingham 129 (no quota).

Number of applicants (**a** UK **b** EU (non-UK) **c** non-EU **d** mature) Bristol **ab**633 **c**83 **d**148; Glasgow **a**437 **b**45 **c**70 **d**79; Leeds **a**877 **b**42 **c**97 **d**158; Liverpool **a**704 **b**46 **c**73 **d**143; London (King's) **ab**137 **c**25; Manchester **a**1290 **b**81 **c**152 **d**331.

Advice to applicants and planning the UCAS personal statement UCAS applications listing four choices only should be submitted by 15 October. Applicants may add up to two alternative (non-Dentistry) courses. However, if they receive offers for these courses and are rejected for Dentistry, they will not be considered for Dentistry courses in Clearing if they perform better than expected in the examinations.

On your UCAS application show evidence of your manual dexterity, work experience and awareness of problems experienced by dentists. Details should be provided of discussions with dentists and workshadowing in dental surgeries. Employment (paid or voluntary) in any field, preferably dealing with people in an environment widely removed from your home or school, could be described. Discuss any specialised fields of dentistry in which you might be interested. See also **Appendix 4**. **Bristol** Applications are not segregated by type of educational institution. Candidates are assessed on general presentation. At least 20 days of work experience is expected, if possible in different fields of dentistry. Re-sit candidates only considered if they failed to get the grades by a small margin and they had originally placed Bristol as their first firm choice. **Cardiff** Applicants must be able to demonstrate (a) evidence of, and potential for, high academic achievement, (b) an understanding of the demands of dental training and practice, (c) a caring and committed attitude towards people, (d) a willingness to accept resonsibility, (e) an ability to communicate effectively, (f) evidence of broad social, cultural or sporting interests. **Glasgow** Applicants invited to submit portfolio as evidence of their suitability. This will be assessed against the BDS Person Specification available from the Dental School. Candidiates who do not submit a portfolio are not invited to selection interview. **London (King's)** School activities desirable, for example, general reading, debating, theological interests. Community activities very desirable. General activities desirable, for example, sport, first-aid, handiwork (which can be shown at interview to demonstrate manual dexterity). Work shadowing and paid or voluntary work very desirable (check website). **Manchester** Resit offers normally only made to students who firmly accepted an offer the previous year. Resit offers AAA. Applicants are required to have observed a general dental practitioner at work before applying; a minimum of two weeks is expected. **Newcastle** Applications from students with disabilities welcomed.

Misconceptions about this course **Cardiff (UWIC)** (Dntl Tech) Some think that the course allows them to practise as a dentist. Some think the degree is entirely practical.

Selection interviews (Dentistry) Most dental schools will interview candidates. **Yes** Birmingham (400–450 applicants and only 50% of applicants get through the initial sort); Bristol; Cardiff; Dundee; Glasgow; Leeds; London (King's), (QM); Newcastle; Sheffield; **Some** Cardiff (UWIC). (Other Dental courses) Dundee, Portsmouth.

Interview advice and questions Dental work experience or work shadowing is essential (check with university websites) and, as a result, questions will be asked on your reactions to the work and your understanding of the different types of treatment that a dentist can offer. In the past questions at interview have included: What is conservative dentistry? What does integrity mean? Do you think the first-year syllabus is a good one? What qualities are required by a dentist? What are prosthetics, periodontics, orthodontics? What causes tooth decay? Questions asked on the disadvantages of being a dentist, the future of dentistry and how you could show that you are manually dexterous. Other questions on personal attributes and spare time activities. What are the careers within the profession open to dentists? Questions on the future of dentistry (preventative and cosmetic dentistry), the problems facing dentists, the skills needed and the advantages and disadvantages of fluoride in water. How do you relax? How do you cope with stress?

Bristol All candidates called for interview must attend in order to be considered for a place; 200 are selected for interview for the five-year course and 15 for the six-year course. Offers are made to 180 and six respectively. An essay is set on a dental subject and will be assessed for spontaneity, written content and clear thought processes. Candidates at interview are assessed on general presentation, response to questions, knowledge of dentistry, evidence of teamwork, leadership, general interests and manual dexterity. Examples of practical work, for example, art work, needlework etc may be taken to interview as evidence of manual dexterity. **Leeds** The interview assesses personality, verbal and communication skills and knowledge of dentistry. **London (King's)** 220 applicants are interviewed of whom 180 will receive offers. All applicants receiving offers will have been interviewed. Applicants complete a questionnaire prior to interview and the interviews last about 20 minutes. Applicants may take to interview any examples of practical work, for example, art, woodwork, needlework etc as evidence of manual dexterity. See also **Chapter 5**.

Reasons for rejection (non-academic) Lack of evidence of a firm commitment to Dentistry. Lack of breadth of interests. Lack of motivation for a health care profession. Unprofessional attitude. Poor manual dexterity. Poor communication skills. Poor English. Lack of evidence of ability to work in groups. Not for the faint-hearted! More interested in running a business and making money than in caring for people. **Cardiff (UWIC)** (Dntl Tech) Target numbers need to be precise so the course fills at a late stage.

AFTER-RESULTS ADVICE

Offers to applicants repeating A-levels **Higher** Bristol (AAA), Cardiff (preference given to students who previously applied), Dundee, Leeds (very few), Manchester (AAA – only to previous applicants who firmly accepted offer of a place); **Same** Cardiff (UWIC) (Dntl Tech), Queen's Belfast.

GRADUATE DESTINATIONS AND EMPLOYMENT (2007/8 HESA)

Graduates (Clinical) surveyed 670 **Employed** 550 **In further study** 5 **Assumed unemployed** 5.

Career note The great majority of Dental Technology graduates gain employment in this career with job opportunities excellent in both the UK and Europe. There are openings in the NHS, commercial dental laboratories and the armed services.

OTHER DEGREE SUBJECTS FOR CONSIDERATION

Anatomy; Biochemistry; Biological Sciences; Biomedical Materials Science; Chemistry; Medical Sciences; Medicine; Nursing; Optometry; Pharmacy; Physiology; Physiotherapy; Radiography; Speech Therapy/Sciences; Veterinary Medicine/Science.

DEVELOPMENT STUDIES

Development Studies courses are multi-disciplinary and cover a range of subjects including economics, geography, sociology, social anthropology, politics, natural resources, with special reference to countries overseas.

Useful websites www.devstud.org.uk; www.dfid.gov.uk; www.ids.ac.uk; see also **Politics**.

NB The points totals shown to the left of the institutions are for ease of reference only. It must not be assumed that Tariff points are always used by institutions or that they can be substituted for an offer in grades. The level of an offer is not necessarily indicative of the quality of a course.

COURSE OFFERS INFORMATION

Subject requirements/preferences **GCSE** Mathematics, English and a foreign language may be required. **AL** Science or social science subjects may be required or preferred for some courses.

NB In 2011 universities and colleges will differ in their use of GCE AL/AS unit grade information, A* grades, the Extended Project (EPQ), the Advanced Diploma and the Cambridge Pre-U examination when considering applicants and making offers. An EPQ may be accepted in place of an AS subject. Check websites of universities and colleges for the latest offers information.

Your target offers and examples of courses provided by each institution

360 pts **London (SOAS)** – AAA (Dev Econ) (IB 38 pts HL 766)
340 pts **Bath** – AAB (Econ Int Dev) (IB 38 pts)
320 pts **Leeds** – ABB 320 pts (Int Dev courses) (IB 34 pts HL 16 pts)
Manchester – ABB (Dev St; Dev St Econ; Dev St Pol; Dev St Sociol) (IB 32–34 pts)
Sussex – ABB–BBB (Dev St) (IB 32–34 pts)

300 pts **Birmingham** – BBB–BCC (Af St Dev) (IB 30–32 pts)
East Anglia – BBB 300 pts (Int Dev Ovrs Exp; Int Dev; Int Dev Soc Anth Pol; Int Dev Env Soty) (IB 31 pts)
280 pts **Bradford** – 280 pts (Dev Pce St)
240 pts **Chester** – 240 pts (Int Dev St courses)
London Met – 240 pts (Int Dev; Int Dev Int Rel)
220 pts **Leeds Met** – 220 pts (Glob Dev Pol Econy; Glob Dev Int Rel; Glob Dev Pce St;)
Northampton – 220–260 pts (Third Wrld Dev courses)
200 pts **East London** – 200 pts (Int Dev Third Wrld NGO Mgt)
180 pts **Derby** – 180–240 pts (Int Rel Glob Dev; Third Wrld Dev courses)
80 pts **London (Birk)** – 80 pts (p/t Dev St)

Alternative offers
See **Chapter 7** and **Appendix 1** for grades/UCAS Tariff points information for the International Baccalaureate, Scottish Highers/Advanced Highers, the Welsh Baccalaureate, the Irish Leaving Certificate, the Cambridge Pre-U Diploma, the Advanced Diploma and the Extended Project.

CHOOSING YOUR COURSE (SEE ALSO CH.1)

Some course features

Bradford Development Studies is offered with Economics or Peace Studies.

Derby (Int Rel Glob Dev) Course explores environmental, geographical, political, social, cultural and economic aspects of international relations and global development. Work Placement in final year, visits to key development organisations.

Leeds This is an interdisciplinary degree course with opportunity to study second subject alongside (such as Geography or Politics). Depending on first year grade average (2.1) and on second subject, there are opportunities to study abroad in, for example, Ghana or Turkey in Year 2.

Manchester (Dev St) Students start to specialise in Year 2, choosing options from 10 study areas; in Year 3 they take a single or a joint specialisation with another area of study, for example, politics, economics.

Sussex Development Studies is also offered with French or Spanish, Geography, Economics, International Relations and Sociology.

Universities and colleges teaching quality See www.qaa.ac.uk; www.unistats.com.

Top research universities and colleges (RAE 2008) Oxford; Manchester; East Anglia; Bath; London (SOAS); Birmingham.

ADMISSIONS INFORMATION

Number of applicants per place (approx) Bradford 6; East Anglia 8; Leeds 8.

Advice to applicants and planning the UCAS personal statement Discuss aspects of development studies which interest you, for example in relation to geography, economics, politics. Interests in Third World countries should be mentioned. Knowledge of current events.

Misconceptions about this course Some students think that Development Studies has something to do with property, with plants or with childhood. It is none of these and is about international processes of change, development, progress and crisis.

Interview advice and questions Since this is a multi-disciplinary subject, questions will vary considerably. Initially they will stem from your interests and the information given on your UCAS application and your reasons for choosing the course. In the past, questions at interview have included: Define a Third World country. What help does the United Nations provide in the Third World? Could it do too much? What problems does the United Nations face in its work throughout the world? Why Development Studies? What will you do in your gap year, and what do you want to achieve? See also **Chapter 5**.

AFTER-RESULTS ADVICE

Offers to applicants repeating A-levels **Same** East Anglia.

GRADUATE DESTINATIONS AND EMPLOYMENT (2007/8 HESA)

No data available.

Career note The range of specialisms offered on these courses will encourage graduates to make contact with and seek opportunities in a wide range of organisations, not necessarily limited to the Third World and government agencies.

OTHER DEGREE SUBJECTS FOR CONSIDERATION

Economics; Environmental Science/Studies; Geography; Government; International Relations; Politics; Sociology; Sustainable Development.

DIETETICS

(see also **Food Science/Studies and Technology** and **Nutrition**)

In addition to the scientific aspects of dietetics covering biochemistry, human physiology, food and clinical medicine, students are also introduced to health promotion, psychology, counselling and management skills. Accredited Dietetics courses qualify graduates for registration with the Health Professions Council and to practise as a dietitian in the National Health Service. (See **Appendix 4**.)

Useful websites www.nutrition.org; www.bda.uk.com; www.dietetics.co.uk.

NB The points totals shown to the left of the institutions are for ease of reference only. It must not be assumed that Tariff points are always used by institutions or that they can be substituted for an offer in grades. The level of an offer is not necessarily indicative of the quality of a course.

COURSE OFFERS INFORMATION

Subject requirements/preferences **GCSE** English, mathematics and science usually required. **AL** Biology and/or chemistry may be required. **Other** Health and CRB checks required and possible immunisation against hepatitis-B for practice placements.

NB In 2011 universities and colleges will differ in their use of GCE AL/AS unit grade information, A* grades, the Extended Project (EPQ), the Advanced Diploma and the Cambridge Pre-U examination when considering applicants and making offers. An EPQ may be accepted in place of an AS subject. Check websites of universities and colleges for the latest offers information.

Your target offers and examples of courses provided by each institution

340 pts **London (King's)** – ABB+AS (Nutr Diet) (IB 34 pts)
320 pts **Nottingham** – ABB–BBB (Nutr St (Diet)) (IB 32–34 pts)
Surrey – ABB–BBB 320–300 pts (Nutr Diet) (IB 34–32 pts)
300 pts **London Met** – 300 pts (Hum Nutr Diet)
Ulster – BBB +HPAT (Dietetics) (see **Ch 5**)
280 pts **Chester** – 280 pts (Nutr Diet) (IB 30 pts)
Hertfordshire – 280 pts (Dietetics)
Plymouth – 280 pts (Dietetics)
260 pts **Cardiff (UWIC)** – 260 pts (Hum Nutr Diet)
Coventry – 260 pts (Dietetics)
Leeds Met – BCC (Dietetics)
240 pts **Robert Gordon** – CCC 240 pts (Nutr Diet) (IB 28 pts)
220 pts **Bath Spa** – 220–260 pts (Diet Hlth)
195 pts **Queen Margaret** – 195 pts (Dietetics)
160 pts **Glasgow Caledonian** – CC (Hum Nutr Diet)

Alternative offers
See **Chapter 7** and **Appendix 1** for grades/UCAS Tariff points information for the International Baccalaureate, Scottish Highers/Advanced Highers, the Welsh Baccalaureate, the Irish Leaving Certificate, the Cambridge Pre-U Diploma, the Advanced Diploma and the Extended Project.

CHOOSING YOUR COURSE (SEE ALSO CH.1)

Some course features

Bath Spa (Diet Hlth) Course focuses on the impact of diet, nutrition and lifestyle on health. It is not a Dietetics course and is aimed at students without a science background.

Hertfordshire Three-year course leading to registration with the Health Professions Council to practise as a dietitian.

London (King's) Clinical placements in Years 2, 3 and 4.

Nottingham This is a four-year Master of Nutrition course. Graduates with 2.1 degree in relevant subjects such as Biochemistry accepted into Year 3 to train as dietitians.

Plymouth Supervised clinical practice in Year 2.

Surrey A professional training year is included.

Universities and colleges teaching quality See www.qaa.ac.uk; www.unistats.com.

Examples of sandwich degree courses Cardiff (UWIC); Glasgow Caledonian; Leeds Met; Surrey; Ulster.

ADMISSIONS INFORMATION

Number of applicants per place (approx) Glasgow Caledonian 11; Nottingham 7; Queen Margaret 5; Surrey 1.

Advice to applicants and planning the UCAS personal statement Discuss the work with a hospital dietitian and describe fully work experience gained in hospital dietetics departments or with the schools meals services, and the problems of working in these fields. Admissions tutors expect applicants to have at least visited a dietetics department, and to be outgoing with good oral and written communication skills. Contact the British Dietetic Association (see **Appendix 4**). **Bath Spa** £1000 scholarships available.

Selection interviews All institutions.

Interview advice and questions Your knowledge of a career in dietetics will be fully explored and questions will be asked on your work experience and how you reacted to it. See also **Chapter 5**.

AFTER-RESULTS ADVICE

Offers to applicants repeating A-levels **Possibly higher** Glasgow Caledonian.

GRADUATE DESTINATIONS AND EMPLOYMENT (2007/8 HESA)

No data available.

Career note Dietitians are professionally trained to advise on diets and aspects of nutrition and many degree courses combine both subjects. They may work in the NHS as hospital dietitians collaborating with medical staff on the balance of foods for patients, or in local health authorities working with GPs, or in health centres or clinics dealing with infant welfare and ante-natal problems. In addition, dietitians advise consumer groups in the food industry and government and may be involved in research. Courses can lead to professional registration: check with admissions tutors.

OTHER DEGREE SUBJECTS FOR CONSIDERATION

Biological Sciences; Biochemistry; Biology; Consumer Studies; Food Science; Health Studies; Hospitality Management; Human Nutrition; Nursing; Nutrition.

DRAMA

(including **Performing Arts/Studies, Theatre Arts, Theatre Studies** and **Theatre Design**; see also **Art and Design (General)**)

Drama courses are popular, with twice as many women as men applying each year. Lack of confidence in securing appropriate work at the end of the course, however, tends to encourage many applicants to bid for joint courses although these are usually far more competitive since there are fewer places available. Most Schools of Acting and Drama provide a strong vocational bias whilst University Drama departments offer a broader field of studies combining theory and practice. The choice of course will depend on personal preferences, either practical or theoretical, or a combination of both.

Useful websites www.equity.org.uk; www.abtt.org.uk; www.thestage.co.uk; www.uktw.co.uk; www.ukperformingarts.co.uk; www.arts.org.uk; www.stagecoach.co.uk.

NB The points totals shown to the left of the institutions are for ease of reference only. It must not be assumed that Tariff points are always used by institutions or that they can be substituted for an offer in grades. The level of an offer is not necessarily indicative of the quality of a course.

COURSE OFFERS INFORMATION

Subject requirements/preferences GCSE English usually required. **AL** English, drama, theatre studies may be required or preferred. (Theatre Arts) English, theatre studies or drama may be required for some courses. **Other** CRB clearance required for some courses: check websites.

NB In 2011 universities and colleges will differ in their use of GCE AL/AS unit grade information, A* grades, the Extended Project (EPQ), the Advanced Diploma and the Cambridge Pre-U examination when considering applicants and making offers. An EPQ may be accepted in place of an AS subject. Check websites of universities and colleges for the latest offers information.

Your target offers and examples of courses provided by each institution

390 pts **Warwick** – AABb–ABBb (Thea Perf St; Engl Thea St) (IB 36 pts)
380 pts **Cambridge** – A*AA college offers may vary (Educ Engl Dr)
360 pts **Bristol** – AAA–AAB (Dr; Dr Engl; Dr Fr/Ger/Ital/Port/Span) (IB 37–35 pts)
Exeter – AAA–ABB (Drama) (IB 36–31 pts)
340 pts **Birmingham** – AAB–ABB (Dr Thea Arts; Dr Mus; Dr Class Lit Civ; Media Cult Soty) (IB 34 pts)
East Anglia – AAB–BBB (Engl Lit Dr; Dr; Scrpt Perf) (IB 33–31 pts)
Glasgow – AAB (Thea St courses) (IB 34 pts)
Kent – 340 pts (Dr Thea St; Dr Film St) (IB 36 pts)
Lancaster – 340 pts (Thea St Engl Lit) (IB 31 pts)
Leeds – AAB (Engl Lit Thea St; Thea Perf Des) (IB 36 pts)
London (RH) – AAB 340 pts (Dr Thea St; Dr Engl; Dr Mus; Dr Fr/Ger/Ital; Dr Crea Writ; Dr Phil) (IB 35 pts)
Loughborough – 340 pts (Dr; Dr Engl) (IB 34 pts HL Engl, Thea St)
Manchester – AAB–BBB (Dr; Dr Scrn St; Dr Engl Lit) See **Advice to applicants and planning the UCAS personal statement** (IB 35–32 pts)
Sussex – AAB–ABB (Dr St Film St; Dr St Fr/Ger/Ital/Span) (IB 34–36 pts)
320 pts **Brunel** – BBC +AS/EPQ c 320 pts (Dr Engl) (IB 30 pts)
York – ABB (Writ Dir Perf) (IB 31 pts)
300 pts **Brunel** – BCC +AS/EPQ c 300 pts (Dr Film TV; Dr Mus; Dr Gms Des; Dr Modn Dr St)
Essex – 300 pts (Dr; Dr Lit) (IB 32 pts)
Glamorgan – 300–360 pts (Dr (Thea Media); Perf Media)
Hull – BBB 300 pts (Dr Engl; Dr Hist Art; Am St Dr; Dr Thea Prac)
Lancaster – 300 pts (Thea St) (IB 30 pts)
Leeds – BBB (Perf Des) (IB 32 pts)
London (Central Sch SpDr) – BBB (Dr App Thea Educ)

London (Gold) – BBB (Dr Thea Arts)
London (QM) – 300–320 pts (Dr; Engl Dr; Fr/Ger/Russ Dr; Hisp St Dr; Film St Dr) (IB 32 pts)
Oxford Brookes – BBB (Dr Comb Hons) (IB 33 pts)
Queen's Belfast – BBB–BBCb (Dr courses)
Reading – 300–340 pts (Film Thea)
Salford – 300 pts (Perf Arts) (IB 31 pts)
Surrey – BBB (Thea St) (IB 32 pts)

295 pts **Queen Margaret** – 295 pts (Dr Perf; Actg Perf)

280 pts **Birmingham City** – 280 pts (Thea Perf Evnt Des; Engl Dr; Dr P Educ)
Bristol UWE – 280–340 pts (Dr; Dr Film St) (IB 28–32 pts)
Cumbria – 280 pts (Musl Thea Perf; Perf Arts)
Essex – 280 pts (Dr Modn Langs) (IB 30 pts)
Kingston – 280–320 pts (Dr courses)
London (Central Sch Sp/Dr) – BBC (Thea Prac (Cstm Constr) (Pptry) (Perf Arts) (Prod Ltg) (Tech Prod Mgt))
Northumbria – 280 pts (Dr; Perf)
Roehampton – 280–340 pts (Dr Thea Perf St)
Salford – 280 pts (Contemp Thea Prac)

260 pts **Aberystwyth** – 260–280 pts (Dr Thea St; Perf St; Scnograph Thea Des) (IB 24–26 pts)
Brighton – 260 pts (Perf Vis Arts)
Chichester – BCC Offers may vary (Dr; Perf Arts (Thea Perf)) (IB 28–30 pts)
Huddersfield – 260 pts (Dr; Dr Engl)
Liverpool Hope – 260 pts (Dr Thea St; Crea Perf Arts)
Liverpool John Moores – 260 pts (Dr courses)
London Met – 260 pts (Perf Arts; Thea St courses)
Manchester Met – 260–240 pts (Dr; Contemp Thea Perf; Actg) (IB 24 pts)
Northumbria – 260 pts (Dr Script)`
Plymouth – 260 pts (Thea Perf)
Ulster – 260–240 pts (Dr; Dr Ir; Dr Dance; Dr Psy; Dr Mark)
Winchester – 260–300 pts (Drama) (IB 24 pts)

240 pts **Bangor** – 240–300 pts (Engl Thea St)
Birmingham City (Sch Actg) – 240 pts (Commun App Thea; Stg Mgt)
Bristol UWE – 240–300 pts (Dr Psy)
Central Lancashire – 240 pts (Contemp Thea Perf; Dr Thea St)
Chester – 240–280 pts (Dr Thea St courses) (IB 30 pts)
Coventry – 240 pts (Thea Prof Prac)
De Montfort – 240 pts (Dr St courses; Perf Arts)
Falmouth (UC) – 240 pts (Thea (Dir) (Perf))

Lincoln – 240 pts (Dr; Dr Hist)
Manchester Met – 240 pts (Acting)
Newport – 240–260 pts (Perf Arts)
Nottingham Trent – 240 pts (Thea Des)
Portsmouth – 240–300 pts (Engl Dr; Dr Perf; Crea Perf Arts)
Rose Bruford (Coll) – 240 pts (Am Thea Arts; Euro Thea Arts; Actg; Actr Mushp)
Salford – 240 pts (Engl Dr Perf St)
Winchester – 240–280 pts (Stg Mgt Dr; Strt Arts; Dr Educ St)
Worcester – 240–260 pts (Dr; Dr Perf)

220 pts **Bath Spa** – 220–260 pts (Crea Writ Dr St; Perf Arts; Dr St Educ; Dr St)
Edge Hill – 220–260 pts (Dr; Dr Physl Thea Dance; Dr Mus Snd; Dr Vis Thea)
Newman (UC) – 220–260 pts (Engl Dr)
Newport – 220–260 pts (App Dr)
Northampton – 220–260 pts (Dr courses; Actg)
Queen Margaret – CCD 220 pts (Cstm Des Constr)
Sunderland – 220 pts (Drama)
UCP Marjon – 220 pts (Dr Crea Writ)

200 pts **Anglia Ruskin** – 200–240 pts (Dr; Dr Engl; Media St Dr; Mus Dr; Phil Dr; Writ Dr)
Bucks New – 200–240 pts (Perf Arts)
Canterbury Christ Church – 200 pts (Perf Arts (Dr))
Central Lancashire – 200–260 pts (Contemp Thea Perf; Act; Mus Thea)
Cumbria – 200 pts (Dr Joint Hons)
East London – 200 pts (Thea St)
Glyndŵr – 200 pts (Thea TV Perf)
Middlesex – 200–280 pts (Thea Arts (Perf))
Southampton Solent – 200 pts (Perf Cmdy Writ; Perf)
St Mary's Twickenham (UC) – 200 pts (Dr; Dr Thea Arts; Dr Physl Thea; Dr App Thea Dr)
Staffordshire – 200–260 pts (Dr Perf Thea Arts; Thea St Tech Stg Prod)
Swansea Met – 200 pts (Perf Arts Thea St)
York St John – 200–220 pts (Theatre)

180 pts **Bedfordshire** – 180 pts (Perf Arts; Thea Prof Prac)
Derby – 180–240 pts (Thea Arts courses)
Greenwich – 180 pts (Dr courses)
Liverpool (LIPA) – 180 pts (Commun Dr)
Newman (UC) – 180 pts (Drama)
UCP Marjon – 180 pts (Dr Educ St)
Wolverhampton – 180 pts (Dr Df St; Dr Film St)

160 pts **Doncaster (Coll)** – 160 pts (Engl Thea Prac)
London (Central Sch SpDr) – CC (Actg courses)
London South Bank – CC 160 pts (Dr Perf St; Thea Prac Crea Prodg)
Reading – 160 pts (Thea Arts Educ Df St)
Thames Valley – 160 pts (Actg; Musl Thea; Dr (Actg Stg Media))

140 pts **Birmingham City (Sch Actg)** – 140 pts (Actg; Actg (Musl Thea))
Bishop Grosseteste (UC) – 140 pts (Dr Commun; Educ St Dr)

120 pts **Blackpool and Fylde (Coll)** – 120 pts (Musl Thea)
Royal Welsh (CMusDr) – 120–200 pts (Actg; Stg Mgt; Thea Des)

80 pts **and below** **(Some Theatre Schools and Drama departments do not select on the basis of academic qualifications)**
ALRA – (Acting)
Arts Educ London – entry by audition (Actg; Musl Thea)
Arts London (Central Saint Martins CAD) – interview+portfolio+audition (Actg; Dir; Thea; Des Perf)
Arts London (CFash) – 80 pts (Cstm Tech Effct Mkup)
Bournemouth Arts (UC) – (Acting)
Brighton – interview+portfolio+Fdn Dip (Perf Vis Arts (Thea))

Bristol Old Vic (Thea Sch) – 80 pts (Acting)
Croydon (Coll) – 80–100 pts (Des Crft Stg Scrn)
Edinburgh (CA) – 80 pts (Perf Cost)
Essex (East 15 Loughton) – EE–E +audition (Actg; Actg Contemp Thea)
Grimsby (IFHE) – (Dr St)
GSA (Cons) – audition (Actg; Musl Thea)
London (Arts Educ Sch) – (Acting)
London (Birk) – (p/t Dr Thea St)
London (RADA) – audition (BA Dr)
London Arts – interview+portfolio+Fdn Dip (Actg; Set Des Stg Scrn; Thea Des Perf)
London Mountview (Ac Thea Arts) – audition (Musl Thea; Actg; Tech Thea)
Manchester (Coll) – 80–160 pts (Actg Prof Stg Prac)
Middlesex – audition + interview (Thea Arts courses)
Royal Scottish (RSAMD) – 80 pts min b (Contemp Perf Prac; Actg; Tech Prod Arts)
Trinity Laban Consv – (Dance Thea)

Alternative offers
See **Chapter 7** and **Appendix 1** for grades/UCAS Tariff points information for the International Baccalaureate, Scottish Highers/Advanced Highers, the Welsh Baccalaureate, the Irish Leaving Certificate, the Cambridge Pre-U Diploma, the Advanced Diploma and the Extended Project.

EXAMPLES OF FOUNDATION DEGREES IN THE SUBJECT FIELD
Arts London (Wimbledon CAD); Bath Spa; Bedfordshire; Blackpool and Fylde (Coll); Bournemouth; Bournemouth Arts (UC); Bradford (Coll); Bristol City (Coll); Bucks New; Chichester; Colchester (Inst); Cornwall (Coll); Craven (Coll); Cumbria; Exeter (Coll); Farnborough (CT); Greenwich; Hereford (CA);

Hertfordshire; Huddersfield; Hull (Coll); Kirklees (Coll); Leeds City (Coll); Leeds Met; Manchester (Coll); NEW (Coll); Newcastle (Coll); Northbrook (Coll); Norwich City (Coll); Nottingham New (Coll); Rose Bruford (Coll); Rotherham (CAT); St Helens (Coll); Sheffield (Coll); South Devon (Coll); South Essex (Coll); Staffordshire (Reg Fed); Suffolk (Univ Campus); Sunderland; Teesside; Truro (Coll); Wigan and Leigh (Coll).

CHOOSING YOUR COURSE (SEE ALSO CH.1)

Some course features

Anglia Ruskin (Drama) The course content depends on the options chosen, for example dramatic performance, technical theatre, drama in theory and practice, directing and TV drama.
Bedfordshire (Perf Arts) Focus on dance and theatre.
Brunel (Drama) A strong practical emphasis.
De Montfort (Perf Arts) A highly practical programme covering acting, directing, dance, film, arts management and community education.
Edge Hill (Drama) Options in directing, design, writing, educational or community drama.
Lincoln (Drama) A balanced course covering acting, directing, history and technical aspects.
Liverpool Hope (Crea Perf Arts) There are two main strands – artistic and vocational. The course covers drama, music, dance, visual art, writing and work-related skills.
London (RH) (Int Thea) Practical and theoretical studies, with study in Australia. Year's study abroad also possible in other programmes.
Loughborough (Drama) Six optional modules in Years 2 and 3.
Newport (Perf Arts) Performance for film, radio, TV, theatre and drama.

Universities and colleges teaching quality See www.qaa.ac.uk; www.unistats.com.

Top research universities and colleges (RAE 2008) (Drama, Dance and Performing Arts) Warwick (Film and TV Studies); Roehampton (Dance); London (QM); St Andrews; Manchester; Bristol; Glasgow; Warwick (Theatre Performance and Cultural Policy Studies); Exeter; London (RH); Roehampton (Drama, Theatre and Performance Studies).

ADMISSIONS INFORMATION

Number of applicants per place (approx) Aberystwyth 10; Arts London (Central Saint Martins CAD) (Actg) 32, (Dir) 10; Birmingham 15; Bishop Grosseteste (UC) 4; Bristol 29; Brunel 9; Chester 14; Cumbria 4; De Montfort (Perf Arts) 5; East Anglia 13; Edge Hill 8; Essex 15; Exeter 20; Glamorgan 6; Huddersfield 5; Hull 16; Hull (Scarborough) 2; Kent 24; Lancaster 18; Leeds 10; Liverpool (LIPA) (Perf Arts (Actg)) 48; Liverpool John Moores 10; London (Central Sch SpDr) (Thea Prac) 5, (Gold) 28, (RH) 10; London Met 20; London Mountview (Ac Thea Arts) (Musl Thea) 8; Loughborough 6; Manchester (Dr) 6, (Dr Engl Lit) 8; Manchester (Coll) 10; Manchester Met 48; Middlesex 26; Northampton 3; Northumbria 25; Nottingham Trent 4; Queen Margaret 4; Reading 17; Roehampton 6; Royal Welsh (CMusDr) (Actg) 50, (Stg Mgt) 10; Warwick 18; Winchester (Dr) 6; Worcester 4; York 4; York St John 9.

Advice to applicants and planning the UCAS personal statement List the plays in which you have performed and specify the characters played. Indicate any experience in other areas of theatre, especially directing or writing. Add any information on projects you have initiated or developed or worked on in theatre craft, such as set design, costume design, lighting design, prop-making, scene painting. List any community arts projects such as work with youth clubs, hospital radio, amateur dramatics, music/drama workshops and voluntary work within the arts. Show your strengths in dance and theatre, and your commitment to drama in all its aspects. See **Chapter 6** and also **Appendix 4**.
London (Central Sch SpDr) (Dr App Thea Educ) We look for an interest in theatre and performance in different social and cultural settings, for example, community, schools, prisons. We also look for an enquiring mind, practical drama skills, flexibility and focus. **Manchester** Due to the detailed nature of entry requirements for Drama courses, the University is unable to include full details in the prospectus. For complete and up-to-date information on the entry requirements for these courses, please visit the website at www.manchester.ac.uk/ugcourses. **Warwick** Gap year only acceptable in exceptional circumstances. **York** (Writ Dir Perf) Strong analytical ability plus experience in a related field, eg stage management/design, drama, writing are important factors.

Misconceptions about this course That a Theatre Studies course is a training for the stage: it is not. **Arts London (Central Saint Martins CAD)** provides a long-established classical conservatoire-type training for actors, and not Theatre Studies or Performance Arts courses, contrary to the views of some students. It is no longer a private school and home and EU students pay the standard degree fee. **De Montfort** (Perf Arts) Students are unaware that the course involves music. **Kent** This is not like an acting school. **Staffordshire** We stress to applicants that this is not a drama school course. **Winchester** This is not an Acting course although practical work is involved. **York St John** This is not a course for intending actors.

Selection interviews Yes Most institutions, usually with auditions which are likely to involve solo and group tests; **Some** Anglia Ruskin, Bristol, Bucks New, Chester, St Mary's Twickenham (UC).

Interview advice and questions Arts London (Central Saint Martins CAD) (Actg) Two three-minute speeches or scenes, one of which must be from the classical repertoire. (Dir) Interview and practical workshop which may involve directing actors. **Bristol** Assesses each case on its merits, paying attention to candidate's educational and cultural opportunities. Particularly interested in applicants who have already shown some evidence of commitment in their approach to drama in practical work, theatre-going, film viewing or reading. One fifth of applicants are called for interview and take part in practical sessions. They may present any art work, photography or similar material. (London Board Practical Music not acceptable for Drama/Music unless offered with theoretical music + one other A-level.) **Brunel** All applicants to whom an offer may be made will be auditioned, involving a practical workshop, voice, movement improvisation and a short prepared speech. Offers unlikely to be made to those with less than a grade B in drama or theatre studies. **Chichester** Applicants will be asked to prepare a set-piece in advance and to perform it before a group. **De Montfort** (Perf Arts) What do you hope to gain on a three-year course in Performing Arts? Interviews involve practical workshops in drama and theatre and a written paper. **East Anglia** Looks for candidates with a sound balance of academic and practical skills. Applicants will be expected to analyse performance and to understand what is entailed in the production of a drama. **Hull** Interviews two groups of 18 for whole day which presents a mini-version of the course, with entire staff and number of current students present. Offers then made to about half. Selection process is all-important. More applicants for the Joint Honours courses with English, Theology, American Studies or Modern Language who have a conventional half-hour interview. Drama/English is the most popular combination and the offer includes a B in English. **Kent** No Single Honours candidate accepted without interview. Emphasis equally on academic and practical abilities. Questions asked to probe the applicant's creative and analytical grasp of theatre. **Lancaster** (Thea St) Candidates invited for interview and should be prepared to take part in a workshop with other candidates. We are just as interested in backstage people as actors and now have an arts administration option. **Loughborough** Candidates judged as individuals. Applicants with unconventional subject combinations and mature students considered. Final selection based on interview and audition. Applicants ought to show experience of practical drama, preferably beyond school plays. **Royal Welsh (CMusDr)** BA Acting – audition; BA Stage Management – interview; BA Theatre Design – interview and portfolio presentation. All applicants are charged an audition/interview fee. **Warwick** Interview is important to assess academic potential and particularly commitment to, and suitability for, teaching; offers therefore variable. See also **Chapter 5**.

Reasons for rejection (non-academic) Poor ambition. Wrong expectations of the course. Several students clearly want a drama school acting training rather than a degree course. Not enough background reading. **Arts London (Central Saint Martins CAD)** Insufficient clarity about career aims. **De Montfort** (Perf Arts) Candidate more suitable for a drama or dance school than for a degree course. No genuine engagement with the subject. Evidence of poor attendance at school.

AFTER-RESULTS ADVICE

Offers to applicants repeating A-levels Higher Bristol, Glasgow (AAA), Hull, Warwick; **Possibly higher** London (RH); **Same** Brunel, Chichester, De Montfort (Perf Arts), East Anglia, GSA (Cons), Huddersfield, Kent, Leeds (further audition required), Liverpool Hope, Liverpool John Moores, Loughborough, Manchester (Coll), Newman (UC), Nottingham Trent, Roehampton, Royal Welsh (CMusDr), St Mary's Twickenham (UC), Staffordshire, Sunderland, Winchester, York St John.

GRADUATE DESTINATIONS AND EMPLOYMENT (2007/8 HESA)

Graduates surveyed 3775 **Employed** 2020 **In further study** 350 **Assumed unemployed** 335.

Career note Some graduates develop careers in performance, writing, directing and producing as well as wider roles within the theatre. Others go on to careers such as teaching, media management and retail where their creativity and communication skills are valued.

OTHER DEGREE SUBJECTS FOR CONSIDERATION

Art and Design (Costume Design, Stage Design); Arts Management; Dance; Education (Primary); English; Performance Studies.

ECONOMICS

Economics is about how society makes good use of the limited resources available. Degree courses cover all aspects of finance, taxation and monetary union between countries, aiming to equip the student to analyse economic problems in a systematic way and thus acquire an understanding of how economic systems work. Economics involves mathematics and statistics, and applicants without economics at A- or AS-level should be prepared for this.

Useful websites www.bized.co.uk; www.iea.org.uk; www.res.org.uk; www.economist.com; www.neweconomics.org; see also **Finance**.

NB The points totals shown to the left of the institutions are for ease of reference only. It must not be assumed that Tariff points are always used by institutions or that they can be substituted for an offer in grades. The level of an offer is not necessarily indicative of the quality of a course.

COURSE OFFERS INFORMATION

Subject requirements/preferences **GCSE** English, mathematics and occasionally a foreign language required. A*/A/B may be stipulated by some universities. **AL** Mathematics, economics or business studies may be required or preferred. Business studies may be preferred if economics is not offered. Applicants should note that many courses will accept students without economics (check prospectuses and websites).

NB In 2011 universities and colleges will differ in their use of GCE AL/AS unit grade information, A* grades, the Extended Project (EPQ), the Advanced Diploma and the Cambridge Pre-U examination when considering applicants and making offers. An EPQ may be accepted in place of an AS subject. Check websites of universities and colleges for the latest offers information.

Your target offers and examples of courses provided by each institution

430 pts **Warwick** – AAAb (Econ; Ind Econ; Econ Pol Int St; Econ Econ Hist; PPE) (IB 38 pts)

380 pts **Cambridge** – A*AA college offers may vary (Econ; Land Econ) (IB 38–42 pts HL 766–777)

London (UCL) – A*AA+AS–AAA+AS (Econ; Econ Stats; Phil Econ) (IB 38–39 pts)

360 pts **Bath** – AAA (Econ; Econ Pol; Econ Int Dev) (IB 38 pts HL 766)

Bristol – AAA–AAB (Econ; Econ Euro; Econ Ecomet; Econ Fin; Econ Pol; Phil Econ) (IB 37–35 pts)

Durham – AAA (Nat Sci (Econ); Bus Econ; Econ Pol; Econ; PPE; Econ Fr) (IB 38 pts)

East Anglia – AAA–AAB (Econ Econ Psy) (IB 34–35 pts)

Lancaster – AAA 360 pts (Econ Abrd) (IB 32 pts)

London (RH) – AAA–AAB (Econ; Fin Bus Econ; Econ Fr/Ger/Ital/Span; Econ Mgt; Econ Pol St; Econ Maths; Econ Mus) (IB 33–35 pts)

London (SOAS) – AAA (Econ; Dev Econ) (IB 38 pts)

London (UCL) – AABe–ABBe (Econ Bus E Euro St) (IB 34–36 pts)

London LSE – AAA (Econ; Econ Econ Hist; Ecomet Mathem Econ; Maths Econ) (IB 38 pts HL 766)

Nottingham – AAA (Econ; Econ Chin Ct; Econ Ecomet; Econ Hisp St) (IB 38 pts)

Oxford – AAA (Econ Mgt; Hist Econ; Mat Econ Mgt; Eng Econ Mgt; PPE) (IB 38–40 pts)

340 pts **Aston** – 340–320 pts (Econ Mgt; Int Bus Econ) (IB 34 pts HL 665)
Birmingham – AAB (Econ; Econ Lang; Pol Econ; Econ Russ St)
Cardiff – AAB (Bus Econ; Econ; Econ Euro Lang; Bus Econ Euro Lang; Econ Fin)
Exeter – AAB–ABB (Econ; Econ Fin; Econ Ecomet; Econ Pol; Bus Econ) (IB 36–33 pts)
Glasgow – AAB (Econ courses; Bus Econ courses) (IB 36–34 pts)
Lancaster – AAB (Economics)
Leeds – AAB (Bus Fin Econ; Econ; Chin Econ; Bus Econ; Econ Mgt) (IB 35 pts HL 17 pts)
London (QM) – AAB (Econ; Econ Fin Mgt; Econ Maths Stats courses) (IB 34 pts)
London LSE – AAB (Gov Econ; Geog Econ) (IB 37 pts HL 666)
Loughborough – AAB (Econ; Econ Acc; Maths Econ) (IB 34–36 pts)
Manchester – AAB (Econ; Econ Fin) (IB 35–34 pts)
Newcastle – AAB (Econ; Econ Bus Mgt; Fin Bus Econ) (IB 34 pts)
Nottingham – AAB (Ind Econ; Ind Econ Ins) (IB 38 pts)
Queen's Belfast – AAB–ABBa (PPE)
St Andrews – AAB (Econ courses) (IB 37 pts)
Sheffield – AAB (Econ Pol; Econ)
Southampton – AAB–ABBb (Econ; Econ Act Sci; Econ Fin; Econ Mgt Sci; Pol Econ; Acc Econ) (IB 34 pts)
York – AAB–ABB (Econ; Econ Fin; Econ Ecomet Fin; Econ Econ Hist; Maths Econ) (IB 36 pts H666)

320 pts **Birmingham** – ABB–BBB (Plan Econ)
Brunel – BBC +AS/EPQ c 320 pts (Econ Bus Fin; Bus Econ) (IB 32 pts)
Cardiff – ABB (Econ Mgt St; Econ Soc Phil App Eth)
City – ABB 320 pts (Econ; Econ Acc; Fin Econ) (IB 34 pts)
East Anglia – ABB–BBB (Econ; Econ Acc; Bus Econ; Bus Fin Econ; PPE) (IB 32–31 pts)
Essex – 320 pts (Econ; Fin Econ; Int Econ; Mgt Econ; Econ Langs)
Kent – 320 pts (Econ; Econ Lang; Fin Econ; Econ Comp; Fin Ecomet) (IB 34 pts H16 pts)
Lancaster – ABB 320 pts (Econ Int Rel; Econ Maths; Econ Geog; Econ Pol; Bus Econ) (IB 30 pts)
Leicester – ABB (Econ Law; Econ; Fin Econ; Bus Econ) (IB 32 pts)
Liverpool – ABB (Econ Maths; Econ; Bus Econ) (IB 33 pts)
London (Gold) – ABB (Pol Econ; Econ Pol Pblc Pol)
London LSE – ABB (Env Pol Econ; Soc Plcy Econ) (IB 37 pts)
Loughborough – ABB (Geog Econ) (IB 34 pts)
Manchester – ABB (BA Econ; Econ Pol; Econ Sociol; Econ Crim; Econ Econ Soc Hist) (IB 34 pts)
Newcastle – ABB (Econ Stats)
Queen's Belfast – ABB–BBBb (Econ Acc)
Reading – 320 pts (Econ; Bus Econ; Econ Ecomet)
Sheffield – ABB–BBB (Econ; Econ Geog; Econ Soc Plcy; Econ) (IB 32 pts)
Strathclyde – ABB (Econ Maths Stats; Econ Psy; Econ Mgt)
Surrey – ABB–BBB 320–300 pts (Bus Econ Fin; Econ; Bus Econ) (IB 34–32 pts)
Sussex – ABB–BBB (Econ; Econ Dev St; Econ Int Rel; Econ Mgt St; Econ Pol) (IB 32–34 pts)

300 pts **Aston** – BBB (Maths Econ) (IB 31 pts)
Brunel – BCC +AS/EPQ c 300 pts (Pol Econ)
City – 300 pts (Mathem Sci Fin Econ)
Dundee – BBB 2nd yr entry (MA/BSc Econ; Bus Econ; Fin Econ courses)
Edinburgh – BBB/AAA (Econ; Econ Acc; Econ Law; Econ Pol; Econ Chin; Econ Env St; Econ Mgt Sci) (IB 34 pts HL 555)
Edinburgh – ABC/AAA (Econ Maths; Econ Stats)
Heriot-Watt – BBB 2nd yr entry (Economics)
Keele – 300–360 pts inc AB/BB (Bus Econ)
Liverpool – BBB/ABB (Economics) (IB 32 pts)
Oxford Brookes – BBB–BBC (Econ Law; Econ Int Rel; Econ Pol)
Queen's Belfast – BBB–BBCb (Bus Econ; Econ Mgt; Econ Fin; Econ Fr/Ger/Span; Econ) (IB 35 pts)
Sheffield – ABC (Econ Maths)
Stirling – BBB 2nd yr entry (Econ Env Sci; Econ Mgt Sci; Econ)
Swansea – 300–280 pts (Econ; Bus Econ; Econ Pol; Bus Mgt Econ) (IB 30–32 pts)
Westminster – BBB (Bus Econ) (IB 28 pts)

280 pts **Brighton** – BBC 280 pts (Econ Fin)
De Montfort – 280 pts (Econ Fin)
Keele – 280–320 pts (Econ courses) (IB 28–30 pts)
Northumbria – 280 pts (Bus Econ)
Reading – 280 pts (Fd Mark Bus Econ)

260 pts **Aberystwyth** – 260 pts (Econ; Bus Econ; Econ Mark) (IB 29 pts)
Birmingham City – 260 pts (Econ courses)
Bristol UWE – 260–300 pts (Bus St Econ; Econ (Econ Mny Bank Fin); Econ) (IB 24–28 pts)
Coventry – 260–320 pts (Econ; Fin Econ; Bus Econ; Int Econ Trd)
Heriot-Watt – BCC 1st yr entry (Economics)
Hertfordshire – 260 pts (Econ courses; Bus Econ)
Hull – 260 pts (Econ; Int Econ; Econ Bus Econ; Int Bus Econ; Econ Log; Bus Econ courses)
Kingston – 260 pts (Econ; Bus Econ; Fin Econ; App Econ)
Oxford Brookes – BCC (Econ; Econ Fin Int Bus) (IB 29 pts)
Portsmouth – 260–300 pts (Econ Fin Bank; Econ; Bus Econ; App Econ)
Staffordshire – BCC–BB 260 pts (Bus Econ; Econ Leg St)
Staffordshire – 260 pts (Econ Modn Hist; Econ Phil)
Stirling – BCC 1st yr entry (Econ; Econ Mgt Sci; Econ Env Sci; PPE)

240 pts **Aberdeen** – CCC 1st yr entry (Econ courses) (IB 28 pts)
Bangor – 240–280 pts (Bus Econ; Econ joint courses) (IB 28 pts)
Bradford – 240–260 pts (Econ; Fin Econ; Econ Mark; Econ Psy; Int Econ)
Cardiff (UWIC) – 240 pts (Economics)
De Montfort – 240 pts (Econ Gov)
Dundee – CCC 1st yr entry (MA/BSc Bus Econ; Econ; Fin Econ courses) (IB 29 pts)
Edinburgh Napier – 240 pts (Econ Mgt)
Liverpool John Moores – 240 pts (Bus Econ)
Manchester Met – CCC 240 pts (Econ; Econ Tour; Bus Econ) (IB 27 pts)
Newport – 240 pts (Econ Law; Acc Econ; Bus Econ)
Nottingham Trent – 240 pts (Econ; Bus Econ)
Plymouth – 240 pts (Econ courses; Bus Econ courses; Fin Econ Bus Econ)
Robert Gordon – CCC (Mgt Econ)
Stirling – CCC (PPE) (IB 28 pts)
Ulster – CCC 240 pts (Econ; Econ Prcrmt; Int Pol Econ St; Econ Mark; Econ Soc Pol)
Worcester – 240 pts (Bus Acc Econ; Bus Econ Adv; Bus Econ PR)

230 pts **Buckingham** – 230 pts (Economics)
Edinburgh Napier – 230 pts (Acc Econ)

220 pts **Birmingham City** – 220 pts (Constr Mgt Econ)
Central Lancashire – 220–260 pts (Econ courses)
Leeds Met – 220 pts (Econ Bus; Gbl Dev Pol Econ)
London Met – 220 pts (Econ; Econ St; Fin Econ; Int Econ)
Northampton – 220–260 pts (Econ courses)

200 pts **Anglia Ruskin** – 200 pts (Bus Econ)
East London – 200 pts (Bus Econ courses)
Middlesex – 200–280 pts (Bus Econ; Bus Econ Stats)

180 pts **Greenwich** – 180–220 pts (Bus Econ; Econ; Int St Econ)

160 pts **West Scotland** – CC–CD (Bus Econ; Econ)

80 pts **London (Birk)** – 80 pts for under 21s (over 21 varies) (p/t Econ Soc Pol; Fin Econ)

Open University – (Econ Maths Sci; Pol Phil Econ – contact +44 (0)845 300 6090 or www.openuniversity.co.uk/you)

Alternative offers

See **Chapter 7** and **Appendix 1** for grades/UCAS Tariff points information for the International Baccalaureate, Scottish Highers/Advanced Highers, the Welsh Baccalaureate, the Irish Leaving Certificate, the Cambridge Pre-U Diploma, the Advanced Diploma and the Extended Project.

CHOOSING YOUR COURSE (SEE ALSO CH.1)

Some course features

Bath One-year sandwich placements with leading financial organisations.
Durham Economics is offered as a Single or Joint Honours subject or as part of the Combined Honours (Social Sciences) or Natural Sciences programmes.
Greenwich Options to specialise in business or banking subjects.
Hertfordshire Work placement in Year 3.
Lancaster A third subject from another department can be studied in Year 1.
London LSE One subject option each year can be taken in other subjects offered at LSE.
Manchester The Economics and Social Studies programmes give extensive choice and flexibility for students to put together their preferred programme of study.
Warwick Some option modules can be taken from other departments, eg Law, Politics, Mathematics and International Studies.
York A modular Economics course with a wide range of options including some which can be taken from other departments.

Universities and colleges teaching quality See www.qaa.ac.uk; www.unistats.com.

Top research universities and colleges (RAE 2008) (Economics and Econometrics) London LSE; London (UCL); Essex; Oxford; Warwick; Bristol; Nottingham; London (QM); Cambridge; Manchester; Glasgow; London (RH); Southampton.

Examples of sandwich degree courses Aberystwyth; Aston; Bath; Birmingham City; Bristol UWE; Brunel; Hertfordshire; Kingston; Leeds Met; Loughborough; Middlesex; Newcastle; Nottingham Trent; Oxford Brookes; Plymouth; Portsmouth; Reading; Staffordshire; Surrey; Ulster; West Scotland; Westminster; Worcester.

ADMISSIONS INFORMATION

Number of applicants per place (approx) Aberystwyth 3; Anglia Ruskin 10; Aston 8; Bangor 4; Bath 12; Birmingham 10; Birmingham City 16; Bradford 5; Bristol 11; Brunel 12; Buckingham 4; Cambridge 6; Cardiff 8; Central Lancashire 5; City 18, (Econ Acc) 12; Coventry 10; Dundee 5; Durham (Econ) 10; East Anglia 15; Essex 6; Exeter 12; Greenwich 8; Heriot-Watt 4; Hull 15; Kent 11; Kingston 9; Lancaster 14; Leeds 16; Leicester 10; Liverpool 4; Liverpool John Moores 8; London (UCL) 12; London LSE (Econ) 10, (Econ Econ Hist) 8, (Ecomet Mathem Econ) 20; Loughborough 15; Manchester (Econ) 7, (Econ Fin) 22, (Econ Pol) 27, (Econ Sociol) 27; Manchester Met 5; Middlesex 8; Newcastle 11, (Econ Bus Mgt) 27; Northampton 8; Northumbria 16; Nottingham (Econ Chin) 8; Nottingham Trent 2; Oxford Brookes 51; Plymouth 4; Portsmouth 6; Queen's Belfast 10; St Andrews 5; Salford 6; Sheffield 10; Southampton 7; Staffordshire 4; Stirling 6; Surrey 5; Swansea 7; Warwick 16; West Scotland 7; York 4.

Number of applicants (**a** UK **b** EU (non-UK) **c** non-EU **d** mature) **Aston a**300 **b**30 **c**50 **d**20; **Leeds a**433 **b**5 **c**70 **d**33.

Advice to applicants and planning the UCAS personal statement Visits, work experience and work shadowing in banks, insurance companies, accountants' offices etc should be described. Keep up-to-date with economic issues by reading *The Economist* and *The Financial Times* and find other sources of information. Describe any particular aspects of economics which interest you – and why. Make it clear on the statement that you know what economics is and why you want to study it. Give evidence of your interest in economics and your reasons for choosing the course and provide information about your sport/extra-curricular activities and positions of responsibility.

Misconceptions about this course **Bradford** That the Economics course is very mathematical and that students will not get a good job, eg management. **Kent** That the Economics course is mathematical, has a high failure rate and has poorer job prospects than Business Studies courses. **London (UCL)** Some think the Economics course is a Business course.

Selection interviews **Yes** Bristol, Bristol UWE, Brunel, Cambridge, Coventry, East London, Edinburgh, Essex, Keele, London (RH), (UCL), Manchester Met, Middlesex, Nottingham Trent, Oxford, Southampton (Acc Econ) (interviews influence level of offer), Surrey; **Some** Aberystwyth, Anglia

Ruskin, Bangor, Buckingham, Dundee, East Anglia, Kent, Leeds, London LSE, London Met (mature students), Loughborough, Staffordshire, Swansea.

Interview advice and questions If you have studied economics at A-level or in other examinations, expect to be questioned on aspects of the subject. This is a subject which is constantly in the news, so keep abreast of developments and be prepared to be asked questions such as: What is happening to sterling at present? What is happening to the dollar? How relevant is economics today? What are your views of the Government's economic policy? Do you think that the family is declining as an institution? Discuss Keynesian economics. Is the power of the Prime Minister increasing? What is a recession? How would you get the world out of recession? What causes a recession? **Cambridge** What is the point of using NHS money to keep old people alive? What would you say if Gordon Brown were to take a report which shows that people who go to university earn more than those who did not and then proclaims that university causes you to earn more? **Oxford** (Econ Mgt) 'I was asked questions on a newspaper article I had been given to read 45 minutes beforehand, followed by a few maths problems and an economics question.' Explain why teachers might be changing jobs to become plumbers. (Econ Mgt) What is the difference between the buying and selling of slaves and the buying and selling of football players? Should a Wal-Mart store be opened in the middle of Oxford? See also **Chapter 5**.

Reasons for rejection (non-academic) Lack of knowledge about the course offered and the subject matter; lack of care in preparing personal statement; poor written English; the revelation on the statement that they want a course different from that for which they have applied! **Aberystwyth** Would have trouble fitting into the unique environment at Aberystwyth.

AFTER-RESULTS ADVICE

Offers to applicants repeating A-levels **Higher** Birmingham City, City, East Anglia, Essex, Leeds, Newcastle, Northumbria, Nottingham, Queen's Belfast, St Andrews, Warwick, York; **Possibly higher** Bradford, Brunel, Durham, Lancaster, Oxford Brookes; **Same** Aberystwyth, Anglia Ruskin, Bangor, Bath, Buckingham, Cambridge, Cardiff, Coventry, Dundee, East London, Edinburgh Napier, Heriot-Watt, Hull, Kingston, Liverpool, Liverpool John Moores, London (RH), London Met, Loughborough, Nottingham Trent, Salford, Sheffield, Staffordshire, Surrey, Swansea, Ulster.

GRADUATE DESTINATIONS AND EMPLOYMENT (2007/8 HESA)

Graduates surveyed 3310 **Employed** 1585 **In further study** 495 **Assumed unemployed** 295.

Career note Most graduates work within areas of business and finance, and in a range of jobs including management and administration posts across both public and private sectors.

OTHER DEGREE SUBJECTS FOR CONSIDERATION

Accountancy; Actuarial Studies; Administration; Banking; Business Studies; Development Studies; Estate Management; Financial Services; Government; Politics; Management Sciences/Studies; Property Development; Quantity Surveying; Social Sciences; Sociology; Statistics.

EDUCATION STUDIES and TEACHER TRAINING

(see also **Physical Education** and **Social Sciences/Studies**)

There are two types of degree courses in Education – those which cover the history, philosophy and theory of education but which are not necessarily teacher training courses, and those which prepare the student for a career in the teaching profession. Read prospectuses carefully. For teaching, candidates should be well motivated towards both teaching and education – the interview is important. Interview panels look for candidates with confidence in their own ability, a lively personality, patience and optimism. Experience of working with children is important. Students planning to follow a degree with a Postgraduate Certificate in Education (PGCE) are advised that problems may arise if their first degree subject is not a National Curriculum subject.

Teacher training courses are offered in the following subject areas: Art and Design (P); Biology (P S); Business Studies (S); Chemistry (P S); Childhood (P); Computer Education (P); Creative and Performing Arts (P); Dance (P S); Design and Technology (P S); Drama (P S); English (P S); Environmental Science (P S); Environmental Studies (P); French (P S); General Primary; Geography (P S); History (P S); Maths (P S); Music (P S); Physical Education/Movement Studies (P S); Religious Studies (P); Science (P S); Sociology (P); Textile Design (P); Welsh (P). Two-year BEd courses are also offered for holders of HND or equivalent qualifications (minimum age in some cases 23–25) in the following subject areas: Business Studies (S); Chemistry (S); Design and Technology (S); English (P); French (S); General Primary; German (S); Language Studies (P); Mathematics (S); Music (S); Physics (S); Science (S); Spanish (S); Welsh (S). For further information on teaching as a career see websites below and **Appendix 4** for contact details. Over 50 taster courses are offered each year to those considering teaching as a career. Early Childhood Studies has been introduced in recent years by a number of universities. The courses focus on child development, from birth to eight years of age, and the provision of education for children and their families. It is a multi-disciplinary subject and can cover social problems and legal and psychological issues. Note that many institutions listed below also offer one-year Postgraduate Certificate in Education (PGCE) courses which qualify graduates to teach other subjects.

Useful websites www.tda.gov.uk; www.gtcs.org.uk; www.gttr.ac.uk; http://educationcymru.org; www.dcsf.gov.uk.

NB The points totals shown to the left of the institutions are for ease of reference only. It must not be assumed that Tariff points are always used by institutions or that they can be substituted for an offer in grades. The level of an offer is not necessarily indicative of the quality of a course.

COURSE OFFERS INFORMATION

Subject requirements/preferences **GCSE** English, mathematics and a science subject for those born after 1 September 1979. **AL** One A-level is usually required in the main subject of choice plus one or two other subjects. **Other** CRB Enhanced Level clearance and health checks required.

NB In 2011 universities and colleges will differ in their use of GCE AL/AS unit grade information, A* grades, the Extended Project (EPQ), the Advanced Diploma and the Cambridge Pre-U examination when considering applicants and making offers. An EPQ may be accepted in place of an AS subject. Check websites of universities and colleges for the latest offers information.

The following table is divided into two sections: **Education Studies** including **Childhood Studies**, and **Teacher Training Courses**.

EDUCATION STUDIES

Your target offers and examples of courses provided by each institution

360 pts **Cambridge** – A*AA college offers may vary (Educ St courses) (IB 38–42 pts)

340 pts **Durham** – AAB (BA Educ St (Biol Sci) (Engl St) (Geog) (Hist) (Maths) (Mus) (Phil) (Psy) (Sociol) (Theol)) (IB 34 pts)

Lancaster – AAB (Psy Educ)

320 pts **Bath** – ABB (Coach Educ Spo Dev; Chld Yth Educ St) (IB 35 pts)

Birmingham – ABB (Engl Lang Lit Educ)

Bristol – ABB–BBC (Child St)

Liverpool – ABB (Maths Educ)

Warwick – BBCc (Ely Chld St) (IB 30 pts)

300 pts **Birmingham** – BBB (Chld Cult Educ) (IB 32 pts)

East Anglia – BBB (Educ St)

Edinburgh – BBB (Commun Educ)

Glasgow – BBB (Commun Dev)

Gloucestershire – 300 pts (Spo Educ)

Stranmillis (UC) – BBB (Ely Chld St)

York – BBB–BCC (Lang Lit Educ; Educ St) (IB 31–30 pts)

280 pts **Leeds** – BBC (Chld St) (IB 30 pts)

Oxford Brookes – BBC (Educ St courses; Ely Chld St) (IB 30 pts)

260 pts **Aberystwyth** – 260–300 pts (Educ joint Hons courses) (IB 26–30 pts)

Brighton – BCC (Educ courses) (IB 28 pts)

Bristol UWE – 260 pts (Ely Chld St Ling)

Cardiff (UWIC) – 260 pts (Educ St (Ely Chld St) (Engl) (Modn Hist) (Psy) (Spo) (Welsh))

Keele – 260–320 pts (Educ St courses) (IB 28–30 pts)

Liverpool Hope – 260 pts (Educ St courses; Disab St courses; Inclsn Educ)

London (Gold) – BCC (Educ Cult Soty) (IB 28 pts)

Newport – 260 pts (Crea Thera Educ)

Northumbria – 260 pts (Ely Yrs Chld St Gdnc Cnslg; Chld St Hlth Contemp Soty)

Strathclyde – BCC (Commun Educ)

Teesside – 260 pts (Psy Educ St)

240 pts **Brighton** – CCC/BCD (Educ Engl Lit)

Bristol – CCC 300 pts (Df St) (IB 28 pts)

Chester – 240 pts (Educ St courses) (IB 30 pts)

De Montfort – 240 pts (Educ St courses)

Gloucestershire – 240 pts (Ely Chld St; Educ St courses)

Hull – 240 pts (Educ courses)

Liverpool John Moores – 240–280 pts (Educ St Ely Yrs; Ely Chld St)

London Met – 240 pts (Educ St courses)

Manchester Met – 240 pts (Ely Chld St)

Plymouth – 240 pts (Ely Chld St)

Portsmouth – 240–300 pts (Ely Chld St; Educ Engl Lang; Educ Hist; Educ Langs)

Staffordshire – 240 pts (Ely Chld St)

Stranmillis (UC) – CCC (Hlth Leis Educ)

Sunderland – 240 pts (Chld St)

Ulster – 240–220 pts (Educ Geog; Bus Educ; Ir Educ; Euro St Educ)

Winchester – 240–280 pts (Educ St courses; Ely Chld St; Chld Yth Commun St)

220 pts **Aberystwyth** – 220 pts (Chld St)

Bangor – CCD 220–260 pts (Addysg; Astudiaethau Plentyndod Joint Hons)

Bangor – 220–240 pts (Chld St)

Bath Spa – 220–260 pts (Educ St courses; Ely Yrs Educ courses; Int Educ)

Bristol UWE – 220–300 pts (Ely Chld St) (IB 32 pts)

Central Lancashire – 220–240 pts (Df St; Educ courses)

Chichester – CCD (Ely Chld St)

Edge Hill – 220 pts (Ely Chld St; Child Yth St)
Glamorgan – 220–260 pts (Ely Yrs Dev Educ)
Hertfordshire – 220 pts (Educ St)
Liverpool John Moores – 220–260 pts (Out Educ Env Educ)
Newport – 220 pts (Ely Yrs; Educ St)
Leeds Met – 220 pts (Educ St)
Newman (UC) – 220–260 pts (Educ St courses)
Northampton – 220–240 pts (Educ St courses; Ely Chld St; Chld Yth)
Nottingham Trent – 220–200 pts (Chld St; Ely Yrs Educ Dev; Educ joint courses)
Plymouth – 220–240 pts (Educ St; Ely Chld St)
Sheffield Hallam – 220–200 pts (Educ St; Educ Disab St; Chld St)
Teesside – 220 pts (Ely Chld St; Yth Chld St)

200 pts **Birmingham City** – 200 pts (Ely Chld St)
Bolton – 200 pts (Educ St courses)
Bristol UWE – 200–300 pts (Educ St)
Canterbury Christ Church – 200 pts (Infml Educ; Educ St)
Chester (Warrington) – 200–240 pts (Ely Chld St)
Chichester – CDD (Advntr Educ)
Cumbria – 200 pts (Ely Chld St)
Dundee – BB 200 pts (Commun Lrng Dev) (IB 29 pts)
East London – 200 pts (Educ Commun Dev courses; Educ St; Ely Chld St; SEN)
Glyndŵr – 200 pts (Educ St courses)
Manchester Met – 200 pts (Ely Chld St) (IB 28 pts)
Middlesex – 200–240 pts (Educ St courses; Ely Chld St)
Roehampton – 200–300 pts (Educ courses)
Suffolk (Univ Campus) – 200 pts (Ely Chld St)
Worcester – 200 pts (Educ St)
York St John – 200–220 pts (Educ St)

180 pts **Anglia Ruskin** – 180 pts (Educ Chld)
Derby – 180–240 pts (Educ St)
Leeds Trinity (UC) – 180 pts (Educ St)
Swansea Met – 180 pts (Educ St)
UCP Marjon – 180 pts (Educ St Comb)

160 pts **Bedfordshire** – 160–220 pts (Disab St; Ely Yrs Educ; Educ St)
Bishop Grosseteste (UC) – 160 pts (Educ St courses; Ely Chld St)
Greenwich – 160 pts (Chld St; Educ St)
St Mary's Twickenham (UC) – 160–200 pts (Educ Soc Sci)
UHI Millennium Inst (NHC) – CC (Chld Yth St)
Wolverhampton – 160–220 pts (Df St Educ St; Chld Fmly St Educ St; Spec Nds Inclsn St; Cond Educ)

140 pts **Bradford (Coll)** – 140 pts (BA Educ St)

Open University – (Chld Yth St; Ely Yrs – contact +44 (0)845 300 6090 or www.openuniversity.co.uk/you)

TEACHER TRAINING

Subjects attracting the most applicants include Drama, History, Physical Education, Social Science, English and Art. Subjects attracting the fewest applicants include Modern Languages, Sciences, Craft Design and Technology, Music, Religious Education, Mathematics and Home Economics. The choice of subject will affect the level of the offer made. See also separate subject tables.

Subject requirements/preferences **GCSE** Grades A–C in English, mathematics and a science subject. **AL** One subject is usually required in the main subject of choice. **Other** CRB Enhanced Level clearance and health checks required and registration with the Independent Safeguarding Authority – check websites.

NB In 2011 universities and colleges will differ in their use of GCE AL/AS unit grade information, A* grades, the Extended Project (EPQ), the Advanced Diploma and the Cambridge Pre-U examination when considering applicants and making offers. An EPQ may be accepted in place of an AS subject. Check websites of universities and colleges for the latest offers information.

Abbreviations used in this table ITE – Initial Teacher Education; ITT – Initial Teacher Training; P – Primary Teaching; QTS – Qualified Teacher Status; S – Secondary Teaching; STQ – Scottish Teaching Qualification.

Your target offers and examples of courses provided by each institution

380 pts **Cambridge** – A*AA college offers may vary (BA Educ (Biol Sci) (Class) (Engl) (Engl Dr) (Geog) (Hist) (Maths) (Modn Langs) (Mus) (Phys Sci) (Relig St))

320 pts **Brunel** – BBC +AS/EPQ c 320 pts (BSc S PE)
Sussex – ABB–BBB (Engl ELT) (IB 32–34 pts)

300 pts **Durham (Stockton)** – BBB (BA/BSc P Teach Gen)
Edinburgh – BBB (BEd P; PE BEd P)
Glasgow – BBB (MA P STQ)
Hertfordshire – 300 pts (BEd P)
Liverpool Hope – 300 pts (BA P QTS Educ)
Roehampton – 300–360 pts (BA/BSc P Educ QTS; Educ courses)
Stranmillis (UC) – BBB (P BEd)

280 pts **Edge Hill** – 280 pts (Educ QTS ICT; Educ QTS Maths; Educ QTS Modn Lang; Educ QTS RE; Educ QTS Sci; S Educ QTS Maths; S Educ QTS ICT; S Educ QTS Des Tech; S Educ QTS Sci; P Educ)
Leeds Trinity (UC) – BBC (BA P Educ (7–11))
Liverpool John Moores – 280–320 pts (P BA QTS Educ Ely Yrs)
Manchester Met – 280 pts (BA P)
Newman (UC) – 280–320 pts (BA P QTS S (Art) (Engl))
Northampton – 280 pts (BA P QTS Educ; Ely Yrs Educ QTS)
Oxford Brookes – BBC (BA P Educ)
Sunderland – 280 pts (BA P)

260 pts **Brighton** – BCC (BA P Engl/ICT/Maths/Sci QTS (KS 2/3); S Educ QTS; PE QTS)
Leeds Met – 260 pts (BA P; Ely Yrs Educ QTS)
Liverpool John Moores – 260 pts (BA P Ely Yrs QTS)
Northumbria – 260 pts (BA Ely Educ)
Nottingham Trent – BCC 260 pts (BA P)
Nottingham Trent – 260 pts (TESOL (Engl) (Fr) (Ger) (Ital) (Span) (Glob St) (Int Rel); Des Tech Educ)
Strathclyde – BCC (BEd P)

240 pts **Anglia Ruskin** – 240 pts (BA P; Educ Modn Langs; BA P Educ ITT)
Bangor – 240 pts (BA P Educ QTS)
Bedfordshire – 240 pts (BEd P Educ QTS)
Brighton – CCC/BCD (Media Prod Educ)
Canterbury Christ Church – 240–200 pts (BA QTS P Educ; BSc Maths S Educ QTS)
Chester – 240 pts (BEd Ely Yrs; Gen P)
Chichester – CCC (BA P QTS)
Chichester – CCD 260–320 pts (Maths Teach KS 2+3) (IB 26 pts)
Cumbria – 240 pts (Ely Yrs Educ QTS; BA P Educ QTS)
Derby – 240–280 pts (BEd courses)
Glasgow (RSAMD) – AA–DD (Mus BEd)
Gloucestershire – 240 pts (BEd P QTS)
Leeds Trinity (UC) – 240 pts (BA P Educ)
Liverpool John Moores – 240–280 pts (P BA QTS Educ Fr Educ)
Manchester Met – 220 pts (BA Maths S Educ QTS)
Newman (UC) – 240–280 pts (BSc P ICT Sci (KS 2/3) QTS)
Plymouth – 240 pts (BEd P courses)

Sheffield Hallam – 240 pts (Ely Yrs Educ QTS; BA P S)
Stirling – CCC (Prof Educ (Modn Langs/Env) BA/BSc P S; Educ P; Educ S)
220 pts **Aberdeen** – AB–CC (Educ P; Educ S)
Central Lancashire – 220 pts (Df St; Brit Sign Lang)
Glamorgan – 220–260 pts (Ely Yrs Dev)
Newport – 220 pts (BA P St QTS; S Des Tech)
Sunderland – 220 pts (BA S (Engl Educ) (Geog Educ) (Hist Educ) (ICT Educ) (Sci Educ) (Des Tech Educ) (Maths Educ) (Spo Educ))
West Scotland – CCD/DDDD (BEd P)
200 pts **Bangor** – 200–240 pts (BSc S QTS Des Tech Educ)
Bristol UWE – 200–300 pts (BA P ITE/Ely Yrs Chld Educ)
Bristol UWE – 200–300 pts (Educ St +PGCE P)
Canterbury Christ Church – 200 pts (BA P Educ QTS)
Cumbria – 200 pts (BA S Educ Prof St QTS)
Dundee – BB (BEd P Educ)
Edinburgh – BB (Des Tech BEd)
Greenwich – 200 pts (BA P Educ QTS)
Hull – 200–260 pts (BA P Educ QTS)
Kingston – 200 pts (BA P Educ QTS)
Nottingham Trent – 200 pts (BA S Des Tech Educ QTS)
UCP Marjon – 200–240 pts (BEd P QTS)
Wolverhampton – 200–260 pts (BEd P)
180 pts **Middlesex** – 180 pts (BA Educ P)
St Mary's Twickenham (UC) – 180–200 pts (BA P Educ QTS)
160 pts **Bishop Grosseteste (UC)** – CC 160 pts (BA P QTS)
Greenwich – 160 pts (BA S Educ Des Tech QTS)
Sheffield Hallam – 160 pts (BSc QTS S (Des Tech) (Sci) (Maths))
140 pts **Royal Welsh (CMusDr)** – 140 pts (BA S)

Queen's Belfast – contact St Mary's (UC) **or** Stranmillis (UC) (BEd P)

Alternative offers

See **Chapter 7** and **Appendix 1** for grades/UCAS Tariff points information for the International Baccalaureate, Scottish Highers/Advanced Highers, the Welsh Baccalaureate, the Irish Leaving Certificate, the Cambridge Pre-U Diploma, the Advanced Diploma and the Extended Project.

EXAMPLES OF FOUNDATION DEGREES IN THE SUBJECT FIELD

Bangor; Bath City (Coll); Bath Spa; Bedfordshire; Bishop Grosseteste (UC); Blackburn (Coll Univ Centre); Blackpool and Fylde (Coll); Bournemouth; Bradford; Bradford (Coll); Brighton; Bristol City (Coll); Bristol UWE; Bucks New; Central Lancashire; Chichester; Cornwall (Coll); Cumbria; Derby; Duchy (Coll); East London; Edge Hill; Exeter (Coll); Farnborough (CT); Glamorgan; Gloucestershire; Glyndŵr; Greenwich; Grimsby (IFHE); Guildford (Coll); Havering (Coll); Hopwood Hall (Coll); Huddersfield; Kingston; Kirklees (Coll); Lakes (Coll); Leeds City (Coll); Leeds Met; Leeds Trinity (UC); London Met; Loughborough (Coll); Manchester (Coll); Mid-Cheshire (Coll); Myerscough (Coll); NEW (Coll); Newman (UC); North Devon (Coll); Northbrook (Coll); Norwich City (Coll); Oxford Brookes; Peterborough Reg (Coll); Plymouth; Plymouth City (Coll); Reading; Riverside Halton (Coll); Roehampton; St Mary's Twickenham (UC); Sheffield (Coll); South Cheshire (Coll); South Devon (Coll); South Essex (Coll); Southport (Coll); Stockport (Coll); Stranmilllis (UC); Stratford upon Avon (Coll); Suffolk (Univ Campus); Sunderland; Teesside; Truro (Coll); UCP Marjon; Wakefield (Coll); Warrington (Coll); West Anglia (Coll); Wigan and Leigh (Coll); Wirral Met (Coll); Worcester.

CHOOSING YOUR COURSE (SEE ALSO CH.1)

Some course features

Education Studies

Bristol (Chld St) This new course is provided in the Department of Social Policy and Social Work. It

focuses on children, their communities and on the political and economic environment. A study of children, social policy and psychology (not a teacher training course).
Cambridge Education Studies is combined with a range of other subjects which can lead on to a PGCE qualification.
Durham A study of educational issues plus the opportunity to study one of seven subjects from other departments.
Keele Two main strands – education for training or education for social policy.
York A study of educational ideas and issues.

Teaching
Chester Early years and primary teaching degrees.
Chichester Primary teacher training, and postgraduate courses in Primary and Secondary Education.
Durham A three-year teaching course is offered at Queen's campus.
Edge Hill Primary and secondary teaching courses.
Liverpool Hope Education Studies plus the option to take primary teaching courses in mathematics or modern languages.
Middlesex Education Studies can be taken with a National Curriculum subject as a route to a PGCE in Primary or Secondary Education.

Top teacher training providers See www.tda.gov.uk (England); www.shefc.ac.uk (Scotland); www.elwa.org.uk (Wales); www.unistats.com.

Top research universities and colleges (RAE 2008) London (Inst Ed); Oxford; Cambridge; London (King's); Bristol; Leeds; Exeter; Manchester Met; Warwick; York; Durham; Sussex; Stirling.

ADMISSIONS INFORMATION

Number of applicants per place (approx) Aberystwyth 6; Anglia Ruskin 1; Bangor 5; Bath 17; Bath Spa 5; Birmingham 8; Bishop Grosseteste (UC) 12; Bristol (Df St) 2, (Ely Chld St) 9; Bristol UWE 20; Brunel (PE) 5; Cambridge 2.5; Canterbury Christ Church 15; Cardiff (Educ) 8; Cardiff (UWIC) 3; Central Lancashire 5; Chester 25; Chichester 12; Cumbria 5; Derby 13; Dundee 5; Durham 8; Edge Hill 17; Edinburgh (P) 3; Gloucestershire 20; Glyndŵr 15; Greenwich 3; Hull 7; Hull (Scarborough) 4; Kingston 9; Leeds 4; Liverpool Hope 5; Liverpool John Moores 3; London (Gold) 5, (Des Tech) 4; Manchester Met 23, (Maths) 4; Middlesex 7; Newman (UC) (S Engl) 3, (Theol) 3, (Ely Yrs) 5, (Biol) 7, (Geog) 3, (PE) 6, (Sci) 1; Northampton 7; Northumbria 8; Nottingham Trent 11; Oxford Brookes 6; Plymouth 14; Roehampton 6; St Mary's Twickenham (UC) 19; Sheffield Hallam 7, (PE) 60; Strathclyde 7; Swansea Met 10; Trinity (UC) 10; UCP Marjon 5; West Scotland 7; Winchester 4; Wolverhampton 4; Worcester 21, (Engl) 51; York 3.

Advice to applicants and planning the UCAS personal statement Any application for teacher training courses requires candidates to have experience of observation in schools and with children relevant to the choice of age range. Describe what you have learned from this. Any work with young people should be described in detail, indicating any problems which you may have seen which children create for the teacher. Applicants are strongly advised to have had some teaching practice prior to interview and should give evidence of time spent in primary school and give an analysis of activity undertaken with children. Give details of music qualifications, if any. Admissions tutors look for precise, succinct, well-reasoned, well-written statements (no mistakes!). **Chichester** Applicants should have spent a minimum of two weeks observing/helping out in a state school.
NB All appplicants for Initial Teacher Training (ITT) courses in England leading to Qualified Teacher Status must register provisionally with the General Teaching Council for England. Check with www.gtce.org.uk for full details. See **Chapter 5**.

Misconceptions about this course That Childhood Studies is a childcare, child health or teaching course: it is not. That Educational Studies leads to a teaching qualification – it does not. **Bath Spa** (Educ St) Applicants should note that this is not a teacher training course – it leads on to PGCE teacher training (this applies to other Education Studies courses). **Newman (UC)** That the Theology course only concentrates on the Christian/Catholic religions – all major religions are covered. **UHI**

Millennium Inst (NHC) Candidates are unaware that on-line methods form a significant part of the course delivery.

Selection interviews **Yes** Bishop Grosseteste (UC), Brighton, Bristol UWE, Brunel, Cambridge, Cardiff (UWIC), Chichester, Derby, Durham, Kingston, London (Gold), Manchester Met (group interviews), Newman (UC), Nottingham Trent, Oxford Brookes, Plymouth, Stockport (CFHE), Worcester, York St John. Check all institutions. It is a requirement that all candidates for teacher education are interviewed. Many institutions offering Education Studies also interview selected applicants. Additionally, candidates are asked to compose a short written statement on a given topic at interview in order to ensure an acceptable standard of written English; **Some** Anglia Ruskin, Bangor, Bristol (Df St), Cardiff, Dundee, Lincoln, Liverpool John Moores, Roehampton, UCP Marjon, West Scotland, Winchester, York.

Interview advice and questions Questions invariably focus on why you want to teach and your experiences in the classroom. In some cases you may be asked to write an essay on these topics. Questions in the past have included: What do you think are important issues in education at present? Discussion of course work will take place for Art applicants. **Cambridge** The stage is a platform for opinions or just entertainment? **Derby** Applicants are asked about an aspect of education. **Liverpool John Moores** Discussion regarding any experience the applicant has had with children. **Worcester** Interviewees are asked to write a statement concerning their impressions of the interview. See also **Chapter 5**.

Reasons for rejection (non-academic) Unable to meet the requirements of written standard English. Ungrammatical personal statements. Lack of research about teaching at primary or secondary levels. Lack of experience in schools. Insufficient experience of working with people; tendency to be racist.

AFTER-RESULTS ADVICE

Offers to applicants repeating A-levels **Higher** Oxford Brookes, Warwick; **Possibly higher** Cumbria; **Same** Anglia Ruskin, Bangor, Bishop Grosseteste (UC), Brighton, Brunel, Cambridge, Canterbury Christ Church, Cardiff, Chester, Chichester, De Montfort, Derby, Dundee, Durham, East Anglia, Lincoln, Liverpool Hope, Liverpool John Moores, London (Gold), Manchester Met, Newman (UC), Northumbria, Nottingham Trent, Roehampton, St Mary's Twickenham (UC), Stirling, Sunderland, UCP Marjon, UHI Millennium Inst (NHC), Winchester, Wolverhampton, Worcester, York, York St John; **Not considered** Kingston.

GRADUATE DESTINATIONS AND EMPLOYMENT (2007/8 HESA)

Teaching courses graduates surveyed 5615 **Employed** 4315 **In further study** 120 **Assumed unemployed** 145.

Education courses graduates surveyed 2700 **Employed** 1120 **In further study** 220 **Assumed unemployed** 118.

Career note Education Studies degrees prepare graduates for careers in educational administration although many will move into more general areas of business or into aspects of work with Social Services. If courses in Education include Qualified Teacher Status (QTS), graduates can enter the teaching profession. Prospects are generally good. Courses in Childhood Studies could lead to work in health or childcare-related posts, in social work or administration.

OTHER DEGREE SUBJECTS FOR CONSIDERATION

Psychology; Social Policy; Social Sciences; Social Work.

ENGINEERING/ENGINEERING SCIENCES

(including **Forensic Engineering, General Engineering, Integrated Engineering, Engineering Product Design** and **Robotics**; see also **Art and Design (Industrial and Product Design)** and **Technologies**)

Many of these Engineering courses listed below enable students to delay their decision of their final Engineering specialism. Mathematics and physics provide the basis of all Engineering courses although several universities and colleges now provide one-year Foundation courses for applicants without science A-levels. Many institutions offer sandwich courses and firms also offer sponsorships. In prospectuses it will be noted that some courses are 'subject to approval'. The problem which can arise is that the examinations taken on these courses may not be accepted by the professional body overseeing that particular branch of engineering and examinations set by these professional bodies (see **Appendix 4**) will have to be retaken in order that graduates can obtain Chartered Engineer status.

Useful websites www.ukrc4setwomen.org.uk; www.ergonomics.org.uk; www.scicentral.com; www.engc.org.uk; www.noisemakers.org.uk; www.yini.org.uk; www.enginuity.org.uk.

ENGINEERING COUNCIL UK (ECUK) STATEMENT

Recent developments in the engineering profession and the regulations that govern registration as a professional engineer (UK-SPEC) mean that MEng and Bachelors degrees are the typical academic routes to becoming registered.

Chartered Engineers (CEng) develop solutions to engineering problems, using new or existing technologies, through innovation, creativity and change. They might develop and apply new technologies, promote advanced designs and design methods, introduce new and more efficient production techniques, marketing and construction concepts, and pioneer new engineering services and management methods.

Incorporated Engineers (IEng) act as exponents of today's technology through creativity and innovation. They maintain and manage applications of current and developing technology, and may be involved in engineering design, development, manufacture, construction and operation.

Both Chartered and Incorporated Engineers are variously engaged in technical and commercial leadership and possess effective interpersonal skills.

You should confirm with universities whether their courses are accredited for CEng or IEng by relevant professional engineering institutions. To become a Chartered or Incorporated Engineer, you will have to demonstrate competence and commitment appropriate to the registration category. On top of your academic knowledge, you will also need to demonstrate your professional development and experience. Most of this will come after you graduate but placements in industry during your degree course are also available. Both Chartered and Incorporated Engineers usually progress to become team leaders or to take other key management roles. For full information check www.engc.org.uk/ukspec.

NB The points totals shown to the left of the institutions are for ease of reference only. It must not be assumed that Tariff points are always used by institutions or that they can be substituted for an offer in grades. The level of an offer is not necessarily indicative of the quality of a course.

COURSE OFFERS INFORMATION

Subject requirements/preferences GCSE English, mathematics and a science subject required. **AL** Mathematics and/or physics, engineering or another science usually required. Design technology may be acceptable or in some cases required. **Cambridge** (Churchill, Peterhouse) May use STEP as part of conditional offer; (Trinity) If not further mathematics then a merit in AEA mathematics is required. **Oxford** Maths mechanics modules recommended, further mathematics helpful. (See **Chapter 6**.) **All institutions** Check with universities on the acceptability of the Advanced Engineering Diploma and see also **Chapter 4 Universities Admissions Policies**.

NB In 2011 universities and colleges will differ in their use of GCE AL/AS unit grade information, A* grades, the Extended Project (EPQ), the Advanced Diploma and the Cambridge Pre-U examination when considering applicants and making offers. An EPQ may be accepted in place of an AS subject. Check websites of universities and colleges for the latest offers information.

Biochemical Engineering – *the challenge to sixth formers in creating health and wealth from new life science discoveries*

The discovery of penicillin was a momentous achievement. It took 15 years and an international effort to find a way to produce it in the quantities needed for medical treatment and led to the birth of the discipline of biochemical engineering.

The medicines of the future – human proteins, therapeutic vaccines and human tissue for repair – are even more complex than penicillin. They address previously intractable conditions and are generating many opportunities spanning the initial discovery, to point of care. Those who are numerate and have gained engineering team and leadership skills are translating these opportunities into new medicines. It is also such people who are managing the billions of pounds of investment required and who are dealing with the social and environmental issues that all big endeavours must address.

Those seeking a professional career in a subject that is demanding, and who want a life at the cutting edge that is highly rewarded, should consider the excitement of biochemical engineering as a degree option.

Information on courses can be found in UCAS guides both under biochemical engineering and chemical engineering and more information is on the web. Visits can be arranged to explore in more detail the A level requirements, the courses and the careers available.

Your target offers and examples of courses provided by each institution

380 pts **Cambridge** – A*AA college offers may vary (Engineering) (IB 38–42 pts)
London (UCL) – AAA+AS–AAB+AS (MEng Eng Bus Fin) (IB 34–36 pts)

360 pts **Bath** – AAA (Innov Eng Des; Innov Eng Des Fr/Ger) (IB 36 pts HL maths phys 6)
Bristol – AAA–AAB (Eng Des) (IB 37–35 pts)
London (UCL) – AAB+AS (BEng Eng Bus Fin) (IB 34–36 pts)
Oxford – AAA (Eng Sci; Eng Econ Mgt) (IB 38–42 pts)

340 pts **Birmingham** – AAB–BBB (Eng Bus Mgt) (IB 32–36 pts)
Bristol – AAB (Eng Maths) (IB 36 pts)
Cardiff – AAB (MEng Integ Eng)
Durham – AAB (MEng Gen Eng) (IB 38 pts)
Exeter – AAB–ABB (MEng Eng Mgt; Eng) (IB 32–29 pts)
Liverpool – AAB (MEng Eng; Eng Prod Des) (IB 35 pts HL 555)
Loughborough – AAB (MEng Prod Des Manuf) (IB 34 pts)
Warwick – AAB (MEng Eng) (IB 35–37 pts)

320 pts **Brunel** – BBC +AS/EPQ c 320 pts (Prod Des Eng) (IB 32 pts)
Exeter – ABB–BBB (BEng Eng; Eng Mgt) (IB 32–29 pts)
Lancaster – ABB 320 pts (MEng Eng Yr in USA/Aus) (IB 30 pts)
Leicester – ABB (MEng Gen Eng; Gen Eng Ind/Euro/USA)
Reading – 320 pts (Cyber inc Fdn Yr)
Sussex – ABB–BBC (MEng Prod Des (Eng Des)) (IB 34–30 pts)
Swansea – 320–360 pts (MEng Prod Des Eng)

300 pts **Aberdeen** – BBB 300 pts 2nd yr entry (MEng Eng; Eng Sfty Rlblty Eng) (IB 24 pts)
Aston – BBB 300 pts (BSc Auto Prod Des; BEng Des Eng) (IB 31–32 pts)
Bournemouth – 300 pts (Prod Des)
Brighton – BBB (Prod Des; Spo Prod Des; Sust Prod Des Prof Expnc)
Cardiff – BBB 300 pts (BEng Integ Eng) (IB 28 pts)
Durham – BBB (BEng Gen Eng)
Liverpool – BBB (BEng Eng; Eng Prod Des) (IB 32 pts HL 555)
Nottingham – BBB (MEng Eng inc Fdn Yr) (IB 28–30 pts)
Plymouth – BBB 300 pts (MEng Robotics)
Queen's Belfast – BBB (MEng Prod Des Dev)
Strathclyde – BBB (MEng Eng; Spo Eng; Prod Des Innov; Prod Des Eng)
Ulster – 300 pts (MEng Eng; Eng Dip Ing)
Warwick – BBB–BBC (BEng Eng; Eng Bus Mgt; BSc Eng Bus St) (IB 34 pts)

280 pts **Aberdeen** – BBC 280 pts 2nd yr entry (BEng Eng)
Lancaster – BBC (BEng Eng) (IB 30 pts)
Leicester – BBC (BEng Gen Eng; Gen Eng Ind/Euro/USA) (IB 30 pts)
Liverpool John Moores – 280 pts (Ener Mgt Sust)
London (QM)/(Gold) – BBC (MEng/BEng Des Innov)
Loughborough – BBC (Prod Des Tech; Ind Des Tech; Des Eng Mgt) (IB 28–30 pts)
Nottingham Trent – 280 pts (Prod Des)
Salford – 280 pts (Pros Orthot) (IB 28 pts)
Strathclyde – BBC (Pros Orthot) (IB 32 pts)

260 pts **Aberdeen** – BCC 260 pts 1st yr entry (MEng Eng Integ Eng) (IB 32 pts)
Bristol UWE – 260–300 pts (Robotics)
London (QM) – 260–340 pts (Eng; Eng Bus Mgt; Des Innov; Sust Ener Eng; Med Eng) (IB 30–32 pts)
Loughborough – 260–300 pts (Ind Des Tech) (IB 30–32 pts)
Northumbria – 260–280 pts (Prod Des Tech; Eng Bus St)
Queen's Belfast – BCC (BEng Prod Des Dev)
Plymouth – BCC 260 pts (BEng Robotics)
Salford – 260 pts (Prod Des) (IB 26 pts)
Swansea – 260–300 pts (BEng Prod Des Eng; Prod Des Tech)
Ulster – 260 pts (BEng Eng)

240 pts **Bradford** – 240 pts (BEng Eng Mgt; Ind Eng)
Central Lancashire – 240 pts (Comp Aid Eng)
Heriot-Watt – CCC (BEng Eng)
Leicester – CCC–DDD (Gen Eng inc Fdn)
Manchester Met – 240–220 pts (Prod Des Tech) (IB 26 pts)
Plymouth – 240 pts (BSc Robotics)
Staffordshire – 240 pts (Robot Eng; Robot Tech)
Strathclyde – CCC (BEng Prod Des Eng; Prod Spo Eng; Des Innov; Eng Ent Mgt)

230 pts **Edinburgh Napier** – 230–220 pts (Eng Mgt; Prod Des Eng)

220 pts **Aberdeen** – CCD 1st yr entry (BEng Eng)
Birmingham City – 220–240 pts (Eng Prod Des)
Bristol UWE – 220–240 pts (BSc Eng)
Coventry – 220 pts (Eng Maths)
Hull – 220–260 pts (Prod Innov; Med Prod Des)
Northampton – 220–260 pts (BSc Eng)
Robert Gordon – CCD (BEng Eng) (IB 24 pts)
Staffordshire – 220–280 pts (Robot Tech; Robot Eng) (IB 26 pts)
Ulster – 220 pts (BEng Hons Eng Mgt)

200 pts **Coventry** – 200 pts (Vrtl Eng)
Glamorgan – 200–240 pts (Eng Tech Mgt)
Sheffield Hallam – 200 pts (Foren Eng)

180 pts **Cardiff (UWIC)** – BC (Prod Des)
Southampton Solent – 180 pts (Eng Bus; Prod Des)
Ulster – 180 pts (BEng Eng Mgt)

160 pts **East London** – 160–200 pts (BSc Prod Des courses)
Southampton Solent – 160 pts (Prod Des)
Wolverhampton – 160–240 pts (Eng Des Mgt)

150 pts **Anglia Ruskin** – 150 pts (Integ Eng)

140 pts **West Scotland** – CD (Eng Mgt)

120 pts **Aberdeen** – DD (BSc Eng)
London South Bank – 120–160 pts (Eng Prod Des; Prod Des Comp)
Ulster – 120 pts (Eng Integ Fdn Yr)

Leicester – contact University (Fdn Eng)
Open University – (BEng – contact +44 (0)845 300 6090 or www.openuniversity.co.uk/you)

Alternative offers

See **Chapter 7** and **Appendix 1** for grades/UCAS Tariff points information for the International Baccalaureate, Scottish Highers/Advanced Highers, the Welsh Baccalaureate, the Irish Leaving Certificate, the Cambridge Pre-U Diploma, the Advanced Diploma and the Extended Project.

EXAMPLES OF FOUNDATION DEGREES IN THE SUBJECT FIELD

Blackburn (Coll Univ Centre); Bolton; Bournemouth; Bradford (Coll); Bristol City (Coll); Central Lancashire; Colchester (Inst); De Montfort; Doncaster (Coll); Exeter (Coll); Greenwich; Harper Adams (UC); Hull (Coll); London Met; Manchester (Coll); Mid-Cheshire (Coll); Middlesex; Newcastle (Coll); Newman (UC); Newport; Northumbria; Oxford Brookes; Queen's Belfast; Sheffield Hallam; Somerset (CAT); Suffolk (Univ Campus); Tyne Met (Coll); Warwickshire (Coll); West Thames (Coll); Wolverhampton.

CHOOSING YOUR COURSE (SEE ALSO CH.1)

Some course features

Bath, Durham, Warwick All Engineering courses share the first two years, with the choice of specialisation made in Year 3.

Bristol Thirteen specialisations follow a study of core subjects.

Cardiff The first year is common to all nine Engineering programmes.

Lancaster All students follow a common first year followed by a choice from six Engineering specialisations.

London (QM)/(Gold) (MEng/BEng Des Innov) The course is run jointly by the Engineering Departments at London (QM) and the Department of Design at London (Goldsmiths). It consists of core studio practice (at QM), design context study (at Goldsmiths) and design engineering (at QM). Applications are to London (QM), via UCAS.

Universities and colleges teaching quality www.qaa.ac.uk; www.unistats.com.

Top research universities and colleges (RAE 2008) (General, Mineral and Mining Engineering) Cambridge; Oxford; Nottingham; Leeds; Imperial London; Swansea; Manchester; Surrey; Warwick.

Examples of sandwich degree courses (General courses) Aston; Bath; Bournemouth; Bradford; Bristol UWE; Brunel; Cardiff; Coventry; Leicester; London South Bank; Loughborough; Manchester Met; Northumbria; Sheffield Hallam; Ulster; Wolverhampton.

ADMISSIONS INFORMATION

Number of applicants per place (approx) Aberdeen 6; Aston 8; Bath 15; Birmingham 6; Bournemouth 5; Bristol (Eng Des) 3, (Eng Maths) 5; Brunel (Ind Des Eng) 10; Cambridge 4; Cardiff 5; City 3; Coventry 6; Durham 9; Edinburgh 5; Exeter 6; Hull 6; Lancaster 15; Leicester 10; London (UCL) 5; Loughborough 9; Manchester Met 2; Northampton 3; Robert Gordon 2; Salford (Pros Orthot) 3; Sheffield Hallam 6; Strathclyde 5; Warwick 10.

Advice to applicants and planning the UCAS personal statement Details of careers in the various engineering specialisms should be obtained from the relevant engineering institutions (see **Appendix 4**). This will enable you to describe your interests in various aspects of engineering. Contact engineers to discuss their work with them. Try to arrange a visit to an engineering firm relevant to your choice of specialism.

Selection interviews **Yes** Brunel, Cambridge, Coventry, Durham, Lancaster, Leicester, London (QM), (UCL), Loughborough, Manchester Met, Oxford, Oxford Brookes (English test for overseas students), Robert Gordon, Salford, Sheffield Hallam, Strathclyde; **Some** Bristol, Cardiff.

Interview advice and questions Since mathematics and physics are important subjects, it is probable that you will be questioned on the applications of these subjects to, for example, the transmission of electricity, nuclear power, aeronautics, mechanics etc. Past questions have included: Explain the theory of an arch; what is its function? What is the connection between distance and velocity and acceleration and velocity? How does a car ignition work? **Nottingham Trent** What is Integrated Engineering? See also separate **Engineering** tables and **Chapter 5**.

Reasons for rejection (non-academic) Made no contribution whatsoever to the project discussions during the UCAS interview. Forged reference! Poor work ethic. Lack of motivation towards the subject area. Better suited to an alternative Engineering course. Failure to attend interview. Poor interview preparation. **Salford** (Pros Orthot) Lack of sympathy with people with disabilities.

AFTER-RESULTS ADVICE

Offers to applicants repeating A-levels Higher Loughborough, Warwick; **Possibly higher** Coventry, Edinburgh, Lancaster, Manchester Met, Robert Gordon, Sheffield Hallam; **Same** Birmingham City, Brunel (good reasons needed for repeating), Cambridge, Cardiff, Derby, Durham, Exeter, Edinburgh Napier, Heriot-Watt, Hull, Liverpool, London (UCL), Nottingham Trent.

GRADUATE DESTINATIONS AND EMPLOYMENT (2007/8 HESA)

Graduates surveyed 855 **Employed** 535 **In further study** 85 **Assumed unemployed** 50.

Career note A high proportion of Engineering graduates go into industry as engineers, technicians, IT specialists or managers, irrespective of their engineering speciality. However, the transferable skills gained during their courses are also valued by employers in other sectors.

OTHER DEGREE SUBJECTS FOR CONSIDERATION

Computer Science; Materials Science; Mathematics; Physics; Technology; all branches of Engineering (see also following **Engineering** tables).

ENGINEERING (ACOUSTICS and SOUND)

(including **Audio Engineering** and **Sound Technology**; see also **Film, Radio, Video and TV Studies** and **Media Studies**)

Apart from the scientific aspect of sound, these courses also involve the measurement of sound, hearing, environmental health and legal aspects of sound and vibration. Acoustics topics are also included in some Music and Media Technology courses.

Useful websites www.ioa.org.uk; www.engc.org.uk; www.enginuity.org.uk.

NB The points totals shown to the left of the institutions are for ease of reference only. It must not be assumed that Tariff points are always used by institutions or that they can be substituted for an offer in grades. The level of an offer is not necessarily indicative of the quality of a course.

Engineering Council Statement: See **Engineering/Engineering Sciences**.

COURSE OFFERS INFORMATION

Subject requirements/preferences AL mathematics and physics usually required; music is also required for some courses. See also **Engineering/Engineering Sciences**.

NB In 2011 universities and colleges will differ in their use of GCE AL/AS unit grade information, A* grades, the Extended Project (EPQ), the Advanced Diploma and the Cambridge Pre-U examination when considering applicants and making offers. An EPQ may be accepted in place of an AS subject. Check websites of universities and colleges for the latest offers information.

Your target offers and examples of courses provided by each institution

340 pts **Glasgow** – AAB (MEng Faster Route AV Eng)
Surrey – AAB 340 pts (Mus Snd Rec (Tonmeister))
York – AAB–ABB (MEng Mus Tech Sys)
320 pts **Bournemouth** – 320 pts (Sndtrk Prod)
Glasgow – ABB (MEng AV Eng)
Southampton – ABB (MEng/BEng Acoust Eng; Acoust Mus) (IB 32–30 pts)
300 pts **Glasgow** – BBB (AV Eng)
Salford – 300 pts (MPhys Phys Acoust)
York – BBB–BBC (BEng Mus Tech Sys)
280 pts **Liverpool John Moores** – 280 pts (Aud Mus Prod)
Salford – 280 pts (Acoust; Aud Tech)
260 pts **Birmingham City** – 260–280 pts (Snd Multim Tech; Snd Eng Rec)

Bristol UWE – 260–280 pts (Aud Mus Tech)
Liverpool (LIPA) – 260 pts (Snd Tech)
London (QM) – 260 pts (Aud Sys Eng)
Salford – 260 pts (BSc Phys Acoust)

240 pts **Bolton** – 240 pts (Snd Eng Sys; Snd Eng Des)
Lincoln – 240 pts (Aud Prod)
Oxford Brookes – CCC (Snd Tech Dig Mus) (IB 29 pts)

220 pts **London Met** – 220 pts (Mus Tech (Aud Sys) (Snd Media))

200 pts **Glyndŵr** – 200 pts (Snd Broad Eng; Std Rec Perf Tech)

170 pts **Glasgow Caledonian** – 170 pts (Aud Tech Electron)

160 pts **Southampton Solent** – 160 pts (Aud Tech; Snd Eng; Liv Std Snd; Mus Std Tech; Snd Film TV Gms)

150 pts **Anglia Ruskin** – 150 pts (Aud Tech Electron)

Alternative offers
See **Chapter 7** and **Appendix 1** for grades/UCAS Tariff points information for the International Baccalaureate, Scottish Highers/Advanced Highers, the Welsh Baccalaureate, the Irish Leaving Certificate, the Cambridge Pre-U Diploma, the Advanced Diploma and the Extended Project.

EXAMPLES OF FOUNDATION DEGREES IN THE SUBJECT FIELD

Brighton; Glyndŵr; Lincoln; Ravensbourne (CDC); St Helens (Coll); Salford; Thames Valley.

CHOOSING YOUR COURSE (SEE ALSO CH.1)

Some course features
Bournemouth (Sndtrk Prod) The course combines moving images, music and audio production in a project-based practical course.
Brighton (Aud Electron) A very broad course covering electronics, engineering design and communications technology with a bias towards audio systems. The sandwich course is optional.
Salford (Acoust) Course includes electronics, computing, maths and specialist acoustic topics, for example musical acoustics, psychoacoustics and acoustics of performance spaces.
Southampton (Acoust Eng) The course involves engineering design to minimise noise and vibration, ocean acoustics and sonar and sound reproduction and musical instrument acoustics. There are 10-week industrial placements. The Acoustics and Music degree allows students to weight their studies in favour of either subject 75/25 or 25/75.
Surrey (Mus Snd Rec (Tonmeister)) This well-established course comprises three areas of study: the technical aspects of audio, practical experience of recording, and music theory and practice.

Universities and colleges teaching quality See www.qaa.ac.uk; www.unistats.com.

ADMISSIONS INFORMATION

Number of applicants per place (approx) Anglia Ruskin 5; Salford 4; Southampton 4.

Advice to applicants and planning the UCAS personal statement See **Engineering/Engineering Sciences**. See also **Appendix 4**.

Misconceptions about this course **Anglia Ruskin** Failure to appreciate the emphasis that the course gives to science and technology.

Selection interviews Salford, Southampton; **Some** Anglia Ruskin.

Interview advice and questions What interests you about Acoustics Engineering? What career do you have in mind on graduating? See also **Chapter 5**.

Reasons for rejection (non-academic) See **Engineering/Engineering Sciences**.

AFTER-RESULTS ADVICE

Offers to applicants repeating A-levels **Same** Anglia Ruskin, Salford.

GRADUATE DESTINATIONS AND EMPLOYMENT (2007/8 HESA)

No data available.

Career note Specialist topics on these courses will enable graduates to make decisions as to their future career destinations.

OTHER DEGREE SUBJECTS FOR CONSIDERATION

Audiology; Broadcast Engineering; Communications Engineering; Computer Engineering; Computer Science; Media Technology; Music; Radio and TV; Technology; Telecommunications Engineering and Electronic Engineering.

ENGINEERING (AERONAUTICAL and AEROSPACE)

Courses cover the manufacture of military and civil aircraft, theories of mechanics, thermodynamics, electronics, computing and engine design. Avionics courses include flight and energy control systems, airborne computing, navigation, optical and TV displays, airborne communications, and radar systems for navigation and power.

Useful websites www.raes.org.uk; www.engc.org.uk; www.enginuity.org.uk.

NB The points totals shown to the left of the institutions are for ease of reference only. It must not be assumed that Tariff points are always used by institutions or that they can be substituted for an offer in grades. The level of an offer is not necessarily indicative of the quality of a course.

Engineering Council statement See **Engineering/Engineering Sciences**.

COURSE OFFERS INFORMATION

Subject requirements/preferences See **Engineering/Engineering Sciences**.

NB In 2011 universities and colleges will differ in their use of GCE AL/AS unit grade information, A* grades, the Extended Project (EPQ), the Advanced Diploma and the Cambridge Pre-U examination when considering applicants and making offers. An EPQ may be accepted in place of an AS subject. Check websites of universities and colleges for the latest offers information.

Your target offers and examples of courses provided by each institution

380 pts **Cambridge** – A*AA college offers may vary (Aerosp Aeroth Eng) (IB 38–42 pts)
Imperial London – A*mathsAA (Aero Eng; Aero Eng Abrd) (IB 39 pts)

370 pts **Brunel** – ABB +AS/EPQ b 370 pts (MEng Avn Eng; Avn Eng Plt St; Aerosp Eng; Mech Eng Aero) (IB 34 pts)

360 pts **Bath** – AAA (Aerosp Eng; Aerosp Eng Fr; Aerosp Eng Ger) (IB 36 pts HL maths phys 6)
Bristol – AAA–AAB (Aero Eng; Aero Eng Euro) (IB 36 pts)
Imperial London – AAA (Aerosp Mat) (IB 36 pts)
Loughborough – AAA (MEng Aero Eng) (IB 36 pts)
Southampton – AAA (MEng/BEng Aero Astnaut; Aero Astnaut (Eng Mgt) (Spcrft Eng) (Advncd Mats); Spc Sys Eng) (IB 36 pts)

340 pts **Glasgow** – AAB (MEng Faster Route Aerosp Sys)
Leeds – AAB (MEng/BEng Aero Aerosp Eng; Avn Tech Mgt; Avn Tech Plt St) (MEng IB 36 pts HL 17 pts)
Liverpool – AAB (MEng Aerosp Eng; Aerosp Eng Plt St; Avion Sys; Avion Sys Plt St) (IB 34 pts)
Manchester – AAB (MEng Aerosp Eng; Aerosp Eng Ind; Aerosp Eng Mgt) (IB 35–33 pts)
Sheffield – AAB (MEng Aerosp Eng; Aerosp Eng PPI; Aerosp Eng Ind N Am; Aerosp Mats) (IB 32 pts HL maths phys 6)
Strathclyde – AAB (MEng Aero Mech Eng; Mech Eng Aero) (IB 32 pts)
Surrey – AAB 340 pts (Aerosp Eng) (IB 30 pts)
York – AAB–ABB (MEng Avionics) (IB 34 pts)

320 pts **Brunel** – BBC +AS/EPQ c 320 pts (BEng Avn Eng; Avn Eng Plt St; Aerosp Eng) (IB 32 pts)
City – 320 pts (MEng Aero Eng; Air Trans Eng) (IB 30 pts)
Glasgow – ABB (MEng Aerosp Sys)
Hertfordshire – 320 pts (MEng Aerosp Eng; Aerosp Sys Eng Plt St; Aerosp Sys Eng) (IB 30 pts)
Leicester – ABB (MEng Aerosp Eng)
Manchester – ABB (BEng Aerosp Eng) (IB 35–33 pts)
Queen's Belfast – ABB–BBB (MEng Aero Eng)
Sheffield – ABB 320 pts (BEng Aerosp Eng; Aerosp Mat; Aerosp Eng PPI; Aerosp Eng Ind) (IB 31 pts)
Swansea – 320–380 pts (MEng Aerosp Eng; Aerosp Eng Prplsn)

300 pts **Glasgow** – BBB 300 pts (BEng Aero Sys)
Kingston – 300 pts (MEng Aerosp Eng; Aerosp Eng Astnaut Spc Tech) (IB 30 pts)
Liverpool – BBB–BBC (BEng Aerosp Eng courses; Avion Sys Plt St; Avion Sys) (IB 32 pts)
London (QM) – 300–340 pts (MEng Aerosp Eng; Avion Spc Sys) (IB 30–32 pts)
Loughborough – BBB (BEng Aero Eng) (IB 30 pts)
Salford – 300 pts (MEng Aero Eng) (IB 27–32 pts)
Strathclyde – BBB (BEng Aero Mech Eng; Mech Eng Aero)
Surrey – BBB 300 pts (BEng Aerosp Eng) (IB 30 pts)
York – BBB–BBC (BEng Avionics) (IB 31 pts)

280 pts **Bristol UWE** – 280–300 pts (Aerosp Sys Eng; Aerosp Des Eng; Aerosp Manuf Eng)
City – 280 pts (BEng Air Trans Eng; Aero Eng; Air Trans Ops) (IB 28–30 pts HL maths 6)
Glasgow – BBC (Aero Eng)
Leicester – BBC (BEng Aerosp Eng)
Queen's Belfast – BBC–BCC (BEng Aero Eng)

260 pts **Brighton** – 260–280 pts (MEng Aero Eng)
Coventry – 260 pts (Aerosp Sys Eng; Avn Tech; Avn Mgt)
Glamorgan – 260–300 pts (Aero Eng Sys Avion)
Hertfordshire – 260 pts (BEng Aerosp Eng; Aerosp Sys Eng Plt St; Aerosp Sys Eng)
London (QM) – 260–340 pts (BEng Aerosp Eng Avn; Avion Spc Sys) (IB 30–32 pts)
Salford – 260 pts (BEng Aero Eng; Aircft Eng Plt St; Phys Plt St)
Swansea – 260–300 pts (BEng Aerosp Eng; Aerosp Eng Prplsn)

240 pts **Bristol UWE** – 240–260 pts (BEng Aerosp Sys Eng; Aerosp Des Eng; Aerosp Manuf Eng)
City – 240 pts (BSc Air Trans Ops Mgt)
Glamorgan – 240–300 pts (Aero Eng)
Kingston – 240 pts (Aerosp Eng Astnaut Spc Tech; Aerosp Eng)
London Met – 240 pts (Avn Mgt)
Staffordshire – 240 (Aero Tech) (IB 26 pts)

220 pts **Birmingham City** – 220–240 pts (Aero Prod Dev)
Salford – 220 pts (Avn Tech Plt St)

200 pts **Coventry** – 200 pts (Aerosp Tech; Avn Mgt; Avn Tech)
Glamorgan – 200–260 pts (Aircrft Mntnc Eng)
Glyndŵr – 200 pts (Aero Electron Eng (Avion); Aero Mech Eng)
Hertfordshire – 200 pts (Aerosp Tech Mgt; Aerosp Tech Plt St) (IB 24–26 pts)

160 pts **Kingston** – 160 pts (BSc Aerosp Eng)
Salford – 160 pts (Avn Tech Plt St; Aerosp Bus Sys)

80 pts **Farnborough (CT)** – 80–160 pts (Aero Eng)
Kingston – 80 pts (Aircrft Eng Fdn)
UHI Millennium Inst (PC) – 80 pts (Aircrft Eng)

Alternative offers

See **Chapter 7** and **Appendix 1** for grades/UCAS Tariff points information for the International Baccalaureate, Scottish Highers/Advanced Highers, the Welsh Baccalaureate, the Irish Leaving Certificate, the Cambridge Pre-U Diploma, the Advanced Diploma and the Extended Project.

EXAMPLES OF FOUNDATION DEGREES IN THE SUBJECT FIELD

Bristol UWE; Bristol City (Coll); Farnborough (CT); Glyndŵr; Hertfordshire; Kingston; London Met; Sheffield Hallam.

CHOOSING YOUR COURSE (SEE ALSO CH.1)

Some course features

Bath All courses have sandwich placements.
Brunel, **Hertfordshire**, **Liverpool**, **Sheffield** Pilot Studies available in some Aeronautical or Aerospace Engineering courses.
Durham A common course for Years 1 and 2 and then two years specialising in the chosen discipline.
Imperial London Fourth year students may take the European option spending four months research in universities in France or Germany.
Loughborough The first two years are common for all BEng and MEng students allowing the former to transfer to the MEng course at the end of the second year.
Manchester A year out in industry or in Europe are options.
Swansea Aerospace Engineering can be combined with a study of aircraft and spacecraft propulsion systems.
York All Electronics courses have a common first year with specialisation following in Avionics in Year 2 or allowing students to transfer to one of eight Electronics courses.

Universities and colleges teaching quality See www.qaa.ac.uk; www.unistats.com.

Top research universities and colleges (RAE 2008) See **Engineering (Mechanical)**.

Examples of sandwich degree courses Bath; Brighton; Bristol UWE; Brunel; City; Coventry; Glamorgan; Hertfordshire; Kingston; Liverpool; London (QM); Loughborough; Manchester; Queen's Belfast; Salford; Staffordshire; Surrey.

ADMISSIONS INFORMATION

Number of applicants per place (approx) Bath 13, (MEng) 18; Bristol 11; Bristol UWE 4; City 17; Coventry 7; Farnborough (CT) 7; Glyndŵr 5; Hertfordshire 17; Imperial London 7; Kingston 9; London (QM) 8; Loughborough 10; Queen's Belfast 6; Salford 6; Southampton 10; York 3 ave.

Advice to applicants and planning the UCAS personal statement Interest in engineering and aerospace. Work experience in engineering. Flying experience. Personal attainments. Relevant hobbies. Membership of Air Training Corps. See also **Engineering/Engineering Sciences** and **Appendix 2**.

Misconceptions about this course That Aeronautical Engineering is not a highly analytical subject: it is.

Selection interviews **Yes** Bristol, Cambridge, Farnborough (CT), Hertfordshire, Imperial London, Kingston, London (QM), Loughborough, Salford, Southampton.

Interview advice and questions Why Aeronautical Engineering? Questions about different types of aircraft and flight principles of helicopters. Range of interests in engineering. **Imperial London** Deferred entry acceptable. See also **Chapter 5**.

Reasons for rejection (non-academic) See **Engineering/Engineering Sciences**.

AFTER-RESULTS ADVICE

Offers to applicants repeating A-levels **Higher** Bristol, Queen's Belfast; **Possibly higher** Hertfordshire; **Same** Bath, City, Farnborough (CT), Kingston, Liverpool, Loughborough, Salford, Southampton, York; **No offers made** Cambridge.

GRADUATE DESTINATIONS AND EMPLOYMENT (2007/8 HESA)

Graduates surveyed 720 **Employed** 395 **In further study** 110 **Assumed unemployed** 80.

Career note Specialist areas of study on these courses will open up possible career directions. See also Engineering/Engineering Sciences.

OTHER DEGREE SUBJECTS FOR CONSIDERATION

Astronomy; Astrophysics; Computer Science; Electronics and Systems Engineering; Materials Science; Mathematics; Naval Architecture; Physics.

ENGINEERING (CHEMICAL)

(Including **Fire Engineering** and **Fire Safety**)

Courses cover chemistry, microbiology, physics and mathematics. Management, economics, process dynamics, process design and safety are introduced in Years 2 and 3.

Useful websites www.icheme.org; www.engc.org.uk; www.enginuity.org.uk; www.whynotchemeng.com.

NB The points totals shown to the left of the institutions are for ease of reference only. It must not be assumed that Tariff points are always used by institutions or that they can be substituted for an offer in grades. The level of an offer is not necessarily indicative of the quality of a course.

Engineering Council Statement See **Engineering/Engineering Sciences**.

COURSE OFFERS INFORMATION

Subject requirements/preferences **AL** Mathematics and chemistry required. See also **Engineering/Engineering Sciences**.

NB In 2011 universities and colleges will differ in their use of GCE AL/AS unit grade information, A* grades, the Extended Project (EPQ), the Advanced Diploma and the Cambridge Pre-U examination when considering applicants and making offers. An EPQ may be accepted in place of an AS subject. Check websites of universities and colleges for the latest offers information.

Your target offers and examples of courses provided by each institution

380 pts **Cambridge** – A*AA college offers may vary (Chem Eng 2nd yr entry only via Eng or Nat Sci) (IB 38–42 pts HL 766–777)

Imperial London – A*mathsAA (Chem Eng; Chem Eng Yr Abrd; Chem Nucl Eng) (IB 39 pts H maths chem phys 6 pts)

360 pts **Edinburgh** – AAA 2nd yr entry (Chem Eng; Chem Eng Env Eng; Chem Eng Mgt; Struct Fire Sfty Eng) (IB 36 pts)

Oxford – AAA (Eng Sci (Chem Eng)) (IB 38–40 pts)

340 pts **Aston** – AAB (MEng Chem Eng; Chem Eng App Chem) (IB 32 pts)

Bath – AAB (MEng Chem Eng; Bioch Eng) (IB 36 pts HL maths chem 6)

Birmingham – AAB (Chem Eng; Chem Eng Bus Mgt; Chem Eng Int St; Chem Ener Eng) (IB 32–34 pts)

Heriot-Watt – AAB 2nd yr entry (Brew Distil)

Leeds – AAB (Petrol Eng; Chem Eng; Chem Ener Eng; Chem Mat Eng; Chem Nucl Eng; Chem Pharml Eng) (IB 36 pts HL 17 pts)

London (UCL) – ABB+AS (Chem Eng courses; Chem Bioch Eng) (IB 36 pts)

Loughborough – 340 pts (Chem Eng; Chem Eng Mgt) (IB 36 pts HL maths, phys chem 17 pts)

Manchester – AAB (Chem Eng; Chem Eng Biotech; Chem Eng Env Tech; Chem Eng (Bus Mgt); Petrol Eng) (IB 35 pts)

Newcastle – AAB–ABB (MEng Chem Eng; Mat Proc Eng; Bioproc Eng) (IB 36 pts HL chem maths 5)

320 pts **Bath** – ABB (BEng Chem Eng; Chem Bioproc Eng) (IB 34 pts HL maths chem 6)

Edinburgh – ABB 1st yr entry (Chem Eng; Chem Eng Env Eng; Chem Eng Mgt; Struct Fire Sfty Eng) (IB 34 pts)

Lancaster – ABB 320 pts (Nucl Eng) (IB 30 pts)

Leeds – ABB (Chem Eng; Chem Eng Ener; Chem Eng Mat; Chem Eng Min; Chem Eng Pharml)

Loughborough – 320 pts (BEng Chem Eng; Chem Eng Env Prot; Chem Eng Mgt) (IB 34 pts)
Nottingham – ABB–BBB (MEng/BEng Chem Eng; Chem Eng Env Eng) (IB 32 pts)
Sheffield – ABB–BBB (Chem Eng Fuel Tech; Chem Eng Lang; Chem Eng Mgt) (IB 32–33 pts)
Strathclyde – ABB (MEng Chem Eng; App Chem Chem Eng) (IB 34 pts)
Surrey – ABB (Chem Eng) (IB 32 pts)

300 pts **Aberdeen** – BBB 300 pts 2nd yr entry (MEng Chem Eng)
Aston – BBB (BEng Chem Eng; Chem Eng App Chem)
Heriot-Watt – BBB 1st yr entry (Brew Distil)
Newcastle – BBB (BEng Chem Eng; Biopharml Tech; Mat Proc Eng) (IB 30 pts HL chem maths 5)
Queen's Belfast – BBB (MEng Chem Eng)
Strathclyde – BBB (BEng Chem Eng; App Chem Chem Eng) (IB 31 pts)
Surrey – BBB (Chem Eng; Chem Eng inc Fdn Yr) (IB 30 pts)
Swansea – 300 pts (MEng Chem Bioproc Eng)

280 pts **Aberdeen** – BBC 280 pts 2nd yr entry (BEng Chem Eng)
Central Lancashire – 280 pts (Fire Ldrshp St)
Heriot-Watt – BBC 2nd yr entry (Chem Eng; Chem Eng Ener Eng; Chem Eng Oil Gas Tech; Chem Eng Pharml Chem)
Teesside – 280 pts (Chem Eng) (IB 30 pts)

270 pts **Glasgow Caledonian** – 270 pts (Fire Risk Eng)

260 pts **Aberdeen** – BCC 260 pts 1st yr entry (MEng Chem Eng)
Central Lancashire – 260 pts (Fire Eng) (IB 28 pts)
Queen's Belfast – BCC (BEng Chem Eng)
Swansea – 260 pts (BEng Chem Bioproc Eng)

240 pts **Edinburgh Napier** – 240 pts (Poly Eng)
Newport – 240 pts (Fire Sfty Eng)

220 pts **Aberdeen** – CCD 220 pts 1st yr entry (BEng Chem Eng)
Heriot-Watt – CCD 1st yr entry (Chem Eng; Chem Eng Pharml Chem; Chem Eng Ener Eng; Chem Eng Oil Gas Tech) (IB 27 pts)
Huddersfield – 220 pts (Chem Chem Eng)
London South Bank – 220 pts (Chem Proc Eng; Petrol Eng) (IB 24 pts)

200 pts **London Met** – 200 pts (Poly Eng) (IB 28 pts)

160 pts **Central Lancashire** – 160 pts (Fire Sfty Risk Mgt)
Swansea – 160 pts (Chem Bioproc Eng Fdn)

140 pts **West Scotland** – CD (BSc Chem Eng)

Alternative offers

See **Chapter 7** and **Appendix 1** for grades/UCAS Tariff points information for the International Baccalaureate, Scottish Highers/Advanced Highers, the Welsh Baccalaureate, the Irish Leaving Certificate, the Cambridge Pre-U Diploma, the Advanced Diploma and the Extended Project.

EXAMPLES OF FOUNDATION DEGREES IN THE SUBJECT FIELD

Cumbria; Lakes (Coll).

CHOOSING YOUR COURSE (SEE ALSO CH.1)

Some course features

Aberdeen Close contacts with the oil and gas industries.
Birmingham One third of the course with Business Management is devoted to management subjects.
Heriot-Watt Direct entry to Year 2 depending on A-level results. Courses have a common structure up to Year 3 allowing for a change in specialisation.
London (UCL) The MEng course leads directly to Chartered Engineer status. Students taking the BEng course will need to complete a period of further training to achieve this.
Newcastle Stages 1 and 2 are common for all nine courses in the department.
Nottingham Mining can be combined with Chemical Engineering.

Universities and colleges teaching quality See www.qaa.ac.uk; www.unistats.com.

Top universities and colleges (Research) Cambridge; Imperial London; Manchester; London (UCL); Birmingham; Sheffield; Newcastle; Bath.

Examples of sandwich degree courses Aston; Bath; London South Bank; Loughborough; Manchester; Queen's Belfast; Surrey; Teesside.

ADMISSIONS INFORMATION

Number of applicants per place (approx) Aston 4; Bath 8; Birmingham 8; Heriot-Watt 8; Huddersfield 7; Imperial London 4, (MEng) 4; Leeds 9; London (UCL) 8; Loughborough 7; Newcastle (MEng/BEng) 6; Nottingham 6; Sheffield 14; Strathclyde 6; Surrey 5; Swansea 3.

Misconceptions about this course **Surrey** That chemical engineering is chemistry on a large scale: physics is as applicable as chemistry.

Selection interviews **Yes** Bath, Cambridge, Imperial London, Leeds, London (UCL), London South Bank, Newcastle, Nottingham, Oxford, Surrey, Sussex, Teesside; **Some** Loughborough.

Interview advice and questions Past questions have included the following: How would you justify the processing of radioactive waste to people living in the neighbourhood? What is public health engineering? What is biochemical engineering? What could be the sources of fuel and energy in the year 2020? Discuss some industrial applications of chemistry. Regular incidents occur in which chemical spillage and other problems affect the environment. Be prepared to discuss these social issues. **Imperial London** Interviews can be conducted in South East Asia if necessary. See also **Chapter 5**.

Reasons for rejection (non-academic) See **Engineering/Engineering Sciences**.

AFTER-RESULTS ADVICE

Offers to applicants repeating A-levels **Higher** Swansea; **Possibly higher** Bath, Leeds, London South Bank, Queen's Belfast; **Same** Aston, Birmingham, Cambridge, Loughborough, Newcastle, Nottingham, Sheffield, Surrey, Teesside.

GRADUATE DESTINATIONS AND EMPLOYMENT (2007/8 HESA)

Graduates surveyed 430 **Employed** 260 **In further study** 75 **Assumed unemployed** 45.

Career note Chemical engineering is involved in many aspects of industry and scientific development. In addition to the oil and chemical-based industries, graduates enter a wide range of careers including the design and construction of chemical process plants, food production, pollution control, environmental protection, energy conservation, waste recovery and recycling, medical science, health and safety, and alternative energy sources.

OTHER DEGREE SUBJECTS FOR CONSIDERATION

Biochemistry; Biotechnology; Chemistry; Colour Chemistry; Cosmetic Science; Environmental Science; Food Science and Technology; Materials Science; Mathematics; Nuclear Engineering; Physics.

ENGINEERING (CIVIL)

(including **Architectural, Coastal, Disaster Management, Environmental, Offshore, Structural** and **Transportation Engineering**; see also **Building and Construction**)

Civil engineering is concerned with the science and art of large-scale projects. This involves the planning, design, construction, maintenance and environmental assessment of roads, railways, bridges, airports, tunnels, docks, offshore structures, dams, high rise buildings and other major works. Specialist courses may also involve water, drainage, irrigation schemes and waste engineering, traffic and coastal engineering.

Useful websites www.ice.org.uk; www.engc.org.uk; www.enginuity.org.uk.

NB The points totals shown to the left of the institutions are for ease of reference only. It must not be assumed that Tariff points are always used by institutions or that they can be substituted for an offer in grades. The level of an offer is not necessarily indicative of the quality of a course.

Engineering Council statement See **Engineering/Engineering Sciences**.

COURSE OFFERS INFORMATION

Subject requirements/preferences See **Engineering/Engineering Sciences**.

NB In 2011 universities and colleges will differ in their use of GCE AL/AS unit grade information, A* grades, the Extended Project (EPQ), the Advanced Diploma and the Cambridge Pre-U examination when considering applicants and making offers. An EPQ may be accepted in place of an AS subject. Check websites of universities and colleges for the latest offers information.

Your target offers and examples of courses provided by each institution

380 pts **Cambridge** – A*AA college offers may vary (Eng (Part II specialism Civ Eng)) (IB 38–42 pts)
Imperial London – A*mathsAA (Civ Eng; Civ Eng Yr Abrd) (IB 38 pts)
London (UCL) – AAA+AS (MEng/BEng Civ Eng) (IB 38 pts)

370 pts **Brunel** – ABB +AS/EPQ b 370 pts (MEng Mech Eng Bld Serv; Civ Eng Sust)

360 pts **Bath** – AAA (Civ Archit Eng; Civ Eng) (IB 36 pts HL maths 6)
Birmingham – AAA–AAB (Civ Eng; Civ Eng Ind; Civ Ener Eng; Civ Eng Bus Mgt) (IB 30–34 pts)
Bristol – AAA (Civ Eng; Civ Eng Euro) (IB 37 pts HL 666)
Edinburgh – AAA 2nd yr entry (MEng/BEng Civ Eng; Civ Eng Constr Mgt; Civ Env Eng) (IB 36 pts)
Newcastle – AAA (MEng Civ Eng; Civ Struct Eng) (IB 36 pts HL maths 5)
Oxford – AAA (Civ Eng) (IB 38–40 pts)
Sheffield – AAA (Struct Eng Archit) (IB 37–32 pts)
Southampton – AAA (Civ Eng; Civ Eng Archit) (IB 36 pts)

340 pts **Cardiff** – AAB (MEng Civ Eng; Civ Env Eng; Archit Eng) (IB 30 pts)
Durham – AAB (MEng Civ Eng) (IB 36 pts)
Glasgow – AAB–ABB (MEng Civ Eng; Civ Eng Archit)
Heriot-Watt – AAB 340 pts 2nd yr entry (MEng/BEng Civ Eng; Civ Eng Struct Eng; Civ Env Eng) (IB 35 pts)
Leeds – AAB (MEng Civ Struct Eng; Civ Env Eng; Civ Eng Constr Mgt; Archit Eng) (IB 36 pts HL 17 pts)
Loughborough – AAB (MEng Civ Eng) (IB 34 pts)
Manchester – AAB (MEng Civ Eng; Civ Struct Eng; Civ Eng (Ent); Civ Eng N Am) (IB 35–33 pts)
Nottingham – AAB–ABB (MEng Civ Eng; Civ Eng Fr/Ger; Civ Env Eng) (IB 36 pts)
Sheffield – AAB (Civ Eng; Civ Struct Eng; Civ Eng Modn Lang; Civ Eng Bus Mgt; Struct Eng; Struct Eng Archit St) (IB 32–33 pts)
Strathclyde – AAB (MEng Archit Eng; Civ Eng; Civ Eng Env Eng) (IB 36 pts)
Warwick – AAB (MEng Civ Eng; Civ Eng Fl Dynmcs; Civ Eng Bus Mgt; Civ Eng Sust) (IB 34–36 pts)

320 pts **Brunel** – BBC +AS/EPQ c 320 pts (BEng Mech Eng Bld Serv) (IB 32 pts)
City – 320 pts (MEng Civ Eng Surv; Civ Eng Archit; Civ Eng) (IB 30–32 pts)
Dundee – ABB 2nd yr entry (MEng Civ Eng Mgt)
Edinburgh – ABB 1st yr entry (MEng/BEng Civ Eng; Civ Eng Constr Mgt; Civ Env Eng)
Exeter – ABB–BBB (Civ Eng; Civ Env Eng) (IB 29–30 pts)
Liverpool – ABB (MEng Civ Eng; Civ Struct Eng) (IB 35 pts)
Loughborough – ABB (BEng Civ Eng) (IB 34 pts)
Manchester – ABB (BEng Civ Eng) (IB 34 pts)
Nottingham – ABB–BBB (Env Eng)

Queen's Belfast – ABB (MEng Civ Eng; Env Civ Eng; Struct Eng Archit)
Strathclyde – ABB (MEng Civ Eng; Archit Eng)
Surrey – ABB 320 pts (MEng Civ Eng)
Swansea – 320 pts (MEng Civ Eng)

300 pts **Aberdeen** – BBB 2nd yr entry (MEng Civ Eng; Civ Struct Eng; Civ Env Eng; Off Eng) (IB 24 pts)
Anglia Ruskin – 300 pts (MEng Civ Eng)
Birmingham – BBB (Civ Eng inc Fdn Yr) (IB 28 pts)
Bradford – 300 pts (MEng Civ Struct Eng) (IB 28–32 pts)
Brunel – BCC +AS/EPQ c 300 pts (BEng Civ Eng Sust) (IB 28 pts)
Dundee – BBB 2nd yr entry (BEng Civ Eng; Civ Eng Mgt)
Durham – BBB (BEng Civ Eng)
Edinburgh Napier – BBB 300 pts (MEng Civ Trans Eng; Civ Eng)
Glasgow – BBB (BEng Civ Eng; Civ Eng Archit) (IB 28 pts)
Liverpool – BBB (BEng Civ Eng)
Newcastle – BBB (BEng Civ Eng; Civ Struct Eng; MEng Off Eng) (IB 32 pts HL maths 5)
Nottingham – ABC–BBC (BEng Civ Eng; Civ Eng Fr/Ger; Civ Struct Eng) (IB 32 pts)
Plymouth – 300 pts (MEng Civ Eng; Civ Cstl Eng)
Portsmouth – 300 pts (MEng Civ Eng)
Salford – 300 pts (MEng Civ Eng; Civ Archit Eng) (IB 35 pts)
Sheffield – BBB (Civ Struct Eng inc Fdn Yr)
Southampton – BBB (Eng inc Fdn Yr (Civ Eng))
Strathclyde – BBB (BEng Archit Eng; Civ Eng; Civ Eng Env Eng) (IB 32 pts)
Surrey – BBB 300 pts (BEng Civ Eng)
Warwick – BBB (BEng Civ Eng; Civ Eng (Bus Mgt) (Eng Sust)) (IB 34 pts)

280 pts **Aberdeen** – BBC 280 pts 2nd yr entry (BEng Civ Env Eng; Civ Struct Eng; Civ Eng; Civ Eng Mgt)
Brighton – BBC/ABC (MEng Civ Eng; BEng Civ Env Eng) (IB 32 pts)
City – 280 pts (BEng Civ Eng Surv; Civ Eng Archit) (IB 28 pts)
Heriot-Watt – BBC 1st yr entry (Civ Eng; Civ Eng Struct Eng; Civ Env Eng) (IB 29 pts)
Loughborough – 280 pts (Archit Eng Des Mgt) IB 30 pts)
Queen's Belfast – BBC (BEng Civ Eng)
Swansea – 280 pts (BEng Civ Eng)
Teesside – 280 pts (BEng Civ Eng; Civ Eng Disas Mgt) (IB 30 pts)

270 pts **Glasgow Caledonian** – 270 pts (Env Civ Eng; Fire Risk Eng)
Liverpool John Moores – 270 pts (MEng Civ Eng)

260 pts **Aberdeen** – BCC 260 pts 1st yr entry (MEng Civ Env Eng; Civ Struct Eng)
Brighton – BCC 260 pts (BEng Civ Eng) (IB 28 pts)
Bristol UWE – 260–300 pts (Rvr Cstl Eng)
Coventry – 260 pts (BEng Civ Eng; Civ Struct Eng; Civ Eng Mgt)
Dundee – BCC 1st yr entry (MEng Civ Eng Mgt)
Liverpool – BCC–BBB (Civ Eng inc Fdn)
Nottingham Trent – 260 pts (BEng Civ Eng) (IB 28 pts)
Plymouth – 260 pts (BEng Civ Eng)
Salford – 260 pts (BEng Civ Eng; Civ Archit Eng)
Ulster – BCC 260 pts (BEng Civ Eng; Env Eng) (IB 24 pts)

240 pts **Bolton** – 240 pts (Civ Eng)
Bradford – 240 pts (BEng Civ Struct Eng) (IB 26 pts)
Dundee – CCC 1st yr entry (BEng Civ Eng; Civ Eng Mgt)
Edinburgh Napier – 240 pts (BEng Civ Trans Eng; Civ Eng)
Glamorgan – 240–300 pts (BEng Civ Eng)
Greenwich – 240 pts (BEng Civ Eng; Civ Eng Proj Mgt; Civ Eng Wtr Env Mgt)
Kingston – 240 pts (BEng Civ Eng)
London South Bank – 240 pts (BEng Civ Eng) (IB 24 pts)
Newport – 240 pts (Civ Constr Eng)
Portsmouth – 240 pts (BEng Civ Eng)

225 pts **East London** – 225 pts (BEng Civ Eng) (IB 26 pts)
220 pts **Aberdeen** – CCD 220 pts 1st yr entry (BEng Civ Eng; Civ Struct Eng; Civ Env Eng; Civ Eng Mgt) (IB 22 pts)
Bristol UWE – 220–260 pts (BSc Civ Eng) (IB 24–28 pts)
Coventry – 220 pts (Civ Eng Constr; Civ Eng Des)
Edinburgh Napier – 220 pts (BSc Civ Eng; Civ Tmbr Eng)
Ulster – 220 pts (BSc Civ Eng (Tech Ops))
Wolverhampton – 220 pts (Civ Eng)
200 pts **Abertay Dundee** – CDD 200 pts (Civ Eng) (IB 26 pts)
Anglia Ruskin – 200 pts (BSc Civ Eng) (IB 26 pts)
East London – 200 pts (Civ Eng Surv)
Glamorgan – 200–240 pts (BSc Civ Eng; Civ Eng Int St)
Leeds Met – 200 pts (Civ Eng)
Nottingham Trent – 200 pts (BSc Civ Eng St) (IB 24 pts)
180 pts **Greenwich** – 180 pts (BSc Civ Eng)
Plymouth – 180 pts (BSc Civ Eng; Civ Cstl Eng)
160 pts **Kingston** – 160 pts (BSc Civ Eng) (IB 24 pts)
Swansea – 160–260 pts (Civ Eng inc Fdn Yr)
Swansea Met – 160 pts (Civ Eng Env Mgt; Constr Mgt)
West Scotland – CC–CD (Civ Eng)
140 pts **Robert Gordon** – CD (Constr Des Mgt (Civ Eng)) (IB 24 pts)
120 pts **Aberdeen** – DD 120 pts (BSc Eng (Civ Eng))
Bradford – 120–180 pts (Civ Struct Eng inc Fdn Yr)
Kingston – 120 pts (BSc Civ Eng)
London South Bank – 120 pts (BSc Civ Eng) (IB 24 pts)
80 pts **Bolton** – 80 pts (Civ Eng inc Fdn Yr)
Salford – 80 pts (Civ Eng inc Fdn Yr)
40 pts **East London** – 40 pts (Civ Eng Ext)

Alternative offers
See **Chapter 7** and **Appendix 1** for grades/UCAS Tariff points information for the International Baccalaureate, Scottish Highers/Advanced Highers, the Welsh Baccalaureate, the Irish Leaving Certificate, the Cambridge Pre-U Diploma, the Advanced Diploma and the Extended Project.

EXAMPLES OF FOUNDATION DEGREES IN THE SUBJECT FIELD

Bedfordshire; Blackburn (Coll Univ Centre); Bolton; Bristol UWE; Derby; Glamorgan; Kent; Kingston; Northampton; Nottingham Trent; Somerset (CAT); Suffolk (Univ Campus); Swansea Met.

CHOOSING YOUR COURSE (SEE ALSO CH.1)

Some course features
Cardiff The first year is common to all nine Engineering programmes.
Durham A common course for Years 1 and 2 and then two years specialising in the chosen discipline.
Exeter A multidisciplinary first year before specialising in Year 2.
Liverpool John Moores Projects include highways, railways, airports, flood control and sports stadia.
Portsmouth Opportunities for language study and vacation training in France, Germany and Spain.
Southampton Options to take a year in industry or Europe.

Universities and colleges teaching quality See www.qaa.ac.uk; www.unistats.com.

Top research universities and colleges (RAE 2008) Imperial London; Swansea; Cardiff; Nottingham; Newcastle; Southampton; Sheffield; Bristol; Dundee.

Examples of sandwich degree courses Bath; Bradford; Brighton; Cardiff; City; Coventry; East London; Glamorgan; Kingston; London South Bank; Loughborough; Nottingham Trent; Portsmouth; Queen's Belfast; Salford; Southampton; Surrey; Teesside; Ulster; West Scotland.

ADMISSIONS INFORMATION

Number of applicants per place (approx) Abertay Dundee 8; Bath 13; Birmingham 6; Bradford (BEng) 5; Bristol 10; Brunel 4; Cardiff 5; City 11; Coventry 10, (Civ Eng) 11; Dundee 5; Durham 8; Edinburgh Napier 4; Glamorgan 6; Glasgow Caledonian 4; Greenwich 11; Heriot-Watt 7; Imperial London 4; Kingston 8; Leeds 10; Liverpool John Moores 16; London (UCL) 5; London South Bank 5; Loughborough 6; Newcastle 11, (Off Eng) 9; Nottingham 6; Nottingham Trent 11; Plymouth 3; Portsmouth 3; Queen's Belfast 6; Salford 5; Sheffield 7; Southampton 8; Strathclyde 4; Surrey 5; Swansea 3; Teesside 6; West Scotland 4; Wolverhampton 3.

Advice to applicants and planning the UCAS personal statement See **Engineering/Engineering Sciences**. Also read the magazine *The New Civil Engineer* and discuss articles which interest you on your application. See also **Appendix 4**.

Selection interviews **Yes** Bath, Brighton, Bristol, Brunel, Cambridge, Coventry, Durham, Edinburgh Napier, Glamorgan, Greenwich, Heriot-Watt, Imperial London, Kingston, Leeds, London (UCL), London South Bank, Loughborough, Newcastle, Nottingham, Oxford, Queen's Belfast, Southampton, Surrey, Sussex, Warwick; **Some** Abertay Dundee, Anglia Ruskin, Cardiff, Dundee, Nottingham Trent, Salford.

Interview advice and questions Past questions have included: Why have you chosen Civil Engineering? Have you contacted the Institution of Civil Engineers/Institution of Structural Engineers? How would you define the difference between the work of a civil engineer and the work of an architect? What would happen to a concrete beam if a load were applied? Where would it break and how could it be strengthened? The favourite question: Why do you want to be a civil engineer? What would you do if you were asked to build a concrete boat? Do you know any civil engineers? What problems were faced in building the Channel Tunnel? **Cambridge** Why did they make mill chimneys so tall? See also **Chapter 5**.

Reasons for rejection (non-academic) Lack of vitality. Lack of interest in buildings, the built environment or in civil engineering. Poor communication skills. See also **Engineering/Engineering Sciences**.

AFTER-RESULTS ADVICE

Offers to applicants repeating A-levels **Higher** East London, Kingston, Liverpool John Moores, Nottingham, Queen's Belfast, Teesside, Warwick; **Possibly higher** Portsmouth, Southampton; **Same** Abertay Dundee, Bath, Birmingham, Bradford, Brighton, Bristol, Cardiff, City, Coventry, Dundee, Durham, Greenwich, Heriot-Watt, Leeds, London (UCL), London South Bank, Loughborough, Newcastle, Nottingham Trent, Salford, Sheffield, Wolverhampton; **No offers made** Cambridge.

GRADUATE DESTINATIONS AND EMPLOYMENT (2007/8 HESA)

Graduates surveyed 1520 **Employed** 1020 **In further study** 130 **Assumed unemployed** 115.

Career note The many aspects of this subject will provide career directions for graduates with many openings with local authorities and commercial organisations.

OTHER DEGREE SUBJECTS FOR CONSIDERATION

Architecture; Building; Surveying; Town and Country Planning.

ENGINEERING (COMMUNICATIONS)

(Including **Mobile Communications**; see also **Engineering (Computer, Control, Software and Systems)** and **Engineering (Electrical and Electronic)**)

Communications Engineering impacts on many aspects of the engineering and business world. Courses overlap considerably with Electronic, Computer, Digital, Media and Internet Engineering and provide graduates with expertise in such fields as telecommunications, mobile communications and microwave engineering, optoelectronics, radio engineering and internet technology. Sandwich courses and sponsorships are offered by several universities.

Useful websites See **Computer Courses** and **Engineering (Electrical and Electronic)**.

NB The points totals shown to the left of the institutions are for ease of reference only. It must not be assumed that Tariff points are always used by institutions or that they can be substituted for an offer in grades. The level of an offer is not necessarily indicative of the quality of a course.

Engineering Council Statement See **Engineering/Engineering Sciences**.

COURSE OFFERS INFORMATION

Subject requirements/preferences See **Engineering/Engineering Sciences**.

NB In 2011 universities and colleges will differ in their use of GCE AL/AS unit grade information, A* grades, the Extended Project (EPQ), the Advanced Diploma and the Cambridge Pre-U examination when considering applicants and making offers. An EPQ may be accepted in place of an AS subject. Check websites of universities and colleges for the latest offers information.

Your target offers and examples of courses provided by each institution

380 pts **London (UCL)** – AAA+AS–ABB+AS (Electron Eng Comm Eng) (IB 34–38 pts)
370 pts **Brunel** – ABB +AS/EPQ b 370 pts (MEng Comm Net Eng) (IB 33 pts HL maths 6)
360 pts **Edinburgh** – AAA–AAB (Electronic Elec Eng (Comms))
Southampton – AAA (Electron Eng Wrlss Comms) (IB 36 pts)
340 pts **Bath** – AAB (MEng Electron Comm Eng) (IB 36 pts HL maths phys 6)
Birmingham – AAB–ABB (Comm Sys Eng; Comm Sys Eng Bus Mgt; Electron Comm Eng) (IB 32–36 pts)
Bristol – AAB (Comm Multim Eng; Electron Comm Eng courses) (IB 35 pts)
Durham – AAB (MEng Comm Eng) (IB 36 pts)
Leeds – AAB (Electron Comm Eng) (IB 36pts HL 17 pts)
Manchester – AAB–ABB (Comm Sys Eng) (IB 35–33 pts)
Nottingham – AAB–BBB (Electron Comm Eng) (IB 30 pts)
Sheffield – AAB–ABB (Electron Comms Eng) (IB 33–35 pts)
Strathclyde – AAB 2nd yr entry (MEng Dig Comm Multim Sys)
Surrey – 340–320 pts (Telecomm Sys; Electron Sat Eng) (IB 34–32 pts)
Warwick – AAB–ABB (MEng Electron Eng (Comm)) (IB 36 pts)
York – AAB–ABB (MEng Electron Comm Eng) (IB 34 pts)
320 pts **Brunel** – BBC +AS/EPQ c 320 pts (BEng Comm Net Eng) (IB 31 pts)
Hertfordshire – 320 pts (MEng Dig Comm Electron)
Kent – 320–300 pts (Electron Comm Eng)
Lancaster – ABB 320 pts (MEng/MSci Telecomm Mgt; Electron Comm Sys) (IB 30 pts)
Leicester – ABB (MEng Comm Electron Eng) (IB 32 pts)
Liverpool – ABB (MEng Electron Comm Eng) (IB 34 pts)
Newcastle – ABB (MEng Electron Comm) (IB 34 pts HL maths phys 5)
Strathclyde – ABB 2nd yr entry (BEng Dig Comm Multim Sys)
Sussex – ABB–BBC (MEng Electron Comm Eng) (IB 30–34 pts)
300 pts **Aston** – BBB 300 pts (Comm Eng) (IB 29 pts)
Bath – BBB (BEng Electron Comm Eng) (IB 34 pts)
Bradford – BBB 300 pts (MEng Electron Telecomm Intnet Eng) (IB 28–32 pts)
Brunel – BCC +AS/EPQ c 300 pts (BEng Electron Elec Eng (Comm Sys)) (IB 30 pts)
Essex – 300 pts (Telecomm Eng) (IB 29 pts)
Lancaster – BBB (BEng Elec Comm Sys) (IB 29 pts)
Liverpool – BBB (BEng Electron Comm Eng) (IB 32 pts)
London (QM) – 300–340 pts (MEng Comm Eng; Telecomm Eng) (IB 34 pts)
Newcastle – BBB (BEng Electron Comm) (IB 32 pts HL maths phys 5)
Portsmouth – 300–360 pts (MEng Comm Sys)
Strathclyde – BBB 1st yr entry (MEng Dig Comm Multim Sys)
Swansea – 300 pts (MEng Comm Sys)
Warwick – BBB (BEng Electron Eng (Comm)) (IB 34 pts)
York – BBB–BBC (BEng Electron Comm Eng) (IB 31 pts)

280 pts **City** – 280–260 pts (BEng Media Comm Sys; Telecomm; Multim Intnet Sys Eng) (IB 28 pts)
Glamorgan – 280 pts (Electron Comm Eng; Mbl Telecomm)
Kent – 280–300 pts (Electron Comm Eng) (IB 31 pts)
Leicester – BBC (BEng Comm Electron Eng) (IB 30 pts)
Liverpool John Moores – 280 pts (Telecomm Eng)
260 pts **Birmingham City** – 260–280 pts (Telecomm Net)
Brighton – BCC (Dig Electron Comp Comm)
Hertfordshire – 260 pts (BEng Dig Comm Electron)
London (QM) – 260–300 pts (BEng Telecomm Eng; Comm Eng)
Northumbria – 260 pts (Comm Electron Eng) (IB 28 pts)
Strathclyde – BCC 1st yr entry (BEng Dig Comm Multim Sys) (IB 30 pts)
Swansea – 260 pts (BEng Comm Sys; Telecomms Eng)
240 pts **Bradford** – 240 pts (Mbl Comp)
Central Lancashire – 240 pts (Dig Comm)
Edinburgh Napier – 240 pts (Electron Comm Eng)
London Met – 240 pts (Electron Comm Eng)
London South Bank – 240 pts (Telecomm Comp Net Eng)
Manchester Met – 240 pts (Comm Electron Eng) (IB 26 pts)
Newport – 240 pts (Electron Comm Eng)
Plymouth – 240 pts (Electron Comm Sys)
Portsmouth – 240–280 pts (BEng Comm Eng)
Westminster – AA–CCC (Comp Net Comms)
220 pts **Aberdeen** – CCD 4 yr Eng (Electron Eng Comm)
East London – 220 pts (Elec Electron Eng (Comm))
200 pts **Bradford** – 200 pts (BEng Electron Telecomm Intnet Eng) (IB 26 pts)
Central Lancashire – 200 pts (Dig Sgnl Imag Proc) (IB 26 pts)
Coventry – 200 pts (Comp Net Comm Tech; Comm Eng)
London Met – 200 pts (Comm Sys; Mbl Sat Comm) (IB 28 pts)
Plymouth – 200 pts (BEng Electron Comm Eng) (IB 26 pts)
Wolverhampton – 200 pts (Electron Comm Eng)
180 pts **City** – DDD 180 pts (BSc Multim Interact Sys Eng) (IB 25 pts)
160 pts **Kent** – 160 pts (Electron Comm Eng inc Fdn Yr)
Kingston – 160–280 pts (Comm Sys)
140 pts **Glasgow Caledonian** – CD (Telecomm Eng)
120 pts **Northumbria** – 120 pts (Comm Electron Eng inc Fdn Yr) (IB 24 pts)

Alternative offers

See **Chapter 7** and **Appendix 1** for grades/UCAS Tariff points information for the International Baccalaureate, Scottish Highers/Advanced Highers, the Welsh Baccalaureate, the Irish Leaving Certificate, the Cambridge Pre-U Diploma, the Advanced Diploma and the Extended Project.

EXAMPLES OF FOUNDATION DEGREES IN THE SUBJECT FIELD

Plymouth.

CHOOSING YOUR COURSE (SEE ALSO CH.1)

Some course features

Durham A common course for Years 1 and 2 and then two years specialising in the chosen discipline.
Leicester Communications and Electronic Engineering combined. Options to study for a year in industry or in Europe.
London (QM) There are 16 degree programmes offered in the Department of Electronic Engineering, and there is some flexibility and overlap.
Portsmouth A Foundation Year can lead to a number of Engineering and Technological degree courses.

Universities and colleges teaching quality See www.qaa.ac.uk; www.unistats.com.

Examples of sandwich degree courses Aston; Bath; Bradford; Brunel; Central Lancashire; Glamorgan; Kingston; Manchester Met; Northumbria; Plymouth; Portsmouth; Surrey; Westminster; York.

ADMISSIONS INFORMATION

Number of applicants per place (approx) Birmingham 10; Bradford 9; Bristol 2; Coventry 7; Hull 8; London Met 5; London South Bank 3; Northumbria 7; Plymouth 4; York 8 ave.

Advice to applicants and planning the UCAS personal statement See **Engineering (Electrical and Electronic)**. See also **Appendix 4**.

Selection interviews **Yes** Bradford, Bristol, Hertfordshire, Kent, London Met, London South Bank, Sunderland.

Interview advice and questions See **Engineering (Electrical and Electronic)**.

Reasons for rejection (non-academic) See **Engineering (Electrical and Electronic)**.

AFTER-RESULTS ADVICE

Offers to applicants repeating A-levels **Same** Loughborough.

GRADUATE DESTINATIONS AND EMPLOYMENT (2007/8 HESA)

See **Engineering (Electrical and Electronic)** and **Engineering/Engineering Sciences**.

Career note Many commercial organisations offer opportunities in the specialist areas described at the top of this table. Work placements and sandwich courses have, in the past, resulted in over 60% of graduates gaining employment with their firms.

OTHER DEGREE SUBJECTS FOR CONSIDERATION

Computer Science; Engineering (Computer, Control, Electrical, Electronic Systems); Physics.

ENGINEERING (COMPUTER, CONTROL, SOFTWARE and SYSTEMS)

(see also **Computer Courses** and **Engineering (Electrical and Electronic)**)

The design and application of modern computer systems is fundamental to a wide range of disciplines which also include electronic, software and computer-aided engineering. Most courses give priority to reinforcing the essential 'transferable skills' consisting of management techniques, leadership skills, literacy, presentation skills, business skills and time management. At many universities Computer Engineering is offered as part of a range of Electronics degree programmes when the first and even the second year courses are common to all students who choose to specialise later. A year in industry is a common feature of many of these courses.

Useful websites See **Computer Courses** and **Engineering/Engineering Sciences**.

NB The points totals shown to the left of the institutions are for ease of reference only. It must not be assumed that Tariff points are always used by institutions or that they can be substituted for an offer in grades. The level of an offer is not necessarily indicative of the quality of a course.

Engineering Council statement See **Engineering/Engineering Sciences**.

COURSE OFFERS INFORMATION

Subject requirements/preferences See **Engineering/Engineering Sciences**.

NB In 2011 universities and colleges will differ in their use of GCE AL/AS unit grade information, A* grades, the Extended Project (EPQ), the Advanced Diploma and the Cambridge Pre-U examination when considering applicants and making offers. An EPQ may be accepted in place of an AS subject. Check websites of universities and colleges for the latest offers information.

Your target offers and examples of courses provided by each institution

380 pts **Cambridge** – A*AA college offers may vary (Eng (Inf Comp Eng) yrs 3 and 4 specialisation via Engineering Tripos) (IB 38–42 pts)
Imperial London – A*mathsAA (Inf Sys Eng; Inf Sys Eng Abrd)

370 pts **Brunel** – ABB +AS/EPQ b 370 pts (MEng Comp Sys Eng; Electron Comptng)

360 pts **Bristol** – AAA–AAB (MEng Comp Sci; Comp Sci Electron) (IB 35 pts)
Edinburgh – AAA 2nd yr entry (MEng Electron Soft Eng; Electron Comp Sci) (IB 36 pts)
Oxford – AAA (Inf Eng) (IB 38–42 pts)
Southampton – AAA (MEng Soft Eng; Comp Sci; Comp Sci Artif Intel) (IB 34 pts)

340 pts **Aberystwyth** – 340 pts (MEng Soft Eng) (IB 28 pts)
Bath – AAB (MEng Comp Sys Eng) (IB 36 pts HL maths phys 6)
Birmingham – AAB–BBB (Comp Sys Eng; Comp Sci Soft Eng; Comp Interact Sys) (IB 32–36 pts)
Durham – AAB (MEng Comp Eng)
Glasgow – AAB (MEng Faster Route Microcomp Sys Eng)
Leeds – AAB (Electron Comp Eng) (IB 36 pts HL 17 pts)
Loughborough – AAB 340 pts (MEng Sys Eng; Electron Comp Sys Eng) (IB 35 pts)
Manchester – AAB (Comp Sys Eng courses) (IB 35–33 pts)
Surrey – AAB 340 pts (MEng Dig Media Eng)
Warwick – AAB (MEng Sys Eng courses; Comp Inf Eng; Comp Sci (Eng); Comp Sys) (IB 35–37 pts)
York – AAB (MEng Electron Comp Eng; Comp Sys Soft Eng; Comp Sci Embd Sys)

320 pts **Cardiff** – ABB 320 pts (MEng Comp Sys Eng) (IB 30 pts)
Dundee – ABB 2nd yr entry (MEng Electron Eng Microcomp Sys)
Durham – ABB (Soft Eng Euro St)
Edinburgh – ABB 1st yr entry (MEng Electron Soft Eng; Electron Comp Sci) (IB 32 pts)
Glasgow – ABB (MEng Microcomp Sys Eng)
Lancaster – ABB 320 pts (MEng Comp Sys Eng) (IB 30 pts HL 16 pts)
Leicester – ABB (MEng Soft Electron Eng)
Liverpool – ABB (MEng Comp Sci Electron Eng; BSc Soft Dev) (IB 34 pts)
Newcastle – ABB (MEng Electron Comp Eng) (IB 34 pts HL maths phys 5)
Reading – 320 pts (MEng Comp Sci Cyber; Cyber)
Sheffield – ABB (Comp Sys Eng courses; Soft Eng; Sys Cntrl Eng courses) (IB 33 pts)
Strathclyde – AAB 2nd yr entry (MEng Soft Eng; Comp Electron Sys; Dig Comm Multim Sys)
Surrey – ABB 320 pts (BEng Dig Media Eng; Comp Sci Eng)
Sussex – ABB–BBC (Comp Sys Eng) (IB 30–34 pts)

300 pts **Aberdeen** – BBB 300 pts 2nd yr entry (MEng Electron Comp Eng)
Aston – 300 pts (Intnet Sys; Multim Comp) (IB 29 pts)
Bangor – 300–320 pts (Comp Sys Eng)
Bath – BBB (BEng Comp Sys Eng) (IB 34 pts HL maths phys 6)
Bournemouth – 300 pts (Soft Eng; Soft Eng Mgt; Soft Prod Des; Soft Sys Frmwk)
Bradford – 300 pts (MEng Electron Telecomm Intnet Eng; Electron Comp Eng)
Brunel – BCC +AS/EPQ c 300 pts (Intnet Eng; BEng Comp Sys Eng) (IB 30 pts)
Dundee – 300 pts 2nd yr entry (BEng Electron Eng Microcomp Sys) (IB 32 pts)
East Anglia – BBB 300 pts (BSc Comp Sys Eng; Soft Eng) (IB 31 pts)
Essex – 300 pts (Comp Electron; Comp Sys Eng; Comp Net; Soft Eng) (IB 32 pts)
Glamorgan – 300–320 pts (MEng Comp Sys Eng)
Glasgow – BBB (BEng Microcomp Sys Eng; Electron Soft Eng)
Greenwich – 300 pts (Comp Sys Soft Eng)
Heriot-Watt – ABC 2nd yr entry (Comp Electron)
Kingston – 300 pts (MComp Soft Eng)
Liverpool – BBB (BEng Comp Sci Electron Eng) (IB 32 pts)
London (QM) – 300–340 pts (MEng Comp Eng; e-Commer Eng; Dig Aud Mus Sys Eng; Intnet Comp) (IB 34 pts)
Newcastle – BBB/ABC (BEng Comp Sci (Soft Eng); BEng Electron Comp Eng) (IB 32 pts HL maths phys 5)

	Portsmouth – 300–360 pts (MEng Comp Eng) (IB 30 pts)
	Reading – 300–340 pts (BSc Comp Eng; Soft Eng) (IB 30 pts)
	Strathclyde – BBB 1st yr entry (MEng Comp Electron Sys; Dig Comm Multim Sys; Soft Eng)
	Warwick – BBB (BEng Electron Comp Eng; Sys Eng; Comp Inf Eng) (IB 34 pts)
	Westminster – BBB (MEng Comp Sys Eng) (IB 32 pts)
	York – BBB–BBC (BEng Electron Comp Eng; Dig Media Sys)
280 pts	**Aberystwyth** – 280 pts (BEng Soft Eng; Intnet Eng) (IB 24 pts)
	Cardiff – BBC 280 pts (BEng Comp Sys Eng) (IB 30 pts)
	Central Lancashire – 280 pts (MEng Comp Aid Eng)
	City – 280 pts BCC (BEng Comp Sys Eng) (IB 28 pts)
	Glamorgan – 280–320 pts (BEng Comp Sys Eng)
	Huddersfield – 280 pts (Comp Contr Sys) (IB 30 pts)
	Kent – 280–300 pts (Comp Sys Eng)
	Lancaster – BBC (BEng Comp Sys Eng) (IB 28 pts HL 14 pts)
	Leicester – BBC (Soft Electron Eng)
	Liverpool John Moores – 280–240 pts (Comp Eng; Soft Eng)
	Loughborough – BBC 280 pts (BEng Sys Eng; Comp Sys Eng) (IB 32 pts)
	Plymouth – 280 pts (Comp Sys Net)
	Teesside – 280 pts (Comp Aid Des Eng)
	Westminster – BBC (BEng Comp Sys Eng) (IB 30 pts)
260 pts	**Aberdeen** – BCC 260 pts 1st yr entry (MEng Electron Comp Eng)
	Brighton – BCC/BBD 260–280 pts (MEng Dig Electron Comp Comm)
	Bristol UWE – 260 pts (Comp Sys Integ; Soft Eng) (IB 24–28 pts)
	Dundee – BCC 1st yr entry (MEng Electron Eng Microcomp Sys)
	Heriot-Watt – BCC 1st yr entry (Comp Electron)
	London (QM) – 260–280 pts (BEng Comp Eng; Intnet Eng) (IB 30 pts)
	Manchester Met – 260 pts (Comp Comm Soft Eng) (IB 26 pts)
	Northumbria – 260 pts (Comp Net Tech)
	Oxford Brookes – BCC (Soft Eng) (IB 29 pts)
	Portsmouth – 260 pts (BSc Comp Eng)
	Reading – 260 pts (Sys Eng) (IB 30 pts)
	Strathclyde – BCC 1st yr entry (Comp Electron Sys; Soft Eng; Dig Comm Multim Sys)
240 pts	**Bangor** – 240–260 pts (BEng Comp Sys Eng)
	Bradford – 240 pts (BEng Soft Eng; Electron Telecomm Intnet Eng)
	Central Lancashire – 240 pts (BEng Comp Aid Eng)
	Coventry – 240 pts (Soft Eng)
	Dundee – CCC 240 pts 1st yr entry (BEng Electron Eng Microcomp Sys)
	Edinburgh Napier – 240 pts (Electron Comp Eng)
	Greenwich – 240 pts (MEng Soft Eng)
	Huddersfield – 240 pts (Comp Cntrl Sys; Comp Sys Eng) (IB 26 pts)
	Newport – 240 pts (Robot Intel Sys Eng)
	Nottingham Trent – 240 pts (Comp Sys Eng)
	Oxford Brookes – CCC (Soft Eng; Comp Aid Mech Eng)
	Plymouth – 240 pts (Comp Sys Eng)
	Portsmouth – 240–280 pts (BEng Comp Eng) (IB 28 pts)
	Sheffield Hallam – 240 pts (Soft Eng)
	Staffordshire – 240 pts (MEng Comp Scrty (Eng))
	Ulster – 240 pts (Electron Soft)
230 pts	**Edinburgh Napier** – 230 pts (Embd Comp Sys)
220 pts	**Birmingham City** – 220 pts (Soft Des Net) (IB 28 pts)
	Hull – 220–260 pts (Comp Sys Eng; Inf Comp Cntr Tech)
	Robert Gordon – 220–240 pts (Comp Net Mgt Des)
	Teesside – 220–280 pts (Soft Dev)
200 pts	**Aberystwyth** – 200 pts (Intnet Comp)
	Bolton – 200 pts (Electron Comp Eng; Comp Aid Eng)

Coventry – 200 pts (Comp Net Comm Tech; Comp Hard Soft Eng; Sys Eng; Vrtl Eng)
East London – 200 pts (Soft Eng)
Heriot-Watt – CDD 1st yr entry (BEng Comp Electron)
Hertfordshire – 200 pts (BSc Comp Sci (Soft Eng))
Northampton – 200–240 pts (Comp (Comp Sys Eng))
Sheffield Hallam – 200 pts (Comp Net Eng)

180 pts **Greenwich** – 180 pts (BSc Comp Sys Soft Eng)

170 pts **Glasgow Caledonian** – 170 pts CD/DDE (Comp Eng; Comp Aid Mech Eng)
London South Bank – 170 pts (Comp Sys Netg)

160 pts **Bedfordshire** – 160 pts (Comp Sci Soft Eng)
Birmingham City – 160–180 pts (Soft Eng Net Tech)
Greenwich – 160 pts (Embd Comp Sys)
Kent – 160 pts (Comp Sys Eng inc Fdn Yr)
Sheffield Hallam – 160 pts (Comp Aid Eng Des)
South Essex (Coll) – 160 pts (Net Tech)
Southampton Solent – 160 pts (Comp Sys Net)
West Scotland – CC (Comp Net)
Wolverhampton – 160–220 pts (Comp Sci (Soft Eng))

150 pts **Anglia Ruskin** – 150 pts (Electron Intnet Tech)

120 pts **London South Bank** – 120 pts (Comp Aid Eng)
Swansea Met – 120 pts (Comp Sys Electron)

Alternative offers
See **Chapter 7** and **Appendix 1** for grades/UCAS Tariff points information for the International Baccalaureate, Scottish Highers/Advanced Highers, the Welsh Baccalaureate, the Irish Leaving Certificate, the Cambridge Pre-U Diploma, the Advanced Diploma and the Extended Project.

EXAMPLES OF FOUNDATION DEGREES IN THE SUBJECT FIELD
Bedfordshire; Bournemouth; Manchester (Coll); Swansea Met.

CHOOSING YOUR COURSE (SEE ALSO CH.1)
Some course features
Bristol UWE (Comp Sys Integ) A practical course covering all aspects of computer systems, but also focuses on networks, CPU architecture and embedded systems development.
Cardiff The first year is common to all nine Engineering programmes.
Durham (MEng courses) A common course for Years 1 and 2 and then two years specialising in one of four streams, with a major design project (from design to manufacture) in Year 3.
Heriot-Watt The Software Engineering course involves a study of computer science in the first three years followed in Year 4 and 5 by specialist studies in software technology.
London (QM) The MEng programme covers all the material of the BEng programme with more time spent on professional development and advanced studies.
Plymouth Four final year pathways from which to choose your specialisation.

Universities and colleges teaching quality See www.qaa.ac.uk; www.unistats.com.

Top research universities and colleges (RAE 2008) See **Computer Courses**.

Examples of sandwich degree courses Aston; Bath; Brighton; Bristol UWE; Brunel; Cardiff; City; Coventry; Greenwich; Hertfordshire; Kingston; Liverpool John Moores; London South Bank; Loughborough; Manchester; Manchester Met; Portsmouth; Queen's Belfast; Sheffield Hallam; Staffordshire; Surrey; Teesside; York.

ADMISSIONS INFORMATION
Number of applicants per place (approx) Aberystwyth 6; Aston 6; Bangor 5; Birmingham 10; Birmingham City 6; Bournemouth 3; Bradford 6; Bristol 4; Bristol UWE 12; Cardiff 6; Central Lancashire 12; Coventry 2; Durham 6; East Anglia 4; Edinburgh 3; Huddersfield 2; Imperial London 5; Kent 5; Lancaster 12; Liverpool John Moores 2; London South Bank 3; Loughborough 17; Sheffield 10;

Sheffield Hallam 8; Southampton 4; Staffordshire 5; Stirling 7; Strathclyde 7; Surrey (MEng, BEng) 3; Swansea Met 4; Teesside 3; Westminster 5; York 3 ave.

Advice to applicants and planning the UCAS personal statement See **Computer Courses** and **Engineering (Electrical and Electronic)**. See also **Appendix 4**.

Selection interviews **Yes** Aston, Bath, Bradford, Cardiff, Durham, East Anglia, Glamorgan, Hertfordshire, Huddersfield, Kent, Liverpool John Moores, London South Bank, Nottingham Trent, Sheffield Hallam, Swansea Met, Westminster, York; **Some** Aberystwyth, Exeter, Loughborough, Manchester.

Interview advice and questions **See Computer Courses** and **Engineering (Electrical and Electronic)** and **Chapter 5**.

Reasons for rejection (non-academic) Lack of understanding that the course involves engineering. See also **Computer Courses** and **Engineering (Electrical and Electronic)**.

AFTER-RESULTS ADVICE

Offers to applicants repeating A-levels **Higher** Bristol, Strathclyde, Warwick, York; **Possibly higher** City, Huddersfield, Sheffield; **Same** Aston, Bath, Birmingham, Coventry, East Anglia, Exeter, Lancaster, Liverpool John Moores, London South Bank, Loughborough, Salford, Teesside, Ulster; **No offers made** Cambridge.

GRADUATE DESTINATIONS AND EMPLOYMENT (2007/8 HESA)

Software Engineering graduates surveyed 603 **Employed** 375 **In further study** 60 **Assumed unemployed** 93.

Career note Career opportunities extend right across the whole field of electronics, telecommunications, control and systems engineering.

OTHER DEGREE SUBJECTS FOR CONSIDERATION

Computer Science; Computing; Engineering (Aeronautical, Aerospace, Communications, Electrical and Electronic); Mathematics; Media (Systems/Engineering/Technology); Physics.

ENGINEERING (ELECTRICAL and ELECTRONIC)

(See also **Engineering (Acoustics and Sound) (Aeronautical and Aerospace) (Communications) (Computer, Control, Software and Systems)** and **Technologies**)

Electrical and Electronic Engineering courses provide a sound foundation for those looking for a career in electricity generation and transmission, communications or control systems, including robotics. All courses cater for students wanting a general or specialist Engineering education and options should be considered when choosing degree courses. These could include optoelectronics and optical communication systems, microwave systems, radio frequency engineering and circuit technology. Many courses have common first years, allowing transfer in Year 2. Most universities and colleges have good industrial contacts and can arrange industrial placements, in some cases abroad.

Useful websites www.theiet.org; www.engc.org.uk; www.enginuity.org.uk.

NB The points totals shown to the left of the institutions are for ease of reference only. It must not be assumed that Tariff points are always used by institutions or that they can be substituted for an offer in grades. The level of an offer is not necessarily indicative of the quality of a course.

Engineering Council statement See **Engineering/Engineering Sciences**.

COURSE OFFERS INFORMATION

Subject requirements/preferences See **Engineering/Engineering Sciences**.

NB In 2011 universities and colleges will differ in their use of GCE AL/AS unit grade information, A* grades, the Extended Project (EPQ), the Advanced Diploma and the Cambridge Pre-U examination when considering applicants and making offers. An EPQ may be accepted in place of an AS subject. Check websites of universities and colleges for the latest offers information.

Your target offers and examples of courses provided by each institution

380 pts **Cambridge** – A*AA college offers may vary (Eng (Elec Inf Sci) (Elec Electron Eng)) (IB 38–42 pts)

Imperial London – A*mathsAA (MEng/BEng Elec Electron Eng; Elec Electron Eng Mgt; Elec Electron Eng Yr Abrd; Inf Sys Eng; Inf Sys Eng Yr Abrd) (IB 38 pts)

London (UCL) – AAA+AS–AAB+AS (Electron Elec Eng; Electron Eng Comm Eng; Electron Eng Comp Sci; Electron Eng Nanotech) (IB 34–38 pts)

370 pts **Brunel** – ABB +AS/EPQ b 370 pts (MEng Electron Comp Eng; Elec Eng Renew Ener Sys; Electron Elec Eng) (IB 33 pts)

360 pts **Edinburgh** – AAA 2nd yr entry (Elec Electron Eng; Elec Eng; Electron; Elec Eng Renew Ener) (IB 36 pts)

Leeds – AAA (MEng/BEng Electron Nano)

Oxford – AAA (Elec Eng) (IB 38–42 pts)

Southampton – AAA (MEng Electron Eng; Electron Eng Artif Intel; Electron Eng Nano; Electron Eng Mbl Scr Sys) (IB 36 pts HL 18 pts)

Strathclyde – AAA 2nd yr entry (MEng Elec Ener Sys; Electron Dig Sys; Electron Elec Eng Bus St)

340 pts **Bath** – AAB (MEng Electron Elec Eng; Electron Spc Sci Tech; Electron Comm Eng; Elec Pwr Eng) (IB 36 pts HL maths phys 6)

Birmingham – AAB–ABB (Electron Eng; Electron Comp Eng; Electron Comm Eng; Electron Eng Bus Mgt; Elec Ener Eng) (IB 32–36 pts)

Bristol – AAB (Electron Eng; Elec Electron Eng; Elec Electron Eng Euro; Elec Electron Eng Mgt; Comp Sci Electron) (IB 35 pts)

Durham – AAB (MEng Electron Eng) (IB 38 pts)

Edinburgh – AAB–ABB 1st yr entry (MEng/BEng Electron Elec Eng; Electron; Elec Eng Renew Ener) (IB 32 pts)

Exeter – AAB–ABB (Electron Eng; Electron Eng Comp Sci) (IB 30–29 pts)

Glasgow – AAB (MEng Faster Route Electron Elec Eng)

Leeds – AAB (MEng Electron Elec Eng; Electron Eng; Electron Comm Eng) (IB 36 pts HL 17 pts)

Loughborough – 340 pts (Electron Comp Sys; Electron Elec Eng; Electron Commer Comp; Electron courses) (IB 35 pts)

Manchester – AAB (MEng/BEng Elec Electron Eng; Electron Sys Eng; Mecha Eng) (IB 35–33 pts)

Nottingham – AAB–BBB (MEng/BEng Elec Eng; Elec Eng Renew Ener Sys; Elec Electron Eng courses; Electron Eng courses) (IB 30–32 pts)

Sheffield – AAB–ABB (MEng Elec Eng courses; Med Sys Eng Mgt; Electron Eng courses) (IB 32–35 pts)

Southampton – AAB (MEng/BEng Elec Eng; Electromech Eng) (IB 34 pts HL 17 pts)

Strathclyde – AAB 2nd yr entry (MEng Elec Ener Sys; Elec Electron Eng; Elec Dig Sys; Electron Eng Bus St) (IB 36 pts)

Surrey – AAB 340 pts (MEng Electron Eng; Electron Comp Eng; Electron Sat Eng) (IB 35 pts)

Warwick – AAB (MEng Electron Eng) (IB 35–37 pts)

York – AAB–ABB (MEng Electron Eng; Electron Eng Nano; Electron Comm Eng; Electron Comp Eng)

320 pts **Cardiff** – ABB 320 pts (MEng Elec Electron Eng; Electron Comm Eng) (IB 30 pts)

City – 320 pts (Ener Eng) (IB 30 pts HL maths 6)

Dundee – ABB 2nd yr entry (MEng Electron Elec Eng; Electron Eng Mgt; Electron Eng Microcomp Sys; Electron Eng Phys) (IB 32 pts)

Exeter – ABB–BBB (BEng Elec Electron Eng) (IB 26–30 pts)
Glasgow – ABB (MEng Electron Elec Eng)
Hertfordshire – 320 pts (MEng Dig Comms Electron)
Lancaster – ABB (MEng Electron Sys Eng; Mecha Eng) (IB 30 pts)
Leicester – ABB (MEng Elec Electron Eng courses) (IB 32 pts)
Liverpool – ABB (MEng Elec Eng Electron courses; Elec Electron Eng; Med Electron Instr) (IB 34 pts)
Newcastle – ABB–BBB (MEng Electron Comm; Elec Electron Eng; Electron Comp Eng; Electron Eng) (IB 34 pts HL maths phys 5)
Queen's Belfast – ABB (MEng Elec Electron Eng) (IB 31–32 pts)
Strathclyde – ABB 2nd yr entry (BEng Elec Ener Sys; Electron Dig Sys; Electron Eng Bus St) (IB 36 pts)
Surrey – ABB 320 pts (BEng Electron Eng; Electron Sat Eng; Electron Comp Eng)
Sussex – ABB–BBC (MEng Elec Electron Eng; Electron Eng)

300 pts **Aberdeen** – BBB 300 pts 2nd yr entry (MEng Elec Electron Eng; Electron Eng Ocnc Instr; Electron Eng Photon)
Aston – BBB (Electron Eng Comp Sci; Elec Electron Eng; Electromech Eng)
Bath – BBB (BEng Electron Elec Eng; Electron Spc Sci Tech; Elec Pwr Eng; Electron Comm Eng) (IB 34 pts maths phys 6)
Bristol UWE – 300 pts (MEng Elec Electron Eng; Electron Eng) (IB 28–30 pts)
Brunel – BCC +AS/EPQ c 300 pts (BEng Electron Elec Eng courses; Electron Microelec Eng) (IB 28 pts)
Dundee – BBB 2nd yr entry (BEng Electron Elec Eng; Electron Eng Microcomp Sys; Electron Phys; Electron Mgt)
Durham – BBB (BEng Electron Eng)
Essex – 300 pts (Electron Eng; Comp Electron) (IB 29 pts)
Glasgow – BBB (BEng Elec Electron Eng)
Heriot-Watt – ABC 2nd yr entry (MEng Elec Electron Eng) (IB 28 pts)
Lancaster – BBB (BEng Electron Sys Eng; Mecha Eng) (IB 29 pts)
Liverpool – BBB (BEng Elec Electron Eng; Elec Eng; Med Electron Instr; Elec Eng Electron courses) (IB 28 pts)
London (QM) – 300–340 pts (MEng Electron Eng courses) (IB 30–36 pts)
Newcastle – BBB (BEng Elec Electron Eng; Electron Comm; Electron Comp Eng Electron Eng) (IB 32 pts HL maths phys 5)
Plymouth – 300 pts (MEng Elec Electron Eng; Electron Comm Eng) (IB 26 pts)
Portsmouth – 300 pts (MEng Electron Elec Eng)
Reading – 300 pts (MEng Electron Eng courses; Electron Eng Cyber) (IB 29–32 pts)
Sheffield – BBB–BCC (MEng Med Sys Eng; BEng Electron Eng; Elec Eng) (IB 32 pts)
Sheffield Hallam – 300 pts (MEng Elec Electron Eng)
Southampton – BBB (Elec Electron/Electromech Eng + Fdn Yr) (IB 30 pts HL 16 pts)
Strathclyde – BBB 1st yr entry (MEng Elec Ener Sys; Electron Dig Sys; Electron Eng Bus St) (IB 30 pts)
Swansea – 300 pts (MEng Electron Elec Eng; Nanoelectron)
Warwick – BBB (BEng Electron Eng) (IB 34 pts)
Westminster – BBB (MEng Electron Eng) (IB 32 pts)
York – BBB–BBC (BEng Electron Eng; Electron Comp Eng; Electron Comm Eng; Electron Eng Nano) (IB 32 pts)

280 pts **Aberdeen** – BBC 2nd yr entry (BEng Elec Electron Eng; Electron Eng Ocnc Instr; Electron Eng Photon)
Bristol UWE – 280–300pts (MEng Electron Eng) (IB 28–30 pts)
Cardiff – BBC 280 pts (BEng Electron Comm Eng; Elec Electron Eng) (IB 28 pts)
City – 280 pts (BEng Elec Electron Eng; Ener Eng) (IB 28 pts)
Glamorgan – 280–320 pts (Elec Electron Eng; Electron Eng; Ltg Des Tech)
Huddersfield – 280 pts (MEng Electron Eng)
Hull – 280–320 pts (MEng Electron Eng)

Kent – 280–300 pts (BEng Electron Comm Eng) (IB 33 pts)
Leicester – BBC (BEng Elec Electron Eng courses) (IB 30 pts)
Liverpool John Moores – 280 pts (MEng Elec Electron Eng)
London (QM) – 280 pts (BSc Elec Electron Eng courses)
Loughborough – 280 pts (BEng Electron Elec Eng; Electron Comp Sys Eng) (IB 32 pts)
Queen's Belfast – BBC–BCC (BEng Elec Electron Eng) (IB 29–30 pts)
Teesside – 280 pts (Elec Electron Eng) (IB 30 pts)
Westminster – BBC (BEng Electron Eng)

260 pts **Aberdeen** – BCC 1st yr entry (MEng Elec Electron Eng; Electron Eng Photon; Electron Eng Ocnc Instr) (IB 24 pts)
Bristol UWE – 260–280 pts (BEng Electron Eng)
Dundee – BCC 2nd yr entry (MEng Electron Eng Mgt; Electron Eng Phys; Electron Eng Microcomp Sys; Electron Elec Eng)
Heriot-Watt – BCC 260 pts 1st yr entry (Elec Electron Eng courses)
Hertfordshire – 260 pts (BEng Elec Electron Eng)
London (QM) – 260–280 pts (BEng Electron Eng courses)
Manchester Met – 260 pts (Elec Electron Eng; Electron Sys Des) (IB 24 pts)
Northumbria – 260–280 pts (Elec Electron Eng)
Plymouth – 260 pts (BEng Elec Electron Eng; Electron Comm Eng)
Reading – 260 pts (BEng Electron Eng Cyber; Electron Eng)
Robert Gordon – BCC (MEng Electron Elec Eng)
Strathclyde – BCC 1st yr entry (BEng Elec Ener Sys; Electron Dig Sys; Electron Eng Bus St; Electron Elec Eng courses) (IB 30 pts)
Swansea – BCC 260 pts (BEng Electron Elec Eng; Med Eng; Elec Eng; Nanoelectron)
Ulster – 260 pts (Electron Comp Sys; BEng Electron Eng)

240 pts **Bangor** – 240–260 pts (MEng/BEng Electron Eng)
Bolton – 240 pts (Electron Comp Eng)
Bradford – 240 pts (Elec Electron Eng; Electron Telecomm Intnet Eng; Med Eng)
Brighton – CCC/BCD (Elec Electron Eng; Dig Electron Comp Comm) (IB 28 pts)
Central Lancashire – 240 pts (Electron Eng)
De Montfort – 240 pts (Electron Eng; Electron Gms Tech; Electron Eng (Telecomm) (Broad Sys))
Dundee – 240 pts 1st yr entry (BEng Electron Elec Eng; Electron Eng Mgt; Electron Comp (Sat Electron Sys); Electron Eng Microcomp Sys; Electron Eng Phys) (IB 28 pts)
Edinburgh Napier – 240 pts (Elec Eng; Electron Elec Eng; Electron Comm Eng)
Greenwich – 240 pts (BEng Electron Eng; Elec Eng)
Huddersfield – 240 pts (BSc Electron Des; Electron Mus Tech; BEng Electron Eng)
Liverpool John Moores – 240 pts (BEng Elec Electron Eng)
London Met – 240 pts (Electron Comm Eng)
Newport – 240 pts (Elec Eng; Electron Comm Eng)
Plymouth – 240 pts (BSc Elec Electron Eng)
Sheffield Hallam – 240 pts (BEng Elec Electron Eng)
Staffordshire – 240 pts (BEng Elec Eng; Electron Eng)
Sunderland – 240 pts (Electron Elec Eng)

230 pts **Glasgow Caledonian** – BC 230 pts (Elec Pwr Eng; Electron Eng)

220 pts **Aberdeen** – CCD 220 pts (BEng Electron; Elec Eng; Electron Eng Ocnc Instr; Electron Eng Photon)
East London – 220 pts (BEng Elec Electron Eng; Elec Electron Eng (Contr) (Pwr) (Comms))
Hull – 220–260 pts (BEng Electron Eng)
Robert Gordon – CCD (BEng Electron Elec Eng) (IB 26 pts)
Ulster – 220 pts (Electron Soft)

200 pts **Bangor** – 200 pts (BSc Electron (Hard Sys))
Coventry – 200 pts (Electron Eng; Elec Sys Eng)
Glyndŵr – 200 pts (Elec Electron Eng; Aero Electron Eng; Perf Car Electron Tech)
Heriot-Watt – CDD 1st yr entry (BEng Elec Electron Eng courses)
London Met – 200 pts (Electronics)

180 pts **Derby** – 180–240 pts (Elec Electron Eng)
170 pts **London South Bank** – 170 pts (Elec Electron Eng)
160 pts **Sussex** – CC (Elec Electron Eng + Fdn Yr)
150 pts **Anglia Ruskin** – 150 pts (Elec Comp Sci)
140 pts **Glasgow Caledonian** – CD (BSc Electron Eng)
Robert Gordon – CD (BSc Elec Electron Eng)
120 pts **Glamorgan** – 120–160 pts (BSc Elec Electron Eng)
Northumbria – 120 pts (Ext Comm Electron Eng)
Sheffield Hallam – 120 pts (BSc Electron Elec Eng)
Southampton Solent – 120 pts (BSc Electron Eng)
Swansea Met – 120–340 pts (Comp Sys Electron)
100 pts **Birmingham City** – 100 pts (Electron Eng Fdn)

Alternative offers

See **Chapter 7** and **Appendix 1** for grades/UCAS Tariff points information for the International Baccalaureate, Scottish Highers/Advanced Highers, the Welsh Baccalaureate, the Irish Leaving Certificate, the Cambridge Pre-U Diploma, the Advanced Diploma and the Extended Project.

EXAMPLES OF FOUNDATION DEGREES IN THE SUBJECT FIELD

Arts London; Bedfordshire; Bolton; Bournemouth; Brighton; De Montfort; Exeter (Coll); Farnborough (CT); Glamorgan; Greenwich; Havering (Coll); Hertfordshire; Leeds Met; London South Bank; Manchester (Coll); Newcastle (Coll); Northbrook (Coll); Plymouth; Ravensbourne (CDC); St Helens (Coll); South Cheshire (Coll); Southampton Solent; Swansea Met; Thames Valley; Walsall (Coll); York (Coll).

CHOOSING YOUR COURSE (SEE ALSO CH.1)

Some course features

Bath After a common two-year introduction covering electronics, communications, electrical engineering, mathematics and design, students specialise in Years 3 and 4, choosing from a range of optional and core modules. Individual and group project and design work and placement opportunities are key features of these modular courses.
Exeter A multidisciplinary first year before specialising in Year 2.
Leicester Options to study for a year in industry, in Europe or the USA.
London (QM) The MEng and BEng courses include modules on telecoms, programming, digital systems, multimedia systems, wireless networks and video and image processing.
London (UCL) (Electron Eng Nanotech) Course has solid foundation of traditional electronics and specialisation in Years 3 and 4 in fast-developing field of nanotechnology (a research specialisation at UCL).
Loughborough There is a common first year for all students in the Department, followed by a choice of five degrees.
Manchester (Electron Sys Eng) Course focuses on embedded computer systems, for example in engine management systems, MP3 players and mobile phones, with emphasis on system design.

Universities and colleges teaching quality See www.qaa.ac.uk; www.unistats.com.

Top research universities and colleges (RAE 2008) (Electrical and Electronic Engineering) Leeds; Surrey; Bangor; Manchester; Imperial London; Sheffield (Automatic Control and Systems Engineering); Southampton; London (UCL); Glasgow; Bath.

Examples of sandwich degree courses Aston; Bath; Birmingham City; Bournemouth; Bradford; Brighton; Bristol UWE; Brunel; Cardiff; Central Lancashire; City; Coventry; De Montfort; East London; Glamorgan; Glasgow Caledonian; Hertfordshire; Huddersfield; Leicester; Liverpool John Moores; London Met; London South Bank; Loughborough; Manchester Met; Northumbria; Plymouth; Portsmouth; Queen's Belfast; Reading; Sheffield Hallam; Staffordshire; Sunderland; Surrey; Teesside; Ulster; Westminster; York.

ADMISSIONS INFORMATION

Number of applicants per place (approx) Aston 6; Bath 8; Birmingham 18; Birmingham City 11; Bolton 3; Bournemouth 3; Bradford (Elec Electron Eng) 8; Bristol 5; Bristol UWE 8; Cardiff 7; Central Lancashire 4; City 10; Coventry 8; De Montfort 1; Derby 8; Dundee 5; Edinburgh Napier 8; Glamorgan 2; Glasgow Caledonian 5; Greenwich 10; Hertfordshire 7; Heriot-Watt 6; Huddersfield 5; Hull 8; Kent 5; Kingston 8; Leeds 15; Lancaster 7; Leicester 15; Lincoln 8; Liverpool John Moores 2; London (UCL) 9; London South Bank 5; Manchester Met 5; Newcastle 9; Northumbria 7; Nottingham 8; Plymouth 22; Portsmouth 4; Robert Gordon 3; Salford 5; Sheffield 15; Sheffield Hallam 2; Southampton 8; Staffordshire 7; Strathclyde 7; Sunderland 6; Surrey (BEng) 6, (MEng) 3; Swansea 3; Teesside 4; Westminster 5; Warwick 8; York 5.

Advice to applicants and planning the UCAS personal statement Enthusiasm for the subject, for example career ambitions, hobbies, work experience, attendance at appropriate events, competitions etc. Evidence of good ability in mathematics and also a scientific mind. Applicants should show that they can think creatively and have the motivation to succeed on a demanding course. See also Engineering/Engineering Sciences and **Appendix 4**.

Selection interviews **Yes** Aston, Bangor (Electron Eng only), Bath, Bournemouth, Bradford, Bristol, Bristol UWE, Brunel, Cambridge, Central Lancashire, De Montfort, Derby, Durham, Essex, Heriot-Watt, Hertfordshire, Huddersfield, Hull, Imperial London, Kingston, Lancaster, Liverpool, London (UCL), London South Bank, Newcastle, Nottingham, Oxford, Plymouth, Portsmouth, Queen's Belfast, Southampton, Strathclyde, Sunderland, Surrey, Thames Valley, Westminster, York; **Some** Anglia Ruskin, Brighton, Cardiff, Dundee, Kent, Leicester, Liverpool John Moores, Loughborough, Salford, Staffordshire.

Interview advice and questions Past questions have included: How does a combustion engine work? How does a trumpet work? What type of position do you hope to reach in five to ten years' time? Could you sack an employee? What was your last physics practical? What did you learn from it? What are the methods of transmitting information from a moving object to a stationary observer? Wire bending exercise – you are provided with an accurate diagram of a shape that could be produced by bending a length of wire in a particular way. You are supplied with a pair of pliers and the exact length of wire required and you are given 10 minutes to reproduce as accurately as possible the shape drawn. A three-minute talk had to be given on one of six subjects (topics given several weeks before the interview); for example, 'The best is the enemy of the good'. Is there a lesson here for British industry? 'I was asked to take my physics file and discuss some of my conclusions in certain experiments.' Explain power transmission through the National Grid. How would you explain power transmission to a friend who hasn't done physics? **York** Questions based on a mathematical problem. See also **Chapter 5**.

Reasons for rejection (non-academic) Poor English. Inability to communicate. Frightened of technology or mathematics. Poor motivation and work ethic. Better suited to a less specialised engineering/science course. Some foreign applicants do not have adequate English. **Surrey** Can't speak English (it has happened!). See also **Engineering/Engineering Sciences**.

AFTER-RESULTS ADVICE

Offers to applicants repeating A-levels **Higher** Brighton, Central Lancashire, Greenwich, Huddersfield, Kingston, Newcastle, Queen's Belfast, Strathclyde, Warwick; **Possibly higher** Aston, City, De Montfort, Derby, Glasgow, Hertfordshire, London Met, Portsmouth, Sheffield; **Same** Anglia Ruskin, Bangor, Bath, Birmingham, Bolton, Bradford, Cardiff, Coventry, Dundee, Durham, Hull, Kent, Leeds, Liverpool, Liverpool John Moores, London South Bank, Loughborough, Northumbria, Nottingham (usually), Nottingham Trent, Robert Gordon, Salford, Southampton, Staffordshire, Surrey, Thames Valley, Wolverhampton, York; **No offers made** Cambridge.

GRADUATE DESTINATIONS AND EMPLOYMENT (2007/8 HESA)

Graduates surveyed 2025 **Employed** 1210 **In further study** 215 **Assumed unemployed** 235.

Career note Electrical and Electronic Engineering is divided into two main fields – heavy current (electrical machinery, distribution systems, generating stations) and light current (computers, control engineering, telecommunications). Opportunities exist with many commercial organisations.

OTHER DEGREE SUBJECTS FOR CONSIDERATION

Computer Science; Engineering (Aeronautical, Communications, Computer, Control); Mathematics; Physics.

ENGINEERING (MANUFACTURING)

(See also **Art and Design (Industrial and Product Design)** and **Engineering/Engineering Sciences**)

Manufacturing engineering is sometimes referred to as production engineering. It is a branch of the subject concerned with management aspects of engineering such as industrial organisation, purchasing, and the planning and control of operations. Manufacturing Engineering courses are therefore geared to providing the student with a broad-based portfolio of knowledge in both the technical and business areas.

Useful websites www.engc.org.uk; www.imeche.org; www.enginuity.org.uk.

NB The points totals shown to the left of the institutions are for ease of reference only. It must not be assumed that Tariff points are always used by institutions or that they can be substituted for an offer in grades. The level of an offer is not necessarily indicative of the quality of a course.

Engineering Council statement See **Engineering/Engineering Sciences**.

COURSE OFFERS INFORMATION

Subject requirements/preferences See **Engineering/Engineering Sciences**.

NB In 2011 universities and colleges will differ in their use of GCE AL/AS unit grade information, A* grades, the Extended Project (EPQ), the Advanced Diploma and the Cambridge Pre-U examination when considering applicants and making offers. An EPQ may be accepted in place of an AS subject. Check websites of universities and colleges for the latest offers information.

Your target offers and examples of courses provided by each institution

380 pts **Cambridge** – A*AA college offers may vary (Eng (Manuf Eng)) (IB 38–42 pts)
360 pts **Bath** – AAA (Manuf; Manuf Fr/Ger; Spo Eng) (IB 36 pts HL maths phys 6)
Loughborough – AAA (MEng Innov Manuf Eng) (IB 33 pts)
340 pts **Durham** – AAB (MEng Des Manuf Mgt) (IB 36 pts)
Newcastle – AAB (Mech Manuf Eng) (IB 34 pts)
Nottingham – AAB (MEng Manuf Eng Mgt) (IB 30 pts)
Warwick – AAB (MEng Manuf Mech Eng) (IB 35–37 pts)
320 pts **Brunel** – BBC +AS/EPQ c 320 pts (BA Ind Des Tech) (IB 32 pts)
Nottingham – ABB (MEng Prod Des Manuf; BEng Manuf Eng Mgt)
Queen's Belfast – ABB–BBB (Mech Manuf Eng)
300 pts **Aston** – BBB (BSc Eng Prod Des; Ind Prod Des; Prod Des Mgt; Sust Prod Des) (IB 29 pts)
Loughborough – BBB (Manuf Eng)
Strathclyde – BBB (Prod Des Eng)
Warwick – BBB (BEng Manuf Mech Eng)
280 pts **Bristol UWE** – 280–300 pts (Aerosp Manuf Eng) (IB 28–30 pts)
Nottingham – BBC (BEng Prod Des Manuf)
Queen's Belfast – BBC–BCC (BEng Manuf Eng) (IB 29–30 pts)
260 pts **Birmingham City** – 260–280 pts (Mgt Manuf Sys) (IB 28 pts)
240 pts **Bradford** – 240 pts (Ind Eng) (IB 26 pts)
Greenwich – 240 pts (BEng Manuf Sys Eng)
Newport – 240 pts (Mech Manuf Eng)
230 pts **Glasgow Caledonian** – 230 pts (Manuf Sys Eng)
200 pts **Glamorgan** – 200–240 pts (BSc Mech Manuf Eng)

Portsmouth – 200 pts (Mech Manuf Eng) (IB 24 pts)
Swansea Met – 200 pts (Manuf Sys Eng; Auto Manuf)
160 pts **Loughborough** – 160–200 pts (Manuf Eng Mgt inc Fdn Yr) (IB 25 pts)
Plymouth – 160 pts (BSc Mech Des Manuf)
140 pts **Liverpool John Moores** – 140 pts (Robotics)
West Scotland – CD (Des (Manuf Sys))
120 pts **Southampton Solent** – 120 pts (Manuf Mech Eng; Mech Des)
80 pts **Greenwich** – 80 pts (Manuf Sys Eng inc Fdn Yr)
Portsmouth – 80 pts (Eng Tech inc Fdn Yr (Mech Manuf Eng))
Southampton Solent – 80 pts (Mech Des inc Fdn Yr)
60 pts **Swansea Met** – 60–360 pts (Mtrspo Manuf Eng; Manuf Sys Eng; Mech Manuf Eng)

Alternative offers
See **Chapter 7** and **Appendix 1** for grades/UCAS Tariff points information for the International Baccalaureate, Scottish Highers/Advanced Highers, the Welsh Baccalaureate, the Irish Leaving Certificate, the Cambridge Pre-U Diploma, the Advanced Diploma and the Extended Project.

EXAMPLES OF FOUNDATION DEGREES IN THE SUBJECT FIELD

Blackpool and Fylde (Coll); Brighton; Bristol City (Coll); Exeter (Coll); Havering (Coll); Myerscough (Coll); Somerset (CAT); Sunderland; Swansea Met; York (Coll).

CHOOSING YOUR COURSE (SEE ALSO CH.1)

Some course features
Greenwich The degree programme in Manufacturing Systems Engineering shares the first two years with Mechanical Engineering, opening doors to a wide range of engineering technologies, eg aeronautical, automotive and process engineering.
Loughborough Courses include an industrial placement year leading to both a degree and a Diploma in Industrial Studies.
Newcastle Mechanical or Manufacturing Engineering is an option which is chosen after the first two years.
Nottingham (Manuf Eng Mgt) Management and business modules support studies in engineering science and design.

Universities and colleges teaching quality See www.qaa.ac.uk; www.unistats.com.

Top research universities and colleges (RAE 2008) See **Engineering (Mechanical)**.

Examples of sandwich degree courses Aston; Bath; Birmingham City; Bradford; Brunel; Glamorgan; Glasgow Caledonian; London South Bank; Loughborough; Queen's Belfast; Staffordshire; Ulster.

ADMISSIONS INFORMATION

Number of applicants per place (approx) Aston 6; Bath 18; Huddersfield 1; Loughborough 6; Nottingham 5; Strathclyde 8; Warwick 8.

Advice to applicants and planning the UCAS personal statement Work experience or work shadowing in industry should be mentioned. See **Engineering/Engineering Sciences**. See also **Appendix 4**.

Selection interviews **Yes** Cambridge, Nottingham, Strathclyde; **Some** Loughborough.

Interview advice and questions Past questions include: What is the function of an engineer? Describe something interesting you have recently done in your A-levels. What do you know about careers in manufacturing engineering? Discuss the role of women engineers in industry. Why is a disc brake better than a drum brake? Would you be prepared to make people redundant to improve the efficiency of a production line? See also **Chapter 5**.

Reasons for rejection (non-academic) Mature students failing to attend interview are rejected. One applicant produced a forged reference and was immediately rejected. See also **Engineering/Engineering Sciences**.

AFTER-RESULTS ADVICE

Offers to applicants repeating A-levels **Higher** Strathclyde; **Same** Cambridge, Huddersfield, Loughborough, Nottingham.

GRADUATE DESTINATIONS AND EMPLOYMENT (2007/8 HESA)

Graduates surveyed 490 **Employed** 275 **In further study** 55 **Assumed unemployed** 60.

Career note Graduates with experience in both technical and business skills have the flexibility to enter careers in technology or business management.

OTHER DEGREE SUBJECTS FOR CONSIDERATION

Business Studies; Computer Science; Engineering (Electrical, Mechanical); Physics; Technology.

ENGINEERING (MECHANICAL)

(including **Agricultural Engineering, Automotive Engineering** and **Motorsport Engineering**)

Mechanical Engineering is one of the most wide-ranging engineering disciplines. All courses involve the design, installation and maintenance of equipment used in industry. Several universities include a range of Engineering courses with a common first year allowing students to specialise from Year 2. Agricultural Engineering involves all aspects of off-road vehicle design and maintenance of other machinery used in agriculture.

Useful websites www.imeche.org; www.engc.org.uk; www.iagre.org.

NB The points totals shown to the left of the institutions are for ease of reference only. It must not be assumed that Tariff points are always used by institutions or that they can be substituted for an offer in grades. The level of an offer is not necessarily indicative of the quality of a course.

Engineering Council statement See **Engineering/Engineering Sciences**.

COURSE OFFERS INFORMATION

Subject requirements/preferences (Product Design courses) Design technology or art may be required or preferred. See also **Engineering/Engineering Sciences**.

NB In 2011 universities and colleges will differ in their use of GCE AL/AS unit grade information, A* grades, the Extended Project (EPQ), the Advanced Diploma and the Cambridge Pre-U examination when considering applicants and making offers. An EPQ may be accepted in place of an AS subject. Check websites of universities and colleges for the latest offers information.

Your target offers and examples of courses provided by each institution

380 pts **Cambridge** – A*AA college offers may vary (Eng (Mech Eng)) (IB 38–42 pts)
Imperial London – A*mathsAA (Mech Eng (Ttl Tech); Mech Nucl Eng courses) (IB 38 pts)

370 pts **Brunel** – ABB +AS/EPQ b 370 pts (MEng Mech Eng Bld Serv; Mech Eng Auto Des; Mech Eng Aero; Mech Eng; MEng Mech Eng Auto Des) (IB 33 pts)

360 pts **Bath** – AAA (Aerosp Eng; Auto Eng; Innov Eng Des; Mech Eng; Manuf Eng; Integ Mech Elec Eng) (IB 35–37 pts HL maths phys 6)
Bristol – AAA–AAB (MEng Mech Eng Euro; Mech Eng) (IB 35 pts)
Edinburgh – AAA 2nd yr entry (Mech Eng; Mech Eng Mgt; Mech Eng Renew Ener; Elec Mech Eng) (IB 36 pts)
London (UCL) – AAB+AS–ABB+AS (MEng Mech Eng) (IB 34–38 pts)
Loughborough – AAA (MEng Mech Eng courses) (IB 34 pts)
Oxford – AAA (Mech Eng) (IB 38–42 pts)
Southampton – AAA (MEng Mech Eng; Mech Eng Bioeng; Mech Eng Auto; Mech Eng Sust Ener Sys) (IB 36 pts)

340 pts **Aston** – AAB 340 pts (MEng Mech Eng) (IB 32 pts)

Birmingham – AAB (Mech Eng; Mech Mat Eng; Mech Eng (Auto) (Biomed)) (IB 34–36 pts)
Birmingham – AAB–BCC (Mech Eng inc Fdn Yr)
Durham – AAB (MEng Mech Eng) (IB 38 pts)
Exeter – AAB–ABB (MEng Mech Eng; Min Eng) (IB 30–34 pts)
Glasgow – AAB–ABB (MEng Mech Eng; Mech Eng Aero; Prod Des Eng; Mech Des Eng) (IB 32 pts)
Leeds – AAB (MEng Mech Eng; Auto Eng; Med Eng; Mecha Robot) (IB 36 pts HL 17 pts)
Liverpool – AAB (MEng Mech Eng; Mech Eng Bus; Mech Sys Des Eng; Mecha Robot Eng) (IB 35 pts HL maths phys Engl 5)
London (UCL) – ABB+AS–BBB+AS (BEng Mech Eng) (IB 32 pts)
Loughborough – AAB (MEng Auto Eng) (IB 36 pts)
Manchester – AAB (MEng Mech Eng; Mech Eng Mgt; Mecha Eng) (IB 35–33 pts)
Newcastle – AAB (MEng Mech Manuf Eng; Mech Auto Eng; Mech Eng; Mech Des Eng; Mech Eng Mathem Mdl) (IB 36 pts HL maths phys 5)
Nottingham – AAB (MEng Mech Eng) (IB 30–34 pts)
Sheffield – AAB (MEng Mech Eng; Mech Eng Ind Mgt; Mech Eng N Am; Mtrspo Eng Mgt; Spo Eng; Mech Eng Lang) (IB 32 pts HL maths 6)
Strathclyde – AAB (MEng Mech Eng; Mech Eng Aero; Mech Eng Fin Mgt; Mech Eng Mat Eng) (IB 36 pts)
Surrey – AAB 340 pts (MEng Mech Eng; Med Eng) (IB 34–30 pts)
Warwick – AAB (MEng Mech Eng; Manuf Mech Eng; Mech Eng (Sust) (Auto Eng)) (IB 35–37 pts)

320 pts **Birmingham** – ABB (Mech Mat Eng)
Brunel – BBC +AS/EPQ c 320 pts (BEng Mech Eng Bld Serv; Mech Eng; Mech Eng Auto Des; Mech Eng Aero; BEng Mech Eng Auto Des) (IB 31 pts)
Cardiff – ABB 320 pts (MEng Mech Eng) (IB 30 pts)
City – 320 pts (MEng Auto Mtrspo Eng; Mech Eng) (IB 30 pts)
Edinburgh – ABB 1st yr entry (Mech Eng; Mech Eng Mgt; Mech Eng Renew Ener; Elec Mech Eng) (IB 32 pts)
Exeter – ABB–BBB (BEng Mech Eng) (IB 32–29 pts)
Glasgow (SA) – ABB (MEng Prod Des Eng) (Check with Admissions)
Hertfordshire – 320 pts (MEng Auto Eng; Auto Eng Mtrspo) (IB 30 pts)
Lancaster – ABB (MEng Eng (Mech); Mecha) (IB 30 pts)
Leicester – ABB (MEng Mech Eng courses) (IB 32 pts)
Manchester – ABB (BEng Mech Eng Mgt; Mech Eng) (IB 33 pts)
Nottingham – ABB–BBB (BEng Mech Eng)
Sheffield – ABB (BEng Mech Eng; MEng Mech Sys Eng) (IB 32 pts HL maths 6)
Sussex – ABB–BBC (Auto Eng; Mech Eng) (IB 30–34 pts)
Swansea – 320–380 pts (MEng Mech Eng; Med Eng)

300 pts **Aberdeen** – BBB 300 pts 2nd yr entry (MEng Mech Eng; Mech Eng Mgt; Mech Eng Euro St; Mech Eng Contr; Mech Eng Mat; Mech Eng Petrol) (IB 30 pts)
Aston – BBB 300 pts (BEng Mech Eng; Electromech Eng) (IB 29 pts)
Bradford – 300 pts (MEng Mech Eng; Mech Auto Eng) (IB 28–32 pts)
Bristol UWE – BBB–BBC (Min Eng)
Coventry – 300 pts (MEng Auto Eng)
Dundee – BBB 300 pts 2nd yr entry (Mech Eng)
Durham – BBB (BEng Mech Eng)
Exeter – BBB–BBC (Min Eng) (IB 30–28 pts)
Glasgow – BBB (BEng Mech Eng; Mech Des Eng; Mech Eng Euro; Mech Eng Aero) (IB 30 pts)
Glasgow (SA) – BBB (BEng Prod Des Eng) (Check with Admissions)
Greenwich – 300 pts (MEng/BEng Mech Eng)
Harper Adams (UC) – 300 pts (Agric Eng) (IB 30 pts)
Heriot-Watt – BBB (MEng Mech Eng Ener Eng; Mech Eng courses)
Huddersfield – 300 pts (MEng Auto Eng; Auto Des; Mech Eng)
Liverpool – BBB (BEng Mech Eng; Mech Mat Eng; Mech Eng Bus; Mech Sys Des Eng; Mecha Robot Eng)

London (QM) – 300 pts (MEng Mech Eng) (IB 32 pts)
Loughborough – BBB (BEng Mech Eng courses: Mech Eng inc Fdn; Auto Eng)
Newcastle – BBB (BEng Mech Eng inc Fdn Yr) (IB 30 pts HL maths phys 5)
Oxford Brookes – BBB (MEng Auto Eng; Mech Eng; Mtrspo Eng)
Plymouth – 300 pts (MEng Mech Eng) (IB 30 pts)
Portsmouth – 300 pts (MEng Mech Eng) (IB 30 pts)
Queen's Belfast – BBB (MEng Mech Manuf Eng; Mech Eng; BSc Agric Tech) (IB 31–32 pts)
Robert Gordon – 300 pts (MEng Mech Eng) (IB 30 pts)
Salford – 300 pts (MEng Mech Eng) (IB 32 pts)
Sheffield – BBB 300 pts (Fdn Mech Eng)
Sheffield Hallam – 300 pts (MEng Mech Eng)
Strathclyde – BBB (MEng Mech Eng; Mech Eng Aero; Mech Eng Fin Mgt; Mech Eng Mat Eng) (IB 32 pts)
Surrey – BBB 300 pts (BEng Mech Eng; Med Eng) (IB 27 pts)
Warwick – BBB (BEng Mech Eng; Manuf Mech Eng; Auto Eng) (IB 34 pts)

280 pts **Aberdeen** – BBC 280 pts 2nd yr entry (BEng Eng (Mech Oil Gas St); Petrol Eng; Mech Eng Contr; Mech Eng Euro St; Mech Eng Mat; Mech Eng Petrol Eng) (IB 26 pts)
Bristol UWE – 280–300 pts (Mech Eng; Mtrspo Eng) (IB 28–30 pts)
Cardiff – BBC (BEng Mech Eng) (IB 28 pts)
Central Lancashire – 280 pts (MEng Mtrspo Eng)
City – BBC 280 pts (BEng Auto Mtrspo Eng; Mech Eng) (IB 28 pts)
Hull – 280–320 pts (MEng Mech Eng; Mech Med Eng)
Lancaster – BBC (BEng Eng (Mech); Mecha) (IB 28 pts)
Leicester – BBC (BEng Mech Eng) (IB 30 pts)
Liverpool John Moores – 280 pts (MEng Mech Eng; Mech Mar Eng; Auto Eng)
Strathclyde – BBC (BEng Elec Mech Eng) (IB 30 pts)
Teesside – 280 pts (Mech Eng)

260 pts **Aberdeen** – BCC 260 pts 1st yr entry (MEng Mech Eng; Mech Eng Mgt; Mech Eng Euro St; Mech Eng Contr; Mech Eng Mat; Mech Eng Petrol) (IB 24 pts)
Birmingham City – 260–280 pts (Mech Eng; Mtrspo Tech; Auto Eng) (IB 28 pts)
Brighton – BCC–BBD (Mech Eng; Auto Eng) (IB 30 pts)
Coventry – 260 pts (Mech Eng; Auto Eng; Auto Eng Des)
Edinburgh Napier – 260 pts (MEng Mech Eng)
Hertfordshire – 260 pts (BEng Auto Eng; Mech Eng; Auto Eng Mtrspo)
London (QM) – 260 pts (BEng Mech Eng) (IB 32 pts)
Manchester Met – 260 pts (Mech Eng courses; Mech Eng (Auto Contr) (Auto Eng); Mech Eng Net) (IB 26 pts)
Northumbria – 260–280 pts (Mech Eng)
Plymouth – BCC 260 pts (BEng Mech Eng; Mech Eng Cmpsts; Mar Tech) (IB 26 pts)
Queen's Belfast – BCC (BEng Mech Eng; Mech Manuf Eng) (IB 29–30 pts)
Salford – 260 pts (BEng Mech Eng) (IB 30 pts)
Swansea – 260–300 pts (BEng Mech Eng courses; Med Eng)

240 pts **Bolton** – 240 pts (Autombl Eng; Mech Eng)
Bradford – 240 pts (BEng Mech Eng; Mech Auto Eng; Mech Veh Tech) (IB 26 pts)
Central Lancashire – 240 pts (BEng Mtrspo Eng)
Coventry – 240 pts (Auto Des; Mtrspo courses)
De Montfort – 240 pts (Mech Eng; Mecha)
Dundee – CCC (BEng 4 yr Hons Mech Eng)
Huddersfield – 240 pts (BEng Auto Eng; Auto Des; Mech Eng; Auto Des Tech) (IB 26 pts)
Kingston – 240 pts (BEng Mech Eng)
Liverpool John Moores – 240 pts (BEng Mech Mar Eng; Mech Eng; Auto Eng; Mecha)
Manchester Met – 240 pts (Mech Tech Net)
Newport – 240 pts (Mech Manuf Eng)
Oxford Brookes – CCC (Auto Eng; Mech Eng; Mtrspo Eng)
Portsmouth – 240 pts (BEng Mech Eng) (IB 28 pts)

Staffordshire – 240 pts (Mecha; Mech Eng)
Strathclyde – CCC (Spo Eng)

230 pts **Glasgow Caledonian** – BC 230 pts (Mech Electron Sys Eng)

220 pts **Aberdeen** – CCD 220 pts 1st yr entry (BEng Eng (Mech Oil Gas St); Petrol Eng; Mech Eng Contr; Mech Eng Euro St; Mech Eng Mat; Mech Eng Petrol Eng) (IB 22 pts)
Heriot-Watt – CCD (BEng Mech Eng; Auto Eng; Mech Eng Ener Eng)
Hull – 220–260 pts (BEng Mech Eng; Mech Med Eng)
London South Bank – 220 pts (BEng Mech Eng; Mecha)
Robert Gordon – CCD (Mech Elec Eng; Mech Off Eng; Mech Eng)
Sheffield Hallam – 220–280 pts (Mech Comp Aid Eng)
Sunderland – 220 pts (Auto Eng; Mech Eng)

200 pts **Coventry** – 200 pts (BSc Mech Eng; BEng Mtrspo Eng; Auto Eng; Sust Prod Eng)
Dundee – CDD (BEng 3 yr non-Hons Mech Eng) (IB 28 pts)
Glamorgan – 200–240 pts (BSc Mech Manuf Eng)
Glyndŵr – 200 pts (Aero Mech Eng; Mtrspo Des Mgt; Perf Car Tech)
Hertfordshire – 200 pts (BSc Auto Tech Mgt) (IB 24–26 pts)
Portsmouth – 200 pts (Mech Manuf Eng) (IB 24 pts)
Southampton Solent – 200 pts (Mech Des)
Swansea Met – 200 pts (Auto Eng; Mtrspo Eng Des; Mtrcycl Eng)
Ulster – 180 pts CC (Mech Eng)

180 pts **Greenwich** – 180 pts (Mech Eng Tech)
Plymouth – 180 pts (BSc Mar Spo Tech; Mech Des Manuf; Mech Eng Comp Aid Des) (IB 24 pts)

170 pts **Glasgow Caledonian** – DDE 170 pts (Mechatronics)

160 pts **Blackburn (Coll Univ Centre)** – 160 pts (Mech Eng; Mecha)
Harper Adams (UC) – 160–180 pts (Offrd Veh Des Mark Mgt; BSc Agric Eng Mark Mgt) (IB 24 pts)
Kingston – 160 pts (Mtrcycl Engs; Mech Eng; Auto Eng; Mtrspo Eng)
Sheffield Hallam – 160 pts (Mech Eng; Mech Des Eng; Auto Des Tech; Mech Auto Eng)
Sussex – CC/BCC (Eng inc Fdn Yr)
West Scotland – CC (Mtrspo Des Eng)

140 pts **Robert Gordon** – CD (BSc Mech Eng)

120 pts **Glamorgan** – 120–160 pts (BSc Mecha Eng)
Northumbria – 120 pts (Mech Eng inc Fdn Yr)
Sheffield Hallam – 120 pts (BSc Mech Des Eng)

80 pts **Swansea Met** – 80–340 pts (Mech Manuf Eng 4 yrs)

40 pts **Hertfordshire** – 40–80 pts (BEng Eng Ext)

Alternative offers

See **Chapter 7** and **Appendix 1** for grades/UCAS Tariff points information for the International Baccalaureate, Scottish Highers/Advanced Highers, the Welsh Baccalaureate, the Irish Leaving Certificate, the Cambridge Pre-U Diploma, the Advanced Diploma and the Extended Project.

EXAMPLES OF FOUNDATION DEGREES IN THE SUBJECT FIELD

Bath; Blackburn (Coll Univ Centre); Blackpool and Fylde (Coll); Brighton; Bristol City (Coll); Bristol UWE; Derby; Exeter (Coll); Glyndŵr; Greenwich; Havering (Coll); Kingston; Loughborough (Coll); Myerscough (Coll); Oxford Brookes; Plymouth; Queen's Belfast; Sheffield Hallam; Somerset (CAT); South Cheshire (Coll); Staffordshire; Sunderland; Swansea Met; Warwickshire (Coll).

Agricultural Engineering Bicton (Coll); Harper Adams (UC).

CHOOSING YOUR COURSE (SEE ALSO CH.1)

Some course features

Brunel (Mech Eng) Course combines fundamental elements of mechanical engineering and design with study in associated disciplines including computing, electronics, environment and energy systems. All courses emphasise importance of industrial and commercial insight and awareness.

Cardiff The first year is common to all Engineering programmes. Core subjects include mathematics, dynamics, properties of materials, electrical engineering, electronics and business management. Option to study French or German or Spanish.
Durham A common course for Years 1 and 2 and then two years specialising in the chosen discipline.
Exeter A multidisciplinary first year before specialising in Year 2. Emphasis on design skills practice and development.
Leicester Options to study for a year in industry, in Europe or the USA.
Newcastle Eleven mechanical engineering options with common first and second years for all students.
Salford (MEng Mech Eng) Programme has broad engineering themes built around study of transport, energy, structures and communication.
Surrey Mechanical, medical and aerospace programmes have a common first year allowing for a final choice of degree in Year 2.
Strathclyde (MEng Mech Eng) Opportunity for year abroad in either Year 3 or 5.

Universities and colleges teaching quality See www.qaa.ac.uk; www.unistats.com.

Top research universities and colleges (RAE 2008) (Mechanical, Aeronautical and Manufacturing Engineering) Imperial London; Sheffield; Bristol (Aerospace Engineering); Greenwich; Nottingham; Bristol (Mechanical Engineering); Leeds; Loughborough; Birmingham; Cardiff.

Examples of sandwich degree courses Aston; Bath; Birmingham City; Bradford; Brighton; Bristol UWE; Brunel; Cardiff; Central Lancashire; City; Coventry; De Montfort; East London; Glamorgan; Glasgow Caledonian; Harper Adams (UC); Hertfordshire; Huddersfield; Kingston; Leicester; Liverpool John Moores; London (QM); London South Bank; Loughborough; Manchester Met; Northumbria; Oxford Brookes; Plymouth; Portsmouth; Queen's Belfast; Salford; Sheffield Hallam; Staffordshire; Sunderland; Surrey; Teesside; Ulster; West Scotland.

ADMISSIONS INFORMATION

Number of applicants per place (approx) Abertay Dundee 4; Aston 8; Bath (MEng) 13; Birmingham 6; Bradford 4; Brighton 10; Bristol 8; Bristol UWE 17; Brunel 12; Cardiff 8; Coventry 8; City 13; Dundee 5; Durham 8; Glamorgan 6; Glyndŵr 4; Heriot-Watt 9; Hertfordshire 10; Huddersfield 1; Hull 11; Kingston 8; Lancaster 8; Leeds 15; Leicester 11; Liverpool 6; Liverpool John Moores (Mech Eng) 2; London (QM) 6; London South Bank 4; Loughborough 8, (Mech Eng) 12, (Auto Eng) 7; Manchester Met 6, (Mech Eng) 6; Newcastle 10; Northumbria 4; Nottingham 8; Plymouth 6; Portsmouth 6; Sheffield 10; Southampton 8; Staffordshire 6; Strathclyde 6; Surrey 9; Teesside 7; Warwick 8; Westminster 11.

Advice to applicants and planning the UCAS personal statement Work experience; hands-on skills. An interest in solving mathematical problems related to physical concepts. Enjoyment in designing mechanical devices or components. Interest in engines, structures, dynamics or fluid flow and efficient use of materials or energy. Apply for the Year in Industry Scheme (www.yini.org.uk) for placement. Scholarships are available to supplement the scheme. See **Engineering/Engineering Sciences**. See also **Appendix 4**.

Misconceptions about this course **Loughborough** Although organised by the Wolfson School of Manufacturing and Mechanical Engineering, the degree does not include manufacturing.

Selection interviews **Yes** Aston, Birmingham, Bolton, Bradford, Brighton, Bristol, Brunel, Cambridge, Cardiff, Durham, Harper Adams (UC), Hertfordshire, Huddersfield, Imperial London, Kingston, Lancaster, Leeds, Leicester, Liverpool John Moores, London (QM), London South Bank, Loughborough (Auto Eng), Manchester Met, Newcastle, Nottingham, Oxford, Queen's Belfast, Sheffield, Sheffield Hallam, Strathclyde, Sunderland, Surrey, Sussex; **Some** Blackpool and Fylde (Coll), Dundee, Liverpool, Staffordshire.

Interview advice and questions Past questions include: What mechanical objects have you examined and/or tried to repair? How do you see yourself in five years' time? What do you imagine you would be doing (production, management or design engineering)? What engineering interests do you have? What qualities are required to become a successful mechanical engineer? Do you like sixth form work? Describe the working of parts on an engineering drawing. How does a fridge work? What is design in the context of mechanical engineering? What has been your greatest achievement to date? What are your career plans? **Hertfordshire** All interviewees receive a conditional offer. **Sunderland** Provide an example of working as part of a team, meeting a deadline, working on your own. See also **Engineering/Engineering Sciences** and **Chapter 5**.

Reasons for rejection (non-academic) See **Engineering/Engineering Sciences**.

AFTER-RESULTS ADVICE

Offers to applicants repeating A-levels **Higher** Brighton, Dundee, Kingston, Newcastle, Queen's Belfast, Swansea, Warwick; **Possibly higher** City, Huddersfield; **Same** Aston, Bath, Bradford, Bristol, Brunel, Coventry, Derby, Durham, East London, Edinburgh Napier, Harper Adams (UC), Heriot-Watt, Leeds (usually), Lincoln, Liverpool, Liverpool John Moores, London South Bank, Loughborough, Manchester Met, Northumbria, Nottingham, Nottingham Trent, Oxford Brookes, Sheffield, Sheffield Hallam, Southampton, Staffordshire, Sunderland, Surrey, Teesside, Wolverhampton; **No offers made** Cambridge.

GRADUATE DESTINATIONS AND EMPLOYMENT (2007/8 HESA)

Graduates surveyed 1985 **Employed** 1195 **In further study** 225 **Assumed unemployed** 215.

Career note Mechanical Engineering graduates have a wide choice of career options. Apart from design and development of plant and machinery, they are also likely to be involved in production processes and working at various levels of management. Mechanical engineers share interests such as structures and stress analysis with civil and aeronautical engineers, and electronics and computing with electrical and software engineers.

OTHER DEGREE SUBJECTS FOR CONSIDERATION

Engineering (Aeronautical/Aerospace, Building, Computer (Control, Software and Systems), Electrical/Electronic, Manufacturing, Marine); Materials Science; Mathematics; Physics; Product Design; Technologies.

ENGLISH

(including **Creative Writing**)

English courses continue to be extremely popular and competitive. They are an extension of school studies in literature and language and may cover topics ranging from Anglo-Saxon literature to writing in the present day. Most courses, however, will focus on certain areas such as the Medieval or Renaissance periods of literature or on English language studies. Admissions tutors will expect students to have read widely outside their A-level syllabus.

Useful websites www.bl.uk; www.lrb.co.uk; www.literature.org; www.bibliomania.com; www.online-literature.com.

NB The points totals shown to the left of the institutions are for ease of reference only. It must not be assumed that Tariff points are always used by institutions or that they can be substituted for an offer in grades. The level of an offer is not necessarily indicative of the quality of a course.

COURSE OFFERS INFORMATION

Subject requirements/preferences **GCSE** English language, literature required and a foreign language may be preferred. Grades may be stipulated. **AL** English with specific grades usually stipulated. Modern languages required for joint courses with languages.

NB In 2011 universities and colleges will differ in their use of GCE AL/AS unit grade information, A* grades, the Extended Project (EPQ), the Advanced Diploma and the Cambridge Pre-U examination when considering applicants and making offers. An EPQ may be accepted in place of an AS subject. Check websites of universities and colleges for the latest offers information.

Your target offers and examples of courses provided by each institution

390 pts **London (King's)** – AABb (Engl Lang Lit; Hisp St Engl; Lat Engl; Port Braz St Engl) (IB 36 pts)
Warwick – AABb (Engl Lit; Engl Lit Crea Writ; Engl Thea St) (IB 36 pts)

380 pts **Cambridge** – A*AA college offers may vary (Engl; A-Sxn Nrs Celt; Educ Engl) (IB 38–42 pts)
London (UCL) – AAA+AS (English) (IB 38 pts)

360 pts **Bristol** – AAA–ABB no pts offer (Engl; Engl Class St; Dr Engl) (IB 38–37 pts)
Durham – AAA (Engl Lit; Engl Lit Hist; Engl Lit Phil; Engl Lit Comb Hons) (IB 37 pts)
East Anglia – AAA–AAB (Engl Lit Crea Writ) (IB 34–33 pts)
Exeter – AAA–AAB (Engl; Engl Film St; Engl N Am; Engl Fr) (IB 36–33 pts)
London (King's) – AAB+AS (Class St Engl)
Manchester – AAA–ABB (Engl Lit courses) (IB 37–35 pts)
Newcastle – AAA (Engl Lit) (IB 35 pts)
Oxford – AAA (Engl Lang Lit; Class Engl; Engl Modn Langs; Hist Engl) (IB 38–42 pts)
Sussex – AAA–AAB (Engl Art Hist; Engl Film St; Engl Engl Lang Teach; Engl Hist; Engl)
Warwick – ABBc (Engl Lat Lit)
York – AAA–AAB (Engl; Engl Ling; Engl Hist Art; Engl Pol; Engl Hist; Engl Phil; Engl Lang Ling) (IB 36 pts)

340 pts **Birmingham** – AAB (Engl; Engl Crea Writ) (IB 34–36 pts)
Cardiff – AAB (Engl Lit Anc Hist; Engl Lit Arch; Cult Crit Engl Lit)
Durham – AAB (Arts Comb Hons; Educ St Engl Lit)
East Anglia – AAB–ABB (Engl Lit)
East Anglia – AAB–BBB (Engl Lit Dr; Script Perf)
Exeter – AAB–ABB (Engl Fr/Ger/Ital/Russ/Span) (IB 34–36 pts)
Glasgow – AAB (Engl Lit courses; Engl Lang courses; Gael Engl Lang; Gael Engl Lit; Scot Lit) (IB 34 pts)
Leeds – AAB (Engl Lang Lit; Engl Lang; Engl Lit Thea St; Arbc Engl) (IB 35 pts HL Engl 6)
Lancaster – AAB–ABB 340–320 pts (Engl Lang; Engl Lang Lit; Engl Lit Mus; Engl Lang Crea Writ) (IB 32–34 pts)
Leicester – AAB–ABB (Engl courses)
Liverpool – AAB (Engl; Engl Comm St; Engl Modn Hist) (IB 35 pts)
London (RH) – AAB (Engl Fr/Ger/Ital; Engl Crea Writ; Engl Dr) (IB 33 pts)
Loughborough – AAB–ABB 340 pts (Engl; Engl Spo Sci; Hist Engl)
Manchester – AAB–BBC (Engl Lang Chin; Engl Lang Scrn St; Engl Lang Russ)
Newcastle – AAB (Engl Lang Lit) (IB 35 pts HL Engl 6)
Nottingham – AAB–ABB (Engl St Phil; Engl Lang Hist; Engl Crea Writ; Engl Hist) (IB 34–36 pts)
St Andrews – AAB (Engl courses) (IB 36 pts)
Sheffield – AAB–ABB (Engl Lang Lit; Engl Lit; Engl courses) (IB 35–32 pts)
Southampton – AAB (Engl; Engl Hist; Engl Phil) (IB 34 pts)

320 pts **Birmingham** – ABB (Engl Lang courses; Mediev Engl Hist; Engl Lit Modn Langs)
Brunel – BBC +AS/EPQ b 320 pts (Engl; Engl Crea Writ; Engl Mus; Engl Film TV St) (IB 31 pts)
Cardiff – ABB (Engl Lang Fr/Ger; Cult Crit Engl Lang)
East Anglia – ABB–BBB (Engl Am Lit; Lit Hist)
Kent – 320–340 pts (Engl Lang (Compar Lit) (Hist) (Pol); Engl Am Lit joint courses)
Kingston – 320 pts (Engl Lang courses; Engl Lit; Crea Writ)
Leeds – ABB (Class Lit Engl) (IB 33 pts)
London (Gold) – ABB (Engl; Engl Crea Writ; Engl Compar Lit)
Newcastle – ABB (Engl Lang) (IB 34 pts HL Engl 6)
Oxford Brookes – ABB (English) (IB 34 pts)
Queen's Belfast – ABB–BBB (Engl courses)
Sheffield – ABB–BBB (Engl Lang Ling; Engl Lang Sociol)
Southampton – ABB (Lang Soty; Engl Mus) (IB 32 pts)
Surrey – ABB 320 pts (Engl Lit; Engl Crea Writ)
Sussex – ABB (Am St Engl)
Swansea – 320–300 pts (Engl courses; Engl Lit Lang St)
Warwick – ABB 320 pts (Engl Ital Lit; Engl Ger Lit)

300 pts **Aston** – 300–320 pts (Engl Lang; Engl Lang Int Rel; Engl Lang Fr/Ger) (IB 32–33 pts)
Bournemouth – 300 pts (Engl; Engl Hist)
Brighton – 300 pts (Engl Lit) (IB 28–30 pts)
Bristol UWE – 300–320 pts (English)
Cardiff – BBB (Engl Lang Ital/Welsh; Cult Crit)
Dundee – 300 pts 2nd yr entry (Engl courses)
East Anglia – BBB (Am Engl Lit)
Edinburgh – BBB (Engl Lang courses; Engl Lit courses; Engl Scot Lit; Engl Lang)
Essex – 300 pts (Engl Lit; Lit Myth; Crea Writ; Engl Lang; Engl Lang Lit) (IB 29 pts)
Gloucestershire – 300 pts (Engl Lit; Engl Lang)
Kent – 300–320 pts (Engl Am Lit courses; Engl Lang; Engl Lit) (IB 33–35 pts)
Liverpool – BBB (Engl Fr/Ger; Engl Hisp St) (IB 30 pts)
London (Gold) – BBB (Media Modn Lit; Engl Dr)
London (King's) – BBB (Engl Comm)
London (QM) – 300–340 pts (Engl Lit Ling; Engl Film St; Engl Dr) (IB 32 pts)
Northumbria – 300 pts (Engl Lit; Engl Lang Lit; Engl Crea Writ)
Nottingham – BBB (Vkng St)
Nottingham – ABC (Engl Russ E Euro Civ)
Oxford Brookes – BBB (Engl Comb Hons) (IB 33 pts)
Reading – 300–340 pts (Engl Lang courses; Engl Lit courses) (IB 31–32 pts)
Sheffield – BBB (Engl Lang Sociol)
Stirling – BBB 2nd yr entry (Engl St)
Strathclyde – BBB 2nd yr entry (Engl St)

280 pts **Aberystwyth** – 280 pts (Engl Lit courses; Crea Writ Engl Lit) (IB 30 pts)
Birmingham City – 280 pts (Engl Lit; Engl Dr; Engl Crea Writ; Engl Lang St)
Bristol UWE – 280–320 pts (Engl Hist)
Hertfordshire – 280 pts (Engl Lang Comm courses; Engl Lit courses)
Hull – 280–320 pts (English)
Loughborough – 280 pts (Pub Engl) (IB 32–35 pts)
Manchester – BBC (Lang Lit Comm) (IB 30–28 pts)
Nottingham Trent – 280–260 pts (Engl; Engl Comm Soty; Engl Crea Writ)
Oxford Brookes – BBC (Engl Lang Comm)
Salford – 280 pts (Engl Jrnl; Engl Film)

260 pts **Brighton** – BCC (Engl Lang Lit; Engl Lang Media) (IB 28 pts)
Cardiff (UWIC) – 260 pts (Engl Crea Writ)
Central Lancashire – 260 pts (Engl Lang; Jrnl Engl)
Chichester – BCC 260–300 pts (Engl; Engl Crea Writ) (IB 28–30 pts)
Coventry – 260–280 pts (Engl; Engl Jrnl St)
Huddersfield – 260 pts (Engl St; Engl Lang; Engl Lit courses; Engl Lit Crea Writ)
Hull – 260–300 pts (Engl; Engl Am Lit Cult)
Keele – 260–320 pts (Engl courses; Engl Am Lit) (IB 30–32 pts)
Lincoln – 260 pts (Engl; Engl Pol)
Liverpool – BCC (Ir St Engl)
Liverpool Hope – 260 pts (Engl Lang courses; Engl Lit courses)
Newport – 260 pts (Crea Writ Engl)
Plymouth – 260 pts (Engl courses)
Salford – 260–240 pts (Engl Cult St; Engl Crea Writ; Engl Lit; Engl Lit Engl Lang) (IB 31 pts)
Stirling – BCC 1st yr entry (Engl St)
Strathclyde – BCC/BB (Engl Psy; Engl HR; Engl Geog)
Ulster – 260 pts (English)
Westminster – BCC/BB (Engl Lit Cult St; Engl Lang) (IB 30 pts)
Winchester – 260–300 pts (Engl courses; Engl Lit courses; Crea Writ courses) (IB 24–26 pts)

240 pts **Aberdeen** – CCC (Engl courses; Engl Scot Lit; Celt Civ Engl) (IB 28 pts)
Bangor – 240–280 pts (Engl courses; Engl Lang courses)
Bath Spa – 240–280 pts (Engl Lit courses; Crea Writ courses)

Bolton – 240 pts (Crea Wri courses; Engl courses; Media Writ Prod)
Brighton – CCC/BCD (Engl Lit Commun Hist)
Buckingham – CCC 240 pts (Engl Lit courses; Engl St courses)
Cardiff (UWIC) – 240 pts (Engl Pop Cult; Engl Dr; Modn Hist Engl)
Chester – 240–280 pts (Engl courses; Crea Writ courses) (IB 30 pts)
De Montfort – 240 pts (Engl; Engl Lang courses; Crea Writ joint Hons)
Dundee – 240 pts 1st yr entry (Engl courses)
Edinburgh Napier – 240 pts (Engl; Engl Film)
Glamorgan – 240–280 pts (Engl Lit; Crea Prof Writ; Engl Lang)
Liverpool John Moores – 240 pts (Crea Writ courses; Engl courses)
London Met – 240 pts (Crea Writ Engl Lit; Crea Writ; Engl Lit)
Manchester Met – 240–280 pts (Engl Am Lit; Engl; Engl Crea Writ courses)
Portsmouth – 240–300 pts (Engl Lang courses; Engl Lit courses; Crea Writ Dr)
Roehampton – 240–340 pts (Engl Lit; Engl Lang Ling; Crea Writ courses)
Sheffield Hallam – 240 pts (Engl; Engl Scrn St; Engl Educ St; Crea Writ)
Salford – 240 pts (Engl Cult St)
Southampton Solent – 240 pts (Engl Writ Contemp Fctn; Engl Adv; Engl PR)
Ulster – 240–260 pts (Engl Euro St; Engl Int Dev; Engl Compar Lit)
Worcester – 240–260 pts (Engl Lang courses; Engl Lit St courses)
York St John – 240–220 pts (Engl Lang courses; Engl Lit courses)

220 pts **Bishop Grosseteste (UC)** – 220 pts (Engl Lit; Educ St Engl)
East London – 220 pts (Engl Lang courses; Engl Lit courses; Crea Prof Writ courses)
Edge Hill – 220–260 pts (Engl; Crea Writ courses; Engl Lang courses; Engl Lit courses)
Falmouth (UC) – 220 pts (Writ Engl Media St; Engl Crea Writ)
Leeds Met – 220–180 pts (Engl Lit; Engl Hist)
Leeds Trinity (UC) – 220–240 pts (Engl; Engl Hist; Engl Media; Engl Writ)
Newman (UC) – 220–260 pts (Engl courses)
Northampton – 220–260 pts (Engl courses; Crea Writ courses)
Sunderland – 220 pts (Engl; Engl Crea Writ; Engl Dr; Engl Lang Lit; Engl St courses)
Teesside – 220–260 pts (Engl Media St; Engl St Hist; Engl St Crea Writ)

200 pts **Anglia Ruskin** – 200–240 pts (Engl courses; Engl Lang courses; Writ courses)
Bedfordshire – 200–240 pts (Engl courses; Crea Writ)
Blackburn (Coll Univ Centre) – 200–240 pts (Engl (Lang Lit St))
Blackpool and Fylde (Coll) – 200 pts (Engl Lang Lit Writ)
Bucks New – 200–240 pts (Crea Writ; Script)
Canterbury Christ Church – 200 pts (Engl courses; Engl Lang Comm courses)
Central Lancashire – 200–240 pts (Engl Lang Ling; Engl Thea St)
Cumbria – 200–240 pts (Engl courses; Crea Writ)
Glyndŵr – 200 pts (Engl; Engl Writ; Engl Media Comms)

Middlesex – 200–240 pts (Engl Lit courses; Engl Lang Lit)
Southampton Solent – 200 pts (Cmdy Writ Perf)
Staffordshire – 200–260 pts (Engl Lit courses; Script) (IB 28 pts)
Suffolk (Univ Campus) – 200 pts (Engl; Engl Hist)
Trinity Saint David – 200 pts (Modn Lit courses; Crea Writ)
UCP Marjon – 200–220 pts (Engl Lit courses; Crea Writ courses; Engl Lang Ling)

180 pts **Aberystwyth** – 180 pts (Inf Lib St Engl Lit)
Blackburn (Coll Univ Centre) – 180–220 pts (Engl courses)
Bradford – 180–220 pts (Engl; Crea Writ)
Derby – 180–240 pts (Engl courses; Crea Writ courses; Media Writ courses)
Hull – 180–240 pts (Engl Lit Cult St)
St Mary's Twickenham (UC) – 180–200 pts (Engl courses; Crea Writ)
Trinity Saint David – 180 pts (Welsh Engl Lit; Engl Lit Anth; Engl Modn Lit courses)

160 pts **Doncaster (Coll)** – 160 pts (Engl courses)
Greenwich – 160 pts (Engl courses; Crea Writ courses)
London South Bank – 160 pts (Engl Dr Perf; Crea Writ Engl; Engl Comb)
Wolverhampton – 160–220 pts (Engl courses; Crea Prof Writ courses)

120 pts **Arts London** – 120 pts (Mag Pub)
Peterborough Reg (Coll) – 120 pts (Hist Engl; Engl Sociol)
Swansea Met – 120 pts (Engl St Psy; Engl St Art Hist)
Trinity Saint David – 120 pts (Engl courses; Crea Writ courses)

100 pts **Bournemouth (Yeovil)** – 100 pts (Engl Hist)

80 pts **London (Birk)** – 80 pts for under 21s (over 21s varies) (p/t English)

Alternative offers

See **Chapter 7** and **Appendix 1** for grades/UCAS Tariff points information for the International Baccalaureate, Scottish Highers/Advanced Highers, the Welsh Baccalaureate, the Irish Leaving Certificate, the Cambridge Pre-U Diploma, the Advanced Diploma and the Extended Project.

EXAMPLES OF FOUNDATION DEGREES IN THE SUBJECT FIELD

Greenwich; Plymouth.

CHOOSING YOUR COURSE (SEE ALSO CH.1)

Some course features

Bangor (Engl) A wide choice of modules in a variety of periods, from 900AD to the present from wide range of English and American texts.
Birmingham Literature and language foundation modules are offered in Year 1 with a choice of pathway commencing in Year 2.
East Anglia Opportunity to study abroad in Europe or Australia for one or both semesters of Year 2.
Essex (Lit Myth) An unusual course focusing on the role and function of myth in literature through a study of key literary and mythological texts from a range of cultures.
Loughborough (Engl) Very flexible course enabling students to construct their own programmes covering literature and language from the sixteenth century.
Portsmouth (Engl Lang) Opportunity to obtain Trinity Certificate in Teaching English to Speakers of other Languages.
Queen's Belfast Creative writing modules offered as part of the English degree. Other options include Irish fiction in the twentieth century, contemporary Irish poetry and modern Indian fiction in English.
Warwick Eight Literature courses offered including the popular English with Creative Writing.

Universities and colleges teaching quality See www.qaa.ac.uk; www.unistats.com.

Top research universities and colleges (RAE 2008) (English Language and Literature) York; London (QM); Edinburgh; Manchester; Exeter; Oxford; Nottingham; Cambridge; De Montfort; Leeds; Warwick; Glasgow; St Andrews; Queen's Belfast; Liverpool; Aberdeen; Newcastle.

Examples of sandwich degree courses Brighton; East London; Glamorgan; Huddersfield; Lancaster; Loughborough; Nottingham Trent; Oxford Brookes; Westminster.

ADMISSIONS INFORMATION

Number of applicants per place (approx) Aberystwyth 7; Anglia Ruskin 5; Bangor 5; Bath Spa 8; Birmingham 7, (Engl Educ) 4; Birmingham City 9; Blackpool and Fylde (Coll) 2; Bristol 28, (Engl Dr) 45; Bristol UWE 4; Brunel 10; Buckingham 2; Cambridge (A-Sxn Nrs Celt) 2, (Engl) 4.9; Cardiff (Engl Lit) 6; Central Lancashire 10; Chester 20; Chichester 4; Cumbria 24; De Montfort 7; Derby 6; Dundee 6; Durham 20; East Anglia (Engl Lit Dr) 22, (Engl Lit Crea Writ) 17, (Engl St) 12; Edge Hill 4; Exeter 13; Glamorgan 8; Gloucestershire 35; Glyndŵr 2; Hertfordshire 6; Huddersfield 5; Hull 14; Hull (Scarborough) 1; Kingston 6; Lancaster 12; Leeds 10; Leeds Trinity (UC) 7; Leicester 7; Liverpool (Engl Comm St) 7; London (Gold) 9, (King's) (Engl Film) 15, (QM) 9, (RH) 9, (UCL) 13; London South Bank 5; Loughborough 40; Manchester (Engl Lit) 11; Manchester Met 7; Middlesex 8; Newman (UC) 3; Northampton 3; Nottingham 22; Nottingham Trent 21; Oxford (success rate 25%), (Magdalen) 15; Oxford Brookes 15; Portsmouth 8; Reading 11; Roehampton 5; Salford 12; Sheffield 12; Sheffield Hallam 4; Southampton 4; Stirling 9; Sunderland 10; Swansea Met 4; Teesside 5; Trinity Saint David 4; Warwick 15, (Engl Thea) 26; Winchester 3; York 8; York St John 3.

Advice to applicants and planning the UCAS personal statement Applicants should read outside their subject. Details of any writing you have done (for example poetry, short stories) should be provided. Theatre visits and play readings are also important. Keep up to date by reading literary and theatre reviews in the national newspapers (keep a scrapbook of reviews for reference). Evidence is needed of a good writing style. Favourite authors, spare-time reading. Ability to write lucidly, accurately and succinctly. Evidence of literary enthusiasm. General interest in communications – verbal, visual, media. **Manchester** Due to the detailed nature of entry requirements for English Literature and American Studies courses, we are unable to include full details in the prospectus. For complete and up-to-date information on our entry requirements for these courses, please visit our website at www.manchester.ac.uk/ugcourses.

Misconceptions about this course **Birmingham City** The study of English language means descriptive linguistics – the course won't necessarily enable students to speak or write better English. **Buckingham** Native speakers of English often do not realise that the EFL degree courses are restricted to non-native speakers of English. **East Anglia** (Engl Lit Crea Writ) This is not simply a creative writing course: English literature is the predominant element. **Liverpool** (Engl Comm St) The course is not a training in journalism, although some students go on to work in the press, radio or TV.

Selection interviews **Yes** Bangor (mature students), Brunel, Cambridge, Canterbury Christ Church, Exeter, Gloucestershire, Huddersfield, Hull, Hull (Scarborough), Kingston, Lancaster, Leeds Trinity (UC), London (Gold), (RH), London South Bank, Middlesex, Newcastle, Newport, Oxford, Portsmouth, Reading, Roehampton, Trinity Saint David, Warwick; **Some** Aberystwyth, Anglia Ruskin, Bangor, Bath Spa, Birmingham City, Blackburn (Coll Univ Centre), Blackpool and Fylde (Coll), Bristol, Cardiff (UWIC), Chester, De Montfort, Derby, Dundee, East Anglia, Leeds, Liverpool (Engl Comm St), London (King's), London Met, Loughborough, Salford, Southampton, Swansea Met, Truro (Coll), Wolverhampton.

Interview advice and questions Questions will almost certainly be asked on set A-level texts and any essays which have been submitted prior to the interview. You will also be expected to have read outside your A-level subjects and to answer questions about your favourite authors, poets, dramatists etc. Questions in the past have included: Do you think that class discussion plays an important part in your English course? What is the value of studying a text in depth rather than just reading it for pleasure? What is the difference between satire and comedy? Are books written by women different from those written by men? Why would you go to see a production of *Hamlet*? What are your views on the choice of novels for this year's Booker Prize? Short verbal tests and a précis may be set. **Buckingham** It is useful to know if there is any particular reason why students want a particular programme; for example, for the TEFL degree is a member of the family a teacher? **Cambridge** We look for interviewees who respond positively to ideas, can think on their feet, engage intelligently with critical issues and sustain an argument. If they don't evince any of these we reject them. What books are bad for you? **East Anglia** (Engl Lit Dr) How do you reconcile yourself to an academic interest in literature on the one hand and the belief in practical performance on the other? Interviews are accompanied by auditions. **Leeds** Interview questions based on information supplied in the personal ststement. One third of the applicants are interviewed. Academic ability; current reading interests. **Liverpool** (Engl Comm St) General questions only. Reading interests, general interests, career ambitions. **London (King's)** Interview questions are based on the information in the personal statement. Applicants are asked to prepare a short literary text which will be discussed at interview. **(UCL)** The interview will focus on an ability to discuss literature in terms of language, plot, characters and genre. Following the interview applicants will be asked to write a critical commentary on an example of unseen prose or verse. **Oxford** Is there a difference between innocence and naivety? If you could make up a word, what would it be? Why? Do you think *Hamlet* is a bit long? No? Well I do. Is the Bible a fictional work? Was Shakespeare a rebel? **Roehampton** Samples of work taken to interview and discussed. **Warwick** We may ask students to sight-read or to analyse a text. **York** Written essays are required to be submitted at interview. See also **Chapter 5**.

Reasons for rejection (non-academic) Some are well-informed about English literature – others are not. Inability to respond to questions about their current studies. Lack of enthusiasm for the challenge of studying familiar subjects from a different perspective. Must be able to benefit from the course. Little interest in how people communicate with each other. They don't know a single thing about our course. **Bangor** We reject those who decline interviews. **Bristol** Not enough places to make offers to all those whose qualifications deserve one. **Cambridge** See **Interview advice and questions**. **East Anglia** (Engl Am Lit) Personal statement unconvincing in its commitment to American literature. (Other courses) Poor examples of work submitted. **Leeds** Unsuitable predictions. **Liverpool** (Engl Comm St) Student more suited to a practical course. Ungrammatical Personal Statement. **Oxford** (1) The essay she submitted was poorly written, careless and reductive and, in general, lacking in attention to the subject. She should be encouraged to write less and think more about what she is saying. She seems to put down the first thing that comes into her head. (2) We had the feeling that he rather tended to dismiss texts which did not satisfy the requirements of his personal canon and that he therefore might not be happy pursuing a course requiring the study of texts from all periods. (3) In her essay on Bronte she took a phrase from Arnold which was metaphorical (to do with hunger) and applied it literally, writing at length about the diet of the characters. **Reading** None. If they have reached the interview we have already eliminated all other factors. **Sheffield Hallam** Apparent lack of eagerness to tackle all three strands of the course (literature, language and creative writing). **Southampton** Insufficient or patchy academic achievement. Applicants coming from non-standard academic backgrounds are assessed in terms of their individual situations.

AFTER-RESULTS ADVICE

Offers to applicants repeating A-levels **Higher** Aberystwyth, Sheffield Hallam, Southampton (varies), Warwick; **Possibly higher** Lancaster, Newcastle, Oxford Brookes; **Same** Anglia Ruskin, Bangor, Birmingham City, Blackpool and Fylde (Coll), Bristol, Cambridge, Cardiff, Cardiff (UWIC), Chester, Chichester, Cumbria, De Montfort, Derby, Dundee, Durham, East Anglia, Edge Hill, Hull, Leeds, Leeds Trinity (UC), Liverpool, Liverpool Hope, London (Gold), (RH), Loughborough, Manchester Met, Newman (UC), Newport, Nottingham, Nottingham Trent, Portsmouth, Reading, Roehampton, St Mary's Twickenham (UC), Salford, Sheffield, Staffordshire, Stirling, Suffolk (Univ Campus), Trinity Saint David, Ulster, Winchester, Wolverhampton, York, York St John.

GRADUATE DESTINATIONS AND EMPLOYMENT (2008 HESA)

English graduates surveyed 7785 **Employed** 3385 **In further study** 1780 **Assumed unemployed** 645.

Creative Writing graduates surveyed 495 **Employed** 220 **In further study** 60 **Assumed unemployed** 65.

Career note English graduates work in the media, management, public and social services, business, administration and IT, sales retail, the cultural industries and the teaching profession. Those who have undertaken courses in creative writing could aim for careers in advertising, public relations, journalism or publishing.

OTHER DEGREE SUBJECTS FOR CONSIDERATION

Communication Studies; Drama; Language courses; Linguistics; Literature; Media Studies.

ENVIRONMENTAL SCIENCES/STUDIES

(including **Conservation, Ecology, Environmental Health** and **Environmental Management**; see also **Biological Sciences, Biology, Engineering (Civil), Geography, Geology/Geological Sciences** and **Town and Country Planning**)

Environmental Science/Studies courses need to be considered with care as, depending on their content and specialisms, they lead to very different careers. Environmental Health courses usually focus on the training of environmental health officers whilst Environmental Studies or Science degrees cover a range of subjects with options which may include biology, geography, geology, oceanography, chemistry, legal, social and political issues.

Useful websites www.cieh.org; www.ends.co.uk; www.enn.com; www.iagre.org.uk; www.defra.gov.uk; www.socenv.org.uk; www.ies-uk.org.uk; www.noc.soton.ac.uk.

NB The points totals shown to the left of the institutions are for ease of reference only. It must not be assumed that Tariff points are always used by institutions or that they can be substituted for an offer in grades. The level of an offer is not necessarily indicative of the quality of a course.

COURSE OFFERS INFORMATION

Subject requirements/preferences GCSE English, mathematics and a science (often chemistry or biology) usually required. **AL** One or two science subjects are usually stipulated; mathematics may be required. **Meteorology** Mathematics, physics and another science may be required sometimes with specified grades, eg **Reading** mathematics and physics grade B.

NB In 2011 universities and colleges will differ in their use of GCE AL/AS unit grade information, A* grades, the Extended Project (EPQ), the Advanced Diploma and the Cambridge Pre-U examination when considering applicants and making offers. An EPQ may be accepted in place of an AS subject. Check websites of universities and colleges for the latest offers information.

Your target offers and examples of courses provided by each institution

380 pts **Cambridge** – A*AA college offers may vary (Lnd Econ; Nat Sci (Geol Sci)) (IB 38–42 pts)
London (UCL) – AAAe–ABBe (Env Geosci) (IB 36–38 pts)

360 pts **Birmingham** – AAA (Env Geosci Int Yr) (IB 34–38 pts)
East Anglia – AAA–AAB (MSci Env Sci; Env Earth Sci; Clim Sci; Ecol; Env Geophys; Meteor Ocean) (IB 34–33 pts)
Leeds – AAA (Int Env Mgt) (IB 38 pts)
Nottingham – AAA (Archit Env Des) (IB 28 pts)

340 pts **Bristol** – AAB (Env Geosci) (IB 35 pts)
Cardiff – AAB–ABB 340–320 pts (Ecol; Env Geosci) (IB 34 pts)
Edinburgh – AAB 2nd yr entry (Ecol Sci; Ecol Sci (Cons Ecol Mgt) (Ecol) (Env Sci) (Frsty); Env Arch) (IB 34 pts)
Exeter (Cornwall) – AAB–BBB (Cons Biol Ecol; Renew Ener) (IB 34–29 pts))
Imperial London – AAB (Ecol Env Biol; Env Geosci)
Lancaster – AAB 340 pts (Env Sci N Am/Aus; MEng Sust Eng; MChem Env Chem Abrd; Earth Env Sci Abrd) (IB 30 pts)
Leeds – AAB (Ener Env Eng) (IB 36 pts)
Manchester – AAB–BBB (Blt Nat Env courses) (IB 32–35 pts)
St Andrews – AAB (MA Sust Dev; Ecol Cons) (IB 36 pts)
Sheffield – AAB (MBiol Sci Ecol) (IB 35 pts)
Southampton – AAB (MEnvSci Env Sci) (IB 34 pts)

320 pts **Birmingham** – ABB–BBC (Env Geosci)
Durham – ABB (Env Geosci) (IB 34 pts)
East Anglia – ABB–BBB 320 pts (BSc Env Earth Sci; Env Sci; Clim Sci; Meteor Ocean; Meteor Clim; Geophys Sci; Ecol) (IB 32–31 pts)
Glasgow – ABB (Env Biogeochem; Env Chem Geog) (IB 32 pts)
Lancaster – ABB 320 pts (Env Biol Abrd; Ecol Abrd; MEng Sust Eng)
Leeds – ABB–BBB 320–300 pts (Ecol Env Biol) (IB 34–32 pts)
Liverpool – ABB–BBB (Ecol Env) (IB 33–30 pts HL biol 6)
London LSE – ABB (Env Plcy Econ; Env Plcy) (IB 37 pts HL 666)
Loughborough – 320 pts (Chem Eng Env Prot) (IB 34 pts)
Newcastle – ABB–BBB (Env Sci; Mar Env Eng) (IB 32 pts)
Nottingham – ABB (Env Sci; Env Sci Euro) (IB 24–30 pts)
Reading – 320 pts (Meteor Yr Okl; App Ecol Cons; MEnv Env Sci) (IB 31 pts)
St Andrews – ABB (Env Geosci) (IB 30 pts)
Sheffield – ABB (Env Sci; Ecol) (IB 33 pts)
Southampton – ABB (BSc Env Sci) (IB 34–32 pts)
Sussex – ABB–BBC (Ecol Cons; Env Sci) (IB 32–34 pts)
York – ABB–BBB (Ecol Cons Euro; Env Econ Env Mgt; Env Geog; Env Sci) (IB 34 pts)

300 pts **Aberdeen** – BBB 300 pts 2nd yr entry (Env Sci; Anim Ecol; Ecol; Wldlf Mgt)
Bangor – 300 pts (MEnvSci Env Sci) (IB 28 pts)
Birmingham – BBB (BSc Env Mgt; Env Sci) (IB 30–32 pts)
Cardiff – BBB 300 pts (BSc Env Geosci; Ecol) (IB 32 pts)
Dundee – BBB 300 pts 2nd yr entry (Env Sust Bus; Env Sci; Env Sci Geog; Renew Ener) (IB 26 pts)
Edinburgh – BBB 1st yr entry (Ecol Sci; Ecol Sci (Cons Ecol Mgt) (Ecol) (Env Sci) (Frsty); Arch Env) (IB 32 pts)
Essex – 300–260 pts (Ecology) (IB 26–28 pts)
Lancaster – BBB (Env Chem; Env Biol; Ecol; Env Sci) (IB 29 pts)
Lancaster – ABC (Env Maths) (IB 28 pts)
Leeds – BBB (Env Cons; Env Sust; Env Sci; Env Bus; BA Env Mgt) (IB 32 pts)
London (QM) – 300–340 pts (Env Sci; Env Geog; Glob Chng Env Econ Dev) (IB 32 pts)
London (RH) – BBB 300 pts (Env Geol) (IB 34 pts)
Manchester – BBB (Env Sci; Env St) (IB 32 pts)
Newcastle – BBB–BBC (Cntry Mgt; Rur St) (IB 30 pts)
Plymouth – 300–360 pts (Mar Biol Cstl Ecol) (IB 28 pts)
Queen's Belfast – BBB (Env Biol) (IB 30 pts)
Reading – 300 pts (Env Foren; Env Cntry Mgt; Meteor Clim)
Southampton – BBB–BCC (Sci Fdn Yr) (IB 30–28 pts HL 16 pts)
Stirling – BBB 2nd yr entry (Env Sci; Ecol; Cons Sci)
Warwick – BBB (Biol Sci (Env Res); Env Biol) (IB 32 pts)

280 pts **Aberystwyth** – 280 pts (Biol Sci (Env Biol)) (IB 28 pts)
Coventry – 280–300 pts (Clim Chng; Glob Sust; Geog Nat Haz)
Huddersfield – 280 pts (Bus St Env Mgt)
Keele – 280–300 pts (Env Sust; App Env Sci)
Lancaster – BBC 280 pts (BEng Sust Eng)
Liverpool – BBC 280 pts (Env Plan)
Liverpool John Moores – 280 pts (Ener Mgt Sust)
Manchester – BBC (Env Mgt)
Northumbria – 280 pts (Env Mgt; Env Hlth)
Nottingham – BBC (Sust Blt Env)
Oxford Brookes – BBC (Env Sci courses) (IB 30 pts)
Staffordshire – 280 pts (Env Sust; Env Cons) (IB 24 pts)
Teesside – 280 pts (Env Sust)
Ulster – 280 pts (Env Hlth) (IB 32 pts)

270 pts **Glasgow Caledonian** – 270 pts (Env Mgt Plan)

260 pts **Bradford** – 260 pts (Env Sci)
Brighton – BCC (Env Haz; Env Sci) (IB 28 pts)
Bristol UWE – 260–300 pts (Env Biol; Tour Env Mgt; Env Sci; Cons Biol) (IB 24–28 pts)
Liverpool Hope – 260 pts (Env Biol Comb; Env Mgt Comb)
Nottingham – BCC (Env Biol) (IB 24–30 pts)
Strathclyde – BCC 1st yr entry (Env Hlth)

240 pts **Aberdeen** – CCC 240 pts 1st yr entry (Env Sci; Ecol; Anim Ecol; Wldlf Mgt) (IB 28 pts)
Anglia Ruskin – 240 pts (Env Plan) (IB 24 pts)
Bangor – 240–300 pts (Env Cons; Env Sci; Ecol; Env Mgt; Sust Dev; Agric Cons Env; App Ter Mar Ecol; Env Plan Mgt; Env Chem) (IB 28 pts)
Bolton – 240 pts (Env St courses)
Bournemouth – 240 pts (Mar Cstl Mgt; Ecol Wldlf Cons; Env Foren)
Brighton – CCC/BCD 240–280 pts (Env Biol Educ)
Chester – 240 pts (Nat Haz Mgt)
Coventry – 240 pts (Env Hlth)
Cumbria – 240 pts (Anim Cons Sci)
De Montfort – 240 pts (Grn Ener Tech)
Dundee – CCC 240 pts 1st yr entry (Env Sci; Env Sci Geog; Env Sust Int Bus; Renew Ener)
Edinburgh Napier – 240 pts (Ener Env Eng)
Glamorgan – 240–280 pts (Int Wldlf Biol)
Greenwich – 240 pts (Env Sci; Sust Dev) (IB 24 pts)
Hertfordshire – 240 pts (Env Mgt courses) (IB 24–26 pts)
Hull – 240–300 pts (Env Mgt)
Kent – 240 pts (Env Soc Sci) (IB 27 pts)
Kingston – 240–280 pts (Env Mgt; Env Sci; Env Haz Disas Mgt; Sust Dev; App Env Geol)
Liverpool John Moores – 240 pts (Pblc Hlth (Env))
Manchester Met – 240 pts (Clim Chng; Ecol Cons; Env Sci) (IB 24–28 pts)
Northampton – 240–280 pts (Env Sci (Clim Chng) (Lnd Ecol) (Wst Mgt); App Cons Biol) (IB 24 pts)
Nottingham Trent – 240 pts (Env Cons Cntry Mgt) (IB 24 pts)
Plymouth – 240–280 pts (Env Sci; Env Sci (Biodiv Cons) (Clim Chng) (Env Sust) (Env Hlth) (Mar Cons) (Res Sust)) (IB 28 pts)
Portsmouth – 240–300 pts (Mar Env Sci; Env Sci)
Roehampton – 240–300 pts (Cons Biol)

230 pts **Sheffield Hallam** – 230 pts (Env Mgt; Env St; Env Cons)

220 pts **Bangor** – 220–260 pts (Mar Env St) (IB 28 pts)
Bath Spa – 220–260 pts (Env Sci)
Cardiff (UWIC) – 220 pts (Env Hlth)
Central Lancashire – 220 pts (Env Mgt; Env Haz)
Edge Hill – 220 pts (Env Sci)
Edinburgh Napier – 220 pts (Ecotour; Env Biol)
Harper Adams (UC) – 220–240 pts (Cntry Env Mgt)
Hull – 220–280 pts (Ecol; Env Sci)
Liverpool John Moores – 220 pts (Env Sci)
Liverpool John Moores – 220–260 pts (Out Educ Env Educ)
Nottingham Trent – 220 pts (Wldlf Cons)
Stirling – CCD 1st yr entry (Env Sci; Cons Sci; Ecol)
Ulster – 220 pts (Env Sci courses) (IB 24 pts)
Worcester – 220 pts (Ecol; Env Mgt) (IB 26 pts)

200 pts **Anglia Ruskin** – 200 pts (Nat Hist Ecol Cons)
Canterbury Christ Church – 200 pts (Ecol Cons)
Central Lancashire – 200–240 pts (Env Haz Sci Plcy Mgt)
Glyndŵr – 200 pts (Env St Mgt; Env Sci; Sust Dev; Renew Ener Sust Tech)
Kingston – 200–280 pts (Env St courses)
Leeds Met – 200 pts (Pblc Hlth Env Hlth) (IB 26 pts)

Middlesex – 200–280 pts (Env Pblc Hlth)
Nottingham Trent – 200 pts (Env Sci)
Plymouth – 200 pts (Env Constr Surv)
Salford – 200 pts (Env Mgt; Wldlf Prac Cons; Env Geog; Env Hlth) (IB 24 pts)
Wolverhampton – 200–260 pts (Env Sci Mgt; Env Hlth)

180 pts **Derby** – 180–240 pts (Env Haz)
Southampton Solent – 180 pts (Geog Env St)
Trinity Saint David – 180–240 pts (Env Arch) (IB 26 pts)
Writtle (Coll) – 180 pts (Cons Env (Biol Surv))

160 pts **Blackpool and Fylde (Coll)** – 160 pts+portfolio (Des Wldlf Env Photo)
London South Bank – 160 pts (Urb Env Plan)
SAC (Scottish CAg) – CC (Sust Env Mgt)
Swansea Met – 160–340 pts (Env Cons)
UHI Millennium Inst – CC (Env Herit St; Sust Frsty Mgt Frst Cons)

Open University – (Env St – contact +44 (0)845 300 6090 or www.openuniversity.co.uk/you)

Alternative offers
See **Chapter 7** and **Appendix 1** for grades/UCAS Tariff points information for the International Baccalaureate, Scottish Highers/Advanced Highers, the Welsh Baccalaureate, the Irish Leaving Certificate, the Cambridge Pre-U Diploma, the Advanced Diploma and the Extended Project.

EXAMPLES OF FOUNDATION DEGREES IN THE SUBJECT FIELD

Askham Bryan (Coll); Bournemouth; Cumbria; Glyndŵr; Leeds City (Coll); Manchester (Coll); Nottingham Trent; Suffolk (Univ Campus); Writtle (Coll).

CHOOSING YOUR COURSE (SEE ALSO CH.1)

Some course features
East Anglia A wide range of Environmental Science courses with free choice options from other subject areas, eg music, drama, languages, and opportunities to study in Australia, New Zealand, USA, Canada, France and Spain.
Lancaster Some courses focus on environmental biology, chemistry or mathematics.
London LSE The course in Environmental Policy focuses on social science issues unlike most courses which offer a natural sciences perspective.
Reading The BSc course offers pathways in environmental change, habitat management, earth systems and earth and atmospheric science. There is also a course in Meteorology with some Met Office scholarships available for 'end of first year' students on the basis of academic performance.
Stirling One or two semesters can be taken at Guelph University in Canada.
Sussex A flexible degree with the option to specialise in development studies focusing on the developing world, eg colonialism, global cultures, nationalism, race.

Universities and colleges teaching quality See www.qaa.ac.uk; www.unistats.com.

Top research universities and colleges (RAE 2008) (**Geography and Environmental Studies**) Bristol; Cambridge; Durham; Oxford; London (QM); Leeds; London (King's), (UCL); London LSE; Sheffield; London (RH); Aberystwyth. (**Earth Systems and Environmental Sciences**) Cambridge; Oxford; London (Birk), (UCL); Reading; Bristol; East Anglia; London (RH); Manchester; Southampton.

Examples of sandwich degree courses Birmingham; Bangor; Bradford; Brighton; Bristol UWE; Cardiff; Cardiff (UWIC); Coventry; Edinburgh Napier; Glasgow Caledonian; Harper Adams (UC); Hertfordshire; Kingston; Liverpool John Moores; Loughborough; Manchester Met; Nottingham Trent; Reading; Salford; Southampton Solent; Teesside; Ulster; West Scotland; Wolverhampton.

ADMISSIONS INFORMATION

Number of applicants per place (approx) Abertay Dundee 5; Aberystwyth 3; Bangor 3; Bath Spa 2; Birmingham 5; Bournemouth 4; Bradford 3; Bristol 7; Bristol UWE 1; Cardiff (UWIC) 4; Coventry 9; De

Montfort 9; Dundee 6; Durham 5; East Anglia 7; Edinburgh 1; Essex 3; Glamorgan 1; Glasgow Caledonian 1; Gloucestershire 11; Glyndŵr 3; Greenwich 2; Harper Adams (UC) 5; Hertfordshire 5; Hull 8; Kingston 3; Lampeter 3; Lancaster 11; Leeds (Env Sci Ener) 2; Liverpool John Moores 5; London (King's) 5, (RH) 8; London LSE 4; Manchester Met (Env Sci) 5; Northampton 4; Northumbria 8; Nottingham 6; Nottingham Trent 3; Oxford Brookes 13; Plymouth 8; Portsmouth 5; Roehampton 3; Salford 8; Sheffield Hallam 8; Southampton 5; Stirling 10; Strathclyde 1; Ulster 16; Wolverhampton 2; Worcester 7; York 4.

Advice to applicants and planning the UCAS personal statement 'We want doers, not just thinkers' is one comment from an admissions tutor. Describe any field courses which you have attended; make an effort to visit one of the National Parks. Discuss these visits and identify any particular aspects which impressed you. Outline travel interests. Give details of work as a conservation volunteer and other outside-school activities. Strong communication skills, people-oriented work experience. Watch your spelling and grammar! What sparked your interest in Environmental Science? Discuss your field trips. (**Env Hlth courses**) A basic knowledge of environmental health as opposed to environmental sciences. Work experience in an environmental health department is looked upon very favourably. See also **Appendix 4**.

Misconceptions about this course **Bangor** Students should note that only simple mathematical skills are required for this course. **Leeds** (Ener Env Sci) Note that the course is closer to environmental technology than to environmental science. **Southampton** This is not just a course for environmentalists, for example links with BP, IBM etc. **Wolverhampton** This is a course in Environmental Science, not Environmental Studies: there is a difference. **York** (Env Econ Env Mgt) Some students worry that the economics part of the course will be too difficult which is not the case.

Selection interviews **Yes** Bradford, Bristol UWE, Cambridge, Coventry, Durham, Glamorgan, Gloucestershire, Greenwich, Harper Adams (UC) (advisory), Hertfordshire, Kingston, Lampeter, Manchester Met, Newcastle, Newport, Nottingham, Nottingham Trent, Oxford Brookes, Sheffield Hallam, Strathclyde, Sussex; **Some** Anglia Ruskin, Bangor, Bath Spa, Birmingham, Cardiff (UWIC), Derby, Dundee, East Anglia, London (King's), Plymouth, Salford, Southampton, Staffordshire, York.

Interview advice and questions Environmental issues are constantly in the news, so keep abreast of developments. You could be asked to discuss any particular environmental problems in the area in which you live and to justify your stance on any environmental issues on which you have strong opinions. **Bath Spa** Questions on school work, current affairs and field courses. **East Anglia** Can you display an informed interest in any aspect of environmental science? See also **Chapter 5**.

Reasons for rejection (non-academic) Inability to be aware of the needs of others.

AFTER-RESULTS ADVICE

Offers to applicants repeating A-levels **Higher** Greenwich, Lancaster, London (King's), Nottingham, Nottingham Trent, Strathclyde; **Possibly higher** Aberystwyth, Bradford, Northumbria; **Same** Birmingham, Bangor, Brighton, Cardiff (UWIC), Derby, Dundee, East Anglia, Leeds, Liverpool John Moores, Manchester Met, Plymouth, SAC (Scottish CAg), Salford, Southampton, Ulster, Wolverhampton.

GRADUATE DESTINATIONS AND EMPLOYMENT (2007/8 HESA)

Graduates surveyed 2715 **Employed** 1355 **In further study** 565 **Assumed unemployed** 140.

Career note Some graduates find work with government departments, local authorities, statutory and voluntary bodies in areas like land management and pollution control. Others go into a range of non-scientific careers.

OTHER DEGREE SUBJECTS FOR CONSIDERATION

Biological Sciences; Biology; Chemistry; Earth Sciences; Environmental Engineering; Geography; Geology; Meteorology; Ocean Sciences/Oceanography; Town and Country Planning.

EUROPEAN STUDIES

(see also **Business Courses, Languages** and **Russian and East European Studies**)

European Studies is an increasingly popular subject and in many cases offers the language student an opportunity to study modern languages within the context of a European country (for example, economics, politics, legal, social and cultural aspects). In these courses there is usually a strong emphasis on the written and spoken word. It is important to note, also, that many courses in other subjects offer the opportunity to study in Europe.

Useful websites www.europa.eu; www.eaces.net; www.britishcouncil.org/erasmus; see also Languages.

NB The points totals shown to the left of the institutions are for ease of reference only. It must not be assumed that Tariff points are always used by institutions or that they can be substituted for an offer in grades. The level of an offer is not necessarily indicative of the quality of a course.

COURSE OFFERS INFORMATION

Subject requirements/preferences GCSE English and a foreign language for all courses and possibly mathematics. Grades may be stipulated. **AL** A modern language usually required.

NB In 2011 universities and colleges will differ in their use of GCE AL/AS unit grade information, A* grades, the Extended Project (EPQ), the Advanced Diploma and the Cambridge Pre-U examination when considering applicants and making offers. An EPQ may be accepted in place of an AS subject. Check websites of universities and colleges for the latest offers information.

Your target offers and examples of courses provided by each institution

380 pts **London (UCL)** – A*AA (Euro Soc Pol St) (IB 39 pts)

360 pts **Exeter** – AAA–AAB (Bus Econ Euro St) (IB 30–32 pts)
Lancaster – AAA (Euro Lgl St) (IB 32 pts)
London (King's) – AAB+AS (Euro St (Fr/Ger/Span)) (IB 34 pts)

340 pts **Birmingham** – AAB (Econ Cnt E Euro St) (IB 34 pts)
Birmingham – AAB–ABB (Euro Bus Mgt; Euro Pol Soty Econ) (IB 33–36 pts)
Cardiff – AAB (Euro Pol Int Rel)
Durham – AAB (Comp Sci (Euro St); Maths (Euro St); Theol (Euro St)) (IB 36–32 pts)
Glasgow – AAB (Cnt E Euro St) (IB 34 pts)
Lancaster – AAB (Euro Mgt Fr/Ger/Ital/Span)
Newcastle – AAB–BBB (Gov EU St) (IB 32–36 pts)
Sussex – AAB–ABB (Pol Contemp Euro St)

320 pts **Bath** – ABB–BBB (Modn Langs Euro St) (IB 34 pts HL lang 6)
Cardiff – ABB–BBB (EU St) (IB 33 pts)
East Anglia – ABB–BBB (Int Rel Euro Pol; Euro St Lang)
Kent – 320 pts (Euro Econ; Euro St (Hum) courses)
Lancaster – ABB (Euro Langs Mgt) (IB 30 pts)
Leeds – ABB (Euro Pol)
Leicester – ABB (Euro St) (IB 28–30 pts)
Manchester – ABB–BBC (Euro St Fr/Ger/Ital/Port/Russ/Span) (IB 33–30 pts)
Southampton – ABB 320 pts (Langs Contemp Euro St) (IB 32 pts)

300 pts **Aston** – 300–320 pts (Euro St Fr/Ger/Span) (IB 31–33 pts)
Birmingham – 300 pts (Modn Langs Euro St (Soty Cult Hist) (Pol)) (IB 32 pts)
Bristol UWE – 300–340 pts (Euro Int Law) (IB 26–32 pts)
Dundee – BBB–CCC 300–240 pts (Euro St courses; Euro Pol; Transat St Euro St) (IB 29 pts)
Edinburgh – BBB (Modn Euro Lang EU St)
Lancaster – BBB (Euro Langs Film St) (IB 33 pts)
London (RH) – ABC–BBB 300 pts (Euro St Fr/Ger/Ital/Span)
Nottingham – ABC (Modn Euro St) (IB 32 pts)
Reading – 300–320 pts (Euro St; Euro Cult Hist)

Stirling – BBB 2nd yr entry (Euro Soc Plcy) (IB 30 pts)
Strathclyde – BBB–BCC (Civ Eng Euro St) (IB 30–34 pts)
Swansea – 300 pts (Geog Euro St)

280 pts **Aberystwyth** – 280 pts (Euro St) (IB 29 pts)
Essex – 280 pts (Euro St; Euro St Fr/Ger/Ital/Span; Euro St Pol) (IB 27 pts)
Kent – 280 pts (Euro St (Soc Sci) courses) (IB 28–32 pts)
London (QM) – 280 pts (Euro St courses) (IB 32 pts)
Loughborough – 280–320 pts (Euro St) (IB 32 pts)
Portsmouth – 280–300 pts (Euro Bus (Fr/Ger/Span); Euro St)
Stirling – BBC (Euro Film Media)

260 pts **Nottingham Trent** – 260 pts (Euro St courses) (IB 24 pts)

240 pts **Aberdeen** – CCC (Euro St) (IB 28 pts)
Manchester Met – 240 pts (Euro Film; Int Bus (Euro Mgt)) (IB 26 pts)
Stirling – CCC 1st yr entry (Euro Soc Plcy)
Ulster – 240 pts (Euro St courses) (IB 24 pts)

220 pts **Southampton Solent** – 220 pts (Law Euro St)

200 pts **Manchester Met** – 200 pts (Euro St Comb Hons)
Portsmouth – 200–280 pts (Euro St Int Rel)

160 pts **London South Bank** – 160 pts (Euro Pol St)

Open University – (Euro St – contact +44 (0)845 300 6090 or www.openuniversity.co.uk/you)

Alternative offers
See **Chapter 7** and **Appendix 1** for grades/UCAS Tariff points information for the International Baccalaureate, Scottish Highers/Advanced Highers, the Welsh Baccalaureate, the Irish Leaving Certificate, the Cambridge Pre-U Diploma, the Advanced Diploma and the Extended Project.

CHOOSING YOUR COURSE (SEE ALSO CH.1)

Some course features
Bath Two modern languages are offered with European Studies, the third year is spent abroad.
East Anglia In the School of International and European Studies a foundation (first) year leads to a wide range of options.
Glasgow (Cnt E Euro St) The course focuses on the history, economics, politics and sociology of the countries in Central and Eastern Europe; Czech, Polish or Russian can also be studied.
Lancaster The course has the option to study one or two European languages.
Loughborough Major studies in International Relations and minor studies in, eg business, media studies, languages, psychology. One semester in Year 2 is spent in a partner institution in the Czech Republic, Sweden or Finland.
Portsmouth European Studies can be taken with or without a European language.

Universities and colleges teaching quality See www.qaa.ac.uk; www.unistats.com.

Top research universities and colleges (RAE 2008) Southampton; Sussex; Birmingham; Portsmouth; Cardiff; Bath; Liverpool; Aberystwyth.

ADMISSIONS INFORMATION

Number of applicants per place (approx) Aberystwyth 10; Aston 5; Cardiff 5; Dundee 6; Durham 2; East Anglia 11; Hull 6; Kent 11; Lancaster 9; Leicester 15; London (King's) 7, (UCL) 2; London South Bank 6; Loughborough 4; Northumbria 7; Nottingham 6; Nottingham Trent 12; Portsmouth 5.

Advice to applicants and planning the UCAS personal statement Try to identify an interest you have in the country relevant to your studies. Visits to that country should be described. Read the national newspapers and magazines and keep up to date with political and economic developments. Show your interest in the culture and civilisation of Europe as a whole, through, for example, European travel. Show your motivation for choosing the course and give details of your personal achievements and any future career plans, showing your international awareness and perspective.

Selection interviews **Yes** Durham, East Anglia, Hull, London (Gold), London Met, London South Bank, Stirling, Sussex; **Some** Cardiff, Dundee, Kent (not usually), Liverpool John Moores, Loughborough, Portsmouth.

Interview advice and questions Whilst your interest in studying a language may be the main reason for applying for this subject, the politics, economics and culture of European countries are constantly in the news. You should keep up-to-date with any such topics concerning your chosen country and be prepared for questions. A language test may occupy part of the interview. **Loughborough** No tests. Interview designed to inform students about the course. See also **Chapter 5**.

Reasons for rejection (non-academic) Poor powers of expression. Lack of ideas on any issues. Lack of enthusiasm.

AFTER-RESULTS ADVICE

Offers to applicants repeating A-levels **Higher** Aberystwyth, East Anglia; **Same** Aston, Cardiff, Dundee, Liverpool John Moores, London South Bank, Loughborough.

GRADUATE DESTINATIONS AND EMPLOYMENT (2007/8 HESA)

Graduates surveyed 75 **Employed** 30 **In further study** 20 **Assumed unemployed** 5. See also **Languages** and separate language tables.

Career note See **Languages**.

OTHER DEGREE SUBJECTS FOR CONSIDERATION

Business and Management; History; International Relations; Politics; Language courses.

FILM, RADIO, VIDEO and TV STUDIES

(see also **Communication Studies/Communication, Media Studies** and **Photography**)

A wide range of courses in this field are on offer although applicants should be aware that many courses cover theoretical or historical aspects of the subject. Students wishing to follow courses with practical applications must check with the institution beforehand to determine how much time in the course is spent on actual film-making or video production.

Useful websites www.bfi.org.uk; www.film.com; www.allmovie.com; www.bksts.com; www.imdb.com; www.fwfr.com; www.bafta.org; www.movingimage.us; www.britfilms.com; www.filmsite.org; www.festival-cannes.com/en; www.bbc.co.uk/jobs; http://rogerebert.suntimes.com; www.radiostudiesnetwork.org.uk.

NB The points totals shown to the left of the institutions are for ease of reference only. It must not be assumed that Tariff points are always used by institutions or that they can be substituted for an offer in grades. The level of an offer is not necessarily indicative of the quality of a course.

COURSE OFFERS INFORMATION

Subject requirements/preferences **GCSE** English usually required. Courses vary, check prospectuses. **AL** English may be stipulated for some courses.

NB In 2011 universities and colleges will differ in their use of GCE AL/AS unit grade information, A* grades, the Extended Project (EPQ), the Advanced Diploma and the Cambridge Pre-U examination when considering applicants and making offers. An EPQ may be accepted in place of an AS subject. Check websites of universities and colleges for the latest offers information.

Your target offers and examples of courses provided by each institution

390 pts **Warwick** – AABb (Film TV St; Film Lit) (IB 36 pts)
360 pts **Exeter** – AAA–AAB (Engl Film St) (IB 32 pts)
London (King's) – AAB+AS (Film St) (IB 34 pts)
340 pts **East Anglia** – AAB–BBB (Film TV St; Film Engl St; Film Am St; Film St Art Hist; Span Film TV) (IB 31–33 pts)
Exeter – AAB–ABB (Film St Fr/Ger/Ital/Russ/Span) (IB 31–29 pts)
Glasgow – AAB (Film TV St courses) (IB 34 pts)
Kent – 340 pts (Film St) (IB 35–33 pts)
Manchester – AAB–BBB (Film St Lit St Dr; Film St Langs; Film St Sci Psy; Film St Blt Nat Env) (IB 35–32 pts)
Southampton – AAB–ABB (Film Phil; Film Hist; Film Span) (IB 34 pts HL 17 pts)
Sussex – AAB–BBB (Am St Film St; Dr St Film St; Film St) (IB 32–36 pts)
320 pts **Birmingham** – ABB (Modn Lang Film St)
Bournemouth – 320 pts (TV Script Film)
Brunel – BBC/BCC +AS/EPQ c 300 pts (Film TV St Gms; Film TV St Mus) (IB 31 pts)
Kent – 320–280 pts (Film St Hist Phil Art; Film St Comp; Film St Engl Am Postcol Lit)
Lancaster – ABB–BBB (Film St Cult St; Film St Sociol; Film St Engl Lit) (IB 29–30 pts)
Leeds – ABB (Broad Jrnl)
London (RH) – ABB–ABbb (Film TV)
St Andrews – ABB (Film St; Film St Arbc; Film St Psy; Film St Art Hist; Film St Scot Hist) (IB 32 pts)
Westminster – ABB (Film TV Prod) (IB 30 pts)
York – ABB (Film TV Prod) (IB 34 pts)
300 pts **Dundee** – BBB 2nd yr entry (Engl Film St)
Essex – BBB 300 pts (Film St; Film St Lit; Hist Film St Hist) (IB 32 pts)
Leeds – BBB (TV Prod; Cnma Photo) (IB 32 pts)
Leicester – BBB (Film St Engl; Modn Langs Film St) (IB 30–32 pts)
Liverpool – BBB (inc B/C lang) (Film St (Euro) Lang) (IB 30 pts)
London (QM) – 300–320 pts (Film St; Compar Lit Film St; Film St Dr) (IB 32 pts)
Nottingham – ABC/BBB (Film TV St Mus; Film TV St Cult Sociol; Film TV St Russ) (IB 32 pts)
Nottingham Trent – 300 pts (Broad Jrnl)
Queen's Belfast – BBB–BBCb (Film St courses)
Reading – 300–340 pts (Engl Lit Film Thea; Film Thea)
Surrey – BBB 300 pts (Film St; Film St Crea Writ)
Westminster – BBB (Rad Prod)
295 pts **Queen Margaret** – 295 pts (Stg Scrn)
280 pts **Aberystwyth** – 280 pts (Film TV St courses; Scngrph St courses) (IB 24–26 pts)
Chester – 280 pts (Rad Prod) (IB 24 pts)
Glamorgan – 280–320 pts (Film Vid; Film St)
Hertfordshire – 280–300 pts (Film TV (Fctn) (Doc) (Enter); Engl Lang Comm Film)
Lincoln – 280 pts (Film TV; Film TV Jrnl joint courses)
Liverpool John Moores – 280–320 pts (Film St; Film St Crea Writ; Film St Dr)
Manchester Met – 280 pts (Engl Film)
Nottingham Trent – 280 pts (Media (Film TV) (Crea Ind) (Comms))
Oxford Brookes – BBC (Film St; Film St Jap St) (IB 33–30 pts)
Reading – 280–300 pts (Film Thea (Ger)) (IB 32 pts)
Staffordshire – 280 pts (Film Prod Tech Mgt; Film Prod Mus Tech)
Stirling – BBC (Film Media courses; Euro Film Media; Glob Cnma Cult) (IB 32 pts)
Swansea – 280 pts (Scrn St joint courses)
260 pts **Aberdeen** – BCC 1st yr entry (Film Vis Cult courses) (IB 28 pts)
Bangor – 260–300 pts (Film St courses)
Birmingham City – 260–280 pts (Film Tech Prod; TV Tech Prod; Media Comm (Rad Prod) (TV Vid))
Bradford – 260 pts (TV Prod)

Brighton – BCC (Film Scrn St) (IB 28 pts)
Bristol UWE – 260–300 pts (Film St Joint Hons)
Gloucestershire – 260 pts (Film St; Dig Film Prod; Film St Crea Writ)
Hull – 260–300 pts (Film St courses)
Liverpool Hope – 260 pts (Film St Comb; Film TV Prod)
Manchester Met – 260 pts (Film TV Cult St)
Middlesex – 260 pts (TV Prod; Film Crea Writ)
Newport – 260 pts (Film Vid; Doc Film TV)
Northumbria – 260 pts (Film TV St)
Queen Margaret – 260 pts (Film Media)
Sheffield Hallam – 260 pts (Film Media Prod; Engl Scrn St; Film Vis Effcts)

240 pts **Bolton** – 240 pts (Film Prod Adv Mus Ind)
Canterbury Christ Church – CCC–BCC (Film Rad TV St (Film) (Rad) (TV) (Broad) (Animat))
Central Lancashire – 240 pts (TV Prod; Film TV Scrnwrit; Film Prod)
Chester – 240–280 pts (Film St courses; Rad Prod courses; TV Prod courses) (IB 24 pts)
Cumbria – 240 pts (Film TV Prod)
De Montfort – 240 pts (Photo Vid; Rad Prod; Film St Photo Vid; Aud Rec Tech)
Dundee – CCC 1st yr entry (Engl Film St)
Edinburgh Napier – 240 pts (Photo Film)
Glamorgan – 240–280 pts (TV Film Set Des)
Hertfordshire – 240 pts (3D Dig Animat)
London Met – 240–260 pts (Film Broad Prod; Film St)
Manchester Met – 240 pts (Contemp Film Vid; Film TV St; Euro Film Comb Hons)
Nottingham Trent – 240 pts (Film TV St; Des Film TV; Film TV joint Hons)
Portsmouth – 240–300 pts (Film St courses)
Roehampton – 240–320 pts (Film)
Sheffield Hallam – 240 pts (Engl Scrn St)
Southampton Solent – 240 pts (Film TV St; Film; Engl Film; Scrnwrit; TV Vid Prod; TV Std Prod)
Sunderland – 240 pts (Film Media (TV Rad); Dig Film Prod; Media Prod (TV Rad))
Ulster – 240 pts (Film St courses)
Winchester – 240–280 pts (Film Cnma Tech; Film St)
Worcester – 240–260 pts (Film St)
York St John – 240 pts (Film TV Prod;)

220 pts **Bath Spa** – 220–260 pts (Film Scrn St courses)
Bournemouth – 220 pts (Film Prod Cnma)
Edge Hill – 220–260 pts (Film St; Film St TV Prod; Film TV Prod; TV Prod Mgt)
Huddersfield (Barnsley) – 220 pts (Dig Film Vis Efcts Prod; Film Animat Mus Ent)
Kingston – 220 pts (Film St courses)
Leeds Trinity (UC) – 220 pts (Film St courses; Film TV St)
Northampton – 220–260 pts (Film TV St)
Sunderland – 220–280 pts (Engl Film; Film Media; TV St)
Teesside – 220–260 pts (Film TV Prod; Broad Media Prod)
Worcester – 220–260 pts (Dig Film Prod)

200 pts **Bucks New** – 200–240 pts (Film TV Prod; Dig Film Art)
Central Lancashire – 200 pts (Film Media St)
Creative Arts – 200 pts (Film Prod; Dig Film Scrn Arts) (IB 30 pts)
Cumbria – 200 pts (Film St joint Hons)
East London – 200 pts (Film St; Film Vid (Theor Prac))
Glyndŵr – 200 pts (Des (Crea Lens Media); Rad Prod Comm; TV)
Hereford (CA) – 200 pts (Film Scren Media Des)
Hertfordshire – 200 pts (Dig Film TV Tech)
Leeds Met – 200 pts (Film Mov Imag Prod)
Middlesex – 200–220 pts (Film St; Film Media Cult St)
Portsmouth – 200–280 pts (TV Film Prod; Vid Broad)
Staffordshire – 200 pts (Adv Commer Film Prod)

Swansea Met – 200 pts (Doc Vid; Vid Arts)
Thames Valley – 200 pts (Film Vid Prod Film St; TV)
180 pts **Anglia Ruskin** – 180–220 pts (Film St; Film TV Prod; Film TV St)
Derby – 180–240 pts (Film TV St; Film St; Film Vid Prod)
St Mary's Twickenham (UC) – 180–200 pts (Film Pop Cult)
Trinity Saint David – 180–300 pts (Film St Welsh; Film St Theol)
West Scotland – BC–CC (Film Scrnwrit; Broad Prod)
160 pts **Bedfordshire** – 160 pts (TV Prod)
Bournemouth Arts (UC) – 160 pts (Film Prod; Animat Prod)
Creative Arts – 160 pts (Photo Vid) (IB 24 pts)
London South Bank – 160 pts (Film St; Dig Film Vid)
South Essex (Coll) – 160 pts (TV Prod Scrn Media)
Southampton Solent – 160 pts (Snd Film TV Gms; Outsd Broad (Prod Ops))
Suffolk (Univ Campus) – 160 pts (Film Media St)
Wolverhampton – 160–220 pts (Film St courses)
120 pts **Arts London** – 120 pts (Film TV)
80 pts **Royal Scottish (RSACM)** – 80 pts min (Dig Film TV)

Keele – (Film St; new course – contact University)

Alternative offers

See **Chapter 7** and **Appendix 1** for grades/UCAS Tariff points information for the International Baccalaureate, Scottish Highers/Advanced Highers, the Welsh Baccalaureate, the Irish Leaving Certificate, the Cambridge Pre-U Diploma, the Advanced Diploma and the Extended Project.

EXAMPLES OF FOUNDATION DEGREES IN THE SUBJECT FIELD

Arts London; Bath Spa; Bournemouth; Bucks New; Cleveland (CAD); Colchester (Inst); Croydon; Derby; Falmouth (UC); Farnborough (CT); Glamorgan; Grimsby (IFHE); Hull (Coll); Leeds Met; Leicester (Coll); Manchester (Coll); Newcastle (Coll); Norwich Arts (UC); Norwich City (Coll); Nottingham New (Coll); Plymouth (CAD); St Helens (Coll); South Cheshire (Coll); South Essex (Coll); Stockport (Coll).

CHOOSING YOUR COURSE (SEE ALSO CH.1)

Some course features

East Anglia Emphasis on the history and theory of film with practical units offered in Years 2 and 3. Study abroad available in Europe, USA and Australia.
Manchester Met Practical work is the main focus of the Contemporary Film and Video programme whilst the other degree courses on offer here are predominantly critical and textual academic studies.
Oxford Brookes Film Studies can be taken as a Single Honours course or combined with one of nine other subjects including Japanese language, Marketing or Music.

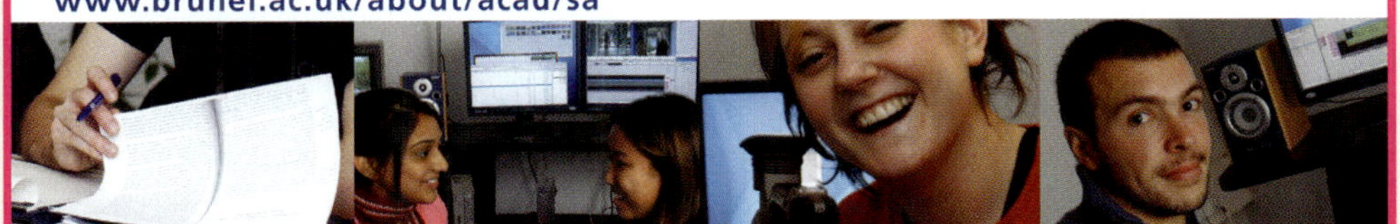

Portsmouth (Film St) The course allows students to combine their interests in reading, writing and the use of language.
Southampton Solent (Film Vid Tech) Practical production units in film and digital video-making alongside academic study.
York (Film TV Prod) This new BSc course combines practical production work with theoretical and historical understanding, involving students in a wide range of technical roles.

Universities and colleges teaching quality See www.qaa.ac.uk; www.unistats.com.

Top research universities and colleges (RAE 2008) See **Drama**.

Examples of sandwich degree courses See **Media Studies**.

ADMISSIONS INFORMATION

Number of applicants per place (approx) Anglia Ruskin 3; Bournemouth 30; Bournemouth Arts (UC) 9; Brunel 10; Canterbury Christ Church 50; Cardiff 11; Central Lancashire 5; East Anglia (Film Engl St) 7, (Film Am St) 5; Kent 30; Leicester 5; Liverpool John Moores 17; London Met 7; Portsmouth 20; Sheffield Hallam 60; Southampton 5; Southampton Solent 7; Staffordshire 31; Stirling 12; Warwick 18; Westminster 41; York 4; York St John 6.

Advice to applicants and planning the UCAS personal statement Any experience in film-making (beyond home videos) should be described in detail. Knowledge and preferences of types of films and the work of some producers should be included on the UCAS application. Read film magazines and other appropriate literature to keep informed of developments. Show genuine interest in a range of film genres and be knowledgeable about favourite films, directors and give details of work experience or film projects undertaken. You should also be able to discuss the ways in which films relate to broader cultural phenomena, social, literary, historical. See also **Appendix 4**.

Misconceptions about this course That an A-level film or media studies is required; it is not. That it's Film so it's easy! That the course is all practical work. Some applicants believe that these are Media courses. Some applicants believe that Film and TV Studies is a training for production work. **Bournemouth Arts (UC)** (Animat Prod) This is not a Film Studies course but a course based on traditional animation with supported computer image processing. **De Montfort** Some believe that this is a course in practical film-making: it is not, it is for analysts and historians. **Winchester** That graduation automatically leads to a job in broadcasting!

Selection interviews Most institutions will interview some applicants in this subject. **Yes** Bournemouth, Bournemouth Arts (UC), Brunel, Canterbury Christ Church, Chichester, Liverpool John Moores, Newport, York, York St John; **Some** Anglia Ruskin, East Anglia, Staffordshire, Wolverhampton.

Interview advice and questions Questions will focus on your chosen field. In the case of films be prepared to answer questions not only on your favourite films but on the work of one or two directors you admire and early Hollywood examples. **Anglia Ruskin** We ask for an original review of a film recently seen. **Bournemouth** (TV Script Film) Successful applicants will be required to submit a 20-page screenplay. A good applicant will have the ability to discuss media issues in depth, to have total commitment to TV and video production and will have attempted to make programmes. **Bournemouth Arts (UC)** Written piece prior to interview. Questions at interview relevant to the portfolio/reel. **Staffordshire** We assess essay-writing skills. See also **Chapter 5**.

Reasons for rejection (non-academic) Not enough drive or ambition. No creative or original ideas. Preference for production work rather than practical work. Inability to articulate the thought process behind the work in the applicant's portfolio. Insufficient knowledge of media affairs. Lack of knowledge of film history. Wrong course choice, wanted more practical work.

AFTER-RESULTS ADVICE

Offers to applicants repeating A-levels **Higher** Bournemouth Arts (UC), Glasgow, Manchester Met; **Same** Anglia Ruskin, De Montfort, East Anglia, Liverpool Hope, St Mary's Twickenham (UC), Staffordshire, Stirling, Winchester, Wolverhampton, York St John.

GRADUATE DESTINATIONS AND EMPLOYMENT (2007/8 HESA)

Cinematics and Photography graduates surveyed 2180 **Employed** 1175 **In further study** 140 **Assumed unemployed** 250.

Career note Although this is a popular subject field, job opportunities in film, TV and radio are limited. Successful graduates frequently have gained work experience with companies during their undergraduate years. The transferable skills (verbal communication etc) will open up other career opportunities.

OTHER DEGREE SUBJECTS FOR CONSIDERATION

Animation; Communication Studies; Creative Writing; Media Studies; Photography.

FINANCE

(including **Banking, Financial Services, Insurance**; see also **Accountancy/Accounting**)

Financial Services courses provide a comprehensive view of the world of finance and normally cover banking, insurance, investment, building societies, international finance, accounting and economics. Major banks offer sponsorships for some of the specialised Banking courses.

Useful websites www.cii.co.uk; www.secinst.co.uk; www.financialadvice.co.uk; www.efinancialnews.com; www.worldbank.org; www.ifslearning.ac.uk; www.ft.com.

NB The points totals shown to the left of the institutions are for ease of reference only. It must not be assumed that Tariff points are always used by institutions or that they can be substituted for an offer in grades. The level of an offer is not necessarily indicative of the quality of a course.

COURSE OFFERS INFORMATION

Subject requirements/preferences **GCSE** Most institutions will require English and mathematics grade C minimum. **AL** Mathematics may be required or preferred.

NB In 2011 universities and colleges will differ in their use of GCE AL/AS unit grade information, A* grades, the Extended Project (EPQ), the Advanced Diploma and the Cambridge Pre-U examination when considering applicants and making offers. An EPQ may be accepted in place of an AS subject. Check websites of universities and colleges for the latest offers information.

Your target offers and examples of courses provided by each institution

410 pts **London (UCL)** – AAAb–BBBe (MEng/BEng Eng Bus Fin)
360 pts **Bristol** – AAA–AAB (Econ Fin) (IB 33–37 pts)
Exeter – AAA–AAB (Econ Fin)
London (RH) – AAA–ABB (Fin Bus Econ) (IB 33–35 pts)
Newcastle – AAA–AAB (Bus Acc Fin) (IB 36–38 pts)
Reading – 360–340 pts (Fin Invest Bank)
340 pts **Aston** – 340–320 pts (Finance) (IB 34 pts)
Birmingham – AAB 340 pts (Mny Bank Fin; Mny Fin Bank Lang) (IB 34–36 pts)
Cardiff – AAB (Bank Fin; Bank Fin Euro Lang)
City – AAB (Bank Int Fin; Invest Fin Risk Mgt; Rl Est Fin Invest; Invest Analys Ins) (IB 35 pts)
Glasgow – AAB (Stats Fin)
Heriot-Watt – AAB 2nd yr entry (Fin Maths)
Lancaster – AAB 340 pts (Fin; Fin Econ; Fin Mgt St) (IB 31 pts)
Leeds – AAB (Maths Fin; Acc Fin; Int Bus Fin) (IB 35 pts HL 17 pts)
London (QM) – AAB (Econ Fin) (IB 34 pts)
Loughborough – AAB (Bank Fin Mgt; Bus Econ Fin; Acc Fin Mgt; Fin Maths) (IB 36 pts)
Manchester – AAB (Fin; Econ Fin) (IB 35 pts)
Newcastle – AAB (Fin Bus Econ) (IB 34 pts)
Nottingham – AAB (Ind Econ Ins; Fin Acc Mgt) (IB 32 pts)

Cass Business School
CITY UNIVERSITY LONDON

Cass Business School Student Profile: Greg Drach

20 year old Greg Drach, is a second year investment and financial risk management student at City University's Cass Business School. He's already demonstrated his passion for business and his entrepreneurial experience at Cass by setting up his own venture. Greg and two friends launched TGT Education, which promotes the study of foreign languages in primary schools. Running a business while studying full time is a tremendous feat, but this is by no means Greg's greatest achievement. Greg also secured a finalist spot in the nPower Future Leaders Challenge, a nationwide competition to find the UK's top four keenest and greenest university students, and is vice-president of AIESEC, a student organisation which develops leadership and team working skills.

Greg says "I chose this course because I believed it would allow me to make the most of my analytical skills and equip me with highly technical skills, I have not been disappointed. My course is very well structured, provides a good insight into the financial industry and gives me a chance to do a one year business placement in my third year." Greg also rates Cass Business School for its diversity.

After graduating in 2011, Greg hopes to launch his career on a fast paced graduate training programme with a major financial institution.

www.cass.city.ac.uk/undergrad

Reading – 340–370 pts (Invest Fin Prop)
Sheffield – AAB–AAbb (Fin Maths)
Southampton – AAB (Econ Fin) (IB 34 pts)

320 pts **Brunel** – BBC +AS/EPQ c – BCC +AS/EPQ c 320–300 pts (Fin Comp; Fin Maths; Fin Acc; Econ Bus Fin) (IB 30 pts)
Durham – ABB–BBB (Acc Fin; Bus Fin) (IB 30 pts)
Heriot-Watt – ABB 320 pts 1st yr entry (Fin Maths)
Lancaster – ABB (Fin Maths) (IB 30 pts)
Leicester – ABB (Bank Fin)
Liverpool – ABB (e-Fin; Maths Fin) (IB 33 pts)
Queen's Belfast – ABB (Finance)
Sheffield – ABB–BBB (Acc Fin Mgt; Acc Fin Mgt Inf Mgt; Acc Fin Mgt Maths)
Surrey – ABB 320 pts (Acc Fin Mgt)

300 pts **Aberystwyth** – 300 pts (Fin Maths) (IB 28 pts)
Bournemouth – 300 pts (Fin Bus; Econ Fin)
Essex – 300 pts (Fin Mgt; Fin; Fin Maths) (IB 32 pts)
Heriot-Watt – BBB 2nd yr entry (Econ Fin; Fin Bus Law)
Strathclyde – ABC–BBC (Fin courses)
Westminster – BBB 300 pts (Bus Sgt (Fin Serv) (Fin)) (IB 28 pts)

280 pts **Brighton** – BBC 280–320 pts (Econ Fin; Fin Invest) (IB 30 pts)
De Montfort – 280 pts (Fin; Fin Mgt)
East Anglia – ACC–BBC (Fin Acc)
Keele – 280–340 pts (Fin courses) (IB 28–30 pts)
Kent – 280 pts (Fin Maths)
Lincoln – 280 pts (Law Fin)
Northumbria – 280 pts (Bus Fin; Fin Invest Mgt)
Plymouth – 280 pts (Maths Fin)
Portsmouth – 280 pts (Finance – check with University)
Salford – 280 pts (Fin Acc) (IB 28 pts)
Swansea – 280 pts (Fin Econ Acc) (IB 30 pts)

260 pts **Aberystwyth** – 260 pts (Bus Fin; Acc Fin)
Birmingham City – 260 pts (Acc Fin; Bus Fin)
Bristol UWE – 260–300 pts (Econ Mny Bank Fin)
Coventry – 260–320 pts (Fin Invest)
Heriot-Watt – BCC 260 pts 1st yr entry (Econ Fin; Fin Bus Law)
Hertfordshire – 260 pts (Fin courses)
Hull – 260 pts (Fin Mgt courses)
Kingston – 260 pts (Fin Econ)
Lincoln – 260 pts (Bus Fin)
Manchester Met – 260 pts (Fin Mgt courses)
Oxford Brookes – BCC (Econ Fin Int Bus) (IB 29 pts)
Portsmouth – 260–280 pts (Fin Bus; Int Fin Tr)
Staffordshire – 260 pts (Finance)
Stirling – 260 pts (Mny Bank Fin) (IB 30 pts)
Winchester – 260–300 pts (Bus Mgt Fin Econ)

240 pts **Aberdeen** – CCC (Fin courses) (IB 28 pts)
Bangor – 240–280 pts (Bank Fin)
Bradford – 240 pts (Fin Plan - check with University)
Buckingham – 240 pts (Acc Fin Mgt)
Derby – 240 pts (Fin Acc)
Dundee – CCC (Finance) (IB 29 pts)
Edinburgh Napier – 240 pts (Fin Serv)
Glasgow Caledonian – CCC (Fin Invest Risk)
Nottingham Trent – 240 pts (Fin Maths; Bus Mgt Fin Serv Plan; Econ Fin Bank)
Plymouth – 240 pts (Int Fin Serv; Fin Econ)

For a quick reference offers calculator, fold out the inside back cover.

Robert Gordon – CCC (Mgt Fin)
Sheffield Hallam – 240 pts (Bank Fin Mgt; Bus Fin Mgt; Acc Fin Mgt; Bus Fin Servs)
Stirling – CCC (Finance)
Teesside – 240 pts (Econ Crim Mgt)

220 pts **Hertfordshire** – 220–280 pts (Comp Fin Maths)
Huddersfield – 220–280 pts (Bus Fin Serv)
Leeds Met – 220 pts (Acc Fin)
Northampton – 220–260 pts (Finance)
Southampton Solent – 220 pts (Bus Mgt Fin)
Sunderland – 220 pts (Bus Fin Mgt)
York St John – 220 pts (Bus Mgt (Fin))

200 pts **Bucks New** – 200–240 pts (Acc Fin; Bus Fin)
East London – 200 pts (Fin Mny Bank)
Leeds Trinity (UC) – 200 pts (Bus Fin)
London Met – 200 pts (Bank; Bank Fin; Fin; Fin Econ; Fin Servs)
Middlesex – 200–280 pts (Mny Bank Fin)
Southampton Solent – 200 pts (Fin Bus Mgt; Fin Entre)
Suffolk (Univ Campus) – 200 pts (Bus Mgt Fin)

180 pts **Abertay Dundee** – DDD (Fin Bus)
Greenwich – 180–220 pts (Acc Fin Inf Sys)

100 pts **Bradford (Coll)** – 100–140 pts (Fin Serv)

80 pts **London Sch Bus Comp** – 80 pts (Bank Fin)

Regents Bus Sch London – check with School (Int Fin Acc)

Alternative offers
See **Chapter 7** and **Appendix 1** for grades/UCAS Tariff points information for the International Baccalaureate, Scottish Highers/Advanced Highers, the Welsh Baccalaureate, the Irish Leaving Certificate, the Cambridge Pre-U Diploma, the Advanced Diploma and the Extended Project.

EXAMPLES OF FOUNDATION DEGREES IN THE SUBJECT FIELD

Blackburn (Coll Univ Centre); Blackpool and Fylde (Coll); Bournemouth; Cardiff (UWIC); Cornwall (Coll); Croydon (Coll); Cumbria; Glamorgan; Hertfordshire; Highbury (Coll); Kensington Bus (Coll); Leeds Met; Manchester (Coll); Northbrook (Coll); Salford; Sheffield (Coll); Suffolk (Univ Campus); Thames Valley; Truro (Coll); West Cheshire (Coll); West Kent (Coll); Westminster Kingsway (Coll); Wirral Met (Coll); Weymouth (Coll).

CHOOSING YOUR COURSE (SEE ALSO CH.1)

Some course features
Brighton (Fin Invest) The course in Finance and Investment shares a common first year with the Economics and Finance degree, making transfers possible.
City An excellent portfolio of courses covering banking, insurance, investment and property.
Durham The degrees in Business, Business Finance and Accounting and Finance share a common first year, allowing for later specialisation.
London Met Financial Services covers banking, insurance and investment with opportunities to specialise.
Sheffield Hallam Overseas placements possible in the Banking with Finance degree.
Teesside (Econ Crim Mgt) The only Honours course to deal specifically with economic crime management, focusing on accountancy, audit, fraud investigation, financial crime, criminal behaviour and law.

Universities and colleges teaching quality See www.qaa.ac.uk; www.unistats.com.

Top research universities and colleges (RAE 2008) See **Accountancy/Accounting**.

Examples of sandwich degree courses Abertay Dundee; Bath; Birmingham City; Bournemouth; Brighton; Bristol UWE; Brunel; City; Coventry; De Montfort; Glamorgan; Gloucestershire; Hertfordshire;

Huddersfield; Kingston; Lancaster; Leeds Met; London Met; Loughborough; Manchester Met; Middlesex; Nottingham Trent; Plymouth; Portsmouth; Sheffield Hallam; Surrey; Swansea Met; Teesside; Westminster; Wolverhampton; Worcester.

ADMISSIONS INFORMATION

Number of applicants per place (approx) Aberystwyth 4; Bangor 10; Birmingham 3; Birmingham City 13; Bristol UWE 4; Buckingham 4; Cardiff 10; Central Lancashire 6; City 10; Dundee 5; Durham 4; Glamorgan 3; Loughborough 35; Middlesex 3; Northampton 3; Portsmouth 4; Sheffield Hallam 4.

Advice to applicants and planning the UCAS personal statement Visits to banks or insurance companies should be described, giving details of any work experience or work shadowing done in various departments. Discuss any particular aspects of finance etc which interest you. See also **Appendix 4**.

Misconceptions about this course Many applicants believe that they can only enter careers in banking and finance when they graduate in fact, business and industry provide wide-ranging opportunities.

Selection interviews **Yes** Buckingham (pref), Huddersfield; **Some** Dundee, Staffordshire, Stirling; **No** City.

Interview advice and questions Banking involves both high street and merchant banks, so a knowledge of banking activities in general will be expected. In the past mergers have been discussed and also the role of the Bank of England in the economy. The work of the accountant may be discussed. See also **Chapter 5**.

Reasons for rejection (non-academic) Lack of interest. Poor English. Lacking in motivation and determination to complete the course.

AFTER-RESULTS ADVICE

Offers to applicants repeating A-levels **Higher** Glasgow; **Possibly higher** Bangor; **Same** Birmingham, Birmingham City, Bradford, Cardiff, City, Dundee, Edinburgh Napier, London Met, Loughborough, Northumbria, Stirling.

GRADUATE DESTINATIONS AND EMPLOYMENT (2007/8 HESA)

Graduates surveyed 1155 **Employed** 550 **In further study** 120 **Assumed unemployed** 110.

Career note Most graduates enter financial careers. Further study is required to qualify as an accountant and to obtain other professional qualifications, eg Institute of Banking.

OTHER DEGREE SUBJECTS FOR CONSIDERATION

Accountancy; Actuarial Studies; Business Studies; Economics.

FOOD SCIENCE/STUDIES and TECHNOLOGY

(see also **Agricultural Sciences/Agriculture, Biochemistry, Consumer Studies, Dietetics** and **Nutrition**)

Biochemistry, microbiology, dietetics, human nutrition, food processing and technology are components of Food Science courses as well as being degree courses in their own right (and appropriate alternative courses). The study depends for its understanding on a secure foundation of several pure sciences – chemistry and two subjects from physics, mathematics, biology, botany or zoology. Only students offering subjects from these fields are likely to be considered. Food Technology covers the engineering aspects of food processing and management. A number of bursaries are offered by the food industry. Check with admissions tutors. See also **Appendix 4**.

Useful websites www.scienceyear.com; www.sofht.co.uk; www.ifst.org; www.defra.gov.uk; www.iagre.org.

NB The points totals shown to the left of the institutions are for ease of reference only. It must not be assumed that Tariff points are always used by institutions or that they can be substituted for an offer in grades. The level of an offer is not necessarily indicative of the quality of a course.

COURSE OFFERS INFORMATION

Subject requirements/preferences **GCSE** English, mathematics and a science. **AL** One or two mathematics/science subjects; chemistry may be required.

NB In 2011 universities and colleges will differ in their use of GCE AL/AS unit grade information, A* grades, the Extended Project (EPQ), the Advanced Diploma and the Cambridge Pre-U examination when considering applicants and making offers. An EPQ may be accepted in place of an AS subject. Check websites of universities and colleges for the latest offers information.

Your target offers and examples of courses provided by each institution

340 pts **Heriot-Watt** – AAB 2nd yr entry (Fd Sci Tech Mgt; Biol Sci (Fd Sci); Brew Distil)
320 pts **Newcastle** – ABB (Fd Hum Nutr) (IB 32 pts)
300 pts **Heriot-Watt** – BBB 1st yr entry (Fd Sci Tech Mgt; Biol Sci (Fd Sci); Brew Distil)
Leeds – BBB (Fd Sci courses; Fd St Nutr) (IB 32 pts HL 15 pts)
Nottingham – BBB–BCC (Fd Sci; Nutr Fd Sci; Fd Microbiol) (IB 24–30 pts)
Reading – 300 pts (Fd Sci; Fd Sci Bus; Fd Mark Bus Econ)
Surrey – BBB–BBC (Fd Sci Microbiol; Nutr Fd Sci) (IB 32–28 pts)
280 pts **Northumbria** – 280 pts (Fd Sci Nutr)
Queen's Belfast – BBC (Fd Qual Sfty Nutr)
Reading – 280 pts (Fd Tech) (IB 30 pts)
260 pts **Brighton** – BCC 260 pts (Vit Oeno; Mark Fd Drink) (IB 28 pts)
240 pts **Cardiff (UWIC)** – 240 pts (Pblc Hlth Nutr)
Coventry – 240 pts (Fd Sci Nutr)
Liverpool John Moores – 240–280 pts (Fd Nutr; Home Econ (Fd Des Tech))
Royal (CAg) – 240 pts (Fd Prod Sply Mgt)
Teesside – 240 pts (Fd Nutr Hlth Sci)
Ulster – 240 pts (Fd Nutr)
220 pts **Bath Spa** – 220–260 pts (Fd Nutr)
200 pts **Birmingham (UC)** – 200 pts (Fd Consum Rtl Mgt; Culn Arts Mgt; Fd Mark Mgt; Fd Media Comm Mgt)
Cardiff (UWIC) – 200 pts (Fd Sci Tech)
Huddersfield – 200 pts (Fd Nutr Hlth)
Leeds Trinity (UC) – 200 pts (Nutr Fd)
Manchester Met – 200 pts (Fd Nutr; Fd Mgt; Fd Tech) (IB 28 pts)
Sheffield Hallam – 200 pts (Fd Nutr; Fd Mark Mgt; Int Fd Mark Mgt)
Thames Valley – 200 pts (Hosp Mgt Fd St)
180 pts **Abertay Dundee** – DDD (Fd Consum Sci; Fd Nutr Hlth; Fd Prod Des)
Harper Adams (UC) – 180–220 pts (Fd Nutr Wlbng; Consum St)
160 pts **Glasgow Caledonian** – CC–DDD (Fd Biosci)
London Met – 160 pts (Fd Consum St; Fd Med Microbiol)
SAC (Scottish CAg) – CC (Rur Bus Mgt (Fd))
120 pts **London South Bank** – 120 pts (Fd Des Tech; Fd Nutr; Fd Sci; Fd St)

Alternative offers

See **Chapter 7** and **Appendix 1** for grades/UCAS Tariff points information for the International Baccalaureate, Scottish Highers/Advanced Highers, the Welsh Baccalaureate, the Irish Leaving Certificate, the Cambridge Pre-U Diploma, the Advanced Diploma and the Extended Project.

EXAMPLES OF FOUNDATION DEGREES IN THE SUBJECT FIELD

Askham Bryan (Coll); Birmingham (UC); Bournemouth; Bradford (Coll); Brighton; Bristol City (Coll); Bristol UWE; CAFRE; Cornwall (Coll); Derby; Duchy (Coll); Harper Adams (UC); Leeds Met; London South

Bank; Loughborough; Nottingham New (Coll); Stratford upon Avon (Coll); Westminster Kingsway (Coll); Worcester; Worcester (CT).

CHOOSING YOUR COURSE (SEE ALSO CH.1)

Some course features

Brighton (Vit Oeno) The only undergraduate degree course in wine production in the United Kingdom includes biological sciences, practical winegrowing and wine making.
Heriot-Watt (Biol Sci (Fd Sci)) Course is biology-based and has less emphasis on management and commercial aspects of food science and nutrition than the degree course in Food Science, Technology and Management.
Leeds (Fd Sci) A broad-based science degree focusing on the nature of food materials, food quality and food safety. The Department has a pilot plant and taste panel facilities for product testing.
Liverpool John Moores The Home Economics course qualifies graduates to work in the consumer and services industries and also to teach (Design and Technology).
Manchester Met All courses focus on nutrition, technology, marketing and economics.
Reading (Fd Tech) The course focuses on food products manufacture, food engineering and food materials, chemicals and microbiology.
Teesside Specialism is possible in either nutrition and health sciences or on food technology.

Universities and colleges teaching quality See www.qaa.ac.uk; www.unistats.com.

Top research universities and colleges (RAE 2008) See **Agricultural Sciences/Agriculture** and **Nutrition**.

Examples of sandwich degree courses Birmingham (UC); Bournemouth; Brighton; Cardiff (UWIC); Coventry; Glamorgan; Harper Adams (UC); Huddersfield; London South Bank; Manchester Met; Newcastle; Northumbria; Queen's Belfast; Reading; Royal (CAg); Sheffield Hallam; Surrey; Teesside; Ulster.

ADMISSIONS INFORMATION

Number of applicants per place (approx) Bath Spa 4; Cardiff (UWIC) 1; Dundee 3; Huddersfield (Fd Nutr Hlth) 4; Leeds 5; Liverpool John Moores 2; London Met 5; London South Bank 3; Manchester Met 3; Newcastle 13; Nottingham 7; Oxford Brookes 20; Queen's Belfast 10; Robert Gordon 4; Sheffield Hallam 4; Surrey 17.

Advice to applicants and planning the UCAS personal statement Visits, work experience or work shadowing in any food manufacturing firm, or visits to laboratories, should be described on your UCAS application. Keep up-to-date with developments by reading journals relating to the industry. See also **Appendix 2**.

Misconceptions about this course Some applicants confuse food technology with catering or hospitality management. Applicants under-estimate the job prospects. **Leeds** (Fd Sci) Food Science is not food technology, catering or cooking. It aims to understand why food materials behave in the way they do, in order to improve the nutritive value, safety and quality of the food we eat.

Selection interviews **Yes** London South Bank, Nottingham (depends on application), Queen's Belfast, Reading, Surrey; **Some** Abertay Dundee, Bath Spa, Leeds (applicants with non-standard qualifications), Liverpool John Moores, Manchester Met, Salford.

Interview advice and questions Food science and technology is a specialised field and admissions tutors will want to know your reasons for choosing the subject. You will be questioned on any experience you have had in the food industry. More general questions may cover the reasons for the trends in the popularity of certain types of food, the value of junk food and whether scientific interference with food is justifiable. **Leeds** Questions asked to ensure that the student understands, and can cope with, the science content of the course. See also **Chapter 5**.

Reasons for rejection (non-academic) Too immature. Unlikely to integrate well. Lack of vocational commitment.

AFTER-RESULTS ADVICE

Offers to applicants repeating A-levels **Higher** Leeds; **Possibly higher** Nottingham; **Same** Abertay Dundee, Liverpool John Moores, Manchester Met, Queen's Belfast, Salford, Sheffield Hallam, Surrey, Wolverhampton.

GRADUATE DESTINATIONS AND EMPLOYMENT (2007/8 HESA)

Graduates surveyed 255 **Employed** 160 **In further study** 25 **Assumed unemployed** 15.

Career note Employment levels for food graduates are high mainly in manufacturing and retailing and increasingly with large companies.

OTHER DEGREE SUBJECTS FOR CONSIDERATION

Biochemistry; Biological Sciences; Biology; Biotechnology; Chemistry; Consumer Studies; Crop Science; Dietetics; Health Studies; Hospitality Management; Nutrition; Plant Science.

FORESTRY

(see also **Agricultural Sciences/Agriculture**)

Forestry is concerned with the establishment and management of woodlands and forests for timber production, environmental, conservation and amenity purposes.

Useful websites www.iagre.org.uk; www.forestry.gov.uk; www.rfs.org.uk; www.charteredforesters.org; www.iwsc.org.uk; www.british-trees.com; www.woodland-trust.org.uk.

NB The points totals shown to the left of the institutions are for ease of reference only. It must not be assumed that Tariff points are always used by institutions or that they can be substituted for an offer in grades. The level of an offer is not necessarily indicative of the quality of a course.

COURSE OFFERS INFORMATION

Subject requirements/preferences **GCSE** English, Mathematics or science usually required. Check prospectuses. **AL** Two science subjects are usually stipulated which can include mathematics, geography or geology.

NB In 2011 universities and colleges will differ in their use of GCE AL/AS unit grade information, A* grades, the Extended Project (EPQ), the Advanced Diploma and the Cambridge Pre-U examination when considering applicants and making offers. An EPQ may be accepted in place of an AS subject. Check websites of universities and colleges for the latest offers information.

Your target offers and examples of courses provided by each institution

340 pts **Edinburgh** – AAB 2nd yr entry (Ecol Sci (Frsty)) (IB 34 pts)
300 pts **Aberdeen** – BBB 2nd yr entry (Frsty; Frst Sci)
Edinburgh – BBB 1st yr entry (Ecol Sci (Frsty))
240 pts **Aberdeen** – CCC 1st yr entry (Frsty; Frst Sci)
Bangor – 240 pts (Frst; Cons Frst Ecosys) (IB 28 pts)
Cumbria – 240 pts (Frst Wdlnd Mgt; Frsty Wdlnd Cons)
200 pts **Worcester** – 200 pts (Sust Wdlnd Mgt)
160 pts **UHI Millennium Inst** – CC (Sust Frst Mgt (Frst Cons) (Arb Urb Frsty))

Alternative offers

See **Chapter 7** and **Appendix 1** for grades/UCAS Tariff points information for the International Baccalaureate, Scottish Highers/Advanced Highers, the Welsh Baccalaureate, the Irish Leaving Certificate, the Cambridge Pre-U Diploma, the Advanced Diploma and the Extended Project.

EXAMPLES OF FOUNDATION DEGREES IN THE SUBJECT FIELD

Askham Bryan (Coll); Bolton; Brighton; Cumbria; Northampton; Sparsholt (Coll); Sunderland; Warwickshire (Coll); Worcester.

CHOOSING YOUR COURSE (SEE ALSO CH.1)

Some course features

Bangor Students on the four-year Conservation and Forest Ecosystems course spend 7–12 months of practical work with a forestry organisation.

Edinburgh Applicants may apply for Ecological Science (C900), deciding on the Forestry specialisation at a later stage.

UHI Millennium Inst This applied fieldwork-based course focuses on the practical aspects of either forest or arboricultural conservation and management. It provdes a technical management qualification and includes wood technology, woodland ecology and conservation, environmental economics, environmental change and capital project planning.

Universities and colleges teaching quality See www.qaa.ac.uk; www.unistats.com.

Examples of sandwich degree courses Bangor, Cumbria.

ADMISSIONS INFORMATION

Number of applicants per place (approx) Bangor 2; Edinburgh 9.

Advice to applicants and planning the UCAS personal statement Contact the Forestry Commission and the Woodland Trust and try to arrange visits to forestry centres, local community woodlands and forests and to the Woodland Trust's sites. Discuss the work with forest officers and learn about future plans for specific forest areas and describe any visits made. Mention any experience of forestry or wood processing industries (for example, visits to forests and mills, work experience in relevant organisations). See **Appendix 4**.

Misconceptions about this course **Bangor** That the course provides practical training in forestry (for example, in the use of chainsaws and pesticides) or wood processing. It does not: it is intended to educate future managers, for example, not to train forestry or mill workers.

Selection interviews Most institutions.

Interview advice and questions Work experience or field courses attended are likely to be discussed and questions asked such as: What is arboriculture? On a desert island how would you get food from wood? How do you see forestry developing in the next hundred years? What aspects of forestry are the most important? **Bangor** Why are you interested in forestry? See also **Chapter 5**.

AFTER-RESULTS ADVICE

Offers to applicants repeating A-levels **Same** Bangor.

GRADUATE DESTINATIONS AND EMPLOYMENT (2007/8 HESA)

Graduates surveyed 40 **Employed** 30 **In further study** 5 **Assumed unemployed** 5.

Career note Opportunities exist with the Forestry Commission as supervisors, managers and in some cases, scientists. Other employers include private landowners (especially in Scotland), co-operative forest societies, local authorities and commercial firms.

OTHER DEGREE SUBJECTS FOR CONSIDERATION

Agriculture; Biological Sciences; Countryside Management; Crop Science; Ecology; Environmental Sciences; Woodland and Wildlife Management

FRENCH

(see also **European Studies** and **Languages**)

Applicants should select courses according to the emphasis which they prefer. Courses could focus on literature or language (or both), or on the written and spoken word, as in the case of interpreting and translating courses, or on the broader study of French culture, political and social aspects found on European Studies courses.

Useful websites http://europa.eu; www.visavis.org; www.bbc.co.uk/languages; http://languageadvantage.com; www.languagematters.co.uk; www.iol.org.uk; www.reed.co.uk/multilingual; www.cilt.org.uk; www.lemonde.fr; www.institut-francais.org.uk; www.academie-francaise.fr; www.institut-de-france.fr; www.sfs.ac.uk; http://fs.oxfordjournals.org.

NB The points totals shown to the left of the institutions are for ease of reference only. It must not be assumed that Tariff points are always used by institutions or that they can be substituted for an offer in grades. The level of an offer is not necessarily indicative of the quality of a course.

COURSE OFFERS INFORMATION

Subject requirements/preferences **GCSE** French, mathematics (for business courses), grade levels may be stipulated. **AL** French is usually required at a specific grade and in some cases a second language may be stipulated.

NB In 2011 universities and colleges will differ in their use of GCE AL/AS unit grade information, A* grades, the Extended Project (EPQ), the Advanced Diploma and the Cambridge Pre-U examination when considering applicants and making offers. An EPQ may be accepted in place of an AS subject. Check websites of universities and colleges for the latest offers information.

Your target offers and examples of courses provided by each institution

410 pts **London (King's)** – AAAb (Fr Hist) (IB 36 pts)

380 pts **Cambridge** – A*AA college offers may vary (Modn Mediev Lang (Fr)) (IB 38–42 pts HL 766–777)

360 pts **Bath** – AAA (Innov Eng Des Fr) (IB 36 pts HL maths phys Fr 6)
Birmingham – AAA (Law Fr) (IB 30–32 pts)
Exeter – AAA–AAB (Engl Fr) (IB 36–33 pts HL66)
Imperial London – AAA (Chem Fr Sci)
Leicester – AAA (Law Fr Law Lang)
London (King's) – AAB+AS (Fr courses except under **410 pts**) (IB 36 pts)
London (UCL) – AAB+AS–ABB+AS (Fr courses) (IB 34–36 pts)
Nottingham – AAA +LNAT for Law course (Econ Fr; Law Fr)
Oxford – AAA (Fr courses) (IB 38–42 pts)
St Andrews – AAA (Fr Int Rel) (IB 32 pts)
York – AAA (Fr Hist)

350 pts **Warwick** – 350 pts (Fr Ger St)

340 pts **Aston** – AAB–ABB 340–320 pts (Int Bus Fr)
Bath – AAB (Int Mgt Fr) (IB 34–36 pts)
Birmingham – AAB–ABB (Int Bus Fr; Fr Mus; Fr Hist Art; Fr Maths) (IB 30–32 pts)
Bristol – AAB–BBC (Fr Port/Russ/Span) (IB 35–30 pts)
Durham – AAB (Modn Lang)
East Anglia – AAB–BBB (Fr Film TV)
Imperial London – AAB 340 pts (Biol Fr Sci)
Lancaster – AAB (Euro Mgt (Fr))
Manchester – AAB–ABC (Fr courses) (IB 35–30 pts)
St Andrews – AAB (Fr courses except under **360 pts**) (IB 36 pts)
Sheffield – AAB 340 pts (Law Fr; Mech Eng Fr)
Southampton – AAB–ABB (Fr courses) (IB 32 pts)
Warwick – AAB (Fr Hist) (IB 34–35 pts)

320 pts **Bath** – ABB–BBB (Euro St Modn Lang (Fr Ital) (Fr Russ) (Fr Ger) (Fr Span)) (IB 34 pts HL Fr 6)
Cardiff – ABB–ABC (Fr; Fr joint courses)
East Anglia – ABB–BBB (Transl Interp Dbl Hons Langs)
Essex – 320 pts (Econ Fr) (IB 30 pts)
Exeter – AAB–ABB (Fr courses except under **360 pts**) (IB 30 pts)
Glasgow – ABB (Fr courses) (IB 30 pts)
Kent – 320 pts (Fr Lic de Let; Fr Single/Joint Hons)

Lancaster – ABB (Fr St Pol; Fr St Thea St; Fr St Psy) (IB 30 pts)
Leeds – ABB (Fr courses) (IB 34 pts HL Fr 6)
Leicester – ABB (Fr Engl; Fr Ital joint courses)
London (Inst in Paris) – ABB (Fr St)
London (RH) – ABB–BBB (Fr courses) (IB 32 pts H Fr 6)
Newcastle – ABB (Fr; Fr Bus St; Fr Pol) (IB 32 pts HL Fr 6)
Nottingham – ABB (Fr Hist; Fr Span; Fr Pol)
Sheffield – ABB–BBB (Fr courses except under **340 pts**) (IB 36–32 pts)
Strathclyde – ABB 1st yr entry (Fr courses)
Surrey – ABB 320 pts (Law Fr Law)
Sussex – ABB–BBB (Fr courses) (IB 32–34 pts)
Warwick – ABB (Fr St; Fr Thea St; Fr Int St)
York – ABB (Fr courses except under **360 pts**) (IB 32 pts)

300 pts **Aston** – BBB–ABB 300–320 pts (Fr courses except under **340 pts**) (IB 31–33 pts)
Bristol – BBB–BBC (French) (IB 32–30 pts)
Bristol UWE – 300–340 pts (LLB Fr)
Coventry – 300 pts (Law Fr)
East Anglia – BBB–BBC (Transl Media Fr)
Edinburgh – BBB (Fr courses)
Hull – 300 pts (Dr Fr)
Liverpool – BBB (Fr; Fr Hisp St; Fr Ger; Bus St Fr) (IB 30 pts HL Fr 6)
London (QM) – 300 pts (Fr courses) (IB 32 pts HL Fr 6)
Newcastle – ABC/BBB (Ling Fr)
Northumbria – 300–280 pts (Fr Bus; Int Bus Mgt Fr)
Nottingham – ABC (Fr Contemp Chin St; Fr Int Media Comm St; Fr Can St) (IB 30–32 pts)
Queen's Belfast – BBB–BBCb (Fr courses)
Reading – 300–320 pts (Fr courses) (IB 28 pts)
Salford – 300 pts (Modn Lang Transl Interp St (Fr) (Ger) (Ital) (Port) (Span); Modn Lang Ling)
Stirling – BBB 2nd yr entry (Fr Jrnl St; Fr Mgt Sci; Fr Comp Sci)
Strathclyde – ABC 2nd yr entry (Fr courses)
Surrey – BBB 300 pts (Bus Mgt Fr; Langs Transl) (IB 32 pts)
Swansea – BBB 300 pts (Fr courses)

280 pts **Essex** – 280 pts (Fr St Modn Langs) (IB 30 pts)
Heriot-Watt – BBC (App Langs Transl (Fr/Ger); Langs (Interp Transl) Fr/Ger)
Hull – 280–300 pts (Phil Fr)
Westminster – BBC–BCC 280 pts (Fr Ling; Transl St (Fr); Hist Fr)

260 pts **Aberystwyth** – 260 pts (Fr courses) (IB 29 pts)
Essex – 260 pts (Euro St Fr) (IB 28 pts)
Hull – 260–280 pts (Fr Joint courses except under **280/300 pts**)
Nottingham Trent – 260 pts (Fr Euro St; Fr Comm Soty; Fr Media)
Oxford Brookes – BCC (Fr Comb Hons courses) (IB 30 pts)

240 pts **Aberdeen** – CCC (Fr courses) (IB 28 pts)
Bangor – 240–260 pts (Fr courses)
Buckingham – CCC 240 pts (Mark Fr; Engl Lit Fr)
Coventry – 240–260 pts (Fr courses except under **300 pts**)
Hull – 240–300 pts (Sociol Anth Fr)
Kingston – 240–320 pts (Int Bus Fr; Media Cult St Fr)
Liverpool John Moores – 240–280 pts (P Educ Fr; Fr PR; Int Bus St Fr)
Manchester Met – 240 pts (Fr + 2nd Lang; Fr St) (IB 26 pts)
Portsmouth – 240 pts (Law Fr)
Sheffield Hallam – 240 pts (Int Bus Fr)
Stirling – CCC 1st yr entry (Fr Jrnl St; Fr Mgt Sci; Fr Comp Sci) (IB 28 pts)
Ulster – 240 pts (Fr courses)
Winchester – 240–280 pts (Fr P Teach)

220 pts **Chester** – 220–260 pts (Fr courses) (IB 24 pts)
Kingston – 220 pts (Vis Mat Cult Fr)
Leeds Met – 220 pts (Fr Int Rel; Fr Glob Dev; Fr PR; Fr Mark; Fr Tour Mgt)
Northampton – 220–260 pts (Fr courses)
200 pts **Canterbury Christ Church** – 200 pts (Fr courses)
Central Lancashire – 200 pts (Fr Bus Fr)
80 pts **London (Birk)** – 80 pts for under 21s (p/t Fr Ger; Fr Span; Fr Mgt; Fr St)

London LSE – optional course offered by the language centre: check with admissions tutor (Fr/Ger/Span/Russ)

Alternative offers
See **Chapter 7** and **Appendix 1** for grades/UCAS Tariff points information for the International Baccalaureate, Scottish Highers/Advanced Highers, the Welsh Baccalaureate, the Irish Leaving Certificate, the Cambridge Pre-U Diploma, the Advanced Diploma and the Extended Project.

CHOOSING YOUR COURSE (SEE ALSO CH.1)

Some course features
Bangor A three-language Honours course is offered with languages chosen from French, German, Italian or Spanish. This is an exclusively practical language course, two semesters being spent at universities appropriate to the languages chosen.
Bath (Euro St Modn Langs) French is studied with a second, equally weighted, language. The course has a contemporary focus and a wide range of options.
Cardiff (Fr) The course has a vocational emphasis, and the opportunity to sit the Paris Chamber of Commerce examination and to gain a French language qualification recognised in France.
Chester French can be studied as a Single Honours degree or as part of a Combined Honours programme.
Heriot-Watt (Langs (Interp Transl) (App Langs Transl)) Both degrees enable two main foreign languages to be studied to the same level throughout the course: the second language can be studied either from beginners' or post-beginners' level.
Leeds A large department offering a range of single, combined and major/minor courses.
Salford (Modn Langs Transl Interp St) Three languages are chosen from French, German, Italian, Portuguese, Spanish, and English as a Foreign Language.

Universities and colleges teaching quality See www.qaa.ac.uk; www.unistats.com.

Top research universities and colleges (RAE 2008) Oxford; London (King's); Warwick; Cambridge; Aberdeen; St Andrews; Sheffield; Nottingham; Kent; Leeds; Exeter; London (UCL).

ADMISSIONS INFORMATION

Number of applicants per place (approx) Aston 6; Bangor 4; Bath (Euro St Modn Langs) 6; Birmingham 5; Bradford 3; Bristol 7; Cardiff 6; Central Lancashire 5; Durham 8; Exeter 8; Huddersfield 3; Hull 12; Kent 10; Kingston 4; Lancaster 7; Leeds (Joint Hons) 8; Leicester (Fr Ital) 5; Liverpool 5; Liverpool John Moores 8; London (Inst in Paris) 9, (King's) 9, (RH) 5, (UCL) 8; Manchester Met 13; Middlesex 6; Newcastle 17; Northampton 3; Nottingham 16; Oxford Brookes 8; Portsmouth 20; Roehampton 5; Warwick 7; York 8.

Advice to applicants and planning the UCAS personal statement Visits to France (including exchange visits) should be described, with reference to any particular cultural or geographical features of the region visited. Providing information about your contacts with French friends and experience in speaking the language are also important. Express your willingness to work/live/travel abroad and show your interests in French life and culture. Read French newspapers and magazines and keep up-to-date with news stories etc. See also **Appendix 4**.

Misconceptions about this course **Leeds** See **Languages**. **Swansea** Some applicants are not aware of the range of subjects which can be combined with French in our flexible modular system. They sometimes do not know that linguistics and area studies options are also available as well as literature options in French.

Selection interviews **Yes** Bangor, Birmingham, Cambridge, Canterbury Christ Church, Durham, East Anglia (after offer), Essex, Exeter, Heriot-Watt, Huddersfield, Hull, Kingston, Lancaster, Liverpool, Liverpool John Moores, London (RH), (UCL), Oxford, Portsmouth, Reading, Surrey, Sussex, Warwick; **Some** Brighton, Leeds.

Interview advice and questions Questions will almost certainly be asked on your A-level texts, in addition to your reading outside the syllabus – books, magazines, newspapers etc. Part of the interview may be conducted in French and written tests may be involved (see **Chapter 5**). **Leeds** See **Languages**.

Reasons for rejection (non-academic) Unstable personality. Known alcoholism. Poor motivation. Candidate unenthusiastic, unmotivated, ill-informed about the nature of the course (had not read the prospectus). Not keen to spend a year abroad.

AFTER-RESULTS ADVICE

Offers to applicants repeating A-levels **Higher** Aberystwyth, Bristol (Fr), Glasgow, Leeds, Oxford Brookes, Warwick; **Possibly higher** Aston (Fr; Fr Ger); **Same** Aston, Bradford, Brighton, Bristol (Phil Fr; Fr Lat), Chester, Durham, East Anglia, Lancaster, Liverpool, London (RH), Newcastle, Nottingham (Fr Ger; Fr Lat), Sheffield, Surrey, Sussex, Ulster; **No offers made** Cambridge.

GRADUATE DESTINATIONS AND EMPLOYMENT (2007/8 HESA)

Graduates surveyed 1235 **Employed** 620 **In further study** 260 **Assumed unemployed** 85.

Career note See **Languages**.

OTHER DEGREE SUBJECTS FOR CONSIDERATION

European Studies; International Business Studies; Literature; other language tables.

GENETICS

(see also **Biological Sciences**)

Over the years genetics, the science of heredity, has developed into a detailed and wide-ranging science. It involves, on the one hand, population genetics, and on the other, molecular interactions. Studies may therefore cover microbial, plant, animal and human genetics.

Useful websites www.genetics.org; www.nature.com/genetics; www.genetics.org.uk; see also Biological Sciences.

NB The points totals shown to the left of the institutions are for ease of reference only. It must not be assumed that Tariff points are always used by institutions or that they can be substituted for an offer in grades. The level of an offer is not necessarily indicative of the quality of a course.

COURSE OFFERS INFORMATION

Subject requirements/preferences **GCSE** English, mathematics and science subjects. **AL** Chemistry and/or biology are usually required or preferred.

NB In 2011 universities and colleges will differ in their use of GCE AL/AS unit grade information, A* grades, the Extended Project (EPQ), the Advanced Diploma and the Cambridge Pre-U examination when considering applicants and making offers. An EPQ may be accepted in place of an AS subject. Check websites of universities and colleges for the latest offers information.

Your target offers and examples of courses provided by each institution

380 pts **Cambridge** – A*AA college offers may vary (Nat Sci (Genet)) (IB 38–42 pts)

360 pts **Edinburgh** – AAA 2nd yr entry (Genetics)

Glasgow – AAA (Genet – fast route) (IB 38 pts HL 665)

London (UCL) – AABe–ABBe (Biol Sci (Genet) (Hum Genet)) (IB 34–36 pts)

340 pts **Birmingham** – AAB–BBB (Biol Sci (Genet); Bioch (Genet)) (IB 32–34 pts)
Cardiff – AAB–ABB (Genetics) (IB 34 pts)
London (King's) – ABB+AS (Mol Genet; Pharmacol Mol Genet) (IB 34 pts HL chem 5)
Manchester – AAB–BBB (Genet; Genet Ind; Genet Modn Lang) (IB 35–32 pts)
Nottingham – AAB–BBB (Bioch Genet)
Sheffield – AAB–ABB (Bioch Genet; Genet; Genet Microbiol; Genet Mol Cell Biol; Med Genet) (IB 35–33 pts)

320 pts **Brunel** – 320 pts BBC +AS/EPQ c (Biomed Sci (Genet)) (IB 32 pts)
East Anglia – ABB–BBB (Mol Biol Genet) (IB 31–32 pts)
Glasgow – ABB (Genetics) (IB 32 pts)
Leeds – ABB–BBB 320–300 pts (Genetics) (IB 34–32 pts HL 15–16 pts)
Leicester – ABB (Med Genet; Biol Sci (Genet)) (IB 32 pts)
Liverpool – ABB–BBB (Genet; Genet Ind; Genet Comb Hons) (IB 33–30 pts HL biol 6)
Newcastle – ABB (Hum Genet; Genet) (IB 32 pts)
Nottingham – ABB–BBB (Genet; Hum Genet) (IB 32 pts)
York – ABB (Genet; Genet Euro; Genet Ind) (IB 32 pts)

300 pts **Aberdeen** – BBB 2nd yr entry (Genet; Genet (Immun); Genet Psy)
Dundee – BBB 2nd yr entry (Mol Genet) (IB 34 pts)
Edinburgh – BBB 1st yr entry (Genetics) (IB 30 pts)
Essex – 300–260 pts inc BB–BC (Genet 3 yrs) (IB 30 pts)
Lancaster – BBB (Bioch Genet) (IB 29 pts)
Queen's Belfast – BBB (Genetics) (IB 28 pts)
Sussex – BBB–BBC (Mol Genet) (IB 32 pts)
Warwick – BBB (Biol Sci (Mol Genet))

280 pts **London (QM)** – 280–320 pts (Genet; Med Genet) (IB 28 pts)
Swansea – 280–300 pts (Genet; Med Genet; Genet Zool; Genet Bioch; Genet Mar Biol)

240 pts **Aberystwyth** – 240–280 pts (Genet Hum Hlth; Genet; Genet Bioch) (IB 26 pts)
Dundee – CCC 1st yr entry (Mol Genet 4 yrs)

220 pts **Liverpool John Moores** – 220–260 pts (Mol Biol Genet)
Westminster – CCD (Mol Biol Genet) (IB 26 pts)

200 pts **Anglia Ruskin** – 200 pts (Genet Med Biol; Genet Microbiol)
London Met – 200 pts (Genetics) (IB 28 pts)
Wolverhampton – 200–260 pts (Genet Mol Biol) (IB 28 pts)

160 pts **Essex** – 160 pts inc DD (Genet 4 yrs) (IB 24 pts)
Westminster – CC (Mol Biol Genet 4 yrs inc Fdn) (IB 26 pts)

Alternative offers

See **Chapter 7** and **Appendix 1** for grades/UCAS Tariff points information for the International Baccalaureate, Scottish Highers/Advanced Highers, the Welsh Baccalaureate, the Irish Leaving Certificate, the Cambridge Pre-U Diploma, the Advanced Diploma and the Extended Project.

CHOOSING YOUR COURSE (SEE ALSO CH.1)

Some course features

Brunel Genetics is offered as part of the Biomedical Sciences programme.
Liverpool Modules are offered in genetic engineering, human and medical genetics. The year in industry/research enables students to work in the UK, Europe or the USA.
London (UCL) After a common first year for all Biological Sciences students, Genetics and Human Genetics are two of the degree specialisms offered for the following years of the BSc and MSci courses. The Genetics programme focuses on genomic, evolutionary and population genetics, while cytology, pre-natal diagnosis and genetic counselling are options in the Human Genetics programme.
Manchester Transfer possible between most life sciences degree programmes at the end of the first year; students can also opt on, or off, sandwich placement year, and a foundation year is also available.
Nottingham Human Genetics is offered as a three- or four-year programme.
York Genetics is available as a specialist degree programme in the Biology degree programme, with an opportunity to spend a year abroad or in industry.

Universities and colleges teaching quality See www.qaa.ac.uk; www.unistats.com.

Top research universities and colleges (RAE 2008) See **Biological Sciences**.

Examples of sandwich degree courses Bristol UWE; Brunel; Cardiff; Huddersfield; Sussex; York; see also **Biological Sciences**.

ADMISSIONS INFORMATION

Number of applicants per place (approx) Cardiff 8; Dundee 5; Leeds 7; Leicester (for all Biol Sci courses) 10; Newcastle 8; Nottingham 6; Swansea 7; Wolverhampton 4; York 9.

Advice to applicants and planning the UCAS personal statement See **Biological Sciences**.

Misconceptions about this course **York** Some fail to realise that chemistry (beyond GCSE) is essential to an understanding of genetics.

Selection interviews **Yes** Cambridge, Liverpool, Swansea; **Some** Anglia Ruskin, Cardiff, Dundee, Wolverhampton, York.

Interview advice and questions Likely questions will focus on your A-level science subjects, particularly biology, why you wish to study genetics, and on careers in genetics. See also **Chapter 5**.

AFTER-RESULTS ADVICE

Offers to applicants repeating A-levels **Higher** Aberystwyth, Leeds, Newcastle, Nottingham, Swansea; **Same** Anglia Ruskin, Cardiff, Dundee, London (UCL), Wolverhampton, York; **No offers made** Cambridge.

GRADUATE DESTINATIONS AND EMPLOYMENT (2007/8 HESA)

Graduates surveyed 295 **Employed** 85 **In further study** 105 **Assumed unemployed** 75.

Career note See **Biological Sciences**.

OTHER DEGREE SUBJECTS FOR CONSIDERATION

Biochemistry; Biological Sciences; Biology; Biotechnology; Human Sciences; Immunology; Life Sciences; Medical Biochemistry; Medical Biology; Medicine; Microbiology; Molecular Biology; Natural Sciences; Physiology; Plant Sciences.

GEOGRAPHY

(including **Meteorology**)

Students following BA and BSc Geography courses often choose options from the same range of modules, but the choice of degree will depend on the arts or science subjects taken at A-level (or equivalent). The content and focus of courses will vary between universities and could emphasise the human, physical, economic or social aspects of the subject.

Useful websites www.metoffice.gov.uk; www.ccw.gov.uk; www.rgs.org; www.ordnancesurvey.co.uk; www.geographical.co.uk; www.nationalgeographic.com; www.cartography.org.uk; www.naturalengland.org.uk; www.geography.org.uk; www.thepowerofgeography.co.uk; www.spatial-literacy.org; www.gis.com.

NB The points totals shown to the left of the institutions are for ease of reference only. It must not be assumed that Tariff points are always used by institutions or that they can be substituted for an offer in grades. The level of an offer is not necessarily indicative of the quality of a course.

COURSE OFFERS INFORMATION

Subject requirements/preferences **GCSE** Geography usually required. Mathematics/sciences often required for BSc courses. **AL** Geography is usually required for most courses. Mathematics/science subjects required for BSc courses. (Meteorology) Mathematics, physics and another science may be required sometimes with specified grades, eg **Reading** mathematics and physics grade B.

NB In 2011 universities and colleges will differ in their use of GCE AL/AS unit grade information, A* grades, the Extended Project (EPQ), the Advanced Diploma and the Cambridge Pre-U examination when considering applicants and making offers. An EPQ may be accepted in place of an AS subject. Check websites of universities and colleges for the latest offers information.

Your target offers and examples of courses provided by each institution

380 pts **Cambridge** – A*AA college offers may vary (Geography) (IB 38–42 pts)
London (UCL) – AAA+AS–ABB+AS (Geog; Env Geog; Econ Geog) (IB 34–38 pts)

360 pts **Bristol** – AAA–ABB (Geog; Geog Euro) (IB 37–36 pts)
Durham – AAA (Nat Sci (Geog); BA/BSc Geog; Geog Comb Hons)
East Anglia – AAA–AAB (MSci Env Geog Int Dev; Meteor Ocean Abrd) (IB 34–33 pts)
Glasgow – AAA faster route (Geog courses) (IB 38 pts)
Leeds – AAA (Meteor Atmos Sci Int) (IB 38 pts)
London (SOAS) – AAA (Pol Geog) (IB 38 pts)
Manchester – AAA–AAB (Geography)
Oxford – AAA (Geography) (IB 38–42 pts)
St Andrews – AAA (Geog Int Rel; Geog Psy; Geog Mgt) (IB 36 pts)

340 pts **Durham** – AAB (Educ St (Geog))
Exeter – AAB–ABB (BA/BSc Geog; Geog Euro St) (IB 34–31 pts)
Hull – 340 pts (MPhys Geog)
Lancaster – AAB 340 pts (Physl Geog Abrd)
Leeds – AAB (BA Geog; Geog Pol)
London (King's) – ABB+AS (Geography) (IB 32 pts)
London LSE – AAB (Geog; Geog Econ) (IB 37 pts)
Loughborough – AAB–ABB (Geog Spo Sci; Geog Spo Mgt) (IB 34 pts)
Newcastle – AAB–ABB (Physl Geog; Geog; Geog Maths) (IB 30–38 pts)
Nottingham – AAB–ABB (Geog Bus; Geog Chin St; BA/BSc Geog) (IB 32–36 pts)
St Andrews – AAB (Geog; Geog Scot Hist; Geog Langs; Geog Mid E St) (IB 32–36 pts)
Southampton – AAB–ABB (Geog; Geog Geol; Geog Ocean) (IB 36–30 pts)

320 pts **Birmingham** – ABB (Geog Econ; Geog Hist; Geog Urb Reg Plan; Geog) (IB 32–34 pts)
Cardiff – 320 pts (Geog (Hum) Plan)
East Anglia – ABB–BBB (Meteor Ocean courses except under **360 pts**)
Exeter (Cornwall) – ABB-BBB (BA/Bsc Geog; Geog Euro Mgt; Geog Engl; Cons Biol Geog)
Glasgow – ABB (BA Geog courses) (IB 32 pts)
Lancaster – ABB (Geog; Physl Geog; Hum Geog; Geog (Env Chng))
Leeds – ABB (BSc Geog; Geog Mgt) (IB 34 pts HL 16 pts)
Leicester – ABB (Geog; Geog Arch; Hum Geog; Physl Geog) (IB 32 pts)
Liverpool – ABB (Geog; Geog Mgt; Geol Physl Geog) (IB 32 pts)
London (RH) – ABB 320 pts (Geog; Hum Geog; Physl Geog; Geog Pol Int Rel; Physl Geog Geol) (IB 37 pts HL 666)
London (SOAS) – ABB (BA/BSc Geog Joint Hons) (IB 34 pts)
Loughborough – ABB 320 pts (Geog Spo Sci; Geog; Geog Econ; Geog Mgt) (IB 34 pts)
Newcastle – ABB–BBB (BA/BSc Geog; Physl Geog) (IB 35 pts HL geog 6)
Reading – 320 pts (Hum Geog; Physl Geog; Hum Physl Geog; Geog Econ (Reg Sci); Meteor) (IB 34–31 pts)
St Andrews – ABB (Env Geosci) (IB 32 pts)
Sheffield – ABB (BA/BSc Geog; Geog Maths; Geog Pol; Geog Sociol; Geog Plan) (IB 33 pts)
Strathclyde – ABB 2nd yr entry (Geography) (IB 34 pts)
Sussex – ABB–BBB (Geog; Geog Anth; Geog Dev St; Geog Ecol) (IB 32–34 pts)

300 pts **Aberystwyth** – 300 pts (Hum Geog courses; Physl Geog; Geog) (IB 30 pts)
Cardiff – BBB pts (Mar Geog)
Dundee – BBB 2nd yr entry (Geog Env Sci; Geog; Geog Pol Int Rel; Geog Plan) (IB 34 pts)
Edinburgh – BBB (MA Geog; BSc Geog; Geog Soc Anth) (IB 32 pts)
Leeds – BBB (BSc Geog Trans Plan; Meteor Atmos Sci; Geog Geol)
Leicester – BBB (Geog Geol)

Liverpool – BBB (Ocns Clim Physl Geog; Ocns Clim; Geog Arch) (IB 30 pts)
London (QM) – 300–340 pts (BA/BSc Geog; Hum Geog; Physl Geog; Env Geog) (IB 32 pts)
London (RH) – ABC–BBC (Physl Geog Geol)
Manchester – BBB (Geog Geol)
Newcastle – BBB–BBC (Geog Plan; Geog Inf Sci; Surv Map Sci) (IB 30–32 pts)
Reading – 300 pts (Meteor Clim)
Southampton – BBB (Arch Geog; Geol Physl Geog) (IB 30 pts)
Stirling – BBB 2nd yr entry (Geography)
Strathclyde – ABC 1st yr entry (Geography)
Swansea – 300 pts (Geog; Geog Econ; Geog Euro St; Geog Geoinf)
York – BBB (Env Geog)

280 pts **Coventry** – 280–300 pts (Glob Sust; Clim Chng; Geog; Geog Nat Haz; Disas Mgt Emer Plan)
Gloucestershire – 280 pts (Geog courses)
Keele – 280–300 pts (Geog; Physl Geog; Hum Geog; Geosci) (IB 26–28 pts)
Newman (UC) – 280–320 pts (P Educ Hum)
Northumbria – 280 pts (Geog; Geog Env Mgt) (IB 28 pts)
Portsmouth – 280 pts (BA/BSc Geog; Hum Geog; Physl Geog; Env Geog)
Queen's Belfast – BBC–BBCb (Arch Palae Geog; Geog Euro; Geog)
Staffordshire – 280 pts (Geog; Physl Env Geog; Hum Env Geog; Geog Mntn Ldrshp; Geog joint courses) (IB 28 pts)

260 pts **Aberdeen** – BCC (Geog (Arts) (Sci); Geog Inf Sys)
Bradford – 260 pts (Geog; Geog Env Mgt; Physl Env Geog; Geog Arch)
Brighton – BCC (Geog; Geog Geol) (IB 28 pts)
Bristol UWE – 260–300 pts (Geog; Geog Env Mgt; Geog Plan) (IB 26–32 pts)
Coventry – 260–300 pts (BA/BSc Geog)
Coventry – 260–280 pts (Disas Mgt; Disas Reconstr Mgt)
Liverpool Hope – 260 pts (Geog courses)
Oxford Brookes – BCC (Geog Comb Hons) (IB 29 pts)
Plymouth – 260–280 pts (BA/BSc Geog; Geog Media Arts; Geog Langs; Geog Tour Mgt)
Sheffield Hallam – 260 pts (Geog Plan; Geog)

240 pts **Bangor** – 240–300 pts (Geography) (IB 28 pts)
Bournemouth – 240 pts (App Geog)
Brighton – CCC/BCD (Ecol Biogeog; Geog Geol; Env Haz) (IB 28 pts)
Chester – 240–280 pts (Geog courses) (IB 30 pts)
Dundee – CCC 1st yr entry (Geog Env Sci; Geog; Geopol Int Rel; Geog Plan) (IB 29 pts)
Greenwich – 240 pts (BA/BSc Geog)
Hull – 240–300 pts (Geog Arch; Geog Spo Sci; BSc Physl Geog; Hum Geog)
Kingston – 240–280 pts (Geog Single Hons courses; Hum Geog Single Hons; Geog Inf Sys Single Hons; Env Haz Disas Mgt)
Leeds Met – 240 pts (Hum Geog; Hum Geog Plan)
Manchester Met – 240–260 pts (Geog N Am/Aus; Hum Geog; Physl Geog) (IB 24 pts)
Northampton – 240–280 pts (Hum Geog; Physl Geog; Geog)
Worcester – 240–260 pts (Geog; Hum Geog; Physl Geog courses)

220 pts **Bangor** – 220–260 pts (Cstl Geog)
Bath Spa – 220–260 pts (Geog; Geog Inf Sys)
Edge Hill – 220 pts (Geog; Biogeog; Geotour)
Glamorgan – 220–280 pts (Geog; Hum Geog; Physl Geog)
Hertfordshire – 220 pts (Geog courses)
Liverpool John Moores – 220–260 pts (BSc/BA Geog; Physl Geog)
Stirling – CCD 1st yr entry (Geography) (IB 26 pts)
Sunderland – 220 pts (Geog courses; Geog Educ)
Ulster – 220–240 pts (Geog; Geog Int Dev; Geog Educ; Geog Ir; Geog Langs)

200 pts **Canterbury Christ Church** – 200 pts (Geog courses)
Central Lancashire – 200–240 pts (BA/BSc Geog; Env Haz Sci Plcy Mgt)

	Derby – 200–240 pts (Geog courses)
	East London – 200 pts (Geog Inf Sys)
	Kingston – 200–280 pts (Geog Joint Hons; Hum Geog Joint Hons; Geog Inf Sys Joint Hons)
	Nottingham Trent – 200–220 pts (Geog; Physl Geog)
	Salford – 200 pts (Env Geog; BA/BSc Geog) (IB 24 pts)
	Wolverhampton – 200–260 pts (Geog courses)
180 pts	**Southampton Solent** – 180 pts (Geog Env St; Geog Mar St)
160 pts	**Bishop Grosseteste (UC)** – 160 pts (Educ St Geog)
	St Mary's Twickenham (UC) – 160–200 pts (Geog courses)
80 pts	**London (Birk)** – 80 pts for under 21s (over 21s varies) (p/t Geog Env)

Alternative offers
See **Chapter 7** and **Appendix 1** for grades/UCAS Tariff points information for the International Baccalaureate, Scottish Highers/Advanced Highers, the Welsh Baccalaureate, the Irish Leaving Certificate, the Cambridge Pre-U Diploma, the Advanced Diploma and the Extended Project.

EXAMPLES OF FOUNDATION DEGREES IN THE SUBJECT FIELD
Bournemouth; Truro (Coll).

CHOOSING YOUR COURSE (SEE ALSO CH.1)
Some course features
East Anglia (MSci Meteor Ocean) A new (2010) four-year course integrates a study of the Earth's oceans and atmosphere, their interactions and external influence on them and is run jointly by the Schools of Environmental Sciences and Mathematics, together with the School of Computing.
Lancaster The Geography degree schemes are flexible so students can specialise in human or physical geography, or geography, or study an outside related subject, in the second and third years. There are study abroad opportunities an an option to teach geography in a local school.
Newcastle Geography can be taken in the Combined Studies degree with three other subjects in Stage 1 and two in Stage 2.
Reading A leading university for the study of meteorology with opportunities for placement at the University of Oklahoma equally renowned for this subject.

Universities and colleges teaching quality See www.qaa.ac.uk; www.unistats.com.

Top research universities and colleges (RAE 2008) See **Environmental Science/Studies**.

Examples of sandwich degree courses Aberystwyth; Bradford; Cardiff; Coventry; Glamorgan; Hertfordshire; Kingston; Loughborough; Manchester Met; Nottingham Trent; Oxford Brookes; Plymouth; Queen's Belfast; Salford; Ulster; Wolverhampton.

ADMISSIONS INFORMATION
Number of applicants per place (approx) Aberystwyth 3; Birmingham 6; Bristol 9; Bristol UWE 10; Cambridge 3; Cardiff 5; Central Lancashire 3; Chester 10; Coventry 12; Derby 4; Dundee 5; Durham 8; East Anglia (Meteor Ocean) 7; Edge Hill 8; Edinburgh 8; Exeter 10; Glamorgan 5; Gloucestershire 40; Greenwich 2; Hull 10; Kent 15; Kingston 7; Lancaster 13; Leeds 12; Leicester (BA) 19, (BSc) 17; Liverpool 3; Liverpool John Moores 6; London (King's) 5, (QM) 5, (RH) 7, (SOAS) 5; London LSE (Geog) 5 (Geog Econ) 4, Loughborough 6, (Geog Spo Sci) 20; Newcastle 14; Newman (UC) 2; Northampton 4; Northumbria 16; Nottingham 7; Portsmouth (Geog) 5; St Mary's Twickenham (UC) 4; Salford 3; Sheffield (BA) 13, (BSc) 10; Southampton (Geog) 7; Staffordshire 10; Strathclyde 8; Swansea 5; Wolverhampton 2; Worcester 5.

Advice to applicants and planning the UCAS personal statement Visits to, and field courses in, any specific geographical region should be fully described. Study your own locality in detail and get in touch with the area Planning Office to learn about any future developments. Read geographical magazines and describe any special interests you have – and why. Awareness of world issues and travel experience.

Misconceptions about this course **Birmingham** Some students think that the BA and BSc Geography courses are very different: in fact they do not differ from one another. All course options are available for both degrees. **East Anglia** (Meteor Ocean) Some applicants don't realise that the course is a very mathematical and physics-based subject. **Liverpool** Some applicants assume that a BSc course restricts them to physical geography modules. This is not so since human geography modules can be taken. Some students later specialise in human geography.

Selection interviews **Yes** Bristol UWE, Cambridge, Canterbury Christ Church, Central Lancashire, Coventry, Durham (essential for overseas applicants), East Anglia, Edge Hill, Greenwich, Kingston, London (King's), (QM), (RH), (SOAS), (UCL), Manchester Met, Northumbria, Oxford; **Some** Bath Spa, Bristol, Cardiff, Dundee, Liverpool, Loughborough, Newcastle, Nottingham, Salford, Southampton, Staffordshire.

Interview advice and questions Geography is a very broad subject and applicants can expect to be questioned on their syllabus and those aspects which they find of special interest. Some questions in the past have included: What fieldwork have you done? What are your views on ecology? What changes in the landscape have you noticed on the way to the interview? Explain in simple meteorological terms today's weather. Why are earthquakes almost unknown in Britain? What is the value of practical work in geography to primary school children? (BEd course) What do you enjoy about geography and why? Are there any articles of geographical importance in the news at present? Discuss the current economic situation in Britain and give your views. Questions on the Third World, on world ocean currents and drainage and economic factors world-wide. Expect to comment on local geography and on geographical photographs and diagrams. **Cambridge** What do you think about those who regard global warming as nonsense? Are Fair-Trade bananas really fair? Imagine you are hosting the BBC radio show on New Year's day, what message would you send to listeners? **Liverpool** Looks for why students have chosen Geography and the aspects of the subject they enjoy. **Oxford** Is nature natural? **Southampton** Applicants selected on academic ability only. See **Chapter 5**.

Reasons for rejection (non-academic) Lack of awareness of the content of the course. Failure to attend interview. Poor general knowledge. Lack of geographical awareness. **Hull** (BSc) Usually insufficient science background. **Liverpool** Personal statement gave no reason for choosing Geography.

AFTER-RESULTS ADVICE

Offers to applicants repeating A-levels **Higher** Bournemouth, Glasgow, Hull, Kingston, Nottingham, St Andrews, Sussex (Geog Lang); **Possibly higher** Edinburgh; **Same** Aberystwyth, Birmingham, Bradford, Brighton, Bristol, Cardiff, Chester, Coventry, Derby, Dundee, Durham, East Anglia, Edge Hill, Lancaster, Leeds (applicants consider which A-levels to resit for the BSc course), Liverpool, Liverpool Hope, Liverpool John Moores, London (RH), (SOAS), Loughborough, Manchester Met, Newcastle, Newman (UC), Newport, Northumbria, Oxford Brookes, St Mary's Twickenham (UC), Salford, Southampton, Staffordshire, Ulster, Wolverhampton; **No offers made** Cambridge.

GRADUATE DESTINATIONS AND EMPLOYMENT (2007/8 HESA)

Human and Social Geography graduates surveyed 2925 **Employed** 1410 **In further study** 595 **Assumed unemployed** 210.

Career note Geography graduates enter a wide range of occupations, many in business and administrative careers. Depending on specialisations, areas could include agriculture, forestry, hydrology, transport, market research and retail. Teaching is also a popular option.

OTHER DEGREE SUBJECTS FOR CONSIDERATION

Agriculture; Anthropology; Civil Engineering; Countryside Management; Development Studies; Environmental Engineering/Science/Studies; Forestry; Geology; Geomatic Engineering; Surveying; Town Planning; Urban Land Economics; Urban Studies.

GEOLOGY/GEOLOGICAL SCIENCES

(including **Earth Sciences, Geophysics** and **Geoscience**)

Topics in Geology courses include the physical and chemical constitution of the earth, exploration geophysics, oil and marine geology (oceanography) and seismic interpretation. Earth Sciences cover geology, environmental science, physical geography and can also include business studies and language modules. No previous knowledge of geology is required for most courses.

Useful websites www.geolsoc.org.uk; www.bgs.ac.uk; www.noc.soton.ac.uk; www.scicentral.com.

NB The points totals shown to the left of the institutions are for ease of reference only. It must not be assumed that Tariff points are always used by institutions or that they can be substituted for an offer in grades. The level of an offer is not necessarily indicative of the quality of a course.

COURSE OFFERS INFORMATION

Subject requirements/preferences GCSE English, mathematics and a science required. **AL** One or two mathematics/science subjects usually required. Geography may be accepted as a science subject.

NB In 2011 universities and colleges will differ in their use of GCE AL/AS unit grade information, A* grades, the Extended Project (EPQ), the Advanced Diploma and the Cambridge Pre-U examination when considering applicants and making offers. An EPQ may be accepted in place of an AS subject. Check websites of universities and colleges for the latest offers information.

Your target offers and examples of courses provided by each institution

380 pts **Cambridge** – A*AA college offers may vary (Nat Sci (Geol)) (IB 38–42 pts)
London (UCL) – AAAe–AABe (Earth Sci (Int)) (IB 36–38 pts)
London (UCL) – AAAe–ABBe (Geol; Earth Sci; Env Geosci; Pal; Planet Sci) (IB 34–38 pts)

360 pts **Birmingham** – AAA (MSci Geol Int Yr; Res App Geol Int Yr; Env Geosci Int Yr) (IB 34–38 pts)
East Anglia – AAA–AAB (MSci Env Earth Sci; Meteor Ocean; Clim Sci; Env Geophys) (IB 34–33 pts)
Glasgow – AAA (Faster route – Arch Earth Sci; Earth Sci) (IB 38 pts HL 665)
Leeds – AAA (MGeophys Geophysl Sci Int; Geol Sci (Int)) (IB 36 pts HL 18 pts)
Oxford – AAA (Earth Sci (Geol)) (IB 38–42 pts)
Southampton – AAA–ABB (MGeol Geol; Geophys) (IB 32–36 pts)

340 pts **Bristol** – AAB (Geol; Geol Biol; Palae Evol) (IB 33 pts)
Cardiff – AAB (MESci Geol (Int); Earth Sci (Int); Env Geosci (Int); Explor Res Geol (Int))
East Anglia – AAB (BSc Env Earth Sci N Am; Geophys Sci N Am; Meteor Ocean N Am; Clim Sci N Am) (IB 33 pts)
Edinburgh – AAB 2nd yr entry (BSc Geol; Geophys Geol; Geophys Meteor; MESci Geol) (IB 34 pts)
Glasgow – ABB (Arch Earth Sci; Env Biogeochem) (IB 32 pts)
Imperial London – AAB 340 pts (Geol; Env Geosci; Geol Geophys; Petrol Geosci)
Lancaster – AAB 340 pts (Earth Env Sci Abrd Earth Sci Abrd) (IB 31 pts)
Leicester – AAB (MGeol App Env Geol; MGeol Geol; Geol Geophys; Geol; Geol Pal)
Liverpool – AAB (MSci Geophys N Am) (IB 33 pts)

320 pts **Birmingham** – ABB–BBC (Geol Arch; Geol Geog; Geol; Env Geosci) (IB 28–34 pts)
Cardiff – ABB (MESci Geol; Earth Sci; Env Geosci; Explor Res Geol)
East Anglia – ABB–BBB (Geophys Sci; Env Earth Sci; Clim Sci; Meteor Ocean) (IB 32–31 pts)
Exeter – ABB–BBB (App Geol; Eng Geol Geotech) (IB 30–28 pts)
Liverpool – ABB (MSci Geol; Geol Geophys) (IB 31 pts)
London (RH) – ABB 320 pts (Geoscience)
St Andrews – ABB (Geosci courses; Env Geosci courses) (IB 30–32 pts)

300 pts **Aberdeen** – BBB 2nd yr entry (Geol Petrol Geol; Geosci; Arch Geosci) (IB 32 pts)
Cardiff – BBB (BSc Explor Res Geol; Env Geosci)
Durham – BBB (Earth Sci; Geosci; Geol; Env Geosci; Geophys Geol)

Edinburgh – BBB 1st yr entry (BSc Geol; Geophys Geol; Geophys Meteor; MESci Geol) (IB 34 pts)
Lancaster – BBB (Earth Sci; Earth Sci Geog;) (IB 29 pts)
Leeds – BBB (BSc Geol Sci; Geophys Sci) (IB 32 pts HL 16 pts)
Leicester – BBB (Geol; Geol Phys) (IB 28–30 pts)
Liverpool – BBB (BSc Geol; Geol Physl Geog; Geophys (Geol)) (IB 30 pts)
London (RH) – BBB 300 pts (BSc Env Geol; Geol; Geosci) (IB 38 pts HL 66)
Manchester – BBB 300 pts (Geol; Geol Planet Sci; Earth Sci; Env Res Geol; Geochem) (IB 32 pts)
Pymouth – 300 pts (MGeol Geol)
Southampton – BBB (BSc Geol; Geol Mar Biol; Geophysl Sci) (IB 30 pts HL 16 pts)
Southampton – BBB–BCC (Geol inc Sci Fdn Yr) (IB 30–28 pts)

280 pts **Aberystwyth** – 280 pts (Env Earth Sci) (IB 30 pts)
Keele – 280–300 pts (Geol courses; Geosci) (IB 26–30 pts)

260 pts **Brighton** – BCC 260 pts (Geol; Geog Geol; Earth Ocn Sci) (IB 28 pts)
Plymouth – 260pts (Geol Ocn Sci; App Geol; BSc Physl Geog Geol; Mar Geosci)

240 pts **Kingston** – 240–280 pts (Earth Sys Sci; App Geol courses; Geol; App Env Geol; Env Haz Disas Mgt)
Portsmouth – 240–300pts (Eng Geol Geotech; Earth Sci; Geol; Geol Haz; Pal Evol)
St Andrews – CCC 1st yr entry (Geol Petrol Geol; Geosci; Arch Geosci) (IB 28 pts)

220 pts **Bangor** – 220–260 pts (Geol Ocean)

200 pts **Derby** – 200–240 pts (Geology)
Glamorgan – 200–260 pts (Geol courses)

140 pts **West Scotland** – CD (App Biosci Earth Sci)

80 pts **London (Birk)** – 80 pts for under 21s (over 21s varies) (p/t Geol; Env Geol; Earth Sci)

Open University – (Geol St – contact +44 (0)845 300 6090 or www.openuniversity.co.uk/you)

Alternative offers
See **Chapter 7** and **Appendix 1** for grades/UCAS Tariff points information for the International Baccalaureate, Scottish Highers/Advanced Highers, the Welsh Baccalaureate, the Irish Leaving Certificate, the Cambridge Pre-U Diploma, the Advanced Diploma and the Extended Project.

CHOOSING YOUR COURSE (SEE ALSO CH.1)

Some course features
Cardiff (Explor Res Geol) Course provides a grounding in applied geology and the evaluation and exploration of the Earth's natural resources. During the second summer, an industrial placement is offered with an exploration company in the UK or overseas.
East Anglia A strong department of Environmental Sciences incorporating courses in Geophysical Sciences with opportunities to study abroad and in industry. A new range of integrated masters' degrees is introduced in 2010 and includes a new MSci in Climate Science.
Exeter Camborne School of Mines is a leader in the field of Engineering Geology and Geotechnics and Mining Engineering. £2000 scholarships are offered on the basis of academic excellence, together with some sponsorships.
Leeds Geological and Geophysical Sciences can be studied with placements in Europe or worldwide or with industrial placement.

Universities and colleges teaching quality See www.qaa.ac.uk; www.unistats.com.

Top research universities and colleges (RAE 2008) See **Environmental Science/Studies**.

Examples of sandwich degree courses Cardiff; Glamorgan; Greenwich; Kingston; West Scotland.

ADMISSIONS INFORMATION

Number of applicants per place (approx) Aberystwyth 5; Bangor 4; Birmingham 4; Bristol 7; Cardiff 7; Derby 4; Durham 4; East Anglia 7; Edinburgh 5; Exeter 5; Imperial London 5; Kingston 19, (Earth

Sys Sci) 3; Leeds 8; Liverpool 5; London (RH) 5, (UCL) 3; Oxford 1.2; Plymouth 7; Portsmouth (Eng Geol Geotech) 2, (Geol) 2; Southampton 5.

Advice to applicants and planning the UCAS personal statement Visits to any outstanding geological sites and field courses you have attended should be described in detail. Apart from geological formations, you should also be aware of how geology has affected humankind in specific areas in the architecture of the region and artefacts used. Evidence of social skills could be given. See also **Appendix 4**.

Misconceptions about this course **East Anglia** Many applicants fail to realise that environmental earth science extends beyond geology to the links between the solid earth and its behaviour and society in general. **London (UCL)** Environmental geoscience is sometimes mistaken for environmental science; they are two different subjects.

Selection interviews **Yes** Birmingham, Cambridge, Durham, Edinburgh, Kingston, Liverpool, London (RH), Oxford, Southampton, Sunderland; **Some** Aberystwyth (mature students only), Cardiff, Derby, East Anglia.

Interview advice and questions Some knowledge of the subject will be expected and applicants could be questioned on specimens of rocks and their origins. Past interviews have included questions on the field courses attended, and the geophysical methods of exploration in the detection of metals. How would you determine the age of this rock (sample shown)? Can you integrate a decay curve function and would it help you to determine the age of rocks? How many planes of crystallisation could this rock have? What causes a volcano? What is your local geology? **Oxford** (Earth Sci) Candidates may be asked to comment on specimens of a geological nature, based on previous knowledge of the subject. See **Chapter 5**.

Reasons for rejection (non-academic) Misconceptions about the course. **Exeter** Outright rejection uncommon but some applicants advised to apply for other programmes.

AFTER-RESULTS ADVICE

Offers to applicants repeating A-levels **Higher** Bristol, St Andrews; **Possibly higher** Portsmouth; **Same** Aberystwyth, Cardiff, Derby, Durham, East Anglia, Leeds, London (RH), Plymouth, Southampton; **No offers made** Cambridge.

GRADUATE DESTINATIONS AND EMPLOYMENT (2007/8 HESA)

Geology graduates surveyed 855 **Employed** 395 **In further study** 225 **Assumed unemployed** 95.

Career note Areas of employment include mining and quarrying, the oil and gas industry, prospecting and processing.

OTHER DEGREE SUBJECTS FOR CONSIDERATION

Archaeology; Civil and Mining Engineering; Environmental Science; Geography; Meteorology; Oceanography; Physics.

GERMAN

(see also **European Studies** and **Languages**)

Language, literature, practical language skills or a broader study of Germany and its culture (European Studies) are alternative study approaches. See also **Appendix 4** under Languages.

Useful websites www.cilt.org.uk; www.goethe.de; www.bbc.co.uk/languages; www.iol.org.uk; http://languageadvantage.com; www.languagematters.co.uk; www.reed.co.uk/multilingual; www.deutsch-online.com; www.faz.net; www.sueddeutsche.de; http://europa.eu; www.gslg.org.uk; www.amgs.org.uk; www.wigs.ac.uk.

NB The points totals shown to the left of the institutions are for ease of reference only. It must not be assumed that Tariff points are always used by institutions or that they can be substituted for an offer in grades. The level of an offer is not necessarily indicative of the quality of a course.

COURSE OFFERS INFORMATION

Subject requirements/preferences **GCSE** English and German are required. **AL** German required usually at a specified grade.

NB In 2011 universities and colleges will differ in their use of GCE AL/AS unit grade information, A* grades, the Extended Project (EPQ), the Advanced Diploma and the Cambridge Pre-U examination when considering applicants and making offers. An EPQ may be accepted in place of an AS subject. Check websites of universities and colleges for the latest offers information.

Your target offers and examples of courses provided by each institution

380 pts **Cambridge** – A*AA college offers may vary (Modn Mediev Lang (Ger))
360 pts **Bath** – AAA–ABB (MEng Manuf Ger; Int Mgt Modn Langs (Ger))
Birmingham – AAA +LNAT (Law Ger)
Bristol – AAA +LNAT (Law Ger) (IB 37 pts)
Bristol – AAA–ABB (Phil Ger; Pol Ger) (IB 37–33 pts)
Imperial London – AAA (Chem Ger Sci)
London (King's) – AAB+AS (Ger Hist) (IB 32 pts)
London (UCL) – AAB+AS–BBB+AS (Ger courses) (IB 32–36 pts)
Manchester – AAA–AAB (MML Ger Chin; Ger Russ; Ger Jap) (IB 35–37 pts)
Nottingham – AAA +LNAT (Law Ger)
Oxford – AAA (Ger courses)
St Andrews – AAA (Ger Int Rel; Ger Mgt; Ger Psy)

340 pts **Aston** – 340–320 pts (Int Bus Ger)
Bath – AAB (Ger Pol) (IB 34–36 pts)
Durham – AAB (Comb St; Modn Lang)
East Anglia – AAB (Law Euro Leg Sys) (IB 33 pts)
Exeter – AAB–ABB (Ger; Class St Ger; Ger Arbc; Int Rel Ger) (IB 29 pts)
Glasgow – AAB (Ger courses) (IB 34 pts)
Imperial London – AAB (Biol Ger Sci)
Lancaster – AAB 340 pts (Euro Mgt (Ger)) (IB 31 pts)
Manchester – AAB–BBC (BA Ger Chin; Ger Russ; Ger Jap; Ger St) (IB 30–35 pts)
Queen's Belfast – AAB–ABBa (Acc Ger)
St Andrews – AAB (Ger courses except under **360 pts**) (IB 34 pts)
Sheffield – AAB (Law Ger; Mech Eng Ger) (IB 35 pts)
Southampton – AAB–ABB (Ger courses) (IB 34–32 pts)
Warwick – 340–320 pts (Ger St courses) (IB 32–34 pts)

320 pts **Bath** – ABB–BBB (Modn Langs Euro St (Fr/Ger/Ital/Russ/Span); Ger Fr/Ital/Span)
Birmingham – ABB (Ger St joint courses) (IB 32–34 pts)
Cardiff – ABB–BBC (Ger Jap; Ger Relig St; Ger Welsh)
Hull – 320 pts (Law Ger Law Lang)
Lancaster – ABB 320 pts (Ger Maths; Ger Pol; Ger Psy)
Leeds – ABB (Ger joint courses)
London (King's) – BBB+AS (Ger Hisp St) (IB 32 pts HL Ger Span 6)
London (RH) – ABB–BBB (Ger courses) (IB 32 pts HL lang 6)
Newcastle – ABB (Ger; Ger Bus St; Ger Pol; Ling Ger) (IB 32 pts HL Ger 6)
Reading – ABB (Int Mgt Bus Admin Ger)
Sheffield – ABB (Ger Bus Mgt; Ger Phil) (IB 32–33 pts)
Surrey – ABB 320 pts (Law Ger Law; Bus Mgt Ger)
York – ABB (Ger Ling; Ger Span) (IB 32 pts)

300 pts **Aston** – 300–320 pts (Ger courses except under **340 pts**)
Birmingham – BBB (Ger St) (IB 30–32 pts)
Bristol – BBB–BCC (Ger; Ger Cz/Fr/Ital/Port/Russ/Span; Mus Ger) (IB 29–32 pts)
Cardiff – BBB (Ger; Engl Lit Ger)
Dundee – BBB (Law Ger; Int Bus Ger; Phil Ger; Psy Ger; Scot Hist Ger)
Edinburgh – BBB (Ger courses)
Lancaster – BBB 300 pts (Ger St; Ger St Geog; Ger St Comp) (IB 29 pts)
Leeds – BBB (German) (IB 32 pts HL 15 pts)
Liverpool – BBB (Ger courses) (IB 30 pts)
London (King's) – BBC+AS (German) (IB 30 pts HL Ger 6)
London (QM) – 300–340 pts (Ger Ling Comp Sci; Ger Compar Lit; Ger; Ger Geog) (IB 32–36 pts)
Nottingham – ABC–BBB (Ger; Ger Hist; Ger Russ; Ger Mus) (IB 32 pts)
Queen's Belfast – BBB–BBCb (Ger courses except under **340 pts**)
Reading – 300–320 pts (Ger courses except under **320 pts**) (IB 28 pts)
Salford – 300 pts (Modn Langs Transl Interp: Ger with 2nd Lang)
Sheffield – BBB (Ger St; Ger Polh; Ger Dutch; Ger Ling; Ger Econ)
Surrey – BBB 300 pts (Ger Engl Int Comm; Ger Transl; Ger Fr/Span) (IB 32–28 pts)
Swansea – BBB (Ger courses)
Westminster – BBB 300 pts (Int Bus Ger) (IB 28 pts)

280 pts **Essex** – 280 pts (Ger St Modn Lang) (IB 30 pts)
Heriot-Watt – BBC (Langs (Interp Transl) (Fr/Ger) (Ger/Span)) (IB 28 pts)
Hull – 280–300 pts (Dr Ger; Phil Ger)
Kent – 280–320 pts (Ger Joint Hons courses) (IB 31–35 pts)
Northumbria – 280–300 pts (Int Bus Mgt Ger; Ger Bus) (IB 26 pts)
Westminster – BBC (Engl Lit Ger; Int Rel Ger; Ling Ger)

260 pts **Aberystwyth** – 260 pts (Ger courses) (IB 27 pts)
Hull – 260–280 pts (Ger Mgt; Ger Transl St; Ger St; Ger Mark)

Nottingham Trent – 260 pts (Ger Euro St; Ger Glob St; Ger Media)
240 pts **Aberdeen** – CCC (Ger courses) (IB 28 pts)
Bangor – 240–260 pts (Ger courses)
Dundee – CCC 240 pts (Ger courses except under **300 pts**)
Manchester Met – 240 pts (Ger St; Ger Fr/Ital/Span) (IB 28 pts)
Portsmouth – 240 pts (Euro Bus (UK Ger))
Ulster – 240 pts (Ger courses)
220 pts **Central Lancashire** – 220 pts (Ger Bus Ger)
Chester – 220–260 pts (Ger courses) (IB 30 pts)
Leeds Met – 220 pts (Ger Glob Dev; Ger Int Rel; Ger Mark; Ger PR; Ger Tour Mgt)
Northampton – 220–260 pts (Ger courses)
Sunderland – 220 pts (Ger Comb courses)
200 pts **Anglia Ruskin** – 200 pts (Int Bus (Berlin))
Portsmouth – 200–280 pts (Ger St)
80 pts **London (Birk)** – 80 pts (p/t Ger Mgt; Modn Ger St)

London LSE – optional course offered by language centre (check with admissions tutor) (Fr/Ger/Russ/Span)

Alternative offers
See **Chapter 7** and **Appendix 1** for grades/UCAS Tariff points information for the International Baccalaureate, Scottish Highers/Advanced Highers, the Welsh Baccalaureate, the Irish Leaving Certificate, the Cambridge Pre-U Diploma, the Advanced Diploma and the Extended Project.

CHOOSING YOUR COURSE (SEE ALSO CH.1)

Some course features
Bangor German is offered with two other languages from French, Italian and Spanish.
Durham (Modn Lang) Students take core language module each year and options from a range of modules, including film, history, literature, translation, interpreting and cultural studies.
East Anglia German can be taken as part of the Law course with European Legal Systems.
Heriot-Watt The course focuses on practical language skills, linguistics and translation studies, communication studies and European studies.
Salford The only university to offer a course combining media, a language and business studies.

Universities and colleges teaching quality See www.qaa.ac.uk; www.unistats.com.

Top research universities and colleges (RAE 2008) (German, Dutch and Scandinavian languages) Oxford; Cambridge; London (King's); Leeds; London (UCL) (German); Durham; London (RH); St Andrews; Manchester; Birmingham; London (UCL) (Scandinavian Studies).

ADMISSIONS INFORMATION

Number of applicants per place (approx) Aston 4; Bangor 6; Birmingham 6; Bradford 6; Bristol 3; Cardiff 6; Central Lancashire 2; Durham 4; East Anglia 4; Exeter 4; Heriot-Watt 10; Hull 12; Kent 10; Lancaster 7; Leeds (Joint Hons) 8; Leicester 4; London (King's) 5, (QM) 6, (RH) 5, (UCL) 4; Newcastle 6; Nottingham 5; Portsmouth 5; Salford 5; Staffordshire 5; Stirling 6; Surrey 2; Swansea 4; Warwick (Ger Bus St) 16, (Ger) 8; York 6.

Advice to applicants and planning the UCAS personal statement Describe visits to Germany or a German-speaking country and the particular cultural and geographical features of the region. Contacts with friends in Germany and language experience should also be mentioned, and if you are bilingual, say so. Read German newspapers and magazines and keep up-to-date with national news.

Misconceptions about this course **Leeds** See **Languages**. **Swansea** Some students are afraid of the year abroad, which is actually one of the most enjoyable parts of the course.

Selection interviews **Yes** Bangor, Birmingham (short conversation in German), Bradford, Cambridge, Durham, East Anglia, Exeter, Heriot-Watt, Hull, Liverpool, London (RH), (UCL), Newcastle, Oxford, Sheffield, Southampton, Surrey (always); **Some** Cardiff, Leeds, Portsmouth, Swansea.

Interview advice and questions Questions asked on A-level syllabus. Part of the interview may be in German. What foreign newspapers and/or magazines do you read? Questions on German current affairs, particularly politics and reunification problems, books read outside the course, etc. **Leeds** See **Languages**. See **Chapter 5**.

Reasons for rejection (non-academic) Unstable personality. Poor motivation. Insufficient commitment. Unrealistic expectations. Not interested in spending a year abroad.

AFTER-RESULTS ADVICE

Offers to applicants repeating A-levels **Higher** Birmingham, Glasgow, Leeds, Warwick; **Same** Aston, Cardiff, Chester, Durham, East Anglia, London (RH), Newcastle (not always), Nottingham, Salford, Surrey, Swansea, Ulster, York; **No offers made** Cambridge.

GRADUATE DESTINATIONS AND EMPLOYMENT (2007/8 HESA)

Graduates surveyed 480 **Employed** 240 **In further study** 90 **Assumed unemployed** 40.

Career note See **Languages**.

OTHER DEGREE SUBJECTS FOR CONSIDERATION

East European Studies; European Studies; International Business Studies.

GREEK

(see also **Classical Studies/Classical Civilisation** and **Classics**)

Courses are offered in Ancient and Modern Greek, covering the language and literature from ancient times to the present day. Classics and Classical Studies courses (see separate tables) also focus on Greek language and literature, and many provide the opportunity to learn Greek (and/or Latin) from scratch.

Useful websites www.greek-language.com; www.arwhead.com/Greeks; www.greekmyth.org; www.fhw.gr; www.culture.gr; www.greeklanguage.gr.

NB The points totals shown to the left of the institutions are for ease of reference only. It must not be assumed that Tariff points are always used by institutions or that they can be substituted for an offer in grades. The level of an offer is not necessarily indicative of the quality of a course.

COURSE OFFERS INFORMATION

Subject requirements/preferences **GCSE** English and a foreign language required. Greek required by some universities. **AL** Latin, Greek or a foreign language may be specified by some universities.

NB In 2011 universities and colleges will differ in their use of GCE AL/AS unit grade information, A* grades, the Extended Project (EPQ), the Advanced Diploma and the Cambridge Pre-U examination when considering applicants and making offers. An EPQ may be accepted in place of an AS subject. Check websites of universities and colleges for the latest offers information.

Your target offers and examples of courses provided by each institution

380 pts **Cambridge** – A*AA college offers may vary (Modn Mediev Lang (Class Gk); Class Gk Lat) (IB 38–42 pts)

360 pts **London (King's)** – AABe (Gk Engl) (IB 36 pts)
Oxford – AAA (Modn Gk courses)

340 pts **Durham** – AAB (Class (Gk/Lat Lang option); Comb Hons Arts (Gk))
Exeter – AAB–ABB (Gk Arbc St) (IB 34–31 pts)
Glasgow – AAB (Gk courses)
London (King's) – ABB+AS (Gk; Modn Gk Byz St; Modn Gk Port Braz St) (IB 36 pts)
London (UCL) – ABB+AS (Gk Lat) (IB 31 pts)

Newcastle – AAB (Comb St (Gk)) (IB 34 pts)
St Andrews – AAB (Gk courses) (IB 36 pts)

320 pts **Leeds** – ABB (Gk; Engl Gk Civ; Arbc Gk Civ) (IB 33 pts)
London (RH) – ABB 320 pts (Gk; Gk Ital; Fr/Ger Gk)
Manchester – ABB–BBB (Gk; Gk Engl Lit) (IB 33–32 pts)
Nottingham – ABB (Gk (Anc))
Swansea – ABB–BBB 320–300 pts (Greek)

300 pts **Edinburgh** – BBB (Gk St; Class Arch Gk; Phil Gk; Sansk Gk) (IB 34 pts)
Leeds – BBB (Gk Civ Phil; Gk Civ Theol Relig St) (IB 32 pts)

Alternative offers
See **Chapter 7** and **Appendix 1** for grades/UCAS Tariff points information for the International Baccalaureate, Scottish Highers/Advanced Highers, the Welsh Baccalaureate, the Irish Leaving Certificate, the Cambridge Pre-U Diploma, the Advanced Diploma and the Extended Project.

CHOOSING YOUR COURSE (SEE ALSO CH.1)

Some course features
Durham Classics courses have a common first year which allows the student to begin or continue a study of Greek.
Edinburgh (Gk St) The course covers archaeology, art, literature of Greek civilisation, with an intensive Greek course in the first term for beginners.
London (King's) The Modern Greek with English course focuses on studying the classical world through reading ancient texts in the original Greek. A-level Greek is required for entry.
Nottingham (Gk (Anc)) The course combines Greek language learning thoughout (no prior knowledge required) with a study of Greek literature, history, society and culture. Intensive language study is provided so at each level of the course students can read texts in the original Greek.

Universities and colleges teaching quality See www.qaa.ac.uk; www.unistats.com.

Top research universities and colleges (RAE 2008) See **Classics**.

ADMISSIONS INFORMATION

Number of applicants per place (approx) Leeds 2; London (King's) 3.

Advice to applicants and planning the UCAS personal statement See **Classical Studies/Classical Civilisation**.

Selection interviews **Yes** Cambridge, London (RH).

Interview advice and questions Questions asked on A-level syllabus. Why do you want to study Greek? What aspects of this course interest you? (Questions will develop from answers.) See also **Chapter 5**.

Reasons for rejection (non-academic) Poor language ability.

AFTER-RESULTS ADVICE

Offers to applicants repeating A-levels **Higher** St Andrews; **Same** Leeds; **No offers made** Cambridge.

GRADUATE DESTINATIONS AND EMPLOYMENT (2007/8 HESA)

Classical Greek graduates surveyed 5 **Employed** 5 **In further study** none **Assumed unemployed** none.

Career note See **Languages**.

OTHER DEGREE SUBJECTS FOR CONSIDERATION

Ancient History; Classical Studies; Classics; European Studies; Philosophy.

HEALTH SCIENCES/STUDIES

(including **Audiology, Chiropractic, Orthoptics, Osteopathy, Paramedic Science**; see also **Community Studies, Environmental Science/Studies, Nursing and Midwifery, Optometry, Physiotherapy, Podiatry, Radiography, Social Work, Speech Pathology/Sciences/Therapy** and **Sports Science/Studies**)

Health Sciences/Studies is a broad subject-field which offers courses covering both practical applications concerning health and well-being (some of which border on nursing) and also the administrative activities involved in the promotion of health in the community. Also included are some specialised careers which include Chiropractic, involving the healing process by way of manipulation, mainly in the spinal region, and Osteopathy in which joints and tissues are manipulated to correct abnormalities. Audiology is concerned with the treatment and diagnosis of hearing and balance disorders while Prosthetics involves the provision and fitting of artificial limbs and Orthotics is concerned with making and fitting braces, splints and special footwear to ease pain and to assist movement.

Useful websites www.rsph.org.uk; www.bmj.com; www.reflexology.org; www.baap.org.uk; www.chiropractic-uk.co.uk; www.osteopathy.org.uk; www.who.int; www.csp.org.uk; www.scienceyear.com; www.intute.ac.uk.

NB The points totals shown to the left of the institutions are for ease of reference only. It must not be assumed that Tariff points are always used by institutions or that they can be substituted for an offer in grades. The level of an offer is not necessarily indicative of the quality of a course.

COURSE OFFERS INFORMATION

Subject requirements/preferences **GCSE** English, mathematics and a science important or essential for some courses. **AL** Mathematics, chemistry or biology may be required for some courses. **Other** Health checks and CRB clearance required for many courses.

NB In 2011 universities and colleges will differ in their use of GCE AL/AS unit grade information, A* grades, the Extended Project (EPQ), the Advanced Diploma and the Cambridge Pre-U examination when considering applicants and making offers. An EPQ may be accepted in place of an AS subject. Check websites of universities and colleges for the latest offers information.

Your target offers and examples of courses provided by each institution

340 pts **London (UCL)** – ABB+AS–BBB+AS (Audiology) (IB 32–34 pts)

320 pts **Anglo-Euro (Coll Chiro)** – ABB–BBC 320–280 pts (Chiropractic)
Brunel – BBC +AS/EPQ c 320 pts (Biomed Sci (Hum Hlth)) (IB 32 pts)
Glasgow – ABB (Spo Med) (IB 32 pts)
Manchester – ABB–BBB (Audiology) (IB 33–30 pts)
Southampton – ABB (Audiology) (IB 32 pts)

300 pts **Aberdeen** – BBB 2nd yr entry (Hlth Sci (Hlth Soty) (Hlth Spo) (Hlth Nutr) (Hlth Prom) (Hlth Serv Rsch))
Aston – BBB (Audiology)
Bristol – BBB (Audiology) (IB 32 pts)
Essex – 300–280 pts (Hlth Hum Sci; Hlth St; Hlth St Sociol) (IB 32–30 pts)
Glamorgan – 300 pts (Chiropractic)
Glasgow – BBB (Hlth Soc St)
Hull – 300 pts (Glob Hlth Dis)
Oxford Brookes – BBB (Osteopathy)
Sheffield – BBB (Orthoptics) (IB 32 pts)

295 pts **Queen Margaret** – 295 pts (Audiology)

280 pts **Abertay Dundee** – BBC (Mntl Hlth Cnslg)
Bradford – 280 pts (Clin Sci – optional transfer to Medicine at **Leeds**)
Brighton – BBC 280 pts (Hlth Soc Cr Soc Plcy) (IB 30 pts)

British Sch Ost – BBC–CCC (Osteopathy)
De Montfort – 280 pts (Audiology)
Durham – BBC (Hlth Hum Sci) (IB 30 pts)
Hertfordshire – 280 pts (Paramed Sci) (IB 28–30 pts)
Leeds – BBC (Audiology)
NESCOT – 280 pts (Ost Med)
Newport – 280 pts (Hlth Exer Nutr)
Northumbria – 280 pts (Env Hlth)
Plymouth – 280–320 pts (Tox Hlth) (IB 26 pts)
Queen Margaret – 280 pts (Hlth Psy)
Salford – 280 pts (Pros Orthot) (IB 28 pts)
Strathclyde – BBC (Pros Orthot) (IB 32 pts)
Swansea – BBC 280 pts (Audiology)
Worcester – 280 pts (Hlth Psy)

260 pts **Kent** – 260 pts (Hlth Soc Cr Prac) (IB 31 pts)
Liverpool Hope – 260 pts (Hlth Nutr Fit)
Manchester Met – 260–240 pts (Hlth St Comb courses; Env Hlth)
Northumbria – 260 pts (Hlth Contemp Soty Gdnc Cnslg)
Sheffield – BCC (Hlth Hum Sci) (IB 29 pts)
Surrey – 260–300 pts (Paramed Prac)
Ulster – 260 pts (Hlth Soc Cr Plcy)

240 pts **Aberdeen** – CCC 1st yr entry (Hlth Sci (Hlth Nutr) (Hlth Spo) (Hlth Soty) (Hlth Prom))
Arts London (CFash) – 240 pts (Cos Sci)
Bristol – CCC (Df St) (IB 28 pts)
Central Lancashire – 240 pts (Hlth St courses)
Chester – 240 pts (Hlth Soc Cr)
Coventry – 240 pts (Hum Biosci)
Dundee – CCC (Oral Hlth Sci)
Edge Hill – 240 pts (Wmns Hlth; Hlth Soc Wlbng)
European Sch Ost/Greenwich – 240 pts (Osteopathy)
Glamorgan – 240–280 pts (Hlth Soc Cr)
Leeds Met – 240 pts (Osteopathy)
Liverpool – CCC (Orthoptics) (IB 28 pts)
Liverpool John Moores – 240–280 pts (Commun Nutr; Env Hlth)
Manchester – CCC (Oral Hlth Sci)
Manchester Met – 240 pts (Env Hlth)
Nottingham Trent – 240 pts (Exer Nutr Hlth)
Teesside – 240 pts (Fd Nutr Hlth Sci)

220 pts **Bangor** – 220–260 pts (Hlth Soc Cr)
Bath Spa – 220–260 pts (Diet Hlth; Hlth St courses)
British Coll Ost Med – 220–260 pts (Ost Med)
Cardiff (UWIC) – 220 pts (Env Hlth)
Central Lancashire – 220 pts (Df St; Sex Hlth St)
Coventry – 220–240 pts (Hlth Lfstl Mgt)
Hertfordshire – 220–260 pts (Hlth St joint courses)
Kingston – 220–280 pts (Exer Nutr Hlth)
Northampton – 220–260 pts (Hlth St courses; Hlth Exer; Hum Biosci)
Southampton Solent – 220 pts (Hlth Exer Physl Actvt; Hlth Prom Fit)
Sunderland – 220 pts (Hlth Soc Cr; Commun Hlth)
UCP Marjon – 220 pts (Hlth Exer Phys Actvt)
Westminster – CCD (Hlth Sci (Complem Thera) (Herb Med) (Nutr Thera); Chin Med Acu) (IB 26 pts)

200 pts **Birmingham City** – 200 pts (Hlth Wlbng)
Bolton – 200 pts (Commun Hlth Wlbng)
Bradford – 200 pts (Clin Sci Fdn)
Canterbury Christ Church – 200 pts (Hlth St courses)
Cardiff (UWIC) – 200 pts (Complem Thera)
Cumbria – 200 pts (Hlth Phys)
De Montfort – 200 pts (Pharml Cos Sci)
East London – 200 pts (Hlth Fit; Hlth Prom; Hlth St; Herb Med)
Gloucestershire – 200 pts (Hlth Commun Soc Cr)
Glyndŵr – 200 pts (Complem Med Prac; Chin Med)
Greenwich – 200 pts (Hlth; Pblc Hlth; Complem Thera)
Huddersfield – 200 pts (Hlth Commun St)
Leeds Trinity (UC) – 200 pts (Hlth Prom Dev)
Lincoln – 200 pts (Hlth Soc Cr)
London Met – 200 pts (Hlth St; Hlth St Soc Plcy)
Middlesex – 200–240 pts (Trad Chin Acu; Trad Chin Med; Complem Hlth Sci; Herb Med)
Nottingham Trent – 200 pts (Hlth Soc Cr courses)
Oldham (Coll Univ Centre) – 200–220 pts (Hlth Commun St)
Plymouth – 200 pts (Hlth Soc Cr St)
Portsmouth – 200–220 pts (Clin Hlth Sci)
Salford – 200 pts (Env Hlth; Exer Physl Actvt Hlth) (IB 24 pts)
Sheffield Hallam – 200 pts (Pblc Hlth Nutr)
Suffolk (Univ Campus) – 200 pts (Hlth Wlbng)
Sunderland – 200 pts (Hlth Soc Cr)
Thames Valley – 200 pts (Hlth St)

180 pts **Anglia Ruskin** – 180 pts (Exer Hlth)
Derby – 180–200 pts (Hlth Soc Cr)
Greenwich – 180 pts (Pblc Hlth)
Manchester Met – 180 pts (Soc Chng (Hlth Soc Cr))

160 pts **Colchester (Inst)** – 160 pts (Hlth Soc Cr)
Cumbria – 160 pts (Complem Thera)
De Montfort – 160 pts (Hlth St)
Derby – 160–280 pts (Complem Thera)
Leeds Met – 160 pts (Pblc Hlth; Complem Thera; Hlth Cr Sci; Acpntr)
London Met – 160 pts (Hlth Prom; Cos Sci; Hrbl Medcnl Sci)
Roehampton – 160–200 pts (Hlth Hum Sci)
St Mary's Twickenham (UC) – 160–200 pts (Hlth Exer Physl Actvts)
UHI Millennium Inst – CC (Hlth St; Hlth St (Hlth Welf) (Rur Hlth))
Wolverhampton – 160–220 pts (Complem Thera; Hlth St Soc Cr; Hlth St; Df St)

100 pts **Newport** – 100–120 pts (Commun Hlth)

Brighton – offers may vary (Acpntr; Ost)
Kingston – preference given to applicants 21 yrs and over with 2 A-levels (Acupuncture)
Open University – (Hlth Soc Cr – contact +44 (0)845 300 6090 or www.openuniversity.co.uk/you)

Alternative offers
See **Chapter 7** and **Appendix 1** for grades/UCAS Tariff points information for the International Baccalaureate, Scottish Highers/Advanced Highers, the Welsh Baccalaureate, the Irish Leaving Certificate, the Cambridge Pre-U Diploma, the Advanced Diploma and the Extended Project.

EXAMPLES OF FOUNDATION DEGREES IN THE SUBJECT FIELD
(See also **Social and Public Policy and Administration**)

Bedfordshire; Blackburn (Coll Univ Centre); Bradford; Brighton; Bristol City (Coll); Bristol UWE; Bucks New; Cardiff (UWIC); Central Lancashire; Chichester; Cornwall (Coll); Coventry; Cumbria; Durham New (Coll); East London; Edge Hill; Farnborough (CT); Greenwich; Grimsby (IFHE); Harper Adams (UC); Hereford (CA); Hopwood Hall (Coll); Huddersfield; Hugh Baird (Coll); Hull (Coll); Kendal (Coll); Kingston; Kirklees (Coll); Leeds Trinity (UC); Lincoln; Loughborough (Coll); Manchester (Coll); Newport; Norwich City (Coll); Plymouth; Portsmouth; Riverside Halton (Coll); St Helens (Coll); Stratford upon Avon (Coll); Stockton Riverside (Coll); Suffolk (Univ Campus); Swansea (Coll); Thames Valley; Truro (Coll); Wakefield (Coll); Wigan and Leigh (Coll); York St John.

CHOOSING YOUR COURSE (SEE ALSO CH.1)
Some course features
Aberdeen The Health Sciences programme is based in the Medical School and combines courses on social, life and medical sciences. In the third year students are attached to a health or social care agency in the community.
Bath Spa Health Studies is a part of the Combined Honours programme choosing one other subject from 17 options. In addition to health subjects the course covers education, public health, child, disability and mental health.
Brunel Human Health is one of five options chosen at the end of Year 1 as part of the Biomedical Sciences programme.
Essex (Hlth Hum Sci) A multi-disciplinary course involving a study of psychology, sociology and biology relevant to health and communication skills.

Universities and colleges teaching quality See www.qaa.ac.uk; www.unistats.com.

Top research universities and colleges (RAE 2008) (Allied Health Professions and Studies) London (UCL); Lancaster; Surrey; Bristol UWE; Hull; Cardiff; Swansea; Glasgow; Strathclyde; Queen's Belfast.

ADMISSIONS INFORMATION
Number of applicants per place (approx) Bangor 2; Bath Spa 1; Bournemouth 4; Bournemouth Anglo-Euro (Coll) 1; Bristol (Audiol) 5, (Df St) 2; British Sch Ost 5; Brunel 2; Central Lancashire 6; Chester 6; Chichester 5; Cumbria 4; European Sch Ost/Greenwich 3; Liverpool John Moores 10; London Met 7; Manchester 18; Manchester Met 10; Middlesex 4; Northampton 3; Portsmouth 12; Roehampton 10; Salford 8; Southampton 4; Swansea 1; Worcester 3.

Advice to applicants and planning the UCAS personal statement You should describe any work with people you have done, particularly in a caring capacity, for example, working with the elderly, nursing, hospital work. Show why you wish to study this subject. You should give evidence of your ability to communicate and to work in a group. Evidence needed of applicants' understanding of the NHS and health care systems. Osteopathy applicants should provide clear evidence of why they want to work as an osteopath: work shadowing in an osteopath's practice is important and should be described. Give details of any work using your hands.

Misconceptions about this course There is a mistaken belief that Health Science courses include nursing. **Bangor** (Hlth Soc Cr) This is an administration course, not a nursing course. **Brit Coll Ost Med** Some students think that we offer an orthodox course in medicine. **European Sch Ost/**

Greenwich Some applicants think we teach in French: we do not although we do have a franchise with a French school based in St Etienne and a high percentage of international students. All lectures are in English. Applicants should note that cranial osteopathy – one of our specialisms – is only one aspect of the programme.

Selection interviews **Yes** Birmingham, Bristol, Central Lancashire, Chichester, Coventry, European Sch Ost/Greenwich, Glamorgan, Middlesex, Nottingham Trent, Worcester; **Some** Abertay Dundee, Bath Spa, Canterbury Christ Church, Cardiff (UWIC) (Complem Thera), Derby, Huddersfield (mature students), Liverpool John Moores, Salford, Swansea.

Interview advice and questions Courses vary considerably and you are likely to be questioned on your reasons for choosing the course at that university or college. If you have studied biology then questions are possible on the A-level syllabus and you could also be asked to discuss any work experience you have had. (Osteopathy) What personal qualities would you need to be a good osteopath? What have you done that you would feel demonstrates a sense of responsibility? What would you do if you were not able to secure a place on an Osteopathy course this year? **Liverpool John Moores** Interviews are informal. It would be useful for you to bring samples of coursework to the interview. See **Chapter 5**.

Reasons for rejection (non-academic) Some students are mistakenly looking for a professional qualification in, for example, occupational therapy, nursing. Inability to be aware of the needs of others (in the environmental health field). **Coventry** Inadequate mathematics.

AFTER-RESULTS ADVICE

Offers to applicants repeating A-levels **Same** Abertay Dundee, Aston, Bangor, Brighton, Chester, Derby, European Sch Ost/Greenwich, Huddersfield, Lincoln, Liverpool John Moores, Nottingham Trent (Hlth Env), Roehampton, Salford, Surrey, Swansea.

GRADUATE DESTINATIONS AND EMPLOYMENT (2007/8 HESA)

Complementary Medicine graduates surveyed 575 **Employed** 360 **In further study** 15 **Assumed unemployed** 40.

Aural and Oral Sciences graduates surveyed 535 **Employed** 410 **In further study** 15 **Assumed unemployed** 20.

See also **Dentistry**, **Medicine**, **Nursing and Midwifery**, **Nutrition** and **Optometry**.

Career note Graduates enter a very broad variety of careers depending on their specialism. Opportunities exist in the public sector, for example, management and administrative positions with health and local authorities and in health promotion.

OTHER DEGREE SUBJECTS FOR CONSIDERATION

Audiology; Biological Sciences; Biology; Community Studies; Consumer Studies; Dentistry; Dietetics; Medicine; Nursing; Nutrition; Occupational Therapy; Optometry; Physiotherapy; Psychology; Podiatry; Radiography; Speech Therapy; Sport Science.

HISTORY

(including **Heritage Management** and **Medieval Studies**; see also **History (Ancient), History (Economic and Social)** and **History of Art**)

Degrees in History cover a very broad field with many courses focusing on British and European history. However, specialised History degrees are available which cover other regions of the world and, in addition, all courses will offer a wide range of modules.

Useful websites www.english-heritage.org.uk; www.historytoday.com; www.genealogyarchives.com; www.historynet.com; www.archives.org.uk; www.royalhistoricalsociety.org; www.nationalarchives.gov.uk; www.historesearch.com.

NB The points totals shown to the left of the institutions are for ease of reference only. It must not be assumed that Tariff points are always used by institutions or that they can be substituted for an offer in grades. The level of an offer is not necessarily indicative of the quality of a course.

COURSE OFFERS INFORMATION

Subject requirements/preferences GCSE English and a foreign language may be required or preferred. **AL** History usually required at a specified grade. (Medieval Studies) History or English literature required for some courses. (Viking Studies) English or history.

NB In 2011 universities and colleges will differ in their use of GCE AL/AS unit grade information, A* grades, the Extended Project (EPQ), the Advanced Diploma and the Cambridge Pre-U examination when considering applicants and making offers. An EPQ may be accepted in place of an AS subject. Check websites of universities and colleges for the latest offers information.

Your target offers and examples of courses provided by each institution

410 pts London (King's) – AAAb (Hist courses) (IB 36–37 pts)
400 pts London (UCL) – A*AA+AS–AAA+AS (Hist V100; Hist Euro Lang; Hist Yr Abrd) (IB 38–39 pts)
380 pts Cambridge – A*AA college offers may vary (Hist; Educ Hist) (IB 38–42 pts)
Warwick – AABc (Hist (Modn); Hist Cult courses; Hist Pol) (IB 37–38 pts)
360 pts Bristol – AAA–AAB (Hist St Ger; Hist) (IB 34–35 pts)
Durham – AAA (Hist; Engl Lit Hist; Modn Langs Hist; Hist Comb Hons) (IB 32 pts)
Exeter – AAA–ABB 360–340 pts (Hist; Hist Fr; Hist Int Rel; Hist Arbc St) (IB 36–31 pts)
Leeds – AAA–AAB (History) (IB 37 HL 18 pts hist 7)
London (UCL) – AAB+AS–BBB+AS (Hist V101; Hist Phil Sci) (IB 32–36 pts)
Manchester – AAA–AAB (Hist; Hist Am St) (IB 32–37 pts)
Newcastle – AAA–AAB (Pol Hist; Hist Arch) (IB 37 pts)
Nottingham – AAA (Hist; Hist Pol) (IB 34 pts)
Oxford – AAA (Hist Econ; Anc Modn Hist; Hist Engl; Hist Modn Langs; Hist Pol) (IB 38–42 pts)
St Andrews – AAA (History) (IB 37 pts)
Sheffield – AAA (History)
Sussex – AAA–AAB (Engl Hist) (IB 36–34 pts)
York – AAA (Hist; Hist Pol; Hist Engl) (IB 36 pts)
340 pts Birmingham – AAB (Hist; Hist joint courses) (IB 34–36 pts)
Cardiff – AAB (Modn Hist Pol; Hist)
Durham – AAB (Educ St (Hist))
East Anglia – AAB–ABB (Hist; Modn Hist; Hist Land Arch) (IB 32–34 pts)
Glasgow – AAB (Scot Hist; Hist) (IB 34 pts)
Lancaster – AAB 340 pts (History)
Liverpool – AAB (History) (IB 33 pts HL hist 6)
London (QM) – AAB 340 pts (Hist; Mediev Hist; Hist Compar Lit; Modn Contemp Hist) (IB 32 pts)
London (RH) – AAB (Hist courses) (IB 36 pts)
London LSE – AAB (Hist; Int Rel Hist; Gov Hist) (IB 37 pts HL 666)
Manchester – AAB–BBB (Hist St courses; Mediev St; Modn Hist Econ)
Newcastle – AAB (History) (IB 35 pts HL hist 6 pts)
Reading – 340–360 pts (Hist; Modn Hist Int Rel; Hist Euro Lit Cult) (IB 32 pts HL 666)
St Andrews – AAB (Mediev Hist courses; Modn Hist courses; Scot Hist courses) (IB 36–38 pts)
Sheffield – AAB (Int Hist Int Pol) (IB 35–32 pts)
Southampton – AAB (Hist; Modn Hist Pol) (IB 34 pts)
Sussex – AAB–BBB (Hist; Hist Anth; Hist Film St; Hist Lang)
320 pts Birmingham – ABB (War St; Mediev Engl Hist)
Cardiff – ABB (Hist Mus; Hist Soc Pol Phil App Eth; Hist Welsh Hist) (IB 28–30 pts)
Kent – 320 pts (Ger Hist; Hist; Hist Phil; War St) (IB 33 pts)
Lancaster – ABB 320 pts (Hist Phil Pol; Hist Mus) (IB 30 pts)

Leeds – ABB (Hist Phil Sci courses; Hist joint courses) (IB 35–37 pts)
Leicester – ABB 320–300 pts (Engl Hist; Hist) (IB 34 pts)
Liverpool – ABB (Modn Hist Pol) (IB 33 pts)
London (Gold) – ABB (Hist; Hist Hist Ideas; Hist Sociol; Hist Anth)
London (SOAS) – ABB (Hist courses) (IB 30–32 pts)
Nottingham – ABB (Hist Contemp Chin St)
Swansea – ABB–BBB (Euro Hist courses; Mediev St courses)

300 pts **Birmingham** – BBB (E Medit Hist)
Brunel – 300 pts 3AL+AS/EPQ (History) (IB 31 pts)
Dundee – BBB 2nd yr entry (Hist; Scot Hist St; Hist Bus Econ Mark) (IB 34 pts HL 18 pts)
East Anglia – BBB (Am Hist Engl Hist) (IB 29–30 pts)
Edinburgh – BBB (Hist; Archit Hist; Celt Scot Hist; Chin Hist; Soc Hist) (IB 34 pts)
Essex – 300 pts (Hist; Contemp Hist; Modn Hist; Soc Cult Hist) (IB 32 pts)
Gloucestershire – 300 pts (History)
Hull – 300 pts (Hist; Hist Marit Hist; Hist Soc Hist)
Leicester – BBB (Contemp Hist; Hist Pol; Hist Arch) (IB 34 pts)
Liverpool – BBB (Hist Fr/Ger; Hist Hisp St)
London (UCL) – BBB (Jew Hist)
Northumbria – 300 pts (Hist; Engl Lit Hist) (IB 26 pts)
Nottingham – ABC (Hist Russ)
Nottingham – BBB (Vkg St) (IB 32 pts)
Oxford Brookes – BBB (Hist courses) (IB 32 pts)
Queen's Belfast – ABB/BBBb (Modn Hist)
Sheffield – BBB (Hist Dutch; Hist Russ; Hist Hisp St)
Stirling – BBB 2nd yr entry (Hist; Scot Hist; Hist Jrnl St) (IB 28 pts)
Stranmillis (UC) – BBB (Hist Educ)
Strathclyde – ABC 1st yr entry (History)

280 pts **Aberystwyth** – 280 pts (Hist; Hist Welsh Hist; Mediev Ely Modn Hist; Modn Contemp Hist) (IB 30 pts)
Bristol UWE – 280–320 pts (Hist courses; Int Hist Int Pol) (IB 28–30 pts)
Hertfordshire – 280 pts (Hist courses)
Huddersfield – 280–320 pts (Hist; Hist Jrnl)
Northumbria – 280 pts (Hist Pol) (IB 25 pts)
Nottingham Trent – 280 pts (History)

260 pts **Brighton** – BCC (Cult Hist Lits; Hist Des Cult Soty; Engl Lit Commun Hist) (IB 30 pts)
Chichester – BCC (History)
Coventry – 260–280 pts (Hist courses)
Glamorgan – 260–300 pts (Hist courses)
Glasgow – BCC (Ir St Hist) (IB 27 pts)
Hull – 260–280 pts (Hist Fr/Ger/Ital/Span; Am St Hist)
Keele – 260–320 pts (Am St Hist; Hist courses) (IB 28–30 pts)
Lincoln – 260 pts (Engl Hist)
Liverpool – BCC (Ir St Hist) (IB 27 pts)
Liverpool Hope – 260 pts (Hist courses)
Newport – 260 pts (Hist; Engl Hist)
Nottingham Trent – 260 pts (Hist joint courses)
Oldham (Coll Univ Centre) – 260 pts (Hist Eng Lit)
Stirling – BCC 1st yr entry (Hist; Scot Hist; Hist Jrnl St) (IB 28 pts
Westminster – BCC/BB (Modn Hist; Engl Lit Hist) (IB 28 pts)
Winchester – 260–300 pts (Hist; Hist Mediev Wrld)

240 pts **Aberdeen** – CCC (Hist courses; Scot St)
Bangor – 240–260 pts (Hist; Herit Arch Hist; Mediev Ely Modn Hist; Modn Contemp Hist; Welsh Hist Arch; Welsh Hist – also available in Welsh)
Bolton – 240 pts (History)
Bournemouth – 240 pts (Arch Prehist; Herit Cons)

Bradford – 240 pts (Hist Law; Hist Pol; Modn Euro Hist)
Buckingham – CCC (Engl Lit Hist) (IB 27 pts)
Cardiff (UWIC) – 240 pts (Modn Hist Pol; Modn Hist Engl)
Chester – 240–280 pts (History)
Cumbria – 240 pts (Educ Hist)
De Montfort – 240 pts (Hist; Hist Joint Hons)
Dundee – 240 pts 1st yr entry (Hist; Scot Hist St; Hist Bus Econ Mark) (IB 29 pts HL 15 pts)
Lincoln – 240 pts (Cons Restor; Hist; Hist Pol)
Liverpool John Moores – 240 pts (History)
London Met – 240 pts (Hist courses; Restor Cons)
Plymouth – 240 pts (Hist courses) (IB 27 pts)
Portsmouth – 240–300 pts (Hist; Am St Hist; Engl Hist)
Roehampton – 240–320 pts (Hist courses)
Salford – 240 pts (Contemp Hist Pol; Contemp Mltry Int Hist) (IB 27 pts)
Ulster – CCC 240 pts (Irish Hist courses; Hist courses)

220 pts **Bath Spa** – 220–260 pts (History)
Central Lancashire – 220 pts (Hist Musm Herit; Modn Wrld Hist; Hist)
Edge Hill – 220–260 pts (Hist courses)
Kingston – 220–320 pts (Hist; Hist Joint Hons)
Manchester Met – 220 pts (Modn Hist)
Newman (UC) – 220–260 pts (Hist courses)
Sunderland – 220 pts (Hist; Hist Pol; Hist Media St courses)
Teesside – 220–260 pts (Hist courses)
Worcester – 220–260 pts (Hist courses)
York St John – 220 pts (Hist courses)

200 pts **Anglia Ruskin** – 200 pts (Hist; Hist Engl)
Canterbury Christ Church – 200 pts (Hist courses)
Cumbria – 200 pts (History)
East London – 200 pts (Hist courses)
Glyndŵr – 200 pts (Hist; Hist Engl)
Northampton – 200–240 pts (Hist courses)
Suffolk (Univ Campus) – 200 pts (Hist; Fmly Lcl Commun Hist)
Trinity Saint David – 200–300 pts (Hist courses; Mediev St; Welsh Hist Hist; Hist Mgt)

180 pts **Derby** – 180–240 pts (Hist courses)
Leeds Met – 180 pts (History)
Leeds Trinity (UC) – 180 pts (History)
Salford – 180–200 pts (Contemp Hist Pol; Contemp Mltry Int Hist) (IB 27 pts)

160 pts **Bishop Grosseteste (UC)** – 160 pts (Educ St Hist)
Greenwich – 160 pts (History)
St Mary's Twickenham (UC) – 160–200 pts inc BC (Hist courses)
UHI Millennium Inst – CC (Scot Hist)
Wolverhampton – 160–220 pts (Hist; War St)

140 pts **Bishop Grosseteste (UC)** – 140 pts (Herit St)

120 pts **West Anglia (Coll)** – DD (Engl Hist; Sociol Hist)

100 pts **Bournemouth** – 100 pts (Engl Hist)

80 pts **London (Birk)** – 80 pts for under 21s (over 21s varies) (p/t Hist; Hist Arch)

Staffordshire – contact University (Modn Hist courses; Int Hist courses)

Alternative offers

See **Chapter 7** and **Appendix 1** for grades/UCAS Tariff points information for the International Baccalaureate, Scottish Highers/Advanced Highers, the Welsh Baccalaureate, the Irish Leaving Certificate, the Cambridge Pre-U Diploma, the Advanced Diploma and the Extended Project.

EXAMPLES OF FOUNDATION DEGREES IN THE SUBJECT FIELD

Bath Spa; Blackpool and Fylde (Coll); Cumbria; Truro (Coll); Winchester.

CHOOSING YOUR COURSE (SEE ALSO CH.1)

Some course features

Kent History can be taken with an optional deferred subject. The Single Honours programme provides the opportunity of a work placement in a museum, a cathedral workshop or a year abroad in Europe.
Leicester A very large department offering specialisms in a wide range of subjects. The subject is also part of the Combined Studies programme in which, from a choice of 17 subjects, two subjects are studied for three years and one subject for two years.
Manchester The History programme enables students to study course units across the whole range of history topics including the history of science. There are opportunities to spend part of the course studying abroad.
Ulster In addition to the Single Honours course, History is offered as a joint course (two subjects) or under the Combined Arts programme when students choose three subjects in Year 1 continuing with a study of two subjects or one major and one minor subject.

Universities and colleges teaching quality See www.qaa.ac.uk; www.unistats.com.

Top research universities and colleges (RAE 2008) Imperial London; Essex; Kent; Liverpool; Oxford; Warwick; Cambridge; London (UCL), (Birk); Southampton; Hertfordshire; London LSE; Sheffield.

ADMISSIONS INFORMATION

Number of applicants per place (approx) Aberystwyth 6; Anglia Ruskin 4; Bangor 6; Bath Spa 6; Birmingham 8, (E Medit Hist) 3, (War St) 4; Bournemouth (Herit Cons) 3; Bristol 15; Bristol UWE 6; Brunel 6; Buckingham 10; Cambridge 3; Cardiff 7; Central Lancashire 5; Chichester 4; Cumbria 5; De Montfort 10; Dundee 6; Durham 15; East Anglia 8; Edge Hill 8; Exeter 9; Gloucestershire 26; Glyndŵr 2; Huddersfield 4; Hull 5; Kent 12; Kingston 6; Lancaster 11; Leeds 12; Leeds Trinity (UC) 14; Leicester 7; Liverpool 6; London (Gold) 6, (King's) 10, (QM) 5, (RH) 9, (UCL) 13; London LSE 10, (Gov Hist) 10; London Met 2; Manchester Met 8; Middlesex 10; Newcastle 13; Newman (UC) 2; Northampton 4; Nottingham 20; Oxford Brookes 25; Portsmouth 5; Roehampton 3; St Mary's Twickenham (UC) 5; Sheffield Hallam 21; Southampton 5; Staffordshire 8; Stirling 2; Teesside 4; Trinity Saint David 6; Warwick 17; York 7; York St John 3.

Advice to applicants and planning the UCAS personal statement Show your passion for the past! Visits to places of interest should be mentioned, together with any particular features which impressed you. Read historical books and magazines outside your A-level syllabus. Mention these and describe any special areas of study which interest you. (Check that these areas are covered in the courses for which you are applying!) **Manchester** Due to the detailed nature of entry requirements for History courses, we are unable to include full details in the prospectus. For complete and up-to-date information on our entry requirements for these courses, please visit our website at www.manchester.ac.uk/ugcourses.

Misconceptions about this course Students sometimes under-estimate the amount of reading required. **Lincoln** Some students expect the subject to be assessed only by exams and essays. It is not – we use a wide range of assessment methods. **Liverpool John Moores** Some applicants think that they have to study ancient and medieval history as well as modern; we actually only cover post-1750 history. **Stirling** Some applicants think that we only teach British history. We also cover European, American, African and Environmental History.

Selection interviews **Yes** Bangor, Birmingham (E Medit Hist), Bishop Grosseteste (UC), Brighton, Bristol, Brunel, Cambridge, Canterbury Christ Church, Edge Hill, Essex, Hertfordshire, Hull, Lancaster, Leeds Trinity (UC), Lincoln (Cons Restor), London (King's), (QM), (RH), (UCL), London Met, London South Bank, Middlesex, Oxford, Oxford Brookes, Portsmouth, Roehampton, Sussex, Warwick; **Some** Anglia Ruskin, Bath Spa, Buckingham, Cardiff, Chichester, De Montfort, Dundee, Exeter, Huddersfield, Kent, Lincoln, Liverpool, London LSE (rarely), Salford, Sheffield Hallam, Southampton, Staffordshire, Trinity Saint David, Winchester, Wolverhampton, York.

Interview advice and questions Questions are almost certain to be asked on those aspects of the history A-level syllabus which interest you. Examples of questions in previous years have included:

Why did imperialism happen? If a Martian arrived on Earth what aspect of life would you show him/her to sum up today's society? Has the role of class been exaggerated by Marxist historians? What is the difference between power and authority and between patriotism and nationalism? Did Elizabeth I have a foreign policy? What is the relevance to history in modern society? Who are your favourite monarchs? How could you justify your study of history to the taxpayer? **Cambridge** How would you compare Henry VIII to Stalin? In the 1920s did the invention of the Henry Ford car lead to a national sub-culture or was it just an aspect of one? Is there such a thing as 'race'? Should historians be allowed to read sci-fi novels? **Cumbria** Questions about interest in research, analysis, argument, information gathering, future plans after study, motivation. **De Montfort** Why History? Why is history important? **Oxford** Questions on submitted work and the capacity to think independently. **Oxford** What are the origins of your name? Why are you sitting in this chair? **Sheffield** Written work may be required. **Swansea** We ask applicants to explain something – a hobby, an historical problem or a novel. The subject is less important than a coherent and enthusiastic explanation.
See **Chapter 5**.

Reasons for rejection (non-academic) Personal statements which read like job applications, focusing extensively on personal skills and saying nothing about the applicant's passion for history. Poor use of personal statement combined with predicted grades. Little commitment and enthusiasm. No clear reason for choice of course. Little understanding of history. Absence or narrowness of intellectual pursuits. Deception or concealment on the UCAS application. Knowledge of 19th century history (chosen subject) did not have any depth. Unwillingness to learn. Narrow approach to subject. Failure to submit requested information. **Birmingham** Commitment insufficient to sustain interest over three years. **London (King's)** Inability to think analytically and comparatively. **(UCL)** The vast majority of applications are of a very high standard, many applicants being predicted AAA grades. We view each application as a complete picture, taking into account personal statement, reference and performance at any interview as well as actual and predicted academic performance. There is no single rule by which applicants are selected and therefore no single reason why they are rejected. **Nottingham** No discrimination against Oxbridge applicants.

AFTER-RESULTS ADVICE

Offers to applicants repeating A-levels **Higher** Exeter, Glasgow, Huddersfield, Leeds, Liverpool, St Andrews, Trinity Saint David, Warwick; **Possibly higher** Aberystwyth, Birmingham, Cambridge, Portsmouth; **Same** Anglia Ruskin, Bangor, Buckingham, Bristol, Cardiff, Chester, Chichester, De Montfort, Dundee, Durham, East Anglia, Edge Hill, Hull, Kent, Lancaster, Lincoln, Liverpool Hope, Liverpool John Moores, London (QM), (RH), (SOAS), Newcastle, Newman (UC), Newport, Nottingham Trent, Oxford Brookes, Roehampton, St Mary's Twickenham (UC), Staffordshire, Stirling, Suffolk (Univ Campus), Winchester, Wolverhampton, York, York St John.

GRADUATE DESTINATIONS AND EMPLOYMENT (2007/8 HESA)

Graduates surveyed 6330 **Employed** 2630 **In further study** 1495 **Assumed unemployed** 655.

Career note Graduates enter a broad spectrum of careers. Whilst a small number seek positions with museums and galleries, most will enter careers in management, public and social services and retail as well as the teaching profession.

OTHER DEGREE SUBJECTS FOR CONSIDERATION

Ancient History; Anthropology; Archaeology; Economic and Social History; Government; History of Art; International Relations; Medieval History; Politics.

HISTORY (ANCIENT)

(see also **Archaeology** and **History**)

Ancient History covers the Greek and Roman world, the social, religious, political and economic changes taking place in the Byzantine period and the medieval era which followed.

Useful websites www.royalhistoricalsociety.org; www.guardians.net; www.arwhead.com/Greeks; www.ancientworlds.net; www.bbc.co.uk/history/ancient; www.historesearch.com/ancient.html.

NB The points totals shown to the left of the institutions are for ease of reference only. It must not be assumed that Tariff points are always used by institutions or that they can be substituted for an offer in grades. The level of an offer is not necessarily indicative of the quality of a course.

COURSE OFFERS INFORMATION

Subject requirements/preferences **GCSE** A foreign language or classical language may be required. **AL** History or classical civilisation may be preferred subjects.

NB In 2011 universities and colleges will differ in their use of GCE AL/AS unit grade information, A* grades, the Extended Project (EPQ), the Advanced Diploma and the Cambridge Pre-U examination when considering applicants and making offers. An EPQ may be accepted in place of an AS subject. Check websites of universities and colleges for the latest offers information.

Your target offers and examples of courses provided by each institution

360 pts **Durham** – AAA (Anc Mediev Modn Hist; Anc Hist Comb Hons; Anc Hist Arch)
Exeter – AAA–ABB (Anc Hist) (IB 36–31 pts)
London (King's) – AAB+AS (Anc Hist) (IB 32 pts)
London (UCL) – AAB+AS (Anc Hist; Anc Hist Egypt) (IB 36 pts)
Oxford – AAA (Anc Modn Hist; Anc Hist Class Arch)
St Andrews – AAA (Anc Hist Econ; Anc Hist Maths)
Warwick – ABBc/ABbbc (Anc Hist Class Arch)

340 pts **Bristol** – AAB (Anc Hist) (IB 35 pts)
Exeter – AAB–BBB (Anc Hist Arch) (IB 34–29 pts)
London (UCL) – ABB+AS (Anc Wrld St) (IB 34 pts)
Newcastle – AAB–BBC (Anc Hist Arch) (IB 30–35 pts)
St Andrews – AAB (Anc Hist; Anc Hist Arch; Anc Hist Joint Hons except under **360 pts**) (IB 36 pts)

320 pts **Birmingham** – ABB (Hist Anc Mediev; Anc Hist) (IB 34 pts)
Cardiff – ABB (Anc Hist; Anc Mediev Hist; Anc Hist Cult Crit)
Manchester – ABB–BBB (Anc Hist; Anc Hist Arch) (IB 33–32 pts)
Newcastle – ABB (Anc Hist) (IB 32 pts)
Nottingham – ABB (Anc Hist; Anc Hist Hist; Anc Hist Lat) (IB 34 pts)
Swansea – ABB–BB 320–300 pts (Anc Hist; Egypt Anc Hist; Anc Mediev Hist; Egypt)

300 pts **Birmingham** – BBB (Arch Anc Hist) (IB 32 pts)
Cardiff – BBB (Anc Hist; Anc Hist Welsh)
Edinburgh – BBB (Anc Hist; Anc Hist Class Arch; Anc Hist Gk/Lat; Anc Mediev Hist)
Leicester – BBB (Anc Hist Hist; Anc Hist Arch; Comb St)
Liverpool – BBB (Anc Hist; Egypt; Arch Anc Civ; Anc Hist Arch) (IB 30 pts)
Nottingham – BBB (Vkg St) (IB 32 pts)
Queen's Belfast – BBB–BBCb (Anc Hist courses; Byz St)
Reading – 300–320 pts (Anc Hist; Anc Hist Hist)

280 pts **Reading** – 280–300 pts (Anc Hist Arch)

180 pts **Trinity Saint David** – 180–200 pts (Anc Mediev Hist; Anc Hist Media St; Anc Hist)

Alternative offers

See **Chapter 7** and **Appendix 1** for grades/UCAS Tariff points information for the International Baccalaureate, Scottish Highers/Advanced Highers, the Welsh Baccalaureate, the Irish Leaving Certificate, the Cambridge Pre-U Diploma, the Advanced Diploma and the Extended Project.

CHOOSING YOUR COURSE (SEE ALSO CH.1)

Some course features

Birmingham (Anc Hist) Course focuses on social history and the lives, work, trade and leisure of everyday people from around 1000 BC to AD 1500.

Cardiff (Anc Hist) Archaeological modules can be studied as well as language modules in Greek or Latin at beginners and advanced levels.
Leicester (Anc Hist Arch) The course centres on Ancient Greece and Rome, with particular reference to the interpretation of classical texts and material remains. There is an optional module in classical and post-classical Latin.
Swansea Egyptian language study is essential for Egyptology students but optional for the Ancient History and Egyptology course. Students use the resources of the Egypt Centre, with over 3000 Egyptian antiquities.

Universities and colleges teaching quality See www.qaa.ac.uk; www.unistats.com.

Top research universities and colleges (RAE 2008) See **Classics**.

ADMISSIONS INFORMATION

Number of applicants per place (approx) Birmingham 7; Bristol 11; Cardiff 4; Durham 12; Leicester 32; London (RH) 3; Manchester 5; Newcastle 10; Nottingham 10; Oxford 2.

Advice to applicants and planning the UCAS personal statement Any information about experience of excavation or museum work should be given. Visits to Greece and Italy to study archaeological sites should be described. Show your interest in, for example, Ancient Egypt developed through, for example reading, television and the Internet. Be aware of the work of the career archaeologist, for example, sites and measurement officers, field officers and field researchers (often specialists in pottery, glass, metalwork). See also **History**.

Misconceptions about this course **Liverpool** (Egypt) Some students would have been better advised looking at V400 Archaeology or VV16 Ancient History and Archaeology, both of which offer major pathways in the study of Ancient Egypt.

Selection interviews **Yes** Birmingham, Durham, Leeds, London (RH), Oxford; **Some** Cardiff, Newcastle.

Interview advice and questions See **History**.

Reasons for rejection (non-academic) **Liverpool** (Egypt) Egyptology used to fill a gap on the UCAS application. Applicant misguided in choice of subject.

AFTER-RESULTS ADVICE

Offers to applicants repeating A-levels **Same** Birmingham, Cardiff, Durham, Newcastle.

GRADUATE DESTINATIONS AND EMPLOYMENT (2007/8 HESA)

See **History**.

Career note See **History**.

OTHER DEGREE SUBJECTS FOR CONSIDERATION

Anthropology; Archaeology; Classical Studies; Classics; Greek; History of Art; Latin.

HISTORY (ECONOMIC and SOCIAL)

(see also **History**)

Economic and Social History is a study of societies and economies and explores the changes that have taken place in the past and the causes and consequences of those changes. The study can cover Britain, Europe and other major powers.

Useful websites www.royalhistoricalsociety.org; www.ehs.org.uk; see also **Economics** and **History**.

NB The points totals shown to the left of the institutions are for ease of reference only. It must not be assumed that Tariff points are always used by institutions or that they can be substituted for an offer in grades. The level of an offer is not necessarily indicative of the quality of a course.

COURSE OFFERS INFORMATION

Subject requirements/preferences **GCSE** Mathematics usually required and a language may be preferred. **AL** History preferred.

NB In 2011 universities and colleges will differ in their use of GCE AL/AS unit grade information, A* grades, the Extended Project (EPQ), the Advanced Diploma and the Cambridge Pre-U examination when considering applicants and making offers. An EPQ may be accepted in place of an AS subject. Check websites of universities and colleges for the latest offers information.

Your target offers and examples of courses provided by each institution

410 pts	**Warwick** – AAAb (Econ Econ Hist)
360 pts	**York** – AAA (Hist Econ) (IB 36 pts)
340 pts	**Glasgow** – AAB (Econ Soc Hist) (IB 34 pts)
	London LSE – AAB (Econ Hist; Econ Hist Econ; Econ Econ Hist) (IB 37 pts HL 666)
	York – AAB (Econ Econ Hist) (IB 36 pts)
320 pts	**Manchester** – ABB–BBB (Econ Hist Econ; Econ Soc Hist) (IB 32–34 pts)
	Swansea – ABB–BBB 320–300 pts (Econ Soc Hist; Econ Hist Econ)
300 pt	**Birmingham** – BBB (Econ Soc Hist) (IB 32 pts)
	Edinburgh – BBB (Econ Hist; Econ Soc Hist; Econ Soc Hist Env St)
	Essex – 300 pts (Soc Cult Hist) (IB 32 pts)
	Liverpool – BBB (Hist (Soc Econ)) (IB 30 pts)
280 pts	**Aberystwyth** – 280 pts (Hist Econ Soc Hist) (IB 30 pts)

Alternative offers

See **Chapter 7** and **Appendix 1** for grades/UCAS Tariff points information for the International Baccalaureate, Scottish Highers/Advanced Highers, the Welsh Baccalaureate, the Irish Leaving Certificate, the Cambridge Pre-U Diploma, the Advanced Diploma and the Extended Project.

CHOOSING YOUR COURSE (SEE ALSO CH.1)

Some course features

Birmingham The course in History and Social Science offers a study of two social sciences from economics, sociology, politics and psychology.

Manchester The subject features in three degree courses within the overall Economic and Social Studies programme of 28 degree courses. All students follow a general and broad course in Year 1 specialising in their chosen field in Years 2 and 3.

Warwick (Econ Econ Hist) The course combines economic analysis with an historical understanding of economic development and policies, the causes of economic flutuations and unemployment, the conditions for exchange rate flexibility and European integration.

Universities and colleges teaching quality See www.qaa.ac.uk; www.unistats.com.

ADMISSIONS INFORMATION

Number of applicants per place (approx) Birmingham 3; Liverpool 3; London LSE (Econ Hist) 3, (Econ Hist Econ) 5; York 8.

Advice to applicants and planning the UCAS personal statement See **History**.

Selection interviews **Yes** Aberystwyth, Birmingham, Liverpool, Warwick (rarely).

Interview advice and questions See **History**.

AFTER-RESULTS ADVICE

Offers to applicants repeating A-levels **Higher** Warwick, York; **Possibly higher** Liverpool.

GRADUATE DESTINATIONS AND EMPLOYMENT (2007/8 HESA)

See **History**.

Career note See **History**.

OTHER DEGREE SUBJECTS FOR CONSIDERATION

Economics; Government; History; Politics; Social Policy and Administration; Sociology.

HISTORY OF ART

History of Art (and Design) courses differ slightly between universities although most will focus on the history and appreciation of European art and architecture from the 14th to 20th centuries. Some courses also cover the Egyptian, Greek and Roman periods and at London (SOAS), Asian, African and European Art. The history of all aspects of design and film can also be studied in some courses. There has been an increase in the popularity of these courses in recent years.

Useful websites www.artchive.com; www.artcyclopedia.com; www.artguide.org; www.artefact.co.uk; www.fine-art.com; www.nationalgallery.org.uk; www.britisharts.co.uk; www.tate.org.uk.

NB The points totals shown to the left of the institutions are for ease of reference only. It must not be assumed that Tariff points are always used by institutions or that they can be substituted for an offer in grades. The level of an offer is not necessarily indicative of the quality of a course.

COURSE OFFERS INFORMATION

Subject requirements/preferences GCSE English required and a foreign language usually preferred. **AL** History is preferred for some courses.

NB In 2011 universities and colleges will differ in their use of GCE AL/AS unit grade information, A* grades, the Extended Project (EPQ), the Advanced Diploma and the Cambridge Pre-U examination when considering applicants and making offers. An EPQ may be accepted in place of an AS subject. Check websites of universities and colleges for the latest offers information.

Your target offers and examples of courses provided by each institution

380 pts **Cambridge** – A*AA college offers may vary (Hist Art) (IB 38–42 pts)

360 pts **Bristol** – AAA–ABB (Hist Art; Hist Art Fr/Ger/Ital/Port/Russ/Span) (IB 37–33 pts)
London (UCL) – AAB+AS–ABB+AS (Hist Art; Hist Art Mat St) (IB 34–36 pts)
Oxford – AAA (Hist Art) (IB 38–42 pts)
Warwick – ABBc–BBBc (Hist Art; Hist Art Fr St) (IB 32–34 pts)

340 pts **Birmingham** – AAB–BBB (Hist Art joint courses)
East Anglia – AAB–BBB (Hist Hist Art; Hist Art Gllry Musm St)
St Andrews – AAB (Art Hist Class St; Art Hist; Art Hist Ital; Art Hist Mid E St; Art Hist Mediev Hist; Art Hist Mgt) (IB 34–40 pts)
York – AAB–ABB (Hist Hist Art; Hist Art) (IB 32–34 pts)

320 pts **Birmingham** – ABB (Hist Art; Modn Langs Hist Art) (IB 34 pts)
Essex – 320–300 pts (Hist Art; Lit Hist Art; Film St Hist Art) (IB 34–32 pts)
Glasgow – ABB (Hist Art courses) (IB 30 pts)
Leeds – ABB (Hist Art Ital/Span; Hist Art Phil) (IB 33 pts)
London (Gold) – ABB (Hist Art)
London (SOAS) – ABB (Hist Art (As Af Euro))
Manchester – ABB–BBB (Hist Art; Arch Art Hist; Hist Art Modn Lang) (IB 33–32 pts)
Nottingham – ABB (Art Hist Engl St) (IB 34 pts)
Sussex – ABB–BBB (Art Hist; Art Hist Arch; Art Hist Lang; Art Hist Cult St) (IB 32–34 pts)

300 pts **Edinburgh** – BBB (Hist Art Archit Hist; Hist Art Chin St; Hist Art Hist Mus)
Kent – 300 pts (Hist Phil Art; Hist Phil Art Cult St; Hist Phil Art Class Arch St)
Leeds – BBB (Hist Art; Hist Art Musm St; Hist Art Mus; Hist Art Theol Relig St) (IB 32 pts)
Leicester – BBB (Hist Art; Hist Art (EU); Hist Art Engl)
London (Court) – BBB (Hist Art)
Nottingham – BBB–ABC (Art Hist) (IB 32 pts)
Reading – 300–320 pts (Hist Art Archit) (IB 30 pts)

280 pts **Essex** – 280 pts (Hist Art Modn Langs) (IB 30 pts)
London (SOAS) – BBC (Hist Art; Hist Art Arch) (IB 30 pts)
Nottingham – BBC (Arch Art Hist) (IB 30 pts)
Oxford Brookes – BBC (Hist Art; Hist Art Anth; Hist Art Pub Media; Hist Hist Art)
Reading – 280–300 pts (Hist Art Hist; Art Hist Art Archit)
Roehampton – 280–340 pts (Crea Writ Art Hist)
260 pts **Aberystwyth** – 260 pts (Art Hist Fine Art; Art Hist; Musm Gllry St)
Brighton – BCC 260 pts (Musm Herit St; Hist Decr Arts Crfts; Hist Des Cult Soty; Fash Drs Hist) (IB 28 pts)
Central Lancashire – 260 pts (Contemp Vis Arts (Hist Theor))
Hull – 260–300 pts (Hist Hist Art; Engl Hist Art; Hist Art Dr)
240 pts **Aberdeen** – CCC 1st yr entry (Hist Art courses)
Lincoln – 240 pts (Cons Restor)
Liverpool John Moores – 240 pts (Hist Art Musm St)
Manchester Met – 240 pts (Hist Art Des)
Plymouth – 240 pts (Art Hist)
Roehampton – 240–320 pts (Photo Art Hist)
80 pts **London (Birk)** – 80 pts for under 21s (over 21s varies) (p/t Hist Art)

Alternative offers
See **Chapter 7** and **Appendix 1** for grades/UCAS Tariff points information for the International Baccalaureate, Scottish Highers/Advanced Highers, the Welsh Baccalaureate, the Irish Leaving Certificate, the Cambridge Pre-U Diploma, the Advanced Diploma and the Extended Project.

CHOOSING YOUR COURSE (SEE ALSO CH.1)

Some course features
Aberystwyth (Art Hist) The course combines the study of art history and visual culture. In the second and third years students choose from a wide range of core and optional modules, including history of graphic art, history of photography, contemporary art and Renaissance art.
Kent (Hist Phil Art) The course has streams in art history, contemporary arts, philosophy of art or photographic studies.
Leeds (Hist Art Musm St) An unusual course focusing on art history, fine art and museum and gallery collections and country houses, with opportunities for related work experience.
Leicester (Hist Art) A wide range of supplementary subjects (including languages) can be studied including practical art which explores artistic techniques and problems.
Manchester (Hist Art) A study of art history, visual culture, architecture and theory from antiquity to the present day. The course focuses on mainly European art but there are opportunities to study non-Western cultures.
Manchester Met (Hist Art Des) Course has a studio practice unit.

Universities and colleges teaching quality See www.qaa.ac.uk; www.unistats.com.

Top research universities and colleges (RAE 2008) (History of Art, Architecture and Design) Glasgow; London (Court); East Anglia; Sussex; Manchester; York; Birmingham; London (UCL); Essex; Nottingham; London (Birk); Warwick.

ADMISSIONS INFORMATION

Number of applicants per place (approx) Aberystwyth 9; Birmingham 14; Brighton 8; Cambridge 4; East Anglia 7; Essex 5; Kent 3; Kingston 4; Leeds 29; Leicester 10; London (Gold) 10, (SOAS) 4; Manchester Met 10; Nottingham 10; York 4.

Advice to applicants and planning the UCAS personal statement Applicants for History of Art courses should have made extensive visits to art galleries, particularly in London, and should be familiar with the main European schools of painting. Evidence of lively interest required. Discuss your preferences and say why you prefer certain types of work or particular artists. You should also describe any visits to museums and any special interests in furniture, pottery or other artefacts.
London (Court) A-levels in history, history of art, English, and modern European languages are the

most relevant, however other subjects are considered. Art offered as an A-level should include a history of art paper (see also **Appendix 4**).

Misconceptions about this course **Kent** The History of Art is not a practical course in fine arts. **York** Students do not need a background in art or art history. It is not a course with a studio element in it.

Selection interviews **Yes** Brighton, Cambridge, East Anglia (majority), London (UCL), Manchester Met, Warwick; **Some** Bristol, Buckingham, Kent.

Interview advice and questions Some universities set slide tests on painting and sculpture. Those applicants who have not taken history of art at A-level will be questioned on their reasons for choosing the subject, their visits to art galleries and museums and their reactions to the art work which has impressed them. **Kent** Do they visit art galleries? Have they studied art history previously? What do they expect to get out of the degree? Sometimes they are given images to compare and discuss. See **Chapter 5**.

Reasons for rejection (non-academic) Poorly presented practical work. Students who do not express any interest or enthusiasm in contemporary visual arts are rejected.

AFTER-RESULTS ADVICE

Offers to applicants repeating A-levels **Possibly higher** St Andrews; **Same** Aberystwyth, East Anglia, Kent, Leeds, Warwick, York; **No offers made** Cambridge.

GRADUATE DESTINATIONS AND EMPLOYMENT (2007/8 HESA)

No data available.

Career note Work in galleries, museums and collections will be the objective of many graduates who should try to establish contacts by way of work placements and experience during their undergraduate years. The personal skills acquired during their studies however, open up many opportunities in other careers.

OTHER DEGREE SUBJECTS FOR CONSIDERATION

Art; Archaeology; Architecture; Classical Studies; Photography.

HORTICULTURE

(including **Garden Design**; see also **Agricultural Sciences/Agriculture, Landscape Architecture** and **Plant Sciences**)

Horticulture is a broad subject area covering amenity or landscape horticulture, production horticulture and retail horticulture.

Useful websites www.iagre.org; www.rhs.org.uk; www.horticulture.org.uk.

NB The points totals shown to the left of the institutions are for ease of reference only. It must not be assumed that Tariff points are always used by institutions or that they can be substituted for an offer in grades. The level of an offer is not necessarily indicative of the quality of a course.

COURSE OFFERS INFORMATION

Subject requirements/preferences **GCSE** Mathematics sometimes required. **AL** A science subject may be required or preferred for some courses.

NB In 2011 universities and colleges will differ in their use of GCE AL/AS unit grade information, A* grades, the Extended Project (EPQ), the Advanced Diploma and the Cambridge Pre-U examination when considering applicants and making offers. An EPQ may be accepted in place of an AS subject. Check websites of universities and colleges for the latest offers information.

Your target offers and examples of courses provided by each institution

300 pts **Aberdeen** – BBB 2nd yr entry (Plnt Soil Sci)
Edinburgh – BBB (Plnt Sci) (IB 30 pts)
240 pts **Aberdeen** – CCC 1st yr entry (Plnt Soil Sci)
180 pts **Worcester** – 180 pts (Horticulture)
160 pts **Bristol UWE (Hartpury (Coll))** – 160–200 pts (Amen Hort Mgt) (IB 28 pts)
Greenwich – 160 pts (Commer Hort; Medcnl Hort)
Hadlow (Coll) – CC 160 pts (Commer Hort; Medcnl Hort; Gdn Des)
SAC (Scottish CAg) – CC (Hort Plntsmn; Hort)
140 pts **Writtle (Coll)** – 140 pts (Hort; Hort (Plntsmn) (Tree Mgt) (Glob Crop Prot); Hort Bus Mgt; Soc Thera Hort; Grn Spc Mgt)

Warwickshire (Coll Pershore) [Horticulture – contact college]

Alternative offers

See **Chapter 7** and **Appendix 1** for grades/UCAS Tariff points information for the International Baccalaureate, Scottish Highers/Advanced Highers, the Welsh Baccalaureate, the Irish Leaving Certificate, the Cambridge Pre-U Diploma, the Advanced Diploma and the Extended Project.

EXAMPLES OF FOUNDATION DEGREES IN THE SUBJECT FIELD

Askham Bryan (Coll); Bicton (Coll); Bolton; Bournemouth; Brighton; Bristol UWE; CAFRE; Glyndŵr; Greenwich; Harper Adams (UC); Myerscough (Coll); Nottingham Trent; Plymouth; South Devon (Coll); Sparsholt (Coll); Warwickshire (Coll); Welsh (CHort); Wolverhampton; Worcester; Writtle (Coll).

CHOOSING YOUR COURSE (SEE ALSO CH.1)

Some course features

Bristol UWE (Amen Hort Mgt) Course lasts four years including a one-year work placement. Alternatively, two years on a Foundation degree can be followed by one year to the BA degree.
SAC (Scottish CAg) (Hort Plntsmn) The course combines a study of the diversity of plants and their cultivation, with practical horticultural skills, and is delivered in partnership with the Royal Botanic Garden, Edinburgh.
Worcester (Hort) Course based at Pershore College and enables students to gain practical experience in the horticultural industry in the UK or overseas at the end of the first and second years.
Writtle (Coll) The College, the largest provider of horticultural education in the country, encourages students to take a sandwich placement during their course, in the UK or overseas. Twelve-month practical training placements are available with the Royal Horticultural Society.

Examples of sandwich degree courses Greenwich; Writtle (Coll).

ADMISSIONS INFORMATION

Number of applicants per place (approx) Greenwich 4; SAC (Scottish CAg) 1; Writtle (Coll) 3.

Advice to applicants and planning the UCAS personal statement Practical experience is important and visits to botanical gardens (the Royal Botanic Gardens, Kew or Edinburgh and the Royal Horticultural Society gardens at Wisley) could be described. Contact your local authority offices for details of work in parks and gardens departments. See also **Appendix 4**.

Misconceptions about this course **Greenwich** (Commer Hort) Students are unaware of the scope of this degree. The course covers commercial horticulture – plants, plant products, ornamentals, bedding plants, hardy trees and shrubs, salads, vegetables, fruit and organic crops from production to marketing.

Selection interviews **Yes** Greenwich, SAC (Scottish CAg), Worcester.

Interview advice and questions Past questions have included: How did you become interested in horticulture? How do you think this course will benefit you? Could you work in all weathers? What career are you aiming for? Are you interested in gardening? Describe your garden. What plants do you grow? How do you prune rose trees and fruit trees? Are there any EU policies at present affecting the horticulture industry? Topics relating to the importance of science and horticulture. See **Chapter 5**.

AFTER-RESULTS ADVICE

Offers to applicants repeating A-levels **Same** Greenwich, SAC (Scottish CAg).

GRADUATE DESTINATIONS AND EMPLOYMENT (2007/8 HESA)

See **Agricultural Sciences/Agriculture**.

Career note Graduates seeking employment in horticulture will look towards commercial organisations for the majority of openings. These will include positions as growers and managers with fewer vacancies for scientists involved in research and development and advisory services.

OTHER DEGREE SUBJECTS FOR CONSIDERATION

Agriculture; Biology; Crop Science; Ecology; Forestry; Landscape Architecture; Plant Sciences.

HOSPITALITY and HOTEL MANAGEMENT

(including **Events Management**; see also **Business Courses (Section C), Consumer Studies/Sciences, Food Science/Studies and Technology, Leisure and Recreation Management/Studies** and **Tourism and Travel**)

Courses cover the full range of skills required for those working in the industry. Specific studies include management, food and beverage supplies, equipment design, public relations and marketing. Depending on the course, other topics may include events management, tourism and the international trade.

Useful websites www.baha.org.uk; www.cordonbleu.net; www.instituteofhospitality.org; www.people1st.co.uk.

NB The points totals shown to the left of the institutions are for ease of reference only. It must not be assumed that Tariff points are always used by institutions or that they can be substituted for an offer in grades. The level of an offer is not necessarily indicative of the quality of a course.

COURSE OFFERS INFORMATION

Subject requirements/preferences **GCSE** English and mathematics usually required together with a foreign language for International Management courses. **AL** No specified subjects.

NB In 2011 universities and colleges will differ in their use of GCE AL/AS unit grade information, A* grades, the Extended Project (EPQ), the Advanced Diploma and the Cambridge Pre-U examination when considering applicants and making offers. An EPQ may be accepted in place of an AS subject. Check websites of universities and colleges for the latest offers information.

Your target offers and examples of courses provided by each institution

300 pts **Bournemouth** – 300 pts (Evnts Mgt)

280 pts **Plymouth** – 280 pts (Evnts Mgt)
Strathclyde – BBC (Hspty Tour Mgt)
Surrey – BBC 280 pts (Int Hspty Mgt; Int Hspty Tour Mgt) (IB 30–32 pts)

260 pts **Brighton** – BCC (Int Hspty Mgt) (IB 28 pts)
Bournemouth – 260 pts (Hspty Mgt)
Gloucestershire – 260 pts (Evnts Mgt) (IB 26–30 pts)
Huddersfield – 260 pts (Evnts Mgt)
Manchester Met – 260 pts (Evnts Mgt)
Oxford Brookes – BCC (Int Hspty Mgt) (IB 29 pts)

Salford – BCC 260 pts (Hspty Mgt; Leis Tour Mgt) (IB 26 pts)
Staffordshire – 260 pts (Evnts Mgt)
240 pts **Cardiff (UWIC)** – 240 pts (Hspty Mgt courses; Evnts Mgt; Int Tour Hspty Mgt)
Chichester – CCC (Evnt Mgt courses)
Coventry – 240–260 pts (Evnt Mgt)
De Montfort – 240 pts (Arts Fstvl Mgt; Arts Fstvl Mgt Dr)
Glamorgan – 240–280 pts (Evnt Mgt)
Gloucestershire – 240 pts (Hspty Mgt)
Huddersfield – CCC (Evnts Mgt)
Leeds Met – 240 pts (Hspty Ldrshp Mgt)
Liverpool John Moores – 240–280 pts (Evnts Mgt)
Robert Gordon – CCC (Evnts Mgt)
Ulster – CCC–CCD 240 pts (Int Hspty Mgt; Leis Evnts Mgt; Int Htl Tour Mgt)
Winchester – 240–280 pts (Evnt Mgt)
230 pts **Edinburgh Napier** – 230–240 pts (Hspty Mark Mgt; Hspty Tour Mgt; Hspty Mgt Entre; Fstvl Evnts Mgt courses)
220 pts **Central Lancashire** – 220–260 pts (Hspty Mgt; Int Hspty Mgt; Evnt Mgt; Evnts)
Derby – 220 pts (Hspty Mgt)
London Met – 220 pts (Evnts Mgt Mus Media Mgt; Evnts Mgt PR; Int Hspty Mgt)
Northampton – 220–260 pts (Evnts Mgt courses; Enter Mark)
Plymouth – 220 pts (Cru Mgt; Int Hspty Mgt; Hspty Mgt)
Portsmouth – 220 pts (Hspty Mgt; Hspty Mgt Tour)
Southampton Solent – 220 pts (Evnt Mgt; Evnt Mgt (Spo) (Tour))
Sunderland – 220 pts (Evnts Mgt; Int Tour Hspty Mgt)
200 pts **Birmingham (UC)** – 200 pts (Evnts Mgt; Hspty Bus Mgt; Hspty Fd Mgt; Hspty Tour Bus Admin; Culn Arts Mgt)
Bucks New – 200–240 pts (Evnt Fstvl Mgt; Corp Evnts Conf Mgt)
Canterbury Christ Church – 200 pts (Evnts Mgt)
Chester – 200–240 pts (Evnts Mgt)
East London – 200 pts (Evnts Mgt courses)
Huddersfield – 200 pts (Hspty Mgt Modn Lang)
Manchester Met – 200–240 pts (Hspty Bus Mgt; Hspty Mgt Tour; Hspty Mgt Culn Arts; Hspty Evnts Mgt; Hspty Lic Rtl Mgt; Int Hspty Mgt) (IB 28 pts)
Suffolk (Univ Campus) – 200 pts (Evnt Mgt)
Thames Valley – 200 pts (Hspty Mgt; Hspty Mgt Fd St; Evnts Mgt Hspty; Culn Arts Mgt; Evnts Mgt Tour) (IB 28 pts)
195 pts **Queen Margaret** – 195 pts (Int Hspty Mgt; Evnts Mgt; Hspty Tour Mgt)
180 pts **Greenwich** – 180 pts (Evnts Mgt)
Huddersfield – 180 pts (Hspty Mgt Tour Leis)
Leeds Met – 180 pts (Enter Mgt)
Wolverhampton – 180 pts (Int Hspty Mgt Langs)
160 pts **Bedfordshire** – 160 pts minimum (Evnts Mgt)
Bournemouth Arts (UC) – 160 pts (Arts Evnt Mgt)
Derby – 160–240 pts (Evnts Mgt; Prof Culn Arts)
Glasgow Caledonian – CC (Enter Evnts Mgt)
Robert Gordon – CC 160 pts (Int Hspty Mgt) (IB 24 pts)
West Scotland – CC (Evnt Mgt)
120 pts **Colchester (Inst)** – DD 120 pts (Mgt Hspty)
Llandrillo Cymru (Col) – 120 pts (Htl Hspty Mgt)

Alternative offers

See **Chapter 7** and **Appendix 1** for grades/UCAS Tariff point information for the International Baccalaureate, Scottish Highers/Advanced Highers, the Welsh Baccalaureate, the Irish Leaving Certificate, the Cambridge Pre-U Diploma, the Advanced Diploma and the Extended Project.

EXAMPLES OF FOUNDATION DEGREES IN THE SUBJECT FIELD

Birmingham (UC); Bishop Grosseteste (UC); Blackburn (Coll Univ Centre); Blackpool and Fylde (Coll); Bournemouth; Bradford (Coll); Brighton; Bristol City (Coll); Bromley (CFHE); Bucks New; Cardiff (UWIC); Central Lancashire; Cornwall (Coll); Greenwich; Guildford (Coll); Highbury (Coll); Loughborough (Coll); Manchester (Coll); Newcastle (Coll); Norwich City (Coll); Nottingham New (Coll); Plymouth; Salford; South Devon (Coll); Stratford upon Avon (Coll); Suffolk (Univ Campus); Ulster; Warrington (Coll); Warwickshire (Coll); Westminster Kingsway (Coll).

CHOOSING YOUR COURSE (SEE ALSO CH.1)

Some course features

Edinburgh Napier (Fstvl Evnts Mgt courses) Students learn how to plan, design, market, operate and develop events and how they can be used to help local economies. There are opportunities to study a European language and to study abroad.

Manchester Met The wide range of courses includes options in culinary arts and licensed retail management.

Oxford Brookes (Int Hspty Mgt) A Single Honours course with a paid placement year and opportunities to study abroad. In addition, Hospitality Management can be studied as part of the Combined Honours programme.

Surrey Opportunities for professional training places with leading UK and overseas companies.

Examples of sandwich degree courses Birmingham (UC); Bournemouth; Brighton; Cardiff (UWIC); Central Lancashire; Derby; Edinburgh Napier; Gloucestershire; Huddersfield; Leeds Met; Manchester Met; Oxford Brookes; Portsmouth; Sheffield Hallam; Sunderland; Surrey; Ulster; Wolverhampton.

ADMISSIONS INFORMATION

Number of applicants per place (approx) Bournemouth 9; Cardiff (UWIC) 12; Central Lancashire 8; Edinburgh Napier 17; London Met 10; Manchester Met (Hspty Mgt) 12, (Hspty Mgt Tour) 20; Middlesex 4; Oxford Brookes 9; Portsmouth 10; Robert Gordon 3; Strathclyde 8; Surrey 12.

Advice to applicants and planning the UCAS personal statement Experience in dealing with members of the public is an important element in this work which, coupled with work experience in cafés, restaurants or hotels, should be described fully. All applicants are strongly recommended to obtain practical experience in catering or hotel work. Admissions tutors are likely to look for experience in industry and for people who are ambitious, sociable and team players. See also **Appendix 4**.

Misconceptions about this course **Cardiff (UWIC)** (Hspty Mgt) The course is not about cooking! We are looking to create managers, not chefs.

Selection interviews **Yes** Manchester Met, Portsmouth, Robert Gordon, Surrey; **Some** Bucks New, Salford.

Interview advice and questions Past questions have included: What books do you read? What do you know about hotel work and management? What work experience have you had? What kind of job do you have in mind when you have qualified? How did you become interested in this course? Do you eat in restaurants? What types of restaurants? Discuss examples of good and bad restaurant organisation. What qualities do you have which make you suitable for management? See **Chapter 5**.

Reasons for rejection (non-academic) Lack of suitable work experience or practical training. Inability to communicate. Lack of awareness of workload, for example shift working, weekend work. **Cardiff (UWIC)** Students looking specifically for licensed trade courses or a cookery course. **Oxford Brookes** Lack of commitment to the hotel and restaurant industry.

AFTER-RESULTS ADVICE

Offers to applicants repeating A-levels **Higher** Bournemouth, Huddersfield, Oxford Brookes, Surrey; **Same** Brighton, Cardiff (UWIC), Manchester Met, Salford, Strathclyde, Suffolk (Univ Campus), Thames Valley, Ulster, Wolverhampton.

GRADUATE DESTINATIONS AND EMPLOYMENT (2007/8 HESA)

(Including **Leisure** and **Tourism**)

Graduates surveyed 2500 **Employed** 1470 **In further study** 180 **Assumed unemployed** 240.

Career note These business-focused hospitality programmes open up a wide range of employment and career opportunities in both hospitality and other business sectors. The demand for employees has been high in recent years. Events Management is currently a growth area with graduates working in sports and the arts, tourist attractions, hospitality, business and industry.

OTHER DEGREE SUBJECTS FOR CONSIDERATION

Business; Consumer Studies; Dietetics; Food Science; Health Studies; Leisure and Recreation Management; Management; Tourism and Travel.

HOUSING

(see also **Building and Construction, Community Studies, Property Management/Development** and **Town and Country Planning**)

These courses prepare students for careers in housing management although topics covered will also be relevant to other careers in business and administration. Modules will be taken in housing, law, finance, planning policy, public administration and construction.

Useful websites www.housingcorp.gov.uk; www.communities.gov.uk/housing; www.rtpi.org.uk; www.freeindex.co.uk/categories/property/construction/Property_Development.

NB The points totals shown to the left of the institutions are for ease of reference only. It must not be assumed that Tariff points are always used by institutions or that they can be substituted for an offer in grades. The level of an offer is not necessarily indicative of the quality of a course.

COURSE OFFERS INFORMATION

Subject requirements/preferences **GCSE** English and mathematics required. **AL** No specified subjects.

NB In 2011 universities and colleges will differ in their use of GCE AL/AS unit grade information, A* grades, the Extended Project (EPQ), the Advanced Diploma and the Cambridge Pre-U examination when considering applicants and making offers. An EPQ may be accepted in place of an AS subject. Check websites of universities and colleges for the latest offers information.

Your target offers and examples of courses provided by each institution

280 pts **Staffordshire** – 280 pts (Sust Commun)
240 pts **Ulster** – 240 pts (Hous Mgt)
230 pts **Sheffield Hallam** – 230 pts (Hous Prof St)
200 pts **Birmingham City** – 200 pts (Prof Hous St)
Glyndŵr – 200 pts (Sust Dev; Est Agncy; Est Mgt)
Middlesex – 200–280 pts (Hous St)
160 pts **London South Bank** – 160 pts (Hous St; Sust Commun)
140 pts **Cardiff (UWIC)** – 140 pts (Hous (Supptd Hous) (Hous Plcy Prac))

Alternative offers

See **Chapter 7** and **Appendix 1** for grades/UCAS Tariff points information for the International Baccalaureate, Scottish Highers/Advanced Highers, the Welsh Baccalaureate, the Irish Leaving Certificate, the Cambridge Pre-U Diploma, the Advanced Diploma and the Extended Project.

EXAMPLES OF FOUNDATION DEGREES IN THE SUBJECT FIELD

Anglia Ruskin; Birmingham City; Blackburn (Coll Univ Centre); Bradford (Coll); Bristol UWE; Glyndŵr; Grimsby (IFHE); Middlesex; St Helens (Coll).

CHOOSING YOUR COURSE (SEE ALSO CH.1)

Some course features

Cardiff (UWIC) (Hous (Supptd Hous)) The course involves social, emotional and/or lifestyle support for a variety of client needs, for example, learning disabilities, mental health, vulnerable people.

London South Bank (Hous St) The course focuses on the policy, management and economic aspects of housing, and on housing in the European context.

Sheffield Hallam A long-established course with work placement in Year 3 and the option to study a European language.

Ulster (Hous Mgt) The course, involving research, practical placements and links with practitioners, focuses on how housing management affects individuals in society, on the built environment, housing needs and the development and implementation of housing policy. The course links to others in the built environment, including Environmental Health, Construction Engineering and Management.

ADMISSIONS INFORMATION

Number of applicants per place (approx) Cardiff (UWIC) 1; Sheffield Hallam 2.

Advice to applicants and planning the UCAS personal statement An interest in people, housing problems, social affairs and the built environment is important for this course. Contacts with local housing managers (through local authority offices or housing associations) are important. Describe any such contacts and your knowledge of the housing types and needs in your area. The planning department in your local council office will be able to provide information on the various types of developments taking place in your locality and how housing needs have changed during the past 50 years. See also **Appendix 4**.

Misconceptions about this course Applicants do not appreciate that the course is very close to social work/community work and is most suitable for those wishing to work with people.

Selection interviews **Some** Birmingham City, Cardiff (UWIC).

Interview advice and questions Since the subject is not studied at school, questions are likely to be asked on reasons for choosing this degree. Other past questions include: What is a housing association? Why were housing associations formed? In which parts of the country would you expect private housing to be expensive and, by comparison, cheap? What is the cause of this? Have estates of multi-storey flats fulfilled their original purpose? If not, why not? What causes a slum? What is an almshouse? **Sheffield Hallam** An informal discussion of the course focusing on the student's interest in housing and any experience of working with the public. See **Chapter 5**.

Reasons for rejection (non-academic) Lack of awareness of current social policy issues.

AFTER-RESULTS ADVICE

Offers to applicants repeating A-levels **Same** Birmingham City, Cardiff (UWIC), London South Bank, Sheffield Hallam.

GRADUATE DESTINATIONS AND EMPLOYMENT (2007/8 HESA)

No data available.

Career note Graduates aiming for openings in housing will be employed mainly as managers with local authorities; others will be employed by non-profit-making housing associations and trusts and also by property companies owning blocks of flats.

OTHER DEGREE SUBJECTS FOR CONSIDERATION

Architecture; Building; Business Studies; Community Studies; Environmental Planning; Estate Management; Property Development; Social Policy and Administration; Social Studies; Surveying; Town Planning; Urban Regeneration.

HUMAN RESOURCE MANAGEMENT

(see also **Business Courses**)

This is one of the many branches of the world of business and has developed from the role of the personnel manager. HR managers may be involved with the induction and training of staff, disciplinary and grievance procedures, redundancies and equal opportunities issues. In large organisations some HR staff may specialise in one or more of these areas. Work experience dealing with the public should be stressed in the UCAS personal statement.

Useful websites www.hrmguide.co.uk; www.humanresourcemanagement.co.uk.

NB The points totals shown to the left of the institutions are for ease of reference only. It must not be assumed that Tariff points are always used by institutions or that they can be substituted for an offer in grades. The level of an offer is not necessarily indicative of the quality of a course.

COURSE OFFERS INFORMATION

Subject requirements/preferences **GCSE** English and mathematics at C or above. **AL** No subjects specified.

NB In 2011 universities and colleges will differ in their use of GCE AL/AS unit grade information, A* grades, the Extended Project (EPQ), the Advanced Diploma and the Cambridge Pre-U examination when considering applicants and making offers. An EPQ may be accepted in place of an AS subject. Check websites of universities and colleges for the latest offers information.

Your target offers and examples of courses provided by each institution

340 pts **Aston** – AAB–ABB 340–320 pts (HR Mgt) (IB 34 pts)
Cardiff – AAB (Bus Mgt (HR))
London (RH) – AAB 340 pts (Mgt HR) (IB 35 pts)
Manchester – AAB (Mgt (HR)) (IB 35–34 pts)

320 pts **Bournemouth** – 320 pts (Bus St (HR Mgt))
Lancaster – ABB (Mgt Org (HR Mgt)) (IB 30 pts)
Leeds – ABB (HR Mgt) (IB 33 pts HL 16 pts)
London LSE – ABB (HR Mgt Emp Rel) (IB 37 pts HL 666)
Staffordshire – 320 pts (Law (HR Mgt))
Ulster – ABB (Law HR Mgt) (IB 26 pts)

300 pts **Bath** – BBB (Sociol HR Mgt) (IB 32 pts)
Essex – 300 pts (Mark HR Mgt)
Heriot-Watt – BBB 2nd yr entry (Mgt HR Mgt)
Stirling – BBB 2nd yr entry (HR Mgt)
Strathclyde – BBB (HR Mgt) (IB 32 pts)

280 pts **Gloucestershire** – 280 pts (Bus Mgt (HR Mgt))
Keele – 280–340 pts (HR Mgt courses) (IB 28–30 pts)
Kingston – 280–320 pts (HR Mgt) (IB 31 pts)
Northumbria – BBC 280 pts (HR Mgt) (IB 28 pts)

260 pts **Birmingham City** – 260–280 pts (Mgt HR Mgt; Bus Law HR Mgt; PR HR Mgt) (IB 28 pts)
Coventry – 260–280 pts (HR Mgt)
Edge Hill – 260 pts (Bus Mgt HR Mgt)
Heriot-Watt – BCC 1st yr entry (Mgt HR Mgt) (IB 28–30 pts)
Hertfordshire – 260 pts (HR Mgt; Bus HR; HR Mand)
Lincoln – 260 pts (HR Mgt Mark; HR Mgt Pr)
Staffordshire – 260 pts (HR Mgt)
Stirling – BCC (HR Mgt) (IB 30 pts)
Winchester – 260–300 pts (Bus Mgt HR Mgt)
Worcester – 260 pts (HR Mgt courses)

240 pts **Bradford** – 240 pts (Bus Mgt (HR Mgt))

Bristol UWE – 240–300 pts (Bus St HR Mgt)
Cardiff (UWIC) – 240 pts (Bus Mgt St HR Mgt)
Cumbria – 240 pts (Bus HR Mgt)
De Montfort – 240 pts (HR Mgt courses)
Derby – 240 pts (HR Mgt)
Glamorgan – 240–280 pts (HR Mgt)
Liverpool John Moores – 240 pts (HR Mgt)
Manchester Met – 240 pts (HR Mgt; HR Mgt Comb Hons)
Newport – 240 pts (Bus (HR Mgt))
Nottingham Trent – 240 pts (Bus Mgt HR)
Portsmouth – 240 pts (HR Mgt; HR Mgt Psy)
Robert Gordon – CCC (Mgt HR Mgt)
Roehampton – 240–280 pts (Bus Mgt (HR Mgt))
Sheffield Hallam – 240 pts (Bus HR Mgt)
Ulster – 240 pts (Adv HR Mgt; HR Mgt Mark)
Westminster – CCC (Bus HR Mgt) (IB 28 pts)

230 pts **Edinburgh Napier** – 230 pts (Acc HR)

220 pts **Central Lancashire** – 220 pts (HR Mgt Comb Hons) (IB 28 pts)
Chichester – 220 pts (HR Mgt)
Leeds Met – 220 pts (Bus HR Mgt)
London Met – 220 pts (HR Mgt courses)
Northampton – 220–260 pts (HR Mgt courses)
Southampton Solent – 220 pts (Bus Mgt (HR Mgt))
Sunderland – 220 pts (Bus HR Mgt)
Wolverhampton – 220–240 pts (HR Mgt; HR Mgt Law; Mark HR Mgt)

200 pts **Anglia Ruskin** – 200 pts (HR Mgt) (IB 24 pts)
Bedfordshire – 200 pts (Int HR Mgt)
Bucks New – 200–240 pts (HR Mgt; Bus HR Mgt)
Canterbury Christ Church – 200 pts (HR Mgt Bus; HR Mgt Mark)
East London – 200 pts (HR Mgt)
Middlesex – 200–240 pts (Bus HR Mgt; HR Mgt; HR Mgt Mark)
Suffolk (Univ Campus) – 200 pts (Bus HR Mgt)

180 pts **Abertay Dundee** – DDD (HR Mgt)
Greenwich – 180 pts (HR Mgt courses)

160 pts **London South Bank** – 160 pts (HR Mgt Mark)
West Scotland – CC (HR Mgt)

120 pts **Bradford (Coll)** – 120 pts (HR Mgt)
Norwich City (Coll) – 120 pts (Bus Mgt (HR Mgt))
Swansea Met – DD (HR Mgt)

80 pts **Euro Bus Sch London** – 80 pts (Int Bus HR Mgt 2 Langs)

Alternative offers

See **Chapter 7** and **Appendix 1** for grades/UCAS Tariff points information for the International Baccalaureate, Scottish Highers/Advanced Highers, the Welsh Baccalaureate, the Irish Leaving Certificate, the Cambridge Pre-U Diploma, the Advanced Diploma and the Extended Project.

EXAMPLES OF FOUNDATION DEGREES IN THE SUBJECT FIELD

Croydon (Coll); Glamorgan; Glyndŵr; Hertfordshire; Leeds Met; Middlesex; Plymouth.

CHOOSING YOUR COURSE (SEE ALSO CH.1)

Some course features

Bath The course with Sociology has a compulsory placement year.
Cardiff Human Resources is an option within the Business programme which offers several specialist routes. The course provides the flexibility for students to transfer between degree programmes in the first year.

Lancaster (Mgt Org (HR Mgt)) The course focuses on social scientific concepts and an analysis of HR techniques, including recruitment, motivation, development and strategic planning. Students can opt to spend third year in industry.
London LSE (HR Mgt Emp Rel) This is a three-year full-time course with options from the first year which include economics, statistics, sociology, psychology, government, anthropology, information technology and language.
Portsmouth Optional industrial placement in Year 3.

Universities and colleges teaching quality See www.qaa.ac.uk; www.unistats.com.

Examples of sandwich degree courses Aston; Bath; Birmingham City; Bournemouth; Bradford; Bristol UWE; Central England; Coventry; De Montfort; East London; Edinburgh Napier; Glamorgan; Gloucestershire; Hertfordshire; Lancaster; Leeds Met; Lincoln; Liverpool John Moores; London Met; Northumbria; Plymouth; Portsmouth; Sheffield Hallam; Staffordshire; Sunderland; Swansea Met; Ulster; West Scotland; Westminster; Wolverhampton; Worcester.

ADMISSIONS INFORMATION

Number of applicants per place (approx) Aston 10; Anglia Ruskin 10; London LSE 13; see also Business Courses.

Advice to applicants and planning the UCAS personal statement See under **Business Courses**.

Selection interviews **Yes** De Montfort; **Some** Anglia Ruskin; see also **Business Courses**.

Interview advice and questions See **Business Courses**.

Reasons for rejection (non-academic) See **Business Courses**.

AFTER-RESULTS ADVICE

Offers to applicants repeating A-levels **Higher** Anglia Ruskin.

GRADUATE DESTINATIONS AND EMPLOYMENT (2007/8 HESA)

Graduates surveyed 490 **Employed** 285 **In further study** 40 **Assumed unemployed** 55.

Career note See **Business Courses**.

OTHER DEGREE SUBJECTS FOR CONSIDERATION

Business Studies; Information Systems; Management Studies/Sciences; Marketing; Psychology; Retail Management; Sociology; Sports Management.

HUMAN SCIENCES/HUMAN BIOSCIENCES

Human Sciences is a multi-disciplinary study relating to biological and social sciences and focuses on social and cultural behaviour. Topics range from genetics and evolution to health, disease, social behaviour and industrial societies.

Useful websites www.scienceyear.com; www.becominghuman.org; see also Biology and Geography.

NB The points totals shown to the left of the institutions are for ease of reference only. It must not be assumed that Tariff points are always used by institutions or that they can be substituted for an offer in grades. The level of an offer is not necessarily indicative of the quality of a course.

COURSE OFFERS INFORMATION

Subject requirements/preferences **GCSE** Science essential and mathematics usually required. **AL** Chemistry/biology usually required or preferred for some courses.

NB In 2011 universities and colleges will differ in their use of GCE AL/AS unit grade information, A* grades, the Extended Project (EPQ), the Advanced Diploma and the Cambridge Pre-U examination when considering applicants and making offers. An EPQ may be accepted in

place of an AS subject. Check websites of universities and colleges for the latest offers information.

Your target offers and examples of courses provided by each institution

360 pts **London (UCL)** – AAB+AS (Hum Sci) (IB 36 pts)
Oxford – AAA (Hum Sci) (IB 38–42 pts)
340 pts **Exeter** – AAB–BBB (Hum Biosci)
London (King's) – ABB+AS (Hum Sci) (IB 34 pts)
Sussex – AAB–ABB (Hum Sci) (IB 34–36 pts)
300 pts **Sheffield** – BBB (Hum Comm Sci) (IB 32 pts)
280 pts **Durham** – BBC (Hlth Hum Sci) (IB 30 pts)
Loughborough – 280–300 pts (Ergonomics) (IB 30–32 pts)
Plymouth – 280–320 pts (Hum Biosci) (IB 26 pts)
260 pts **Northumbria** – 260 pts (Hum Biosci) (IB 24 pts)
Sheffield – BCC (Hlth Hum Sci) (IB 29 pts)
240 pts **Bolton** – 240 pts (Hum Sci courses)
Coventry – 240 pts (Hum Biosci)
Roehampton – 240–300 pts (Hum Biosci courses)
220 pts **Northampton** – 220–260 pts (Hum Biosci)
200 pts **Thames Valley** – 200 pts (Hum Sci; Hum Sci pre-Med Yr 1: optional transfer to Medicine at **London (UCL)**) (IB 30 pts)
180 pts **Bradford** – 180–220 pts (Interd Hum St)
Glasgow Caledonian – DDD (Hum Biosci)
160 pts **Roehampton** – 160–200 pts (Hlth Hum Sci)

Alternative offers
See **Chapter 7** and **Appendix 1** for grades/UCAS Tariff points information for the International Baccalaureate, Scottish Highers/Advanced Highers, the Welsh Baccalaureate, the Irish Leaving Certificate, the Cambridge Pre-U Diploma, the Advanced Diploma and the Extended Project.

CHOOSING YOUR COURSE (SEE ALSO CH.1)

Some course features
Bradford (Interd Hum St) The course covers philosophy, psychology and sociology.
Exeter The subject is taught equally between the Schools of Biosciences and Sport and Health Sciences and has a strong scientific element.
London (UCL) (Hum Sci) The course combines biological and social studies and covers such topics as anatomy, physiology, genetics, anthropology, geography and psychology.
Loughborough (Ergon) The course deals with human reactions to technical and social environments, and includes anatomy, physiology, bio-mechanics, human psychology, the principles of design and organisational behaviour.
Oxford (Hum Sci) The degree focuses on the biological, social and cultural aspects of human life. A-level or AS-level biology or mathematics may be helpful but are not a requirement.
Sussex (Hum Sci) The core of the degree is made up of anthropology, biology, psychology, linguistics and philosophy.

ADMISSIONS INFORMATION

Number of applicants per place (approx) Bradford 7; Oxford 4–5.

Advice to applicants and planning the UCAS personal statement See **Biology** and **Anthropology.** See also **Appendix 2**.

Selection interviews **Yes** London (UCL), Oxford.

Interview advice and questions Past questions have included: What do you expect to get out of a degree in Human Sciences? Why are you interested in this subject? What problems do you think you will be able to tackle after completing the course? Why did you drop PE as an A-level given that it's relevant to Human Sciences? How do you explain altruism, given that we are surely programmed by our genes to be selfish? How far is human behaviour determined by genes? What do you think are the key differences between animals and human beings? **Oxford** Are there too many people in the world? See **Chapter 5**.

AFTER-RESULTS ADVICE

Information not available from institutions.

GRADUATE DESTINATIONS AND EMPLOYMENT (2007/8 HESA)

No data available.

Career note As a result of the multi-disciplinary nature of these courses, graduates could focus on openings linked to their special interests or look in general at the scientific and health sectors. Health administration and social services work and laboratory-based careers are some of the more common career destinations of graduates.

OTHER DEGREE SUBJECTS FOR CONSIDERATION

Anthropology; Biology; Community Studies; Environmental Sciences; Life Sciences; Psychology; Sociology.

INFORMATION MANAGEMENT and LIBRARIANSHIP

(Including **Information Systems/Technology**; see also **Business Courses, Communications, Computer Courses** and **Media Studies**)

Information Management and Library Studies covers the very wide field of information. Its organisation, retrieval, indexing, computer and media technology, classification and cataloguing are all included in these courses.

Useful websites www.aslib.co.uk; www.ukoln.ac.uk; www.cilip.org.uk; www.bl.uk.

NB The points totals shown to the left of the institutions are for ease of reference only. It must not be assumed that Tariff points are always used by institutions or that they can be substituted for an offer in grades. The level of an offer is not necessarily indicative of the quality of a course.

COURSE OFFERS INFORMATION

Subject requirements/preferences **GCSE** English, mathematics and occasionally a foreign language. **AL** No specified subjects.

NB In 2011 universities and colleges will differ in their use of GCE AL/AS unit grade information, A* grades, the Extended Project (EPQ), the Advanced Diploma and the Cambridge Pre-U examination when considering applicants and making offers. An EPQ may be accepted in place of an AS subject. Check websites of universities and colleges for the latest offers information.

Your target offers and examples of courses provided by each institution

340 pts **Exeter** – AAB–BBB (IT Mgt Bus) (IB 34–29 pts)
London (UCL) – ABB+AS (Inf Mgt Bus) (IB 34 pts)
320 pts **Lancaster** – ABB 320 pts (MSci Inf Comm Sys) (IB 30 pts)
Loughborough – 320 pts (Inf Mgt Bus St) (IB 32 pts)
300 pts **Keele** – 300 pts (IT Mgt Bus)
Lancaster – BBB 300 pts (BSc Inf Comm Sys) (IB 29 pts)
Loughborough – BBB–AAB (IT Mgt Bus) (IB 32 pts)
Sheffield – BBB (Inf Mgt) (IB 32 pts)
280 pts **Bristol UWE** – 280–300 pts (IT Mgt Bus)
Greenwich – 280 pts (ICT Bus)

	Heriot-Watt – BBC 2nd yr entry (Inf Sys courses)
	London (QM) – 280 pts (ICTs; ICTs Bus Env)
	Loughborough – 280 pts (Inf Mgt Comp) (IB 30 pts)
260 pts	**Aberystwyth** – 260 pts (Musm Gllry St) (IB 29 pts)
	Birmingham City – 260 pts (ICT)
	Glamorgan – 260–300 pts (IT)
	Kent – 260 pts (IT courses; Bus IT courses)
	Liverpool Hope – 260 pts (IT)
	Newport – 260 pts (Inf Scrty)
	Plymouth – 260 pts (IT Mgt)
240 pts	**Aberdeen** – CCC 1st yr entry (Inf Sys Mgt)
	Bradford – 240 pts (ICT courses)
	Cardiff (UWIC) – 240 pts (Int Inf Sys Mgt)
	De Montfort – 240 pts (ICT)
	Heriot-Watt – CCC 1st yr entry (Inf Sys courses)
	Huddersfield – 240 pts (ICT)
	Lincoln – 240 pts (Des Exhib Mus; Doc Prod)
	Liverpool John Moores – 240 pts (Bus Mgt Inf; Hist Art Musm St)
	Northumbria – 240 pts (Electron Pub Inf Mgt) (IB 24 pts)
	Nottingham Trent – 240 pts (Bus Inf Mgt)
	Plymouth – 240 pts (Bus Econ Inf Mgt)
220 pts	**Bristol UWE** – 220–260 pts (Bus Inf Sys)
	Gloucestershire – 220 pts (IT)
	Manchester Met – 220 pts (Libshp; Inf Mgt)
	Stirling – CCD 1st yr entry (Inf Sys) (IB 26 pts)
200 pts	**Chester** – 200–240 pts (Inf Sys Mgt) (IB 24 pts)
	Chichester – CDD (IT Mgt Bus)
	East London – 200 pts (Inf Scrty Sys; ICT Int Dev)
	Liverpool John Moores – 200 pts (IT Multim Comp)
195 pts	**Glasgow Caledonian** – 195 pts inc CC (IT Mgt Bus)
180 pts	**Aberystwyth** – 180 pts (Inf Mgt; Inf Lib St) (IB 26 pts)
	Greenwich – 180 pts (ICT)
	Wolverhampton – 180 pts (Trvl Bus Inf Mgt)
160 pts	**Bedfordshire** – 160 pts (Inf Sys)
	Greenwich – 160 pts (Bus Inf Sys; Bus IT; IT Scrty)
	Southampton Solent – 160 pts (Bus Inf Sys; ICT; Knwl Mgt)
	West Scotland – CC (Inf Mgt)
	Aberystwyth – contact University (Hist Arcvl St)

Alternative offers

See **Chapter 7** and **Appendix 1** for grades/UCAS Tariff points information for the International Baccalaureate, Scottish Highers/Advanced Highers, the Welsh Baccalaureate, the Irish Leaving Certificate, the Cambridge Pre-U Diploma, the Advanced Diploma and the Extended Project.

EXAMPLES OF FOUNDATION DEGREES IN THE SUBJECT FIELD

Edge Hill; Peterborough Reg (Coll); Truro (Coll).

CHOOSING YOUR COURSE (SEE ALSO CH.1)

Some course features

Aberystwyth Information Management can be taken with a special focus on library studies. A new course is available in Historical and Archival Studies.
London (UCL) The Information Management degree has a strong business base.
Loughborough The course provides a balance of business and information management subjects. The four-year programme includes a professional placement and is accredited by the Chartered Institute of Library and Information Professionals.

Manchester Met (Libshp) The course combines the knowledge and skills of librarianship, information handling skills in a range of media and formats, together with integral professional experience. **Sheffield** Information Management can be taken with business or accounting and financial management.

Universities and colleges teaching quality See www.qaa.ac.uk; www.unistats.com.

Top research universities and colleges (RAE 2008) Sheffield; London (King's), (UCL); Wolverhampton; City; Robert Gordon; Glasgow; Brunel; Loughborough; Edinburgh Napier.

Examples of sandwich degree courses Bristol UWE; Loughborough; Northumbria; Nottingham Trent; Plymouth; Staffordshire; West Scotland.

ADMISSIONS INFORMATION

Number of applicants per place (approx) Aberystwyth 4; London (UCL) 7; Loughborough 5; Manchester Met 4; Sheffield 30.

Advice to applicants and planning the UCAS personal statement Work experience or work shadowing in local libraries is important but remember that reference libraries provide a different field of work. Visit university libraries and major reference libraries and discuss the work with librarians. Describe your experiences on the form. See also **Appendix 4**.

Misconceptions about this course Read the prospectus carefully. The course details can be confusing. Some courses have a bias towards the organisation and retrieval of information, others towards information systems technology.

Selection interviews **Yes** London (UCL), Loughborough.

Interview advice and questions Past questions include: What is it about librarianship that interests you? Why do you think you are suited to be a librarian? What does the job entail? What is the role of the library in school? What is the role of the public library? What new developments are taking place in libraries? Which books do you read? How often do you use a library? What is the Dewey number for the history section in the library? (Applicant studying A-level History.) See **Chapter 5**.

AFTER-RESULTS ADVICE

Offers to applicants repeating A-levels **Higher** Loughborough; **Same** Sheffield.

GRADUATE DESTINATIONS AND EMPLOYMENT (2007/8 HESA)

Graduates surveyed 150 **Employed** 80 **In further study** 15 **Assumed unemployed** 20.

Career note Graduates in this subject area and in communications enter a wide range of public and private sector jobs where the need to process information as well as to make it easily accessible and user-friendly, is very high. Areas of work could include web content, design and internet management and library management.

OTHER DEGREE SUBJECTS FOR CONSIDERATION

Business Information Systems; Communication Studies; Computer Science; Geographic Information Systems; Media Studies.

INTERNATIONAL RELATIONS

(including **International Development, Peace Studies** and **War Studies**; see also **Development Studies, European Studies** and **Politics**)

A strong interest in international affairs is a pre-requisite for these courses which often allow students to focus on a specific area such as African, Asian, West European politics.

Useful websites www.sipri.org; www.un.org; www.un.int; www.irc-online.org; see also **Politics**.

NB The points totals shown to the left of the institutions are for ease of reference only. It must not be assumed that Tariff points are always used by institutions or that they can be substituted for an offer in grades. The level of an offer is not necessarily indicative of the quality of a course.

COURSE OFFERS INFORMATION

Subject requirements/preferences **GCSE** English; a foreign language usually required. **AL** No specified subjects. (War Studies) History may be required.

NB In 2011 universities and colleges will differ in their use of GCE AL/AS unit grade information, A* grades, the Extended Project (EPQ), the Advanced Diploma and the Cambridge Pre-U examination when considering applicants and making offers. An EPQ may be accepted in place of an AS subject. Check websites of universities and colleges for the latest offers information.

Your target offers and examples of courses provided by each institution

410 pts **Warwick** – AAAb (Econ Pol Int St; Pol Int St)
380 pts **London (King's)** – AAA+AS–AAB+AS (War St courses) (IB 36–37 pts)
360 pts **Bath** – AAA (Econ Int Dev; Pol Int Rel) (IB 38 pts)
Exeter – AAA–AAB (Hist Int Rel; Int Rel) (IB 36–33 pts)
London (RH) – AAA–ABB 360–320 pts (Econ Pol Int Rel; Hist Int Rel) (IB 32–35 pts)
Nottingham – AAA (Int Rel Glob Is) (IB 38 pts)
St Andrews – AAA (Int Rel courses) (IB 38 pts)
340 pts **Cardiff** – AAB (Euro Pol Int Rel) (IB 35 pts)
Exeter – AAB–ABB (Int Rel Fr/Ger/Ital/Russ/Span) (IB 31–34 pts)
London LSE – AAB (Int Rel) (IB 37 pts HL 666)
Manchester – AAB (Pol Int Rel) (IB 35 pts)
Reading – 340–360 pts (Modn Hist Int Rel)
Sheffield – AAB (Int Rel Pol)
Southampton – AAB/ABBb 340 pts (Int Rel; Pol Int Rel) (IB 34 pts)
Sussex – AAB–ABB (Int Rel; Int Rel Dev St; Int Rel Contemp Euro St) (IB 34–36 pts)
York – AAB (Pol Int Rel) (IB 36 pts)
320 pts **Birmingham** – ABB (Int Rel; Int Rel joint courses; War St; Int St Pol Sci) (IB 34 pts)
East Anglia – ABB–BBB (Int Rel) (IB 31–32 pts)
Essex – 320 pts (Int Rel) (IB 34 pts)
Hull – 320 pts (Glob Gov; Pol Int Rel) (IB 34–36 pts)
Kent – 320 pts (Int Rel Fr/Ger/Ital; Pol Int Rel Jap; Cnflct Pce Scrty; War St) (IB 33 pts)
Lancaster – ABB (Int Rel Strat St; Pce St Int Rel) (IB 30 pts)
Leeds – ABB (Int Rel; Int Rel Thai SE As St; Int Rel Chin/Ital/Jap/Port/Russ/Span) (IB 34 pts HL 16 pts)
London (Gold) – ABB (Int St)
London (QM) – ABB 320 pts (Int Rel) (IB 32 pts)
Loughborough – ABB–AAB (Hist Int Rel) (IB 32–34 pts)
Surrey – ABB (Law Int St) (IB 32 pts)
300 pts **Aston** – 300–320 pts (Int Rel Langs; Int Rel Pol) (IB 31–33 pts)
Birmingham – BBB (Int St Lang) (IB 32 pts)
Brunel – 300 pts (Int Pol)
Dundee – BBB 300 pts 2nd yr entry (Transat St Int Rel; Geopol Int Rel; Int Rel Euro St; Int Rel Am St)
East Anglia – BBB (Int Dev courses) (IB 31 pts)
Edinburgh – BBB (Int Rel) (IB 34 pts)
Leicester – BBB (Int Rel Hist; Int Rel)
Loughborough – 300–320 pts (Int Rel)
Queen's Belfast – BBB–BBCb (Int Pol Cnflct St)
Reading – 300–320 pts (Ger Int Rel)
Swansea – BBB 300 pts (Int Rel; Int Rel Welsh; Int Rel Am St; War Soty)
280 pts **Aberdeen** – BBC 2nd yr entry (Pol Int Rel; Int Rel Mgt St; Int Rel Fin) (IB 28 pts)

Aberystwyth – 280 pts (Int Pol; Int Rel Intel St; Int Pol Strat St; Int Rel) (IB 28 pts)
Bradford – 280 pts (Pce St; Cnflct Resoln; Dev Pce St; Int Rel Scrty St) (IB 30 pts)
Keele – 280–300 pts (Int Rel) (IB 28–30 pts)
Nottingham Trent – 280 pts (Int Rel)
Oxford Brookes – BBC (Int Rel) (IB 31 pts)
Reading – 280–300 pts (Int Rel Econ)
Salford – 280 pts (Int Rel Pol; Jrnl War St) (IB 31 pts)
Westminster – BBC/BC (Int Rel Arbc; Int Rel Chin) (IB 28 pts)

260 pts **Brighton** – BCC (Hum: War Cnflct Modnty) (IB 28 pts)
Coventry – 260–280 pts (Int Rel Pol)
Keele – 260–320 pts (Int Rel Joint Hons)
Lincoln – 260 pts (Crimin Int Rel)
Nottingham Trent – 260 pts (Glob St Joint Hons; Int Rel Joint Hons)

240 pts **Aberdeen** – CCC 1st yr entry (Pol Int Rel; Int Rel Mgt St; Int Rel Fin) (IB 28 pts)
Bristol UWE – 240–300 pts (Int Rel courses) (IB 26–32 pts)
Chester – 240 pts (Int Dev St) (IB 24 pts)
De Montfort – 240 pts (Int Rel; Int Rel Pol)
Dundee – CCC 240 pts 1st yr entry (Geopol Int Rel; Int Rel Am St; Int Rel Euro St)
Kingston – 240–280 pts (Int Rel courses)
London Met – 240 pts (Int Rel Pce Cnflct St; Int Rel Law)
Plymouth – 240–300 pts (Int Rel Bus; Int Rel Span)
Portsmouth – 240–300 pts (Int Rel)
Ulster – 240 pts (Am St Int Dev; Ir Int Dev)
Winchester – 240–280 pts (Pol Glob St)

220 pts **Leeds Met** – 220 pts (Glob Dev Int Rel; Pce St Int Rel)

200 pts **Canterbury Christ Church** – 200 pts (Pol Int Rel; Int Rel Joint/Comb Hons)
East London – 200 pts (Int Dev: Thrd Wrld NGO Mgt)
Lincoln – 200 pts (Int Rel Soc Pol)
Portsmouth – 200–280 pts (Int Dev St)

180 pts **Derby** – 180–240 pts (Int Rel Glob Devl; Thrd Wrld Dev)

160 pts **Wolverhampton** – 160–220 pts (War St courses)

Open University – (Int St – contact +44 (0)845 300 6090 or www.openuniversity.co.uk/you)

Alternative offers

See **Chapter 7** and **Appendix 1** for grades/UCAS Tariff points information for the International Baccalaureate, Scottish Highers/Advanced Highers, the Welsh Baccalaureate, the Irish Leaving Certificate, the Cambridge Pre-U Diploma, the Advanced Diploma and the Extended Project.

CHOOSING YOUR COURSE (SEE ALSO CH.1)

Some course features

Cardiff There is also a Joint degree in Politics and International Relations with Turin University.
East London (Int Dev: Thrd Wrld NGO Mgt) An interdisciplinary course, this draws on economics, politics, sociology, history and cultural studies to focus on the role of NGOs, their functions and relationships. Students are encouraged to travel to Africa, Asia, Central and Latin America; there is also a final-year work placement scheme.
Exeter International Relations can be studied with a modern language and the third year is spent abroad.
London (King's) A unique range of courses in War Studies includes topics in strategy, security and intelligence.
London LSE The subject can be taken as a Single Honours degree or jointly with History. High percentage of international students.

Top research universities and colleges (RAE 2008) See **Politics**.

Examples of sandwich degree courses Aston; Loughborough; Nottingham Trent; Oxford Brookes; Plymouth; Portsmouth; Surrey.

ADMISSIONS INFORMATION

Number of applicants per place (approx) Aberystwyth 6; Birmingham 10; De Montfort 6; Derby 3; Exeter 8; Leeds 13; London (King's) 6; London LSE (Int Rel) 17; Nottingham 5; Portsmouth 2; Reading 5; Southampton (Int Rel) 6.

Advice to applicants and planning the UCAS personal statement Describe any special interests you have in the affairs of any particular country. Contact embassies for information on cultural, economic and political developments. Follow international events through newspapers and magazines. Give details of any voluntary work you have done. **London (King's)** Substantial experience required in some area of direct relevance to War Studies. **St Andrews** Give reasons for choice of course and evidence of your interest.

Misconceptions about this course Some students think that this degree will give direct entry into the Diplomatic Service.

Selection interviews **Yes** Birmingham, London (King's), London Met, Nottingham Trent; **Some** De Montfort, Kent, Wolverhampton.

Interview advice and questions Applicants are likely to be questioned on current international events and crises between countries. **Nottingham Trent** Be prepared to be challenged on your existing views! See **Chapter 5**.

AFTER-RESULTS ADVICE

Offers to applicants repeating A-levels **Same** Chester, De Montfort, Exeter, Lincoln, Wolverhampton.

GRADUATE DESTINATIONS AND EMPLOYMENT (2007/8 HESA)

See **Politics**.

Career note See **Politics**.

OTHER DEGREE SUBJECTS FOR CONSIDERATION

Development Studies; Economics; European Studies; Government; Politics.

ITALIAN

(see also **Languages**)

The language and literature of Italy will feature strongly on most Italian courses. The majority of applicants have no knowledge of Italian. They will need to give convincing reasons for their interest and to show that they have the ability to assimilate language quickly. See also **Appendix 4** under **Languages**.

Useful websites http://europa.eu; www.italia.gov.it; www.bbc.co.uk/languages; http://languageadvantage.com; www.sis.ac.uk; www.italianstudies.org; www.languagematters.co.uk; www.reed.co.uk/multilingual; see also Languages.

NB The points totals shown to the left of the institutions are for ease of reference only. It must not be assumed that Tariff points are always used by institutions or that they can be substituted for an offer in grades. The level of an offer is not necessarily indicative of the quality of a course.

COURSE OFFERS INFORMATION

Subject requirements/preferences **GCSE** English and a foreign language required. **AL** Italian may be required for some courses.

NB In 2011 universities and colleges will differ in their use of GCE AL/AS unit grade information, A* grades, the Extended Project (EPQ), the Advanced Diploma and the Cambridge Pre-U examination when considering applicants and making offers. An EPQ may be accepted in place of an AS subject. Check websites of universities and colleges for the latest offers information.

Your target offers and examples of courses provided by each institution

380 pts **Cambridge** – A*AA college offers may vary (Modn Mediev Lang (Ital)) (IB 38–42 pts)
360 pts **Durham** – AAA–AAB (Comb Hons Arts; Modn Langs (Ital)) (IB 33–34 pts)
London (UCL) – AAB+AS–ABB+AS (Ital; Ital Des) (IB 34–36 pts)
Manchester – AAA–AAB (MML Ital Chin; Ital Jap; Ital Russ) (IB 35–37 pts)
Oxford – AAA (Modn Langs) (IB 38–42 pts)
340 pts **Bath** – AAB–ABB (Ital Pol) (IB 34–36 pts)
Birmingham – AAB–ABB (Int Bus Ital; Econ Ital)
Bristol – AAB–BBC (Ital Russ; Ital Port; Ital Span; Dr Ital) (IB 35 pts)
Exeter – AAB–ABB (Ital Comb Hons; Modn Euro Langs) (IB 29 pts)
Glasgow – AAB (Ital courses) (IB 34 pts)
Liverpool – AAB–BBB (Ital Comb Hons) (IB 36–30 pts)
Reading – 340–360 pts (Hist Ital)
St Andrews – AAB (Ital courses) (IB 36 pts)
Sheffield – AAB (Mech Eng Ital)
Sussex – AAB–BBB (Anth Ital; Dr St Ital; Geog Ital)
Warwick – BBBc (Ital Thea St; Ital Euro Lit; Ital) (IB 32–34 pts)
320 pts **Bath** – ABB–BBB (Modn Lang Euro St)
Birmingham – ABB–BBC (Ital Joint Hons) (IB 34 pts)
Cardiff – ABB (Ital Econ)
Essex – 320 pts (Econ Ital) (IB 30 pts)
Lancaster – ABB–BBB (Ital courses) (IB 29–30 pts)
Leeds – ABB (Ital; Ital joint courses) (IB 34 pts HL 16 pts)
Leicester – ABB (Ital joint courses) (IB 30 pts)
London (RH) – ABB–BBB (Ital courses) (IB 32 pts HL lang 6)
Manchester – ABB–BBC (BA Ital Chin; Ital Jap; Ital Russ; Ital Ling)
Strathclyde – ABB 1st yr entry (Ital courses)
300 pts **Birmingham** – BBB (Class Lit Civ Ital St) (IB 32–34 pts)
Bristol – BBB–BBC (Ital; Ital Port/Russ/Span; Cz Ital; Fr Ital; Ger Ital) (IB 29–32 pts)
Cardiff – BBB (Ital; Ital Mus; Anc Hist Ital) (IB 30–32 pts)
Edinburgh – BBB (Ital; Ital Ling; Ital Class) (IB 34 pts)
Kent – 300–320 pts (Ital Joint Hons) (IB 33–35 pts)
Lancaster – BBB 300 pts (Ital St Span St; Ital St Comp)
Liverpool – BBB (Bus St Ital; Comm St Ital) (IB 30 pts)
Manchester – BBB–BCC (Ital St) (IB 32–28 pts)
Reading – 300–320 pts (Ital Class St; Ital Hist Art)
Strathclyde – ABC 2nd yr entry (Ital courses)
Swansea – BBB 300 pts (Ital courses)
280 pts **Bangor** – 280 pts (Law Ital) (IB 28 pts)
Birmingham – BBC (Ital St) (IB 30–32 pts)
Essex – 280 pts (Ital St Modn Langs) (IB 28 pts)
Reading – 280–300 pts (Ital St)
Salford – 280–300 pts (Euro Langs (Ital+2 Langs); Modn Lang St (Ital))
260 pts **Essex** – 260 pts (Euro St Ital) (IB 28 pts)
Hull – 260–300 pts (Ital St; Ital Mgt; Ital Transl St; Ital Mark)
Nottingham Trent – 260 pts (Ital Joint Hons)
240 pts **Bangor** – 240–260 pts (Ital Joint Hons)
Manchester Met – 240 pts (Ital; Ital Fr/Ger/Span; Ital Comb Hons) (IB 26 pts)
Portsmouth – 240–300 pts (App Lang; Comb Modn Langs)
230 pts **Edinburgh Napier** – 230 pts (Langs Intercult Comm)
200 pts **European Bus Sch London** – 200 pts (Int Bus Ital)
180 pts **Greenwich** – 180–160 pts (Ital Comb courses)

Alternative offers

See **Chapter 7** and **Appendix 1** for grades/UCAS Tariff points information for the International

Baccalaureate, Scottish Highers/Advanced Highers, the Welsh Baccalaureate, the Irish Leaving Certificate, the Cambridge Pre-U Diploma, the Advanced Diploma and the Extended Project.

CHOOSING YOUR COURSE (SEE ALSO CH.1)

Some course features

Bangor Italian can be studied with two other languages or with Law, Journalism or Media Studies.
Bath Italian is taken with a second European language as part of the European Studies course.
Hull In addition to modern language combinations, Italian can be studied with a choice from 17 other subjects.
London (UCL) (Ital Des) The first and second years are spent at UCL mostly studying Italian, while the third and fourth years are spent at Milan's Politecnico following specialist design courses.
Reading The History with Italian degree does not involve a year abroad.

Universities and colleges teaching quality See www.qaa.ac.uk; www.unistats.com.

Top research universities and colleges (RAE 2008) Cambridge; Leeds; Warwick; Reading; Oxford; Bristol; Manchester; Birmingham; London (UCL); Exeter.

ADMISSIONS INFORMATION

Number of applicants per place (approx) Birmingham 5; Bristol 4; Cardiff 3; Hull 8; Lancaster 8; Leeds 3; London (RH) 4.

Advice to applicants and planning the UCAS personal statement Describe any visits to Italy and experience of speaking the language. Interests in Italian art, literature, culture, society and architecture could also be mentioned. Read Italian newspapers and magazines and give details if you have a bilingual background. Give evidence of your interest and your reasons for choosing the course. See also **Appendix 2** under **Languages**.

Misconceptions about this course **Leeds** See **Languages**.

Selection interviews **Yes** Birmingham (majority receive offers), Cambridge, London (RH), Oxford.

Interview advice and questions Past questions include: Why do you want to learn Italian? What foreign newspapers or magazines do you read (particularly if the applicant has taken A-level Italian)? Have you visited Italy? What do you know of the Italian people, culture, art? **Leeds** See **Languages**. See **Chapter 5**.

AFTER-RESULTS ADVICE

Offers to applicants repeating A-levels **Higher** Birmingham, Glasgow, Warwick; **Same** Cardiff, Hull, Leeds; **No offers made** Cambridge.

GRADUATE DESTINATIONS AND EMPLOYMENT (2007/8 HESA)

Graduates surveyed 210 **Employed** 110 **In further study** 35 **Assumed unemployed** 25.

Career note See **Languages**.

OTHER DEGREE SUBJECTS FOR CONSIDERATION

European Studies; International Business Studies; other languages.

JAPANESE

(see also **Asia-Pacific Studies, Business Courses** and **Languages**)

A strong interest in Japan and its culture is expected of applicants. A number of four-year joint courses are now offered, all of which include a period of study in Japan. Potential employers are showing an interest in Japanese. Students report that 'it is not a soft option'. They are expected to be firmly committed to a Japanese degree (for example, by listing only Japanese on the UCAS application), to have an interest in using their degree in employment and to be prepared for a lot of hard work. See **Appendix 2** under **Languages**.

Useful websites www.cilt.org.uk; www.iol.org.uk; www.bbc.co.uk/languages; http://languageadvantage.com; www.languagematters.co.uk; www.reed.co.uk/multilingual; www.japanese-online.com; www.japaneselifestyle.com.au; www.thejapanesepage.com; www.japanesestudies.org.uk.

NB The points totals shown to the left of the institutions are for ease of reference only. It must not be assumed that Tariff points are always used by institutions or that they can be substituted for an offer in grades. The level of an offer is not necessarily indicative of the quality of a course.

COURSE OFFERS INFORMATION

Subject requirements/preferences **GCSE Edinburgh**: English and a foreign language usually required. **AL** Modern language required for some courses.

NB In 2011 universities and colleges will differ in their use of GCE AL/AS unit grade information, A* grades, the Extended Project (EPQ), the Advanced Diploma and the Cambridge Pre-U examination when considering applicants and making offers. An EPQ may be accepted in place of an AS subject. Check websites of universities and colleges for the latest offers information.

Your target offers and examples of courses provided by each institution

380 pts **Cambridge** – A*AA college offers may vary (As Mid E St (Jap)) (IB 38–42 pts)
360 pts **Oxford** – AAA (Japanese) (IB 38–42 pts)
340 pts **Bath** – AAB (Comp Sci Jap)
Birmingham – AAB–ABB (Int Bus Jap; Econ Jap) (IB 32–34 pts)
London (SOAS) – AAB (Jap; Jap St) (IB 36 pts)
Manchester – AAB–BBC (Jap St; Jap Scrn St; Ling Jap) (IB 35–30 pts)
Southampton – AAB (Modn Lang) (IB 34 pts HL 17 pts)
320 pts **Cardiff** – ABB (Bus St Jap; Fr/Ger/Ital Jap) (IB 32 pts)
Leeds – ABB (Jap courses) (IB 34 pts HL 16 pts)
Newcastle – ABB–ABC (Jap Cult St; Ling Jap) (IB 32 pts)
Sheffield – ABB (Jap St courses) (IB 32 pts)
300 pts **Edinburgh** – BBB (Jap; Jap Ling) (IB 34 pts)
280 pts **Leeds** – BBC (Chin St Jap)
Oxford Brookes – BBC (Jap St; Jap St Comb Hons)
240 pts **Central Lancashire** – 240 pts (Jap Comb Hons courses) (IB 26 pts)
Manchester Met – 240 pts (Jap Modn Lang)
Liverpool John Moores – 240 pts (Jap PR; Int Bus St Jap) (IB 26 pts)

Alternative offers

See **Chapter 7** and **Appendix 1** for grades/UCAS Tariff points information for the International Baccalaureate, Scottish Highers/Advanced Highers, the Welsh Baccalaureate, the Irish Leaving Certificate, the Cambridge Pre-U Diploma, the Advanced Diploma and the Extended Project.

CHOOSING YOUR COURSE (SEE ALSO CH.1)

Some course features

Cardiff Courses are offered with Business or a choice of four European languages.
Manchester (Jap Scrn St) The course combines Japanese language and culture with core course units in understanding film, its history and pre-history, and its development across other media including television, DVD and the internet. The third year is spent abroad.
Newcastle (Jap Cult St) Course covers language, sociology, anthropology and Modern East and South East Asian History.
Sheffield Japanese can be studied in combination with 13 other subjects including Chinese, Korean and Business Management.

Universities and colleges teaching quality See www.qaa.ac.uk; www.unistats.com.

Examples of sandwich degree courses Oxford Brookes.

ADMISSIONS INFORMATION

Number of applicants per place (approx) Cardiff 8; London (SOAS) 9; Sheffield 10.

Advice to applicants and planning the UCAS personal statement Discuss your interest in Japan and your reasons for wishing to study the language. Know Japan, its culture and background history. Discuss any visits you have made or contacts with Japanese nationals. **Leeds** See **Languages**. See also **Appendix 4** under **Languages**.

Misconceptions about this course **Leeds** See **Languages**.

Selection interviews **Yes** Cambridge, Oxford, Southampton; **Some** Leeds.

Interview advice and questions Japanese is an extremely demanding subject and applicants are most likely to be questioned on their reasons for choosing this degree. They will be expected also to have some knowledge of Japanese culture, history and current affairs. See **Chapter 5**.

Reasons for rejection (non-academic) Insufficient evidence of genuine motivation.

AFTER-RESULTS ADVICE

Offers to applicants repeating A-levels **No offers made** Cambridge.

GRADUATE DESTINATIONS AND EMPLOYMENT (2007/8 HESA)

Graduates surveyed 85 **Employed** 45 **In further study** 10 **Assumed unemployed** 10.

Career note See **Languages**.

OTHER DEGREE SUBJECTS FOR CONSIDERATION

Asia-Pacific Studies; International Business Studies; Oriental Languages; South East Asia Studies.

LANDSCAPE ARCHITECTURE

(including **Garden Design** and **Landscape Design and Management**; see also **Art and Design (Industrial and Product Design)** and **Horticulture**)

Landscape architecture is a specialised branch of architecture for which an ability in art and design is sought and for some of these courses a portfolio of art work may be required. Courses focus on the design of the environment and surrounding buildings. Landscape architecture should not be confused with the work of a garden centre.

Useful websites www.landscape.co.uk; www.laprofession.org.

NB The points totals shown to the left of the institutions are for ease of reference only. It must not be assumed that Tariff points are always used by institutions or that they can be substituted for an offer in grades. The level of an offer is not necessarily indicative of the quality of a course.

COURSE OFFERS INFORMATION

Subject requirements/preferences **GCSE** English, geography, art and design, mathematics and at least one science usually required. **AL** Preferred subjects for some courses include biology, geography, environmental science. A portfolio may also be required.

NB In 2011 universities and colleges will differ in their use of GCE AL/AS unit grade information, A* grades, the Extended Project (EPQ), the Advanced Diploma and the Cambridge Pre-U examination when considering applicants and making offers. An EPQ may be accepted in place of an AS subject. Check websites of universities and colleges for the latest offers information.

Your target offers and examples of courses provided by each institution

360 pts **Sheffield** – AAA+portfolio (Archit Land) (IB 37 pts)

280 pts **Birmingham City** – 280 pts (Land Archit) (IB 26 pts)
Edinburgh (CA) – BBC (Land Archit) (IB 30 pts)
Gloucestershire – 280 pts (Land Archit)
Kingston – 280 pts (Land Archit; Land Plan) (IB 28 pts)
Leeds Met – 280–320 pts (Land Plan Des; Land Archit)
Madlow (Coll) – CC 160 pts (Lnd Mgt; Gdn Des; Sust Land Mgt)
Sheffield – BBC (Land Archit Plan; Land Archit Ecol) (IB 30 pts)
260 pts **Manchester Met** – 260–300 pts (Land Archit) (IB 28 pts)
240 pts **Greenwich** – 240 pts (Land Archit)
Leeds Met – 240–280 pts (Gdn Art Des)
160 pts **Hadlow (Coll)** – CC 160 pts (Land Mgt; Gdn Des; Sust Land Mgt)
Writtle (Coll) – 160 pts (Land Gdn Des; Gdn Des Restor Mgt; Land Archit)
140 pts **Writtle (Coll)** – 140 pts (Grn Spc Mgt Hort (Tree Mgt))

Alternative offers
See **Chapter 7** and **Appendix 1** for grades/UCAS Tariff points information for the International Baccalaureate, Scottish Highers/Advanced Highers, the Welsh Baccalaureate, the Irish Leaving Certificate, the Cambridge Pre-U Diploma, the Advanced Diploma and the Extended Project.

EXAMPLES OF FOUNDATION DEGREES IN THE SUBJECT FIELD

Askham Bryan (Coll); Bishop Burton (Coll); Bournemouth; Brighton; CAFRE; Capel Manor (Coll); Cumbria; East Anglia; Falmouth (UC); Glyndŵr; Guildford (Coll); Greenwich; Harper Adams (UC); Hereford (CA); Moulton (Coll); Myerscough (Coll); Northampton; Sparsholt (Coll); Warwickshire (Coll); Welsh (CHort); Writtle (Coll).

CHOOSING YOUR COURSE (SEE ALSO CH.1)

Some course features
Birmingham City (Land Archit) The course is accredited by the Landscape Institute and combines a strong study of design with a focus on environmental and cultural issues and technical skills.
Gloucestershire Joint Honours courses are offered with relevant subjects such as geography, garden design, landscape management and heritage management.
Manchester Met The three-year BA course can be followed by a one-year Bachelor of Landscape Architecture for those wanting to enter the profession of landscape architecture. The course focuses on the design of outdoor space and includes a European study tour and offers study opportunities in American and European universities.
Sheffield A multi-disciplinary course providing a comprehensive training in landscape architecture with a specialism in either planning or ecology. The Ecology pathway focuses on habitat restoration, urban regeneration and green technologies, while the Planning pathway centres on the political, social and economic facors of urban and rural environments.

Universities and colleges teaching quality See www.qaa.ac.uk; www.unistats.com.

Examples of sandwich degree courses Edinburgh (CA); Writtle (Coll).

ADMISSIONS INFORMATION

Number of applicants per place (approx) Edinburgh (CA) 7; Gloucestershire 9; Greenwich 3; Kingston 4; Manchester Met 9; Writtle (Coll) 5.

Advice to applicants and planning the UCAS personal statement Knowledge of the work of landscape architects is important. Arrange a visit to a landscape architect's office and try to organise some work experience. Read up on historical landscape design and visit country house estates with examples of outstanding designs. Describe these visits in detail and your preferences. Membership of the National Trust could be useful. See also **Appendix 4**.

Selection interviews **Yes** Gloucestershire, Greenwich, Manchester Met, Sheffield, Writtle (Coll); **Some** Birmingham City.

Interview advice and questions Applicants will be expected to have had some work experience and are likely to be questioned on their knowledge of landscape architectural work and the subject. Historical examples of good landscaping could also be asked for. See **Chapter 5**.

Reasons for rejection (non-academic) Lack of historical knowledge and awareness of current developments. Poor portfolio.

AFTER-RESULTS ADVICE

Offers to applicants repeating A-levels **Same** Birmingham City, Greenwich, Edinburgh (CA), Manchester Met.

GRADUATE DESTINATIONS AND EMPLOYMENT (2007/8 HESA)

Graduates surveyed 170 **Employed** 95 **In further study** 25 **Assumed unemployed** 15.

Career note Opportunities at present in landscape architecture are good. Openings exist in local government or private practice and may cover planning, housing, environmental and conservation.

OTHER DEGREE SUBJECTS FOR CONSIDERATION

Architecture; Art and Design; Environmental Planning; Forestry; Horticulture.

LANGUAGES

(including **Hebrew** and **Modern Languages**; see also **African and Caribbean Studies, Arabic and Near and Middle Eastern Studies, Asia-Pacific Studies, Chinese, English, French, German, Greek, Italian, Japanese, Latin, Linguistics, Russian and East European Studies, Scandinavian Studies, Spanish** and **Celtic, Irish, Scottish and Welsh Studies**)

Modern Language courses usually offer three main options: a single subject degree commonly based on literature and language, a European Studies course, or two-language subjects which can often include languages different from those available at school (such as Scandinavian Studies, Russian and the languages of Eastern Europe, the Middle and Far East).

Useful websites www.iol.org.uk; www.iti.org.uk; http://europa.eu; www.cilt.org.uk; www.bbc.co.uk/languages; http://languageadvantage.com; www.omniglot.com; www.languagematters.co.uk; www.reed.co.uk/multilingual.

NB The points totals shown to the left of the institutions are for ease of reference only. It must not be assumed that Tariff points are always used by institutions or that they can be substituted for an offer in grades. The level of an offer is not necessarily indicative of the quality of a course.

COURSE OFFERS INFORMATION

Subject requirements/preferences **GCSE** English and a modern language required. In some cases grades A and/or B may be stipulated. **AL** A modern foreign language required usually with specified grades.

NB In 2011 universities and colleges will differ in their use of GCE AL/AS unit grade information, A* grades, the Extended Project (EPQ), the Advanced Diploma and the Cambridge Pre-U examination when considering applicants and making offers. An EPQ may be accepted in place of an AS subject. Check websites of universities and colleges for the latest offers information.

Your target offers and examples of courses provided by each institution

380 pts **Cambridge** – A*AA college offers may vary (Modn Mediev Lang) (IB 38–42 pts)
London (UCL) – AAA+AS–BBB+AS (Modn Lang; Lang Cult) (IB 32–38 pts)

360 pts **Durham** – AAA–AAB (Modn Langs; Comb Hons)
Oxford – AAA (Euro Mid E Langs; Class Modn Langs; Engl Modn Langs; Modn Langs; Modn Langs Ling; Phil Modn Langs; Hist Modn Langs) (IB 38–42 pts)
St Andrews – AAA–AAB (Modn Lang courses; Heb) (IB 38–40 pts)
Sussex – AAA–AAB (Fr/Ger/Ital/Span courses)

340 pts **Bath** – AAB (Euro St Modn Langs Fr/Span) (IB 36 pts)
Bristol – AAB–BCC (see separate language tables) (Cz; Fr; Ger; Ital; Port; Russ; Span) (IB 29–35 pts)
Cardiff – AAB–ABB (Euro Langs)
Exeter – AAB–ABB (see separate language tables) (Comb Lang courses)
Manchester – AAB–BBB (Modn Lang Bus Mgt; Langs App Engl Lang St; Modn lang Lf Sci; Lang joint courses; Comb St courses) (IB 35 pts)
Southampton – AAB (Lang Learn; Lang Soty; Modn Langs) (IB 34 pts HL 17 pts)
Sussex – ABB–BBB (Lang Contemp Euro St)
York – AAB–ABB (Modn Lang Ling; Ling courses) (IB 34 pts)

320 pts **Bath** – ABB–BBB (Modn Langs Euro St courses except under **340 pts**) (IB 34 pts)
Birmingham – ABB 320 pts (Modn Langs joint courses) (IB 32–34 pts)
Leeds – ABB–BBB (Modn Langs Joint Hons (see separate language tables))
Lancaster – ABB 320 pts (Euro Langs Mgt St)
Leicester – ABB (Modn Lang St; Modn Langs Film St) (IB 28–30 pts)
Liverpool – ABB (Modn Euro Langs) (IB 30 pts)
London (RH) – ABB–BBB (Multiling St) (IB 32 pts)
London (SOAS) – ABB (Arbc; Bngli; Burm; Chin; Grgn; Guj; Hsa; Hindi; Indsn; Jap; Kor; Npli; Pers; Sansk; Swli; Thai; Tbtn; Turk; Viet; Heb Isrl St) (IB 30 pts)
Newcastle – ABB (Modn Langs; Modn Lang Ling; Modn Langs Mgt St) (IB 32 pts HL Fr/Ger/Span 6)
Nottingham – ABB–ABC/BBB (Modn Langs St; Modn Euro St; Fr Dutch; Fr Port; Fr Russ) (IB 32 pts)
Surrey – ABB–BBB 320–300 pts (Bus Mgt Lang; Langs St)

300 pts **Aston** – 300–320 pts (Transl St Fr/Ger/Span; Modn Langs courses) (IB 31–33 pts)
Birmingham – BBB 300 pts (Modn Lang Euro St (Pol) (Soty Cult Hist)) (IB 32–34 pts)
East Anglia – ABC–ACC (Transl Media Fr/Span 3 yrs)
East Anglia – BBB (Langs Mgt St)
Edinburgh – BBB (Modn Euro Langs; Modn Euro Langs EU St (2 langs from Fr/Ger/Ital/Russ St/Scand St/Span)) (IB 34 pts)
Lancaster – BBB (Euro Langs Film St) (IB 29 pts)
Leeds – BBB (Thai SE As St) (IB 32 pts)
London (QM) – 300 pts (Fr/Ger/Russ Euro St; Modn Langs)
London (UCL) – BBB (Dutch courses) (IB 32 pts)
Salford – 300–280 pts (Modn Lang Ling; Euro Langs; Modn Langs; Modn Langs Transl Interp St)
Sheffield – BBB (Modn Langs) (IB 32 pts HL lang 6)
Strathclyde – BBB 1st yr entry (Int Bus Modn Lang; Modn Langs)
Swansea – BBB 300 pts (Lang courses; Lang Comm)

280 pts **East Anglia** – BBC (Transl Media Fr/Span 4 yrs; Modn Langs 4 yrs)
Essex – 280 pts (Modn Lang; Lang St) (IB 30 pts)
Heriot-Watt – BBC (App Langs Transl; Langs (Interp Transl); Int Mgt Langs)
Roehampton – 280–340 pts (Modn Langs Transl Interp)

260 pts **Aberystwyth** – 260 pts (Euro Lang; Rmnc Langs) (IB 29 pts)
Bristol UWE – 260–300 pts (Int Bus Lang)
Hull – 260–280 pts (Modn Lang St; Modn Langs)
Nottingham Trent – 260 pts (Modn Langs courses; Chin/Fr/Ger/Ital/Span courses)
Ulster – 260 pts inc BC (Lang Ling Comm; Lang Ling PR)
Westminster – BCC (Transl St) (IB 28 pts)

240 pts **Aberdeen** – CCC 1st yr entry (Euro Langs 20th Cent Cult; Lang Ling courses; Langs Lit Scot)
Bangor – 240 pts (Fr/Ger/Ital/Span Joint Hons)
Coventry – 240–260 pts (Fr courses; Span courses)
Glamorgan – 240–280 pts (App Lang St)
London Met – 240 pts (App Transl)
Manchester Met – 240 pts (Joint Hons Langs)

Plymouth – 240 pts (Modn Langs courses; Modn Langs; Int Bus Modn Langs) (IB 24 pts)
Portsmouth – 240–300 pts (Comb Modn Langs; App Langs)
Sheffield Hallam – 240 pts (Bus St Langs Fr/Ger/Span; Langs Mark; Langs Tour)
Stirling – CCC (Modn Langs (Fr/Ger/Span); Modn Langs Mark; Int Mgt St Euro Langs Soty; Euro Langs Psy) (IB 28 pts)

230 pts **Edinburgh Napier** – 230 pts (Lang Joint courses)
220 pts **Leeds Met** – 220 pts (Lang St)
200 pts **Middlesex** – 200–240 pts (Transl; Int Bus Langs)
180 pts **Central Lancashire** – 180–200 pts (Modn Langs courses)
160 pts **Greenwich** – 160 pts (Int St Lang Cult)
West Scotland – CC (Langs Fr/Span)
Wolverhampton – 160–220 pts (Interp (Brit Sign Lang Engl))

Open University – (Modn Lang St – contact +44 (0)845 300 6090 or www.openuniversity.co.uk/you)

Alternative offers
See **Chapter 7** and **Appendix 1** for grades/UCAS Tariff points information for the International Baccalaureate, Scottish Highers/Advanced Highers, the Welsh Baccalaureate, the Irish Leaving Certificate, the Cambridge Pre-U Diploma, the Advanced Diploma and the Extended Project.

CHOOSING YOUR COURSE (SEE ALSO CH.1)

Some course features
See separate language tables.

Universities and colleges teaching quality See www.qaa.ac.uk; www.unistats.com.

Top research universities and colleges (RAE 2008) See separate language tables.

ADMISSIONS INFORMATION

Number of applicants per place (approx) Aston 4; Bangor 5; Birmingham 5; Brighton 4; Bristol 15; Bristol UWE 4; Cambridge 3; Cardiff 6; Durham 6; East Anglia 15; Heriot-Watt 5; Huddersfield 12; Lancaster 10; Leeds (Joint Hons) 8; Leicester 5; Liverpool 5; Newcastle 22; Northumbria 4; Roehampton 3; Salford 6; Swansea 4; Wolverhampton 10; York 4.

Advice to applicants and planning the UCAS personal statement Discuss any literature studied outside your course work. Students applying for courses in which they have no previous knowledge (for example, Italian, Portuguese, Modern Greek, Czech, Russian) would be expected to have done a considerable amount of language work on their own in their chosen language before starting the course. See also **Appendix 4**.

Misconceptions about this course **Leeds** (Joint Hons) Some applicants think that studying languages means studying masses of literature – wrong. At Leeds, generally speaking, it's up to you; you study as much or as little literature as you choose. Residence abroad does not inevitably mean a university course (except where you are taking a language from scratch). Paid employment is usually another option.

Selection interviews **Yes** Aston, Cambridge, Coventry, Durham, East Anglia, Heriot-Watt, Hertfordshire, Huddersfield, Liverpool (Open Day invitation), London (RH), Roehampton; **Some** Brighton, Bristol UWE, Leeds, Salford, Swansea.

Interview advice and questions **Bangor** All applicants invited for interview after offer when a lower offer may be made. **Cambridge** Think of a painting of a tree. Is the tree real? **Leeds** (Joint Hons) Give an example of something outside your studies that you have achieved over the past year. **London (RH)** Conversation in the appropriate language. See **Chapter 5**.

Reasons for rejection (non-academic) Lack of commitment to spend a year abroad. Poor references. Poor standard of English. No reasons for why the course has been selected. Poor communication skills. Incomplete applications, for example missing qualifications and reference.

AFTER-RESULTS ADVICE

Offers to applicants repeating A-levels **Higher** Bristol UWE; **Possibly higher** Aston; **Same** Bangor (usually), Birmingham, Bristol, Durham, East Anglia, Leeds, Liverpool, Newcastle, Nottingham Trent, Salford, Stirling, Wolverhampton, York; **No offers made** Cambridge.

GRADUATE DESTINATIONS AND EMPLOYMENT (2007/8 HESA)

See separate language tables.

Career note The only career-related fields for language students are teaching which attracts some graduates and the demanding work of interpreting and translating to which only a small number aspire. The majority will be attracted to work in management and administration, financial services and a host of other occupations which may include the social services, law and property development.

OTHER DEGREE SUBJECTS FOR CONSIDERATION

Communication Studies; Linguistics; Modern Languages Education/Teaching.

LATIN

(see also **Classical Studies/Classical Civilisation, Classics** and **Greek**)

Latin courses provide a study of the language, art, religion and history of the Roman world. This table should be read in conjunction with the **Classical Studies/Classical Civilisation** and **Classics** tables.

Useful websites www.thelatinlibrary.com; www.la.wikipedia.org; www.arlt.co.uk.

NB The points totals shown to the left of the institutions are for ease of reference only. It must not be assumed that Tariff points are always used by institutions or that they can be substituted for an offer in grades. The level of an offer is not necessarily indicative of the quality of a course.

COURSE OFFERS INFORMATION

Subject requirements/preferences **GCSE** English, a foreign language and Latin may be stipulated. **AL** Check courses for Latin requirement.

NB In 2011 universities and colleges will differ in their use of GCE AL/AS unit grade information, A* grades, the Extended Project (EPQ), the Advanced Diploma and the Cambridge Pre-U examination when considering applicants and making offers. An EPQ may be accepted in place of an AS subject. Check websites of universities and colleges for the latest offers information.

Your target offers and examples of courses provided by each institution

380 pts **Cambridge** – A*AA college offers may vary (Class Gk Lat; Modn Mediev Lang (Class Lat)) (IB 38–42 pts)

360 pts **Exeter** – AAA–ABB (Lat; Lat Arbc St) (IB 36–31 pts)
London (King's) – AAB+AS (Lat Engl)
Oxford – AAA (Classics) (IB 38–42 pts)
Warwick – ABBc/ABbbc (Engl Lat Lit)

340 pts **Exeter** – AAB–ABB (Fr Lat) (IB 34–31 pts)
Glasgow – AAB (Latin) (IB 34 pts)
London (UCL) – ABB+AS (Lat Gk)
St Andrews – AAB (Lat Mediev Hist; Lat; Lat Maths) (IB 36 pts)

320 pts **Leeds** – ABB (Lat Class; Lat Phil; Lat Theol Relig St; Lat Russ)
London (RH) – ABB (Fr Lat; Ger Lat; Lat; Engl Lat) (IB 34 pts)
Manchester – ABB–BBB (Lat; Lat Fr/Ital/Span; Lat Engl Lit; Lat Ling)
Nottingham – ABB (Anc Hist Lat; Lat; Engl St Lat) (IB 32 pts)
Swansea – ABB–BBB 320–300 pts (Mediev St Lat; Lat Lang St; Class Civ Lat)

300 pts **Edinburgh** – BBB (Lat St; Anc Hist Lat) (IB 34 pts)
200 pts **Trinity Saint David** – 200–300 pts (Lat; Phil St Lat; Lat Arch) (IB 24 pts)

Alternative offers
See **Chapter 7** and **Appendix 1** for grades/UCAS Tariff points information for the International Baccalaureate, Scottish Highers/Advanced Highers, the Welsh Baccalaureate, the Irish Leaving Certificate, the Cambridge Pre-U Diploma, the Advanced Diploma and the Extended Project.

CHOOSING YOUR COURSE (SEE ALSO CH.1)

Some course features
Edinburgh An intensive Latin course is offered to beginners.
Exeter (Lat) The course focuses on the language and society of Rome, with modules in literature, history and culture, and translation from set books from and into Latin.
Leeds Joint Honours Latin students focus on Latin language and literature, and an intensive beginners' language course. There may be opportunities for study abroad.
St Andrews Latin is available as a Single Honours degree or in a wide range of Joint Honours subjects. The Single Honours course combines Latin language study (beginners' and post A-level/Highers) with an in-depth reading and understanding of Latin classics and other texts.
Swansea Latin is offered as a Joint Honours course with ancient history, classical civilisation or modern languages.
Trinity Saint David Latin is offered at beginners', intermediate and advanced levels.

Universities and colleges teaching quality See www.qaa.ac.uk; www.unistats.com.

Top research universities and colleges (RAE 2008) See **Classics**.

ADMISSIONS INFORMATION

Number of applicants per place (approx) Leeds 2; Nottingham 6; Trinity St David 6.

Advice to applicants and planning the UCAS personal statement See **Classical Studies/Classical Civilisation** and **Classics**.

Selection interviews **Yes** Cambridge, Exeter, London (RH), (UCL), Nottingham, Oxford, Trinity Saint David.

Interview advice and questions See **Classical Studies/Classical Civilisation** and **Classics**.

AFTER-RESULTS ADVICE

Offers to applicants repeating A-levels **Higher** Leeds, St Andrews, Warwick.

GRADUATE DESTINATIONS AND EMPLOYMENT (2007/8 HESA)

Graduates surveyed 10 **Employed** 5 **In further study** None **Assumed unemployed** None.

Career note Graduates enter a broad range of careers within management, the media, commerce and tourism as well as social and public services. Some graduates choose to work abroad and teaching is a popular option.

OTHER DEGREE SUBJECTS FOR CONSIDERATION

Ancient History; Archaeology; Classical Studies; Classics.

LATIN AMERICAN STUDIES

(including **Hispanic Studies**; see also **American Studies** and **Spanish**)

Latin American courses provide a study of Spanish and of Latin American republics, covering both historical and present-day conditions and problems. Normally a year is spent in Latin America.

Useful websites www.iol.org.uk; www.bbc.co.uk/languages; http://languageadvantage.com; www.languagematters.co.uk; www.reed.co.uk/multilingual; www.cilt.org.uk; www.latinworld.com; www.wola.org; www.latinamericalinks.com; www.latinamericanassoc.org; see also **Languages** and **Spanish**.

NB The points totals shown to the left of the institutions are for ease of reference only. It must not be assumed that Tariff points are always used by institutions or that they can be substituted for an offer in grades. The level of an offer is not necessarily indicative of the quality of a course.

COURSE OFFERS INFORMATION

Subject requirements/preferences **GCSE Aberdeen**: English, mathematics or science and a foreign language. English and a foreign language required by most universities. **AL** Spanish may be required for some courses.

NB In 2011 universities and colleges will differ in their use of GCE AL/AS unit grade information, A* grades, the Extended Project (EPQ), the Advanced Diploma and the Cambridge Pre-U examination when considering applicants and making offers. An EPQ may be accepted in place of an AS subject. Check websites of universities and colleges for the latest offers information.

Your target offers and examples of courses provided by each institution

360 pts **London (UCL)** – AAB+AS–ABB+AS (Lat Am St; Hisp St) (IB 34–36 pts)
340 pts **Essex** – 340–300 pts (Lat Am St Hum Rts) (IB 31–29 pts)
Glasgow – AAB (Hisp St courses) (IB 34 pts)
Manchester – AAB–ABC (Span Port Lat Am St)
Southampton – AAB (Span Lat Am St) (IB 32 pts)
320 pts **Birmingham** – ABB–BBB (Hisp St Joint Hons)
Bristol – ABB–BBC (Hisp St) (IB 30–33 pts)
Kent – 320 pts (Hisp St Cult St; Hisp St; Hisp St Comp; Hisp St Film St) (IB 33 pts)
Leeds – ABB (Hisp Lat Am St) (IB 32 pts)
London (King's) – BBB+AS **or** BBbbb (Hisp St Port Braz St; Hisp St; Hisp St Engl)
Newcastle – ABB (Span Port Lat Am St) (IB 32 pts HL Span 6)
Sheffield – ABB (Hisp St Pol)
300 pts **Birmingham** – BBB–BBC (Hisp St) (IB 32 pts)
Liverpool – BBB–BBC (Lat Am St; Lat Am Hisp St; Hisp St) (IB 32 pts)
London (QM) – 300–320 pts (Film St Hisp St) (IB 32 pts)
London (QM) – BBB 300 pts (Hisp St Bus Mgt; Hisp St Ling Comp Sci)
Nottingham – ABC/BBB (Hisp St; Hisp St Hist; Am St Lat Am St) (IB 32 pts)
Sheffield – BBB (Hisp St; Hisp St Econ; Hisp St Jap) (IB 32 pts)
280 pts **Essex** – 280–260 pts (Lat Am St; Lat Am St Bus Mgt)
Manchester – BBC (Lat Am St Scrn St)
260 pts **Hull** – 260–280 pts (Hisp St Relig)
240 pts **Aberdeen** – CCC (Hisp St (Lat Am) (Spn); Hisp St Geog; Hisp St Fin) (IB 30 pts)
London Met – 240 pts (Span Lat Am St)
200 pts **Portsmouth** – 200–280 pts (Span Lat Am Dev St; Span Lat Am St)

Alternative offers

See **Chapter 7** and **Appendix 1** for grades/UCAS Tariff points information for the International Baccalaureate, Scottish Highers/Advanced Highers, the Welsh Baccalaureate, the Irish Leaving Certificate, the Cambridge Pre-U Diploma, the Advanced Diploma and the Extended Project.

CHOOSING YOUR COURSE (SEE ALSO CH.1)

Some course features

Birmingham (Hisp St) The first two years of the course focus on Spanish language skills and Hispanic literature and culture. The third year is spent in Spain or Latin America while the fourth year centres on students' individual programme interests, for example advanced translation skills or cultural studies.

Liverpool (Hisp St) Three Iberian Romance languages (Catalan, Portuguese or Galician) are studied in addition to the main degree of Spanish. The degree programme also focuses on Spanish, Portuguese, Galician and Latin American culture.
London (UCL) (Hisp St) Course combines a study of Spanish language with courses in film history and literature. (Lat Am St) The course focuses on a study of Spanish and Portuguese and the literature and history of Spain, Portugal and Latin America.
Portsmouth (Span Lat Am Dev St) Students study the language and culture of contemporary Latin American societies, taking Spanish throughout the course. Half the placement year is in Spain and the other half at a partner institution in Latin America.

Top research universities and colleges (RAE 2008) See **Spanish**.

ADMISSIONS INFORMATION

Number of applicants per place (approx) Essex 3; Liverpool 3; Newcastle 25; Nottingham 7; Portsmouth 5.

Advice to applicants and planning the UCAS personal statement Visits and contacts with Spain and Latin American countries should be described. An awareness of the economic, historical and political scene of these countries is also important. Information may be obtained from respective embassies.

Selection interviews **Yes** Newcastle; **Some** Portsmouth.

Interview advice and questions Past questions include: Why are you interested in studying Latin American Studies? What countries related to the degree course have you visited? What career are you planning when you finish your degree? Applicants taking Spanish are likely to be asked questions on their syllabus and should also be familiar with some Spanish newspapers and magazines. See **Chapter 5**.

AFTER-RESULTS ADVICE

Offers to applicants repeating A-levels **Higher** Essex; **Same** Newcastle, Portsmouth.

GRADUATE DESTINATIONS AND EMPLOYMENT (2007/8 HESA)

No data available.

Career note See **Languages**.

OTHER DEGREE SUBJECTS FOR CONSIDERATION

American Studies; Brazilian; Portuguese; Spanish.

LAW

(for **Criminology** and **Criminal Justice** courses see also **Social Sciences/Studies**)

Law courses are usually divided into two parts. Part I occupies the first year and introduces the student to criminal and constitutional law and the legal process. Thereafter many different specialised topics can be studied in the second and third years. The course content is very similar for most courses. Applicants are advised to check with universities for their current policies concerning their use of the National Admissions Test for Law (LNAT). See **Subject requirements/preferences** below and also **Chapter 5**.

Useful websites www.barcouncil.org.uk; www.ilex.org.uk; www.lawcareers.net; www.lawsociety.org.uk; www.cps.gov.uk; www.hmcourts-service.gov.uk; www.lawscot.org.uk; www.lawsoc-ni.org; www.rollonfriday.com; www.lnat.ac.uk.

NB The points totals shown to the left of the institutions are for ease of reference only. It must not be assumed that Tariff points are always used by institutions or that they can be substituted for an offer in grades. The level of an offer is not necessarily indicative of the quality of a course.

COURSE OFFERS INFORMATION

Subject requirements/preferences **GCSE** Many universities will expect high grades. **Manchester** Requirements are often higher than normal – minimum of five A-grades. **AL** Arts, humanities, social sciences and sciences plus languages for courses combined with a foreign language. **All universities** Applicants offering art and music A-levels should check whether these subjects are acceptable.

NB In 2011 universities and colleges will differ in their use of GCE AL/AS unit grade information, A* grades, the Extended Project (EPQ), the Advanced Diploma and the Cambridge Pre-U examination when considering applicants and making offers. An EPQ may be accepted in place of an AS subject. Check websites of universities and colleges for the latest offers information.

The National Admissions Test for Law (LNAT) may be required by universities other than those indicated in the table below – check university websites and prospectuses and see also **Chapter 5**.

Your target offers and examples of courses provided by each institution

410 pts **London (King's)** – AAAb +LNAT (Law) (IB 38 pts HL 555–554)
400 pts **Warwick** – AAAc +LNAT (Law 3yr/4yr) (IB 36–38 pts)
390 pts **Brunel** – 390 pts AAB+AS/EPQ b (Law)
Warwick – AABb/c–AAAb/c (Euro Law)
380 pts **Cambridge** – A*AA college offers may vary (Law; Lnd Econ) (IB 38–42 pts) (see **Ch.5**)
London (UCL) – AAA+AS +LNAT (Law; Law Advnc St; Law Fr/Ger/Hisp/Ital) (IB 38 pts)
Warwick – AABc (Law Bus St)
360 pts **Birmingham** – AAA +a good LNAT (Law; Law Bus St; Law Fr/Ger) (IB 36 pts)
Bristol – AAA +LNAT (Law; Law Fr/Ger Law) (IB 37 pts HL 666)
Cardiff – AAA (Law; Law Crimin)
City – AAA (Law; Law Prop Val) (IB 35 pts)
Durham – AAA +LNAT (Law) (IB 37 pts)
East Anglia – AAA (Law Am Law) (IB 35 pts)
Exeter – AAA–AAB (Law; Law (Euro); Law Euro St) (IB 36–33 pts)
Lancaster – AAA 360 pts (Law (Int); Law; Euro Leg St) (IB 32 pts HL 17–18 pts)
Leeds – AAA +LNAT (Law; Law Mgt; Law Fr) (IB 38 pts HL 18 pts)
Leicester – AAA (Law; Law Fr Law Lang; Maîtrise Engl Fr Law)
Liverpool – AAA (Law) (IB 35 pts)
London (QM) – AAA (Law; Engl Euro Law) (IB 36 pts HL 666)
London (SOAS) – AAA (Law) (IB 38 pts HL 766)
London LSE – AAA (Law) (IB 38 pts HL 766/666)
Manchester – AAA (Law; Engl Law Fr Law; Law Crimin) (IB 37–35 pts)
Newcastle – AAA (Law) (IB 38 pts HL 666)
Nottingham – AAA +LNAT (Law; Law Fr/Ger/Span) (IB 40 pts HL 7 in subj)
Oxford – AAA +LNAT (Law; Law Euro Law) (IB 39 pts)
Queen's Belfast – AAA–AABa (Law; Law Pol; Cmn Civ Law Fr/Span) (IB 34 pts HL 666)
Sheffield – AAA (Law; Law (Euro Int)) (IB 37 pts HL 666)
Southampton – AAA–AAB (Law; Law (Euro Leg St) (Int Leg St); Marit Law) (IB 36 pts HL 18 pts)
Warwick – ABBc (Law Sociol)
York – AAA (Law) (IB 36 pts)
340 pts **Aston** – AAB–ABB 340–320 pts (Law Mgt) (IB 34 pts)
Bristol – AAB–ABB (Law Chem)
Cardiff – AAB (Law Sociol; Law Pol; Law Fr)
East Anglia – AAB (Law; Law Euro Leg Sys) (IB 33 pts)
Essex – AAB (Law; Engl Fr Law; Law Phil; Law Pol; Law Hum Rts) (IB 36 pts)
Glasgow – AAB +LNAT (Law courses)
Keele – 340–360 pts (Law Single Hons)
Kent – AAB (Law; Engl Fr/Ger/Ita/Span Law; Euro Leg St) (IB 33 pts)
Lancaster – AAB 340 pts (Law Crimin)

Leeds – AAB (Law Acc) (IB 38 pts)
Manchester – AAB (Law Pol)
Reading – AAB (Law; Law Leg St Euro)
Sheffield – AAB (Law Crimin; Law Fr/Ger/Span)
Strathclyde – AAB (LLB Law; Law Modn Lang)
Sussex – AAB–ABB (Law; Law Int Rel; Law Contemp Euro St) (IB 34–36 pts)

320 pts **Bournemouth** – 320 pts (Law; Law Tax; Bus Law; Enter Law)
Durham – ABB (Sociol Law)
East Anglia – ABB (Law Fr Law Lang) (IB 32 pts)
Hertfordshire – 320–300 pts (Law)
Huddersfield – 320–300 pts (Bus Law; Law)
Hull – ABB 320 pts (Law; Law Fr/Ger Law Lang; Law Pol; Law Lit)
Keele – 320 pts (Law Dual Hons)
Kingston – 320 pts (Law; Int Law Bus; Law Crimin)
Liverpool – ABB (BA Law Bus) (IB 32 pts)
London (QM) – ABB 320 pts (Law Pol)
London LSE – ABB (Anth Law) (IB 37 pts)
London Met – 320–280 pts (LLB Law; Bus Law; Law Int Dev; Law Int Rel)
Manchester – ABB (Chem Pat Law)
Northumbria – ABB 320 pts (Law (Exempting)) (IB 32 pts)
Oldham (Coll Univ Centre) – 320 pts (Law)
Portsmouth – 320 pts (Law; Law Crimin)
Salford – ABB–BBB 320–300 pts (Law Chin; Law; Law Fin St)
Salford – 320 pts (LLB Law) (IB 31 pts)
Staffordshire – 320 pts (LLB Law; Law (Spo) (Hum Rts) (HR Mgt); Bus Law)
Strathclyde – ABB (BA Law)
Surrey – ABB 320 pts (Law; Law Fr/Ger/Span Law; Law Int St) (IB 34 pts)
Swansea – 320 pts (Law Bus)
Ulster – ABB (Law; Law Acc; Law Int Pol; Law HR Mgt; Law Ir; Law Mark)
Westminster – ABB–ABC (Commer Law; Euro Leg St; LLB Law) (IB 32 pts)

300 pts **Aberdeen** – BBB (Law) (IB 34 pts)
Bradford – 300 pts (Law)
Bristol UWE – 300–340 pts (Law; Law (Euro Int))
Buckingham – 300 pts (Law; Law Bus Fin; Law Econ; Law Mgt St; Law Pol)
Cardiff – BBB (Law Welsh)
Central Lancashire – BBB (Law Arbc; LLB Law)
Coventry – 300 pts (Law; Law Bus; Law Fr/Span)
De Montfort – 300 pts (LLB Law; Law Hum Rts Soc Just)
Derby – 300 pts (LLB Law; Law Crimin; Law (Bus Law) (Int Law) (Soc Pblc Law))
Dundee – BBB 300 pts (Scots Law; Law (Engl NI); Law Fr/Ger/Span)
Edinburgh – BBB (Law courses)
Glamorgan – 300–340 pts (Law; Commer Law; Crim Law)
Glasgow Caledonian – BBB (LLB Law)
Huddersfield – 300 pts (Bus Law)
Nottingham Trent – 300–280 pts (Law; Law Bus; Law Crimin; Law Psy) (IB 24 pts)
Oxford Brookes – BBB (Law courses) (IB 32 pts)
Plymouth – 300–360 pts (Law; Law Bus St; Law Int Rel)
Salford – 300 pts (Law Fin; Law Crim)
Stirling – BBB (LLB Law)
Westminster – ABC (Law Fr Law) (IB 30 pts)

280 pts **Aberystwyth** – 280 pts (Law; Crim Law; Euro Law; Bus Law; Law Langs) (IB 32 pts)
Bangor – 280 pts (Law; Law Acc Fin) (IB 28 pts)
Birmingham City – 280 pts (Law; Law Am Leg St; Law Hum Rts; Law Bus Law)
Brighton – BBC 280 pts (Law Bus)
Gloucestershire – 280–300 pts (Law)

Lincoln – 280 pts (Law; Law Fin; Law Bus)
Liverpool John Moores – 280 pts (Law) (IB 30 pts)
Middlesex – 280 pts (LLB Law)
Teesside – 280 pts (Law; Law Pol)

260 pts **Abertay Dundee** – BCC (LLB Hons Law)
Birmingham City – 260 pts (Bus Bus Law; Bus Law Fin) (IB 30 pts)
Bolton – 260 pts (Law; Law Comb Hons)
Canterbury Christ Church – 260–200 pts (Law)
Coventry – 260–280 pts (Law Int St)
Cumbria – BCC 260 pts (Law)
Derby – 260 pts (BA Law)
Edge Hill – 260 pts (Law; Law Crim; Law Mgt)
Edinburgh Napier – 260 pts (LLB Law)
Leeds Met – 260 pts (Law; Law Crim)
Liverpool Hope – 260 pts (Law Comb Hons)
Manchester Met – 260 pts (Leg St Comb Hons)
Portsmouth – 260–300 pts (Law Euro St; Law Int Rel; Law Bus)
Sheffield Hallam – 260 pts (Law; Law Crim; Law Maîtrise Fr; Bus Law)
Stirling – BCC (BA Law; Bus Law; Law) (IB 30 pts)
Sunderland – 260–220 pts (Law courses)
Winchester – 260–300 pts (Law)

240 pts **Aberdeen** – CCC (Leg St courses)
Anglia Ruskin – 240 pts (LLB Law)
Bradford – 240 pts (Bus St Law)
Bradford (Coll) – 240 pts (Law; Acc Law; Law Soc Welf; Mark Law)
Bristol UWE – 240–300 pts (Law Crim; Law Lang; Law joint courses)

LJMU Law School

The School of Law at Liverpool John Moores University (LJMU) offers a broad portfolio of undergraduate, postgraduate and professional programmes in law, legal practice and criminal justice.

The following undergraduate degree programmes are available within the School of Law:

- **LLB (Hons) Law**
- **LLB (Hons) Law and Criminal Justice**
- **BA Single Honours Criminal Justice**
- **BSc Single Honours Forensic Psychology and Criminal Justice**

Graduate skills development and work-related learning are embedded in all of our programmes, helping you gain the essential skills and experience demanded by today's employers. Lectures are delivered within the Mount Pleasant Campus, which also comprises an award-winning learning resource centre.

Student Lawyers at LJMU have done very well over the years in national competitions. The teams won the 2007 English Speaking Union – Essex Court Chambers National Mooting Competition, 2008 National Negotiation Championship and 2008 International Mediation Event. Additionally, the Student Law Society is a vibrant organisation of law students supporting law students.

If you want to have a great university experience, graduate with a respected qualification and secure the skills and 'know-how' that will help you climb the professional career ladder, then you should choose the School of Law at LJMU.

For more information about the LJMU School of Law contact the BLW Admissions Team:

tel: 0151 231 3999
email: blwadmissions@ljmu.ac.uk
website: www.ljmu.ac.uk/law

	Bucks New – 240–280 pts (Law; Bus Law)
	Central Lancashire – 240 pts (Law Crimin)
	Chester – 240–300 pts (Law; Law Jrnl; Law Crimin) (IB 24 pts)
	De Montfort – 240 pts (BA Law)
	East London – 240 pts (Law)
	Greenwich – 240 pts (LLB Law)
	London Met – 240 pts (BA Law)
	London South Bank – 240 pts (LLB Law)
	Middlesex – 240 pts (BA Law)
	Newport – 240 pts (Acc Law; Bus Law courses)
	Northampton – 240–260 pts (Law courses)
	Plymouth – 240 pts (Marit Bus Marit Law)
	Robert Gordon – CCC (Law; Law Mgt)
	Winchester – 240–280 pts (Law Comb Hons)
	Wolverhampton – 240–220 pts (Fin Law; Bus Law)
230 pts	**Edinburgh Napier** – 230 pts (Acc Law)
228 pts	**Glasgow Caledonian** – BC 228 pts (Bus Law)
220 pts	**Anglia Ruskin** – 220 pts (Law Crim)
	Blackburn (Coll Univ Centre) – 220 pts (Commer Law; Crim Law)
	Hertfordshire – 220–260 pts (Law joint courses)
	Northampton – 220–260 pts (Law Joint Hons)
	Southampton Solent – 220–200 pts (Law; Commer Law; Law Bus Mgt)
200 pts	**Canterbury Christ Church** – 200 pts (Leg St courses)
	Leeds Trinity (UC) – 200 pts (Bus Law)
	London Met – 200–280 pts (Bus Law courses)
	Peterborough Reg (Coll) – 200 pts (Bus Law)
	Plymouth – 200 pts (Marit Bus Marit Law)
	Thames valley – 200 pts (Crimin Law)
160 pts	**Bedfordshire** – 160 pts (Law; Acc Law)
	Doncaster (Coll) – 160 pts (Law Crim)
	St Mary's Twickenham (UC) – 160–200 pts (Bus Law)
	Wolverhampton – 160–220 pts (Law; Law Phil)
120 pts	**Croydon (Coll)** – 120 pts (Law)
80 pts	**Holborn (Coll)** – 80 pts (Law)
	London (Birk) – degree reqd (not Law) interview+reasoning test (p/t Accelerated Law)
	Open University – contact +44 (0)845 300 6090 or www.openuniversity.co.uk/you

Alternative offers

See **Chapter 7** and **Appendix 1** for grades/UCAS Tariff points information for the International Baccalaureate, Scottish Highers/Advanced Highers, the Welsh Baccalaureate, the Irish Leaving Certificate, the Cambridge Pre-U Diploma, the Advanced Diploma and the Extended Project.

EXAMPLES OF FOUNDATION DEGREES IN THE SUBJECT FIELD

Blackpool and Fylde (Coll); Bournemouth; Bradford; Bristol City (Coll); Croydon (Coll); Exeter (Coll); Glyndŵr; Kingston; Nottingham New (Coll); Peterborough Reg (Coll); Portsmouth; Shrewsbury (Coll); Southampton Solent; Truro (Coll); Walsall (Coll); Weston (Coll).

CHOOSING YOUR COURSE (SEE ALSO CH.1)

Some course features

Bournemouth All Law degrees have a common first year, with specialisation options made at the end. A minimum of 40 weeks is spent in industry.
Dundee English Law and Scots Law are both offered.
Edinburgh Twelve joint courses with Law are offered including accountancy, business studies and languages.
Exeter (Law (Euro)) The fourth year is spent either at Rennes following a French Maîtrise en Droit

programme or at Saabrucken following the German Magister programme. Graduates obtain a dual qualification, are exempt from the academic stages of UK professional training and are ready for the aptitude test to practise as a lawyer in France or Germany.
London (King's) English Law can be studied with American, French, German or Australian Law. Transfers to these programmes take place only after completion of the first year.
London (UCL) Law can be studied with another legal system with a year spent at a host university in Australia, Singapore, Hong Kong, or, for the European degree, in France, Germany, Italy or Spain.

Universities and colleges teaching quality See www.qaa.ac.uk; www.unistats.com.

Top research universities and colleges (RAE 2008) London LSE; London (UCL); Oxford; Durham; Nottingham; Kent; Cambridge; Cardiff; Queen's Belfast; Edinburgh; London (QM); Reading; Strathclyde; Ulster; Birmingham.

Examples of sandwich degree courses Abertay Dundee; Aston (compulsory); Birmingham City; Bournemouth; Bradford; Brighton; Brunel; City; De Montfort; Edinburgh Napier; Hertfordshire; Huddersfield; Lancaster; Nottingham Trent; Plymouth; Surrey; Teesside; Westminster.

ADMISSIONS INFORMATION

Number of applicants per place (approx) Abertay Dundee 3; Aberystwyth 8; Anglia Ruskin 10; Aston 10; Bangor 3; Birmingham 4; Birmingham City 20; Bournemouth 9; Bradford (Coll) 2; Bristol 20; Bristol UWE 27; Brunel 2; Buckingham 3; Cambridge 7; Cardiff 12; Central Lancashire 36; City 23; Coventry 15; De Montfort 6; Derby 7; Dundee 6; Durham 14; East Anglia 14; East London 13; Edinburgh 5; Edinburgh Napier 7; Essex 26; Exeter 15; Glamorgan 3; Glasgow 8; Glasgow Caledonian 10; Huddersfield 10; Hull 15; Kent 11; Kingston 25; Lancaster 8; Leeds 15; Leicester 14; Liverpool 10; Liverpool John Moores 10; London (King's) 14, (QM) 17, (SOAS) 8, (UCL) 21; London LSE 14; London Met 13; London South Bank 4; Manchester 11; Manchester Met 21; Middlesex 25; Newcastle 13; Northampton 4; Northumbria 12; Nottingham 9; Nottingham Trent 15; Oxford Brookes 18; Plymouth 14; Robert Gordon 4; Sheffield 16; Sheffield Hallam 6; Southampton 7; Southampton Solent 5; Staffordshire 16; Strathclyde (Law) 10; Sussex 10; Teesside 3; Thames Valley 18; Warwick 20; Westminster 29; Wolverhampton 12; York 8.

Advice to applicants and planning the UCAS personal statement Visit the law courts and take notes on cases heard. Follow leading legal arguments in the press. Read the law sections in *The Independent*, *The Times* and *The Guardian*. Discuss the career with lawyers and, if possible, obtain work shadowing in lawyers' offices. Describe these visits and experiences and indicate any special areas of law which interest you. (Read *Learning the Law* by Glanville Williams.) Commitment is essential to the study of law as an academic discipline, not necessarily with a view to taking it up as a career.

When writing to admissions tutors, especially by email, take care to present yourself well: text language is not acceptable. You should use communication as an opportunity to demonstrate your skill in the use of English. Spelling mistakes, punctuation errors and bad grammar suggest that you will struggle to develop the expected writing ability (see **Misconceptions about this course**) and may lead to your application being rejected. When writing to an admissions tutor do not demand an answer 'immediately' or 'by return' or 'urgently'. If your query is reasonable the tutor will respond without such urging. Adding these demands is bad manners and suggests that you are doing everything at the last minute and increases your chances of a rejection.

The criteria for admission are: motivation and capacity for sustained and intense work; the ability to analyse and solve problems using logical and critical approaches; the ability to draw fine distinctions, to separate the relevant from the irrelevant; the capacity for accurate and critical observation, for sustained and cogent argument; creativity and flexibility of thought and lateral thinking; competence in English; the ability to express ideas clearly and effectively, a willingness to listen and to be able to give considered responses. See also **Appendix 4**.

Misconceptions about this course **Aberystwyth** Some applicants believe that all Law graduates enter the legal profession – this is incorrect. **Birmingham** Students tend to believe that success in the law centres on the ability to learn information. Whilst some information does necessarily have to be learnt, the most important skills involve (a) developing an ability to select the most relevant pieces of information and (b) developing the ability to write tightly argued, persuasively reasoned essays on the basis of such information. **Bristol** Many applicants think that most of our applicants have been privately educated: the reverse is true. **Derby** Many applicants do not realise the amount of work involved to get a good degree classification.

Selection interviews Approximately four well-qualified candidates apply for every place on undergraduate Law courses in the UK and the National Admissions Test for Law (LNAT) is used by a number of universities (see **Your target offers and examples of courses provided by each institution** above and **Chapter 5**). Only candidates performing well in this test will be called for interview at universities requiring LNAT, but a good performance in this test, however, does not guarantee an interview or admission (see www.lnat.ac.uk). **Yes** Anglia Ruskin, Aberystwyth, Birmingham, Bristol, Bristol UWE, Buckingham, Cambridge, Canterbury Christ Church, Central Lancashire, Coventry, Durham, East London, Edinburgh Napier, Essex, Exeter, Glasgow, Lancaster, Liverpool, Liverpool John Moores, London (King's), (UCL), London South Bank, Northumbria, Nottingham, Oxford, Queen's Belfast, Southampton Solent, Surrey, Teesside, Warwick, York; **Some** Bangor, Cardiff (Law Lang), Derby, Dundee, East Anglia, Huddersfield, Kent (mature/Access students), Nottingham Trent (mature students), Oxford Brookes (mature students), Sheffield Hallam, Southampton (mature students), Staffordshire, Sunderland; **No** Sussex.

Interview advice and questions Law is a highly competitive subject and applicants will be expected to have a basic awareness of aspects of law and to have gained some work experience, on which they are likely to be questioned. It is almost certain that a legal question will be asked at interview and applicants will be tested on their responses. Questions in the past have included: What interests you in the study of law? What would you do to overcome the problem of prison overcrowding if you were (a) a judge (b) a prosecutor (c) the Prime Minister? What legal cases have you read about recently? What is jurisprudence? What are the causes of violence in society? A friend bought a bun which, unknown to him, contained a stone. He gave it to you to eat and you broke a tooth. Could you sue anyone? Have you visited any law courts? What cases did you see? A person arrives in England unable to speak the language. He lights a cigarette in a restaurant where smoking is not allowed. Can he be charged and convicted? What should be done in the case of an elderly person who steals a bar of soap? What, in your opinion, would be the two basic laws in Utopia? Describe, without using your hands, how you would do the butterfly stroke. What would happen if there were no law? Should we legalise euthanasia? If you could change any law, what would it be? How would you implement the changes? If a person tries to kill someone using black magic, are they guilty of attempted murder? If a jury uses a ouija board to reach a decision, is it wrong? If so, why? Jane attends a university interview. As she enters the building she sees a diamond brooch on the floor. She hands it to the interviewer who hands it to the police. The brooch is never claimed. Who is entitled to it? Jane? The interviewer? The police? The University authorities? The Crown? Mr Grabbit who owns the building? **Cambridge** Logic questions. If I returned to the waiting room and my jacket had been taken and I then took another one, got home and actually discovered it was mine, had I committed a crime? If the interviewer pulled out a gun and aimed it at me, but missed as he had a bad arm, had he committed a crime? If the interviewer pulled out a gun and aimed it at me, thinking it was loaded but, in fact, it was full of blanks and fired it at me with the intention to kill, had he committed a crime? Which of the three preceding situations are similar and which is the odd one out? If a law is immoral, is it still a law and must people abide by it? For example, when Hitler legalised the systematic killing of Jews, was it still law?

For joint courses: what academic skills are needed to succeed? Why have you applied for a joint degree? Where does honesty fit into law? **Oxford** Should the use of mobile phones be banned on public transport? Is wearing school uniform a breach of human rights? If you could go back in time to any period of time, when would it be and why? Would you trade your scarf for my bike, even if you have no idea what state it's in or if I even have one? Is someone guilty of an offence if they did not set out to commit a crime but ended up doing so? Does a girl-scout have a political agenda? See also **Chapter 5**.

Reasons for rejection (non-academic) 'Dreams' about being a lawyer! Poorly informed about the subject. Badly drafted application. Under-estimate of work load. Poor communication skills. **Manchester Met** Some were rejected because they were obviously more suited to Psychology.

AFTER-RESULTS ADVICE

Offers to applicants repeating A-levels **Higher** Aberystwyth, Bristol UWE, Coventry, Dundee, Essex, Glamorgan, Glasgow, Hull, Leeds, London Met, Manchester Met, Newcastle, Nottingham, Oxford Brookes, Queen's Belfast, Sheffield, Sheffield Hallam, Strathclyde, Warwick; **Possibly higher** Liverpool; **Same** Anglia Ruskin, Bangor, Birmingham, Bradford (Coll), Brighton, Bristol, Brunel, Cardiff, De Montfort, Derby, Durham, East Anglia, Huddersfield, Kingston, Lincoln, Liverpool Hope, Liverpool John Moores, Northumbria, Nottingham Trent, Staffordshire, Stirling, Sunderland, Surrey, Wolverhampton; **No offers made** Cambridge.

GRADUATE DESTINATIONS AND EMPLOYMENT (2007/8 HESA)

Graduates surveyed 9125 **Employed** 2535 **In further study** 3975 **Assumed unemployed** 515.

Career note Many graduates seek to practise in the legal profession after further training. However, a Law degree provides a good starting point for many other careers in industry, commerce and the public services. The study of consumer protection can lead to specialisation and qualification as a trading standards officer.

OTHER DEGREE SUBJECTS FOR CONSIDERATION

Criminology; Economics; Government; History; International Relations; Politics; Social Policy and Administration; Sociology.

LEISURE and RECREATION MANAGEMENT/STUDIES

(see also **Hospitality and Event Management, Sports Sciences/Studies** and **Tourism and Travel**)

The courses cover various aspects of leisure and recreation. Specialist options include recreation management, tourism and countryside management, all of which are offered as individual degree courses in their own right. There is also an obvious link with Sports Studies, Physical Education and Tourism and Travel courses. See also Appendix 2.

Useful websites www.ispal.org.uk; www.bized.co.uk; www.leisuremanagement.co.uk; www.baha.org.uk; www.leisureopportunities.co.uk; www.recmanagement.com; www.isrm.co.uk; www.uksport.gov.uk; www.london2012.com.

NB The points totals shown to the left of the institutions are for ease of reference only. It must not be assumed that Tariff points are always used by institutions or that they can be substituted for an offer in grades. The level of an offer is not necessarily indicative of the quality of a course.

COURSE OFFERS INFORMATION

Subject requirements/preferences **GCSE** Normally English and mathematics grades A–C. **AL** No specified subjects. **Other** CRB clearance and health checks required for some courses.

NB In 2011 universities and colleges will differ in their use of GCE AL/AS unit grade information, A* grades, the Extended Project (EPQ), the Advanced Diploma and the Cambridge Pre-U examination when considering applicants and making offers. An EPQ may be accepted in place of an AS subject. Check websites of universities and colleges for the latest offers information.

Your target offers and examples of courses provided by each institution

300 pts **Manchester** BBB-BBC (Mgt Leis) (IB 30–28 pts)
280 pts **Bournemouth** – 280 pts (Leis Mark) (IB 30 pts)
Cardiff (UWIC) – 280 pts (Spo Mgt)
260 pts **Brighton** – BCC 260–300 pts (Spo Leis Mgt) (IB 30–28 pts)
Liverpool Hope – 260 pts (Leis Comp; Leis Dance; Leis Disab St; Leis Media; Leis Mus)

	Manchester Met – 260 pts (Spo Leis Evnt Mgt)
	Oxford Brookes – BCC (Leis Plan Comb courses)
	Salford – 260 pts (Leis Tour Mgt; Spo Leis Mgt) (IB 26 pts)
240 pts	**Creative Arts** – 240 pts (Leis Jrnl) (IB 30 pts)
	Edinburgh Napier – 240 pts (Fstvl Evnts Mgt courses)
	Gloucestershire – 240 pts (Leis Spo Mgt)
	Leeds Met – 240 pts (Spo Leis Cult)
	Liverpool John Moores – 240–280 pts (Tour Leis Mgt) (IB 25 pts)
	Manchester Met – 240 pts (Leis Mgt; Leis Mgt (Spo Dev) (Out Actvts)) (IB 28 pts)
	Nottingham Trent – 240 pts (Spo Leis Out Mgt)
	Sheffield Hallam – 240 pts (Evnts Leis Mgt)
	Stranmillis (UC) – CCC 240 pts (Hlth Leis St)
	Ulster – 240 pts (Leis Evnts Mgt)
	Worcester – 240 pts (Out Advntr Ldrshp Mgt
220 pts	**Cumbria** – 220 pts (Out St; Out Ldrshp)
	Harper Adams (UC) – 220–240 pts (Advntr Recr Mgt; Leis Tour Mgt)
	Nottingham Trent – 220 pts (Spo Leis Psy Educ; Spo Leis Educ Dev)
	Southampton Solent – 220 pts (Out Advntr Mgt; Wtrspo St Mgt; Extrm Spo Mgt)
200 pts	**Aberystwyth** – 200 pts (Cntry Recr Tour) (IB 28 pts)
	Bolton – 200 pts (Spo Leis Mgt) (IB 20 pts)
	Canterbury Christ Church – 200 pts (Tour Leis St courses)
	Hull – 200 pts (Spo Leis Mgt courses)
	Suffolk (Univ Campus) – 200 pts (Leis Mgt)
160 pts	**SAC (Scottish CAg)** – CC (Spo Recr Mgt; Out Prsts Mgt)
120 pts	**Swansea Met** – 120 pts (Leis Mgt)
	Staffordshire – contact University (Media Leis Ind)

Alternative offers
See **Chapter 7** and **Appendix 1** for grades/UCAS Tariff points information for the International Baccalaureate, Scottish Highers/Advanced Highers, the Welsh Baccalaureate, the Irish Leaving Certificate, the Cambridge Pre-U Diploma, the Advanced Diploma and the Extended Project.

EXAMPLES OF FOUNDATION DEGREES IN THE SUBJECT FIELD

(see also Tourism and Travel) Aberystwyth; Blackpool and Fylde (Coll); Bournemouth; Bucks New; Chichester; Colchester (Inst); Cornwall (Coll); Cumbria; Derby; Duchy (Coll); East Lancashire (IHE); Edge Hill; Glamorgan; Guildford (Coll); Harper Adams (UC); Leeds City (Coll); Liverpool (CmC); Loughborough (Coll); Manchester (Coll); Myerscough (Coll); Newcastle (Coll); Norwich City (Coll); Salford; Sheffield (Coll); Wirral (Coll); Writtle (Coll); Yorkshire Coast (Coll).

CHOOSING YOUR COURSE (SEE ALSO CH.1)

Some course features

Brighton (Spo Leis Mgt) The course has options in sport psychology, performance and marketing.
Creative Arts (Leis Jrnl) This unique course is taught alongside the Sports Journalism and the Motoring Journalism courses. A multimedia degree, it targets the leisure magazine sector and specialist sports and leisure websites and has particular strengths in practical production training.
Cumbria (Out St; Out Ldrshp) The courses involve climbing, canoeing, sailing and mountaineering and are based in the centre of the Lake District.
Southampton Solent Courses focus on principles of coaching, event and activity safety and operations, customer service management, leisure marketing and business management.

Universities and colleges teaching quality See www.qaa.ac.uk; www.unistats.com.

Top research universities and colleges (RAE 2008) See **Sports Sciences/Studies**.

Examples of sandwich degree courses Aberystwyth; Bournemouth; Brighton; Gloucestershire; Harper Adams (UC); Ulster.

ADMISSIONS INFORMATION

Number of applicants per place (approx) Brighton 10; Cardiff (UWIC) 3; Gloucestershire 7; Hull 3; Liverpool John Moores 3; SAC (Scottish CAg) 4.

Advice to applicants and planning the UCAS personal statement Work experience, visits to leisure centres and national parks and any interests you have in particular aspects of leisure should be described, for example, art galleries, museums, countryside management, sport. An involvement in sports and leisure as a participant or employee is an advantage. See also **Appendix 4**.

Misconceptions about this course The level of business studies in leisure management courses is higher than many students expect.

Selection interviews **Some** Liverpool John Moores, Salford.

Interview advice and questions In addition to sporting or other related interests, applicants will be expected to have had some work experience and can expect to be asked to discuss their interests. What do you hope to gain by going to university? See **Chapter 5**.

Reasons for rejection (non-academic) Poor communication or presentation skills. Relatively poor sporting background or knowledge.

AFTER-RESULTS ADVICE

Offers to applicants repeating A-levels **Same** Cardiff (UWIC), Liverpool John Moores, Salford.

GRADUATE DESTINATIONS AND EMPLOYMENT (2007/8 HESA)

See **Hospitality and Event Management**.

Career note Career opportunities exist in public and private sectors within leisure facilities, health clubs, the arts, leisure promotion, marketing and events management. Some graduates work in sports development and outdoor activities.

OTHER DEGREE SUBJECTS FOR CONSIDERATION

Business Studies; Events Management; Hospitality Management; Sports Studies; Tourism.

LINGUISTICS

(see also **English**)

Linguistics covers the study of language structure and function, and also includes areas such as children's language, slang, language handicap, advertising language, language styles and the learning of foreign languages.

Useful websites www.iol.org.uk; www.cal.org; http://web.mit.edu/linguistics; www.applij.oxfordjournals.org; www.lsadc.org; www.sil.org; www.baal.org.uk.

NB The points totals shown to the left of the institutions are for ease of reference only. It must not be assumed that Tariff points are always used by institutions or that they can be substituted for an offer in grades. The level of an offer is not necessarily indicative of the quality of a course.

COURSE OFFERS INFORMATION

Subject requirements/preferences **GCSE** English required and a foreign language preferred. **AL** English may be required or preferred for some courses.

NB In 2011 universities and colleges will differ in their use of GCE AL/AS unit grade information, A* grades, the Extended Project (EPQ), the Advanced Diploma and the Cambridge Pre-U examination when considering applicants and making offers. An EPQ may be accepted in place of an AS subject. Check websites of universities and colleges for the latest offers information.

Your target offers and examples of courses provided by each institution

380 pts **Cambridge** – A*AA college offers may vary (Modn Mediev Lang (Ling) (Part II subject, taken after Part I in another, usually language-related, subject)) (IB 38–42 pts)
London (UCL) – AAA+AS–ABB+AS (Linguistics) (IB 34–38 pts)

360 pts **Oxford** – AAA (Modn Lang Ling) (IB 38–42 pts)

340 pts **Lancaster** – AAB 340 pts (Ling; Ling Psy; Ling N Am) (IB 31 pts)
Manchester – AAB–BBB (Ling courses; Comb St courses) (IB 35–30 pts)
St Andrews – AAB–ABB (Bib St Ling; Engl Ling)
Southampton – AAB (Fr/Ger/Span Ling St) (IB 32 pts)
York – AAB (Engl Ling; Fr/Ger/Span Ling) (IB 32 pts)

320 pts **Lancaster** – ABB (Socioling; Ling Phil) (IB 30 pts)
Leeds – ABB (Ling joint courses) (IB 34 pts HL 16 pts)
London (SOAS) – ABB (Ling courses) (IB 36 pts)
Queen's Belfast – ABB–BBCb (Ling Joint Hons)

300 pts **Edinburgh** – BBB (Ling; Ling Artif Intel; Celt Ling; Mnd Lang; Ling Soc Anth) (IB 34 pts H555)
Essex – 300 pts (Ling; Engl Lang Ling) (IB 32 pts)
London (QM) – BBB 300 pts (Compar Lit Ling; Fr Ling) (IB 32 pts)
Newcastle – ABC–BBB (Ling; Ling Chin/Jap; Ling Fr/Ger/Span) (IB 32 pts HL Engl 5)
Salford – 300 pts (Ling Arbc/Chin/Fr/Ger/Ital/Port/Span)
Sheffield – BBB (Ling Jap St; Ling Kor St; Ling Hisp St) (IB 32–35 pts)

280 pts **Essex** – 280 pts (Modn Langs Ling) (IB 30 pts)
Westminster – BBC/BC (Chin Ling; Russ Ling)

260 pts **Aberdeen** – BCC (Lang Ling courses)
Brighton – BCC (Engl Lang Ling) (IB 28 pts)
Bristol UWE – 260–300 pts (Ely Chld St Ling; Engl Lang Ling) (IB 26–32 pts)
Nottingham Trent – 260 pts (Ling Joint Hons)
Ulster – 260 pts (Ling Adv; Ling Comm; Ling PR) (IB 24 pts)
Westminster – BCC/BB (Ling Crea Writ) (IB 30 pts)

240 pts **Bangor** – 240–280 pts (Ling Engl Lang; Ling; Ling Engl Lit)
Central Lancashire – 240 pts (Engl Lang Ling Comb Hons)
Manchester Met – 240 pts (Fr/Ger/Ital/Span Ling; Comb Hons Ling)
Roehampton – 240–320 pts (Engl Lang Ling)

220 pts **Sunderland** – 220 pts (Ling courses)
UCP Marjon – 220 pts (Engl Lang Ling Educ St)

160 pts **Wolverhampton** – 160–220 pts (Ling courses)

London (Birk) – no A-level reqs (p/t Ling Lang)

Alternative offers

See **Chapter 7** and **Appendix 1** for grades/UCAS Tariff points information for the International Baccalaureate, Scottish Highers/Advanced Highers, the Welsh Baccalaureate, the Irish Leaving Certificate, the Cambridge Pre-U Diploma, the Advanced Diploma and the Extended Project.

CHOOSING YOUR COURSE (SEE ALSO CH.1)

Some course features

Edinburgh The University is regarded as a world leader in the study of linguistics. Opportunity to take an MA in Linguistics or as the lead subject combined with a second subject.
Lancaster (Ling N Am) The course focuses on the sound, grammar and meaning systems of different languages, and has a wide range of options. Study in a North American institution may be possible.
Leeds Linguistics and Phonetics can be taken as a single subject, a major subject or as part of a Joint Honours programme.
London (QM) (Compar Lit Ling) Students divide their time between the two subjects, the former making connections with literature and film, music, the visual arts and popular culture.

Universities and colleges teaching quality See www.qaa.ac.uk; www.unistats.com.

Top research universities and colleges (RAE 2008) London (QM); Edinburgh; York; Essex; Sheffield; Wolverhampton; London (UCL); Manchester; Lancaster; Central Lancashire; Cambridge; Bristol UWE.

ADMISSIONS INFORMATION

Number of applicants per place (approx) Bangor 3; East London 3; Essex 1; Lancaster 12; Leeds 12; York 11.

Advice to applicants and planning the UCAS personal statement Give details of your interests in language and how it works, and about your knowledge of languages and their similarities and differences.

Selection interviews **Yes** Brighton, Cambridge, East London, Essex, Lancaster, Newcastle, Reading; **Some** Salford, Sheffield.

Interview advice and questions Past questions include: Why do you want to study Linguistics? What does the subject involve? What do you intend to do at the end of your degree course? What answer do you give to your parents or friends when they ask why you want to study the subject? How and why does language vary according to sex, age, social background and regional origins? See also **Chapter 5**.

Reasons for rejection (non-academic) Lack of knowledge of linguistics. Hesitation about the period to be spent abroad.

AFTER-RESULTS ADVICE

Offers to applicants repeating A-levels **Higher** Essex; **Same** Brighton, Leeds, Newcastle, Salford, York.

GRADUATE DESTINATIONS AND EMPLOYMENT (2007/8 HESA)

Graduates surveyed 490 **Employed** 220 **In further study** 110 **Assumed unemployed** 45.

Career note Students enter a wide range of careers, with information management and editorial work in publishing offering some interesting and useful outlets.

OTHER DEGREE SUBJECTS FOR CONSIDERATION

Cognitive Science; Communication Studies; Education Studies; English; Psychology; Speech Sciences.

LITERATURE

(see also **English**)

This is a very broad subject introducing many aspects of the study of literature and aesthetics. Courses will vary in content. Degree courses in English and foreign languages will also include a study of literature.

Useful websites www.lrb.co.uk; www.literature.org; www.bibliomania.com; www.bl.uk; www.acla.org; http://icla.byu.edu.

NB The points totals shown to the left of the institutions are for ease of reference only. It must not be assumed that Tariff points are always used by institutions or that they can be substituted for an offer in grades. The level of an offer is not necessarily indicative of the quality of a course.

COURSE OFFERS INFORMATION

Subject requirements/preferences **GCSE** English and a foreign language usually required. **AL** English may be required or preferred for some courses.

NB In 2011 universities and colleges will differ in their use of GCE AL/AS unit grade information, A* grades, the Extended Project (EPQ), the Advanced Diploma and the Cambridge Pre-U examination when considering applicants and making offers. An EPQ may be accepted in place of an AS subject. Check websites of universities and colleges for the latest offers information.

Your target offers and examples of courses provided by each institution

390 pts **Warwick** – AABb (Film Lit; Phil Lit; Ital Euro Lit; Engl Lit)
360 pts **Durham** – AAA (Engl Lit)
London (King's) – AAB+AS (Compar Lit; Compar Lit Film St) (IB 35 pts)
Warwick – ABBc/ABbbc (Engl Lat Lit)
340 pts **East Anglia** – AAB–BBB (Engl Lit; Art Hist Lit)
Glasgow – AAB (Scot Lit; Compar Lit courses) (IB 30 pts)
Manchester – AAB–ABB (Lit St Dr Hlcst St; Lit St Dr App Engl St; Comb St courses) (IB 35–32 pts)
320 pts **East Anglia** – ABB–BBB (Lit; Lit Hist; Engl Am Lit) (IB 32–31 pts)
Essex – 320–300 pts (Lit Hist Art; Lit Myth; Lit Sociol) (IB 29 pts)
London (Gold) – ABB (Engl Compar Lit) (IB 32 pts)
London (RH) – ABB–BBB (Compar Lit Cult courses) (IB 32 pts)
Warwick – ABB (Engl Ital Lit)
Warwick – 320 pts (Engl Ger Lit)
York – ABB–BBB (Ling Lit)
300 pts **Edinburgh** – BBB (Scot Ethnol Scot Lit; Scot Lit Scot Hist)
Kent – 300–320 pts (Compar Lit St courses) (IB 28 pts)
London (Gold) – BBB (Media Modn Lit; Engl Am Lit)
London (QM) – 300 pts (Compar Lit; Compar Lit Film St; Russ Compar Lit)
London (UCL) – BBB (Ital Euro Lit)
Reading – 300–320 pts (Engl Lit Euro Lit Cult)
Stirling – BBB 2nd yr entry (Engl St Scot Lit)
280 pts **Aberystwyth** – 280 pts (Engl Lit) (IB 30 pts)
Birmingham City – 280 pts (Engl Lit courses)
Hertfordshire – 280 pts (Engl Lit courses)
260 pts **Edge Hill** – 260 pts (Engl Lit courses)
Stirling – BCC 1st yr entry (Engl St Scot Lit)
240 pts **Aberdeen** – CCC (Langs Lit Scot; Lit Wrld Cntxt)
Aberystwyth – 240 pts (Ir Lang Lit)
Buckingham – CCC (Engl Lit courses)
Ulster – 240 pts (Ir Lang Lit)
Worcester – 240–260 pts (Engl Lit St courses)
200 pts **Trinity Saint David** – 200 pts (Welsh Engl Lit)

Staffordshire – contact University (Lit Contemp Cult)

Alternative offers

See **Chapter 7** and **Appendix 1** for grades/UCAS Tariff points information for the International Baccalaureate, Scottish Highers/Advanced Highers, the Welsh Baccalaureate, the Irish Leaving Certificate, the Cambridge Pre-U Diploma, the Advanced Diploma and the Extended Project.

EXAMPLES OF FOUNDATION DEGREES IN THE SUBJECT FIELD

Bath Spa; Truro (Coll); Winchester.

CHOOSING YOUR COURSE (SEE ALSO CH.1)

Some course features

Glasgow (Scot Lit) Course covers poetry, drama, fiction and prose of Scotland in English and Scots from the 14th century to the present day.
London (Gold) (Engl Compar Lit) There is an option to specialise in the literature of other countries, for example America, Europe, the Caribbean.
Reading (Engl Lit Euro Lit Cult) The course explores the inter-relationship between the literatures and cultures of different European countries to gain a comparative perspective on English literature, culture and history. All works are in translation for those without foreign language skills.
Ulster (Ir Lang Lit) Course focuses on an in-depth study of the literary and historical traditions of Gaelic Ireland from the Bardic period to the present day and gaining a high level of competence in written and spoken Irish. Applicants need at least grade C (or equivalent) in A-level Irish.

Top research universities and colleges (RAE 2008) See **English**.

ADMISSIONS INFORMATION

Number of applicants per place (approx) East Anglia 12; Essex 4.

Advice to applicants and planning the UCAS personal statement **Kent** Interest in literatures other than English. See **English**.

Misconceptions about this course **Kent** Some students think that a foreign language is required – it is not.

Selection interviews **Yes** Trinity Saint David.

Interview advice and questions **Kent** Which book would you take on a desert island, and why? What is the point of doing a Literature degree in the 21st century? See **English**. See also **Chapter 5**.

Reasons for rejection (non-academic) **Kent** Perceived inability to think on their feet.

AFTER-RESULTS ADVICE

Information not available from institutions.

GRADUATE DESTINATIONS AND EMPLOYMENT (2007/8 HESA)

Graduates surveyed 150 **Employed** 70 **In further study** 50 **Assumed unemployed** 10.

Career note See **English**.

OTHER DEGREE SUBJECTS FOR CONSIDERATION

Arts; English; Linguistics; Welsh and Celtic Studies.

MARINE/MARITIME STUDIES

(including **Oceanography**; see also **Biology (for Marine Biology courses), Environmental Sciences/Studies** and **Naval Architecture**)

Marine and Maritime Studies can involve a range of subjects such as marine business, technology, navigation, nautical studies, underwater rescue and transport.

Useful websites www.bized.co.uk; www.british-shipping.org; www.uk-sail.org.uk; www.rya.org.uk; www.royalnavy.mod.uk; www.sstg.org; www.noc.soton.ac.uk; www.nautinst.org; www.mcsuk.org; www.nmm.ac.uk; www.imo.org; www.mcga.gov.uk.

NB The points totals shown to the left of the institutions are for ease of reference only. It must not be assumed that Tariff points are always used by institutions or that they can be substituted for an offer in grades. The level of an offer is not necessarily indicative of the quality of a course.

COURSE OFFERS INFORMATION

Subject requirements/preferences **GCSE** Mathematics and science are required for several courses. **AL** Science or mathematics will be required or preferred for some courses.

NB In 2011 universities and colleges will differ in their use of GCE AL/AS unit grade information, A* grades, the Extended Project (EPQ), the Advanced Diploma and the Cambridge Pre-U examination when considering applicants and making offers. An EPQ may be accepted in place of an AS subject. Check websites of universities and colleges for the latest offers information.

Your target offers and examples of courses provided by each institution

360 pts **East Anglia** – AAA–AAB (MSci Meteor Ocean courses) (IB 34–33 pts HL 666 inc maths)
Southampton – AAA–ABB (MOcean Ocean courses) (IB 36–33 pts)

340 pts **Cardiff** – AAB–ABB (Mar Geosci courses)

Heriot-Watt – AAB 2nd yr entry (App Mar Biol)
Newcastle – AAB (MEng Mar Eng; Off Eng; Sml Crft Tech) (IB 36 pts HL maths phys 5)
320 pts **East Anglia** – ABB–BBB (BSc Meteor Ocean) (IB 32–31 pts)
Liverpool – ABB–BBB (Mar Biol) (IB 33–30 pts)
300 pts **Aberdeen** – BBB 2nd yr entry (Mar Biol)
Cardiff – BBB (Mar Geog) (IB 32 pts)
Heriot-Watt – BBB 1st yr entry (App Mar Biol)
Liverpool – BBB 300 pts (Ocn Sci; Ocn Clim; Ocn Clim Physl Geog) (IB 30 pts)
Newcastle – BBB (BEng Mar Eng; Off Eng; Sml Crft Tech; Mar Biol Ocean; Mar Zool) (IB 32 pts HL maths phys 5)
Plymouth – BBB 300–360 pts (Mar Biol Cstl Ecol; Mar Biol Ocean) (IB 24 pts)
Southampton – BBB (BSc Ocean; Ocn Chem) (IB 32 pts HL 15 pts)
280 pts **Swansea** – 280–300 pts (Mar Biol)
260 pts **Bangor** – 260–320 pts (App Mar Biol; Mar Biol Zool) (IB 28 pts)
Bournemouth – 260 pts (Mar Arch; Mar Cstl Mgt)
Brighton – BCC (Earth Ocean Sci) (IB 28 pts)
Plymouth – BCC 260 pts (BEng Mar Tech; Mar Geosci)
Portsmouth – 260–300 pts (Mar Env Sci; Mar Biol; Marit Bus Log)
240 pts **Aberdeen** – 240 pts 1st yr entry (Mar Biol) (IB 28 pts)
Bangor – 240 pts (App Trstrl Mar Ecol; Mar Biol Ocean)
Hull – 240–280 pts (Aqua Zool; Mar Frshwtr Biol)
Liverpool John Moores – 240 pts (Marit St; Marit Bus Mgt; Naut Sci)
Plymouth – 240–280 pts (Env Sci (Marit Cons); Marit Bus Marit Law; Ocn Explor; Ocn Sci)
Southampton Solent – 240 pts (App Spo Sci (Wtrspo Out Actvts))
220 pts **Bangor** – 220–260 pts (Ocn Sci; Ocean Comp; Geol Ocean; Cstl Geog; Mar Chem; Mar Env St) (IB 28 pts)
Hull – 220–280 pts (Cstl Mar Biol)
Plymouth – 220 pts (Cru Mgt)
Southampton Solent – 220 pts (Wtrspo St Mgt)
Ulster – 220 pts (Mar Sci) (IB 24 pts)
200 pts **Plymouth** – 200 pts (Surf Sci Tech; App Mar Spo Sci; Mar St (Ocn Ycht) (Navig))
Portsmouth – 200 pts (Mar Spo Tech)
180 pts **Plymouth** – 180 pts (Mar Spo Tech; Mar Cmpstes Tech)
Southampton Solent – 180 pts (Geog Mar St; Ycht Prod Surv; Ycht Pwrcrft Des)
160 pts **Essex** – 160 pts (Mar Frshwtr Biol) (IB 24 pts)
120 pts **Southampton Solent** – 120 pts (Marit Bus; Ship Port Mgt)

UHI Millennium Inst (NHC) – check with admissions tutor (Mar Sci)

Alternative offers
See **Chapter 7** and **Appendix 1** for grades/UCAS Tariff points information for the International Baccalaureate, Scottish Highers/Advanced Highers, the Welsh Baccalaureate, the Irish Leaving Certificate, the Cambridge Pre-U Diploma, the Advanced Diploma and the Extended Project.

EXAMPLES OF FOUNDATION DEGREES IN THE SUBJECT FIELD
Blackpool and Fylde (Coll); Bournemouth; Cornwall (Coll); Liverpool John Moores; Plymouth; South Tyneside (Coll); Southampton Solent; Suffolk (Univ Campus).

CHOOSING YOUR COURSE (SEE ALSO CH.1)
Some course features
Bangor A large department covering marine sciences, coastal geography and ocean sciences.
Liverpool John Moores (Marit St) A broad-based programme for students with a general interest in ships and sea, with a wide range of optional maritime subjects (for example, freight operations, navigation, marine engineering, meteorology, international trade and finance). Students can build their own degree course as their interests develop, based on core modules such as port and cargo operations, management of people and goods, management science and law. Part of the final year

can be spent in Norway and all Maritime courses have an optional placement year.
Plymouth (App Mar Spo Sci) A unique course involving the study of human performance, equipment use and design, the nature of the marine environment and practical work. An optional professional diving module is available in the second year.
Southampton Solent Unique courses in Yacht and Powercraft Design and Yacht Production and Surveying.

Universities and colleges teaching quality See www.qaa.ac.uk; www.unistats.com.

Examples of sandwich degree courses Bangor; Cardiff; Greenwich; Liverpool John Moores; Plymouth; Portsmouth; South Tyneside (Coll); Southampton Solent.

ADMISSIONS INFORMATION

Number of applicants per place (approx) Glasgow 2; Liverpool John Moores (Marit St) 3; Southampton (Ocean) 6, (Ocn Chem) 6.

Advice to applicants and planning the UCAS personal statement This is a specialised field and, in many cases, applicants will have experience of marine activities. Describe these experiences, for example, sailing, snorkelling, fishing. See also **Appendix 4**.

Selection interviews **Yes** UHI Millennium Inst (NHC).

Interview advice and questions Most applicants will have been stimulated by their studies in science or will have strong interests or connections with marine activities. They are likely to be questioned on their reasons for choosing the course. See **Chapter 5**.

AFTER-RESULTS ADVICE

Offers to applicants repeating A-levels **Same** Bangor, Liverpool John Moores, Plymouth, UHI Millennium Inst (NHC).

GRADUATE DESTINATIONS AND EMPLOYMENT (2007/8 HESA)

Maritime Technology graduates surveyed 85 **Employed** 50 **In further study** 10 **Assumed unemployed** 10.

Ocean Sciences graduates surveyed 815 **Employed** 405 **In further study** 165 **Assumed unemployed** 180.

Career note This subject area covers a wide range of vocational courses, each offering graduates an equally wide choice of career openings in either purely scientific or very practical areas.

OTHER DEGREE SUBJECTS FOR CONSIDERATION

Biology; Civil Engineering; Environmental Studies/Sciences; Geography; Marine Engineering; Marine Transport; Naval Architecture; Oceanography.

MARKETING

(including **Public Relations**; see also **Art and Design (Fashion)** and **Business Courses**)

Marketing courses are very popular and applications should include evidence of work experience or work shadowing. Marketing is a subject also covered in most Business Studies courses and in specialist (and equally relevant) courses such as Leisure Marketing and Food Marketing for which lower offers are often made. Most courses offer the same subject content.

Useful websites www.adassoc.org.uk; www.cim.co.uk; www.camfoundation.com; www.ipa.co.uk; www.ipsos-mori.com; www.marketingstudies.net; www.marketingtoday.com.

NB The points totals shown to the left of the institutions are for ease of reference only. It must not be assumed that Tariff points are always used by institutions or that they can be substituted for an offer in grades. The level of an offer is not necessarily indicative of the quality of a course.

COURSE OFFERS INFORMATION

Subject requirements/preferences **GCSE** English and mathematics. **AL** No specified subjects required.

NB In 2011 universities and colleges will differ in their use of GCE AL/AS unit grade information, A* grades, the Extended Project (EPQ), the Advanced Diploma and the Cambridge Pre-U examination when considering applicants and making offers. An EPQ may be accepted in place of an AS subject. Check websites of universities and colleges for the latest offers information.

Your target offers and examples of courses provided by each institution

360 pts **Exeter** – AAA–AAB (Mgt Mark) (IB 36–33 pts)
Lancaster – AAA 360 pts (Mark Abrd; Mark Mgt Abrd) (IB 32 pts)
Ulster – AAA (Comm Adv Mark)

350 pts **Brunel** – 350 pts (Bus Mgt (Mark)) (IB 32 pts)

340 pts **Aston** – 340–320 pts (Marketing) (IB 34 pts HL 665)
Cardiff – AAB (Bus Mgt (Mark))
Lancaster – AAB 340 pts (Mark; Mark Mgt; Adv Mark) (IB 32 pts)
Leeds – AAB (Mgt Mark) (IB 35 pts)
London (RH) – AAB 340 pts (Mgt Mark) (IB 35 pts)
Loughborough – AAB (Rtl Mark Mgt)
Manchester – AAB (Mgt (Mark))

320 pts **Bournemouth** – 320 pts (Bus St Mark)
Lancaster – ABB 320 pts (Mark Des; Mark Psy) (IB 30 pts)
Liverpool – ABB (Marketing) (IB 32 pts)
Newcastle – ABB (Mark; Mark Mgt) (IB 34 pts)
Northumbria – ABB 320 pts (Mark Mgt)

300 pts **Bournemouth** – 300 pts (Adv Mark Comm; Mark; PR)
Dundee – BBB 2nd yr entry (MA Bus Econ Mark)
Essex – 300 pts (Mark Innov; Mark Fin; Mark; Mgt Mark) (IB 32 pts)
Heriot-Watt – BBB 2nd yr entry (Mgt Mark)
Kent – 300 pts (Bus Admin (Mark)) (IB 33 pts)
Manchester – ABC 300 pts (Mgt Mark Tex)
Nottingham Trent – 300 pts (Fash Mark Brnd; Fash Comm Prom)
Oxford Brookes – BBB (Bus Mark Mgt)
Reading – 300 pts (Consum Bhv Mark; Bus Stats Mark)
Royal (CAg) – 300 pts (Prop Agncy Mark)
Stirling – BBB 2nd yr entry (Mark; Rtl Mark)
Strathclyde – BBB (Mark courses)

280 pts **Bournemouth** – 280 pts (Leis Mark; PR) (IB 30 pts)
Brighton – BBC (Bus Mgt Mark)
Huddersfield – 280 pts (Mark Brnd Mgt; Mark; Mark PR)
Keele – 280–340 pts (Mark courses)
Kingston – 280 pts (Mark Mgt) (IB 31 pts)
Manchester Met – 280 pts (Int Fash Mark)
Northumbria – 280 pts (Fash Mark; Bus Mark) (IB 25 pts)
Portsmouth – 280–300 pts (Mark; Mark Psy)
Swansea – 280 pts (Bus Mgt (Mark))
Worcester – 280 pts (Bus Mgt Mark; Mark; Mark Adv Web Des; Mark Adv PR)

260 pts **Aberystwyth** – 260 pts (Mark courses) (IB 27 pts)
Birmingham City – 260–280 pts (Mark Econ; Mark; Mark Bus Law; Mark Adv PR) (IB 24 pts)
Bolton – 260 pts (Bus Mgt (Mark)) (IB 24 pts)
Brighton – BCC (Rtl Mark; Trav Tour Mark) (IB 28 pts)
Bristol UWE – 260–300 pts (Bus St Mark; Mark; Mark Comm)
Coventry – 260–280 pts (Mark; Adv Mark; Mark Mgt)

Heriot-Watt – BCC 1st yr entry (Mgt Mark)
Hertfordshire – 260 pts (Mark; Mark Comb courses)
Hull – 260 pts (Mgt Mark; Mark courses; Int Mark)
Leeds Met – 260 pts (PR Mark)
Lincoln – 260 pts (Mark; Mark PR)
Liverpool Hope – 260 pts (Mark courses)
Plymouth – 260 pts (Marketing)
Queen Margaret – 260 pts (PR Mark; PR Media)
Staffordshire – BCC (Mark Mgt)
Ulster – 260 pts (Marketing)
Westminster – BCC–CCC (Bus Mark Mgt; Glob Mark; Mark Comms) (IB 28 pts)

240 pts **Bangor** – 240–280 pts (Mark Fr/Ger/Ital/Span)
Bradford – 240 pts (Marketing) (IB 24 pts)
Bradford (Coll Univ Centre) – 240 pts (Mark Law)
Buckingham – 240 pts (Mark Media Comm; Mark Psy) (IB 26 pts)
Cardiff (UWIC) – 240 pts (Mark Mgt)
Chester – 240 pts (Mark; PR)
Coventry – 240–260 pts (Spo Mark; Des Mark)
Cumbria – 240–280 pts (Mark Bus; Mark PR)
De Montfort – 240 pts (Mark; Int Mark Bus; Mark Mgt)
Derby – 240 pts (Int Mark Mgt)
Dundee – CCC 240 pts 1st yr entry (MA Bus Econ Mark)
Edinburgh Napier – 240 pts (Mark Mgt; Mark Dig Media; Mark Mgt Consum St)
Glamorgan – 240–280 pts (Mark Tour; Mark)
Glasgow Caledonian – CCC–CCD (Mark; Fash Mark)
Gloucestershire – 240 pts (Mark Mgt Brnd; Mark Adv Comms)
Liverpool John Moores – 240 pts (Mark; Bus PR)
Manchester Met – 240 pts (Mark Mgt; Rtl Mark Mgt; Spo Mark Mgt; Dig Mark Comms)
Newport – 240 pts (Marketing)
Nottingham Trent – 240 pts (Mark Des Comm; Bus Mgt Mark)
Plymouth – 240 pts (Bus Econ Mark)
Robert Gordon – CCC 240 pts (Mgt Mark)
Roehampton – 240–280 pts (Mark; Mark Multim)
Sheffield Hallam – 240–200 pts (Bus Mark; Fd Mark Mgt; Mark Rtl)
Southampton Solent – 240 pts (PR Comm)
Stirling – CCC 1st yr entry (Mark; Rtl Mark)
Ulster – 240 pts (Mark Int Pol)

230 pts **Greenwich** – 230–240 pts (PR)

220 pts **Chester** – 220–260 pts (Mark Comb Hons courses)
Chichester – CCD 220–240 pts (Marketing) (IB 26 pts)
Creative Arts – 220–260 pts (Des Brnd Mark; Fash Mgt Mark) (IB 24 pts)
Edge Hill – 220–260 pts (Marketing)
Leeds Met – 220 pts (Mark; Mark Adv Mgt; Rtl Mark Mgt; Spo Mark PR)
London Met – 220 pts (Mark; Fash Mark; PR)
Northampton – 220–260 pts (Mark; Mark Psy; Mark Joint Hons)
Southampton Solent – 220 pts (Mark Adv Mgt; Mark Entre; Mark Evnt Mgt; Mark Tour St)
Sunderland – 220 pts (Bus Mark Mgt)
Teesside – 220 pts (Mark Adv)
Wolverhampton – 220 pts (Mark Mgt; Mark HR Mgt)
York St John – 220 pts (Mark Mgt Web Techs)

200 pts **Anglia Ruskin** – 200 pts (Marketing)
Birmingham (UC) – 200 pts (Mark Mgt; Mark Evnts Mgt; Mark Tour Mgt)
Bucks New – 200–240 pts (Mark; Bus Mark Mgt; PR Mark Comm) (IB 24 pts)
Canterbury Christ Church – 200 pts (Mark courses) (IB 24 pts)
Central Lancashire – 200–260 pts (Mark Mgt; Mark Mgt Fash; Adv Mark Comms) (IB 28 pts)

De Montfort – 200 pts (Crea Mgt Mark)
East London – 200 pts (Marketing)
European Bus Sch London – 200–160 pts (Int Bus Mark Lang)
Glyndŵr – 200 pts (Marketing)
Middlesex – 200–280 pts (Mark; Mark Mgt; Mark Comms)
Portsmouth – 200 pts (Prop Mark Des Dev)
Suffolk (Univ Campus) – 200 pts (Bus Mgt Mark)
Thames Valley – 200 pts (Mark Bus)
195 pts **Queen Margaret** – 195 pts (Mark Mgt)
180 pts **Abertay Dundee** – DDD (Mark Bus)
Greenwich – 180 pts (Adv Mark Comm; Glob Mark Langs; Mark)
Harper Adams (UC) – 180–240 pts (Agri-Fd Mark Bus St; Agric Mark; Bus Mgt Mark)
Writtle (Coll) – 180 pts (Bus Mgt (Mark Sply Chn Mgt))
160 pts **Bedfordshire** – 160–240 pts (Mark; Adv Mark Comm; Mark Media Prac; PR)
Leeds Trinity (UC) – 160–240 pts (Mark; Media Mark; Bus Mark)
London South Bank – 160–240 pts (Mark Comb courses)
Swansea Met – 160 pts (Marketing)
West Scotland – CC (Int Mark)
100 pts **Bradford (Coll)** – 100–140 pts (Mark Sls)

Regents Bus Sch London – contact admissions tutor (Glob Mark Mgt)

Alternative offers
See **Chapter 7** and **Appendix 1** for grades/UCAS Tariff points information for the International Baccalaureate, Scottish Highers/Advanced Highers, the Welsh Baccalaureate, the Irish Leaving Certificate, the Cambridge Pre-U Diploma, the Advanced Diploma and the Extended Project.

EXAMPLES OF FOUNDATION DEGREES IN THE SUBJECT FIELD
Arts London; Bath Spa; Bedfordshire; Birmingham (UC); Bournemouth; Central Lancashire; Cornwall (Coll); Croydon; Glamorgan; Glyndŵr; Grimsby (IFHE); Guildford (Coll); Harper Adams (UC); Kirklees (Coll); Leeds (CAD); Manchester (Coll); Nottingham New (Coll); Plymouth; Salford; Sheffield (Coll); Somerset (CAT); Southampton Solent; Truro (Coll); Writtle (Coll).

CHOOSING YOUR COURSE (SEE ALSO CH.1)
Some course features
Brunel Marketing is offered as a pathway in the Business and Management programme and can be taken as a three-year full-time or four-year sandwich course.
Lancaster (Mark Mgt) There is a one-year work placement between the second and third years.
Loughborough (Rtl Mark Mgt) The third year is spent on a salaried business placement as a trainee manager in a UK retail or marketing organisation.
Oxford Brookes (Mark Mgt) The course can be taken as a Single Honours degree or combined with one of 18 other subjects.
Portsmouth (Mark) The course is recognised by the Chartered Institute of Marketing. The four-year sandwich course involves a paid marketing placement.
Westminster Students are expected to find employment for a period during the course, ideally abroad. Work placement officers have contacts with institutions overseas.

Universities and colleges teaching quality See www.qaa.ac.uk; www.unistats.com.

Examples of sandwich degree courses Abertay Dundee; Aston; Birmingham City; Bournemouth; Bradford; Brighton; Bristol UWE; Brunel; Central Lancashire; De Montfort; Glamorgan; Gloucestershire; Greenwich; Harper Adams (UC); Hertfordshire; Huddersfield; Lancaster; Leeds Met; Liverpool John Moores; Manchester Met; Newcastle; Northumbria; Nottingham Trent; Plymouth; Portsmouth; Sheffield Hallam; Staffordshire; Swansea Met; Ulster; Westminster; Wolverhampton; Worcester.

ADMISSIONS INFORMATION
Number of applicants per place (approx) Abertay Dundee 6; Aberystwyth 3; Anglia Ruskin 5;

Aston 9; Birmingham City 4; Bournemouth 10; Brunel 10; Central Lancashire 13; De Montfort 3; Derby 5; Glasgow Caledonian 15; Harper Adams (UC) 3; Huddersfield 7; Lancaster 28; Lincoln 3; London Met 10; Northampton 4; Northumbria 8; Nottingham Trent 2; Plymouth 12; Portsmouth 4; Staffordshire 6; Stirling 10; Teesside 3.

Advice to applicants and planning the UCAS personal statement See **Business Courses.** See also **Appendix 4.**

Selection interviews **Yes** Harper Adams (UC) (advisory), Manchester Met, Middlesex, Northbrook (Coll), Writtle (Coll); **Some** Abertay Dundee, Aberystwyth, Anglia Ruskin, Aston, Buckingham, De Montfort, Queen Margaret, Staffordshire.

Interview advice and questions Past questions include: What is marketing? Why do you want to take a Marketing degree? Is sales pressure justified? How would you feel if you had to market a product which you considered to be inferior? **Buckingham** What job do you see yourself doing in five years' time? See **Chapter 5**.

Reasons for rejection (non-academic) Little thought of reasons for deciding on a Marketing degree. Weak on numeracy and problem-solving. Limited commercial awareness. Poor inter-personal skills. Lack of leadership potential. No interest in widening their horizons, either geographically or intellectually. 'We look at appearance, motivation and the applicant's ability to ask questions.' Not hungry enough. Limited understanding of the career. No clear reasons for wishing to do the course.

AFTER-RESULTS ADVICE

Offers to applicants repeating A-levels **Same** Abertay Dundee, Aberystwyth, Anglia Ruskin, Aston, Buckingham, De Montfort, Lincoln, Manchester Met, Queen Margaret, Staffordshire.

GRADUATE DESTINATIONS AND EMPLOYMENT (2007/8 HESA)

Graduates surveyed 2170 **Employed** 1360 **In further study** 110 **Assumed unemployed** 215.

Career note See **Business Courses**.

OTHER DEGREE SUBJECTS FOR CONSIDERATION

Advertising; Art and Design; Business courses; Communications; Graphic Design; Psychology; Public Relations.

MATERIALS SCIENCE/METALLURGY

Materials Science is a broad subject which mainly covers physics, chemistry and engineering at one and the same time! From its origins in metallurgy, materials science has now moved into the processing, structure and properties of materials – ceramics, polymers, composites and electrical materials. Materials science and metallurgy are perhaps the most misunderstood of all careers and applications for degree courses are low with very reasonable offers. Valuable bursaries and scholarships are offered by the Institute of Materials, Minerals and Mining (check with Institute – see **Appendix 4**).

Polymer Science is a branch of materials science and is often studied in conjunction with Chemistry and covers such topics as polymer properties and processing relating to industrial applications with, for example, plastics, paints, adhesives. Other courses under this heading include Fashion and Leather Technology. See also **Appendix 4**.

Useful websites www.scienceyear.com; www.eef.org.uk/uksteel; www.iom3.org; www.noisemakers.org.uk; www.imm.org.

NB The points totals shown to the left of the institutions are for ease of reference only. It must not be assumed that Tariff points are always used by institutions or that they can be substituted for an offer in grades. The level of an offer is not necessarily indicative of the quality of a course.

COURSE OFFERS INFORMATION

Subject requirements/preferences **GCSE** (for Engineering/Science courses) Science/mathematics subjects. **AL** Mathematics, physics and/or chemistry required for most courses. (Polymer Science) Mathematics and/or physics usually required; design technology encouraged.

NB In 2011 universities and colleges will differ in their use of GCE AL/AS unit grade information, A* grades, the Extended Project (EPQ), the Advanced Diploma and the Cambridge Pre-U examination when considering applicants and making offers. An EPQ may be accepted in place of an AS subject. Check websites of universities and colleges for the latest offers information.

Your target offers and examples of courses provided by each institution

380 pts **Cambridge** – A*AA college offers may vary (Nat Sci (Mat Sci)) (IB 38–42 pts)

360 pts **Imperial London** – AAA (MEng Mat Sci Eng; Aerosp Mat; Biomat Tiss Eng; Mat Nucl Eng)
London (UCL) – AABe (Hist Art Mat St) (IB 34 pts)
Oxford – AAA (Mat Sci; Mat Econ Mgt) (IB 38–42 pts)
Southampton – AAA (MEng Mech Eng Advnc Mat) (IB 36 pts)

340 pts **Exeter** – AAB–ABB (MEng Mat Eng) (IB 34–31 pts)
Imperial London – AAB (BEng Mat Mgt; Mats; Mat Sci Eng)
Leeds – AAB (Mat Sci Eng; Chem Mat Eng; Chem Miner Eng) (IB 36 pts HL 17 pts)
Loughborough – 340 pts (MEng Mat Eng; Auto Mat) (IB 32 pts)
Manchester – AAB–ABC (Mat Sci Eng courses; Biomed Mat Sci; Tex Sci Tech) (IB 35–32 pts)
Newcastle – AAB (MEng Mech Mat Eng) (IB 36 pts)
St Andrews – AAB 2nd yr entry (Mat Sci; Chem Mat Chem) (IB 34 pts)
Sheffield – AAB (Mat Sci Eng Yr in Jap) (IB 33–30 pts)
Strathclyde – AAB (MEng Mech Eng Mat Eng) (IB 36 pts)

320 pts **Birmingham** – ABB (Metal Mat Eng; Mat Sci Ener Eng; Mat Sci Bus Mgt; Spo Mat Sci) (IB 32 pts)
Exeter – ABB–BBB (BEng Mat Eng) (IB 32–29 pts)
Liverpool – ABB (BEng Mech Mat Eng) (IB 30 pts)
London (QM) – 320 pts (MEng Mat Eng Med; Dntl Mat; Mat Bus; Mat Sci Eng; Env Mat Tech) (IB 32 pts)
St Andrews – ABB 1st yr entry (Mat Sci; Chem Mat Chem) (IB 32 pts)
Sheffield – ABB (MEng Mat Sci Eng courses; Metal; Biomat Sci Tiss Eng; Aerosp Mat) (IB 30–33 pts)

300 pts **Birmingham** – BBB (Biomed Mat Sci)
Bradford – 300 pts (MEng Med Eng)
Edinburgh – BBB (Chem Mat Chem) (IB 32 pts)
Exeter – BBB–BBC (Min Eng)
Liverpool – BBB (BEng Mat Eng; Mat Des Manuf) (IB 28 pts)
Nottingham – BBB (Biomed Mat Sci) (IB 30–32 pts)
Sheffield – BBB–BBC (BEng Mat Sci Eng; Biomat Sci Tiss Eng; Aerosp Mat) (IB 30–33 pts)
Swansea – 300 pts (MEng Mat Sci Eng)

280 pts **Birmingham City** – 280 pts (Fash Des Gmnt Tech)
London (QM) – 280 pts (BEng Biomed Mat Sci Eng; Env Mat Tech; Mat Bus; Dntl Mat; Mat Sci Eng) (IB 28 pts)
Loughborough – 280 pts (BEng Mat Eng; Auto Mat; Des Eng Mat) (IB 28–30 pts)

260 pts **Central Lancashire** – 260 pts (Fire Eng)
Heriot-Watt – BCC 2nd yr entry (Chem Mats; Chem Nanotech) (IB 28 pts)
London (QM) – 260 pts (BSc Mat Sci Eng; Biomat) (IB 26 pts)
Northampton – 260 pts (Mat Tech (Lea))
Swansea – 260 pts (BEng Mat Sci Eng)

240 pts **Bradford** – 240 pts (BEng Med Eng)
De Montfort – 240 pts (Fash Tech)
Edinburgh Napier – 240 pts (Poly Eng)
Manchester Met – 240 pts (Cloth Des Tech; Tex)

220 pts **Heriot-Watt** – CCD–CDD 1st yr entry (Chem Mats; Chem Nanotech)
200 pts **London Met** – 200 pts (Poly Eng)
180 pts **Plymouth** – 180 pts (Mar Cmpstes Tech) (IB 24 pts)

Alternative offers
See **Chapter 7** and **Appendix 1** for grades/UCAS Tariff points information for the International Baccalaureate, Scottish Highers/Advanced Highers, the Welsh Baccalaureate, the Irish Leaving Certificate, the Cambridge Pre-U Diploma, the Advanced Diploma and the Extended Project.

EXAMPLES OF FOUNDATION DEGREES IN THE SUBJECT FIELD
Arts London; Bradford (Coll); Bucks New; De Montfort; Kirklees (Coll); Leeds (CAD); Leeds Met; Leicester (Coll); Liverpool (CmC); London Met; West Anglia (Coll).

CHOOSING YOUR COURSE (SEE ALSO CH.1)
Some course features
Birmingham The courses with Technology, Engineering and Business Management share a common first two years prior to specialisation.
Imperial London All Materials courses are the same for all students in the first two years, with specialisation in the final year, with additional options including management, finance and languages. One-year relevant placements for MEng students.
London (QM) (Dntl Mat) MEng and BEng programmes focus on maxillofacial anatomy, biomaterials, dental materials and materials properties and structures. The MEng fourth year has advanced topics in ceramics and biomaterials with an optional one-year industrial placement after the third year.
Manchester (Biomed Mat Sci) Half the course is shared in common with the Materials Science programme, while half focuses on biology, biochemistry, anatomy and cytology, to study the interactions between materials and different tissue structures of the human body.
Northampton (Mat Tech (Lea)) This course is unique. The University is the UK's leading provider of leather technology courses, and is the only one to have a tannery.

Universities and colleges teaching quality See www.qaa.ac.uk; www.unistats.com.

Top research universities and colleges (RAE 2008) (Metallurgy and Materials) Cambridge; Liverpool; Kent; Oxford; Manchester; Birmingham; Sheffield; Imperial London; Swansea; London (QM).

Examples of sandwich degree courses Loughborough; Manchester; Plymouth; Portsmouth.

ADMISSIONS INFORMATION
Number of applicants per place (approx) Birmingham 8; Imperial London 3; Liverpool 3; Manchester Met 7; Nottingham 7; Southampton 8; Swansea 4.

Advice to applicants and planning the UCAS personal statement Read scientific and engineering journals and describe any special interests you have. Try to visit chemical or technological installations (rubber, plastics, glass etc) and describe your visits. See also **Appendix 4**.

Misconceptions about this course Students are generally unaware of what this subject involves or the opportunities within the industry.

Selection interviews **Yes** Birmingham, Imperial London, Oxford; **Some** Leeds.

Interview advice and questions Questions are likely to be based on A/AS-level science subjects. Recent examples include: Why did you choose Materials Science? How would you make each part of this table lamp (on the interviewer's desk)? Identify this piece of material. How was it manufactured? How has it been treated? (Questions related to metal and polymer samples.) What would you consider the major growth area in materials science? **Birmingham** We try to gauge understanding; for example, an applicant would be unlikely to be questioned on specific facts, but might be asked what they have understood from a piece of coursework at school. **Oxford** Tutors look for an ability to apply logical reasoning to problems in physical science and an enthusiasm for thinking about new concepts in science and engineering. See **Chapter 5**.

AFTER-RESULTS ADVICE

Offers to applicants repeating A-levels **Higher** Swansea; **Same** Birmingham, Leeds, Liverpool, Manchester Met; **No offers made** Cambridge.

GRADUATE DESTINATIONS AND EMPLOYMENT (2007/8 HESA)

Including **Metallurgy**, **Ceramics** and **Polymers**

Materials Science graduates surveyed 480 **Employed** 305 **In further study** 40 **Assumed unemployed** 40.

Career note Materials scientists are involved in a wide range of specialisms in which openings are likely in a range of industries. These include manufacturing processes in which the work is closely linked with that of mechanical, chemical, production and design engineers.

OTHER DEGREE SUBJECTS FOR CONSIDERATION

Aerospace Engineering; Biotechnology; Chemistry; Dentistry; Engineering Sciences; Mathematics; Mechanical Engineering; Medical Engineering; Plastics Technology; Physics; Product Design and Materials; Prosthetics and Orthotics; Sports Technology.

MATHEMATICS

(including **Mathematical Sciences/Studies**)

Mathematics at degree level is an extension of A-level mathematics, covering pure and applied mathematics, statistics, computing, mathematical analysis and mathematical applications. Mathematics is of increasing importance and is used in the simplest of design procedures and not only in applications in the physical sciences and engineering. It also plays a key role in management, economics, medicine and the social and behavioural sciences.

Useful websites www.ima.org.uk; www.gchq.gov.uk/codebreaking; www.orsoc.org.uk; www.scienceyear.com; www.m-a.org.uk; www.mathscareers.org.uk; www.imo.math.ca; www.bmoc.maths.org; www.maths.org; www.ukmt.org.uk.

NB The points totals shown to the left of the institutions are for ease of reference only. It must not be assumed that Tariff points are always used by institutions or that they can be substituted for an offer in grades. The level of an offer is not necessarily indicative of the quality of a course.

COURSE OFFERS INFORMATION

Subject requirements/preferences **GCSE** English often required and mathematics is obviously essential at a high grade for leading universities. **AS** further mathematics may be required. **AL** Mathematics, in several cases with a specified grade, required for all courses. **Other** Maths AEA or STEP papers may be required by some universities (eg **Imperial**, **Warwick**). See also **Chapter 5**. **NB** The level of an offer may depend on whether an applicant is taking AS/AL further maths; check websites.

NB In 2011 universities and colleges will differ in their use of GCE AL/AS unit grade information, A* grades, the Extended Project (EPQ), the Advanced Diploma and the Cambridge Pre-U examination when considering applicants and making offers. An EPQ may be accepted in place of an AS subject. Check websites of universities and colleges for the latest offers information.

Your target offers and examples of courses provided by each institution

440 pts **Warwick** – A*AAa–AAAa (MMaths Maths; Maths Bus St; Maths Econ; Maths Phil; Maths Stats; Maths Phys; MORSE) (IB 39 pts HL maths 6) See **Advice to applicants and planning the UCAS personal statement** below and **Chapter 5**.

Imperial London A*A*A (Maths Comp Sci)

400 pts **London (UCL)** – A*AA+AS (Maths; Maths Modn Langs; Maths Phys; Maths Mgt St; Maths Econ) (IB 36–38 pts HL 766)

380 pts **Cambridge** – A*AA+STEP college offers may vary (Maths; Maths Phys; Educ Maths) (IB 38–42 pts HL 766–777) See **Chapter 5**.

London (King's) – AAA+AS (Maths; Maths Mgt Fin; Maths Phil; Maths Phys) (IB 38 pts H maths 6)

360 pts **Bath** – AAA–AAB (Maths; Mathem Sci; Maths Stats; Comp Sci Maths; Maths Phys) (IB 36 pts HL maths 6)

Birmingham – AAA–AAB (Mathem Eng; Maths; Maths Bus Mgt; Maths Spo Sci) (IB 34 pts HL maths 6)

Bristol – AAA–AAB (Maths; Maths Stats; Maths Comp Sci; Maths Phil; Maths Phys; Biol Maths; Eng Maths) (IB 36 pts HL 666)

Cardiff – AAA (MMaths Maths) (IB 35 pts)

Durham – AAA (Nat Sci (Maths)) (IB 35 pts HL maths 7)

Exeter – AAA–ABB (Maths; Maths Acc; Maths Fin; Maths Mgt) (IB 36 pts)

Imperial London – AAA (Maths; Maths (Pure); Maths Stats; Maths Euro; Maths Mathem Comput) (IB 38 pts)

Leeds – AAA (Maths; Comp Sci Maths) (IB 34 pts HL maths 6)

London LSE – AAA (Bus Maths Stats; Maths Econ)

Loughborough – AAA–AAB (Maths Spo Sci) (IB 36 pts)

Manchester – AAA–AAB (maths A+AB in modules C3/C4) (Maths; Maths Mgt; Maths Bus Mgt; Maths Fin; Maths Fin Maths; Maths Modn Lang) (IB 37–35 pts)

Nottingham – AAA–AAB (Maths; Mathem Phys; Maths Comp Sci; Maths As/Chin St; Maths Eng; Maths Mgt St) (IB 35–38 pts HL maths 6)

Oxford – AAA (Maths; Maths Phil; Maths Comp Sci; Maths Stats) (IB 38–42 pts)

St Andrews – AAA (App Maths; Maths; PMaths; Maths Langs; Arbc Maths)

Sheffield – AAA (Maths Abrd)

Southampton – AAA–AAB (Maths; Mathem St; Maths OR; Maths Act Sci; Maths Langs; Maths Astron; Maths Mus) (IB 36 pts HL 17 pts)
Strathclyde – AAA 2nd yr entry (MMaths Maths) (IB 36 pts)
Surrey – AAA–AAB 360–340 pts (MMaths Maths courses) (IB 34–36 pts)
Sussex – AAA–AAB (MMaths Maths; Maths Econ; Maths Comp Sci) (IB 36 pts)
York – AAA–AABa (MMaths Maths; Maths Phys; Maths Comp Sci) (IB 34–32 pts)

350 pts **Brunel** – 350 pts (MMaths Maths) (IB 33 pts HL maths 6)

340 pts **Aberystwyth** – 340 pts (MMaths Maths) (IB 31 pts)
Cardiff – AAB (BSc Maths; Maths Apps; Maths OR Stats; Maths Welsh; Maths Relig St) (IB 33 pts HL maths 6)
Durham – AAB (MMaths; BSc Maths; Maths (Euro St); Educ St Maths) (IB 35 pts HL maths 7)
East Anglia – AAB (MMath Maths; Maths Euro; Maths Aus/N Am) (IB 33 pts)
Edinburgh – AAB (MA Maths)
Heriot-Watt – AAB 2nd yr entry (Fin Maths)
Lancaster – AAB (Maths Abrd) (IB 30–31 pts)
Leeds – AAB (Maths St; Act Maths; Mathem St)
Leicester – AAB (Maths; Fin Maths; Comput Maths; Maths Astron; Maths Mgt; Maths Euro/USA) (IB 28–32 pts)
London (QM) – 340 pts (MSci Maths) (IB 32 pts HL maths 6)
Loughborough – AAB–AAC (Maths Mgt; Maths; Maths Acc Fin Mgt; Fin Maths)
Newcastle – AAB (MMaths Maths; Maths; Fin Maths Mgt; Mathem Sci; Maths Biol; Maths Psy) (IB 34–36 pts HL maths 6)
Queen's Belfast – AAB (MSci Maths Comp Sci; Maths; Maths Stats OR; App Maths Phys)
Sheffield – AAB (MMaths Maths; Fin Maths) (IB 32–37 pts)
Strathclyde – AAB 1st yr entry (MMaths Maths) **and** 2nd yr entry (BSc Maths courses)
Surrey – AAB–ABB 340–320 pts (BSc Maths; Fin Maths; Maths Mus; Maths Mgt)
Sussex – AAB–ABB (BSc Maths) (IB 34–36 pts)
York – AAB–ABBa (Maths 3 yrs; Maths Stats; Ling Maths; Maths Fin; Maths Phys)

320 pts **Aston** – ABB–BBB 320 pts (Maths; Maths Comp; Maths Joint Hons) (IB 31–33 pts)
Brunel – 320 pts (Fin Maths) (IB 32 pts)
East Anglia – ABB (BSc Maths; Maths Mgt St; Maths Econ; Maths Stats; Maths Comp) (IB 32 pts HL maths 6)
Edinburgh – ABB (PMaths; Maths Mus; BSc Maths; Maths Stats; Maths Mgt) (IB 32 pts)
Glasgow – ABB (Mathematics) (IB 28 pts)
Heriot-Watt – ABB 1st yr entry (Fin Maths; App Maths; PMaths; Mathem Sci)
Lancaster – ABB (BSc Maths; Maths Stats; Maths Phil) (IB 30–31 pts)
Liverpool – ABB (Maths; Mathem Sci; Mathem Phys; PMaths; Maths Mgt) (IB 33 pts)
London (RH) – ABB 320 pts (Maths courses) (IB 33 pts HL maths 6)
London (QM) – 320 pts (BSc Maths; Maths Bus Mgt Fin; Maths Psy; Maths Stats Fin Econ)
Reading – 320–340 pts (Maths; Maths App Stats; Maths Meteor; Maths Stats Comput Maths)
Sheffield – ABB–BBB (BSc Maths; Maths Astron; Maths Phil; Maths Phys; Maths Euro; Maths Fr/Ger/Span) (IB 32–37 pts HL maths 5)
Swansea – 320 pts (MMaths Maths)

300 pts **Aberystwyth** – 300 pts (BSc Maths; PMaths; App Maths; Fin Maths) (IB 27 pts)
Bristol UWE – 300 pts (Mathematics) (IB 24–28 pts)
Brunel – 300 pts (Maths Comp; Mathem Mgt St; Maths Stats Mgt) (IB 30 pts)
City – BBB 300 pts (Maths Fin; Mathem Sci; Mathem Sci Fin Econ) (IB 28 pts)
Dundee – BBB 300 pts 2nd yr entry (Maths courses) (IB 28 pts)
Essex – 300–320 pts (Maths; Maths Biol; Maths Hum courses; Maths Crypt Net Scrty) (IB 29–32 pts)
Keele – 300 pts (Maths courses)
Liverpool Hope – 300 pts (Maths Educ QTS)
Northumbria – 300 pts (Maths; Maths Bus) (IB 30 pts)

Plymouth – 300 pts (Maths; Maths Fin)
Queen's Belfast – ABC (BSc Comput Maths; Maths; Maths Stats OR; App Maths Phys; Maths Euro)
Stirling – BBB 2nd yr entry (Maths Apps)
Strathclyde – BBB 1st yr entry (BSc Maths courses)
Swansea – 300 pts (BSc Maths; PMaths; App Maths; Maths Langs; Maths Spo Sci; Maths Geoinform; Maths Fin)

280 pts **Central Lancashire** – 280 pts (Mathematics)
Glamorgan – 280–320 pts (Maths courses)
Kent – 280–300 pts (MMaths/BSc/BA Maths; Bus Maths; Fin Maths; Maths Stats) (IB 28 pts)
Staffordshire – 280 pts (Maths courses)
Stranmillis (UC) – BBC (Maths Educ)

260 pts **Bolton** – 260 pts (Maths courses)
Brighton – BCC 260 pts (Maths; Maths Fin; Maths Bus; Maths Comp) (IB 28 pts)
Canterbury Christ Church – BCC (Maths Educ QTS)
Kingston – 260 pts (Mathem Sci; Act Maths Stats; Maths; Fin Maths) (IB 26–28 pts)
Manchester Met – 260 pts (Maths Fin Maths)
Oxford Brookes – BCC (Mathematics) (IB 30 pts)
Portsmouth – 260 pts (Maths; Maths Stats; Maths Fin Mgt)

240 pts **Aberdeen** – CCC (Maths courses)
Bradford – 240 pts (Comput Maths)
Bristol UWE – 240–300 pts (Comp App Maths)
Central Lancashire – 240 pts (Maths Joint/Comb Hons)
Coventry – 240 pts (Mathematics)
Cumbria – 240–200 pts (Maths Educ)
Derby – 240–180 pts (Mathem St; Maths; Mathem St Educ)
Dundee – CCC 1st yr entry (Maths courses)
Nottingham Trent – 240 pts (Maths; Spo Sci Maths)
Oxford Brookes – CCC (Mathem Sci; Maths Comb Hons)

220 pts **Chester** – 220–260 pts (Maths courses) (IB 24 pts)
Chichester – CCD 220–280 pts (Maths Educ QTS)
Coventry – 220 pts (Maths Comp; Maths Stats; Eng Maths)
Hertfordshire – 220–260 pts (Comput Maths; Maths; Fin Maths Psy)
Liverpool John Moores – 220–260 pts (Maths Stats Comp; Bus Maths; Maths Educ QTS)
Stirling – CCD 1st yr entry (Maths Apps)
Winchester – 220–280 pts (Maths P Educ)

200 pts **Coventry** – 200 pts (Mathem Sci)
London Met – 200 pts (Maths; Mathem Sci)
Manchester Met – 200 pts (Maths Comb Hons)
Sheffield Hallam – 200 pts (Mathematics)

160 pts **Bishop Grosseteste (UC)** – 160 pts (Educ St Maths)
Greenwich – 160–180 pts (Fin Maths; Maths Comp)
Wolverhampton – 160–220 pts (Mathem Sci; Maths)

140 pts **West Scotland** – CD (Mathem Sci)

80 pts **London (Birk)** – 80 pts for under 21s (over 21s varies) (p/t Maths Stats)

Open University – contact +44 (0)845 300 6090 or www.openuniversity.co.uk/you

Alternative offers

See **Chapter 7** and **Appendix 1** for grades/UCAS Tariff points information for the International Baccalaureate, Scottish Highers/Advanced Highers, the Welsh Baccalaureate, the Irish Leaving Certificate, the Cambridge Pre-U Diploma, the Advanced Diploma and the Extended Project.

EXAMPLES OF FOUNDATION DEGREES IN THE SUBJECT FIELD

London Met.

CHOOSING YOUR COURSE (SEE ALSO CH.1)

Some course features
East Anglia Six courses are offered in which one third of the time is spent on a subsidiary subject.
Lancaster The Mathematics degree course is for those students wanting to specialise in Pure Mathematics whilst having the option to include some statistics or another subject.
London (QM) A wide range of joint courses are available offering specialisms in accounting, business, computing and finance.
Sheffield Mathematics can be studied with modern languages, astronomy and computer science and with placements in Europe.
York In the four-year programme students spend a third of the year at one of several European universities (a language at AS-level is normally required).

Universities and colleges teaching quality See www.qaa.ac.uk; www.unistats.com.

Top research universities and colleges (RAE 2008) (Pure Maths) Imperial London; Warwick; Oxford; Cambridge; Bristol; Edinburgh; Heriot-Watt; Bath; Aberdeen; London (King's); Manchester; London (UCL); Durham; East Anglia; Sheffield; London (QM); (Applied Maths) Cambridge; Oxford; Bristol; St Andrews; Bath; Portsmouth; Warwick; Manchester; Imperial London; Durham; Southampton; Nottingham; Surrey.

Examples of sandwich degree courses Aston; Bath; Bradford; Brighton; Bristol UWE; Brunel; Cardiff; Coventry; East Anglia; Glamorgan; Greenwich; Hertfordshire; Kingston; Liverpool John Moores; Loughborough; Manchester Met; Northumbria; Nottingham Trent; Portsmouth; Reading; Staffordshire; Surrey; West Scotland; Wolverhampton; York.

ADMISSIONS INFORMATION

Number of applicants per place (approx) Aberystwyth 8, (App Maths) 5; Anglia Ruskin 6; Aston 8; Bangor 4; Bath 6; Birmingham 4; Bristol 7; Brunel 5; Cambridge 4; Cardiff 5; Central Lancashire 7; City 6; Coventry 8; Cumbria 9; Derby 4; Dundee 5; Durham 5; East Anglia 5; East London 2; Edinburgh 4; Exeter 6; Glamorgan 3; Greenwich 2; Hertfordshire 9; Heriot-Watt 5; Kent 8; Lancaster 12; Leeds (Maths) 5, (Maths Fin) 4; Leicester 8; Liverpool 5; London (Gold) 5, (King's) 8, (QM) 5, (RH) 8, (UCL) 8; London LSE (Maths Econ) 10, (Bus Maths Stats) 10; London Met 3; Manchester Met 3; Middlesex 5; Newcastle 7; Northumbria 7; Nottingham 7; Oxford Brookes 21; Plymouth 8; Portsmouth 7; Sheffield 5; Sheffield Hallam 3; Southampton 9–10; Strathclyde 6; Surrey 7; Warwick 6; Westminster 3; York 6.

Advice to applicants and planning the UCAS personal statement Any interests you have in careers requiring mathematical ability could be mentioned – for example, engineering, computers (hardware and software) and business applications. Show determination, love of mathematics and an appreciation of the rigour of the course. Give details of your skills, work experience, positions of responsibility. A variety of non-academic interests to complement the applicant's academic abilities preferred. For non-EU students fluency in oral and written English required. **Manchester** Unit grades may form part of an offer. **Warwick** The Mathematics offer will not be decided until the autumn of 2010, but it is likely to include at least one A* in one of the standard offers. Offers for courses in Statistics (MORSE, Mathematics and Statistics) may include achievement requirements in selected unit grades. Check University website for latest information. See also **Appendix 4**.

Misconceptions about this course **London (QM)** Some believe that a study of mechanics is compulsory – it is not. **Surrey** Maths is not just about calculations: it focuses on reasoning, logic and applications. **York** Further maths is not required.

Selection interviews **Yes** Aberystwyth, Bath, Birmingham, Bishop Grosseteste (UC), Bristol UWE, Brunel, Cambridge, Cardiff, Central Lancashire, City, Coventry, Durham, East London, Essex, Exeter, Glamorgan, Heriot-Watt, Imperial London, Kent, Kingston, Lancaster, Leeds, Liverpool, Liverpool John Moores, London (Gold), (King's), (RH), (UCL), London Met, Manchester Met, Newcastle, Northampton, Northumbria, Nottingham, Oxford, Reading, Salford, Sheffield, Southampton, Sussex, Warwick, York; **Some** Brighton, Bristol, East Anglia, Greenwich, London LSE (rarely), Loughborough.

Interview advice and questions Questions are likely to be asked arising from the information you have given in your UCAS application and about your interests in the subject. Questions in recent years have included: How many ways are there of incorrectly setting up the back row of a chess board? A ladder on a rough floor leans against a smooth wall. Describe the forces acting on the ladder and give the maximum possible angle of inclination possible. There are three particles connected by a string; the middle one is made to move – describe the subsequent motion of the particles. What mathematics books have you read outside your syllabus? Why does a ball bounce? Discuss the work of any renowned mathematician. Balance a pencil on your index fingers and then try to move both towards the centre of the pencil. Explain what is happening in terms of forces and friction. **Cambridge** If you could spend half an hour with any mathematician past or present, who would it be? **Oxford** (Maths Phil) What makes you think I'm having thoughts? What was the most beautiful proof in A-level mathematics? I am an oil baron in the desert and I need to deliver oil to four different towns which happen to lie in a straight line. In order to deliver the correct amount to each town I must visit each town in turn, returning to my warehouse in between each visit. Where would I position my warehouse in order to drive the shortest possible distance? Roads are no problem since I have a friend who will build me as many roads as I like for free. **Southampton** Personal statements generate discussion points. Our interviews are informal chats and so technical probing is kept low key. See **Chapter 5**.

Reasons for rejection (non-academic) Usually academic reasons only. Lack of motivation. We were somewhat uneasy about how much mathematics he will remember after a gap year running a theatre in South Africa. **Birmingham** A poorly-written and poorly-organised personal statement.

AFTER-RESULTS ADVICE

Offers to applicants repeating A-levels **Higher** Brighton, Coventry, Essex, Glasgow, London Met, Salford, Strathclyde, Swansea, Surrey, Warwick; **Possibly higher** Cambridge (Hom), Durham, Lancaster, Leeds, Newcastle, Sheffield; **Same** Aberystwyth, Aston, Bath, Birmingham, Bristol, Brunel, Chester, East Anglia, Liverpool, Liverpool Hope, London (RH), Loughborough (usually), Manchester Met, Nottingham, Nottingham Trent, Oxford Brookes, Sheffield Hallam, Southampton, Stirling, Ulster, Wolverhampton, York; **No offers made** Cambridge.

GRADUATE DESTINATIONS AND EMPLOYMENT (2007/8 HESA)

Mathematics graduates surveyed 3345 **Employed** 1365 **In further study** 795 **Assumed unemployed** 295.

Operational research graduates surveyed 50 **Employed** 25 **In further study** 15 **Assumed unemployed** none.

Career note Graduates enter a range of careers. Whilst business, finance and retail areas are popular options, mathematicians also have important roles in the manufacturing industries. Mathematics offers the pleasure of problem-solving, the satisfaction of a rigorous argument and the most widely employable non-vocational degree subject. A student's view: 'Maths trains you to work in the abstract, to think creatively and to come up with concrete conclusions'. These transferable skills are much sought-after by employers. Employment prospects are excellent, with high salaries.

OTHER DEGREE SUBJECTS FOR CONSIDERATION

Accountancy; Actuarial Studies; Astronomy; Astrophysics; Computer Science; Economics; Engineering Sciences; Operational Research; Physics; Statistics.

MEDIA STUDIES

(including **Broadcasting** and **Journalism**; see also **Art and Design (General), Communication Studies/Communication, Computer Courses, Engineering (Acoustics and Sound)** and **Film, Radio, Video and TV Studies**)

Intending Media applicants need to check course details carefully since this subject area can involve graphic design, illustration and other art courses as well as the media in the fields of TV, radio and journalism. Courses in Journalism include block and day release, evening/weekend magazine journalism, and photo-journalism. Full details can be obtained by referring to www.nctj.com/courses.

Useful websites www.bbc.co.uk/jobs; www.newspapersoc.org.uk; www.ppa.co.uk; http://careers.thomsonreuters.com; www.arts.org.uk; www.nctj.com; www.ipa.co.uk; www.camfoundation.com; www.mediastudies.com.

NB The points totals shown to the left of the institutions are for ease of reference only. It must not be assumed that Tariff points are always used by institutions or that they can be substituted for an offer in grades. The level of an offer is not necessarily indicative of the quality of a course.

COURSE OFFERS INFORMATION

Subject requirements/preferences **GCSE** English and mathematics often required. **AL** No specified subjects required.

NB In 2011 universities and colleges will differ in their use of GCE AL/AS unit grade information, A* grades, the Extended Project (EPQ), the Advanced Diploma and the Cambridge Pre-U examination when considering applicants and making offers. An EPQ may be accepted in place of an AS subject. Check websites of universities and colleges for the latest offers information.

Your target offers and examples of courses provided by each institution

360 pts **London (UCL)** – AABe–BBBe (Sci Comm Plcy) (IB 32–36 pts)

340 pts **Brunel** – BBB +AS/EPQ c (Jrnl; Broad Media (Des Tech)) (IB 32 pts)
East Anglia – AAB–BBB (Media St)
London (Gold) – AAB (Media Comm) (IB 34 pts)
Newcastle – AAB (Media Comm Cult St) (IB 30–32 pts)
Strathclyde – AAB (Jrnl Crea Writ courses)

320 pts **Birmingham** – ABB (Media Cult Soty courses) (IB 32–34 pts)
Bournemouth – 320 pts (Multim Jrnl; Multim Bus Entre; Comm Media)
Cardiff – ABB (Jrnl Media Cult St) (IB 36 pts)
Central Lancashire – ABB–BBB (Spo Jrnl)
City – ABB 320 pts (Jrnl; Jrnl Soc Sci)
East Anglia – ABB–BBB (Soty Cult Media; Pol Media) (IB 31–32 pts)
Leeds – ABB (Broad Jrnl)
Leicester – ABB (Comm Media Soty)
Liverpool – ABB (Comm Media Pop Mus courses)
London (RH) – ABB (Media Arts) (IB 34 pts)
Loughborough – ABB (Comm Media St) (IB 34 pts)
Sheffield – ABB (Jrnl St) (IB 34–32 pts)
Surrey – ABB–BBB 320–300 pts (Media St)
Sussex – ABB–BBB (Media courses) (IB 32–34 pts)

300 pts **Bournemouth** – 300 pts (Multim Comm Sys; Dig Media Dev; Interact Media Prod)
Brighton – BBB 300 pts (Broad Jrnl)
Brunel – 300 pts (Comm Media St)
Central Lancashire – 300 pts (Web Multim)
Hastings (Univ Centre) – BBB (Broad Jrnl) (IB 32 pts)
Kent – BBB (Jrnl News Ind) (IB 33 pts HL 15 pts)
Kingston – 300–320 pts (Journalism)
Lancaster – BBB (Media Cult St) (IB 29 pts)
Leicester – BBB (Media Sociol) (IB 30 pts)
Lincoln – 300 pts (Media Prod)
London (Gold) – BBB (Media Sociol)
Northumbria – 300 pts (Jrnl; Jrnl Engl Lit; Media Jrnl)
Nottingham Trent – 300 pts (Broad Jrnl)
Oldham (Coll Univ Centre) – 300 pts (Dig Jrnl)
Salford – 300 pts (Media Perf)

Sheffield – BBB (Jrnl Fr/Ger St/Hisp St/Russ) (IB 34–32 pts)
Swansea – 300 pts (Media St courses)
Westminster – BBB (Jrnl; Jrnl Contemp Arbc/Chin St) (IB 30 pts)

285 pts **Cardiff (UWIC)** – 285 pts (Media St Vis Cult)

280 pts **Birmingham City** – 280 pts (Media Comm courses) (IB 32 pts)
Brighton – BBC 280 pts (Dig Media; Media St) (IB 30 pts)
Bristol UWE – 280–340 pts (Jrnl Media Cult St; Int Rel Jrnl)
City – BBC 280 pts (Sociol Media St) (IB 30 pts)
Glamorgan – 280–320 pts (Jrnl; Media Comm; Media Prod)
Huddersfield – 280 pts (Adv Media Rel)
Kingston – 280–320 pts (Media Cult St)
Liverpool John Moores – 280–320 pts (Broad Media Prod; Jrnl)
Nottingham – BBC (Int Media Comm St)
Oxford Brookes – BBC–BCC (Comm Media Cult courses)
Roehampton – 280–340 pts (Jrnl News Media)
Salford – 280 pts (Jrnl courses)
Staffordshire – 280 pts (Jrnl courses)
Stirling – BBC (pre-application experience req) (Jrnl St courses; Film Media courses)
Teesside – 280 pts (Multim Jrnl (Prof Prac))

260 pts **Bangor** – 260–300 pts (Media St courses)
Birmingham City – 260–280 pts (Multim Tech)
Canterbury Christ Church – 260 pts (Jrnl; Multim)
Central Lancashire – 260–240 pts (Engl Lang Jrnl; Jrnl)
Glasgow Caledonian – BCC (Jrnl; Media Comm)
Gloucestershire – 260–220 pts (Media Comm Cult courses; Multim Web Des; Jrnl)
Leeds Met – 260 pts (Journalism)
Lincoln – 260 pts (Jrnl courses)
Liverpool Hope – 260 pts (Media courses)
Northumbria – 260 pts (Media Cult Soty; Media Prod)
Plymouth – 260 pts (Media Arts) (IB 28 pts)
Queen Margaret – 260 pts (Media; PR Media)

240 pts **Abertay Dundee** – 240 pts (Vis Comm Media Des)
Bangor – 240–260 pts (Jrnl Media St)
Bolton – 240 pts (Media Writ Prod; Film Media St)
Bradford – 240 pts (Media St courses)
Brighton – CCC/BCD 240–280 pts (Media Engl St; Env Broad Media Prod) (IB 28 pts)
Chester – 240–280 pts (Media St courses; Jrnl) (IB 24 pts)
Coventry – 240–280 pts (Comm Cult Media; Jrnl Media; Media Prod)
De Montfort – 240 pts (Media Comm courses; Jrnl courses)
Derby – 240 pts (Broad Media courses; Jrnl; Media St)

Dundee – CCC (Inter Media Des)
Edinburgh Napier – 240 pts (Journalism)
Leeds Trinity (UC) – 240–200 pts (Jrnl; Media courses)
Liverpool John Moores – 240–280 pts (Int Jrnl; Media Cult Comm)
Nottingham Trent – 240–280 pts (Media; Media Joint Hons; Prnt Jrnl)
Nottingham Trent – 240 pts (Multimedia)
Plymouth – 240 pts (Multim Prod Tech)
Portsmouth – 240–300 pts (Media St joint courses)
Robert Gordon – CCC (Jrnl; Media)
Roehampton – 240–320 pts (Media Cult courses)
Sheffield Hallam – 240–260 pts (Media St; Jrnl)
Southampton Solent – 240 pts (Jrnl; Media Comm; Spo Jrnl; Jrnl Engl Media)
Sunderland – 240 pts (Broad Jrnl; Media Cult Comm; Fash Jrnl; Int Jrnl; Mag Jrnl; Spo Jrnl)
Ulster – 240–280 pts (Media St courses; Jrnl courses)
Winchester – 240–300 pts (Media Prod; Jrnl; Media St Comb courses) (IB 26–28 pts)

220 pts **Bath Spa** – 220–260 pts (Media Comm)
Chichester – CCD 240–220 pts (Media St courses; Media Prod courses) (IB 28 pts)
Creative Arts – 220–240 pts (Media Arts; Fash Jrnl; Mus Jrnl; Spo Jrnl; Mtrg Jrnl) (IB 24–30 pts)
Edge Hill – 220–260 pts (Media Joint Hons; Jrnl St; Jrnl (Prof Prac))
Falmouth (UC) – 220 pts (Dig Media)
Hertfordshire – 220–280 pts (Jrnl Media Cult Comb St; Scrn Cult Media Prac)
Leeds Met – 220 pts (Media Pop Cult)
Manchester Met – 220–280 pts (Dig Media)
Newman (UC) – 220–260 pts (Psy Media Comm)
Northampton – 220–260 pts (Media St courses; Media Prod)
Teesside – 220–260 pts (Media St; Broad Media Prod)
Winchester – 220–260 pts (Dig Media Dev)
Worcester – 220–260 pts (Media Cult St courses; Crea Dig Media)

200 pts **Bucks New** – 200–240 pts (Jrnl; Spo Media Mgt)
Canterbury Christ Church – 200–240 pts (Dig Media courses; Media Cult St joint courses)
Chester – 200–240 pts (Multim Tech courses)
East London – 200 pts (Media Crea Ind; Media St; Jrnl; Spo Jrnl)
Glyndŵr – 200 pts (Broad Jrnl Media Comms; Broad Jrnl Crea Writ)
Kingston – 200–280 pts (Media Tech)
London Met – 200–240 pts (Media Arts courses; Dig Media courses; Mass Comms; Jrnl)
Middlesex – 200–240 pts (Crea Media Writ; Media Cult St; Jrnl Comm; Pub Jrnl Media)
Portsmouth – 200–280 pts (Dig Media)
Suffolk (Univ Campus) – 200 pts (Film Media)
Thames Valley – 200 pts (Media St; Mus Media; Broad Jrnl)
UCP Marjon – 200 pts (Writ Media; Media St courses; Media Prod; Spo Media)
York St John – 200–240 pts (Media courses)

190 pts **Buckingham** – 190 pts (Comm Media Jrnl)

180 pts **Anglia Ruskin** – 180–220 pts (Media courses)
Huddersfield – 180–240 pts (Multim courses; Interact Media)
Newman (UC) – 180 pts (Media Comm courses except under **220 pts**)
St Mary's Twickenham (UC) – 180–200 pts (Media Arts)
Trinity Saint David – 180–240 pts (Media St courses; Media Prod)
Westminster – BC (Contemp Media Prac) (IB 26 pts)

160 pts **Abertay Dundee** – CC (Media Cult Soty)
Arts London – 160 pts (Jrnl; Media Cult St)
Bedfordshire – 160 pts (Media Prac courses; Jrnl)
East London – 160 pts (Media Tech)
Greenwich – 160 pts (Media Writ)

Grimsby (IFHE) – 160 pts (Journalism)
London South Bank – 160 pts (Media Cult St; Mgt Media St; Prnt Onln Jrnl)
South Essex (Coll) – 160 pts (Journalism)
Southampton Solent – 160 pts (Media Tech)
Swansea Met – 160 pts (Multimedia)
West Scotland – CC (Multim Tech)
Wolverhampton – 160–220 pts (Media Cult St; Media Comm St; Broad Jrnl)
120 pts **Wirral Met (Coll)** – DD (Media St)
80 pts **Farnborough (CT)** – 80–160 pts (Media Prod)

Alternative offers
See **Chapter 7** and **Appendix 1** for grades/UCAS Tariff points information for the International Baccalaureate, Scottish Highers/Advanced Highers, the Welsh Baccalaureate, the Irish Leaving Certificate, the Cambridge Pre-U Diploma, the Advanced Diploma and the Extended Project.

EXAMPLES OF FOUNDATION DEGREES IN THE SUBJECT FIELD
Arts London (CComm); Bath Spa; Blackpool and Fylde (Coll); Bournemouth; Brighton; Bristol City (Coll); Bucks New; City; Cornwall (Coll); East Riding (Coll); Exeter (Coll); Falmouth (UC); Farnborough (CT); Glyndŵr; Highbury (Coll); Hull (Coll); Liverpool (CmC); Llandrillo Cymru (Coll); Manchester (Coll); Neath Port Talbot (Coll); Newcastle (Coll); Norwich City (Coll); Nottingham New (Coll); Plymouth; Plymouth City (Coll); Sheffield (Coll); South Cheshire (Coll); South Devon (Coll); South Essex (Coll); South Nottingham (Coll); Stockport (Coll); Suffolk (Univ Campus); Truro (Coll); Westminster Kingsway (Coll); Wolverhampton.

CHOOSING YOUR COURSE (SEE ALSO CH.1)
Some course features
City The Journalism course is a vocational programme in which students are encouraged to spend their third year doing work placements or paid employment in the industry.
London (RH) (Media Arts) Course offers theoretical studies and practical production including drama documentaries, performance pieces and art projects.
Loughborough (Comm Media St) A broad course which includes options in public relations, political marketing, the magazine business and the book trade. French, German and Spanish are offered in Year 1.

Universities and colleges teaching quality See www.qaa.ac.uk; www.unistats.com.

Top research universities and colleges (RAE 2008) See **Communication Studies/Communication**.

Examples of sandwich degree courses Bournemouth; Bradford; Brighton; Brunel; City; De Montfort; Gloucestershire; Greenwich; Hertfordshire; Huddersfield; Kingston; Leeds Met; Lincoln; Liverpool John Moores; Plymouth; Sheffield Hallam; Staffordshire; Surrey; Ulster; Worcester; York.

ADMISSIONS INFORMATION
Number of applicants per place (approx) Birmingham 10; Bournemouth (Interact Media Prod) 24, (Multim Jrnl) 30; Bradford 13; Bristol UWE 20; Canterbury Christ Church 23; Cardiff 11; Cardiff (UWIC) 3; Central Lancashire 33; Chichester 6; City 50; Creative Arts 3; Cumbria 4; De Montfort 11; East London 27; Falmouth (UC) 4; Gloucestershire 25; Greenwich 12; Lincoln 4; London (Gold) 13, (RH) 11; London South Bank 11; Newport 12; Northampton 4; Northumbria 14; Nottingham Trent 5; Plymouth City (Coll) 33; Portsmouth 5; Sheffield Hallam 56; South Essex (Coll) 10; Southampton Solent (Jrnl) 20, (Media Tech) 6; Strathclyde (Jrnl) 20; Swansea Met 5; Teesside 33; Winchester 7; West Scotland 6; Westminster 44.

Advice to applicants and planning the UCAS personal statement Work experience or work shadowing is important. Contact local newspaper offices to meet journalists and to discuss their work. Contact local radio stations and advertising agencies, read newspapers (all types) and be able to describe the different approaches of newspapers. Watch TV coverage of news stories and the way in which the interviewer deals with politicians or members of the public. Give your opinions on the various forms of media. School magazine and/or any published work should be mentioned. A balance of academic and practical skills preferred. Creativity, problem-solving, cultural awareness, communication skills and commitment required. (International students: Fluency in written and spoken English required.) See also **Communication Studies/Communication** and **Appendix 4**.

Misconceptions about this course **Birmingham City** That Media courses are soft options: they are not! **Cardiff (UWIC)** Some applicants believe that the course will automatically lead to a job in the media – it won't. This depends on the student developing other employment skills and experience. **Cumbria** This is not a Media Studies course: it is a highly practical media production course. **Lincoln** (Media Prod) BTEC applicants may think that this is a technology-based course.

Selection interviews **Yes** Anglia Ruskin, Bournemouth, Brunel, Creative Arts, Dundee, East Anglia, Glamorgan, Huddersfield, Liverpool John Moores, London (Gold), (RH), London South Bank, Portsmouth, Sheffield Hallam, Solihull (Coll), South Essex (Coll), Staffordshire, Swansea Met, Thames Valley (group interview), UCP Marjon, York; **Some** Abertay Dundee, Bath Spa, Cardiff, Cardiff (UWIC), Chichester, City, Nottingham Trent, Salford, Sunderland, Wolverhampton.

Interview advice and questions Past questions include: Which newspapers do you read? Discuss the main differences between the national daily newspapers. Which radio programmes do you listen to each day? Which television programmes do you watch? Should the BBC broadcast advertisements? What do you think are the reasons for the popularity of EastEnders? Film or video work, if required, should be edited to a running time of 15 minutes unless otherwise stated. **Cardiff (UWIC)** What is your favourite area in respect of popular culture? Are you considering taking up the work placement module? If so where would you plan to go? **Cumbria** Role of journalism in society. What is today's main news story? Who is Rupert Murdoch? **Lincoln** Give a written or verbal critique of a media product. See **Chapter 5**.

Reasons for rejection (non-academic) No clear commitment (to Broadcast Journalism) plus no evidence of experience (now proving to be essential). Mistaken expectations of the nature of the course. Can't write and doesn't work well in groups. Too specific and narrow areas of media interest, for example, video or script-writing. Lack of knowledge of current affairs. **Cardiff (UWIC)** Lack of experience in the field. Application arrived too late. **City** Inadequate English language.

AFTER-RESULTS ADVICE

Offers to applicants repeating A-levels **Same** Abertay Dundee, Birmingham City, Cardiff, Cardiff (UWIC), Chester, Chichester, City, De Montfort, Huddersfield, Lincoln, Loughborough, Manchester Met, Nottingham Trent, St Mary's Twickenham (UC), Salford, South Essex (Coll), Staffordshire, Sunderland, Winchester, Wolverhampton.

GRADUATE DESTINATIONS AND EMPLOYMENT (2007/8 HESA)

Media Studies graduates surveyed 4035 **Employed** 2190 **In further study** 275 **Assumed unemployed** 515.

Journalism graduates surveyed 1175 **Employed** 690 **In further study** 90 **Assumed unemployed** 140.

Career note See **Film, Radio, Video and TV Studies**.

OTHER DEGREE SUBJECTS FOR CONSIDERATION

Advertising; Communication; English; Film, Radio and TV Studies; Journalism; Photography; Public Relations.

MEDICINE

(for **Medical Sciences** see **Biological Sciences**)

Medicine is a highly popular choice of degree subject and career. All courses listed below include the same areas of study and training and all lead to a qualification and career in medicine.

Medical schools aim to produce doctors who are clinically competent, who are able to see patients as people and have a holistic and ethical approach (including the ability to understand and manage each patient's case in a family and social context as well as in hospital), who treat patients and colleagues with respect, dignity and sensitivity, are skilled at teamwork and are prepared for continual learning. These aims in several ways reflect the qualities which selectors seek when interviewing applicants. In all cases, close attention will be paid to the confidential report on the UCAS application to judge the applicant's personality, communication skills, academic potential and commitment to a medical career. Methods of teaching may vary slightly, depending on the medical school. To achieve these aims, some medical schools adopt the system of self-directed learning (SDL) in which objectives are set to assess students' progress, and problem-based learning (PBL) which helps students to develop critical thinking and clinical problem-solving skills.

Whilst there is a core curriculum of knowledge, the first three years integrate scientific and clinical experience, and there are fewer formal lectures than before, with more group and individual work. For outstanding students without science A-levels, some pre-medical courses are available. Thereafter for all, a period of pre-clinical studies leads on to clinical studies. Most medical schools also offer an extra year of study, usually in the middle of the medical degree, to enable students to research a scientific subject leading to an 'intercalated' BSc degree. Additionally, elective periods abroad in the final year can sometimes be taken.

Useful websites www.scicentral.com; www.ipem.org.uk; www.bmj.com; www.admissionstests.cambridgeassessment.org.uk; www.gmc-uk.org; www.nhscareers.nhs.uk.

Applicants for places in Medicine may select only **four** universities or medical schools.

COURSE OFFERS INFORMATION

Subject requirements/preferences **GCSE** In all cases a good spread of science and non-science subjects will be expected at high grades.

Aberdeen English, mathematics, biology, physics or dual award science. Combinations of AB grades, especially in sciences.

Birmingham Seven GCSEs at A* including chemistry, English language and mathematics normally at grade A. Dual science award grade A acceptable as an alternative to physics and biology.

Brighton and Sussex (MS) Mathematics and English at grade B, biology and chemistry.

Bristol Five A/A* grades to include mathematics, English and two sciences.

Cambridge Mathematics, physics, chemistry or dual science award.

Cardiff English or Welsh at grade B, mathematics at grade B or above, grades AA in dual science or AAA in three sciences.

Dundee Chemistry and biology or human biology essential.

Durham See **Newcastle**

East Anglia Six GCSE subjects at grade A including science, mathematics and English.

Edinburgh English, mathematics, biology, chemistry or dual science award at grade B or higher.

Glasgow English, chemistry, biology (preferred), mathematics and physics.

Hull York (MS) Six subjects grades A*-C: English and mathematics at grade B or higher plus chemistry and biology.

Imperial London Chemistry, biology, physics (or dual science award) plus mathematics and English. At least three subjects are required at grade A, and two subjects at grade B.

Keele Chemistry, physics, biology (dual science award acceptable, grades BB minimum), English language and mathematics at grade B minimum. A broad spread of subjects is expected with a minimum of four at grade A.

Lancaster (see **Liverpool**)

Leeds Six subjects at grade B minimum including English, mathematics, chemistry and biology or dual science award.

Leicester English language and sciences (including chemistry) or dual science award.

Liverpool Nine subjects grades A–C, including dual science (or biology, chemistry and physics), English language and mathematics at grade B minimum.

London (King's) Grade B (minimum) in chemistry, biology and physics (or dual science award), English and mathematics.

London (QM) Six subjects at AB minimum grades including English, mathematics and science subjects.

London (St George's) 416 pts required (A* 58 pts, A 52 pts, B 46 pts, C 40 pts, D 34 pts, E 28 pts). Eight subjects including English, mathematics, physics, chemistry, biology (or dual science award) minimum.

London (UCL) English and mathematics at grade B minimum.

Manchester Seven subjects with five at grades A/A*. Chemistry, biology and physics required at either AS or GCSE grade C minimum, with English and mathematics at grade B minimum.

Newcastle and Durham At least five subjects with grades AAAAB to include English, mathematics and either biology, chemistry, physics or dual science award.

Nottingham Six subjects at grade A/A* to include biology, chemistry and physics or dual science award. (Grade A AS physics can compensate for a B at GCSE.)

Oxford Chemistry, mathematics, biology and physics or dual science award acceptable.

Peninsula (MS) Seven subjects at grades A/B including biology, chemistry or physics or dual science award, English and mathematics or dual science award.

Queen's Belfast Chemistry, biology, mathematics and either physics or dual science award.

Sheffield At least six subjects at grade A. English, mathematics, chemistry and a science required.

Southampton Seven subjects at grade B or above including English, mathematics and dual science award or equivalent. (Widening Access course BM6) Five GCSEs at grade C including English, mathematics and dual science award or equivalent. (Students join the five-year programme on completion of Year Zero.)

St Andrews Chemistry, biology, mathematics and physics. If mathematics and biology are not offered at A2 then each must have been passed at grade B or higher. English is required at grade B or higher.

AL See Your target offers and examples of courses provided by each institution below. Candidates applying for A104 courses at **Bristol**, **Cardiff**, **Dundee**, **East Anglia**, **Edinburgh**, **London (King's)**, **Manchester**, **Sheffield** and **Southampton** are not accepted if they are offering more than one laboratory-based subject (check with University). **Cambridge (Emmanuel)** AEA in one science subject when only two are taken may be required. **London (UCL)** Mathematics and further mathematics will not both be counted towards three AL subjects. **Other requirements** See **Health Requirements** below; CRB clearance is also required.

NB In 2011 universities and colleges will differ in their use of GCE AL/AS unit grade information, A* grades, the Extended Project (EPQ), the Advanced Diploma and the Cambridge Pre-U examination when considering applicants and making offers. An EPQ may be accepted in place of an AS subject. Check websites of universities and colleges for the latest offers information.

NB Home and EU-funded students applying for entry to Medicine are required by many universities to sit either the UKCAT or BMAT tests before applying. See Your target offers and examples of courses provided by each institution below, Chapter 6 and Chapter 5 for further information.

NB The points totals shown to the left of the institutions are for ease of reference only. It must not be assumed that Tariff points are always used by institutions or that they can be substituted for an offer in grades. The level of an offer is not necessarily indicative of the quality of a course.

Your target offers and examples of courses provided by each institution

420 pts **Queen's Belfast** – AAAa +UKCAT (inc AL chem+sci/maths subj; AS biol b min) (Medicine 5 yrs) (IB 37 pts H666)

410 pts **Edinburgh** – AAAb +UKCAT (inc AL chem+1 from maths/phys/biol; AS biol min) (Medicine 5/6 yrs) (IB 37 pts HL 766)

Hull York (MS) – AAAb +UKCAT (inc chem, biol) (Medicine) (IB 36 pts HL 665)

Imperial London – AAAb +BMAT (inc AL biol/chem+sci/maths) (Medicine) (IB HL 655)

London (King's) – AAAb **or** AAaab +UKCAT (inc AL chem/biol or AS b chem/biol) (Medicine 5 yrs) (IB 38 pts HL 655)

London (King's) – AAAb +UKCAT (Med Conversion Entry Prog 6 yrs)

London (QM) – AAAb +UKCAT (inc chem and/or biol to at least AS b with 1 of these (or both) to A2 +1 other sci) (Medicine 5 yrs) (IB 36 pts HL 665)

London (St George's) – AAAb +UKCAT (BBCb for schools with AL average 245 pts and below) (inc AL chem+biol or AS chem/biol b) (Medicine 5 yrs) (IB HL 665)

London (UCL) – AAAb +BMAT (inc AL chem+biol; some pref to applicants offering a contrasting 3rd subj, eg English, music, history) (Medicine 6 yrs) (IB 38 pts HL 665)

390 pts **East Anglia** – AABb +UKCAT (inc AL A biol) (Medicine 5 yrs) (IB 33–34 pts HL 666)

Lancaster – AABb 390 pts (inc chem+biol at AL/AS) (Medicine – application through Liverpool University. See **Admissions Information** below)

Liverpool – AABb 390 pts (inc chem+biol at AL/AS) (Medicine 6 yrs) (IB 38 pts HL 676)

380 pts **Cambridge** – A*AA +BMAT college offers may vary (inc AL biol/chem/maths/phys; chem reqd at least at AS; some colleges may require 3 sci ALs) (Medicine 6 yrs) (IB 38–42 pts)

370 pts **Peninsula (MS)** – 370–400 pts inc 320–340 pts AL +UKCAT (inc biol/chem/phys +2AL inc 1 non-sci pref) (Medicine 5 yrs)

360 pts **Birmingham** – AAA 360 pts (inc AL chem+1 from biol/maths/phys; AS biol grade b if not offered at AL: hum biol acceptable) (Medicine 5 yrs) (IB 36 pts)

Brighton and Sussex (MS) – AAA 360 pts UKCAT (inc AS biol/chem+AL) (Medicine 5 yrs) (IB 37 pts HL 17 pts)

Dundee – AAA +UKCAT (inc chem +any sci +any subj at grade A) (Medicine 5 yrs) (IB 37 pts HL 766)

Dundee – AAA (Medicine 6 yrs Pre-Med Year) (IB 34 pts HL 766)

Durham and Newcastle – See **Newcastle and Durham** below

Newcastle and Durham – AAA +UKCAT (inc AL chem/biol pref 1 non-sci at AL/AS) (Medicine 5 yrs) (IB 38 pts HL chem 6)

Oxford – AAA +BMAT (inc AL chem+1 from biol/phys/maths) (Medicine 6 yrs) (IB 38–40 pts)

340 pts **Aberdeen** – AAB +UKCAT (chem required+1 from biol/maths/phys +1 other) (Medicine 5 yrs) (IB 36 pts HL 666)

Bristol – AAB (A106: A chem +2 subjs biol pref inc 4AS; A104: 3AL 1 sci accepted) (Medicine 5 yrs; 1st/2nd MB) (IB 35 pts HL 666)

Bristol – AAB (Medicine 6 yrs Pre-Med Yr)

Cardiff – AAB (Medicine 6 yrs Fdn course)

Cardiff – AAB +UKCAT (inc 2 subjs from chem, biol, phys, stats inc chem/biol at AS if not at AL) (Medicine 6 yrs) (IB 36 pts HL 18 pts)

Glasgow – AAB +UKCAT (inc AL chem+1 subj from maths/phys/biol; biol/hum biol pref; 4AS in yr 12; pts not accepted) (Medicine 5 yrs) (IB 36 pts)

Keele – AAB +UKCAT (inc AL chem+1 from biol/phys/maths+1 from a rigorous academic subj if only 2 sci subjs are offered) (Medicine) (IB 34 pts)

Leeds – AAB +UKCAT 3AL (inc AL chem) (Medicine 5 yrs) (IB 36 pts HL chem 6)

Leicester – AAB +UKCAT 3AL or 340–400 pts +UKCAT (inc 4AS in yr 12 inc A chem, biol at AL/AS) (Medicine 5 yrs) (IB 36 pts HL chem biol 6)

Understanding How to Make the New Medicines – 5th/6th UCAS Choices

The discovery of penicillin was a huge achievement. It took 15 years and an international effort to find a way to produce it in the quantities needed for medical treatment and led to the birth of the discipline of biochemical engineering.

The medicines of the future – human proteins, therapeutic vaccines, human cells and tissue for repair – are much more complex than penicillin. The challenges to biochemical engineers in understanding how to bring such new discoveries to fruition have never been greater, nor the rewards higher.

All who apply for a medical place through UCAS are asked to choose additional fifth and sixth places in other fields. Those seeking a professionally recognised qualification in a subject that is demanding, and who want a life at the cutting edge that is highly regarded, should consider the excitement of biochemical engineering as a degree option.

Details of courses can be found in UCAS guides, or on the web and visits can be arranged to explore in more detail the A level requirements, the courses and the careers available.

Manchester – AAB +UKCAT (inc AL chem+1 from biol/hum biol/phys/maths +1 other subj) (Medicine 5 yrs)
Nottingham – AAB +UKCAT (inc AL chem+biol) (Medicine 5 yrs) (IB 36 pts)
St Andrews – AAB +UKCAT (inc AL chem+biol/maths/phys) (Medicine 5 yrs; Fdn Yr 6 yrs) (IB 37 pts HL 766)
Sheffield – AAB +UKCAT (inc AB chem+sci subjs) (Medicine; BSc 3 yrs) (IB 34 pts HL 666)
Southampton – AAB 340 pts +UKCAT (inc AS chem+biol or AL chem) (Medicine 5 yrs)

320 pts **Manchester** – ABB (Medicine Fdn Yr 6 yrs)

240 pts **Southampton** – CCC +UKCAT (Medicine (Widening Access))

220 pts **Thames Valley** – CCD (inc C min chem) (Hum Sci (Pre-Med option))
London (St George's) – check with admissions tutor, min age 21 GCSE sci, Engl, maths (Fdn Med)

Medicine Foundation courses These are designed for students who have demonstrated high academic potential but who have taken non-science subjects or a combination including no more than one of biology, chemistry and physics.

Alternative offers

See **Chapter 7** and **Appendix 1** for grades/UCAS Tariff points information for the International Baccalaureate, Scottish Highers/Advanced Highers, the Welsh Baccalaureate, the Irish Leaving Certificate, the Cambridge Pre-U Diploma, the Advanced Diploma and the Extended Project.

OTHER HIGHER EDUCATION COURSES IN THE SUBJECT FIELD

Foundation and other courses (contact the institutions for details) Bradford (Clin Sci Fdn 200 pts); Brighton and Sussex (MS) (260 pts); Cardiff (370 pts); Coventry; Hertfordshire (Paramed Sci); London (King's) (St George's) (Nat Sci ABBc); Portsmouth.

CHOOSING YOUR COURSE (SEE ALSO CH.1)

NB See **Chapter 5** for details of admissions tests to be taken **before** application.

Some course features

Cambridge As with several other medical schools, the courses consist of Pre-Clinical Studies in Years 1 and 2 and Clinical Studies in Years 3, 4 and 5. Fifty per cent of students remain in Cambridge for their clinical training whilst the remainder go to other medical schools, usually Oxford or London.
Hull York (MS) This is an integrated course (also provided by other medical schools) with early clinical placements in Phase 1 (Years 1 and 2). Students are based in Hull or York with their clinical placements in Phase 2 throughout the region.
Leicester Clinical studies start in Phase 1 (two years and six months) followed by long clinical attachments in Phase 2.
Peninsula (MS) Seventy per cent of the degree programme focuses on core knowledge and skills, and 30% is spent in special study units, allowing students to select areas of special interest.
St Andrews Students undertake the first three years of their medical course, leading to a BSc degree. They then choose between Manchester or another medical school in Scotland to complete their course. Overseas students are recommended to choose Manchester where more places are available.

Universities and colleges teaching quality See www.qaa.ac.uk; www.unistats.com.

Top research universities and colleges (RAE 2008) (Pre-clinical and Human Biological Sciences) Oxford; London (UCL); Manchester; London (QM), (King's); Bristol; Liverpool; Sussex; (Hospital-based Clinical subjects) Edinburgh; Cambridge; London (UCL); Oxford; Imperial London; London (King's); Birmingham; London (QM); Aberdeen; Manchester; Newcastle; Southampton; Bristol.

ADMISSIONS INFORMATION

Number of applicants per place and places (**a** UK **b** EU (non-UK) **c** non-EU **d** mature). Note that numbers quoted of applicants per place are approximate, and that all medical schools have a limited quota of places for non-EU applicants.

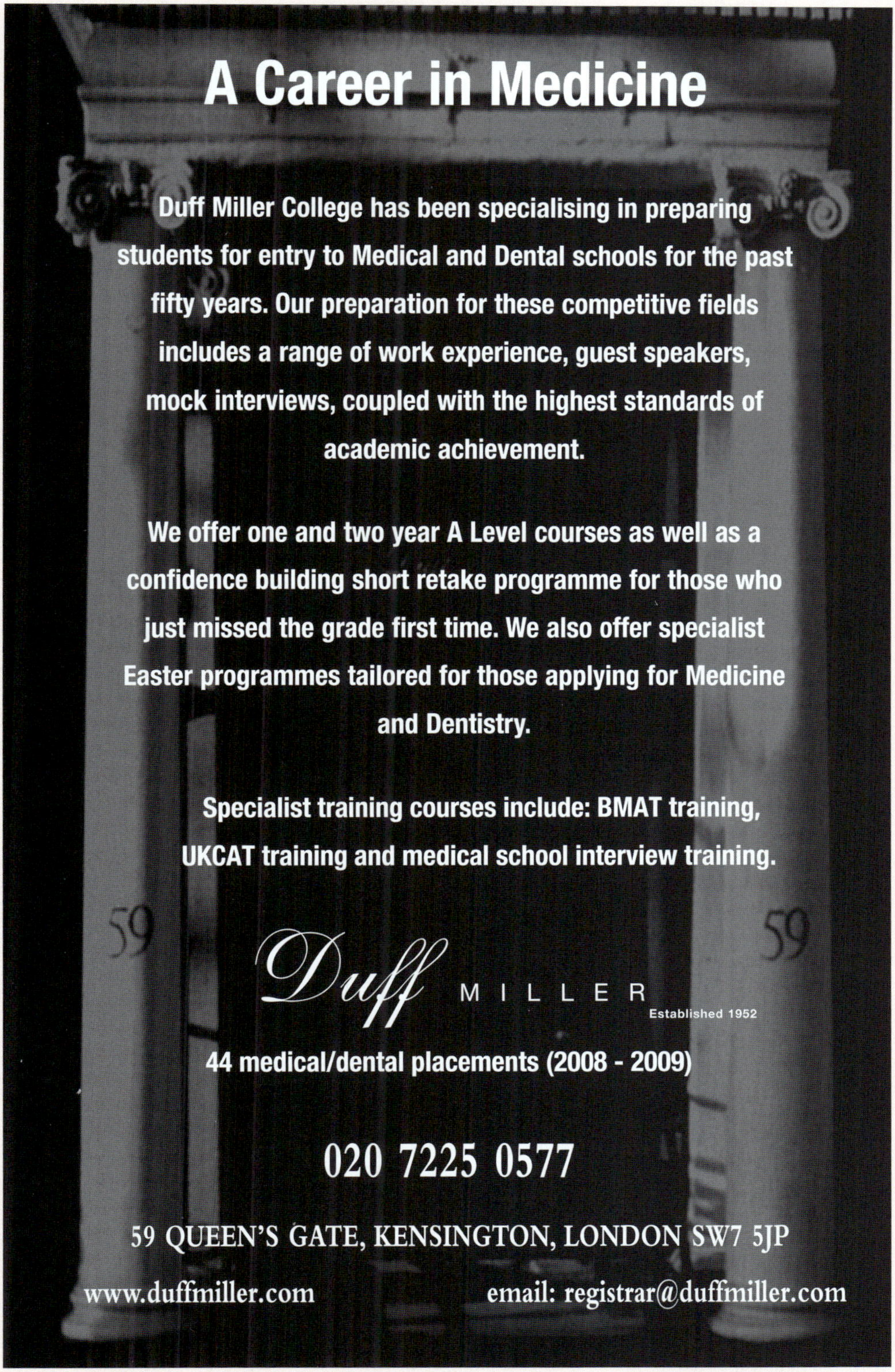
A Career in Medicine
Duff Miller College has been specialising in preparing students for entry to Medical and Dental schools for the past fifty years. Our preparation for these competitive fields includes a range of work experience, guest speakers, mock interviews, coupled with the highest standards of academic achievement.
We offer one and two year A Level courses as well as a confidence building short retake programme for those who just missed the grade first time. We also offer specialist Easter programmes tailored for those applying for Medicine and Dentistry.
Specialist training courses include: BMAT training, UKCAT training and medical school interview training.
59
59
Duff MILLER
Established 1952
44 medical/dental placements (2008 - 2009)
020 7225 0577
59 QUEEN'S GATE, KENSINGTON, LONDON SW7 5JP
www.duffmiller.com
email: registrar@duffmiller.com

Aberdeen ab1513 for 162 places; **c**270 for 13 places (preference given to applicants from countries unable to provide a medical training); **Birmingham a**5, **c**25 Grad entry 12; **Brighton and Sussex (MS) a**10 **c**10; **Bristol** 216 places (5yr course), 10 places (6yr course), 19 places (graduate entry); **Cambridge a**5; **Cardiff a**20 (6-year course) **c**22 (preference given to applicants from countries not providing a medical training); **Dundee a**7 (Pre-Med yr 11); **East Anglia a**7; **Edinburgh a**11 (international applicants not normally called for interview); **Glasgow a**6, **c**20; **Hull York (MS) ab**130 **c**10; **Imperial London a**7 **c**25; **Leeds a**2156 **b**97 **c**352 **d**488; **Leicester a**7; **Liverpool a**8; **London (King's) ab**311 places **c**25 places; **London (QM) a**8 **c**20; **London (St George's)** 19 (**a**3200 **b**250 **c**260 **d**1950: total places 292); **London (UCL) c**24; **Manchester a**8 **c**10; **Newcastle and Durham a**10 (Pre-Med yr 27) **c**14; **Nottingham a**9 **c**15; **Oxford a**26% success rate **c**10; **Peninsula (MS) a**9; **Queen's Belfast a**4 **c**(a small number of places are allocated); **St Andrews a**8; **Sheffield a**17. (For six-year courses the number of applicants per place averages 30)

Admissions tutors' advice Policies adopted by all medical schools are very similar. However, a brief outline of the information provided by admissions tutors is given below. Further information should be obtained direct from institutions. Applicants wishing to contact medical schools should do so either by letter or by telephone and not by e-mail.

Aberdeen Applicants must take the UKCAT in the year of application. This also applies to those students seeking deferred entry and those who are reapplying. In the past, students with scores between 513 and 776 have been called for interview. Interviews for some applicants. Applicants to show a knowledge of the core qualities required by doctors and evidence of teamwork and non-academic pursuits. Overseas applicants may be interviewed abroad. Interviews last about 15 minutes. Most offers made in March. Points equivalent results not accepted. Re-sits not normally accepted. International students English language entry requirement (or equivalent): IELTS 7.0. Minimum age on entry 17 years 5 months. Clinical teaching and patient contact in Year 2.

Birmingham Non-academic interests and extra-curricular activities noted in addition to academic factors. General studies not accepted, but points equivalent results may be accepted. Interviews last about 15 minutes with three interviewers – a GP, a surgeon and a student. Approximately 1000 called for interview; 10% take a year off which does not jeopardise the chances of an offer but candidates must be available for interview. Re-sit candidates who failed by a small margin are only considered in exceptional circumstances. Transfers of undergraduates from other medical schools not considered. International applicants must show a good standard of written and spoken English.

Brighton and Sussex (MS) An average UKCAT score is considered an advantage, a lower score is not regarded as a disadvantage. General studies not accepted. No offers made without an interview. Interviews last about 15 minutes with three selectors. Students are members of both universities. Years 3–5 take place in the Medical Education Centre at the Royal Sussex Hospital in Brighton. Clinical experience from Year 1.

Bristol No places offered without an interview. Top 10% of applicants called for interview lasting 15 minutes, remainder grouped into three categories: 'high reserve', 'hold' and 'unsuccessful' – some from the first two categories will be interviewed. Full details of the interview process are offered on the Bristol website. Widening participation panel considers appropriate candidates, 50 of whom will be interviewed. Criteria for selection: realistic and academic interest in medicine, commitment to helping others, wide range of interests, contribution to school/college activities, personal achievements. Interview criteria: reasons for wanting to study Medicine, awareness of current developments, communication skills, self-confidence, enthusiasm and determination to study, ability to cope with stress, awareness of the content of the course and career. General studies not acceptable. Deferred entry welcomed but applicants must be available for interview. Points equivalent results not accepted. International students English language requirement (or equivalent): IELTS 7.0.

Cambridge Some colleges insist on three science/maths subjects. Normally two interviews, each of 20 minutes each. Films of interviews on www.cam.ac.uk/admissions/undergraduate/interviews. Gap year acceptable but for positive reasons. Clinical studies from Year 4; 50% of students continue at the Cambridge Clinical School (Addenbrooke's Hospital).

Cardiff Great emphasis placed on evidence of a caring nature and exposure to hospital/health environments. Applicant's comment: 'Two interviewers and a 15-minute interview. Mainly questions on "Why Medicine?" Very helpful students'. Points-equivalent results not accepted. Clinical studies from Year 1.

Dundee Preference given to candidates who achieve the right grades at the first sitting. A system of mini interviews has been introduced which enable students separate opportunities to sell themselves. Deferred entry acceptable. Clinical attachments in Year 4.

Durham (see also **Newcastle**) The medical course is offered in partnership with Newcastle University. Study is at Queen's Campus, Stockton. Preference given to applicants with relevant work experience in caring environment, hospital, voluntary capacity or through previous employment. Particular interest in recruiting local students, either school leavers or mature students. Interviews at Stockton with two selectors; may include a written personal qualities assessment test (PQA). Graduate applicants with a 2(ii) degree are not accepted even if they possess a Masters degree or a PhD. Applicants from non-EU countries must apply to Newcastle where there is a quota of places for overseas students. Clinical contact begins in Year 1.

East Anglia Criteria include academic requirements, capacity to cope with self-directed learning, team work, responsibility, motivation. Interview regarded as the acid test; seven stations are used for the interviews, candidates visit each station for one question with six minutes at each station. Two scenario questions, see www.med.uea.ac.uk/mbbs/mbbs application). English entry requirements IELTS 7.5. Clinical experience from Year 1.

Edinburgh All examination grades must be achieved at the first sitting; only in extenuating circumstances will re-sits be considered. Equal weighting given to academic and non-academic criteria. Non-academic criteria score based on personal qualities and skills, evidence of career exploration prior to application, breadth and level of non-academic achievements and interests. Work experience and work shadowing viewed positively but the admissions panel recognise that not all applicants have equal opportunities to gain such experience. Most school-leaving applicants are not interviewed. Graduate and mature applicants may be interviewed; 202 places available, one in seven receive an offer. International applicants not normally called for interview. Clinical experience from Year 1.

Glasgow General studies not accepted. Formal work experience expected. (Work experience scheme operated by staff at Monklands Hospital, Lanarkshire.) All interviews held in Glasgow including those for overseas students. Interviewers assess candidates' performance on five points (i) knowledge of the medical course and experience of self-directed learning, (ii) experience of teamwork, (iii) communication skills, (iv) understanding of a medical career, (v) enthusiasm and commitment to medicine. Only in extenuating circumstances (family illness etc) will second-time applications be considered. Points-equivalent results not accepted. Feedback available to all candidates who fail to achieve admission. Transfers from other medical schools not accepted. Clinical experience from Year 1.

Hull York (MS). Students apply to HYMS not to Hull or York universities. Students allocated places at Hull or York by ballot in Years 1 and 2. Non-EU applicants English language (or equivalent requirement) IELTS 7.0. Transfers from other medical schools not accepted. Disabilities listed on UCAS application do not affect the assessment of the application; 600 called for interview, 340 offered places. Interviews of 20 minutes with two people. Article to be read beforehand, with a question to follow. Formally structured interviews exploring academic ability, motivation, understanding of healthcare issues, communication skills, conscientiousness, empathy, tolerance and maturity. Questions are drawn from a bank of possible topics (available online prior to interview). Re-sits acceptable but with higher grades. Feedback to unsuccessful candidates after February. Clinical placements from Year 1.

Imperial London Fifteen-minute interviews with panel of four or five selectors. Not aimed at being an intimidating experience – an evaluation of motivation, capacity to deal with stress, evidence of working as a leader and team member, ability to multitask, likely contribution to university life, communication skills and maturity. Admissions tutor's comment: 'We look for resourceful men and women with wide interests and accomplishments, a practical concern for others and for those who will make a contribution to the life of the school and hospital.' Results within two weeks. Re-sit candidates must have applied to Imperial School of Medicine previously, have achieved at least CCC and have predictions of AAA in the winter re-sit examinations and have extenuating circumstances to explain previous failure in the referee's statement. Candidates may also write directly to the School. Clinical contact in Year 1.

Keele Keele is no longer in partnership with the Manchester Medical School. All applications are now submitted to Keele. There are 130 places available, 10 for international students. There are three entry routes for Medicine: there is a Health Foundation Year (A104) for home and international applicants without the science A-levels required for the five-year course (chemistry or biology and one subject from chemistry, biology, mathematics or physics) and with grades of AAB (not including chemistry beyond GCSE) although A-level biology is acceptable with non-science A-levels. Four GCSEs are also required at grades A/A* including English and mathematics at grade C or above. Successful completion of this course gives automatic entry to Year 1 of the five-year Medicine degree; 10 places are available on the graduate entry course for home/EU applicants who enter directly into Module 2 of the five-year course. Graduates must offer a 2i honours degree or better in a biomedically-related science for entry to this course although applicants with other backgrounds can be successful with appropriate prior study and preparation for GAMSAT. Resit candidates must achieve AAA. English requirement for international applicants is IELTS 7.0.

Lancaster The University delivers the curriculum of the Medical School of Liverpool University, with the academic base at Lancaster University and clinical placements in Lancashire and Cumbria. To apply, use Liverpool University's UCAS code and see www.liv.ac.uk/sme for course and application information.

Leeds Admissions tutors' comment: 'Consider your motivation carefully – we do!' Good verbal, non-verbal and presentational skills required. Candidates should: (i) be able to report on some direct experience of what a career in medicine is about; (ii) show evidence of social activities on a regular basis (eg, part-time employment, organised community experiences); (iii) show evidence of positions of responsibility and interests outside medical and school activities. Gap years encouraged but candidates must be available for interview, 20% of all applicants interviewed. Points equivalent results not accepted. International students English language requirement (or equivalent): IELTS 7.5. Re-applications accepted from students who have achieved the right grades. Re-sits only considered in exceptional circumstances and with good supporting evidence; offer AAA. Transfers from other medical schools not encouraged. Clinical practice begins in Year 4.

Leicester Final award is a combined degree from both universities. Interview lasts 20 minutes with two selectors (one doctor and one final-year medical student; both have had interview training). Interview not an academic test. Selectors each score independently on motivation, communication skills and suitability for a career in medicine. Gap years acceptable. Re-sits considered only in exceptional circumstances; offer AAA. Transfers from other medical schools not accepted. Clinical work commences in Year 1.

Liverpool Fifty medical places for the five-year medical course are offered at Lancaster University. Students follow the Liverpool curriculum and graduate with a Liverpool degree. Applications are made to Liverpool University (Code L41, course code 105). Evidence required of healthcare experience. Gap Year acceptable for positive reasons but applicants must be available for interview. Gap Year not possible for overseas students. First year Foundation programme offered for under-qualified international students. English language requirement (or equivalent): IELTS 7.5. Clinical contact from Year 1.

London (King's) Personal statement a significant factor in selection. Emphasis placed on appreciation of academic, physical and emotional demands of the course, commitment, evidence of working in a caring environment, communication skills and interaction with the general public. Approximately 1200 applicants (35%) called for interview. Clinical contact in Year 1.

London (QM) Personal statement a significant factor in selection. 'You are expected to write your own, with an honest reflection of your strengths and interests and you will be closely questioned on

For a quick reference offers calculator, fold out the inside back cover.

this statement at interview. We don't want people who are simply good at science. High grades are no guarantee of a place. For interview applicants are ranked by their UKCAT score – no predetermined scores. Interview of 15–20 minutes. Re-sits only considered in exceptional cases; offer AAAb. Clinical experience from Year 1.

London (St George's) Applicants must be taking A-level chemistry and biology (or one to A-level and the other to AS-level). You will be required to complete your A-levels within two years of study and be predicted between BBC and AAA and have taken a fourth distinct AS-level in which you have achieved (or are predicted) a B. If not, your application will be unsuccessful. However, if you are predicted AABb and have at least 416 pts from 8 subjects at GCSE including mathematics, English and dual award science (ie average of grade A) then you will be called for interview. All applicants expected to have work experience in a medical environment. No offers without an interview – predicted grades important in selecting candidates for interview. Four selectors and an interview of 15–20 minutes. Some students who are not predicted to get the grades of the offer are also interviewed and considered for a place. Transfers from other medical schools rare. International students English language requirement (or equivalent): IELTS 7.0. Deferred entry welcomed. Clinical experience commences in Year 3. (Fdn Med) This course is for mature non-graduate students only.

London (UCL) Three selectors interview applicants, each interview lasting 15–20 minutes; 30% of applicants interviewed. Qualities sought include motivation, awareness of scientific and medical issues, ability to express and defend opinions, maturity and individual strengths. Deferred entry for good reason is acceptable. Repeat applications only considered if candidate has previously received and held a firm offer from Royal Free or University College Medical School. Minimum age of entry 18 years. Transfers from other medical schools not accepted. International students may take the University Preparation Certificate for Science and Engineering (UPCSE) which is the minimum entry requirement for entry to Medicine. Clinical attachments start in Year 3.

Manchester Minimum age of entry 17 years; 341 places. Interviews with three selectors last about 15 minutes. Mitigating circumstances regarding the health or disposition of the candidate should appear on the referee's report. If you feel unwell before the interview inform the admissions tutor and the interview will be re-scheduled; pleas of infirmity cannot be accepted after the interview! Candidates should be aware of the advantages and disadvantages of problem-based learning and opinions may be asked. Ethical questions may be raised. Decisions will be made by the end of March. Re-sit offers only made to applicants who received an offer after interview the previous year and who marginally failed to achieve the required grades; increasingly such offers are only made in the light of extenuating circumstances. Second-time applicants should include their previous UCAS number on their statement. Clinical attachments from Year 3.

Newcastle (see also **Durham**) 225 places at Newcastle; 102 places at Durham. Applicants' comments (Durham): 'Two interviewers and a 25 minute interview. Very relaxed interview. Stockton campus small. Good community spirit but some way from Durham'; (Newcastle): 'I had an interview with two selectors who had a gentle, helpful manner. I didn't feel under pressure but felt stretched'. Retakes not considered except in special circumstances. Deferred entry accepted. Consideration given to candidates who have overcome significant disadvantages (eg caring for parents with ill health). Clinical experience from Year 3.

Nottingham Critical thinking and general studies not acceptable. Candidates requesting deferred entry are expected to undertake a constructive year. No offers are made without an interview. Candidates receive preliminary online questionnaire to be completed. Interviews 15 minutes with two selectors. Re-sit applicants who have previously applied will be reconsidered but only in extenuating circumstances. Deferred entry acceptable. International students English language requirement (or equivalent): IELTS 7.0. No transfers accepted from other medical schools. Clinical experience from Year 1. Applicant's comments: 'I had one interview. There were two interviewers: the first asked me questions based on my personal statement, the second asked no scientific questions, focusing on the problems of the NHS and asking how I would deal with certain problems. He finally asked me to convince him why he should offer me a place.'

Oxford Critical thinking and general studies are not acceptable. Biology is recommended at AS-level. 425 applicants called for interview on the basis of academic performance, test score and information on the application form. Ratio of interviewees to places approximately 2.5 to 1. No student admitted without an interview. All colleges use a common set of selection criteria. Candidate's comment (Lincoln College): 'Two interviewers and two interviews. Questions covered my hobbies and social life, and scientific topics to test my logical train of thought. A great university, but it's not the be-all and end-all if you don't get in'. Clinical experience commences in Year 4.

Peninsula (MS) In the first two years students will be based at either the Exeter or Plymouth universities, allocation taking place on a random basis. Qualities sought on the application and at interview: (i) integrity and honesty; (ii) motivation and commitment; (iii) empathy and non-judgemental attitudes; (iv) communication and listening skills; (v) teamwork; (vi) ability to cope with stress; (vii) problem-solving skills; (viii) awareness of one's strengths and weaknesses; (ix) reflectiveness; (x) suitable approach to life and people. Applicant's comment: 'I was asked to stand in the middle of the room and to demonstrate my commitment to Medicine in one minute! They then asked me to write my responses to a series of questions.' Clinical skills training commences in the first year.

Queen's Belfast Majority of applicants are school-leavers; 95% from Northern Ireland. When considering applicants' GCSE performance, the best nine subjects will be scored on the basis of 4 points for an A* and 3 points for an A. Points will also be given or deducted on each UKCAT paper. Offers for resitting applicants will be restricted. These applicants will have been expected to have missed their offer by one grade. A proportion of candidates will be called for interview. Interviews last about 15 minutes. A small number of places are allocated to non-EU applicants. Number of places restricted for re-sit applicants who have narrowly missed an offer at Queen's. Clinical experience from Year 1.

St Andrews Medical Science students take full three-year programme leading to BSc (Hons), followed by clinical studies at Manchester University. Interviews last about 20 minutes with two or three selectors. Special attention given to international students and those who achieve qualifications at more than one sitting. As far as possible the interview panel will reflect the gender and ethnic distribution of candidates for interview.

Sheffield Applications processed between October and end of March. Candidates may send additional information concerning extenuating circumstances or health problems. Interviews last 20 minutes with up to three selectors. Candidates re-sitting for the first time may be considered: offer AAA. Gap year acceptable; medicine-related work very helpful. Clinical experience from Year 1.

Southampton Only mature, non-graduate applicants are selected for interview. All applicants should show in their UCAS personal statement and reference that they are (i) self-motivated and have initiative, (ii) literate and articulate, (iii) able to interact successfully with others, (iv) that they have learnt from their experiences with people in health and social care settings. Deferred entry accepted. Candidates who wish to change their year of entry should submit requests before mid-March. Patient contact from Year 1.

Warwick Graduate entry only to Medicine.

Advice to applicants and planning the UCAS personal statement (See also **Admissions Tutors' advice**).
Nearly all universities now require either the UKCAT or BMAT entry tests to be taken before applying for Medicine. Check websites (www.ukcat.ac.uk; www.bmat.org.uk) for details of test dates and test centres and with universities for their requirements. It is essential that you check for the latest information before applying and that you give yourself plenty of time to make arrangements for sitting these tests (see also **Chapter 5**).

Admissions tutors look for certain personal qualities (see **Admissions information** above) and these will emerge in your personal statement, at the interview and on your school or college reference. There should be evidence of scientific interest, commitment, enthusiasm, determination, stability, self-motivation, ability to organise your own work, interest in the welfare of others, communication skills, modesty (arrogance and over-confidence could lead to rejection!), breadth of interest, leadership skills, stamina, good physical and mental health.

Some kind of first-hand experience in a medical setting is almost obligatory for those applying for Medicine (see also under **Admissions tutors' advice**). Depending on your personal contacts in the medical profession, this could include observing operations (for example, orthopaedic surgery), working in hospitals and discussing the career with your GP. Remember that your friends and relatives may have medical conditions that they would be willing to discuss with you – and all this will contribute to your knowledge and show that you are informed and interested. Read medical and scientific magazines and keep up-to-date with important current issues – AIDS, swine 'flu, assisted dying, abortion. Community work, clubs, societies, school and social activities should be mentioned. Show that you have an understanding of the role of health professionals in society and the social factors that influence health and disease. And finally, a comment from one admissions tutor 'Don't rush around doing things just for your CV. If you are a boring student, be an incredibly well-read boring student! You can play netball, rugby, hockey, make beautiful music and paint with your feet, but if you fail to get the grades you'll be rejected.'

Misconceptions about this course **Liverpool** Some applicants think that three science subjects at A-level are required to study Medicine – wrong! **London (St George's)** That you should be white, middle class and male: 60% of medical students are now female and 53% of our students are not white.

Selection interviews All medical schools interview candidates. See **Admissions tutors' advice** and also **Chapter 5**.

Interview advice and questions Questions will vary between applicants, depending on their UCAS statements and their A/AS-level subjects. Questions are likely to relate to A-level specific subjects, general medicine topics and unconnected topics (see also **Admissions tutors' advice**). The following questions will provide a guide to the range of topics covered in past interviews. Outline the structure of DNA. What is meant by homeostasis? Is a virus a living organism? What has been the most important advance in biology in the last 50 years? What interests you about (i) science, (ii) biology, (iii) chemistry? Why did you choose the particular AS/A-level subjects you are doing? Why do you want to study Medicine/become a doctor? Do you expect people to be grateful? Why do you want to study here? Why should we take you? What do you do to relax? What do you do when you have three or four things to do, and they are all equally urgent? How do you balance work and all the outside activities you do? Do you agree with the concept of Foundation hospitals? What do you think about polyclinics? Do you think NHS doctors and staff should be able to take private patients? If you were in charge of finances for a large health authority, what would be your priorities for funding? If you had to decide between saving the life of a young child and that of an old person, what would you do? Would you treat lung cancer patients who refuse to give up smoking? What do you understand by 'gene therapy'? Can you give any examples? In your opinion what is the most serious cause for concern for the health of the UK? What do you want to do with your medical degree? What do you think the human genome project can offer medicine? Should we pay for donor organs? Where do you see yourself in 15 years' time? What was the last non-technical book you read? What is your favourite piece of classical music? List your top five novels. What is your favourite play? What politician do you admire the most? Who made the most valuable contribution to the 20th century? Why do you think research is important? Why is teamwork important? What do you think about the NHS's problems?? Do you think that sport is important? What did you gain from doing work experience in a nursing home? What were the standards like? How does the medical profession deal with social issues? What societies will you join at university? How could you compare your hobby of rowing with medicine? Do you agree that it is difficult to balance the demands of being a doctor with those of starting a family? In doing a medical course, what would you find the most emotionally challenging aspect? How would you cope with emotional strain? What do you think about going to war with Iraq? Who should have priority for receiving drugs in a 'flu epidemic/ pandemic? How would you deal with the death of a patient? What are stem cells? Why are they controversial? How is cloning done? What constitutes a human being? Describe an egg. How can you measure intelligence? How do we combat genetic diseases? How are genes actually implanted? What do you want to talk about? If you were a cardiothoracic surgeon, would you perform a heart by-pass operation on a smoker? What are the negative aspects of becoming a doctor? At some interviews essays may be set, eg (i) 'A scientific education is a good basis for a medical degree: discuss'; (ii) 'Only drugs that are safe and effective should be prescribed to patients: discuss'. Occasionally applicants at interview may be given scenarios to discuss (see **East Anglia** under **Admissions tutors' advice**). **Oxford** Tell me about drowning. What do you think of assisted suicide? Would you give a 60-year-old woman IVF treatment? When are people dead? See **Chapter 5**.

Reasons for rejection (non-academic) Insufficient vocation demonstrated. No steps taken to gain practical experience relevant to medicine. Doubts as to the ability to cope with the stress of a medical career. Not enough awareness about the career. Lack of knowledge about the course. Applicant appears dull and lacking in enthusiasm and motivation. Lacking a caring, committed attitude towards people. No evidence of broad social, cultural or sporting interests or of teamwork. Poor or lack of communication skills. Arrogance. Over-confident at interview. Unrealistic expectations about being a doctor.

Age at entry Applicants must be 17 years old on 30 September of the year of entry. However, some medical schools stipulate 17 years 6 months, and a small number stipulate 18 years. Those considering entry at 17 would probably be advised to take a gap year.

Health requirements Medical schools require all students to have their immunity status for hepatitis B, tuberculosis and rubella checked on entry. Offers are usually made subject to satisfactory health screening for hepatitis B. In line with advice from the General Medical Council, students will not be admitted to courses who are found to be e-antigen positive when screened within the first week of the course. Candidates accepting offers should assure themselves of their immunity status. **Dyslexia** Applicants with dyslexia should contact the admissions office prior to application. It is expected that most students will have successfully adapted to their situation. Whilst some medical schools may allow a limited amount of extra time for purely academic examinations, eg essays and multiple choice questions, the British Dyslexia Association and medical schools generally take the view that absolutely no concessions should be made in the conduct of clinical examinations.

Advice to mature students Medical schools usually accept a small number of mature students each year. However, several, if not the majority, reject applicants over 30 years of age. Some medical schools accept non-graduates although A-level passes at high grades are usually stipulated. The majority of applicants accepted are likely to be graduates with a first or upper second honours degree. **Birmingham**, **Bristol**, **Leeds** Maximum age at entry is 30 years. **Leeds** Applicants should hold the required A-level grades or a high class science degree; 15–20 places. **Southampton** 36 places available, maximum age 40; GCSE mathematics, physics, biology or double science required. Applicants with nursing qualifications should hold two grade B A-levels including chemistry. Mature students taking Access courses must achieve 70% in A2 chemistry.

Advice to graduate applicants Graduate applicants are considered by all medical schools. At some medical schools the Graduate Australian Medical Schools Admission Test (GAMSAT) and the Medical Schools Admissions Test (MSAT) are now being used to assess the aptitude of prospective applicants. Applicants, for example, at **Peninsula (MS)** are selected on the basis of three criteria: (i) an Honours degree at 2.2 or above; (ii) the GAMSAT score; (iii) performance at interview. All applicants must be EU students. **London (St George's)** Some students think that science graduates are the only ones to do well in GAMSAT: 40% of those on the course do not have a science degree or A-levels; however, work experience is essential.

GRADUATE DESTINATIONS AND EMPLOYMENT (2007/8 HESA)

Graduates surveyed 4830 **Employed** 4525 **In further study** 230 **Assumed unemployed** 25.

Career note Applicants should also bear in mind that while most doctors do work in the NHS, either in hospital services or in general practice, not a few graduates choose to work in other fields such as public health, pharmacology, the environment, occupational medicine with industrial organisations, the armed services and opportunities abroad.

OTHER DEGREE SUBJECTS FOR CONSIDERATION

Biomedical/Medical Materials Science; Biology; Biotechnology; Clinical Sciences; Dentistry; Dietetics; Genetics; Health Sciences; Immunology; Medical Biochemistry; Medical Engineering; Medical Microbiology; Medical Physics; Medical Product Design; Medical Sciences; Medicinal Chemistry; Midwifery; Nursing; Nutrition; Occupational Therapy; Optometry; Osteopathy; Pharmacology; Pharmacy; Physiology; Physiotherapy; Psychology; Radiography; Speech Sciences; Sports Medicine; Veterinary Medicine; Virology – and Law! (The work of doctors and lawyers is similar: both are required to identify the relevant information – clinical symptoms or legal issues!)

MICROBIOLOGY

(see also **Biological Sciences, Biology, Biotechnology** and **Genetics**)

Microbiology is a branch of biological science specialising in the study of micro-organisms: bacteria, viruses and fungi. The subject covers the relationship between these organisms and disease and industrial applications such as food and drug production, waste-water treatment and future biochemical uses.

Useful websites www.scienceyear.com; www.sgm.ac.uk; www.nature.com/micro; www.microbes.info; www.asm.org; www.microbiol.org; see also **Biochemistry**, **Biological Sciences** and **Biology**.

NB The points totals shown to the left of the institutions are for ease of reference only. It must not be assumed that Tariff points are always used by institutions or that they can be substituted for an offer in grades. The level of an offer is not necessarily indicative of the quality of a course.

COURSE OFFERS INFORMATION

Subject requirements/preferences GCSE English and mathematics and science subjects. **AL** One or two mathematics/science subjects including chemistry and/or biology, required or preferred; grades sometimes specified.

NB In 2011 universities and colleges will differ in their use of GCE AL/AS unit grade information, A* grades, the Extended Project (EPQ), the Advanced Diploma and the Cambridge Pre-U examination when considering applicants and making offers. An EPQ may be accepted in place of an AS subject. Check websites of universities and colleges for the latest offers information.

Your target offers and examples of courses provided by each institution

360 pts **Glasgow** – AAA Faster route (Microbiology) (IB 38 pts HL 665)

340 pts **Birmingham** – AAB–BBB (Biol Sci (Microbiol)) (IB 32–34 pts)
Cardiff – AAB–ABB 340–300 pts (Microbiology) (IB 32 pts HL biol chem 55)
Heriot-Watt – AAB 2nd yr entry (Biol Sci (Microbiol))
Imperial London – AAB 340 pts (Microbiology) (IB 36 pts HL 66)
Manchester – AAB–BBB (Microbiol; Microbiol Ind; Microbiol Modn Lang) (IB 33–35 pts)
Sheffield – AAB–ABB (Microbiol; Med Microbiol; Bioch Microbiol; Genet Microbiol) (IB 35–32 pts)

320 pts **Bristol** – ABB (Path Microbiol; Med Microbiol; Microbiol) (IB 32 pts HL 655)
East Anglia – ABB (Microbiology) (IB 32 pts HL 555)
Glasgow – ABB–BBC (Microbiology) (IB 32 pts)
Leeds – ABB–BBB 320–300 pts (Microbiol; Med Microbiol; Microbiol Immun; Microbiol Virol) (IB 34–32 pts HL 16–15 pts)
Leicester – ABB (Biol Sci (Microbiol); Med Microbiol) (IB 32 pts HL 66)
Liverpool – ABB–BBB (Microbiol; Microbl Biotech) (IB 33–30 pts)
Newcastle – ABB (Med Microbiol Immun) (IB 32 pts)
Surrey – ABB–BBB (Microbiol; Microbiol (Med); Microbl Genet; Fd Sci Microbiol; Bioch (Tox)) (IB 32–28 pts)

300 pts **Aberdeen** – BBB 2nd yr entry (Microbiology)
Aston – BBB (Infec Immun) (IB 33 pts)
Dundee – BBB 2nd yr entry (Microbiology)
Heriot-Watt – BBB 1st yr entry (Biol Sci (Microbiol))
Nottingham – BBB (Microbiol; Microbiol St Euro) (IB 28 pts)
Queen's Belfast – BBB (Microbiology) (IB 28 pts HL 555)
Reading – 300 pts (Microbiology)
Warwick – BBB (Microbiol Virol; Med Microbiol Virol) (IB 32 pts)
280 pts **Aberystwyth** – 280 pts (Microbiol; Zool Microbiol) (IB 26 pts HL biol 5)
Strathclyde – BBC 2nd yr entry (Bioch Microbiol; Immun Microbiol)
260 pts **Bradford** – 260 pts (Biomed Sci (Med Microbiol))
Staffordshire – 260 pts (Bioch Microbiol)
Strathclyde – BCC 1st yr entry (Immun Microbiol; Bioch Microbiol)
240 pts **Aberdeen** – CCC 1st yr entry (Microbiology)
Bristol UWE – 240–300 pts (Microbiology)
Dundee – CCC 1st yr entry (Microbiology)
Huddersfield – 240 pts (Microbl Sci)
Manchester Met – 240 pts (Microbiology)
220 pts **Edinburgh Napier** – 220 pts (Microbiol Biotech)
Nottingham Trent – 220 pts (Biol Sci (Microbiol))
Westminster – CCD (Microbiology)
200 pts **Anglia Ruskin** – 200 pts (Microbiol; Genet Microbiol)
East London – 200 pts (Med Microbiol)
Wolverhampton – 200–260 pts (Microbiology)
180 pts **Glasgow Caledonian** – DDD (Microbiology)
160 pts **London Met** – 160 pts (Microbiology)
140 pts **West Scotland** – CD (App Biosci Microbiol)
120 pts **London South Bank** – 120 pts (Biosci (Microbiol))

Alternative offers
See **Chapter 7** and **Appendix 1** for grades/UCAS Tariff points information for the International Baccalaureate, Scottish Highers/Advanced Highers, the Welsh Baccalaureate, the Irish Leaving Certificate, the Cambridge Pre-U Diploma, the Advanced Diploma and the Extended Project.

EXAMPLES OF FOUNDATION DEGREES IN THE SUBJECT FIELD
St Helens (Coll).

CHOOSING YOUR COURSE (SEE ALSO CH.1)
Some course features
Aston (Infec Immun) Course is included in the Biology programmes and offers a placement year in industry.
Bristol Within the field of cellular and molecular medicine there is a range of courses which include medical and pathological microbiology. The courses are flexible and allow students to transfer between them as their interests develop.
Leeds Specialisation in Immunology or Virology starts in Year 2. There is an optional year abroad or in industry in Year 3.
Liverpool John Moores (Microbiol; App Microbiol) These courses can be taken as three-year full-time or four-year sandwich courses.
Surrey The Microbiology programmes cover a broad range of biological science, from molecular biology to the biochemistry of micro-organisms and disease pathogenesis. Students can choose the general pathway, or specialise in medical, genetics or biotechnological applications, transferring between programmes at any stage up to the start of the third year.

Universities and colleges teaching quality See www.qaa.ac.uk; www.unistats.com.

Top research universities and colleges (RAE 2008) See **Biological Sciences**.

Examples of sandwich degree courses Aston; Bristol; Bristol UWE; Cardiff; De Montfort; Glamorgan; Leeds; London South Bank; Manchester; Nottingham Trent; West Scotland. See also **Biochemistry** and **Biological Sciences**.

ADMISSIONS INFORMATION

Number of applicants per place (approx) Aberystwyth 5; Bradford 6; Bristol 6; Cardiff 4; Dundee 5; Leeds 7; Liverpool 3; Nottingham 7; Strathclyde 10; Surrey 4; Swansea 5; Wolverhampton 4.

Advice to applicants and planning the UCAS personal statement Relevant experience, particularly for mature students. See **Biological Sciences** and also **Appendix 4**.

Selection interviews **Yes** Bristol, London South Bank, Nottingham (depends on application), Surrey, Swansea; **Some** Aberystwyth (mature applicants only), Cardiff, Leeds, Wolverhampton.

Interview advice and questions Examples of past questions include: Is money spent on the arts a waste? How much does the country spend on research and on the armed forces? Discuss reproduction in bacteria. What do you particularly like about your study of biology? What would you like to do after your degree? Do you have any strong views on vivisection? Discuss the differences between the courses you have applied for. What important advances have been made in the biological field recently? How would you describe microbiology? Do you know anything about the diseases caused by micro-organisms? What symptoms would be caused by which particular organisms? See **Chapter 5**.

AFTER-RESULTS ADVICE

Offers to applicants repeating A-levels **Higher** Bristol, Strathclyde, Swansea, Warwick; **Possibly higher** East Anglia, Nottingham; **Same** Aberystwyth, Anglia Ruskin, Bradford, Cardiff, Leeds, Liverpool, Wolverhampton.

GRADUATE DESTINATIONS AND EMPLOYMENT (2006/7 HESA)

Graduates surveyed 460 **Employed** 165 **In further study** 170 **Assumed unemployed** 35.

Career note See **Biology**.

OTHER DEGREE SUBJECTS FOR CONSIDERATION

Animal Sciences; Biochemistry; Biological Sciences; Biology; Biotechnology; Genetics; Medical Sciences; Medicine; Molecular Biology; Pharmacology; Physiology.

MUSIC

(including **Music Technology**)

Theory and practice are combined to a greater or lesser extent in most university Music courses and from which about 50 per cent or more of graduates will go on to non-music careers. However, courses are also offered by Conservatoires and Schools of Music where the majority of applicants are aiming to become professional musicians. For these courses the ability to perform on an instrument is more important than academic ability and offers are therefore likely to be lower. See also Appendix 2.

Useful websites www.arts.org.uk; www.communitymusic.org; www.ism.org; www.bpi-med.co.uk; www.roh.org.uk; www.nyo.org.uk; www.bbc.co.uk/youngmusican; www.cukas.ac.uk.

NB The points totals shown to the left of the institutions are for ease of reference only. It must not be assumed that Tariff points are always used by institutions or that they can be substituted for an offer in grades. The level of an offer is not necessarily indicative of the quality of a course.

COURSE OFFERS INFORMATION

Subject requirements/preferences GCSE A foreign language and mathematics may be required. A good range of As and Bs for popular universities. **AL** Music plus an instrumental grade usually required.

NB In 2011 universities and colleges will differ in their use of GCE AL/AS unit grade information, A* grades, the Extended Project (EPQ), the Advanced Diploma and the Cambridge Pre-U examination when considering applicants and making offers. An EPQ may be accepted in place of an AS subject. Check websites of universities and colleges for the latest offers information.

NB Some applications are made through the Conservatoires Admissions Service (CUKAS): see **Chapter 6** for details.

Music examinations Additional points will be awarded for Music examinations from the Associated Board of the Royal Schools of Music (ABRSM), the Guildhall School of Music and Drama, the London College of Music Examinations (LCMM) and Trinity College of Music (music examinations at grades 6, 7, 8 (D=Distinction; M=Merit; P=Pass)).

Practical:	Grade 6 – D 45 pts; M 40 pts; P 25 pts.
	Grade 7 – D 60 pts; M 55 pts; P 40 pts.
	Grade 8 – D 75 pts; M 70 pts; P 55 pts.
Theory:	Grade 6 – D 15 pts; M 10 pts; P 5 pts.
	Grade 7 – D 20 pts; M 15 pts; P 10 pts.
	Grade 8 – D 30 pts; M 25 pts; P 20 pts.

Your target offers and examples of courses provided by each institution

380 pts **Cambridge** – A*AA college offers may vary (Music) (IB 38–42 pts HL 766–777)
London (King's) – AAA+AS **or** AAaab (Mus; Ger Mus) (IB 38 pts HL mus 7)

360 pts **Durham** – AAA (Mus Comb Arts) (IB 37 pts)
Oxford – AAA (Music) (IB 38–42 pts)
Southampton – AAA–AAB (Maths Mus) (IB 36 pts HL 17 pts)

340 pts **Birmingham** – AAB–ABB (Mus courses) (IB 36 pts)
Bristol – AAB–BBC (inc ABRSM gr 5 piano) (Mus; Mus Fr/Ger/Ital) (IB 35–30 pts)
Cardiff – AAB–BBC (inc gr 8 theor+gr 8 prac) (Mus; Mus Relig St; Mus Welsh) (IB 33 pts)
Durham – AAB (Mus; Educ St Mus)
Glasgow – AAB (+ gr 8 for BMus) (BMus Mus; MA Mus courses) (IB 34 pts)
Leeds – AAB +ABRSM (Mus Multim Electron) (IB 36 pts HL 17 pts)
Manchester – AAB (inc gr 8D inst/voice, gr 6 piano) (Mus; Mus Dr) (IB 35 pts)
Surrey – AAB 340 pts (Snd Rec (Tonmeister))
Sussex – AAB–ABB (Phil Mus)

320 pts **City** – ABB–BBC (Mus; Wrld Mus St)
East Anglia – ABB–BBC (Mus; Mus Tech; Mus Maths) (IB 30 pts)
Edinburgh – ABB (Maths Mus)
Leeds – ABB +80% gr 8 ABRSM for perf (Mus; Mus joint courses) (IB 33 pts HL mus 6)
Leeds – ABB +audition (Mus (Perf)) (IB 33 pts HL mus 6)
Leeds – ABB (Pop Wrld Mus) (IB 33 pts)
Liverpool – ABB 320 pts (Mus Pop Mus) (IB 33 pts)
London (Gold) – ABB (Mus; Pop Mus; Mus Comp) (IB 32 pts)
London (RH) – ABB 320 pts (inc gr 7 instr) (Mus Fr/Ger/Ital/Span; Mus Pol St) (IB 35 pts HL mus 6)
London (SOAS) – ABB (Ling Mus)
Newcastle – AAB (BA Mus Mus) (IB 35 pts HL mus 5)
Nottingham – ABB (BA Music) (IB 34 pts)
Southampton – ABB (Mus Mgt Sci; Mus; Engl Mus; Accoust Mus) (IB 32 pts HL 16 pts)
Sussex – ABB–BBB (inc gr 7) (Mus; Mus Inform) (IB 32–34 pts)
York – ABB (Music) (IB 34 pts HL mus 6)

300 pts **Bournemouth** – 300 pts (Mus Aud Tech)
Brunel – 300 pts (inc gr 6/7 instr/vocal) (Mus; Mus joint courses; Dr Mus; Musl Perf; Musl Cmpsn; Snc Arts) (IB 31 pts)
Edinburgh – BBB (Mus; Hist Art Hist Mus) (IB 34 pts HL 555)
Glamorgan – 300–360 pts (Mus Tech)
Huddersfield – 300–280 pts (Mus Hist; Mus Dr; Mus Tech; Mus; Mus Jrnl)
Lancaster – BBB–BBC 300–280 pts (Mus; Mus Tech) (IB 28–29 pts)
London (SOAS) – BBB (Mus St; Mus Arbc; Mus Dev St; Mus Jap)
Newcastle – BBB (BMus Folk Trad Mus) (IB 32 pts)
Nottingham – ABC (Mus Phil) (IB 36 pts)
Queen's Belfast – BBB–BBCb (Mus; Ethnomus; Mus Tech) (IB 29 pts HL 655)
Sheffield – ABC (Music) (IB 35–30 pts)
Sheffield – BBB–BBC (Mus Hisp St; Mus E As St)
Surrey – ABC 300 pts (inc gr 7) (Music) (IB 32 pts)
York – BBB–BBC (BEng Mus Tech Sys)

280 pts **Birmingham City** – 280 pts (Media Comm Mus Ind)
Chester (Warrington) – 280 pts (Commer Mus Prod) (IB 24 pts)
Cumbria – 280 pts (Mus Thea Perf courses)
Glamorgan – 280–320 pts (Pop Mus)
Gloucestershire – 280 pts (Pop Mus; Mus Media Mgt)
Kent – 280 pts (Mus Tech)
Leeds (CMus) – BBC 280 pts (Mus Prod)
Staffordshire – 280 pts (Crea Mus Tech; Mus Tech; e Mus)
Stranmillis (UC) – BBC (Mus Educ)
Surrey – BBC (inc gr 5 theory) (Crea Mus Tech) (IB 32 pts)
Teesside – 280 pts (Mus Tech)
Ulster – 280–240 pts (Mus; Mus Dance; Mus Ir; Mus Psy)

260 pts **Bangor** – 260–280 pts (Music) (IB 28 pts)
Brighton – BCC 260 pts (Dig Mus Snd Arts)
Bristol UWE – 260–300 pts (Aud Mus Tech; Crea Mus Tech; Mus Sys Eng)
Hertfordshire – 260–240 pts (Mus Cmpsn Tech; Mus Tech)
Hull – 260–280 pts (inc gr 7 or above on 1st study instr/voice) (Mus Fr/Ger/Ital/Span)
Keele – 260 pts (Mus courses; Mus Tech)
Liverpool (LIPA) – 260 pts (Mus; Mus (Perf Arts); Snd Tech)
Liverpool Hope – 260–300 pts (Mus courses)
Manchester Met – 260 pts (Crea Mus Prod; Mus Comb Hons; Pop Mus courses)
Salford – 260 pts (Music)
Strathclyde – BCC (App Mus)

240 pts **Aberdeen** – CCC (BMus Mus; Mus St courses)
Anglia Ruskin – 240 pts (Mus; Mus Dr)

Bangor – 240–300 pts (Engl Sng Writ)
Bradford – 240 pts (Media St Mus Tech)
Chester – 240–280 pts (Pop Mus courses)
Coventry – 240 pts (Mus Prof Prac; Mus Cmpsn Prof Prac; Mus Tech)
De Montfort – 240 pts (Mus Tech Innov; Mus Tech; Mus Tech Perf)
Edinburgh Napier – 240 pts (Mus; Pop Mus)
Hull (Scarborough) – 240 pts (Crea Mus Tech courses)
Leeds (CMus) – 240 pts (Mus; Jazz; Pop Mus St)
Lincoln – 240 pts (Aud Prod)
Liverpool John Moores – 240 pts (Pop Mus St)
Oxford Brookes – CCC–CCD (Dig Mus Snd Tech)
Plymouth – 240 pts (BEd P Mus)
Southampton Solent – 240 pts (Mus Prom; Pop Mus Jrnl)

220 pts **Bath Spa** – 220–260 pts (+ gr 8) (Mus; Crea Mus Tech)
Creative Arts – 220 pts (Mus Jrnl)
Edge Hill – 220–260 pts (Dr Mus Snd)
Manchester Met – 220 pts (Comp Mus Tech Comb Hons)
Northampton – 220–260 pts (Pop Mus courses)
Oxford Brookes – CCD (Mus; Mus Comb Hons)
Salford – 220 pts (Pop Mus Rec) (IB 24 pts)
Sunderland – 220 pts (Commun Mus)
Teesside – 220–280 pts (Mus Gms Des; Mus Vis Media)
York St John – 220 pts (Mus courses)

200 pts **Bucks New** – 200–240 pts (Aud Mus Prod; Mus Arts Mgt; Mus Mgt Arts Dev)
Canterbury Christ Church – 200 pts (Mus courses)
Central Lancashire – 200–260 pts (Mus Prac; Mus Prod; Mus Prod Arts; Mus Thea)
East London – 200 pts (Mus Cult Theor Prod)
Kingston – 200–260 pts (Mus; Mus Tech)
London Met – 200–240 pts (Musl Instr courses; Mus Media Mgt)
Portsmouth – 200–280 pts (Mus Snd Tech)
Salford – 200 pts (Music)
Swansea Met – 200 pts (Mus Tech)
Thames Valley – 200 pts (Mus (Perf Comp); Mus Tech Pop Mus Perf)
UCP Marjon – 200 pts (Live Mus)

180 pts **Chichester** – DDD 180 pts +gr 8 (Mus; Mus joint courses)
Derby – 180–240 pts (Pop Mus Prod joint courses)
Liverpool (LIPA) – 180 pts (Mus Thea Ent Mgt)
Plymouth – 180 pts (Music)
Wolverhampton – 180 pts (Mus; Mus Pop Mus)

160 pts **Bishop Grosseteste (UC)** – DDE 160 pts (Educ St Mus)
Colchester (Inst) – BD 160 pts (Mus; Musl Thea)
Doncaster (Coll) – 160 pts (Crea Mus Tech)
Grimsby (IFHE) – 160 pts (Crea Mus)
Leeds Met – 160 pts (Music)
Rose Bruford (Coll) – 160 pts individual interview/audition (Actr Mus; Mus Tech)
Southampton Solent – 160–120 pts (Mus Std Tech; Dig Mus)
Truro (Coll) – 160 pts (Contemp Wrld Jazz)
West Scotland – CC (Commer Mus)
Westminster – CC (Commer Mus; Mus Inform) (IB 24 pts)

150 pts **Anglia Ruskin** – 150 pts (Aud Tech Crea Mus Tech)

120 pts **RCMus** – 120 pts (Music)

100 pts and below
Birmingham City/Birmingham Consv – 80 pts (Mus; Jazz)
Guildhall (Sch Mus Dr) – 100 pts (Mus; Thea)
London (RAcMus) – EE (BMus Mus)

Manchester (RNCM) – 80–120 pts (BMus; Mus)
Middlesex – (Mus Arts Mgt; Jazz; Mus Perf; Mus Comp; Snc Arts)
Trinity Laban Consv – (inc gr 8) (BMus (Perf); MMus (Perf St))
UHI Millennium Inst – (Gael Trad Mus; Pop Mus Perf)

Falmouth (UC) – contact College (Mus courses)
Havering (Coll) – contact the College (Mus Prac Tech)
Royal Scottish (RSAMD) – check with College (Mus; BA Scot Mus; Mus Thea; BEd Mus)
Royal Welsh (CMusDr) – contact College and apply direct (Mus (gr 8 principal inst); Pop Mus; Perf Prod)

Alternative offers

See **Chapter 7** and **Appendix 1** for grades/UCAS Tariff points information for the International Baccalaureate, Scottish Highers/Advanced Highers, the Welsh Baccalaureate, the Irish Leaving Certificate, the Cambridge Pre-U Diploma, the Advanced Diploma and the Extended Project.

EXAMPLES OF FOUNDATION DEGREES IN THE SUBJECT FIELD

Bath Spa; Bournemouth; Brighton; Bucks New; Canterbury Christ Church; Creative Arts; Central Lancashire; Colchester (Inst); Exeter (Coll); Farnborough (CT); Hereford (CA); Hull (Coll); Kent; Leeds City (Coll); Manchester (Coll); Newcastle (Coll); North Lindsey (Coll); Northbrook (Coll); Norwich City (Coll); Nottingham New (Coll); Plymouth; Rotherham (CAT); St Helens (Coll); South Essex (Coll); South Tyneside (Coll); Suffolk (Univ Campus); Sunderland; Thames Valley; Truro (Coll); West Anglia (Coll); Westminster City (Coll).

CHOOSING YOUR COURSE (SEE ALSO CH.1)

Some course features

Brunel (Mus) The course centres on an academic study of music, ranging from early music history to the development of Western music in the 20th and 21st centuries. Students also follow their own interests in, for example, composition, performance, computer music, improvisation.
Central Lancashire (Mus Thea) This is a practice-based course involving acting and movement, voice, music composition, production and the creation and production of students' own works.
Oxford Brookes (Dig Mus Snd Tech) An interdisciplinary course, accredited by the Institution of Engineering and Technology, it includes sound recording and production, music and electroacoustic composition, studio design, video production, electronics and business management.
Surrey (Crea Mus Tech) This new degree focuses on creative practice for composers and performers. Compositional modules include composing for TV, film, advertising and computer games. Students can take performance as part of their degree if they have at least grade 7 (ABRSM) in their chosen instrument. Qualifying applicants receive paid instrumental lessons.

Universities and colleges teaching quality See www.qaa.ac.uk; www.unistats.com.

Top research universities and colleges (RAE 2008) London (RH); Birmingham; Manchester; Southampton; Cambridge; London (King's); Sheffield; Oxford; York; Newcastle; Nottingham.

Examples of sandwich degree courses Birmingham City; Bournemouth; Bristol UWE; Brunel; City; Glamorgan; Gloucestershire; Hertfordshire; Huddersfield; London Met; Portsmouth; Staffordshire; Surrey; Teesside.

ADMISSIONS INFORMATION

Number of applicants per place (approx) Aberystwyth 5; Anglia Ruskin 5; Bangor (BA) 4; Bath Spa 8; Birmingham 8; Bristol 8; Brunel 7; Cambridge 3; Cambridge (Hom) 4; Cardiff 6; Chichester 4; City 7; Colchester (Inst) 4; Cumbria 7; Dartington (CA) 8; Durham 5; East Anglia 12; Edinburgh 11; Edinburgh Napier 3; Glasgow 4; Huddersfield 2; Hull 21; Kingston 18; Lancaster 8; Leeds 18; Liverpool 9; Liverpool (LIPA) 12; London (Gold) 7, (King's) 10, (RAcMus) 7, (RH) 7, (SOAS) 4; London Met 10; Manchester (RNCM) 8; Middlesex 23; Newcastle 24; Northampton 3; Northumbria 12; Nottingham 7; Oxford Brookes 12; Queen's Belfast 6; Roehampton 4; Rose Bruford (Coll) 15; RCMus 10; Royal Scottish (RSAMD) 6; Salford 5; Southampton 5; Strathclyde 15; Surrey average 6, (Tonmeister) 12; Trinity Laban Consv 4; Ulster 8; Worcester 8; York 8; York St John 2.

Interview advice and questions

NB See also **Chapter 5** under Music.

Anglia Ruskin In addition to A-levels, we also require Grade 7 (good pass, first study) plus Grade 5 minimum keyboard standard.

Bangor Offer depends on proven ability in historical or compositional fields plus acceptable performance standard. Options include music therapy, recording techniques, jazz.

Bath Spa Some candidates interviewed. Required to perform and sight-read on main instrument, and given aural and critical listening tests. Discussion of previous performing, composing and academic experience. (Fdn Commer Mus) All applicants must submit a self-composed audio prior to interview. (Mus Tech) Applicants will be required to submit an audio portfolio demonstrating technical and creative skills.

Bristol (Mus Fr/Ger/Ital) No in-depth interviews; candidates invited to Open Days.

Cambridge (St Catharine's) At interview candidates may have to undergo some simple keyboard or aural tests (such as harmonisation of an unseen melody or memorisation of a rhythm). More importantly, they will have to comment on some unseen musical extracts from a stylistic and analytical point of view. Candidates are asked to submit some examples of work before the interview, from the fields of harmony and counterpoint, history, and analysis; they are also encouraged to send any other material such as compositions, programme notes or an independent essay on a subject of interest to the candidate. (Taking the STEP examination is not a requirement for admission.) Above all this, though, the main prerequisite for reading Music at St Catharine's is an academic interest in the subject itself.

Canterbury Christ Church Associated Board examinations in two instruments (or one instrument and voice); keyboard competence essential, particularly for the BEd course.

Colchester (Inst) Great stress laid on candidate's ability to communicate love of the subject.

Cumbria Admission by live performance or on tape. QTS applicants interviewed for teaching suitability. See **Chapter 6**.

Durham We also require Grade 6 piano (Associated Board) and a foreign language (GCSE grade A–C), A-level music grade B.

East Anglia Only unusual and mature candidates are interviewed. Applicants are expected to perform music with insight and show genuine intellectual curiosity about music and its cultural background. At interview candidates will be asked to perform on their principal instrument. Those who play orchestral instruments or sing will also be expected to play simple music on the piano. At interview we look for applicants with proficiency in instrumental or vocal performance (preferably at Grade 8 standard or above), range of experience of music of many types and an intelligent attitude towards discussion.

Edinburgh Most candidates are called for interview, although very well qualified candidates may be offered a place without interview. All are asked to submit samples of their work. Associated Board Grade 7 on piano is usually expected.

Huddersfield Have an open and inquisitive outlook with regard to all aspects of music from performing to composing, musicology to listening. Candidates auditioned on their principal instrument or voice. They will be asked about playing technique, interpretation and interests.

Hull Good instrumental grades can improve chances of an offer and of confirmation in August. Students are not normally required to attend an audition/interview. Decisions will be made according to the information supplied on the UCAS application. Successful applicants will be invited to attend a departmental Open Day. We welcome applications from mature students and those with unconventional qualifications: in such cases an interview may be required.

Kingston Associated Board Grade 8 on main instrument is required, with at least Grade 4 on a keyboard instrument (where this is not the main instrument). Audition and interview may be required. Candidates with non-standard qualifications are interviewed and asked to bring samples of written work.

Lancaster Grade 8 Associated Board required on an instrument or voice and some keyboard proficiency (grade 6) usually expected. We do not accept candidates without interview. For the Music degree, instrumental or vocal skills equivalent to Grade 8 required. For Music Technology, applicants should hold music theory grade 5 or be able to demonstrate the ability to read a score. Applicants wishing to take practical studies will need instrumental or vocal skills equivalent to Grade 8.

Leeds Intending students should follow an academic rather than practical-oriented A-level course. The University is experimenting with abandoning the formal interview in favour of small group Open Days for those holding offers made on the UCAS information, to focus on a practical exchange of information relevant to the applicant's decision to accept or reject the offer. Grade 8 Associated Board on an instrument is a normal expectation.

Leeds (CMus) There will be an audition and an essay on music theory.

Liverpool (LIPA) In addition to performing in orchestras etc, give details of any compositions you have completed (the number and styles). Instrumentalists (including vocalists) should describe any performance/gig experience together with any musical instrument grades achieved. (Mus) Candidates should prepare two pieces of contrasting music to play on their chosen instrument. Candidates who have put song-writing/composition as either first or second choice should have a cassette, CD or minidisc of their work to play to the panel. (Snd Tech) Applicants must prepare a critical review of a sound recording of their choice which highlights the technical and production values that they think are the most important. Examples of recorded work they have undertaken should also be available at interview eg on CD, cassette or DAT.

London (Gold) The interview will include an aural discussion of music and the personal interests of the applicant.

London (RAcMus) All candidates are called for audition, and those who are successful are called for a further interview; places are offered later, subject to the minimum GCSE requirements being achieved. (BMus) Applicants sit a 50-minute written paper, and may also be tested on keyboard and aural performance.

London (RH) Candidates are tested with an aural test, a harmony/counterpoint test, a conceptual essay, and a viva at which they are asked questions and asked to perform. On the basis of the results in these tests we make offers. There is a tradition of caring for each individual and we strive to give each applicant a fair hearing. Musicality, a good intellect and real enthusiasm are the qualities we look for.

London (SOAS) Candidates are judged on individual merits. Applicants are expected to have substantial practical experience of musical performance, but not necessarily Western music.

Manchester (RNCM) All applicants are called for audition. Successful applicants proceed to an academic interview which will include aural tests and questions on music theory and history. Student comment: 'A 45-minute interview with a panel of three. Focus was on portfolio of compositions sent in advance. Prior to interview was asked to harmonise a short passage and study an orchestral excerpt followed up at interview. Aural test waived.'

Newcastle We expect a reasonable background knowledge of musical history, basic harmony and counterpoint and keyboard skills of approximately Grade 8 standard; if the main instrument is not piano or organ – Grade 5. While practical skills are important, academic ability is the primary requisite. Practical Music or Music Technology accepted in place of Music.

Nottingham A high standard of aural ability is expected. Interviewees take two short written papers, intellectual enquiry and attainment are looked for, together with a good range of knowledge and sense of enterprise. No places are offered without interview – each offer is tailored to the student at interview: we do not just use the points system. Only borderline/mature students are interviewed, successful applicants are invited to an Open Day.

Nottingham Trent Music students require Grade 6 on two instruments. Candidates submit a marked sample of harmony and/or counterpoint and two marked essays on any areas or aspects of music.

Candidates may also submit a portfolio of compositions if they wish, but it is not possible to return any copies. Candidates will take the following tests at interview: (i) A one-hour harmony or counterpoint written test (candidates will not have access to a piano); there is no composition option; (ii) A 40-minute aural test in three parts: dictation of a Bach chorale (bass given)/melodic dictation, and identification of errors heard in a two-part piece; (iii) Performance of a prepared piece on the candidate's principal instrument or voice (organists, percussionists and candidates requiring an accompanist should inform the Faculty in advance of the interview period); (iv) Keyboard skills in three parts: score reading of a string quartet; keyboard harmony; and sight-reading (sight-reading examples will take into account candidates' keyboard proficiency).

RCMus All UK and Eire candidates are required to attend for audition in person but tapes are acceptable from overseas applicants. It must be stressed, however, that personal audition is preferable and those students offered places on the basis of a tape audition may be required to take a confirmatory audition on arrival. Candidates are required to perform on the principal study instrument as well as undertaking sight-reading, aural tests and paperwork. There is also an interview. Potential scholars sometimes proceed to a second audition, usually on the same day. The academic requirement for the BMus (RCM) course is two A-levels at pass grades. Acceptance is ultimately based on the quality of performance at audition, performing experience and perceived potential as a performer. As a guide, applicants should be of at least Grade 8 distinction standard.

Royal Welsh (CMus Dr) All UK and Eire applicants are called to audition in person; overseas candidates may audition by tape. Candidates are required to perform on their sight-reading ability. Candidates who are successful in the audition proceed to interview in which there will be a short aural test. Candidates for the BA (Music) course are required to bring recent examples of harmony, counterpoint and essays.

Surrey (Music) Applicants may expect to be questioned in the interview about their musical experience, enthusiasm and any particular compositions they have studied. They will also be asked to perform on their first instrument. (Snd Rec (Tonmeister)) Applicants can expect to be questioned about their recording interests and motivation and show an ability to relate A-level scientific knowledge to simple recording equipment. They may be asked to perform on their first instrument.

Trinity Laban Consv Applicants for the BMus degree must attend an audition and show that they have attained a certain level of competence in their principal and second studies, musical subjects and in musical theory. Grade 8 practical and theory can count as one A-level, but not if the second A-level is in music. Overseas applicants may submit a tape recording in the first instance when a place may be offered for one year. Thereafter they will have to undergo a further test. They must also show evidence of good aural perception in musical techniques and musical analysis.

Wolverhampton The audition will involve playing/singing a piece of own-choice music (up to five minutes – no longer). Accompanists may be brought along or the department may be able to provide one if requested in advance. Candidates will be requested to produce a short piece of written work. It would be helpful to see any music certificates and a Record of Achievement if available, together with examples of recent work in music (an essay, harmony, composition etc).

Advice to applicants and planning the UCAS personal statement In addition to your ability and expertise with your chosen musical instrument(s), it is also important to know your composers and to take a critical interest in various kinds of music. Reference should be made to these, visits to concerts listed and any special interests indicated in types of musical activity, for example, opera, ballet. Work with orchestras, choirs and other musical groups should also be included and full details given of any competitions entered and awards obtained. **Guildhall (Sch Mus Dr)** International applicants sending extra documentation from overseas must make sure that for Customs purposes they indicate that they will pay any import tax charged. **London (Gold)** We encourage students to bring examples of their written and creative work. **Royal Welsh (CMus Dr)** Evidence of performance-related experience, eg youth orchestras, solo work, prizes, scholarships etc. Our course is a conservatoire course as opposed to a more academic university course. We offer a very high standard of performance tuition balanced with academic theory modules. **Surrey** (Snd Rec (Tonmeister)) Demonstration of motivation towards professional sound recording. **NB** See **Chapter 6** for details of applications for Music courses at Conservatoires.

Misconceptions about this course **Cardiff** Some mistakenly think that the BMus scheme is either performance-based or something inferior to the principal music-based degree. **Salford** (Pop Mus Rec) This is not a specialised music technology degree: it is a music degree with specialisation in music technology and production. Specialisation can be significant in Year 3. BTEC Popular Music students must be prepared for the rigours of an academic degree. Some students expect the course to make them famous! **Surrey** Some believe that the Music course is exclusively performance-based (the course includes substantial academic and compositional elements).

Selection interviews **Yes** Most institutions, plus audition to include a performance of a prepared piece (or pieces) on main instrument or vocal study; **Guildhall (Sch Mus Dr)** Interviews mostly held at the School but also at Newcastle and in the USA. **Some** Anglia Ruskin, Bath Spa, Bucks New, Cardiff, Coventry (Proforma used prior to interview – some students rejected at this stage), Liverpool (LIPA), Staffordshire (Mus Tech), Surrey. See also **Chapter 5** under **Music**.

Reasons for rejection Usually academic (auditions, practical, aural/written test). Dull, unenthusiastic students, ignorant about their subject, showing lack of motivation and imagination. **Cambridge** Her harmony was marred by elementary technical errors and her compositions lacked formal and stylistic focus. **London (King's)** Apparent lack of interest, performance not good enough, lack of music history knowledge. Foreign students: language skills inadequate. **Royal Welsh (CMus Dr)** Performing/technical ability not of the required standard.

AFTER-RESULTS ADVICE

Offers to applicants repeating A-levels **Higher** Aberystwyth, Leeds; **Same** Anglia Ruskin, Bath Spa, Bristol, Cardiff, City, Colchester (Inst), De Montfort, Durham, East Anglia, Guildhall (Sch Mus Dr), Huddersfield, Hull, Kingston, Leeds (CMus), London (RAcMus), (RH), Nottingham, Rose Bruford (Coll), Royal Welsh (CMus Dr), Salford, Staffordshire, Surrey, York, York St John.

GRADUATE DESTINATIONS AND EMPLOYMENT (2007/8 HESA)

Graduates surveyed 2995 **Employed** 1275 **In further study** 675 **Assumed unemployed** 235.

Career note Some graduates go into performance-based careers, many enter the teaching profession and others go into a wide range of careers requiring graduate skills.

OTHER DEGREE COURSES FOR CONSIDERATION

Acoustics; Drama; Musical Theatre; Performance Arts.

NATURAL SCIENCES

(see also **Biological Sciences** and **Science**)

Natural Sciences degrees allow the student to obtain a broad view of the origins and potential of science in general, and then to focus on one specialist area of scientific study.

Useful websites www.scienceyear.com; www.scicentral.com; www.nature.com; see also **Biology**, **Chemistry** and **Physics**.

NB The points totals shown to the left of the institutions are for ease of reference only. It must not be assumed that Tariff points are always used by institutions or that they can be substituted for an offer in grades. The level of an offer is not necessarily indicative of the quality of a course.

COURSE OFFERS INFORMATION

Subject requirements/preferences **GCSE** **Cambridge** Mainly grade As. **AL** Science subjects required. **Cambridge** (Emmanuel) One AEA science may be required when only two sciences taken; (Peterhouse) STEP may be used as part of conditional offer (see **Chapter 5**).

NB In 2011 universities and colleges will differ in their use of GCE AL/AS unit grade information, A* grades, the Extended Project (EPQ), the Advanced Diploma and the Cambridge Pre-U examination when considering applicants and making offers. An EPQ may be accepted in place of an AS subject. Check websites of universities and colleges for the latest offers information.

Your target offers and examples of courses provided by each institution

380 pts **Cambridge** – A*AA college offers may vary (Nat Sci courses) (IB 38–42 pts HL 766–777)
London (UCL) – AAAe–ABBe (Nat Sci) (IB 34–38 pts)
360 pts **Bath** – AAA (Nat Sci; Nat Sci Yr Ind) (IB 36 pts HL 666)
Durham – AAA (Nat Sci courses) (IB 38 pts)
East Anglia – AAA (MSci Nat Sci; Nat Sci Yr Abrd) (IB 34 pts)
East Anglia – AAA–ABB (BSc Nat Sci) (IB 34–32 pts)
Leeds – AAA (Nat Sci)
Nottingham – AAA–AAB (Nat Sci) (IB 34 pts)
Southampton – AAA (Nat Sci) (IB 36 pts)
340 pts **Birmingham** – AAB (Nat Sci; Nat Sci Euro) (IB 34 pts)
Leicester – AAB (MSci Interd Sci) (IB 30 pts)
320 pts **Lancaster** – ABB 320 pts (Nat Sci N Am) (IB 30 pts)
Newcastle – ABB (Nat Sci) (IB 34 pts)
300 pts **Leicester** – BBB (BSc Interd Sci) (IB 28 pts)
London (QM) – 300 pts (Nat Sci) (IB 30–32 pts)
Strathclyde – BBB 2nd yr entry (Nat Sci)
280 pts **Lancaster** – BBC 280 pts (Nat Sci) (IB 30 pts)
260 pts **Strathclyde** – BCC 1st yr entry (Nat Sci)
160 pts **UHI Millennium Inst** – CC (Nat Env Sci)

Open University – (Nat Sci – contact +44 (0)845 300 6090 or www.openuniversity.co.uk/you)

Alternative offers
See **Chapter 7** and **Appendix 1** for grades/UCAS Tariff points information for the International Baccalaureate, Scottish Highers/Advanced Highers, the Welsh Baccalaureate, the Irish Leaving Certificate, the Cambridge Pre-U Diploma, the Advanced Diploma and the Extended Project.

CHOOSING YOUR COURSE (SEE ALSO CH.1)

Some course features
Bath A flexible range of courses, with opportunity to transfer between the three and four-year degree programmes and the new undergraduate Master's degree. Students can also apply for transfer to a Single Honours programme in Biology, Chemistry or Physics.
Cambridge (Nat Sci) Courses focus on the biological and physical sciences with 17 final year specialist subjects from which to choose, including Genetics, History and Philosophy of Science, Materials Science and Plant Sciences.
Durham (Nat Sci) A very flexible degree programme, with specialisation in 15 subjects, ranging from Anthropology and Astronomy to Earth Sciences, Mathematics, Psychology and Statistics. Students take modules from the Faculties of Arts, Humanities and Social Sciences.
Lancaster (Nat Sci) Two or three science subjects can be studied throughout the course. There is an option to spend Year 2 in North America.
Newcastle (Nat Sci) Two major science subjects are studied with modules offered in practical and vocational skills in computing, languages, business or economics.

Top research universities and colleges (RAE 2008) See separate science tables.

Examples of sandwich degree courses Bath; Nottingham Trent; Surrey.

ADMISSIONS INFORMATION

Number of applicants per place (approx) Bath 7; Birmingham 10; Cambridge 3; Durham 5; Nottingham 7.

Advice to applicants and planning the UCAS personal statement See **Biology**, **Chemistry** and **Physics**. See also **Appendix 4**.

Selection interviews **Yes** Bath, Cambridge.

Interview advice and questions **Cambridge** Questions depend on subject choices and studies at A-level and past questions have included the following: Discuss the setting up of a chemical engineering plant and the probabilities of failure of various components. Questions on the basic principles of physical chemistry, protein structure and functions and physiology. Questions on biological specimens. Comment on the theory of evolution and the story of the Creation in Genesis. What are your weaknesses? Questions on electro-micrographs. What do you talk about with your friends? How would you benefit from a university education? What scientific magazines do you read? Questions on atoms, types of bonding and structures. What are the problems of being tall? What are the differences between metals and non-metals? Why does graphite conduct? Questions on quantum physics and wave mechanics. How could you contribute to life here? What do you see yourself doing in five years' time? Was the Second World War justified? If it is common public belief that today's problems, for example industrial pollution, are caused by scientists, why do you wish to become one? Questions on the gyroscopic motion of cycle wheels, the forces on a cycle in motion and the design of mountain bikes. What do you consider will be the most startling scientific development in the future? What do you estimate is the mass of air in this room? If a carrot can grow from one carrot cell, why not a human? See **Chapter 5**.

AFTER-RESULTS ADVICE

Offers to applicants repeating A-levels **No offers made** Cambridge.

GRADUATE DESTINATIONS AND EMPLOYMENT (2007/8 HESA)

See **Biology**, **Chemistry**, **Mathematics** and **Physics**.

Career note These courses offer a range of science and in some cases non-scientific subjects, providing students with the flexibility to develop particular interests as they progress through the course.

OTHER DEGREE SUBJECTS FOR CONSIDERATION

Anatomy; Anthropology; Archaeology; Astrophysics; Biochemistry; Biological Sciences; Biology; Chemistry; Earth Sciences; Ecology; Genetics; Geography; Geology; History and Philosophy of Science; Neuroscience; Pharmacology; Physics; Plant Sciences; Psychology; Zoology.

NAVAL ARCHITECTURE

(including **Marine Engineering** and **Ship Science**; see also **Marine/Maritime Studies**)

Professional naval architects or marine engineers are responsible for the design, construction and repair of cruise liners, yachts, submarines, container ships and oil tankers. Ship Science focuses on, for example, vehicles and structures that use the oceans for transport, recreation and energy generation. Courses cover marine structures, transport and operations, design, propulsion and mathematics. Ship design has many similarities to the design of aircraft. See **Appendix 2**.

Useful websites www.rina.org.uk; www.na-me.ac.uk; www.naval-architecture.co.uk.

NB The points totals shown to the left of the institutions are for ease of reference only. It must not be assumed that Tariff points are always used by institutions or that they can be substituted for an offer in grades. The level of an offer is not necessarily indicative of the quality of a course.

COURSE OFFERS INFORMATION

Subject requirements/preferences **GCSE** Grades A–C in mathematics and physics are normally required. **AL** Mathematics and physics usually required.

NB In 2011 universities and colleges will differ in their use of GCE AL/AS unit grade information, A* grades, the Extended Project (EPQ), the Advanced Diploma and the Cambridge Pre-U examination when considering applicants and making offers. An EPQ may be accepted in place of an AS subject. Check websites of universities and colleges for the latest offers information.

Your target offers and examples of courses provided by each institution

340 pts **Newcastle** – AAB (MEng Mar Tech; Mar Eng; Off Eng; Nvl Archit; Sml Crft Tech) (IB 36 pts HL maths phys 5)
Southampton – AAB (MEng Ship Sci Nvl Archit; Ship Sci Nvl Eng; Ship Sci Ycht Sml Crft; MEng/BEng Ship Sci; Ship Sci Advnc Mats) (IB 34 pts HL 17 pts)

320 pts **Strathclyde/Glasgow** – ABB 2nd yr entry (MEng Nvl Archit Mar Eng; Nvl Archit; Nvl Archit Ocn Eng; Nvl Archit Sml Crft Eng) (IB 34 pts)

300 pts **Newcastle** – BBB (BEng Mar Tech; Nvl Archit; Mar Eng; Off Eng; Sml Crft Tech) (IB 32 pts HL maths phys 5)

280 pts **Liverpool John Moores** – 280 pts (MEng Mech Mar Eng)
Strathclyde/Glasgow – BBC 1st yr entry (MEng Nvl Archit Mar Eng; Nvl Archit; Nvl Archit Ocn Eng; Nvl Archit Sml Crft Eng) (IB 34 pts)
Strathclyde/Glasgow – BBC 2nd yr entry (BEng Nvl Archit; Nvl Archit Mar Eng; Nvl Archit Ocn Eng; Nvl Archit Sml Crft Eng)

260 pts **Plymouth** – 260 pts (Mar Tech)

240 pts **Liverpool John Moores** – 240 pts (BEng Mech Mar Eng; BSc Naut Sci)
Strathclyde/Glasgow – CCC 1st yr entry (BEng Nvl Archit Mar Eng; Nvl Archit Ocn Eng; Nvl Archit Sml Crft Eng) (IB 30 pts)

200 pts **Plymouth** – 200 pts (Mar St (Ocn Ycht))

180 pts **Southampton Solent** – 180 pts (Ycht Prod Surv; Ycht Pwrcrft Des)

Alternative offers
See **Chapter 7** and **Appendix 1** for grades/UCAS Tariff points information for the International Baccalaureate, Scottish Highers/Advanced Highers, the Welsh Baccalaureate, the Irish Leaving Certificate, the Cambridge Pre-U Diploma, the Advanced Diploma and the Extended Project.

EXAMPLES OF FOUNDATION DEGREES IN THE SUBJECT FIELD

Blackpool and Fylde (Coll); Cornwall (Coll); Liverpool John Moores; Plymouth City (Coll); South Devon (Coll); Southampton Solent.

CHOOSING YOUR COURSE (SEE ALSO CH.1)

Some course features
Newcastle (Mar Tech; Off Eng; Sml Crft Tech; Nvl Archit) All MEng and BEng courses take a common Stage 1 first year and then follow their specialised degree programmes. Transfer is possible between MEng courses and to the Marine Technology BEng degree.
Southampton Solent (Ycht Pwrcrft Des) The course is fully accredited by the Royal Institution of Naval Architects. A foundation year is available.
Strathclyde/Glasgow (Nvl Archit) A broad-based engineering course covering engineering science, flotation and stability, ship and offshore structures design. Topics also include resistance and propulsion, ship structural analysis, marine engineering systems, business and management. Some opportunities for sponsorship and work experience.

Top research universities and colleges (RAE 2008) (Naval Architecture and Marine Engineering) Glasgow; Strathclyde.

ADMISSIONS INFORMATION

Number of applicants per place (approx) Newcastle 9; Southampton 4.

Advice to applicants and planning the UCAS personal statement Special interests in this subject area should be described fully. Visits to shipyards and awareness of ship design from the *Mary Rose* in Portsmouth to modern speed boats should be fully explained and the problems noted. See also **Engineering/Engineering Sciences** and **Marine/Maritime Studies**. See also **Appendix 4**.

Selection interviews **Yes** Newcastle, Southampton.

Interview advice and questions Because of the highly vocational nature of this subject, applicants will naturally be expected to discuss any work experience and to justify their reasons for choosing the course. See **Chapter 5**.

AFTER-RESULTS ADVICE

Offers to applicants repeating A-levels **Higher** Newcastle.

GRADUATE DESTINATIONS AND EMPLOYMENT (2007/8 HESA)

Graduates surveyed 30 **Employed** 20 **In further study** 5 **Assumed unemployed** none.

Career note A small proportion of naval architects work in the shipbuilding and repair industry, others are involved in the construction of oil rigs or may work for ship-owning companies. There are also a number of firms of marine consultants employing naval architects as managers or consultants.

OTHER DEGREE SUBJECTS FOR CONSIDERATION

Aeronautical Engineering; Civil Engineering; Electrical/Electronic Engineering; Geography; Marine Biology; Marine Engineering; Marine/Maritime Studies; Marine Technology; Mechanical Engineering; Oceanography; Physics; Shipping Operations; Transport Management.

NURSING and MIDWIFERY

(including **Paramedic Science**; see also **Biological Sciences, Community Studies** and **Health Sciences/Studies**)

Nursing and Midwifery courses are designed to equip students with the scientific and caring skills demanded by medical science in the 21st century. Courses follow a similar pattern with an introductory programme of study covering clinical skills, nursing practice and the behavioural and social sciences. Thereafter, specialisation starts in adult, child or mental health nursing, or with patients with learning disabilities. Throughout the three-year course students gain extensive clinical experience in hospital wards, clinics, accident and emergency and high-dependency settings.

Useful websites www.scicentral.com; www.nhscareers.nhs.uk; www.nursingtimes.net; see also **Health Sciences/Studies** and **Medicine**.

NB The points totals shown to the left of the institutions are for ease of reference only. It must not be assumed that Tariff points are always used by institutions or that they can be substituted for an offer in grades. The level of an offer is not necessarily indicative of the quality of a course.

APPLICATIONS FOR NURSING AND MIDWIFERY

UCAS handles applications for Nursing degree and diploma courses.

COURSE OFFERS INFORMATION

Subject requirements/preferences **GCSE** English and a science subject. Mathematics required at several universities. **AL** Science subjects required for some courses. **Other requirements** All applicants holding firm offers will require an occupational health check and Criminal Records Bureau (CRB) clearance and are required to provide documentary evidence that they have not been infected with hepatitis-B. (Paramed Sci) Full clean manual UK driving licence with at least a provisional C1 category.

NB In 2011 universities and colleges will differ in their use of GCE AL/AS unit grade information, A* grades, the Extended Project (EPQ), the Advanced Diploma and the Cambridge Pre-U examination when considering applicants and making offers. An EPQ may be accepted in place of an AS subject. Check websites of universities and colleges for the latest offers information.

Abbreviations used in this table A - Adult; C - Child; LD - Learning Disability; MH - Mental Health.

Your target offers and examples of courses provided by each institution

320 pts **Southampton** – ABB 320 pts (Midwifery)
300 pts **Bournemouth** – 300 pts (Midwifery))
Edinburgh – BBB (Nurs St) (IB 34 pts HL 555)
Glasgow – BBB (Nurs A/C/LD/MH)

Leeds – BBB (Midwifery)
London (King's) – BBCe (Midwif St; Nurs A/C/MH)
Surrey – BBB–BCC 300–260 pts (Paramed Prac; Nurs St A/C/MH; Midwif St)

280 pts **Abertay Dundee** – BBC (Nursing)
Birmingham – BBC (Nurs A/MH) (IB 28–30 pts)
Bradford – 280 pts (Midwif St)
Central Lancashire – 280 pts (Midwifery)
East Anglia – BBC (Midwifery)
Hertfordshire – 280 pts (Paramed Sci)
Manchester – BBC (Midwifery) (IB 30 pts)
Northumbria – 280 pts (Midwif St))
Oxford Brookes – BBC (Midwifery)
Salford – 280 pts (Midwifery)
Sheffield Hallam – 280 pts (Midwifery)
Southampton – BBC 300–280 pts (Nurs A/C/LD/MH)
Ulster – 280 pts (Nurs A/MH)

260 pts **Bournemouth** – 260 pts (Nurs A/C/LD/MH)
Brighton – BCC 260 pts offers may vary (Paramed Sci) (IB 28 pts)
Coventry – 260 pts (Midwifery)
East Anglia – BCC (Nurs A/C/LD/MH)
Huddersfield – BCC (Midwif St)
Kingston (London St George's) – BCC (Midwifery)
Liverpool – BCC (Nursing) (IB 28 pts)
Liverpool John Moores – 260 pts (Nurs A/MH; Midwif)
Manchester – BCC (Nurs A/C/MH) (IB 28 pts)
Northumbria – 260 pts (Nurs A/C/LD/MH) (IB 26 pts)
Nottingham – BCC (MNurs Sci A/C/MH) (IB 30 pts HL 55 biol 6)
Oxford Brookes – BCC (Nurs A)
Teesside – 260–360 pts (Midwifery)
York – BCC/CCC (Midwif; Nurs Prac A/C/LD/MH) (IB 28 pts)

240 pts **Bangor** – 240 pts (Midwifery)
Birmingham City – 240 pts (Nurs A/C/LD/MH; Midwif)
Brighton – CCC (Midwif; Nurs A/C/MH) (IB 28 pts)
Bristol UWE – 240–280 pts (Midwifery)
Canterbury Christ Church – CCC (Midwifery)
Cardiff – CCC 240 pts (Nurs A/C/MH; Midwif) (IB 26 pts)
Chester – 240 pts (Nurs A/C/LD/MH; Midwif)
Cumbria – 240 pts (Nurs A/MH)
De Montfort – 240 pts (Nurs A/C/MH; Midwif)
Glamorgan – 240 pts (Nurs A/C/LD/MH; Midwif)
Leeds – CCC (Nurs A/C/LD/MH)
Lincoln – 240 pts (Nurs A)
Northampton – 240 pts (Midwifery)
Oxford Brookes – CCC (Nurs C/LD/MH)
Plymouth – 240 pts (Paramed Practnr)
Robert Gordon – CCC–BC (Nurs A/C/MH)
Staffordshire – 240 pts (Nurs Prac A/C/MH; Midwif Prac)
Suffolk (Univ Campus) – 240 pts (Midwifery)
Swansea – 240 pts (Nurs A/C/MH; Midwif)
Teesside – 240 pts (Nurs St A/C/MH)
Wolverhampton – 240 pts (Midwifery)

230 pts **Queen Margaret** – 230 pts (Nursing)

220 pts **Bedfordshire** – 220 pts (Midwifery)
City (St Bartholomew's) – 220 pts (Nurs A/C/MH; Midwif)
Edge Hill – 220–260 pts (Nurs A/C/MH/LD; Midwif)

Kingston (London St George's) – 220 pts (Nurs A/C/LD/MH) (IB 27 pts)
Salford – 220 pts (Nurs A/C/MH; Prof St Nurs Soc Wk) (IB 26 pts)

200 pts **Anglia Ruskin** – 200 pts (Midwifery)
Bangor – 200 pts 2AL (Nurs A/C/MH/LD)
Bedfordshire – 200 pts (Nurs A/C/LD/MH)
Bristol UWE – 200–240 pts (Nurs A/C/MH/LD) (IB 24 pts)
Central Lancashire – 200 pts (Nurs A/C/MH)
Glyndŵr – 200 pts (Nursing)
Greenwich – 200 pts (Nurs A/C/LD/MH; Midwif)
Hertfordshire – 200 pts (Nurs LD Soc Wk; Midwif) (IB 26–28 pts)
Hull – 200 pts (Nurs A/C/MH/LD)
Leeds Met – 200 pts (Nurs A/MH)
Manchester Met – 200 pts (Nurs A/MH)
Northampton – 200–220 pts (Nurs A/C/MH/LD)
Plymouth – 200–240 pts (Midwif; Nurs A/C/MH)
Queen's Belfast – BB–CCD (Midwif; Nurs A/C/LD/MH)
Sheffield Hallam – 200 pts (Nurs St A/C/MH)
Wolverhampton – 200 pts (Nurs A/C/MH)

180 pts **Edinburgh Napier** – 180 pts (Nurs A/C/MH/LD; Midwif)

160 pts **Abertay Dundee** – CC (Nurs; Nurs MH)
Anglia Ruskin – 160 pts (Nurs A/C/LD/MH)
Canterbury Christ Church – 160 pts (Nurs A/C/MH)
Glasgow Caledonian – CC (Nurs A/LD/MH; Nurs St; Midwif)
Keele – 160 pts (Nurs A/C/MH/LD)
London South Bank – CC (Nurs A/C/LD/MH; MH Nurs Soc Wk)
Worcester – CC (Midwifery)

120 pts **Bucks New** – 120 pts (Nurs A/C/MH)
Robert Gordon – DD (Midwifery)
Middlesex – 2AL (Nurs A/C/MH; Euro Nurs; Midwif)

Open University – (Nurs top-up – contact +44 (0)845 300 6090 or www.openuniversity.co.uk/you)

Alternative offers

See **Chapter 7** and **Appendix 1** for grades/UCAS Tariff points information for the International Baccalaureate, Scottish Highers/Advanced Highers, the Welsh Baccalaureate, the Irish Leaving Certificate, the Cambridge Pre-U Diploma, the Advanced Diploma and the Extended Project.

EXAMPLES OF FOUNDATION DEGREES IN THE SUBJECT FIELD

Bournemouth; Bristol UWE; Cornwall (Coll); Coventry 200 pts (Paramed Sci); Cumbria; East London; Essex; Greenwich; Grimsby (IFHE); Liverpool John Moores; London (St George's); South Devon (Coll); Wigan and Leigh (Coll); Worcester.

CHOOSING YOUR COURSE (SEE ALSO CH.1)

Some course features

Cardiff (Midwif) Practical experience throughout the three-year course.
Hertfordshire (Paramed Sci) The course runs over four extended academic years and leads to qualifying and registering as a professional paramedic. Theoretical studies are interspersed with clinical practice placements. The third year is a sandwich/practice year when students are paid employees of the London Ambulance Service NHS Trust.
Manchester (Midwifery) This degree course is for non-nurses. Students are expected to work early and late shifts including some weekends, bank holidays and night duty.
Southampton (Nurs) The course is 50% theory and 50% practice with hands-on experience from Year 1.
Surrey (Nurs St) The course has strong scientific and clinical foundations with placements in hospital and community settings.

Universities and colleges teaching quality See www.qaa.ac.uk; www.unistats.com.

Top research universities and colleges (RAE 2008) (Nursing and Midwifery) Manchester; Southampton; Ulster; York; City; Hertfordshire; Leeds; Nottingham; Stirling.

ADMISSIONS INFORMATION

Number of applicants per place (approx) Abertay Dundee 10; Anglia Ruskin 10; Bangor 10; Birmingham 8; Birmingham City 15; Bournemouth 9; Brighton 3; Bristol UWE 27; Cardiff 12, (non-EU) 6; Central Lancashire (Midwif) 14; City (Nurs MH) 4, (Nurs C) 8, (Midwif) 5; Cumbria 8; De Montfort 10; Glasgow Caledonian 12; Glynd̂wr 4; Huddersfield (Midwif St) 10; Hull 10; Leeds (Midwif) 12; Liverpool John Moores (Nurs) 5; London (King's) 4; London South Bank 16; Middlesex 10; Northampton 17; Northumbria 16; Nottingham 3; Queen Margaret 3; Salford 10, (Midwif) 11; Sheffield Hallam 8; Staffordshire (Midwif Prac) 10; Surrey 10; Swansea 10; York (Nurs) 8, (Midwif Prac) 2.

Advice to applicants and planning the UCAS personal statement Experience of care work – for example in hospitals, old people's homes, children's homes – is important. Describe what you have done and what you have learned. Read nursing journals in order to be aware of new developments in the treatment of illnesses. Note, in particular, the various needs of patients and the problems they experience. Try to compare different nursing approaches with, for example, children, people with learning disabilities, old people and terminally ill people. If you under-performed at GCSE, give reasons. If you have had work experience or a part-time job, describe how your skills have developed, for example responsibility, communication, team-building, organisational skills. How do you spend your spare time? Explain how your interests help with stress and pressure. See also **Appendix 4**. Admission is subject to eligibility for an NHS bursary. Contact NHS Student Grants Unit, tel 01253 655655.

Misconceptions about this course That Nursing programmes are not demanding. Midwives and nurses don't do shift work and are not involved in travelling! **City** Midwives are only involved at the birth stage and not at the ante-natal and post-natal stages, or in education and support.

Selection interviews **Yes** Most institutions, Anglia Ruskin, Birmingham, Bournemouth (Midwif), Brighton, Cardiff, City, East Anglia, Hertfordshire, Sheffield Hallam, Surrey, Swansea, Wolverhampton, York; **Some** Abertay Dundee, Bucks New, Salford.

Interview advice and questions Past questions have included: Why do you want to be a nurse? What experience have you had in nursing? What do you think of the nurses' pay situation? Should nurses go on strike? What are your views on abortion? What branch of nursing most interests you? How would you communicate with someone who can't speak English? What is the nurse's role in the community? How should a nurse react in an emergency? How would you cope with telling a patient's relative that the patient was dying? Admissions tutors look for communication skills, team interaction and the applicant's understanding of health/society-related subjects. (Some applicants have difficulty with maths – multiplication and division – used in calculating dosage for medicines.) **London South Bank** What do you understand by equal opportunities? **Swansea** What is your perception of the role of the nurse? What qualities do you have that would be good for nursing? See **Chapter 5**.

Reasons for rejection (non-academic) Insufficient awareness of the roles and responsibilities of a midwife or nurse. Lack of motivation. Poor communication skills. Lack of awareness of nursing developments through the media. (Detailed knowledge of the NHS or nursing practice not usually required.) Failed medical. Unsatisfactory health record. Not fulfilling the hepatitis B requirements or police check requirements. Poor preparation for the interview. Too shy. Only wants nursing as a means to something else, for example commission in the armed forces. Too many choices on the UCAS application, for example Midwifery, Physiotherapy, Occupational Therapy. No care experience. **Birmingham** No work experience. **De Montfort** No insight as to nursing as a career or the various branches of nursing. **Swansea** Poor communication skills.

AFTER-RESULTS ADVICE

Offers to applicants repeating A-levels **Higher** Bristol UWE, Cardiff, Hull, Liverpool John Moores (Midwif); **Same** De Montfort, Huddersfield, Liverpool John Moores, London South Bank, Queen Margaret, Salford, Staffordshire, Stirling, Suffolk (Univ Campus), Surrey, Swansea, Wolverhampton.

GRADUATE DESTINATIONS AND EMPLOYMENT (2007/8 HESA)

Graduates surveyed 5960 **Employed** 4660 **In further study** 80 **Assumed unemployed** 140.

Career note The majority of graduates aim to enter the nursing profession.

OTHER DEGREE SUBJECTS FOR CONSIDERATION

Audiology; Biological Sciences; Biology; Community Studies; Dietetics; Education; Health Studies; Medicine; Nutrition; Occupational Therapy; Optometry; Pharmacology; Pharmacy; Physiotherapy; Podiatry; Psychology; Radiography; Social Policy and Administration; Social Work; Sociology; Speech Therapy; Veterinary Nursing.

NUTRITION

(see also **Dietetics** and **Food Science/Studies and Technology**)

Nutrition attracts a great deal of attention in society and whilst controversy, claim and counter-claim seem to focus daily on the merits and otherwise of food and its value, it is, nevertheless, a scientific study in itself. Courses involve topics relating to diet, health, nutrition and food policy and are designed to prepare students to enter careers as specialists in nutrition and dietetics.

Useful websites www.nutrition.org.uk; www.nutritionsociety.org; see also under **Dietetics**.

NB The points totals shown to the left of the institutions are for ease of reference only. It must not be assumed that Tariff points are always used by institutions or that they can be substituted for an offer in grades. The level of an offer is not necessarily indicative of the quality of a course.

COURSE OFFERS INFORMATION

Subject requirements/preferences **GCSE** Mathematics and science usually required. **AL** Science subjects required for most courses, biology and/or chemistry preferred.

NB In 2011 universities and colleges will differ in their use of GCE AL/AS unit grade information, A* grades, the Extended Project (EPQ), the Advanced Diploma and the Cambridge Pre-U examination when considering applicants and making offers. An EPQ may be accepted in place of an AS subject. Check websites of universities and colleges for the latest offers information.

Your target offers and examples of courses provided by each institution

340 pts **London (King's)** – ABB+AS (Nutr Diet) (IB 34 pts)
320 pts **Glasgow** – ABB (Physiol Spo Sci Nutr) (IB 32 pts)
Leeds – ABB (Nutrition)
Newcastle – ABB (Fd Hum Nutr) (IB 32–35 pts)
Nottingham – ABB–BBB (MNutr Nutr (Diet)) (IB 32–34 pts)
Reading – 320 pts (Nutr Fd Consum Sci)
Surrey – ABB–BBB 320–300 pts (Nutr Diet) (IB 34–32 pts)
300 pts **Aberdeen** – BBB 2nd yr entry (Hlth Sci (Hlth Nutr))
Leeds – BBB (Fd St Nutr) (IB 32 pts HL 15 pts)
London (King's) – BBB (Nutrition) (IB 32 pts)
London Met – 300 pts (Hum Nutr Diet)
Nottingham – BBB–BBC (Nutr; Nutr Fd Sci (Euro St); Nutr Bioch) (IB 28–32 pts)
Queen's Belfast – BBB (Fd Qual Sfty Nutr)
Reading – 300 pts (Fd Sci)
Surrey – BBB–BBC 300–280 pts (Nutrition)
280 pts **Northumbria** – 280 pts (Hum Nutr; Fd Sci Nutr; Spo Exer Nutr) (IB 25 pts)
Oxford Brookes – BBC (Nutrition) (IB 30 pts)
Plymouth – 280–300 pts (Exer Nutr Hlth; Pblc Hlth Nutr)

260 pts **Cardiff (UWIC)** – 260 pts (Hum Nutr Diet)
Leeds Met – BCC (Dietetics)
Liverpool Hope – 260 pts (Nutr Hlth Prom; Hlth Nutr Comb Hons) (IB 25 pts)
240 pts **Aberdeen** – CCC 1st yr entry (Hlth Sci (Hlth Nutr))
Bournemouth – 240 pts (Nutrition)
Cardiff (UWIC) – 240 pts (Pblc Hlth Nutr; Spo Biomed Nutr)
Central Lancashire – 240 pts (Exer Nutr Hlth)
Chester – 240 pts (Hum Nutr)
Greenwich – 240 pts (Hum Nutr)
Leeds Trinity (UC) – 240 pts (Nutr Hlth Psy; Spo Hlth Exer Nutr)
Liverpool John Moores – 240–280 pts (Fd Nutr; Commun Nutr)
Manchester Met – 240 pts (Hum Nutr)
Nottingham Trent – 240 pts (Exer Nutr Hlth)
Robert Gordon – CCC (Nutr Diet)
Staffordshire – 240 pts (Spo Exer Nutr)
Teesside – 240 pts (Fd Nutr Hlth Sci)
Ulster – CCC 240 pts (Hum Nutr)
220 pts **Bath Spa** – 220–260 pts (Hum Nutr; Fd Nutr)
Coventry – 220–240 pts (Fd Sci Nutr)
Glamorgan – 220–260 pts (Nutr Phys; Actvty Commun Hlth) (IB 28 pts)
Huddersfield – 220 pts (Fd Nutr Hlth; Nutr Pblc Hlth)
Lincoln – 220 pts (Hum Nutr)
Suffolk (Univ Campus) – 220 pts (Nutr Hum Hlth)
Westminster – CCD (Hum Nutr; Hlth Sci (Nutr Thera); Nutr Exer Sci) (IB 26 pts)
Worcester – 220–240 pts (Hum Nutr)
200 pts **Kingston** – 200–280 pts (Nutr Spo Sci; Nutr; Hum Biol Nutr; Bioch Nutr)
Leeds Met – 200 pts (Nutr Pblc Hlth)
Leeds Trinity (UC) – 200 pts (Nutr Fd)
London Met – 200 pts (Hum Nutr)
Middlesex – 200 pts (Spo Exer Sci (Spo Nutr))
Roehampton – 200–240 pts (Nutr Hlth)
Sheffield Hallam – 200 pts (Pblc Hlth Nutr; Nutr Hlth Lfstl; Fd Nutr)
180 pts **Abertay Dundee** – 180 pts (Fd Nutr Hlth; Spo Exer Nutr) (IB 26 pts)
Harper Adams (UC) – 180–220 pts (Fd Nutr Wlbng)
165 pts **Queen Margaret** – 165 pts (Nutrition)
160 pts **Glasgow Caledonian** – CC (Hum Nutr Diet)
London Met – 160 pts (Pblc Hlth Nutr)
Robert Gordon – CC (Nutrition)
St Mary's Twickenham (UC) – 160–200 pts (Nutr courses)
120 pts **London South Bank** – 120 pts (Fd Nutr)

Bradford (Coll) – contact admissions (Diet Nutr Hlth)
Central Lancashire – contact admissions (Hum Nutr)

Alternative offers
See **Chapter 7** and **Appendix 1** for grades/UCAS Tariff points information for the International Baccalaureate, Scottish Highers/Advanced Highers, the Welsh Baccalaureate, the Irish Leaving Certificate, the Cambridge Pre-U Diploma, the Advanced Diploma and the Extended Project.

EXAMPLES OF FOUNDATION DEGREES IN THE SUBJECT FIELD
CAFRE; Duchy (Coll); Glamorgan.

CHOOSING YOUR COURSE (SEE ALSO CH.1)
Some course features
London (King's) (Nutr Diet) Graduates are eligible to be employed as dietitians in the NHS.
Newcastle (Fd Hum Nutr) Stages 1 and 2 focus on biology and biological chemistry, with an

emphasis on nutrition and food science. After a work placement, Stage 3 covers nutrition, health and disease, biotechnology in the food industry, plants as food, and sport and exercise nutrition.
Reading (Nutr Fd Sci) Course is normally four years with a placement year in Year 3.
Sheffield Hallam (Pblc Hlth Nutr) Course includes business elements covering human resources and project management.

Top research universities and colleges (RAE 2008) (Nutritional Sciences) London (King's); see also **Agricultural Sciences/Agriculture**.

Examples of sandwich degree courses Cardiff (UWIC); Coventry; Glamorgan; Glasgow Caledonian; Harper Adams (UC); Huddersfield; Kingston; Leeds Met; London South Bank; Manchester Met; Newcastle; Northumbria; Queen's Belfast; Reading; Sheffield Hallam; Surrey; Teesside; Ulster.

ADMISSIONS INFORMATION

Number of applicants per place (approx) Cardiff (UWIC) 5; Glasgow Caledonian 8; Liverpool John Moores 10; London (King's) 6; London Met 9; London South Bank 5; Newcastle 5; Nottingham 7; Robert Gordon 4; Surrey 5.

Advice to applicants and planning the UCAS personal statement Information on relevant experience, reasons for wanting to do the degree and careers sought would be useful. **Surrey** Overseas students not eligible for Nutrition and Dietetics course. See also **Dietetics** and **Appendix 4**.

Misconceptions about this course Some applicants do not realise that this is a science course.

Selection interviews **Yes** London Met, London South Bank, Nottingham (depends on application), Robert Gordon, Surrey; **Some** Liverpool John Moores, Roehampton.

Interview advice and questions Past questions have focused on scientific A-level subjects studied and aspects of subjects enjoyed by the applicants. Questions then arise from answers. Extensive knowledge expected of nutrition as a career and candidates should have talked to people involved in this type of work, for example dietitians. They will also be expected to discuss wider problems such as food supplies in developing countries and nutritional problems resulting from famine. **Liverpool John Moores** Interviews are informal. It would be useful for you to bring samples of coursework to the interview. See **Chapter 5**.

AFTER-RESULTS ADVICE

Offers to applicants repeating A-levels **Possibly higher** Nottingham; **Same** Liverpool John Moores, Manchester Met, Roehampton, St Mary's Twickenham (UC), Surrey.

GRADUATE DESTINATIONS AND EMPLOYMENT (2007/8 HESA)

Graduates surveyed 565 **Employed** 345 **In further study** 75 **Assumed unemployed** 35.

Career note Nutritionists work in retail, health promotion and sport whilst others specialise in dietetics.

OTHER DEGREE SUBJECTS FOR CONSIDERATION

Biological Sciences; Biology; Consumer Studies; Dietetics; Food Sciences; Health Studies/Sciences.

OCCUPATIONAL THERAPY

Contrary to common belief, occupational therapy is not an art career although art and craftwork may be involved as a therapeutic exercise. Occupational therapists assess the physical, mental and social needs of ill or disabled people and help them regain lost skills and manage their lives to the best of their circumstances. Most courses include anatomy, physiology, physical rehabilitation, psychology, sociology, mental health and ethics. Selectors look for maturity, initiative, enterprise, tact, sound judgement and organising ability.

Useful websites www.cot.co.uk; www.otdirect.co.uk.

NB The points totals shown to the left of the institutions are for ease of reference only. It must not be assumed that Tariff points are always used by institutions or that they can be substituted for an offer in grades. The level of an offer is not necessarily indicative of the quality of a course.

COURSE OFFERS INFORMATION

Subject requirements/preferences **GCSE** English, mathematics and science grade A–C. **AL** A social science or science subjects required or preferred for most courses. **Other** All applicants need to pass an occupational health check and obtain Criminal Records Bureau (CRB) clearance.

NB In 2011 universities and colleges will differ in their use of GCE AL/AS unit grade information, A* grades, the Extended Project (EPQ), the Advanced Diploma and the Cambridge Pre-U examination when considering applicants and making offers. An EPQ may be accepted in place of an AS subject. Check websites of universities and colleges for the latest offers information.

Your target offers and examples of courses provided by each institution

320 pts **Cardiff** – ABB (Occ Thera) (IB 28 pts)
300 pts **Bournemouth** – 300 pts (Occ Thera)
Brunel – 300 pts (Occ Thera) (IB 31 pts)
Southampton – BBB (Occ Thera) (IB 30 pts)
Ulster – BBB +HPAT (Occ Thera) (See **Ch.5**)
280 pts **Bristol UWE** – 280–320 pts (Occ Thera) (IB 28 pts)
Northumbria – 280 pts (Occ Thera) (IB 25 pts)
270 pts **Glyndŵr** – 270 pts (Occ Thera)
260 pts **East Anglia** – BCC (Occ Thera) (IB 30 pts)
240 pts **Bradford** – CCC (Occ Thera)
Coventry – 240 pts (Occ Thera)
Cumbria – 240 pts (Occ Thera)
Derby – 240 pts (Occ Thera)
Huddersfield – CCC 240 pts (Occ Thera)
Liverpool – CCC 240 pts (Occ Thera) (IB 28 pts)
Northampton – 240 pts (Occ Thera)
Oxford Brookes – CCC 240 pts (Occ Thera)
Plymouth – 240 pts (Occ Thera)
Robert Gordon – CCC 240 pts (Occ Thera)
Salford – 240 pts (Occ Thera) (IB 24 pts)
Sheffield Hallam – 240 pts (Occ Thera)
Teesside – 240–280 pts (Occ Thera)
York St John – CCC 240 pts (Occ Thera)
230 pts **Queen Margaret** – 230 pts (Occ Thera)
200 pts **Canterbury Christ Church** – 200 pts (Occ Thera)
160 pts **Glasgow Caledonian** – CC (Occ Thera)

Brighton – indiv offers may vary (p/t Occ Thera)

NHS bursaries are available for all courses.

Alternative offers

See **Chapter 7** and **Appendix 1** for grades/UCAS Tariff points information for the International Baccalaureate, Scottish Highers/Advanced Highers, the Welsh Baccalaureate, the Irish Leaving Certificate, the Cambridge Pre-U Diploma, the Advanced Diploma and the Extended Project.

CHOOSING YOUR COURSE (SEE ALSO CH.1)

Some course features

Brunel (Occ Thera) Course can also be taken as a four- to six-year part-time course.
East Anglia (Occ Thera) Practice placements in hospitals and the community. Advanced units in Year 3 include paediatrics and orthotics.

Liverpool (Occ Thera) Six placements take place throughout the course. 1000 hours required in practice settings for professional registration.

See also **Health Sciences/Studies**.

Universities and colleges teaching quality See www.qaa.ac.uk; www.unistats.com.

ADMISSIONS INFORMATION

Number of applicants per place (approx) Canterbury Christ Church 5; Cardiff 10; Coventry 15; Cumbria 20; Derby 5; East Anglia 5; Northampton 4; Northumbria 4; Oxford Brookes 12; Queen Margaret 7; Robert Gordon 6; Salford 5; Sheffield Hallam 7; Southampton 7; Ulster 13; York St John 5.

Advice to applicants and planning the UCAS personal statement Contact your local hospital and discuss this career with the occupational therapists. Try to obtain work shadowing experience and make notes of your observations. Describe any such visits in full (see **Reasons for rejection (non-academic)**). Applicants are expected to have visited two occupational therapy departments, one in a physical or social services setting, one in the mental health field. Good interpersonal skills. Breadth and nature of health-related work experience is important. Also skills, interests (for example, sports, design). Applicants should have a high standard of communication skills and experience of working with people with disabilities. **York St John** Contact with the profession essential; very competitive course. See also **Appendix 4**.

Selection interviews East Anglia; most institutions.

Interview advice and questions Since this a vocational course, work experience is nearly always essential and applicants are likely to be questioned on the types of work involved and the career. Some universities may use admissions tests: check websites and see **Chapter 5**.

Reasons for rejection (non-academic) Poor communication skills. Lack of knowledge of occupational therapy. Little evidence of working with people. Uncertain about their future career. Lack of maturity. Indecision regarding the profession. **Salford** Failure to function well in groups and inability to perform practical tasks.

AFTER-RESULTS ADVICE

Offers to applicants repeating A-levels **Same** Derby, Salford, York St John.

GRADUATE DESTINATIONS AND EMPLOYMENT (2007/8 HESA)

No data available.

Career note Occupational therapists (who work mostly in hospital departments) are involved in the rehabilitation of those who have required medical treatment and involve the young, aged and, for example, people with learning difficulties.

OTHER DEGREE SUBJECTS FOR CONSIDERATION

Audiology; Community Studies; Dietetics; Education; Health Studies/Sciences; Nursing; Nutrition; Physiotherapy; Podiatry; Psychology; Radiography; Social Policy and Administration; Social Work; Sociology; Speech Sciences.

OPTOMETRY (OPHTHALMIC OPTICS)

(including **Ophthalmic Dispensing** and **Orthoptics**)

Optometry courses (which are increasingly popular) lead to qualification as an optometrist (previously known as an ophthalmic optician). They provide training in detecting defects and diseases in the eye and in prescribing treatment with, for example, spectacles, contact lenses and other appliances to correct or improve vision. Orthoptics includes the study of general anatomy, physiology and normal child development and leads to a career as an orthoptist. This involves the investigation, diagnosis and treatment of binocular vision and other eye conditions. The main components of degree courses include the study of the eye, the use of diagnostic and measuring equipment and treatment of eye abnormalities. See also **Appendix 4**.

Useful websites www.optical.org; www.orthoptics.org.uk.

NB The points totals shown to the left of the institutions are for ease of reference only. It must not be assumed that Tariff points are always used by institutions or that they can be substituted for an offer in grades. The level of an offer is not necessarily indicative of the quality of a course.

COURSE OFFERS INFORMATION

Subject requirements/preferences GCSE Good grades in English and science subjects usually required. **AL** Science subjects required for all Optometry courses. Mathematics usually acceptable.

NB In 2011 universities and colleges will differ in their use of GCE AL/AS unit grade information, A* grades, the Extended Project (EPQ), the Advanced Diploma and the Cambridge Pre-U examination when considering applicants and making offers. An EPQ may be accepted in place of an AS subject. Check websites of universities and colleges for the latest offers information.

Your target offers and examples of courses provided by each institution

360 pts **Aston** – AAA (Optometry) (IB 34–35 pts)
Cardiff – AAA (Optometry) (IB 34 pts)
340 pts **Bradford** – AAB 340 pts (Optometry) (IB 33 pts)
City – AAB (Optometry) (IB 33 pts)
Glasgow Caledonian – AAB (Optometry)
Manchester – AAB (Optometry) (IB 35 pts)
Ulster – AAB 340 pts (Optometry) (IB 37 pts)
320 pts **Anglia Ruskin** – ABB (Optometry) (IB 33 pts HL chem biol maths 6)
300 pts **Sheffield** – BBB (Orthoptics) (IB 32 pts)
240 pts **Liverpool** – CCC 240 pts (Orthoptics) (IB 26 pts)
200 pts **Anglia Ruskin** – 200 pts (Oph Disp; Opt Mgt)
160 pts **Glasgow Caledonian** – CC (Oph Disp)
120 pts **Bradford (Coll)** – 120–160 pts (Oph Disp Mgt)

Alternative offers

See **Chapter 7** and **Appendix 1** for grades/UCAS Tariff points information for the International Baccalaureate, Scottish Highers/Advanced Highers, the Welsh Baccalaureate, the Irish Leaving Certificate, the Cambridge Pre-U Diploma, the Advanced Diploma and the Extended Project.

EXAMPLES OF FOUNDATION DEGREES IN THE SUBJECT FIELD

City; Nottingham Castle (Coll).

CHOOSING YOUR COURSE (SEE ALSO CH.1)

Some course features

Aston The course offers an integration of teaching and professional practice and a hospital placement scheme.
Bradford Placements take place after graduation during the Pre-registration Year.
Cardiff This is a three-year course after which graduates undertake a one-year pre-registration course.
City Extensive patient contact takes place in Year 3.

Universities and colleges teaching quality See www.qaa.ac.uk; www.unistats.com.

Top research universities and colleges (RAE 2008) Bradford (Optometry); Glasgow Caledonian (Biomedical and Vision Sciences); City (Optometry and Vision Science).

ADMISSIONS INFORMATION

Number of applicants per place (approx) Anglia Ruskin 12; Aston 7; Bradford 6; Cardiff 13; City 11; Glasgow Caledonian 9.

Number of applicants (**a** UK **b** EU (non-UK) **c** non-EU **d** mature) **Anglia Ruskin ab**431; **Aston a**700 **b**50 c**70** d**10**; **Bradford ab**600 **c**90; **Glasgow Caledonian a**548 **c**23

Advice to applicants and planning the UCAS personal statement For Optometry courses contact with optometrists is essential, either work shadowing or gaining some work experience. Make notes of your experiences and the work done and report fully on the UCAS application on why the career interests you. See also **Appendix 4**.

Selection interviews Yes Bradford, City, Glasgow Caledonian; **Some** Anglia Ruskin, Aston, Cardiff.

Interview advice and questions Optometry is a competitive subject requiring applicants to have had some work experience on which they will be questioned. **Anglia Ruskin** Why will you make a good optometrist? Describe the job. See **Chapter 5**.

AFTER-RESULTS ADVICE

Offers to applicants repeating A-levels Higher City; **Possibly higher** Aston; **Same** Anglia Ruskin, Cardiff.

GRADUATE DESTINATIONS AND EMPLOYMENT (2007/8 HESA)

Optometry graduates surveyed 515 **Employed** 325 **In further stud**y 15 **Assumed unemployed** 5.

Career note The great majority of graduates enter private practice either in small businesses or in larger organisations (which have been on the increase in recent years). A small number work in eye hospitals. Orthoptists tend to work in public health and education dealing with children and the elderly.

OTHER DEGREE SUBJECTS FOR CONSIDERATION

Health Studies; Nursing; Occupational Therapy; Physics; Physiotherapy; Radiography; Speech Studies.

PHARMACOLOGY

(including **Toxicology**; see also **Biological Sciences, Health Sciences/Studies** and **Pharmacy**)

Pharmacology is the study of drugs and medicines and courses focus on physiology, biochemistry, toxicology, immunology, microbiology and chemotherapy. Pharmacologists are not qualified to work as pharmacists. Toxicology involves the study of the adverse effects of chemicals on living systems. See also **Appendix 4** under **Pharmacology**.

Useful websites www.thebts.org; www.scienceyear.com; www.pharmacology.com.

NB The points totals shown to the left of the institutions are for ease of reference only. It must not be assumed that Tariff points are always used by institutions or that they can be substituted for an offer in grades. The level of an offer is not necessarily indicative of the quality of a course.

COURSE OFFERS INFORMATION

Subject requirements/preferences GCSE English, science and mathematics. **AL** Chemistry and/or biology required for most courses.

NB In 2011 universities and colleges will differ in their use of GCE AL/AS unit grade information, A* grades, the Extended Project (EPQ), the Advanced Diploma and the Cambridge Pre-U examination when considering applicants and making offers. An EPQ may be accepted in place of an AS subject. Check websites of universities and colleges for the latest offers information.

Your target offers and examples of courses provided by each institution

410 pts **Imperial London** – AAAb +BMAT (Pharmacol Transnl Med Sci)

380 pts **Cambridge** – A*AA college offers may vary (Nat Sci (Pharmacol)) (IB 38–42 pts HL 766–777)

London (UCL) – AAB+AS–ABB+AS (Pharmacology) (IB 34–36 pts)

360 pts **Edinburgh** – AAA 2nd yr entry (Pharmacology) (IB 36 pts)
340 pts **Leeds** – AAB–BBB (Pharmacology) (IB 36–32 pts HL 17–15 pts)
London (King's) – ABB+AS (Pharmacol; Pharmacol Mol Genet; Physiol Pharmacol) (IB 34 pts HL 5 chem biol)
Manchester – AAB–BBB (Pharmacol Physiol Ind; Pharmacol; Pharmacol Ind; Pharmacol Modn Lang) (IB 35–32 pts)
Newcastle – AAB (Drug Dev) (IB 36 pts)
St Andrews – AAB (Chem Pharmacol) (IB 36 pts)
Southampton – AAB–BBB 340–300 pts (Pharmacology)
320 pts **Bath** – ABB (Pharmacology) (IB 34 pts HL 666)
Birmingham – ABB–BBC (Chem Pharmacol) (IB 31 pts HL chem 5)
Bristol – ABB (Pharmacol; Pharmacol Ind) (IB 33 pts HL 665 inc 2 sci)
Cardiff – ABB 320–300 pts (Med Pharmacol) (IB 32 pts)
Glasgow – ABB (Pharmacology) (IB 32 pts)
Leicester – ABB (Biol Sci (Physiol Pharmacol))
Liverpool – ABB–BBB (Pharmacol; Medcnl Chem Pharmacol) (IB 33 pts)
Newcastle – ABB (Pharmacology) (IB 30–32 pts HL 5 chem)
Surrey – ABB–BBB (Bioch (Pharmacol) (Tox))
300 pts **Aberdeen** – BBB 2nd yr entry (Pharmacol; Immun Pharmacol)
Dundee – BBB 2nd yr entry (Pharmacol; Bioch Pharmacol; Pharmacol Physiol Sci) (IB 34 pts)
Edinburgh – BBB 1st yr entry (Pharmacology) (IB 30 pts)
Nottingham – BBB (Neuro Pharmacol) (IB 32 pts)
280 pts **Plymouth** – 280–320 pts (Tox Hlth) (IB 26 pts)
Strathclyde – BBC–BCC (Bioch Pharmacol; Immun Pharmacol) (IB 28 pts)
260 pts **Bradford** – 260 pts (Biomed Sci (Pharmacol))
Nottingham Trent – 260 pts (Pharmacology)
240 pts **Aberdeen** – CCC 1st yr entry (Pharmacol; Immun Pharmacol) (IB 28 pts)
Central Lancashire – 240–260 pts (Physiol Pharmacol)
Coventry – 240 pts (Med Pharmacol Sci)
Dundee – CCC 1st yr entry (Pharmacol; Bioch Pharmacol; Pharmacol Physiol Sci) (IB 28 pts)
Hertfordshire – 240 pts (Pharmacol; Pharmacol Euro/N Am)
Manchester Met – 240 pts (Physiol Pharmacol)
Portsmouth – 240 pts (Pharmacology)
220 pts **Nottingham Trent** – 220 pts (Biol Sci (Pharmacol))
Westminster – CCD/CC (Physiol Pharmacol) (IB 26 pts)
200 pts **East London** – 200 pts (Pharmacol courses; Tox courses)
Edinburgh Napier – CDD 220 pts (Immun Tox)
Kingston – 200–280 pts (Pharmacol; Pharmacol Bus)
Wolverhampton – 200–260 pts (Pharmacology)
180 pts **London Met** – 180 pts (Pharmacol; Herb Medcnl Sci)
165 pts **Queen Margaret** – 165 pts (App Pharmacol)
160 pts **Leeds Met** – 160 pts (Biomed Sci (Physiol Pharmacol))

Middlesex – 2–3 AL contact University (Trad Chin Med)

Alternative offers

See **Chapter 7** and **Appendix 1** for grades/UCAS Tariff points information for the International Baccalaureate, Scottish Highers/Advanced Highers, the Welsh Baccalaureate, the Irish Leaving Certificate, the Cambridge Pre-U Diploma, the Advanced Diploma and the Extended Project.

CHOOSING YOUR COURSE (SEE ALSO CH.1)

Some course features

Aberdeen (Pharmacol; Immun Pharmacol) Both courses have industrial placement options.
Cardiff Pharmacology shares a common first year in the Biomedical Science programme with seven other subjects; the decision to specialise takes place in Year 2.

Kingston There is an optional sandwich year in full-time employment.
Liverpool Studies include physiology, biology and biochemistry.
Manchester Pharmacology is part of the extensive Life Sciences programme and can be taken with modern languages or with industrial or professional experience.
Newcastle (Drug Dev) This new course focuses on science and engineering, covering chemistry, genetics, biology and pharmacology as well as bioprocessing for the large-scale manufacture of biopharmaceuticals.
Surrey Pharmacology and Toxicology are options in the Biochemistry degree programme.

Universities and colleges teaching quality See www.qaa.ac.uk; www.unistats.com.

Examples of sandwich degree courses (including Pharmaceutical Sciences, Pharmacology and Pharmacy) Bath (Pharmacol); Bradford (Pharm); Bristol (Pharmacol); Bristol UWE (Pharmacol); Cardiff (Pharmacol); Coventry (Pharm Sci); De Montfort (Pharml Sci); East London (Pharmacol); Hertfordshire (Pharml Sci); Huddersfield (Pharml Sci); Imperial London (Pharmacol Transnl Med Sci); Kingston (Pharml Sci; Pharmacol); London Met (Pharmacol); Manchester (Pharmacol); Manchester Met (Physiol Pharmacol St); Nottingham Trent (Physiol Pharmacol); Sheffield Hallam (Pharml Sci); Southampton (Pharmacol); Sunderland (Pharmacol).

ADMISSIONS INFORMATION

Number of applicants per place (approx) Bath 6; Birmingham 6; Bradford 20; Bristol 8; Cardiff 8; Dundee 5; East London 4; Hertfordshire 10; Leeds 7; Liverpool 5; London (King's) 6; Portsmouth 4; Southampton 8; Strathclyde 10; Sunderland 12; Wolverhampton 4.

Advice to applicants and planning the UCAS personal statement Contact with the pharmaceutical industry is important in order to be aware of the range of work undertaken. Read pharmaceutical journals (although note that Pharmacology and Pharmacy courses lead to different careers). **Bath** Interests outside A-level studies. Important to produce evidence that there is more to the student than A-level ability. **Bristol** Be aware that a Pharmacology degree is mainly biological rather than chemical although both subjects are important. See also **Pharmacy**.

Misconceptions about this course Mistaken belief that Pharmacology and Pharmaceutical Sciences is the same as Pharmacy and that a Pharmacology degree will lead to work as a pharmacist.

Selection interviews **Yes** Bath, Birmingham (don't be anxious – this is an opportunity for you to see us!), Cambridge, Newcastle; **Some** Cardiff, Dundee, Portsmouth, Sunderland.

Interview advice and questions Past questions include: Why do you want to do Pharmacology? Why not Pharmacy? Why not Chemistry? How are pharmacologists employed in industry? What are the issues raised by anti-vivisectionists on animal experimentation? Questions relating to the A-level syllabus in chemistry and biology. See **Chapter 5**.

Reasons for rejection (non-academic) Confusion between Pharmacology, Pharmacy and Pharmaceutical Sciences. One university rejected two applicants because they had no motivation or understanding of the course (one had A-levels at AAB!). Insurance against rejection for Medicine. Lack of knowledge about pharmacology as a subject.

AFTER-RESULTS ADVICE

Offers to applicants repeating A-levels **Higher** Bristol, Glasgow, Leeds; **Same** Bath, Bradford, Cardiff, Dundee, Portsmouth, Sunderland.

GRADUATE DESTINATIONS AND EMPLOYMENT (2007/8 HESA)

Pharmacology, Toxicology and Pharmacy graduates surveyed 1830 **Employed** 1165 **In further study** 235 **Assumed unemployed** 60.

Career note The majority of pharmacologists work with the large pharmaceutical companies involved in research and development. A small number are employed by the NHS in medical research and clinical trials. Some will eventually diversify and become involved in marketing, sales and advertising.

OTHER DEGREE SUBJECTS FOR CONSIDERATION

Biochemistry; Biological Sciences; Biology; Biotechnology; Chemistry; Life Sciences; Medical Biochemistry; Medicinal Chemistry; Microbiology; Natural Sciences; Pharmaceutical Sciences; Pharmacy; Physiology; Toxicology.

PHARMACY and PHARMACEUTICAL SCIENCES

(including **Herbal Medicine**; see also **Biochemistry, Chemistry** and **Health Sciences/Studies**)

Pharmacy is the science of medicines, involving research into chemical structures and natural products of possible medicinal value, the development of dosage and the safety testing of products. This table also includes information on courses in Pharmaceutical Science (which should not be confused with Pharmacy) which is a multi-disciplinary subject covering chemistry, biochemistry, pharmacology and medical issues. Pharmaceutical scientists apply their knowledge of science and the biology of disease to the design and delivery of therapeutic agents. Note: All Pharmacy courses leading to MPharm are four years.

Useful websites www.pharmweb.net; www.scienceyear.com; www.pharmacycareers.org; www.chemistanddruggist.co.uk.

NB The points totals shown to the left of the institutions are for ease of reference only. It must not be assumed that Tariff points are always used by institutions or that they can be substituted for an offer in grades. The level of an offer is not necessarily indicative of the quality of a course.

NB Only Pharmacy degree courses accredited by the Royal Phamaceutical Society of Great Britain lead to a qualification as a pharmacist. Check prospectuses and websites.

COURSE OFFERS INFORMATION

Subject requirements/preferences **GCSE** English, mathematics and science subjects. **AL** Chemistry and one or two other sciences required for most courses.

NB In 2011 universities and colleges will differ in their use of GCE AL/AS unit grade information, A* grades, the Extended Project (EPQ), the Advanced Diploma and the Cambridge Pre-U examination when considering applicants and making offers. An EPQ may be accepted in place of an AS subject. Check websites of universities and colleges for the latest offers information.

Your target offers and examples of courses provided by each institution

340 pts **Bath** – AAB (MPharm Pharm) (IB 36 pts HL 666)
Cardiff – AAB–ABB (MPharm Pharm) (IB 34 pts HL chem 6 +1 sci)
Leeds – AAB (Cheml Pharml Eng)
London (King's) – ABB+AS–BBB+AS (MPharm Pharm) (IB 34 pts HL 655)
Manchester – AAB–ABB (MPharm Pharm) (IB 35 pts HL 766)
Nottingham – AAB (MPharm Pharm) (IB 36 pts)
Queen's Belfast – AAB–ABBa (MPharm Pharm) (IB 34 pts HL 666)

320 pts **Aston** – ABB (MPharm Pharm) (IB 34 pts)
Brighton – ABB (MPharm Pharm) (IB 34 pts HL 5 chem)
East Anglia – ABB–BBB (MPharm Pharm) (IB 31–32 pts)
Hertfordshire – 320 pts (MPharm Pharm)
Huddersfield – 320 pts (MPharm Pharm)
Leicester – ABB (Pharml Chem Ind)
London (Sch Pharm) – ABB (MPharm Pharm) (IB 32 pts HL 655)
Strathclyde – ABB–BBB (MPharm Pharm)

300 pts **Bradford** – 300 pts (MPharm Pharm) (IB 30 pts)
Central Lancashire – 300 pts (Pharmacy) (IB 32 pts)
De Montfort – 300 pts (MPharm Pharm)

Dundee – BBB 300 pts 2nd yr entry (Biomol Drug Dscvry; Drug Des Mechnsms) (IB 34 pts)
East Anglia – BBB (Pharml Chem)
Hull – BBB–CCC 300–240 pts (Pharml Sci) (IB 30 pts)
Keele – BBB (MPharm Pharm) (IB 32 pts)
Kent (Medway Sch Pharm) – BBB 300 pts (MPharm Pharm) (IB 32 pts)
Kingston – 300 pts (MPharm Pharm)
Loughborough – 300–280 pts (Medcnl Pharml Chem) (IB 34 pts)
Portsmouth – BBB (MPharm Pharm) (IB 30 pts)
Reading – BBB (MPharm Pharm)
Robert Gordon – BBB (MPharm Pharm)
Sunderland – 300 pts (MPharm Pharm)
Wolverhampton – 300–360 pts (MPharm Pharm)

280 pts **London (QM)** – 280 pts (Pharml Chem) (IB 28 pts)
Northumbria – 280 pts (Pharml Chem)

260 pts **Bradford** – 260 pts (Chem Pharml Foren Sci)
Brighton – BCC (Pharml Chem Sci) (IB 28 pts)
Leicester – BCC (Pharml Chem) (IB 30 pts)
Nottingham Trent – 260 pts (Pharml Medicin Chem)
Sheffield Hallam – 260 pts (Pharml Sci)

240 pts **Bradford** – 240 pts (Pharml Mgt)
Dundee – CCC 240 pts 1st yr entry (Biomol Drug Dscvry; Drug Des Mechansms) (IB 28 pts)
Greenwich – 240 pts (Pharml Sci)
Hertfordshire – 240 pts (Pharml Sci)
Manchester Met – 240 pts (Pharml Chem)

220 pts **Huddersfield** – 220 pts (Pharml Sci)

200 pts **De Montfort** – 200 pts (Pharml Cos Sci)
East London – 200 pts (Herb Med)
Kingston – 200–280 pts (Pharml Sci)
Lincoln – 200 pts (Herb Med)
London Met – 200 pts (Pharml Sci)
Wolverhampton – 200–260 pts (Pharml Sci)

160 pts **Westminster** – CC–CD (Hlth Sci (Herb Med))

140 pts **West Scotland** – CD (Pharml Sci)

Liverpool John Moores – offers vary: contact University (MPharm Pharm)
Middlesex – contact University (Herb Med)

Alternative offers
See **Chapter 7** and **Appendix 1** for grades/UCAS Tariff points information for the International Baccalaureate, Scottish Highers/Advanced Highers, the Advanced Diploma and the Extended Project.

EXAMPLES OF FOUNDATION DEGREES IN THE SUBJECT FIELD
Aston; Birmingham Met (Coll); Kent (Medway Sch Pharm); Kingston; Merton (Coll); Preston (Coll); Sunderland City (Coll).

CHOOSING YOUR COURSE (SEE ALSO CH.1)
Some course features
Aston One of the largest Pharmacy Schools which includes hospital-based clinical teaching.
Brighton (Pharm) Studies include behavioural sciences, social pharmacy, health promotion and business studies reflecting the changing role of the pharmacist.
East Anglia (Pharm) Professional placements begin in Year 1.
Hertfordshire (Pharml Sci) Students not meeting the normal entry requirements can apply for an Extended degree which leads to Year 1 entry.
Keele Hospital, industrial and community placements take place throughout the course.

Universities and colleges teaching quality See www.qaa.ac.uk; www.unistats.com.

Top research universities and colleges (RAE 2008) Nottingham; Manchester; London (Sch Pharm); Bath; Queen's Belfast; East Anglia; London (King's); Strathclyde; Bradford; Cardiff.

Examples of sandwich degree courses See **Pharmacology**.

ADMISSIONS INFORMATION

Number of applicants per place (approx) Aston 10; Bath 6; Bradford 10; Brighton 24 (apply early); Cardiff 5; De Montfort 14; Liverpool John Moores (Pharm) 7; London (King's) 15, (Sch Pharm) 6; Nottingham 8; Portsmouth 20; Robert Gordon 11; Strathclyde 10; Sunderland 20.

Number of applicants (**a** UK **b** EU (non-UK) **c** non-EU **d** mature) **Aston a**1400 **b**100 **c**300 **d**180; **Bradford ab**1200 **c**200.

Advice to applicants and planning the UCAS personal statement Work experience and work shadowing with a retail and/or hospital pharmacist is important, and essential for Pharmacy applicants. Read pharmaceutical journals, extend your knowledge of well known drugs and antibiotics. Read up on the history of drugs. Attendance at Open Days or careers conference. See also **Appendix 4**. **Manchester** Students giving preference for Pharmacy are likely to be more successful than those who choose Pharmacy as an alternative to Medicine or Dentistry.

Misconceptions about this course That a degree in Pharmaceutical Science is a qualification leading to a career as a pharmacist. It is not: it is a course which concerns the application of chemical and biomedical science to the design, synthesis and analysis of pharmaceuticals for medicinal purposes. See also **Pharmacology**.

Selection interviews Yes Bath, Bradford, Brighton, Bristol, De Montfort, East Anglia, Liverpool John Moores, London (Sch Pharm), Manchester (most), Nottingham, Robert Gordon, Strathclyde, Wolverhampton; **Some** Aston, Cardiff, Portsmouth.

Interview advice and questions As work experience is essential for Pharmacy applicants, questions are likely to focus on this and what they have discovered. Other relevant questions could include: Why do you want to study Pharmacy? What types of work do pharmacists do? What interests you about the Pharmacy course? What branch of pharmacy do you want to enter? Name a drug – what do you know about it (formula, use etc)? Name a drug from a natural source and its use. Can you think of another way of extracting a drug? Why do fungi destroy bacteria? What is an antibiotic? Can you name one and say how it was discovered? What is insulin? What is its source and function? What is diabetes? What type of insulin is used in its treatment? What is a hormone? What drugs are available over the counter without prescription? What is the formula of aspirin? What is genetic engineering? **Bath** Informal and relaxed; 400 approx selected for interview – very few rejected at this stage. **Cardiff** Interviews cover both academic and vocational aspects; candidates must reach a satisfactory level in both areas. **Liverpool John Moores** What are the products of a reaction between an alcohol and a carboxylic acid? **Manchester** Candidates failing to attend interviews will have their applications withdrawn. The majority of applicants are called for interview. See also **Chapter 5**.

Reasons for rejection (non-academic) Poor communication skills. Poor knowledge of pharmacy and the work of a pharmacist.

AFTER-RESULTS ADVICE

Offers to applicants repeating A-levels Higher Bradford, Cardiff, De Montfort, Liverpool John Moores, London (Sch Pharm) AAB, Nottingham (offers rarely made), Portsmouth, Queen's Belfast, Strathclyde; **Possibly higher** Aston, Robert Gordon; **Same** Bath, Brighton, East Anglia, Sunderland, Wolverhampton.

GRADUATE DESTINATIONS AND EMPLOYMENT (2007/8 HESA)

See **Pharmacology**.

Career note The majority of Pharmacy graduates proceed to work in the commercial and retail fields, although opportunities also exist with pharmaceutical companies and in hospital pharmacies. There are also opportunities in agricultural and veterinary pharmacy.

OTHER DEGREE SUBJECTS FOR CONSIDERATION

Biochemistry; Biological Sciences; Biology; Biotechnology; Chemistry; Drug Development; Life Sciences; Medicinal Chemistry; Microbiology; Natural Sciences; Pharmacology; Physiology.

PHILOSOPHY

(see also **Physiology** and **Psychology**)

Philosophy is one of the oldest and most fundamental disciplines, which examines the nature of the universe and humanity's place in it. Philosophy seeks to discover the essence of the mind, language and physical reality and discusses the methods used to investigate these topics.

Useful websites www.iep.utm.edu; www.philosophypages.com; www.philosophy.eserver.org; see also **Religious Studies**.

NB The points totals shown to the left of the institutions are for ease of reference only. It must not be assumed that Tariff points are always used by institutions or that they can be substituted for an offer in grades. The level of an offer is not necessarily indicative of the quality of a course.

COURSE OFFERS INFORMATION

Subject requirements/preferences **GCSE** English and mathematics. A foreign language may be required. **AL** No specific subjects except for joint courses.

NB In 2011 universities and colleges will differ in their use of GCE AL/AS unit grade information, A* grades, the Extended Project (EPQ), the Advanced Diploma and the Cambridge Pre-U examination when considering applicants and making offers. An EPQ may be accepted in place of an AS subject. Check websites of universities and colleges for the latest offers information.

Your target offers and examples of courses provided by each institution

410 pts **Warwick** – AAAb (PPE) (IB 38–40 pts)

390 pts **Warwick** – AABb/AAbbb (Phil; Phil Lit; Phil Class Civ; Phil Comp Sci) (IB 36–38 pts)

380 pts **Cambridge** – A*AA college offers may vary (Philosophy) (IB 38–42 pts)
London (King's) – AAA+AS–AAB+AS (Maths Phil) (IB 38 pts HL maths 6)
London (UCL) – AAA+AS–AAB+AS (Phil; Phil Gk; Phil Econ; Phil Hist Art) (IB 36–38 pts)

360 pts **Birmingham** – AAA–AAB (Maths Phil) (IB 34–36 pts)
Bristol – AAA–ABB (Phil; Phil Econ; Phil Theol) (IB 37–33 pts HL 665)
Durham – AAA (Nat Sci (Phil); Phil; Phil Psy; Phil Comb Hons) (IB 38 pts)
London (King's) – AAB+AS **or** AAbbb (Phil; Phys Phil; Fr/Ger/Hisp St Phil; War St Phil) (IB 36 pts)
London LSE – AAA (Phil Econ; Phil Lgc Sci Meth) (IB 38 pts HL 766)
Nottingham – AAA–AAB (Econ Phil; Maths Phil) (IB 38 pts)
Oxford – AAA (PPE; Maths Phil; Phys Phil; Phil; Phil Theol; Psy Phil Physiol (PPP); Phil Modn Langs) (IB 38–40 pts)
St Andrews – AAA (Lgc Phil Sci Maths; Mgt Phil; Phil Psy) (IB 36–40 pts)

340 pts **Bristol** – AAB–ABB (Class St Phil) (IB 35–33 pts)
Cardiff – AAB (Phil Cult Crit)
East Anglia – AAB–BBB (Art Hist Phil; Econ Phil; Phil Hist; Phil Film St) (IB 35 pts)
Essex – AAB (Law Phil)
Exeter – AAB–ABB (Phil Arbc St; Phil Pol Econ; Phil Langs)
Glasgow – AAB (Phil MA courses; Phil MA Soc Sci courses; Phil BSc courses) (IB 34–32 pts)
Liverpool – AAB–ABB (Phil; Engl Phil; Maths Phil) (IB 35 pts HL 555)
London (King's) – ABB+AS **or** BBB+AS (Relig Phil Eth) (IB 34 pts HL 6)
London (RH) – AAB–ABB (Mus Phil; Phil; Anc Hist Phil; Dr Phil; Langs Phil)
Manchester – AAB–BBB (Phil; Phil Hlcst St; Phil Langs; Phil Blt Nat Env; Phil Class Civ Art Hist; Phil Comb St courses) (IB 35–32 pts)
St Andrews – AAB (Phil Scot Hist; Phil Soc Anth; Phil Theol St) (IB 36 pts)

Sheffield – AAB–ABB (Phil; Bib St Phil; Phil Psy; Ling Phil courses) (IB 32–35 pts)
Southampton – AAB–ABB 340–320 pts (Phil; Phil Maths; Phil Pol; Phil Sociol) (IB 34 pts HL 16 pts)
Sussex – AAB–ABB (Phil; Phil Cog Sci; Phil Langs; Hist Phil) (IB 34–36 pts)
York – AAB–BBB (Phil; Phil Ling; Phil Pol) (IB 34 pts)

320 pts **Birmingham** – ABB (Phil; Phil Joint Hons) (IB 32–34 pts)
Cardiff – ABB (Phil; Phil Welsh; Phil Sociol) (IB 32 pts)
Essex – 320–300 pts (Phil; Phil Hist; Phil Film; PPE; Phil Law) (IB 29 pts)
Hull – 320–300 pts (Phil; Phil Pol; Phil Relig; Phil Langs; Law Phil) (IB 30 pts)
Kent – 320–280 pts (Phil; Phil Soc Psy; Phil Pol) (IB 31–35 pts)
Lancaster – ABB 320 pts (Phil; Phil Pol Econ; Hist Phil) (IB 30 pts)
Leeds – ABB–BBC (Phil; Hist Phil Sci courses; Mind Knwl; Phil joint courses) (IB 32 pts)
Newcastle – ABB (Phil St) (IB 32 pts HL 555)
Reading – 320–340 pts (Phil; Art Phil)

300 pts **Dundee** – BBB 2nd yr entry (Phil; Euro Phil courses; Art Phil Contemp Prac; Am St Phil) (IB 34 pts)
Edinburgh – BBB (Phil; Artif Intel Phil; Mnd Lang; Phil Gk) (IB 34 pts HL 555)
Gloucestershire – 300 pts (Relig Phil Eth)
Keele – 300–320 pts (Law Phil)
Lancaster – BBB–BBC 300–280 pts (Phil Relig St; Eth Phil Relig) (IB 29 pts)
Liverpool – BBB (Phil Fr/Ger/Hisp St/Ital) (IB 30 pts)
Nottingham – ABC–BBB (Phil; Phil Theol; Mus Phil; Fr/Ger Phil) (IB 32 pts)
Queen's Belfast – BBB–BBCb (Phil courses; PPE) (IB 29 pts HL 655)

280 pts **Essex** – 280 pts (Phil Modn Langs)
Hertfordshire – 280 pts (Phil Crea Writ; Phil Media Cult; Phil)
London (Hey) – 280 pts (Phil; Phil Relig Eth; Psy Phil)
Middlesex – 280 pts (Phil; Phil Relig St)
Oxford Brookes – BBC (Phil; Phil Comb Hons courses)

260 pts **Bristol UWE** – 260–300 pts (Phil; Phil Media Cult St; Phil Jrnl)
Keele – 260–320 pts (Phil Fin; Chem Phil; Astro Phil; Educ St Phil)
Liverpool Hope – 260 pts (Phil Eth courses)
Manchester Met – 260 pts (Psy Phil Slf; Analyt App Phil)
Nottingham Trent – 260 pts (Phil Media; Phil Lang; Phil Euro St)

240 pts **Aberdeen** – CCC (Phil Hist Art; Phil; Nat Phil (Phys)) (IB 30 pts HL 15 pts)
Central Lancashire – 240–200 pts (Phil Comb Hons; Phil)
Dundee – 240 pts 1st yr entry (Phil; Euro Phil courses; Art Phil Contemp Prac; Am St Phil) (IB 29 pts)
London Met – 240 pts (Phil Bus Econ; Phil Hist)
St Mary's Twickenham (UC) – 240 pts (Phil Joint Hons)
Stirling – CCC (Phil; Comp Sci Phil; Phil Psy; Phil Crimin)

220 pts **Bath Spa** – 220–280 pts (Phil Eth)
Newman (UC) – 220–260 pts (Phil Relig Eth courses; Phil Theol courses)

200 pts **Anglia Ruskin** – 200 pts (Phil; Phil Dr; Phil Engl)
Northampton – 200–260 pts (Phil; Phil Joint Hons)
Staffordshire – 200 pts (Phil Psy; Eth Phil Soty; Int Hist Phil)
Trinity Saint David – 200–240 pts (Phil; Phil Joint Hons)

180 pts **Bradford** – 180–220 pts (Interd Hum St (Phil Engl Psy Sociol))
Greenwich – 180 pts (Phil Int St; Phil Law; Phil Langs)

160 pts **Wolverhampton** – 160–220 pts (Phil Sociol; Relig St Phil; War St Phil)

80 pts **London (Birk)** – 80 pts for under 21s (over 21s varies) (p/t Philosophy)

Open University – (Phil Psy; Pol Phil Econ – contact +44 (0)845 300 6090 or www.openuniversity.co.uk/you)

Alternative offers

See **Chapter 7** and **Appendix 1** for grades/UCAS Tariff points information for the International

Baccalaureate, Scottish Highers/Advanced Highers, the Welsh Baccalaureate, the Irish Leaving Certificate, the Cambridge Pre-U Diploma, the Advanced Diploma and the Extended Project.

CHOOSING YOUR COURSE (SEE ALSO CH.1)

Some course features
Kent A very wide range of options in Stages 2 and 3. Optional year abroad.
Leeds Elective modules include the history and philosophy of science.
London (Hey) One of the largest faculties. Philosophy can also be studied with Theology, Psychology or Religion and Ethics.
Sussex Eleven joint courses with Philosophy.

Universities and colleges teaching quality See www.qaa.ac.uk; www.unistats.com.

Top research universities and colleges (RAE 2008) London (UCL); St Andrews; London (King's); Sheffield; Reading; Cambridge (History and Philosophy of Science); London LSE; Oxford; Stirling; Bristol; Essex; London (Birk); Cambridge (Philosophy); Nottingham; Leeds; Middlesex; Edinburgh.

ADMISSIONS INFORMATION

Number of applicants per place (approx) Birmingham 6; Bradford 7; Bristol 20; Cambridge 6; Cardiff 8; Dundee 6; Durham 14 (all courses); East Anglia 6; Hull 19; Kent 9; Lancaster 6; Leeds 10; Liverpool 5; London (Hey) 4, (King's) 6; London LSE (Phil Lgc Sci Meth) 4, (Phil Econ) 32; London Met 3; Manchester (Phil) 10; Middlesex 8; Northampton 3; Nottingham 7; Oxford (success rate 44%, (PPE) 29%); Sheffield 6; Southampton 7; Staffordshire 8; Trinity Saint David 4; Warwick 9; York 6.

Advice to applicants and planning the UCAS personal statement Read Bertrand Russell's *Problems of Philosophy*. Refer to any particular aspects of philosophy which interest you (check that these are offered on the courses for which you are applying). Since Philosophy is not a school subject, selectors will expect applicants to have read around the subject. Explain what you know about the nature of studying philosophy. Say what you have read in philosophy and give an example of a philosophical issue that interests you. Universities do not expect applicants to have a wide knowledge of the subject, but evidence that you know what the subject is about is important.

Misconceptions about this course Applicants are sometimes surprised to find what wide-ranging Philosophy courses are offered.

Selection interviews **Yes** Bangor, Birmingham, Bristol (mature students), Cambridge, Durham, Kingston, Lancaster, Leeds, Liverpool, London (Hey), (UCL), Newcastle, Oxford, Southampton, Staffordshire, Trinity Saint David, Warwick; **Some** Cardiff, Dundee, Hull, London LSE (rare), York.

Interview advice and questions Philosophy is a very wide subject and initially applicants will be asked for their reasons for their choice and their special interests in the subject. Questions in recent years have included: Is there a difference between being tactless and being insensitive? Can you be tactless and thin-skinned? Define the difference between knowledge and belief. Was the vertical distortion of El Greco's paintings a product of a vision defect? What is the point of studying philosophy? What books on philosophy have you read? Discuss the work of a renowned philosopher. What is a philosophical novel? Who has the right to decide your future – yourself or another? What do you want to do with your life? What is a philosophical question? John is your husband, and if John is your husband then necessarily you must be his wife; if you are necessarily his wife then it is not possible that you could not be his wife; so it was impossible for you not to have married him – you were destined for each other. Discuss. What is the difference between a man's entitlements, his deserts and his attributes? What are morals? A good understanding of philosophy is needed for entry to degree courses, and applicants are expected to demonstrate this if they are called to interview. As one admissions tutor stated, 'If you find Bertrand Russell's *Problems of Philosophy* unreadable – don't apply!' **Cambridge** If you were to form a government of philosophers what selection process would you use? Is it moral to hook up a psychopath (whose only pleasure is killing) to a really stimulating machine so that he can believe he is in the real world and kill as much as he likes? **Oxford** If you entered a teletransporter and your body was destroyed and instantly recreated on Mars in exactly the same way with all your memories intact etc, would you be the same person? Tutors are not so much concerned with what you know as how you think about it. Evidence required concerning social and political topics and the ability to discuss them critically. (PPE) Is being hungry the same thing as wanting to eat? Why is there not a global government? What do you think of teleport machines? Should there be an intelligence test to decide who should vote? **York** Do human beings have free will? Do we perceive the world as it really is? See also **Chapter 5**.

Reasons for rejection (non-academic) Evidence of severe psychological disturbance, criminal activity, drug problems (evidence from referees' reports). Lack of knowledge of philosophy. **Oxford** He was not able to explore his thoughts deeply enough or with sufficient centrality. **York** No evidence of having read any philosophical literature.

AFTER-RESULTS ADVICE

Offers to applicants repeating A-levels **Higher** Bristol (Phil Econ), Essex, Glasgow, Leeds, Nottingham (in some cases), Warwick; **Same** Bangor, Birmingham, Bristol, Cardiff, Dundee, Durham, East Anglia, Hull, Liverpool Hope, Newcastle, Newport, Nottingham (for previous applicants), Nottingham Trent, Southampton, St Mary's Twickenham (UC), Staffordshire, Stirling, Wolverhampton, York; **No offers made** Cambridge.

GRADUATE DESTINATIONS AND EMPLOYMENT (2007/8 HESA)

Graduates surveyed 1615 **Employed** 685 **In further study** 385 **Assumed unemployed** 165.

Career note Graduates have a wide range of transferable skills that can lead to employment in many areas, eg management, public administration, publishing, banking and social services.

OTHER DEGREE SUBJECTS FOR CONSIDERATION

Divinity; History and Philosophy of Science; History of Art; Human Sciences; Psychology; Religious Studies; Science; Theology.

PHOTOGRAPHY

(see also **Art and Design (General) (Fine Art), Film, Radio, Video and TV Studies** and **Media Studies**)

Photography courses offer a range of specialised studies involving commercial, industrial and still photography, portraiture and film, digital and video work. Increasingly this subject is featuring in Media courses. See also **Appendix 4**.

Useful websites http://hub.the-aop.org; www.rps.org; www.bjp-online.com.

NB The points totals shown to the left of the institutions are for ease of reference only. It must not be assumed that Tariff points are always used by institutions or that they can be substituted for an offer in grades. The level of an offer is not necessarily indicative of the quality of a course.

COURSE OFFERS INFORMATION

Subject requirements/preferences **GCSE** Art and/or a portfolio usually required. **AL** One or two subjects may be required, including an art/design or creative subject.

NB In 2011 universities and colleges will differ in their use of GCE AL/AS unit grade information, A* grades, the Extended Project (EPQ), the Advanced Diploma and the Cambridge Pre-U examination when considering applicants and making offers. An EPQ may be accepted in place of an AS subject. Check websites of universities and colleges for the latest offers information.

Your target offers and examples of courses provided by each institution

360 pts **Glasgow SA** – AAA–AAB (Fine Art (Photo))

300 pts **Heriot-Watt** – ABC/BCC 2nd yr entry (MEng/BEng Electron Eng Imag Sci Tech)
Leeds – BBB 300 pts (Cnma Photo)

280 pts **Birmingham City** – 280 pts (Media Comm (Media Photo))
Nottingham Trent – 280 pts (Photo Photo Euro)
Plymouth – 280–320 pts (Photography) (IB 26 pts)
Sheffield Hallam – 280 pts (Photography)
260 pts **Coventry** – 260 pts (Photography)
Gloucestershire – 260 pts (Photojrnl Doc Photo)
Heriot-Watt – BCC/CDD 1st yr entry (MEng/BEng Electron Eng Imag Sci Tech)
Huddersfield – 260 pts (Photography)
Northumbria – 260 pts (Contemp Photo Prac)
240 pts **Bolton** – 240 pts (Photo; Photo Comb Hons)
Bournemouth – 240 pts (Photography)
Chester – 240 pts (Photo Comb courses)
Cumbria – 240 pts (Photography)
De Montfort – 240 pts (Photo Vid)
Edinburgh Napier – 240 pts (Photo Film)
Lincoln – 240 pts (Contemp Lns Media courses)
London Met – 240 pts (Fine Art (Photo))
Manchester Met – 240 pts (Photography)
Newport – 240–260 pts (Doc Photo; Photo Fash Adv; Photo Art)
Roehampton – 240–320 pts (Photo joint courses)
Wolverhampton – 240 pts (Photography)
220 pts **Anglia Ruskin** – 220 pts (Photography)
Glamorgan – 220 pts (Photography)
Northampton – 220–260 pts (Photo Prac)
200 pts **Canterbury Christ Church** – 200 pts (Photo Comb Hons; Photo Joint Hons)
Creative Arts – 200–160 pts (Photo Media Arts; Photo Vid; Photo) (IB 30 pts)
Hereford (CA) – 200 pts (Photography)
Portsmouth – 200–280 pts/Fdn Art (Photography)
Suffolk (Univ Campus) – 200 pts (Photo Dig Media; Photo)
Thames Valley (London CMusMedia) – 200 pts (Photo Dig Imag)
Westminster – BB (Photo Arts)
180 pts **Derby** – 180–240 pts (Photo; Commer Photography)
Sunderland – 180–220 pts (Photo Vid Dig Imag; Photo)
165 pts **Staffordshire** – 165–200 pts (Photo; Photojrnl; Photo Phil; Fine Art (Photo))
160 pts **Blackpool and Fylde (Coll)** – 160 pts (Photo; Wldlf Photo)
Bournemouth Arts (UC) – 160 pts (Photography)
Central Lancashire – 160–220 pts (Photo; Photo Jrnl; Photo Fash Brnd Prom)
Glasgow (SA) – CC (Fine Art (Photo))
London South Bank – CC (Dig Photo)
Middlesex – 160 pts/Fdn Art (Photography)
Robert Gordon – 160 pts (Photo Electron Media) (IB 24 pts)
Southampton Solent – 160–200 pts (Fash Photo; Photo)
Ulster – 160 pts (Photography)
Westminster – CC (Clin Photo; Photo Dig Imag) (IB 26 pts)
120 pts **Cleveland (CAD)** – 120 pts (Photography)
Northbrook (Coll) – 120 pts (Contemp Photo Arts (Prac))
Stockport (CFHE) – 120 pts (Photography)
80 pts **Bristol UWE** – 80 pts (Photography)
Croydon (Coll) – 80 pts (Photography)

Arts London – contact admissions (Photography)
Bedfordshire – contact admissions (Dig Photo Vid Art)
Brighton – contact admissions (Photography)
East London – Fdn Art (Photography)
Edinburgh (CA) – contact admissions (Photography)

Falmouth (UC) – contact admissions (Press Edit Photo; Mar Nat Hist Photo)
Gloucestershire – Fdn Art (Photo Edit Adv; Fine Art (Photo))
Kingston – Fdn Art (Graph Des Photo; Photo)
Norwich Arts (UC) – (Photography)
Swansea Met – contact admissions (Photo Arts)

Alternative offers
See **Chapter 7** and **Appendix 1** for grades/UCAS Tariff points information for the International Baccalaureate, Scottish Highers/Advanced Highers, the Welsh Baccalaureate, the Irish Leaving Certificate, the Cambridge Pre-U Diploma, the Advanced Diploma and the Extended Project.

EXAMPLES OF FOUNDATION DEGREES IN THE SUBJECT FIELD

Anglia Ruskin; Arts London; Bath Spa; Bedfordshire; Blackburn (Coll Univ Centre); Blackpool and Fylde (Coll); Bournemouth Arts (UC); Brighton; Bristol City (Coll); Bucks New; Cleveland (CAD); Cornwall (Coll); Exeter (Coll); Farnborough (CT); Gloucestershire; Greenwich; Grimsby (IFHE); Guildford (Coll); Hereford (CA); Hertfordshire; Hull (Coll); Kirklees (Coll); Leeds (CAD); Manchester (Coll); Mid-Cheshire (Coll); Nescot; Nottingham New (Coll); Plymouth (CAD); St Helens (Coll); Sheffield (Coll); Staffordshire (Reg Fed); Truro (Coll).

CHOOSING YOUR COURSE (SEE ALSO CH.1)

Some course features
Falmouth (UC) Specialist courses in Press, Marine and Natural History Photography are also offered.
Nottingham Trent Courses in Photography are offered focusing on social documentary, art practice, fashion work or with a year in Europe.
Westminster (Clin Photo) The only full-time degree in clinical photography in the UK, it combines a study of photography and digital imaging with science, anatomy, physiology, biology and clinical practice. Work-based learning in a clinical setting forms a large part of the course.

Universities and colleges teaching quality See www.qaa.ac.uk; www.unistats.com.

Examples of sandwich degree courses Birmingham City; Portsmouth; Staffordshire.

ADMISSIONS INFORMATION

Number of applicants per place (approx) Arts London 10; Birmingham City 6; Blackpool and Fylde (Coll) 3; Bournemouth Arts (UC) 7; Cleveland (CAD) 2; Croydon (Coll) 15; Derby 20; Edinburgh Napier 33; Falmouth (UC) 3; Newport 2; Nottingham Trent 4; Plymouth 2; Plymouth (CAD) 7; Portsmouth 4; Staffordshire 3; Stockport (CFHE) 6; Swansea Met 12.

Advice to applicants and planning the UCAS personal statement Discuss your interest in photography and your knowledge of various aspects of the subject, for example, digital, video, landscape, medical, wildlife and portrait photography. Read photographic journals to keep up-to-date on developments, particularly in photographic technology. You will also need first-hand experience of photography and to be competent in basic skills. **Croydon (Coll)** Broad range of interests. **Derby** (Non-EU students) Fluency in written and spoken English important. Portfolio of work essential. See also **Appendix 4**.

Misconceptions about this course Some believe that courses are all practical work with no theory. **Cumbria** They didn't realise the facilities were so good! **Kirklees (Coll)** Some applicants think that it's a traditional photography course. It's as digital as the individual wants it to be.

Selection interviews **Yes** Most institutions will interview applicants and expect to see a portfolio of work.

Interview advice and questions Questions relate to the applicant's portfolio of work which, for these courses, is of prime importance. Who are your favourite photographers? What is the most recent exhibition you have attended? Have any leading photographers influenced your work? Questions regarding contemporary photography. Written work sometimes required. See **Chapter 5**.

Reasons for rejection (non-academic) Lack of passion for the subject. Lack of exploration and creativity in practical work. Poorly presented portfolio.

AFTER-RESULTS ADVICE

Offers to applicants repeating A-levels **Same** Birmingham City, Blackpool and Fylde (Coll), Chester, Cumbria, Manchester Met, Nottingham Trent, Staffordshire.

GRADUATE DESTINATIONS AND EMPLOYMENT (2007/8 HESA)

Cinematics and Photography graduates surveyed 2115 **Employed** 1025 **In further study** 175 **Assumed unemployed** 270.

Career note Opportunities for photographers exist in a range of specialisms including advertising and editorial work, fashion, medical, industrial, scientific and technical photography. Some graduates also go into photojournalism and other aspects of the media.

OTHER DEGREE SUBJECTS FOR CONSIDERATION

Art and Design; Digital Animation; Film, Radio, Video and TV Studies; Media Studies; Moving Image; Radiography.

PHYSICAL EDUCATION

(see also **Sports Sciences/Studies**)

Physical Education courses are very popular and unfortunately restricted in number. Ability in gymnastics and involvement in sport are obviously important factors. See also Appendix 2.

Useful websites www.afpe.org.uk; www.uksport.gov.uk; see also **Education Studies and Teacher Training**.

NB The points totals shown to the left of the institutions are for ease of reference only. It must not be assumed that Tariff points are always used by institutions or that they can be substituted for an offer in grades. The level of an offer is not necessarily indicative of the quality of a course.

COURSE OFFERS INFORMATION

Subject requirements/preferences **GCSE** English, mathematics and a science. **AL** PE, sports studies and science are preferred subjects and for some courses one of these may be required. **Other** Enhanced Disclosure (criminal record check) before starting the course. Declaration of Health usually required.

NB In 2011 universities and colleges will differ in their use of GCE AL/AS unit grade information, A* grades, the Extended Project (EPQ), the Advanced Diploma and the Cambridge Pre-U examination when considering applicants and making offers. An EPQ may be accepted in place of an AS subject. Check websites of universities and colleges for the latest offers information.

Abbreviations used in this table P - Primary Teaching; S - Secondary Teaching; QTS - Qualified Teacher Status.

Your target offers and examples of courses provided by each institution

340 pts **Brighton** – AAB 340–380 pts (PE QTS) (IB 36 pts)
320 pts **Birmingham** – ABB–BBB (Spo PE Coach Sci)
Brunel – 320–300 pts (Spo Sci (PE Yth Spo); S PE) (IB 30 pts)
Leeds – ABB–BBB (Spo Exer Sci)
300 pts **Bangor** – 300–260 pts (Spo Sci (PE); Spo Hlth PE)
Brighton – BBB (Spo Coach)
Edinburgh – BBB (PE)
Roehampton – 300–360 pts (P Educ (PE) QTS)
Stranmillis (UC) – BBB (PE Educ)
280 pts **Edge Hill** – 280 pts (PE Sch Spo)
Hull – 280 pts (PE Spo Sci Psy; PE Spo Sci Mgt)

Leeds Met – 280–260 pts (PE S; PE)
Liverpool John Moores – 280–320 pts (Spo Dev PE; PE QTS P/S; Educ St PE)
Newman (UC) – 280–320 pts (Ely Yrs P Educ PE; Ely Chld P Educ PE)
Sheffield Hallam – 280 pts (PE Yth Spo)
Worcester – 280 pts (PE Comb Hons)

260 pts **Cardiff (UWIC)** – 260 pts (Educ St Spo Physl Actvt) (IB 28 pts)
Chichester – BCC (PE QTS S)
Manchester Met – 260 pts (Exer PE Comb Hons; Coach St Comb Hons)
Stirling – BCC (Spo St PE Educ) (IB 30 pts)

240 pts **Bedfordshire** – 240–320 pts (PE QTS S)
Cumbria – 240 pts (PE QTS P/S)
Greenwich – 240 pts (Spo Sci Coach)
Leeds Trinity (UC) – 240 pts (PE P Spo Dev)
Plymouth – 240 pts (PE P)
UCP Marjon – 240 pts (Coach PE; PE S Educ)

220 pts **Liverpool John Moores** – 220–260 pts (Out Educ PE)
UCP Marjon – 220 pts (Chld PE)
Wolverhampton – 220–260 pts (PE QTS P)

180 pts **St Mary's Twickenham (UC)** – 180–200 pts (PE QTS S)

160 pts **Bedfordshire** – 160 pts (Spo PE)
Bishop Grosseteste (UC) – 160 pts (Educ St Spo)

Alternative offers
See **Chapter 7** and **Appendix 1** for grades/UCAS Tariff points information for the International Baccalaureate, Scottish Highers/Advanced Highers, the Welsh Baccalaureate, the Irish Leaving Certificate, the Cambridge Pre-U Diploma, the Advanced Diploma and the Extended Project.

CHOOSING YOUR COURSE (SEE ALSO CH.1)

Some course features
Birmingham (Spo PE Coach Sci) A practical and theoretical programme in sport, physical education and leisure with a placement module in education or the leisure industry.
Chichester (PE QTS S) Course covers games, gymnastics, dance, aquatic, athletic fitness and health and outdoor adventure activities. Placements take place in Years 2 and 3 and the final year.
Liverpool John Moores Courses are offered for those wanting to train as PE teachers or with specialist studies in sport development and management.
UPC Marjon (Coach PE) Course covers coach and sport education and also leads to a PGCE in PE teaching.

Top research universities and colleges (RAE 2008) See **Sports Sciences/Studies**.

ADMISSIONS INFORMATION

Number of applicants per place (approx) Bangor 19; Birmingham 5; Brunel 10; Chichester 5; Edge Hill 40; Leeds Trinity (UC) 33; Liverpool John Moores 4; Newman (UC) 5; St Mary's Twickenham (UC) 9; Sheffield Hallam 60; UCP Marjon 18; Worcester 31.

Advice to applicants and planning the UCAS personal statement Ability in gymnastics, athletics and all sports and games is important. Full details of these activities should be given on the UCAS application – for example, teams, dates and awards achieved, assisting in extra-curricular activities. Involvement with local sports clubs, health clubs, summer camps, gap year. Relevant experience in coaching, teaching, community and youth work. **Liverpool John Moores** Commitment to working with children and a good sports background.

Selection interviews **Yes** Most institutions. In most cases, applicants will take part in physical education practical tests and games/gymnastics, depending on the course. The results of these tests could affect the level of offers. See **Chapter 5**.

Interview advice and questions The applicant's interests in physical education will be discussed, with specific questions on, for example, sportsmanship, refereeing, umpiring and coaching. Questions in the past have also included: What qualities should a good netball goal defence possess? How could you encourage a group of children into believing that sport is fun? Do you think that physical education should be compulsory in schools? Why do you think you would make a good teacher? What is the name of the education minister? **Liverpool John Moores** Questions on what the applicant has gained or learned through experiences with children.

Reasons for rejection (non-academic) Poor communication and presentational skills. Relatively poor sporting background or knowledge. Lack of knowledge about the teaching of physical education and the commitment required. Lack of ability in practicalities, for example, gymnastics, dance when relevant. Poor self-presentation. Poor writing skills.

AFTER-RESULTS ADVICE

Offers to applicants repeating A-levels **Same** Liverpool John Moores, Newman (UC), St Mary's Twickenham (UC).

GRADUATE DESTINATIONS AND EMPLOYMENT (2007/8 HESA)

No data available.

Career note The majority of graduates go into education although, depending on any special interests, they may also go on into the sport and leisure industry.

OTHER DEGREE SUBJECTS FOR CONSIDERATION

Coach Education; Exercise and Fitness; Exercise Physiology; Human Biology; Leisure and Recreation; Physiotherapy; Sport and Exercise Science; Sport Health and Exercise; Sport Studies/Sciences; Sports Coaching; Sports Development; Sports Engineering; Sports Psychology; Sports Therapy.

PHYSICS

(see also **Astronomy/Astrophysics**)

There is a considerable shortage of applicants for Physics courses. Many courses have flexible arrangements to enable students to follow their own interests and specialisations, for example circuit design, microwave devices, cosmology, medical physics, solid state electronics.

Useful websites www.scienceyear.com; www.scicentral.com; www.ipem.org.uk; www.iop.org; www.noisemakers.org.uk; www.NewScientistJobs.com; www.physics.org; www.nature.com/physics.

NB The points totals shown to the left of the institutions are for ease of reference only. It must not be assumed that Tariff points are always used by institutions or that they can be substituted for an offer in grades. The level of an offer is not necessarily indicative of the quality of a course.

COURSE OFFERS INFORMATION

Subject requirements/preferences **GCSE** English, mathematics and science. **AL** Physics and mathematics are required for most courses.

NB In 2011 universities and colleges will differ in their use of GCE AL/AS unit grade information, A* grades, the Extended Project (EPQ), the Advanced Diploma and the Cambridge Pre-U examination when considering applicants and making offers. An EPQ may be accepted in place of an AS subject. Check websites of universities and colleges for the latest offers information.

Your target offers and examples of courses provided by each institution

380 pts **Cambridge** – A*AA college offers may vary (Nat Sci (Phys) (Physl Sci) (Astro)) (IB 38–42 pts HL 766–777)

Imperial London – A*mathsAA (Phys; Phys St Musl Perf; Phys Yr Euro; Phys Theor Phys) (IB 38 pts HL 666)

360 pts **Bath** – AAA (Nat Sci) (IB 36 pts HL 666)

Bristol – AAA–AAB (MSci/BSc Phys; Phys Astro; Maths Phys; Phys Phil) (IB 37–35 pts)

Durham – AAA (Nat Sci Phys) (IB 38–40 pts HL maths phys 6–7)

Durham – AAA–AAB (Phys; Phys Astron; Theor Phys; Chem Phys; Phys Joint Hons) (IB 36–40 pts)

Edinburgh – AAA 2nd yr entry (Cheml Phys; Comput Phys; Phys; Mathem Phys) (IB 36 pts HL 666)

Leeds – AAA–AAB (MPhys Phys; Phys Nano; Med Phys; Theor Phys; Phys Astro) (IB 36–34 pts HL maths phys 6)

Liverpool – AAA–ABB (MPhys Phys; Mathem Phys; Astro) (IB 32 pts)

London (King's) – AAA (Maths Phys)

London (King's) – AAB+AS (Phys; Phys Phil; Phys Med Apps) (IB 36 pts HL maths phys 5)

London (RH) – AAA–ABB (MSci/BSc Phys; App Phys; Theor Phys; Phys Mus; Phys Prtcl Phys) (IB 36 pts)

London (UCL) – AAB+AS–ABB+AS (Phys; Cheml Phys; Theor Phys) (IB 34–36 pts HL 6 maths phys)

London (UCL) – AAB+AS–BBB+AS (Med Phys; Phys Med Sci; Cheml Phys) (IB 32–36 pts)

Manchester – AAA–AAB (Phys; Phys Photon; Phys Astro; Phys Bus Mgt; Phys Phil) (IB 37–33 pts)

Nottingham – AAA–AAB (Nat Sci) (IB 34–36 pts)

Oxford – AAA (Phys; Phys Phil) (IB 38–42 pts)

St Andrews – AAA (Phys Langs; Phys Photon; Comp Sci Phys; Phys; Lgc Phil Sci (Phys)) (IB 36 pts)

Sussex – AAA (MPhys Phys Rsch) (IB 36 pts)

Warwick – AAA–AAB (Maths Phys; Phys; Phys Bus St) (IB 36 pts)

340 pts **Bath** – AAB–ABB (Phys; Maths Phys) (IB 34–36 pts HL maths phys 5–6)
Birmingham – AAB–ABB (Phys; Phys Astro; Phys Bus Mgt; Phys Nanoscl Phys; Phys Prtcl Phys Cosmo) (IB 32–34 pts)
Bristol – AAB–ABB (Cheml Phys) (IB 34 pts HL 665 maths phys chem)
Cardiff – AAB–ABB (MPhys Phys; Phys Astron; Phys Maths) (IB 32 pts HL 6 maths phys)
Edinburgh – AAB–ABB 1st yr entry (Cheml Phys; Comput Phys; Phys; Mathem Phys) (IB 34 pts)
Edinburgh – AAB 2nd yr entry (Geophys; Geophys Meteor) (IB 34 pts)
Exeter – AAB–ABB (Phys; Phys Astro; Phys Med Apps; Phys Aus/N Am/NZ) (IB 34–31 pts)
Lancaster – AAB–ABB 340–320 pts (MPhys Phys; Phys Prtcl Phys Cosmo; Phys Biomed Phys; BSc Phys Spc Sci; Theor Phys Maths) (IB 31 pts HL 16 pts)
Leicester – AAB (MPhys Phys; Phys Planet Sci; Phys Spc Sci Tech; Phys Nano Tech) (IB 34 pts)
Liverpool – AAB–BBB (BSc Phys; Mathem Phys; Geophys; Theor Phys; Phys Med Apps; Phys Nucl Sci) (IB 26 pts)
London (QM) – 340 pts (MSci Phys; Astro; Theor Phys; Phys Prtcl Phys) (IB 32 pts)
Nottingham – AAB–ABB (Phys Theor Phys; Mathem Phys; Phys; Phys Euro Lang; Phys Nano; Phys Med Phys) (IB 35 pts)
Queen's Belfast – AAB (MSci Phys; Phys Med Apps; Theor Phys)
Southampton – AAB (Phys; Phys Astron; Phys Nano; Phys Maths; Phys Spc Sci) (IB 36–34 pts)
Surrey – AAB 340 pts (MPhys Phys; Phys Nucl Astro; Phys Sat Tech; Phys Fin)
Sussex – AAB–ABB (MPhys Phys; Phys Astro; Theor Phys) (IB 36 pts)
Swansea – 340 pts (MPhys Phys; Theor Phys; Phys Nano; Phys Spo Sci)
York – AAB–ABB (Phys; Phys Astro; Phys Bus Mgt; Maths Phys; Phys Phil) (IB 34–32 pts)

320 pts **East Anglia** – ABB–BBB (Cheml Phys) (IB 31 pts)
Glasgow – ABB (Phys Astron; Phys; Phys Theor Phys) (B 32 pts)
Leeds – ABB (Hist Phil Sci (Phys); Chem Phys)
Liverpool – ABB (BSc Phys Ocn Clim St) (IB 33 pts)
Liverpool John Moores – ABB 320 pts (Astrophysics)
Loughborough – 320–300 pts (Eng Phys; Phys Maths; Phys Mgt; Spo Sci Phys) (IB 30 pts)
Newcastle – ABB (Nat Sci) (IB 34 pts)
Sheffield – ABB (Theor Phys; Phys Aus/N Am; Phys Comp Sci; Phys Med Phys) (IB 33 pts)
Strathclyde – ABB–BBB (Phys; Phys QTS) (IB 30–32 pts)
Surrey – ABB 320 pts (Phys; Phys Nucl Astro; Phys Sat Tech; Phys Fin) (IB 28 pts)
Sussex – ABB–BBB (Phys; Phys Astro; Theor Phys) (IB 34 pts)

300 pts **Cardiff** – 300 pts (Phys Med Phys; Phys Mus) (IB 30 pts)
Dundee – BBB–CDD (Phys; App Phys; Electron Eng Phys) (IB 28–32 pts)
Edinburgh – BBB 1st yr entry (Geophys; Geophys Meteor) (IB 30 pts)
Keele – 300–320 pts (Phys courses)
Leicester – BBB (BSc Phys; Phys Nano Tech; Phys Spc Sci Tech; Phys Planet Sci)
Liverpool John Moores – BBB 300 pts (Phys Astron)
London (QM) – 300 pts (BSc Phys; Theor Phys; Phys Prtcl Phys) (IB 28 pts)
Nottingham Trent – 300–260 pts (Phys; Phys Astro; Phys Nucl Tech)
Salford – 300–260 pts (Phys; Pure App Phys; Phys Plt St; Phys Acoust)
Swansea – 300 pts (BSc Phys; Phys Nano; Phys Spo Sci)

280 pts **Aberystwyth** – 280 pts (Spc Sci Robot) (IB 27 pts HL phys comp-sci maths 5)
Cardiff – BBC (BSc Phys Astron; Astro; Phys Med Phys; Theor Comput Phys)
Central Lancashire – 280–320 pts (Physics)
Hertfordshire – 280 pts (Phys courses)
Kent – BBC (Phys; Phys Foren Sci; Phys Spc Sci Sys; Phys Astro) (IB 30 pts)
Queen's Belfast – BBC (BSc Phys; Phys Med Apps; Phys Comp Sci)

240 pts **Aberdeen** – CCC 240 pts (Nat Phil Sci; Phys Langs; Phys Geol)
Aberystwyth – 240–280 pts (Phys Planet Spc Phys; Mathem Theor Phys) (IB 29 pts)
Hull – 240–300 pts (BSc App Phys; Phys; Phys Nano)

220 pts **Heriot-Watt** – BB+AS 2nd yr entry (Comput Phys; Eng Phys; Mathem Phys; Phys)
Nottingham Trent – 220 pts (Phys Foren Apps)

180 pts **Heriot-Watt** – CC+AS 1st yr entry (Comput Phys; Eng Phys; Mathem Phys; Phys)

160 pts **Canterbury Christ Church** – 160 pts (Integ Sci)

140 pts **West Scotland** – CD–DD **or** bbc (Phys; Phys Med Tech; Phys Multim)

120 pts **Sussex** – DD (Phys Astron courses +Fdn Yr)

100 pts **London (Birk)** – 100 pts (p/t Phys)

Open University – (Phys Sci – contact +44 (0)845 300 6090 or www.openuniversity.co.uk/you)

Alternative offers
See **Chapter 7** and **Appendix 1** for grades/UCAS Tariff points information for the International Baccalaureate, Scottish Highers/Advanced Highers, the Welsh Baccalaureate, the Irish Leaving Certificate, the Cambridge Pre-U Diploma, the Advanced Diploma and the Extended Project.

EXAMPLES OF FOUNDATION DEGREES IN THE SUBJECT FIELD

Cumbria; Hull (Coll); Nottingham Trent.

CHOOSING YOUR COURSE (SEE ALSO CH.1)

Some course features
Bath After a first year on the Natural Sciences programme or the Mathematics and Physics course it is possible to transfer to Single Honours Physics in Year 2.
Durham Several courses are offered which include Theoretical Physics and Astronomy. Physics can also be taken jointly with seven other subjects and is also offered as part of the Natural Sciences programme.
Lancaster A wide range of degree courses is offered with considerable flexibility to tailor the course to individual interests.
Leicester Students can follow several routes, for example specialising in space science, planetary science or astrophysics in this leading department.
Loughborough An optional year in paid employement is offered either in the UK or abroad.

Universities and colleges teaching quality See www.qaa.ac.uk; www.unistats.com.

Top research universities and colleges (RAE 2008) Lancaster; Cambridge; Nottingham; St Andrews; Bath; Edinburgh; Durham; Imperial London; Sheffield; London (UCL); Glasgow; Birmingham; Exeter; Sussex.

Examples of sandwich degree courses Bath; Bristol; Hertfordshire; London South Bank; Loughborough; Nottingham Trent; Surrey; West Scotland.

ADMISSIONS INFORMATION

Number of applicants per place (approx) Bath 6; Birmingham 6; Bristol 9; Cardiff 4, (Phys Astron) 6; Dundee 5; Durham 6; Edinburgh 9; Exeter 5; Heriot-Watt 5; Hull 7; Imperial London 3; Kent 8; Lancaster 8; Leeds 7; Leicester 7; Liverpool 4; London (King's) 7, (QM) 6, (RH) 9, (UCL) 6; Loughborough 6; Nottingham 10; Salford 5; Southampton 6; Strathclyde 5; Surrey 5; Swansea 3; Warwick 8; York 5.

Advice to applicants and planning the UCAS personal statement Work experience should be mentioned, together with interests in maths and physics. Admissions tutors look for potential, enthusiasm and interest in the subject. The Institute of Physics can provide information on the work of the physicist. An awareness of the range of careers in which physics is involved should also be mentioned on the UCAS application, together with an explanation of any particular interests and details of books read on physics or mathematics (not science fiction!), and attendance at courses, for example, summer schools or day conferences for physics or engineering. See **Appendix 4**.

Selection interviews **Yes** Bath, Birmingham, Cambridge, Durham, Exeter, Heriot-Watt, Hull, Imperial London, Lancaster, Liverpool, London (QM), (RH), Loughborough, Nottingham, Oxford, Sheffield, Strathclyde, Surrey, Swansea, Warwick, York; **Some** Cardiff, Dundee, East Anglia, Salford.

Interview advice and questions Questions will almost certainly focus on those aspects of the physics A/AS-level course which the student enjoys. **Bristol** Why Physics? Questions on mechanics, physics and pure maths. Given paper and calculator and questions asked orally; best to take your own calculator. Tutors seek enthusiastic and highly motivated students and the physicist's ability to apply basic principles to unfamiliar situations. See **Chapter 5**.

AFTER-RESULTS ADVICE

Offers to applicants repeating A-levels **Higher** Bristol, Glasgow, St Andrews, Warwick; **Possibly higher** Aberystwyth, Hull, Leeds, Loughborough, York; **Same** Birmingham, Cardiff, Dundee, Durham, East Anglia, Exeter, Lancaster, Leicester, Liverpool, Salford, Swansea; **No offers made** Cambridge.

GRADUATE DESTINATIONS AND EMPLOYMENT (2007/8 HESA)

Graduates surveyed 1600 **Employed** 535 **In further study** 590 **Assumed unemployed** 150.

Career note Many graduates go into scientific and technical work in the manufacturing industries. However, in recent years, financial work, management and marketing have also attracted many seeking alternative careers.

OTHER DEGREE SUBJECTS FOR CONSIDERATION

Astronomy; Astrophysics; Computer Science; Earth Sciences; Engineering subjects; Geophysics; Materials Science and Metallurgy; Mathematics; Meteorology; Natural Sciences; Oceanography; Optometry; Radiography.

PHYSIOLOGY

(see also **Animal Sciences, Philosophy** and **Psychology**)

Physiology is a study of body function. Courses in this wide-ranging subject will cover the central nervous system, special senses and neuro-muscular mechanisms, and body-regulating systems such as exercise, stress and temperature regulation.

Useful websites www.scienceyear.com; www.physoc.org; www.physiology.org; see also **Biological Sciences**.

NB The points totals shown to the left of the institutions are for ease of reference only. It must not be assumed that Tariff points are always used by institutions or that they can be substituted for an offer in grades. The level of an offer is not necessarily indicative of the quality of a course.

COURSE OFFERS INFORMATION

Subject requirements/preferences **GCSE** Science and mathematics at grade A. **AL** Two science subjects are usually required; chemistry and biology are the preferred subjects. **Other requirements** **Oxford** (Biomed Sci) Applicants take the BioMedical Admissions Test (BMAT) (see **Chapter 5**).

NB In 2011 universities and colleges will differ in their use of GCE AL/AS unit grade information, A* grades, the Extended Project (EPQ), the Advanced Diploma and the Cambridge Pre-U examination when considering applicants and making offers. An EPQ may be accepted in place of an AS subject. Check websites of universities and colleges for the latest offers information.

Your target offers and examples of courses provided by each institution

380 pts **Cambridge** – A*AA college offers may vary (Nat Sci (Physiol Dev Neuro)) (IB 38–42 pts)
360 pts **Edinburgh** – AAA 2nd yr entry (Physiology) (IB 36 pts)
Oxford – AAA +BMAT (Biomed Sci; Physiol Psy; Physiol Phil) (IB 38–42 pts)
Oxford – AAA (Psy Physiol Phil (PPP)) (IB 38–42 pts)
340 pts **Cardiff** – AAB–ABB 340–320 pts (Biomed Sci (Physiol)) (IB 34 pts)
Leeds – AAB–BBB (Hum Physiol; Spo Sci Physiol) (IB 34–32 pts)
London (King's) – ABB+AS (Physiol; Physiol Pharmacol) (IB 34 pts)
Manchester – AAB–BBB (Physiol; Physiol Ind; Physiol Modn Lang) (IB 35–32 pts)
320 pts **Aberdeen** – ABB–BCC (Biomed Sci (Physiol))
Bristol – ABB (Physiol Sci) (IB 33 pts HL 6–5 inc sci)
Glasgow – ABB (Physiol; Physiol Spo Sci Nutr; Physiol Psy) (IB 32 pts)
Leicester – ABB (Med Physiol; Biol Sci (Physiol Pharmacol)) (IB 32–34 pts)
Liverpool – ABB–BBB (Physiology) (IB 31 pts)
Newcastle – ABB (Physiol Sci) (IB 32 pts)
300 pts **Dundee** – BBB 2nd yr entry (Physiol Sci; Physiol Spo Biomed; Anat Physiol Sci; Bioch Physiol Sci) (IB 34 pts)
Edinburgh – BBB 1st yr entry (Physiology) (IB 30 pts)

280 pts **Swansea** – 280 pts (Med Sci Hum)
260 pts **Edinburgh Napier** – BCC 260 pts (Spo Exer Sci (Exer Physiol))
Ulster – 260 pts (Clin Physiol courses)
Wolverhampton – 260–320 pts (Hum Physiol)
240 pts **Central Lancashire** – 240–260 pts (Physiol Pharmacol)
Dundee – CCC 1st yr entry (Physiol Sci; Physiol Spo Biomed; Anat Physiol Sci; Bioch Physiol Sci) (IB 28 pts)
Leeds – CCC (Clin Physiol (Cardio))
Manchester Met – 240 (Physiol Pharmacol; Clin Physiol; App Biomed Sci (Clin))
220 pts **Westminster** – CCD/CC (Physiol Pharmacol) (IB 26 pts)
200 pts **Portsmouth** – 200–220 pts (Clin Hlth Sci)
180 pts **Bristol UWE** – DDD–CCD 180–220 pts (App Physiol Pharmacol)
Salford – 180–200 pts (Physiol Bioch)
120 pts **Wolverhampton** – 120–180 pts (Clin Physiol)

Alternative offers
See **Chapter 7** and **Appendix 1** for grades/UCAS Tariff points information for the International Baccalaureate, Scottish Highers/Advanced Highers, the Welsh Baccalaureate, the Irish Leaving Certificate, the Cambridge Pre-U Diploma, the Advanced Diploma and the Extended Project.

EXAMPLES OF FOUNDATION DEGREES IN THE SUBJECT FIELD
Middlesex; Nescot.

CHOOSING YOUR COURSE (SEE ALSO CH.1)
Some course features
Bristol In the first two years Physiology is studied with two other subjects, for example anatomy, pharmacology, psychology, philosophy or a language.
Leeds (Hum Physiol) Course has an optional year in industry or abroad.
Leicester (Med Physiol) Students with first class performance in the first year can apply to transfer to Medicine. Study abroad through the Erasmus scheme is also possible, and a four-year sandwich course is also available.
Newcastle The Biomedical Sciences programme offers seven science subjects, all of which have a common first year. The decision to take Physiology, or any other subject, takes place in Year 2.
See also **Biological Sciences**.

Universities and colleges teaching quality See www.qaa.ac.uk; www.unistats.com.

Top research universities and colleges (RAE 2008) See **Biological Sciences**.

Examples of sandwich degree courses Bristol UWE; Cardiff; Manchester Met; Portsmouth; Salford; Wolverhampton.

ADMISSIONS INFORMATION
Number of applicants per place (approx) Birmingham 9; Bristol 7; Cardiff 8; Dundee 5; Leeds 4; Leicester 5; Liverpool 10; London (King's) 5; Newcastle 6; Sheffield 25.

Advice to applicants and planning the UCAS personal statement See **Anatomical Science/Anatomy** and **Biological Sciences**.

Selection interviews **Yes** Birmingham, Cambridge, Leeds, Newcastle, Oxford, Sheffield; **Some** Bristol, Cardiff, Dundee.

Interview advice and questions Past questions include: What made you decide to do a Physiology degree? What experimental work have you done connected with physiology? What future career do you have in mind? What is physiology? Why not choose Medicine instead? What practicals do you do at school? **Cardiff** Interviewer expects to see outside interests and ability to mix with people as well as an interest in biological sciences. **Oxford** Over 85% of applicants interviewed. What food (out of choice) was the best to eat before an interview? See **Chapter 5**.

AFTER-RESULTS ADVICE

Offers to applicants repeating A-levels **Higher** Bristol, Glasgow, Leeds, Leicester, Newcastle, St Andrews, Sheffield; **Same** Cardiff, Dundee; **No offers made** Cambridge.

GRADUATE DESTINATIONS AND EMPLOYMENT (2007/8 HESA)

(including **Anatomical Science/Anatomy**)
Graduates surveyed 2730 **Employed** 1620 **In further study** 480 **Assumed unemployed** 160.

Career note See **Biology**.

OTHER DEGREE SUBJECTS FOR CONSIDERATION

Anatomy; Biochemistry; Biological Sciences; Biotechnology; Dentistry; Genetics; Health Studies; Medicine; Microbiology; Nursing; Optometry; Pharmacology; Radiography; Sports Science.

PHYSIOTHERAPY

Physiotherapists work as part of a multi-disciplinary team with other health professionals and are involved in the treatment and rehabilitation of patients of all ages and with a wide variety of medical problems. On successful completion of the three-year course, graduates are eligible for State Registration and Membership of the Chartered Society of Physiotherapy. (See **Appendix 2**)

Useful websites www.csp.org.uk; www.thephysiotherapysite.co.uk; www.nhscareers.nhs.uk; www.physiotherapy.co.uk.

NB The points totals shown to the left of the institutions are for ease of reference only. It must not be assumed that Tariff points are always used by institutions or that they can be substituted for an offer in grades. The level of an offer is not necessarily indicative of the quality of a course.

COURSE OFFERS INFORMATION

Subject requirements/preferences **GCSE** English, mathematics and science subjects. Many universities stipulate A/B grades in specific subjects. **AL** One or two science subjects are required. **Other requirements** Occupational health check and Criminal Records Bureau (CRB) clearance.

NB In 2011 universities and colleges will differ in their use of GCE AL/AS unit grade information, A* grades, the Extended Project (EPQ), the Advanced Diploma and the Cambridge Pre-U examination when considering applicants and making offers. An EPQ may be accepted in place of an AS subject. Check websites of universities and colleges for the latest offers information.

Your target offers and examples of courses provided by each institution

370 pts **Southampton** – ABBb 370 pts (Physiotherapy) (IB 33 pts)
360 pts **Ulster** – 360 pts +HPAT (Physiotherapy – see **Ch 5**)
355 pts **Queen Margaret** – 355 pts (Physiotherapy)
350 pts **Coventry** – 350 pts (Physiotherapy – see **Advice to applicants and planning the UCAS personal statement**)
340 pts **Bournemouth** – 340 pts (Physiotherapy)
Cardiff – AAB–BBBc (Physiotherapy) (IB 27 pts)
London (King's) – BBBc (Physiotherapy) (IB 32 pts HL 5 in 2 sci)
320 pts **Birmingham** – ABB 320 pts (Physiotherapy) (IB 34 pts)
Brunel – 320 pts inc BBC (Physiotherapy) (IB 31 pts)
Northumbria – 320 pts (Physiotherapy) (IB 32 pts)
Nottingham – ABB (Physiotherapy) (IB 32 pts HL biol 6)
300 pts **Bradford** – BBB 300 pts (Physiotherapy) (IB 32 pts)
Brighton – BBB (Physiotherapy) (IB 32 pts)
Central Lancashire – BBB (Physiotherapy) (IB 30 pts)
Cumbria – 300 pts (Physiotherapy)

East Anglia – BBB (Physiotherapy) (IB 31 pts)
Glasgow Caledonian – BBB (Physiotherapy)
Hertfordshire – 300 pts (Physiotherapy)
Keele – BBB (Physiotherapy) (IB 27 pts)
Kingston – 300 pts (Physiotherapy)
Liverpool – 300 pts (Physiotherapy) (IB 30 pts)
London (St George's) – BBB 300 pts (Physiotherapy)
Manchester Met – 300 pts (Physiotherapy)
Oxford Brookes – BBB (Physiotherapy)
Plymouth – 300 pts (Physiotherapy)
Robert Gordon – BBB (Physiotherapy) (IB 32 pts)
Salford – BBB 300 pts (Physiotherapy) (IB 32 pts)
Sheffield Hallam – 300 pts (Physiotherapy)
Teesside – 300 pts (Physiotherapy)
York St John – 300 pts (Physiotherapy)

280 pts **Bristol UWE** – 280–340 pts (Physiotherapy)
East London – 280 pts (Physiotherapy) (IB 28 pts)
Huddersfield – BBC (Physiotherapy)
Leeds Met – 280 pts (Physiotherapy)

160 pts **London South Bank** – 160 pts (Physiotherapy)

Alternative offers
See **Chapter 7** and **Appendix 1** for grades/UCAS Tariff points information for the International Baccalaureate, Scottish Highers/Advanced Highers, the Welsh Baccalaureate, the Irish Leaving Certificate, the Cambridge Pre-U Diploma, the Advanced Diploma and the Extended Project.

EXAMPLES OF FOUNDATION DEGREES IN THE SUBJECT FIELD

Salford.

CHOOSING YOUR COURSE (SEE ALSO CH. 1)

Some course features
East London Physiotherapy is available as full-time, or part-time university-based courses, or as full-time situated learning where one third of the course is practice-based and two-thirds is university-based.
Hertfordshire (Physiotherapy) One third of the course is spent on practice placements in hospitals and health care units.
Nottingham (Physiotherapy) 32 weeks of supervised clinical practice split into eight four-week blocks take place in Years 2 and 3.
Southampton A four-year part-time course is offered to school leavers.
NHS bursaries are available for all Physiotherapy courses.

Universities and colleges teaching quality See www.qaa.ac.uk; www.unistats.com.

ADMISSIONS INFORMATION

Number of applicants per place (approx) Birmingham 9; Bradford 22; Brighton 30 (6 places for overseas candidates); Bristol UWE 12; Brunel 11; Cardiff 17; Coventry 15; East Anglia 14; East London 10; Glasgow Caledonian 12; Hertfordshire 13; Huddersfield 18; Kingston 9; Liverpool 20; London (King's) 16; Manchester 18; Northumbria 37; Queen Margaret 11; Robert Gordon 13; Salford 28; Sheffield Hallam 12; Southampton 15; Teesside 33; Ulster 12.

Advice to applicants and planning the UCAS personal statement Visits to, and work experience in, hospital physiotherapy departments are important although many universities publicly state that this is not necessary. However, with the level of competition for this subject I would regard this as doubtful (see **Reasons for rejection**). Applicants must demonstrate a clear understanding of the nature of the profession. Give details of voluntary work activities. Take notes of the work done and the different aspects of physiotherapy. Explain your experience fully on the UCAS application. Outside interests and teamwork are considered important. Good communication skills. Observation placement within a physiotherapy department. **Coventry** The University of Leicester part-delivers a BSc Physiotherapy degree. This course is a Coventry University degree that has 30 places based at the Leicester campus. Teaching takes place at Leicester and Coventry. Students are admitted by Coventry but live and mostly study at Leicester. **Manchester Met** We need to know why you want to be a physiotherapist. We also look for work shadowing a physiotherapist or work experience in another caring role. Evidence is also required of good communication skills, ability to care for people and of teamwork and leadership. **Salford** Essential for applicants to seek experience in as wide a range of settings as possible. See also **Appendix 4**.

Advice to overseas (non-EU) applicants Places for students from overseas are limited and applicants must be able to read, speak and write English fluently. Information on the minimum educational qualifications required by overseas students and details concerning grants and funding are available from the Chartered Society of Physiotherapy (see **Appendix 4**). **Brunel**, **Glasgow Caledonian** Proficiency in English essential. **Queen Margaret** Several overseas students recruited each year. **Ulster** Exams and continuous assessment.

Misconceptions about this course Some applicants think that physiotherapy has a sports bias.

Selection interviews **Yes** Most institutions including Birmingham, Bradford, Brighton, Coventry, East Anglia, East London, Huddersfield, Nottingham, Robert Gordon, Salford, Sheffield Hallam; **Some** Brunel (mature students), Cardiff (mature students), Kingston, Queen Margaret, Southampton (mature students, who are asked to write about their life experience).

Interview advice and questions Physiotherapy is one of the most popular courses at present and work experience is very important, if not essential. A sound knowledge of the career, types of treatment used in physiotherapy and some understanding of the possible problems experienced by patients will be expected. Past interview questions include: How does physiotherapy fit into the overall health care system? If one patient was a heavy smoker and the other not, would you treat them the same? What was the most emotionally challenging thing you have ever done? Give an example of teamwork in which you have been involved. Why should we make you an offer? What is chiropractic? What is osteopathy? See **Chapter 5**.

Reasons for rejection (non-academic) Lack of knowledge of the profession. Failure to convince the interviewers of a reasoned basis for following the profession. Failure to have visited a hospital physiotherapy unit. Lack of awareness of the demands of the course. Other subjects listed on the UCAS application. **Birmingham** Poor communication skills. Lack of career insight. **Bristol UWE** Applicants re-sitting A-levels are not normally considered. **Cardiff** Lack of knowledge of physiotherapy; experience of sports injuries only.

AFTER-RESULTS ADVICE

Offers to applicants repeating A-levels **Higher** Bristol UWE (candidates who fail at interview will not normally be reconsidered), East Anglia, East London, Glasgow Caledonian, Kingston, Teesside; **Same** Coventry, Queen Margaret, Salford, Southampton.

GRADUATE DESTINATIONS AND EMPLOYMENT (2007/8 HESA)

No data available.

Career note The professional qualifications gained on graduation enable physiotherapists to seek posts in the Health Service where the majority are employed. A small number work in the community health service, particularly in rural areas, whilst others work in residential homes. In addition to private practice, there are also some opportunities in professional sports clubs.

OTHER DEGREE SUBJECTS FOR CONSIDERATION

Anatomy; Audiology; Biological Sciences; Health Studies; Leisure and Recreation; Nursing; Occupational Therapy; Osteopathy; Physical Education; Psychology; Sport Science/Studies.

PLANT SCIENCES

(including **Botany**; see also **Biological Sciences, Biology** and **Horticulture**)

Plant Sciences cover such areas as plant biochemistry, plant genetics, plant conservation and plant geography. Botany encompasses all aspects of plant science and also other subject areas including agriculture, forestry and horticulture. Botany is basic to these subjects and others including pharmacology and water management. As with other biological sciences, some universities introduce Plant Sciences by way of a common first year with other subjects.

Useful websites www.kew.org; www.anbg.gov.au; www.scienceyear.com; www.botany.net; www.botany.org.

NB The points totals shown to the left of the institutions are for ease of reference only. It must not be assumed that Tariff points are always used by institutions or that they can be substituted for an offer in grades. The level of an offer is not necessarily indicative of the quality of a course.

COURSE OFFERS INFORMATION

Subject requirements/preferences **GCSE** Mathematics if not offered at A-level. **AL** One or two science subjects are usually required.

NB In 2011 universities and colleges will differ in their use of GCE AL/AS unit grade information, A* grades, the Extended Project (EPQ), the Advanced Diploma and the Cambridge Pre-U examination when considering applicants and making offers. An EPQ may be accepted in place of an AS subject. Check websites of universities and colleges for the latest offers information.

Your target offers and examples of courses provided by each institution

380 pts **Cambridge** – A*AA college offers may vary (Nat Sci (Plnt Sci)) (IB 38–42 pts)

360 pts **Bristol** – AAA–ABB (Botany) (IB 34 pts HL 666 inc 2 sci)

Edinburgh – AAA 2nd yr entry (Plnt Sci) (IB 36 pts)

340 pts **Birmingham** – AAB–BBB (Biol Sci (Plnt Biol)) (IB 32–34 pts)

Imperial London – AAB 340 pts (Plant Biol) (IB 38 pts HL 665)

Manchester – AAB–BBB (Plnt Sci; Plnt Sci Modn Lang; Plnt Sci Ind) (IB 35–32 pts)

Sheffield – AAB–ABB (Plnt Sci courses) (IB 35–33 pts)

320 pts **East Anglia** – ABB (MSci Plnt Sci) (IB 32 pts)

East Anglia – ABB–BBB (BSc Plant Sci) (IB 31 pts)

Glasgow – ABB (Plnt Sci) (IB 32 pts)

300 pts **Aberdeen** – BBB 2nd yr entry (Plnt Biol; Plnt Soil Sci)

Edinburgh – BBB (Plnt Sci) (IB 30 pts)

Nottingham – BBB–BBC (Plnt Sci; Plnt Sci (Euro St)) (IB 28–32 pts)

280 pts **Aberystwyth** – 280 pts (Plnt Biol) (IB 26 pts)

240 pts **Aberdeen** – CCC 1st yr entry (Plnt Biol; Plnt Soil Sci)

220 pts **Worcester** – 220 pts (Biol (Plnt Sci))

Alternative offers

See **Chapter 7** and **Appendix 1** for grades/UCAS Tariff points information for the International Baccalaureate, Scottish Highers/Advanced Highers, the Welsh Baccalaureate, the Irish Leaving Certificate, the Cambridge Pre-U Diploma, the Advanced Diploma and the Extended Project.

CHOOSING YOUR COURSE (SEE ALSO CH.1)

Some course features

Aberystwyth After a common first year focusing on plant structure, function, physiology and classification, students can tailor their degree scheme through their choice of module options. Field studies in Northern Spain and Western Ireland are available.

Birmingham Plant Biology is an option in the Biological Sciences programme. Specialisation can take place at the beginning of the course or in Year 2.

East Anglia It is possible to start on the flexible Biological Sciences programme in which modules are chosen depending on the student's preference.
See also **Biology** and **Horticulture**.

Top research universities and colleges (RAE 2008) See **Biological Sciences**.

Examples of sandwich degree courses Greenwich; Manchester; Warwickshire (Coll); Writtle (Coll).

ADMISSIONS INFORMATION

Number of applicants per place (approx) Bristol 5; Edinburgh 6; Glasgow 4; Nottingham 7; Reading 3; Sheffield 5.

Advice to applicants and planning the UCAS personal statement Visit botanical gardens. See **Biological Sciences.** See also **Appendix 2**.

Selection interviews **Yes** Cambridge, Durham, Nottingham (depends on application).

Interview advice and questions You are likely to be questioned on your biology studies, your reasons for wishing to study Plant Sciences and your ideas about a possible future career. In the past questions have been asked about Darwin's theory of evolution, photosynthesis and DNA and the value of gardening programmes on TV! See **Chapter 5**.

AFTER-RESULTS ADVICE

Offers to applicants repeating A-levels **Possibly higher** Nottingham; **Same** Birmingham, Sheffield; **No offer made** Cambridge.

GRADUATE DESTINATIONS AND EMPLOYMENT (2007/8 HESA)

Graduates surveyed 25 **Employed** 10 **In further study** 10 **Assumed unemployed** none.

Career note See **Biology** and **Horticulture**.

OTHER DEGREE SUBJECTS FOR CONSIDERATION

Agriculture; Biochemistry; Biological Sciences; Biology; Crop Science (Agronomy); Ecology; Food Science; Forestry; Herbal Medicine; Horticulture; Landscape Architecture; Traditional Chinese Medicine.

PODIATRY (CHIROPODY)

Podiatry is a relatively new term for chiropody and deals with the management of disease and disorders of the ankle and foot. Podiatrists diagnose nail, skin and movement problems, devise treatment plans and carry out treatment for all age groups. Courses lead to state registration and some work shadowing prior to application is preferred by admissions tutors.

Useful websites www.feetforlife.org; www.nhscareers.nhs.uk; www.podiatrynetwork.com; www.podiatrytoday.com; www.podiatrychannel.com.

NB The points totals shown to the left of the institutions are for ease of reference only. It must not be assumed that Tariff points are always used by institutions or that they can be substituted for an offer in grades. The level of an offer is not necessarily indicative of the quality of a course.

COURSE OFFERS INFORMATION

Subject requirements/preferences **GCSE** Mathematics and science subjects. **AL** Biology usually required or preferred. **Other requirements** Hepatitis B, tuberculosis and tetanus immunisation; Criminal Records Bureau (CRB) clearance (a pre-existing record could prevent a student from participating in the placement component of the course and prevent the student from gaining state registration).

NB In 2011 universities and colleges will differ in their use of GCE AL/AS unit grade information, A* grades, the Extended Project (EPQ), the Advanced Diploma and the Cambridge

Pre-U examination when considering applicants and making offers. An EPQ may be accepted in place of an AS subject. Check websites of universities and colleges for the latest offers information.

Your target offers and examples of courses provided by each institution

300 pts	**Southampton** – BBB (Podiatry) (IB 30 pts)
	Ulster – BBB +HPAT (Podiatry) (See **Ch.5**)
280 pts	**Huddersfield** – BBC (Podiatry)
260 pts	**Brighton** – BCC 260 pts (Podiatry) (IB 28 pts)
	Cardiff (UWIC) – 260 pts (Podiatry)
245 pts	**Queen Margaret** – 245 pts (Podiatry)
240 pts	**East London** – 240 pts (Pod Med) (IB 26 pts)
	Plymouth – 240–260 pts (Podiatry)
	Salford – 240 pts (Podiatry) (IB 24 pts)
220 pts	**Birmingham Met (Coll)** – 220 pts (Podiatry)
	Northampton – 220–240 pts (Podiatry)
160 pts	**Durham New (Coll)** – 160 pts (Podiatry)
	Glasgow Caledonian – CC (Podiatry)

Alternative offers

See **Chapter 7** and **Appendix 1** for grades/UCAS Tariff points information for the International Baccalaureate, Scottish Highers/Advanced Highers, the Welsh Baccalaureate, the Irish Leaving Certificate, the Cambridge Pre-U Diploma, the Advanced Diploma and the Extended Project.

EXAMPLES OF FOUNDATION DEGREES IN THE SUBJECT FIELD

Salford.

CHOOSING YOUR COURSE (SEE ALSO CH.1)

Some course features

Northampton Students manage their own patient cases during the course.
Plymouth Supervised placements in NHS Trusts from Year 1.
Southampton A modular programme with six units studied in each semester, these include local anaesthesia and prescription-only medicines.
See also **Health Sciences/Studies**.
NHS bursaries are available for all Podiatry courses.

Universities and colleges teaching quality See www.qaa.ac.uk; www.unistats.com.

ADMISSIONS INFORMATION

Number of applicants per place (approx) Birmingham Met (Coll) 4; Cardiff (UWIC) 8; Huddersfield 2–3; Northampton 2; Salford 3; Southampton 4.

Advice to applicants and planning the UCAS personal statement Visit a podiatrist's clinic to gain work experience/work shadowing experience. Applicants need the ability to communicate with all age ranges, to work independently, to be resourceful and to possess a focussed approach to academic work. Admissions tutors look for evidence of an understanding of podiatry, some work experience, good people skills, and effective communication. Mature applicants must include an academic reference (not an employer reference). See also **Appendix 4**.

Misconceptions about this course **Cardiff (UWIC)** Prospective students are often not aware of the demanding requirements of the course: 1000 practical clinical hours augmented by a rigorous academic programme. Applicants are often unaware that whilst the elderly are a significant sub-population of patients with a variety of foot problems, increasingly the role of the podiatrist is the diagnosis and management of biomechanical/developmental disorders as well as the management of the diabetic or rheumatoid patient and those who require surgical intervention for nail problems. **Huddersfield** Many people think that podiatry is limited in its scope of practice to treating toe nails, corns and calluses: FALSE. As professionals, we do treat such pathologies but the scope of practice is much wider. It now includes surgery, biomechanics, sports injuries, treating children and high risk patients. Because offers are low it is considered an easier course than, for example, Physiotherapy: FALSE. The course is academically demanding in addition to the compulsory clinical requirement.

Selection interviews **Yes** Most institutions; Huddersfield, Southampton; **Some** Cardiff (UWIC).

Interview advice and questions Past questions include: Have you visited a podiatrist's surgery? What do your friends think about your choice of career? Do you think that being a podiatrist could cause you any physical problems? With which groups of people do podiatrists come into contact? What are your perceptions of the scope of practice of podiatry? What transferable skills do you think you will need? **Cardiff (UWIC)** What made you consider podiatry as a career? Have you researched your career choice and where did you find the information? What have you discovered and has this altered your original perception of podiatry? What personal characteristics do you think you possess which might be useful for this work? See **Chapter 5**.

Reasons for rejection (non-academic) Unconvincing attitude; poor communication and interpersonal skills; lack of motivation; medical condition or physical disabilities which are incompatible with professional practice; no knowledge of chosen profession; lack of work experience.

AFTER-RESULTS ADVICE

Offers to applicants repeating A-levels **Same** Cardiff (UWIC), Huddersfield, Salford.

GRADUATE DESTINATIONS AND EMPLOYMENT (2007/8 HESA)

No data available.

Career note Many state-registered podiatrists are employed by the NHS whilst others work in private practice or commercially run clinics.

OTHER DEGREE SUBJECTS FOR CONSIDERATION

Audiology; Biological Sciences; Health Studies; Nursing; Occupational Therapy; Osteopathy; Physiotherapy.

POLITICS

(including **Government**; see also **Development Studies** and **International Relations**)

Politics is often described as the study of 'who gets what, where, when and how'. Courses have become increasingly popular in recent years and usually cover the politics and government of the major powers. Because of the variety of degree courses on offer, it is possible to study the politics of almost any country in the world.

Useful websites http://europa.eu; www.fco.gov.uk; www.psa.ac.uk; www.parliament.uk; www.whitehouse.gov; www.amnesty.org; www.direct.gov.uk; www.un.org; www.un.int.

NB The points totals shown to the left of the institutions are for ease of reference only. It must not be assumed that Tariff points are always used by institutions or that they can be substituted for an offer in grades. The level of an offer is not necessarily indicative of the quality of a course.

COURSE OFFERS INFORMATION

Subject requirements/preferences **GCSE** English, mathematics and a foreign language may be required. **AL** No subjects specified; history useful but an arts or social science subject an advantage.

NB In 2011 universities and colleges will differ in their use of GCE AL/AS unit grade information, A* grades, the Extended Project (EPQ), the Advanced Diploma and the Cambridge Pre-U examination when considering applicants and making offers. An EPQ may be accepted in place of an AS subject. Check websites of universities and colleges for the latest offers information.

Your target offers and examples of courses provided by each institution

410 pts **Warwick** – AAAb (Phil Pol Econ (PPE))
400 pts **London (UCL)** – A*AAe (Euro Soc Pol St) (IB 39 pts)
390 pts **Warwick** – AABb (Pol; Phil Pol Econ; Pol Int St; Pol Fr) (IB 38–40 pts)
380 pts **Cambridge** – A*AA college offers may vary (Pol Psy Sociol) (IB 38–42 pts HL 766–777)
360 pts **Bath** – AAA (Pol Int Rel) (IB 38 pts)
Bristol – AAA–AAB (Pol; Pol Fr/Ger/Ital/Port/Russ/Span) (IB 37–34 pts HL 666)
Durham – AAA–AAB (Pol; Pol (Euro St); PPE; Comb Hons) (IB 36 pts HL 17 pts)
Exeter – AAA–ABB (Pol; Hist Pol) (IB 36–31 pts)
London (King's) – AAB+AS **or** AAbb+AS (War St courses)
London (SOAS) – AAA (Pol Af St; Pol SE As St; Pol Dev St) (IB 34 pts)
London (UCL) – AAB+AS–ABB+AS (Pol E Euro St) (IB 34–36 pts)
Newcastle – AAA–BBB (Pol; Pol Econ) (IB 35 pts)
Nottingham – AAA (Int Rel Glob Is) (IB 38 pts)
Oxford – AAA (Hist Pol; PPE) (IB 38–40 pts)
Queen's Belfast – AAA/AABa (Law Pol)
York – AAA (Hist Pol) (IB 36 pts)
340 pts **Bath** – AAB–ABB (Pol Econ; Euro Lang Pol) (IB 34–36 pts)
Cardiff – AAB (Pol; Pol Soc Phil App Eth; Euro Pol Int Rel)
Essex – AAB 340–300 pts (Law Pol) (IB 36 pts)
Exeter – AAB–ABB (Pol Arbc St; Pol Langs; Pol Geog; Pol Law) (IB 34–29 pts)
Glasgow – AAB (Pol; Pol Langs; Pol Psy; Pol Bus Mgt)
Leeds – AAB (Pol Parl St; Pol) (IB 36 pts HL 17 pts)
London LSE – AAB (Gov; Gov Econ; Gov Hist; Pol Phil) (IB 37 pts)
Manchester – AAB–ABB (Pol Modn Hist; Pol Int Rel; Pol) (IB 35–34 pts)
Newcastle – AAB–BBB (Gov EU St) (IB 32–36 pts)
Nottingham – AAB (Politics) (IB 36 pts)
Queen's Belfast – AAB–ABB (Pol Econ Phil)
Sheffield – AAB (Econ Pol; Pol Phil; Pol Sociol; Int Pol E As St) (IB 35 pts)
Southampton – AAB (Pol courses) (IB 34 pts)
Sussex – AAB–ABB (Pol Contemp Euro St; Pol; Pol Dev St) (IB 34–36 pts)
Swansea – AAB (PPE)
York – AAB–ABB (Engl Pol; Pol Sci; Soc Pol) (IB 34–32 pts)
320 pts **Birmingham** – ABB (Pol Sci; Pol Econ; Int St Pol Sci) (IB 32–34 pts)
Birmingham – ABB–BBB (Euro Pol Soty Econ) (IB 34–32 pts)
Brunel – 320–300 pts (Int Pol; Pol Econ; Pol Hist) (IB 31 pts)
Cardiff – ABB (Pol Welsh) (IB 35 pts)
Durham – ABB (Pol Sociol)
East Anglia – ABB–BBB (Pol; Pol Sociol; Pol Media; Cult Lit Pol; Int Rel Euro Pol) (IB 35 pts)
Essex – 320–300 pts (Pol; Econ Pol; Pol Sociol) (IB 32–36 pts)
Hull – 320–280 pts (Pol; PPE; Glob Gov)
Kent – 320–300 pts (Pol; Pol Phil Econ Euro; Cnflct Pce Scrty; Pol Int Rel courses) (IB 32 pts)
Lancaster – ABB 320 pts (Pol; Pol N Am; Pol Relig St; Pol Int Rel) (IB 30 pts)
Leeds – ABB (Euro Pol; Pol Port/Russ/Span; Chin Pol; Euro Pol Fr/Ger/Ital; Int Dev) (IB 34 pts)
Leicester – ABB (Mgt St Pol; Pol Econ)
Liverpool – ABB (Int Pol Plcy; Pol Int Bus; Pol Comm St) (IB 33 pts)
London (Gold) – ABB (Pol; Econ Pol Pblc Plcy; Int St) (IB 28 pts)
London (QM) – ABB (Pol; Pol Bus Mgt; Law Pol) (IB 32 pts)
London (RH) – ABB 320 pts (Pol; Pol Phil; Pol Int Rel) (IB 34–32 pts)
Loughborough – ABB–AAB (Hist Pol) (IB 32–34 pts)
Nottingham – ABB (Pol Am St; Euro Pol)
Strathclyde – ABB/ABC (Pol courses) (IB 34 pts)
Surrey – ABB (Law Int St)
Ulster – ABB (Law Int Pol)

300 pts **Aston** – BBB–ABB 300–320 pts (Pol; Pol Pblc Plcy Mgt; Pol Comb Hons; Pol Int Rel) (IB 32–33 pts)
Buckingham – 300 pts (Law Pol)
Cardiff – BBB (Pol Span)
City – BBB 300 pts (Int Pol) (IB 32 pts)
Dundee – BBB 2nd yr entry (Pol courses; Euro Pol courses)
Edinburgh – BBB (Pol; Russ St Pol; Scand St Pol) (IB 34 pts HL 555)
Lancaster – BBB 300 pts (Pol Sociol) (IB 33 pts)
Leicester – BBB (Hist Pol; Pol)
Northumbria – 300–280 pts (Politics)
Queen's Belfast – BBB–BBCb (Pol joint courses) (IB 29 pts HL 655)
Reading – 300–320 pts (Pol Int Rel; War Pce Int Rel)
Surrey – BBB 300 pts (Pol; Int Pol; Pol Plcy St) (IB 32 pts)
Swansea – BBB 300 pts (Pol; Pol Soc Hist; Pol Langs; Pol Comms)

280 pts **Aberystwyth** – 280 pts (Pol St; Int Pol courses; Euro Pol; Pce Cnflct Scrty)
Bradford – BBC 280 pts (Pol; Pol Pce St; Pol Law; Cnflct Res)
Oxford Brookes – BBC (Pol courses) (IB 31 pts)
Reading – 280–320 pts (Pol Econ)
Salford – 280 pts (Pol Arbc)

260 pts **Brighton** – BCC (Pol App Psy; Pol Soc Plcy; Pol Crimin)
Bristol UWE – 260–300 pts (Pol; Engl Pol)
Coventry – 260–280 pts (Pol Hist; Pol)
Huddersfield – 260–280 pts (Pol; Pol Contemp Hist; Pol Media)
Keele – 260–320 pts (Am St Pol; Pol; Mus Pol)
Liverpool Hope – 260 pts (Pol; Pol Tour; Pol Geog)
Nottingham Trent – 260 pts (Pol Hist; Pol Int Rel)
Westminster – BCC–BB (Pol Comb Hons; Pol) (IB 28 pts)

240 pts **Aberdeen** – CCC 240 pts (Pol; Pol Hist Art; Pol Educ; Pol Fin; Pol Int Rel)
Bangor – 240–260 pts (Pol Soc Sci)
Buckingham – 240 pts (Pol Econ Law; Int St)
Cardiff (UWIC) – 240 pts (Modn Hist Pol)
Central Lancashire – 240–220 pts (Pol; Pol Int Rel)
De Montfort – 240 pts (Pol; Pol Hist; Pol Jrnl; Pol Int Rel)
Dundee – 240 pts 1st yr entry (Pol courses; Euro Pol courses)
London Met – 240 pts (Pol; Pol Bank; Pol Pce Cnflct St)
Plymouth – 240 pts (Pol Int Rel)
Portsmouth – 240–300 pts (Pol; Pol Sociol)
Stirling – CCC (PPE; Pol; Pol (Int Pol))
Ulster – CCC 240 pts (Pol; Pol Crimin; Pol Soc Plcy) (IB 24 pts)
Worcester – 240–260 pts (Pol Ppl Pwr)

220 pts **Liverpool John Moores** – 220 pts (Politics)
Northampton – 220–240 pts (Pol; Pol Joint Hons)
Nottingham Trent – 220–200 pts (Pol; Sociol Pol)
Sunderland – 220 pts (Contemp Hist Pol; Pol courses)
Winchester – 220–260 pts (Pol Glob St courses) (IB 24 pts)

200 pts **Canterbury Christ Church** – 200 pts (Pol Gov; Pol Glob Gov courses; Glob Pol courses)
East London – 200 pts (Int Pol courses)
Kingston – 200–320 pts (Pol Jrnl; Int Rel; Pol App Econ)
Leeds Met – 200–220 pts (Pol; Pol Int Rel; Glob Dev Pol; Pce St Pol)
Lincoln – 200–260 pts (Pol; Crimin Pol; Int Rel Pol)
Manchester Met – 200–220 pts (Pol courses; Int Pol courses)
Middlesex – 200–280 pts (Int Pol St courses)
Sheffield Hallam – 200 pts (Pol; Pol Crimin; Pol Sociol)

180 pts **Blackburn (Coll Univ Centre)** – 180–220 pts (Pol Engl)
Salford – 180–280 pts (Pol; Contemp Hist Pol) (IB 29 pts)

160 pts **Greenwich** – 160 pts (Politics)
London South Bank – CC (Int Pol courses)
Wolverhampton – 160–220 pts (Pol PRl; Pol Hist)
140 pts **West Scotland** – CD (Soc Sci (Pol))
80 pts **London (Birk)** – 80 pts for under 21s (over 21s varies) (p/t Pol Soc; Pol Phil Hist)

Open University – (Pol Phil Econ – contact +44 (0)845 300 6090 or www.openuniversity.co.uk/you)

Alternative offers
See **Chapter 7** and **Appendix 1** for grades/UCAS Tariff points information for the International Baccalaureate, Scottish Highers/Advanced Highers, the Welsh Baccalaureate, the Irish Leaving Certificate, the Cambridge Pre-U Diploma, the Advanced Diploma and the Extended Project.

CHOOSING YOUR COURSE (SEE ALSO CH.1)

Some course features
Durham Politics can be taken as part of the PPE course or with European Studies with a year in France, Italy, Spain, Holland, Germany, Norway or Sweden.
East Anglia Opportunities for parliamentary or other internships.
London (SOAS) Seventeen degree courses are offered with Politics including 12 language options covering African and Far Eastern languages.
Southampton The Social Sciences programme offers Politics with Economics, International Relations and Sociology.
Warwick Various opportunities for overseas study as part of the degree course. Students can apply for a second year in the US completing their course in the UK in the third year.

Universities and colleges teaching quality See www.qaa.ac.uk; www.unistats.com.

Top research universities and colleges (RAE 2008) (Politics and International Studies) Essex; Sheffield; Aberystwyth; Oxford; London LSE; London (UCL), (SOAS); Sussex (International Relations); Warwick; Exeter; Nottingham; Manchester; Cambridge.

Examples of sandwich degree courses Aston; Bath; Brunel; Coventry; De Montfort; Huddersfield; Lancaster; Leeds Met; Loughborough; Nottingham Trent; Oxford Brookes; Plymouth; Portsmouth; Surrey; Westminster.

ADMISSIONS INFORMATION

Number of applicants per place (approx) Aberystwyth 4; Aston 4; Bath 2; Birmingham 6; Bradford 10; Bristol 18; Brunel 5; Buckingham 2; Cardiff 14; Cardiff (UWIC) 3; De Montfort 6; Dundee 6; Durham 11 (all courses); East Anglia 15; Exeter 8; Hull 11, (PPE) 20; Kent 14; Lancaster 14; Leeds 18; Leicester 10; Liverpool 9; Liverpool John Moores 6; London (QM) 10, (SOAS) 5; London LSE (Gov) 17, (Gov Econ) 10, (Gov Hist) 17; London Met 5; Loughborough 4; Newcastle 9; Northampton 4; Nottingham 5; Nottingham Trent 3; Oxford (PPE) 7; Oxford Brookes 12; Portsmouth 6; Salford 7; Southampton 10; Staffordshire 10; Stirling 9; Swansea 3; Warwick 10; York 8.

Advice to applicants and planning the UCAS personal statement Study the workings of government in the UK, Europe and other areas of the world, such as the Middle East, the Far East, America and Russia. Describe visits to the Houses of Commons and Lords and the debates taking place. Attend council meetings – county, town, district, village halls. Describe these visits and agendas. Read current affairs avidly. Be aware of political developments in the major countries and regions of the world including the Middle East, South America, the UK, Europe, USA, China, Korea and Russia. Keep abreast of developments in theatres of war, for example, Afghanistan. Explain your interests in detail. **Aberystwyth** We look for degree candidates with a strong interest in political and social issues and who want to inquire into the way in which the world is organised politically, socially and economically. **De Montfort** Demonstration of active interest in current affairs and some understanding of how politics affects our daily lives.

Misconceptions about this course **Aberystwyth** Many students believe that they need to study politics at A-level for Politics courses – this is not the case. **Cardiff (UWIC)** Some consider that Politics is a narrow subject, only relevant to those who want a political career. **De Montfort** Some applicants believe that a Politics course only covers the mechanics of government and parliament.

Selection interviews **Yes** Bath (mature students), Birmingham, Cambridge, Durham, Exeter, Huddersfield, Hull, Leeds (Pol Parl St), Leicester, Liverpool, London (Gold), (SOAS), London Met, London South Bank, Nottingham, Oxford, Portsmouth, Sheffield, Sussex, Swansea, Ulster, Warwick; **Some** Aberystwyth, Bristol, Cardiff (UWIC), De Montfort, Dundee, Liverpool John Moores, London LSE, Loughborough, Salford, Staffordshire, York.

Interview advice and questions Questions may stem from A/AS-level studies but applicants will also be expected to be up-to-date in their knowledge and opinions of current events. Questions in recent years have included: What constitutes a 'great power'? What is happening at present in the Labour Party? Define capitalism. What is a political decision? How do opinion polls detract from democracy? Is the European Union a good idea? Why? What are the views of the present government on the European Union? What is a 'spin doctor'? Are politicians hypocrites? **De Montfort** Why Politics? What political issues motivate your interests, for example environmentalism, human rights? See also **Chapter 5**.

AFTER-RESULTS ADVICE

Offers to applicants repeating A-levels **Higher** Essex, Glasgow, Leeds, Newcastle, Nottingham, Warwick, York; **Possibly higher** Hull, Lancaster, Oxford Brookes, Swansea; **Same** Aberystwyth, Birmingham, Bristol, Buckingham, Cardiff (UWIC), De Montfort, Dundee, Durham, East Anglia, Lincoln, Liverpool Hope, Liverpool John Moores, London (SOAS), London Met, London South Bank, Loughborough, Nottingham Trent, Portsmouth, Richmond (Am Int Univ), Salford, Staffordshire, Stirling, Sussex, Wolverhampton; **No offer made** Cambridge.

GRADUATE DESTINATIONS AND EMPLOYMENT (2007/8 HESA)

Graduates surveyed 3670 **Employed** 1675 **In further study** 785 **Assumed unemployed** 335.

Career note The transferable skills gained in this degree open up a wide range of career opportunities. Graduates seek positions in management, public services and administration and in some cases in political activities.

OTHER DEGREE SUBJECTS FOR CONSIDERATION

Development Studies; Economics; Government; History; International Relations; Public Policy and Administration; Social Policy and Administration; Sociology.

PROPERTY MANAGEMENT/DEVELOPMENT

(including **Estate, Land and Valuation Surveying**; see also **Building Surveying (under Building and Construction), Housing** and **Quantity Surveying**)

Property degree courses cover a wide range of subjects relevant to careers in managing, planning and implementing the development of property and regeneration of cities. Surveying is also a very broad subject (and career) and includes several specialisms, for example building surveying, quantity surveying, land valuation, surveying and architecture: this table focuses on degrees in general surveying, land and valuation surveying. Most Property and Real Estate courses are accredited by the RICS . . . but check!

Useful websites www.rics.org/careers; www.cqsa.co.uk.

NB The points totals shown to the left of the institutions are for ease of reference only. It must not be assumed that Tariff points are always used by institutions or that they can be substituted for an offer in grades. The level of an offer is not necessarily indicative of the quality of a course.

COURSE OFFERS INFORMATION

Subject requirements/preferences **GCSE** English and mathematics required and for some institutions, a science subject (for Chartered Surveyor registration). **AL** No subjects specified.

NB In 2011 universities and colleges will differ in their use of GCE AL/AS unit grade information, A* grades, the Extended Project (EPQ), the Advanced Diploma and the Cambridge Pre-U examination when considering applicants and making offers. An EPQ may be accepted in place of an AS subject. Check websites of universities and colleges for the latest offers information.

Your target offers and examples of courses provided by each institution

380 pts **Cambridge** – A*AA (Lnd Econ)
360 pts **City** – AAA (Law Prop Val)
340 pts **City** – AAB (Rl Est Fin Invest) (IB 35 pts)
Heriot-Watt – AAB 2nd yr entry (Rl Est Mgt; Plan Prop Dev) (IB 35 pts)
Reading – 340 pts (Rl Est; Invest Fin Prop; Rur Prop Mgt)
320 pts **Oxford Brookes** – ABB (Rl Est Mgt)
Ulster – 320–300 pts (Prop Invest Dev; Plan Prop Dev)
300 pts **Kingston** – 300 pts (Rl Est Mgt; Prop Plan Dev) (IB 28 pts)
Northumbria – 300 pts (Est Mgt; Plan Dev Surv) (IB 30 pts)
Royal (CAg) – 300 pts (Prop Agncy Mark)
280 pts **Bristol UWE** – 280–320 pts (Prop Mgt Invest; Prop Dev Plan; Bus Prop) (IB 24–28 pts)
Heriot-Watt – BBC 1st yr entry (Rl Est Mgt; Plan Prop Dev) (IB 29 pts)
Nottingham Trent – 280–240 pts (Plan Prop Dev; Prop Invest Fin; Rl Est Mgt) (IB 31 pts)
Salford – 280 pts (Prop Mgt Invest)
Westminster – BBC 280 pts (Bus Prop; Prop Urb Dev; Urb Est Mgt) (IB 26 pts)
270 pts **Glasgow Caledonian** – 270 pts (Int Rl Est; Rl Est Bus Mgt; Rl Est Econ Invest)
Liverpool John Moores – 270 pts (Rl Est Mgt courses)
Portsmouth – 270 pts (Prop Dev; Prop Dev Quant Surv) (IB 28 pts)
Sheffield Hallam – 270 pts (Bus Prop Mgt; Prop Dev; Urb Lnd Econ)
240 pts **Aberdeen** – CCC 1st yr entry (Prop Spat Plan; Prop)
Bolton – 240 pts (Bld Surv Prop Mgt)
Edinburgh Napier – 240 pts (Prop Dev Val)
230 pts **Greenwich** – 230 pts (Rl Est)
Wolverhampton – 230–260 pts (Rl Est)
220 pts **Glamorgan** – 220–260 pts (Rl Est Apprsl Mgt)
Sheffield Hallam – 220 pts (Rl Est)
200 pts **Glyndŵr** – 200 pts (Est Agncy; Est Mgt)
Portsmouth – 200 pts (Prop Mark Des Dev)
180 pts **Anglia Ruskin** – 180 pts (Prop Surv)
Bristol UWE – 180–220 pts (Rl Est (Val Mgt))
Derby – 180–240 pts (Prop Dev Joint Hons)
160 pts **London South Bank** – 160 pts (Prop Mgt (Bld Surv))
120 pts **Huddersfield** – 120 pts (Prop Dev)
Oldham (Coll Univ Centre) – 120 pts (Prop Dev)

Alternative offers

See **Chapter 7** and **Appendix 1** for grades/UCAS Tariff points information for the International Baccalaureate, Scottish Highers/Advanced Highers, the Welsh Baccalaureate, the Irish Leaving Certificate, the Cambridge Pre-U Diploma, the Advanced Diploma and the Extended Project.

EXAMPLES OF FOUNDATION DEGREES IN THE SUBJECT FIELD

Anglia Ruskin; Birmingham City; Bolton; Bradford; Glamorgan; Glyndŵr; Middlesex; Moulton (Coll); Northampton; Northumbria; Royal (CAg).

CHOOSING YOUR COURSE (SEE ALSO CH.1)

Some course features
City A-level mathematics is preferred for the Real Estate course.
Kingston (Prop Plan Dev) Economics, business and law are studied on the course. (Rl Est Mgt) Prepares students for entry to membership of the Royal Institution of Chartered Surveyors (RICS).
Oxford Brookes (Rl Est Mgt) Possible to also take with a Diploma in Planning. Apply early for both courses.
Reading All the degree courses in the Real Estate and Property programme are recognised by the Royal Institution of Chartered Surveyors.

Universities and colleges teaching quality See www.qaa.ac.uk; www.unistats.com.

Examples of sandwich degree courses Bradford; Bristol UWE; Ulster.

ADMISSIONS INFORMATION

Number of applicants per place (approx) Bristol UWE 11; Cambridge 4; City 20; Glamorgan 6; Glyndŵr 3; Harper Adams (UC) 4; Heriot-Watt 6; Kingston 22; Liverpool John Moores 15; London South Bank 2; Newcastle 6; Northumbria 17; Nottingham Trent 3; Portsmouth 5; Royal (CAg) 3; Salford 3; Sheffield Hallam 5; Westminster 10.

Advice to applicants and planning the UCAS personal statement There are different specialisms in this subject area. If you have any special interests, list and discuss them. Give details of all the contacts you have made, especially with, for example, property developers or surveying practices in your locality. Discuss the careers and try to arrange work experience or work shadowing. **Nottingham Trent** Candidates should demonstrate that they have researched the employment opportunities in the property and construction sectors and should have sought some practical experience. **Oxford Brookes** (Non-EU students) Written and spoken English must be good.

Misconceptions about this course Students under-estimate the need for numerical competence.

Selection interviews **Yes** Bristol UWE, Cambridge, Edinburgh, Glamorgan, Harper Adams (UC), Heriot-Watt, Newcastle, Royal (CAg); **Some** Anglia Ruskin, East London, Nottingham Trent, Salford.

Interview advice and questions Some work experience will be expected and questions will be asked on the applicant's course and career interests. **Cambridge** Questions on subsidies and the euro, economics, dynamic efficiency. Who owns London? How important is the modern-day church in town planning? How important are natural resources to a country? Is it more important to focus on poverty at home or abroad? Is the environment a bigger crisis than poverty? Do you think that getting involved with poverty abroad is interfering with others' 'freedoms'? (Questions based on information given in the personal statement.) See **Chapter 5**.

Reasons for rejection (non-academic) **Nottingham Trent** Incoherent and badly written application forms.

AFTER-RESULTS ADVICE

Offers to applicants repeating A-levels **Same** Nottingham Trent, Salford.

GRADUATE DESTINATIONS AND EMPLOYMENT (2007/8 HESA)

No data available.

Career note Property development until recently has been a rapidly expanding field and attracts graduates from a range of disciplines. These courses, however, provide exemptions in many cases from the examinations of the Royal Institution of Chartered Surveyors, opening up a wide range of opportunities.

OTHER DEGREE SUBJECTS FOR CONSIDERATION

Architecture; Building Surveying; Civil Engineering; Construction; Estate Management; Housing; Quantity Surveying; Town Planning; Urban Studies.

PSYCHOLOGY

(including **Behavioural Science, Cognitive Sciences, Counselling** and **Neuroscience**; see also **Biological Sciences, Philosophy** and **Physiology**)

Psychology is a very popular subject, with the number of applications rising by 40,000 in the last ten years. The study attracts three times more women than men. It covers studies in development, behaviour, perception, memory, language, learning, personality as well as social relationships and abnormal psychology. Psychology is a science and you will be involved in experimentation and statistical analysis. The degree is usually offered as a BSc or a BA course and there are many similarities between them. The differences are in the elective subjects which can be taken in the second and third years. It is not a training to enable you to psycho-analyse your friends – psychology is not the same as psychiatry!

To qualify as a chartered psychologist (for which a postgraduate qualification is required) it is necessary to obtain a first degree (or equivalent) qualification which gives eligibility for both Graduate Membership (GM) and the Graduate Basis for Registration (GBR) of the British Psychological Society (BPS). A full list of courses accredited by the British Psychological Society is available on the Society's website www.bps.org.uk. The website also provides careers information and information about all the qualifications needed for careers in the wide-ranging field of psychology. (See **Appendix 4**).

Behavioural Science covers the study of animal and human behaviour and offers an overlap between Zoology, Sociology, Psychology and Biological Sciences. Psychology, however, also crosses over into Education, Management Sciences, Human Resource Management, Counselling, Public Relations, Advertising, Artificial Intelligence, Marketing, Sales and Social Studies.

Useful websites www.psychology.org; www.bps.org.uk; www.socialpsychology.org; www.psychcentral.com.

NB The points totals shown to the left of the institutions are for ease of reference only. It must not be assumed that Tariff points are always used by institutions or that they can be substituted for an offer in grades. The level of an offer is not necessarily indicative of the quality of a course.

COURSE OFFERS INFORMATION

Subject requirements/preferences **GCSE** English, mathematics and a science. **AL** A science subject is usually required.

NB In 2011 universities and colleges will differ in their use of GCE AL/AS unit grade information, A* grades, the Extended Project (EPQ), the Advanced Diploma and the Cambridge Pre-U examination when considering applicants and making offers. An EPQ may be accepted in place of an AS subject. Check websites of universities and colleges for the latest offers information.

Your target offers and examples of courses provided by each institution

400 pts **London (UCL)** – A*AA+AS–AAA+AS (Psychology) (IB 38–39 pts)
390 pts **Warwick** – AABb/AAbbb (Phil Psy; Psy) (IB 36 pts)
380 pts **Cambridge** – A*AA college offers may vary (Nat Sci (Psy) (Neuro); Pol Psy Sociol) (IB 38–42 pts HL 766–777)
360 pts **Bath** – AAA (Psychology) (IB 38 pts HL 766)
Birmingham – AAA–ABB (Psy; Psy Fr/Ger/Russ/Span; Psy Maths) (IB 34 pts)
Bristol – AAA–AAB (Psy; Psy Phil; Psy Zool) (IB 36 pts HL 18 pts)
Cardiff – AAA (Psychology)
Durham – AAA (Nat Sci (Psy); Phil Psy) (IB 38–40 pts)
Exeter – AAA–AAB (Psy courses) (IB 36–33 pts)
London (UCL) – AAB+AS–ABB+AS (Neuroscience) (IB 34–36 pts)
Loughborough – AAA–ABB (Psy; Soc Psy) (IB 34 pts)
Oxford – AAA (Expmtl Psy; Psy Phil Physiol) (IB 38–40 pts)
Reading – AAA–AAB (Psy Chld Age; Psy Mntl Phys Hlth)
St Andrews – AAA (Psy; Art Hist Psy; Comp Sci Psy; Econ Psy; Psy Theol St) (IB 36 pts)

350 pts **Brunel** – BBB +AS/EPQ b 350 pts (Psy; Psy Anth; Psy Sociol) (IB 33 pts)
340 pts **Cardiff** – AAB–ABB 340–320 pts (Biomed Sci (Neuro))
Durham – AAB (Psy Comb Soc Sci; Comb Arts; App Psy; Phil Psy; Educ St Psy) (IB 36 pts)
Glasgow – AAB (BA Psy courses) (IB 34 pts)
Heriot-Watt – AAB 2nd yr entry (Psy courses)
Lancaster – AAB–ABB (Psy; Psy Educ; Org St Psy) (IB 31 pts)
Leeds – AAB–BBB (Psy; Mnd Knwl; Neuro) (IB 35 pts)
Leicester – AAB–ABB (Psy; Psy Cog Neuro; Psy Sociol) (IB 33 pts)
Liverpool – AAB (Psychology) (IB 34 pts)
London (RH) – AAB–ABB (Maths Psy; Biol Psy)
Manchester – AAB (Psychology) (IB 35–33 pts)
Newcastle – AAB–BBB (Psy; Psy Stats; Biol Psy) (IB 34 pts HL 666)
Nottingham – AAB (Psy; Psy Cog Neuro) (IB 32 pts)
Reading – AAB–ABBb (Psy; Art Psy; Psy Biol)
St Andrews – AAB (Neuroscience) (IB 32 pts)
Sheffield – AAB (Psy; Phil Psy) (IB 35 pts)
Southampton – AAB 340 pts (Psychology) (IB 34 pts HL 17 pts)
Surrey – AAB 340 pts (Psychology) (IB 34 pts)
Sussex – AAB–ABB (Psy; Psy Sociol; Neuro Cog Sci; Med Neuro) (IB 34–36 pts)
York – AAB–ABB (Psychology) (IB 34 pts)
320 pts **Aston** – ABB (Hum Psy courses) (IB 33–34 pts)
Bournemouth – 320 pts (Spo Psy Coach Sci; Psy)
Bristol – ABB (Neuroscience)
Bristol UWE – 320–360 pts (Psychology)
City – ABB 320 pts (Psychology) (IB 34 pts)
Edinburgh – ABB (Artif Intel Psy; Cog Sci)
Glasgow – ABB (Neuroscience) (IB 32 pts)
Hertfordshire – 320 pts (Psychology)
Kent – ABB–AAC 320 pts (Psy; Psy Clin Psy; Soc Psy; App Psy; Clin Psy) (IB 35 pts)
London (Gold) – ABB (Psychology) (IB 30 pts)
Nottingham – ABB–BBB (Neuro; Neuro Bioch; Neuro Pharmacol) (IB 32 pts)
Oxford Brookes – ABB offers vary depending on 2nd subj (Psy; Psy Comb courses) (IB 33 pts)
Portsmouth – 320 pts (Psy; Foren Psy) (IB 30 pts)
Queen's Belfast – ABB–BBBb (Psychology)
Reading – 320–340 pts (Maths Psy)
Southampton – ABB (App Soc Sci (Crimin Psy St))
Strathclyde – ABB–ABC (Psychology) (IB 34 pts)
300 pts **Aberdeen** – BBB 2nd yr entry (Neuro Psy; Psy)
Aston – 300–340 pts (Psy Bus; Psy Chem; Psy Comp Sci) (IB 32 pts)
Bangor – 300–260 pts (Psy; Psy Neuropsy; Psy Chld Lang Dev) (IB 28 pts)
Birmingham City – 300 pts (Psychology)
Brighton – BBB 300 pts (App Psy Sociol; App Psy Crimin) (IB 32 pts)
City – BBB (Jrnl Psy)
Dundee – BBB 2nd yr entry (MA Psy courses) (IB 34 pts)
East Anglia – BBB (Psychology) (IB 32 pts)
Edinburgh – BBB (MA Psy; Biol Sci (Psy); Psy Bus St) (IB 34 pts)
Essex – 300–280 pts (Psy; Soc Psy Sociol) (IB 29 pts)
Heriot-Watt – BBB 1st yr entry (Psy courses)
Keele – 300–320 pts (Neuro Psy)
Manchester Met – 300–280 pts (Psy; Psy Sp Path)
Northumbria – 300 pts (Psy Ling) (IB 32 pts)
Stirling – BBB 2nd yr entry (Psy; Psy Comb Hons)
Swansea – 300–320 pts (Psy; Psy Law)
Westminster – BBB–AB (Psychology) (IB 32 pts)
280 pts **Brighton** – BBC–BCC 280–260 pts (Pol App Psy; Hlth Soc Cr App Psy) (IB 28 pts)

City – BBC 280 pts (Sociol Psy) (IB 30 pts)
Coventry – 280 pts (Psy; Spo Psy; Psy Commun)
Huddersfield – 280–300 pts (Psy; Psy Crimin; Psy Cnslg)
Hull – 280 pts (Psy; Psy Phil; Psy Crimin; Psy Spo Sci)
Lincoln – 280 pts (Psy; Engl Psy; Psy Chld St; Psy Mark)
London (Hey) – 280 pts (Psy Phil; Psy Theol)
London Met – 280 pts (Psy; Hlth St Psy; HR Mgt Psy)
Loughborough – 280–300 pts (Ergonomics) (IB 30–32 pts)
Middlesex – 280 pts (Psychology)
Newport – 280 pts (Psy Cnslg St Soty)
Nottingham Trent – BBC 280 pts (Psy; Law Psy)
Queen Margaret – 280 pts (Psy; Hlth Psy)
Roehampton – 280–340 pts (Psy Cnslg; Psy; Psy Hlth)
Salford – BBC 280 pts (Psy Crimin; Psy St Cnslg St) (IB 27 pts)
Sheffield Hallam – 280 pts (Psy; Psy Law)
Staffordshire – 280 pts (Psy; Foren Psy; Hlth Psy)
Swansea – 280–300 pts (Psy Fr/Ger/Ital/Span/Welsh)
Worcester – 280 pts (Psychology)

260 pts **Aberystwyth** – 260 pts (Psy Engl Lit; Psy Mark; Psy Pol)
Birmingham City – 260 pts (Bus Psy Adv; Bus Psy HR Mgt; Bus Psy PR)
Bolton – 260 pts (Psy; Cnslg Psy; Crimin Foren Psy; Spo Exer Psy)
Bristol UWE – 260–300 pts (Psy Foren Sci; Psy Spo Biol)
Central Lancashire – 260 pts (Neuroscience)
Chichester – BCC–CCC 260–240 pts (Psy; Spo Exer Psy)
Leeds Met – 260–240 pts (Psy; Psy Soty; Psy Spo Exer)
Liverpool Hope – 260 pts (Psy; Psy Comb Hons)
Liverpool John Moores – 260–300 pts (App Psy; App Spo Psy)

Teesside – 260 pts (Psy; Foren Psy; Psy Cnslg; Psy Educ St)
Ulster – 260 pts (Psy courses)
240 pts **Aberdeen** – CCC 240 pts 1st yr entry (Neuro Psy; Psy)
Anglia Ruskin – 240–220 pts (Psy; Psy Mus; Psy Crimin)
Bath Spa – 240–280 pts (Psy; Psy Comb Hons)
Bradford – 240 pts (Psy; Psy Mgt; Sociol Psy)
Buckingham – 240 pts (Psychology)
Bucks New – 240–280 pts (Psy; Crimin Psy; Psy Sociol)
Canterbury Christ Church – CCC 240 pts (Psy; Spo Exer Psy)
Central Lancashire – 240 pts (Crs Cult Psy; Foren Psy; Hlth Psy; Psy; Spo Psy)
Chester – 240–280 pts (Psy courses; Cnslg)
De Montfort – 240 pts (Psy; Psy App Crimin; Educ St Psy; Mark Psy; HR Mgt Psy)
Dundee – CCC 1st yr entry (Psy courses) (IB 29 pts)
Glamorgan – 240–280 pts (App Psy; Psy; Dev Psy; Spo Psy)
Glasgow Caledonian – CCC 240 pts (Psychology)
Glyndŵr – 240 pts (Psychology)
Leeds Trinity (UC) – 240 pts (Psy Nutr Hlth; Psy; Foren Psy)
London South Bank – 240 pts (Psy Clin Psy; Psy; Psy Chld Dev)
Manchester Met – 240–260 pts (Biol Biomed Psy; Psy Spo Exer)
Nottingham Trent – 240 pts (Psy Spo Sci)
Portsmouth – 240–300 pts (Crimin Psy)
St Mary's Twickenham (UC) – 240 pts (Psy courses)
Southampton Solent – 240 pts (Psy; Hlth Psy; Cnslg Psy; Psy (Crim Bhv))
Stirling – CCC 1st yr entry (Psy; Psy Comb Hons)
Sunderland – 240 pts (Psy; Psy Cnslg; Spo Exer Psy)
Winchester – 240–300 pts (Jrnl Psy; Media St Psy; Psy Bus Mgt)
York St John – 240 pts (Psy; Psy Bus Mgt; Psy Cnslg Sk)
230 pts **Edinburgh Napier** – 230 pts (Psy; Psy Sociol; Psy Spo Exer)
Queen Margaret – 230 pts (Psy Sociol)
220 pts **Cardiff (UWIC)** – 220 pts (Psy; Educ St Psy)
Derby – 220–240 pts (Psy; Cnslg Psy)
Edge Hill – 220–260 pts (Psy Educ; Hlth Psy)
Glasgow Caledonian – CCD 216 pts (Psy Interact Enter)
Hertfordshire – 220–280 pts (Psy Hlth St; Psy Spo St; Bus Psy; Psy Fin Maths; Psy Law)
Kingston – 220–320 pts (Psy courses; Psy joint courses) (IB 30 pts)
Liverpool John Moores – 220–260 pts (Psy Foren Sci)
Newman (UC) – 220–260 pts (Psy courses)
Northampton – 220–260 pts (Psy Joint Hons)
Nottingham Trent – 220 pts (Eqn Spo Sci (Eqstrn Psy))
Plymouth – 220 pts (App Psy; Psy; Psy Sociol)
Westminster – CCD (Psy Neuro) (IB 26 pts)
Wolverhampton – 220–240 pts (Psy; Cnslg Psy)
200 pts **Anglia Ruskin** – 200 pts (Psysoc St; Anim Bhv Psy)
East London – 200 pts (Psy; Dev Psy; Foren Psy)
Gloucestershire – 200–280 pts (Anim Bhv Psy; Educ St Psy; Engl Lit Psy)
Huddersfield – 200 pts (Psy St)
Leeds Met – 200 pts (Psy Sociol; Psy Pol)
Middlesex – 200–280 pts (Psy HR Mgt; Psy Mark; Psy Crimin)
Newport – 200–240 pts (Psychology)
Suffolk (Univ Campus) – 200 pts (Psy Sociol; Psy Bus Mgt; Psy Yth St)
Thames Valley – 200 pts (Psychology)
180 pts **Abertay Dundee** – DDD 180–168 pts (Spo Psy)
Bradford – 180–220 pts (Psy Crim; Psy Mgt)
Greenwich – 180–200 pts (Stats Psy; Educ Psy; Hlth Psy)
Westminster – BC (Cog Sci) (IB 26 pts)

160 pts **Abertay Dundee** – CC 168 pts (Psychology)
Bedfordshire – 160 pts (Psy; App Psy; Hlth Psy; Psy Crim Bhv; Psy St)
Cumbria – 160 pts (App Psy)
Derby – 160–240 pts (Spo Psy)
Oldham (Coll Univ Centre) – 160 pts (Psy St)
Swansea Met – CC (Educ Psy; Cnslg Psy)
140 pts **West Scotland** – CD (Psy; Psy Joint Hons)
120 pts **Blackburn (Coll Univ Centre)** – 120 pts (App Psy Cnslg Hlth)
Grimsby (IFHE) – 120 pts (Psy St)
100 pts **Bradford (Coll)** – 100–140 pts (Cnslg Psy Commun Set)
80 pts **London (Birk)** – 80 pts for under 21s (over 21s varies) (p/t Psychology)
West Anglia (Coll) – 80–160 pts (Psysoc St)

London LSE – (Soc Psy – subject option for students registered in other degree subjects, check with admissions tutor)
Norwich City (Coll) – contact College (Psy Soty)
Open University – (Psychology – contact +44 (0)845 300 6090 or www.openuniversity.co.uk/you)

Alternative offers
See **Chapter 7** and **Appendix 1** for grades/UCAS Tariff points information for the International Baccalaureate, Scottish Highers/Advanced Highers, the Welsh Baccalaureate, the Irish Leaving Certificate, the Cambridge Pre-U Diploma, the Advanced Diploma and the Extended Project.

EXAMPLES OF FOUNDATION DEGREES IN THE SUBJECT FIELD

Bedfordfordshire; Edge Hill; Plymouth; Somerset (CAT); Welsh (CHort).

CHOOSING YOUR COURSE (SEE ALSO CH.1)

Some course features
Bangor A leading Psychology department with courses which include clinical and health psychology, neuropsychology and child and language development.
Exeter The course with Sport and Exercise Science will interest students aiming for a career as psychologists focusing on health maintenance.
London (UCL) Apply early – 1600 applicants each year with 250 from overseas.
Loughborough (Ergonomics) This practical course centres on providing solutions to improve the ways in which people interact with their technical and social environment, for example by finding out how aircraft can be made more safe, by designing workplaces to be more efficient. Students acquire a broad understanding of human stucture, function and behaviour and spend a third year on a relevant industrial placement.

Universities and colleges teaching quality See www.qaa.ac.uk; www.unistats.com.

Top research universities and colleges (RAE 2008) Cambridge; Oxford; Birmingham; London (UCL), (Birk); Cardiff; St Andrews; London (RH); York; Glasgow; Bangor; (Psychiatry, Neuroscience and Clinical Psychology) Cambridge; Cardiff; London (UCL), (King's); Oxford; Imperial London; Edinburgh; Bristol.

Examples of sandwich degree courses Aston; Bath; Bedfordshire; Birmingham City; Bournemouth; Bradford; Bristol UWE; Brunel; Cardiff; De Montfort; Hertfordshire; Huddersfield; Kent; Lancaster; Liverpool John Moores; London Met; Loughborough; Manchester; Manchester Met; Middlesex; Portsmouth; Sheffield Hallam; Surrey; Swansea Met; Ulster; West Scotland; Westminster; Wolverhampton.

ADMISSIONS INFORMATION

Number of applicants per place (approx) Abertay Dundee 5; Aston 6; Bangor 5; Bath 10; Birmingham 9; Bolton 5; Bournemouth 4; Bradford 14; Bradford (Coll) 2; Bristol 17; Bristol UWE 12; Brunel 20; Buckingham 1; Cardiff 10; Cardiff (UWIC) 5; Central Lancashire 13; Chester 20; City 6; Coventry 7; De Montfort 10; Derby 6; Dundee 6; Durham 20; East Anglia (Psysoc St) 6; Edinburgh

Napier 6; Exeter 14; Glamorgan 6; Glasgow Caledonian 15; Gloucestershire 50; Greenwich 8; Hertfordshire 22; Huddersfield 3; Hull 14; Kent 15; Lancaster 20; Leeds 12; Leeds Trinity (UC) 13; Leicester 22; Liverpool 21; Liverpool John Moores 8; London (RH) 10, (UCL) 18; London South Bank 7; Loughborough 8; Manchester Met 27, (Psy p/t) 2; Middlesex 10; Newcastle 20; Newman (UC) 3; Northampton 4; Northumbria 2; Nottingham 9; Nottingham Trent 3; Oxford Brookes 29; Plymouth 5; Portsmouth 10; Roehampton 7; Salford 4; Sheffield 12; Sheffield Hallam 10; Southampton 10; Staffordshire 6; Stirling 9; Surrey 10; Sussex 5; Swansea 7; Teesside 10; Warwick 13; Westminster 6; Worcester 9; York 9; York St John 3.

Number of applicants (**a** UK **b** EU (non-UK) **c** non-EU **d** mature) **Aston a**800 **b**100 **c**70 **d**90; **Bradford ab**200 **c**20; **Bristol ab**1421 **c**91 **d**156; **Derby a**407 **b**152 **c**5; **Leeds a**1758 **b**36 **c**37 **d**165; **London (UCL) a**1500 **c**250; **Manchester Met abc**14 **d**14; **Swansea ab**800 **c**50.

Advice to applicants and planning the UCAS personal statement Psychology is heavily over-subscribed so prepare well in advance by choosing suitable AS- and A-level subjects. Contact the Education and Social Services departments in your local authority office to arrange meetings with psychologists to gain a knowledge of the work. Make notes during those meetings and of any work experience gained and describe these fully on the UCAS application. Reference to introductory reading in psychology is important (many students have a distorted image of it). Demonstrate your interest in psychology through, for example, voluntary or other work experience. See also **Appendix 4**.

Misconceptions about this course Some believe a Psychology course will train them as therapists or counsellors – it will not. **Bath** They think that they are going to learn about themselves. **Birmingham** Some applicants underestimate the scientific nature of the course. **Exeter** It's scientific! **Lincoln** Applicants should be aware that this is a science-based course. Academic psychology is an empirical science requiring research methodologies and statistical analysis. **Reading** Not all applicants are aware that it is a science-based course and are surprised at the high science and statistics content. **Sussex** Applicants should note that the BSc course is not harder than the BA course. Many students mistakenly believe that psychology consists of counselling and that there is no maths. Psychology is a science. **York** Some students think psychology means Freud which it hasn't done for 50 years or more. They do not realise that psychology is a science in the same vein as biology, chemistry or physics. Only 20 per cent of Psychology graduates become professional psychologists. This involves taking a postgraduate degree in a specialist area of psychology.

Selection interviews Yes Bolton, Brunel, Buckingham, Cambridge, Durham, Glamorgan, Glasgow Caledonian, Leeds Trinity (UC), London (UCL) 300 out of 1500 applicants, London Met, London South Bank, Middlesex, Newcastle, Northampton, Norwich City (Coll), Oxford, Oxford Brookes, Plymouth, Swansea; **Some** Anglia Ruskin, Aston, Bangor, Bristol, Cardiff, Derby (non-standard applications), Dundee, East Anglia, Exeter (mature students), Huddersfield (mature students), Keele, Leeds (mature students), Liverpool John Moores, Nottingham Trent (for non-standard applications), Roehampton, Salford, Sunderland.

Interview advice and questions Although some applicants will have studied the subject at A-level and will have a broad understanding of its coverage, it is still essential to have gained some work experience or to have discussed the career with a professional psychologist. Questions will focus on this and in previous years they have included: What have you read about psychology? What do you expect to gain by studying psychology? What are your parents' and teachers' views on your choice of subject? Are you interested in any particular branch of the subject? Is psychology an art or a science? Do you think you are well suited to this course? Why? Do you think it is possible that if we learn enough about the functioning of the brain we can create a computer that is functionally the same? What is counselling? Is it necessary? Know the differences between the various branches of psychology and discuss any specific interests, for example, in clinical, occupational, educational, criminal psychology and cognitive, neuro-, social or physiological psychology. What influences young children's food choices? What stereotypes do we have of people with mental illness? **Bangor** Each application is treated individually and considered on its own merits. **Oxford** Ability to evaluate evidence and to have the capacity for logical and creative thinking. See **Chapter 5**.

Reasons for rejection (non-academic) Lack of background reading and lack of awareness of psychology; poor communication skills; misunderstanding of what is involved in a degree course. Poor personal statement. Poor grades, especially in GCSE maths. **Exeter** Competition for places – we can select those with exceptional grades. **Sheffield** Poor predicted grades. **Surrey** Inarticulate. **Warwick** (BSc) Lack of science background.

AFTER-RESULTS ADVICE

Offers to applicants repeating A-levels **Higher** Birmingham, City, Loughborough, Newcastle, Portsmouth, Southampton, Swansea, Warwick, York; **Possibly higher** Aston, Northampton; **Same** Aston (Comb Hons), Bangor, Bolton, Brunel, Cardiff, Cardiff (UWIC), Chester, Derby, Dundee, Durham, East Anglia, Huddersfield, Hull, Lincoln, Liverpool Hope, Liverpool John Moores, London (RH), London South Bank, Manchester Met, Newman (UC), Nottingham, Nottingham Trent, Oxford Brookes, Roehampton, Salford, Sheffield Hallam, Staffordshire, Stirling, Suffolk (Univ Campus), Sunderland, Surrey, Thames Valley, Ulster, Wolverhampton, York St John; **No offers made** Cambridge.

GRADUATE DESTINATIONS AND EMPLOYMENT (2007/8 HESA)

Graduates surveyed 8495 **Employed** 4060 **In further study** 1320 **Assumed unemployed** 655.

Career note Clinical, educational and occupational psychology are the three main specialist careers for graduate psychologists, all involving further study. Ergonomics, human–computer interaction, marketing, public relations, human resource management, advertising, the social services, the prison and rehabilitation services also provide alternative career routes.

OTHER DEGREE SUBJECTS FOR CONSIDERATION

Anthropology; Behavioural Science; Cognitive Sciences; Education; Health Studies; Neuroscience; Sociology

QUANTITY SURVEYING

(see also **Building and Construction**)

Quantity Surveying is a specialised field of surveying which focuses on the costing of the built environment. Students are introduced to construction studies, measurement cost studies, economics and law. The work is similar, in some aspects, to the work of an accountant and requires the same attention to detail. See also **Architecture**, **Building** and **Surveying** courses.

Useful website www.rics.org/careers.

NB The points totals shown to the left of the institutions are for ease of reference only. It must not be assumed that Tariff points are always used by institutions or that they can be substituted for an offer in grades. The level of an offer is not necessarily indicative of the quality of a course.

COURSE OFFERS INFORMATION

Subject requirements/preferences **GCSE** English and mathematics grade A–C. **AL** No subjects specified; mathematics useful.

NB In 2011 universities and colleges will differ in their use of GCE AL/AS unit grade information, A* grades, the Extended Project (EPQ), the Advanced Diploma and the Cambridge Pre-U examination when considering applicants and making offers. An EPQ may be accepted in place of an AS subject. Check websites of universities and colleges for the latest offers information.

Your target offers and examples of courses provided by each institution

340 pts **Heriot-Watt** – AAB 2nd yr entry (Quant Surv) (IB 35 pts)
320 pts **Ulster** – 320 pts (Quant Surv)
300 pts **Kingston** – 300 pts (Quant Surv Cnsltncy) (IB 32 pts)
Loughborough – 300 pts (Commer Mgt Quant Surv) (IB 32 pts)
Reading – 300–320 pts (Quant Surv)

280 pts **Heriot-Watt** – BBC 1st yr entry (Quant Surv) (IB 29 pts)
Northumbria – 280–260 pts (Quant Surv; Commer Quant Surv) (IB 25 pts)
Salford – 280 pts (Quant Surv)
Westminster – BBC (Quant Surv) (IB 26 pts)
270 pts **Anglia Ruskin** – 270 pts (Quant Surv) (IB 26 pts)
Glasgow Caledonian – 270 pts (Quant Surv)
Liverpool John Moores – 270 pts (Quant Surv)
Portsmouth – 270 pts (Prop Dev Quant Surv)
Sheffield Hallam – 270 pts (Quant Surv)
260 pts **Birmingham City** – 260 pts (Quant Surv) (IB 27 pts)
Bristol UWE – 260–300 pts (Quant Surv Commer Mgt) (IB 24–28 pts)
240 pts **Bolton** – 240 pts (Quant Surv Commer Mgt)
Central Lancashire – 240 pts (Commer Mgt Quant Surv)
Edinburgh Napier – 240 pts (Quant Surv)
Leeds Met – 240 pts (Quant Surv) (IB 28 pts)
Nottingham Trent – 240–280 pts (Quant Surv; Quant Surv Constr Commer Mgt) (IB 28 pts)
230 pts **Coventry** – 230 pts (Quant Surv Commer Mgt)
Robert Gordon – 230 pts (Surv (Quant Surv))
Wolverhampton – 230 pts (Commer Mgt Quant Surv)
220 pts **Glamorgan** – 220–260 pts (Quant Surv)
180 pts **Greenwich** – 180 pts (Quant Surv)
160 pts **London South Bank** – CC (Commer Mgt (Quant Surv))
Wolverhampton – 160–220 pts (Quant Surv)

Thames Valley – contact University (Blt Env (Quant Surv))

Alternative offers
See **Chapter 7** and **Appendix 1** for grades/UCAS Tariff points information for the International Baccalaureate, Scottish Highers/Advanced Highers, the Welsh Baccalaureate, the Irish Leaving Certificate, the Cambridge Pre-U Diploma, the Advanced Diploma and the Extended Project.

EXAMPLES OF FOUNDATION DEGREES IN THE SUBJECT FIELD
Bolton; Glamorgan; Northumbria; Swansea Met.

CHOOSING YOUR COURSE (SEE ALSO CH.1)
Some course features
Anglia Ruskin (Quant Surv) The course shares many common themes with the Building Surveying course but also focuses on management practice, project management and procurement.
Loughborough (Commer Mgt Quant Surv) The course is accredited by the Royal Institution of Chartered Surveyors and the Institution of Civil Engineering Surveying. Sponsorship is a condition of entry to the course: all suitable applicants are interviewed by the sponsors.
Nottingham Trent Three-year full-time, four-year sandwich and five-year part-time courses are offered.
Portsmouth (Prop Dev Quant Surv) The course combines the business bias in property development with a professional qualification in quantity surveying.
Westminster A five-year part-time course is available.

Universities and colleges teaching quality See www.qaa.ac.uk; www.unistats.com.

Examples of sandwich degree courses Bristol UWE; Coventry; Kingston; London South Bank; Loughborough; Northumbria; Nottingham Trent; Sheffield Hallam; Ulster.

ADMISSIONS INFORMATION
Number of applicants per place (approx) Anglia Ruskin 2; Birmingham City 14; Edinburgh Napier 2; Glamorgan 4; Glasgow Caledonian 3; Greenwich 11; Kingston 13; Liverpool John Moores 10; Loughborough 9; Northumbria 11; Nottingham Trent 10; Robert Gordon 5; Salford 16; Sheffield Hallam 7; Wolverhampton 6.

Advice to applicants and planning the UCAS personal statement Surveyors work with architects and builders as well as in their own consultancies and these organisations should be approached to discuss quantity surveying or to obtain work experience. Explain your interests fully. Read *The Chartered Quantity Surveyor* magazine. See also **Appendix 4**.

Selection interviews **Yes** Birmingham City, Glamorgan, Glasgow Caledonian, Heriot-Watt, Kingston, Liverpool John Moores, Nottingham Trent, Robert Gordon, Ulster; **Some** Abertay Dundee, Anglia Ruskin.

Interview advice and questions Past questions have included: What is quantity surveying? What is the scope of the work? How do you qualify to do this work? Have you spoken to a quantity surveyor or spent any time in a quantity surveyor's office? See **Chapter 5**.

AFTER-RESULTS ADVICE

Offers to applicants repeating A-levels **Higher** Bolton, Nottingham Trent; **Possibly higher** Glamorgan, Liverpool John Moores; **Same** Abertay Dundee, Salford.

GRADUATE DESTINATIONS AND EMPLOYMENT (2007/8 HESA)

No data available.

Career note See **Building and Construction** and **Property Management**.

OTHER DEGREE SUBJECTS FOR CONSIDERATION

Architectural Technology; Architecture; Building; Civil Engineering; Construction Management; Surveying.

RADIOGRAPHY

(including **Medical Imaging** and **Radiotherapy**; see also **Health Sciences/Studies**)

Many institutions offer both Diagnostic and Therapeutic Radiography but applicants should check this, and course entry requirements, before applying. Information on courses is also available from the Society of Radiographers (see **Appendix 4**). **Diagnostic Radiography** The demonstration on film (or other imaging materials) of the position and structure of the body's organs using radiation or other imaging media. **Therapeutic Radiography** The planning and administration of treatment for patients suffering from malignant and non-malignant disease using different forms of radiation. Courses lead to state registration.

Useful websites www.sor.org; www.radiographycareers.co.uk; www.nhscareers.nhs.uk.

NB The points totals shown to the left of the institutions are for ease of reference only. It must not be assumed that Tariff points are always used by institutions or that they can be substituted for an offer in grades. The level of an offer is not necessarily indicative of the quality of a course.

COURSE OFFERS INFORMATION

Subject requirements/preferences **GCSE** Five subjects including English, mathematics and a science subject (usually at one sitting). **AL** One or two sciences required; mathematics may be acceptable. (Radiotherapy) One science subject required for some courses. Psychology may not be considered a science subject at some institutions. **Other requirements** Applicants required to have an occupational health check and a Criminal Records Bureau (CRB) clearance. Visit to, or work experience in, hospital imaging department often required/expected.

NB In 2011 universities and colleges will differ in their use of GCE AL/AS unit grade information, A* grades, the Extended Project (EPQ), the Advanced Diploma and the Cambridge Pre-U examination when considering applicants and making offers. An EPQ may be accepted in place of an AS subject. Check websites of universities and colleges for the latest offers information.

Your target offers and examples of courses provided by each institution

320 pts **Exeter** – ABB–BBC (Med Imag (Diag Radiog)) (IB 32–28 pts)
300 pts **Cardiff** – 300 pts (Radiog (Diag Radiog Imag)) (IB 24 pts)
Portsmouth – 300 pts (Diag Radiog; Ther Radiog)
Ulster – BBB +HPAT (Radiog (Diag) (Ther)) (IB 25 pts) (See **Ch.5**)
280 pts **Bradford** – 280 pts (Diag Radiog)
Salford – 280 pts (Diag Radiog) (IB 30 pts)
Suffolk (Univ Campus) – 280 pts (Onc Radiothera Tech)
260 pts **Cardiff** – 260 pts (Radiothera Onc) (IB 24 pts)
Glasgow Caledonian – BCC (Rdtn Onc Sci; Diag Imag Sci)
Leeds – BCC (Radiog (Diag))
London (St George's) – 260 pts (Diag Radiog; Ther Radiog)
Sheffield Hallam – 260 pts (Diag Radiog)
240 pts **Bangor** – 240–260 pts (Diag Radiog Imag) (IB 28 pts)
Birmingham City – 240 pts (Radiothera; Diag Radiog)
Bristol UWE – 240–280 pts (Diag Imag; Radiothera) (IB 26 pts)
City – CCC 240 pts (Radiog (Diag Imag) (Radiothera Onc))
Cumbria – 240 pts BCC (Diag Radiog)
Hertfordshire – 240 pts (Diag Radiog Imag; Radiothera Onc)
Liverpool – CCC (Diag Radiog; Radiothera) (IB 28 pts)
Robert Gordon – CCC 240 pts (Diag Radiog) (IB 26 pts)
Suffolk (Univ Campus) – 240 pts (Diag Radiog)
Teesside – 240–300 pts (Diag Radiog)
220 pts **Sheffield Hallam** – 220 pts (Radiothera Onc)
200 pts **Canterbury Christ Church** – 200 pts (Diag Radiog)
Derby – 200–240 pts (Diag Radiog)
195 pts **Queen Margaret** – 195 pts (Diag Radiog; Ther Radiog)
160 pts **London South Bank** – 160 pts (Diag Radiog; Thera Radiog)

Alternative offers
See **Chapter 7** and **Appendix 1** for grades/UCAS Tariff points information for the International Baccalaureate, Scottish Highers/Advanced Highers, the Welsh Baccalaureate, the Irish Leaving Certificate, the Cambridge Pre-U Diploma, the Advanced Diploma and the Extended Project.

EXAMPLES OF FOUNDATION DEGREES IN THE SUBJECT FIELD
Anglia Ruskin; City; Portsmouth; Salford.

CHOOSING YOUR COURSE (SEE ALSO CH.1)
Some course features
Cardiff The year is divided into seven academic and seven clinical blocks. Placements are in radiography departments throughout South Wales.
City A Foundation degree in Radiotherapy Practice is offered.
Cumbria Fifty-four weeks of clinical placements in the three-year course are spent in hospitals in Northen England. Students' preferences are taken into account.
Exeter (Med Imag (Diag Radiog)) This is a specialist course leading to a career as a diagnostic radiographer.
Portsmouth There is a seven-week exchange programme working in hospitals in Hong Kong.

Universities and colleges teaching quality See www.qaa.ac.uk; www.unistats.com.

ADMISSIONS INFORMATION
Number of applicants per place (approx) Bangor 7; Birmingham City (Radiothera) 8; Bradford 8; Cardiff 3; Derby 6; Glasgow Caledonian 7; Hertfordshire (Diag Radiog Imag) 8; Leeds 10; Liverpool 13; London (St George's) 7; London South Bank 9; Portsmouth 10; Robert Gordon 5; Salford 10; Sheffield Hallam 8, (Radiothera Onc) 3; Southampton 5; Suffolk (Univ Campus) 3; Teesside 10.

Advice to applicants and planning the UCAS personal statement Contacts with radiographers and visits to the radiography departments of hospitals should be discussed in full on the UCAS application. **Birmingham City** Evidence needed of a visit to at least one imaging department or oncology (radiotherapy) department before completing UCAS application. Evidence of good research into career. **Liverpool** Decision to choose between therapeutic and diagnostic pathways should be made before applying. **Salford** Selectors look for evidence of communication skills, teamwork, work experience in public areas. See also **Appendix 4**.

Misconceptions about this course There is often confusion between radiotherapy and diagnostic imaging and between diagnostic and therapeutic radiography.

Selection interviews **Yes** Birmingham City, Cardiff, City, Derby, Hertfordshire, London South Bank, Queen Margaret, Portsmouth, Salford, Sheffield Hallam; **Some** Bangor, London (St George's).

Interview advice and questions All applicants should have discussed this career with a radiographer and visited a hospital radiography department. Questions follow from these contacts. Where does radiography fit into the overall health care system? See **Chapter 5**.

Reasons for rejection (non-academic) Lack of interest in people. Poor communication skills. Occasionally students may be unsuitable for the clinical environment, for example, they express a fear of blood and needles; poor grasp of radiography as a career. Unable to meet criteria for employment in the Health Service, for example, health factors, criminal convictions, severe disabilities.

AFTER-RESULTS ADVICE

Offers to applicants repeating A-levels **Higher** London (St George's); **Same** Derby, Salford.

GRADUATE DESTINATIONS AND EMPLOYMENT (2007/8 HESA)

No data available.

Career note Most radiographers work in the NHS in hospital radiography departments undertaking diagnostic or therapeutic treatment. Others work in private healthcare.

OTHER DEGREE SUBJECTS FOR CONSIDERATION

Audiology; Forensic Engineering; Health Studies; Medical Physics; Nursing; Occupational Therapy; Physics; Podiatry; Speech Sciences.

RELIGIOUS STUDIES

(including **Biblical Studies, Divinity, Jewish Studies** and **Theology**)

Religious Studies courses cover four degree course subjects: Religious Studies, Divinity, Theology and Biblical Studies. The subject content of these courses varies and students should check prospectuses carefully. They are not intended as training courses for church ministry; an adherence to a particular religious denomination is not a necessary qualification for entry. (NB Religious studies is an acceptable second or third A-level for any non-scientific degree course.)

Useful websites www.guardian.co.uk/religion; www.cwmission.org; www.miraclestudies.net; www.academicinfo.net/religindex.html; www.theologywebsite.com; www.jewishstudies.org; www.jewishstudies.virtualave.net; www.jewfaq.org; www.virtualreligion.net; www.jis.oxfordjournals.org.

NB The points totals shown to the left of the institutions are for ease of reference only. It must not be assumed that Tariff points are always used by institutions or that they can be substituted for an offer in grades. The level of an offer is not necessarily indicative of the quality of a course.

COURSE OFFERS INFORMATION

Subject requirements/preferences **GCSE** English and mathematics. For teacher training, English and mathematics and science. **AL** Religious studies or theology may be required or preferred for some courses.

NB In 2011 universities and colleges will differ in their use of GCE AL/AS unit grade information, A* grades, the Extended Project (EPQ), the Advanced Diploma and the Cambridge Pre-U examination when considering applicants and making offers. An EPQ may be accepted in place of an AS subject. Check websites of universities and colleges for the latest offers information.

Your target offers and examples of courses provided by each institution

380 pts **Cambridge** – A*AA college offers may vary (Theol Relig St; BA Educ Relig St) (IB 38–42 pts)

360 pts **Bristol** – AAA–AAB (Phil Theol) (IB 37–33 pts)
Durham – AAA (Theol Phil)
Oxford – AAA (Theol; Theol Orntl St; Phil Theol) (IB 38–40 pts)

340 pts **Birmingham** – AAB–BBB (Hist Art Theol)
Bristol – AAB–BBB (Theol Relig St) (IB 35–32 pts)
Durham – AAB (Theol; Theol (Euro St))
Exeter – AAB–BBB (Class St Theol) (IB 34–29 pts)
Glasgow – AAB (Theol Relig St) (IB 34 pts)
London (King's) – ABB+AS–BBB+AS (Relig Contemp Wrld; Relig Phil Eth) (IB 34 pts)
St Andrews – AAB (Theol St; Theol Bib St courses) (IB 30 pts)

320 pts **Exeter** – ABB–BBB (Theol Arbc St; Theol Islam St; Theol) (IB 32–29 pts)
Kent – 320 pts (Relig St)
Kent – 320–280 pts (Relig St Hist; Relig St Phil)
Leeds – ABB (Theol Relig St)
London (UCL) – BBBe (Heb Jew St; Jew Hist) (IB 32 pts)
Manchester – ABB–BBB (Compar Relig Soc Anth; St Relig Theol (Jew St) (Bib St) (Relig Soty) (S As St)) (IB 33–32 pts)
Manchester – ABB–BBC (Islam St Arbc) (IB 30–32 pts)
Nottingham – ABB (Engl St Theol) (IB 34 pts)
St Andrews – ABB (Bib St Ling) (IB 32 pts)
Sheffield – ABB–BBB (Bib St Mus; Bib St; Bib St Phil) (IB 35–32 pts)

300 pts **Birmingham** – BBB–BBC (E Medit Hist Theol)
Cardiff – BBB 300 pts (Relig Theol St)
Edinburgh – BBB (MA Relig St; Div) (IB 26–28 pts)
Gloucestershire – 300 pts (Relig Phil Eth)
Lancaster – BBB–BBC 300–280 pts (Relig St; Relig St Sociol) (IB 28–29 pts)
Nottingham – ABC (Theology) (IB 32 pts)
Queen's Belfast – BBB–BBCb (Theol; Div) (IB 29 pts)
Sheffield – BBB (Bib St Fr/Ger) (IB 35–32 pts)
Stranmillis (UC) – BBB (Relig St Educ)

280 pts **Aberdeen** – BBC (Theology) (IB 30 pts)
Birmingham – BBC (Islam St) (IB 30 pts)
Cardiff – BBC 280 pts (Relig St Ital/Span)
London (Hey) – 280 pts (Phil Relig Eth; St Relig; Div; Theol) (IB 28–32 pts)
London (SOAS) – BBC (St Relig)
Oxford Brookes – BBC (Relig Theol)
Stirling – BBC–CCC (Relig St Comb Hons)
Winchester – 280–320 pts (Theol Relig St; Relig St Arch; Relig St Bus Mgt)

260 pts **Chester** – 260 pts (Relig St; Theol Relig St) (IB 24 pts)
Huddersfield – 260 pts (Relig Educ)
Liverpool Hope – 260 pts (Theol Relig St)
Newport – 260 pts (Relig St; Relig St Joint Hons)

240 pts **Aberdeen** – CCC (Relig St; Div)
Bangor – 240–300 pts (Relig St; BA/BD Theol courses)
Central Lancashire – 240 pts (Islam St Comb Hons; Relig Cult Soty Comb Hons)
Hull – 240–280 pts (Relig courses)
UHI Millennium Inst (HTC) – CCC (Theol St)

220 pts **Bath Spa** – 220–260 pts (St Relig)
Newman (UC) – 220–260 pts (Theol courses)
York St John – 220 pts (Theol Relig St)
200 pts **Canterbury Christ Church** – 200–240 pts (Theol courses; Relig St courses)
Chichester – CDD 220–260 pts (Theology) (IB 26 pts)
Cumbria – 200 pts (Relig St)
Leeds Trinity (UC) – 200 pts (Relig St; Theol)
180 pts **Trinity Saint David** – 180–240 pts (Theol courses; Relig St courses; Islam St; Div)
160 pts **Bishop Grosseteste (UC)** – 160 pts (Educ St Theol)
St Mary's Twickenham (UC) – 160–200 pts (Theol Relig St)
Wolverhampton – 160–220 pts (Relig St courses)

Alternative offers

See **Chapter 7** and **Appendix 1** for grades/UCAS Tariff points information for the International Baccalaureate, Scottish Highers/Advanced Highers, the Welsh Baccalaureate, the Irish Leaving Certificate, the Cambridge Pre-U Diploma, the Advanced Diploma and the Extended Project.

EXAMPLES OF FOUNDATION DEGREES IN THE SUBJECT FIELD

Newman (UC); York St John.

CHOOSING YOUR COURSE (SEE ALSO CH.1)

Some course features

Birmingham (Islam St) The course provides a critical investigation of Islamic history with options in Arabic, Islamic Law and introductions to Christianity and Judaism.
Durham (Theol) The course combines aspects of philosophy, history and social sciences and includes a detailed study of the Old and New Testaments.
Edinburgh MA and Honours and BA General degrees are offered in Religious Studies and Divinity. There is also a Bachelor of Divinity course equipping students for the ordained ministry.
Lancaster (Relig St) A distinguished course offering core and over 40 optional modules in such diverse areas as Islam, Sanskrit, pilgrimage, practical anthropology, myth and mysticism. There is a second year placement programme in the USA and an optional four-week summer course in India.
Sheffield (Bib St) The only course in England looking at the development of the Bible and its place in contemporary society, politics, art, film, literature and music.

Universities and colleges teaching quality See www.qaa.ac.uk; www.unistats.com.

Top research universities and colleges (RAE 2008) (Theology, Divinity and Religious Studies) Durham; Aberdeen; Cambridge; Oxford; London (UCL); Manchester; Sheffield; Edinburgh; Nottingham.

ADMISSIONS INFORMATION

Number of applicants per place (approx) Bangor 5; Birmingham 4; Bristol 7; Cambridge 2; Chichester 6; Cumbria 12; Durham 6; Edinburgh 3; Exeter 7; Glasgow 4; Hull 10; Kent 13; Lancaster 6; Leeds 4; Leeds Trinity (UC) 4; Liverpool Hope 6; London (Hey) 4, (King's) 6; Middlesex 4; Newman (UC) 2; Nottingham 10; Sheffield 7; Trinity Saint David 7; Winchester 6; York St John 2.

Advice to applicants and planning the UCAS personal statement An awareness of the differences between the main religions is important as is any special research you have done to help you decide on your preferred courses. Interests in the religious art and architecture of various periods and styles should be noted. Applicants should have an open-minded approach to studying a diverse range of religious traditions.

Misconceptions about this course Some students think that you must be religious to study Theology – in fact, people of all faiths and none study the subject. A study of religions is not Christian theology. **Leeds** Some applicants are not aware of the breadth of the subject. We offer modules covering New Testament, Christian theology, Islamic studies, Hinduism, Buddhism, Sikhism, Christian ethics, sociology of religion.

Selection interviews **Yes** Aberystwyth, Cambridge, Chester, Durham, Edinburgh, Glasgow, Hull, Lancaster, Leeds, Leeds Trinity (UC), London (Hey), (SOAS), Nottingham, Oxford, Oxford Brookes, Sheffield, Trinity Saint David, Winchester; **Some** Bristol, Cardiff, Southampton.

Interview advice and questions Past questions have included: Why do you want to study Theology/Biblical Studies/Religious Studies? What do you hope to do after obtaining your degree? Questions relating to the A-level syllabus. Questions on current theological topics. Do you have any strong religious convictions? Do you think that your religious beliefs will be changed at the end of the course? Why did you choose Religious Studies rather than Biblical Studies? How would you explain the miracles to a 10-year-old? (BEd course). Do you agree with the National Lottery? How do you think you can apply theology to your career? **Cambridge** There is a Christian priest who regularly visits India and converted to a Hindu priest. When he is in England he still practises as a Christian priest. What problems might this pose? Do you believe we should eradicate Christmas on the basis that it offends other religious groups? **Oxford** The ability to defend one's opinions and willingness to engage in a lively dialogue are both important. See **Chapter 5**.

Reasons for rejection (non-academic) Students not attending Open Days may be rejected. Too religiously conservative. Failure to interact. Lack of motivation to study a subject which goes beyond A-level. **Cardiff** Insufficiently open to an academic study of religion.

AFTER-RESULTS ADVICE

Offers to applicants repeating A-levels **Higher** Hull, Manchester, St Andrews; **Possibly higher** Cambridge (Hom); **Same** Bangor, Birmingham, Cardiff, Chester, Durham, Glasgow, Greenwich, Lancaster, Leeds, Liverpool Hope, London (SOAS), Nottingham, St Mary's Twickenham (UC), Sheffield, Stirling, Trinity Saint David, Winchester, Wolverhampton, York St John; **No offers made** Cambridge.

GRADUATE DESTINATIONS AND EMPLOYMENT (2007/8 HESA)

Graduates surveyed 1070 **Employed** 405 **In further study** 320 **Assumed unemployed** 65.

Career note Although a small number of graduates may regard these courses as a preparation for entry to religious orders, the great majority enter other careers, with teaching particularly popular.

OTHER DEGREE SUBJECTS FOR CONSIDERATION

Community Studies; Education; History; Philosophy; Psychology; Social Policy and Administration; Social Work.

RETAIL MANAGEMENT

(see also **Marketing**)

This subject attracts a large number of applicants each year and it is necessary to have work experience before applying. The work itself varies depending on the type of retail outlet. After completing their courses graduates in a large department store will be involved in different aspects of the business, for example supervising shop assistants, warehouse and packing staff. They could also receive special training in the sales of particular goods, for example food and drink, clothing, furniture. Subsequently there may be opportunities to become buyers. In more specialised shops, for example shoes, fashion and food, graduates are likely to work only with these products, with opportunities to reach senior management.

Useful websites www.brc.org.uk; www.retailweek.com; www.theretailbulletin.com; www.retailcareers.co.uk; www.retailchoice.com; www.nrf.com.

NB The points totals shown to the left of the institutions are for ease of reference only. It must not be assumed that Tariff points are always used by institutions or that they can be substituted for an offer in grades. The level of an offer is not necessarily indicative of the quality of a course.

COURSE OFFERS INFORMATION

Subject requirements/preferences **GCSE** English and mathematics at grade C or above. **AL** No subjects specified.

NB In 2011 universities and colleges will differ in their use of GCE AL/AS unit grade information, A* grades, the Extended Project (EPQ), the Advanced Diploma and the Cambridge Pre-U examination when considering applicants and making offers. An EPQ may be accepted in place of an AS subject. Check websites of universities and colleges for the latest offers information.

Your target offers and examples of courses provided by each institution

340 pts **Loughborough** – AAB (Rtl Mark Mgt) (IB 36 pts)
320 pts **Manchester** – ABB (Des Mgt Fash Rtl)
300 pts **Stirling** – BBB 2nd yr entry (Rtl Mark)
Surrey – BBB 300 pts (Bus Rtl Mgt) (IB 30 pts)
Westminster – BBB 300 pts (Bus Mgt (Rtl); Bus St Rtl) (IB 28 pts)
280 pts **Birmingham City** – 280 pts (Fash Rtl Mgt) (IB 28 pts)
Bournemouth – 280 pts (Rtl Mgt)
Huddersfield – 280 pts (Rtl Mark Mgt)
260 pts **Brighton** – 260 pts (Rtl Mgt; Rtl Mark) (IB 28 pts)
Liverpool John Moores – 260 pts (Rtl Mgt)
Stirling – BCC 1st yr entry (Rtl Mark)
240 pts **Cardiff (UWIC)** – 240 pts (Mark Mgt)
De Montfort – 240 pts (Rtl Buy (Tex) (Fash); Rtl Mgt)
Leeds Met – 240 pts (Rtl Mark Mgt)
Manchester Met – 240 pts (Rtl Mark Mgt; Hspty Lic Rtl Mgt)
Roehampton – 240–280 pts (Bus Mgt (Rtl Mgt Mark))
Ulster – 240 pts (Bus Rtl St; Comp Rtl St)
220 pts **Central Lancashire** – 220–260 pts (Rtl Mgt (Buy) (E-Commer) (Entre) (Fash) (Mark); Rtl Mgt Comb Hons) (IB 28 pts)
London Met – 220 pts (Rtl Mgt courses)
Northampton – 220–260 pts (Rtl Mark; Rtl Joint Hons)
200 pts **Bucks New** – 200–240 pts (Bus Rtl Mgt)
Canterbury Christ Church – 200 pts (Bus Mgt (Rtl))
195 pts **Queen Margaret** – 195 pts (Rtl Mgt)
160 pts **Robert Gordon** – CC (Rtl Mgt) (IB 24 pts)

Alternative offers

See **Chapter 7** and **Appendix 1** for grades/UCAS Tariff points information for the International Baccalaureate, Scottish Highers/Advanced Highers, the Welsh Baccalaureate, the Irish Leaving Certificate, the Cambridge Pre-U Diploma, the Advanced Diploma and the Extended Project.

EXAMPLES OF FOUNDATION DEGREES IN THE SUBJECT FIELD

Arts London; Bedfordshire; Birmingham (UC); Blackburn (Coll Univ Centre); Bournemouth; Brighton; Cornwall (Coll); Exeter (Coll); Grimsby (IFHE); Kent; Middlesex; Norwich City (Coll); Plymouth; Suffolk (Univ Campus); Wolverhampton.

CHOOSING YOUR COURSE (SEE ALSO CH.1)

Some course features

Birmingham City (Fash Rtl Mgt) The course focuses on the global fashion industry and design management. It includes fabric sourcing, pattern cutting and manufacturing, and fashion forecasting.
Bournemouth (Rtl Mgt) The course has paid industrial placements and overseas opportunities.
Loughborough (Rtl Mark Mgt) This four-year sandwich course includes a placement year leading to a Diploma in Professional Studies. Retailers are closely involved throughout and provide lectures, case studies, skills workshops and company visits.
Queen Margaret (Rtl Mgt) Course options in the third year include e-marketing, advertising and marketing communications, fashion marketing and market planning.
Surrey (Rtl Mgt) A long-established course with industrial work placements and high graduate employment.

Universities and colleges teaching quality See www.qaa.ac.uk; www.unistats.com.

Top research universities and colleges (RAE 2008) See **Business Courses**.

Examples of sandwich degree courses Birmingham (UC); Bournemouth; Bradford; Brighton; Central Lancashire; De Montfort; Huddersfield; Manchester Met.

ADMISSIONS INFORMATION

Number of applicants per place (approx) Bournemouth 8; Manchester Met 10; See also **Business Courses**.

Advice to applicants and planning the UCAS personal statement **Manchester Met** (Rtl Mark Mgt) Evidence of working with people or voluntary work experience (department unable to assist with sponsorships); see also **Business Courses**.

Misconceptions about this course See **Business Courses.**

Selection interviews See **Business Courses.**

Interview advice and questions See **Business Courses.**

Reasons for rejection (non-academic) See **Business Courses.**

AFTER-RESULTS ADVICE

Offers to applicants repeating A-levels See **Business Courses.**

GRADUATE DESTINATIONS AND EMPLOYMENT (2007/8 HESA)

No data available.

Career note The majority of graduates work in business involved in marketing and retail work. Employment options include brand design, product management, advertising, PR, sales and account management.

OTHER DEGREE SUBJECTS FOR CONSIDERATION

Business Studies; Consumer Sciences/Studies; E-Commerce; Human Resource Management; Psychology; Supply Chain Management.

RUSSIAN and EAST EUROPEAN STUDIES

(including **Bulgarian, Croatian, Czech, Finnish, Georgian, Hungarian, Polish, Romanian, Russian** and **Serbian**; see also **European Studies** and **Languages**)

East European Studies cover a wide range of the less popular language courses and should be considered by anyone with a love of and gift for languages. Many natural linguists often devote themselves to one of the popular European languages studied up to A-level, when their language skills could be extended to the more unusual languages, thereby increasing their future career opportunities.

Useful websites www.basees.org.uk; www.iol.org.uk; www.bbc.co.uk/languages; http://languageadvantage.com; www.languagematters.co.uk; www.reed.co.uk/multilingual; www.cilt.org.uk.

NB The points totals shown to the left of the institutions are for ease of reference only. It must not be assumed that Tariff points are always used by institutions or that they can be substituted for an offer in grades. The level of an offer is not necessarily indicative of the quality of a course.

COURSE OFFERS INFORMATION

Subject requirements/preferences **GCSE** A foreign language. **AL** One or two modern languages may be stipulated.

NB In 2011 universities and colleges will differ in their use of GCE AL/AS unit grade information, A* grades, the Extended Project (EPQ), the Advanced Diploma and the Cambridge Pre-U examination when considering applicants and making offers. An EPQ may be accepted in place of an AS subject. Check websites of universities and colleges for the latest offers information.

Your target offers and examples of courses provided by each institution

380 pts **Cambridge** – A*AA college offers may vary (Modn Mediev Lang (Russ)) (IB 38–42 pts HL 776–777)

360 pts **Manchester** – AAA–AAB (MML Russ Chin; Russ Jap; Russ Span) (IB 35–37 pts)

Oxford – AAA (Modn Langs (Russ +2nd Lang); Modn Lang Ling (Russ); Euro Mid E Langs (Cz/Russ); Engl Russ) (IB 38–42 pts)

St Andrews – AAA–AAB (Russ; Modn Hist Russ; Econ Russ) (IB 32 pts)

340 pts **Bath** – AAB–ABB (Russ Pol) (IB 34–36 pts)

Bristol – AAB–BBC (Cz Fr/Ger/Ital/Port/Russ/Span; Russ) (IB 35–30 pts HL 655)

Durham – AAB (Modn Langs (Russ +1–2 Langs)) (IB 34 pts)

Exeter – AAB–ABB (Russ; Russ Arbc; Hist Russ; Int Rel Russ) (IB 29 pts)

Glasgow – AAB (Cnt E Euro St; Cz; Russ; Polh; Slav St) (IB 34 pts)

320 pts **Bath** – ABB–BBB (Euro St Modn Lang (Russ Fr/Ger/Span)) (IB 34 pts HL lang 6)

Birmingham – ABB–BBB (Russ St; Russ Psy; Int Bus Russ; Russ Thea St)

Leeds – ABB (Russ Sociol; Russ Span; Russ Civ Theol Relig St; Russ A/B courses) (IB 32 pts)

London (SOAS) – ABB (Georg Pol)

London (UCL) – BBB+AS (E Euro St; E Euro St Bulg/Cz/Finn/Hung/Slov/Polh/Romn/Serb Cro/Ukr; Russ St; Russ Hist) (IB 32 pts)

Manchester – ABB–BBC (BA Russ Chin; Russ Jap; Russ Port) (IB 30–33 pts)

300 pts **Edinburgh** – BBB (Russ St; Russ St Phil; Russ St Pol; Russ St Hist Art) (IB 34 pts)

London (QM) – 300–340 pts (Russ Bus Mgt; Russ Geog; Russ Pol) (IB 32 pts)

Manchester – BBB–BCC (Russ St; Russ Scrn St) (IB 32–28 pts)

Sheffield – BBB–BBC (Russ St; Russ Mus; Russ Pol; Russ Mgt) (IB 30–33 pts)

Westminster – BBB (Int Bus Russ)

280 pts **Nottingham** – BBC–ABC (Russ St; Russ E Euro Civ; Serb Cro St) (IB 28–30 pts)

Westminster – BBC (Int Rel Russ)

200 pts **European Bus Sch London** – CDD 200 pts check with Bus Sch (Int Bus (Russ))

Alternative offers

See **Chapter 7** and **Appendix 1** for grades/UCAS Tariff points information for the International Baccalaureate, Scottish Highers/Advanced Highers, the Welsh Baccalaureate, the Irish Leaving Certificate, the Cambridge Pre-U Diploma, the Advanced Diploma and the Extended Project.

CHOOSING YOUR COURSE (SEE ALSO CH.1)

Some course features

Durham Russian is only offered as one of two or three other subjects in the Combined Honours course.

Glasgow At all levels language tuition is given by Russian native language speakers.

London LSE Full degrees in languages are not offered by LSE, but Russian Language and Society can be taken as a degree option on most undergraduate courses.

Nottingham Beginners' courses are offered in Russian which can also be combined with another subject taken from the very wide range available, from Serbo-Croat to Contemporary Chinese Studies).

See also **Languages**.

Universities and colleges teaching quality See www.qaa.ac.uk; www.unistats.com.

Top research universities and colleges (RAE 2008) (Russian, Slavonic and East European languages) Manchester; Oxford; Sheffield; Cambridge; Bristol; Nottingham; Exeter.

ADMISSIONS INFORMATION

Number of applicants per place (approx) Birmingham 3; Bristol 3; Durham 7; Leeds 3; London (UCL) (E Euro St Bulg) 1; Nottingham 5.

Advice to applicants and planning the UCAS personal statement Visits to Eastern Europe should be mentioned, supported by your special reasons for wishing to study the language. A knowledge of the cultural, economic and political scene could be important. Fluent English important for non-UK students. Evidence of wide reading, travel and residence abroad. See also **Appendix 4** under **Languages**.

Selection interviews **Yes** Cambridge, Durham, Exeter, London (UCL), Oxford; **Some** Nottingham.

Interview advice and questions Since many applicants will not have taken Russian at A-level, questions often focus on their reasons for choosing a Russian degree, and their knowledge of, and interest in, Russia. Those taking A-level Russian are likely to be questioned on the course and on any reading done outside A-level work. East European Studies applicants will need to show some knowledge of their chosen country/countries and any specific reasons why they wish to follow the course. **Leeds** See **Languages.** See also **Chapter 5**.

Reasons for rejection (non-academic) Lack of perceived commitment for a demanding *ab initio* subject.

AFTER-RESULTS ADVICE

Offers to applicants repeating A-levels **Higher** Bristol, Glasgow, Leeds, St Andrews, Surrey (if candidate is re-sitting 2 A-levels); **Same** Durham; **No offers made** Cambridge.

GRADUATE DESTINATIONS AND EMPLOYMENT (2007/8 HESA)

Graduates surveyed 115 **Employed** 55 **In further study** 25 **Assumed unemployed** 10.

Career note See **Languages**.

OTHER DEGREE SUBJECTS FOR CONSIDERATION

Economics; European Studies; International Relations; Linguistics; Politics; other languages.

SCANDINAVIAN STUDIES

Scandinavian Studies provides students who enjoy languages with the opportunity to extend their language expertise to learn a modern Scandinavian language – Danish, Norwegian or Swedish – from beginner's level to Honours level in four years, including a year in Scandinavia. The three languages are very similar to each other and a knowledge of one makes it possible to access easily the literature and cultures of the other two. Viking Studies includes Old Norse, runology and archaeology.

Useful websites www.cilt.org.uk; www.iol.org.uk; www.bbc.co.uk/languages; http://languageadvantage.com; www.languagematters.co.uk; www.reed.co.uk/multilingual; www.scandinaviahouse.org; www.scandinavianstudy.org; www.nordicstudies.com.

NB The points totals shown to the left of the institutions are for ease of reference only. It must not be assumed that Tariff points are always used by institutions or that they can be substituted for an offer in grades. The level of an offer is not necessarily indicative of the quality of a course.

COURSE OFFERS INFORMATION

Subject requirements/preferences **GCSE** Foreign language preferred for all courses. **AL** A modern language may be required.

NB In 2011 universities and colleges will differ in their use of GCE AL/AS unit grade information, A* grades, the Extended Project (EPQ), the Advanced Diploma and the Cambridge Pre-U examination when considering applicants and making offers. An EPQ may be accepted in place of an AS subject. Check websites of universities and colleges for the latest offers information.

Your target offers and examples of courses provided by each institution

380 pts **Cambridge** – A*AA college offers may vary (A-Sxn Nrs Celt) (IB 38–42 pts)

360 pts **London (UCL)** – AAB+AS–BBB+AS (Modn Langs (Scand (Dan/Ice/Norw/Swed)); Scand St; Ice; Vkg St; Scand St Hist) (IB 32–36 pts)

300 pts **Edinburgh** – BBB (Scand St (Dan Norw Swed); Scand St; Scand St Hist; Scand St Pol; Scot Ethnol Scand St; Celt Scand St) (IB 34 pts HL 555)

Nottingham – BBB (Vkg St) (IB 32 pts)

Alternative offers

See **Chapter 7** and **Appendix 1** for grades/UCAS Tariff points information for the International Baccalaureate, Scottish Highers/Advanced Highers, the Welsh Baccalaureate, the Irish Leaving Certificate, the Cambridge Pre-U Diploma, the Advanced Diploma and the Extended Project.

CHOOSING YOUR COURSE (SEE ALSO CH.1)

Some course features

Cambridge (A-Sxn Nrs Celt) Old Norse is offered as part of this degree.

Edinburgh Beginners are provided with a concentrated course in the spoken and written language of their choice from Danish, Norwegian or Swedish. Year 3 is spent in a university in one of the Scandinavian countries.

London (UCL) Danish, Icelandic, Norwegian and Swedish are taught from scratch on the Scandinavian Studies courses. Icelandic and one other Scandinavian language are taught on the Icelandic course. No prior knowledge of the languages is required.

Nottingham (Vkg St) Course covers languages, literature, history and archaeology.

See also **Languages**.

Universities and colleges teaching quality See www.qaa.ac.uk; www.unistats.com.

Top research universities and colleges (RAE 2008) See **German**.

ADMISSIONS INFORMATION

Number of applicants per place (approx) London (UCL) 3.

Advice to applicants and planning the UCAS personal statement Visits to Scandinavian countries could be the source of an interest in studying these languages. You should also be aware of cultural, political, geographical and economic aspects of Scandinavian countries. Knowledge of these should be shown in your statement.

Selection interviews **Yes** Cambridge.

Interview advice and questions Applicants in the past have been questioned on why they have chosen this subject area, on their visits to Scandinavia and on their knowledge of the country/countries and their people. Future career plans are likely to be discussed. See **Chapter 5**.

Reasons for rejection (non-academic) One applicant didn't know the difference between a noun and a verb.

AFTER-RESULTS ADVICE

Offers to applicants repeating A-levels **No offers made** Cambridge.

GRADUATE DESTINATIONS AND EMPLOYMENT (2007/8 HESA)

Graduates surveyed 10 **Employed** 5 **In further study** none **Assumed unemployed** none.

Career note See **Languages**.

OTHER DEGREE SUBJECTS FOR CONSIDERATION

Archaeology; European History/Studies; History; other modern languages, including, for example, Russian and East European languages.

SCIENCE

(including **Combined** and **General Science**; see also **Biological Sciences** and **Natural Sciences**)

This table includes a range of specialised and general science degree subjects. General science degrees are interdisciplinary programmes, often giving a variety of subject combinations and a range of scientific skills.

Useful websites www.planet-science.com; www.scicentral.com; www.noisemakers.org.uk; www.intute.ac.uk; see also **Biology**, **Chemistry** and **Physics**.

NB The points totals shown to the left of the institutions are for ease of reference only. It must not be assumed that Tariff points are always used by institutions or that they can be substituted for an offer in grades. The level of an offer is not necessarily indicative of the quality of a course.

COURSE OFFERS INFORMATION

Subject requirements/preferences **GCSE** Science/mathematics subjects. Teacher Training courses English, mathematics. **AL** One or two sciences may be required but courses in the History and Philosophy of Science may not necessarily require a science subject at A-level.

NB In 2011 universities and colleges will differ in their use of GCE AL/AS unit grade information, A* grades, the Extended Project (EPQ), the Advanced Diploma and the Cambridge Pre-U examination when considering applicants and making offers. An EPQ may be accepted in place of an AS subject. Check websites of universities and colleges for the latest offers information.

Your target offers and examples of courses provided by each institution

380 pts **Cambridge** – A*AA (Nat Sci) (IB 38–42 pts)
London (UCL) – AAA+AS–ABB+AS (Hist Phil Sci; Hist Phil Soc St Sci; Sci Comm Pol; Nat Sci) (IB 34–38 pts)

360 pts **Bath** – AAA (Nat Sci; Nat Sci Yr Ind/Yr Abrd) (IB 36 pts)
Durham – AAA (Nat Sci) (IB 38 pts)
East Anglia – AAA (MNat Sci Nat Sci) (IB 34 pts)
East Anglia – AAA–ABB (BSc Nat Sci; Nat Sci Ind/Abrd) (IB 34 pts HL 66)
Exeter – AAA–AAB–BBC (BSc Flex Comb Hons) (IB 36–28 pts)
Leeds – AAA (Nat Sci)
London (UCL) – AAB+AS–BEB+AS (Hist Phil Sci; Sci Comm Plcy) (IB 32–36 pts)
Nottingham – AAA–AAB (Nat Sci) (IB 34 pts)

340 pts **Birmingham** – AAB (Nat Sci) (IB 34 pts)
Leicester – AAB/BBB (MSci Interd Sci) (IB 30 pts)
Liverpool – AAB–BBC (Sci Comb Hons) (IB 30–32 pts)
Manchester – AAB–BBB (Biol Sci Soty; Sci Psy Hlcst St) (IB 35–32 pts)

320 pts **Lancaster** – ABB 320 pts (Nat Sci N Am) (IB 30 pts)
Leeds – ABB (Hist Phil Sci courses) (IB 33 pts)
Newcastle – ABB (Nat Sci) (IB 34 pts)

300 pts **Leicester** – BBB (BSc Interd Sci) (IB 28 pts)
London (QM) – 300 pts (Nat Sci) (IB 30–32 pts)
Strathclyde – BBB 2nd yr entry (Nat Sci)

280 pts **Lancaster** – BBC 280 pts (Nat Sci) (IB 30 pts)
Liverpool John Moores – 280 pts (Sci Ftbl)
Southampton – BBC–BCC (Sci Fdn)

260 pts **Strathclyde** – BCC 1st yr entry (BSc Hons Nat Sci)

240 pts **Heriot-Watt** – CCC/BCE (BSc Comb St)

220 pts **Bradford** – 220 pts (BSc Comb St)
Glamorgan – 220–260 pts (Comb Sci)

160 pts **Canterbury Christ Church** – 160 pts (Integ Sci)
London South Bank – 160 pts (App Sci)

Suffolk (Univ Campus) – 160 pts (Sci Fdn)
UHI Millennium Inst – CC (Nat Env Sci)
120 pts **Huddersfield** – 120 pts (Sci Fdn)
80 pts **East London** – 80 pts (Extd Hlth Biosci)
Keele – 80 pts (Sci Fdn)
40 pts **Kingston** – 40 pts (Sci Fdn)

Liverpool John Moores – contact admissions (Fdn Nat Sci)
West Scotland – contact admissions (Gen Sci)

Alternative offers
See **Chapter 7** and **Appendix 1** for grades/UCAS Tariff points information for the International Baccalaureate, Scottish Highers/Advanced Highers, the Welsh Baccalaureate, the Irish Leaving Certificate, the Cambridge Pre-U Diploma, the Advanced Diploma and the Extended Project.

EXAMPLES OF FOUNDATION DEGREES IN THE SUBJECT FIELD

Cumbria.

CHOOSING YOUR COURSE (SEE ALSO CH.1)

Some course features
Cambridge (Nat Sci) There are 17 final year science options in the programme.
Lancaster (Nat Sci) Degree consists of three subjects, two of which are taken at major level and one at minor level. Subjects offered cover 10 science and 13 non-science areas.
Liverpool John Moores (Sci Ftbl) Course covers player development, social science aspects and science and applied science applications of the game.
London (UCL) The three science courses cover the historical, philosophical and social studies of science and technology.

Top research universities and colleges (RAE 2008) See science subjects and **Philosophy**.

Examples of sandwich degree courses East London; Huddersfield; London South Bank; Teesside.

ADMISSIONS INFORMATION

Number of applicants per place (approx) Glamorgan 9; Heriot-Watt 2; Lancaster 7; Liverpool John Moores (Sci Ftbl) 10; West Scotland 4.

Advice to applicants and planning the UCAS personal statement **Liverpool John Moores** (Sci Ftbl) This is a lab-based course examining physical stress. See **Biology**, **Biological Sciences**, **Chemistry**, **Physics**. See also **Appendix 4**.

Misconceptions about this course **Liverpool John Moores** (Sci Ftbl) Some applicants believe that scientific ability is not needed for the course: this is not true. Both scientific and practical ability are essential.

Selection interviews **Yes** Cambridge, London (UCL).

Interview advice and questions Past applicants have been questioned on their A-level work and aspects they particularly enjoyed. See **Chapter 5**.

Reasons for rejection (non-academic) Lack of an active interest in scientific issues.

AFTER-RESULTS ADVICE

Offers to applicants repeating A-levels **No offers made** Cambridge.

GRADUATE DESTINATIONS AND EMPLOYMENT (2007/8 HESA)

See separate science tables.

Career note See separate science tables.

OTHER DEGREE SUBJECTS FOR CONSIDERATION
Biochemistry; Biological Sciences; Biology; Health Sciences; Life Sciences; Natural Sciences; Physics; Sports Sciences.

SOCIAL and PUBLIC POLICY and ADMINISTRATION

(see also **Community Studies** and **Social Work**)

Social Policy is a multi-disciplinary degree that combines elements from sociology, political science, social and economic history, economics, cultural studies and philosophy. It is a study of the needs of society and how best to provide such services as education, housing, health and welfare services.

Useful websites www.lga.gov.uk; www.ippr.org.uk; www.swap.ac.uk.

NB The points totals shown to the left of the institutions are for ease of reference only. It must not be assumed that Tariff points are always used by institutions or that they can be substituted for an offer in grades. The level of an offer is not necessarily indicative of the quality of a course.

COURSE OFFERS INFORMATION
Subject requirements/preferences **GCSE** English and mathematics normally required. **AL** No subjects specified.

NB In 2011 universities and colleges will differ in their use of GCE AL/AS unit grade information, A* grades, the Extended Project (EPQ), the Advanced Diploma and the Cambridge Pre-U examination when considering applicants and making offers. An EPQ may be accepted in place of an AS subject. Check websites of universities and colleges for the latest offers information.

Your target offers and examples of courses provided by each institution

350 pts **Queen's Belfast** – BBBb–BBCb (Soc Plcy courses)
340 pts **Glasgow** – AAB (Pblc Plcy courses)
Loughborough – AAB (Econ Soc Pol) (IB 34 pts)
Warwick – BBBc–BBCc (Sociol (Soc Plcy))
320 pts **Birmingham** – ABB–BBB (Plan Soc Plcy Joint Hons)
London LSE – ABB–BBB (Soc Plcy; Soc Plcy Crimin; Soc Plcy Gov) (IB 36–37 pts)
Loughborough – 320 pts (Crimin Soc Plcy) (IB 32 pts)
Southampton – ABB (Soc Plcy Sociol) (IB 33 pts)
300 pts **Aston** – BBB 300–320 pts (Pblc Plcy Mgt courses) (IB 31–33 pts)
Bath – BBB (Soc Plcy; Sociol Soc Plcy) (IB 34 pts)
Brighton – BBB–BCC (Pol Soc Plcy; Crimin Soc Plcy; Hlth Soc Cr Soc Plcy) (IB 28 pts)
Bristol – ABC–BBB (Soc Plcy; Soc Plcy Sociol) (IB 32 pts)
Cardiff – BBB (Educ Soc Plcy; Crimin Soc Plcy; Soc Plcy)
Edinburgh – BBB (Geog Soc Plcy; Soc Plcy Soc Pol St; Soc Plcy Law)
Leeds – BBB (Soc Plcy Crm; Phil Soc Plcy) (IB 32 pts HL 15 pts)
Liverpool – BBB (Sociol Soc Plcy) (IB 30 pts) (IB 30 pts)
Nottingham – ABC–BBB (Soc Pol Admin; Soc Cult St)
Nottingham – ABC–BBB (Soc Wk Soc Pol) (IB 30–32 pts)
Sheffield – BBB–BBC (Soc Plcy Crimin; Soc Plcy Sociol) (IB 32 pts)
Stirling – BBB 2nd yr entry (Soc Plcy Sociol)
280 pts **Bangor** – 280 pts (Law Soc Plcy)
Birmingham – BBC (Soc Plcy; Soc Plcy Joint Hons) (IB 30–32 pts)
Kent – 280–320 pts (Soc Plcy; Soc Plcy Law Welf) (IB 31–33 pts)
Leeds – BBC (Soc Pol Sociol; Soc Plcy) (IB 30 pts HL 14 pts)
Lincoln – 280–260 pts (Psy Soc Plcy; Crimin Soc Plcy)
York – BBC (Soc Plcy) (IB 30 pts)

260 pts **Swansea** – 260 pts (Soc Plcy; Soc Plcy Crimin; Soc Hist Soc Plcy) (IB 30 pts)
240 pts **Bradford** – 240 pts (Soc Plcy Sociol) (IB 24 pts)
Central Lancashire – 240 pts (Soc Plcy Comb Hons)
Stirling – CCC 1st yr entry (Soc Plcy Sociol) (IB 28 pts)
Ulster – 240 pts (Soc Plcy; Soc Plcy Pol; Soc Plcy Econ)
220 pts **Anglia Ruskin** – 220–260 pts (Soc Plcy Crimin; Soc Plcy Law)
Bangor – 220–260 pts (Soc Plcy Joint Hons courses except under **280 pts**)
Worcester – 220–260 pts (Soc Welf)
200 pts **De Montfort** – 200 pts (Pblc Plcy Gov Mgt; Pblc Plcy Joint Hons)
Glyndŵr – 200 pts (Pblc Soc Plcy)
Lincoln – 200 pts (Soc Plcy; Soc Plcy Mgt)
London Met – 200 pts (Soc Plcy Joint Hons)
Manchester Met – 200 pts (Pblc Serv; Pblc Mgt St)
Middlesex – 200–280 pts (Dev St Soc Plcy)
180 pts **Salford** – 180–240 pts (Soc Plcy; Cnslg St Soc Plcy) (IB 24 pts)
160 pts **London South Bank** – 160 pts (Soc Plcy; Euro Plcy St courses; Int Soc Plcy)
Swansea Met – 160 pts (Pblc Admin; Pblc Serv)
Wolverhampton – 160–220 pts (Soc Cr Soc Plcy; Soc Plcy Df St; Soc Plcy Pol; Sociol Soc Plcy)
140 pts **Anglia Ruskin** – 140 pts (Soc Plcy)
West Scotland – CD (Soc Plcy)

Open University – (Soc Plcy Sociol) contact +44(0)845 300 6090 or www.openuniversity.co.uk/you

Alternative offers
See **Chapter 7** and **Appendix 1** for grades/UCAS Tariff points information for the International Baccalaureate, Scottish Highers/Advanced Highers, the Welsh Baccalaureate, the Irish Leaving Certificate, the Cambridge Pre-U Diploma, the Advanced Diploma and the Extended Project.

EXAMPLES OF FOUNDATION DEGREES IN THE SUBJECT FIELD

Anglia Ruskin; Bath; Bedfordshire; Bishop Burton (Coll); Bishop Grosseteste (UC); Blackburn (Coll Univ Centre); Blackpool and Fylde (Coll); Bournemouth; Bradford; Brighton; Bristol City (Coll); Bristol UWE; Carmarthenshire (Coll); City; Colchester (Inst); Cornwall (Coll); Coventry; Craven (Coll); Cumbria; De Montfort; Derby; Duchy (Coll); Durham New (Coll); East London; Edge Hill; Essex; Exeter (Coll); Farnborough (CT); Glamorgan; Gloucestershire; Glyndŵr; Greenwich; Grimsby (IFHE); Havering (Coll); Hertfordshire; Hopwood Hall (Coll); Huddersfield; Kent; Kirklees (Coll); Lakes (Coll); Lancaster; Leeds City (Coll); Leeds Met; Leeds Trinity (UC); Lincoln; Llandrillo Cymru (Col); Manchester (Coll); Newman (UC); Newport; Northbrook (Coll); Northumberland (Coll); Norwich City (Coll); Nottingham Trent; Peterborough Reg (Coll); Plymouth; Riverside Halton (Coll); Ruskin Oxford (Coll); St Helens (Coll); Sheffield (Coll); Somerset (CAT); Staffordshire; Stockport (Coll); Stranmillis (UC); Sunderland; Sunderland City (Coll); Truro (Coll); Tyne Met (Coll); Uxbridge (Coll); Walsall (Coll); Warwickshire (Coll); West Anglia (Coll); Westminster Kingsway (Coll); Weymouth (Coll); Wigan and Leigh (Coll); Wirral Met (Coll); Wolverhampton; Worcester; Worcester (CT); York (Coll); York St John.

CHOOSING YOUR COURSE (SEE ALSO CH.1)

Some course features
Anglia Ruskin (Soc Plcy courses) In addition to an optional semester abroad in Year 2 there is also an internship module in which students can gain vocational experience with an organisation.
Kent (Soc Plcy Pblc Sctr Mgt) Course has an option to study a language and many other subjects in Year 1.
London LSE (Soc Plcy) An outside option of special interest to the student is taken in each year of the course.
Sheffield (Soc Plcy Crimin) There is a Year Abroad scheme in the USA and Australia.

Universities and colleges teaching quality See www.qaa.ac.uk; www.unistats.com.

Top research universities and colleges (RAE 2008) See **Social Work**.

Sandwich degree courses Aston; Bath; Central Lancashire; De Montfort; Loughborough; Middlesex.

ADMISSIONS INFORMATION

Number of applicants per place (approx) Aston 8; Bangor 6; Bath 6; Birmingham 5; Bristol 4; Cardiff 4; Central Lancashire 6; De Montfort 5; Hull 9; Kent 5; Leeds 10; London LSE (Soc Plcy) 6, (Soc Plcy Sociol) 8, (Soc Plcy Econ) 7, (Soc Plcy Gov) 14; Loughborough 5; Manchester Met 4; Middlesex 12; Nottingham 3; Southampton 6; Stirling 11; Swansea 6; York 3.

Advice to applicants and planning the UCAS personal statement Careers in public and social administration are covered by this subject; consequently a good knowledge of these occupations and contacts with the social services should be discussed fully on your UCAS application. Gain work experience if possible. **Aston** The course is specially tailored for students aiming for careers in NHS management, the civil service and local government. **Bangor** Ability to communicate and work in a group. **York** Work experience, including voluntary work relevant to social policy. (See **Appendix 4** for contact details of some relevant organisations.)

Misconceptions about this course **York** Some applicants imagine that the course is vocational and leads directly to social work – it does not. Graduates in this field are well placed for a wide range of careers.

Selection interviews **Yes** Birmingham, London LSE, Swansea; **Some** Anglia Ruskin, Bangor, Bath (mature applicants), Cardiff, Kent, Leeds (mature students), Loughborough, Salford, Southampton, York.

Interview advice and questions Past questions have included: What relevance has history to social administration? What do you understand by 'public policy'? What advantage do you think studying social science gives when working in policy fields? How could the image of public management of services be improved? Applicants should be fully aware of the content and the differences between all the courses on offer, why they want to study Social Policy and their career objectives. See **Chapter 5**.

Reasons for rejection (non-academic) Some universities require attendance when they invite applicants to Open Days (check). Lack of awareness of current social issues. **Bath** Applicant really wanted Business Studies: evidence that teacher, careers adviser or parents are pushing the applicant into the subject or higher education. See also **Social Work**.

AFTER-RESULTS ADVICE

Offers to applicants repeating A-levels **Higher** Glasgow, Leeds, Newcastle; **Same** Anglia Ruskin, Bangor, Bath, Birmingham, Brighton, Cardiff, Loughborough, Salford, Southampton, York.

GRADUATE DESTINATIONS AND EMPLOYMENT (2007/8 HESA)

Graduates surveyed 920 **Employed** 455 **In further study** 120 **Assumed unemployed** 100.

Career note See **Social Sciences/Studies**.

OTHER DEGREE SUBJECTS FOR CONSIDERATION

Behavioural Science; Community Studies; Criminology; Economic and Social History; Economics; Education; Government; Health Studies; Human Resource Management; Law; Politics; Psychology; Social Work; Sociology; Women's Studies.

SOCIAL SCIENCES/STUDIES

(including **Criminology, Criminal Justice** and **Human Rights**; see also specific subject tables in the Social Sciences field (eg **Anthropology, Politics, Psychology, Social and Public Policy and Administration** and **Sociology**), **Community Studies** and **Health Sciences/Studies**)

Most Social Sciences/Studies courses take a broad view of aspects of society, for example, economics, politics, history, social psychology and urban studies. Applied Social Studies usually focuses on practical and theoretical preparation for a career in social work. These courses are particularly popular with mature students and some universities and colleges offer shortened degree courses for those with relevant work experience.

Useful websites www.csv.org.uk; www.intute.ac.uk.

NB The points totals shown to the left of the institutions are for ease of reference only. It must not be assumed that Tariff points are always used by institutions or that they can be substituted for an offer in grades. The level of an offer is not necessarily indicative of the quality of a course.

COURSE OFFERS INFORMATION

Subject requirements/preferences **GCSE** Usually English and mathematics; a science may be required. **AL** No subjects specified. **Other requirements** A Criminal Records Bureau (CRB) check and relevant work experience required for some courses.

NB In 2011 universities and colleges will differ in their use of GCE AL/AS unit grade information, A* grades, the Extended Project (EPQ), the Advanced Diploma and the Cambridge Pre-U examination when considering applicants and making offers. An EPQ may be accepted in place of an AS subject. Check websites of universities and colleges for the latest offers information.

Your target offers and examples of courses provided by each institution

400 pts **London (UCL)** – A*AA+AS (Euro Soc Pol St) (IB 39 pts)
360 pts **Durham** – AAA (Comb Soc Sci)
340 pts **Essex** – 340–300 pts (Sociol Crimin; Law Hum Rts; Sociol Hum Rts; Crimin) (IB 34–32 pts)
Lancaster – AAB (Law Crimin)
Manchester – AAB–BBB (Soc Sci Blt Nat Env; Soc Sci Sci Psy; Comb St courses) (IB 35–32 pts)
320 pts **Birmingham** – ABB (Hist Soc Sci) (IB 33 pts)
Cardiff – ABB–BBB (Crimin; Crimin Sociol; Crimin Educ)
Durham – ABB (Criminology) (IB 34 pts)
East Anglia – ABB–BBB (Soty Cult Media)
Kent – 320–280 pts (Crimin Joint Hons) (IB 33–31 pts)
Leeds – ABB (Crim Just Crimin) (IB 34 pts)
Loughborough – 320 pts (Crimin Soc Pol) (IB 32 pts)
Manchester – ABB (Criminology) (IB 33 pts)
Queen's Belfast – ABB–BBBb (Criminology)
Southampton – ABB (App Soc Sci courses; Popn Sci) (IB 33–32 pts)
Staffordshire – 320 pts (Criminology)
Strathclyde – ABB/ABC (Arts Soc Sci)
300 pts **Bath** – BBB (Soc Sci) (IB 34 pts)
Cardiff – BBB (Soc Sci)
De Montfort – 300 pts (Law Hum Rts Soc Just)
Gloucestershire – 300 pts (Criminology)
Lancaster – BBB (Crimin; Crimin Sociol) (IB 29 pts)
Leicester – BBB (Criminology)
London LSE – BBB (Soc Plcy Crimin)
Sheffield – BBB (Soc Plcy Crimin)
Stirling – BBB 2nd yr entry (Criminology)
Ulster – 300 pts (Crimin Crim Just)
280 pts **Aberystwyth** – 280 pts (Criminology) (IB 32 pts)
Brighton – BBC 280 pts (Crimin Soc Plcy; Crimin Sociol; Soc Sci) (IB 30 pts)
Bristol UWE – 280–320 pts (Crimin; Crimin Jrnl)
City – BBC 280 pts (Crimin Sociol) (IB 30 pts)
Newport – 280 pts (Crimin Crim Just; Cnslg St Soty)

Northumbria – 280 pts (Crimin; Crimin Foren Sci) (IB 25 pts)
Salford – 280–240 pts (Crimin; Crimin Cult St)
York – BBC (App Soc Sci (Child Yng Ppl) (Crm); Crim Just; App Soc Sci) (IB 30 pts)

260 pts **Bolton** – 260 pts (Crimin Foren Psy)
Coventry – 260 pts (Crimin; Crimin Psy; Crimin Law)
Derby – 260 pts (Crim Just)
Glasgow Caledonian – BBD 288 pts (Criminology)
Keele – 260–320 pts (Crimin courses) (IB 32 pts)
Lincoln – 260 pts (Crimin; Crimin Hist; Crimin Int Rel)
Liverpool Hope – 260 pts (Criminology)
Manchester Met – 260 pts (Criminology)
Plymouth – 260–300 pts (Crimin Crim Just St courses)
Swansea – 260–320 pts (Crimin Soc Plcy; Crim Psy; Crimin Crim Just)
Westminster – BCC/BB (Soc Sci) (IB 28 pts)

240 pts **Bangor** – 240–260 pts (Crimin Crim Just; Crimin Crim Just Joint Hons) (IB 28 pts)
Birmingham City – 240 pts (Crimin Sociol; Crim Invstg; Crimin Scrty St; Crimin Plc)
Brighton – CCC (App Soc Sci) (IB 28 pts)
Bristol UWE – 240–320 pts (Crimin Joint Hons)
Central Lancashire – CCC (Crimin Joint Hons; Law Crimin)
East London – 240 pts (Crimin Crim Just)
Glamorgan – 240–280 pts (Crimin Crim Just; Crimin Foren Sci; Crimin Comb Hons)
Hastings (Coll Univ Centre) – CCC/BCD 240–280 pts (App Soc Sci) (IB 28 pts)
Hull – 240–300 pts (Crimin courses)
Leeds Met – 240 pts (Criminology)
Liverpool John Moores – 240 pts (Crimin; Crim Just)
London Met – 240 pts (Crimin Media St)
Newport – 240 pts (Soc Welf)
Nottingham Trent – 240 pts (Criminology)
Portsmouth – 240–300 pts (Crimin Psy; Crimin Foren St)
Roehampton – 240–280 pts (Criminology)
Sheffield Hallam – 240 pts (Crimin; Crim Sociol)
Southampton Solent – 240 pts (Crimin; Crim Invstg Psy)
Stirling – CCC 1st yr entry (Criminology) (IB 28 pts)
Suffolk (Univ Campus) – 240 pts (Crimin; Crimin Yth St)
Teesside – 240–220 pts (Crim courses; Yth St)
Wolverhampton – 240 pts (Crim Just Crimin)

220 pts **Anglia Ruskin** – 220–280 pts (Crimin courses) (IB 30 pts)
Chester – 220–260 pts (Crimin; Crimin Comb courses) (IB 30 pts)
Edge Hill – 220–260 pts (Crimin Crim Just courses)
Kingston – 220–320 pts (Crimin Joint Hons; Hum Rts Joint Hons)
Northampton – 220–260 pts (Criminology)
Sunderland – 220 pts (Criminology)
Worcester – 220–260 pts (Soc Welf)

200 pts **Canterbury Christ Church** – 200 pts (App Crimin courses) (IB 24 pts)
Central Lancashire – 200 pts (Crimin Crim Just)
Coventry – 200 pts (Yth Wk)
Cumbria – 200–240 pts (Soc Sci Crimin)
De Montfort – 200 pts (App Crimin; App Crimin Foren Sci)
Glyndŵr – 200 pts (Crim Just)
Huddersfield – 200 pts (Soc Sci)
Kent – 200 pts (Soc Sci; Crim Just St) (IB 27 pts)
Lincoln – 200 pts (Soc Sci)
London Met – 200 pts (Crimin Yth St)
Middlesex – 200–280 pts (Glob Soc Sci; Crim Just Crimin; Crimin Psy; Yth Just)
Nottingham Trent – 200 pts (Yth St)

Oldham (Coll Univ Centre) – 200 pts (Soc Sci)
Roehampton – 200–240 pts (Hum Rts)
Sheffield Hallam – 200 pts (Pol Crimin; App Soc Sci)
Staffordshire – 200 pts (Crim Dvnc Soc)
Thames Valley – 200 pts (Crimin Sociol)

180 pts **Blackburn (Coll Univ Centre)** – 180–200 pts (Soc Sci)
Derby – 180–240 pts (Crimin Joint Hons)
Glasgow Caledonian – BC/CCD 228 pts (Soc Sci)
Leeds Met – 180 pts (Soc Sci) (IB 24 pts)

160 pts **Abertay Dundee** – CC 168 pts (Crimin St; Soc Sci)
Bedfordshire – 160 pts (Crimin; App Soc St)
Bucks New – 160–200 pts (Plc St; Crimin)
Doncaster (Coll) – CC 160 pts (Law Crimin; App Soc Sci)
Greenwich – 160 pts (Yth Commun St; Crimin)
London (Gold) – CC–EE (App Soc Sci Commun Dev Yth Wk)
London South Bank – CC 160 pts (Crimin Soc Pol; Citzn St courses)
Robert Gordon – CC (App Soc Sci)
South Essex (Coll) – 160 pts (Soc St)
UHI Millennium Inst (IC) – CC (Soc Sci)
Wolverhampton – 160–220 pts (Policing)
Worcester – 160 pts (Yth Commun St)

150 pts **Swansea Met** – 150 pts (Pblc Serv; Pblc Admin)

140 pts **West Scotland** – CD (Soc Sci)

120 pts **Cornwall (Coll)** – 120 pts (Comb Soc Sci)

Liverpool Hope – contact University (App Soc Sci)
Open University – (Crimin Psy St; Soc Sci Econ; Soc Sci Geog; Soc Sci Media St; Soc Sci Pol; Soc Sci Psy St) contact +44(0)845 300 6090 or www.openuniversity.co.uk/you

Alternative offers

See **Chapter 7** and **Appendix 1** for grades/UCAS Tariff points information for the International Baccalaureate, Scottish Highers/Advanced Highers, the Welsh Baccalaureate, the Irish Leaving Certificate, the Cambridge Pre-U Diploma, the Advanced Diploma and the Extended Project.

EXAMPLES OF FOUNDATION DEGREES IN THE SUBJECT FIELD

(see also **Social and Public Policy and Administration**) Barnfield (Coll); Bath; Bedford (Coll); Bedfordshire; Blackburn (Coll Univ Centre); Blackpool and Fylde (Coll); Boston (Coll); Bournemouth; Bradford; Bradford (Coll); Brighton; Bristol City (Coll); Canterbury Christ Church; Central Lancashire; Croydon (Coll); Cumbria; De Montfort; Derby; Duchy (Coll); Exeter (Coll); Grantham (Coll); Grimsby (IFHE); Hartlepool (CFE); Huddersfield; Hull (Coll); Leeds City (Coll); Leicester; Leicester (Coll); Liverpool Hope; London Met; Newcastle (Coll); Newman (UC); Newport; Northampton; Northbrook (Coll); Nottingham Castle (Coll); Nottingham Trent; Oaklands (Coll); Open University; Oxford and Cherwell Valley (Coll); Oxford Brookes; Peterborough Reg (Coll); Plymouth; Plymouth City (Coll); Portsmouth; Runshaw (Coll); Ruskin Oxford (Coll); St Helens (Coll); Sir Gâr (Col); South Tyneside (Coll); Staffordshire (Reg Fed); Stratford upon Avon (Coll); Sunderland City (Coll); Sussex Downs (Coll); Teesside; Truro (Coll); Warrington (Coll); West Anglia (Coll); Worcester; Winchester; York St John; Yorkshire Coast (Coll).

CHOOSING YOUR COURSE (SEE ALSO CH.1)

Some course features

Brighton (Soc Sci) Course explores areas of social policy, crime, health and social care.
Cumbria (Soc Sci Crimin) Degree covers sociology, social policy, psychology, ethics and criminology.
Essex (Sociol Hum Rts) Human Rights focuses on law, politics, social science and also on the definition, development, defence and abuse of rights worldwide.
Lincoln (Soc Sci) The programme has five strands: criminology, political economy, social policy, social science in context, and the University skills and capabilities curriculum. There is a strong emphasis on research methods.

Universities and colleges teaching quality See www.qaa.ac.uk; www.unistats.com.

Top research universities and colleges (RAE 2008) See **Social Work**.

Examples of sandwich degree courses Bath; Gloucestershire.

ADMISSIONS INFORMATION

Number of applicants per place (approx) Abertay Dundee 1; Aston 5; Bangor 2; Bath 6; Bath Spa 4; Bradford 15; Cornwall (Coll) 2; Coventry 7; Cumbria 4; De Montfort 1; Durham 3; East London 10; Edge Hill 5; Edinburgh 12; Glasgow Caledonian 9; Hull 5; Kingston 5; Liverpool 13; London (King's) 5; London LSE (all progs) 14; London South Bank 3; Manchester Met 10; Middlesex 26; Northampton 5; Nottingham 16; Nottingham Trent 2; Portsmouth 3; Roehampton 6; Salford 12; Sheffield Hallam 7; Southampton 6; Staffordshire 2; Sunderland 11; Swansea 8; West Scotland 5; Westminster 14; Winchester 3; York 5.

Advice to applicants and planning the UCAS personal statement The Social Sciences/Studies subject area covers several topics. Focus on these (or some of these) and state your main areas of interest, outlining your work experience, personal goals and motivation to follow the course. Show your interest in current affairs and especially in social issues and government policies.

Misconceptions about this course **Cornwall (Coll)** That students transfer to Plymouth at the end of Year 1: this is a three-year course in Cornwall.

Selection interviews **Yes** Anglia Ruskin, Bangor, Birmingham, Brunel, Coventry, Cumbria, Doncaster (Coll), Durham, East London, Edge Hill, Essex, Glasgow Caledonian, Hull, Kingston, London South Bank, Newcastle, Newport, Nottingham Trent, Oxford, Roehampton, Salford, Sunderland, Thames Valley, Westminster; **Some** Abertay Dundee, Bath (mature students), Bristol, Cornwall (Coll), East Anglia, Robert Gordon, Staffordshire, Winchester, York.

Interview advice and questions Past questions have included: Define democracy. What is the role of the Church in nationalistic aspirations? Does today's government listen to its people? Questions on current affairs. How would you change the running of your school? What are the faults of the Labour Party/Conservative Party? Do you agree with the National Lottery? Is money from the National Lottery well spent? Give examples of how the social services have failed. What is your understanding of the social origins of problems? See also **Chapter 5**.

Reasons for rejection (non-academic) Stated preference for other institutions. Incompetence in answering questions.

AFTER-RESULTS ADVICE

Offers to applicants repeating A-levels **Higher** Aston, Essex, Glasgow, Salford (possibly), Swansea; **Same** Abertay Dundee, Anglia Ruskin, Bangor, Bath Spa, Bradford, Chester, Cornwall (Coll), Coventry, Cumbria, Durham, East Anglia, Gloucestershire, Leeds, Liverpool, London Met, London South Bank, Manchester Met, Newport, Nottingham Trent, Roehampton, Sheffield Hallam, Staffordshire, Stirling, Winchester, Wolverhampton.

GRADUATE DESTINATIONS AND EMPLOYMENT (2007/8 HESA)

Graduates surveyed 745 **Employed** 360 **In further study** 115 **Assumed unemployed** 85.

Career note Graduates find careers in all aspects of social provision, for example health services, welfare agencies such as housing departments, the probation service, police forces, the prison service, personnel work and residential care and other careers not necessarily linked with their degree subjects.

OTHER DEGREE SUBJECTS FOR CONSIDERATION

Business Studies; Community Studies; Economics; Education; Geography; Government; Health Studies; Law; Politics; Psychology; Public Administration; Social Policy; Social Work; Sociology; Urban Studies.

SOCIAL WORK

(see also **Community Studies** and **Social and Public Policy and Administration**)

Social Work courses (which lead to careers in social work) have similarities to those in Applied Social Studies, Social Policy and Administration, Community Studies and Health Studies. If you are offered a place on a Social Work course which leads to registration as a social worker, you must undergo the Criminal Records Bureau (CRB) disclosure check. You will also have to provide health information and certification. Check for full details of training and careers in social work with the General Social Care Council (see **Appendix 4**). Students from England receive full payment of fees and student bursaries from the General Social Care Council.

Useful websites www.gscc.org.uk; www.swap.ac.uk; www.ageconcern.org.uk; www.samaritans.org; www.ccwales.org.uk; www.sssc.uk.com; www.niscc.info; www.socialworkandcare.co.uk.

NB The points totals shown to the left of the institutions are for ease of reference only. It must not be assumed that Tariff points are always used by institutions or that they can be substituted for an offer in grades. The level of an offer is not necessarily indicative of the quality of a course.

COURSE OFFERS INFORMATION

Subject requirements/preferences **GCSE** English and mathematics usually required. **AL** No subjects specified. **Other** An Enhanced Criminal Records Bureau check and an occupational health check required. Check also minimum age requirements.

NB In 2011 universities and colleges will differ in their use of GCE AL/AS unit grade information, A* grades, the Extended Project (EPQ), the Advanced Diploma and the Cambridge Pre-U examination when considering applicants and making offers. An EPQ may be accepted in place of an AS subject. Check websites of universities and colleges for the latest offers information.

Your target offers and examples of courses provided by each institution

320 pts **Brunel** – BBC +AS/EPQ c 320 pts (Soc Wk) (IB 32 pts)
Queen's Belfast – ABB (Soc Wk)
Sussex – ABB–BBB (Soc Wk) (IB 34 pts)

300 pts **Brighton** – BBB 300 pts (Soc Wk)
Edinburgh – BBB (Soc Wk) (IB 34 pts)
Ulster – BBB 300 pts (Soc Wk)

280 pts **Bath** – BBC (Soc Wk App Soc St) (IB 32 pts)
Birmingham – BBC (Soc Wk)
Bournemouth – 280 pts (Soc Wk)
Bucks New – 280 pts (Soc Wk)
Coventry – 280 pts (Soc Wk)
East Anglia – BBC (Soc Wk) (IB 30 pts)
Lancaster – BBC 280–300 pts (Soc Wk) (IB 28 pts)
Leeds – BBC (Soc Wk)
London (Gold) – BBC (Soc Wk) (IB 30 pts)
Newport – 280–160 pts (Soc Wk; Soc Welf)
Nottingham – BBC 280 pts (Soc Wk Soc Plcy) (IB 30–32 pts)
Salford – 280 pts (Soc Wk St)
Sheffield – BBC (Soc Wk) (IB 30 pts)
York – BBC (Soc Wk) (IB 30 pts)

260 pts **Bangor** – 260 pts (Soc Wk)
Bradford – 260 pts (Soc Wk)
Edge Hill – 260 pts (Soc Wk)
Keele – 260–280 pts (Soc Wk) (IB 26–28 pts)
Liverpool John Moores – 260 pts (Soc Wk)
London (RH) – 260 pts (Soc Wk)

Northumbria – 260 pts (Soc Wk)
Portsmouth – 260 pts (Soc Wk)
Strathclyde – BCC (Soc Wk) (IB 28 pts)
Wiltshire (Coll) – 260 pts (Soc Wk)

240 pts **Anglia Ruskin** – 240 pts (Soc Wk)
Birmingham City – 240 pts (Soc Wk)
Chester – 240 pts (Soc Wk) (IB 24 pts)
Chichester – CCC (Soc Wk) (IB 28 pts)
De Montfort – 240 pts (Soc Wk)
Glamorgan – 240 pts (Soc Wk)
Gloucestershire – 240 pts (Soc Wk)
Huddersfield – 240 pts (Soc Wk)
Hull – 240 pts (Soc Wk)
Lincoln – 240 pts (Soc Wk)
London Met – 240 pts (Soc Wk)
Nottingham Trent – CCC 240 pts (Soc Wk)
Robert Gordon – CCC 240 pts (Soc Wk)
Stirling – CCC (Soc Wk)
Suffolk (Univ Campus) – 240 pts (Soc Wk)
Sunderland – 240 pts (Soc Wk)
Swansea – 240 pts (Soc Wk)
Teesside – 240 pts (Soc Wk)

220 pts **Dundee** – CCD (Soc Wk)
Glyndŵr – 220–260 pts (Soc Wk)
Hertfordshire – 220 pts (Soc Wk)
Northampton – 220–260 pts (Soc Cr courses; Soc Wk)
Worcester – 220–260 pts (Soc Welf courses)

200 pts **Bristol UWE** – 200–240 pts (Soc Wk)
Canterbury Christ Church – 200 pts (Soc Wk)
Cumbria – 200 pts (Soc Wk)
Hull – 200 pts (Soc Wk)
Kent – 200 pts (Soc Wk) (IB 27 pts)
Kingston – 200 pts (Soc Wk)
Leeds Met – 200 pts (Soc Wk)
Lincoln – 200 pts (Hlth Soc Cr)
Manchester Met – 200 pts (Soc Wk) (IB 24 pts)
NEW (Coll) – 200 pts (Soc Wk)
Oxford Brookes – 200 pts (Soc Wk)
Plymouth – 200 pts (Soc Wk)
Sheffield Hallam – 200 pts (Soc Wk)
Southampton Solent – 200 pts (Soc Wk)
Sunderland – 200 pts (Soc Wk (Hlth Soc Cr))
Thames Valley – 200 pts (Soc Wk)
Winchester – 200–240 pts (Soc Cr St courses)

180 pts **Liverpool (CmC)** – 180 pts (Soc Wk)
Staffordshire – 180–240 pts (Soc Wk)
UCP Marjon – 180 pts (Yth Commun Wk; Chld Welf Soty; Commun Wk; Wk Chld Yng Ppl)

160 pts **Bedfordshire** – 160 pts (Soc Wk; Hlth Soc Cr)
Cardiff (UWIC) – 160 pts (Soc Wk; Hlth Soc Cr)
Central Lancashire – CC (Soc Wk)
Chester – 160–200 pts (Chr Yth Wk; Mslm Yth Wk)
Colchester (Inst) – 160 pts (Hlth Soc Cr)
Cornwall (Coll) – 160 pts (Soc Wk)
Glasgow Caledonian – CC (Soc Wk)
London (Gold) – CC (App Soc Sci Commun Dev Yth Wk)

London South Bank – 160 pts (Soc Wk)
Middlesex – CC (Soc Wk)
Roehampton – 160–200 pts (Hlth Soc Cr)
South Essex (Coll) – 160 pts (Soc Wk)
Wolverhampton – 160–220 pts (Soc Wk)
140 pts **West Scotland** – CD (Soc Wk)
120 pts **Bradford (Coll)** – 120 pts (Soc Wk)
80 pts **Derby** – 80–120 pts (App Soc Wk)
Havering (Coll) – 80 pts (check with admissions tutor) (Soc Wk)
Stockport (CFHE) – 80 pts (check with admissions tutor) (Soc Wk)

Open University – (Soc Wk) www.openuniversity.co.uk/you
Trinity Saint David – contact admissions (Yth Commun Wk)

Alternative offers
See **Chapter 7** and **Appendix 1** for grades/UCAS Tariff points information for the International Baccalaureate, Scottish Highers/Advanced Highers, the Welsh Baccalaureate, the Irish Leaving Certificate, the Cambridge Pre-U Diploma, the Advanced Diploma and the Extended Project.

EXAMPLES OF FOUNDATION DEGREES IN THE SUBJECT FIELD
See **Social and Public Policy and Administration**.

CHOOSING YOUR COURSE (SEE ALSO CH.1)
Some course features
Brunel Students are required to attend university and placements each day between 9am and 5pm. Placements are in Years 2 and 3, occupying 2½ to 3 days each week, with the remaining time at university.
Coventry The course covers law, human growth and development, communication skills and partnership working.
East Anglia (Soc Wk) 200 days spent on placements with social work agencies.

Universities and colleges teaching quality See www.qaa.ac.uk; www.unistats.com.

Top research universities and colleges (RAE 2008) (**Social Work** and **Social Policy and Administration**) London LSE; Bath; Leeds; Kent; Edinburgh; York; City; Oxford; Sheffield; Lancaster; Keele; Bristol; Birmingham; London South Bank; Nottingham Trent; Sussex.

Examples of sandwich degree courses Bath.

ADMISSIONS INFORMATION
Number of applicants per place (approx) Bangor 2; Bath 8; Birmingham 13; Bradford 10; Coventry 22; Dundee 6; London Met 27; Northampton 7; Nottingham Trent 6; Sheffield Hallam 4; Southampton 10; Staffordshire 3.

Advice to applicants and planning the UCAS personal statement The statement should show motivation for social work, relevant work experience, awareness of the demands of social work and give relevant personal information, for example disabilities. Awareness of the origins of personal and family difficulties, commitment to anti-discriminatory practice. Most applicants for these courses will have significant experience of a statutory care agency or voluntary/private organisation providing a social work or social care service. See also **Social and Public Policy and Administration** and **Appendix 2**.

Selection interviews **Yes** Most courses; Anglia Ruskin, Bangor, Birmingham, Bradford, Brunel, Chichester, Coventry, Liverpool Hope, Nottingham, Nottingham Trent, Portsmouth, Robert Gordon, Salford, Sheffield Hallam, Staffordshire, Thames Valley, Wolverhampton, York; **Some** Cardiff (UWIC), Dundee.

Interview advice and questions What qualities are needed to be a social worker? What use do you think you will be to society as a social worker? Why should money be spent on prison offenders?

Your younger brother is playing truant and mixing with bad company. Your parents don't know. What would you do? See also **Social and Public Policy and Administration** and **Chapter 5**.

Reasons for rejection (non-academic) Criminal convictions.

AFTER-RESULTS ADVICE

Offers to applicants repeating A-levels **Same** Bangor, Lincoln, Liverpool Hope, Salford, Staffordshire, Suffolk (Univ Campus), Wolverhampton.

GRADUATE DESTINATIONS AND EMPLOYMENT (2007/8 HESA)

Graduates surveyed 3690 **Employed** 2505 **In further study** 190 **Assumed unemployed** 215.

Career note See **Social Sciences/Studies**.

OTHER DEGREE SUBJECTS FOR CONSIDERATION

Community Studies; Conductive Education; Criminology; Economics; Education; Health Studies; Law; Psychology; Public Sector Management and Administration; Social Policy; Sociology; Youth Studies.

SOCIOLOGY

(see also **Anthropology, Social and Public Policy and Administration** and **Social Studies/Science**)

Sociology is the study of social organisation, social structures, systems, institutions and practices. Courses are likely to include the meaning and structure of, for example, race, ethnicity and gender, industrial behaviour, crime and deviance, health and illness. **NB** Sociology is not a training course for social workers, although some graduates take additional qualifications to qualify in social work.

Useful websites www.britsoc.co.uk; www.asanet.org; www.sociology.org.uk; www.sociology.org.

NB The points totals shown to the left of the institutions are for ease of reference only. It must not be assumed that Tariff points are always used by institutions or that they can be substituted for an offer in grades. The level of an offer is not necessarily indicative of the quality of a course.

COURSE OFFERS INFORMATION

Subject requirements/preferences **GCSE** English and mathematics usually required. **AL** No subjects specified.

NB In 2011 universities and colleges will differ in their use of GCE AL/AS unit grade information, A* grades, the Extended Project (EPQ), the Advanced Diploma and the Cambridge Pre-U examination when considering applicants and making offers. An EPQ may be accepted in place of an AS subject. Check websites of universities and colleges for the latest offers information.

Your target offers and examples of courses provided by each institution

380 pts **Cambridge** – A*AA college offers may vary (Pol Psy Sociol (PPS)) (IB 38–42 pts HL 766–777)

360 pts **Durham** – AAA (Comb Hons Soc Sci) (IB 37 pts)

Warwick – ABBc–BBBc (Hist Sociol; Law Sociol; Fr Sociol)

350 pts **Brunel** – BBB +AS/EPQ b 350 pts (Psy Sociol) (IB 33 pts)

340 pts **Durham** – AAB–ABB (Educ St Sociol; Sociol Law; Sociol; Anth Sociol)

Exeter – AAB–BBB (Sociol; Sociol Mid E St; Sociol Fr/Ger/Ital/Russ/Span) (IB 29–28 pts)

Glasgow – AAB (Sociol courses) (IB 34 pts)

Southampton – AAB (Sociol; Phil Sociol) (IB 34 pts HL 17 pts)

320 pts **Birmingham** – ABB–BBC (Sociol; Sociol Pol Sci; Sociol Phil; Sociol Soc Plcy) (IB 32 pts)

Bristol – ABB (Sociol; Sociol Phil; Pol Sociol; Theol Sociol) (IB 33 pts)

Cardiff – ABB (Sociol Jrnl; Soc Phil App Eth)

East Anglia – ABB–BBB (Soty Cult Media)
Essex – 320–300 pts (Sociol (Soc Sci) (Hum); Sociol Mgt; Sociol Law) (IB 30–32 pts)
Lancaster – ABB 320 pts (Sociolinguistics) (IB 30 pts)
London (Gold) – ABB (Hist Sociol)
Loughborough – 320–330 pts (Econ Sociol)
Manchester – ABB–BBB (Sociol courses) (IB 34–33 pts)
Southampton – ABB (Sociol Soc Psy; Soc Sci (Sociol)) (B 33 pts)
Strathclyde – ABB/ABC (Sociology)
Warwick – BBCc–BBBc (Sociology) (IB 32–33 pts)

300 pts **Aston** – BBB–ABB 300 pts (Sociol courses) (IB 32–33 pts)
Bath – BBB (Sociol; Sociol Soc Pol; Sociol HR Mgt) (IB 34 pts)
Brunel – 3AL +AS/EPQ 300 pts (Sociol; Anth Sociol; Sociol Media St) (IB 31–32 pts)
Cardiff – BBB (Sociol; Soc Plcy Sociol; Sociol Welsh)
Edinburgh – BBB (Sociol; Sociol Soc Econ Hist; Sociol Soc Anth)
Lancaster – BBB 300 pts (Sociology) (IB 29 pts)
Leeds – BBB (Sociol; Sociol Theol Relig St) (IB 32 pts HL 15 pts)
Leicester – BBB (Sociol; Media Sociol) (IB 28–30 pts)
Liverpool – BBB–BBC (Sociol; Sociol Cult St; Crimin Sociol) (IB 30 pts)
London (Gold) – BBB (Sociol; Media Sociol) (IB 28 pts)
London LSE – BBB (Sociology) (IB 36 pts)
Loughborough – 300 pts (Sociology) (IB 32 pts)
Newcastle – BBB (Sociol; Pol Sociol) (IB 32 pts)
Nottingham – ABC–BBB (Sociol; Sociol Soc Pol; Cult Sociol) (IB 32 pts)
Queen's Belfast – BBB–BBCb (Sociol courses)
Sheffield – BBB (Sociol courses) (IB 30–33 pts)
Stirling – BBB 2nd yr entry (Sociol Soc Plcy)
Surrey – BBB 300 pts (Sociol; Sociol Cult Media) (IB 32 pts)
Sussex – BBB (Sociol; Sociol Dev St) (IB 32 pts)
York – BBB (Sociol; Sociol Soc Psy; Sociol Educ)

280 pts **City** – BBC 280 pts (Sociol; Sociol Psy) (IB 30 pts)
Gloucestershire – 280 pts (Sociol; Engl Lit Sociol)
Kent – 280–300 pts (Sociol; Sociol Yr Abrd; Sociol Econ) (IB 31–33 pts)
Northumbria – 280 pts (Sociol courses)
Oxford Brookes – BBC (Sociol courses) (IB 31 pts)
Salford – 280–240 pts (Sociol Jrnl; Sociol Cult St) (IB 29 pts)

260 pts **Coventry** – 260–280 pts (Sociol; Sociol Psy; Sociol Crimin)
Huddersfield – 260 pts (Sociol; Sociol Educ)
Keele – 260–320 pts (Sociol courses) (IB 30 pts)
Manchester Met – 260–240 pts (Sociol; Sociol Comb Hons) (IB 24 pts)
Plymouth – 260–300 pts (Sociology)
Westminster – BCC/BB (Sociology) (IB 28 pts)

240 pts **Aberdeen** – CCC (Sociol courses)
Birmingham City – 240 pts (Sociol; Sociol Crimin; Sociol Psy)
Brighton – CCC (Sociol Commun Hist; Sociol Engl Lit) (IB 28 pts)
Bristol UWE – 240–300 pts (Sociol; Hist Sociol; Ely Chld St Sociol) (IB 28 pts)
Bucks New – 240–280 pts (Psy Sociol)
Central Lancashire – 240 pts (Sociol courses except under **200 pts**)
Hastings (Coll Univ Centre) – CCC/BCD 240–280 pts (Sociol Commun Hist)
Hull – 240–300 pts (Sociol; Sociol Anth; Sociol Film St)
Kingston – 240 pts (Sociology)
Newport – 240 pts (Sociol; Sociol Yth Just; Sociol Soc Welf; Sociol Crim)
Nottingham Trent – 240 pts (Sociol; Sociol Pol)
Portsmouth – 240–300 pts (Sociol; Sociol Media St; Sociol Psy)
St Mary's Twickenham (UC) – 240 pts (Sociology)
Stirling – CCC 1st yr entry (Sociol Soc Plcy) (IB 28 pts)

Suffolk (Univ Campus) – 240 pts (Sociol Yth St; Sociol Crimin)
Ulster – 240 pts (Sociol; Sociol Ir Hist; Sociol Commun Dev)

230 pts **Queen Margaret** – 230 pts (Psy Sociol)

220 pts **Bangor** – 220–260 pts (Sociol; Sociol Crimin Joint Hons) (IB 24 pts)
Bath Spa – 220–260 pts (Sociol; Sociol Comb courses)
Chester – 220–260 pts (Sociology)
Edge Hill – 220–260 pts (Sociol; Sociol Chld Yth St; Engl Sociol; Hist Sociol)
Glamorgan – 220–260 pts (Sociol Educ; Sociol Hist)
Liverpool John Moores – 220 pts (Sociol; Sociol Crimin)
Sheffield Hallam – 220 pts (Sociol; App Soc Sci (Psy Sociol))
Sunderland – 220 pts (Sociol courses)
Teesside – 220 pts (Sociol; Sociol Yth St; Sociol Pol)
Worcester – 220–260 pts (Sociology)

200 pts **Anglia Ruskin** – 200 pts (Sociol; Sociol Engl; Sociol Media St)
Bucks New – 200–240 pts (Psysoc St)
Canterbury Christ Church – 200 pts (Sociol Soc Sci courses)
Central Lancashire – 200 pts (Sociology)
Derby – 200–220 pts (Sociology)
Leeds Met – 200–180 pts (Crimin Sociol; Pol Sociol; Psy Sociol)
London Met – 200 pts (Sociology)
Middlesex – 200–280 pts (Sociology)
Northampton – 200–240 pts (Sociology)
Staffordshire – 200 pts (Sociol courses)
Thames Valley – 200 pts (Crimin Sociol)

180 pts **Bedfordshire** – 180–220 pts (Crimin Sociol)
Bradford – 180–220 pts (Sociology)
Derby – 180–240 pts (Sociol Joint Hons)

160 pts **Abertay Dundee** – CC 168 pts (Sociology)
East London – 160–200 pts (Sociol courses)
Greenwich – 160 pts (Sociol courses)
London South Bank – CC (Sociol; Int Pol Sociol)
Roehampton – 160–200 pts (Sociol courses)
Wolverhampton – 160–220 pts (Sociol Pol; Relig St Sociol; Sociol)

140 pts **West Scotland** – CD (Sociology)

Alternative offers
See **Chapter 7** and **Appendix 1** for grades/UCAS Tariff points information for the International Baccalaureate, Scottish Highers/Advanced Highers, the Welsh Baccalaureate, the Irish Leaving Certificate, the Cambridge Pre-U Diploma, the Advanced Diploma and the Extended Project.

EXAMPLES OF FOUNDATION DEGREES IN THE SUBJECT FIELD
Blackburn (Coll Univ Centre); Bradford; De Montfort; London Met; Plymouth; Truro (Coll); Winchester.

CHOOSING YOUR COURSE (SEE ALSO CH.1)
Some course features
Brunel (Sociol) Full-time and thin sandwich courses are offered; past placements range from advertising agencies to psychiatric day centres.
Cardiff The School of Social Science offers full or half degrees in Sociology. Half degrees are taken one from a choice of some 22 other subjects.
City (Sociol) The elective modules in each year cover such topics as criminology, media studies, psychology, policing and race and racism.
Manchester Met (Sociol) The Sociology element of the courses focuses on social policy, health and crime and includes topics such as schooling and youth, social welfare, criminology, family history, and the sociology of health.

UCP Marjon Sociology can be taken as a major or minor subject in combination with a second subject. For students majoring in the subject there is an optional exchange programme with a university in the USA.

Universities and colleges teaching quality See www.qaa.ac.uk; www.unistats.com.

Top research universities and colleges (RAE 2008) Manchester; Essex; London (Gold); York; Lancaster; Surrey; Edinburgh; Warwick; Cardiff; Exeter; Oxford; Cambridge.

Examples of sandwich degree courses Aston; Bath; Brunel; Middlesex; Northumbria; Nottingham Trent; Surrey.

ADMISSIONS INFORMATION

Number of applicants per place (approx) Aston 8; Bangor 1; Bath 6; Birmingham 8; Birmingham City 12; Bristol 8; Brunel 24; Cardiff 5; Cardiff (UWIC) 4; City 11; Durham 13; East Anglia 15; East London 8; Exeter 5; Gloucestershire 8; Greenwich 5; Hull 11; Kent 10; Kingston 9; Lancaster 12; Leeds 14; Leicester 6; Liverpool 9; Liverpool John Moores 10; London (Gold) 5; London LSE 6; London Met 3; Loughborough 10; Northampton 3; Northumbria 18; Nottingham 7; Plymouth 9; Portsmouth 12; Roehampton 4; Sheffield Hallam 7; Southampton 4; Staffordshire 10; Sunderland 5; Surrey 6; Swansea 8; Warwick 20; Worcester 5; York 5.

Advice to applicants and planning the UCAS personal statement Show your ability to communicate and work as part of a group and your curiosity about issues such as social conflict and social change between social groups. Discuss your interests in sociology on the personal statement. Demonstrate an intellectual curiosity about sociology and social problems. (International students) Good command of written and spoken English required. See **Social Sciences/Studies**.

Misconceptions about this course Some applicants believe that all sociologists want to become social workers. **Birmingham** Students with an interest in crime and deviance may be disappointed that we do not offer modules in this area. **London Met** That it is the stamping ground of student activists and has no relevance to the real world.

Selection interviews **Yes** Aston, Birmingham City, Brunel, Cambridge, City, Derby, Durham, East London, Exeter, Hull, Lancaster, Leeds, Leicester, Liverpool, London (Gold), Loughborough, Newcastle, Nottingham, Portsmouth, St Mary's Twickenham (UC), Surrey, Swansea, Warwick; **Some** Anglia Ruskin, Bath (mature applicants), Bath Spa, Birmingham (mature applicants), Bristol, Cardiff, Kent, Liverpool John Moores, London Met, Nottingham Trent, Salford, Sheffield Hallam, Southampton, Staffordshire.

Interview advice and questions Past questions have included: Why do you want to study Sociology? What books have you read on the subject? How do you see the role of women changing in the next 20 years? **London Met** Questions will focus on existing level of interest in the subject and the applicant's expectations about studying. See also **Chapter 5**.

Reasons for rejection (non-academic) Evidence of difficulty with written work. Non-attendance at Open Days (find out from your universities if your attendance will affect their offers). 'In the middle of an interview for Sociology a student asked us if we could interview him for Sports Studies instead!' **Durham** No evidence of awareness of what the course involves. **London Met** References which indicated that the individual would not be able to work effectively within a diverse student group; concern that the applicant had not put any serious thought into the choice of subject for study. See also **Social and Public Policy and Administration**.

AFTER-RESULTS ADVICE

Offers to applicants repeating A-levels **Higher** Brunel, East London, Essex, Glasgow, Hull, Newcastle, Nottingham Trent, Swansea, Warwick, York; **Possibly higher** Leeds, Liverpool, Portsmouth; **Same** Aston, Bangor, Bath, Birmingham, Birmingham City, Bristol, Cardiff, Coventry, Derby, Durham, Gloucestershire, Kingston, Lancaster, Liverpool John Moores, London Met, Loughborough, Northumbria, Roehampton, St Mary's Twickenham (UC), Salford, Sheffield Hallam, Southampton, Staffordshire; **No offers made** Cambridge.

GRADUATE DESTINATIONS AND EMPLOYMENT (2007/8 HESA)

Graduates surveyed 3945 **Employed** 1935 **In further study** 560 **Assumed unemployed** 350.

Career note See **Social Sciences/Studies**.

OTHER DEGREE SUBJECTS FOR CONSIDERATION

Anthropology; Economic and Social History; Economics; Education; Geography; Government; Health Studies; History; Law; Politics; Psychology; Social Policy; Social Work.

SPANISH

(including **Hispanic Studies** and **Portuguese**; see also **Languages** and **Latin American Studies**)

Spanish can be studied by focusing on the language and literature of Spain. Broader courses in Hispanic Studies (see also **Latin American Studies**) are available which also include Portuguese and Latin American studies. See also **Appendix 4** under **Languages**.

Useful websites www.donquijote.co.uk; http://europa.eu; www.cilt.org.uk; www.iol.org.uk; www.bbc.co.uk/languages; http://languageadvantage.com; www.languagematters.co.uk; www.reed.co.uk/multilingual; www.studyspanish.com; www.spanishlanguageguide.com; see also Latin American Studies.

NB The points totals shown to the left of the institutions are for ease of reference only. It must not be assumed that Tariff points are always used by institutions or that they can be substituted for an offer in grades. The level of an offer is not necessarily indicative of the quality of a course.

COURSE OFFERS INFORMATION

Subject requirements/preferences **GCSE** English, mathematics or science and a foreign language. **AL** Spanish required for most courses.

NB In 2011 universities and colleges will differ in their use of GCE AL/AS unit grade information, A* grades, the Extended Project (EPQ), the Advanced Diploma and the Cambridge Pre-U examination when considering applicants and making offers. An EPQ may be accepted in place of an AS subject. Check websites of universities and colleges for the latest offers information.

Your target offers and examples of courses provided by each institution

380 pts **Cambridge** – A*AA college offers may vary (Modn Mediev Langs (Span) (Port)) (IB 38–42 pts HL 766–777)
London (UCL) – AAA+AS–BBB+AS (Modn Lang Plus (Span Mgt St) (Span Lat) (Span Hist Art); Modn Langs (Span)) (IB 32–38 pts)
Warwick – AABc–ABBc (Hist Lit Cult Ams)

360 pts **Bristol** – AAA–ABB (Pol Span; Pol Port; Phil Span/Port; Hist Art Span/Port) (IB 37–34 pts)
Imperial London – AAA (Chem Span Sci) (IB 38 pts)
Manchester – AAA–AAB (MML Span Chin/Jap)
Nottingham – AAA (Econ Hisp St) (IB 38 pts)
Oxford – AAA (Port courses; Span courses) (IB 38–42 pts)
Queen's Belfast – AAA–AABa (Cmn Civ Law Span)
St Andrews – AAA (Mgt Span; Maths Span; Int Rel Span) (IB 38 pts)

340 pts **Aston** – AAB–ABB 340–320 pts (Int Bus Span) (IB 34 pts)
Bath – AAB–ABB (Comp Sci Span; Pol Span)
Birmingham – AAB (Port/Span Econ; Port Mny Bank Fin) (IB 34–36 pts)
Bristol – AAB–BBC (Span courses except under **360 pts**; Span Port; Port courses; Hisp St) (IB 30–33 pts)
East Anglia – AAB–BBB (Span Film TV St)
Exeter – AAB–ABB (Film St Span; Int Rel Span; Span) (IB 32–29 pts)
Glasgow – AAB (Span courses; Hisp St) (IB 34 pts)

Imperial London – AAB (Biol Span Sci) (IB 38 pts)
Lancaster – AAB 340 pts (Euro Mgt (Span)) (IB 31 pts)
London (UCL) – ABB+AS (Hisp St Modn Gk St) (IB 34 pts)
Manchester – AAB–BBB (BA Span Chin/Jap/Port) (IB 35–30 pts)
St Andrews – AAB (Span; Arbc Span; Ital Span; Mediev Hist Span) (IB 36 pts)
Southampton – AAB (Span Ling St; Mgt Sci Span; Span Port Lat Am St) (IB 34 pts)
320 pts **Bath** – ABB–BBB (Modn Langs Euro St; Span Fr/Ger/Ital/Russ) (IB 34 pts HL lang 6)
Birmingham – ABB (Span Engl Lit; Span Hist Art; Span Thea St) (IB 32–34 pts)
Cardiff – ABB (Cult Crit Span; Span) (IB 30 pts)
Exeter – ABB–BBB (Sociol Span) (IB 32–29 pts)
East Anglia – ABB (Transl Media Span)
Kent – 320 pts (Hisp St) (IB 35 pts)
Leeds – ABB (Span; Hisp Lat Am St; Port Span; Span Wrld Cnma) (IB 34 pts HL 16 pts)
Leicester – ABB (Fr Span; Ital Span; Span Engl) (IB 28–30 pts)
London (King's) – BBB+AS (Hisp St; Hisp St Port Braz St) (IB 32 pts)
London (RH) – ABB–BBB (Span Mus; Span Fr/Ger/Ital; Span Int Rel) (IB 32 pts)
Manchester – ABB–BBC (Port Chin Jap) (IB 30–33 pts)
Newcastle – ABB (Span Bus St; Span Port Lat Am St; Span Pol) (IB 32 pts HL Span 6)
Surrey – ABB (Bus Mgt Span)
Sussex – ABB–BBB (Anth Span; Dev St Span; Dr St Span) (IB 32–34 pts)
York – ABB (Span Ling) (IB 32 pts)
300 pts **Aston** – 300–320 pts (Euro St Span; Span Comb Hons) (IB 31–33 pts)
Birmingham – BBB–BBC (Hisp St courses) (IB 32 pts)
Cardiff – BBB (Anc Hist Span)
Coventry – 300 pts (Law Span)
Dundee – BBB 2nd yr entry (Span courses)
East Anglia – BBB–BBC (Transl Media Fr Span; Span It Dev St)
Edinburgh – BBB (Span Port EU St; Span Engl Lit; Span Class; Hisp St Hist)
Heriot-Watt – ABC–BBC (App Langs Transl (Fr Span) (Ger Span); Maths Span) (IB 28 pts)
Lancaster – BBB–BBC 300–280 pts (Span St Geog; Span St Mus) (IB 30–29 pts)
Liverpool – BBB 300 pts (Hisp St courses) (IB 30 pts)
London (QM) – 300–340 pts (Hisp St; Hisp St Geog; Hisp St Pol; Hisp St Ctln Lang)
Northumbria – 300 pts (Span Bus) (IB 26 pts)
Nottingham – ABC–BBB (Span Ger; Port Russ; Hisp St; Span Contemp Chin St) (IB 32 pts)
Nottingham – ABC (Span Int Media Comms)
Queen's Belfast – BBB–BBCb (Span St; Span Port St)
Salford – 300 pts (Law Span)
Sheffield – BBB (Hisp St courses) (IB 35–32 pts)
Swansea – BBB 300 pts (Span Leg St; Span; Span Pol; Span Comp Sci)
Westminster – BBB (Int Bus Span) (IB 28 pts)
280 pts **Essex** – 280 pts (Span St Modn Langs; Port St Modn Langs) (IB 30 pts)
Hertfordshire – 280–260 pts (Hist Span; Mark Span; Tour Span)
Nottingham Trent – 280–260 pts (Law Span; Media Span; Span Ital)
260 pts **Aberystwyth** – 260 pts (Span courses) (IB 29 pts)
Birmingham – BCC (Port Joint Hons)
Hull – 260–300 pts (Span courses)
Oxford Brookes – BCC (Span minor field) (IB 30 pts)
Westminster – BCC/BC (Transl St (Span)) (IB 28 pts)
240 pts **Aberdeen** – CCC (Hisp St courses; Span courses)
Bangor – 240–280 pts (Span courses)
Buckingham – 240–300 pts (Psy Span; Span Mark)
Coventry – 240–260 pts (Span; Span Bus; Span Int Rel)
Dundee – CCC 1st yr entry (Span courses)
Glamorgan – 240–280 pts (Bus Span; Engl Span; Law Span)
Liverpool John Moores – 240 pts (Int Bus St Span)

London Met – 240 pts (Span Lat Am St)
Manchester Met – 240 pts (Span St; Span Comb Hons)
Plymouth – 240–260 pts (Acc Span; Geog Span)
Roehampton – 240–320 pts (Span; Span Media Cult)
Sheffield Hallam – 240 pts (Int Bus Span; Span Mark; Span Tour)
Stirling – CCC (Span Educ; Euro Film Media Span; Span Psy) (IB 28 pts)
Ulster – 240 pts (Euro St Span; Span Comp; Span Acc; Span Rtl St)
230 pts **Edinburgh Napier** – 230 pts (Tour Mgt Span)
220 pts **Chester** – 220–260 pts (Span courses)
Kingston – 220–320 pts (Dr Span; Hum Rts Span; App Econ Span)
Leeds Met – 220 pts (Span PR; Span Glob Dev)
Sunderland – 220 pts (Span Comb Hons)
200 pts **Central Lancashire** – 200 pts (Span joint courses)
Middlesex – 200–280 pts (Span Int Bus)
Portsmouth – 200–280 pts (Span St)
180 pts **European Bus Sch London** – DDD (Int Bus Span)
Greenwich – 180–160 pts (Span courses)
80 pts **London (Birk)** – 80 pts (p/t Span Lat Am St; Span Port)

Alternative offers
See **Chapter 7** and **Appendix 1** for grades/UCAS Tariff points information for the International Baccalaureate, Scottish Highers/Advanced Highers, the Welsh Baccalaureate, the Irish Leaving Certificate, the Cambridge Pre-U Diploma, the Advanced Diploma and the Extended Project.

CHOOSING YOUR COURSE (SEE ALSO CH.1)

Some course features
East Anglia For particularly able students, Spanish courses are offered over three years, not the usual four-year courses.
Heriot-Watt Spanish can be taken with Interpreting and Translating, International Management and teaching English to speakers of other languages.
London (King's) The University offers a very wide range of courses covering Hispanic, Portuguese and Brazilian Studies.
London Met There is an Open Language programme offered to students to continue a study of a preferred language irrespective of their chosen degree course (see also Languages).
Warwick (Hist Lit Cult Ams) A four-year interdisciplinary course, with the third year spent at a university in the Americas. Spanish language is taught throughout, with beginners following an introductory course in Year 1, and students with A-level Spanish taking one more advanced course. There are opportunities to study Spanish American literature as poetry.

Universities and colleges teaching quality See www.qaa.ac.uk; www.unistats.com.

Top research universities and colleges (RAE 2008) (Iberian and Latin American languages) Manchester; Nottingham; Cambridge; London (King's) (Portuguese); London (Birk); Durham; London (King's) (Spanish); London (QM); Leeds; St Andrews; Newcastle; Queen's Belfast.

ADMISSIONS INFORMATION

Number of applicants per place (approx) Birmingham 9; Bristol 3; Cardiff 3; Exeter 5; Hull 14; Leeds 10; Liverpool 3; London (King's) 6, (QM) 5, (UCL) 6; Middlesex 2; Newcastle 12; Nottingham 7; Portsmouth 4; Salford 5.

Advice to applicants and planning the UCAS personal statement Visits to Spanish-speaking countries should be discussed. Study the geography, culture, literature and politics of Spain (or Portugal) and discuss your interests in full. Further information could be obtained from embassies in London. See also **Appendix 4** under **Languages**.

Selection interviews **Yes** Cambridge, Hull, London (RH), (UCL), Nottingham, Oxford; **Some** Cardiff, Leeds, Roehampton, Swansea.

Interview advice and questions Candidates offering A-level Spanish are likely to be questioned on their A-level work, their reasons for wanting to take the subject and on their knowledge of Spain and its people. Interest in Spain important for all applicants. 'Mostly questions about the literature I had read and I was given a poem and asked questions on it.' Questions were asked in the target language. 'There were two interviewers for the Spanish interview; they did their best to trip me up and to make me think under pressure by asking aggressive questions.' See **Chapter 5**.

AFTER-RESULTS ADVICE

Offers to applicants repeating A-levels **Higher** Glasgow, Leeds; **Same** Cardiff, Chester, Hull, Liverpool, London (RH), Newcastle, Nottingham, Roehampton, Swansea; **No offers made** Cambridge.

GRADUATE DESTINATIONS AND EMPLOYMENT (2007/8 HESA)

Graduates in Spanish surveyed 765 **Employed** 370 **In further study** 145 **Assumed unemployed** 55.
Graduates in Portuguese surveyed 45 **Employed** 30 **In further study** 5 **Assumed unemployed** 5.

Career note See **Languages**.

OTHER DEGREE SUBJECTS FOR CONSIDERATION

International Business Studies; Latin American Studies; Linguistics; see other Language tables.

SPEECH PATHOLOGY/SCIENCES/THERAPY

(including **Deaf Studies**)

Speech Pathology/Sciences/Therapy is the study of speech defects caused by accident, disease or psychological trauma. These can include failure to develop communication at the usual age, voice disorders, physical and learning disabilities and stammering. Courses lead to qualification as a speech therapist. This is one of many medical courses. See also **Medicine** and **Appendix 4**.

Useful websites www.rcslt.org; www.speechteach.co.uk; www.asha.org.

NB The points totals shown to the left of the institutions are for ease of reference only. It must not be assumed that Tariff points are always used by institutions or that they can be substituted for an offer in grades. The level of an offer is not necessarily indicative of the quality of a course.

COURSE OFFERS INFORMATION

Subject requirements/preferences **GCSE** English language, modern foreign language and biology/dual award science at grade B or above. **AL** At least one science subject; biology may be stipulated, psychology and English language may be preferred. **Other requirements** Criminal Records Bureau (CRB) and occupational health checks essential for speech sciences/speech therapy applicants.

NB In 2011 universities and colleges will differ in their use of GCE AL/AS unit grade information, A* grades, the Extended Project (EPQ), the Advanced Diploma and the Cambridge Pre-U examination when considering applicants and making offers. An EPQ may be accepted in place of an AS subject. Check websites of universities and colleges for the latest offers information.

Your target offers and examples of courses provided by each institution

380 pts **London (UCL)** – AAA+AS–ABB+AS (Sp Sci) (IB 36–37 pts)
355 pts **Queen Margaret** – 355 pts (Sp Lang Thera) (IB 32 pts)
320 pts **Leeds** – ABB (Ling Phon) (IB 32 pts)
Manchester – ABB (Sp Lang Thera) (IB 33 pts)
Newcastle – ABB (Sp Lang Sci) (IB 35 pts HL 555 biol 6)
Reading – 320 pts (Sp Lang Thera)
Sheffield – ABB **or** ABab (Sp Sci) (IB 33 pts)
300 pts **Cardiff (UWIC)** – BBB 300–320 pts (Sp Lang Thera) (IB 25 pts)

City – BBB (Sp Lang Thera) (IB 32 pts HL 555)
East Anglia – BBB (Sp Lang Thera) (IB 31 pts HL 555)
Essex – 300 pts (Engl Lang Lang Acq Diso) (IB 29 pts)
Leeds Met – BBB (Clin Lang Sci (Sp Lang Thera)) (IB 32 pts)
Manchester Met – BBB (Sp Path Thera; Psy Sp Path)
Sheffield – BBB (Hum Comm Sci)
Strathclyde – BBB (Sp Lang Path) (IB 30 pts)
UCP Marjon – 300 pts (Sp Lang Thera)
Ulster – BBB +HPAT (Sp Lang Thera)

280 pts **Birmingham City** – 280 pts (Sp Lang Thera) (IB 35 pts)
De Montfort – BBC 280 pts (Hum Comm (Sp Lang Thera)) (IB 28 pts)

240 pts **Bristol** – CCC (Df St)

220 pts **Central Lancashire** – 220 pts (Df St) (IB 28 pts)

160 pts **Reading** – 160 pts (Thea Arts Educ Df St)
Wolverhampton – 160–220 pts (Ling Df St courses)

Alternative offers
See **Chapter 7** and **Appendix 1** for grades/UCAS Tariff points information for the International Baccalaureate, Scottish Highers/Advanced Highers, the Welsh Baccalaureate, the Irish Leaving Certificate, the Cambridge Pre-U Diploma, the Advanced Diploma and the Extended Project.

EXAMPLES OF FOUNDATION DEGREES IN THE SUBJECT FIELD

Portsmouth.

CHOOSING YOUR COURSE (SEE ALSO CH.1)

Some course features
Cardiff (UWIC) Course includes a module in bi-lingual studies which focuses on the needs of multi-cultural and multi-lingual groups.
London (UCL) Clinical work begins in the first year. Organised clinical placements take place throughout the course, mostly in London and south-east England.
Manchester Met Placements are four and eight weeks and may be anywhere in the Manchester region, so temporary accommodation may be needed.
Reading (Sp Lang Thera) Clinics are run on campus in collaboration with the local authority. The course involves the use of computer-assisted analyses of language.
Sheffield (Sp Sci) Course leads to qualification as a speech therapist. (Hum Comm Sci) Focuses on the use of speech and language and how the process fails, for example in autism and dyslexia, but is not a professional qualification in speech therapy.

Universities and colleges teaching quality See www.qaa.ac.uk; www.unistats.com.

Top research universities and colleges (RAE 2008) (Language and Communication Science) City.

ADMISSIONS INFORMATION

Number of applicants per place (approx) Birmingham City 28; Cardiff (UWIC) 10; City 16; De Montfort 5; London (UCL) 9; Manchester Met 21; Newcastle 23; Queen Margaret 12.

Advice to applicants and planning the UCAS personal statement Contact with speech therapists and visits to their clinics are an essential part of the preparation for this career. Discuss your contacts in full, giving details of any work experience or work shadowing you have done and your interest in helping people to communicate, showing evidence of good 'people skills'. **Manchester** Selectors look for some practical experience with individuals who have communication or swallowing difficulties. (International students) Good English required because of placement periods. See also **Appendix 4** and **Chapter 5**.

Misconceptions about this course Some students fail to differentiate between speech therapy, occupational therapy and physiotherapy. They do not realise that to study speech and language therapy there are academic demands, including the study of linguistics, psychology, medical sciences and clinical dynamics, so the course is intensive. **Cardiff (UWIC)** Some are under the impression that good grades are not necessary, that it is an easy option and one has to speak with a standard pronunciation.

Selection interviews **Yes** De Montfort, London (UCL), Manchester Met, Queen Margaret, Sheffield, UCP Marjon.

Interview advice and questions Have you visited a speech therapy clinic? What made you want to become a speech therapist? What type of speech problems are there? What type of person would make a good speech therapist? Interviews often include an ear test (test of listening ability). What did you see when you visited a speech and language therapy clinic? **Cardiff (UWIC)** Interviewees must demonstrate an insight into communication problems and explain how one speech sound is produced. See also **Chapter 5**.

Reasons for rejection (non-academic) Insufficient knowledge of speech and language therapy. Lack of maturity. Poor communication skills. Written language problems.

AFTER-RESULTS ADVICE

Offers to applicants repeating A-levels **Higher** Birmingham City, Cardiff (UWIC); **Possibly higher** Manchester Met; **Same** City, De Montfort, Newcastle.

GRADUATE DESTINATIONS AND EMPLOYMENT (2007/8 HESA)

No data available.

Career note Speech therapists work mainly in NHS clinics, some work in hospitals and others in special schools or units for the mentally or physically handicapped. The demand for speech therapists is high.

OTHER DEGREE SUBJECTS FOR CONSIDERATION

Audiology; Communication Studies; Deaf Studies; Education; Health Studies; Linguistics; Psychology.

SPORTS SCIENCES/STUDIES

(see also **Physical Education**)

In addition to the theory and practice of many different sporting activities, Sports Sciences/Studies courses also cover the psychological aspects of sports and of sports business administration. The geography, economics and sociology of recreation may also be included.

Centres of Cricketing Excellence The England and Wales Cricket Board has introduced the Universities Centres of Cricketing Excellence scheme (UCCE). Details can be obtained from the following centres of excellence: Cambridge Centre www.mccuniversities.org/cambridge; Cardiff/Glamorgan Centre www.mccuniversities.org/cardiff-glamorgan; Durham Centre www.mccuniversities.org/durham; Leeds/Bradford Centre www.mccuniversities.org/leeds-bradford; Loughborough Centre www.mccuniversities.org/loughborough; Oxford Centre www.mccuniversities.org/oxford. See also **Appendix 4**.

Useful websites www.isrm.co.uk; www.uksport.gov.uk; www.laureus.com; www.wsf.org.uk; www.sta.co.uk; www.olympic.org; www.sportscotland.org.uk; www.baha.org.uk; www.planet-science.com; www.london2012.com.

NB The points totals shown to the left of the institutions are for ease of reference only. It must not be assumed that Tariff points are always used by institutions or that they can be substituted for an offer in grades. The level of an offer is not necessarily indicative of the quality of a course.

COURSE OFFERS INFORMATION

Subject requirements/preferences **GCSE** English, mathematics and, often, a science subject; check prospectuses. **AL** Science required for Sport Science courses. PE required for some Sport Studies courses. **Other requirements** Enhanced Criminal Records Bureau (CRB) disclosure required for many courses. Evidence of commitment to sport.

NB In 2011 universities and colleges will differ in their use of GCE AL/AS unit grade information, A* grades, the Extended Project (EPQ), the Advanced Diploma and the Cambridge Pre-U examination when considering applicants and making offers. An EPQ may be accepted in place of an AS subject. Check websites of universities and colleges for the latest offers information.

Your target offers and examples of courses provided by each institution

360 pts **Bath** – AAA (Spo Exer Sci; Spo Eng) (IB 36 pts)
Exeter – AAA–AAB (Psy Spo Exer Sci) (IB 36–33 pts)
Loughborough – AAA–AAB (Spo Exer Sci; Spo Tech) (IB 36 pts)

340 pts **Bath** – AAB (Coach Educ Spo Dev) (IB 35–36 pts)
Birmingham – AAB–ABB 340–320 pts (Spo Mat Sci; Spo Exer Sci; App Glf Mgt St; Maths Spo Sci) (IB 32–34 pts)
Exeter – AAB–BBB (Exer Spo Sci; Hum Biosci) (IB 34–29 pts)
Heriot-Watt – AAB 2nd yr entry (Spo Exer Sci Psy)
Loughborough – 340–320 pts (Engl Spo Sci; Spo Mgt) (IB 34–32 pts)
Sheffield – AAB (Spo Eng; Mtr Spo Eng Mgt)

320 pts **Bournemouth** – 320 pts (Spo Mgt; Spo Dev Coach Sci)
Brunel – 320 pts BBC +AS/EPQ c (Spo Sci; Spo Sci (Hum Perf); Mgt Spo Dev) (IB 32 pts)
Cardiff (UWIC) – 320 pts (Spo Exer Sci) (IB 25 pts)
Central Lancashire – ABB–BBB (Spo Jrnl) (IB 32 pts)
Durham – ABB (Sport) (IB 32–30 pts)
Essex – 320–280 pts (Spo Exer Sci; Spo Sci Biol) (IB 30–28 pts)
Glasgow – ABB (Spo Med) (IB 32 pts)
Leeds – ABB–BBB (Spo Sci Physiol; Spo Exer Sci) (IB 32–34 HL 16–15 pts)
Liverpool John Moores – 320–280 pts (Spo Sci; Spo Dev PE; Spo Tech)
Ulster – ABB (Spo Exer Sci)

300 pts **Aberdeen** – BBB 2nd yr entry (Spo Exer Sci; Spo St (Exer Hlth))
Bangor – 300–260 pts (Spo Sci courses; Spo Hlth Exer Sci; Spo Hlth PE)
Brighton – BBB 300–340 pts (Spo Jrnl; Spo Exer Sci; Spo Coach) (IB 32 pts)
Cardiff (UWIC) – 300 pts (Spo PE; Spo Condit Rehab Msg)
Dundee – BBB 2nd yr entry (Spo Biomed) (IB 34 pts)
Gloucestershire – 300 pts (Spo Thera; Spo Sci; Spo Dev)
Heriot-Watt – BBB 1st yr entry (Spo Exer Sci Psy)
Hertfordshire – 300–280 pts (Spo Thera; Spo Exer Sci; Spo St)
Kent – 300 pts (Spo Thera Hlth Fit) (IB 33 pts)
Loughborough – 300 pts (Spo Sci Phys; Chem Spo Sci) (IB 34 pts)
Salford – 300 pts (Spo Rehab) (IB 29 pts)
Sheffield Hallam – 300–280 pts (Spo Exer Sci; Spo Sci Perf Coach)
Southampton – BBB (Spo St) (IB 30 pts)
Strathclyde – BBB (Spo Eng)

280 pts **Bristol UWE** – 280–340 pts (Spo Thera Rehab)
Cardiff (UWIC) – 280 pts (Spo Dev; Spo Mgt)
Edinburgh – BBC (App Spo Sci) (IB 32 pts)
Huddersfield – 280 pts (Spo Mark PR; Spo Jrnl; Spo Prom Mark)
Hull – 280 pts (Spo Coach Perf; Spo Exer Sci; Spo Rehab)
Leeds Met – 280–240 pts (Spo Exer Sci; Spo Bus Mgt; Spo Leis Cult) (IB 28 pts)
Manchester Met – 280–260 pts (Spo Dev; Psy Spo Exer; Spo Exer Sci; Coach St) (IB 28 pts)
Newport – 280 pts (Spo St; Spo Yth Commun St)
Northumbria – 280–260 pts (Spo Mgt; Spo Coach; Spo Exer Nutr) (IB 25 pts)
Nottingham Trent – 280–240 pts (Spo Exer Sci; Spo Sci Mgt; Coach Spo Sci; Spo Leis Out Mgt) (IB 28 pts)
Oxford Brookes – BBC (Exer Nutr Hlth; Spo Coach St; Spo Sci; Spo Exer Sci) (IB 30 pts)

Portsmouth – 280 pts (Spo Dev; Spo Exer Sci)
Swansea – 280–300 pts (Spo Sci)
Teesside – 280–300 pts (Spo Thera)
Worcester – 280 pts (Spo Thera; Spo St; Spo Bus Mgt)

260 pts **Bolton** – 260 pts (Spo Exer Psy)
Brighton – BCC (Spo St)
Bristol UWE – 260–300 pts (Spo Biol; Spo Biomed; Spo Coach) (IB 26–28 pts)
Central Lancashire – 260–240 pts (Spo Psy; Spo Tech; Spo Evnt Mgt; Advntr Spo Sci; Spo Coach; Spo Thera; Spo Sci)
Edge Hill – 260 pts (Spo Thera; Spo Dev; Spo Exer Sci)
Edinburgh – BCC (Spo Recr Mgt) (IB 32 pts)
Edinburgh Napier – 260–240 pts (Spo Exer Sci courses; Spo Tech)
Kent – 260 pts (Spo Sci; Spo Exer Mgt) (IB 29 pts)
Liverpool Hope – 260 pts (Spo Psy; Spo St)
Liverpool John Moores – 260 pts (App Spo Psy)
Sheffield Hallam – 260 pts (Spo Dev Coach; Spo Coach)
Stirling – BCC (Spo St; Spo Exer Sci) (IB 30 pts)
Strathclyde – BCC (Spo Physl Actvt)
Swansea – 260 pts (Spo Mats)
Teesside – 260 pts (Spo Exer Psy; Spo Exer; Spo Exer (Coach Sci) (App Exer Sci))

240 pts **Aberdeen** – CCC 1st yr entry (BSc Spo Exer Sci; Spo St (Exer Hlth); App Spo Sci Educ)
Aberystwyth – 240 pts (Eqn Hum Spo Sci; Spo Exer Sci) (IB 28 pts)
Bournemouth – 240 pts (Exer Sci)
Cardiff (UWIC) – 240 pts (Spo Biomed Nutr) (IB 24 pts)
Chester – 240–280 pts (Spo Exer Sci courses) (IB 24 pts)
Chichester – CCC 240–300 pts (Spo Coach Sci; Spo Exer Psy)

Coventry – 240–260 pts (Spo Tour; Spo Mgt; Spo Mark; Spo Thera)
Cumbria – 240 pts (Spo St; Spo Mgt; Spo Exer Sci; Coach Spo Dev)
Dundee – CCC 1st yr entry (Spo Biomed)
Glamorgan – 240–280 pts (Spo Psy; Spo Mgt; Spo Dev)
Glyndŵr – 240 pts (Spo Coach; Spo Exer Sci)
Greenwich – 240 pts (Spo Sci Coach; Spo Sci)
Leeds Trinity (UC) – 240–260 pts (Spo Dev PE; Spo Exer Psy; Spo Jrnl)
London Met – 240–160 pts (Spo; Spo Dance Thera)
Manchester Met – 240 pts (Spo Mgt)
Robert Gordon – 240 pts (Spo Exer Sci)
Roehampton – 240–280 pts (Spo Sci Comb Hons; Spo Exer Sci)
Salford – 240–260 pts (App Spo Sci courses; Spo Leis Mgt)
Staffordshire – 240 pts (Spo St; Spo Exer Sci)
Suffolk (Univ Campus) – 240 pts (Spo Exer Sci)
Sunderland – 240 pts (Spo Exer Dev; Spo Exer Sci; Spo St)
UCP Marjon – 240 pts (App Spo Sci Coach courses)
Ulster – 240 pts (Spo Tech) (IB 24 pts)
Winchester – 240–280 pts (Spo Coach Dev; Spo Mgt)

220 pts **Birmingham (UC)** – 220 pts (Spo Thera)
Central Lancashire – 220–260 pts (Spo; Spo PR)
Edge Hill – 220 pts (Spo Exer Psy)
Kingston – 220–280 pts (Spo Sci; Spo Analys Coach)
Lincoln – 220–280 pts (Ecn Spo Sci; Glf Sci Dev; Spo Mark; Spo Exer Sci)
Newman (UC) – 220–260 pts (Spo St courses)
Northampton – 220–260 pts (Spo Exer Sci; Spo Dev; Spo Mark)
Nottingham Trent – 220 pts (Eqn Spo Sci)
St Mary's Twickenham (UC) – 220–240 pts (Spo Coach Sci; Spo Rehab; Spo Sci; Clin Exer Sci)
Southampton Solent – 220 pts (Spo St Bus; Extrm Spo Mgt; Wtrspo St Mgt)
Teesside – 220 pts (Spo Mgt)
Warwickshire (Coll) – 220 pts (Spo Sci (Equit Coach))
York St John – 220 pts (Spo Soty Dev; Spo Perf Condit; Spo Sci Injry Mgt)

200 pts **Bolton** – 200–240 pts (Spo Rehab; Spo Dev; Spo Sci Coach)
Bristol UWE – 200–240 pts (Eqn Spo Sci; Spo Bus Mgt) (IB 24 pts)
Bucks New – 200–240 pts (Spo Mgt Coach St; Spo Mgt Ftbl St)
Central Lancashire – 200–220 pts (Mtr Spo)
Chester (Warrington) – 200–240 pts (Spo Dev)
Derby – 200–240 pts (Spo Exer St)
East London – 200 pts (Spo Coach; Spo Dev)
Glamorgan – 200 pts (Spo Sci Rgby; Spo Exer Sci; Spo St)
Middlesex – 200–220 pts (Spo Exer Sci; Spo Rehab)
Plymouth – 200 pts (App Mar Spo Sci; Srf Sci Tech)
Sheffield Hallam – 200 pts (Spo Bus Mgt; Spo Tech)

180 pts **Abertay Dundee** – DDD 168–180 pts (Spo Exer courses)
Anglia Ruskin – 180 pts (Spo Sci) (IB 24 pts)
UCP Marjon – 180 pts (Spo Dev; Out Advntr Educ St)
Wolverhampton – 180–200 pts (Spo Coach; Spo St; Spo Mgt)

160 pts **Bedfordshire** – 160–240 pts (App Spo St; Spo Sci Coach; Spo Exer Sci)
Bishop Grosseteste (UC) – 160 pts (Educ St Spo)
London South Bank – 160 pts CC (Spo Exer Sci)
South Essex (Coll) – 160 pts (Spo St)

140 pts **Writtle (Coll)** – 140–240 pts (Spo Exer Perf courses)

120 pts **Swansea Met** – 120 pts (Spo Mgt; Spo Exer Sci)

80 pts **Farnborough (CT)** – 80 pts (Spo Sci (Exer Hlth Mgt))

Alternative offers
See **Chapter 7** and **Appendix 1** for grades/UCAS Tariff points information for the International Baccalaureate, Scottish Highers/Advanced Highers, the Welsh Baccalaureate, the Irish Leaving Certificate, the Cambridge Pre-U Diploma, the Advanced Diploma and the Extended Project.

EXAMPLES OF FOUNDATION DEGREES IN THE SUBJECT FIELD

Arts London (CComm); Askham Bryan (Coll); Bath; Bath City (Coll); Bedfordshire; Birmingham (UC); Bishop Burton (Coll); Blackpool and Fylde (Coll); Bournemouth; Bradford (Coll); Brighton; Bristol UWE; Bucks New; Cardiff (UWIC); Central Lancashire; Chester; Chesterfield (Coll); Chichester; Colchester (Inst); Cornwall (Coll); Coventry; Cumbria; Duchy (Coll); Durham New (Coll); East Anglia; Edge Hill; Exeter (Coll); Farnborough (CT); Glamorgan; Grimsby (IFHE); Hertfordshire; Hopwood Hall (Coll); Huddersfield; Hull (Coll); Kirklees (Coll); Leeds City (Coll); Leeds Trinity (UC); Lincoln (Coll); Llandrillo (Coll); London Met; London South Bank; Loughborough (Coll); Manchester (Coll); Mid-Cheshire (Coll); Middlesex; Milton Keynes (Univ Centre); Myerscough (Coll); Neath Port Talbot (Coll); Nescot; Newcastle (Coll); Newport; North Lindsey (Coll); Norwich City (Coll); Petroc (Coll); Plymouth; Reaseheath (Coll); Riverside Halton (Coll); St Helens (Coll); Sheffield (Coll); Somerset (CAT); South Devon (Coll); South Nottingham (Coll); Southport (Coll); Suffolk (Univ Campus); Sunderland; Sunderland City (Coll); Teesside; Thames Valley; Truro (Coll); Tyne Met (Coll); Ulster; Wakefield (Coll); Warwickshire (Coll); Wigan and Leigh (Coll); Wolverhampton; Worcester (CT); Writtle (Coll); Yeovil (Univ Centre); York (Coll).

CHOOSING YOUR COURSE (SEE ALSO CH.1)

Some course features
Birmingham (Spo Mat Sci) This course focuses on the design and materials used in the manufacture of sports equipment. Research placements are offered during summer vacations.
Brighton (Spo Jrnl) A placement project takes place in the final year. The course is accredited by the National Council for the Training of Journalists with graduates receiving the Certificate in Newspaper Journalism.
Brunel After a common first year students select their preferred specialisation in administration, coaching, exercise and fitness, physical education or a multi-disciplinary route.
Central Lancashire A wide range of sport and related courses are provided, some specialising in Adventure Sports and Motor Sport.
Exeter (Hum Biosci) The course combines molecular biology and biochemistry with exercise and sports science, including biomechanics and human exercise physiology.
Loughborough The University has a national and international reputation in sport, leisure management and physical education.

Top research universities and colleges (RAE 2008) (Sports-related Studies) Birmingham; Loughborough; Bristol; Liverpool John Moores; Stirling; Bath; Leeds Met; Brunel; Bangor; Exeter; Leeds.

Examples of sandwich degree courses Bath; Bournemouth; Brighton; Bristol UWE; Brunel; Coventry; Glamorgan; Gloucestershire; Hertfordshire; Huddersfield; Kingston; London Met; London South Bank; Loughborough; Nottingham Trent; Sheffield Hallam; Swansea Met; Ulster; Warwickshire (Coll); Wolverhampton; Writtle (Coll).

ADMISSIONS INFORMATION

Number of applicants per place (approx) Aberystwyth 5; Bangor 15; Bath (Coach Educ Spo Dev) 8; Birmingham 7; Brunel 6; Canterbury Christ Church 30; Cardiff (UWIC) 10; Chichester 4; Cumbria 14, (Spo St) 6; Durham 6; Edinburgh 11; Exeter 23; Gloucestershire 8; Kingston 13; Leeds 25; Leeds Trinity (UC) 35; Liverpool John Moores 4; Loughborough 20; Manchester Met 16; Northampton 4; Northumbria 30; Nottingham Trent 8; Portsmouth 12; Roehampton 8; St Mary's Twickenham (UC) 4; Salford 30; Sheffield Hallam 7; South Essex (Coll) 1; Southampton 8; Staffordshire 12; Stirling 10; Strathclyde 28; Sunderland 2; Swansea 6; Teesside 15; Winchester 5; Wolverhampton 4; Worcester 10; York St John 4.

Advice to applicants and planning the UCAS personal statement **Cardiff (UWIC)** A strong personal statement required which clearly identifies current performance profile and indicates a balanced lifestyle. **Salford** Previous experience in a sporting environment will be noted. Previous study is preferred in biology/human biology, physics, chemistry, physical education/sports studies. Psychology is preferred. Other comments (Coach Sci) For these courses applicants must have proven coaching skills to gain a place. (Spo Sci) These are lab-based courses examining the physical stress of sport on the human body. A sound scientific aptitude is required. Although professional sporting qualifications and high level practical experience cannot take the place of scientific entry qualifications, they will be considered in any borderline applicants holding a conditional offer. Comment on any coaching or competitive experience. See also **Physical Education**. See also **Appendix 4**.

Misconceptions about this course **Bath** (Spo Exer Sci) This is not a sports course with a high component of practical sport: it is a science programme with minimal practical sport. (Coach Educ Spo Dev) This is not necessarily a course for elite athletes. **Birmingham** (App Glf Mgt St) Applicants do not appreciate the academic depth required across key areas (it is, in a sense, a multiple Honours course – business management, sports science, coaching theory, materials science). **Sheffield Hallam** (Spo Tech) Some applicants expect an engineering course! **Swansea** (Spo Sci) Applicants underestimate the quantity of maths on the course. Many applicants are uncertain about the differences between Sports Studies and Sports Science.

Selection interviews **Yes** Bath, Birmingham, Bristol UWE, Cumbria, Durham, Edinburgh, Leeds, Leeds Trinity (UC), Nottingham Trent, Swansea; **Some** Anglia Ruskin, Cardiff (UWIC), Chichester, Derby, Liverpool John Moores, Roehampton, St Mary's Twickenham (UC), Salford, Sheffield Hallam, Staffordshire, Wolverhampton.

Interview advice and questions Applicants' interests in sport and their sporting activities are likely to be discussed at length. Past questions include: How do you strike a balance between sport and academic work? How many, and which, sports do you coach? For how long? Have you devised your own coaching programme? What age-range do you coach? Do you coach unsupervised? **Loughborough** A high level of sporting achievement is expected. See **Chapter 5**.

Reasons for rejection (non-academic) Not genuinely interested in outdoor activities. Poor sporting background or knowledge. Personal appearance. Inability to apply their science to their specialist sport. Illiteracy. Using the course as a second option to physiotherapy. Arrogance. Expectation that they will be playing sport all day. When the course is explained to them some applicants realise that a more arts-based course would be more appropriate.

AFTER-RESULTS ADVICE

Offers to applicants repeating A-levels **Higher** Swansea; **Same** Cardiff (UWIC), Chichester, Derby, Dundee, Lincoln, Liverpool John Moores, Loughborough, Plymouth, Roehampton, St Mary's Twickenham (UC), Salford, Sheffield Hallam, Staffordshire, Stirling, Suffolk (Univ Campus), Sunderland, Winchester, Wolverhampton, York St John.

GRADUATE DESTINATIONS AND EMPLOYMENT (2007/8 HESA)

Graduates surveyed 5360 **Employed** 2595 **In further study** 935 **Assumed unemployed** 310.

Career note Career options include sport development, coaching, teaching, outdoor centres, sports equipment development, sales, recreation management and professional sport.

OTHER DEGREE SUBJECTS FOR CONSIDERATION

Anatomy; Biology; Human Movement Studies; Leisure and Recreation Management; Nutrition; Physical Education; Physiology; Physiotherapy; Sports Equipment Product Design.

STATISTICS

(see also **Business Courses** and **Mathematics**)

Statistics has mathematical underpinnings but is primarily concerned with the collection, interpretation and analysis of data. Statistics are used to analyse and solve problems in a wide range of areas, particularly in the scientific, business, government and public services.

Useful websites www.rss.org.uk; www.statistics.gov.uk.

NB The points totals shown to the left of the institutions are for ease of reference only. It must not be assumed that Tariff points are always used by institutions or that they can be substituted for an offer in grades. The level of an offer is not necessarily indicative of the quality of a course.

COURSE OFFERS INFORMATION

Subject requirements/preferences GCSE English and mathematics. **AL** Mathematics required for all courses.

NB In 2011 universities and colleges will differ in their use of GCE AL/AS unit grade information, A* grades, the Extended Project (EPQ), the Advanced Diploma and the Cambridge Pre-U examination when considering applicants and making offers. An EPQ may be accepted in place of an AS subject. Check websites of universities and colleges for the latest offers information.

Your target offers and examples of courses provided by each institution

440 pts **Warwick** – A*AAa (Maths OR Stats Econ (MORSE); Maths Stats) (IB 39 pts HL maths 6)

400 pts **London (UCL)** – A*AA+AS–AAB+AS (Stats; Stats Sci; Stats Mgt Bus; Stats Econ Lang) (IB 39–36 pts)

360 pts **Bath** – AAA–AAB (Stats; Maths Stats) (IB 36 pts HL maths 6)
Bristol – AAA–AAB (Maths Stats) (IB 36 pts HL 665)
Durham – AAA (Nat Sci (Stats)) (IB 38–42 pts HL maths 6/7)
Glasgow – AAA Faster route (Stats courses)
Imperial London – AAA (Maths Stats; Maths Stats Fin) (IB 38 pts HL maths phys 6)
London LSE – AAA (Bus Maths Stats) (IB 38 pts HL 766)
Manchester – AAA–AAB (Maths Stats) (IB 36 pts)
Oxford – AAA (Maths Stats) (IB 38–40 pts)
St Andrews – AAA (Stats; Mgt Sci Stats; Lgc Phil Sci Stats) (IB 34 pts)
Southampton – AAA (Maths Stats) (IB 36 pts HL 17 pts)
York – AAA–AAB (Maths Stats) (IB 34 pts)

340 pts **Birmingham** – AAB (Mathem Econ Stats) (IB 34 pts)
Heriot-Watt – AAB 2nd yr entry (Stats Mdl)
Lancaster – AAB 340 pts (Stats N Am/Aus) (IB 31 pts)
London (QM) – 340 pts (MSci Maths Stats) (IB 34 pts)
Newcastle – AAB–ABB (Stats; Maths Stats; Stats Mgt; Acc Stats) (IB 34–32 pts)
Strathclyde – AAB 2nd yr entry (Maths Stats; Maths Stats Fin) (IB 32 pts)
Surrey – AAB–ABB 340–320 pts (Maths Stats) (IB 30–32 pts)

320 pts **East Anglia** – ABB–ABC (Maths Stats; Bus Stats) (IB 32 pts HL maths 6)
Edinburgh – ABB–ABC (Econ Stats; Maths Stats) (IB 32 pts)
Glasgow – ABB (Stats courses) (IB 32 pts)
Heriot-Watt – ABB 1st yr entry (Stats Mdl)
Heriot-Watt – ABB 2nd yr entry (Maths Stats)
Lancaster – ABB 320 pts (BSc Stats; Maths Stats) (IB 30 pts HL maths 6)
Leeds – ABB (Biol Stats; Geog Stats; Fr/Ger Stats; Stats)
Liverpool – ABB (Maths Stats) (IB 33 pts HL maths 6)
London (QM) – 320 pts (Maths Stats Fin Econ; Maths Stats) (IB 32 pts HL maths 6)
London (RH) – ABB 320 pts (Maths Stats) (IB 33 pts HL maths 6)

300 pts **Aberystwyth** – 300 pts (Educ Stats; Geog Stats) (IB 29 pts)
Brunel – 300 pts BCC +AS/EPQ c (Maths Stats Mgt) (IB 31 pts)
City – 300 pts (Mathem Sci Stats) (IB 28 pts)
Heriot-Watt – BBB 1st yr entry (Maths Stats)
Reading – 300 pts (Bus Stats Mark; App Stats; Stats) (IB 36 pts)
Strathclyde – BBB 1st yr entry (Maths Stats; Maths Stats Fin) (IB 32 pts)
Strathclyde – BBB 2nd yr entry (Nat Sci (Stats))

280 pts **Kent** – 280 pts (Maths Stats) (IB 28 pts)

Plymouth – 280 pts (App Stats) (IB 29 pts)
Staffordshire – 280 pts (Maths App Stats) (IB 26 pts)
260 pts **Bristol UWE** – 260–300 pts (Statistics) (IB 26–28 pts)
Kingston – 260 pts (Stats Bus Mgt; Med Stats; Act Maths Stats) (IB 26–28 pts)
Portsmouth – 260 pts (Maths Stats)
Strathclyde – BCC 1st yr entry (Nat Sci (Stats))
220 pts **Coventry** – 220 pts (Maths Stats)
200 pts **London Met** – 200 pts (Stats joint courses)
Middlesex – 200–280 pts (Bus Stats)
160 pts **Greenwich** – 160 pts (Stats; Maths Stats Comp; Stats Comp)
Liverpool John Moores – CC (Maths Stats Comp)
Oxford Brookes – CC (Stats; Bus Stats) (IB 24 pts)
80 pts **London (Birk)** – 80 pts for under 21s (over 21s varies) (p/t Stats Econ; Stats Mgt)

Alternative offers
See **Chapter 7** and **Appendix 1** for grades/UCAS Tariff points information for the International Baccalaureate, Scottish Highers/Advanced Highers, the Welsh Baccalaureate, the Irish Leaving Certificate, the Cambridge Pre-U Diploma, the Advanced Diploma and the Extended Project.

EXAMPLES OF FOUNDATION DEGREES IN THE SUBJECT FIELD
Blackpool and Fylde (Coll).

CHOOSING YOUR COURSE (SEE ALSO CH.1)
Some course features
Kingston (Med Stats courses) An optional professional placement year is offered to students.
Oxford Brookes Statistics is only offered as a joint course but with 12 other subjects.
Warwick (MORSE) Course has a statistics specialisation in Years 3 and 4 of the BSc and MMORSE courses.

Universities and colleges teaching quality See www.qaa.ac.uk; www.unistats.com.

Top research universities and colleges (RAE 2008) (Statistics and Operational Research) Oxford; Imperial London; Bristol; Warwick; Nottingham; Leeds; Kent; Bath; Southampton; Lancaster.

Examples of sandwich degree courses Bath; Bristol UWE; Coventry; Kingston; Portsmouth; Reading; Staffordshire; Surrey; Ulster; Wolverhampton.

ADMISSIONS INFORMATION
Number of applicants per place (approx) Bath 10; Bristol UWE 2; Coventry 3; East London 3; Heriot-Watt 6; Lancaster 11; Liverpool John Moores 6; London (UCL) 9; Newcastle 5; Southampton 10; York 5.

Advice to applicants and planning the UCAS personal statement Love mathematics, don't expect an easy life. See **Mathematics**. See also **Appendix 4**.

Selection interviews **Yes** Bath, Birmingham, Liverpool, Liverpool John Moores, London (UCL), Newcastle, Sheffield; **Some** Greenwich.

Interview advice and questions Questions could be asked on your A-level syllabus (particularly in mathematics). Applicants' knowledge of statistics and their interest in the subject are likely to be tested, together with their awareness of the application of statistics in commerce and industry. See **Chapter 5**.

AFTER-RESULTS ADVICE
Offers to applicants repeating A-levels **Higher** Kent, Leeds, Liverpool, Liverpool John Moores, Newcastle, Swansea; **Same** Birmingham.

GRADUATE DESTINATIONS AND EMPLOYMENT (2007/8 HESA)
Graduates surveyed 180 **Employed** 65 **In further study** 40 **Assumed unemployed** 10.

Career note See **Mathematics**.

OTHER DEGREE SUBJECTS FOR CONSIDERATION

Accountancy; Actuarial Sciences; Business Information Technology; Business Studies; Computer Science; Economics; Financial Services; Mathematical Studies; Mathematics.

TECHNOLOGIES

(see also technology courses, eg **Architecture, Biotechnology, Broadcast, Business Information, Communications, Design, Education, Engineering, Fashion, Food, Information, Internet, Materials, Media, Music, Sound** and **Sport** under relevant subject tables)

Technology covers a wide range of activities and is commonly associated with the engineering industries although there are also scientific and artistic applications. The courses listed below give an insight into the range of technology courses available and see also individual subject tables.

Useful websites www.techreview.com; www.intute.ac.uk.

NB The points totals shown to the left of the institutions are for ease of reference only. It must not be assumed that Tariff points are always used by institutions or that they can be substituted for an offer in grades. The level of an offer is not necessarily indicative of the quality of a course.

COURSE OFFERS INFORMATION

Subject requirements/preferences **GCSE** English and mathematics required. **AL** Mathematics and/or a science may be required.

NB In 2011 universities and colleges will differ in their use of GCE AL/AS unit grade information, A* grades, the Extended Project (EPQ), the Advanced Diploma and the Cambridge Pre-U examination when considering applicants and making offers. An EPQ may be accepted in place of an AS subject. Check websites of universities and colleges for the latest offers information.

Your target offers and examples of courses provided by each institution

340 pts **Leeds** – AAB (Avn Tech Mgt; Avn Tech Plt St)
Newcastle – AAB (Spo Tech) (IB 32 pts)
Surrey – AAB–ABB (Spc Tech Planet Explor)
York – AAB–ABB (MEng Mus Tech Sys)

320 pts **Birmingham** – ABB (Spo Sci Mat Tech)
Bournemouth – 320 pts (Crea Tech; Gms Tech)
Brunel – 320 pts BBC +AS/EPQ c (Multim Tech Des) (IB 31 pts)

300 pts **Aston** – 300 pts (Tech Ent Mgt) (IB 32 pts)
Glasgow – BBB (Technol Educ)
Manchester – ABC (Tex Tech (Bus Mgt)) (IB 32 pts)
Newcastle – BBB (Biopharml Tech) (IB 32 pts)
Queen's Belfast – BBB (Agric Tech)
Strathclyde – BBB (Tech Bus St) (IB 32 pts)
York – BBB–BBC (BEng Mus Tech Sys)

280 pts **Birmingham City** – 280–260 pts (Fash Des Gmnt Tech; TV Tech Prod)
Bournemouth – 280 pts (Advnc Tech Bus Innov)
Glamorgan – 280–320 pts (Crea Tech)
Suffolk (Univ Campus) – 280 pts (Onc Radiother Tech)
Teesside – 280 pts (Sust Des Tech)

260 pts **Bristol UWE** – 260–300 pts (Crea Mus Tech)
Lincoln – 260 pts (Web Tech)

240 pts **Bangor** – 240–280 pts (Crea Tech; Des Tech S Educ)
Bolton – 240 pts (Comp Tech)
Bristol UWE – 240–300 pts (Prod Des Tech)

De Montfort – 240 pts (Fash Tech)
Huddersfield – 240 pts (Eng Tech Mgt)
Hull – 240 pts (Crea Mus Tech)
Manchester Met – 240 pts (Cloth Des Tech)
Staffordshire – 240 pts (Aero Tech; Auto Tech; Robot Tech)
Stranmillis (UC) – CCC (Tech Des Educ)
Ulster – 240–220 pts (Cln Tech; Tech Des)

220 pts **Abertay Dundee** – CCD 216–220 pts (Env Tech)
Liverpool John Moores – 220–260 pts (Des Tech P S Educ)
Northampton – 220–260 pts (Mat Tech (Lea))
Sunderland – 220 pts (Des Tech Educ)

200 pts **Bradford** – 200 pts (BSc Tech Mgt)
Chester – 200–240 pts (Multim Tech courses) (IB 24 pts)
Glasgow – BB (Tech Mgt)
Hertfordshire – 200 pts (Aerosp Tech Plt St; Intnet Tech e-Commer; Dig Rts Tech)

180 pts **Cardiff (UWIC)** – 180 pts (Dntl Tech)
Derby – 180–240 pts (Snd Lt Lv Evnt Tech)
Plymouth – 180–160 pts (Mar Spo Tech; Mar Cmpstes Tech) (IB 24 pts)

160 pts **SAC (Scottish CAg)** – CC (Grn Tech)
Sheffield Hallam – 160 pts (Des Tech S Educ; Rlwy Tech)
West Scotland – CC (Multim Tech; Bus Tech)

Aberdeen – check with admissions tutor (Tech Educ)
Open University – (Technology) contact +44(0)845 300 6090 or www.openuniversity.co.uk/you

Alternative offers
See **Chapter 7** and **Appendix 1** for grades/UCAS Tariff points information for the International Baccalaureate, Scottish Highers/Advanced Highers, the Welsh Baccalaureate, the Irish Leaving Certificate, the Cambridge Pre-U Diploma, the Advanced Diploma and the Extended Project.

EXAMPLES OF FOUNDATION DEGREES IN THE SUBJECT FIELD

Askham Bryan (Coll); Bath Spa; Bristol City (Coll); Central Lancashire; Leeds Met; Manchester Met; Milton Keynes (Univ Centre); Petroc (Coll).

CHOOSING YOUR COURSE (SEE ALSO CH.1)

Some course features
Aston (Tech Ent Mgt) The course covers product design, computing and engineering management.
Bangor (Crea Tech) The course is made up of two-thirds core computer science modules and one-third creative industries modules; scholarship and sponsorship opportunities are avaialble on a competitive basis.
Birmingham (Spo Sci Mat Tech) The course focuses on the design and materials of sports equipment for athletes, essential to peak performance.
Newcastle (Biopharml Tech) A new course focusing on the science and processes of developing and large-scale manufacturing of biopharmaceuticals, with opportunities for an industrial placement.

Top research universities and colleges (RAE 2008) See **Engineering/Engineering Sciences** and **Materials Science/Metallurgy**.

Examples of sandwich degree courses Aston; Bradford; De Montfort; Glamorgan; Huddersfield; Sheffield Hallam; Teesside; Ulster; West Scotland.

ADMISSIONS INFORMATION

Number of applicants per place (approx) Aston 6.

Advice to applicants and planning the UCAS personal statement See **Engineering** courses and **Physics**.

Selection interviews **Yes** Aston, Glasgow, Staffordshire.

Interview advice and questions See **Engineering/Engineering Sciences** and **Chapter 5**.

AFTER-RESULTS ADVICE
Offers to applicants repeating A-levels **Same** Aston, Staffordshire.

GRADUATE DESTINATIONS AND EMPLOYMENT (2007/8 HESA)
See **Engineering/Engineering Sciences**.

Career note See **Engineering/Engineering Sciences**.

OTHER DEGREE SUBJECTS FOR CONSIDERATION
Architectural Technology; Biotechnology; Design Technology; Digital Technology; Engineering Sciences; Environmental Materials Technology; Fashion Technology; Food Technology; Information Technology; Internet Technology; Marine Technology; Mechanical Engineering; Motorsport Technology; Multimedia Technology; Music Technology; Nanotechnology; Sound Technology; Space Technology; Sports Technology; Web Technology.

TOURISM and TRAVEL

(see also **Business Courses, Hospitality and Event Management** and **Leisure and Recreation Management/Studies**)

Tourism and Travel courses are popular; some are combined with Hospitality Management which provides students with specialisms in two areas. Courses involve business studies and a detailed study of tourism and travel. Industrial placements are frequently involved and language options are often included. See also **Appendix 4**.

Useful websites www.wttc.org; www.abta.com; www.baha.org.uk.

NB The points totals shown to the left of the institutions are for ease of reference only. It must not be assumed that Tariff points are always used by institutions or that they can be substituted for an offer in grades. The level of an offer is not necessarily indicative of the quality of a course.

COURSE OFFERS INFORMATION
Subject requirements/preferences **GCSE** English and mathematics required. **AL** No subjects specified.

NB In 2011 universities and colleges will differ in their use of GCE AL/AS unit grade information, A* grades, the Extended Project (EPQ), the Advanced Diploma and the Cambridge Pre-U examination when considering applicants and making offers. An EPQ may be accepted in place of an AS subject. Check websites of universities and colleges for the latest offers information.

Your target offers and examples of courses provided by each institution

360 pts **Exeter** – AAA–AAB (Mgt Tour) (IB 36–33 pts)
320 pts **Strathclyde** – ABB (Mgt Hspty Tour)
280 pts **Bournemouth** – 280 pts (Tour Mgt)
Kent – 280 pts (Tour Mgt; Tour Mgt Ind) (IB 31 pts HL 14 pts)
Middlesex – 280–200 pts (Int Tour Mgt)
Northumbria – 280 pts (Bus Tour; Trav Tour Mgt) (IB 28 pts)
Surrey – BBC 280 pts (Tour Mgt) (IB 30–32 pts)
260 pts **Bolton** – 260 pts (Bus Mgt (Tour); Int Tour Mgt)
Brighton – BCC (Int Tour Mgt; Trav Tour Mark) (IB 28 pts)
Bristol UWE – 260–280 pts (Tour Env Mgt)
Hertfordshire – 260 pts (Int Tour Mgt; Tour Mgt Tour Langs)
Lincoln – 260–200 pts (Int Tour Mgt; Spo Tour Mgt; Tour Mgt; Tour Mark)
Liverpool Hope – 260 pts (Tourism)
Oxford Brookes – BCC (Int Tour Mgt) (IB 29 pts)
Salford – BCC 260 pts (Tour Mgt; Leis Tour Mgt; Hspty Tour Mgt)

	Staffordshire – 260 pts (Tour Mgt)
	Westminster – BCC (Tour Bus; Tour Plan) (IB 26 pts)
240 pts	**Cardiff (UWIC)** – 240 pts (Tour Mgt courses; Int Tour Hspty Mgt)
	Central Lancashire – 240–220 pts (Int Tour Mgt; Tour Mgt)
	Coventry – 240–280 pts (Tour Mgt; Tour Fr/Span; Spo Tour)
	Edinburgh Napier – 240 pts (Tour Mgt; Tour Entre Mgt; Tour Mgt HR Mgt)
	Glamorgan – 240–280 pts (Tour Mgt; Tour Mark)
	Gloucestershire – 240 pts (Tour Mgt)
	Liverpool John Moores – 240–280 pts (Tour Leis Mgt)
	Manchester Met – 240 pts (Tour Mgt; Tour Mgt Evnts; Tour Comb Hons)
	Plymouth – 240–220 pts (Tour Mgt; Cru Mgt; Bus Tour; Int Tour Mgt)
	Sheffield Hallam – 240 pts (Int Bus St Tour; Tour Hspty Bus Mgt)
	Suffolk (Univ Campus) – 240 pts (Tour Mgt)
	Ulster – 240 pts (Int Trav Tour Mgt; Int Trav Tour St Langs)
220 pts	**Bath Spa** – 220–260 pts (Tour Mgt)
	Birmingham (UC) – 220 pts (Tour Bus Mgt; Int Tour Mgt; Advntr Tour Mgt)
	Chichester – CCD 240–260 pts (Tour Mgt courses)
	Edinburgh Napier – 220 pts (Ecotourism)
	Harper Adams (UC) – 220–240 pts (Leis Tour)
	Hertfordshire – 220–280 pts (Tour Joint Hons)
	Leeds Met – 220–200 pts (Lang Tour Mgt; Int Tour Mgt)
	Liverpool John Moores – 220–260 pts (Out Educ Advntr Tour)
	London Met – 220 pts (Int Tour Mgt; Int Tour Mgt Trav Mgt)
	Northampton – 220–260 pts (Tour courses; Herit Mgt; Trav Tour Mgt courses)
	Plymouth – 220 pts (Cru Mgt)
	St Mary's Twickenham (UC) – 220 pts (Tour; Tour Mgt)
	Southampton Solent – 220 pts (Tour Mgt; Cru Ind Mgt; Int Tour Mgt; Out Advntr Mgt)
	Sunderland – 220 pts (Tour Int Hspty Mgt; Tour Comb Hons; Tour Mgt)
200 pts	**Aberystwyth** – 200 pts (Tour Mgt; Tour Mgt Lang) (IB 26 pts)
	Anglia Ruskin – 200 pts (Tour Mgt)
	Canterbury Christ Church – 200 pts (Tour Leis St; Tour Mgt) (IB 24 pts)
	Chester – 200–240 pts (Tour; Tour Mgt) (IB 24–28 pts)
	East London – 200 pts (Int Tour Mgt)
	Greenwich – 200 pts (Tour Mgt; Tour Mgt Comb Hons)
	Huddersfield – 200 pts (Tour Leis Mgt)
	York St John – 200 pts (Tour Mgt; Int Tour Mgt; Tour Mgt Mark)
195 pts	**Queen Margaret** – 195 pts (Hspty Tour Mgt; Tour Mgt)
190 pts	**Aberystwyth** – 190–220 pts (Cntry Recr Tour)
180 pts	**Abertay Dundee** – DDD (Tour Mgt)
	Derby – 180–240 pts (Trav Tour; Advntr Tour courses)
	Hull – 180 pts (Tour Mgt; Int Tour Mgt)
	Thames Valley – 180 pts (Trav Tour Mgt)
	Wolverhampton – 180 pts (Tour Mgt)
160 pts	**Bedfordshire** – 160 pts (Trav Tour; Int Tour Mgt)
	London South Bank – CC 160 pts (Tour Hspty; Mark Trav St courses)
	SAC (Scottish CAg) – CC 160 pts (Fd Tour Mgt; Out Prsts Mgt; Eqn Tour Mgt; Nat Tour Mgt)
	West Scotland – CC (Tourism)
140 pts	**Blackpool and Fylde (Coll)** – 140 pts (Int Rsrt Tour Mgt)
	Trinity Saint David – 140 pts (Tour; Tour Mgt)
120 pts	**Grimsby (IFHE)** – 120–240 pts (Tour Bus Mgt)
	Llandrillo Cymru (Col) – 120 pts (Mgt Trav Tour)
	Swansea Met – 120 pts (Int Trav Tour Mgt; Tour Mgt)
	Bucks New – contact University (Tour 21st Cnty; Int Trav Tour Mgt)

Alternative offers
See **Chapter 7** and **Appendix 1** for grades/UCAS Tariff points information for the International Baccalaureate, Scottish Highers/Advanced Highers, the Welsh Baccalaureate, the Irish Leaving Certificate, the Cambridge Pre-U Diploma, the Advanced Diploma and the Extended Project.

EXAMPLES OF FOUNDATION DEGREES IN THE SUBJECT FIELD

Aberystwyth; Arts London (CComm); Bath Spa; Bicton (Coll); Birmingham (UC); Bishop Grosseteste (UC); Blackpool and Fylde (Coll); Bolton; Bournemouth; Bradford (Coll); Brighton; Bristol City (Coll); Bucks New; Central Lancashire; Chesterfield (Coll); Colchester (Inst); Cornwall (Coll); Craven (Coll); Cumbria; Doncaster (Coll); Duchy (Coll); Ealing, Hammersmith and West London (Coll); Edge Hill; Exeter (Coll); Greenwich; Grimsby (IFHE); Guildford (Coll); Harper Adams (UC); Hereford (CA); Hertfordshire; Hugh Baird (Coll); Hull (Coll); Leeds City (Coll); Liverpool (CmC); Llandrillo Cymru (Coll); London Met; Loughborough (Coll); Manchester (Coll); Mid-Kent (Coll); Myerscough (Coll); Newcastle (Coll); North Hertfordshire (Coll); Northampton; Northampton (Coll); Northbrook (Coll); Norwich City (Coll); Nottingham Castle (Coll); Oaklands (Coll); Pembrokeshire (Coll); Pershore (Coll); Plymouth; Plymouth City (Coll); Preston (Coll); Riverside Halton (Coll); Runshaw (Coll); Somerset (CAT); South Devon (Coll); Southport (Coll); Sunderland; Sunderland City (Coll); Teesside; Trinity Saint David; Tyne Met (Coll); Westminster Kingsway (Coll); Weston (Coll); Writtle (Coll).

CHOOSING YOUR COURSE (SEE ALSO CH.1)

Some course features
Bristol UWE (Tour Env Mgt) Field courses are UK-based in the first year and overseas in the second. Students contribute to the costs of these. There are options to study a European language, and to take a year out on placement.
Plymouth (Cru Mgt) The course focuses on the study of cruise tourism and the management of cruise operations. There is an optional year on a cruise ship.
Southampton Solent Courses are offered in the Outdoor Adventure and Watersports activities.
Thames Valley In addition to airline travel the course includes modules in retail travel, customer relations, human resources management and transport management.

Examples of sandwich degree courses Aberystwyth; Bedfordshire; Birmingham (UC); Bournemouth; Brighton; Bristol UWE; Cardiff (UWIC); Central Lancashire; Coventry; Glamorgan; Gloucestershire; Greenwich; Harper Adams (UC); Hertfordshire; Huddersfield; Leeds Met; Llandrillo Cymru (Col); London Met; London South Bank; Manchester Met; Middlesex; Northumbria; Oxford Brookes; Plymouth; Portsmouth; Sheffield Hallam; Staffordshire; Sunderland; Surrey; Swansea Met; Teesside; Ulster; West Scotland; Wolverhampton; Writtle (Coll).

ADMISSIONS INFORMATION

Number of applicants per place (approx) Aberystwyth 3; Bath Spa 5; Birmingham (UC) 10; Bournemouth 16; Derby 4; Glamorgan 8; Liverpool John Moores 10; Northumbria 6; Sheffield Hallam 12; Sunderland 2.

Advice to applicants and planning the UCAS personal statement Work experience in the travel and tourism industry is important – in agencies, in the airline industry or hotels. This work could be described in detail. Any experience with people in sales work, dealing with the public – their problems and complaints – should also be included. Travel should be outlined, detailing places visited. Genuine interest in travel, diverse cultures and people. Good communication skills required. See also **Appendix 4**.

Misconceptions about this course **Bath Spa** The course is not purely vocational and operational: it also involves management issues. **Wolverhampton** Some applicants are uncertain whether or not to take a Business Management course instead of Tourism Management. They should be aware that the latter will equip them with a tourism-specific knowledge of business.

Selection interviews **Yes** Brighton, Derby, Sunderland; **Some** Abertay Dundee, Anglia Ruskin, Lincoln, Liverpool John Moores, Salford.

Interview advice and questions Past questions have included: What problems have you experienced when travelling? Questions on places visited. Experiences of air, rail and sea travel. What is marketing? What special qualities do you have that will be of use in the travel industry? See **Chapter 5**.

Reasons for rejection (non-academic) **Wolverhampton** English language competence.

AFTER-RESULTS ADVICE

Offers to applicants repeating A-levels **Same** Abertay Dundee, Anglia Ruskin, Birmingham (UC), Chester, Derby, Lincoln, Liverpool John Moores, Manchester Met, Northumbria, St Mary's Twickenham (UC), Salford, Wolverhampton.

GRADUATE DESTINATIONS AND EMPLOYMENT (2007/8 HESA)

Graduates surveyed 1240 **Employed** 850 **In further study** 65 **Assumed unemployed** 25.

Career note See **Business Courses**.

OTHER DEGREE SUBJECTS FOR CONSIDERATION

Airline and Airport Management; Business Studies; Events Management; Heritage Management; Hospitality Management; Leisure and Recreation Management; Travel Management.

TOWN and COUNTRY PLANNING

(including **Environmental Planning** and **Urban Studies**; see also **Development Studies, Environmental Science/Studies, Housing, Property Management/Development** and **Transport Management and Planning**)

Town and Country Planning courses are very similar and some lead to qualification or part of a qualification as a member of the Royal Town Planning Institute (RTPI). Further information from the RTPI (see **Appendix 4**).

Useful websites www.rtpi.org.uk; www.townplanningreview.lupjournals.org.

NB The points totals shown to the left of the institutions are for ease of reference only. It must not be assumed that Tariff points are always used by institutions or that they can be substituted for an offer in grades. The level of an offer is not necessarily indicative of the quality of a course.

COURSE OFFERS INFORMATION

Subject requirements/preferences **GCSE** English and mathematics required. **AL** Geography may be specified.

NB In 2011 universities and colleges will differ in their use of GCE AL/AS unit grade information, A* grades, the Extended Project (EPQ), the Advanced Diploma and the Cambridge Pre-U examination when considering applicants and making offers. An EPQ may be accepted in place of an AS subject. Check websites of universities and colleges for the latest offers information.

Your target offers and examples of courses provided by each institution

340 pts **Heriot-Watt** – AAB 2nd yr entry (Urb Reg Plan) (IB 35 pts)
Reading – 340–370 pts (Rl Est inc Dip Plan Dev; Rl Est; Rur Prop Mgt)

320 pts **Birmingham** – ABB–BBB (Geog Urb Reg Plan Joint Hons; Plan Soc Plcy; Plan Econ) (IB 32–34 pts)
London (UCL) – BBB+AS (Urb St; Urb Plan Des Mgt) (IB 32 pts)
Manchester – ABB (MTCP Twn Cntry Plan) (IB 32 pts)
Sheffield – ABB (Geog Plan) (IB 30–33 pts)

300 pts **Bristol UWE** – 300–360 pts (Archit Plan)
Cardiff – 300–320 pts (Geog (Hum) Plan; Cty Reg Plan) (IB 32 pts)

Dundee – BBB 2nd yr entry (Plan Geog; Plan Transat St; Spat Econ Dev) (IB 34 pts)
Leeds – BBB (Geog Trans Plan)
Liverpool – BBB (MPlan Twn Reg Plan)
London (QM) – 300–340 pts (Cts Econ Soc Chng) (IB 32 pts)
Newcastle – BBB–BCC (Twn Plan; Geog Plan) (IB 28 pts)
Northumbria – 300 pts (Plan Dev Surv)
Queen's Belfast – BBB–BBCb (Env Plan)
Sheffield – BBB (Urb St Plan) (IB 32 pts)
Ulster – 300 pts (Urb Plan Prop Dev)

280 pts **Bristol UWE** – 280–320 pts (Prop Dev Plan; Geog Plan)
Heriot-Watt – BBC 1st yr entry (Urb Reg Plan)
Leeds Met – 280–320 pts (Lnd Plan Des)
Liverpool – BBC (Env Plan; Urb Reg Plan)
Manchester – BBC (Twn Cntry Plan; Cty Reg Dev; Env Mgt) (IB 28 pts)
Oxford Brookes – BBC (Cty Reg Plan) (IB 28 pts)

270 pts **Sheffield Hallam** – 270 pts (Int Rl Est)

260 pts **Oxford Brookes** – BCC (Cts Env Des Dev) (IB 28 pts)
Sheffield Hallam – 260 pts (Geog Plan)

240 pts **Anglia Ruskin** – 240 pts (Env Plan)
Bangor – 240–280 pts (Env Plan Mgt)
Bristol UWE – 240–280 pts (Plan Commun; Twn Cntry Plan) (IB 26–30 pts)
Dundee – CCC 1st yr entry (Twn Reg Plan; Plan Geog; Plan Transat St; Spat Econ Dev) (IB 29 pts)
Leeds Met – 240 pts (Hum Geog Plan)

230 pts **Edinburgh Napier** – 230 pts (Blt Env)
Sheffield Hallam – 230 pts (MPlan Plan; Plan Trans)

220 pts **Birmingham City** – 220 pts (Plan Dev)

160 pts **London South Bank** – 160 pts (Urb Env Plan)

Alternative offers

See **Chapter 7** and **Appendix 1** for grades/UCAS Tariff points information for the International Baccalaureate, Scottish Highers/Advanced Highers, the Welsh Baccalaureate, the Irish Leaving Certificate, the Cambridge Pre-U Diploma, the Advanced Diploma and the Extended Project.

EXAMPLES OF FOUNDATION DEGREES IN THE SUBJECT FIELD

Anglia Ruskin; Birmingham City; Blackburn (Coll Univ Centre); Bradford; Bradford (Coll); Derby; Glyndŵr; Grimsby (IFHE); Middlesex; Northampton; Royal (CAg).

CHOOSING YOUR COURSE (SEE ALSO CH.1)

Some course features

Bristol UWE There is an optional six-month study abroad in a European university and a six-week work placement in the final year.

Cardiff (City Reg Plan) Course is recognised by The Royal Town Planning Institute as a qualification for those entering the profession.

Liverpool The three courses each cover the same curriculum in the first two years with extra modules taken by MPlan students aiming for a career in town planning.

London (UCL) (Urb St; Urb Plan Des Mgt) These degrees share common core courses enabling students to move freely between courses before making their choice of degree in the final year.

Universities and colleges teaching quality See www.qaa.ac.uk; www.unistats.com.

Top research universities and colleges (RAE 2008) Cambridge; Sheffield; Cardiff; Newcastle; Leeds; Reading; Manchester; Aberdeen; Glasgow; London (UCL).

Examples of sandwich degree courses Bristol UWE; Liverpool John Moores; Manchester Met; Newcastle; Ulster.

ADMISSIONS INFORMATION

Number of applicants per place (approx) Birmingham 2; Birmingham City 6; Bristol UWE 6; Cardiff 6; Dundee 5; London (UCL) 6; London South Bank 3; Newcastle 9; Sheffield Hallam 6.

Advice to applicants and planning the UCAS personal statement Visit your local planning office and discuss the career with planners. Know plans and proposed developments in your area and any objections to them. Study the history of town planning worldwide and the development of new towns in the United Kingdom during the 20th century, for example Bournville, Milton Keynes, Port Sunlight, Welwyn Garden City, Cumbernauld, and the advantages and disadvantages which became apparent. See also **Appendix 4**.

Selection interviews **Yes** Bristol UWE, London (UCL), London South Bank, Newcastle; **Some** Abertay Dundee, Anglia Ruskin, Birmingham City, Cardiff, Dundee.

Interview advice and questions Since Town and Country Planning courses are vocational, work experience in a planning office is relevant and questions are likely to be asked on the type of work done and the problems faced by planners. Questions in recent years have included: If you were re-planning your home county for the future, what points would you consider? How are statistics used in urban planning? How do you think the problem of inner cities can be solved? Have you visited your local planning office? See **Chapter 5**.

Reasons for rejection (non-academic) Lack of commitment to study for a professional qualification in Town Planning.

AFTER-RESULTS ADVICE

Offers to applicants repeating A-levels **Higher** Bristol UWE, Newcastle; **Same** Abertay Dundee, Birmingham City, Cardiff, Dundee, London South Bank, Oxford Brookes.

GRADUATE DESTINATIONS AND EMPLOYMENT (2007/8 HESA)

Graduates surveyed 760 **Employed** 365 **In further study** 160 **Assumed unemployed** 75.

Career note Town planning graduates have a choice of career options within local authority planning offices. In addition to working on individual projects on urban development, they will also be involved in advising, co-ordinating and adjudicating in disputes and appeals. Planners also work closely with economists, surveyors and sociologists and their skills open up a wide range of other careers.

OTHER DEGREE SUBJECTS FOR CONSIDERATION

Architecture; Countryside Management; Environmental Studies; Geography; Heritage Management; Housing; Land Economy; Property; Public Administration; Real Estate; Sociology; Surveying; Transport Management.

TRANSPORT MANAGEMENT and PLANNING

(including **Logistics and Supply Chain Management**; see also **Business Courses, Engineering/Engineering Sciences** and **Town and Country Planning**)

Transport Management and Planning is a specialised branch of business studies with many applications on land, sea and air. It is not as popular as the less specialised Business Studies courses but is just as relevant and will provide the student with an excellent introduction to management and its problems.

Useful websites www.cilt-international.com; www.transportweb.com; www.nats.co.uk; www.ciltuk.org.uk.

NB The points totals shown to the left of the institutions are for ease of reference only. It must not be assumed that Tariff points are always used by institutions or that they can be substituted for an offer in grades. The level of an offer is not necessarily indicative of the quality of a course.

COURSE OFFERS INFORMATION

Subject requirements/preferences **GCSE** English and mathematics required. Birmingham Mathematics grade B. **AL** No subjects specified.

NB In 2011 universities and colleges will differ in their use of GCE AL/AS unit grade information, A* grades, the Extended Project (EPQ), the Advanced Diploma and the Cambridge Pre-U examination when considering applicants and making offers. An EPQ may be accepted in place of an AS subject. Check websites of universities and colleges for the latest offers information.

Your target offers and examples of courses provided by each institution

340 pts **Cardiff** – AAB (Bus Mgt (Log Ops))
Leeds – AAB (Econ Trans St; Mgt Trans St) (IB 35 pts)
300 pts **Aston** – BBB 300 pts (Trans Mgt; Log) (IB 32 pts)
Edinburgh – 300 pts (Civ Trans Eng)
Leeds – BBB (Geog Trans Plan) (IB 32 pts)
280 pts **Loughborough** – 280 pts (Trans Bus Mgt; Air Trans Mgt) (IB 30 pts)
Northumbria – 280 pts+portfolio (Trans Des)
Northumbria – 280 pts (Bus Log Sply Chn Mgt)
260 pts **Bolton** – 260 pts (Bus Mgt (Sply Chn Mgt))
City – BCC 260–240 pts (Air Trans Ops ATPL) (IB 28 pts) See **Advice to applicants and planning the UCAS personal statement** below
Huddersfield – 260 pts (Trans Des)
Hull – 260 pts (Log; Acc Log; Mark Log; Bus Log)
240 pts **Bucks New** – 240–280 pts (Air Trans Plt Trg)
City – 240 pts (Air Trans Ops Mgt) (IB 26 pts)
Coventry – 240 pts (Auto Trans Des (Bike) (Boat) (Veh) (Trans))
Edinburgh Napier – 240 pts (Civ Trans Eng)
Liverpool John Moores – 240 pts (Mgt Trans Log)
Manchester Met – 240 pts (Log Comb Hons)
230 pts **Sheffield Hallam** – 230 pts (Plan Trans courses)
220 pts **Plymouth** – 220 pts (Cru Mgt)
Southampton Solent – 220 pts (Cru Ind Mgt)
Ulster – 220 pts inc CC (Trans courses)
200 pts **Coventry** – 200 pts (Log Bus Mgt)
Huddersfield – 200–280 pts (Trans Log Mgt; Air Trans Log Mgt; Log Sply Chn Mgt; Euro Log Mgt)
Plymouth – 200 pts (Mar St (Navig) (Ocn Ychtg) (Mrchnt Ship))
190 pts **Writtle (Coll)** – 190–240 pts (Bus Mgt (Mark Sply Chn Mgt))
180 pts **Greenwich** – 180–220 pts (Bus Log Trans Mgt; Bus Prchsg Sply Chn Mgt)
120 pts **Swansea Met** – 120–160 pts (Trans Mgt; Log Sply Chn Mgt)

Bucks New – contact University (Airln Airpt Mgt)
Staffordshire – contact University (Trans Des)

Alternative offers
See **Chapter 7** and **Appendix 1** for grades/UCAS Tariff points information for the International Baccalaureate, Scottish Highers/Advanced Highers, the Welsh Baccalaureate, the Irish Leaving Certificate, the Cambridge Pre-U Diploma, the Advanced Diploma and the Extended Project.

EXAMPLES OF FOUNDATION DEGREES IN THE SUBJECT FIELD

Derby; Greenwich; London South Bank; Suffolk (Univ Campus); Teesside.

CHOOSING YOUR COURSE (SEE ALSO CH.1)

Some course features
Aston (Log Mgt) This is a business course focusing on the supply chain and distribution industry. There is a four-year course involving paid professional experience.
Bucks New (Air Trans Plt Trg) Students on this course will only be finally accepted on to the Commercial pilot training route at the end of a successful first year and with a Class 1 medical certificate. There is also an Airline and Airport Management course.
Liverpool John Moores (Mgt Trans Log) The course is accredited by the Chartered Institute of Logistics and Transport; there is an option for a placement/sandwich year in industry.
Loughborough (Trans Bus Mgt; Air Trans Mgt) Courses include a year in industry. French, German and Spanish modules can be selected.

Examples of sandwich degree courses Aston; Bristol UWE; City; Huddersfield; Liverpool John Moores; Loughborough; Plymouth; Sheffield Hallam; Staffordshire.

ADMISSIONS INFORMATION

Number of applicants per place (approx) Aston 5; Coventry 5; Huddersfield 5; Loughborough 11.

Advice to applicants and planning the UCAS personal statement Air, sea, road and rail transport are the main specialist areas. Contacts with those involved and work experience or work shadowing should be described in full. **City** (Air Trans Ops ATPL) Applicants need a Class 1 Medical Certificate from the UK Civil Aviation Authority and preferably to have taken a pilot aptitude test before starting the course. Check with admissions. See also **Appendix 4**.

Selection interviews **Yes** Huddersfield, Loughborough; **Some** Aston, Bucks New.

Interview advice and questions Some knowledge of the transport industry (land, sea and air) is likely to be important at interview. Reading around the subject is also important, as are any contacts with management staff in the industries. Past questions have included: What developments are taking place to reduce the number of cars on the roads? What transport problems are there in your own locality? How did you travel to your interview? What problems did you encounter? How could they have been overcome? See **Chapter 5**.

AFTER-RESULTS ADVICE

Offers to applicants repeating A-levels **Same** Aston.

GRADUATE DESTINATIONS AND EMPLOYMENT (2007/8 HESA)

No data available.

Career note Many graduates will aim for openings linked with specialisms in their degree courses. These could cover air, rail, sea, bus or freight transport in which they will be involved in the management and control of operations as well as marketing and financial operations.

OTHER DEGREE SUBJECTS FOR CONSIDERATION

Air Transport Engineering; Civil Engineering; Environmental Studies; Logistics; Marine Transport; Town and Country Planning; Urban Studies.

VETERINARY SCIENCE/MEDICINE

(including **Bioveterinary Sciences** and **Veterinary Nursing**)

Veterinary Medicine/Science degrees enable students to acquire the professional skills and experience to qualify as veterinary surgeons. Courses follow the same pattern and combine a rigorous scientific training with practical experience. The demand for these courses is considerable (see below) and work experience is essential prior to application. Graduate entry programmes provide a route to qualifying as a vet to graduates with good degrees in specified subjects. See also **Appendix 4**. Veterinary Nursing honours degree courses combine both the academic learning and the nursing training required by the Royal College of Veterinary Surgeons, and can also include practice management. Foundation degrees in Veterinary Nursing are more widely available. Bioveterinary Sciences are usually three-year full-time BSc degree courses focusing on animal biology, management and disease but do not qualify graduates to work as vets.

Useful websites www.rcvs.org.uk; www.admissionstests.cambridgeassessment.org.uk; www.bvna.org.uk; www.spvs.org.uk.

NB The points totals shown to the left of the institutions are for ease of reference only. It must not be assumed that Tariff points are always used by institutions or that they can be substituted for an offer in grades. The level of an offer is not necessarily indicative of the quality of a course.

COURSE OFFERS INFORMATION

Subject requirements/preferences **GCSE** (Vet Sci/Med) Grade B English, mathematics, physics, dual science if not at A-level. **Bristol**, **Glasgow** Grade A or B in physics. **Bristol** Grade A in five or six subjects. **Liverpool** English, mathematics, physics, dual science grade B if not at A-level. (Vet Nurs) Five subjects including English and two science. **AL** (Vet Sci/Med) See offers below. (Vet Nurs) Biology and another science may be required. **Other** Work experience essential for Vet Sci/Med and Vet Nurs courses and preferred for other courses: check requirements. Health checks may be required.

NB In 2011 universities and colleges will differ in their use of GCE AL/AS unit grade information, A* grades, the Extended Project (EPQ), the Advanced Diploma and the Cambridge Pre-U examination when considering applicants and making offers. An EPQ may be accepted in place of an AS subject. Check websites of universities and colleges for the latest offers information.

For places in Veterinary Science/Medicine, applicants may select only **four** universities. Applicants to the University of Cambridge Veterinary School and the Royal Veterinary College, University of London are required to sit the BioMedical Admissions Test (BMAT) (see **Chapter 5**).

Your target offers and examples of courses provided by each institution

390 pts **Liverpool** – AABb (inc biol+chem) (Vet Sci) (IB 36 pts HL 666)

380 pts **Cambridge** – A*AA +BMAT college offers vary (inc AL in 3 sci subjs pref/AL in 2 sci accepted) (Vet Med) (IB 38–42 pts)

360 pts **London (RVC)** – AAA +BMAT (inc AL chem+biol +1 other) (Vet Med)

340 pts **Bristol** – AAB (inc chem+biol) (Vet Sci; Vet Sci+Pre-Vet Yr) (IB 35 pts HL 766)

Edinburgh – AAB (inc chem+biol +maths/phys) (Vet Med) (IB 36 pts)

Glasgow – AAB (inc A chem+biol+phys/maths AB/BA) (Vet Med) (IB 36 pts)

Nottingham – AAB (inc chem+biol) (Vet Med)

Nottingham – AAB (inc biol/chem) (Vet Med+Prelim Yr) (IB 38 pts HL 76)

320 pts **Bristol** – ABB (Anat Sci Vet Anat) (IB 33 pts)

Surrey – ABB–BBB 320–300 pts (inc 2 sci, pref biol+chem) (Vet Biosci) (IB 34–32 pts) check with University

300 pts **Glasgow** – BBB (inc chem+biol+maths/phys) (Vet Biosci) (IB 30 pts)

Harper Adams (UC) – BBB (Biovet Sci)

Liverpool – BBB (inc biol+sci) (Biovet Sci) (IB 32 pts)

London (RVC) – BBB (inc chem+maths/phys/biol +1 other) (BSc Biovet Sci 3yrs; BMAT reqd for Merit Scholarship)

280 pts **Bristol** – BBC (inc BB biol+chem) (Vet Nurs Biovet Sci) (IB 30 pts)
Lincoln – 280 pts (inc biol) (Biovet Sci)
260 pts **Harper Adams (UC)** – 260 pts (Vet Nurs Prac Mgt)
240 pts **Lincoln** – CCC (1 Yr Cert Vet Med Sci for entry to Yr 1 Vet Med course at Nottingham Univ)
London (RVC) – CCC (inc chem+biol) (1 yr Vet Gateway prog)
200 pts **Bristol UWE** – 200–240 pts (inc biol) (Biovet Sci; Eqn Dntl Sci) (IB 24 pts)
180 pts **Bristol UWE** – 180–200 pts (inc biol) (Vet Nurs Sci) (IB 26 pts)
160 pts **London (RVC)** – CC–AA (inc 2 sci pref biol) (Vet Nurs)
Warwickshire (Coll) – 160 pts (Vet Nurs Bus Mgt; Anim Welf)

Edinburgh Napier – 2AL offers vary (Vet Nurs)
Middlesex – 2AL offers vary check with University (Vet Nurs)

ALTERNATIVE OFFERS

See **Chapter 7** and **Appendix 1** for grades/UCAS Tariff points information for the International Baccalaureate, Scottish Highers/Advanced Highers, the Welsh Baccalaureate, the Irish Leaving Certificate, the Cambridge Pre-U Diploma, the Advanced Diploma and the Extended Project.

EXAMPLES OF FOUNDATION DEGREES IN THE SUBJECT FIELD

Askham Bryan (Coll); Bicton (Coll); Brighton; Bristol UWE (Fdn Sci 100–140 pts); Duchy (Coll); Greenwich; Hadlow (Coll); Harper Adams (UC); London (RVC); Myerscough (Coll); Northampton; Nottingham Trent; Reaseheath (Coll); Sparsholt (Coll); Warwickshire (Coll); Worcester.

CHOOSING YOUR COURSE (SEE ALSO CH.1)

Author's note Veterinary Science/Medicine is the most intensely competitive subject and, as in the case of Medicine, one or two offers and three rejections are not uncommon. As a result, the Royal College of Veterinary Surgeons has raised a number of points which are relevant to applicants and advisers:

* Every candidate for a Veterinary Medicine/Sciences degree course should be advised to spend a suitable period with a veterinarian in practice.
* A period spent in veterinary work may reveal a hitherto unsuspected allergy or sensitivity following contact with various animals.
* Potential applicants should be under no illusions about the difficulty of the task they have set themselves . . . at least five applicants for every available place . . . with no likelihood of places being increased at the present time.
* There are so many candidates who can produce the necessary level of scholastic attainment that other considerations have to be taken into account in making the choice. In most cases, the number of GCSE grade As will be crucial. This is current practice. Headteachers' reports and details of applicants' interests, activities and background are very relevant and are taken fully into consideration . . . applicants are reminded to include details of periods of time spent with veterinary surgeons.
* Any applicant who has not received an offer but who achieves the grades required for admission ought to get in touch as soon as the results are known to the schools and enquire about the prospects of entry at the Clearing stage. All courses cover the same subject topics.

Some course features

Edinburgh Veterinary Medicine programmes are also accredited by the American Veterinary Medical Association so graduates can practise as vets in North America.
London (RVC) (Vet Gateway) Course guarantees a place on the five-year Veterinary Medicine programme. Applicants require chemistry and biology and any other subject at A-level (except general studies) and there are other conditions for eligibility (see www.rvc.ac.uk). (BSc Biovet Sci 3 yr) Course does not qualify graduates to practise as veterinary surgeons. There is also a six-year Veterinary Medicine Combined course.

Nottingham The course which involves the Preliminary Year is for students without the required science qualifications but who have high academic achievement in non-science or vocational subjects. Successful completion of the course enables direct entry into Year 1 of the five-year course.

Universities and colleges teaching quality See www.qaa.ac.uk; www.unistats.com.

Top research universities and colleges (RAE 2008) See **Agricultural Sciences/Agriculture**.

Examples of sandwich degree courses Bristol UWE (Vet Nurs); Harper Adams (UC) (Vet Nurs).

ADMISSIONS INFORMATION

Number of applicants per place (approx) Bristol (Vet Sci) 16, (Vet Nurs Biovet Sci) 4; Cambridge 5; Edinburgh 17; Glasgow 20; Liverpool 12; London (RVC) 5; Nottingham 11.

Numbers of applicants (**a** UK **b** EU (non-UK) **c** non-EU **d** mature) **London (RVC)** **a**759 **b**71 **c**156 **d**172.

Advice to applicants and planning the UCAS personal statement Applicants for Veterinary Science must limit their choices to four universities and submit their applications by 15 October. They may add up to two alternative courses. Work experience is almost always essential so discuss this in full, giving information about the size and type of practice and the type of work in which you were involved. **Bristol** Evidence is needed of wide veterinary animal experience, together with evidence of initiative. **Edinburgh** Competition for places is intense: 72 places are available and only one in seven applicants will receive an offer. The strongest candidates are interviewed and are normally required to take with them an additional reference outlining recent work experience. **Liverpool** The selection process involves three areas: academic ability to cope with the course; knowledge of vocational aspects of veterinary science acquired through work experience in veterinary practice and working with animals; personal attributes that demonstrate responsibility and self-motivation. **London (RVC)** Six weeks' hands-on experience needed: two weeks in a veterinary practice; two weeks with large domestic animals; two weeks with other animals, for example riding school, zoo, kennels. See also **Appendix 4**.

Misconceptions about this course **Bristol UWE** (Vet Nurs Sci) Students think that the degree qualifies them as veterinary nurses but in fact RCVS assessment/training is additional. **Liverpool** (Biovet Sci) Some applicants think that the course allows students to transfer to Veterinary Science: it does not.

Selection interviews All institutions; (Vet Sci and Vet Nurs) **Some** Bristol.

Interview advice and questions Past questions have included: Why do you want to be a vet? Have you visited a veterinary practice? What did you see? Do you think there should be a Vet National Health Service? What are your views on vivisection? What are your views on intensive factory farming? How can you justify thousands of pounds of taxpayers' money being spent on training you to be a vet when it could be used to train a civil engineer? When would you feel it your responsibility to tell battery hen farmers that they were being cruel to their livestock? What are your views on vegetarians? How does aspirin stop pain? Why does it only work for a certain length of time? Do you eat beef? Outline the bovine TB problem. Questions on A-level science syllabus. **Glasgow** Applicants complete a questionnaire prior to interview. Questions cover experience with animals, reasons for choice of career, animal welfare, teamwork, work experience, stressful situations. See **Chapter 5**.

Reasons for rejection (non-academic) Failure to demonstrate motivation. Lack of basic knowledge or understanding of ethical and animal issues.

AFTER-RESULTS ADVICE

Offers to applicants repeating A-levels **Higher** London (RVC); **Same** Bristol UWE (Vet Nurs Sci), Liverpool (candidates achieving the necessary grades are welcome to reapply); **Not acceptable** Edinburgh, Glasgow; **No offers made** Cambridge.

GRADUATE DESTINATIONS AND EMPLOYMENT (2007/8 HESA)

Graduates surveyed 425 **Employed** 345 **In further study** 15 **Assumed unemployed** 20.

Career note Over 80% of veterinary surgeons work in private practice with the remainder involved in research in universities, government-financed research departments and in firms linked with farming, foodstuff manufacturers and pharmaceutical companies.

OTHER DEGREE SUBJECTS FOR CONSIDERATION

Agricultural Science; Agriculture; Animal Sciences; Biological Sciences; Biology; Dentistry; Equine Dental Science; Equine Management; Equine Studies; Medicine; Zoology.

ZOOLOGY

(including **Animal Biology**; see also **Agricultural Sciences/Agriculture, Animal Sciences** and **Biology**)

Zoology courses have a biological science foundation and could cover animal ecology, marine and fisheries biology, animal population, development and behaviour and, on some courses, wildlife management and fisheries.

Useful websites www.scienceyear.com; www.zsl.org/ioz; www.zsl.org; www.academicinfo.net/zoo.html.

NB The points totals shown to the left of the institutions are for ease of reference only. It must not be assumed that Tariff points are always used by institutions or that they can be substituted for an offer in grades. The level of an offer is not necessarily indicative of the quality of a course.

COURSE OFFERS INFORMATION

Subject requirements/preferences **GCSE** English and science/mathematics required or preferred. **AL** One or two sciences will be required.

NB In 2011 universities and colleges will differ in their use of GCE AL/AS unit grade information, A* grades, the Extended Project (EPQ), the Advanced Diploma and the Cambridge Pre-U examination when considering applicants and making offers. An EPQ may be accepted in place of an AS subject. Check websites of universities and colleges for the latest offers information.

Your target offers and examples of courses provided by each institution

380 pts **Cambridge** – A*AA college offers may vary (Nat Sci (Zool)) (IB 38–42 pts)
360 pts **Bristol** – AAA–ABB (Zoology) (IB 34 pts HL 666)
Edinburgh – AAA 2nd yr entry (Zoology) (IB 36 pts)
London (UCL) – AABe–ABBe (Biol Sci (Zool)) (IB 34–36 pts)
340 pts **Birmingham** – AAB–BBB (Biol Sci (Zool)) (IB 32–34 pts)
Bristol – AAB–BBB (Psy Zool) (IB 33 pts HL 665)
Cardiff – AAB–ABB 340–320 pts (Zoology) (IB 34 pts HL biol chem 5)
Imperial London – AAB 340 pts (Zoology) (IB 36 pts HL 66)
Manchester – AAB–BBB (Zool; Zool Ind; Zool Modn Lang) (IB 35–32 pts)
St Andrews – AAB (Zoology) (IB 32 pts)
Sheffield – AAB (MBiol Sci Zool) (IB 35 pts)
320 pts **Durham** – ABB (Zool; Zool Ind) (IB 34 pts H55)
Exeter (Cornwall) – ABB–BBB (Zool courses) (IB 34 pts)
Glasgow – ABB (Zool; App Maths Zool) (IB 32 pts)
Leeds – ABB–BBB (Zoology) (IB 34–32 pts HL 16–15 pts)
Leicester – ABB (Biol Sci (Zool)) (IB 32 pts)
Liverpool – ABB–BBB (Zoology) (IB 33–30 pts)
Nottingham – ABB–BBB (MSci/BSc Zoology) (IB 32–34 pts)

	Reading – 320 pts (Zoology)
	Sheffield – ABB (BSc Zoology) (IB 33 pts)
300 pts	**Aberdeen** – BBB 2nd yr entry (Zoology)
	Dundee – BBB 2nd yr entry (Zoology) (IB 34 pts)
	Edinburgh – BBB 1st yr entry (Zoology) (IB 30 pts)
	London (QM) – BBB (Zool; Zool Aqua Biol) (IB 30 pts)
	Newcastle – BBB (Zool; Mar Zool) (IB 32 pts HL biol 6)
	Southampton – BBB (3 sci) ABB (2 sci) (Zoology) (IB 32 pts HL 15 pts)
	Stirling – BBB 2nd yr entry (Anim Biol; Aqua)
280 pts	**Bangor** – 280–340 pts (MZool Zoology)
	Gloucestershire – 280 pts (Anim Biol)
	Queen's Belfast – BBC–BCCb (Zoology) (IB 28 pts HL 555)
	Swansea – 280–300 pts (Zoology)
260 pts	**Hull** – 260–300 pts (Aqua Zool; Zool)
	Staffordshire – 260 pts (Anim Biol Cons)
240 pts	**Aberdeen** – CCC 1st yr entry (Zoology) (IB 28 pts)
	Aberystwyth – 240–280 pts (Zool; Zool Microbiol)
	Bangor – 240–280 pts (Zool; Zool Cons; Zool Mar Zool; Zool Anim Ecol; Zool Anim Bhv) (IB 28 pts)
	Bolton – 240 pts (Biol (Anim Biol))
	Cumbria – 240 pts (Wldlf Media)
	Dundee – CCC 1st yr entry (Zoology) (IB 28 pts)
	Manchester Met – 240 pts (Wldlf Biol)
	Roehampton – 240–300 pts (Zoology)
220 pts	**Edinburgh Napier** – CCD 220 pts (Anim Biol)
	Liverpool John Moores – 220–260 pts (Zoology)
	Nottingham Trent – 220 pts (Zoo Biol)
	Stirling – CCD 1st yr entry (Anim Biol; Aqua)
200 pts	**Anglia Ruskin** – 200 pts (Zool; Wldlf Biol; Mar Biol Nat Hist) (IB 24 pts)
	Derby – 200–220 pts (Zool courses)
	Salford – 200 pts (Zool; Wldlf Cons Zoo Biol)
180 pts	**Hull** – 180–40 pts (Zool inc Fdn Yr)
160 pts	**Blackpool and Fylde (Coll)** – 160 pts (Wldlf Photo)
140 pts	**West Scotland** – CD (App Biosci Zool)
	Liverpool John Moores – contact University (Nat Sci Fdn)

Alternative offers

See **Chapter 7** and **Appendix 1** for grades/UCAS Tariff points information for the International Baccalaureate, Scottish Highers/Advanced Highers, the Welsh Baccalaureate, the Irish Leaving Certificate, the Cambridge Pre-U Diploma, the Advanced Diploma and the Extended Project.

EXAMPLES OF FOUNDATION DEGREES IN THE SUBJECT FIELD

Cornwall (Coll); Sparsholt (Coll); see also **Animal Sciences**.

CHOOSING YOUR COURSE (SEE ALSO CH.1)

Some course features

Anglia Ruskin (Zool) Study in the USA is an option for one semester.
Durham All Biological Sciences degrees have a common first year, with transfers possible to other degrees or to Natural Sciences in the second year. The four-year Zoology degree includes an industrial placement.
Hull (Aqua Zool) Course focuses on the interface between land and water and expands on the animal biology aspects of marine and freshwater biology.
Stirling (Aqua) An exchange programme with universities in Sweden is part of the course.

Universities and colleges teaching quality See www.qaa.ac.uk; www.unistats.com.

Top research universities and colleges (RAE 2008) See **Biological Sciences**.

Examples of sandwich degree courses Cardiff; Durham; Exeter; Manchester; West Scotland.

ADMISSIONS INFORMATION

Number of applicants per place (approx) Aberystwyth 8; Bangor 3; Bristol 13; Cardiff 8; Durham 11; Leeds 7; Liverpool John Moores 6; London (RH) 6, (UCL) 8; Newcastle 15; Nottingham 6; Swansea 6.

Advice to applicants and planning the UCAS personal statement Interests in animals should be described, together with any first-hand experience gained. Visits to zoos, farms, fish farms etc and field courses attended should be described, together with any special points of interest that you noted.

Selection interviews **Yes** Cambridge, Durham, Hull, Liverpool, London (RH), Newcastle; **Some** Cardiff, Derby, Dundee, Roehampton, Swansea.

Interview questions Past questions have included: Why do you want to study Zoology? What career do you hope to follow on graduation? Specimens may be given to identify. Questions usually asked on the A-level subjects. See **Chapter 5**.

AFTER-RESULTS ADVICE

Offers to applicants repeating A-levels **Higher** Bristol, Hull, Leeds, Swansea; **Same** Aberystwyth, Bangor, Cardiff, Derby, Dundee, Durham, Liverpool, Liverpool John Moores, London (RH), Roehampton, Swansea; **No offers made** Cambridge.

GRADUATE DESTINATIONS AND EMPLOYMENT (2007/8 HESA)

Graduates surveyed 665 **Employed** 270 **In further study** 125 **Assumed unemployed** 75.

Career note See **Biology**.

OTHER DEGREE SUBJECTS FOR CONSIDERATION

Animal Ecology; Animal Sciences; Aquaculture; Biological Sciences; Biology; Ecology; Fisheries Management; Marine Biology; Parasitology; Veterinary Science; Wildlife Management.

9 | INFORMATION FOR INTERNATIONAL STUDENTS

The choice of a subject to study (from over 50,000 degree courses) and of a university or college (from more than 300 institutions) is a major task for students living in the United Kingdom (UK). For overseas and European Union (EU) applicants it is even greater, and the decisions that have to be made need much careful planning, preferably beginning two years before the start of the course. **NB** Beware that there are some private institutions offering bogus degrees: check www.ucas.com for your university and college choices.

APPLICATIONS AND THE POINTS-BASED IMMIGRATION SYSTEM

In addition to submitting your application through UCAS (see **Chapter 6**) a new Points-based Immigration System is now in operation for overseas students. The main features of this system include:

- **Visa letters** Students will require a special 'visa letter' from their universities before being admitted. This will be sent to you by the university in time for you to apply for your visa.
- **Maintenance** Students will need to show that they are able to pay for the first year's tuition fees, plus £600 per month for accommodation and living expenses. Additional funds and regulations apply for those bringing dependants into the UK.
- **Proof of qualifications** Your visa letter will list all the qualifications that you submitted to obtain your university place and original proof will be required for these qualifications when submitting your visa application. These documents will be checked by the Home Office. Any fraudulent documents will result in your visa application being rejected and a possible ban from entering the UK for 10 years.
- **Attendance** Once you have started your course, your attendance will be monitored. Non-attending students will be reported to the UK Border Agency.

Full details can be obtained from www.ukcisa.ork.uk/student/pbs_students.php.

SELECTION, ADMISSION AND FINANCE

The first reason for making early contact with your preferred institution is to check their requirements for your chosen subject and their selection policies for overseas applicants. For example, for all Art and some Architecture courses you will have to present a portfolio of work or slides. For Music courses your application often will have to be accompanied by a recording you have made of your playing or singing and, in many cases, a personal audition will be necessary. Attendance at an interview in this country is compulsory for some universities and for some courses. At other institutions the interview may take place either in the UK or with a university or college representative in your own country.

The ability to speak and write good English is essential and many institutions require evidence of competence, for example scores from the International English Language Testing System (IELTS) or from the Test of English as a Foreign Language (TOEFL) (see www.ielts.org and www.ets.org/toefl). For some institutions you may have to send examples of your written work. Each institution provides information about its English language entry requirements and a summary of this is given for each university listed below. International students should note that the recommended threshold for minimum English language requirements is IELTS 6.5–7.0. Recent research indicates that students with a lower score may have difficulty in dealing with their course.

At the end of this book you will find a directory of universities and colleges in the UK, together with their contact details. Most universities and colleges in the UK have an overseas student adviser who can advise you on these and other points you need to consider, such as passports, visas, entry certificates, evidence of financial support, medical certificates, medical insurance, and the numbers of overseas students in the university from your own country. All these details are very important and need to be considered at the same time as choosing your course and institution.

The subject tables in **Chapter 8** provide a comprehensive picture of courses on offer and of comparative entry levels. However, before making an application, other factors should be considered such as English language entry requirements (see above), the availability of English language teaching, living costs, tuition fees and any scholarships or other awards which might be offered. Detailed information about these can be obtained from the international offices in each university or college, from British higher education fairs throughout the world and from the British Council offices abroad and from websites: see www.britishcouncil.org; www.education.org.

Below is a brief summary of the arrangements made by each university in the UK for students aiming to take a full-time degree programme. The information is presented as follows:

- Institution.
- International student numbers.
- English language entry requirements for degree programmes shown in either IELTS or TOEFL scores. These vary between universities and courses. For the IELTS, scores can range from 5.5 to 7.5, and for the TOEFL computer-based test, scores can range from a minimum of 213; for the written TOEFL the usual minimum entry level is 5.0. For full details contact the university or college.
- Arrangements for English tuition.
- International Foundation courses.
- Annual tuition fees (approximate) for full-time undergraduate degree courses. Tuition fees also usually include fees for examinations and graduation. These figures are approximate and are subject to change each year. EU students pay 'home student' fees, except for those from the Channel Islands and the Isle of Man; students from the British Overseas Territories are now treated as home students for fee purposes at universities and other institutions of higher education.
- Annual living costs. These are also approximate and represent the costs for a single student over the year. The living costs shown cover university accommodation (usually guaranteed for the first year only), food, books, clothing and travel in the UK, but not travel to or from the UK. (Costs are likely to rise year by year in line with the rate of inflation in the UK, currently around 3% per year.) Overseas students are normally permitted to take part-time work for a period of up to 20 hours per week.
- Scholarships and awards for non-EU students (most universities offer awards for EU students).

UNIVERSITY INFORMATION AND FEES FOR INTERNATIONAL STUDENTS

Aberdeen International students 14%, 115 nationalities; *English language entry requirement (or equivalent):* IELTS 6.0; for Medicine 7.0. Four-week English course available in August before the start of the academic year. *Fees:* Arts subjects £9250, Science subjects £11,500, Medicine £22,500. *Living costs:* £5000–£6000. Some scholarships and grants.

Abertay Dundee International students 10%; *English language entry requirement (or equivalent):* IELTS 5.5. Pre-sessional English course available, also full-time English course September to May and free English tuition throughout degree course. *Fees:* all courses £8150. *Living costs:* £5000–£6000. Several scholarships available, including special awards for students from India and from some countries in the Far East and the USA.

Aberystwyth A large number of international students. *English language entry requirement (or equivalent):* IELTS 6.5. Full-time tuition in English available. *Fees:* Arts subjects £8500, Science subjects £10,750, joint courses £9500. *Living costs:* £5000–£6000. Awards for students from the Far East.

Anglia Ruskin International students 21%. *English language entry requirement (or equivalent):* IELTS 5.5. A one-year International Foundation programme available. *Fees:* Arts subjects £9300, Science subjects £10,300. *Living costs:* £7000–£7500.

Arts London A large number of international students. *English language entry requirement (or equivalent):* IELTS 6.5. Courses in Fashion Promotion, Acting, Directing require IELTS 7.5. Language Centre courses in academic English for 12, 24, 34 or 36 weeks. *Fees:* degree courses £11,900. *Living costs:* £9500–£10,500.

Aston Over 1000 students from over 80 countries, with 15% of the total student population from overseas. International Orientation programme at the beginning of the academic year. *English language entry requirement (or equivalent):* IELTS 6.0–6.5. International Foundation programme offered as a bridge to the degree courses. Pre-sessional English classes also available of five and 10 weeks duration. *Fees:* non-Science programmes £10,500, Engineering and Science courses £12,200. *Living costs:* £6000–£7000. Scholarships offered, including bursaries for Engineering and Science subjects.

Bangor Ten per cent of the student population is made up of international students from 70 countries. Lower cost of living than many other UK cities. *English language entry requirement (or equivalent):* IELTS 6.0. Pre-study English course starting September, January or April depending on level of English proficiency, leads to International Foundation course. One-month or two-month courses before starting degree course also offered. *Fees:* £8800. *Living costs:* £5700. Scholarships available.

Bath Over 1500 international students from around 100 countries. *English language entry requirement (or equivalent):* IELTS 6.0. Pre-degree language courses offered, ranging from one month to one year. *Fees:* Arts and Social Science subjects £10,600, Science and Engineering courses £13,700. *Living costs:* £7500–£8000. Scholarships and awards available, including residential awards for applicants from the Far East and Kenya.

Bath Spa Students from 40 countries. *English language entry requirement (or equivalent):* IELTS 5.5 for subjects supported by the Undergraduate Course for International Students (UCIS). Foundation courses available for students below this score. Subjects not supported by UCIS, entry level IELTS 6.0. *Fees:* £9000–£9600 (plus studio fees £200–£300 for Art and Design courses). *Living costs:* £7000–£8000.

Bedfordshire Over 3000 EU and international students. *English language entry requirement (or equivalent):* IELTS 6.0. General English programmes are offered, including a summer school. *Fees:* £8500. *Living costs:* £6000–£7000.

Birmingham Over 4000 international students from 152 countries. *English language entry requirement (or equivalent):* IELTS 6.0. Six, 10 and 20-week English language programmes available, depending on language proficiency, ranging from IELTS 4.5 to 5.5. *Fees:* non-laboratory subjects £10,000, laboratory subjects £12,800, clinical programmes £22,350. *Living costs:* £8000–£9000. International Foundation programme available. Awards are offered by some subject departments including Bioscience, Computer Science, Earth Sciences, Law, Psychology; there are also Engineering scholarships for students from Malaysia.

Birmingham City Large number of international students. *English language entry requirement (or equivalent):* IELTS 6.0. Pre-sessional language courses and in-session language support. Orientation programme for all students. *Fees:* £9000, Conservatoire/Acting courses £12,500-£13,000. *Living costs:* £6000–£7000. Music bursaries.

Bolton Over 500 students from 60 countries represented. *English language entry requirement (or equivalent):* IELTS 6.0. Courses start in September, some in January. Pre-sessional and in-session English tuition plus Access and Foundation programmes available in Business Management and Engineering. *Fees:* £8000 with up to £250 discount for prompt payment. *Living costs:* £7000.

Bournemouth A large number of international students. *English language entry requirement (or equivalent):* IELTS 6.0. Preparatory English programme offered, starting in January, April or July depending on applicant's level of English (entry IELTS 4.5/5.0/5.5). Several language schools in the town (see www.englishuk.com.uk or www.baselt.org.uk). Pre-sessional study skills programme also offered. *Fees:* £8000–£10,000. *Living costs:* £7500–£8500. Some subject awards available.

Bradford Over 100 countries represented (22%). *English language entry requirement (or equivalent):* IELTS 6.0. Some students may be admitted to Year 2, depending on qualifications. *Fees:* Science and Engineering courses £11,000, other courses £8500 (lower fees for students taking a sandwich year). *Living costs:* £6000–£8500. Ten scholarships to cover the duration of the course.

Brighton Some 2000 international students from over 100 countries. *English language entry requirement (or equivalent):* IELTS 6.0 (or 5.5 for less linguistically demanding subjects). New four-year degree programme (UK4) includes preparatory year. *Fees:* £10,900–£11,500. Fixed fees possible. *Living costs:* £7000–£8000. Links with other nationals at Brighton. Merit scholarships for students from some countries in the Far East, Africa and Norway.

Bristol Approximately 1100 students from over 100 countries. *English language entry requirement (or equivalent):* IELTS 6.5 (possibly lower for some Science and Engineering subjects). *Fees:* Arts subjects £11,600, Science subjects £14,900, Clinical subjects £25,500. *Living costs:* £6500–£9000. Some bursaries and scholarships for one year from some subject departments including Law, Medicine, Dentistry and Veterinary Science.

Bristol UWE More than 1750 international students. *English language entry requirement (or equivalent):* IELTS 6.0. English language preparatory and pre-sessional courses offered. English modules can also be taken throughout your degree. *Fees:* classroom-based subjects £8250, laboratory subjects £8700. *Living costs:* £6500–£9000. Some partial fee scholarships available in Computing, Mathematics and Engineering, and Law scholarships for students from the Far East, South Africa, the West Indies and North America.

Brunel More than 2000 international students from over 110 countries. *English language entry requirement (or equivalent):* IELTS 6.0 for science/technology subjects, 7.0 for Law, 6.5 for other subjects. English language tuition offered during and before the course but only to improve existing skills. *Fees:* non-laboratory subjects £9200, laboratory subjects £11,100. *Living costs:* £7000–£8000. Twenty bursaries offered.

Buckingham Eighty nationalities represented at this small university. *English language entry requirement (or equivalent):* IELTS 6.0. *Fees:* £3500 (approximately) per term – check with the University. *Living costs:* £6000–£7000. Tuition fee discount for students from the Bahamas, Bulgaria and India. Some scholarships for students from the Far East, Russia and Eastern Europe.

Bucks New (Buckinghamshire New) Some 7.5% of students from overseas. *English language entry requirement (or equivalent):* IELTS 5.5/6.0. *Fees:* £7800–£8800. *Living costs:* £6000–£7000.

Cambridge Over 1000 international undergraduate students. *English language entry requirement (or equivalent):* IELTS 7.0 overall, with minimum of 6.0 in each element. TOEFL (written) 600 (minimum) and at least 5.0 in TOEFL test of written English. *Fees:* classroom-based subjects £10,000, laboratory-based subjects £12,700, clinical subjects £23,500; College fees (average) £3800. *Living costs:* £6000–£7000. Awards available, also scholarships for students from Hong Kong.

Canterbury Christ Church *English language entry requirement (or equivalent):* IELTS 6.0. *Fees:* £7880–£8050. *Living costs:* £6000–£7000.

Cardiff Over 3500 international students from 100 countries. *English language entry requirement (or equivalent):* IELTS 6.5. Comprehensive selection of pre-sessional language courses from three weeks to nine months. Induction course for all students. International Foundation courses for Business, Law, Engineering, Computer Science and Health and Life Sciences. *Fees:* Arts courses £9600, science courses £12,300. *Living costs:* £6000–£8000. Law scholarships offered on the basis of academic merit.

Central Lancashire Large international student population from many countries. *English language entry requirement (or equivalent):* IELTS 6.0. Competence in written and spoken English required on application. *Fees:* £8000–£8700. *Living costs:* £6000–£7000.

Chester *English language entry requirement (or equivalent):* IELTS 6.0. International Foundation year available for Business Studies students. *Fees:* £7400. *Living costs:* £6000–£7000.

Chichester International students from several countries. *English language entry requirement (or equivalent):* IELTS 6.0. *Fees:* £8300–£9500. *Living costs:* £7000–£8000.

City A large international community. *English language entry requirement (or equivalent):* IELTS 6.0 (6.5 for Business, Law and Journalism). August and September pre-sessional English language courses, and in-session English workshops. International Foundation programmes in Law, Business, Engineering and Management. *Fees:* £9000–£12,750. *Living costs:* £9500–£10,500. Scholarships available for applicants for Actuarial Science, Engineering (Cypriot applicants only) and Law.

Coventry About 2500 international students. *English language entry requirement (or equivalent):* IELTS 6.0. *Fees:* £8300. *Living costs:* £6000–£7000. Scholarships available.

Creative Arts *English language entry requirement (or equivalent):* Contact the University. *Fees:* £7124–£9507. *Living costs:* £6500–£7500.

Cumbria A new university (2007). *English language entry requirement (or equivalent):* IELTS 6.0. *Fees:* £8150. *Living costs:* £5000–£6000.

De Montfort Over 1000 international students from more than 100 countries. *English language entry requirement (or equivalent):* IELTS 6.5 (lower for some faculties). In-session English tuition in some degree courses. One-year International Foundation Certificate courses in Business and Law. Orientation programme in September for all students. *Fees:* £8000–£9000. *Living costs:* £8500–£9000. Some scholarships for overseas students.

Derby Students from 70 countries. *English language entry requirement (or equivalent):* IELTS 6.0. Courses offered to those needing tuition in English language. Foundation courses (£5200) and pre-sessional intensive English tuition (£2000), and also language support whilst studying for degree. *Fees:* £7800–£8400. *Living costs:* £4000–£5000. International scholarships available for applicants from some countries in the Far East.

Dundee Students from 83 countries. *English language entry requirement (or equivalent):* IELTS 6.0. Foundation courses in English and for Business and Art and Design courses. *Fees:* classroom-based courses £8500, laboratory-based courses £10,500, clinical courses £22,000. *Living costs:* £6000–£7000. Some awards for overseas students in Arts and Social Sciences, Law, Accountancy, Science and Engineering and Art and Design.

Durham Some 1600 international students from over 120 countries. *English language entry requirement (or equivalent):* IELTS 6.5. Three-day induction programme before the start of the academic year. Intensive English language course is provided if standard of English does not meet the required level. *Fees:* £10,700–£13,700. *Living costs:* £6000, plus college fees (Durham); £2800 (Stockton). Scholarships for nationals from some Far Eastern countries.

East Anglia Over 2000 international students from 120 countries. *English language entry requirement (or equivalent):* IELTS 6.0 (higher for some courses). Four, eight and twelve-week pre-sessional courses in English and tuition during degree courses. *Fees:* classroom-based subjects £9850, laboratory-based subjects £12,350, Medicine £19,260. *Living costs:* £6000–£7000. Scholarships available including awards, based on academic merit, cover part of the cost of tuition fees.

East London About 3300 international students from 120 countries. *English language entry requirement (or equivalent):* IELTS 6.0. One-year full-time preparatory English course available. *Fees:* £9510–£13,140. *Living costs:* £9500–£10,500.

Edge Hill This university near Liverpool has a small number of international students. *English language entry requirement (or equivalent):* IELTS 6.5. *Fees:* £8200. *Living costs:* £5000–£6000.

Edinburgh Some 4000 international students from 120 countries. *English language entry requirement (or equivalent):* IELTS 6.0–6.5. English language support. *Fees:* £11,050–£14,500, Clinical Medicine £23,500. *Living costs:* £6800–£7500. Awards include two India scholarships.

Edinburgh Napier Approximately 2000 international students. *English language entry requirement (or equivalent):* IELTS 5.5. English language programmes in September and January; English language support through Foundation programmes. *Fees:* £8950-£10,390. *Living costs:* £7000–£8000.

Essex International students from over 125 countries. *English language entry requirement (or equivalent):* IELTS 6.0–6.5. English language courses available before entry to degree course. *Fees:* non-Science courses £9750, laboratory courses £11,990. *Living costs:* £6000–£7500. Some funding available for students in need.

Exeter Over 1500 international students from 120 countries. *English language entry requirement (or equivalent):* IELTS 6.5. Full-time Foundation programme in English, with opportunity to specialise in Physical Sciences, Computer Science, Business, Politics, History, Sociology or Law. Also pre-sessional courses in English starting in July, August or September as well as in-session support. *Fees:* non-Science programmes £10,000, Science and Engineering programmes £12,250. *Living costs:* £7500–£8500. Awards available, including some subject and South East Asian scholarships.

Glamorgan Some 1500 international students from 60 different countries. *English language entry requirement (or equivalent):* IELTS from 5.0. Pre-sessional course offered in English, and also a 10–14-week English language skills programme. An International Foundation programme is also offered. *Fees:* £9500. *Living costs:* £6500–£7500.

Glasgow Over 2000 international students. *English language entry requirement (or equivalent):* IELTS 6.0 (higher for some courses). The English as a Foreign Language Unit offers intensive five-week pre-sessional language courses in Foundation programme covering English language and study skills. *Fees:* classroom-based subjects £9800, Engineering, Sciences, Nursing £12,950, Clinical Medicine £22,600, Dentistry £23,450, Veterinary Medicine £18,750. *Living costs:* £6000-£7500. Fee-waiver scholarships and automatic Fourth Year scholarships available (not for Dentistry, Medicine or Veterinary Science).

Glasgow Caledonian Students from 70 countries. *English language entry requirement (or equivalent):* IELTS 6.0. English language programmes available. *Fees:* £9000–£13,000. *Living costs:* £8000.

Gloucestershire *English language entry requirement (or equivalent):* IELTS 5.5. English language support and mentor scheme with other international students. *Fees:* £8500. *Living costs:* £6000–£7500.

Glyndŵr This new university welcomes students from Europe and world-wide. *English language entry requirement (or equivalent):* IELTS 6.0. *Fees:* £7300. *Living costs:* £7500.

Greenwich Over 4500 international students (including those from European countries). *English language entry requirement (or equivalent):* IELTS 6.0. Pre-sessional English courses, Access and International Foundation programmes. *Fees:* classroom-based subjects £8800, laboratory-based subjects £11,500. *Living costs:* £9500–£10,500. Scholarships open to applicants from 25 countries.

Heriot-Watt Twenty-three per cent of the student population comes from over 90 countries. *English language entry requirement (or equivalent):* IELTS 6.5, and 6.8 for language courses. Several English language courses are offered; these range in length depending on students' requirements. *Fees:* £9500–£12,000. *Living costs:* £6000–£7500. Some international scholarships are available worth £1500–£2000 for one year.

Hertfordshire Students from over 90 countries are at present studying at the University. *English language entry requirement (or equivalent):* IELTS 6.0. English language tuition is offered in the one-year International Foundation course, in a course for the Foundation Certificate in English for Academic Purposes, and in a pre-sessional intensive English course held during the summer months. *Fees:* £8400. *Living costs:* £7000–£8000.

Huddersfield International students from over 80 countries. *English language entry requirement (or equivalent):* IELTS 6.0. English language courses available and a one-year International Foundation course in English language with options in Business, Computing, Engineering, Mathematics and Music. Students guaranteed entry to Huddersfield courses on completion. *Fees:* classroom-based subjects £8250, laboratory-based subjects £9250, Foundation programme £7000. *Living costs:* £5500–£6500.

Hull Ten per cent of students from outside the EU. *English language entry requirement (or equivalent):* IELTS 6.0. English summer study programme through the three months before the start of the academic year. In-session study in English also available. Foundation programmes for Business and Management degrees. *Fees:* non-Science-based courses £9500, Science-based programmes £11,500, Medicine £22,000. *Living costs:* £4500–£5500. Hull has one of the best overseas scholarship provision of any British university, including full-tuition and 30 partial-tuition awards (50% of fees).

Imperial London Some 5000 international students from over 110 countries. *English language entry requirement (or equivalent):* IELTS 6.0–7.0. *Fees:* £15,500–£19,450, Pre-clinical Medicine £35,500, Clinical Medicine £35,000, other courses £14,300. *Living costs:* £9500–£10,500 (minimum). Scholarships available.

Keele Large number of overseas students. *English language entry requirement (or equivalent):* IELTS 6.0–6.5. English language summer school before the start of degree course. International Foundation year degree programmes (entry IELTS 4.5). *Fees:* £10,350–£12,590, Medicine £18,000-£22,000. *Living costs:* £8000–£9000. Some bursaries valued at £1300 per annum.

Kent Comprehensive English language support service. *English language entry requirement (or equivalent):* IELTS 5.5. Foundation programmes (entry IELTS 5.0) to prepare students for Arts, Business, Science, Engineering and Law courses. Non-degree courses also offered for one year or less. *Fees:* £9400–£11,800. *Living costs:* £8000–£9000. Certificate of chest X-ray required. Limited number of scholarships available and some general scholarships for students from Hong Kong and Singapore.

Kingston More than 2000 international students from over 70 countries. *English language entry requirement (or equivalent):* IELTS 6.5. Foundation level Science and Technology courses. Pre-sessional English language courses and free English support during degree studies. *Fees:* £9400, and most laboratory-based subjects £10,350. *Living costs:* £9500–£10,500.

Lancaster Twenty per cent of student population from over 100 countries. *English language entry requirement (or equivalent):* IELTS 5.5–6.0. Pre-sessional and in-session English language courses cover reading, writing, listening and speaking skills. On-campus accommodation throughout your degree course. *Fees:* £9200–£11,100. *Living costs:* £7000–£8000.

Leeds Approximately 4000 students from outside the UK. *English language entry requirement (or equivalent):* IELTS 6.0. *Fees:* £10,300–£13,300 and for Clinical Medicine and Dentistry £23,500. Partial scholarships offered. *Living costs:* £8000–£9000.

Leeds Metropolitan Over 2500 international students from 110 countries. *English language entry requirement (or equivalent):* IELTS 6.0 (IELTS 4.0 or 5.0 for the International Foundation programme, starting September or February). Also general English courses. *Fees:* Check with the University. *Living costs:* £8000–£9000. Small number of scholarships.

Leicester Fourteen per cent of full-time students are from outside the UK. *English language entry requirement (or equivalent):* IELTS 6.0 (IELTS 6.5 for Law, Medicine, Arts and Social Science programmes, 5.5 for the Foundation year). English language preparatory programmes and on-going support Foundation programme. *Fees:* £9450–£12,650, Clinical Medicine £22,900. *Living costs:* £7000–£8000. Scholarships and bursaries awarded in a range of subjects, with special awards for students from India and Singapore.

Lincoln Over 2000 students from more than 40 countries. *English language entry requirement (or equivalent):* IELTS 6.0. *Fees:* classroom-based subjects £8524–£9038. *Living costs:* £7000–£8000.

Liverpool Approximately 2600 international students from over 100 countries. *English language entry requirement (or equivalent):* IELTS 6.0–6.5. International Foundation course (IELTS 5.0–5.5). *Fees:* £9400–£12,000, Dentistry and Medicine £18,600, Veterinary Science £18,000. *Living costs:* £7000–£8000. Scholarships available, including special awards for students from Hong Kong and Singapore.

Liverpool Hope Approximately 700 international students. *English language entry requirement (or equivalent):* IELTS 6.0. Language courses available. *Fees:* £6600–£7000. *Living costs:* £7000–£8000.

Liverpool John Moores A large number of overseas students. *English language entry requirement (or equivalent):* IELTS 6.0. Pre-sessional and in-session English tuition available. *Fees:* £9790–£10,450. *Living costs:* £7000–£8000. Some awards available.

London (Central School of Speech and Drama) More than 60 International students from over 40 countries are currently following courses. *Fees:* from £10,000. *Living costs:* £9500–£10,500.

London (Courtauld) Approximately 25–30% students are from overseas. *English language entry requirement (or equivalent):* IELTS 7.0. *Fees:* undergraduate courses £12,000. *Living costs:* £9500–£10,500.

London (Goldsmiths) Some 1500 overseas students. *English language entry requirement (or equivalent):* IELTS 6.5; IELTS 5.5 for Extension degrees and IELTS 5.0 for entry to the one-year Foundation course. Certificate course in Language and Contemporary Culture or pre-sessional programmes available. *Fees:* £10,680–£14,110. *Living costs:* £9500–£10,500.

London (Heythrop College) *English language entry requirement (or equivalent):* IELTS 6.0. *Fees:* £5490. *Living costs:* £9500–£10,500.

London (King's College) A large number of international students (20%). *English language entry requirement (or equivalent):* IELTS 6.5 for Engineering, Nursing, Science courses, 7.0 for Dentistry, Law, Medicine, Physiotherapy and 7.5 for Humanities, Social Sciences. Pre-sessional summer courses and a one-year Foundation course available. *Fees:* £12,000–£15,000, clinically based subjects £28,000. *Living costs:* £9500–£11,500. Awards available, including Hong Kong scholarships.

London (Queen Mary) Large number of international students (20%). *English language entry requirement (or equivalent):* IELTS 6.5. International Foundation course covering English language tuition and specialist courses in Business, Management, Economics, Mathematics, Spanish, Geography and European Studies. The course guarantees progression to linked degree courses including Law. *Fees:*

£9000–£11,500, Medicine Years 1 and 2 £14,600. *Living costs:* £9500–£11,500. Several departments operate scholarship schemes for overseas students.

London (Royal Holloway) Twenty per cent of students from over 120 countries. *English language entry requirement (or equivalent):* IELTS 4.0–5.5 for English language programmes. Ten-month Foundation course with studies in English language and introduction to specialist studies in a range of degree subjects. *Fees:* £10,200–£12,300. *Living costs:* £9500–£10,500. International student scholarships offered.

London (Royal Veterinary College) About 110 international students. *Fees:* £8030–£18,400. *Living costs:* £9500–£10,500. Contact for further information tel 020 7468 5000; Fax 020 7388 2342.

London (St George's) *Fees:* £12,000–£14,000, MBBS £25,875. *Living costs:* £9500–£10,500.

London (School of Oriental and African Studies) Large number of international students (30%). *English language entry requirement (or equivalent):* IELTS 7.0. A one-year Foundation programme and English language courses available with an entry requirement of IELTS 4.0. Three-day International Students' Orientation programme. *Fees:* £12,000. *Living costs:* £9500–£10,500.

London (School of Pharmacy) International students – 20%. *English language entry requirement (or equivalent):* IELTS 6.5. *Fees:* £12,300. *Living costs:* £9500–£10,500. For further information tel 020 7753 5831; Fax 020 7753 5829.

London (University College) Some 7000 students (34% of the total student body) are from countries outside the UK. *English language entry requirement (or equivalent):* Science and Engineering IELTS 6.5, Arts courses 7.0, Speech Science and Law 7.5. *Fees:* £12,300–£16,000, Medicine £24,000. *Living costs:* £9500–£10,500. Scholarships available, including awards for students from Hong Kong and China.

London Metropolitan Over 4000 students from 147 countries. *English language entry requirement (or equivalent):* IELTS 5.5. One-year International Foundation programme (IELTS entry requirement 4.5). Full range of English courses. *Fees:* £8800, Foundation programme £5500. *Living costs:* £9500–£10,500.

London School of Economics and Political Science Approximately 5500 international students represent 150 countries. *English language entry requirement (or equivalent):* TOEFL 627 (paper test). Language Centre courses available. *Fees:* £12,840. *Living costs:* £9500–£10,500.

London South Bank Approximately 2500 international students, including 1300 from the EU. *English language entry requirement (or equivalent):* IELTS 6.0. Pre-study English course and a University Foundation course for overseas students. *Fees:* £8360–£8600. *Living costs:* £9500–£10,500.

Loughborough Some 800 students from outside the UK. *English language entry requirement (or equivalent):* IELTS 6.5. Special courses offered by the English Language Study Unit. One-week residential course for international students before the start of the academic year. *Fees:* £10,400–£13,500. *Living costs:* £4300–£5800. Eight merit-based scholarships offered.

Manchester A high proportion of international students from over 180 countries. *English language entry requirement (or equivalent):* IELTS 6.0–7.5, depending on the high linguistic demands of courses, for example Law, Management and Medicine. Foundation Year programme in Informatics, Engineering, Science and Biological Sciences. English language courses are also offered. *Fees:* £10,500–£12,900, clinical courses in Medicine and Dentistry £23,500. *Living costs:* £8500–£9000. Some scholarships and bursaries are available.

Manchester Metropolitan A large number of international students. *English language entry requirement (or equivalent):* IELTS 6.0. English language courses in January, April and July. *Fees:* £8385–£9065, Architecture £11,200. *Living costs:* £8500–£9000.

Middlesex International students from 30 countries around the world. *English language entry requirement (or equivalent):* IELTS 6.0. Foundation course (IELTS entry requirement 4.5). Extended English language course from September to July. International summer school. *Fees:* £9400. *Living costs:* £9500–£10,500.

Newcastle Over 2500 students from outside the UK. *English language entry requirement (or equivalent):* IELTS 6.5 (7.0 for English, Law and Medicine). English language support and Foundation programmes in Arts and Social Sciences, Business and Finance, Computing, Science and Engineering. *Fees:* £10,215–£13,360, Medicine £13,360–£24,735. *Living costs:* £7500–£8500. Some awards available.

Newport International students from 50 countries. *English language entry requirement (or equivalent):* IELTS 6.0. *Fees:* £7500–£8500. *Living costs:* £5500–£6500.

Northampton Over 700 students from over 100 countries. *English language entry requirement (or equivalent):* IELTS 6.0. English language courses available. *Fees:* £7950-£8250. *Living costs:* £6500–£7500.

Northumbria Approximately 2500 international students from over 80 countries. *English language entry requirement (or equivalent):* IELTS 5.5–6.5. English language and Foundation courses. *Fees:* £7800–£9000. *Living costs:* £7500–£8500. Country scholarships for students from over 15 countries; some merit-based course scholarships.

Nottingham Students from over 130 countries. *English language entry requirement (or equivalent):* IELTS 6.0–6.5 (7.5 for Medicine). *Fees:* £10,610–£13,910, Medicine £14,660–£25,480. *Living costs:* £7500–£8500. Scholarships for siblings and science applicants.

Nottingham Trent Large number of overseas students. *English language entry requirement (or equivalent):* IELTS 6.5. English language courses (19, 10 and 5 weeks) available. *Fees:* £9100–£10,300. *Living costs:* £7500–£8500. Discounted overseas fees for some applicants for Art and Design courses.

Open University Courses are open to students throughout the world with study on-line or with educational partners. Tutorial support is by telephone, fax, computer conferencing or email. Non-EU students' fees vary depending on courses.

Oxford Large proportion of international students. *English language entry requirement (or equivalent):* IELTS 7.5 (minimum), TOEFL 650 (275 in the computer-based TOEFL). *Fees:* £10,500–£14,000, Clinical Medicine £25,500. *Living costs:* £10,500–£13,000. University and college scholarships and awards.

Oxford Brookes Large number of international students. *English language entry requirement (or equivalent):* IELTS scores for Engineering and Construction 5.5; for Business, Social Sciences, Computing and Humanities 6.0; for Law and Psychology 6.5. Large number of English language support courses from two weeks to two years offered by the Centre for English Language Studies. *Fees:* £9780–£11,000. *Living costs:* £9000–£9500. Engineering scholarships and family awards.

Plymouth *English language entry requirement (or equivalent):* IELTS 6.5. 'English for University' courses available with IELTS entry requirement of 4.5. *Fees:* £8750, depending on subject. *Living costs:* £7000–£7500. Scholarships for applicants from Malaysia.

Portsmouth Students from over 100 countries. *English language entry requirement (or equivalent):* IELTS 6.0 (5.5 for Foundation-level study). Induction, academic skills and language courses available. *Fees:* £8350–£9350. *Living costs:* £7500–£8500. Scholarships for first-year students.

Queen Margaret Some 400 international students from 50 countries. *English language entry requirement (or equivalent):* IELTS 5.5. *Fees:* £9250–£10,200. Some partial scholarships for self-funding students. *Living costs:* £6000.

Queen's Belfast Over 60 countries represented by 2400 international students. *English language entry requirement (or equivalent):* IELTS 6.0–6.5. Special English language summer schools and pre-university language courses are provided, also weekly language courses. Three-day orientation programme held before the start of the academic year. *Fees:* £9500–£11,500, Medicine/Dentistry pre-clinical £12,750, clinical £24,000. *Living costs:* £7500–£8500. Awards available.

Reading Over 3000 students from 135 countries. *English language entry requirement (or equivalent):* IELTS 6.5–7.0. International Foundation programme offering English language tuition and specialist studies in a choice of 14 subjects. Other pre-sessional English courses offered. *Fees:* £9600–£11,600 for courses with a significant laboratory content. *Living costs:* £6000–£6500. Some scholarships offered.

Robert Gordon Approximately 500 international students from over 50 countries. *English language entry requirement (or equivalent):* IELTS 6.0. Pre-entry English programme requirement IELTS 5.0 or above. *Fees:* £8700–£10,700. *Living costs:* £5000–£6000. Partial scholarship scheme.

Roehampton *English language entry requirement (or equivalent):* IELTS 5.5–6.0. *Fees:* £9230. *Living costs:* £7500–£8500.

St Andrews Twenty-six per cent of students from overseas. *English language entry requirement (or equivalent):* IELTS 6.5. Pre-entry English and study skills programmes and Foundation courses specialising in Arts, Science or Social Science subjects. *Fees:* £12,200, Medicine £18,600. *Living costs:* £7500–£8500. Scholarships available.

Salford Some 1500 international students. *English language entry requirement (or equivalent):* IELTS 6.0. English study programmes and a very comprehensive International Foundation year. *Fees:* £8600–£10,700. *Living costs:* £8500–£9000.

Sheffield Over 3700 international students. *English language entry requirement (or equivalent):* IELTS 6.0. Preparatory English courses (one–nine months) and an international summer school with English classes. *Fees:* £10,420–£13,700, Clinical Medicine £24,760. *Living costs:* £7000–£8000. Scholarships available for applicants from Africa and the Far East, for siblings and alumni.

Sheffield Hallam Over 80 countries represented by 3000 international students. *English language entry requirement (or equivalent):* IELTS 6.0. English language tuition available on four, eight and 12 week courses (£810, £1700 and £2200 respectively and IELTS entry requirement 4.5). *Fees:* £8400–£11,400. *Living costs:* £7000–£8000.

Southampton Over 2000 international students. *English language entry requirement (or equivalent):* IELTS 6.0–6.5. English courses offered and also an International Foundation course covering Arts, Humanities, Social Sciences and Law. *Fees:* £9660–£12,360, Clinical Medicine £22,240. *Living costs:* £7500–£8500. Awards available in Computer Science, Electronics, Law, Mathematics and Science.

Southampton Solent Students from over 50 countries. *English language entry requirement (or equivalent):* IELTS 6.0. Induction programme and language tuition available. *Fees:* £7900–£8400. *Living costs:* £7500–£8500.

Staffordshire Students from over 70 countries. *English language entry requirement (or equivalent):* IELTS 5.5–6.0. English tuition available. *Fees:* £9350. *Living costs:* £7500–£8000.

Stirling Thirteen per cent overseas students from 70 nationalities. *English language entry requirement (or equivalent):* IELTS 6.0. English language tuition available. *Fees:* £9400–£11,550. *Living costs:* £5500–£6000. Some scholarships for students from South East Asia.

Strathclyde Students from 90 countries. *English language entry requirement (or equivalent):* IELTS 6.5. Pre-entry and pre-sessional English tuition available. *Fees:* £9500–£12,200. *Living costs:* £7500–£8500.

Sunderland A large number of international students. *English language entry requirement (or equivalent):* IELTS 5.5–6.0. English language tuition available. *Fees:* £8300. *Living costs:* £5500–£6500.

Surrey A large international community with 43% from the Far East. *English language entry requirement (or equivalent):* IELTS 6.0. English language courses and summer courses offered. *Fees:* £8300–£10,700. *Living costs:* £7000–£8000. Scholarships and bursaries offered, including awards for students on Civil Engineering courses.

Sussex More than 2500 international students. *English language entry requirement (or equivalent):* IELTS 6.5. English language and study skills courses available. International Foundation courses offered, covering English language tuition and a choice from Humanities, Law, Media Studies, Social Sciences and Cultural Studies and Science and Technology. *Fees:* £9975–£12,750. *Living costs:* £8000–£8500. Forty international scholarships.

Swansea Students from over 100 countries. *English language entry requirement (or equivalent):* IELTS 6.0. Pre-sessional English language courses available and on-going support during degree courses. *Fees:* £9300–£11,900. *Living costs:* £5500–£6500. Some overseas scholarships and prizes.

Swansea Metropolitan A new university (2008). *English language entry requirement (or equivalent):* IELTS 6.5. *Fees:* No information – contact the University. *Living costs:* £5500–£6500.

Teesside Students from over 75 countries. *English language entry requirement (or equivalent):* IELTS 6.5 for Law, English and Humanities, 5.5 for Engineering, Science, Technology and Computing courses and 6.0 for all other courses. Free English courses available throughout the year while following degree programmes. International summer school available. *Fees:* £8500. *Living costs:* £5500–£6500.

Thames Valley A large number of international students. *English language entry requirement (or equivalent):* IELTS 5.0 for the International Foundation programme and 5.5 for undergraduate courses. English language support available and also pre-sessional courses. *Fees:* Arts-based courses £4500–£7800. *Living costs:* £9500–£12,500.

Trinity Saint David International students represented at this new (2010) university created from the merger of Lampeter University and Trinity University College. *English language entry requirement (or equivalent):* IELTS 6.0. International Foundation programme. Accommodation possible for each year at university. *Fees:* £9070. *Living costs:* £5500–£6500.

Ulster Students from over 40 countries. *English language entry requirement (or equivalent):* IELTS 5.5. *Fees:* £8900. *Living costs:* £5500–£6500.

Warwick Over 3500 international students. *English language entry requirement (or equivalent):* IELTS 6.0 for Science courses, 6.5 for Arts courses, 6.5 for MORSE courses, and 7.0 for Social Studies and Business courses. English support available. *Fees:* £10,900–£13,950. *Living costs:* £6500–£7500. More than 20 awards available for overseas students.

West of Scotland Over 1100 international students. *English language entry requirement (or equivalent):* IELTS 6.0. English language Foundation course available. *Fees:* £9350–£10,050. *Living costs:* £6500–£7000. Some first-year scholarships.

Westminster Students from 148 countries (51% Asian). *English language entry requirement (or equivalent):* IELTS 6.0. International Foundation certificate courses available focusing on the Built Environment, Mathematics and Computing or Social Sciences and Literature. *Fees:* £9830. *Living costs:* £9500–£10,500.

Winchester Some 150 international students from 30 countries. *English language entry requirement (or equivalent):* IELTS 6.0. Language courses available. *Fees:* £7890. *Living costs:* £7500–£8500.

Wolverhampton A large number (2500) of international students. *English language entry requirement (or equivalent):* IELTS 6.0. English courses available over one or two months or longer. International student programme. *Fees:* £8850. *Living costs:* £6000–£6500. Twenty Scholarships for Excellence offered.

Worcester *English language entry requirement (or equivalent):* IELTS 6.0. *Fees:* £8400. *Living costs:* £6000–£6500.

York Fifteen per cent of students from outside the UK. *English language entry requirement (or equivalent):* IELTS 6.0. Six-month and pre-sessional English language courses. Intensive vacation courses. *Fees:* £10,271–£13,811. *Living costs:* £6500–£7500. Several scholarships for overseas students.

York St John *English language entry requirement (or equivalent):* IELTS 6.0 (3 year degree course or 4 year course including Foundation year). *Fees:* £8100, 10-week English language course £1900, Pre-sessional 4-week course £760. *Living costs:* £6500–£7500.

BRITISH OVERSEAS TERRITORIES STUDENTS

Students from British Overseas Territories are now treated as home students for fee purposes at universities and other institutions of higher education in the UK. The territories to which this policy applies are:

British Overseas Territories Anguilla, Bermuda, British Antarctic Territory, British Indian Ocean Territory, British Virgin Islands, Cayman Islands, Falkland Islands, Montserrat, Pitcairn Islands, South Georgia and the South Sandwich Islands, St Helena and its Dependencies, Turks and Caicos Islands.

Overseas Territories of other EU member states Greenland, Faroe Islands (Denmark), Netherlands Antilles (Bonaire, Curacao, Saba, St Eustatius, St Marten), Aruba (Netherlands), New Caledonia, French Polynesia, Wallis and Futura, Mayotte, St Pierre et Miquelon (France).

10 | LATE INFORMATION

Universities and higher education colleges have made many changes in their course offers during 2009/10 and these are reflected in the subject tables in **Chapter 8**. At the same time, they are starting to provide typical course offers to be made to candidates offering the Advanced Diploma and the new Cambridge Pre-U, who will be considered on a case-by-case basis for entry in 2011. This chapter has been set aside to include late-arriving information to help students in researching and planning their applications. It is important to read the information in this chapter in conjunction with **Chapter 4** and with the relevant subject tables in **Chapter 8** – and also to check the websites of universities and colleges where their latest offers are given, and where comprehensive information is available about their course requirements. Admissions staff are always willing to deal with queries, and, in particular, to give guidance to applicants with new qualifications such as the Advanced Diploma and the Cambridge Pre-U. See **Appendix 1** for the UCAS 2011 entry tariff points for the Advanced Diploma, the Extended Project, the Progression Diploma, the Pre-U, and Scottish, Welsh and Irish qualifications.

RECENT ADVANCED DIPLOMA OFFERS

NB The Advanced Diploma = Progression Diploma plus Additional and Specialist Learning. See **Appendix 1** for details of grades and UCAS tariff points used in the offers below for Principal Learning (PL), Additional and Specialist Learning (ASL) and the Extended Project (EP). See **Chapter 7** for Course Abbreviations.

Diploma abbreviations

BAF = Business, Administration & Finance; CBE = Construction & the Built Environment; Eng = Engineering; CM = Creative & Media; ELB = Environment & Land-based Studies; H = Hospitality; IT = Information Technology; MPD = Manufacturing & Product Design; SHD = Society, Health & Development; PS = Public Services.

Bath

Acc Fin – A (Eng/IT/BAF) + ASL (AL maths A + EP A)
Biochemistry – B (ELB/Eng) + ASL (AL B chem + EP a/b))
Biology – B (ELB/Eng) + ASL (AL biol + EP a/b)
Bus Admin – A (CM/Eng/IT/SHD/BAF/ELB/PS) + ASL (AL A + EP a)
Chem Eng – A (Eng) + ASL (AL maths + chem, A in one)
Chemistry – A/B (Eng/ELB) + ASL (AL B chem)
Electron Elect Eng – A (MEng) B (BEng) (Eng/IT) + ASL (AL A/B maths or B Maths for Engineering + AS a electron or similar)
Eng (Mech) – A (Eng/MPD) + A specified units + ASL (AL A maths + EP a)
Sociology – B (SHD) + ASL (AL B)

Bristol

Acc Fin – A (Eng) + A specified units + A Maths for Engineers
Arch St – B (CBE/ELB) + ASL (AL A maths/chem/phys)
Audiology – B (SHD) + ASL (AL B sci)
Elect Electron Eng – A + A units 8+9 + specialist maths unit + relevant ALs
Sociology – B (SHD) + ASL (AL)

Brunel

Aerosp Eng – 320pts (Eng) inc ASL Maths for Engineers unit
Anthropology – SHD may be accepted
Avn Eng – 310/320pts (Eng) inc ASL (Maths for Engineers unit)
Biomed Sci – no Diploma subjects currently accepted
Broad Media (Des Tech) – 320pts (CM/IT) inc ASL (AL)
Bus Econ – 320pts (BAF) + ASL (AL maths or AS b maths)
Bus Mgt – 300–350pts (BAF) inc ASL (AL)
Bus Mgt (Fin Acc) – 320pts (BAF) inc ASL (AL maths or AS b maths)
Civ Eng Sust – 300/370pts – (Eng) inc ASL (Maths for Engineers unit)
Comm Media St – 300pts (CM/SHD) inc ASL (AL)
Comp Sci courses – 320pts – Eng/IT inc ASL (AL)
Comp (Mbl) – 300pts (Eng) (no ASL specified)
Crea Writ – 320pts (CM) inc ASL (AL Engl + EP related subject)
Drama – 300pts (CM) inc ASL (AL B drama)
Economics – 320pts (BAF) +inc ASL (AL maths or AS b maths + econ)
Educ (S) – 300pts (all Diploma subjs) inc ASL (AL spo st/PE)
Electron Elec Eng (Comm Sys) – 300pts (Eng) inc ASL (Maths for Engineers unit)
English – 320pts (CM) + ASL (AL Engl + EP (related subject preferred))
Film TV St – 300pts (CM) inc ASL (AL)
Fin Comp – 300pts (IT/BAF) inc ASL (AL)
History – 300pts – (CM/SHD/BAF) inc ASL (AL)
Inf Sys – 320pts (Eng/IT) inc ASL (AL)
Intnet Eng – 320pts (Eng) inc ASL (Maths for Engineers unit)
Journalism – 320pts (CM) inc ASL (AL)
Law – 390pts (SHD/BAF) inc ASL (AL + EP relevant subjects)
Mathematics – 350/360pts (Eng/IT/BAF) inc ASL (AL B maths)
Maths Stats Mgt – 300pts (Eng/IT/BAF) inc ASL (AL B)
Mech Eng – 370/320pts (Eng) inc ASL (Maths for Engineers unit)
Music 300pts (CM) inc ASL (AL C mus/test)
Net Comp – 320pts (Eng/IT) inc ASL (AL)
Occ Ther – 300pts (SHD) inc ASL (AL bio/hum bio)
Politics – 300pts (CM/SHD/BAF) inc ASL (AL)
Prod Des – 320pts (CM/Eng/MPD) inc ASL (AL maths/phys)
Psychology – 350pts (SHD) inc ASL (AL)
Soc Wk – 320pts (SHD) inc ASL (AL)
Sociology – 300pts (SHD) inc ASL (AL)
Snc Arts – 300pts (CM) inc ASL (AL)
Spo Sci – 320pts (SHD) inc ASL (AL sci/soc sci/PE)

Cambridge

Engineering – (Eng) + ASL (AL phys + Maths for Engineering): check grades with Admissions
Manuf Eng – (Eng) + ASL (AL phys +Maths for Engineering): check grades with Admissions

Leeds

Chem Eng – A (Eng) + ASL (AL B min maths/phys)
Electron Comm Eng – A (Eng) + ASL (AL B min maths)

London (Gold)

Advanced Diploma in Society, Health & Development will be accepted on the following courses

Anthropology (Integrated degree)
App Soc Sci Commun Dev Yth Wk BA
Int Fdn Cert Hum Soc Sci
Psychology BSc (Integrated 4 yr degree)
Soc Cult S BA
Soc Wk BA
Thera Cult BA

Advanced Diploma in Creative & Media will be accepted on the following courses

Anth Media BA
Art Prac BA
Art Prac (4 yr Extd degree)
Design BA
Des Innov BA
Dr Thea Arts
Educ Des Tech BA
English (Integrated degree)
Engl Crea Writ
Engl Dr
Fine Art Hist Art BA
History (Integrated)
Hist Art
Int Fdn Cert Hum Soc Sci
Soc Cult Studies BA
Media Comms BA (inc Integrated 4 yr degree)
Media Modn Lit BA
Media Sociol BA
Music + Fdn Yr (integrated degree)
Music BMus
Music (4 yr Extd degree)
Mus Comp BMus
Pop Mus St BSc

Advanced Diploma in Information Technology will be accepted on the following courses

Comp Sci courses
IT courses

London (King's)

Dentistry – A (SHD) + ASL (AL chem A + AS biol a + EP a (health topic))
Medicine – A (SHD) + ASL (AL A chem + AS biol a + EP a (health topic))

Loughborough

Acc Fin Mgt – A (IT) + ASL (AL B)
Aero Eng – A (Eng) + ASL (AL A maths)
Archit Eng Des Mgt – 330pts (Eng/IT/CBE)
Auto Eng – A (Eng) + ASL (AL A maths)
Bank Fin Mgt – A (IT) + ASL (AL B)
Bus Econ Fin – A (IT) + ASL (AL B)
Bus (Int) – A (IT) + ASL (AL B)

Chemistry – 350 pts (Eng/IT) inc ASL (AL B chem)
Economics – A (IT) + ASL (AL B)
Eng Phys – 350pts (Eng) inc ASL (AL B phys)
Euro St – 350pts (IT/CM)
Geography – 350pts (IT/CBE) inc ASL (AL goeg)
Int Rel – 350pts (IT/CM)
History courses– 350pts (IT/CM) inc ASL (AL B hist/geog/Engl)
Ind DesTech – 330pts (IT/Eng/CM) inc ASL (AL art des/des tech/art des + portfolio)
Mathematics – 370pts (Eng/IT) inc ASL (AL maths A)
Physics – 350pts (Eng) inc ASL (AL phys B)
Spo Tech – B (Eng) + ASL (AL maths B)

Newcastle
Agriculture – B (ELB) + ASL (AL B sci + EP b)
Eng (Civ) – A (CBE/Eng) + ASL (AL A maths/Maths for Engineers unit + EP a)

Oxford
Eng Sci – (Eng) + ASL (AL A phys + Maths for Engineering + EP) Check grades with admissions

Portsmouth
*Any Phase 1 Diploma subjects acceptable for the following courses except for **
Accountancy – 300–350pts C ASL (AL B maths/econ pref)
Am St – 300–350pts C ASL (AL B subj relevant to degree)
Animat – 300–350pts C ASL (AL B subj relevant to degree)
App Biomed Sci – 300–350pts inc ASL (AL B sci)
App Econ – 300–350pts C ASL (AL B maths/econ)
Bus Admin – 300–350pts C ASL (AL B maths/Engl/bus-related subj)
Bus Econ – 300–350pts C ASL (AL B maths/econ)
Bus St – 300–350pts C ASL (AL B maths/Engl/bus-related subj)
Clin Hlth Sci – 300–350pts C ASL (AL B sci)
Comb Modn Langs – 300–350pts C ASL (AL B modn lang)
Comm Sys – 300–350pts C ASL (AL B maths/Maths for Engineers)
Comp Sci – 300–350pts C ASL (AL B subj related to degree)
Crea Media Writ – 300–350pts C ASL (AL B subj related to degree)
Crimin Psy – 300–350pts C ASL (AL B subj related to degree)
Dntl Hyg Dntl Thera* – 300–350pts C (SHD only) ASL (AL B biol/chem/phys)
Dia Radiog – 300–350pts C ASL (AL B sci)
Dig Foren – 300–350pts C ASL (AL B subj related to degree)
Dr Perf – 300–350pts C ASL (AL B subj related to degree)
Earth Sci – 300–350pts C ASL (AL B sci)
Econ Fin Bank – 300–350pts C ASL (AL B maths/econ)
Eng (Civ) – 300–350pts C + ASL (AL B maths/Maths for Engineers)
Eng (Comp) – 300–350pts C ASL (AL B maths/Maths for Engineers)
Eng (Electron) – 300–350pts C ASL (AL B maths/Maths for Engineers)
Eng Geol – 300–350pts C ASL (AL B sci)

Warwick
Engineering courses (MEng) – A (Eng) + ASL (AL maths A)
Engineering courses (BEng) – B (Eng) + ASL (AL maths B)
Erly Chld St B (SHD) + ASL (AL B – not AL crit think or gen st)
Env Biol – B (ELB) + ASL (AL biol B)

RECENT PRE-U OFFERS

See **Appendix 1** for details of grades and points used in offers, and **Appendix 3** for information about the Pre-U qualification.

Hull York Medical School
Medicine – D3 D3 D3 (inc chem+biol)

Leicester
Medicine – D3 D3 D3 (inc chem+biol)

London (King's)
Anc Hist – D3 D3 M2 (class herit/hist preferred)
Biochemistry – D3 M2 M2 (inc chem+1 other sci)
Biomed Sci – D3 M2 M2 (inc chem+biol)
Bus Mgt – D3 D3 M2
Class Arch – D3 M2 M2 (class herit/anc hist preferred)
Class St – D3 D3 M2 (class herit/anc hist preferred)
Classics – D3 D3 M2 (inc Latin/class Greek)
Compar Lt – D3 D3 M2 (inc English +relevant modn/anc language)
Comp Sci (BSc) – D3 M2 M2 (inc maths)
Dentistry – D3 D3 M2 (inc chem+biol)
Engl Lang Commun – M2 M2 M2 (inc Engl lang/modn lang)
Engl Lang Lit – D3 D3 M2 (inc D3 Engl)
Engl Fr/Ger Law – D3 D3 D3 (inc Fr/Ger)
Engl Hong Kong Law – D3 D3 D3
Euro St (Fr/Ger/Span) – D3 D3 M2 (inc relevant lang)
Film St – D3 M2 M2 (inc Engl)
French – D3 M2 M2 (inc D3 Fr)
Geography – D3 M2 M2 (inc goeg)
German – M2 M2 P1 (Inc M2 Ger)
Gk Engl – D3 D3 M2 (inc Engl + class Gk)
Hisp St – M2 M2 M2 (inc Span)
History – D3 D3 D3 (inc hist)
Hum Sci – D3 M2 M2 (inc chem+biol)
Law – D3 D3 D3
Mathematics – D3 D3 D3 (inc maths)
Medicine – D3 D3 D3 (inc chem+biol)
Mol Genet – D3 M2 M2 (inc chem +1 other sci)
Music – D3 D3 D3 (inc mus)
Neuroscience – D3 M2 M2 (inc chem+biol)
Pharmacology – D3 M2 M2 (inc chem+biol)
Pharmacy – D3 M2 M2 (inc chem+biol+maths)
Philosophy – D3 D3 M2
Physics – D3 D3 M2 (inc maths+phys)
Physiology – D3 M2 M2 (inc chem+biol)
Physiotherapy – M2 M2 M2 (inc biol or 2 from chem/maths/phys/psy)
Relig Phil Eth – D3 M2 M2 **or** M2 M2 M2
Spanish – M2 M2 M2 (inc Span)
Theology – D3 M2 M2 **or** M2 M2 M2
Turk Modn Gk St – D3 M2 M2 (inc D3 lang)
War St – D3 D3 M2

Newcastle
Bus Mgt – D3 D3 M2
Chem Eng – M2 M2 M2 (inc maths+chem)
Civ Eng – D3 D3 D3 (inc maths+phys)
Dentistry – D3 D3 M2 (inc chem+biol D3)
Economics – D3 D3 M2
Fin Maths – D3 D3 M2
Mathematics – D3 D3 M2 (inc maths D3)
Politics – D3 D3 D3 **or** M2 M2 M2 (inc sci/hum AL)
Sociology – M2 M2 M2

LATE ADMISSIONS INFORMATION

Anglia Ruskin We will accept UCAS tariff points from all lines of learning, including, for example, points from the Advanced Diplomas and Extended Project.
All applicants for the following courses are interviewed before offers are made:

* Art and Design; Education; Midwifery; Nursing; Social Work; TV and Media Studies;
* Some applicants are interviewed for Business courses.

Aston The University interviews applicants for courses only in special cases, for example, mature students, or those with non-standard entry qualifications. For most courses (and 70 per cent of students) there is a one-year placement as part of the degree. This is normally paid, and also has a reduced tuition fee and a placement bursary. Aston is one of only four UK universities with more than 50 per cent of students taking sandwich courses or year-abroad programmes.

Bath Spa All eligible candidates are interviewed for the following courses: Art and Design; Broadcast Media; Creative Media Practice; Music and Performing Arts; Publishing.

Brighton and Sussex Medical School We do not, currently, expect to make A* as part of our offers to candidates applying for 2011 entry to Medicine. We will welcome candidates offering A*, or predicted to achieve A*, and we will account for this level of attainment when we shortlist for interview. The same policy will apply to applicants offering Extended Projects.

Brunel All applicants are interviewed for Design, Electrical Engineering, Social Work and Education courses. No admissions tests will be used for entry in 2011.

Bucks New We accept the full range of the UCAS tariff and currently have no subject requirements. Advanced Diplomas and Extended Projects are accepted as part of the UCAS tariff. Admissions tests will be used for entry to Nursing and Social Work courses.

Chichester Some applicants will be interviewed for Teacher Training, Physical Education, Social Work, Dance, Fine Art, Music, Musical Theatre, Drama, Performing Arts and Childhood Studies courses. Admissions tests will not be used in 2010/11. For entry Chichester will use more grades-based offers than UCAS tariff points offers.

Glyndŵr Some applicants are interviewed for Education, Social Work, Nursing and Art courses. Admissions tests will not be used.

London School of Economics (LSE) All first-year students follow a new course in their degree programme 'Understanding the causes of things' which actively challenges them to analyse questions of current public concern and to develop their critical skills.

London South Bank All applicants are interviewed for Nursing, Allied Health Professions and Architecture courses.

Loughborough All applicants are interviewed prior to making an offer for Aeronautical and Automotive Engineering, Information Science, Design and Technology, Civil Engineering and Art and Design.

Newman (UC) Basic literacy and numeracy tests are required for Humanities, Primary Education and English. A written test is set for applicants to Youth and Community Work.

St Andrews Admissions tutors prefer candidates to achieve their grades at the first sitting and, if they re-apply, to improve their academic attainment if that is the main reason for their rejection.

Suffolk (Univ Campus) We welcome applications from students studying Diploma qualifications and consider the Progression, Advanced and Extended Diplomas to meet the minimum entry requirements for university study. Depending on which University Campus Suffolk course the student applies for, and which Diploma they are studying for, we may require specific Additional and Specialist Learning or, in some cases, additional qualifications. In certain cases, GCSE subjects may be required. For a detailed list of courses and the Diploma subjects acceptable see www.ucas.com. **NB** We are currently reviewing our tariff point entry for 2011 and requirements will be displayed on our website once these are decided.

Warwick Where a department typically makes offers which include a fourth subject at AS level, the Extended Project will normally be considered in lieu of this requirement. All applicants are interviewed for Engineering, English, Film, Theatre and Statistics.

11 DIRECTORY OF UNIVERSITIES AND COLLEGES OFFERING HIGHER EDUCATION COURSES

SECTION 1: UNIVERSITIES

Listed below are universities in the United Kingdom that offer degree and diploma courses at higher education level. Applications to these institutions are submitted through UCAS except for part-time courses, private universities and colleges, and further education courses. For current information refer to the websites shown and also to www.ucas.com and to the UCAS *Big Guide* for a comprehensive list of degree and diploma courses (see **Appendix 5**).

Aberdeen This is a city-centre university on Scotland's east coast. (University of Aberdeen, Students Admissions and School Leavers, University Office, King's College, Aberdeen, Grampian, Scotland AB24 3FX. Tel 01224 272090; www.abdn.ac.uk)

Abertay Dundee The University has a modern city-centre campus. (University of Abertay Dundee, Student Recruitment Office, 40 Bell Street, Dundee, Scotland DD1 1HG. Tel 01382 308000; www.abertay.ac.uk)

Aberystwyth This is a coastal university with a striking campus. (Aberystwyth University, The Admissions Office, Old College, King Street, Aberystwyth, Ceredigion, Wales SY23 2AX. Tel 01970 622021; www.aber.ac.uk)

Anglia Ruskin The University has main campuses in Cambridge and Chelmsford and partner colleges throughout East Anglia. (Anglia Ruskin University, Contact Centre, Bishop Hall Lane, Chelmsford, Essex CM1 1SQ. Tel 0845 271 3333; www.anglia.ac.uk)

Arts London The University consists of four Colleges of Art and Design (Camberwell, Chelsea, Central Saint Martins (including Byam Shaw School of Art) and Wimbledon), the London College of Communication and the London College of Fashion (University of the Arts London, 65 Davies Street, London W1K 5DA. Tel 020 7514 6000; www.arts.ac.uk)

Aston This University has a green campus in the centre of Birmingham with academic, sporting and social activities on site. (Aston University, The Registry (Admissions), Aston Triangle, Birmingham B4 7ET. Tel 0121 204 4444; www.aston.ac.uk)

Bangor The University has a central site in Bangor on the Menai Straits with partner institutions (including Welsh College of Horticulture) throughout North Wales. (Bangor University, Bangor, Gwynedd, Wales LL57 2DG. Tel 01248 351151; www.bangor.ac.uk)

Bath The University is on a rural campus one mile from the centre of Bath, with partner colleges in Bath, Swindon and Wiltshire. (University of Bath, Undergraduate Admissions Office, Claverton Down, Bath, Somerset BA2 7AY. Tel 01225 383019; www.bath.ac.uk)

Bath Spa This University was created in 2005 and is located on two campuses near Bath, with partner colleges in Wiltshire. (Bath Spa University, Admissions Office, Newton Park, Newton St Loe, Bath, Somerset BA2 9BN. Tel 01225 875875; www.bathspa.ac.uk)

Bedfordshire This University was formed in August 2006 from the merger of Luton University and the Bedford campus of De Montfort University. The main campus is in the centre of Luton, with two campuses in Bedford, and four partner colleges. (University of Bedfordshire, The Admissions Office, Park Square, Luton, Bedfordshire LU1 3JU. Tel 01582 489286; www.beds.ac.uk)

Birmingham This is a 'red-brick' university at Edgbaston to the south of the city, with a second campus at Selly Oak. (The University of Birmingham, Admissions, Edgbaston, Birmingham B15 2TT. Tel 0121 414 3344; www.bham.ac.uk)

Birmingham City Situated in Birmingham itself, the University has teaching sites located around the city, each focusing on one subject. Partner colleges in Birmingham and Warwickshire also offer courses. (Birmingham City University, Course Information and Guidance Centre, Perry Bar, Birmingham B42 2SU. Tel 0121 331 5595; www.bcu.ac.uk)

Bolton The University was created in 2005 and is based at Deane Campus, close to the town centre. (The University of Bolton, Recruitment and Admissions, Deane Road, Bolton, Greater Manchester BL3 5AB. Tel 01204 900600; www.bolton.ac.uk)

Bournemouth The University site is in a large coastal resort, with partner colleges in the region also offering courses. (Bournemouth University, The Registry, Lansdowne Campus, 1st Floor Melbury House, 1-3 Oxford Road, Bournemouth BH8 8ES. Tel 01202 524111; www.bournemouth.ac.uk)

Bradford The University's main campus is close to the city centre, with the School of Management two miles away. (The University of Bradford, Course Enquiries Office, Richmond Road, Bradford, West Yorkshire BD7 1DP. Tel 0800 073 1255; www.brad.ac.uk)

Brighton Situated on the south coast, the University has campuses in Brighton and Eastbourne and partner colleges in Sussex. University-validated courses are offered at several partner colleges. (University of Brighton, The Registry (Admissions), Mithras House, Lewes Road, Brighton, East Sussex BN2 4AT. Tel 01273 600900; www.brighton.ac.uk)

Brighton and Sussex Medical School The campus is located at Falmer, just outside Brighton. (BSMS Admissions, Brighton and Sussex Medical School, University of Sussex, Brighton, East Sussex BN1 9PX; Tel 01273 643528; www.bsms.ac.uk)

Bristol This is a city university with halls of residence in Stoke Bishop and Clifton. (University of Bristol, Senate House, Tyndall Avenue, Bristol BS8 1TH. Tel 0117 928 9000; www.bristol.ac.uk)

Bristol UWE The University has four campuses in and around Bristol with an associate Faculty at Hartpury, and regional centres in Bath, Gloucestershire and Swindon. Links with the Bristol Old Vic Theatre School and the Royal West of England Academy. (University of the West of England, Bristol, Admissions Office, Frenchay Campus, Coldharbour Lane. Bristol BS16 1QY. Tel 0117 965 6261; www.uwe.ac.uk)

Brunel The University has a compact campus to the west of London at Uxbridge. Brunel also validates courses at the London School of Theology. (Brunel University, Admissions Office, Uxbridge, Middlesex UB8 3PH. Tel 01895 265265; www.brunel.ac.uk)

Buckingham A small independent university, it has two sites within the town some 40 miles north of London offering two-year (eight-term) degrees. (The University of Buckingham, Admissions Office, Hunter Street, Buckingham MK18 1EG. Tel 01280 820313; www.buckingham.ac.uk)

Bucks New A new university (2007) it has two campuses in High Wycombe and one at Chalfont St Giles and links with partner colleges. (Buckinghamshire New University, Admissions, Queen Alexandra Road, High Wycombe HP11 2JZ. Tel 0800 0565 660; www.bucks.ac.uk)

Cambridge The University has 31 colleges located throughout the city. **Colleges** Lucy Cavendish, Murray Edwards (formerly New Hall) and Newnham (women only); the following admit both men and women undergraduates: Christ's, Churchill, Clare, Corpus Christi, Darwin, Downing, Emmanuel, Fitzwilliam, Girton, Gonville and Caius, Homerton, Hughes, Jesus, King's, Magdalene, Pembroke, Peterhouse, Queens', Robinson, St Catharine's, St John's, Selwyn, Sidney Sussex, Trinity, Trinity Hall, Wolfson. Clare Hall and Darwin admit only graduates. (Enquiries should be addressed to the Tutor for Admissions, ... College,

Cambridge or to the University of Cambridge, Cambridge Admissions Office, Fitzwilliam House, 32 Trumpington Street, Cambridge CB2 1QY. Tel 01223 333308; www.cam.ac.uk)

Canterbury Christ Church The University was created in 2005 with the main campus located near Canterbury city centre and campuses also at Broadstairs, Medway University Centre and Folkestone. (Canterbury Christ Church University, Admissions, North Holmes Road, Canterbury, Kent CT1 1QU. Tel: 01227 782900; www.canterbury.ac.uk)

Cardiff The main (Cathays Park) campus of the University is located in the city centre, with the Heath Park campus a mile to the south. (Cardiff University, Admissions, MacKenzie House, 30–36 Newport Road, Cardiff, Wales CF24 0DE. Tel 029 2087 9999; www.cardiff.ac.uk)

Central Lancashire The University is located on a small campus in the city centre with partner colleges throughout Lancashire. (University of Central Lancashire, Admissions Office, Preston PR1 2HE. Tel 01772 201201; www.uclan.ac.uk)

Chester This university was formed in 2005 and is located on a campus in Chester, with a second campus in Warrington and two partner colleges. (Chester University, Undergraduate Admissions, Parkgate Road, Chester CH1 4BJ. Tel 01244 512528; www.chester.ac.uk)

Chichester This is a small university (2005) with campuses at Chichester and Bognor Regis. (University of Chichester, Admissions, Bognor Regis Campus, Upper Bognor Road, Bognor Regis, West Sussex PO21 1HR. Tel 01243 816002; www.chiuni.ac.uk)

City The University is situated in central London, with Nursing and Midwifery located at St Bartholomew's Hospital. (City University, Undergraduate Admissions Office, Northampton Square, London EC1V 0HB. Tel 020 7040 5060; www.city.ac.uk)

Coventry The University has a 33-acre campus in Coventry and a number of teaching centres throughout the city with courses offered in several partner colleges. (The Student Centre, Coventry University, 1 Gulson Road, Coventry CV1 2JH. Tel 024 7615 2525; www.coventry.ac.uk)

Creative Arts The University has five colleges – three in Kent (Canterbury, Maidstone and Rochester) and two in Surrey (Epsom and Farnham). (University for the Creative Arts, Enquiries Service, Falkner Road, Farnham, Surrey GU9 7DS. Tel 01252 892883; www.ucreative.ac.uk/enquiries)

Cumbria This new university (2007) was created by the merger of St Martin's College and Cumbria Institute of the Arts. There are campuses in Ambleside, Carlisle, Lancaster, Penrith and London. (University of Cumbria, Fusehill Street, Carlisle, Cumbria CA1 2HH. Tel 01228 616234; www.cumbria.ac.uk)

De Montfort The University has two sites in Leicester and nine associated colleges. (De Montfort University, Students Admissions, The Gateway, Leicester LE1 9BH. Tel 0116 255 1551; www.dmu.ac.uk)

Derby The University has two campuses: one close to Derby city centre and the second at Buxton. (University of Derby, Admissions, Kedleston Road, Derby DE22 1GB. Tel 01332 591167; www.derby.ac.uk)

Dundee A city-centre campus, with the Medical School and School of Nursing located at Ninewells Hospital to the west of the city. (University of Dundee, Admissions and Student Recruitment, Nethergate, Dundee, Scotland DD1 4HN. Tel 01382 384160; www.dundee.ac.uk)

Durham The University has two sites, the main site in Durham city and the second, at Stockton, with two colleges on the Queen's Campus. (Durham University, Undergraduate Admissions Office, University Office, Old Elvet, Durham DH1 3HP. Tel 0191 334 6123; www.dur.ac.uk)

East Anglia The University is set in parkland close to Norwich. (University of East Anglia, Admissions Office, Norwich, Norfolk NR4 7TJ. Tel 01603 592092; www.uea.ac.uk)

East London The University has campuses in London at Stratford and Docklands. Courses are also offered at several colleges in Greater London. (University of East London, Admissions/Applicant Enquiries, Docklands Campus, 4–6 University Way, London E16 2RB. Tel 020 8223 3333; www.uel.ac.uk)

Edge Hill This university (formed in 2005) has its campus in Ormskirk near Liverpool. (Edge Hill University, Academic Registry, Ormskirk, Lancashire L39 4QP. Tel 0169 558 4747; www.edgehill.ac.uk)

Edinburgh This university consists of the University Central Area in the city centre and the University King's Buildings on a site a mile to the south. (The University of Edinburgh, Student Recruitment and Admissions, 57 George Square, Edinburgh, Scotland EH8 9JU. Tel 0131 650 4360; www.ed.ac.uk)

Edinburgh Napier The University has six campuses in the centre of Edinburgh and two to the south-west. (Edinburgh Napier University, Information Office, Craiglockart Campus, Edinburgh, Scotland EH14 1DJ. Tel 08452 606040; www.napier.ac.uk)

Essex The University has a parkland campus two miles from Colchester. The University and the South Essex College Partnership also provide degree schemes at the new Southend campus. The University validates degrees offered by Writtle College and by the East 15 Acting School. (University of Essex, Undergraduate Admissions, Wivenhoe Park, Colchester, Essex CO4 3SQ. Tel 01206 873666; www.essex.ac.uk)

Exeter The University has two sites in Exeter: the Streatham campus is the largest, and the St Luke's campus is a mile away. A third campus (University of Exeter in Cornwall campus) is situated at Penryn in Cornwall. (University of Exeter, Admissions Office, 8th Floor, Laver Building, North Park Road, Exeter, Devon EX4 4QE. Tel 01392 263855; www.exeter.ac.uk)

Glamorgan The University has four faculties on two campuses in Pontypridd and a faculty in Cardiff. The main campus is at Glamorgan and the new School of Creative and Cultural Industries is in Cardiff city centre. The University has partnerships with the Royal Welsh College of Music and Drama and several other colleges. (University of Glamorgan, Enquiries and Admissions Unit, Pontypridd, Wales CF37 1DL. Tel 0800 716925; www.glam.ac.uk)

Glasgow The University has three campuses, two on the outskirts of Glasgow and one on the Crichton campus at Dumfries. Glasgow School of Art and the Scottish Agricultural College in Ayr are associated institutions. (The University of Glasgow, Recruitment, Admissions and Participation Service, Fraser Building, 65 Hillhead Street, Glasgow, Strathclyde, Scotland G12 8QF. Tel 0141 330 3282; www.gla.ac.uk)

Glasgow Caledonian The University has a city-centre campus. (Glasgow Caledonian University, City Campus, Admissions Office, Cowcaddens Road, Glasgow, Strathclyde, Scotland G4 0BA. Tel 0141 331 3000; www.gcal.ac.uk)

Gloucestershire Three campuses in Cheltenham and one in Gloucester form the University. It also has partner colleges in Gloucestershire, Herefordshire, Wiltshire and Worcestershire. (The University of Gloucestershire, The Park, Cheltenham, Gloucestershire GL50 2RH. Tel 0844 801 0001; www.glos.ac.uk)

Glyndŵr This is a new university (2008), formerly North East Wales IHE, and is situated in Wrexham town centre. (Glyndŵr University, Plas Coch, Mold Road, Wrexham LL11 2AW. Tel 01978 290666; www.glyndwr.ac.uk)

Greenwich The main campus of the University is at Greenwich, a second is at Avery Hill in south London and a third is at Medway at Chatham Maritime. There are also partner colleges in east London and Kent. (University of Greenwich, Enquiry Unit, Greenwich Campus, Old Royal Naval College, Park Row, London SE10 9LS. Tel 0800 005 006; www.gre.ac.uk)

Heriot-Watt The University has a large parkland campus seven miles west of Edinburgh and a second campus in the Scottish Borders at Galashiels 35 miles to the south. (Heriot-Watt University, Admissions Unit, Edinburgh Campus, Edinburgh, Lothian, Scotland EH14 4AS. Tel 0131 449 5111; www.hw.ac.uk)

Hertfordshire This university has two campuses in Hatfield. Courses are also offered through a consortium of four Hertfordshire colleges and the University has links with all Hertfordshire further education colleges. (University of Hertfordshire, University Admissions Service, College Lane, Hatfield, Hertfordshire AL10 9AB. Tel 01707 284800; www.herts.ac.uk)

Huddersfield This is a town-centre university with University Centres at Barnsley and Oldham and links to colleges of further education throughout the north of England. (University of Huddersfield, Admissions Office, Queensgate, Huddersfield HD1 3DH. Tel 01484 473969; www.hud.ac.uk)

Hull The main campus is in Hull, two miles from the city centre, with a smaller campus at Scarborough. (The University of Hull, Admissions Service, Cottingham Road, Hull, East Yorkshire HU6 7RX. Tel 01482 466100; www.hull.ac.uk)

Hull York Medical School The Medical School is a partnership between the Universities of Hull and York, with teaching facilities on the main campuses of both universities. (Admissions Section, University of York, Heslington, York YO10 5DD. Tel 0870 124 5500, www.hyms.ac.uk)

Imperial London The College became an independent university, separate from the University of London, in 2007. The central site is in South Kensington. Medicine is based mainly at St Mary's Hospital, Paddington, Charing Cross Hospital and Hammersmith Hospital. (Imperial College London, Registry, South Kensington Campus, London SW7 2AZ. Tel 020 7589 5111; www.imperial.ac.uk)

Keele This is a small university on a green campus five miles from Stoke-on-Trent. (Keele University, Academic Registry, Keele, Staffordshire ST5 5BG. Tel 01782 734005; www.keele.ac.uk)

Kent The University has a spacious campus near Canterbury, and also campuses at Medway, Chatham and Wye, with two associate colleges (South Kent College, Mid Kent College) and two partner institutions (West Kent College, Canterbury College). (The University of Kent, The Registry, Canterbury, Kent CT2 7NZ. Tel 01227 764000; www.kent.ac.uk)

Kingston With four campuses in and around the town and 10 partner colleges, the University has easy access to London. (Kingston University, Student Information and Advice Centre, Cooper House, 40–46 Surbiton Road, Kingston upon Thames, Surrey KT1 2HX. Tel 020 8417 3553; www.kingston.ac.uk)

Lampeter The University is merging in 2010 with Trinity University College, Carmarthen, to form the new University of Wales, Trinity Saint David University (see below).

Lancaster The University has a parkland site three miles south of Lancaster city centre. (The University, Undergraduate Admissions Office, Bailrigg, Lancaster LA1 4YW. Tel 01524 592028; www.lancs.ac.uk)

Leeds The University is sited on a campus in the centre of the city. (The University of Leeds, Undergraduate Admissions Office, Leeds LS2 9JT. Tel 0113 243 1751; www.leeds.ac.uk)

Leeds Metropolitan The University has two campuses, one in the city and a second in Headingley on the outskirts of Leeds, and partner colleges throughout the region. (Leeds Metropolitian University, Course Enquiries Office, Civic Quarter, Leeds LS1 3HE. Tel 0113 812 3113; www.lmu.ac.uk)

Leicester The compact campus is located on the southern edge of the city. (University of Leicester, Admissions Office, University Road, Leicester LE1 7RH. Tel 0116 252 5281; www.le.ac.uk)

Lincoln The Brayford and Cathedral campuses are in the city, with the Riseholme Park campus some five miles away. There is also a campus in Hull and associated colleges in Lincolnshire. (University of Lincoln, Admissions, Brayford Pool, Lincoln LN6 7TS. Tel 01522 886097; www.lincoln.ac.uk)

Liverpool The University has a large city-centre campus. (The University of Liverpool, Student Recruitment and Admissions Office, Liverpool L69 3BX. Tel 0151 794 2000; www.liv.ac.uk)

Liverpool Hope This university, created in 2005, is situated outside Liverpool. (Liverpool Hope University, Admissions Office, Hope Park, Liverpool L16 9JD. Tel 0151 291 3295; www.hope.ac.uk)

Liverpool John Moores The University has three campuses in and around Liverpool. (Liverpool John Moores University, Admissions and Information Officer, Byrom Street, Liverpool L3 3AF. Tel 0151 231 2021; www.livjm.ac.uk)

London – Birkbeck (Birk) The College is situated in Bloomsbury in the London University precinct and provides part-time and evening higher education courses. (Birkbeck, University of London, Malet Street, Bloomsbury, London WC1E 7HX. Tel 020 7631 6000; Course Enquiries 0845 601 0174; www.bbk.ac.uk)

London – Central School of Speech and Drama The School's main campus is at the Embassy Theatre, 15 minutes by Underground from Central London. (Central School of Speech and Drama (University of London), Academic Registry, Embassy Theatre, 64 Eton Avenue, London NW3 3HY. Tel 020 7722 8183; www.cssd.ac.uk)

London – Courtauld (Court) The Institute, together with its gallery, is located in Somerset House on the Strand in central London. (The Courtauld Institute of Art (University of London), Somerset House, Strand, London WC2R 0RN. Tel 020 7848 2635/2645; www.courtauld.ac.uk)

London – Goldsmiths (Gold) The College is located on a single campus in south-east London. (Goldsmiths, University of London, Admissions Office, Lewisham Way, New Cross, London SE14 6NW. Tel 020 7919 7766; www.gold.ac.uk)

London – Heythrop College (Hey) The College is on a site in central London. (Heythrop College, University of London, Registry, Kensington Square, London W8 5HN. Tel 020 7795 6600; www.heythrop.ac.uk)

London – Institute in Paris The Institute's Department of French Studies and Comparative Studies is located in central Paris and operates in partnership with Queen Mary and Royal Holloway, University of London. (University of London Institute in Paris, 9–11 rue de Constantine, 75340 Paris, Cedex 07. Tel 00 331 44 117383; www.ulip.lon.ac.uk)

London – King's College (King's) The College has campuses in central and south London (Strand, Waterloo and London Bridge) including the School of Medicine, the Dental Institute and the School of Biomedical and Health Sciences. (King's College London, Enquiries, Strand, London WC2R 2LS. Tel 020 7836 5454; www.kcl.ac.uk)

London – Queen Mary (QM) There is a city campus in the East End of London. (Queen Mary, University of London, Admissions Office, Mile End Road, London E1 4NS. Tel 020 7882 5555; www.qmul.ac.uk)

London – Royal Academy of Music (RAcMus) This is Britain's senior conservatoire, founded in 1822. (Royal Academy of Music, University of London, Marylebone Road, London NW1 5HT. Tel 020 7873 7373; www.ram.ac.uk)

London – Royal Holloway (RH) There is a large campus with halls of residence situated at Egham, 19 miles west from central London and three miles from Windsor. (Royal Holloway, University of London, Admissions Office, Egham, Surrey TW20 0EX. Tel 01784 434455; www.rhul.ac.uk)

London – Royal Veterinary College (RVC) The College has campuses in London and Hertfordshire. (Royal Veterinary College, University of London, Admissions Office, Royal College Street, London NW1 0TU. Tel 020 7468 5147; www.rvc.ac.uk)

London – St George's Located on a compact site in south-west London, St George's is a specialist health sciences university, having extensive links with many hospitals and practices, and with Kingston University and Royal Holloway London. (St George's, University of London, Admissions, Cranmer Terrace, Tooting, London SW17 0RE. Tel 020 87672 9944; www.sgul.ac.uk)

London – School of Oriental and African Studies (SOAS) The School is located in Bloomsbury and Islington in central London. (School of Oriental and African Studies, University of London, Admissions Unit, Thornhaugh Street, Russell Square, London WC1H 0XG. Tel 020 7074 5105; www.soas.ac.uk)

London – School of Pharmacy The School has a central London site close to the London University precinct. (The School of Pharmacy (University of London), Registry, 29–39 Brunswick Square, London WC1N 1AX. Tel 020 7753 5831; www.pharmacy.ac.uk)

London – University College London (UCL) The College is located in Bloomsbury in the London University precinct. (University College London, Study Information Centre, Gower Street, London WC1E 6BT. Tel 020 7679 2000; www.ucl.ac.uk)

London Metropolitan The University has two campuses, one in north London (with the largest (new) science laboratory in Europe) and one in the City, and several partner colleges. (London Metropolitan University, Admissions Office, 166–220 Holloway Road, London N7 8DB. Tel 020 7133 4200; www.londonmet.ac.uk)

London School of Economics and Political Science (LSE) LSE is a university specialising in the whole range of social science subjects (from Economics, Politics and Law to Sociology, Accounting and Finance). Located in the heart of London. LSE entrance examination may be required. (London School of Economics and Political Science, Undergraduate Admissions Office, Houghton Street, London WC2A 2AE. Tel 020 7955 7125; www.lse.ac.uk)

London South Bank The main campus of the University is in Southwark on the south bank of the Thames in London. Other campuses are at Whipps Cross in east London and at Havering in Essex. (London South Bank University, Admissions Office, 103 Borough Road, London SE1 0AA. Tel 020 7815 7815; www.lsbu.ac.uk)

Loughborough On a large rural single-site campus, the University is a mile from the town centre. (Loughborough University, Undergraduate Admissions Office, Loughborough, Leicestershire LE11 3TU. Tel 01509 263171; www.lboro.ac.uk)

Manchester The University has a large precinct one mile south of the city centre. (The University of Manchester, Student Recruitment and Admissions, Oxford Road, Manchester M13 9PL. Tel 0161 275 2077; www.manchester.ac.uk)

Manchester Metropolitan The University has five sites in Manchester and one in Cheshire, at Alsager and Crewe. (The Manchester Metropolitan University, Admissions Office, All Saints Building, All Saints, Manchester M15 6BH. Tel 0161 247 2000; www.mmu.ac.uk)

Middlesex This is a multi-campus university in north London with associate colleges in the region. (Middlesex University, Admissions Enquiries, The Burroughs, Hendon, London NW4 4BT. Tel 020 8411 5555; www.mdx.ac.uk)

Newcastle The University has a single campus in the city centre. (Newcastle University, Admissions Office, 6 Kensington Terrace, Newcastle upon Tyne NE1 7RU. Tel 0191 222 5594; www.ncl.ac.uk)

Newport The University has two campuses, in Newport and Caerleon. (University of Wales, Newport, Admissions Office, Caerleon Campus, Lodge Road, Caerleon, Newport, South Wales NP18 3QT. Tel 01633 432030; www.newport.ac.uk)

Northampton The University (created in 2005) has two campuses close to the town centre. (University of Northampton, Admissions Office, Park Campus, Boughton Green Road, Northampton NN2 7AL. Tel 0800 358 2232; www.northampton.ac.uk)

Northumbria The University has two campuses in and around Newcastle. (Northumbria University, Trinity Building, Northumberland Road, Newcastle upon Tyne NE1 8ST. Tel 0191 232 6002; www.northumbria.ac.uk)

Nottingham This is a large campus university to the west of the city with a second campus two miles from the city centre, and a third at Sutton Bonington for the new School of Veterinary Science and Medicine, 10 miles south of University Park. (The University of Nottingham, Admissions Office, University Park, Nottingham NG7 2RD. Tel 0115 951 5151; www.nottingham.ac.uk)

Nottingham Trent The Clifton campus of the University is four miles from Nottingham city centre and caters for Education, Humanities and Science whilst Brackenhurst, near Southwell, focuses on land-based subjects. (Nottingham Trent University, Registry Admissions, Dryden Centre, Burton Street, Nottingham NG1 4BU. Tel 0115 848 4200; www.ntu.ac.uk)

Open University This is the UK's largest university for part-time and distance-learning higher education, providing supported distance learning for undergraduate (and postgraduate) students who must be over 18. Application and registration is made direct to the OU, and not through UCAS (at present). (The Open University, Student Registration and Enquiry Service, PO Box 197, Milton Keynes MK7 6BJ. Tel 0845 300 6090; www.open.ac.uk)

Oxford The University has 30 colleges and seven private halls admitting undergraduates throughout the city. **Colleges** Balliol, Brasenose, Christ Church, Corpus Christi, Exeter, Harris Manchester (mature students only), Hertford, Jesus, Keble, Lady Margaret Hall, Lincoln, Magdalen, Mansfield, Merton, New, Oriel, Pembroke, St Anne's, St Catherine's, St Edmund Hall, St Hilda's (women only, but has voted to admit men), St Hugh's, St John's, St Peter's, Somerville, Queen's, Trinity, University, Wadham, Worcester. **Permanent Private Halls** Blackfriars, Campion Hall (men only), Greyfriars, Regent's Park College, St Benet's Hall, St Stephen's House, Wycliffe. (Enquiries should be addressed to The Tutor for Admissions .... College, Oxford, or to The Undergraduate Admissions Office, Oxford University, Wellington Square, Oxford OX1 2JD. Tel 01865 288000; www.ox.ac.uk)

Oxford Brookes The University has three main campuses in and around Oxford. (Oxford Brookes University, Admissions Office, Headington Campus, Gipsy Lane, Oxford OX3 0BP. Tel 01865 483040; www.brookes.ac.uk)

Peninsula College of Medicine and Dentistry The College has campuses at Exeter and Plymouth Universities and teaching facilities in Truro. (Peninsula Medical School, The John Bull Building, Tamar Science Park, Research Way, Plymouth, Devon PL6 8BU. Tel 01752 437444; www.pms.ac.uk)

Plymouth The University has two main campuses, one in Plymouth and a second, the Peninsula Allied Health Centre, is four miles north of the main campus. Courses are also offered at eight partner colleges. (University of Plymouth, Central Admissions, Drake Circus, Plymouth PL4 8AA. Tel 01752 588014; www.plymouth.ac.uk)

Portsmouth The main campus of the University is close to the town centre; courses are also taught at colleges in Hampshire and Surrey. (University of Portsmouth, Academic Registry, University House, Winston Churchill Avenue, Portsmouth, Hampshire PO1 2UP. Tel 023 9284 8484; www.port.ac.uk)

Queen Margaret This new university (2007) is located on a new campus on the Firth of Forth east of Edinburgh, with student accommodation on site. (Queen Margaret University, The Admissions Office, Queen Margaret University Drive, Edinburgh EH21 6UU. Tel 0131 474 0000; www.qmu.ac.uk)

Queen's Belfast The University has a large campus in the south of the city. (Queen's University Belfast, Admissions Service, University Road, Belfast, Northern Ireland BT7 1NN. Tel 028 9097 2727; www.qub.ac.uk)

Reading There are three campuses in the University, with the main (Whiteknights) on a rural campus at the edge of the city, and two others within walking distance. Foundation degrees are taught at two partner colleges. (The University of Reading, Student Recruitment Office, PO Box 217, Reading, Berkshire RG6 6AH. Tel 0118 378 8619; www.rdg.ac.uk)

Robert Gordon The University has two campuses in and near Aberdeen city centre. (The Robert Gordon University, Admissions Office, Schoolhill, Aberdeen, Grampian, Scotland AB10 1FR. Tel 01224 262728; www.rgu.ac.uk)

Roehampton Established in 2004, the University is located in south west London, close to Richmond Park, and has four Colleges: Southlands, Digby Stuart, Froebel and Whitelands. (Roehampton University, Enquiries Office, Erasmus House, Roehampton Lane, London SW15 5PU. Tel 020 8392 3232; www.roehampton.ac.uk)

St Andrews Founded in 1413, and the third oldest university in the English-speaking world, this is a town-centre university on the east coast of Scotland. (University of St Andrews, Admissions Application Centre, St Katherine's West, The Scores, St Andrews, Fife, Scotland KY16 9AX. Tel 01334 462150; www.st-andrews.ac.uk)

Salford This is a city-centre campus university for all courses, except for Midwifery at Bury and Nursing at Eccles. (The University of Salford, Admissions Officer, The Crescent, Salford, Greater Manchester M5 4WT. Tel 0161 295 4545; www.salford.ac.uk)

Sheffield The university campus is close to Sheffield's city centre. (The University of Sheffield, Undergraduate Admissions, Western Bank, Sheffield, South Yorkshire S10 2TN. Tel 0114 222 1255, www.shef.ac.uk)

Sheffield Hallam The University has two campuses, one in the city centre, and the second two miles away. (Sheffield Hallam University, Admissions Office, City Campus, Howard Street, Sheffield, South Yorkshire S1 1WB. Tel 0114 225 5555; www.shu.ac.uk)

Southampton The University has six main campuses in Southampton and Winchester. (University of Southampton, University Road, Southampton SO17 1BJ. Tel 023 8059 5000; www.soton.ac.uk)

Southampton Solent The University (created in 2005) is close to Southampton city centre, and has two partner colleges. (Southampton Solent University, Student Recruitment, East Park Terrace, Southampton, Hampshire SO14 0YN. Tel 023 8031 9000; www.solent.ac.uk)

Staffordshire The University has campuses at Stafford, Stoke and Lichfield and several regional colleges. (Staffordshire University, Admissions, College Road, Stoke on Trent, Staffordshire ST4 2DE. Tel 01782 292753; www.staffs.ac.uk)

Stirling The University is situated on a large rural campus. (The University of Stirling, The UG Admissions Office, Stirling, Central Scotland FK9 4LA. Tel 01786 467044; www.stir.ac.uk)

Strathclyde The University's main campus is in Glasgow city centre, with the Jordanhill campus to the west of the city. (The University of Strathclyde, 16 Richmond Street, Glasgow, Scotland G1 1XQ. Tel 0141 552 4400; www.strath.ac.uk)

Sunderland The main campus of the University is in Sunderland city centre, with the Sir Tom Cowie campus across the river accommodating the Business School and Informatics Centre. (University of Sunderland, Student Recruitment, Chester Road, Sunderland SR1 3SD. Tel 0191 515 2000; www.sunderland.ac.uk)

Surrey The University has a modern campus a mile from Guildford city centre. Some foundation-year teaching takes place in local colleges. (University of Surrey, Undergraduate Admissions Office, Stag Hill, Guildford, Surrey GU2 7XH. Tel 01483 689305; www.surrey.ac.uk)

Sussex The University has a single site campus four miles from Brighton. (University of Sussex, Undergraduate Admissions, Sussex House, Falmer, Brighton, Sussex BN1 9RH. Tel 01273 678416; www.sussex.ac.uk)

Swansea The University is situated in a parkland campus outside Swansea. (Swansea University, Admissions, Singleton Park, Swansea, Wales SA2 8PP. Tel 01792 205678; www.swan.ac.uk)

Swansea Metropolitan This new (2008) university (formerly Swansea Institute) is situated in the centre of Swansea. (Swansea Metropolitan University, Admissions Office, Mount Pleasant Campus, Swansea, Wales SA1 6ED. Tel 01792 481000; www.smu.ac.uk)

Teesside This is a city-centre university, with its campus in Middlesbrough. It has links with colleges in the region. (University of Teesside, Admissions Office, Middlesbrough, Tees Valley TS1 3BA. Tel 01642 218121; www.tees.ac.uk)

Thames Valley The University has campuses at Ealing, Reading, Slough and Brentford, and links with four sites in west London and associated colleges. (Thames Valley University, Learning Advice Centre, St Mary's Road, Ealing, London W5 5RF. 0800 036 8888; www.tvu.ac.uk)

Trinity Saint David This is a new university (2010) created by the merger of the University of Wales, Lampeter, and Trinity University College with courses run at Carmarthen and Lampeter. (University of Wales, Trinity Saint David, Academic Registry, Lampeter, Ceredigion, Wales SA48 7ED. Tel 01570 422351; www.lamp.ac.uk)

Ulster The University has four campuses – Belfast, Coleraine, Jordanstown, and Magee in Londonderry. (University of Ulster Coleraine, County Londonderry, Northern Ireland BT52 1SA. Tel 08 700 400 700; www.ulster.ac.uk)

Warwick The University has a single-site campus situated three miles outside Coventry. (The University of Warwick, Student Admissions Office, Coventry, West Midlands CV4 7AL. Tel 024 7652 3723; www.warwick.ac.uk)

West of Scotland This new university (2007) was formed from the merger of the University of Paisley and Bell College. There are four campuses – Paisley, Ayr, Hamilton and Dumfries. (University of The West of Scotland, Admissions Office, High Street, Paisley, Renfrewshire, Scotland PA1 2BE. Tel 0141 8483727; www.uws.ac.uk)

Westminster The University has four campuses (Cavendish, Marylebone and Regent in central London and Harrow) and associated colleges including the British Academy of New Music. (University of Westminster, Central Admissions, 35 Marylebone Road, London NW1 5LS. Tel 020 7911 5020; www.westminster.ac.uk)

Winchester This is a new university (2005) close to the centre of the city with sites in Basingstoke and Bournemouth. (University of Winchester, Course Enquiries, West Hill, Winchester, Hampshire SO22 4NR. Tel 01962 8272334; www.winchester.ac.uk)

Wolverhampton The University has two campuses in Wolverhampton and others in Walsall and Telford. (University of Wolverhampton, Admissions Unit, MX, City Campus North, Camp Street, Wolverhampton, West Midlands WV1 1AD. Tel 01902 323443; www.wlv.ac.uk)

Worcester This small new university (2005) is located on a campus a short distance from Worcester city centre. (University of Worcester, Admissions Office, Henwick Grove, Worcester WR2 6AJ. Tel 01905 855111; www.worcester.ac.uk)

York The University has a parkland campus on the outskirts of York and a second campus in the city centre. (The University of York, Admissions and School Liaison, Heslington, York YO10 5DD. Tel 01904 433533; www.york.ac.uk)

York St John This university (created in 2006) is on a site facing York Minster, five minutes' walk from York city centre. (York St John University, Lord Mayor's Walk, York YO31 7EX. Tel 01904 624624; www.yorksj.ac.uk)

SECTION 2: UNIVERSITY COLLEGES, INSTITUTES, AND SPECIALIST COLLEGES OF AGRICULTURE AND HORTICULTURE, ART, DANCE, DRAMA, MUSIC, OSTEOPATHY AND SPEECH

University Colleges and Institutes provide undergraduate and postgraduate courses in a wide range of subjects and are university-sector institutions. While many universities and university colleges offer courses in art, design, music, drama, agriculture, horticulture and courses connected to the land-based industries, the specialist colleges listed below provide courses at many levels, often part-time, in these separate fields.

It is important that you read prospectuses and check websites carefully and go to Open Days to find out as much as you can about these colleges and about their courses which interest you. Applications for full-time courses at the institutions listed below are through UCAS. Refer to the *Big Guide* for details (see **Appendix 5**).

Abbreviations used below A = Art and Design; **Ag** = Agriculture, Animals and Land-related courses; **C** = Communication; **D** = Drama, Performing and Theatre Arts; **Da** = Dance; **F** = Fashion; **H** = Horticulture and Landscape-related courses; **M** = Music.

ALRA (Academy of Live and Recorded Arts) Studio 1 Royal Victoria Patriotic Building, John Archer Way, London SW18 3SX. Tel 020 8870 6475; www.alra.co.uk [**D**]

Anglo-European College of Chiropractic 13-15 Parkwood Road, Bournemouth, Dorset BH5 2DF. Tel 01202 436200; www.aecc.ac.uk

Architectural Association School of Architecture 36 Bedford Square, London WC1B 3ES. Tel 020 7887 4000; www.aaschool.ac.uk

Arts Educational Schools London Cone Ripman House, 14 Bath Road, Chiswick, London W4 1LY. Tel 020 8987 6666; www.artsed.co.uk [**D**]

Askham Bryan College Admissions Office, Askham Bryan, York YO23 3FR. Tel 01904 772211; www.askham-bryan.ac.uk [**Ag**]

Birmingham Conservatoire (Faculty of Birmingham City University), Paradise Place, Birmingham B3 3HG. Tel 0121 331 5901/2; www.conservatoire.bcu.ac.uk [**M**]

Birmingham Institute of Art and Design (Faculty of Birmingham City University), Gosta Green, Corporation Street, Birmingham B4 7DX. Tel 0121 331 5800/1; www.biad.bcu.ac.uk [**A**]

Birmingham School of Acting (Faculty of Birmingham City University), G2 Millennium Point, Curzon Street, Birmingham, B4 7XG. Tel 0121 331 7220; www.bsa.bcu.ac.uk [**D**]

Birmingham University College Admissions Office, Summer Row, Birmingham, West Midlands B3 1JB. Tel 0121 604 1040; www.ucb.ac.uk

Bishop Burton College Learner Services, York Road, Bishop Burton, Beverley, East Yorkshire HU17 8QG. Tel 01964 553000; www.bishopb-college.ac.uk [**Ag**]

Bishop Grosseteste University College Academic Registry, Newport, Lincoln LN1 3DY. Tel 01522 583658; www.bishopg.ac.uk

Bournemouth Arts University College Wallisdown, Poole, Dorset BH12 5HH. Tel 01202 533011; www.aucb.ac.uk [**A**]

Bristol Old Vic Theatre School 1–2 Downside Road, Clifton, Bristol BS8 2XF. Tel 0117 973 3535; www.oldvic.ac.uk [**D**]

British College of Osteopathic Medicine Lief House, 120–122 Finchley Road, London NW3 5HR. Tel 020 7435 6464; www.bcom.ac.uk

British School of Osteopathy 275 Borough High Street, London SE1 1JE. Tel 020 7407 0222; Student Admissions 020 7089 5316; www.bso.ac.uk

Camberwell College of Arts University of the Arts London, Peckham Road, London SE5 8UF. Tel 020 7514 6302; www.camberwell.arts.ac.uk [**A**]

Capel Manor College Administrative Office, Bullsmore Lane, Enfield, Middlesex EN1 4RQ. Tel 08456 122122; www.capel.ac.uk [**H**]

Cardiff University of Wales Institute Llandaff Campus, Western Avenue, Cardiff, Wales CF5 2YB. Tel 029 2041 6070; www.uwic.ac.uk

Central Saint Martins College of Art and Design University of the Arts London, Southampton Row, Holborn, London WC1B 4AP. Tel 020 7514 7022; www.csm.arts.ac.uk [**A**]

Central School of Speech and Drama, University of London, Embassy Theatre, Eton Avenue, London NW3 3HY. Tel 020 7722 8183; www.cssd.ac.uk [**D**]

Chelsea College of Art and Design University of the Arts London, 16 John Islip Street, London SW1P 4JU. Tel 020 7514 7751; www.chelsea.arts.ac.uk [**A**]

City and Guilds of London Art School 124 Kennington Park Road, London SE11 4DJ. Tel 020 7735 2306; www.cityandguildsartschool.ac.uk [**A**]

Cleveland College of Art and Design Green Lane, Linthorpe, Middlesbrough TS5 7RJ. Tel 01642 288000; Student Recruitment 01642 288888; www.ccad.ac.uk [**A**]

Colchester Institute Course Enquiries, Sheepen Road, Colchester, Essex CO3 3LL. Tel 01206 712777; www.colchester.ac.uk

College of Agriculture, Food and Rural Enterprise (CAFRE) Greenmount Campus, 22 Greenmount Road, County Antrim, Northern Ireland BT41 4PU. Tel 0800 028 4291; www.cafre.ac.uk [**Ag**]

Drama Centre London (part of Central Saint Martins: University of the Arts London), Saffron House, 10 Back Hill, London EC1R 5LQ. Tel 020 7514 8778; www.csm.arts.ac.uk/drama [**D**]

East 15 Acting School Hatfields, Rectory Lane, Loughton, Essex IG10 3RY. Tel 020 8508 5983; www.east15.ac.uk [**D**]

Edinburgh College of Art Lauriston Place, Edinburgh, EH3 9DF. Tel 0131 221 6027; www.eca.ac.uk [**A**]

European School of Osteopathy Boxley House, The Street, Boxley, Maidstone, Kent ME14 3DZ. Tel 01622 671558; www.eso.ac.uk

Falmouth University College (including Dartington College of Arts) Admissions Office, Woodlane, Falmouth, Cornwall TR11 4RH. Tel 01326 211077; www.falmouth.ac.uk

Glasgow School of Art 167 Renfrew Street, Glasgow, Scotland G3 6RQ. Tel 0141 353 4500; www.gsa.ac.uk [**A**]

Gray's School of Art The Robert Gordon University, Garthdee Road, Aberdeen, Scotland AB10 7QD. Tel 01224 263600; www.rgu.ac.uk [**A**]

GSA Conservatoire Guildford School of Acting, Millmead Terrace, Guildford, Surrey GU2 4YT. Tel 01483 560701; www.conservatoire.org [**D**]

Guildhall School of Music and Drama Silk Street, Barbican, London EC2Y 8DT. Tel 020 7628 2571; www.gsmd.ac.uk [**M D**]

Harper Adams University College Admissions Office, Newport, Shropshire TF10 8NB. Tel 01952 820280; www.harper-adams.ac.uk [**Ag**]

Hartpury College (an Associate Faculty of Bristol UWE) Hartpury House, Hartpury, Gloucester GL19 3BE. Tel 01452 702345; www.hartpury.ac.uk [**Ag**]

Heatherley School of Fine Art 75 Lots Road, London SW10 0RN. Tel 020 7351 4190; www.heatherleys.org [**A**]

Hereford College of Arts Folly Lane, Hereford HR1 1LT. Tel 01432 273359; www.hca.ac.uk [**A**]

Leeds College of Art and Design Blenheim Walk, Leeds LS2 9AQ. Tel 0113 202 8039; www.leeds-art.ac.uk [**A**]

Leeds College of Music 3 Quarry Hill, Leeds, West Yorkshire LS2 7PD. Tel Course Enquiries 0113 222 3416; www.lcm.ac.uk [**M**]

Leeds Trinity University College Student Enquiries Office, Brownberrie Lane, Horsforth, Leeds LS18 5HD. Tel 0113 283 7100; www.leedstrinity.ac.uk

Liverpool Institute for Performing Arts (LIPA) Mount Street, Liverpool L1 9HF. Tel 0151 330 3000; www.lipa.ac.uk [**D**]

London Academy of Music and Dramatic Art (LAMDA) 155 Talgarth Road, London W14 9DA. Tel 020 8834 0500; www.lamda.org.uk [**M D**]

London College of Communication, University of the Arts London, Elephant and Castle, London SE1 6SB. Tel 020 7514 6500; www.lcc.arts.ac.uk [**C**]

London College of Fashion, University of the Arts London, 20 John Princes Street, London W1G 0BJ. Tel 020 7514 7400; www.fashion.arts.ac.uk [**F**]

Marjon – University College Plymouth St Mark and St John Admissions Office, Derriford Road, Plymouth, Devon PL6 8BH. Tel 01752 636890; www.marjon.ac.uk

Mountview Academy of Theatre Arts Ralph Richardson Memorial Studios, Clarendon Road, Wood Green, London N22 6XF. Tel 020 8881 2201; www.mountview.org.uk [**D**]

Myerscough College (an Associate College of the University of Central Lancashire) Myerscough Hall, St Michael's Road, Bilsborrow, Preston, Lancashire PR3 0RY. Tel 01995 642222; www.myerscough.ac.uk [**Ag**]

Newman University College Admissions Registrar, Genners Lane, Bartley Green, Birmingham, West Midlands B32 3NT. Tel 0121 476 1181; www.newman.ac.uk

Northern School of Contemporary Dance 98 Chapeltown Road, Leeds LS7 4BH. Tel 0113 219 3000; www.nscd.ac.uk [**Da**]

Norwich University College of the Arts (Formerly Norwich School of Art and Design) Admissions, Francis House, 3–7 Redwell Street, Norwich, Norfolk NR2 4SN. Tel 01603 610561; www.nuca.ac.uk [**A**]

Pershore College (part of Warwickshire College) Avonbank, Pershore, Worcestershire WR10 3JP. Tel 01386 552443; www.pershore.ac.uk [**H**]

Plymouth College of Art Tavistock Place, Plymouth, Devon PL4 8AT. Tel 01752 203434; www.plymouthart.ac.uk [**A**]

Ravensbourne College of Design and Communication Walden Road, Chislehurst, Kent BR7 5SN. Tel 020 8289 4900; www.rave.ac.uk [**C**]

Reaseheath College Reaseheath, Nantwich, Cheshire CW5 6DF. Tel 01270 625131; Course Information 01270 613242; www.reaseheath.ac.uk [**Ag**]

Rose Bruford College Lamorbey Park Campus, Burnt Oak Lane, Sidcup, Kent DA15 9DF. Tel 020 8308 2600; www.bruford.ac.uk [**D**]

Royal Academy of Dance 36 Battersea Square, London SW11 3RA. Tel 020 7326 8000; www.rad.org.uk [**Da**]

Royal Academy of Dramatic Art (RADA) 62–64 Gower Street, London WC1E 6ED. Tel 020 7636 7076; www.rada.org [**D**]

Royal Academy of Music, University of London Marylebone Road, London NW1 5HT. Tel 020 7873 7373; www.ram.ac.uk [**M**]

Royal Agricultural College Stroud Road, Cirencester, Gloucestershire GL7 6JS. Tel 01285 652531; www.rac.ac.uk [**Ag**]

Royal Ballet School 46 Floral Street, Covent Garden, London WC2E 9DA. Tel 020 7836 8899; www.royal-ballet-school.org.uk [**Da**]

Royal College of Music Prince Consort Road, London SW7 2BS. Tel 020 7589 3643; www.rcm.ac.uk [**M**]

Royal Northern College of Music 124 Oxford Road, Manchester M13 9RD. Tel 0161 907 5200; www.rncm.ac.uk [**M**]

Royal Scottish Academy of Music and Drama 100 Renfrew Street, Glasgow, Scotland G2 3DB. Tel 0141 332 4101; www.rsamd.ac.uk [**M D**]

Royal Welsh College of Music and Drama Castle Grounds, Cathays Park, Cardiff, Wales CF10 3ER. Tel 029 2034 2854; www.rwcmd.ac.uk [**M D**]

Ruskin School of Drawing and Fine Art (part of Oxford University) 74 High Street, Oxford OX1 4BG. Tel 01865 276940; www.ruskin-sch.ox.ac.uk [**A**]

St Mary's University College Twickenham Registry, Waldegrave Road, Strawberry Hill, Twickenham, Middlesex TW1 4SX. Tel 020 8240 4027; www.smuc.ac.uk

Scottish Agricultural College (SAC) Student Recruitment and Admissions Office, SAC Ayr Campus, Auchincruive Estate, Ayr, Scotland KA6 5HW. Tel 0800 269453; www.sac.ac.uk [**Ag**]

Sparsholt College Hampshire Westley Lane, Sparsholt, Winchester, Hampshire SO21 2NF. Tel 01962 776441; www.sparsholt.ac.uk [**Ag H**]

Stranmillis University College Academic Registry, Stranmillis Road, Belfast, Northern Ireland BT9 5DY. Tel 028 9038 42631; www.stran.ac.uk

Suffolk University Campus Admissions Office, Waterfront Building, Neptune Quay, Ipswich, Suffolk IP4 1QJ. Tel 01473 338348; www.ucs.ac.uk

Trinity Laban Conservatoire of Music and Dance King Charles Court, Old Royal Naval College, Greenwich, London SE10 9JF. Tel 020 8305 4444; www.tcm.ac.uk [**M D**]

Trinity Laban Conservatoire of Music and Dance Creekside, London SE8 3DZ. Tel 020 8691 8600; www.laban.org [**M D**]

Trinity University College (merged 2010 with the University of Wales, Lampeter, to create the University of Wales, Trinity Saint David) Registry, College Road, Carmarthen, Wales SA31 3EP. Tel 01267 676767; www.trinity-cm.ac.uk

UHI Millennium Institute The UHI is based on a partnership of colleges and research centres, each with its own distinctive character. Full-time undergraduate courses are provided by the following partner colleges (for addresses see **Section 3**). Institutions are shown by initials in the tables in **Chapter 8**: Argyll College (AC), Highland Theological College (HTC), Inverness College (IC), Lews Castle College (LCC), Lochaber College (LOC), Moray College (MC), Ness Foundation (NF), North Atlantic Fisheries College (NAFC), North Highland College (NHC), Orkney College (OC), Perth College (PC), Sabhal Mor Ostaig (SMO), Scottish Association for Marine Science (SAMS) and Shetland College (SC). (UHI Millennium Institute, Course Information Unit, Executive Office, Ness Walk, Inverness, Scotland IV3 5SQ. Tel 01463 279000; www.uhi.ac.uk)

Warwickshire College Leamington Centre, Warwick New Road, Leamington Spa, Warwickshire CV32 5JE. Tel 01926 318000; www.warkscol.ac.uk [**Ag H**]

Welsh College of Horticulture Northop, Holywell Road, Northop, Mold, Flintshire, Wales CH7 6AA. Tel 01352 841000; www.wcoh.ac.uk [**H**]

Wimbledon College of Art, University of the Arts London, Main Building, Merton Hall Road, London SW19 3QA. Tel 020 7514 9641; Admissions 020 7514 9687; www.wimbledon.ac.uk [**A**]

Winchester School of Art University of Southampton, Park Avenue, Winchester, Hampshire SO23 8DL. Tel 023 8059 7141; www.wsa.soton.ac.uk [**A**]

Writtle College (an Associate College of Essex University) Chelmsford, Essex CM1 3RR. Tel 01245 424200; www.writtle.ac.uk [**Ag H**]

SECTION 3: UNIVERSITY CENTRES, FURTHER EDUCATION AND OTHER COLLEGES OFFERING HIGHER EDUCATION COURSES

Changes are taking place fast in this sector, with the merger of colleges and the introduction in 2009 of University Centres. These are linked to further education colleges and to one or more universities, and provide Foundation and Honours degree courses (often part-time) and sometimes postgraduate qualifications.

The following colleges appear under various subject headings in the tables in **Chapter 8** and are in UCAS for some of their courses. See prospectuses and websites for application details.

University Centres

Barnsley University Centre Church Street, Barnsley, South Yorkshire S70 2AN. Tel 01226 606262; Student Admissions and Records Office Tel 01484 473969; www.barnsley.hud.ac.uk

Blackburn College University Centre Feilden Street, Blackburn, Lancashire BB2 1LH. Tel 01254 55144; Student Hotline 01254 292929; www.blackburn.ac.uk

Bradford College University Centre Admissions Office, Great Horton Road, Bradford, West Yorkshire BD7 1AY. Tel 01274 433333; www.bradfordcollege.ac.uk

Doncaster College University Centre The Hub, Chappell Drive, Doncaster DN1 2RF. Tel 01302 553553; www.don.ac.uk

Folkestone University Centre Mill Bay, Folkestone, Kent CT20 1JG. Tel 0800 804 8500; www.ucf.ac.uk

Hastings University Centre Havelock Road, Hastings, East Sussex TN34 1BE. Tel 08456 020607; www.uch.ac.uk

Milton Keynes University Centre 200 Silbury Boulevard, Milton Keynes MK9 1LT. Tel 01908 684444; www.ucmk.ac.uk

Oldham College University Centre Cromwell Street, Oldham, Greater Manchester OL1 1BB. Tel 0800 085 0374; www.hud.ac.uk/oldham

Yeovil University Centre 91 Preston Road, Yeovil, Somerset BA20 2DN. Tel 01935 845454; www.ucy.ac.uk

Other Further Education Colleges

Aberdeen College Gallowgate Centre, Gallowgate, Aberdeen, Grampian AB25 1BN. Tel 01224 612000; Information and Booking Centre 01224 612330; www.abcol.ac.uk

Abingdon and Witney College Abingdon Campus, Wootton Road, Abingdon, Oxfordshire OX14 1GG. Tel 01235 555585; www.abingdon-witney.ac.uk

Accrington and Rossendale College Broad Oak Road, Accrington, Lancashire BB5 2AW. Tel 01254 389933; Information and Care 01254 354354; www.accross.ac.uk

Adam Smith College St Brycedale Campus, St Brycedale Avenue, Kirkcaldy, Fife, Scotland KY1 1EX. Tel 01592 223400; Course Hotline 0800 413280; www.adamsmithcollege.ac.uk

Andover College (Sparsholt College Hampshire) Charlton Road, Andover, Hampshire SP10 1EJ. Tel 01264 360000; www.andover.ac.uk

Angus College Keptie Road, Arbroath, Angus DD11 3EA. Tel 01241 432600; www.angus.ac.uk

Anniesland College Hatfield Campus, 19 Hatfield Drive, Glasgow G12 0YE. Tel 0141 357 3969; www.anniesland.ac.uk

Argyll College (UHI partner college – see **Section 2**) West Bay, Dunoon, Argyll PA23 7HP. Tel 08452 309969; www.argyllcollege.com

Aylesbury College Oxford Road, Aylesbury, Buckinghamshire HP21 8PD. Tel 01296 588588; www.aylesbury.ac.uk

Ayr College Dam Park, Ayr, Strathclyde KA8 0EU. Tel 01292 265184; Admissions 0800 199798; www.ayrcoll.ac.uk

Banff and Buchan College Main Campus, Henderson Road, Fraserburgh, Grampian AB43 9GA. Tel 01346 586100; www.banff-buchan.ac.uk

Barnet College Graseby House, Wood Street, Barnet, Hertfordshire EN5 5UJ. Tel 020 8200 8300; Enrolment/Course Information 020 8266 4000; www.barnet.ac.uk

Barking College Dagenham Road, Romford, Essex RM7 0XU. Tel 01708 770000; www.barkingcollege.ac.uk

Barony College Parkgate, Dumfries, Dumfries and Galloway DG1 3NE. Tel 01387 860251; www.barony.ac.uk

Basingstoke College of Technology Worting Road, Basingstoke, Hampshire RG21 8TN. Tel 01256 354141; www.bcot.ac.uk

Bedford College Cauldwell Street, Bedford MK42 9AH. Tel 01234 291000; www.bedford.ac.uk

Bexley College Tower Road, Belvedere, Kent DA17 6JA. Tel 01322 404000; www.bexley.ac.uk

Bicton College East Budleigh, Budleigh Salterton, Devon EX9 7BY. Tel 01395 562400; www.bicton.ac.uk

Birmingham Metropolitan College (incorpoating Matthew Boulton College of Further and Higher Education and Sutton Coldfield College) Jennens Road, Birmingham, West Midlands B4 7PS. Tel 0121 446 4545; www.bmetc.ac.uk

Bishop Auckland College Woodhouse Lane, Bishop Auckland, County Durham DL14 6JZ. Tel 01388 443000; Course Enquiries 08000 926506; www.bacoll.ac.uk

Blackpool and the Fylde College Central Blackpool Campus, Palatine Road, Blackpool, Lancashire FY1 4DW. Tel 01253 504343; www.blackpool.ac.uk

Borders College Head Office, Scottish Borders Campus, Nether Road, Galashiels TD1 3HE. Tel 08700 505152; www.borderscollege.ac.uk

Boston College Skirbeck Road, Boston, Lincolnshire PE21 6JF. Tel 01205 365701; Course Information 01205 313218; www.boston.ac.uk

Bournemouth and Poole College Customer Enquiry Centre, North Road, Poole, Dorset BH14 0LS. Tel 01202 205205; www.thecollege.co.uk

Bournville College Bristol Road South, Northfield, Birmingham, West Midlands B31 2AJ. Tel 0121 483 1000; Course Enquiries 0121 483 1111; www.bournville.ac.uk

Bracknell and Wokingham College College Information Centre, Church Road, Bracknell, Berkshire RG12 1DJ. Tel 0845 330 3343; www.bracknell.ac.uk

Braintree College Church Lane, Braintree, Essex CM7 5SN. Tel 01376 321711; Course Enquiries 01376 557020; www.braintree.ac.uk

Bridgwater College Bath Road, Bridgwater, Somerset TA6 4PZ. Tel 01278 455464; Course Enquiries 01278 441234; www.bridgwater.ac.uk

Brockenhurst College Lyndhurst Road, Brockenhurst, Hampshire SO42 7ZE. Tel 01590 625555; www.brock.ac.uk

Bromley College of Further and Higher Education Rookery Lane, Bromley, Kent BR2 8HE. Tel 020 8295 7000; Course Enquiries 020 8295 7001; www.bromley.ac.uk

Brooklands College Weybridge Campus, Heath Road, Weybridge, Surrey KT13 8TT. Tel 01932 797797; www.brooklands.ac.uk

Brooksby Melton College Melton Mowbray Campus, Ashfordby Road, Melton Mowbray, Leicestershire LE13 0HJ. Tel 01664 850850; Course Enquiries 01664 855444; www.brooksbymelton.ac.uk

Burnley College Princess Way, Burnley, Lancashire BB12 0AN. Tel 01282 733373; Student Services 01282 733333; www.burnley.ac.uk

Burton College Student Services, Lichfield Street, Burton on Trent, Staffordshire DE14 3RL. Tel 01283 494400; www.burton-college.ac.uk

Bury College Woodbury Centre, Market Street, Bury, Greater Manchester BL9 0BG. Tel 0161 280 8280; Course Information 0161 280 8280; www.burycollege.ac.uk

Calderdale College Francis Street, Halifax, West Yorkshire HX1 3UZ. Tel Course Information 01422 399399; www.calderdale.ac.uk

Calne Campus, Wiltshire College The Green, Calne, Wiltshire SN11 8DJ. Tel Enrolment 01225 350035; www.wiltshire.ac.uk

Cambridge Regional College Kings Hedges Road, Cambridge CB4 2QT. Tel 01223 418200; www.camre.ac.uk

Cannock Campus, South Staffordshire College The Green, Cannock, Staffordshire WS11 1UE. Tel 0300 456 2424; www.southstaffs.ac.uk

Canterbury College New Dover Road, Canterbury, Kent CT1 3AJ. Tel 01227 811111; Learning Advice/Courses 01227 811188; www.cant-col.ac.uk

Cardonald College Mosspark Drive, Glasgow, G52 3AY. Tel 0141 272 3333; www.cardonald.ac.uk

Carlisle College Information Unit, Victoria Place, Carlisle, Cumbria CA1 1HS. Tel 01228 822703; www.carlisle.ac.uk

Carmarthenshire College (see Coleg Sir Gâr)

Carmel College Prescot Road, St Helens, Merseyside WA10 3AG. Tel 01744 452200; www.carmel.ac.uk

Carnegie College (formerly Lauder College) Pittsburgh Road, Halbeath, Dunfermline, Fife KY11 8DY. Tel 0844 248 0155; www.carnegiecollege.ac.uk

Carshalton College Nightingale Road, Carshalton, Surrey SM5 2EJ. Tel 020 8544 4444; www.carshalton.ac.uk

Castle College Nottingham Maid Marian Way, Nottingham NG1 6AB. Tel 08458 450500; www.castlecollege.ac.uk

CECOS London College 59 Crompton Road, Islington, London N1 2YT. Tel 020 7359 3316; www.cecos.co.uk

Central College of Commerce Cathedral Street, Glasgow, G1 2TA. Information Unit 0141 552 3941; www.centralcollege.ac.uk

Chelmsford College 102 Moulsham Street, Chelmsford, Essex CM2 0JQ. Tel 01245 265611; www.chelmsford-college.ac.uk

Chesterfield College Infirmary Road, Chesterfield, Derbyshire S41 7NG. Tel 01246 500500; www.chesterfield.ac.uk

Chichester College Westgate Fields, Chichester, West Sussex PO19 1SB. Tel 01243 786321; www.chichester.ac.uk

Chippenham Campus, Wiltshire College Cocklebury Road, Chippenham, Wiltshire SN15 3QD. Tel Enrolment 01225 350035; www.wiltshire.ac.uk

City of Bath College Student Advice Centre, Avon Street, Bath, Somerset BA1 1UP. Tel 01225 312191; www.citybathcoll.ac.uk

City College, Birmingham 286 Kitts Green Road, Birmingham B33 0BR. Tel 0121 204 0000; Course Enquiries 08450 501144; www.citycol.ac.uk

City College Brighton and Hove Pelham Street, Brighton, East Sussex BN1 4FA. Tel 01273 667788; Course Advisers 01273 667759; www.ccb.ac.uk

City of Bristol College Bedminster Centre, Marksbury Road, Bristol BS3 5JL. Tel 0117 312 5000; www.cityofbristol.ac.uk

City College, Coventry Swanswell Centre, 50 Swanswell Street, Coventry CV1 5DG. Tel 0800 616202; www.covcollege.ac.uk

City College Norwich Ipswich Road, Norwich, Norfolk NR2 2LJ. Tel 01603 773311; www.ccn.ac.uk

City College, Plymouth (formerly Plymouth College of Further Education) Kings Road, Devonport, Plymouth, Devon PL1 5QG. Tel 01752 305300; www.cityplym.ac.uk

City and Islington College The Marlborough Building, 383 Holloway Road, London N7 0RN. Tel 020 7700 9200; www.candi.ac.uk

City of Sunderland College Bede Centre, Durham Road, Sunderland, Tyne and Wear SR3 4AH. Tel 0191 511 6000; HE Admissions 0191 511 6260; www.citysun.ac.uk

City of Westminster College Paddington Basin Campus, North Wharf Road, London W2 1LF. Tel 020 7723 8826; www.cwc.ac.uk

City of Wolverhampton College Paget Road Campus, Paget Road, Wolverhampton, West Midlands WV6 0DU. Tel 01902 836000; www.wolverhamptoncollege.ac.uk

Cliff College Calver, Hope Valley, Derbyshire S32 3XG. Tel 01246 584202; www.cliffcollege.ac.uk

Clydebank College College Square, Queens' Quay, Clydebank, G81 1BF. Tel 0141 951 7400; www.clydebank.ac.uk

Coatbridge College Kildonan Street, Coatbridge, Lanarkshire ML5 3LS. Tel 01236 422316; Admissions 01236 436000; www.coatbridge.ac.uk

Coleg Llandrillo Cymru Llandudno Road, Rhos on Sea, Colwyn Bay, Wales LL28 4HZ. Tel 01492 546666; Admissions 01492 542339; www.llandrillo.ac.uk

Coleg Menai Ffriddoedd Road, Bangor, Gwynedd, Wales LL57 2TP. Tel 01248 370125; www.menai.ac.uk

Coleg Sir Gâr Graig Campus, Sandy Road, Pwll, Llanelli, Wales SA15 4DN. Tel 01554 748000; www.colegsirgar.ac.uk

Coleg Ystrad Mynach Twyn Road, Ystrad Mynach, Hengoed, Wales CF82 7XR. Tel 01443 816888; www.ystrad-mynach.ac.uk

College of North West London Willesden Centre, Dudden Hill Lane, London NW10 2XD. Tel 020 8208 5000; Course Information 020 8208 5050; www.cnwl.ac.uk

College of West Anglia King's Lynn Centre, Tennyson Avenue, King's Lynn, Norfolk PE30 2QW. Tel 01553 761144; www.col-westanglia.ac.uk

CONEL (College of North East London) Tottenham Centre, High Road, London N15 4RU. Tel 020 8802 3111; Course Information 020 8442 3055; www.conel.ac.uk

Cornwall College Camborne Campus, Trevenson Road, Pool, Redruth, Cornwall TR15 3RD. Tel 01209 616161; www.cornwall.ac.uk

Corsham Campus, Wiltshire College 26 Martingate Centre, Corsham, Wiltshire SN13 0HL. Tel Enrolment 01225 350035; www.wiltshire.ac.uk

Craven College High Street, Skipton, North Yorkshire BD23 1JY. Tel 01756 791411; www.craven-college.ac.uk

Crichton Campus (Universities of Glasgow and West Scotland and Dumfries and Galloway College) Rutherford McGowan Building, Dumfries, Scotland DG1 4ZL. Tel 01387 702001; Admissions 01387 702131; www.gla.ac.uk/departments/crichtoncampus

Croydon College College Road, Croydon CR9 1DX. Course Information 020 8760 5914; www.croydon.ac.uk

Cumbernauld College Town Centre, Cumbernauld, Glasgow, Strathclyde G67 1HU. Tel 01236 731811; www.cumbernauld.ac.uk

Darlington College Central Park, Haughton Road, Darlington DL1 1DR. Tel 01325 503050; www.darlington.ac.uk

Dearne Valley College Manvers Park, Wath upon Dearne, Rotherham, South Yorkshire S63 7EW. Tel 01709 513333; www.dearne-coll.ac.uk

Derby College Prince Charles Avenue, Mackworth, Derby DE22 4LR. Tel 01332 520200; Course enquiries 0800 028 0289; www.derby-college.ac.uk

Derwentside College Consett Campus, Front Street, Consett, County Durham DH8 5EE. Tel 01207 585900; www.derwentside.ac.uk

Devizes Campus, Wiltshire College Southbroom, Devizes, Wiltshire SN10 5AB. Tel Enrolment 01225 350035; www.wiltshire.ac.uk

Duchy College Rosewarne Campus, Camborne, Cornwall TR14 0AB. Tel 01209 722100; www.cornwall.ac.uk/duchy

Dudley College The Broadway, Dudley, West Midlands DY1 4AS. Tel 01384 363000; Course Enquiries 01384 363363; www.dudleycol.ac.uk

Dumfries and Galloway College College Gate, Bankend Road, Dumfries DG1 4FD. Tel 01387 7340001; www.dumgal.ac.uk

Dundee College Kingsway Campus, Old Glamis Road, Dundee, Scotland DD3 8LE. Tel 01382 834834; Student Services 01382 834844; www.dundeecollege.ac.uk

Dunstable College Kingsway, Dunstable, Bedfordshire LU5 4HG. Tel 0845 355 2525; www.dunstable.ac.uk

Ealing, Hammersmith and West London College Gliddon Road, Barons Court, London W14 9BL. Tel 020 8741 1688; www.wlc.ac.uk

East Berkshire College Langley Campus, Station Road, Langley, Berkshire SL3 8BY. Tel 0845 373 2500; www.eastberks.ac.uk

East Durham College Peterlee Campus, Willerby Grove, Peterlee, County Durham SR8 2RN. Tel 0191 518 2000; www.eastdurham.ac.uk

East Durham College Houghall Campus, Houghall, Durham DH1 3SG. Tel 0191 375 4700; www.eastdurham.ac.uk

East Riding College Beverley Campus, Gallows Lane, Beverley, East Riding of Yorkshire HU17 7DT. Tel 845 120 0037; www.eastridingcollege.ac.uk

East Surrey College Gatton Point, London Road, Redhill, Surrey RH1 2JT. Tel 01737 788444; www.esc.ac.uk

Eastleigh College Chestnut Avenue, Eastleigh, Hampshire SO50 5FS. Tel 023 8091 1299; www.eastleigh.ac.uk

Easton College Easton, Norwich, Norfolk NR9 5DX. Tel 01603 731200; www.easton-college.ac.uk

Edinburgh's Telford College 350 West Granton Road, Edinburgh, EH5 1QE. Tel 0131 559 4000; www.ed-coll.ac.uk

Enfield College 73 Hertford Road, Enfield, Middlesex EN3 5HA. Tel 020 8443 3434; www.enfield.ac.uk

European Business School London Regent's College, Inner Circle, Regent's Park, London NW1 4NS. Tel 020 7487 7505; www.ebslondon.ac.uk

Exeter College Hele Road, Exeter, Devon EX4 4JS. Tel 0845 111 6000; www.exe-col.ac.uk

Fareham College Bishopsfield Road, Fareham, Hampshire PO14 1NH. Tel 01329 815200; www.fareham.ac.uk

Farnborough College of Technology Boundary Road, Farnborough, Hampshire GU14 6SB. Course Enquiries Tel 01252 407040; www.farn-ct.ac.uk

Filton College Filton Avenue, Filton, Bristol BS34 7AT. Tel 0117 909 2297; www.filton.ac.uk

Forth Valley College Falkirk Campus, Grangemouth Road, Falkirk FK2 9AD. Tel 01324 403000; www.forthvalley.ac.uk

Furness College Channelside, Barrow-in-Furness, Cumbria LA14 2PJ. Tel 01229 825017; www.furness.ac.uk

Gateshead College Baltic Campus, Baltic Business Quarter, Quarryfield Road, Gateshead NE8 3BE. Tel 0191 490 2245; www.gateshead.ac.uk

Glasgow College of Nautical Studies 21 Thistle Street, Glasgow, G5 9XB. Tel 0141 565 2500; www.glasgow-nautical.ac.uk

Glasgow Metropolitan College 60 North Hanover Street, Glasgow, Strathclyde, Scotland G1 2BP. Tel 0141 566 6222; www.glasgowmet.ac.uk

Gloucestershire College Gloucester Campus, Llanthony Road, Gloucester GL2 5JQ. Tel 01452 532000; www.gloscol.ac.uk

Grantham College Stonebridge Road, Grantham, Lincolnshire NG31 9AP. Tel 01476 400200; Course Information 01476 400200; www.grantham.ac.uk

Great Yarmouth College Suffolk Road, Southtown, Great Yarmouth, Norfolk NR31 0ED. Tel 01493 655261; www.gyc.ac.uk

Greenwich School of Management Meridian House, Royal Hill, Greenwich, London SE10 8RD. Tel 020 8516 7800; www.greenwich-college.ac.uk

Grimsby Institute of Further and Higher Education Nuns Corner, Laceby Road, Grimsby, North East Lincolnshire DN34 5BQ. Tel 0800 315002; www.grimsby.ac.uk

Guildford College Stoke Park Campus, Stoke Road, Guildford, Surrey GU1 1EZ. Tel 01483 448500; www.guildford.ac.uk

Hackney Community College Shoreditch Campus, Falkirk Street, London N1 6HQ. Tel 020 7613 9123; www.tcch.ac.uk

Hadlow College Tonbridge Road, Hadlow, Kent TN11 0AL. Tel 01732 850551; Course Enquiry Unit 0500 551434 (free); www.hadlow.ac.uk

Halesowen College Whittingham Road, Halesowen, West Midlands B63 3NA. Tel 0121 602 7777; www.halesowen.ac.uk

Harlow College Valizy Avenue, Harlow, Essex CM20 3LH. Tel 01279 868000; www.harlow-college.ac.uk

Harrow College Harrow on the Hill Campus, Lowlands Road, Harrow, Middlesex HA1 3AQ. Tel 020 8909 6000; www.harrow.ac.uk

Hastings College of Arts and Technology Archery Campus, Archery Road, St Leonards on Sea, East Sussex TN38 0HX. Tel 01424 442222; www.hastings.ac.uk

Havering College Ardleigh Green Road, Hornchurch, Essex RM11 2LL. Tel 01708 455011; www.havering-college.ac.uk

Henley College Coventry Henley Road, Bell Green, Coventry, West Midlands CV2 1ED. Tel 024 7662 6300; www.henley-cov.ac.uk

Hereford College of Technology Folly Lane, Hereford HR1 1LS. Tel 0800 032 1986; www.hct.ac.uk

Hertford Regional College Ware Centre, Scotts Road, Ware, Hertfordshire SG12 9JF. Tel 01992 411400; www.hrc.ac.uk

Highbury College Portsmouth Dovercourt Road, Cosham, Portsmouth, Hampshire PO6 2SA. Tel 023 9238 3131; www.highbury.ac.uk

Highland Theological College (UHI partner college – see **Section 2**) High Street, Dingwall, Scotland IV15 9HA. Tel 01349 780000; www.htc.uhi.ac.uk

Hillcroft College South Bank, Surbiton, Surrey KT6 6DF. Tel 020 8399 2688; www.hillcroft.ac.uk

Holborn College Woolwich Road, London SE7 8LN. Tel 020 8317 6000; www.holborncollege.ac.uk

Hopwood Hall College Rochdale Campus, St Mary's Gate, Rochdale OL12 6RY. Tel 01706 345346; www.hopwood.ac.uk

Hull College The Queen's Gardens Centre, Wilberforce Drive, Hull, East Yorkshire HU1 3DG. Tel 01482 329943; www.hull-college.ac.uk

Huntingdonshire Regional College California Road, Huntingdon PE29 1BL. Tel 01480 379100; www.huntingdon.ac.uk

Inverness College (UHI partner college – see **Section 2**) 3 Longman Road, Inverness IV1 1SA. Tel 01463 273000; www.inverness.uhi.ac.uk

Islamic College for Advanced Studies 133 High Road, Willesden, London NW10 2SW. Tel 020 8451 9993; www.islamic-college.ac.uk

Isle of Wight College Medina Way, Newport, Isle of Wight PO30 5TA. Tel 01983 526631; www.iwcollege.ac.uk

James Watt College Finnart Street, Greenock, Strathclyde PA16 8HF. Tel 01475 724433; Student Information Centre 0800 587 2277; www.jameswatt.ac.uk

Jewel and Esk Valley College Edinburgh Campus, 24 Milton Road East, Edinburgh EH15 2PP. Tel 0131 334 7000; Information Services 08458 500060; www.jec.ac.uk

Keighley College (see Park Lane College Keighley below)

Kendal College (The College of the South Lakes) Milnthorpe Road, Kendal, Cumbria LA9 5AY. Tel 01539 814700; www.kendal.ac.uk

Kidderminster College Market Street, Kidderminster, Worcestershire DY10 1LX. Tel 01562 820811; www.kidderminster.ac.uk

Kilmarnock College Holehouse Road, Kilmarnock, Strathclyde KA3 7AT. Tel 01563 523501; www.kilmarnock.ac.uk

Kingston College Kingston Hall Road, Kingston upon Thames, Surrey KT1 2AQ. Tel 020 8546 2151; www.kingston-college.ac.uk

Kingston Maurward College Kingston Maurward, Dorchester, Dorset DT2 8PY. Tel 01305 215000; Course Enquiries 01305 215032/215025; www.kmc.ac.uk

Kirklees College Huddersfield Centre, New North Road, Huddersfield, West Yorkshire HD1 5NN. Tel 01484 437000; www.huddcoll.ac.uk

Kirklees College (formerly Dewsbury College) Dewsbury Centre, Halifax Road, Dewsbury, West Yorkshire WF13 2AS. Tel 01924 465916; www.dewsbury.ac.uk

Knowsley Community College Kirkby Campus, Cherryfield Drive, Kirkby L32 8SF. Tel 08451 551055; www.knowsleycollege.ac.uk

Lackham Campus, Wiltshire College Laycock, Chippenham, Wiltshire SN15 2NY. Tel Enrolment 01225 350035; www.wiltshire.ac.uk

Lakes College, West Cumbria Hallwood Road, Lillyhall Business Park, Workington, Cumbria CA14 4JN. Tel 01946 839300; www.lcwc.ac.uk

Lambeth College 45 Clapham Common South Side, London SW4 9BL. Tel 020 7501 5010; Course Information 020 7501 5000; www.lambethcollege.ac.uk

Lancaster and Morecambe College Morecambe Road, Lancaster LA1 2TY. Tel 01524 66215; www.lmc.ac.uk

Langside College 50 Prospecthill Road, Glasgow, Strathclyde, Scotland G42 9LB. Tel 0141 272 3600; Student Services 0141 272 3636; www.langside.ac.uk

Lansdowne College 40–44 Bark Place, London W2 4AT. Tel 020 7616 4400; www.lansdownecollege.com

Lauder College (Now Carnegie College)

Leeds City College Park Lane Campus, Park Lane, Leeds LS3 1AA. Admissions 0113 216 2200; Course/General Enquiries 0845 045 7275; www.leedscitycollege.ac.uk

Leeds City College Technology Campus, Cookridge Street, Leeds, West Yorkshire LS2 8BL. Tel 0113 297 6300; Student Services 0113 297 6464; www.leedscitycollege.ac.uk

Leeds City College Thomas Danby Campus, Roundhay Road, Leeds, West Yorkshire LS7 3BG. Tel 0113 249 4912; www.leedscitycollege.ac.uk

Leeds College of Building North Street, Leeds, West Yorkshire LS2 7QT. Tel 0113 222 6000; Student Services 0113 222 6000; www.lcb.ac.uk

Leek College Stockwell Street, Leek, Staffordshire ST13 6DP. Tel 01538 398866; www.leek.ac.uk

Leicester College Freemen's Park Campus, Aylestone Road, Leicester LE2 7LW. Tel 0116 224 2240; www.leicestercollege.ac.uk

Leo Baeck College The Sternberg Centre, 80 East End Road, London N3 2SY. Tel 020 8349 5600; www.lbc.ac.uk

Lewisham College Lewisham Way, London SE4 1UT. Tel 020 8692 0353/0800 834545; www.lewisham.ac.uk

Lews Castle College (Colaisde A' Chaisteil) (UHI partner college – see **Section 2**) Stornoway, Isle of Lewis HS2 0XR. Tel 01851 770000; www.lews.uhi.ac.uk

Lichfield Campus, South Staffordshire College The Friary, Lichfield, Staffordshire WS13 6QG. Tel 0300 456 2424; www.southstaffs.ac.uk

Lincoln College Monks Road, Lincoln LN2 5HQ. Tel 01522 876000; www.lincolncollege.ac.uk

Liverpool Community College Bankfield Road, Liverpool L13 0BQ. Tel 0151 252 1515; www.liv-coll.ac.uk

Lochaber College (UHI partner college – see **Section 2**) Fort William, Inverness-shire, Scotland PH33 6FF. Tel 01397 874000; www.lochaber.uhi.ac.uk

London School of Commerce Chaucer House, White Hart Yard, London SE1 1NX. Tel 020 7357 0077; www.lsclondon.co.uk

Loughborough College Radmoor Road, Loughborough, Leicestershire LE11 3BT. Tel 0845 166 2950; www.loucoll.ac.uk

Lowestoft College St Peters Street, Lowestoft, Suffolk NR32 2NB. Tel 0800 854695; www.lowestoft.ac.uk

Macclesfield College Park Lane, Macclesfield, Cheshire SK11 8LF. Tel 01625 410000; Information/Enrolment 01625 410001; www.macclesfield.ac.uk

(The) Manchester College Ashton Old Road, Openshaw, Manchester M11 2WH. Tel 0800 068 8585; www.themanchestercollege.ac.uk

Matthew Boulton College of Further and Higher Education (now Birmingham Metropolitan College)

Melksham Campus, Wiltshire College Challeymead Business Centre, Melksham, Wiltshire SN12 8BU. Tel Enrolment 01225 350035; www.wiltshire.ac.uk

Mid-Cheshire College Hartford Campus, Chester Road, Northwich, Cheshire CW8 1LJ. Tel 01606 74444; www.midchesh.ac.uk

Mid-Kent College Horsted Centre, Medway Building, Chatham Maritime, Chatham, Kent ME4 4AG. Tel 01634 888800; www.midkent.ac.uk

Middlesbrough College Dock Street, Middlesbrough TS2 1AD. Tel 01642 333333; Course Information 01642 296600; www.mibro.ac.uk

Milton Keynes College Wroughton Campus, Chaffron Way Campus, Leadenhall, Milton Keynes, Buckinghamshire MK6 5LP. Tel 01908 684444; www.mkcollege.ac.uk

Moray College (UHI partner college – see **Section 2**) Moray Street, Elgin, Moray IV30 1JJ. Tel 01343 576216; www.moray.ac.uk

Moulton College West Street, Moulton, Northampton NN3 7RR. Tel 01604 491131; www.moulton.ac.uk

Nazarene Theological College Dene Road, Didsbury, Manchester M20 2GU. Tel 0161 445 3063; www.nazarene.ac.uk

Neath Port Talbot College Dwr-y-Felin Road, Neath SA10 7RF. Tel 01639 648000; www.nptc.ac.uk

Nelson and Colne College Reedyford Site, Scotland Road, Nelson, Lancashire BB9 7YT. Tel 01282 440200; www.nelson.ac.uk

Nescot (North East Surrey College of Technology) Reigate Road, Ewell, Epsom, Surrey KT17 3DS. Tel 020 8394 3038; www.nescot.ac.uk

Ness Foundation (see Lochaber College) (UHI partner college – see **Section 2**) Ness House, Dochfour Business Centre, Dochgarroch, Inverness IV3 8GY. Tel 01463 220407; www.ness-foundation.org.uk

NEW College (North East Worcestershire College) Redditch Campus, Peakman Street, Redditch, Worcestershire B98 8DW. Tel 01527 570020; www.ne-worcs.ac.uk

New College Durham Framwellgate Moor Campus, Framwellgate Moor, County Durham DH1 5ES. Admissions Office Tel 0191 375 4210; www.newcollegedurham.ac.uk

New College Nottingham The Adams Building, Stoney Street, The Lace Market, Nottingham NG1 1NG. Tel 0115 910 0100; www.ncn.ac.uk

New College Stamford Drift Road, Stamford, Lincolnshire PE9 1XA. Tel 01780 484300; www.stamford.ac.uk

New College, Swindon New College Drive, Swindon, Wiltshire SN3 1AH. Tel 0808 172 1721; www.newcollege.ac.uk

New College, Telford King Street, Wellington, Telford, Shropshire TF1 1NY. Tel 01952 641892; www.newcollegetelford.ac.uk

Newbury College Monks Lane, Newbury, Berkshire RG14 7TD. Tel 01635 845000; www.newbury-college.ac.uk

Newcastle College Rye Hill Campus, Scotswood Road, Newcastle upon Tyne NE4 7SA. Tel 0191 200 4000; www.ncl-coll.ac.uk

Newcastle-under-Lyme College Liverpool Road, Newcastle-under-Lyme, Staffordshire ST5 2DF. Tel 01782 254212; www.nulc.ac.uk

Newham College of Further Education East Ham Campus, High Street South, London E6 6ER. Tel 020 8257 4000; www.newham.ac.uk

North Atlantic Fisheries College (UHI partner college – see **Section 2**) NAFC Marine Centre, Port Arthur, Scalloway, Shetland ZE1 0UN. Tel 01595 772000; www.nafc.ac.uk

North Glasgow College 123 Flemington Street, Springburn, Glasgow G21 4TD. Tel 0141 558 9001; www.northglasgowcollege.ac.uk

North Hertfordshire College Monkswood Way, Stevenage, Hertfordshire SG1 1LA. Tel 01462 424242; Courses 01462 424242; www.nhc.ac.uk

North Highland College (UHI partner college – see **Section 2**) Ormlie Road, Thurso, Caithness, Scotland KW14 7EE. Tel 01847 889000; www.northhighland.ac.uk

North Lindsey College Kingsway, Scunthorpe, North Lincolnshire DN17 1AJ. Tel 01724 281111; www.northlindsey.ac.uk

North Nottinghamshire College Carlton Road, Worksop, Nottinghamshire S81 7HP. Tel 01909 504504; Student Services 01909 504500; www.nnotts-col.ac.uk

North Trafford College (See Trafford College below)

North Warwickshire and Hinckley College Nuneaton Campus, Hinckley Road, Nuneaton, Warwickshire CV11 6BH. Tel 024 7624 3000; www.nwhc.ac.uk

Northampton College Booth Lane, Northampton NN3 3RF. Tel 01604 734567; www.northamptoncollege.ac.uk

Northbrook College, Sussex West Durrington Campus, Littlehampton Road, Worthing, West Sussex BN12 6NU. Tel 08451 556060; www.northbrook.ac.uk

Northern Regional College (formerly North East Institute of Further and Higher Education) Ballymena Campus, Trostan Avenue Building, Ballymena, Co Antrim, Northern Ireland BT43 7BN. Tel 028 2563 6221; www.nrc.ac.uk

Northumberland College College Road, Ashington, Northumberland NE63 9RG. Tel 01670 841200; www.northumberland.ac.uk

Norton Radstock College South Hill Park, Radstock, Somerset BA3 3RW. Tel 01761 433161; www.nortcoll.ac.uk

Norwich City College Ipswich Road, Norwich, Norfolk NR2 2LJ. Tel 01603 773005; www.ccn.ac.uk

Oaklands College St Albans Smallford Campus, Hatfield Road, St Albans, Hertfordshire AL4 0JA. Tel 01727 737080; www.oaklands.ac.uk

Oatridge College Information Unit, Ecclesmachan, Broxburn, West Lothian, Scotland EH52 6NH. Tel 01506 864800; www.oatridge.ac.uk

Orkney College (UHI partner college – see **Section 2**) Kirkwall, Orkney KW15 1LX. Tel 01856 569000; www.orkney.uhi.ac.uk

Orpington College The Walnuts, Orpington, Kent BR6 0TE. Tel 01689 899700; www.orpington.ac.uk

Otley College Otley, Ipswich, Suffolk IP6 9EY. Tel 01473 785543; www.otleycollege.ac.uk

Oxford and Cherwell Valley College Banbury Campus, Broughton Road, Banbury, Oxfordshire OX16 9QA. Tel 01865 550550; www.ocvc.ac.uk

Park Lane College (now Leeds City College, Park Lane Campus)

Park Lane College Keighley Cavendish Street, Keighley, West Yorkshire BD21 3DF. Tel 01535 618600; www.parklane.ac.uk

Pembrokeshire College (Coleg Sir Benfro) FREEPOST, Pembrokeshire College, Haverfordwest, Pembrokeshire SA61 1SZ. Tel 01437 753000; Freephone 0800 716236; www.pembrokeshire.ac.uk

Perth College (UHI partner college – see **Section 2**) Admissions Office Freepost, Perth PH1 2BR. Tel 08452 701177; www.perth.ac.uk

Peterborough Regional College Park Crescent, Peterborough, Cambridgeshire PE1 4DZ. Tel 0845 872 8722; www.peterborough.ac.uk

Petroc East Devon College Admissions Department, Bolham Road, Tiverton, Devon EX16 6SH. Tel 01884 235264; www.edc.ac.uk

Plumpton College Ditchling Road, Near Lewes, East Sussex BN7 3AE. Tel 01273 890454; www.plumpton.ac.uk

Plymouth College of Further Education (see City College, Plymouth)

Portsmouth College Tangier Road, Portsmouth, Hampshire PO3 6PZ. Tel 023 9266 7521; www.portsmouth-college.ac.uk

Redbridge College Little Heath, Barley Lane, Romford, Essex RM6 4XT. Tel 020 8548 7400; www.redbridge-college.ac.uk

Redcar and Cleveland College Corporation Road, Redcar TS10 1EZ. Tel 01642 473132; www.cleveland.ac.uk

Regents Business School London Inner Circle, Regent's Park, London NW1 4NS. Tel 020 7487 7505; www.rbslondon.ac.uk

Reid Kerr College Admission Unit, Renfrew Road, Paisley, Renfrewshire PA3 4DR. Tel 0141 581 2222; Course Enquiries 0800 527343; www.reidkerr.net

Richmond upon Thames College Egerton Road, Twickenham, Surrey TW2 7SJ. Tel 020 8607 8000; www.richmond-utcoll.ac.uk

Riverside College Halton Kingsway Campus, Kingsway, Widnes, Cheshire WA8 7QQ. Tel 0151 257 2020; www.riversidecollege.ac.uk

Rodbaston Campus, South Staffordshire College Penkridge, Staffordshire ST19 5PH. Tel 300 456 2424; www.southstaffs.ac.uk

Rotherham College of Arts and Technology Town Centre Campus, Eastwood Lane, Rotherham, South Yorkshire S65 1EG. Tel 08080 722777; www.rotherham.ac.uk

Royal Forest of Dean College Five Acres Campus, Bury Hill, Coleford, Gloucestershire GL16 7JT. Tel 01594 833416; www.rfdc.ac.uk

Royal National College for the Blind College Road, Hereford HR1 1EB. Tel 01432 265725; www.rncb.ac.uk

Runshaw College Adult College, Euxton Lane, Chorley, Lancashire PR7 6AD. Tel 01772 642040; www.runshaw.ac.uk

Ruskin College Oxford Student Enquiry Office, Walton Street, Oxford OX1 2HE. Tel 01865 517832; www.ruskin.ac.uk

Sabhal Mor Ostaig (UHI partner college – see **Section 2**) Teangue, Isle of Skye, Scotland IV44 8RQ. Tel 01471 888000; www.smo.uhi.ac.uk

SAE Institute 297 Kingsland Road, London E8 4DD. Tel 020 7923 301 9159; www.sae.edu

St Helens College Water Street, St Helens, Merseyside WA10 1PP. Tel 01744 733766; www.sthelens.ac.uk

Salford College Worsley Campus, Walkden Road, Worsley M28 7QD. Tel 0161 702 8272; Central Admissions 0161 211 5001/2/3; www.salford-col.ac.uk

Salisbury Campus, Wiltshire College Southampton Road, Salisbury, Wiltshire SP1 2LW. Tel Enrolment 01225 350035; www.wiltshire.ac.uk

Sandwell College Central Enquiries, Oldbury Campus, Pound Road, Oldbury, West Midlands B68 8NA. Tel 0800 622006; www.sandwell.ac.uk

Scottish Association for Marine Science (UHI partner college – see **Section 2**) Dunstaffnage Marine Laboratory, Oban, Argyll PA37 1QA. Tel 01631 559000; www.sams.ac.uk

Selby College Abbot's Road, Selby, North Yorkshire YO8 8AT. Tel 01757 211000; www.selby.ac.uk

(The) Sheffield College PO Box 345, Sheffield S2 2YY. Tel 0114 260 2600; www.sheffcol.ac.uk

Shetland College (UHI partner college – see **Section 2**) Gremista, Lerwick, Shetland ZE1 0PX. Tel 01595 771000; www.shetland.uhi.ac.uk

Shrewsbury College of Arts and Technology London Road, Shrewsbury, Shropshire SY2 6PR. Tel 01743 342342; www.shrewsbury.ac.uk

Shuttleworth College Old Warden Park, Biggleswade, Bedfordshire SG18 9EA. Tel 01767 626222; www.shuttleworth.ac.uk

Skelmersdale and Ormskirk Colleges Westbank Campus, Yewdale, Skelmersdale, Lancashire WN8 6JA. Tel 01695 52300; www.skelmersdale.ac.uk

Solihull College Blossomfield Road, Solihull, West Midlands B91 1SB. Tel 0121 678 7000; www.solihull.ac.uk

Somerset College of Arts and Technology Wellington Road, Taunton, Somerset TA1 5AX. Tel 01823 366366; www.somerset.ac.uk

South Birmingham College Digbeth Campus, High Street, Deritend, Digbeth, Birmingham, West Midlands B5 5SU. Tel 0121 694 5000; www.sbirmc.ac.uk

South Cheshire College Dane Bank Avenue, Crewe, Cheshire CW2 8AB. Tel 01270 654654; www.s-cheshire.ac.uk

South Devon College Vantage Point, Long Road, Paignton, Devon TQ2 7EJ. Tel 01803 540505; www.southdevon.ac.uk

South Downs College College Road, Waterlooville, Hampshire PO7 8AA. Tel 023 9279 7979; www.southdowns.ac.uk

South East Derbyshire College Field Road, Ilkeston, Derbyshire DE7 5RS. Tel 0115 849 2020; www.sedc.ac.uk

South Essex College (formerly South East Essex College merged Jan 2010 with Thurrock and Basildon College) Luker Road, Southend-on-Sea, Essex SS1 1ND. Tel 01702 220400; www.southessex.ac.uk

South Kent College Shorncliffe Road, Folkestone, Kent CT20 2TZ. Tel 0845 207 8220; www.southkent.ac.uk

South Lanarkshire College College Way, East Kilbride G75 0NE. Tel Student Admissions 01355 807780; www.south-lanarkshire-college.ac.uk

South Leicestershire College Station Road, Wigston, Leicestershire LE18 2DW. Tel 0116 288 5051; www.slcollege.ac.uk

South Nottingham College West Bridgford Centre, Greythorne Drive, West Bridgford, Nottingham NG2 7GA. Tel 0115 914 6400; www.snc.ac.uk

South Staffordshire College (with campuses at Cannock, Lichfield, Rodbaston, Tamworth)

South Thames College Wandsworth High Street, London SW18 2PP. Tel Course Enquiries 020 8918 7777; www.south-thames.ac.uk

South Trafford College (now part of Trafford College) Manchester Road, West Timperley, Altrincham, Greater Manchester WA14 5PQ. Tel 0161 244 1050; www.trafford.ac.uk

South Tyneside College St George's Avenue, South Shields, Tyne and Wear NE34 6ET. Tel 0191 427 3500; www.stc.ac.uk

Southampton City College St Mary Street, Southampton, Hampshire SO14 1AR. Tel 023 8048 4848; www.southampton-city.ac.uk

Southern Regional College (Formerly Upper Bann Institute) Portadown Campus, 36 Lurgan Road, Portadown, Armagh, Northern Ireland BT63 5BL. Tel 028 3839 7777; www.src.ac.uk

Southgate College High Street, Southgate, London N14 6BS. Tel 020 8982 5050; www.southgate.ac.uk

Southport College Mornington Road, Southport, Merseyside PR9 0TT. Tel 01704 392704; www.southport.ac.uk

Southwark College Waterloo Centre, The Cut, London SE1 8LE. Tel 020 7815 1500; www.southwark.ac.uk

Spelthorne College (see Brooklands College)

Stafford College Earl Street, Stafford ST16 2QR. Tel 01785 275607; www.staffordcoll.ac.uk

Staffordshire University Regional Federation (SURF) Staffordshire University, College Road, Stoke on Trent ST4 2DE. Tel 01782 294000; www.staffs.ac.uk

Stamford College (See New College Stamford)

Stephenson College Thornborough Road, Coalville, Leicestershire LE67 3TN. Tel 01530 836136; www.stephensoncoll.ac.uk

Stevenson College Edinburgh Bankhead Avenue, Edinburgh, Lothian EH11 4DE. Tel 0131 535 4600; Course Enquiries 0131 535 4700; www.stevenson.ac.uk

Stockport College Town Centre Campus, Wellington Road South, Stockport, Greater Manchester SK1 3UQ. Tel 0161 958 3100; www.stockport.ac.uk

Stourbridge College Hagley Road Centre, Hagley Road, Stourbridge, West Midlands DY8 1QU. Tel 01384 344344; www.stourbridge.ac.uk

Stow College Glasgow 43 Shamrock Street, Glasgow G4 9LD. Tel 0844 249 8585; www.stow.ac.uk

Stratford-upon-Avon College The Willows North, Alcester Road, Stratford-upon-Avon, Warwickshire CV37 9QR. Tel 01789 266245; www.stratford.ac.uk

Strode College Church Road, Street, Somerset BA16 0AB. Tel 01458 844400; www.strode-college.ac.uk

Strode's College High Street, Egham, Surrey TW20 9DR. Tel 01784 437506; www.strodes.ac.uk

Stroud College in Gloucestershire Stratford Road, Stroud, Gloucestershire GL5 4AH. Tel 01453 763424; www.stroud.ac.uk

Sussex Downs College Eastbourne Campus, Cross Levels Way, Eastbourne, East Sussex BN21 2UF. Tel 01323 637637; www.sussexdowns.ac.uk

Sutton Coldfield College (now part of Birmingham Metropolitan College) Lichfield Road, Sutton Coldfield, West Midlands B74 2NW. Tel 0121 355 5671; www.bmetc.ac.uk

Swansea College (Coleg Abertawe) Tycoch Road, Tycoch, Swansea SA2 9EB. Tel 01792 284000; www.swancoll.ac.uk

Swindon College North Star Campus, North Star Avenue, Swindon, Wiltshire SN2 1DY. Tel 01793 491591; www.swindon-college.ac.uk

Tameside College Beaufort Road, Ashton-under- Lyne, Greater Manchester OL6 6NX. Tel 0161 908 6789; www.tameside.ac.uk

Tamworth Campus, South Staffordshire College Croft Street, Upper Gungate, Tamworth, Staffordshire B79 8AE. Tel 0300 456 2424; www.southstaffs.ac.uk

Telford College of Arts and Technology Haybridge Road, Wellington, Telford, Shropshire TF1 2NP. Tel 01952 642237; Student Services 01952 642237; www.tcat.ac.uk

Thanet College Ramsgate Road, Broadstairs, Kent CT10 1PN. Tel 01843 605040; Admissions 01843 605049; www.thanet.ac.uk

Thurrock and Basildon College (now part of South Essex College)

Totton College Calmore Road, Totton, Hampshire SO40 3ZX. Tel 023 8087 4874; www.totton.ac.uk

Trafford College Talbot Road, Stretford, Manchester M32 0XH. Tel 0161 886 7000; www.ntc.ac.uk; www.trafford.ac.uk

Tresham Institute of Further and Higher Education Windmill Avenue, Kettering, Northamptonshire NN15 6ER. Tel 0845 658 8990; www.tresham.ac.uk

Trowbridge Campus, Wiltshire College College Road, Trowbridge, Wiltshire BA14 0ES. Tel Enrolment 01225 350035; www.wiltshire.ac.uk

Truro College College Road, Truro, Cornwall TR1 3XX. General Enquiries 01872 267000; www.trurocollege.ac.uk

Tyne Metropolitan College Embleton Avenue, Wallsend, Tyne and Wear NE28 9NJ. Tel 0191 229 5000; www.tynemet.ac.uk

Upper Bann Institute (see Southern Regional College)

Uxbridge College Park Road, Uxbridge, Middlesex UB8 1NQ. Tel 01895 853333; www.uxbridge.ac.uk

Wakefield College Margaret Street, Wakefield, West Yorkshire WF1 2DH. Tel 01924 789111; www.wakefield.ac.uk

Walford and North Shropshire College Oswestry Campus, Shrewsbury Road, Oswestry, Shropshire SY11 4QB. Tel 01691 688000; www.wnsc.ac.uk

Walsall College Wisemore Campus, Littleton Street, West Walsall, West Midlands WS2 8ES. Tel 01922 657000; www.walsallcollege.ac.uk

Waltham Forest College 707 Forest Road, Walthamstow, London E17 4JB. Tel 020 8501 8501; www.waltham.ac.uk

Warminster Campus, Wiltshire College The Avenue, Warminster, Wiltshire BA12 9AA. Tel Enrolment 01225 350035; www.wiltshire.ac.uk

Warrington Collegiate Winwick Road, Warrington, Cheshire WA2 8QA. Tel 01925 494494; www.warrington.ac.uk

Warwickshire College Leamington Centre, Warwick New Road, Leamington Spa, Warwickshire CV32 5JE. Tel 01926 318000; www.warkscol.ac.uk

West Cheshire College Chester Campus, Eaton Road, Handbridge, Chester CH4 7ER. Tel 01244 670600; Course Information 0151 356 7800; www.west-cheshire.ac.uk

West Herts College Watford Campus, Hempstead Road, Watford, Hertfordshire WD17 3EZ. Tel 01923 812000; www.westherts.ac.uk

West Kent College Brook Street, Tonbridge, Kent TN9 2PW. Tel 01732 358101; www.wkc.ac.uk

West Lothian College Almondvale Crescent, Livingston, West Lothian EH54 7EP. Tel 01506 418181; Information 01506 427605; www.west-lothian.ac.uk

West Nottinghamshire College Derby Road, Mansfield, Nottinghamshire NG18 5BH. Tel 01623 627191; HE Enquiries 01623 413639/0800 100 3626; www.wnc.ac.uk

West Suffolk College Out Risbygate, Bury St Edmunds, Suffolk IP33 3RL. Tel 01284 701301; www.westsuffolk.ac.uk

West Thames College London Road, Isleworth, Middlesex TW7 4HS. Tel 020 8326 2000; www.west-thames.ac.uk

Westbury Campus, Wiltshire College 6-8 High Street, Westbury, Wiltshire BA13 3BW. Tel Enrolment 01225 350035; www.wiltshire.ac.uk

Westminster Kingsway College St James's Park Centre, Castle Lane, London SW1E 6DR. Information 08700 609800; www.westking.ac.uk

Weston College Knightstone Campus Weston College, Knightstone Road, Weston super Mare, Somerset BS23 2AL. Tel 01934 411411; www.weston.ac.uk

Weymouth College Cranford Avenue, Weymouth, Dorset DT4 7LQ. Tel 01305 761100; Course Applications 0870 060 9800/1; www.weymouth.ac.uk

Wigan and Leigh College Parsons Walk, Wigan WN1 1RU. Tel 01942 761111; www.wigan-leigh.ac.uk

Wiltshire College Chippenham Campus, Cocklebury Road, Chippenham, Wiltshire SN15 3QD. Tel 01249 464644; www.wiltshire.ac.uk

Wirral Metropolitan College Conway Park Campus, Europa Boulevard, Conway Park, Birkenhead, Wirral, Merseyside CH41 4NT. Tel 0151 551 7777; www.wmc.ac.uk

Worcester College of Technology Deansway, Worcester WR1 2JF. Tel 01905 725555; www.wortech.ac.uk

Yeovil College Mudford Road, Yeovil, Somerset BA21 4DR. Tel 01935 423921; www.yeovil.ac.uk

York College Sim Balk Lane, York, North Yorkshire YO23 2BB. Tel 01904 770400; www.yorkcollege.ac.uk

Yorkshire Coast College Lady Edith's Drive, Scarborough, North Yorkshire YO12 5RN. Tel 01723 356192; www.yorkshirecoastcollege.ac.uk

APPENDIX 1 UCAS 2011 ENTRY TARIFF POINTS TABLES

GCE A/AS-LEVELS • SCOTTISH HIGHERS/ADVANCED HIGHERS • WELSH BACCALAUREATE • IRISH LEAVING CERTIFICATE • INTERNATIONAL BACCALAUREATE DIPLOMA • CAMBRIDGE PRE-U • PROGRESSION AND ADVANCED DIPLOMA • EXTENDED PROJECT

GCE A/AS-LEVELS

Grade					Tariff Points
GCE & AVCE Double Award	A-level with additional AS (9 units)	GCE A-level and AVCE	GCE AS Double Award	GCE AS and AS VCE	
A*A*					280
A*A					260
AA					240
AB					220
BB	A*A				200
BC	AA				180
	AB				170
CC					160
	BB				150
CD	BC	A*			140
DD	CC	A	AA		120
	CD		AB		110
DE		B	BB		100
	DD		BC		90
EE	DE	C	CC		80
			CD		70
	EE	D	DD	A	60
			DE	B	50
		E	EE	C	40
				D	30
				E	20

Scottish Highers/Advanced Highers

Grade	Higher	Advanced Higher
A	80	130
B	65	110
C	50	90
D	36	72

Welsh Baccalaureate Core

Grade	Tariff points
Pass	120

NB Core points awarded only to candidates obtaining the Welsh Baccalaureate Advanced Diploma

Irish Leaving Certificate

Grade		Tariff points
Higher	Ordinary	
A1		90
A2		77
B1		71
B2		64
B3		58
C1		52
C2		45
C3	A1	39
D1		33
D2	A2	26
D3	B1	20
	B2	14
	B3	7

IB Diploma revised points for 2011 entry

IB Diploma points	UCAS Tariff points
45	720
44	698
43	676
42	654
41	632
40	611
39	589
38	567
37	545
36	523
35	501
34	479
33	457
32	435
31	413
30	392
29	370
28	348
27	326
26	304
25	282
24	260

Cambridge Pre-U (with effect from 2010 entry)

Grade	Principal subject	Global persectives and research	Short course
D1	To be confirmed	To be confirmed	To be confirmed
D2	145	140	To be confirmed
D3	130	126	60
M1	115	112	53
M2	101	98	46
M3	87	84	39
P2	59	56	26
P3	46	42	20

Progression Diploma (with effect from 2010 entry)

Grade	Tariff points
A*	350
A	300
B	250
C	200
D	150
E	100

NB The Advanced Diploma = Progression Diploma plus Additional and Specialist Learning (ASL)

Extended Project – Stand alone (with effect from 2009 entry)

Grade	Tariff points
A*	70
A	60
B	50
C	40
D	30
E	20

Points cannot be counted if taken as part of Advanced Diploma.

NB Full acknowledgement is made to UCAS for this information. For further details of all qualifications awarded UCAS Tariff points see www.ucas.com/students/ucas_tariff/tarifftables. Note that the Tariff is constantly updated and new qualifications are introduced each year.

APPENDIX 2
INTERNATIONAL QUALIFICATIONS

Universities in the UK accept a range of international qualifications and those which normally satisfy the minimum general entrance requirements are listed below. However, the specific levels of achievement or grades required for entry to degree courses with international qualifications will vary, depending on the popularity of the university or college and the chosen degree programme. The subject tables in **Chapter 8** provide a guide to the levels of entry to courses although direct comparisons between A-level grades and international qualifications are not always possible except for the three European examinations listed at the end of this Appendix. Students not holding the required qualifications should consider taking an International Foundation course.

International students whose mother tongue is not English and/or who have not studied for their secondary education in English will be required to pass an English test such as IELTS (International English Language Testing System) or TOEFL (the Test of English as a Foreign Language). Entry requirements vary between universities and courses. For the IELTS, scores can range from 5.5 to 7.5, for the TOEFL computer-based test scores can range from a minimum of 213, and for the TOEFL written test the minimum entry score is 5.0 (see www.ielts.org and www.ets.org/toefl).

Algeria Baccalaureate de l'Enseignement Secondaire
Argentina Completion of Year One of Licenciado/Professional Title
Australia Completion of Year 12 certificates
Austria Reifazeugnis/Maturazeugnis
Bahrain Two-year diploma or associate degree
Bangladesh Bachelor of Arts, Science and Commerce
Belgium Certificat d'Enseignement Secondaire Superieur
Bermuda Diploma of Arts and Science
Bosnia-Herzegovina Secondary School Leaving Diploma
Brazil Completion of Ensino Medio and a good pass in the Vestibular
Brunei Brunei GCE A-level
Bulgaria Diploma za Zavarshino Sredno Obrazovanie (Diploma of Completed Secondary Education)
Canada Completion of Grade 12 secondary/high school certificate or equivalent
Chile Completion of secondary education and a good pass in the Prueba de Conocimientos Especificos
China Completion of one year of a Bachelor degree from a recognised university with good grades
Croatia Matura (Secondary school leaving diploma)
Cyprus Apolytirion/Lise Bitirme Diploma with good grades
Czech Republic Vysvedceni o Maturitni Zkousce/Maturita
Denmark Studentereksamen (HF), (HHX), (HTX)
Egypt Completion of year one of a Bachelor degree or two-year Diploma
Finland Ylioppilastutkinoto/Studentexamen (Matriculation certificate)
France French Baccalaureate
Gambia West African Examinations Council Advanced Level
Georgia Successful completion of Year One of a Bachelor degree
Germany Abitur
Ghana West African High School Certificate/A-levels
Greece Apolytirion of Eniaio Lykeio (previously Apolytirion of Lykeio)

Hong Kong A-levels
Hungary Erettsegi/Matura
Iceland Studentsprof
India High grades from Standard XII School Leaving examinations from certain examination boards
Ireland Irish Leaving Certificate Higher Level
Israel Bagrut
Italy Diploma Conseguito con l'Esame di Stato (formerly the Diploma di Matura) with good grades
Japan Junior College Diploma
Kenya Cambridge Overseas Higher School Certificate
Lebanon Successful completion of year one of Licence
Malaysia Sijil Tinggi Persekolahan Malaysia (STPM, Malaysia Higher School Certificate)
Mauritius Cambridge Overseas Higher School Certificate or A-levels
Mexico Successful completion of year one of Licenciado
Netherlands Voorbereidend Wetenschappelijk Onderwijs (VWO)
Nigeria Successful completion of year one of a Bachelor degree
Norway Diploma of a completed 3-year course of upper secondary education
Pakistan Bachelor degree
Poland Matura/Swiadectwo Dojrzalosci
Portugal Certificado di Fim de Estudos Secundarios with good grades
Russian Federation Diploma of completed Specialised Secondary Education or successful completion of first year of Bakalav
Saudi Arabia Successful completion of first year of a Bachelor degree
Serbia and Montenegro Secondary School Leaving Diploma
Singapore Polytechnic Diploma or A-levels
South Korea Junior College Diploma
Spain Curso de Orientacion Universitaria (COU) with good grades
Sri Lanka A-levels
Sweden Fullstandigt Slutbetyg fran Gymnasieskolan
Taiwan Junior College Diploma
Thailand Successful completion of year one of a Bachelor degree
Turkey Devlet Lise Diplomasi (State High School Diploma) with good grades
Uganda East African Advanced Certificate of Education
Ukraine Successful completion of year one of Bakakavre
USA Good grades from the High School Graduation Diploma with SAT and/or APT

COMPARISONS BETWEEN A-LEVEL GRADES AND THE FOLLOWING EUROPEAN EXAMINATIONS

A-level grades	AAA	AAB	ABB	BBB	BBC	BCC
European Baccalaureate	85%	80%	75%	70%	65%	60%
French Baccalaureate	16 Bien	15 Bien	14 Bien	13 Assez Bien	12 Assez Bien	11 Assez Bien
German Abitur	1.0–1.2	1.3–1.4	1.5–1.8	1.9–2.1	2.2–2.4	2.5–2.7

APPENDIX 3
CAMBRIDGE PRE-U

Cambridge Pre-U is a new post-16 qualification developed by the University of Cambridge International Examinations (CIE). It aims to prepare students from across the world with the skills and knowledge required to make a success of their subsequent studies at university. Representatives from higher education have been involved in writing the syllabi and universities have shown great interest in the qualification.

Students can take individual Cambridge Pre-U subjects and build them up into a portfolio that suits their interests and ambitions. The structure of each Cambridge Pre-U syllabus is linear, and this differentiates it from AS- and A-levels. All the assessment takes place at the end of the two-year course. Students can take a Cambridge Pre-U subject at Subsidiary level (in other words after one year) although the result would not count towards the full (Principal) qualification.

Twenty-four syllabi are now available: Mathematics, Further Mathematics, Economics, Chemistry, Physics, Biology, English, History, Geography, Business Studies, German, French, Spanish, Classical Heritage, Mandarin Chinese, Art History, Sport Science, Greek, Latin, Art and Design, Comparative Government and Politics, Psychology, Music, and Philosophy and Ethics.

Results for individual subjects are decided on a scale of 1 to 10, with a separate grade for the full Diploma. For the full Cambridge Pre-U Diploma students will offer at least three Principal subjects (some will want to offer more). The distinguishing feature is that students will have complete freedom of choice in their subjects, in other words they can specialise in, say, the natural sciences. To qualify for the full Diploma, students offer a programme that includes a core course in Global Perspectives – giving students the opportunity to engage with issues that will face every young person, wherever in the world they live and work.

While the highest grade, D1, has not been allocated a UCAS tariff points value (at the time of this book going to press), the second highest grade (D2) in a Pre-U Principal subject is valued at 145 UCAS tariff points compared to 140 pts for the new A-level A* grade and 120 pts for an A-level grade A. See the Cambridge Pre-U UCAS tariff points table in **Appendix 1**.

Teaching of the Cambridge Pre-U started in September 2008. The first examinations take place in 2010. You can find out more about Cambridge Pre-U at www.cie.org.uk/qualifications/academic/uppersec/preu and if you are planning to apply for university in 2010/11, find out from prospectuses and websites their admissions information for Cambridge Pre-U applicants.

APPENDIX 4 PROFESSIONAL ASSOCIATIONS

Professional associations vary in size and function and many offer examinations to provide members with vocational qualifications. However, many of the larger bodies do not conduct examinations but accept evidence provided by the satisfactory completion of appropriate degree and diploma courses. When applying for courses in vocational subjects, therefore, it is important to check whether your chosen course is accredited by a professional association, since membership of such bodies is usually necessary for progression in your chosen career after graduation.

Information about careers, which you can use as background information for your UCAS application, can be obtained from the organisations below listed under the subject table headings used in **Chapter 8**. Full details of professional associations, their examinations and the degree courses accredited by them are published in *British Qualifications* (see **Appendix 5**).

Some additional organisations that can provide useful careers-related information are listed below under the subject table headings and other sources of relevant information are indicated in the subject tables of **Chapter 8** and in **Appendix 5**.

Accountancy/Accounting

Association of Accounting Technicians www.aat.org.uk
Association of Chartered Certified Accountants www.accaglobal.com
Association of International Accountants www.aiaworldwide.com
Chartered Institute of Management Accountants www.cimaglobal.com
Chartered Institute of Public Finance and Accountancy www.cipfa.org.uk
Chartered Institute of Taxation www.tax.org.uk
Institute of Accounting Technicians in Ireland www.iati.ie
Institute of Chartered Accountants in England and Wales www.icaew.com
Institute of Chartered Accountants in Ireland www.charteredaccountants.ie
Institute of Chartered Accountants of Scotland www.icas.org.uk
Institute of Financial Accountants www.ifa.org.uk
Institute of Internal Auditors www.iia.org.uk

Actuarial Science/Studies

Institute and Faculty of Actuaries www.actuaries.org.uk

Agricultural Sciences/Agriculture

Royal Agricultural Society of England www.rase.org.uk

Animal Sciences

British Horse Society www.bhs.org.uk
British Society of Animal Science www.bsas.org.uk

Anthropology

Association of Social Anthropologists of the UK and Commonwealth www.theasa.org
Royal Anthropological Institute www.therai.org.uk

Archaeology

Council for British Archaeology www.britarch.ac.uk
Institute of Field Archaeologists www.archaeologists.net

Architecture
Chartered Institute of Architectural Technologists www.ciat.org.uk
Royal Incorporation of Architects in Scotland www.rias.org.uk
Royal Institute of British Architects www.architect.com

Art and Design
Arts Council England www.arts.org.uk
Association of Illustrators www.theaoi.com
Association of Photographers http://hub.the-aop.org
British Association of Art Therapists www.baat.org
British Association of Paintings Conservator-Restorers www.bapcr.org.uk
British Institute of Professional Photography www.bipp.com
Chartered Society of Designers www.csd.org.uk
Crafts Council www.craftscouncil.org.uk
Design Council www.designcouncil.org.uk
Institute of Professional Goldsmiths www.ipgold.org.uk
National Society for Education in Art and Design www.nsead.org
Professional Accreditation of Conservator-Restorers www.icon.org.uk
Royal British Society of Sculptors www.rbs.org.uk
Scottish Arts Council www.scottisharts.org.uk
Textile Institute www.texi.org

Astronomy/Astrophysics
Royal Astronomical Society www.ras.org.uk

Biochemistry (see also **Chemistry**)
Association of Clinical Biochemistry www.acb.org.uk
Biochemical Society www.biochemistry.org
British Society for Immunology http://bsi.immunology.org

Biological Sciences/Biology
British Society for Human Genetics www.bshg.org.uk
Genetics Society www.genetics.org.uk
Institute of Biology www.iob.org
Institute of Biomedical Science www.ibms.org

Building
Chartered Institute of Building www.ciob.org.uk
Chartered Institution of Building Services Engineers www.cibse.org
Construction Industry Training Board (CITB) www.cskills.org

Business Courses
Chartered Institute of Personnel and Development www.cipd.co.uk
Chartered Institute of Public Relations www.cipr.org.uk
Chartered Management Institute www.managers.org.uk
Communication, Advertising and Marketing Education Foundation (CAM Foundation) www.camfoundation.com
Council for Administration www.cfa.uk.com
Institute of Administrative Management www.instam.org
Institute of Business Consulting www.ibconsulting.org.uk
Institute of Chartered Secretaries and Administrators www.icsa.org.uk
Institute of Export www.export.org.uk
Institute of Practitioners in Advertising www.ipa.co.uk
Institute of Sales and Marketing Management www.ismm.co.uk

Chemistry

Institute of Nanotechnology www.nano.org.uk
Royal Society of Chemistry www.rsc.org

Computer Courses

BCS The Chartered Institute for IT www.bcs.org
Institute for the Management of Information Systems www.imis.org.uk
Institute of Information Technology Training www.iitt.org.uk
Institution of Analysts and Programmers www.iap.org.uk

Consumer Studies/Sciences

Institute of Consumer Sciences (incorporating Home Economics) www.scenta.co.uk
Trading Standards Institute www.tradingstandards.gov.uk

Dance

Council for Dance Education and Training www.cdet.org.uk

Dentistry

British Association of Dental Nurses www.badn.org.uk
British Association of Dental Therapists www.badt.org.uk
British Dental Association www.bda.org
British Dental Hygienists' Association www.bdha.org.uk
Dental Laboratories Association www.dla.org.uk
Dental Technicians Association www.dta-uk.org
General Dental Council www.gdc-uk.org

Dietetics

British Dietetic Association www.bda.uk.com

Drama

Equity www.equity.org.uk
National Council for Drama Training www.ncdt.co.uk
Society of British Theatre Designers www.theatredesign.org.uk

Economics

Royal Economic Society www.res.org.uk

Education and Teacher Training

Department for Children, Schools and Families www.dcsf.gov.uk
Department for Innovation, Universities and Skills www.dius.gov.uk
General Teaching Council for England www.gtce.org.uk
General Teaching Council for Northern Ireland www.gtcni.org.uk
General Teaching Council for Scotland www.gtcs.org.uk
General Teaching Council for Wales www.gtcw.org.uk
Training and Development Agency for Schools www.tda.gov.uk

Engineering/Engineering Sciences

Energy Institute www.energyinst.org.uk
Engineering Council UK www.engc.org.uk
Institute for Manufacturing www.ifm.eng.cam.ac.uk
Institute of Acoustics www.ioa.org.uk
Institute of Marine Engineering, Science and Technology www.imarest.org
Institution of Agricultural Engineers www.iagre.org
Institution of Civil Engineers www.ice.org.uk

Institution of Engineering Designers www.ied.org.uk
Institution of Engineering and Technology www.theiet.org
Institution of Mechanical Engineers www.imeche.org
Institution of Nuclear Engineers www.nuclearinst.com
Royal Aeronautical Society www.raes.org.uk

Environmental Science/Studies

Chartered Institute of Environmental Health www.cieh.org
Chartered Institution of Wastes Management www.ciwm.co.uk
Chartered Institution of Water and Environmental Management www.ciwem.org
Environment Agency www.environment-agency.gov.uk
Institute of Ecology and Environmental Management www.ieem.net
Institution of Environmental Sciences www.ies-uk.org.uk
Institution of Occupational Safety and Health www.iosh.co.uk
Royal Environmental Health Institute of Scotland www.rehis.org
Society for the Environment www.socenv.org.uk

Film, Radio, Video and TV Studies

British Film Institute www.bfi.org.uk
Skillset (National Training Organisation for broadcast, film, video and multimedia) www.skillset.org

Finance (including Banking and Insurance)

Chartered Institute of Bankers in Scotland www.ciobs.org.uk
Chartered Institute of Loss Adjusters www.cila.co.uk
Chartered Insurance Institute www.cii.co.uk
Financial Services Skills Council www.fssc.org.uk
Institute of Financial Services www.ifslearning.ac.uk
Personal Finance Society www.thepfs.org
Securities and Investment Institute www.secinst.co.uk

Food Science/Studies and Technology

Institute of Food Science and Technology www.ifst.org
Society of Food Hygiene and Technology www.sofht.co.uk

Forensic Science

Forensic Science Society www.forensic-science-society.org

Forestry

Institute of Chartered Foresters www.charteredforesters.org
Institute of Wood Science www.iwsc.org.uk
Royal Forestry Society www.rfs.org.uk

Geography

British Cartographic Society www.cartography.org.uk
Royal Geographical Society www.rgs.org
Royal Meteorological Society www.rmets.org

Geology/Geological Sciences

Geological Society www.geolsoc.org.uk

Health Sciences/Studies

British Academy of Audiology http://theloop.netplan.co.uk
British and Irish Orthoptic Society www.orthoptics.org.uk
British Association of Prosthetists and Orthotists www.bapo.com

British Chiropractic Association www.chiropractic-uk.co.uk
British Occupational Hygiene Society www.bohs.org
British Osteopathic Association and General Osteopathic Council www.osteopathy.org.uk
Institute for Complementary Medicine www.i-c-m.org.uk
Institution of Occupational Safety and Health www.iosh.co.uk
Society of Homeopaths www.homeopathy-soh.org

History

Royal Historical Society www.rhs.ac.uk

Horticulture

Institute of Horticulture www.horticulture.org.uk

Hospitality and Hotel Management

Institute of Hospitality www.instituteofhospitality.org.uk
People 1st www.people1st.co.uk

Housing

Chartered Institute of Housing www.cih.org

Human Resource Management

Chartered Institute of Personnel and Development www.cipd.co.uk

Information Management

Association for Information Management www.aslib.co.uk
Chartered Institute of Library and Information Professionals www.cilip.org.uk

Landscape Architecture

Landscape Institute www.landscapeinstitute.org.uk

Languages

Chartered Institute of Linguists www.iol.org.uk
Institute of Translation and Interpreting www.iti.org.uk

Law

Bar Council www.barcouncil.org.uk
Faculty of Advocates www.advocates.org.uk
Institute of Legal Executives www.ilex.org.uk
Law Society www.lawsociety.org.uk
Law Society of Northern Ireland www.lawsoc-ni.org
Law Society of Scotland www.lawscot.org.uk

Leisure and Recreation Management/Studies

Institute for Sport, Parks and Leisure www.ispal.org.uk

Linguistics

British Association for Applied Linguistics www.baal.org.uk
Royal College of Speech and Language Therapists www.rcslt.org

Marine/Maritime Studies

Nautical Institute www.nautinst.org

Marketing

Chartered Institute of Marketing www.cim.co.uk
Institute of Sales and Marketing Management www.ismm.co.uk

Materials Science/Metallurgy

Institute of Materials, Minerals and Mining www.iom3.org

Mathematics
Council for Mathematical Sciences www.cms.ac.uk
Institute of Mathematics and its Applications www.ima.org.uk
London Mathematical Society www.lms.ac.uk
Mathematical Association www.m-a.org.uk

Media Studies
British Broadcasting Corporation www.bbc.co.uk/jobs
National Council for the Training of Journalists www.nctj.com
Skillset (National training organisation for broadcast, film, video and multimedia) www.skillset.org
Society for Editors and Proofreaders www.sfep.org.uk
Society of Authors www.societyofauthors.org

Medicine
British Medical Association www.bma.org.uk
General Medical Council www.gmc-uk.org
Institute for Complementary Medicine www.i-c-m.org.uk

Microbiology (see also **Biological Sciences/Biology**)
Society for General Microbiology www.sgm.ac.uk

Music
Incorporated Society of Musicians www.ism.org
Institute of Musical Instrument Technology www.imit.org.uk

Naval Architecture
Royal Institution of Naval Architects www.rina.org.uk

Nursing and Midwifery
Community Practitioners' and Health Visitors' Association www.unite-cphva.org
Northern Ireland Practice and Educational Council for Nursing and Midwifery www.n-i.nhs.uk
Nursing and Midwifery Council www.nmc-uk.org
Royal College of Midwives www.rcm.org.uk
Royal College of Nursing www.rcn.org.uk

Nutrition (see **Dietetics**)

Occupational Therapy
British Association/College of Occupational Therapists www.cot.co.uk

Optometry
Association of British Dispensing Opticians www.abdo.org.uk
British and Irish Orthoptic Society www.orthoptics.org.uk
College of Optometrists www.college-optometrists.org
General Optical Council www.optical.org

Pharmacology
British Toxicology Society www.thebts.org
Royal Pharmaceutical Society of Great Britain www.rpsgb.org.uk

Pharmacy
Royal Pharmaceutical Society of Great Britain www.rpsgb.org.uk

Photography
Association of Photographers http://hub.the-aop.org
British Institute of Professional Photography www.bipp.com
Royal Photographic Society www.rps.org

Physical Education (see **Education and Teacher Training** and **Sports Sciences/Studies**)

Physics
Institute of Physics www.iop.org
Institute of Physics and Engineering in Medicine www.ipem.org.uk

Physiotherapy
Association of Chartered Physiotherapists in Animal Therapy www.acpat.org
Chartered Society of Physiotherapy www.csp.org.uk

Plant Sciences (see **Biological Sciences/Biology**)

Podiatry
Society of Chiropodists and Podiatrists www.feetforlife.org

Property Management/Development
Chartered Institute of Building www.ciob.org.uk
Chartered Surveyors Training Trust www.cstt.org.uk
National Association of Estate Agents www.naea.co.uk
Royal Institution of Chartered Surveyors www.rics.org

Psychology
British Psychological Society www.bps.org.uk

Public Relations
Chartered Institute of Public Relations www.cipr.co.uk

Quantity Surveying
Chartered Institute of Building www.ciob.org.uk
Royal Institution of Chartered Surveyors www.rics.org

Radiography
Society and College of Radiographers www.sor.org

Social Work
Care Council for Wales www.ccwales.org.uk
General Social Care Council www.gscc.org.uk
Northern Ireland Social Care Council www.niscc.info
Scottish Social Services Council www.sssc.uk.com

Sociology
British Sociological Association www.britsoc.co.uk

Speech Pathology/Sciences/Therapy
Royal College of Speech and Language Therapists www.rcslt.org

Sports Sciences/Studies
British Association of Sport and Exercise Sciences www.bases.org.uk
English Institute of Sport www.eis2win.co.uk
Institute of Sport and Recreation Management www.isrm.co.uk
Scottish Institute of Sport www.sisport.com
Society of Sports Therapists www.society-of-sports-therapists.org
Sport England www.sportengland.org
Sport Scotland www.sportscotland.org.uk
Sports Council for Wales www.sports-council-wales.co.uk
Sports Institute Northern Ireland www.sini.co.uk
UK Sport www.uksport.gov.uk

Statistics
Royal Statistical Society www.rss.org.uk

Tourism and Travel
Institute for Sport, Parks and Leisure www.ispal.co.uk
Institute of Travel and Tourism www.itt.co.uk

Town and Country Planning
Royal Town Planning Institute www.rtpi.org.uk

Transport Management and Planning
Chartered Institute of Logistics and Transport www.cilt-international.com

Veterinary Science/Medicine/Nursing
Association of Chartered Physiotherapists in Animal Therapy www.acpat.org
British Veterinary Nursing Association www.bvna.org.uk
Royal College of Veterinary Surgeons www.rcvs.org.uk
Royal Veterinary College www.rvc.ac.uk

Zoology
Royal Entomological Society www.royensoc.co.uk
Zoological Society of London www.zsl.org

APPENDIX 5
BOOKLIST AND USEFUL WEBSITES

Unless otherwise stated, the publications in this list are all available from Trotman Publishing (www.trotman.co.uk / 0870 900 2665).

STANDARD REFERENCE BOOKS

Big Guide 2011 Entry – the official universities and colleges entrance guide for 2011 entry, UCAS (www.ucasbooks.com)

British Qualifications, 39th edition, Kogan Page Ltd

British Vocational Qualifications, 10th edition, Kogan Page Ltd

OTHER BOOKS AND RESOURCES

Choosing Your Degree Course and University, 12th edition, Brian Heap, Trotman Publishing

Critical Choices: Applying to University, Trotman Publishing

Destinations of Leavers from Higher Education 2007/8, Higher Education Statistics Agency Services (available from HESA)

Getting Into course guides: US & Canadian Universities, Art & Design Courses, Business, Economics & Management Courses, Dental School, Law, Medical School, Oxford & Cambridge, Physiotherapy Courses, Psychology Courses, Veterinary School, Trotman Publishing

Guide to Student Money 2011, 16th edition, Gwenda Thomas, Trotman Publishing (publishing July 2010)

Guide to UK Universities 2010, 30th edition, Klaus Boehm and Jenny Lees-Spalding, Trotman Publishing

How to Complete Your UCAS Application: 2011 Entry, Trotman Publishing

Insiders' Guide to Applying to University, Karla Fitzhugh, Trotman Publishing

Into Higher Education 2009: The Higher Education Guide for People with Disabilities, Skill – The National Bureau for Students with Disabilities

Study in Europe – UK Socrates-Erasmus Student Guide, UK Socrates-Erasmus Council

Studying and Learning at University, Alan Pritchard, Sage Study Skills Series

Surviving Your First Year at University, Trotman Publishing

The Times Good University Guide 2010, John O'Leary, Times Books

University Scholarships, Awards and Bursaries, 8th edition, Brian Heap, Trotman Publishing

The Virgin 2010 Guide to British Universities, Piers Dudgeon, Virgin Publishing

Which Uni? Find the Best University for You, Karla Fitzhugh, Trotman Publishing

Your Gap Year, 6th edition, Susan Griffith, Crimson Publishing

USEFUL WEBSITES

Education, course and applications information

www.direct.gov.uk/en/EducationAndLearning

www.coursediscover.co.uk

www.direct.gov.uk/studentfinance

www.britishcouncil.org/erasmus

www.hesa.ac.uk

www.opendays.com (information on university and college open days)

www.unistats.com (official information from UK universities and colleges for comparing courses)
www.ucas.com

Careers information

www.armyjobs.mod.uk
www.careerseurope.co.uk
www.connexions.gov.uk
www.enginuity.org.uk
www.insidecareers.co.uk
www.isco.org.uk
www.milkround.com
www.nhscareers.nhs.uk
www.prospects.ac.uk
www.socialworkandcare.co.uk
www.tda.gov.uk
www.trotman.co.uk
www.ucreative.ac.uk

Gap years

www.gapyear.com
www.gap-year.com
www.yini.org.uk (Year in Industry)

Study overseas

www.acu.ac.uk
www.fulbright.co.uk
www.allaboutcollege.com

COURSE INDEX

INDEX OF ADVERTISERS